This modern text is designed to prepare you for your future professional career. While theories, ideas, techniques, and data are dynamic, the information contained in this volume will provide you a quick and useful reference as well as a guide for future learning for many years to come. Your familiarity with the contents of this book will make it an important volume in your professional library.

EX LIBRIS

ORGANIZATIONAL BEHAVIOR AND MANAGEMENT

ORGANIZATIONAL BEHAVIOR AND MANAGEMENT

John M. Ivancevich

Cullen Professor of
Organizational Behavior
and Management
University of Houston

Michael T. Matteson

Professor of Organizational
Behavior and Management
University of Houston

1987

BUSINESS PUBLICATIONS, INC.
Plano, Texas 75075

ISBN 0-256-05608-0

Library of Congress Catalog Card No. 8672712

Printed in the United States of America

1 2 3 4 5 6 7 8 9 0 K 4 3 2 1 0 9 8 7

PREFACE

The major goal of *Organizational Behavior and Management (OBM)* is to encourage students to become involved participants while learning about behavior and management within work settings. To accomplish this goal, we have designed the book with instructional flexibility in mind. *OBM* combines text, readings, diagnostic exercises, group participation exercises, and cases. These elements are aimed at students interested in understanding, interpreting, and attempting to predict the behavior of people working in organizations—the machinists, chief executive officers, apprentices, district managers, administrative assistants, nurses, personnel/human resource directors, and others who make up the labor force.

The complexity of organizational functioning is demonstrated clearly by the fact that no single theory or model of organizational behavior has emerged as the best or most practical. Thus, it is important for managers to be able to probe and diagnose organizational situations when attempting to understand, interpret, and predict behavior. *OBM* devotes considerable space and attention to encouraging the development of these probing and diagnosing skills. The first step in this development is for each reader (student, current manager, trainee) to increase his or her own self-awareness. Before a person can, with enthusiasm and accuracy, probe and diagnose why another person (a friend, subordinate, or competitor) is behaving in a particular way, he or she must conduct a personal introspective analysis. This introspective first step is built into each chapter's content and into the learning elements found at the end of *OBM*'s chapters. The content and these elements encourage the student to relate his or her own knowledge and experience to the text, readings, exercises, and cases in the book.

Framework of the Book

Other books present text, readings, exercises, and cases. However, in most of these works, materials are presented loosely. There is no attempt to integrate, to tie together, to blend the text content and other elements, such as readings or exercises. In *Organizational Behavior and Management* we use a diagnostic model (Figure 1–2) that is the centerpiece of the book's learning involvement focus. The model illustrates how the important pieces (the individual chapters) fit together. The dynamic perspective of the field of organizational behavior and the model are captured when the students become actively involved in the learning process through such elements as the readings, diagnostic exercises, group exercises, and cases. These elements are viewed as learning and skill enhancement (LSE) units.

The book is organized into five parts containing a total of 15 chapters, an epilogue, and an appendix. The main theme of this framework is to highlight behavior, structure, and processes that are part of organizational life. The five parts are as follows:

Part One: *The Field of Organizational Behavior.* The first two chapters of *OMB* introduce the field of organizational behavior. They explore the how, what, why, and when of organizational behavior as viewed and practiced by managers.

Part Two: *The Individual in the Organization* is the focus of four chapters. Chapter 3 is titled "Individual Differences and Work Behavior." Chapter 4 is titled "Motivation." Chapter 5 examines "Rewarding and Punishing Individual Behavior," and Chapter 6 is entitled "Occupational Stress: An Individual View."

Part Three: *Interpersonal Influence and the Group Behavior.* These two topics are explored in a four-chapter sequence. Chapter 7 is titled "Group Behavior." The heading for Chapter 8 is "Intergroup Behavior and Conflict." Chapter 9 is entitled "Organizational Power and Politics," and the title for Chapter 10 is "Leadership."

Part Four: *Organizational Structure and Job Design.* The two chapters in this section are: "Organizational Structure and Design" (Chapter 11) and "Job Design" (Chapter 12).

Part Five: *Organizational Process.* Three chapters examine this area. Chapter 13 is headed "Decision Making," Chapter 14 is titled "Communication," and Chapter 15 is named "Organizational Change and Development."

The textbook's epilogue takes a look back and toward the future. The epilogue raises a number of questions and points to additional managerial and research work that needs to be done. The tools for conducting the needed research, meanwhile, are spelled out in Appendix A, "Quantitative and Qualitative Research Techniques for Studying Organizational Behavior and Management Practice."

Supplementary Materials

OMB includes a variety of supplementary materials, all designed to provide additional classroom support for instructors. These materials are as follows:

Instructor's Manual: The Instructor's Manual is organized to follow each chapter in the text. It includes: chapter objectives; chapter synopses; chapter outlines with tips and ideas; and suggested films to supplement class discussion. Suggested transparencies, term paper topics, and end-of-chapter practical exercises also are included.

Transparencies: Transparency masters are included to highlight illustrations in the text.

Test Bank: This testing resource contains a wide variety of materials, such as true/false, multiple choice, and essay questions. These items are categorized by type of question. Additionally, the test bank includes questions that test the students on the concepts presented in the readings to enhance the integrative nature of the text.

CompuTest II: A complete, high-quality, computerized testing package is provided.

Learning and Skill Enhancement (LSE) Elements

A total of 109 LSE elements are provided. These can be used by instructors in any combination that fits course objectives, teaching style, and classroom situation. The book contains 28 carefully selected classical and contemporary readings from a variety of sources (e.g., *Academy of Management Review, Harvard Business Review, Issues and Observations, Organizational Dynamics*). Each of the readings is tied back to a chapter's content through questions designed as "LEARNING CHECKPOINTS." The readings are indicated by the ▯ notation (e.g., ▯' —the first reading in the chapter).

OBM also includes 27 diagnostic (designated by ▯), or self-learning exercises. These 27 exercises focus on the individual student and ask him or her to participate in a way that enhances self-learning. These self-learning exercises illustrate how to gather and use feedback properly. These exercises emphasize the uniqueness of perception, values, personality, and communication abilities.

There are 27 group exercises in *OBM*. Working in groups is a part of organizational life, so these exercises (designated as ▯) introduce a touch of reality. The exercises take text or content theories, principles, or suggestions and convert them into group activities. This hands-on group interaction can generate debates, lively discussions, the testing of personal ideas, and the sharing of information.

Both the diagnostic (▯) and group (▯) exercises are designed to actively involve the instructor in the learning process. Your participation allows you to try out techniques, patterns of behavior, and integrate exercise materials with the text. None of the exercises require advance preparation on your part. Some do require you to return to a particular section or model in the chapters for information. The main objective is to get you involved. As you become involved, you should start asking yourself questions: "How does this tie in with my experience, the text material, my ideas?"; "What do others think about the exercise?"; "Is this really how I perceive things, feel about things, respond to events?" The exercises will allow you to experience and become involved in the application of *Organizational Behavior and Management* concepts.

OBM contains 27 full-length cases (▯). These realistic, dynamic cases serve as a link between theory, research, and practice. They provide views of various organizational settings. The cases, like the real world, do not have one "right" solution. Each provides opportunities for students to experience the work environment through the eyes of managers. The cases also are an invaluable teaching tool. They encourage the individual student to probe, diagnose, and creatively solve real problems. Group participation and learning, meanwhile, are encouraged through in-class discussion and debate. The questions at the end of each case are used to guide the discussion. A case analysis should follow the following format:

1. Read the case quickly.
2. Reread the case using the following model:

a. Define the major problem in organizational behavior and management terms.
b. If information is incomplete, which it is likely to be, make assumptions that are realistic.
c. Outline the probable causes of the problem.
d. Consider possible solutions in terms of costs and benefits. That is, what are the +'s and −'s of this solution.
e. Choose a solution, and describe how you would implement it.
f. Go over the case again. Make sure the questions at the end are answered and make sure your solution is efficient, feasible, ethical, legally defensible, and can be defended in classroom debate.

Contributors

The authors wish to acknowledge the many scholars, managers, and researchers who contributed to the final preparation of *OBM*. We are indebted to all those individuals who granted permission for the use of readings, exercises, and cases.

In addition, the book was shaped significantly by colleagues such as James Donnelly and James Gibson at the University of Kentucky. These two colleagues have shared, and put into practice, a common belief that teaching and learning about organizational behavior and management can be an exhilarating and worthwhile experience. Roger Blakeney, Sara Freedman, Art Jago, Tim McMahon, and Jim Phillips all at the University of Houston, and Dave Schweiger at the University of South Carolina, and Bob Keller at Louisiana State University have exchanged materials, ideas, and opinions with the authors over the years, and these are reflected in *OBM*.

There also were graduate students (some are now productive faculty members) who—in classes or in discussions—shared ideas and suggestions about teaching organizational behavior and management. We personally thank the following individuals for their suggestions, which have been merged into this integrated text: Kim Stewart, Chris Betts, Carrie Leana, Dennis Duchon, Jim Ragan, Jennifer Ettling, Shel Vernon, Wayne Smeltz, Dave Hunt, Terry Mullins, and Phyllis Finger.

The typing support and efforts of Karen Lytwyn are certainly appreciated. Karen has become, over the years, an expert in reading script that strains the human eye. Finally, the book is dedicated to our former "Organizational Behavior and Management" students at the University of Maryland, the University of Kentucky, and the University of Houston. We also dedicate this textbook to the students who are and will be the managers that are so vital to the improvement of the overall quality of life in society.

John M. Ivancevich
Michael T. Matteson

CONTENTS

**Part V
Organizational Processes   583**

Epilogue   **729**

Appendix A Quantitative and Qualitative Research Techniques for Studying Organizational Behavior and Management Practice   **737**

THE FIELD OF ORGANIZATIONAL BEHAVIOR

1

INTRODUCTION TO ORGANIZATIONAL BEHAVIOR

LEARNING OBJECTIVES

DEFINE the three levels of performance outcomes in an organization.

DESCRIBE the major characteristics of organizational behavior.

DISCUSS the importance of understanding behavior in organizations.

COMPARE the effects of structure and process on organizational behavior.

IDENTIFY the major factors which influence behavior in organizations.

Organizations permeate all levels of our lives. We come into contact with many of them daily. In fact, most of us probably spend most of our lives in—or are affected by—organizations. We expend sizable amounts of our time as members of work, school, social, civic, and church organizations. Or we are involved as employees, students, clients, patients, and citizens of organizations.

At some times, these organizations appear to be efficiently run and responsive to our needs, and at other times they are extremely frustrating and irritating. We may even think they are harassing us. Such personal experiences in or with organizations may have already helped form our sense of what it means to be "organized."

While your attitudes about organizations may be positive or negative, what you understand about them so far can provide a good foundation for examining organizations in a more systematic manner.

Organizations exist for one reason: They can accomplish things that we cannot accomplish individually. Thus, whether the goal is to make a profit, provide education, foster religion, improve health care, put a man or woman on the moon, get a candidate elected, or build a new football stadium, organizations get the job done. Organizations are characterized by their *goal-directed behavior*. They pursue goals and objectives that can be achieved more efficiently and effectively by the concerted action of individuals *and* groups.

The purpose of this book is to help you learn how to manage individuals and groups as resources of organizations. Organizations are essential to the way our society operates. In industry, education, health care, and defense, organizations have created impressive gains for our standard of living and our worldwide image. The size of the organizations with which you deal daily should illustrate the tremendous political, economic, and social powers they separately possess. For example, your college has much economic, political, and social power in its community. If a large firm announced that it was closing its plant in your community, the resulting impact might be devastating economically. On the other hand, if General Motors announced that it was opening an automobile assembly plant in your community, the impact probably would be very positive.

Organizations are, however, much more than means for providing goods and services.[1] They create the settings in which most of us spend our lives. In this respect, they have profound influence on our behavior. However, because large-scale organizations have developed only in recent times, we are just now beginning to recognize the necessity for studying them. Researchers have just begun the process of developing ways to study the behavior of people in organizations.

THE IMPORTANCE OF STUDYING ORGANIZATIONAL BEHAVIOR

Why do employees behave as they do in organizations? Why is one individual or group more productive than another? Why do managers continually seek ways to design jobs and delegate authority? These and similar questions are important to the relatively new field of study known as **organizational behavior.** Understanding the behavior of people in organizations has become increasingly important as management concerns—such as employee productivity, the quality of work life, job stress, and career progression—continue to make front-page news.

The field of organizational behavior can be defined as:

> The study of human behavior, attitudes, and performance within an organizational setting; drawing on theory, methods, and principles from such disciplines as psychology, sociology, and cultural anthropology to learn about *individual* perceptions, values, learning capacities, and actions while working in *groups* and within the total *organization;* analyzing the external environment's effect on the organization and its human resources, missions, objectives, and strategies.

This view of organizational behavior illustrates a number of points. First, organizational behavior is a *way of thinking.* Behavior is viewed as operating at individual, group, and organizational levels. This approach suggests that when studying organizational behavior, we must identify clearly the level of analysis being used—individual, group, and/or organizational. Second, organizational behavior is an *interdisciplinary field.* This means that it utilizes principles, models, theories, and methods from other disciplines. The study of organizational behavior is not a discipline or a generally accepted science with an established theoretical foundation. It is a field that only now is beginning to grow and develop in stature and impact. Third, there is a distinctly *humanistic orientation* within organizational behavior. People and their attitudes, perceptions, learning capacities, feelings, and goals are of major importance to the organization. Fourth, the field of organizational behavior is *performance-oriented.* Why is performance low or high? How can performance be improved? Can training enhance on-the-job performance? These are important issues facing practicing managers. Fifth, the *external environment* is seen as having significant impact on organizational behavior. Sixth, since the field of organizational behavior relies heavily on recognized disciplines, the role of the *scientific method* is deemed important in studying variables

---

[1] See L. F. Urwick, "That Word Organization," *Academy of Management Review,* January 1976, pp. 89–91.

and relationships. As the scientific method has been used in conducting research on organizational behavior, a set of principles and guidelines on what constitutes good research has emerged.[2] Finally, the field has a distinctive *applications orientation;* it is concerned with providing useful answers to questions which arise in the context of managing organizations. Figure 1–1 summarizes the main characteristics of the field of organizational behavior.

FIGURE 1–1

Major
Characteristics of
the Field of
Organizational
Behavior

Characteristic	Focal Point
Three levels of analysis	Individuals, groups, and the organization are equally important in studying and understanding behavior in organizations.
Interdisciplinary nature	Principles, concepts, and models from the behavioral sciences—psychology, sociology, and cultural anthropology—are utilized.
Humanistic orientation	The importance of attitudes and perceptions in understanding behavior within organizations is stressed.
Performance orientation	Continual emphasis is placed on a search for ways to improve, sustain, and encourage effective performance.
Recognition of external environmental forces	The identification and continual monitoring of external environmental forces are important for improving organizational behavior.
Use of the scientific method	Whenever possible, scientific methods are used to supplement experience and intuition.
Application orientation	Knowledge developed in the field of organizational behavior must be useful to practicing managers when they confront individual, group, and organizational problems.

To help you learn how to manage individuals and groups as resources of organizations, this book focuses on the behavior of *individuals, groups,* and *organizations.* Developing the model presented in this book required the use of several assumptions. These assumptions are explained briefly in the following paragraphs, which precede the model.[3]

**ORGANIZA-
TIONAL
BEHAVIOR
FOLLOWS
PRINCIPLES OF
HUMAN
BEHAVIOR**

The effectiveness of any organization is influenced greatly by human behavior. People are a resource common to all organizations. There is no such thing as a peopleless organization.

One important principle of psychology is that each person is different. Each person has unique perceptions, personalities, and life experiences; different capabilities for learning and stress; and different attitudes, beliefs, and aspiration levels. To be effective, managers of organizations must view each employee or member as a unique embodiment of all these behavioral factors.

---

[2] Edward E. Lawler III, "Challenging Traditional Research Assumptions," in Edward E. Lawler III, Allan M. Mohrman, Jr., Susan A. Mohrman, Gerald E. Ledford, Jr., and Thomas G. Cummings (Eds.), *Doing Research That Is Useful for Theory and Practice* (San Francisco: Jossey-Bass, 1985).

[3] See Andrew J. DuBrin, *Fundamentals of Organizational Behavior* (New York: Pergamon Press, 1978), chap. 1; and James R. Meindl, "The Abundance of Solutions: Some Thoughts for Theoretical and Practical Solution Seekers," *Administrative Science Quarterly,* December 1982, pp. 670–85.

ORGANIZATIONS AS SOCIAL SYSTEMS

The relationships among individuals and groups in organizations create expectations for the behavior of individuals. These expectations result in certain roles that must be performed. Some people must perform the role of leader, while others must play the role of follower. Middle managers must perform both roles, because they have both a superior and subordinates. Organizations have systems of authority, status, and power, and people in organizations have varying needs from each system. Groups in organizations also have a powerful impact on individual behavior and on organizational performance.

MANY FACTORS SHAPE ORGANIZATIONAL BEHAVIOR

Our behavior in any situation involves the interaction of our personal characteristics and the characteristics of the situation. Thus, identifying all of the factors is time-consuming and difficult; frequently, the task is impossible.

To help us identify the important managerial factors in organizational behavior, however, we use the **contingency** (or *situational*) **approach.** The basic idea of the contingency approach is that there is no one best way to manage. A method that is very effective in one situation may not even work in others. The contingency approach has grown in popularity over the last two decades because research has shown that, given certain characteristics of a job and certain characteristics of the people doing the job, some management practices work better than others. Thus, when facing a problem, a manager using the contingency approach does not assume that a particular approach will work. Instead, he or she diagnoses the characteristics of the individuals and groups involved, the organizational structure, and his or her own leadership style before deciding on a solution.

HOW STRUCTURE AND PROCESS AFFECT ORGANIZATIONAL BEHAVIOR

An organization's **structure** is the formal pattern of how its people and jobs are grouped. Structure often is illustrated by an organization chart. **Process** refers to activities that give life to the organization chart. Communication, decision making, and organization development are examples of processes in organizations. Sometimes, understanding process problems such as breakdowns in communication and decision making will result in a more accurate understanding of organizational behavior than if you simply examine structural arrangements.

Effective managers know what to look for in a work situation and how to understand what they find. Therefore, managers must develop diagnostic and action abilities. Managers must be trained to identify conditions symptomatic of a problem requiring further attention. A manager's problem indicators include declining profits, declining quantity or quality of work, increases in absenteeism or lateness, and negative employee attitudes. Each of these problems is an issue of organizational behavior.

A MODEL FOR MANAGING ORGANIZATIONS: BEHAVIOR, STRUCTURE, PROCESSES

A model for understanding organizational behavior is presented in Figure 1–2. The model shows how the many topics covered in this book can be combined into a meaningful study of organizational behavior.

FIGURE 1–2

A Framework for the Study of Organizational Behavior and Management

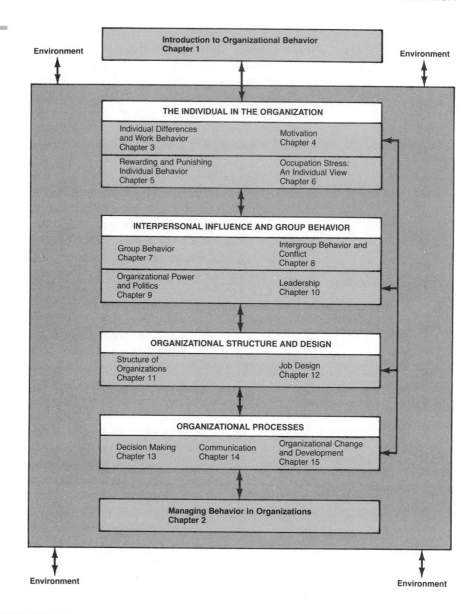

**THE ORGANIZA-
TION'S
ENVIRONMENT**

Organizations exist in societies and are created by societies. Figure 1–2 draws attention to the relationships between organizations and the society which creates and sustains them. Within a society, many factors impinge upon the effectiveness of an organization, and management must be responsive to them. Every organization must respond to the needs of its customers or clients, to legal and political constraints, and to economic and technological changes and developments. The model reflects environmental forces interacting within the organization, and throughout our discussion of each aspect of the model, the relevant environmental factors will be identified and examined.

**THE
INDIVIDUAL
IN THE
ORGANIZATION**

Individual performance is the foundation of organizational performance. Understanding individual behavior therefore is critical for effective management, as illustrated in this account:

> Ted Johnson has been a field representative for a major drug manufacturer since he graduated from college seven years ago. He makes daily calls on physicians, hospitals, clinics, and pharmacies as a representative of the many drugs his firm manufactures. During his time in the field, prescription rates and sales for all of his firm's major drugs have increased, and he has won three national sales awards given by the firm. Yesterday, Ted was promoted to sales manager for a seven-state region. He no longer will be selling but instead will be managing 15 other representatives. Ted accepted the promotion because he believes he knows how to motivate and lead salespeople. He commented: "I know the personality of the salesperson. They are special people. I know what it takes to get them to perform. Remember, I am one. I know their values and attitudes and what it takes to motivate them. I know I can motivate a sales force."

In his new job, Ted Johnson will be trying to maximize the individual performances of 15 sales representatives. In doing so, he will be dealing with several facets of individual behavior. Our model includes four important influences on individual behavior and motivation in organizations: individual characteristics; individual motivation; rewards; and stress.

Individual Characteristics. Because organizational performance depends on individual performance, managers such as Ted Johnson must have more than a passing knowledge of the determinants of individual performance. Psychology and social psychology contribute a great deal of relevant knowledge about the relationships among attitudes, perceptions, personality, values, and individual performance. Understanding individual capacity for learning and for coping with stress has become more and more important in recent years. Managers cannot ignore the necessity for acquiring and acting on knowledge of the individual characteristics of both their subordinates and themselves.

Individual Motivation. Motivation and ability to work interact to determine performance. Motivation theory attempts to explain and predict how the behavior of individuals is aroused, started, sustained, and stopped. Unlike Ted Johnson, not all managers and behavioral scientists agree on what is the "best" theory of motivation. In fact, motivation is so complex that it may be impossible to have an all-encompassing theory of how it occurs. However, managers must still try to understand it. They must be concerned with motivation because they must be concerned with performance.

Rewards. One of the most powerful influences on individual performance is an organization's reward system. Management can use rewards (or punishment) to increase performance by present employees. Management also can use rewards to attract skilled employees to join the organization. Pay checks, raises, and bonuses are important aspects of the reward system, but they are not the only aspects. Ted Johnson makes this point very clear in the account when he states: "I know what it takes to get them to perform." Performance of the work itself can provide employees with rewards, particularly if job performance leads to a sense of personal responsibility, autonomy, and meaningfulness.

Stress. Stress is an important result of the interaction between the job and the individual. Stress in this context is a state of imbalance within an individual that often manifests itself in such symptoms as insomnia, excessive perspiration, nervousness, and irritability. Whether stress is positive or negative depends on the individual's tolerance level. People react differently to situations that outwardly would seem to induce the same physical and psychological demands. Some individuals respond positively through increased motivation and commitment to finish the job. Other individuals respond less desirably by turning to such outlets as alcoholism and drug abuse. Hopefully, Ted Johnson will respond positively to the stresses of his new job.

Management's responsibility in managing stress has not been clearly defined, but there is growing evidence that organizations are devising programs to deal with work-induced stress.

INTERPERSONAL INFLUENCE AND GROUP BEHAVIOR

Interpersonal influence and group behavior are also powerful forces affecting organizational performance. The effects of these forces are illustrated in the following account:

Kelly McCaul spent 2½ years as a teller in the busiest branch of First National Bank. During that time she developed close personal friendships with her co-workers. These friendships extended off the job, as well. Kelly and her friends formed a wine-and-cheese club and the top team in the bank-wide bowling league. In addition, several of the friends took ski trips together each winter.

Two months ago Kelly was promoted to branch manager. She was excited about the new challenge, but was a little surprised that she got the promotion, since some other likely candidates in the branch had been with the bank longer. She began the job with a great deal of optimism and believed her friends would be genuinely happy for her and supportive of her efforts. However, since she became branch manager, things haven't seemed quite the same. Kelly can't spend nearly as much time with her friends because she is often away from the branch attending management meetings at the main office. A training course that she must attend two evenings a week has caused her to miss the last two wine-and-cheese club meetings. And she senses that some of her friends have been acting a little differently toward her lately.

Recently, Kelly said: "I didn't know that being part of the management team could make that much difference. Frankly, I never really thought about it. I guess I was naive. I'm seeing a totally different perspective of the business and have to deal with problems I never knew about."

Kelly McCaul's promotion has made her a member of more than one group. In addition to being a member of her old group of friends at the branch, she also is a member of the management team. She is finding out that group behavior and expectations have a strong impact on individual behavior and interpersonal influence. Our model includes four important aspects of group and interpersonal influence on organizational behavior: leadership; group behavior; intergroup behavior and conflict; and organizational power and politics.

Leadership.   Leaders exist within all organizations. Like the bank's Kelly McCaul, they may be found in formal groups, but they also may be found in informal groups. Leaders may be managers or nonmanagers. The importance of effective leadership for obtaining individual, group, and organizational performance is so critical that it has stimulated a great deal of effort to determine the causes of such leadership. Some people believe that effective leadership depends on traits and certain behaviors—separately and in combination. Other people believe that one leadership style is effective in all situations. Still others believe that each situation requires a specific leadership style.

Group Behavior.   Groups form because of managerial action, but also because of individual efforts. Managers create work groups to carry out assigned jobs and tasks. Such groups, created by managerial decisions, are termed *formal groups.* The group that Kelly McCaul manages at her branch is a formal group.

Groups also form as a consequence of employees' actions. Such groups, termed *informal groups,* develop around common interests and friendships. The wine-and-cheese club at Kelly McCaul's branch is an informal group. Though not sanctioned by management, groups of this kind can affect organizational and individual performance. The effect can be positive or negative, depending on the intention of the group's members. If the group at Kelly's branch decided informally to slow the work pace, this norm would exert pressure on individuals who wanted to remain a part of the group. Effective managers recognize the consequences of individuals' need for affiliation.

Intergroup Behavior and Conflict.   As groups function and interact with other groups, they develop their own unique set of characteristics, including structure, cohesiveness, roles, norms, and processes. As a result, groups may cooperate or compete with other groups, and intergroup competition can lead to conflict. If the management of Kelly's bank instituted an incentive program with cash bonuses to the branch bringing in the most new customers, this might lead to competition and conflict among the branches. While conflict among groups can have beneficial results for an organization, too much or the wrong kinds of intergroup conflict can have very negative results. Thus, managing intergroup conflict is an important aspect of managing organizational behavior.

Power and Politics.   Power is the ability to get someone to do something you want done or to make things happen in the way you want them to happen. Many people in our society are very uncomfortable with the concept of power. Some are very offended by it. This is because the essence of power is control over others. To many Americans, control over others is an offensive thought. However, power is a reality in organizations. Managers derive power from both organizational and individual sources. Kelly McCaul has power by virtue of her position in the formal hierarchy of the bank. She controls performance evaluations and salary increases. However, she also may have power because her co-workers respect and admire the abilities and expertise she possesses. Managers therefore must become comfortable with the concept of power as a reality in organizations and managerial roles.

**ORGANIZA-
TIONAL
STRUCTURE
AND DESIGN**

To work effectively in organizations, managers must have a clear understanding of the organizational structure. Viewing an organization chart on a piece of paper or framed on a wall, one sees only a configuration of positions, job duties, and lines of authority among the parts of an organization. However, organizational structures can be far more complex than that, as illustrated in the following account:

> Dr. John Rice recently was appointed dean of the business school at a major university. Prior to arriving on campus, Rice spent several weeks studying the funding, programs, faculty, students, and organizational structure of the business school. He was trying to develop a list of priorities for things that he believed would require immediate attention during his first year as dean. The president of the university had requested that he have such a list of priorities available when he arrived on campus.
>
> During his first official meeting with the president, Rice was asked the question he fully expected to be asked: "What will be your number one priority?" Rice replied: "Although money is always a problem, I believe the most urgent need is to reorganize the business school. At present, students can major in only one of two departments, accounting and business administration. The accounting department has 20 faculty members. The business administration department has 43 faculty members, including 15 in marketing, 16 in management, and 12 in finance. I foresee a college with four departments—accounting, management, marketing, and finance—each with its own chairperson. First, I believe such a structure will enable us to better meet the needs of our students. Specifically, it will facilitate the development of programs of majors in each of the four areas. Students must be able to major in one of the four functional areas if they are going to be prepared adequately for the job market. Finally, I believe such an organizational structure will enable us to more easily recruit faculty, since they will be joining a group with interests similar to their own."

As this account indicates, an organization's structure is the formal pattern of activities and interrelationships among the various subunits of the organization. Our model includes two important aspects of organizational structure: the actual structure of the organization itself and job design.

Structure of the Organization. The *structure* of the organization refers to the components of the organization and how these components fit together. Dr. Rice plans to alter the basic structure of the business school. The result of his efforts will be a new structure of tasks and authority relationships that he believes will channel the behavior of individuals and groups toward higher levels of performance in the business school.

Job Design. This aspect of structure refers to the processes by which managers specify the contents, methods, and relationships of jobs and specific task assignments to satisfy both organizational and individual needs and requirements. Dr. Rice will have to define the content and duties of the newly created chairperson position and the relationship of that person to the Dean's Office and to the individual faculty members in each department.

ORGANIZA-TIONAL PROCESSES

Certain behavioral processes give life to an organization. When these processes do not function well, unfortunate problems can arise, as illustrated in this account:

> When she began to major in marketing as a junior in college, Connie Vick knew that someday she would work in that field. Once she completed her MBA, she was more positive than ever that marketing would be her life's work. Because of her excellent academic record, she received several outstanding job offers. She decided to accept the job offer that she received from one of the nation's largest consulting firms. She believed that this job would allow her to gain experience in several areas of marketing and to engage in a variety of exciting work. Her last day on campus, she told her favorite professor: "This has got to be one of the happiest days of my life, getting such a great career opportunity."
>
> Recently, while visiting the college placement office, the professor was surprised to hear that Connie had told the placement director that she was looking for another job. Since she had been with the consulting company less than a year, the professor was somewhat surprised. He decided to call Connie and find out why she wanted to change jobs. This is what she told him: "I guess you can say my first experience with the real world was a 'reality shock.' Since being with this company, I have done nothing but gather data on phone surveys. All day long, I sit and talk on the phone, asking questions and checking off the answers. In graduate school I was trained to be a manager, but here I am doing what any high school graduate can do. I talked to my boss, and he said that all employees have to pay their dues. Well, why didn't they tell me this while they were recruiting me? To say there was a conflict between the recruiting information and the real world would be a gross understatement. I'm an adult—why didn't they provide me with realistic job information, then let me decide if I wanted it? A little bit of accurate communication would have gone a long way."

Our model includes three behavioral processes that contribute to effective organizational performance: communication; decision making; and organizational change and development.

Communication Process. Organizational survival is related to the ability of management to receive, transmit, and act on information. The communication process links the organization to its environment as well as to its parts. Information flows to and from the organization and within the organization. Information integrates the activities of the organization with the demands of the environment. But information also integrates the internal activities of the organization. Connie Vick's problem arose because the information that flowed *from* the organization was different from the information that flowed *within* the organization.

Decision-Making Process.   The quality of decision making in an organization depends on selecting proper goals and identifying means for achieving them. With good integration of *behavioral* and *structural* factors, management can increase the probability that high-quality decisions will be made. Connie Vick's experience illustrates inconsistent decision making by different organizational units (personnel and marketing) in the hiring of new employees. Organizations rely on individual decisions as well as group decisions, and effective management requires knowledge of both types of decisions.

Organizational Change and Development Processes.   Managers sometimes must consider the possibility that effective organizational functioning can be improved by making significant changes in the total organization. Organizational change and development represent planned attempts to improve overall individual, group, and organizational performance. Connie Vick might well have been spared the disappointment she experienced had an organizational development effort uncovered and corrected the inconsistent communication and decision making which brought about Connie's unhappiness. Concerted, planned, and evaluative efforts to improve organizational functioning have great potential for success.

PERFORMANCE OUTCOMES: INDIVIDUAL, GROUP, AND ORGANIZA- TIONAL

Individual performance contributes to group performance, which in turn contributes to organizational performance. In truly effective organizations, however, management helps create a positive synergy, that is, a whole that is greater than the sum of its parts.

No one measure, or criterion, adequately reflects performance at any level. The next chapter introduces the idea that organizational performance must be considered in terms of multiple measures within a time frame. But ineffective performance at any level is a signal to management to take corrective actions. All of management's corrective actions will focus on elements of organizational *behavior, structure,* or *processes.*

SUMMARY AND INTRODUCTION

The focus of this book is on the developing subdiscipline of the field of management known as organizational behavior. Organizational behavior studies the behavior of individuals and groups in organizational settings. The framework within which the contents of this book are presented is based on three characteristics common to *all* organizations: the *behavior* of individuals and groups; the *structure* of organizations (that is, the design of the fixed relationships that exist among the jobs in the organization; and the *processes* (for example, communication and decision making) that make the organization "tick" and give it life. Our model, presented in Figure 1–2, has evolved from our concept of what all organizations are.

Thus, our purpose in this book is to review theory and research on what we describe as the behavior, structure, and processes of organizations.[4] A major interest of this book is the behavioral sciences that have produced theory and research concerning human behavior in organizations. However, no attempt has been made here to write a book that will teach the reader "behavioral science." The continuous theme throughout the book is *the management of organizational behavior.* Given this theme, our task is to *interpret* behavioral science materials so that students of management can comprehend the behavior, structure, and process phenomena as these are affected by actions of managers.[5] It is our intention to provide the reader with a basis for applying the relevant contributions of behavioral science to the management of organizations.

Since our goal is to help you become a more effective manager, the next chapter deals with this topic: managing organizations effectively. It serves as the foundation for studying the remainder of the book.

REVIEW AND DISCUSSION QUESTIONS

1. "The effectiveness of any organization is influenced greatly by human behavior." Describe what this may mean in terms of actual experiences you have had with organizations.

2. Why is it useful to distinguish three levels of behavior—individual, group, and organizational—when discussing behavior in organizations?

3. "As organizations increase in size and complexity, managing the behavior of organizational members becomes more difficult." Do you agree or disagree with this statement? Why?

4. Why is organizational behavior considered to be an interdisciplinary field?

5. Organizations are characterized by their goal-directed behavior. So are people. How is the study of organizations similar to the study of people? How is it different?

6. Why is the use of the scientific method a better approach to studying organizational behavior than relying on "common sense"?

7. Frequently, organizations are described in terms used to refer to personality characteristics—dynamic, greedy, creative, conservative, etc. Is this a valid way to describe organizations? Does this mean that the people in the organization possess the same characteristics?

8. Organizations are influenced by the environment in which they operate; in turn, organizations influence their environments. List examples of both types of influence that you can recall from personal experience.

9. "Organizations exist to serve society; society should not have to serve organizations." Do you agree or disagree with this statement? Why or why not?

10. Discuss how organizational structure and processes affect behavior in organizations. If structures and processes are ideal, does that mean behavioral interactions also will be ideal? Explain.

---

[4] See Ronald G. Corwin and Karen Seashore Louis, "Organizational Barriers to the Use of Research," *Administrative Science Quarterly,* December 1982, pp. 623–40.

[5] Paul Shrivastava and Ian I. Mitroff, "Enhancing Organizational Research Utilization: The Role of Decision Makers' Assumptions," *Academy of Management Review,* January 1984, pp. 18–26.

MANAGING BEHAVIOR IN ORGANIZATIONS

LEARNING OBJECTIVES

DEFINE production, efficiency, satisfaction, adaptiveness, and development as effectiveness criteria.

DESCRIBE the goal approach to defining and measuring effectiveness.

DISCUSS the relationship between organizational culture and effectiveness.

COMPARE the meanings of the terms mission, goal, and objectives.

IDENTIFY the major elements of the systems theory approach.

This chapter discusses how managers influence individual, group, and organizational effectiveness. A major purpose of this text is to contribute to the academic preparation of future managers, so this issue must be introduced at this stage to lay the groundwork for the chapters to follow. Whether managers do (or can) influence **effectiveness** is difficult to determine, even though many instances can be cited where corporate excellence was achieved through management excellence. We are reluctant to infer general principles from these instances. Although many writers on management and organizational behavior have attempted to develop a general theory of management, no such theory exists at present. But much is known about management and its role in organizations. This textbook is based on the belief that valuable insights about management can be found in the literature of organizational behavior.

As noted in the previous chapter, the field of organizational behavior identifies three *levels of analysis:* (1) individual, (2) group, and (3) organizational. Theorists and researchers in organizational behavior have accumulated a vast amount of information about each of these levels. These three levels of analysis also coincide with the three levels of managerial responsibility. That is, managers are responsible for the effectiveness of individuals, groups of individuals, and organizations themselves. For example, Lee Iacocca, the widely respected president of Chrysler Corp., took on the difficult task of improving the effectiveness of Chrysler (the organizational level of responsibility). By all accounts, Iacocca met that responsibility. But how did he do it? And by what criteria do we assess the degree to which Chrysler became more effective? Iacocca might respond that Chrysler became more effective because individuals on the assembly lines produced a higher-quality product (the individual level of responsibility), because the engineering divisions designed more reliable automobiles (the group level of responsibility), and because the federal government guaranteed loans that forestalled bankruptcy (the organizational level of responsibility).

Each of these explanations for the improved effectiveness of Chrysler Corp. involves different levels of analysis. Each of these levels involves a different perspective on effectiveness. The next section discusses these perspectives in greater detail.

PERSPECTIVES ON EFFECTIVENESS

Three perspectives on effectiveness can be identified. At the most basic level is *individual* effectiveness. The individual perspective emphasizes the task performance of specific employees or members of the organization. The tasks to be performed are parts of jobs or positions in the organization. Managers routinely assess individual effectiveness through performance evaluation processes. These are the bases for salary increases, promotions, and other rewards available in the organization.

Individuals seldom work in isolation from others in the organization. In fact, the usual situation is for individuals to work together in groups. Thus, you must consider yet another perspective on effectiveness: *group effectiveness.* In some instances, the effectiveness of a group is simply the sum of the contributions of all its members. For example, a group of scientists working on unrelated projects would be effective to the extent that each individual scientist is effective. In other instances, group effectiveness is more than the sum of the individual contributions. An example is an assembly line, which produces a finished product as a result of the contributions of each individual.

The third perspective is that of *organizational* effectiveness. Since organizations consist of individuals and groups, organizational effectiveness is a function of individual and group effectiveness. However, organizational effectiveness is more than the sum of individual and group effectiveness. Organizations are able to obtain higher levels of performance than the sum of the performance of their parts. In fact, the rationale for using organizations as means for doing the work of society is that they can accomplish more than is possible through individual efforts.

From the standpoint of society, the effectiveness of business organizations is critical. Publications that report business and economic events occasionally survey opinions about business performance. One such survey is reported in the following *OBM* Encounter:

 ENCOUNTER

FORTUNE'S SURVEY OF THE MOST ADMIRED COMPANIES

In 1985, *Fortune* magazine reported the results of a poll of 8,000 corporate executives, directors, and financial analysts to determine which companies they held in highest esteem. Half of these officials responded to *Fortune*'s request to rate 10 companies in their respective industries on eight "attributes of reputation," using a 10-point scale running from poor (1)

	Attribute	Company	Score
1.	Quality of Management	IBM	9.15
2.	Quality of products or service	Dow Jones	9.04
3.	Innovativeness	Citicorp	8.93
4.	Long-term investment value	IBM	8.83
5.	Financial soundness	IBM	9.41
6.	Ability to attract, develop and keep talented people	Hewlett-Packard	8.36
7.	Community and environmental responsibility	Eastman Kodak	8.35
8.	Use of corporate assets	IBM	8.52

to excellent (10) on each attribute. The eight attributes, the highest rated company on each attribute, and the companies' scores are listed in the actual article.

Overall, the three most admired companies, according to the *Fortune* survey, were IBM (8.44), Coca-Cola (8.34), and Dow Jones (8.35).   □

Source: Patricia Sellers, "America's Most Admired Corporations," *Fortune,* January 7, 1985, pp. 18–30.

The relationship among the three perspectives on effectiveness is shown in Figure 2–1.[1] The connecting arrows imply that group effectiveness depends on individual effectiveness and that organizational effectiveness depends on group effectiveness. The exact relationships among the three perspectives vary, depending on such factors as the type of organization, the work it does, and the technology used in doing that work. The figure reflects the cumulative effects of the three perspectives. Thus, group effectiveness is larger than the sum of individual effectiveness because of the gains realized through the combined efforts of individuals and groups.

FIGURE 2–1

Three Perspectives on Effectiveness

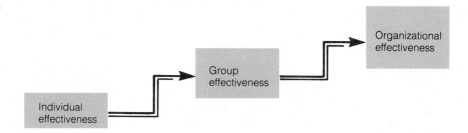

The job of management is to identify the *causes* of organizational, group, and individual effectiveness. As noted in Figure 2–2, each level of effectiveness can be considered a variable that is caused by other variables, namely, the causes of effectiveness. Sources of individual effectiveness include ability, skill, knowledge, attitude, motivation, and stress. Individual differences in these areas account for most of the differences in individual effectiveness. Some of the most common causes of the differences in group and organizational effectiveness are also noted in Figure 2–2.[2] Potential sources of effectiveness are discussed at length in subsequent chapters. However, the reality

---

[1] The following discussion is based on David J. Lawless, *Effective Management: A Social Psychological Approach* (Englewood Cliffs, NJ: Prentice-Hall, 1972), pp. 391–99.

[2] One of the more ambitious attempts to determine the causes of organizational effectiveness is reported in John Child, "Managerial and Organizational Factors Associated with Company Performance—Part I," *Journal of Management Studies,* October 1972, pp. 175–80; and John Child, "Managerial and Organizational Factors Associated with Company Performance—Part II: A Contingency Analysis," *Journal of Management Studies,* February 1975, pp. 12–27. This study did not reach definitive conclusions, due no doubt to the inherent complexity of the organizational effectiveness concept.

FIGURE 2–2

**Causes of
Effectiveness**

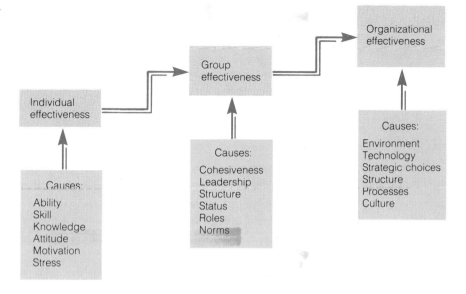

of organizational life is that there are few unambiguous cause-effect relation-ships. In most instances, to make evaluation judgments, you must take into account multiple causes and circumstances.[3]

There is no universal agreement as to what the term *effectiveness* means, in either a theoretical sense or a practical sense. How you define effectiveness, however, can reflect adherence to one of two general approaches: the goal approach and the systems theory approach. These two approaches to defining effectiveness are most often contrasted in both the literature and the practice of organizational behavior.[4]

THE GOAL APPROACH

The **goal approach** to defining and measuring effectiveness is the oldest and most widely used evaluation technique.[5] In the view of this approach, an organization exists to accomplish goals. An early but influential practitioner and writer on management and organizational behavior stated: "What we mean by effectiveness . . . is the accomplishment of recognized objectives of cooperative effort. The degree of accomplishment indicates the degree

---

[3] Jeffrey D. Ford and Deborah A. Schnellenberg, "Conceptual Issues of Linkage in Assessment of Organizational Performance," *Academy of Management Review,* January 1982, pp. 49–58.

[4] Kim Cameron, "Critical Questions in Assessing Organizational Effectiveness," *Organizational Dynamics,* Autumn 1980, pp. 66–80, identifies two other approaches: the internal process approach and the strategic constituencies approach. The former can be subsumed under the systems-theory approach, and the latter is a special case of the multiple-goal approach.

[5] Stephen Strasser, J. D. Eveland, Gaylord Cummins, O. Lynn Deniston, and John H. Romani, "Conceptualizing the Goal and System Models of Organizational Effectiveness," *Journal of Management Studies,* July 1981, p. 323.

of effectiveness."[6] The idea that organizations, as well as individuals and groups, should be evaluated in terms of goal accomplishment has widespread appeal. The goal approach reflects purposefulness, rationality, and achievement—the fundamental tenets of contemporary Western societies.

Many management practices are based on the goal approach. One widely used practice is management by objectives. Using this practice, managers specify in advance the goals that they expect their subordinates to accomplish and periodically evaluate the degree to which the subordinates have accomplished these goals. The actual specifics of management by objectives vary from case to case. In some instances, the manager and subordinate discuss the objectives and attempt to reach mutual agreement. In other instances, the manager simply assigns the goals. The idea of management by objectives is to specify in advance the goals that are to be sought.

Yet the goal approach, for all of its appeal and apparent simplicity, has problems.[7] These are some of its more widely recognized difficulties:

1. Goal achievement is not readily measurable for organizations that do not produce tangible outputs. For example, the goal of a college may be "to provide a liberal education at a fair price." The question is: How would one know whether the college achieves that goal? What is a liberal education? What is a fair price? For that matter, what is education?

2. Organizations attempt to achieve more than one goal, and achievement of one goal often precludes or diminishes their ability to achieve other goals. A business firm may state that its goal is to attain a maximum profit and to provide absolutely safe working conditions. These two goals are in conflict, because each of these goals is achieved at the expense of the other.

3. The very existence of a common set of "official" goals to which all members are committed is questionable. Various researchers have noted the difficulty of obtaining consensus among managers as to the specific goals of their organization.[8]

4. Sometimes, even if stated goals are achieved, the organization is considered to be ineffective. The following *OBM* Encounter illustrates this.

Despite the problems of the goal approach, it continues to exert a powerful influence on the development of management and organizational behavior theory and practice. Saying that managers should achieve the goals of the organization is easy. Knowing *how* to do this is more difficult. The alternative to the goal approach is the systems theory approach. Through systems theory, the concept of effectiveness can be defined in terms that enable managers to take a broader view of the organization and to understand the causes of individual, group, and organizational effectiveness.

---

[6] Chester I. Barnard, *The Functions of the Executive* (Cambridge, MA: Harvard University Press, 1938), p. 55.

[7] E. Frank Harrison, *Management and Organization* (Boston: Houghton Mifflin, 1978), pp. 404–14, is an excellent survey of limitations of the goal approach.

[8] G. H. Gaertner, and S. Ramnarayan, "Organizational Effectiveness: An Alternative Perspective," *Academy of Management Review*, January 1983, pp. 97–107.

ENCOUNTER

WHEN GOAL ATTAINMENT DOESN'T LEAD TO EFFECTIVENESS

Defining organizational effectiveness in terms of goal attainment is a tried-and-true approach. That does not mean, however, that it is always appropriate for all organizations. Sometimes, for example, an organization may be effective in an area in which it has no stated goals. An example of this is NASA, which was successful during the 1960s in producing numerous useful consumer products, even though it had no stated goals relating to this area. More significant, however, is the situation in which stated goals are attained, yet the organization is ineffective. Two examples illustrate this case:

1. Boise Cascade was one of America's fastest-growing organizations in the 1960s. It had set as a goal an annual per-share earnings growth of 20 percent. For an impressive 12 consecutive years, it reached or exceeded this ambitious goal. In order to do so, however, Boise Cascade engaged in practices and undertook projects that were inherently risky and that ignored the concerns of various environmental groups. Eventually, this policy took its toll and brought about bankruptcy and reorganization in 1972.

2. The Nestle Company had an explicit goal of providing nutritional supplements to infants in Third World countries. Nestle was so successful in achieving this goal—and, in the process, replacing natural mother's milk with formula—that the company was boycotted and received a great deal of negative publicity. Nestle was perceived as a prime contributor to starvation and malnutrition in underdeveloped countries. □

Source: Adapted from Kim Cameron, "Critical Questions in Assessing Organizational Effectiveness," *Organizational Dynamics,* Autumn 1980, pp. 66–80.

THE SYSTEMS THEORY APPROACH

Systems theory enables you to describe the behavior of organizations both internally and externally. Internally, you can see how and why people within organizations perform their individual and group tasks. Externally, you can relate the transactions of organizations with other organizations and institutions. All organizations acquire resources from the outside environment of which they are a part and, in turn, provide goods and services demanded by the larger environment. *Managers must deal simultaneously with the internal and external aspects of organizational behavior.* This essentially complex process can be simplified, for analytical purposes, by employing the basic concepts of systems theory.

In systems theory, the organization is seen as one element of a number of elements that act interdependently. The flow of inputs and outputs is the basic starting point in describing the organization. In the simplest terms, the organization takes resources (inputs) from the larger system (environment), processes these resources, and returns them in changed form (output). Figure 2–3 displays the fundamental elements of the organization as a system.

Systems theory can also describe the behavior of individuals and groups. The "inputs" of individual behavior are "causes" that arise from the work-

FIGURE 2–3

**The Basic
Elements of a
System**

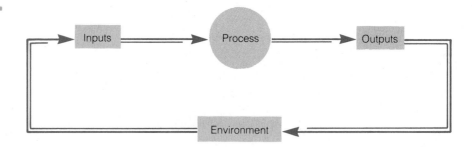

place. For example, the cause could be the directives of a manager to perform a certain task. The input (cause) is then acted on by the individual's mental and psychological processes to produce a particular outcome. The outcome that the manager prefers is, of course, compliance with the directive, but depending on the states of the individual's processes, the outcome could be noncompliance. Similarly, you can describe the behavior of a group in systems-theory terms. For example, the behavior of a group of employees to unionize (outcome) could be explained in terms of perceived managerial unfairness in the assignment of work (input) and the state of the group's cohesiveness (process). We use the terms of systems theory throughout this text to describe and explain the behavior of individuals and groups in organizations.

**SYSTEMS
THEORY AND
FEEDBACK**

The concept of the organization as a system that is related to a larger system introduces the importance of feedback. As mentioned, the organization is dependent on the environment not only for its inputs, but also for the acceptance of its outputs. It is critical, therefore, that the organization develop means for adjusting to environmental demands. The means for adjustment are information channels that enable the organization to recognize these demands. In business organizations, for example, market research is an important *feedback* mechanism. Other forms of feedback are customer complaints, employee comments, and financial reports.

   In simplest terms, feedback refers to information that reflects the outcomes of an act or a series of acts by an individual, a group, or an organization. Throughout this text, you will see the importance of feedback. Systems theory emphasizes the importance of responding to the content of the feedback information.

**EXAMPLES
OF THE INPUT-
OUTPUT CYCLE**

The business firm has two major categories of inputs: *human* and *natural resources.* Human inputs consist of the people who work in the firm. They contribute their time and energy to the organization in exchange for wages and other rewards, tangible and intangible. Natural resources consist of the nonhuman inputs processed or used in combination with the human element to provide other resources. A steel mill must have people and blast furnaces (along with other tools and machinery) to process iron ore into steel and steel products. An auto manufacturer takes steel, rubber, plastics, and fabrics and—in combination with people, tools, and equipment—uses them to make automobiles. A business firm survives as long as its output is purchased in the market in sufficient quantities and at prices that enable it to replenish its depleted stock of inputs.

Similarly, a university uses resources to teach students, to do research, and to provide technical information to society. The survival of a university depends on its ability to attract students' tuitions and taxpayers' dollars in sufficient amounts to pay the salaries of its faculty and staff, as well as the costs of other resources. If a university's output is rejected by the larger environment, so that students enroll elsewhere and taxpayers support other public endeavors, or if a university is guilty of expending too great an amount of resources in relation to its output, it will cease to exist. Like a business firm, a university must provide the right output at the right price if it is to survive.[9]

Systems theory emphasizes two important considerations: (1) the ultimate survival of the organization depends on its ability to *adapt to the demands of its environment,* and (2) in meeting these demands, the *total cycle of input-process-output must be the focus of managerial attention.* Therefore, the criteria of effectiveness must reflect each of these two considerations, and you must define effectiveness accordingly. The systems approach accounts for the fact that resources have to be devoted to activities that have little to do with achieving the organization's primary goal.[10] In other words, *adapting to the environment* and *maintaining the input-process-output flow* require that resources be allocated to activities that are only indirectly related to that goal.

THE TIME DIMENSION MODEL OF ORGANIZATIONAL EFFECTIVENESS

The concept of organizational effectiveness presented in this book relies on the previous discussion of systems theory, but we must develop one additional point: the dimension of time. Recall that two main conclusions of systems theory are: (1) that effectiveness criteria must reflect the entire input-process-output cycle, not simply output; and (2) that effectiveness criteria must reflect the interrelationships between the organization and its outside environment. Thus:

1. Organizational effectiveness is an all-encompassing concept that includes a number of component concepts.
2. The managerial task is to maintain the optimal balance among these components.

Much additional research is needed to develop knowledge about the components of effectiveness. There is little consensus not only about these relevant

---

[9] Kim Cameron, "Measuring Organizational Effectiveness in Institutions of Higher Education," *Administrative Science Quarterly,* December 1978, pp. 604–29.

[10] Amitai Etzioni, "Two Approaches to Organizational Analysis: A Critique and a Suggestion," in *Assessment of Organizational Effectiveness,* ed. Jaisingh Ghorpade (Santa Monica, CA: Goodyear Publishing, 1971), p. 36.

components but about the interrelationships *among them* and about the effects of managerial action on them.[11] In this textbook, we attempt to provide the basis for asking the right questions about what constitutes *effectiveness* and how those qualities that characterize it interact.

According to systems theory, an organization is an element of a larger system, the environment. With the passage of time, every organization takes, processes, and returns resources to the environment. The ultimate criterion of organizational effectiveness is whether the organization survives in the environment. Survival requires adaptation, and adaptation often involves predictable sequences. As the organization ages, it probably will pass through different phases. Some writers suggest that an organization passes through a life cycle. It forms, develops, matures, and declines in relation to environmental circumstances. Organizations and entire industries do rise and fall. Today, the personal computer industry is on the rise and the steel industry is declining. Marketing experts acknowledge the existence of product-market life cycles. Organizations also seem to have life cycles. Consequently, the appropriate criteria of effectiveness must reflect the stage of the organization's life cycle.[12]

Managers and others with interests in the organization must have indicators that assess the probability of the organization's survival. In actual practice, managers use a number of short-run indicators of long-run survival. Among these indicators are measurements of productivity, efficiency, accidents, turnover, absenteeism, quality, rate of return, morale, and employee satisfaction.[13] Any of these criteria can be relevant for particular purposes. For simplicity, we will use three criteria of short-run effectiveness as representative of all such criteria. They are *production, efficiency,* and *satisfaction.*

Two other criteria complete the time dimension model: *adaptiveness* and *development.* These criteria reflect effectiveness in the intermediate time period. The relationships between these criteria and the time dimension are shown in Figure 2–4.

CRITERIA OF EFFECTIVENESS

In the time dimension model, criteria of effectiveness typically are stated in terms of the short run, the intermediate run, and the long run. Short-run criteria are those referring to the results of actions that conclude in a year or less. Intermediate-run criteria are applicable when you judge the effectiveness of an individual, group, or organization for a longer time period, perhaps five years. Long-run criteria are those for which the indefinite future is applicable. We will discuss five general categories of effectiveness criteria, beginning with those of a short-run nature.

---

[11] R. F. Zammuto, "A Comparison of Multiple Constituency Models of Organizational Effectiveness," *Academy of Management Review,* October 1984, pp. 606–616.

[12] Kim S. Cameron and David A. Whetten, "Perceptions of Organizational Effectiveness Over Organizational Life Cycles," *Administrative Science Quarterly,* December 1981, pp. 525–44; and R. E. Quinn and Kim Cameron, "Organizational Life Cycles and Shifting Criteria of Effectiveness: Some Preliminary Evidence," *Management Science,* January 1983, pp. 33–51.

[13] John P. Campbell, "On the Nature of Organizational Effectiveness," in *New Perspectives on Organizational Effectiveness,* ed. Paul S. Goodman and Johannes M. Pennings (San Francisco: Jossey-Bass, 1979), pp. 36–39.

FIGURE 2–4

Time Dimension
Model of
Effectiveness

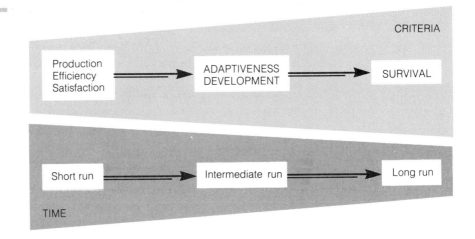

PRODUCTION

As used here, **production** reflects the ability of the organization to produce the quantity and quality of output that the environment demands. The concept excludes any consideration of efficiency, which is defined below. The measures of production include profit, sales, market share, students graduated, patients released, documents processed, clients served, and the like. These measures relate directly to the output that is consumed by the organization's customers and clients.

EFFICIENCY

Efficiency is defined as the ratio of outputs to inputs. This short-run criterion focuses attention on the entire input-process-output cycle, yet it emphasizes the input and process elements. Among the measures of efficiency are rate of return on capital or assets, unit cost, scrappage and waste, downtime, occupancy rates, and cost per patient, per student, or per client. Measures of efficiency must inevitably be in ratio terms; the ratios of benefit to cost or to time are the general forms of these measures.

SATISFACTION

The idea of the organization as a social system requires that some consideration be given to the benefits received by its participants, as well as by its customers and clients. **Satisfaction** and morale are similar terms referring to the extent to which the organization meets the needs of employees. We use the term *satisfaction* to refer to this criterion. Measures of satisfaction include employee attitudes, turnover, absenteeism, tardiness, and grievances.

ADAPTIVENESS

Adaptiveness is the extent to which the organization *can and does* respond to internal and external changes. Adaptiveness in this context refers to management's ability to sense changes in the environment as well as changes within the organization itself. Ineffectiveness in achieving production, efficiency, and satisfaction can signal the need to adapt managerial practices and policies. Or the environment may demand different outputs or provide different inputs, thus necessitating change. To the extent that the organization cannot or does not adapt, its survival is jeopardized.

How can you really know whether the organization is *effectively adaptive?*

There are short-run measures of effectiveness, but there are no specific and concrete measures of adaptiveness. Management can implement policies that encourage a sense of readiness for change, and there are certain managerial practices that, if implemented, facilitate adaptiveness. For example, managers can invest in employee training programs and career counseling. They can encourage and reward innovativeness and risk-taking behavior. Yet, when the time comes for an adaptive response, the organization either adapts or it does not adapt—and that is the ultimate measure.

DEVELOPMENT   This criterion measures the ability of the organization to increase its capacity to deal with environmental demands. An organization must invest in itself to increase its chances of survival in the long run. The usual **development** efforts are training programs for managerial and nonmanagerial personnel. More recently the range of organizational development has expanded to include a number of psychological and sociological approaches.[14]

Time considerations enable you to evaluate effectiveness in the short, intermediate, and long run. For example, you could evaluate a particular organization as effective in terms of production, satisfaction, and efficiency criteria but as ineffective in terms of adaptiveness and development. A manufacturer of buggy whips may be optimally effective because it can produce buggy whips better and faster than any other producer in the short run, but with little chance of survival because no one wants to buy them. Thus, *maintaining optimal balance means, in part, balancing the organization's performance over time.*

The time dimension model effectiveness enables us to understand the work of managers in organizations. The basic job of managers is to identify and influence the causes of individual, group, and organizational effectiveness in the short, intermediate, and long run. Let us examine the nature of managerial work in that light.

THE NATURE OF MANAGERIAL WORK

Theories describing managerial work are many and varied.[15] The first attempts to describe managerial work were undertaken in the early 1900s by writers of the Classical School of Management.[16] The writers of the Classical School

---

[14] Raymond A. Katzell and Richard A. Guzzo, "Psychological Approaches to Productivity Improvement," *American Psychologist,* April 1983, pp. 468–72.

[15] Discussions of the history of management thought can be found in Daniel A. Wren, *The Evolution of Management Thought* (New York: Ronald Press, 1972); and Claude S. George, Jr., *The History of Management Thought (2nd Edition)* (Englewood Cliffs, NJ: Prentice-Hall, 1972).

[16] The term *Classical School of Management* refers to the ideas developed by a group of practitioners who wrote of their experiences in management. Notable contributors to these ideas include Frederick W. Taylor, *Principles of Management* (New York: Harper & Row, 1911); Henri Fayol, *General and Industrial Management,* trans. J. A. Conbrough (Geneva: International Management Institute, 1929); James D. Mooney, *The Principles of Organization* (New York: Harper & Row, 1947); and James D. Mooney, *The Elements of Administration* (New York: Harper & Row, 1944).

proposed that managerial work consists of distinct, yet interrelated, *functions* which, taken together, constitute the *managerial process*. The view has prevailed that management should be defined, described, and analyzed in terms of what managers do.

Management can be defined as a *process*, a series of actions, activities, or operations that lead to some end. The definition of management should also recognize that the process is undertaken by more than one person in most organizations. The definition should be broad enough to describe management wherever it is practiced, yet specific enough to identify differences in the relative importance of the functions associated with a particular manager's job.

The concept of management developed here is based on the assumption that the necessity for managing arises whenever work is specialized and is undertaken by two or more persons. Under such circumstances, the specialized work must be *coordinated*, and this creates the necessity for performing managerial work. The nature of managerial work, then, is to coordinate the work of others by performing four management functions: *planning, organizing, leading,* and *controlling*. In each case, the desired outcome of the function is to improve work performance. The first readings article in this chapter, by Cummings, identifies a performance orientation as being an important element in characterizing the field of organizational behavior. We agree with this and place a great deal of emphasis throughout this text on performance and its improvement.

PLANNING EFFECTIVE PERFORMANCE

The planning function includes defining the ends to be achieved and determining *appropriate means to achieve the defined ends*. Planning activities can be complex or simple, implicit or explicit, impersonal or personal. For example, the sales manager who is forecasting the demand for the firm's major product may rely on complex econometric models or on casual conversations with salespersons in the field. The intended outcomes of planning activities are mutual understandings about what the members of the organization should be attempting to achieve. These understandings may be reflected in the form of complicated plans that specify the intended results, or they may be reflected in a general agreement among the members.

Discussions of planning often are hampered by the absence of definitions of such terms as mission, goal, and objective. In some instances, the terms are used interchangeably, particularly *goal* and *objective*. In other instances, the terms are defined specifically, but there is no general agreement over the definitions. Depending on their backgrounds and purposes, managers and authors use the terms differently. However, the pivotal position of planning as a management function requires us to make very explicit the meanings of these key concepts.

Mission.   Society expects organizations to serve specific purposes. These purposes are the missions of organizations. **Missions** are criteria for assessing the long-run effectiveness of an organization. Effective managers state the mission of their organization in terms of those conditions that, if realized, will assure the organization's survival. Statements of mission are found in laws, articles of incorporation, and other extraorganizational sources. Mission statements are broad, abstract, and value-laden, and thus are subject to various interpretations. For example, the mission of a state public health department—as expressed in the law that created it—mandates the agency to "protect and promote the health and welfare of the citizens of the Commonwealth." It is from this source that the organization will create its specific programs.

Goals.   **Goals** are future states or conditions that contribute to the fulfillment of the organization's mission. A goal is somewhat more concrete and specific than a mission. Goals can be stated in terms of production, efficiency, and satisfaction. For example, one goal of a public health agency could be stated as "the eradication of tuberculosis as a health hazard by the end of 1990." In a business setting, a goal might be "to have viable sales outlets established in every major population center of the country by the end of 1989." It is entirely possible for an organization to have multiple goals that contribute to its mission. For example, a hospital may pursue patient care, research, and training. Universities typically state three significant goals: teaching, research, and community service. The existence of multiple goals places great pressure on managers not only to coordinate the routine operations of the units that strive for these goals but also to plan and allocate scarce resources to the goals.

Objectives.   **Objectives** refer to statements of accomplishment that are to be achieved in the short run, usually one year. The public health agency's objective can be stated as "to reduce the incidence of tuberculosis from 6 per 10,000 to 4 per 10,000 by the end of the current year." The firm seeking to have sales outlets in all major population centers could state its current year's objective as "to have opened and begun operations in Chicago, Los Angeles, Louisville, and New York." Thus, goals are derived from the organization's mission, and objectives are derived from the goals.

A coherent set of missions, goals, and objectives defines the scope and direction of the organization's activities. Planning involves specifying not only where the organization is going, but also how it is to get there. Alternatives must be analyzed and evaluated in terms of criteria that follow from the mission, goals, and objectives. Thus, managers by their own decisions can affect how they and their organizations will be evaluated. Managers determine what ends are legitimate and, therefore, what criteria are relevant. And once the determination of appropriate means has been completed, the next managerial function—organizing—must be undertaken.

ORGANIZING EFFECTIVE PERFORMANCE

The organizing function includes *all managerial activities that are taken to translate the required planned activities into a structure of tasks and authority.* In a practical sense, the organizing function involves specific activities.

Defining the Nature and Content of Each Job in the Organization.   The tangible results of this activity are job specifications, position descriptions, or task definitions. These indicate what is expected of jobholders in terms of responsibilities, outcomes, and objectives. In turn, the skills, abilities, and training required to meet the defined expectations are also specified.

Determining the Bases for Grouping Jobs Together.   The essence of defining jobs is specialization, that is, dividing the work. But once the overall task has been subdivided into jobs, the jobs must be put into groups, or departments. The managerial decision involves selecting the appropriate bases. For example, all of the jobs that require similar machinery may be grouped together, or the manager may decide to group all of the jobs according to the product or service they produce.

Deciding the Size of the Group.   The purpose of grouping jobs is to enable a person to supervise the group's activities. Obviously, there is a limit to the number of jobs that one person can supervise, but the precise number will vary depending on the situation. For example, it is possible to supervise more jobs that are similar and simple, than jobs that are dissimilar and complex. The supervisor of hourly workers can manage up to 25 or 30 employees, but the director of research scientists can manage far fewer, perhaps only 8 to 10.

Delegating Authority to the Assigned Manager.   The preceding activities create groups of jobs with defined tasks. It then becomes necessary to determine the extent to which managers of the groups are allowed to make decisions and use the resources of the group without higher approval. This is **authority.**

Once the structure of task and authority is in place, it must be given life. People perform jobs, and management must recruit and select the appropriate individuals who will perform the jobs. The process of finding and placing people in jobs is termed *staffing*. In some large organizations, specialized units such as personnel perform staffing activities. An important cause of individual *effectiveness* is a good fit between job requirements and individual abilities. Thus, even when staffing is performed by a specialized unit, the activity remains an important management responsibility.

The interrelationships between planning and organizing are apparent. The planning function results in the determination of organizational ends and means; that is, it defines the "whats" and "hows." The organizing function results in the determination of the "whos," that is, *who will do what with whom to achieve the desired end results*. The structure of tasks and authority should facilitate the fulfillment of planned results, if the next management function, leading, is performed properly.

LEADING EFFECTIVE PERFORMANCE

Leading *involves the manager in close, day-to-day contact with individuals and groups*. Thus, leading is uniquely personal and interpersonal. Even though planning and organizing provide guidelines and directives in the form of plans, job descriptions, organization charts, and policies, it is people who do the work. And people frequently are unpredictable. They have unique needs, aspirations, personalities, and attitudes. Thus, they each perceive the workplace and their jobs differently. Managers must take into account these unique perceptions and behaviors and somehow direct them toward common purposes.

Leading places the manager squarely in the arena of individual and group behavior. To function in this arena, you must have knowledge of individual differences and motivation, group behavior, power, and politics. In short, being a leader requires knowledge of ways to influence individuals and groups to accept and pursue organizational objectives, often at the expense of personal objectives.

Leading involves the day-to-day interactions between managers and their subordinates. In these interactions, the full panorama of human behavior is evident: individuals work, play, communicate, compete, accept and reject others, join groups, leave groups, receive rewards, and cope with stress. Of all the management functions, leading is the one most humanly oriented.

CONTROLLING EFFECTIVE PERFORMANCE

The controlling function includes *activities that managers undertake to assure that actual outcomes are consistent with planned outcomes.* Three basic conditions must exist to undertake control: standards, information, and corrective action.

Standards. Norms of acceptable outcomes, standards, must be spelled out. These standards reflect goals and objectives and usually are found in accounting, production, marketing, financial, and budgeting documents. In more specific ways, standards are reflected in procedures, performance criteria, rules of conduct, professional ethics, and work rules. Standards therefore reflect desirable levels of achievement.

Information. Actual and planned outcomes must be compared using appropriate and reliable information. Many organizations have developed sophisticated information systems that provide managers with control data. Prime examples are standard cost accounting and quality control systems used extensively by modern manufacturing firms. In other instances, the sources of information consist of nothing more than managers' observations of the behavior of people assigned to their department.

Corrective Action. If actual outcomes are ineffective, managers must take corrective action. Without the ability to take corrective action, the controlling function has no point or purpose. Corrective action is made possible through the organizing function—if managers have been assigned the authority to take action.

Simply stated, managers undertake control to determine *whether* intended results are achieved and if not, *why* not. The conclusions managers reach because of their controlling activities are that the planning function is faulty or that the organizing function is faulty, or both. Controlling, then, is the completion of a logical sequence. The activities that controlling comprises include employee selection and placement, materials inspection, performance evaluation, financial statement analysis, and other well-recognized managerial techniques.

Describing management in terms of the four functions of planning, organizing, leading, and controlling is certainly not complete. There is nothing in this description that indicates the specific behaviors or activities associated with each function. Nor is there any recognition of the relative importance of these functions for overall organizational effectiveness. However, these four functions conveniently and adequately define management.

The functions of management require the application of technical and administrative skills. They also require the application of human relations skills, the ability to deal with and relate to *people*. The literature of organizational behavior stresses the importance of people. Many observers and practitioners of management believe that managing people effectively is the key to improving the performance of contemporary corporations.

MANAGERIAL WORK AND THE BEHAVIOR, STRUCTURE, AND PROCESSES OF ORGANIZATIONS

The concept of managerial work developed in the preceding pages can now be brought into perspective. This textbook focuses on the *behavior of individuals and groups in organizations*. The purpose of managers in organizations is to achieve coordinated behavior so that an organization is judged effective by those who evaluate its record. Those who evaluate organizations can be concerned with any number of specific or general criteria and with output, process, or input measures.[17] To achieve coordinated behavior and to satisfy evaluators, managers engage in activities intended to *plan, organize, lead,* and *control* behavior. Major factors in determining individual and group behavior are task and authority relationships.[18] Therefore, managers must design organizational *structures* and *processes* to facilitate communication among employees.

The relationships among management, organizations, and effectiveness seem to be straightforward. Effective individual, group, and organizational performance should result from good planning, organizing, leading, and controlling. But organizations are not that simple. Such management writers as Peters and Waterman have focused attention on the importance of organizational *culture*.[19]

ORGANIZA-TIONAL CULTURE

According to Peters and Waterman, effective organizations have internal cultures that reinforce the importance of excellence. *Culture* has various meanings. Kilmann, in the second readings article accompanying this chapter, sees culture as the organization's soul—a style or characteristic that may

---

[17] Frank Hoy and Don Hellriegel, "The Kilmann and Herden Model of Organizational Effectiveness for Small Business Managers," *Academy of Management Journal,* June 1982, pp. 308–22.

[18] Gregory H. Gaertner and S. Ramnarayan, "Organizational Effectiveness: An Alternative Perspective," *Academy of Management Review,* January 1983, pp. 97–107.

[19] Thomas J. Peters and Robert H. Waterman, Jr., *In Search of Excellence* (New York: Harper & Row, 1982).

exert far more influence than any single individual in the organization. For our purpose, culture means a system of shared *values* and *beliefs* that produce *norms* of behavior.[20] Values (what is important) and beliefs (how things work) interact to cause norms (how we *should* do things). Every organization has a culture, and that culture can be either a positive or negative force in achieving effective performance. The following *OBM* Encounter illustrates some examples of organizational culture.

 ENCOUNTER

DIFFERENT ORGANIZATIONS HAVE DIFFERENT CULTURES

Organizational cultures are reflections of values which a company believes are consistent with or necessary for achieving the objectives, goals, and mission it has set for itself. In some organizations the culture is so strong that the company is readily associated with it in the eyes of employees, customers and competitors. For example:

1. IBM's dominant value is customer service. The company keeps a hot line open 24 hours a day, seven days a week, to service IBM products. IBM service engineers will not hesitate to spend their own money for traveling to deal with a customer complaint. The engineers know that the company will reimburse such outlays without hesitation.
2. At Hewlett-Packard, entrepreneurship is a dominant value. Every employee acts as an entrepreneur experimenting with new ideas, taking risks, and courting failure. Similarly, Atlantic-Richfield stresses entrepreneurship. Operating personnel have the autonomy to bid on promising fields with prior approval from above.
3. Digital Equipment Corporation places a great deal of emphasis on innovation, which creates freedom with responsibility. Employees can set their own hours, but are expected to articulate and support their activities with evidence of tangible progress.
4. At Delta Air Lines, where a focus on customer service leads to high value being placed on teamwork, employees will, without hesitation or fear of reprisal, cross job lines to substitute in other task areas to keep planes flying and baggage moving.

Source: Bro Uttal, "The Corporate Culture Vultures," *Fortune*, October 17, 1983, p. 66; and "Corporate Culture: The Hard to Change Values that Spell Success or Failure," *Business Week*, October 27, 1980.

Negative cultures are counterproductive to management efforts to bring about performance improvements. Consider what can happen in the banking industry. Although there are exceptions, the cultures of contemporary banks on the whole emphasize values and beliefs that discourage the behavior required to compete in the recently deregulated banking industry. Bank cultures that value conservative, status quo behavior are incompatible with the need to be aggressive and competitive in the marketplace. Some banks have attempted major overhauls in their corporate cultures to make them

[20] Linda Smircich, "Concepts of Culture and Organizational Analysis," *Administrative Science Quarterly,* September 1983, p. 342.

FIGURE 2–5

**Organizational
Culture and Effectiveness**

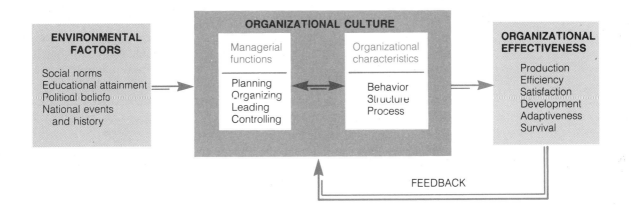

more dynamic. First Chicago and Bank of America are among the major banks that have gone through extensive efforts to redirect their cultures.[21]

The realization that organizational culture is an important cause of organizational effectiveness is widespread in management practice.[22] Not so widespread, however, is understanding of how management can change organizational culture when it inhibits organizational effectiveness. Many management practitioners and consultants in the field are experimenting with alternative change approaches.[23] And much more will be known as managers move into the 1990s. At this point, however, some tentative guidelines for changing culture can be suggested.[24]

First, you must understand that organizational culture—the system of shared values, beliefs, and norms—is the product of the interaction among the managerial functions; the organization's behavior, structure, and process; and the larger environment in which the organization exists. As shown in Figure 2–5, organizational culture encompasses both the managerial functions and organizational characteristics. Management is both a cause of and a part of organizational culture. The existing culture of any organization reflects past and present managerial planning, organizing, leading, and controlling activities. For example, contemporary bank cultures that value operations efficiency (keeping track of the customers' deposits and checking activity) do so because bank managers have stated missions, goals, and objectives

---

[21] Bro Uttal, ''The Corporate Culture Vultures,'' *Fortune,* October 17, 1983, p. 71.

[22] See ''Corporate Culture: The Hard-to-Change Values that Spell Success or Failure,'' *Business Week,* October 27, 1980, pp. 148–60.

[23] Uttal, ''Corporate Culture Vultures.''

[24] Vijay Sathe, ''Some Action Implications of Corporate Culture: A Manager's Guide to Action,'' *Organizational Dynamics,* August 1983, pp. 4–23.

in those terms. These managers evaluate employees in terms of accuracy—for example, "minimum teller errors"—and they publicly proclaim the importance of doing things right. Banking executives have created the culture by virtue of their own managerial actions, and they hire and socialize employees to adopt and accept the important beliefs and values of that culture.

If management can create organizational culture, management should be able to change it by the same means. Or so it would seem. But it is not that simple or easy. Cultures are self-reinforcing. Once in place, cultures provide stability and certainty for their members. Individuals know what is expected, what is important, and what to do. They quite naturally resist any threatened disruption of the existing culture. The issue of changing cultures is addressed in the second readings article in this chapter. Kilmann examines an approach to identify the need to change ("spotting culture gaps") and discusses how the change may be brought about ("closing gaps").

Managers must practice planning, organizing, leading, and controlling that are consistent with the beliefs and values of the desired culture. All four functions can contribute to changing the culture, but it is generally agreed that *leading* is the most important. By personal example and behavior, managers can demonstrate how things should be done. But they must be *capable* managers and *respected* leaders.

The intended effect of organizational structure and process is to predetermine what people will do, with whom they will do it, what decisions they will make, what information they will receive, and when, how, and how often they will perform certain actions and make certain decisions. Managers interact with other managers and with nonmanagers in individual and group settings to establish plans, policies, procedures, rules, job descriptions, reporting channels, and lines of authority and communication. All of these actions and interactions create an organizational culture that will have a significant impact, both positive and negative, on individual, group, and organizational effectiveness.

SUMMARY OF KEYPOINTS

A. Effectiveness, managerial process, and organizational culture are key concepts underlying the practice of management based on organizational behavior theory and research.

B. An overriding consideration documented in many studies of managerial work is that the managerial process is inherently a human process—people relating to people. The recognition of this fact establishes the importance of understanding human behavior in the workplace. The behavior of individuals and groups is important principally for achieving effective organizational performance, but the behavior of managers themselves must also be understood.

C. Managerial techniques are directed toward improving effectiveness. But to understand the impact of these techniques, you must develop an understanding of the concept of effectiveness. Although the term *effectiveness* is widely used, its meaning is not widely understood.

D. Two competing concepts of effectiveness derive from two competing theories of organizations. The goal theory is based on the idea that organizations are rational, purposive entities that pursue specific missions, goals, and objectives. Accordingly, how well organizations function—that is, how effective they are—is reckoned in terms of how successful they are in achieving their purposes. The systems theory assumes that organizations are social entities that exist as parts of a larger environment and that in order to survive they must function to satisfy the demands of that environment.

E. The time-dimension model of effectiveness is based on systems theory and adds to it the effects that occur as the organization moves through time. As the organization does so, there must be short- and intermediate-run indicators of its progress toward long-run survival. These indicators are the criteria of effectiveness, and they apply in the evaluation of individual, group, and organizational effectiveness.

F. Managerial work evolves from the need to coordinate work in organizations. By their nature, organizations exploit the benefits of specialization, but specialization requires coordination. Managers coordinate specialized work through the application of planning, organizing, leading, and controlling functions. These functions require that managers determine and influence the causes of individual, group, and organizational effectiveness.

G. Management work focuses on the behavior of individuals and groups and on the process and structure of organizations. The considerable interdependence of behavior, process, and structure complicates the efforts of management.

H. The interaction of managerial functions and organizational behavior, structure, and processes creates an organizational culture. This culture embodies the values, beliefs, and norms that influence the behavior of individuals and groups. The managerial challenge is to create and maintain organizational cultures that contribute to organizational effectiveness.

REVIEW AND DISCUSSION QUESTIONS

1. Using a university as an example, cite several specific ways of measuring individual, group, and organizational effectiveness.

2. Why should an organization's effectiveness be of concern to people who do not have any direct relationship with it?

3. "If an organization is not effective, its managers have not done their jobs." Do you agree or disagree with this statement? Explain.

4. Discuss the notion that, for some organizations, short-run effectiveness is the most important, while for others, intermediate-run effectiveness is more important, and for others still, long-run effectiveness is the most critical.

5. Is the goal approach to measuring effectiveness suitable for all three time periods and all three levels? Explain.

6. How does systems theory assist in understanding and predicting organizational behavior?

7. Feedback is necessary if organizations are to achieve and maintain effectiveness. Can you think of examples of organizations which failed or experienced great difficulty because they either did not receive or did not respond to feedback?

8. "People are paid to be productive, not to be satisfied." Do you agree with this statement? What are its implications in terms of achieving organizational effectiveness?

9. It has been said that "efficiency is getting anything done right and effectiveness is getting the right thing done." Comment.

10. How might organizational culture influence effectiveness? How might environmental factors influence organizational culture? What role does a manager have in influencing all these factors?

R1 TOWARD ORGANIZATIONAL BEHAVIOR

L. L. CUMMINGS.

Attempting to describe a field as dynamic and as multifaceted, or even as confusing, as Organizational Behavior (OB) is not a task for the timid. It may be a task that only the foolish, yet concerned, would even tackle.

What motivates one toward accepting such an undertaking? Two forces are operating. First, there is a clear need to parcel out knowledge into more understandable and convenient packages. Students, managers, and colleagues in other departments request that we respond to straightforward, honest questions like: What is OB? How is OB different from management? How is it different from human relations? It is difficult for students to understand the philosophy or the systematic nature of a program or curriculum if they cannot define the parts. Our credibility with the managerial world is damaged when OB comes out in executive programs as "a little of everything," as "a combination of behavioral jargon and common sense," or as "touchy-feely" without content. The field's lack of confidence in articulating its structure is occasionally reflected in ambiguous and fuzzy suggestions for improvement in the world that managers face.[1]

[1] This article was first developed as a paper for the 1976 National Academy of Management Convention. The author gratefully acknowledges the comments and critiques of: Michael Aiken, Alan Filley, Barbara Karmel, Johannes Pennings, Jeffrey Pfeffer, Donald Schwab, George Strauss, and Karl Weick.

Source: *Academy of Management Review,* January 1978, pp. 90–98.

Second, identification or assertion of the themes and constructs underlying OB, or any other discipline, represents an important platform for expanding knowledge. Without assumptions about what is included, excluded, and on the boundary, duplication among disciplines results. The efficiency of knowledge generation and transmission is hampered. Until a field is defined in relation to its intellectual cousins, it may develop in redundant directions. This leads to the usual awakening that parallel, and perhaps even superior, developments already have occurred in adjacent fields about which we are ignorant. Repetition of such occurrences in a field lessens its intellectual credibility among scholars. All of this is not to deny the benefits to be gained from cross-fertilization and exchange across subfields once these are delineated and common concerns and interests are discovered.

These are the forces underlying the concern. What is said here represents an unfinished product—a thought in process—not a finished, static, intellectually frozen definition. In fact, the argument is made that stimulating, dynamic fields are defined *in process* and that the processes of emergence and evolution should never end.

Perspectives on Organizational Behavior

Several partitions have been used in attempting to distinguish OB from related disciplines. Tracing some of these provides perspective on our task and builds a critical platform for appraising where the field is today.

Probably the most common segmentation of subfields relating behavior and organization is based on *units of analysis* where the units are differentiated by level of aggregation. Typically, using this framework, OB is defined as the study of individuals and groups within organizations. The units of analysis are individual and micro (e.g., dyadic) interactions among individuals. Organizational characteristics (e.g., structure, process, climate) are seen either as "givens" which assume a constant state or as independent variables whose variations are assumed to covary with or cause variations in the relevant dependent variables. These relevant dependent variables are measures of individual or micro unit affective and/or behavioral reactions.

Organizational Theory (OT) is typically defined by its focus upon the *organization as the unit of analysis*. Organizational structure, process, goals, technology, and, more recently, climate are the relevant dependent variables, assumed to vary systematically with variations in environmental characteristics but not with characteristics embedded within systematically clustered individuals. A comparative, cross-organizational framework is essential for development of knowledge in OT. Studies of single organizations add little to understanding of organizations when the unit of analysis and variation is assumed to be the organization itself. This realization is increasingly reflected in the empirical literature of OT.[2]

[2] Hannan and Freeman (1) have argued quite convincingly that comparative analyses of organizational effectiveness are inappropriate for scientific purposes.

Some have distinguished the field of inquiry based upon an attribution of *typical or modal methodologies* to the respective subfields. OB is defined as studies utilizing laboratory and, occasionally, field experimentation. OT is identified with the predominant use of survey and, occasionally, case designs. While the simplicity of this methodological distinction is attractive, it does not reflect the current diversity of designs underlying current research on people in organizations and on organizations per se.

The adjective pairs "normative-descriptive" and "empirical-theoretical" are attractive labels for describing *epistomological differences*. Certainly, the two predominant versions of classical OT have been characterized, and criticized, as excessively normative and not descriptive of behavioral and organizational realities. Both Taylor and Fayol on the one hand, and Weber on the other, have provided much of the focus for the normative critics. Some OB scholars view their field's mission as adding descriptive, empirically-based facts to what they see as the essentially normative and theoretical biases of classical OT. With the advent of data among OT scholars and the infusion of organizational development (OD) into the OB tent, these distinctions are no longer descriptive of our domain. Descriptive, empirical, theoretical, and normative can each be used to characterize some work in both OB and OT. Complexity now overshadows the simple straw man of yesterday.

As OD began to emerge a few years ago, the theme of several corridor conversations was that OB *was becoming the applied cousin of OT*. After all, some claimed, OT deals with the theory of organizations by definition. For a moment the distinctions between OB and OD became blurred, and that opaqueness was attractive for some. Reading between the lines, OT was to become the reservoir of accepted and evolving constructs, and OB would emerge as the behavioral engineering function. For managers and consultants we would have OB; for scholars, OT. The largest obstacle to enacting such a distinction is that scholars and appliers do not generally read or listen to one another. The OB people must have their own constructs and theories. The OT people need their own applications, their own means of establishing credibility within the world of action. From this insulation, two OD camps have emerged with their own strategies for change. One focuses on change via the individual and micro unit within the organization and the other on change through structural and environmental manipulation. Alas, another simple, definitional distinction melts!

LEARNING CHECKPOINT

The organizing function is discussed by organizational theorists. Name some of the specific activities organizational theorists consider to be important for achieving effective performance.

My preference among these alternative taxonomic bases is the first. The unit of analysis perspective seems cleanest. The most severe problem with this view is finding intellectual bridges to link the subfields. This linkage is crucial for understanding the way organizations function, the impacts they exert, and the opportunities they provide. Some bridges begin to emerge which are at least suggestive. For example, an organization's structure (i.e., number of levels, average span of supervision, degree of horizontal differentiation) can be viewed as a construct linking OT and OB. In OT, structure is typically positioned in a nomological network as a dependent variable. In OB, structure is typically positioned as an independent variable. This differential positioning of the same construct suggests a possible general role that several constructs might take in linking OT and OB. Structure, climate, task design, reward systems, and leader behavior can each be conceived of as intervening between causal forces in the environment of organizations and the behavior and attitudes of persons within organizations. Each is beginning to be modeled as a dependent variable in one context and an independent variable in another.

This differentiation of subfields by unit of analysis and their integration by intervening constructs is subject to limitations. The boundaries of aggregation between levels of analysis are arbitrary, with no fundamental laws underlying the distinctions. That is a limitation shared with the biological and physical sciences, where subfields have arisen as linking mechanisms (e.g., biophysics, biochemistry, psychopharmacology). The conception also lacks feedback loops with reversible intervening constructs. It is likely that such reciprocal causation reflects reality and that models that omit these loops will not provide a full understanding.

If we were to assume this posture of differentiation, what would be the result? Remembering that

LEARNING CHECKPOINT

Development is considered to be a criterion of effectiveness. What is the development criterion?

FIGURE 1

**Distinctions Among Organizational
Behavior, Organizational Psychology,
Organizational Theory and Personnel
and Human Resources.**

Organizational Behavior- Organizational Psychology (OP)	Both fields focus upon explaining human behavior within organizations. Their difference centers on the fact that OP restricts its explanatory constructs to those at the psychological level. OB draws constructs from multiple disciplines. As the domain of OP continues to expand, the difference between OB and OP is diminishing, perhaps to the point of identity between the fields.
Organizational Behavior- Organizational Theory (OT)	The distinction is based on two differences: unit of analysis and focus of dependent variables. OB is defined as the study of individual and group behavior within organizations and the application of such knowledge. OT is the study of structure, processes, and outcomes of the organization per se. The distinction is neither that OB is atheoretical and concerned only with behavior nor that OT is unique or exclusive in its attention to theory. Alternatively, the distinction can be conceived as between micro and macro perspectives on OB. This removes the awkward differentiation of behavior and theory.

Organizational Behavior-
    Personnel and Human Resources
    (P&HR)
	This distinction usually depicts OB as the more basic of the two and P&HR as more applied in emphasis. OB is seen as more concept oriented while P&HR is viewed as emphasizing techniques or technologies. The dependent variables, behavior and affective reactions within organizations, are frequently presented as similar. P&HR can be seen as standing at the interface between the organization and the individual, focusing on developing and implementing the system for attracting, maintaining, and motivating the individual within the organization.

the distinctions are based primarily on levels of analysis with a slight nod toward the other distinctions, we can propose the definitions in Figure 1.

A DIMENSIONAL CHARACTERIZATION OF ORGANIZATIONAL BEHAVIOR

I believe that OB is evolving toward the model presented in Figure 2. The field is being enacted, not defined in some a priori sense, by scholars and teachers in ways that imply the dimensional, thematic conception suggested in that figure.

Three dimensions define the conceptual domain of OB. Most disciplines and emerging fields of inquiry that stand at the interface between science and professional practice are describable in terms of these dimensions. The specific articulation of the dimensions depends significantly upon the underlying epistomological themes adopted by the discipline.

A Way of Thinking

OB is a *way of thinking,* a manner of conceiving problems and articulating research and action solutions which can be characterized by five postures. First, problems and questions are typically formulated within an independent variable(s)-dependent variable(s) framework. Recently, OB has begun to incorporate personal and situational moderators into this framework. OB's assertion that behavior within organizations is subject to systematic study is based on conceptualization of the object of study as nonrandom, systematic, and generally purposive. This way of thinking is significantly influencing our methodologies. The field is engaged in a sometimes painful search for cause and effect within our models.

A second component of OB as a way of thinking is its orientation toward change as a desirable outcome for organizations and persons within organizations. Static phenomena possess diminishing prestige as topics of study. Conditions for stimulating change and models for evaluating change are an increasingly important part of the field.

Third, there is a distinctly humanistic tone within OB, reflected in concern for self development, personal growth, and self actualization. Although its influence on research and teaching seems to ebb and flow, and its reflection in scholarship and pedagogy varies by school, it is there, and its presence is causing both strain (given its positioning adjacent to scienticism) and excitement, even relevance, within OB. The striving is toward humanism without softness. OB shares this dilemma with most of the person-oriented disciplines that attempt to combine basic, good science with a change orientation. Yet this tone of humanism is only one side of the current, slightly schizorphrenic posture of OB. The other side is reflected in a heavy emphasis on operant learning models and behavioral modification techniques, an orientation toward environmental determinism rather than self actualization.

Fourth, OB is becoming increasingly performance oriented, with more studies including a performance-oriented dependent variable. The field is beginning to capture an important distinction between two types of dependent variables. One perspective focuses on description of a behavior, activity, or outcome, that is, the proper focus for scientific analysis and thinking. The other aims at application of a preference function to these behaviors, activities, or outcomes, resulting in a scaling of effectiveness or success. This is the proper focus for an engineering analysis—a managerial mind set.[3]

[3] My thinking here has been significantly influenced by Robert Kahn of the University of Michigan. His comments at the 1976 Carnegie-Mellon Workshop on Organizational Effectiveness have been particularly helpful.

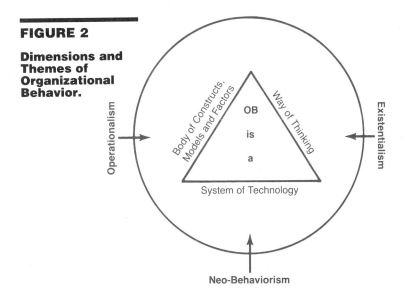

FIGURE 2

Dimensions and Themes of Organizational Behavior.

We are beginning to hear the demands for relevance in our research and teaching. Unless OB can increase its performance payoffs, the field may be in danger of losing some of its hard battles for a niche in the curriculum or a moment in the board room.

Finally, OB uses the discipline imposed by the scientific method. The field is substantially influenced by norms of skepticism, caution, replication, and public exposure of knowledge based on facts. In many ways, this posture of "scientism" confuses some students and clients. It can be seen as the antithesis of several other postures that characterize OB thinking. Yet it is generally accepted as a crucial posture. It helps to keep the field straight, and it is the key ingredient in whatever longevity the field may possess. Scientific method, applied to OB, provides the mechanism for feed-back and self-renewal.

A Body of Constructs, Models, and Facts

Even though OB is characterized by some definitional confusion, an implicit agreement is emerging about some of its components. Differences exist concerning the relative weighting of components and the emphasis given to basic science versus application in transmitting the field to others. But most treatments of the field now include coverage of constructs, models, and facts on: motivation, learning or socialization, group structure and process, leader behavior, task design, interpersonal communication, organizational structure, interpersonal change and conflict, and material on relevant dependent variables (e.g., satisfaction, other attitudes, participation measures, performance dimensions, and other behavior).

LEARNING CHECKPOINT

In the chapter the time dimension model of effectiveness is presented. Describe how the constructs displayed in this model fit in a discussion of organizational behavior.

This emergence of an identity for the field is evidenced by the second generation of OB textbooks, which are more similar in topical coverage than their ancestors. Some models sell and are thus influential in structuring the introductory level curricula underlying our field. Others stretch the field at its boundaries but do not become a part of the core. That core is gradually developing toward an identifiable body of components.

A System of Technology

OB is also a system or a collection of technologies. These have evolved out of the primary areas of study identified as the independent variables of OB. Techniques now exist for: training leaders, designing tasks, designing organizations, evaluating performances, rewarding behaviors, and modeling behaviors.

The uncritical eye might be pleased with OB's tool kit. Superficially, it appears that the field is ready to move into the world of action with vigor and confidence. But our posture of scientism keeps the field honest. These technologies are largely exploratory, unvalidated and, in a few cases, under evaluation. The field has even spawned an occasional technology that has been adopted and later found damaging to an organization and its participants. In most cases, even when the technologies work, the field's theoretical models are not sufficiently developed to explain why they were effective. So, a system or collection of technologies? Yes. A behavioral engineering discipline? No.

THEMES INFLUENCING ORGANIZATIONAL BEHAVIOR

As depicted in Figure 2, three themes span the dimensions defining OB and influence the way each dimension is articulated. The relative emphasis given to each theme over time, by the various schools of thought within OB, determines our ways of thinking, constructs and facts, and development of technologies.

Existentialism

The emphasis here is upon the uncertain, contingent environment of people within organizations (and organizations). Existentialism emphasizes that in the face of this type of environment, persons must exercise self control in pursuit of their own objectives. The ultimate responsibility for designing productive and satisfying organizational environments rests with human beings. It is their responsibility to fashion themselves—to implement self control. This philosophical posture leaves a legacy of concepts within OB—goal, purpose, expectation, expectancy, instrumental, path, and contingency.

This theme is forcing OB to become a more complex discipline. It asserts that no meaning exists in absolutes. All meaning derives from comparison; meaning is always relative. Activities and outcomes within organizations are meaningful only within a context including implicit or explicit statements of purpose. This is at the core of one important, current development in conceptualizing the influence of most of the independent variables treated in OB—the concept of contingency.

With the realization that an independent variable's effects depend, the next logical question becomes: Depends upon what? When? etc. *Why* did *who* do *what* with *whom* with what *outcomes?* This seemingly simple question can be applied to most independent-dependent variable linkages currently of concern in OB. The *why* focuses on the causes, the reasons, the antecedents of variance in the dependent variable. The *who* focuses on the initiating party (individual, group, or organization). The *what* requires description of the behavior in question. The *whom* provides the interaction component, adding dimensionality to the search for meaningfulness. It provides a vertical, horizontal, or diagonal vector to the reality that OB attempts to understand. The *outcomes* provide the ultimate meaning to the field. Existentialism implies that the meaning in any act exists in its consequences, and OB seems to be moving toward this realization.

Operationalism

Operationalism is reflected in three ways. First, the field is searching for theories of the middle range in most of its subareas. The grand, general, abstract models of motivation, leadership, environment-structure interaction, and change are not yielding satisfying, systematic, cumulative data. Some models posit relations between environmental and organizational characteristics and individual attitudes and behaviors. Models are needed to describe the processes through which environment impacts structure and structure impacts attitudes and behavior.

Second, emphasis is being given to the operations or behav-

iors through which people within organizations function. Whether describing what managers do or analyzing the impact of leaders, the importance of formulating the issue in operational terms is being realized. The literature is beginning to be characterized by questions like:

1. Through what operations is structure actually designed?
2. Through what operations does a leader impact a subordinate?
3. Through what operations do rewards and punishments effect change?
4. Through what operations do groups actually make decisions?

In each case, the field is beginning to examine the physiology of behavior within organizations. The anatomy of OB is important, but its study has not led to understanding the processes through which persons and organizations interact.

Third, measurement issues are impacting the field. Questions of reliability and validity must be faced, and questions of scaling and measurement confronted. We are increasingly anxious about our inability to explain large amounts of variance in dependent variables. Three rather lengthy streams of research have reached the point where lack of early attention to how we operationalized constructs and validated measures has caused major problems for continued, meaningful work. Cases in point are research on: the two-factor model of motivation (with faulty measurement procedures); expectancy formulations of motivation (with testing of inappropriate models); and the impact of organizational design on attitudes and behaviors (with designs that confound independent variables). While not completely pessimistic, I believe that the field has been extremely inefficient and

myopic in the research strategies applied in some areas.

Neo-behavioralism

Finally, many causal assumptions and models in OB are moving toward a behavioristic orientation with a cognitive overtone. Motivation theory, under the influence of expectancy models, has moved in this direction. Leadership studies reflect the notion of instrumental, goal-oriented behavior with a significant emphasis on leader behavior being partially a function of the consequences which it produces. The concept of contingency plays a major role in several fields within OB, its general intellectual structure deriving directly from the behavioristic notion of structure and process evolving toward forms that are reinforcing to the organism. The behavioristic perspective also has surfaced in literature dealing with organizational design and organizational control and power. Distributions of influence and power are partially explained by environmental consequences of attempts at influence. The exercise of power generates consequences which, in turn, affect structural configurations of the organization.

Radical behaviorism is not the dominant theme, but rather a combination of general behavioral constructs *and* cognitions. It is not clear what functions are provided by the incorporation of cognitions within OB models. Little research has been addressed to the question of the variance explained in most OB models by cognitions beyond that explained by environmental determinants. Perhaps cognitive concepts do explain added variance, or perhaps they constitute a residual reservoir of unexplained variance to which we inappropriately attribute meaning.

CONCLUSIONS AND IMPLICATIONS

What are the implications of this perspective on the field? First, ultimately the definitions of the domains of OB, OT, OP, and OD are arbitrary. Definitions should be tested by their usefulness in specifying constructs and functional relations. Definitions are needed to guide the field toward middle range and operational theory. Movement toward definition by induction is needed. It may prove fruitful to aim toward definition through describing what is happening in the main streams of research within OB. Definitions established by assertion lead to debate without fruitful results.

Second, realities in organizations change so rapidly that our descriptions (ways of thinking, constructs and technologies) do not keep pace with the rate of change in the objects of our study.[4] I see two implications of this for OB. First, incredibly long periods of time are needed to assess organizations and to identify the fundamental, underlying nature of the field. Second, increasing energy will be devoted to collapsing the time intervals needed to develop relevant constructs and models and to testing these models. This implies that management, as a general field, will accelerate adoption of both simulation and experimental designs. These designs permit the modeling of time lags. Contrary to the usual evaluation of such designs, they will allow us to become more realistic in our modeling and measurement of OB.

Third, what might this line of reasoning mean for the Academy of Management and its members? The Academy is presently the only camp which attempts to house OB, OT, OD, and P&HR. For the moment, these fields have separate tents within the camp, but I believe that the traditional distinctions are beginning to melt. Several examples illustrate this premeability. The 1976 doctoral consortium conducted at the National Academy Convention included topics from both OT and OB. I suspect it is impossible to talk at an advanced level about one domain without the other. The P&HR division's program at the 1976 National Academy Convention consists of about 40 percent OB material. This reflects a healthy trend for both P&HR and OB. It is naive to deal with many of the important issues in P&HR without incorporating OB models and research. The *Academy of Management Journal,* the *Academy of Management Review, Organizational Behavior and Human Peformance,* and *Administrative Science Quarterly* exhibit trends in submissions that reflect an increasing emphasis on *multiple* levels of analysis in both the independent and dependent variable domains.

I believe we are moving toward an enacted field, perhaps best labeled organizational analysis or organizational science (if we wish to emphasize the scientific lineage of our interests and our aspirations). Basically, we now have five divisions within the Academy, composing organizational analysis or science. These are Organizational Behavior, Organization and Management Theory, Personnel and Human Resources, Organization Development, and Organizational Communication. Such segmentation continues to provide important functions for the Academy and its members, but it remains an open question whether segmentation is the most efficient strategy to advance our common interest in behavior *in* and *of* organizations.

As Thurstone said:

> It is the faith of all science that an unlimited number of phenomena can be comprehended in terms of a limited number of concepts or ideal constructs. Without this faith no science could ever have any motivation. To deny this faith is to affirm the primary chaos of nature and the consequent futility of scientific effort. The constructs in terms of which natural phenomena are comprehended are man-made inventions. To discover a scientific law is merely to discover that a man-made scheme serves to unify, and thereby to simplify, comprehension of a certain class of natural phenomena. A scientific law is not to be thought of as having an independent existence which some scientist is fortunate to stumble upon. A scientific law is not a part of nature. It is only a way of comprehending nature.

□

REFERENCES

1. Hannan, M. T. and J. Freeman. "Obstacles for Comparative Studies," in P. S. Goodman and J. M. Pennings (Eds.), *New Perspectives in Organizational Effectiveness* (San Francisco: Jossey-Bass, 1977), pp. 106–131.
2. Thurston, L. S. *Multiple-Factor Analysis* (Chicago: University of Chicago Press, 1947).

[4] I am indebted to Professor Lou Pondy for stimulating this notion.

R² CORPORATE CULTURE

RALPH H. KILMANN

Success in business is determined not by an executive's skills alone, nor by the visible features—the strategy, structure and reward system—of the organization. Rather, the organization itself has an invisible quality—a certain style, a character, a way of doing things—that may be more powerful than the dictates of any one person or any formal system. To understand the soul of the organization requires that we travel below the charts, rule books, machines and buildings into the underground world of corporate cultures.

Culture provides meaning, direction and mobilization, a social energy that moves the corporation into either productive action or destruction. I have encountered many organizations in which this social energy has barely been tapped; whether diffused in all directions or even deactivated, it is not mobilized to help the company. Most members seem apathetic or depressed about their jobs. They no longer pressure one another to do well. Pronouncements by top managers that they will improve the situation fall on the deaf ears of employees who have heard these promises before. Nothing seems to matter. The soul of the organization is slowly dying.

Other companies show considerable energy, but it is driving employees in the wrong direction. The organization lives in an immense culture gap. The social energy pressures members to persist in types

Source: *Psychology Today*, April 1985, pp. 62–68.

of behavior that may have worked well in the past but are clearly dysfunctional today. The gap between the outdated culture and what is needed for organizational success gradually develops into a culture rut—a habitual, unquestioning way of behaving. There is no adaptation or change, only routine motions, despite the fact that the company is unsuccessful. This rut can go on for years, even though morale and performance suffer. Bad habits die hard. Culture shock occurs when the sleeping organization awakes and finds that it has lost touch with its original mission. The new world has left the insulated company behind—a Rip Van Winkle story on a grand scale.

On the other hand, one has merely to experience the energy that flows from shared commitments among group members to know it—the power that emanates from mutual influence and esprit de corps. Why does one organization have a very adaptive culture while another has a culture mired in the past? Is one a case of good fortune and the other a result of bad luck? On the contrary, it seems that any organization can find itself with an outdated culture if the culture itself is not managed explicitly. I have found that, unattended, a company's culture almost always becomes dysfunctional. Normal human fear, insecurity, oversensitivity, dependency and paranoia seem to take over unless there is a concerted effort to establish an adaptive culture. People cope with uncertainty and perceived threats by protecting themselves, by being cautious, by minimizing their risks, by going along with a culture that builds protective barriers around

work units and around the whole organization. An adaptive culture, alternatively, requires risk and trust; employees must actively support one another's efforts to identify problems and adapt to solutions. The latter can be accomplished only by a very conscious, well-planned effort at managing culture.

A company's culture sometimes supports self-defeating individual behavior that persists in spite of its many disruptive effects on morale and performance: doing the minimum to get by; purposely resisting or even sabotaging innovation; and being very negative in general about the organization's capacity to change. Worse, such behavior may even include lying, cheating and stealing as well as intimidating, harassing and hurting others. The most detrimental behavior in the long run, however, is persisting in once-adaptive patterns rather than changing to meet the dynamic complexity of the present. The challenge is to get out of the culture rut.

HOW DO CULTURES FORM?

When an organization is born, a tremendous burst of energy is released as members struggle to make it work. A corporate culture seems to form rather quickly, based on the organization's mission, setting and requirements for success: high quality, efficiency, product reliability, customer service, innovation, hard work and loyalty. The culture captures everyone's drive and imagination. As the reward systems, policies and work procedures are formally documented, they suggest what kinds of behavior and attitudes are important for success.

▨ LEARNING CHECKPOINT

The chapter presents the view that Hewlett-Packard's (H-P) dominant culture is one that encourages every H-P employee to act as an entrepreneur. How can this form of encouragement take place in an organization?

Such situational forces, while important in shaping culture, cannot compete with actions of key individuals. For example, the founder's objectives, principles, values and especially behavior provide important clues as to what is really wanted from all employees, both now and in the future. Carrying on in the traditions of the founder, other top executives affect the culture of the company by their example.

Employees also take note of all critical incidents that stem from management action—such as the time that so-and-so was reprimanded for doing a good job when not asked to do it beforehand or the time that another worker was fired for publicly disagreeing with the company's position. Incidents such as these become an enduring part of the company folklore, indicating what the corporation really wants, what really counts in getting ahead or, alternatively, how to stay out of trouble. They are the unwritten rules of the game.

A culture may be very functional at first. But in time it becomes a separate entity, independent of its initial purpose. The culture becomes distinct from the formal strategy, structure and reward systems of the organization. In a similar vein, culture becomes distinct from workers and even top managers. All members of the organization are taught to follow the cultural norms without questioning them. After employees have been around for

a few years, they have already learned the ropes. Even new top executives who vow that things will be different find out—often the hard way—how the culture is "bigger" and more powerful than they are. A top manager can get individual commitments to some new policy from his subordinates, but after they walk out of the office door and once again become part of the corporate culture, the boss finds the new plan bitterly opposed.

Top management is also caught in the grip of the firm's separate and distinct culture. Employees wonder from below why managers play it so safe, why they refuse to approach things differently, why they keep applying the same old management practices that clearly do not work. They wonder why management is so blind to the world around them. Is management "mean" or just "stupid"?

HOW ARE CULTURES MAINTAINED?

The force controlling group behavior at every level in the organization—a force that can brainwash workers into believing that what they are doing is automatically good for the company, their community and their family—must be very powerful. Is it magic or is it the psychology of group membership that explains the potency of corporate culture? Social scientists speak of "norms" as the unwritten rules of behavior. In a company, for example, a norm might be: Don't disagree with your boss in public. If a norm is violated, there is immediate and strong pressure to get the offending party to change behavior. Consider, for example, an individual who persists in presenting reservations about the company's new product at a group meeting—just after the boss has ar-

gued strongly for investing heavily in its advertising campaign. The bold employee receives stares and frowns, eyes roll—all nonverbal messages to sit down and shut up. If these efforts do not work, the underling will hear about it later, from coworkers if not from the boss.

The human need to be accepted by a group—whether family, friends, co-workers or neighbors—gives the group leverage to demand compliance to its norms. Were such a need not so widespread, groups would have little hold on people other than formal sanctions. The nonconformists and mavericks who defy pressures to adhere to group norms always do so at a considerable price.

Simple experiments conducted by Solomon Asch in the early 1950s demonstrate just how powerfully the group can influence its deviants. The experiments were described to the research subjects as a study in perception. Three lines—A, B and C, all of different lengths—were shown on a single card. Subjects were asked to indicate which of these three lines was identical in length to a fourth line, D, shown on a second card. In one experiment, seven people sat in a row. One by one they indicated their choices. While line C was in fact identical to line D, each of the first six, all confederates of the experimenter, said that line D was identical to A. The seventh person was the unknowing subject. As each person deliberately gave the wrong answer, the seventh subject became increasingly uneasy, anxious and doubtful of his or her own perceptions. When it came time to respond, the seventh subject agreed with the rest almost one-third of the time. Without such group influence there were hardly any errors.

Imagine just how easily such distorted perceptions of reality can be maintained when backed up by formal sanctions—pay, promotions and other rewards. The group can reward its members so that they ignore the disruptive behavior of "troublemakers." The members collectively believe that everything is fine, continue to reinforce the myth and reward one another for maintaining it. In essence, everyone agrees that the dysfunctional ways can continue without question. Any deviant who thinks otherwise is severely punished and eventually banished from the tribe.

Asch's classic study demonstrates that the impact of a group on its members is very powerful indeed. And if the group is cohesive, if there is a strong sense of community and loyalty, there will be even stronger pressures on each member to adopt whatever the cultural norms specify. Other studies have shown that if the cultural norms of a cohesive group support the organization's mission, the workers' performance will be high; the culture is said to be adaptive.

Alternatively, if the norms endorsed by a highly cohesive group oppose the corporate goals, then the culture will foster low performance and morale. It is better to have an uncohesive group with mediocre performance than a highly cohesive counterculture. The latter will result in consistently low performance and headaches for everyone.

LEARNING CHECKPOINT

Suppose you have a highly cohesive group that opposes corporate goals. What organizational effectiveness criteria would be in jeopardy or not met?

Given the crucial role of corporate culture in shaping behavior, and the especially powerful effects of group norms, one way to turn around a maladaptive company is to change its culture by managing its norms. Even norms that dictate appropriate behavior, opinions and facial expressions can be brought to the surface, discussed and altered.

In my corporate consulting work, I have found it helpful to have all group members (generally in a workshop setting) list the actual norms that currently guide their behavior and attitudes. This can be done for one or many groups, departments and divisions. Sometimes it takes a little prodding and a few illustrations to get the process started, but once it begins members are quick to suggest many norms. In fact, they seem to delight in being able to articulate what was never written in any document and rarely mentioned even in casual conversation between themselves.

In an organization with a culture deeply rooted in the past, some of the norms people list are: Don't disagree with your boss; don't rock the boat; treat women as second-class citizens; put down your organization; don't enjoy your work; don't share information with other groups; treat subordinates as incompetent and lazy; cheat on your expense account; look busy even when you're not; don't reward employees on the basis of merit; laugh at those who suggest new ways of doing things; don't smile much; openly criticize company policies to outsiders; complain a lot; don't trust anyone who seems sincere. And, ironically, the one common norm that must be violated in this group process is: Don't make norms explicit.

Other frequently listed norms include: Don't be the bearer of bad news; don't say what the boss doesn't want to hear; don't think of things that are not likely to happen; don't spoil the party; don't be associated with an ugly event; see no evil, hear no evil and speak no evil.

As these norms are listed for everyone to see, there is considerable laughter and amazement. The members become aware that they have been seducing one another into abiding by these counterproductive rules. But no individual made a conscious choice to behave this way; rather, as workers entered the organization, they were taught what was expected—often in quite subtle ways. The more cohesive the group, the more forcefully the sanctions are applied and the more rapidly the learning takes place. In the extreme case, a highly cohesive group that has been around for a long time has members who look, act, think and talk like one another.

In the projects in which I had managers and all employees of a company list their norms, it was surprising to discover that most norms cited were negative. In a number of cases, more than 90 percent of the listed norms had at least mildly negative connotations. It may be, of course, that employees felt I was looking for the dysfunctions in their organizations rather than for the adaptive aspects. Then again, maybe many organizations are plagued with a high proportion of negative norms from their bureaucratic cultures.

The next step is for all group members to discuss where the organization is headed and what type of behavior is necessary to move forward. Even when a corporation has inherited a very dysfunctional culture from the past, individual employees are often aware of what changes are needed in order for the organization to adapt and survive. Similarly, they are aware of what work environment they prefer for their own sanity and satisfaction.

A certain amount of planning and problem solving may have to occur before any new directions can be articulated. In groups that have fallen into a culture rut, members are so absorbed with the negatives that they have not spent much time thinking about or discussing what they would prefer. Sometimes it is helpful to ask them to reflect upon their ideal organization: If they could design their own from scratch, what would it be like? This generally shows what could be changed in the present organization—often things that are accepted merely because they are traditional.

The third step is for all group members to develop a list of new norms for organizational success. What new norms, for example, would encourage a more adaptive stance toward the organization's changing environment? Likewise, what new norms would allow groups to discuss difficult and uncomfortable issues that affect the long-range success of the firm? What cultural norms would bring difficult internal problems out into the open so that they could be resolved?

At this point, employees usually grasp how unwritten rules have affected their behavior. They experience a sense of relief at contemplating a new way of life, realizing that they no longer have to pressure one another to behave in dysfunctional ways. They can create a new social order within their work groups and within their own organization. Part of this sense of relief comes from recognizing that their dissatisfaction and ineffectiveness are not due to their own incompetence: Psychologically, it is much easier to blame the invisible force called culture—as long as they take

responsibility for changing it.

In organizations needing to be more adaptive, flexible and responsive to modern times, some of the norms often listed are: Treat everyone with respect and as a potential source of valuable insight and expertise; be willing to take on responsibility; initiate changes to improve performance; congratulate those who suggest new ideas and new ways of doing things; be cost conscious; speak with pride about your organization and work group; budget your time according to the importance of tasks for accomplishing objectives; don't criticize the organization in front of clients or customers; enjoy your work and show your enthusiasm for a job well done; be helpful and supportive of other groups in the organization.

New norms that directly pertain to complex and difficult problems include: Bring uncomfortable issues out into the open; persist in drawing attention to problems even if others seem reluctant to consider the implications of what you are saying; listen to other members' viewpoints even if you disagree with them; encourage zany and bizarre perspectives to insure that nothing important and possible has been overlooked; make people aware when a topic that should generate a heated debate has not.

SPOTTING CULTURE GAPS

The contrast between desired norms and actual norms can be immense. My colleague, Mary Jane Saxton, and I refer to this contrast as a "culture gap." We have developed a measurement tool for detecting the gap between what the current culture is and what it should be: the Kilmann-Saxton Culture-Gap Survey.

The survey was developed by first collecting more than 400

norms from managers and employees in more than 25 different types of organizations. Many of these norms were also developed through projects in which cultural norms were assessed and changed. The final set of 28 norm pairs that appears on the survey was derived from statistical and clinical analysis of the most consistent norms that were operating in most of the organizations we studied. An example of a norm pair is: A) Share information only when it benefits your own work group versus B) Share information to help the organization make better decisions. Each employee chooses either A) or B) for each norm pair in two ways: first, according to the pressures the work group puts on its members (actual norms); and second, according to which norms should be operating in order to promote high performance and morale (desired norms).

The differences between the actual norms and the desired norms represent the culture gaps. There are four types of culture gaps, each made up of seven norm pairs. First, there are what we call "task support norms" having to do with information sharing, helping other groups and concern with efficiency, such as "Support the work of other groups" versus "Put down the work of other groups." Second, there are "task innovation norms," which stress creativity, such as "Always try to improve" versus "Don't rock the boat." Third, we look at "social relationship norms" for socializing with one's work group and mixing friendships with business, such as "Get to know the people in your work group" versus "Don't bother." Finally, we examine "personal freedom norms" for self-expression, exercising discretion and pleasing oneself, such as "Live for yourself and your family" versus

"Live for your job and career."

Culture gaps can be surveyed in a work group, a department, a division or an entire organization. By calculating the difference between the norms that are actually in force and those that should be, the four culture-gap scores are obtained. The larger the gap, the greater the likelihood that the current norms are hindering both morale and performance. If the assessed culture gaps are allowed to continue, work groups are likely to resist any attempt at change and improvement. Specifically, culture gaps materialize as an unwillingness to adopt new work methods and innovations, as a lack of support for programs to improve quality and productivity, as lip service when changes in strategic directions are announced and, in the extreme, as efforts to maintain the status quo at all costs.

Our use of the Kilmann-Saxton Culture-Gap Survey in numerous for-profit and nonprofit organizations has revealed distinct patterns of culture gaps. For example, in some of the high-technology firms, lack of cooperation and information sharing across groups has resulted in large culture gaps in task support. In the automotive and steel industries, not rewarding creativity and innovation has resulted in large culture gaps in task innovation. In some social-service agencies in which work loads can vary greatly, large gaps in social relationships are found, indicating that too much time is spent socializing rather than looking to get the next job done. Finally, in extremely bureaucratic organizations, such as some banks and government agencies, large gaps in personal freedom are evident. Here, workers' sense of being overly confined and constrained lowers their performance and morale.

The most general finding to date is the presence of large culture gaps in task innovation. It seems that American industry is plagued by significant differences between actual and desired norms in this area—a condition that may relate directly to the frequently mentioned productivity problem in the United States. An industrial culture that pushes for short-term financial results is bound to foster norms that work against efforts at long-term improvement, regardless of what formal documents and publicity statements seem to advocate.

Do all employees of a corporation see the same culture gaps? Apparently not. The smallest culture gaps are found at the top of the organization's hierarchy. Managers believe their own publicity; they say that they reward creativity and innovation but seem to forget that their actions speak louder than their words. By contrast, cultural gaps are largest at the bottom of the hierarchy, where the gaps also reveal alienation and distrust. Here a common norm is: Don't trust management. In essence, workers see management as being up to no good, getting caught up in fads to fool and manipulate employees or thinking that the workers are too stupid to see what's behind management's latest whim.

CLOSING GAPS

Without a supportive culture, every action by top management will be discounted by the groups below— even top-down efforts to change the culture. I have seen cases in which executives have tried dramatic changes in their own behavior coupled with symbolic deeds and fiery speeches in order to dictate a new culture to the company—but to no avail. Only when work-group members encourage one another to be receptive to

overtures by management can the whole change program be successful. For example, various work groups might include such new norms as: Give management another chance; assume good intentions. Managers and consultants, therefore, have to work especially hard to encourage the work groups, including the executive groups, to meet one another halfway.

How can culture gaps be closed? How can an organization move its culture from the actual to the desired? Can a company be taken out of a culture rut and be put back on track for solving present and future problems? Will the organization survive this culture shock?

When the current culture is at least hopeful, the impact of survey results on workers is almost miraculous. In fact, some change from the actual to the desired norms can take place just by listing the new set of norms. Members start "playing out" the new norms immediately after they are discussed. But when the current culture is cynical, depressed and in a deep rut, the response to the survey results is quite different. Even when large gaps are shown or when a listing demonstrates the tremendous differences between actual and desired norms, employees seem apathetic and lifeless. They respond by saying that their work units cannot change for the better until the level of management above them and the rest of the company change. They believe that the external system is keeping them down.

Curiously, when I do a culture-gap survey at the next highest level, the very same argument is heard again: "We have no power to change; we have to wait for the next level to let us change; they have the power!" It is shocking, after conducting the culture-gap survey for an entire organization, to present the results to the top management group only to find the same feelings of helplessness. Here top management is waiting for the economy to change. In actuality, it is the corporate culture that is saying: Don't take on responsibility; protect yourself at all costs; don't try to change until everyone else has changed; don't lead the way, follow; if you ignore the problem, maybe it will go away.

This is the perfect example of a company in a culture rut, where the shock of realizing the discrepancy between actual and desired norms is just too great to confront. Instead, the organization buries its head and hopes everything will be sorted out by itself. Even in the face of strong evidence of a serious problem, time and time again I have witnessed this form of organizational denial—a much more powerful and perhaps destructive force than any case of individual denial. The group's power to define reality clouds everyone's better judgment. The bureaucratic culture "wins" again.

One large industrial organization asked me to present a three-day seminar to the chairman of the board, the chief executive officer and the 10 corporate officers on the topic of corporate culture. I suggested that a representative survey of culture gaps be conducted across all divisions in the company. In this way, I could report on the company's specific culture and thus generate a livelier and more interesting discussion than an abstract lecture would elicit. In a couple of weeks, the vice president for human resources called: "No, we better not do this," he said. "I don't think the executive group really wants to know what is going on in the company. Besides, we can't take the chance of surprising them with your survey results." Who is protecting whom?

Gaining control of the corporate culture is not only possible but necessary for today's organizations. As changes in corporate directions are planned, a new culture may have to replace the old culture—in one or more divisions or for the whole organization. But just as old cultures can become out-of-date and dysfunctional, the same can happen with new ones. Further changes in the organization's setting—and corresponding changes in strategy, structure and reward systems—can make any culture less functional than before. An important part of managing the corporate culture, therefore, is to continue monitoring and assessing norms. If the culture is not managed explicitly, it may be just a matter of time before the organization is once again disrupted. But if it is managed explicitly, the company can expect significant improvements in both morale and performance; it will be, in the best sense of the word, a cultured organization of employees. ☐

LEARNING CHECKPOINT

The chapter states that organizational culture is the product of interaction among managerial functions, organizational behavior, structure, process, and the environment. Is the explicit management of this interaction really possible? Explain.

D INITIAL VIEW OF ORGANIZATIONAL BEHAVIOR

Now that you have completed two chapters that set the tone for the book *Organizational Behavior and Management,* complete the following exercise. This should be used as your beginning *baseline* assumptions, opinions, and understanding of organizational behavior. Once you have completed the course (book) we will again take another look at your assumptions, opinions, and understanding.

This exercise contains 20 pairs of statements about organizational behavior. For each pair, circle the letter preceding the statement which you think is most accurate. Circle only *one* letter in each pair.

After you have circled the letter, indicate how certain you are of your choice by writing 1, 2, 3, or 4 on the line following each item according to the following procedure.

Source: Adapted from Robert Weinberg and Walter Nord, "Coping with 'It's All Common Sense,' " *Exchange: The Organizational Behavior Teaching Journal* 7 no. 2 (1982): 29–32. Used with permission.

Place a "1" if you are *very uncertain* that your choice is correct.

Place a "2" if you are *somewhat uncertain* that your choice is correct.

Place a "3" if you are *somewhat certain* that your choice is correct.

Place a "4" if you are *very certain* that your choice is correct.

Do not skip any pairs.

1. a) A supervisor is well advised to treat, as much as possible, all members of his/her group exactly the same way.
   b) A supervisor is well advised to adjust his/her behavior according to the unique characteristics of the members of his/her group. _____

2. a) Generally speaking, individual motivation is greatest if the person has set goals for himself/herself which are *difficult* to achieve.
   b) Generally speaking, individual motivation is greatest if the person has set goals for himself/herself which are *easy* to achieve. _____

3. a) A major reason why organizations are not so productive as they could be these days is that managers are too concerned with managing the work group rather than the individual.
   b) A major reason why organizations are not so productive as they could be these days is that managers are too concerned with managing the individual rather than the work group. _____

4. a) Supervisors who, sometime prior to becoming a supervisor, have performed the job of the people they are currently supervising are apt to be *more* effective supervisors than those who have never performed that particular job.
   b) Supervisors who, sometime prior to becoming a supervisor, have performed the job of the people they are currently supervising are apt to be *less* effective supervisors than those who have never performed that particular job. _____

5. a) On almost *every* matter relevant to the work, managers are well advised to be completely honest and open with their subordinates.
   b) There are very few matters in the work place where managers are well advised to be completely honest and open with their subordinates. _____

6. a) One's *need for power* is a better predictor of managerial advancement than one's *motivation to do the work well.*
   b) One's *motivation to do the work well* is a better predictor of managerial advancement than one's *need for power.* _____

7. a) When people fail at something, they try harder the next time.
   b) When people fail at something, they quit trying. _____

8. a) Performing well as a manager depends most on how much *education* you have.
   b) Performing well as a manager depends most on how much *experience* you have. _____

9. a) The most effective leaders are those who give more emphasis to *getting the work done* than they do to *relating to people.*
   b) The effective leaders are those who give more emphasis to *relating to people* than they do to *getting the work done.* _____

10. a) It is very important for a leader to "stick to his/her guns."
    b) It is *not* very important for a leader to "stick to his/her guns." _____

11. a) *Pay* is the most important factor in determining how hard people work.
    b) The *nature of the task people are doing* is the most important factor in determining how hard people work. _____

12. a) *Pay* is the most important factor in determining how satisfied people are at work.

b) The *nature of the task people are doing* is the most important factor in determining how satisfied people are at work. _____

13. a) Generally speaking, it is correct to say that a person's *attitudes cause his/her behavior.*
    b) Generally speaking, it is correct to say that a person's *attitudes are primarily rationalizations for his/her behavior.* _____

14. a) Satisfied workers produce *more* than workers who are not satisfied.
    b) Satisfied workers produce *no more* than workers who are not satisfied. _____

15. a) The notion that most semiskilled workers desire work that is interesting and meaningful is most likely *incorrect.*
    b) The notion that most semiskilled workers desire work that is interesting and meaningful is most likely *correct.* _____

16. a) People welcome change for the better.
    b) Even if change is for the better, people will resist it. _____

17. a) Leaders are born, not made.
    b) Leaders are made, not born. _____

18. a) Groups make better decisions than individuals.
    b) *Individuals make better decisions than groups.* _____

19. a) The statement, "A manager's authority needs to be commensurate with his/her responsibility" is, practically speaking, a *very meaningful statement.*
    b) The statement, "A manager's authority needs to be commensurate with his/her responsibility" is, practically speaking, a *basically meaningless statement.* _____

20. a) A major reason for the relative decline in North American productivity is that the division of labor and job specialization *have gone too far.*
    b) A major reason for the relative decline in North American productivity is that the division of labor and job specialization *have not been carried far enough.* _____

APPLIED ORGANIZATIONAL BEHAVIOR

OBJECTIVES

1. To relate individual work experiences to the formal study of organizational behavior.

2. To learn about group interaction and group sharing.

STARTING THE EXERCISE

1. Each individual is to prepare a detailed description of a recent work situation. The description should include reference to the person's attitudes and feelings about the job, the manner in which his/her performance was evaluated, the group culture and norms that existed, and the job's characteristics. Even if the most recent job was only part-time, it still can be used to develop the description. (5 minutes)

2. After preparing the description (a one- or two-page document) prepare another short note (one-half page) on the criteria of organizational effectiveness most stressed in the job (e.g., production, efficiency, satisfaction). (5 minutes)

3. The instructor will form the class into groups of four. Each member then shares his/her description (paraphrases) and criteria of effectiveness with the group. (15 minutes)

4. The group should decide which description and effectiveness criteria is most illustrative of organizational behavior. Why was this particular description selected? This person shares his/her description and effectiveness criteria with the entire class.

5. The instructor will comment on how these descriptions relate to topics that will be covered in the course.

THE CASE OF THE MSWD

Changing the culture of an organization is a difficult, time-consuming, often gut-wrenching process. This is as true in public corporations as it is in the private domain. In fact, effecting such change in a public institution is, if anything, more difficult because of the number of legitimate constituencies—the public, legislators, unions, employees, special-interest groups—that can raise barriers to change. But change can be accomplished if a sufficient level of commitment is applied to the process for a long enough time. One example will reveal all the expenditures—of time, money, and morale—that are involved.

Metropolitan Sewer & Water District (MSWD—a major public wholesaler of these essential services to a large American city) is a public-sector corporation. It employs 2,500 people, has an annual budget of $75 million and spends $200 million a year on capital improvements. MSWD is one of the oldest public agencies of its kind in the country.

Throughout the years, the MSWD carried out its mandate in fine fashion. Its accomplishments were not achieved without difficulty and controversy, however. At times in the history of MSWD, senior officials were charged and convicted of misuse of public funds.

A second problem MSWD faced both internally and in the eyes of the public was patronage. Over the years, administration after administration had found ways to plant favorite sons on MSWD's modest operating-budget payroll.

The third problem MSWD faced was one of rampant bureaucracy—a problem that organization theorist Henry Mintzberg suggests affects all older organizations. The average contract required seventy-two separate signatures and took close to nine months to wind its way through the bureaucracy before being let. Even a minor contract involved a foot-high pile of forms.

Despite the presence of a modern computer system, there were at least six separate manual personnel record systems operating in MSWD. And even with these systems, no one could say with certainty how many people were on the payroll at any time.

All business was conducted by memo, and usually in a prescribed official format rather than face-to-face. Everything was done by the book. If it wasn't on paper, it wouldn't get done. A classic case of the process culture gone awry.

Still, this bureaucracy would not have been a serious problem except for some issues that recently surfaced. Water usage continued to rise and gradually began to exceed the design capacity of the system. Moreover, federal EPA regulations that were enacted required MSWD to upgrade its facilities. Confronted with these problems, the state secretary of the environment was determined to "bring the MSWD into the twentieth century." He recognized that it would be almost irresponsible to launch the MSWD into these major capital expenditures with the organization in its current state of apparent bureaucratic ineptitude. He knew, however, that revitalizing this moribund culture would be difficult and would have to be accomplished without major infusions of new management talent. Nevertheless, he and his new general manager, Ken Dillon (not his real name), were determined to take on the challenge.

Ken Dillon was a key figure in changing MSWD. Dillon was in his mid-fifties, semi-retired, and a successful entrepreneur when he took over the reins at MSWD. He was used to getting things done and making things happen. When he brought this attitude to the career-oriented bureaucratic environment of MSWD, it was like a breath of fresh air.

During the first several months in revitalizing MSWD, Dillon familiarized himself with the organization. What he found was not encouraging. The MSWD's extremely cumbersome superstructure made Dillon officially responsible for running the organization, but most major and many minor decisions were subject to the review of an advisory committee. Decisions required a majority vote of the committee although Dillon did have veto power.

Further crimping his style was the fact that this highly centralized organization reported to a chief operating officer—a career civil servant. Originally this post was intended to help insulate MSWD from self-serving initiatives by politically minded general managers. In

Source: Terrence Deal and Allan Kennedy, *Corporate Culture* 1982, Addison-Wesley, Reading, Massachusetts. pp. 169–174. Reprinted with permission. This case is based on a real consulting assignment carried out by the authors. Names, titles, and a few facts have been changed in the interest of respecting the confidential interests of the client.

practical terms, it meant that Dillon had little direct authority in the day-to-day management of MSWD, since everyone else reported to the chief operating officer who could, in turn, go over Dillon's head to the advisory committee.

In terms of the MSWD's people, there were grounds for encouragement and disappointment. The biggest problem was the average age of the staff: fifty-five or older. The people in the agency had, for the most part, joined right after the war and spent their whole careers with it. The threat of impending retirements and the accompanying loss of the knowledge and skills of those who retired was a serious long-term problem for Dillon to deal with. On the positive side, the loyalty and motivation of the vast majority of the staff was remarkable. Despite public perceptions of a patronage-ridden bureaucracy, these people were dedicated public servants who were sincerely interested in making the MSWD work as well as possible.

Dillon's objective in this change was nothing short of changing MSWD from a reactive, bureaucratic culture to the proactive can-do attitude he was familiar with in his own company—a shift from a process culture to a work hard/play hard culture.

After six months of study, Dillon decided the time had come to act. To reshape the culture, he began by taking two major steps: he engaged consultants to supplement his staff in an aggressive change process, and he announced in a memo to MSWD's permanent complement of 2,500 employees that there would be no firings or layoffs as a result of the process he was launching. His objective, he said, was to work with the talented people of MSWD to improve its effectiveness. This second step turned out to be very significant later in the process since it helped buy time for some basic changes to take hold.

THE CHANGE PROCESS

The team of four consultants spent its first six weeks learning about MSWD. In a meeting at the end of this period, the first gesture in the change process was decided on—to set up three major task forces of MSWD employees to work with the consultants on three commonly agreed-upon problem areas. The three areas selected were:

- **Contracting.** Everyone generally agreed something should be done to speed up contract processing.
- **Operations and Maintenance (O & M).** Over the objections of the chief operating officer's

functional managers, a second task force was assigned responsibility for O & M.
- **Personnel.** All managers in MSWD used personnel constraints as their argument for why things couldn't be done differently no matter what the issue. The chief operating officer, for example, was convinced this task force would prove that nothing could be done.

In all, twenty-five professionals and/or middle managers were assigned to these task forces full-time for their indeterminate duration—a gesture that in itself caused great consternation in the agency. Reservations aside, people in the MSWD were used to following orders, so all twenty-five members dutifully showed up for the initial group meeting that launched their efforts.

Meanwhile, Dillon initiated a weekly series of staff meetings with the chief operating officer, functional officer, functional managers, and their assistants. He specifically excluded these people from membership on the task forces; he would work with them himself.

During their first week of work, the task forces accomplished little. Members were not used to working in this fashion; many of them felt uncomfortable in this new role. By the second week the members began to open up in their meetings. For example, engineers on the contracting task force admitted disappointment when projects they had worked on were not received warmly by operations personnel. They were astonished to learn that the operations people were often distressed when the engineers didn't consult them about projects they were working on and when they delivered equipment that was hard to operate and maintain. Both sides agreed that better communications on projects between the two sides were definitely called for. In the other task forces, similar revelations were occurring—to everyone's amazement.

By the third week, all three task forces were hard at work trying to formulate recommendations to deal with the problems they had identified. Their recommendations—delivered during the seventh week— were reviewed by Dillon, senior management, and the advisory committee.

Awaiting management's response, the task forces had gone back to work on their recommendations. A half dozen more members were added to the task forces. Everyone seemed more and more committed to the change process as time went on.

Six weeks later, the task forces presented their final recommendations—essentially offering details on their original plans. Senior management raised some objections, and modifications were discussed. Then attention turned toward the consultants' recommendations for significant streamlining and decentralization of MSWD. They suggested (1) the elimination of the job of chief operating officer, (2) elimination of the jobs of the assistant functional managers, (3) establishment of a line-of-business (in other words, sewer and water structure), (4) a reassignment of the staffs of major functions such as engineering and environmental planning to create the nucleus of real engineering functions within both the sewer and water divisions, (5) creation of a new director of planning position to run the new planning system, and (6) creation of an office of contract administration to run the new project-management and contracting systems. After some review the package was finally endorsed.

THE IMPLEMENTATION OF CHANGE

With the endorsement in hand, Dillon moved quickly. True to his original pledge, no member of the organization was fired; all were slotted into new jobs. The reorganization was comprehensive enough that, in effect, a new management team was put in place.

Offices were moved on a Monday. On Tuesday, Dillon launched the new planning process that was designed to get the new management groups of each division working together as a team.

The planning process was designed to dovetail with the state budget process, thus creating very tight sched- uling. However, despite weekend and late evening flurries, both divisions made it under the wire. The head of the sewer division, exhausted by the process, said to one of the consultants just after the advisory committee had approved his proposed budget: "This is the best thing that ever happened to the MSWD . . . and the most exhilarating experience I have ever had. We'll never go back to the old way again."

Six months later, no one could doubt that the MSWD was significantly different. There was still too much paper and too much conformance to the book, but there was also a clear set of agreed-upon priorities, a sense of real urgency in pursuing these priorities, and the beginnings of a "we can make it happen" mentality. Dillon believed that with one more year of operation in this new mode, the new culture would really take hold.

The secretary of the environment, the person who launched the whole process, claims it is the greatest organization turnaround he has witnessed in his twenty-five years as a public-sector manager.   □

CASE QUESTIONS

1. Describe the role of Dillon in the change effort.
2. What internal and external threats existed in the change process?
3. What role did training play in the change effort?
4. What potential problems do you see down the road as the change process takes hold?

THE INDIVIDUAL IN THE ORGANIZATION

3 INDIVIDUAL DIFFERENCES AND WORK BEHAVIOR

Any attempt to learn why people behave as they do in organizations requires some understanding of individual differences. Managers spend considerable time making judgments about the fit between individuals, job tasks, and effectiveness. Such judgments are influenced typically by both the manager's and the subordinate's characteristics. Making decisions about who will perform what tasks in a particular manner—without some understanding of behavior—can lead to irreversible long-run problems.

Each employee is different in many respects. A manager needs to ask how such differences influence the behavior and performance of subordinates. This chapter highlights some of the individual differences that can explain why one person is a significantly better performer than another person. Differences among people require forms of adjustment for both the individual and those for whom he or she will work. Managers who ignore such differences often become involved in practices which hinder achieving organizational and personal goals.

THE BASIS FOR UNDERSTANDING BEHAVIOR

A manager's observation and analysis of individual behavior and performance require the consideration of three sets of variables. These variables directly influence individual behavior or what an employee does (e.g., produces output, sells automobiles, services machines). The three sets of variables are classified as being *individual, psychological,* and *organizational.* Within each set are a number of subsets. For example, the individual variables include abilities and skills, background, and demographic variables. Figure 3–1 suggests that an employee's behavior is complex because it is affected by such diverse variables, experiences, and events. In fact, human behavior is far too complex to be explained by a generalization that applies to all people. Consequently, only a sampling of some of the relevant variables that influence human behavior in organizations are presented in Figure 3–1.

FIGURE 3–1

Variables That Influence Behavior and Performance

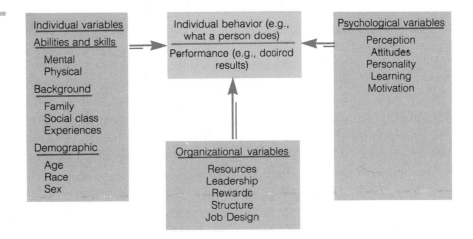

Figure 3–1 suggests that *effective managerial practice requires that individual behavior differences be recognized and, when feasible, taken into consideration while carrying out the job of managing organizational behavior. To understand **individual differences,** a manager must (1) observe and recognize the differences, (2) study relationships between variables that influence individual behavior, and (3) discover relationships. For example, a manager is in a better position to make optimal decisions if he or she knows what the attitudes, perceptions, and mental abilities of employees are, as well as how these and other variables are related. It also is important to know how each variable influences performance. Being able to observe differences, understand relationships, and predict linkages can facilitate managerial attempts to improve performance.

Behavior as outlined in Figure 3–1 is anything that a person does. *Talking* to a manager, *listening* to a co-worker, *filing* a report, *typing* a memo, and *placing* a completed unit in inventory are "behaviors." So are *daydreaming*, *reading* this book, and *learning* how to use a firm's accounting system. The general framework indicates that behavior depends on the types of variables shown in Figure 3–1. Thus, it can be stated that B = f(I, O, P). Figure 3–1 suggests that an employee's behavior (B) is a function of individual (I), organizational (O), and psychological (P) variables. The behavior that results on the job is unique to each individual, but the underlying process is basic to all people.

INDIVIDUAL VARIABLES

The individual variables presented in Figure 3–1 are classified as abilities and skills, background, and demographic. Each of these classes of variables helps explain individual differences in behavior and performance. However, only abilities and skills are examined in this chapter. Background and demographic variables are discussed elsewhere throughout the book.

ABILITIES AND SKILLS

Some employees, though highly motivated, simply do not have the abilities or skills to perform well. Abilities and skills play a major role in individual behavior and performance. An *ability* is a trait (innate or learned) that permits a person to do something mental or physical. For example, various mental abilities such as inductive reasoning, number facility, verbal comprehension, memory span, spatial orientation, and deductive reasoning make up what is commonly referred to as intelligence.[1] *Skills,* on the other hand, are task-related competences, such as the skill to operate a lathe or a computer. Table 3–1 presents a number of physical skills. In most cases, the terms *abilities* and *skills* are used interchangeably in this book. Remember that B = f(I, O, P).

TABLE 3–1

Sample of Physical Skills

Physical Skill	Description
1. Dynamic strength	Muscular endurance in exerting force continuously or repeatedly
2. Extent flexibility	The ability to flex or stretch trunk and back muscles
3. Gross body coordination	The ability to coordinate the action of several parts of the body while the body is in motion
4. Gross body equilibrium	The ability to maintain balance with nonvisual cues
5. Stamina	The capacity to sustain maximum effort requiring cardiovascular exertion

Source: Adapted from Edwin A. Fleishman "On the Relation between Abilities, Learning, and Human Performance," *American Psychologist,* November 1972, pp. 1017–32.

Managers must attempt to match a person with abilities and skills to the job requirements. The matching process is important since no amount of leadership, motivation, or organizational resources can make up for deficiencies in abilities or skills. **Job analysis** is a widely used technique that takes some of the guesswork out of matching. Job analysis is the process of defining and studying a job in terms of tasks or behaviors and specifying the responsibilities, education, and training needed to perform the job successfully.[2]

---

[1] M. D. Dunnette, "Aptitudes, Abilities, and Skills," in *Handbook of Industrial and Organizational Psychology,* Ed. M. D. Dunette (Skokie, IL: Rand McNally, 1976), pp. 481–82.

[2] For a complete discussion of job analysis, see John M. Ivancevich and William F. Glueck, *Foundations of Personnel/Human Resource Management* (Plano, TX: Business Publications, 1986), chap 4, pp. 123–148.

PSYCHOLOGICAL VARIABLES

Unraveling the complexity of psychological variables such as perception, attitudes, and personality is an immense task. Thus, the purpose here is to present basic knowledge about each of these psychological variables. Even psychologists have a difficult time agreeing on the meaning and importance of these variables, so our goal is to provide information that managers can use in solving on-the-job behavior and performance problems.

PERCEPTION

Perception, is the cognitive process by which an individual gives meaning to the environment. Because each person gives his or her own meaning to stimuli, different individuals will "see" the same thing in different ways.[3] The way an employee sees the situation often has much greater meaning for understanding behavior than does the situation itself.

Since perception refers to the acquisition of specific knowledge about objects or events at any particular moment, it occurs whenever stimuli activate the senses. Perception involves cognition (knowledge). Thus, perception includes the interpretation of objects, symbols, and people in the light of pertinent experiences. In other words, perception involves receiving stimuli, organizing the stimuli, and translating or interpreting the organized stimuli so as to influence behavior and form attitudes.

Each person selects various cues that influence his or her perceptions of people, objects, and symbols. Because of these factors and their potential for imbalance, people often misperceive another person, group, or object. To a considerable extent, people interpret the behavior of others in the context of the setting in which they find themselves.

The following are some organizational examples that point out how perception influences behavior:

1. A subordinate's response to a supervisor's request is based on what she thought she heard the supervisor say, not on what was actually requested.
2. The manager considers the product sold to be of high quality, but the customer making a complaint feels that it is poorly made.
3. An employee is viewed by one colleague as a hard worker who gives good effort and by another colleague as a poor worker who expends no effort.
4. The salesperson regards her pay increase as totally inequitable, while the sales manager considers it a very fair raise.
5. A manager considers consulting a psychic an important part of making an impending decision. Another manager scoffs at the idea. (If you feel this example is unrealistic, consider the following OBM Encounter.)

---

[3] W. R. Nord, ed., *Concepts and Controversy in Organizational Behavior* (Santa Monica, CA: Goodyear Publishing, 1976), p. 22.

ENCOUNTER

TOP EXECUTIVES PERCEIVE PSYCHICS, ASTROLOGERS AS VALUABLE

People differ in their perceptions of other people. Some people, for example, perceive politicians as generally dishonest, while others do not. Some see professional athletes as positive role models, while others do not. And some executives view psychics and astrologers as potentially important advice givers, while others clearly do not.

According to Joanne Kaufman of the *New York Times,* many executives consult mentalists of various kinds about important decisions. Examples include:

- H. L. Hunt, oil tycoon, who consulted psychic Jeanne Dixon before starting a series of major oil explorations.
- John DeLorean, who relied heavily on a spiritualist named Sonja in making numerous business decisions.
- Christian Dior, who consults a psychic to determine the best day to show a new fashion collection.

According to Hans Holzer, a parapsychologist at New York Institute of Technology, some of those offering advice are quacks (about 5 percent), some are really good (about 10 percent), and the rest (85 percent) are basically honest, but "just not very good."

Isaac Jaroslawicz, a financial planner for Shearson Lehman Brothers, seeks the advice of his astrologer, Bill Attride, in forecasting Treasury auction rates. Says Jaroslawicz: "Knowing Bill has helped make me money."

Not everyone, of course, believes in the wisdom of consulting psychics and astrologers. But those who do obviously believe it helps them make better decisions. Says Holzer: "It is hit or miss, but it's more than nothing." □

Source: Based on an article by Joanne Kaufman, "Top Executives Turn for Advice to Psychics, Astrologers," *Houston Chronicle,* November 10, 1985, Sec. 5, p. 18.

A study clearly showing that managers and subordinates often have different perceptions was reported by Likert. He examined the perceptions of superiors and subordinates to determine the amounts and types of recognition that subordinates received for good performance. Both supervisors and subordinates were asked how often superiors provided rewards for good work. The results are presented in Table 3–2.

TABLE 3–2

The Perceptual Gap between Supervisors and Subordinates

Types of Recognition	Frequency with which supervisors say they give various types of recognition for good performance	Frequency with which subordinates say supervisors give various types of recognition for good performance
Gives privileges	52%	14%
Gives more responsibility	48	10
Gives a pat on the back	82	13
Gives sincere and thorough praise	80	14
Trains for better jobs	64	9
Gives more interesting work	51	5

Source: Adapted from Rensis Likert, *New Patterns in Management* (New York: McGraw-Hill, 1961), p. 91.

There were significant differences in what the two groups perceived. Each group viewed the type of recognition being given at a different level. The subordinates in most cases reported that very little recognition was being provided by their supervisors and that rewards were provided infrequently. The superiors saw themselves as giving a wide variety of rewards for good performance. The study points out that marked differences existed between the superiors' and the subordinates' perceptions of the superiors' behavior.

Perceptual Organization.   An important aspect of what is perceived involves organization.[4] One of the most elemental organizing principles of perception is the tendency to pattern stimuli in terms of *figure-ground* relationships. Not all stimuli reach one's awareness with equal clarity. The factor focused on is called the *figure*. That which is experienced and is out of focus is called the *ground*. As you read this text, your perceptions are organized in terms of figure and ground. In every perceptual act, the figure-ground principle is operating.[5] A figure-ground workplace example is a union organizer who stands out more than other workers. As the union pushes to organize the work force, the organizer stands out more and more to management. In most cases, a union organizer would stand out and be considered a troublemaker by management.

The organizing nature of perception is also apparent when similar stimuli are grouped together and when stimuli in close proximity are grouped. Another grouping principle that shapes perceptual organization is called *closure*. This refers to the tendency to want to close something with missing parts. There is a strong need in some individuals to complete a configuration, a job, or a project. For example, if a person with a high need for closure is prevented from finishing a job or task, this could lead to frustration or a more drastic behavior such as quitting.

Stereotyping.   The manner in which managers categorize others is often a reflection of a perceptual bias. The term **stereotype** has been used to describe judgments made about people on the basis of their ethnic group membership. Other stereotypes also need to be guarded against.

For example, men stereotype women executives, managers stereotype union stewards, and women stereotype men. Most people engage in stereotyping. Age has been the basis for stereotyping employees. Researchers have found that managerial actions against older workers are influenced by stereotyping.[6] This type of action could proceed as follows: Suppose that a new job opening involves travel, long hours, and attending a lot of meetings. A manager with a negative bias against older candidates might decide that what is needed to accomplish the job is someone with a lot of energy and

[4] M. W. Levine and J. M. Shefner, *Fundamentals of Sensation and Perception* (Reading, MA: Addison-Wesley Publishing, 1981), p. 17.

[5] B. V. H. Gilmer, *Applied Psychology* (New York: McGraw-Hill, 1975), p. 229.

[6] Benson Rosen and Thomas H. Jerdee, "The Influence of Age Stereotypes on Managerial Decisions," *Journal of Applied Psychology,* August 1976, pp. 428–32.

good health. Since the manager assumes that older workers lack energy and usually are not in good health, he or she will not even consider them. Thus, a perceptual bias excludes from consideration any worker past whatever age the manager considers as being old. Such stereotyping can result in implementing improper programs for promotion, motivation, job design, or performance evaluation.

Selective Perception.   The concept of selective perception is important to managers since they often receive large amounts of information and data. Consequently, they may tend to select information that supports their viewpoints. People tend to ignore information or cues that might make them feel discomfort. For example, a skilled manager may be concerned primarily with an employee's final results or output. Since the employee is often cynical and negative when interacting with the manager, other managers may conclude that the employee will probably receive a poor performance rating. However, this manager selects out the negative features or cues and rates the subordinate on the basis of results. This is a form of selective perception.

The Manager's Characteristics.   People frequently use themselves as benchmarks in perceiving others. Research suggests that (1) knowing oneself makes it easier to see others accurately,[7] (2) one's own characteristics affect the characteristics identified in others,[8] and (3) persons who accept themselves are more likely to see favorable aspects of other people.[9]

   Basically, these conclusions suggest that managers perceiving the behavior and individual differences of employees are influenced by their own traits. If they understand that their own traits and values influence perception, they probably can perform a more accurate evaluation of their subordinates. A manager who is a perfectionist tends to look for perfection in subordinates, while a manager who is quick in responding to technical requirements looks for this ability in his subordinates.

Situational Factors.   The press of time, the attitudes of the people a manager is working with, and other situational factors will all influence perceptual accuracy. If a manager is pressed for time and has to immediately fill an order, then her perceptions will be influenced by the time constraints. The press of time literally will force the manager to overlook some details, to rush certain activities, and to ignore certain stimuli such as requests from other managers or from superiors.

---

[7] R. D. Norman, "The Interrelationships Among Acceptance-Rejection, Self-Other Identity, Insight into Self, and Realistic Perception of Others," *Journal of Social Psychology,* May 1953, pp. 205–35.

[8] J. Bossom and A. H. Maslow, "Security of Judges as a Factor in Impressions of Warmth in Others," *Journal of Abnormal and Social Psychology,* July 1957, pp. 147–48.

[9] K. T. Omivake, "The Relation Between Acceptance of Self and Acceptance of Others Shown by Three Personality Inventories," *Journal of Consulting Psychology,* 1954, pp. 443–46.

Needs and Perceptions. Perceptions are influenced significantly by needs and desires. In other words, the employee, the manager, the vice president, and the director see what they want to see. Like the mirrors in the fun house at the amusement park, the world can be distorted; the distortion is related to needs and desires.

The influence of needs in shaping perceptions has been studied in laboratory settings. For instance, subjects at various stages of hunger were asked to report what they saw in ambiguous drawings flashed before them. It was found that as hunger increased up to a certain point, the subjects saw more and more of the ambiguous drawings as articles of food. The hungry subjects saw steaks, salads, and sandwiches, while the subjects who recently had eaten saw nonfood images in the same drawings.[10]

Emotions and Perceptions. A person's emotional state has a lot to do with perceptions. A strong emotion, such as total distaste for an organizational policy, can make a person perceive negative characteristics in most company policies and rules. Determining a person's emotional state is difficult. Yet managers need to be concerned about what issues or practices trigger strong emotions within subordinates. Strong emotions often distort perceptions.

ATTITUDES

Attitudes are determinants of behavior, because they are linked with perception, personality, and motivation. An **attitude** is a mental state of readiness, learned and organized through experience, exerting a specific influence on a person's response to people, objects, and situations with which it is related. Each of us has attitudes on numerous topics—unions, jogging, restaurants, friends, jobs, religion, the government, income taxes.

This definition of attitude has certain implications for the manager. First, attitudes are learned. Second, attitudes define one's predispositions toward given aspects of the world. Third, attitudes provide the emotional basis of one's interpersonal relations and identification with others. And fourth, attitudes are organized and are close to the core of personality. Some attitudes are persistent and enduring. Yet, like each of the psychological variables, attitudes are subject to change.[11]

Attitudes are intrinsic parts of a person's personality. However, a number of theories attempt to account for the formation and change of attitudes. One such theory proposes that people "seek a congruence between their beliefs and feelings toward objects," and suggests that the modification of attitudes depends on changing either the feelings or the beliefs.[12] The theory proposes that affect, cognition, and behavior determine attitudes and that

---

[10] J. A. Deutsch, W. G. Young, and T. J. Kalogeris, "The Stomach Signals Satiety," *Science,* April 1978, pp. 23–33.

[11] D. J. Bem, *Attitudes, Beliefs, and Human Affairs* (Reading, MA: Brooks-Cole, 1982).

[12] M. J. Rosenberg, "A Structural Theory of Attitudes," *Public Opinion Quarterly,* Summer 1960, pp. 319–40.

FIGURE 3–2

The Three Components of Attitudes

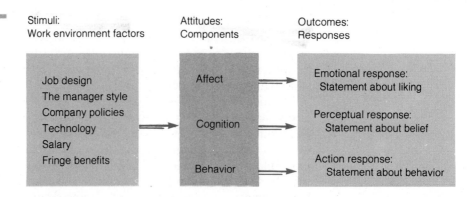

Stimuli: Work environment factors	Attitudes: Components	Outcomes: Responses

Job design
The manager style
Company policies
Technology
Salary
Fringe benefits
	Affect
	
	Cognition
	
	Behavior
		Emotional response:
		  Statement about liking
		Perceptual response:
		  Statement about belief
		Action response:
		  Statement about behavior

attitudes, in turn, determine affect, cognition, and behavior. *Affect,* the emotional, or "feeling," component of an attitude, is learned from parents, teachers, and peer group members. One study displays how the affective component can be measured. A questionnaire was used to survey the attitudes of a group of students toward the church. The students then listened to tape recordings that either praised or disparaged the church. At the time of the tape recordings, the emotional responses of the students were measured with a galvanic skin response (GSR) device. Both prochurch and antichurch students responded with greater emotion (displayed by GSR changes) to statements that contradicted their attitudes than to statements that reflected their attitudes.[13]

The *cognitive* component of an attitude consists of the person's perceptions, opinions, and beliefs. It refers to the thought processes with special emphasis on rationality and logic. An important element of cognition is the evaluative beliefs held by a person. Evaluative beliefs are manifested in the form of favorable or unfavorable impressions that a person holds toward an object or person.

The *behavioral* component of an attitude refers to the tendency of a person to act in a certain way toward someone or something. A person can act toward someone or something in a friendly, warm, aggressive, hostile, or apathetic way or in any of a number of other ways. Such actions could be measured or assessed to examine the behavioral component of attitudes.

Figure 3–2 presents the three components of attitudes in terms of work environment factors such as job design, company policies, and fringe benefits. These stimuli trigger an affect (emotional), cognitive (thought), and behavioral response. In essence, the stimuli result in the formation of attitudes, which then lead to one or more responses—affect, cognitive, or behavioral.

The theory of affective, cognitive, and behavioral components as determinants of attitudes and attitude change has a significant implication for managers. The theory implies that the manager must be able to demonstrate that the positive aspects of contributing to the organization outweigh the negative

---

[13] H. W. Dickson and E. McGinnies, "Affectivity and Arousal of Attitudes as Measured by Galvanic Skin Responses," *American Journal of Psychology,* October 1966, pp. 584–89.

aspects. It is through attempts to develop generally favorable attitudes toward the organization and the job that many managers achieve effectiveness.

Changing Attitudes.   Managers are often faced with the task of changing attitudes because previously structured attitudes hinder job performance. Although many variables affect attitude change, they all can be described in terms of three general factors: trust in the sender; the message itself; and the situation.[14] If employees do not trust the manager, they will not accept the manager's message or change an attitude. Similarly, if the message is not convincing, there will be no pressure to change.

The greater the prestige of the communicator, the greater the attitude change that is produced.[15] A manager who has little prestige and is not shown respect by peers and superiors will be in a difficult position if the job requires changing the attitudes of subordinates so they will work more effectively.

Liking the communicator can lead to attitude change because people try to identify with a liked communicator and tend to adopt attitudes and behaviors of the liked person.[16] Not all managers, however, are fortunate enough to be liked by each of their subordinates. Therefore, it is important to recognize the importance of trust in the manager as a condition for liking the manager.

Even if a manager is trusted, presents a convincing message, and is liked, the problems of changing people's attitudes are not easily solved. An important factor is the strength of the employee's commitment to an attitude. A worker who has decided not to accept a promotion is committed to the belief that it is better to remain in his or her present position than to accept the promotion. Attitudes that have been expressed publicly are more difficult to change because the person has shown commitment, and to change would be to admit a mistake.

How much you are affected by attempts to change your attitude depends in part on the situation. When people are listening to or reading a persuasive message, they sometimes are distracted by other thoughts, sounds, or activities. Studies indicate that if people are distracted while they are listening to a message, they will show more attitude change because the distraction interferes with silent counterarguing.[17]

Distraction is just one of many situational factors that can increase persuasion. Another factor that makes people more susceptible to attempts to change attitudes is pleasant surroundings. The pleasant surroundings may be associated with the attempt to change the attitude.

---

[14] Jonathan L. Freedman, J. Merrill Carlsmith, and David O. Sears, *Social Psychology* (Englewood Cliffs, NJ: Prentice-Hall, 1974), p. 271. Also see D. Coon, *Introduction to Psychology* (St. Paul, MN: West Publishing, 1977), pp. 626–29.

[15] Ibid., p. 272.

[16] H. C. Kelman, "Process of Opinion Change," *Public Opinion Quarterly*, Spring 1961, pp. 57–78.

[17] R. A. Osterhouse and T. C. Brock, "Distraction Increases Yielding to Propaganda by Inhibiting Counterarguing," *Journal of Personality and Social Psychology*, March 1977, pp. 344–58.

Attitudes and Job Satisfaction.   Job satisfaction is an attitude that individuals have about their jobs. It results from their perception of their jobs. Thus, job satisfaction stems from various aspects of the job, such as pay, promotion opportunities, supervisor, and co-workers. Job satisfaction also stems from factors of the work environment, such as the supervisor's style, policies and procedures, work group affiliation, working conditions, and fringe benefits. While numerous dimensions have been associated with job satisfaction, five in particular have crucial characteristics.[18] These five dimensions are:

Pay—the amount of pay received and the perceived equity of pay.

Job—the extent to which job tasks are considered interesting and provide opportunities for learning and for accepting responsibility.

Promotion opportunities—the availability of opportunities for advancement.

Supervisor—the abilities of the supervisor to demonstrate interest in and concern about employees.

Co-workers—the extent to which co-workers are friendly, competent, and supportive.

These five job satisfaction dimensions have been measured in some studies by using the Job Descriptive Index (JDI). Employees are asked to respond "yes," "no," or "?" (can't decide) in describing whether or not a word or phrase reflects their attitudes about their jobs. Of the 72 items on the JDI, 20 are presented in Figure 3–3. A scoring procedure is used to arrive at a score for each of the five dimensions. These five scores then are totaled to provide a measure of overall satisfaction.

A major reason for studying job satisfaction is to provide managers with ways to improve employee attitudes. Many organizations use attitude surveys to determine the levels of employee job satisfaction. National surveys indicate that, in general, workers are satisfied with their jobs.[19] These types of surveys, though interesting, may not reflect the actual degree of job satisfaction in a specific department or organization. There is also a problem that arises simply from asking people how satisfied they are. There is a bias toward giving a positive answer, since declaring anything less indicates that the person is electing to stay in a dissatisfying job. Additionally, to say that workers generally are satisfied with their jobs does not identify the fact that there are differences in satisfaction levels across diverse groups. The following OBM Encounter examines these differences.

---

[18] P. C. Smith, L. M. Kendall, and C. L. Hulin, *The Measurement of Satisfaction in Work and Retirement* (Skokie, IL: Rand McNally, 1969).

[19] Karen E. DeBats, "The Continuing Personnel Challenge," *Personnel Journal*, May 1982, pp. 332–44.

FIGURE 3–3

Sample Items from the 72-Item Job Descriptive Index with "Satisfied" Responses Indicated

Work		Supervision	
N	Routine	Y	Asks my advice
Y	Creative	Y	Praises good work
N	Tiresome	N	Doesn't supervise enough
Y	Gives sense of accomplishment	Y	Tells me where I stand

People		Pay	
Y	Stimulating	Y	Income adequate for normal expenses
Y	Ambitious		
N	Talk too much	N	Bad
N	Hard to meet	N	Less than I deserve
		N	Highly paid

Promotions	
Y	Good opportunity for advancement
Y	Promotion on ability
N	Dead-end job
N	Unfair promotion policy

Source: The Job Descriptive Index is copyrighted by Bowling Green State University. The complete forms, scoring key, instructions, and norms can be obtained from Dr. Patricia C. Smith, Department of Psychology, Bowling Green State University, Bowling Green, Ohio 43404. Reprinted with permission.

ENCOUNTER

JOB SATISFACTION IN THE UNITED STATES

An evaluation of job satisfaction among American workers reveals that there has been no significant change in satisfaction levels in the last two decades. This is the conclusion drawn from results of repeated surveys by the Russell Sage Foundation, the National Science Foundation, and the National Opinion Research Center. Recent findings indicate the following percentage breakdown for a cross section of American workers:

Very satisfied with my job	52%
Somewhat satisfied	36%
A little dissatisfied	9%
Very dissatisfied	3%

Overall figures do not show, however, that there are significant differences in satisfaction levels between various groups. For example:

- Blacks are less satisfied than whites.
- Younger workers are less satisfied than older workers.
- Workers with less education are less satisfied than those with more years of education.
- White-collar workers are more satisfied than blue-collar workers.
- Those with higher incomes are more satisfied than those with lower incomes.

Source: Charles Weaver, "Job Satisfaction in the United States in the 1970s," *Journal of Applied Psychology*, June 1980, pp. 364–367.

Satisfaction and Job Performance.   One of the most debated and controversial issues in the study of job satisfaction is its relationship to job performance. Three views have been advanced: (1) satisfaction causes performance; (2) performance causes satisfaction; and (3) rewards intervene, and there is no inherent relationship.[20] Figure 3–4 shows these three viewpoints.

FIGURE 3–4

**Satisfaction-
Performance
Relationships:
Three Views**

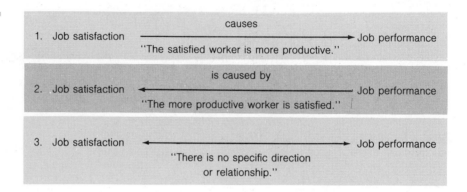

1. Job satisfaction ———————— causes ————————→ Job performance
"The satisfied worker is more productive."

2. Job satisfaction ←———————— is caused by ———————— Job performance
"The more productive worker is satisfied."

3. Job satisfaction ←————————————————————→ Job performance
"There is no specific direction
or relationship."

The first two views are supported weakly by research. A review of 20 studies dealing with the performance-satisfaction relationship found a low association between performance and satisfaction.[21] This evidence is rather convincing that a satisfied worker is not necessarily a high performer. Managerial attempts to make everyone satisfied will not yield high levels of production. Likewise, the assumption that a high-performing employee is likely to be satisfied is not supported.

The third view, that factors such as rewards mediate the performance-satisfaction relationship, *is* supported by research findings.

This means that performance is not a consequence of satisfaction, or vice versa. From a practical standpoint, however, most managers would like to have productive workers who are satisfied and have positive attitudes. In fact, as the following *OBM* Encounter illustrates, managers see a very strong link between attitudes and productivity.

PERSONALITY

The relationship between behavior and personality is perhaps one of the most complex matters that managers have to understand. **Personality** is influenced significantly by cultural and social factors. Regardless of how personality is defined, however, certain principles generally are accepted among psychologists. These are:

---

[20] M. M. Petty, Gail McGee, and Jerry Cavender, "A Meta-Analysis of the Relationship between Individual Job Satisfaction and Individual Performance," *Academy of Management Review,* October 1984, pp. 712–721.

[21] Victor H. Vroom, *Work and Motivation* (New York: John Wiley & Sons, 1964).

PRODUCTIVITY DECLINES AND WORKER ATTITUDES

A growing concern in recent years among organization researchers, managers, and boards of directors has been the nation's declining productivity rate. When management executives are asked for their opinions as to the cause of this decline and they know their reply will be attributed to them by name, they tend to identify a long list of contributing factors, only one of which is labor. Apparently, few executives wish to be known as the person who points the finger at the worker as the villian. Such is not the case, however, when executives are responding to a survey in which they know their views will be anonymous.

In one such survey, more than two-thirds of several hundred business executives queried in the eastern and northeastern sectors of the country felt that productivity declines were due in large part to worker attitudes and habits. The study, conducted by economists from First Pennsylvania Bank, concluded that the decline was *not* a result of governmental overregulation, decreasing technological improvements, inadequate capital investment, or even labor unions. Only two factors showed up as clearly contributing to the decline. One was an increasing cost of energy, and the other was a deterioration in workers' attitudes. ☐

Source: Based on an article by John Cundriff, "Attitudes Blamed for Output Drop," *Lubbock (Texas) Evening Journal*, June 16, 1983, p. 8–A.

1. Personality is an organized whole; otherwise, the individual would have no meaning.
2. Personality appears to be organized into patterns which are, to some degree, observable and measurable.
3. Although personality has a biological basis, its specific development is a product of social and cultural environments.[22]
4. Personality has superficial aspects, such as attitudes toward being a team leader, and a deeper core, such as sentiments about authority or the Protestant work ethic.
5. Personality involves both common and unique characteristics. Every person is different from every other person in some respects, and similar to other persons in other respects.

These five ideas are included in the following definition of personality:

> An individual's personality is a relatively stable set of characteristics, tendencies, and temperaments that have been significantly formed by inheritance and by social, cultural, and environmental factors. This set of variables determines the commonalities and differences in the behavior of the individual.[23]

---

[22] R. A. Price, S. G. Vandenberg, H. Dyer, and J. S. Williams, "Components of Variation in Normal Personality," *Journal of Personality and Social Psychology*, 1982, *43*, pp. 328–340.

[23] This definition is based on Salvatore R. Maddi, *Personality Theories: A Comparative Analysis* (Homewood, IL: Dorsey Press, 1980), p. 41.

The third idea points out some of the forces that are major determinants of personality. These forces are presented in Figure 3–5. Studies of family history, of identical twins, and of early childhood behavior indicate the importance of *hereditary* factors in personality formation. The importance of heredity varies from one personality trait to another. For example, heredity generally is more important in determining a person's temperament than values and ideals.

FIGURE 3–5

Some Major Forces Influencing Personality

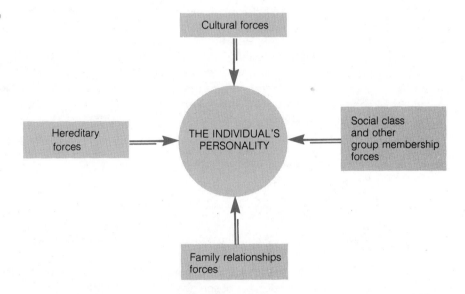

The degree to which every person is molded by *culture* is enormous. We frequently do not comprehend the impact of culture in shaping our personalities. It happens gradually, and usually there is no alternative but to accept the culture. The stable functioning of a society requires that there be shared patterns of behavior among its members and that there be some basis for knowing how to behave in certain situations. To insure this, the society institutionalizes various patterns of behavior. The institutionalization of some patterns of behavior means that most members of a culture will have certain common personality characteristics.

Social class also is important in shaping personality. The various neighborhoods of cities and towns tend to be populated by different social classes, each with its own mores. The neighborhood or community where a child grows up is the setting in which he or she learns about life. Social class influences the person's self-perception, perception of others, and perceptions of work, authority, and money. In terms of such pressing organizational problems as adjustment, quality of work life, and dissatisfaction, the manager attempting to understand employees must give attention to social class factors.

The nature of a person's expectations of others, the ways a person attempts to derive satisfaction, and the manner used to express feelings and resolve emotional conflicts are all formed in an interpersonal context. Family or parent-child relationships are a key factor in this context. They set a pattern of behavior which leaves a significant imprint on all later behavior in the work organization.

A review of each of the determinants that shapes personality (Figure 3–5) will indicate that managers have little control over these determinants. However, no manager should conclude that personality is an unimportant factor in workplace behavior, simply because it is formed outside the organization. The behavior of an employee cannot be understood without considering the concept of personality. In fact, personality is so interrelated with perception, attitudes, learning, and motivation that any analysis of behavior or any attempt to understand behavior is grossly incomplete unless personality is considered.

The importance of personality in shaping organizational behavior is illustrated by Argyris in the chapter readings selection, "The Individual and Organization: Some Problems of Mutual Adjustment." In this article, Argyris argues that a basic incongruency exists between the personality of a mature adult and the demands of the organization. This incongruency explains a great deal of the counterproductive behavior which takes place in work settings.

PERSONALITY AND BEHAVIOR

An issue of interest to behavioral scientists and researchers is whether personality factors such as those measured by inventories or projective tests can predict behavior or performance in organizations. A total inventory or projective test rarely is employed in organizational behavior research. Typically, a few select personality factors such as locus of control, Machiavellianism, or creativity are used, instead, to examine behavior and performance.

Locus of Control. The **locus of control** of individuals determines the degree to which they believe that their behaviors influence what happens to them.[24] Some people believe that they are autonomous—that they are masters of their own fate and bear personal responsibility for what happens to them. They see the control of their lives as coming from inside themselves. Rotter calls these people *internalizers*.[25]

Rotter also holds that many people view themselves as helpless pawns of fate, controlled by outside forces over which they have little, if any, influence. Such people believe that the locus of control is external rather than internal. Rotter calls them *externalizers*.

Rotter devised a scale containing 29 items to identify whether people are internalizers or externalizers.[26] The statements are concerned with success, failure, misfortune, and political events. One statement reflects a belief in

---

[24] P. E. Spector, "Behavior in Organizations as a Function of Employee's Locus of Control," *Psychological Bulletin,* 1982, *91,* pp. 482–497.

[25] J. R. Rotter, "Generalized Expectancies for Internal versus External Control of Reinforcement," *Psychological Monographs 1,* No. 609 (1966), p. 80.

[26] J. R. Rotter, "External Control and Internal Control," *Psychology Today,* June 1971, p. 37.

TABLE 3–3

Sample Items from an Early Version of Rotter's Test of Internal-External Locus of Control

1a	Promotions are earned through hard work and persistence.
1b	Making a lot of money is largely a matter of getting the right breaks.
2a	When I am right, I can convince others.
2b	It is silly to think that one can really change another person's basic attitudes.
3a	In my case, the grades I make are the results of my own efforts; luck has little or nothing to do with it.
3b	Sometimes I feel that I have little to do with the grades I get.
4a	Getting along with people is a skill that must be practiced.
4b	It is almost impossible to figure out how to please some people.

internal control, and the other reflects a belief in external control. Four pairs of statements on the Rotter scale are shown in Table 3–3.

A study of 900 employees in a public utility found that internally controlled employees were more satisfied with their jobs, more likely to be in managerial positions, and more satisfied with a participative management style than were employees who perceived themselves to be externally controlled.[27]

In an interesting study of 90 entrepreneurs, locus of control, perceived stress, coping behaviors, and performance were examined.[28] The study was done in a business district over a 3½-year period following flooding by Hurricane Agnes. Internalizers were found to perceive less stress than did externalizers and to employ more task-centered coping behaviors and fewer emotion-centered coping behaviors. In addition, the task-oriented coping behaviors of internalizers were associated with better performance.

Machiavellianism.   Imagine yourself in the following situation with two other people. Thirty new $1 bills are on the table to be distributed in any way the group decides. The game is over as soon as two of you agree to how it will be divided. Obviously, the fairest distribution would be $10 each. However, a selfish party could cut out the third person, and the other two would each end up with $15. Suppose that one person suggests this alternative to you and that before you can decide, the left-out person offers to give you $16, taking $14 as his or her share and cutting out the other person. What would you do?

Machiavellianism, a concept derived from the writings of Niccolò Machiavelli, helps answer the question.[29] Machiavelli was concerned with the manipulation of people and with the orientations and tactics used by manipulators versus nonmanipulators.[30]

From anecdotal descriptions of power tactics and the nature of influential

---

[27] T. R. Mitchell, C. M. Smyser, and S. E. Weed, "Locus of Control: Supervision and Work Satisfaction," *Academy of Management Journal,* September 1975, pp. 623–31.

[28] C. R. Anderson, "Locus of Control, Coping Behaviors, and Performance in Stress Setting: A Longitudinal Study, *Journal of Applied Psychology,* August 1977, pp. 446–51.

[29] R. Christie and F. L. Geis, eds., *Studies in Machiavellianism* (New York: Academic Press, 1970).

[30] Ibid.

people, various scales have been constructed to measure Machiavellianism. In one scale, the questions are organized around a cluster of beliefs about tactics, people, and morality. The person completing the scale is asked to indicate the extent of their agreement with statements such as: "The best way to handle people is to tell them what they want to hear"; "Anyone who completely trusts someone is asking for trouble"; and, "It is safe to assume that all people have a vicious streak and it will come out when given a chance."[31] In the money allocation game, the individuals who get the lion's share are those who score high on this scale. The low scorers get only slightly less than would be expected by a fair, one-third split.

Creativity. There are a number of ways to view **creativity.** First, you can consider the creative person as mad. Research evidence, however, offers no support for this view. Second, you can see the creative person as being disconnected from the art of creativity. Creativity, in this view, is a mystical act. Third, you can conclude that to be creative, a person must be highly intelligent. Once again, however, the research showing a link between superior intelligence and creativity is generally negative. Finally, you can view creativity as a possibility open to every person—an expression of personality that can be developed.[32]

Many studies have examined creativity. Life histories, personality characteristics, and creativity tests often are scrutinized to determine a person's degree of creativity. In a typical test, subjects might be asked to examine a group of drawings and then indicate what the drawings represent. Novel and unusual responses are rated as being creative.

If creativity is viewed as a personality factor which can be developed, organizations can do a number of things to foster the developmental process.[33] These include:

1. **Buffering.** Managers can look for ways to absorb the risks of creative decisions.
2. **Organizational time-outs.** Give people time off to work on a problem, and allow them to think things through.
3. **Intuition.** Give half-baked ideas a chance.
4. **Innovative attitudes.** Encourage everyone to think of ways to solve problems.
5. **Innovative organizational structures.** Let employees see and interact with many managers and mentors.

Interest in developing creativity in organizations is increasing. The second readings selection in the chapter by Kaplan points out that creativity is an

---

[31] Ibid.

[32] S. S. Gryskiewicz, "Restructuring for Innovation," *Issues and Observations,* November 1981, p. 1; and Isaac Asimov, "Creativity will Dominate Our Time after the Concepts of Work and Fun Have Been Blurred by Technology," *Personnel Administrator,* December 1983, p. 42.

[33] Gryskiewicz, "Restructuring for Innovation," p. 3.

essential element in every managerial job. An important aspect of managerial creativity, according to Kaplan, is the creation of rhythms or alternations between getting caught up in the chaos of work and getting out of it. Whether viewed from Kaplan's perspective or some other, creativity is assuming increasing importance in today's organization.

MOTIVATION AND BEHAVIOR

Now that we have explored the notion of individual differences, it is time that we addressed a specific behavioral concern—motivation (Chapter 4). In order to understand such topics as motivation, rewards, and stress, the psychological and other variables discussed in this chapter must be a part of the manager's knowledge base. Attempting to motivate employees, or to distribute meaningful rewards, or to help subordinates cope with the stresses of work life is like groping in the dark if you do not have a sound, fundamental grasp of, and insight into, abilities, skills, perception, attitudes, and personality. The uninformed manager eventually may find his way, but there will be a lot of bumps, bruises, and wrong turns. The knowledgeable manager, on the other hand, possesses the insight and wisdom needed to move efficiently, to make better decisions, and to be on the lookout for inevitable, individual differences among his or her subordinates. As we proceed through the next four individual-level chapters, think about how abilities, skills, perception, attitudes, and personality help shape the behavior and performance of employees.

SUMMARY OF KEYPOINTS

A. Employees joining an organization must adjust to a new environment, new people, and new tasks. The manner in which people adjust to situations and other people depends largely on their psychological makeup and their personal backgrounds.

B. Individual perceptual processes help the person face the realities of the world. People are influenced by other people and by situations, needs, and past experiences. While a manager is perceiving employees, they are also perceiving the manager.

C. Attitudes are linked with behavioral patterns in a complex manner. They are organized, and they provide the emotional basis for most of a person's interpersonal relations. Changing attitudes is extremely difficult and requires, at the very least, (a) trust in the communicator and (b) strength of message.

D. Job satisfaction is the attitude workers have about their jobs. Managers should be aware of research findings that a satisfied worker is not necessarily a higher performer.

E. Personality is developed long before a person joins an organization. It is influenced by hereditary, cultural, and social determinants. To assume that personality can be modified easily may lead to managerial frustration and ethical problems. The manager should try to cope with personality differences among people and not try to change personalities to fit his or her model of the ideal person.

F. A number of personality variables, such as locus of control and Machiavellianism, have been found to be associated with behavior and performance. Although difficult to measure, these variables appear to be important in explaining and predicting individual behavior.

REVIEW AND DISCUSSION QUESTIONS

1. So many factors influence an individual's behavior that it is impossible to accurately predict what that behavior will be in all situations. Why then should managers take time to understand individual differences?

2. From the standpoint of managing subordinates effectively, which is most important to the manager: subordinates' perceptions of their behavior or the actual behavior itself?

3. It is frequently said that we see what we want to see. Do you agree? What implications does this have for managing people in organizations?

4. Do you have attitudes about school that affect your performance in class? How were these attitudes developed? What would change them?

5. Think of some attitudes you have about work. Identify the three components of these attitudes and indicate what each outcome response would be.

6. For you personally, what seems to be the relationship between performance in school or at work and satisfaction? Does the relationship differ depending on what you are working on? Explain.

7. Personality is shaped by many factors. For each of the factors discussed in the chapter, identify how it influenced your own personality development.

8. Are you an internalizer or externalizer? Would you rather have a boss who is an internalizer or externalizer? Explain.

9. A criticism of some organizations is that all its members have the same personality. Is this a valid criticism in your opinion? How might you explain why this occurs?

10. "If everyone were alike, the task of managing organizations would be much easier." Do you agree or disagree? Explain.

R 1 THE INDIVIDUAL AND ORGANIZATION: SOME PROBLEMS OF MUTUAL ADJUSTMENT*

CHRIS ARGYRIS

It is a fact that most industrial organizations have some sort of formal structure within which individuals must work to achieve the organization's objectives.[1] Each of these basic components of organization (the formal structure and the individuals) has been and continues to be the subject of much research, discussion, and writing. An extensive

* Source: Reprinted from "The Individual and Organization: Some Problems of Mutual Adjustment," by Chris Argyris, published in *Administrative Science Quarterly*, Vol. 2, No. 1 (June 1957), pp. 1–24, by permission of *The Administration Science Quarterly*, Copyright © 1957 *The Administrative Science Quarterly*.

search of the literature leads us to conclude, however, that most of these inquiries are conducted by persons typically interested in one or the other of the basic components. Few focus on both the individual and the organization.

Since in real life the formal structure and the individuals are continuously interacting and transacting, it seems useful to consider a study of their simultaneous impact upon each other. It is the purpose of this paper to outline the beginnings of a systematic framework by which to analyze the nature of the relationship between formal organization and individuals and from which to derive specific hypotheses regarding their mutual impact.[2] Although a much more detailed definition of formal organization will be given later, it is important to

emphasize that this analysis is limited to those organizations whose original formal structure is defined by such traditional principles of organization as "chain of command," "task specialization," "span of control," and so forth. Another limitation is that since the nature of individuals varies from culture to culture, the conclusions of this paper are also limited to those cultures wherein the proposed model of personality applies (primarily American and some Western European cultures).

The method used is a simple one designed to take advantage of the existing research on each component. The first objective is to ascertain the basic properties of each component. Exactly what is known and agreed upon by the experts about each of the components?

Once this information has been collected, the second objective follows logically. When the basic properties of each of these components are known, what predictions can be made regarding their impact upon one another once they are brought together?

SOME PROPERTIES OF HUMAN PERSONALITY

The research on the human personality is so great and voluminous that it is indeed difficult to find agreement regarding its basic properties.[3] It is even more difficult to summarize the agreements once they are inferred from the existing literature. Because of space limitations it is only possible to discuss in detail one of several agreements which seems to the writer to be the most relevant to the problem at hand. The others may be summarized briefly as follows. Personality is conceptualized as (1) being an organization of parts where the parts maintain the whole and the whole maintains the parts; (2) seeking internal balance (usually called adjustment) and external balance (usually called adaptation); (3) being propelled by psychological (as well as physical) energy; (4) located in the need systems; and (5) expressed through the abilities. (6) The personality of the organization may be called "the self" which (7) acts to color all the individual's experiences, thereby causing him to live in "private worlds," and which (8) is capable of defending (maintaining) itself against threats of all types.

 **LEARNING CHECKPOINT**

What are the major forces that shape an individual's personality? Can managers do anything about how an individual's personality is shaped?

The self, in this culture, tends to develop along specific trends which are operationally definable and empirically observable. The basic developmental trends may be described as follows. The human being, in our culture:

1. tends to develop from a state of being passive as an infant to a state of increasing activity as an adult. (This is what E. H. Erikson has called self-initiative and Urie Bronfenbrenner has called self-determination.[4])

2. tends to develop from a state of dependence upon others as an infant to a state of relative independence as an adult. Relative independence is the ability to "stand on one's own two feet" and simultaneously to acknowledge healthy dependencies.[5] It is characterized by the individual's freeing himself from his childhood determiners of behavior (e.g., the family) and developing his own set of behavioral determiners. The individual does not tend to react to others (e.g., the boss) in terms of patterns learned during childhood.[6]

3. tends to develop from being capable of behaving in only a few ways as an infant to being capable of behaving in many different ways as an adult.[7]

4. tends to develop from having erratic, casual, shallow, quickly dropped interests as an infant to possessing a deepening of interests as an adult. The mature state is characterized by an endless series of challenges where the reward comes from doing something for its own sake. The tendency is to analyze and study phenomena in their full-blown wholeness, complexity, and depth.[8]

5. tends to develop from having a short-time perspective (i.e., the present largely determines behavior) as an infant to having a

much longer time perspective as an adult (i.e., the individual's behavior is more affected by the past and the future).[9]

6. tends to develop from being in a subordinate position in the family and society as an infant to aspiring to occupy at least an equal and/or superordinate position relative to his peers.

7. tends to develop from having a lack of awareness of the self as an infant to having an awareness of and control over the self as an adult. The adult who experiences adequate and successful control over his own behavior develops a sense of integrity (Erikson) and feelings of self-worth (Carl R. Rogers).[10]

These characteristics are postulated as being descriptive of a basic multidimensional developmental process along which the growth of individuals in our culture may be measured. Presumably every individual, at any given moment in time, could have his degree of development plotted along these dimensions. The exact location on each dimension will probably vary with each individual and even with the same individual at different times. Self-actualization may now be defined more precisely as the individual's plotted scores (or profile) along the above dimensions.[11]

A few words of explanation may be given concerning these dimensions of personality development:

1. They are only one aspect of the total personality. All the properties of personality mentioned above must be used in trying to understand the behavior of a particular individual. For example, much depends upon the individual's self-concept, his degree of adaptation and adjustment, and the way he perceives his private world.

2. The dimensions are continua, where the growth to be measured is assumed to be continuously changing in degree. An individual is presumed to develop continuously in degree from infancy to adulthood.

3. The only characteristic assumed to hold for all individuals is that, barring unhealthy personality development, they will move from the infant toward the adult end of each continuum. This description is a model outlining the basic growth trends. As such, it does not make any predictions about any specific individual. It does, however, presume to supply the researcher with basic developmental continua along which the growth of any individual in our culture may be described and measured.

4. It is postulated that no individual will ever obtain maximum expression of all these developmental trends. Clearly all individuals cannot be maximally independent, active, and so forth all the time and still maintain an organized society. It is the function of culture (e.g., norms, mores, and so forth) to inhibit maximum expression and to help an individual adjust and adapt by finding his optimum expression.

A second factor that prevents maximum expression and fosters optimum expression are the limits set by the individual's own personality. For example, some people fear the same amount of independence and activity that others desire, and some people do not have the necessary abilities to perform certain tasks. No given individual is known to have developed all known abilities to their full maturity.

5. The dimensions described above are constructed in terms of latent or genotypical characteristics. If one states that an individual

needs to be dependent, this need may be ascertained by clinical inference, because it is one that individuals are not usually aware of. Thus one may observe an employee acting as if he were independent, but it is possible that if one goes below the behavioral surface the individual may be quite dependent. The obvious example is the employee who always seems to behave in a manner contrary to that desired by management. Although this behavior may look as if he is independent, his contrariness may be due to his great need to be dependent upon management which he dislikes to admit to himself and to others.

One might say that an independent person is one whose behavior is not caused by the influence others have over him. Of course, no individual is completely independent. All of us have our healthy dependencies (i.e., those which help us to be creative and to develop). One operational criteria to ascertain whether an individual's desire to be, let us say, independent and active is truly a mature manifestation is to ascertain the extent to which he permits others to express the same needs. Thus an autocratic leader may say that he needs to be active and independent; he may also say that he wants subordinates who are the same. There is ample research to suggest, however, that his leadership pattern only makes him and his subordinates more dependence-ridden.

SOME BASIC PROPERTIES OF FORMAL ORGANIZATION

The next step is to focus the analytic spotlight on the formal organization. What are its properties? What are its basic "givens"? What probable impact will they have upon the human personality? How will the

human personality tend to react to this impact? What sorts of chain reactions are probable when these two basic components are brought together?

Formal Organizations as Rational Organizations

Probably the most basic property of formal organization is its logical foundation or, as it has been called by students of administration, its essential rationality. It is the planners' conception of how the intended consequences of the organization may best be achieved. The underlying assumptions made by the creators of formal organization is that within respectable tolerances man will behave rationally, that is, as the formal plan requires him to behave. Organizations are formed with particular objectives in mind, and their structures mirror these objectives. Although man may not follow the prescribed paths, and consequently the objectives may never be achieved, Herbert A. Simon suggests that by and large man does follow these prescribed paths:

> Organizations are formed with the intention and design of accomplishing goals; and the people who work in organizations believe, at least part of the time, that they are striving toward these same goals. We must not lose sight of the fact that however far organizations may depart from the traditional description . . . nevertheless most behavior in organizations is intendedly rational behavior. By "intended rationality" I mean the kind of adjustment of behavior to goals of which humans are capable—a very incomplete and imperfect adjustment, to be sure, but one which nevertheless does accomplish purposes and does carry out programs.[12]

In an illuminating book, L. Urwick eloquently describes this underlying characteristic.[13] He insists that the creation of a formal organization requires a logical "drawing-office" approach. Although he admits that "nine times out of ten it is impossible to start with a clean sheet," the organizer should sit down and in a "cold-blooded, detached spirit . . . draw an ideal structure." The section from which I quote begins with Urwick's description of how the formal structure should be planned. He then continues:

> Manifestly that is a drawing-office job. It is a designing process. And it may be objected with a great deal of experience to support the contention that organization is never done that way . . . human organization. Nine times out of ten it is impossible to start with a clean sheet. The organizer has to make the best possible use of the human material that is already available. And in 89 out of those 90 percent of cases he has to adjust jobs around to fit the man; he can't change the man to fit the job. He can't sit down in a cold-blooded, detached spirit and draw an ideal structure, an optimum distribution of duties and responsibilities and relationships, and then expect the infinite variety of human nature to fit into it.
>
> To which the reply is that he can and he should. If he has not got a clean sheet, that is no earthly reason why he should not make the slight effort of imagination required to assume that he has a clean sheet. It is not impossible to forget provisionally the personal facts—that old Brown is admirably methodical but wanting in initiative, that young Smith got into a mess with Robinson's wife and that the two men must be kept at opposite ends of the building, that Jones is one of those creatures who can think like a Wrangler about other people's duties but is given to periodic amnesia about certain aspects of his own.[14]

The task of the organizer, therefore, is to create a logically ordered world where, as Fayol suggests, there is a "proper order" and in which there is a "place for everything (everyone)."[15]

The possibility that the formal organization can be altered by personalities, as found by Conrad M. Arensberg and Douglas McGregor[16] and Ralph M. Stogdill and Katheleen Koehler,[17] is not denied by formal organizational experts. Urwick, for example, states in the passage below that the planner must take into account the human element. But it is interesting to note that he perceives these adjustments as "temporary deviations from the pattern in order to deal with idiosyncrasy of personality." If possible, these deviations should be minimized by careful preplanning.

> He [the planner] should never for a moment pretend that these (human) difficulties don't exist. They do exist; they are realities. Nor, when he has drawn up an ideal plan of organization, is it likely that he will be able to fit in all the existing human material perfectly. There will be small adjustments of the job to the man in all kinds of directions. But those adjustments are deliberate and temporary deviations from the pattern in order to deal with idiosyncrasy. There is a world of difference between such modification and drifting into an unworkable organization because Green has a fancy for combining bits of two incompatible functions, or White is "empire-building" . . . or Black has always looked after the canteen, so when he is promoted to Sales Manager, he might as well continue to sell buns internally, though the main product of the business happens to be battleships.
>
> What is suggested is that problems of organization should be handled in the right order. Personal adjustments must be made, insofar as they are necessary. But fewer of them will be necessary and they will

present fewer deviations from what is logical and simple, if the organizer first makes a plan, a design—to which he would work if he had the ideal human material. He should expect to be driven from it here and there. But he will be driven from it far less and his machine will work much more smoothly if he *starts* with a plan. If he starts with a motley collection of human oddities and tries to organize to fit them all in, thinking first of their various shapes and sizes and colors, he may have a patchwork quilt; he will not have an organization.[18]

The majority of experts on formal organization agree with Urwick. Most of them emphasize that no organizational structure will be ideal. None will exemplify the maximum expression of the principles of formal organization. A satisfactory aspiration is for optimum expression, which means modifying the ideal structure to take into account the individual (and any environmental) conditions. Moreover, they urge that the people must be loyal to the formal structure if it is to work effectively. Thus Taylor emphasizes that scientific management would never succeed without a "mental revolution."[19] Fayol has the same problem in mind when he emphasizes the importance of *esprit de corps*.

It is also true, however, that these experts have provided little insight into *why* they believe that people should undergo a "mental revolution," or why an *esprit de corps* is necessary if the principles are to succeed. The only hints found in the literature are that resistance to scientific management occurs because human beings "are what they are" or "because it's human nature." But *why* does "human nature" resist formal organizational principles? Perhaps there is something inherent in the principles which causes human resistance.

Unfortunately too little research specifically assesses the impact of formal organizational principles upon human beings.

Another argument for planning offered by the formal organizational experts is that the organization created by logical, rational design, in the long run, is more human than one created haphazardly. They argue that it is illogical, cruel, wasteful, and inefficient not to have a logical design. It is illogical because design must come first. It does not make sense to pay a large salary to an individual without clearly defining his position and its relationship to the whole. It is cruel because, in the long run, the participants suffer when no clear organizational structure exists. It is wasteful because, unless jobs are clearly predefined, it is impossible to plan logical training, promotion, resigning, and retiring policies. It is inefficient because the organization becomes dependent upon personalities. The personal touch leads to playing politics, which Mary Follett has described as a "deplorable form of coercion."[20]

Unfortunately, the validity of these arguments tends to be obscured in the eyes of the behavioral scientist because they imply that the only choice left, if the formal, rational, predesigned structure is not accepted, is to have no organizational structure at all, with the organizational structure left to the whims, pushes, and pulls of human beings. Some human-relations researchers, on the other hand, have unfortunately given the impression that formal structures are "bad" and that the needs of the individual participants should be paramount in creating and administering an organization. A recent analysis of the existing research, however, points up quite clearly that the importance of the organization is being recognized by those who in the past have focused largely upon the individual.[21]

In the past, and for the most part in the present, the traditional organizational experts based their "human architectural creation" upon certain basic principles or assumptions about the nature of organization. These principles have been described by such people as Urwick,[22] Mooney, Holden et al., Fayol, Dennison, Brown, Gulick, White, Gaus, Stene, Hopf, and Taylor. Although these principles have been attacked by behavioral scientists, the assumption is made in this paper that to date no one has defined a more useful set of formal organization principles. Therefore the principles are accepted as givens. This frees us to inquire about their probable impact upon people, *if they are used as defined.*

Task (Work) Specialization

As James J. Gillespie suggests, the roots of these principles of organization may be traced back to certain principles of industrial economics, the most important of which is the basic economic assumption held by builders of the industrial revolution that "the concentration of effort on a limited field of endeavor increases quality and quantity of output."[23] It follows from the above that the necessity for specialization should increase as the quantity of similar things to be done increases.

If concentrating effort on a limited field of endeavor increases the quality and quantity of output, it follows that organizational and administrative efficiency is increased by the specialization of tasks assigned to the participants of the organization.[24] Inherent in this assumption are three others. The first is that the human personality will behave more efficiently as the task that it is to perform becomes specialized. Second is the assumption that there can be found a one best way to define the job so that it is performed at greater speed.[25] Third is the assumption that any individual differences in the human personality may be ignored by transferring more skill and thought to machines.[26]

A number of difficulties arise concerning these assumptions when the properties of the human personality are recalled. First, the human personality we have seen is always attempting to actualize its unique organization of parts resulting from a continuous, emotionally laden, ego-involving process of growth. It is difficult, if not impossible, to assume that this process can be choked off and the resultant unique differences of individuals ignored. This is tantamount to saying that self-actualization can be ignored. The second difficulty is that task specialization requires the individual to use only a few of his abilities. Moreover, as specialization increases, the less complex motor abilities are used more frequently. These, research suggests, tend to be of lesser psychological importance to the individual. Thus the principle violates two basic givens of the healthy adult human personality. It inhibits self-actualization and provides expression for few, shallow, superficial abilities that do not provide the "endless challenge" desired by the healthy personality.

Harold L. Wilensky and Charles N. Lebeaux correctly point out that task specialization causes what little skill is left in a job to become very important.[27] Now small differences in ability may make enormous differences in output. Thus two machine-shovel operators or two drill-press operators of different degrees of skill can produce dramatically different outputs. Ironically, the increasing importance of this type of skill for the healthy, mature worker means that he should feel he is performing self-satisfying work while using a small number of psychologically unchallenging abilities, when in actuality he may be predisposed to feel otherwise. Task specialization, therefore, requires a healthy adult to behave in a less mature manner, but it also requires that he feel good about it!

Not only is the individual affected, but the social structure as well is modified as a result of the situation described above. Wilensky and Lebeaux, in the same analysis, point out that placing a great emphasis on ability makes "Who you are" become less important that "What you can do." Thus the culture begins to reward relatively superficial, materialistic characteristics.

Chain of Command

The principle of task specialization creates an aggregate of parts, each performing a highly specialized task. An aggregate of parts, each busily performing its particular objective, does not form an organization, however. A pattern of parts must be formed so that the interrelationships among the parts create the organization. Following the logic of specialization, the planners create a new function (leadership) the primary responsibility of which is to control, direct, and coordinate the interrelationships of the parts and to make certain that each part performs its objective adequately. Thus the planner makes the assumption that administrative and organizational efficiency is increased by arranging the parts in a determinate hierarchy of authority in which the part on top can direct and control the part on the bottom.

If the parts being considered are individuals, then they must be motivated to accept direction, control,

and coordination of their behavior. The leader, therefore, is assigned formal power to hire, discharge, reward, and penalize the individuals in order to mold their behavior in the pattern of the organization's objectives.

The impact of such a state of affairs is to make the individuals dependent upon, passive, and subordinate to the leader. As a result, the individuals have little control over their working environment. At the same time their time perspective is shortened because they do not control the information necessary to predict their futures. These requirements of formal organization act to inhibit four of the growth trends of the personality, because to be passive, subordinate, and to have little control and a short time perspective exemplify in adults the dimensions of immaturity, not adulthood.

The planners of formal organization suggest three basic ways to minimize this admittedly difficult position. First, ample rewards should be given to those who perform well and who do not permit their dependence, subordination, passivity, and so forth to influence them in a negative manner. The rewards should be material and psychological. Because of the specialized nature of the worker's job, however, few psychological rewards are possible. It becomes important, therefore, that adequate material rewards are made available to the productive employee. This practice can lead to new difficulties, since the solution is, by its nature, not to do anything about the on-the-job situation (which is what is causing the difficulties) but to pay the individual for the dissatisfactions he experiences. The result is that the employee is paid for his dissatisfaction while at work and his wages are given to him to gain satisfactions outside his work envi-

ronment.

Thus the management helps to create a psychological set which leads the employees to feel that basic causes of dissatisfaction are built into industrial life, that the rewards they receive are wages for dissatisfaction, and that if satisfaction is to be gained, the employee must seek it outside the organization.

To make matters more difficult, there are three assumptions inherent in the above solution that also violate the basic givens of human personality. First, the solution assumes that a whole human being can split his personality so that he will feel satisfied in knowing that the wages for his dissatisfaction will buy him satisfaction outside the plant. Second, it assumes that the employee is primarily interested in maximizing his economic gains. Third, it assumes that the employee is best rewarded as an individual producer. The work group in which he belongs is not viewed as a relevant factor. If he produces well, he should be rewarded. If he does not, he should be penalized even though he may be restricting production because of informal group sanctions.

The second solution suggested by the planners of formal organization is to have technically competent, objective, rational, loyal leaders. The assumption is made that if the leaders are technically competent presumably they cannot have "the wool pulled over their eyes" and that therefore the employees will have a high respect for them. The leaders should be objective and rational and personify the rationality inherent in the formal structure. Being rational means that they must avoid becoming emotionally involved. As one executive states, "We try to keep our personality out of the job." The leader must also be impartial; he must not permit his feelings to operate when he is evaluating others. Finally, the leader must be loyal to the organization so that he can inculcate the loyalty in the employees that Taylor, Fayol, and others believe is so important.

Admirable as this solution may be, it also violates several of the basic properties of personality. If the employees are to respect an individual for what he does rather than for who he is, the sense of integrity based upon evaluation of the total self which is developed in people is lost. Moreover, to ask the leader to keep his personality out of his job is to ask him to stop actualizing himself. This is not possible as long as he is alive. Of course, the executive may want to feel that he is not involved, but it is a basic given that the human personality is an organism always actualizing itself. The same problem arises with impartiality. No one can be completely impartial. As has been shown, the self concept always operates when we are making judgments. In fact, as Rollo May has pointed out, the best way to be impartial is to be as partial as one's needs predispose one to be but to be aware of this partiality in order to correct for it at the moment of decision.[28] Finally, if a leader can be loyal to an organization under these conditions, there may be adequate grounds for questioning the health of his personality make-up.

The third solution suggested by many adherents to formal organizational principles is to motivate the subordinates to have more initiative and to be more creative by placing them in competition with one another for the positions of power that lie above them in the organizational ladder. This solution is traditionally called "the rabble hypothesis." Acting under the assumption that employees will be motivated to ad-

vance upward, the adherents of formal organizations further assume that competition for the increasingly (as one goes up the ladder) scarcer positions will increase the effectiveness of the participants. D. C. S. Williams, conducting some controlled experiments, shows that the latter assumption is not necessarily valid. People placed in competitive situations are not necessarily better learners than those placed in noncompetitive situations.[29] M. Deutsch, as a result of extensive controlled experimental research, supports Williams' results and goes much further to suggest that competitive situations tend to lead to an increase in tension and conflict and a decrease in human effectiveness.[30]

Unity of Direction

If the tasks of everyone in a unit are specialized, then it follows that the objective or purpose of the unit must be specialized. The principle of unity of direction states that organizational efficiency increases if each unit has a single activity (or homogeneous set of activities) that are planned and directed by the leader.[31]

This means that the goal toward which the employees are working, the path toward the goal, and the strength of the barriers they must overcome to achieve the goal are defined and controlled by the leader. Assuming that the work goals do not involve the egos of the employees, (i.e., they are related to peripheral, superficial needs), then ideal conditions for psychological failure have been created. The reader may recall that a basic given of a healthy personality is the aspiration for psychological success. Psychological success is achieved when each individual is able to define his own goals, in relation to his inner needs and the strength of the barriers to be over-

come in order to reach these goals. Repetitive as it may sound, it is nevertheless true that the principle of unity of direction also violates a basic given of personality.

Span of Control

The principle of span of control[32] states that administrative efficiency is increased by limiting the span of control of a leader to no more than five or six subordinates whose work interlocks.[33]

It is interesting to note that Ernest Dale, in an extensive study of organizational principles and practices in one hundred large organizations, concludes that the actual limits of the executive span of control are more often violated than not,[34] while in a recent study James H. Healey arrives at the opposite conclusion.[35] James C. Worthy reports that it is formal policy in his organization to extend the span of control of the top management much further than is theoretically suggested.[36] Finally, W. W. Suojanen, in a review of the current literature on the concept of span of control, concludes that it is no longer valid, particularly as applied to the larger government agencies and business corporations.[37]

In a recent article, however, Urwick criticizes the critics of the span-of-control principle.[38] For example, he notes that in the case described by Worthy, the superior has a large span of control over subordinates whose jobs do not interlock. The buyers in Worthy's organization purchase a clearly defined range of articles; therefore they find no reason to interlock with others.

Simon criticizes the span-of-control principle on the grounds that it increases the "administrative distance" between individuals. An increase in administrative distance violates, in turn, another formal organizational principle that administrative efficiency is enhanced by keeping at a minimum the number of organizational levels through which a matter must pass before it is acted on.[39] Span of control, continues Simon, inevitably increases red tape, since each contact between agents must be carried upward until a common superior is found. Needless waste of time and energy result. Also, since the solution of the problem depends upon the superior, the subordinate is in a position of having less control over his own work situation. This places the subordinate in a work situation in which he is less mature.

Although the distance between individuals in different units increases (because they have to find a common superior), the administrative distance between superior and subordinate within a given unit decreases. As Whyte correctly points out, the principle of span of control, by keeping the number of subordinates at a minimum, places great emphasis on close supervision.[40] Close supervision leads the subordinates to become dependent upon, passive toward, and subordinate to, the leader. Close supervision also tends to place the control in the superior. Thus we must conclude that span of control, if used correctly, will tend to increase the subordinate's feelings of dependence, submissiveness, passivity, and so on. In short, it will tend to create a work situation which requires immature, rather than mature, participants.

AN INCONGRUENCY BETWEEN THE NEEDS OF A MATURE PERSONALITY AND OF FORMAL ORGANIZATION

Bringing together the evidence regarding the impact of formal organizational principles upon the individual, we must conclude that there are some basic incongruencies between the growth trends of a healthy personality in our culture and the requirements of formal organization. If the principles of formal organization are used as ideally defined, then the employees will tend to work in an environment where (1) they are provided minimal control over their work-a-day world, (2) they are expected to be passive, dependent, subordinate, (3) they are expected to have a short-time perspective, (4) they are induced to perfect and value the frequent use of a few superficial abilities, and (5) they are expected to produce under conditions leading to psychological failure.

LEARNING CHECKPOINT

How would social class and culture determinants effect what Arygris calls incongruencies?

All of these characteristics are incongruent to the ones healthy human beings are postulated to desire. They are much more congruent with the needs of infants in our culture. In effect, therefore, formal organizations are willing to pay high wages and provide adequate seniority if mature adults will, for eight hours a day, behave in a less mature manner. If this analysis is correct, this inevitable incongruency increases (1) as the employees are of increasing maturity, (2) as the formal structure (based upon the above principles) is made more clear-cut and logically tight for maximum formal organizational effectiveness, (3) as one goes down the line of command, and (4) as the jobs become more and more mechanized (i.e., take on assembly-line characteristics).

As in the case of the personality developmental trends, this picture of formal organization is also a model. Clearly, no company actually uses the formal principles of organization exactly as stated by their creators. There is ample evidence to suggest that they are being modified constantly in actual situations. Those who expound these principles, however, probably would be willing to defend their position that this is the reason that human-relations problems exist; the principles are not followed as they should be.

In the model of the personality and the formal organization, we are assuming the extreme of each in order that the analysis and its results can be highlighted. Speaking in terms of extremes helps us to make the position sharper. In doing this, we make no assumption that all situations in real life are extreme (i.e., that the individuals will always want to be more mature and that the formal organization will always tend to make people more dependent, passive, and so forth, all the time).[41] The model ought to be useful, however, to plot the degree to which each component tends toward extremes and then to predict the problems that will tend to arise.

Returning to the analysis, it is not difficult to see why some students of organization suggest that immature and even mentally retarded individuals probably would make excellent employees in certain jobs. There is very little documented experience to support such a hypothesis. One reason for this lack of information is probably the delicacy of the subject. Examples of what might be obtained if a systematic study were made may be found in a recent work by Mal Brennan.[42] He cites the Utica Knitting Mill, which made arrangements during 1917 with the Rome Institution for Mentally Defective Girls to employ twenty-four girls whose mental age ranged from six to ten years of age. The girls were such excellent workers that they were employed after the war emergency ended. In fact, the company added forty more in another of their plants. It is interesting to note that the managers praised the subnormal girls highly. According to Brennan, in several important reports they said that:

> when business conditions required a reduction of the working staff, the hostel girls were never "laid off" in disproportion to the normal girls; that they were more punctual, more regular in their habits, and did not indulge in as much "gossip and levity." They received the same rate of pay, and they had been employed successfully at almost every process carried out in the workshops.

In another experiment reported by Brennan, the Works Manager of the Radio Corporation, Ltd., reported that of five young morons employed, "the three girls compared very favourably with the normal class of employee in that age group. The boy employed in the store performed his work with satisfaction. . . . Although there was some doubt about the fifth child, it was felt that getting the most out of him was just a matter of right placement." In each of the five cases, the morons were reported to be quiet, respectful, well behaved, and very obedient. The Works Manager was especially impressed by their truthfulness. A year later the same Works Manager was still able to advise that "in every case, the girls proved to be exceptionally well-behaved, particularly obedient, and strictly honest and trustworthy. They carried out work required of them to such a degree of efficiency that *we were surprised they were classed as subnormals for their age.*"[43]

SUMMARY OF FINDINGS

If one were to put these basic findings in terms of propositions, one could state:

Proposition I. *There Is a Lack of Congruency between the Needs of Healthy Individuals and the Demands of the Formal Organization.*

If one uses the traditional formal principles of organization (*i.e.,* chain of command, task specialization, and so on) to create a social organization, and if one uses as an input agents who tend toward mature psychological development (*i.e.,* who are predisposed toward relative independence, activeness, use of important abilities, and so on), then one creates a disturbance, because the needs of healthy individuals listed above are not congruent with the requirements of formal organization, which tends to require the agents to work in situations where they are dependent, passive, use few and unimportant abilities, and so forth.

Corollary 1. The disturbance will vary in proportion to the degree of incongruency between the needs of the individuals and the requirements of the formal organization.[44]

An administrator, therefore, is always faced with a tendency toward continual disturbance inherent in the work situation of the individuals over whom he is in charge.

Drawing on the existing knowledge of the human personality, a second proposition can be stated.

Proposition II. *The Results of This Disturbance Are Frustration, Failure, Short-Time Perspective, and Conflict.*[45]

If the agents are predisposed to a healthy, mature self-actualization, the following results will occur:

1. They will tend to experience frustration because their self-actualization will be blocked.

2. They will tend to experience failure because they will not be permitted to define their own goals in relation to their central needs, the paths to these goals, and so on.

3. They will tend to experience short-time perspective, because they have no control over the clarity and stability of their future.

4. They will tend to experience conflict, because, as healthy agents, they will dislike the frustration, failure, and short-time perspective which is characteristic of their present jobs. If they leave, however, they may not find new jobs easily, and even if new jobs are found, they may not be much different.[46]

Based upon the analysis of the nature of formal organization, one may state a third proposition.

Proposition III. *The Nature of the Formal Principles of Organization Cause the Subordinate, at Any Given Level, to Experience Competition, Rivalry, Intersubordinate Hostility, and to Develop a Focus toward the Parts Rather than the Whole.*

1. Because of the degree of dependence, subordination, and so on of the subordinates upon the leader, and because the number of positions above any given level always tends to decrease, the subordinates aspiring to perform effectively and to advance will tend to find themselves in competition with, and receiving hostility from, each other.[47]

2. Because, according to the formal principles, the subordinate is directed toward and rewarded for performing his own task well, the subordinate tends to develop an orientation toward his own particular part rather than toward the whole.

3. This part-orientation increases the need for the leader to

coordinate the activity among the parts in order to maintain the whole. This need for the leader, in turn, increases the subordinates' degree of dependence, subordination, and so forth. This is a circular process whose impact is to maintain and/or increase the degree of dependence, subordination, and so on, as well as to stimulate rivalry and competition for the leader's favor.

A BIRD'S-EYE, CURSORY PICTURE OF SOME OTHER RELATED FINDINGS

It is impossible in the short space available to present all of the results obtained from the analysis of the literature. For example, it can be shown that employees tend to adapt to the frustration, failure, short-time perspective, and conflict involved in their work situations by any one or a combination of the following acts:

1. Leaving the organization.
2. Climbing the organizational ladder.
3. Manifesting defense reactions such as daydreaming, aggression, ambivalence, regression, projection, and so forth.
4. Becoming apathetic and disinterested toward the organization, its make-up, and its goals. This leads to such phenomena as: (a) employees reducing the number and potency of the needs they expect to fulfill while at work; (b) employees goldbricking, setting rates, restricting quotas, making errors, cheating, slowing down, and so on.
5. Creating informal groups to sanction the defense reactions and the apathy, disinterest, and lack of self-involvement.
6. Formalizing the informal group.
7. Evolving group norms that perpetuate the behavior outlined in (3), (4), (5), and (6) above.

8. Evolving a psychological set in which human or nonmaterial factors become increasingly unimportant while material factors become increasingly important.
9. Acculturating youth to accept the norms outlined in (7) and (8).

Furthermore, it can also be shown that many managements tend to respond to the employees' behavior by:

1. Increasing the degree of their pressure-oriented leadership.
2. Increasing the degree of their use of management controls.
3. Increasing the number of "pseudo"-participation and communication programs.

These three reactions by management actually compound the dependence, subordination, and so on that the employees experience, which in turn cause the employees to increase their adaptive behavior, the very behavior management desired to curtail in the first place.

Is there a way out of this circular process? The basic problem is the reduction in the degree of dependency, subordination, submissiveness, and so on experienced by the employee in his work situation. It can be shown that job enlargement and employee-centered (or democratic or participative) leadership are elements which, if used correctly, can go a long way toward ameliorating the situation. These are limited, however, because their success depends upon having employees who are ego-involved and highly interested in the organization. This dilemma between individual needs and organization demands is a basic, continual problem posing an eternal challenge to the leader. How is it possible to create an organization in which the individuals may obtain optimum expression and, simultaneously, in

which the organization itself may obtain optimum satisfaction of its demands? Here lies a fertile field for future research in organizational behavior. □

REFERENCES

1. Temporarily, "formal structure" is defined as that which may be found on the organization charts and in the standard operating procedures of an organization.

2. This analysis is part of a larger project whose objectives are to integrate by the use of a systematic framework much of the existing behavioral-science research related to organization. The total report will be published by Harper & Brothers as a book, tentatively entitled *The Behavioral Sciences and Organization*. The project has been supported by a grant from the Foundation for Research on Human Behavior, Ann Arbor, Michigan, for whose generous support the writer is extremely grateful.

3. The relevant literature in clinical, abnormal, child, and social psychology, and in personality theory, sociology, and anthropology was investigated. The basic agreements inferred regarding the properties of personality are assumed to be valid for most contemporary points of view. Allport's "trait theory," Cattell's factor analytic approach, and Kretschmer's somatotype framework are not included. For lay description see the author's *Personality Fundamentals for Administrators*, rev. ed. (New Haven, 1954).

4. E. H. Erikson, *Childhood and Society* (New York, 1950); Urie Bronfenbrenner, "Toward an Integrated Theory of Personality," in Robert R. Blake and Glenn V. Ramsey, *Perception* (New York, 1951), pp. 206–257. See also R. Kotinsky, *Personality in the Making* (New York, 1952), pp. 8–25.

5. This is similar to Erikson's sense of autonomy and Bronfenbrenner's state of creative interdependence.

6. Robert W. White, *Lives in Progress* (New York, 1952), pp. 339 ff.

7. Lewin and Kounin believe that as the individual develops needs and abilities the boundaries between them become more rigid. This explains why an adult is better able than a child to be frustrated in one activity and behave constructively in another. See Kurt Lewin, *A Dynamic Theory of Personality* (New York, 1935) and Jacob S. Kounin, "Intellectual Development and Rigidity," in R. Barker, J. Kounin, and H. R. Wright, eds., *Child Behavior and Development* (New York, 1943), pp. 179–198.

8. Robert White, *op. cit.*, pp. 347 ff.

9. Lewin reminds those who may believe that a long-time perspective is not characteristic of the majority of individuals of the billions of dollars that are invested in insurance policies. Kurt Lewin, *Resolving Social Conflicts* (New York, 1948), p. 105.

10. Carl R. Rogers, *Client-Centered Therapy* (New York, 1951).

11. Another related but discrete set of developmental dimensions may be constructed to measure the protective (defense) mechanisms individuals tend to create as they develop from infancy to adulthood. Exactly how these would be related to the above model is not clear.

12. Herbert A. Simon, *Research Frontiers in Politics and Government* (Washington, D.C., 1955), ch. ii, p. 30.

13. L. Urwick, *The Elements of Administration* (New York, 1944).

14. *Ibid.*, pp. 36–39; quoted by permission of Harper & Brothers.

15. Cited in Harold Koontz and Cyril O'Donnell, *Principles of Management* (New York, 1955), p. 24.

16. Conrad M. Arensberg and Douglas McGregor, Determination of Morale in an Industrial Company, *Applied Anthropology*, Vol. 1 (Jan.–March 1942), 12–34.

17. Ralph M. Stogdill and Katheleen Koehler, *Measures of Leadership Structure and Organization Change* (Columbus, O., 1952).

18. *Ibid.*, pp. 36–39; quoted by permission of Harper & Brothers.

19. For a provocative discussion of Taylor's philosophy, see Reinhard Bendix, *Work and Authority in Industry* (New York, 1956), pp. 274–319.

20. Quoted in *ibid.*, pp. 36–39.

21. Chris Argyris, *The Present State of Research in Human Relations* (New Haven, 1954), ch. i.

22. Urwick, *op. cit.*

23. James J. Gillespie, *Free Expression in Industry* (London, 1948), pp. 34–37.

24. Herbert A. Simon, *Administrative Behavior* (New York, 1947), pp. 80–81.

25. For an interesting discussion see Georges Friedman, *Industrial Society* (Glencoe, Ill., 1955), pp. 54 ff.

26. *Ibid.*, p. 20. Friedman reports that 79 percent of Ford employees had jobs for which they could be trained in one week.

27. Harold L. Wilensky and Charles N. Lebeaux, *Industrialization and Social Welfare* (New York, 1955), p. 43.

28. Rollo May, "Historical and Philosophical Presuppositions for Understanding Therapy," in O. H. Mowrer, *Psychotherapy Theory and Research* (New York, 1953), pp. 38–39.

29. D. C. S. Williams, Effects of Competition between Groups in a Training Situation, *Occupational Psychology*, Vol. 30 (April 1956), 85–93.

30. M. Deutsch, An Experimental Study of the Effects of Cooperation and Competition upon Group Process, *Human Relations*, Vol. 2 (1949), 199–231.

31. The sacredness of these principles is questioned by a recent study. Gunnar Heckscher concludes that the principles of unity of command and unity of direction are formally violated in Sweden: "A fundamental principle of public administration in Sweden is the duty of all public agencies to cooperate directly without necessarily passing through a common superior. This principle is even embodied in the constitution itself, and in actual fact it is being employed daily. It is traditionally one of the most important characteristics of Swedish administration that especially central agencies, but also central and local agencies of different levels, cooperate freely and that this is being regarded as a perfectly normal procedure" (*Swedish Public Administration at Work* [Stockholm, 1955], p. 12).

32. First defined by V. A. Graicunas in an article entitled "Relationship in Organization," in L. Gulick and L. Urwick, eds., *Papers on the Science of Administration*, 2d ed. (New York, 1947), pp. 183–187.

33. L. Urwick, *Scientific Principles and Organization* (New York, 1938), p. 8.

34. Ernest Dale, *Planning and Developing the Company Organization Structure* (New York, 1952), ch. xx.

35. James H. Healey, Coordination and Control of Executive Functions, *Personnel*, Vol. 33 (Sept. 1956), 106–117.

36. James C. Worthy, Organizational Structure and Employee Morale, *American Sociological Review*, Vol. 15 (April 1950), 169–179.

37. W. W. Suojanen, The Span of Control—Fact or Fable?, *Advanced Management*, Vol. 20 (1955) 5–13.

38. L. Urwick, The Manager's Span of Control, *Harvard Business Review*, Vol. 34 (May–June 1956), 39–47.

39. Simon, *op. cit.*, pp. 26–28.

40. William Whyte, "On the Evolution of Industrial Sociology" (mimeographed paper presented at the 1956 meeting of the American Sociological Society).

41. In fact, much evidence is presented in the book from which this article is drawn to support contrary tendencies.

42. Mal Brennan, *The Making of a Moron* (New York, 1953), pp. 13–18.

43. Mr. Brennan's emphasis.

44. This proposition does not hold under certain conditions.

45. In the full analysis, specific conditions are derived under which the basic incongruency increases or decreases.

46. These points are taken, in order, from: Roger G. Barker, T. Dembo, and K. Lewin, "Frustration and Regression: An Experiment with Young Children," *Studies in Child Welfare*, Vol. XVIII, No. 2 (Iowa City, Ia., 1941); John Dollard *et al.*, *Frustration and Aggression* (New Haven, 1939); Kurt Lewin *et al.*, "Level of Aspiration," in J. McV. Hunt, ed., *Personality and the Behavior Disorders* (New York, 1944), pp. 333–378; Ronald Lippitt and Leland Bradford, Employee Success in Work Groups, *Personnel Administration*, Vol. 8 (Dec. 1945), 6–10; Kurt Lewin, "Time Perspective and Morale," in Gertrud Weiss Lewin, ed., *Resolving Social Conflicts* (New York, 1948), pp. 103–124; and Theodore M. Newcomb, *Social Psychology* (New York, 1950), pp. 361–373.

47. These problems may not arise for the subordinate who becomes apathetic, disinterested, and so on.

R² CREATIVITY IN THE EVERYDAY BUSINESS OF MANAGING

ROBERT E. KAPLAN

Asked to list different types of creative professions, the participants in Creativity Week V mentioned writers, scientists, artists, engineers, architects, inventors, musicians, poets, psychologists, creativity specialists, and entrepreneurs. No one mentioned managers. But managers—at least the good ones—are creative all the time. They have to be to meet the confusing, fast-changing procession of demands on their intelligence, adaptability, and people-handling skill.

Creativity is evident in the *process* of management—the moment-to-moment and day-to-day flow of events in the manager's worklife. Claiming that management texts have ignored the management process, Leonard Sayles (1979) described it as:

. . . the actual day-to-day behavior and fragmented give-and-take, and the art of coping and negotiating with the unanticipated, the ambiguous, and the contradictory.

First-rate manager . . . seek to orchestrate . . . the behavior of aggregations of personnel, some motivated, but many obtuse and recalcitrant. The nimble and complex behavior patterns of these superb managers is a delight to behold as they move to motivate, integrate, and modify the structure and personnel that surround them. Yet few texts capture the spirit of excitement and challenge [Sayles might also have said creativity] inherent in these tasks.

Sayles used language that evokes images of management process as an art form. Although often overlooked, the artistic qualities of the effective manager deserve their share of appreciation.

CREATING RHYTHMS IN THE MANAGER'S WORKDAY

Managers are busy, beseiged, harrassed, in demand, and verging out of control. A manager's day is a miscellany of activities: scheduled meetings, impromptu conversations, reading, writing, making presentations, going on tours. Managers jump from one thing to another, from one person or group to another. To fashion order from this potential chaos is a creative act.

What managers create are rhythms, or alternations between giving in to the swirl of events and getting out of the swirl. Three of these rhythms are the alternation between accessibility and inaccessibility, the alternation between activity and reflection, and the alternation between work and leisure.

Rhythm: Accessibility and Inaccessibility

Interruptions pose a dilemma because, although they are the bane of the manager's existence, they are also the lifeline to fresh and necessary information. Managers can afford neither a truly open-door policy, which would rip their workdays to shreds, nor can they afford to close themselves off entirely and miss important news while alienating the very people upon whom they themselves rely for ready accessibility and instant responsiveness.

Effective managers create an ebb and flow; they regulate their boundaries, making them more and then less permeable, admitting intrusions and then resisting or deferring them. The boundaries become more or less permeable depending on the competing pressures—the individual's need to focus on the task at hand versus the pressure to respond to people and events impinging from outside the bounds of the task at hand. Robert Townsend (1970) former president of Avis Rent-A-Car, handled incoming phone calls by having them taken by a secretary until 11:00 A.M., when he returned the calls and accepted additional calls. He used the same method in the afternoon, having calls taken for him from noon to 4:00 P.M., then answering them for the next hour. His was a highly structured way of achieving a rhythm of accessibility and inaccessibility. Other, more flexible methods can be equally effective.

Rhythm: Activity and Reflection

For managers, the time for reflection is hard to come by. Barbara Tuchman (1980), writing about working for the government, observed:

Given schedules broken down into 15 minute appointments and staffs numbering in the hundreds and briefing memos of never less than 30 pages, policy makers never have time to *think*.

For some managers, the only respite from the swift currents of activity comes when they are away from the office—at home, traveling between home and work, on trips. But those who manage their days creatively find havens from activity while at the office. President Nixon had a knack for this (Webber, 1982). He would escape from the White House to a hide-away office across the street in the Executive Office Building where, with his yellow legal pads in front of him, he would concentrate on the larger issues.

As Warren Bennis discovered while he was president of the University of Cincinnati, routine work commonly drives out nonroutine work; only creative managers avoid having the larger issues banished by the details (Bennis, 1976).

Nevertheless, the bustle of the manager's day is not entirely to blame. While sheer activity can overwhelm managers, so can it tempt them. Managers may allow themselves to be seduced by mere activity when the alternative is the anxiety-provoking challenge of reflection and creativity (Ashkenas & Schaffer, 1981). Effective managers find the time to reflect despite being busy and despite the temptation to stay that way.

Alternating rhythmically between action and reflection is partly a matter of making dexterous transitions from one to the other. Managers struggle, after a long bout of activity, to face the unsettling quiet of contemplative work. But activity need not inhibit reflection afterwards, if the period of activity is short. A short burst of activity to start the day can build the momentum needed to glide into reflection later on (Webber, 1982). The key is keeping activity in proportion.

Rhythm: Work and Leisure

Managers work long and hard; "brute persistence" is important to their success (Peters, 1980). Even so, all work and no play can dull a manager's wits and dampen cre-

ativity. According to a board chairman:

> When I hear a man talk about how hard he works, and how he hadn't taken a vacation in 5 years, and how seldom he sees his family, I am almost certain that this man will not succeed in the creative aspects of the business, and most of the important things that have to be done are the result of creative acts. (Mackenzie, 1975, p. 8)

When managers proclaim proudly that they haven't taken a vacation in years, the implication is that they are highly committed to their work and uncommonly loyal to their corporation—qualities that are indeed necessary to career advancement in large organizations (Kanter, 1977). But what does a single-minded devotion to the job sacrifice in the long run? Vaillant (1977) studied 100 men from their college years into their 50's and found that success (in career and family) was associated with, among other things, taking interesting vacations. May (1975) called this pattern the "alternation of the marketplace and the mountain" (p. 65).

Sticking tenaciously to the task can be counterproductive; one can't always attack problems frontally. That may be why Einstein was prompted to ask, "Why is it I get my best ideas in the morning while I'm shaving?" Perhaps because "the mind needs the relaxation of inner controls—needs to be freed in reverie or daydreaming—for the unaccustomed ideas to emerge" (May, 1975, p. 67).

Creative managers achieve this rhythmic interplay between work and diversion in fashioning their workdays and their worklives. If work is fight and diversion is flight, then the diversion considered here is what John Glidewell called constructive flight—not escapism, but

a renewal through involvement in other spheres of activity or inactivity.

With these three rhythms, managers attempt to exercise a modicum of creative control over forces that would control them. The rhythms constitute an order that managers with a talent for orchestrating workday and worklife create out of the disorder of their jobs.

GIVING SHAPE TO PROBLEMS

Despite the play given in the management literature to the solving of problems, managers are equally challenged to find, in the first place, the problems in need of solving. (I mean here, problems as situations to resolve or exploit, difficulties or opportunities.) "Problem finding is no less important a task than problem solving" (Livingston, 1971). This is not to suggest that all of the items in a manager's short- and long-range docket are there because the manager sought them out. Certainly, a sizeable proportion of a manager's work comes already defined. But, to varying degrees, managers are responsible for ferreting out problems—for being attuned to the cues that indicate trouble or opportunity, and for developing a sense of what the cues mean and what action is indicated.

 **LEARNING CHECKPOINT**

The chapter discussed the idea that creativity can be taught. Do you feel that problem finding can be taught? Why?

Finding and defining problems is a creative act with similarities to the visual arts. The manager gives form to a problem in the way a potter sees and then shapes the possibilities in a lump of clay. The difference is that managers practice their craft using an intangible medium—information.

Whether they are employed in an organization that manufactures goods or offers services, managers are more or less removed from the reality of making the product or service. Managers function in a social-informational milieu, in which reality is *constructed*. In other words, managers often decide what is real and what is not. John F. Kennedy and his cabinet interacted in such a way that they came to believe, wrongly, that an invasion of Cuba at the Bay of Pigs would meet with no significant opposition (Janis, 1972). When reality has an indisputable physical basis, there is less room for argument—or construction—although social psychologists have shown that, in a certain percentage of cases, a group can lead an individual to deny the evidence of his or her senses (Asch, 1956). By contrast, social reality is up for grabs. Was the meeting we just attended a productive one or a waste of time? Is morale high, medium or low in this organization? Are women and minorities treated fairly or unfairly in this organization? Does the future of this organization look rosy or bleak? To questions like these, which are the substance of the manager's job, answers are developed—reality is constructed—by a complex mental, emotional, interactive, political process; ultimately, by a creative process.

One way in which managers construct reality is by setting agendas. The notion of agenda setting as a major task of management was developed in an intensive study by Kotter (1982) of 15 general managers. Kotter found that these high-level managers all entered their new positions with only a half-formed idea of what needed to be done. It was in the first 6 to 12 months on the job that these managers developed a firm sense of their short- and long-range goals and the projects that would serve as vehicles to achieve those goals.

The GM's formed their agendas through an elaborate, continuous, and incremental process in which they aggressively collected information—primarily from people, not documents, and to a large extent, from people with whom they already had relationships. In addition they sought information constantly and certainly did not limit their quest to formal planning meetings. Finally, they shaped plans using a combination of analysis and intuition. Out of this searching, sifting, and shaping came a loose and largely unwritten configuration of goals, plans, and projects (Kotter, 1982). In this way the GM's created their sense of what the reality of their organization was and should be.

John DeLorean, whose recent fall from grace should not erase his earlier accomplishments, provides an example of how a GM goes about creating such an agenda (Wright, 1979). Upon taking over the reins as general manager of General Motors' Chevrolet Division in 1969, DeLorean knew the division was in trouble but he didn't know why. Profits were dropping, budgets were being overspent, departments were not coordinating well. To discover the causes of the problem and to give direction to his executive strategy, DeLorean set out on a three-month personal inquiry into the Chevy situation.

What distinguished his search was its inclusiveness. By no means did he limit himself to the people in the immediate organizational vicinity. Instead he visited plants and talked to managers and employees alike; he met with Chevy dealers; he sought out disgruntled employees, even those who had left the division; he consulted with competitors and other informed individuals in and outside of the automobile industry. He neither sat in his office responding to day-to-day problems, nor did he attempt to assess the state of the organization by reading reports. He approached a variety of people and so gave shape to the sources of the division's problems and to a strategy for dealing with those problems.

The urge of managers to make sense of their complex, fast-changing world can be described as a "passion for form" (May, 1975). Fundamentally, it is a wordly version of the artistic instinct that enabled Michelangelo to see and sculpt the statue of David out of Carrera marble.

CREATING SOCIAL ARRANGEMENTS

When we consider the *products* of creative endeavor, we tend to think of *things*—physical objects like industrial products or works of art, or mental objects like ideas. We don't often think of an arrangement as being the creative product itself.

But good managers regularly create social arrangements. Although organizational structure is an obvious example of social creativity, it is a semipermanent structure that becomes an object. More to the point here are the temporary arrangements of people around a task. These arrangements vary from a task force that exists for months, to a group that meets one time on an issue of common concern, to the sequence of people that a manager calls upon during the course of a day to solve a problem.

Creating relationships is a basic form of social creativity, upon which the rest of the manager's work is built. There is no alternative to the developing of relationships; managers depend on a whole host of others without whom they can't perform their jobs at any level of effectiveness (Kaplan & Mazique, 1983). Making up the networks of job-relevant others of the general managers Kotter (1982) studied were hundreds and sometimes thousands of people in and outside of the organization.

Relationships are not bestowed upon a manager; they are developed as a product of individual roles and personalities. A good relationship exists when a manager can depend on another person for a cooperative response. The other person will tend to respond cooperatively when the manager has something to offer. In other words, relationships are based on exchange, whether of tangible or intangible commodities. Effective relationships are reciprocal.

An appreciation of the need to develop reciprocal relationships is shown by an executive who several years ago faced the challenge of introducing computers to the several divisions of his corporation. He headed a new staff function and none of the division heads reported to him. "I spent a lot of time on the opposing forces trying to build credibility—my own and my group's. It was a slam-dunk operation, not loved. I saw us as a change agent, and my approach was to teach a need, induce a need. I tried to build relationships when we weren't in a fight so that when a burning issue came up, you've got money in the bank. When fires broke out, we fought them with face-to-face meetings with our antagonists." This executive had a knack for building relationships under adversity. He gained influence with the division heads by making them aware of how the new func-

tion could meet their needs, built trust by interacting when there wasn't conflict, dealt with conflict by sitting down face to face.

Creating contact is what the manager must do to build or to call upon relationships. The episodes in which a manager and others come together can be likened to a dance. Sayles wrote vividly about how the parties to an effective interaction coordinate their movements. They simultaneously move and respond to the other's movement. As he puts it, "These verbal strokings, this mutual adaptation, appeal to the basic animal nature that calls for rhythmical give-and-take" (1979, p. 67).

LEARNING CHECKPOINT

Can life histories, personality characteristics, and tests provide information on a manager's ability to create contact? Explain.

Just as managers can synchronize their interactions, can dance together, they can also be out-of-step. Managers show a clumsiness on the dance floor of interactions when they only talk and rarely listen, when they only listen and hardly talk, when they can't hold anything but long drawn-out conversations, or when they can only converse on the run.

If contact is dance, then part of creating contact is choosing a suitable stage on which to perform the dance. A plant manager tells the story of how, when he first took over the plant, his predecessor brought him along to a meeting with the union bargaining committee. The adversarial relationship between union and management was demonstrated by the haranguing between the old plant manager

and the union president from opposite ends of a long conference table. After his predecessor had left for good, the new man went to the next union-management meeting and sat down immediately beside the union president, who began as usual to shout and gesture dramatically. But, because it is difficult to yell at a person sitting next to you, the union president moderated his tone and approach, and the relationship between union and management eventually became more cooperative. Thus, by his choice of seating, the manager created a contact with his opposite number that signalled the relationship he wanted. Although his predecessor sought to usher him into the hostile tradition, the new manager saw a choice where others might have thought none existed.

Activating relationships is another dimension of creating social arrangements. With relationships at their disposal, managers get work done by mobilizing these relationships at particular times, in particular ways (some of which have to do with creating contact), around particular tasks.

If contact is dance, then activating relationships is choreography. To begin a project, managers must decide whom to bring on stage to work on which piece of the larger task, in what combinations actors are to be brought together, in what sequence these subgroups are to be convened, and what mode of contact (telephone, written communication, scheduled meeting, impromptu conversation) is to be used among the manager and the others. The manager as choreographer, however, has nothing like a set script to follow, but must improvise the arrangements as he or she goes along.

Something of the quality of the social choreography managers perform is evident in the observation by Bennis (1976):

> To function properly, the leader must have an "executive constellation" [which works] through temporary systems of assembling task forces for a particular assignment, then reassembling others for a different task. (p. 135)

Friend, et al. (1974) also recognize this choreographic talent:

> Knowing how to make effective use of a network is . . . the mobilization of decision networks in an intelligently selective way, which depends on the capacity to understand both the structure of a problem and the structure of organizational and political relations that surround them. (p. 364)

The choreographic art lies in activating relationships in light of the structure of the problem being attacked. Rosebeth Kanter (1982), writing from research on 165 innovative middle managers from five corporations, shows how the success of a project hinges upon the manager's ability to activate relationships. To keep up the commitment of key players over the long course of a project, innovative middle managers make use of briefings, assignments, meeting (both formal and informal), team-building, praise, new structural arrangements, timely appearances by high-level supporters, and the careful management of the impressions of higher-ups (Kanter, 1982). When to resort to which of these and other involvement-building mechanisms is part of the skill of activating relationships.

Thus, managers who are creative in the social sphere invent what we might call microsocial structure—small scale and often ephemeral arrangements of people—designed in such a way as to enlist the help of others in the performance of the bits and pieces of larger tasks.

THE MANAGER AS ARTIST

Managers exhibit creativity in the way they arrange and rearrange, collect and disperse information, ideas, tasks and people. Managers are forever making small departures, and sometimes radical departures, from what has been. Drawing on their talents, energies and history, they make up their responses to situations as they go along. Like the jazz musician, effective managers play variations within a larger thematic framework; they improvise in dealing with problems and people. Ineffective managers replay the same tune, use the same instrument, operate in a narrow band mentally and interpersonally. Versatility separates the effective from the ineffective manager.

But let's not romanticize creativity. It takes *energy* to create, more energy than it does to follow routines. Creative challenges also provoke anxiety. The stress takes a pure form in artists like Giacometti who suffered visibly as he painted, despairing of capturing on canvas his vision of the subject: "Maybe the canvas will become completely empty; then what will become of me? I'll die of it!" (Lord quoted in May, 1975, p. 93). Managers may not agonize as much or as obviously but they do worry about the tough issues that march steadily in their direction. Anxiety in the face of creative tasks can tempt managers to escape into the fast-paced routines of their job.

No joyride for the manager, creativity often carries with it a certain destructive element. Picasso observed that "every act of creation is first of all an act of destruction" (May, 1975, p. 63). For this reason,

established industries tend not to make the next technological advance. The manufacturers of manual typewriters did not invent the electric typewriter, and the manufacturers of electric typewriters did not invent the word processor. The huge capital investment in existing technology works as a disincentive to develop truly new technology (Galbraith, 1982). The next technological breakthrough is, in this sense, destructive. In a small way managers destroy an old idea when they adopt a new one, reject one colleague when they choose another for a desirable assignment.

We can avoid making a fetish of creativity if we recognize the limits of creativity for creativity's sake. Executives with a talent for innovation can do more harm than good if they take over a stable, effective organization and immediately go to work revamping it. Creativity has value to the extent that it is directed to useful purposes. One participant in the Looking Glass simulation, overwhelmed by the material and feeling out of his element, adjusted to his plight by putting on a show of playing his role. Stumped by a question at one point, he excused himself from the meeting and went back to his office to consult his calendar about a time to meet the next day (there was no next day). Observing this, I admired the ingenuity but regretted this manager's response to his ignorance, which was to invent ways to save face. The manager demonstrated creativity, but it was put in the service not of job performance but of defensiveness.

LEARNING CHECKPOINT

Would this manager's creative effort be called an organizational time-out and should it be encouraged? Why?

Effective managers regularly perform unrecognized creative acts. But to develop this underrated talent in the art of managing, and to harness the talent for useful purposes, is no mean feat. Like any artist, the manager puts in years of practice honing skills to a fine edge, but few managers performing their everyday art get the acclaim accorded artists in other fields. ☐

REFERENCES

Asch, S. E. "Studies of Independence of Conformity. A Minority of One Against a Unanimous Majority." *Psychological Monographs 70*(9), 1956, Whole No. 416.

Ashkenas, R. N., and R. H. Schaffer. "Managers Can Avoid Wasting Time." *Harvard Business Review* 60(3), 1982, pp. 84–104.

Bennis, W. *The Unconscious Conspiracy: Why Leaders Can't Lead*. New York: AMACOM, 1976.

Friend, J. K., J. M. Power, and C. J. L. Yewlett. *Public Planning: The Intercorporate Dimension*. London: Tavistock, 1974.

Galbraith, J. R. "Designing the Innovating Organization." *Organizational Dynamics,* Winter 1982, pp. 5–25.

Janis, I. L. *Victims of Groupthink*. Boston: Houghton Mifflin, 1972.

Kanter, R. M., "The Middle Manager as Innovator." *Harvard Business Review,* July-August 1982, pp. 95–105.

Kanter, R. M. *Men and Women of the Corporation.* New York: Basic Books, 1977.

Kaplan, R. E., and M. S. Mazique. *Trade routes: The Manager's Network of Relationships* (Technical Report 22). Greensboro, N.C.: Center for Creative Leadership, February 1983.

Kotter, J. P. *The General Managers.* New York: The Free Press, 1982.

Livingston, J. S. "Myth of the Well-educated manager." *Harvard Business Review* 49(1), 1971, pp. 78–89.

Mackenzie, R. A. *The Time Trap.* New York: AMACOM, 1975.

May, R. *The Courage to Create.* New York: Norton, 1975.

Peters, T. J. "A Style for All Seasons." *The Executive,* Summer, 1980.

Sayles, L. *Leadership.* New York: McGraw-Hill, 1979.

Tuchman, B. "An Inquiry into the Persistence of Unwisdom in Government." *Esquire* 93(5), 1980, pp. 25–31.

Vaillant, G. E. *Adaptation to Life.* Boston: Little, Brown, 1977.

Webber, R. A. "The Art of Construction Procrastination (Manager's Journal)." *The Wall Street Journal,* August 23, 1982.

Wright, J. P. *On a Clear Day You Can See General Motors.* New York: Avon, 1979.

D1 PERSONALITY INSIGHTS

The following 27 statements are designed to provide some insights regarding how you see yourself. In the blank space next to each of these statements, write the number which best describes how strongly you agree or disagree with the statement, or how true or false the statement is as it applies to you. The numbers represent the following:

5 = Strongly Agree, or Definitely True

4 = Generally Agree, or Mostly True

3 = Neither Agree nor Disagree, Neither True or False

2 = Generally Disagree, or Mostly False

1 = Strongly Disagree, or Definitely False

Example:

_2_ You enjoy playing "bridge."

(The "2" in the space next to the statement indicates that you generally disagree: you are more negative than neutral about enjoying "bridge.")

___ 1. In some circumstances in the past you have taken the lead.

___ 2. Everyone should place trust in a supernatural force whose decisions he or she always obeys.

___ 3. You like to perform activities involving selling or salesmanship.

Source: This self-feedback experiential exercise is reprinted with permission from the *Subordinates' Management Styles Survey* by Bernard M. Bass, Enzo R. Valenzi, and Larry D. Eldridge.

____ 4. As a rule you assess your previous actions closely.

____ 5. You often observe those around you to see how your words and actions affect them.

____ 6. What you earn depends on what you know and how hard you work.

____ 7. Generally, those in authority do their share of the unpleasant jobs without passing them on to others.

____ 8. The remedy for social problems depends on eliminating dishonest, immoral, and mentally inferior people.

____ 9. Most people today earn their pay by their own work.

____ 10. The lowest type of person is the one who does not love and respect his parents.

____ 11. There are two kinds of people: the weak and the strong.

____ 12. You are the kind of person who tends to look into and analyze himself or herself.

____ 13. Your promotions depend more on whom you know than on how well you do your job.

____ 14. All children should be taught obedience and respect for authority.

____ 15. Those who are in public offices usually put their own interest ahead of the public interest.

____ 16. Many bosses actually deserve lower pay than their employees.

____ 17. Taking on important responsibilities like starting your own company is something you would like to do.

____ 18. An insult to your good name should never go unpunished.

____ 19. In a meeting you will speak up when you disagree with someone you are convinced is wrong.

____ 20. Thinking about complex problems is enjoyable for you.

____ 21. Generally, people are well paid for their contributions to society.

____ 22. It is better to work for a good boss than for yourself.

____ 23. Many times you would like to know the real reasons why some people behave as they do.

____ 24. In the long run, we each get what we deserve.

____ 25. Most organizations believe in paying a fair day's wages for a fair day's work.

____ 26. Getting ahead is based more on your performance than your politics.

____ 27. You can't expect to be treated fairly by those above you unless you insist on it.

Take your answers to the above questions and enter them below in the appropriate space. In those cases where there is an asterisk before the number, use *reverse scoring* by subtracting your score from six, i.e., a 1 becomes a 5, a 4 becomes a 2, etc. Asterisks indicate that you must change originally high scores to low ones and vice versa.

Group 1	**Group 2**	**Group 3**	**Group 4**
6. ____	1. ____	*2. ____	4. ____
7. ____	3. ____	*8. ____	5. ____
9. ____	17. ____	*10. ____	12. ____
*13. ____	19. ____	*11. ____	20. ____
*15. ____	*22. ____	*14. ____	23. ____
*16. ____	Total ____	*18. ____	Total ____
21. ____		Total ____	
24. ____			
25. ____			
26. ____			
*27. ____			
Total ____			

Now take each of your totals and divide by the number of answers so as to obtain your average responses, i.e., 2.3, 3.2, 4.1, etc. On a scale of 1–5, this measures how you see yourself in each of these four areas.

Average Score The four areas, represented by Groups 1–4 respectively are:

_____ 1. Fair—this score measures the extent to which you see the world as treating you fairly.

_____ 2. Assertive—this score measures the extent to which you see yourself as aggressive.

_____ 3. Equalitarian—this score measures the extent to which you see yourself as nonauthoritarian.

_____ 4. Introspective—this score measures the extent to which you see yourself as thinking about things that go on around you and trying to determine why they occur.

D₂ VALUES ASSESSMENT

A person's values are linked to attitudes. Values serve as a criterion or standard for guiding his or her behavior. In simple terms, values are defined as the constellation of likes, dislikes, viewpoints, shoulds, inner inclinations, rational and irrational judgments, prejudices, and association patterns that determine a person's view of the world.

The following eighteen values are listed in alphabetical order. Your task is to arrange them in order of their importance to *you*, as guiding principles in *your* life. Place a 1 beside the item that is most important, a 2 next to the second most important item, etc., until you have reached number 18.

A Comfortable life a prosperous life	
An Exciting Life a stimulating, active life	
A Sense of Accomplishment lasting contribution	
A World at Peace free of war and conflict	
A World of Beauty beauty of nature and the arts	
Equality brotherhood, equal opportunity for all	

Family Security taking care of loved ones	
Freedom independence, free choice	
Happiness contentedness	
Inner Harmony freedom from inner conflict	
Mature Love sexual and spiritual intimacy	
National Security protection from attack	
Pleasure an enjoyable, leisurely life	
Salvation saved, eternal life	
Self-Respect self-esteem	
Social Recognition respect, admiration	
True Friendship close companionship	
Wisdom a mature understanding of life	

After you have completed the survey, you can compare your ranking with the average for a number of college students who have taken this survey. First, complete the value ranking and then compare your numbers to those of other college students.

ASSUMPTIONS THAT COLOR PERCEPTIONS

OBJECTIVES

1. To gain awareness of the influence of our assumptions on perceptions and evaluations of others.
2. To compare our perceptions with others and to find similarities and differences.

STARTING THE EXERCISE

1. Read the descriptions of the four individuals provided in the *Personal Descriptions* below.
2. Decide which occupation is most likely for each person, and place the name by the corresponding occupation in the *Occupations* list which follows. Each person is in a different occupation and no two people hold the same one.
3. Divide the class into groups of five to seven students each.
a. Share and compare your choices.
b. Compare your choices to the actual occupations. You will receive answers from your instructor.

Discussion

1. What assumptions were made about each person?
2. What assumptions were made about each occupation?
3. Gender was not specified for White or Brown. What gender was assumed? What difference did that make?
4. How could such assumptions influence evaluations?

Your instructor has the identification of theoretical occupations.

Personal Descriptions

R. B. Red is a trim, attractive woman in her early thirties. She holds an undergraduate degree from an eastern woman's college, and is active in several professional organizations. She is an officer (on the national level) of Toastmistress International.

Her hobbies include classical music, opera, and jazz. She is an avid traveler, who is planning a sojourn to China next year.

W. C. White is a quiet, meticulous person. W. C. is tall and thin with blond hair and wire-framed glasses. Family, friends, and church are very important and W. C. devotes any free time to community activities.

W. C. is a wizard with figures but can rarely be persuaded to demonstrate this ability to do mental calculations.

G. A. Green grew up on a small farm in rural Indiana. He is an avid hunter and fisherman. In fact, he and his wife joke about their "deer-hunting honeymoon" in Colorado.

One of his primary goals is to "get back to the land," and he hopes to be able to buy a small farm before he is fifty. He drives a pickup truck and owns several dogs.

B. E. Brown is the child of wealthy professionals who reside on Long Island. Mr. Brown, B. E.'s father, is a "self-made" financial analyst, who made it a point to stress the importance of financial security as B. E. grew up.

B. E. values the ability to structure one's use of time, and can often be found on the golf course on Wednesday afternoons. B. E. dresses in a conservative upper-class manner and professes to be "allergic to polyester."

Occupations

Choose the occupation which seems most appropriate for each person described. Place the names in the spaces next to the corresponding occupations.

____ Banker		____ Clerk	
____ Labor negotiator		____ Army general	
____ Production manager		____ Salesperson	
____ Travel agent		____ Physician	
____ Accountant		____ Truck driver	
____ Teacher		____ Financial analyst	
____ Computer operations manager			

Source: Jerri L. Frantzve, *Behaving in Organizations* (Boston: Allyn & Bacon, 1983), pp. 63–65.

FIRO-B EXERCISE

OBJECTIVES

1. To learn about which needs you prefer to fulfill in your relations with others.
2. To determine how your interpersonal needs relate to the needs of others.

STARTING THE EXERCISE

FIRO-B is an acronym for Fundamental Interpersonal Relations Orientation Behavior. There are no right or wrong answers. Begin step one by completing the FIRO-B scale. The second step, scoring the FIRO-B Instrument will be done with the help of your instructor. Once you have computed your results they are to be entered in the summary matrix. Step three is the interpretation of the FIRO-B results. Step four, the final step, is the group's comparison of the FIRO-B scores.

STEP ONE: COMPLETING THE FIRO-B SCALE

For each statement below, decide which of the following answers best applies to you. Place the number of the answer at the left of the statement.

1. usually   2. often   3. sometimes   4. occasionally   5. rarely   6. never

____ 1. I try to be with people.
____ 2. I let other people decide what to do.
____ 3. I join social groups.
____ 4. I try to have close relationships with people.
____ 5. I tend to join social organizations when I have an opportunity.
____ 6. I let other people strongly influence my actions.
____ 7. I try to be included in informal social activities.
____ 8. I try to have close, personal relationships with people.

____ 9. I try to include other people in my plans.
____ 10. I let other people control my actions.
____ 11. I try to have people around me.
____ 12. I try to get close and personal with people.
____ 13. When people are doing things together, I tend to join them.
____ 14. I am easily led by people.
____ 15. I try to avoid being alone.
____ 16. I try to participate in group activities.

For each of the next group of statements, choose one of the following answers:

1. most people   3. some people   5. one or two people
2. many people   4. a few people   6. nobody

____ 17. I try to be friendly to people.
____ 18. I let other people decide what to do.
____ 19. My personal relations with people are cool and distant.
____ 20. I let other people take charge of things.
____ 21. I try to have close relationships with people.

____ 22. I let other people strongly influence my actions.
____ 23. I try to get close and personal with people.
____ 24. I let other people control my actions.
____ 25. I act cool and distant with people.
____ 26. I am easily led by people.
____ 27. I try to have close, personal relationships with people.

FIRO-B SCORING WORKSHEET (TO BE USED LATER)

$e_i =$	$e_c =$	$e_a =$	$w_i =$	$w_c =$	$w_a =$

Source: Adapted from William Schutz, *The Interpersonal Underworld* (Palo Alto, CA: Science and Behavior Books, 1966).

For each of the next group of statements, choose one of the following answers:

1. most people	2. many people	3. some people	4. a few people	5. one or two people	6. nobody

___ 28. I like people to invite me to things.

___ 29. I like people to act close and personal with me.

___ 30. I try to influence strongly other people's actions.

___ 31. I like people to invite me to join in their activities.

___ 32. I like people to act close toward me.

___ 33. I try to take charge of things when I am with people.

___ 34. I like people to include me in their activities.

___ 35. I like people to act cool and distant toward me.

___ 36. I try to have other people do things the way I want them done.

___ 37. I like people to ask me to participate in their discussions.

___ 38. I like people to act friendly toward me.

___ 39. I like people to invite me to participate in their activities.

___ 40. I like people to act distant toward me.

For each of the next group of statements, choose one of the following answers:

1. usually	2. often	3. sometimes	4. occasionally	5. rarely	6. never

___ 41. I try to be the dominant person when I am with people.

___ 42. I like people to invite me to things.

___ 43. I like people to act close toward me.

___ 44. I try to have other people do things I want done.

___ 45. I like people to invite me to join their activities.

___ 46. I like people to act cool and distant toward me.

___ 47. I try to influence strongly other people's actions.

___ 48. I like people to include me in their activities.

___ 49. I like people to act close and personal with me.

___ 50. I try to take charge of things when I'm with people.

___ 51. I like people to invite me to participate in their activities.

___ 52. I like people to act distant toward me.

___ 53. I try to have other people do things the way I want them done.

___ 54. I take charge of things when I'm with people.

STEP TWO: SCORING THE FIRO-B *(10 minutes)*

Scoring the FIRO-B Instrument will be done with the help of your instructor. After you compute your FIRO-B results, enter them in the following summary matrix:

	Inclusion	Control	Affection
Give (express to others)	$e_i =$	$e_c =$	$e_a =$
Get (want from others)	$w_i =$	$w_c =$	$w_a =$

STEP THREE: INTERPRETING THE RESULTS (*20 minutes*)

Interpret the FIRO-B results. The FIRO-B instrument was designed to measure how much one feels the following needs:

- *Expressed Inclusion* (e_i): The need to include others in one's activities.
- *Wanted Inclusion* (w_i): The need to be included in the activities of others.
- *Expressed Control* (e_c): The need to control others.
- *Wanted Control* (w_c): The need to be controlled by others.
- *Expressed Affection* (e_a): The need to demonstrate your affection toward others.
- *Wanted Affection* (w_a): The need to have others demonstrate affection toward the person feeling the need.

The degree to which the need is felt is indicated by the following scale:

- 0–1: Need felt to a minimum degree. Individual will seldom be making an effort to fulfill need.
- 2–3: Need felt to a slight degree. Individual will occasionally be making an effort to fulfill need.
- 4–5: Need felt to a moderate degree. Individual will be making an effort to fulfill need about 50 percent of the time.
- 6–7: Need felt to a strong degree. Individual will usually be making an effort to fulfill need.
- 8–9: Need felt to a maximum degree. Individual will almost always be making an effort to fulfill need.

The following examples of score combinations will be discussed to further explain the meaning of FIRO-B scores:

Joe				Mac				Pearl				Mae		
	i	*c*	*a*		*i*	*c*	*a*		*i*	*c*	*a*		*i*	*c*	*a*
e	0	0	0	*e*	9	9	9	*e*	0	0	0	*e*	9	9	9
w	0	0	0	*w*	0	0	0	*w*	9	9	9	*w*	9	9	9

The examples given represent extremes seldom encountered in real life, but they dramatically demonstrate differences. More central scores can be interpreted in the same direction but to a lesser degree.

Joe's FIRO-B scores indicate that he tends to be:

i
e 0
w 0

1. A loner who does not want to include others in his activities, nor does he want others to include him in their activities. Apparently, Joe prefers loneliness to rejection.

c
e 0
w 0

2. A free spirit who has no desire to control others and wants no one to control him. Joe probably has a libertarian philosophy and dislikes structure.

a
e 0
w 0

3. A person who needs space. Closeness, body contact, and open expression of affection embarrass Joe. He seldom openly expresses affection and recoils from it if expressed to him. To Joe, expression of affection is being "mushy" or maudlin.

Mac's FIRO-B scores indicate that he tends to be:

	i
e	9
w	0

1. A social activist who organizes and directs the gathering of people for various work and play activities, but one who is very selective about his associates. He doesn't want others to include him in their activities for fear he cannot manipulate his social environment.

	c
e	9
w	0

2. An autocrat who wants to control the behavior of others but who resists direction from others. Mac feels comfortable only if he is running the show without outside interference.

3. An extremely affectionate person who pursues physical and verbal closeness but who recoils from similar expressions of affection that are expressed toward him. Mac takes the same attitude toward affection as the sports person takes toward hunting. Affection is something one does to another.

	a
e	9
w	0

Pearl's FIRO-B scores indicate that she is an unliberated woman who clings to the old-fashioned concepts regarding females. (Some women who answer the FIRO-B scores as they think they should, rather than how they truly feel, obtain results tending toward Pearl's. Males who receive such scores show a tendency toward extreme dependency.) If Pearl answered as she really feels, she would tend to be:

	i
e	0
w	9

1. A telephone and mailbox monitor who patiently waits to be asked to join other's activities and feels hurt if not asked. She does not initiate activities for fear she would appear "pushy."

	c
e	0
w	9

2. A clinging vine who passively looks to others for control and does not ever tell others what to do. She seeks guidance and direction from her parents as a girl, from her husband in midlife, and from her children in her old age.

3. An insecure friend and lover who wants others to aggressively express affection to her, which she would accept passively as if she was doing the other person a favor. If taken for granted, Pearl feels hurt and would probably pout. She considers expressing affection to others as being "unlady-like."

	a
e	0
w	9

Mae's FIRO-B scores indicate that she is a liberated modern woman willing to pursue life to the fullest in spite of the risks involved. Her scores show her with a tendency to be:

	i
e	9
w	9

1. A totally social being who gregariously seeks others to be included in her activities and welcomes invitations of others to be included in their activities. Mae wants to be with others regardless who is running the show. She fears loneliness much more than rejection.

	c
e	9
w	9

2. An organization person who works well in the chain of command and who is willing to work her way up the ladder. She will loyally support and follow the directions of her boss, but also expects the same from those who work for her. She welcomes responsibility and likes to be in total control of her department.

	a
e	9
w	9

3. Assertive friend and lover who wants mutually expressed close and demonstrative relationships with others. She will often be found hugging others she cares for, and she expects a big hug in return.

FIRO-B scores indicate how two individuals will get along with each other and are often used by consultants to forecast boss-employee, work team, and marital compatibility. In our example, Joe would be incompatible with all FIRO-B types except those like him. Often two such loner individuals make a good work or social match. Their relationship is marked with minimum joint activity, each doing his or her own thing without interference from the other and with a great respect for the other's personal space. Joe would not get along well with aggressive Mac, passive Pearl, or assertive Mae.

Mac and Pearl would make a perfect match. Pearl would meet Mac's needs to dominate the situation, and Mac would meet Pearl's need to avoid responsibility, decision-making, and risk-taking.

Mae would not be compatible with Joe, Mac, or Pearl. To Mae, life is a two-way street. She is willing to do her share, but she expects others to carry their load too. Mae gets along best with people like her.

As you interpret your own FIRO-B scores, remember that like all such self-awareness instruments, FIRO-B is not perfect. Therefore, if your scores do not seem to reflect the real you, treat them as you would any other feedback. Give the results an objective but skeptical analysis before accepting or rejecting them.

You will probably have scores in the mid-range rather than in the extremes, and you may find your inclusion, control, and affection scores showing tendencies in different directions. Consistencies as shown in the example are not to be expected. It is possible for a person to have a high need to express control (e_c) and a low need to express affection (e_a), and so on.

STEP FOUR: GROUP COMPARISON OF FIRO-B SCORES
(30 minutes)

Pairs of small group members compare their FIRO-B scores using the following as a guide:

1. What are the inclusion, control, and affection needs or each person?

2. What differences in need patterns exist?

3. What compatibility problems might result from these differences?

4. How might these compatibility problems be solved?

5. Has each person's behavior in your small group reflected his or her FIRO-B need pattern?

6. Predict the nature of your interpersonal relationship if one partner was the boss and the other partner his or her employee.

7. Predict the nature of your interpersonal relationship if you and your partner were close friends.

8. Can you determine what in your backgrounds caused your FIRO-B results?

BOB KNOWLTON

Bob Knowlton was sitting alone in the conference room of the laboratory. The rest of the group had gone. One of the secretaries had stopped and talked for a while about her husband's coming induction into the army and had finally left. Bob, alone in the laboratory, slid a little further down in his chair, looking with satisfaction at the results of the first test run of the new photon unit.

He liked to stay after the others had gone. His appointment as project head was still new enough to give him a deep sense of pleasure. His eyes were on the graphs before him, but in his mind he could hear Dr. Jerrold, the project head, saying again, "There's one thing about this place that you can bank on. The sky is the limit for a man who can produce!" Knowlton felt again the tingle of happiness and embarrassment. Well, dammit, he said to himself, he had produced. He wasn't kidding anybody. He had come to the Simmons Laboratories two years ago. During a routine testing of some rejected Clanson components, he had stumbled on the idea of the photon correlator, and the rest just happened. Jerrold had been enthusiastic: A separate project had been set up for further research and development of the device, and he had gotten the job of running it. The whole sequence of events still seemed a little miraculous to Knowlton.

He shrugged out of the reverie and bent determinedly over the sheets when he heard someone come into the room behind him. He looked up expectantly; Jerrold often stayed late himself and now and then dropped in for a chat. This always made the day's end especially pleasant for Bob. It wasn't Jerrold. The man who had come in was a stranger. He was tall, thin, and rather dark. He wore steel-rimmed glasses and had a very wide leather belt with a large brass buckle. Lucy remarked later that it was the kind of belt the Pilgrims must have worn.

The stranger smiled and introduced himself. "I'm Simon Fester. Are you Bob Knowlton?" Bob said yes, and they shook hands. "Doctor Jerrold said I might find you in. We were talking about your work, and I'm very much interested in what you are doing." Bob waved to a chair.

Fester didn't seem to belong in any of the standard categories of visitors: customer, visiting fireman, stockholder. Bob pointed to the sheets on the table. "There are the preliminary results of a test we're running. We've got a new gadget by the tail and we're trying to understand it. It's not finished, but I can show you the section that we're testing."

He stood up, but Fester was deep in the graphs. After a moment, he looked up with an odd grin. "These look like plots of a Jennings surface. I've been playing around with some autocorrelation functions of surfaces—you know that stuff." Bob, who had no idea what he was referring to, grinned back and nodded, and immediately felt uncomfortable. "Let me show you the monster," he said, and led the way to the workroom.

After Fester left, Knowlton slowly put the graphs away, feeling vaguely annoyed. Then, as if he had made a decision, he quickly locked up and took the long way out so that he would pass Jerrold's office. But the office was locked. Knowlton wondered whether Jerrold and Fester had left together.

The next morning, Knowlton dropped into Jerrold's office, mentioned that he had talked with Fester, and asked who he was.

"Sit down for a minute," Jerrold said. "I want to talk to you about him. What do you think of him?" Knowlton replied truthfully that he thought Fester was very bright and probably very competent. Jerrold looked pleased.

"We're taking him on," he said. "He's had a very good background in a number of laboratories, and he seems to have ideas about the problems we're tackling here." Knowlton nodded in agreement, instantly wishing that Fester would not be placed with him.

"I don't know yet where he will finally land," Jerrold continued, "but he seems interested in what you are doing. I thought he might spend a little time with you by way of getting started." Knowlton nodded thoughtfully. "If his interest in your work continues, you can add him to your group."

"Well, he seemed to have some good ideas even without knowing exactly what we are doing." Knowlton answered. "I hope he stays; we'd be glad to have him."

Knowlton walked back to the lab with mixed feelings. He told himself that Fester would be good for the group. He was no dunce; he'd produce. Knowlton thought again of Jerrold's promise when he had pro-

* This case was prepared by Professor Alex Bavelas for courses in management of research and development conducted at the School of Industrial Management, Massachusetts Institute of Technology, Cambridge, and is used with his permission.

moted him—"the man who produces gets ahead in this outfit." The words seemed to carry the overtones of a threat now.

That day Fester didn't appear until midafternoon. He explained that he had had a long lunch with Jerrold, discussing his place in the lab. "Yes," said Knowlton, "I talked with Jerry this morning about it, and we both thought you might work with us for awhile."

Fester smiled in the same knowing way that he had smiled when he mentioned the Jennings surfaces. "I'd like to," he said.

Knowlton introduced Fester to the other members of the lab. Fester and Link, the mathematician of the group, hit it off well together and spent the rest of the afternoon discussing a method of analysis of patterns that Link had been worrying over the last month.

It was 6:30 when Knowlton finally left the lab that night. He had waited almost eagerly for the end of the day to come—when they would all be gone and he could sit in the quiet rooms, relax, and think it over. "Think what over?" he asked himself. He didn't know. Shortly after 5 P.M. they had all gone except Fester, and what followed was almost a duel. Knowlton was annoyed that he was being cheated out of his quiet period and finally resentfully determined that Fester should leave first.

Fester was sitting at the conference table reading, and Knowlton was sitting at his desk in the little glass-enclosed cubby that he used during the day when he needed to be undisturbed. Fester had gotten the last year's progress reports out and was studying them carefully. The time dragged. Knowlton doodled on a pad, the tension growing inside him. What the hell did Fester think he was going to find in the reports?

Knowlton finally gave up and they left the lab together. Fester took several of the reports with him to study in the evening. Knowlton asked him if he thought the reports gave a clear picture of the lab's activities.

"They're excellent," Fester answered with obvious sincerity. "They're not only good reports, what they report is damn good, too!" Knowlton was surprised at the relief he felt and grew almost jovial as he said good-night.

Driving home, Knowlton felt more optimistic about Fester's presence in the lab. He had never fully understood the analysis that Link was attempting. If there was anything wrong with Link's approach, Fester would probably spot it. "And if I'm any judge," he murmured, "he won't be especially diplomatic about it."

He described Fester to his wife, who was amused

by the broad leather belt and brass buckle.

"It's the kind of belt that Pilgrims must have worn," she laughed.

"I'm not worried about how he holds his pants up," he laughed with her. "I'm afraid that he's the kind that just has to make like a genius twice each day. And that can be pretty rough on the group."

Knowlton had been asleep for several hours when he was jerked awake by the telephone. He realized it had rung several times. He swung off the bed muttering about damn fools and telephones. It was Fester. Without any excuses, apparently oblivious of the time, he plunged into an excited recital of how Link's patterning problem could be solved.

Knowlton covered the mouthpiece to answer his wife's stage-whispered "Who is it?" "It's the genius," replied Knowlton.

Fester, completely ignoring the fact that it was 2:00 in the morning, proceeded in a very excited way to start in the middle of an explanation of a completely new approach to certain of the photon lab problems that he had stumbled on while analyzing past experiments. Knowlton managed to put some enthusiasm in his own voice and stood there, half-dazed and very uncomfortable, listening to Fester talk endlessly about what he had discovered. It was probably not only a new approach, but also an analysis which showed the inherent weakness of the previous experiment and how experimentation along that line would certainly have been inconclusive. The following day Knowlton spent the entire morning with Fester and Link, the mathematician, the customary morning meeting of Bob's group having been called off so that Fester's work of the previous night could be gone over intensively. Fester was very anxious that this be done, and Knowlton was not too unhappy to call the meeting off for reasons of his own.

For the next several days Fester sat in the back office that had been turned over to him and did nothing but read the progress reports of the work that had been done in the last six months. Knowlton caught himself feeling apprehensive about the reaction that Fester might have to some of his work. He was a little surprised at his own feelings. He had always been proud—although he had put on a convincingly modest face—of the way in which new ground in the study of photon measuring devices had been broken in his group. Now he wasn't sure, and it seemed to him that Fester might easily show that the line of research they had been following was unsound or even unimaginative.

The next morning (as was the custom) the members

of the lab, including the girls, sat around a conference table. Bob always prided himself on the fact that the work of the lab was guided and evaluated by the group as a whole, and he was fond of repeating that it was not a waste of time to include secretaries in such meetings. Often, what started out as a boring recital of fundamental assumptions to a naive listener, uncovered new ways of regarding these assumptions that would not have occurred to the researcher who had long ago accepted them as a necessary basis for his work.

These group meetings also served Bob in another sense. He admitted to himself that he would have felt far less secure if he had had to direct the work out of his own mind, so to speak. With the group meeting as the principle of leadership, it was always possible to justify the exploration of blind alleys because of the general educative effect on the team. Fester was there; Lucy and Martha were there; Link was sitting next to Fester, their conversation concerning Link's mathematical study apparently continuing from yesterday. The other members, Bob Davenport, George Thurlow, and Arthur Oliver, were waiting quietly.

Knowlton, for reasons that he didn't quite understand, proposed for discussion this morning a problem that all of them had spent a great deal of time on previously with the conclusion that a solution was impossible, that there was no feasible way of treating it in an experimental fashion. When Knowlton proposed the problem, Davenport remarked that there was hardly any use of going over it again, that he was satisfied that there was no way of approaching the problem with the equipment and the physical capacities of the lab.

This statement had the effect of a shot of adrenalin on Fester. He said he would like to know what the problem was in detail and, walking to the blackboard, began setting down the "factors" as various members of the group began discussing the problem and simultaneously listing the reasons why it had been abandoned.

Very early in the description of the problem it was evident that Fester was going to disagree about the impossibility of attacking it. The group realized this and finally the descriptive materials and their recounting of the reasoning that had led to its abandonment dwindled away. Fester began his statement which, as it proceeded, might well have been prepared the previous night although Knowlton knew this was impossible. He couldn't help being impressed with the organized and logical way that Fester was presenting

ideas that must have occurred to him only a few minutes before.

Fester had some things to say, however, which left Knowlton with a mixture of annoyance, irritation, and at the same time, a rather smug feeling of superiority over Fester in at least one area. Fester was of the opinion that the way that the problem had been analyzed was really typical of group thinking, and with an air of sophistication which made it difficult for a listener to dissent, he proceeded to comment on the American emphasis on team ideas, satirically describing the ways in which they led to a "high level of mediocrity."

During this time Knowlton observed that Link stared studiously at the floor, and he was very conscious of George Thurlow's and Bob Davenport's glances towards him at several points of Fester's little speech. Inwardly, Knowlton couldn't help feeling that this was one point at least in which Fester was off on the wrong foot. The whole lab, following Jerry's lead, talked if not practiced the theory of small research teams as the basic organization for effective research. Fester insisted that the problem could be approached and that he would like to study it for a while himself.

Knowlton ended the morning session by remarking that the meetings would continue and that the very fact that a supposedly insoluble experimental problem was now going to get another chance was another indication of the value of such meetings. Fester immediately remarked that he was not at all averse to meetings for the purpose of informing the group of the progress of its members—that the point he wanted to make was that creative advances were seldom accomplished in such meetings, that they were made by the individual "living with" the problem closely and continuously, a sort of personal relationship to it.

Knowlton went on to say to Fester that he was very glad that Fester had raised these points and that he was sure the group would profit by reexamining the basis on which they had been operating. Knowlton agreed that individual effort was probably the basis for making the major advances but that he considered the group meetings useful primarily because of the effect they had on keeping the group together and on helping the weaker members of the group keep up with the ones who were able to advance more easily and quickly in the analysis of problems.

It was clear as days went by and meetings continued that Fester came to enjoy them because of the pattern which the meetings assumed. It became typical for Fester to hold forth, and it was unquestionably clear that he was more brilliant, better prepared on the various subjects which were germane to the problem being studied, and that he was more capable of going ahead than anyone there. Knowlton grew increasingly disturbed as he realized that his leadership of the group had been, in fact, taken over.

Whenever the subject of Fester was mentioned in occasional meetings with Dr. Jerrold, Knowlton would comment only on the ability and obvious capacity for work that Fester had. Somehow he never felt that he could mention his own discomforts, not only because they revealed a weakness on his own part, but also because it was quite clear that Jerrold himself was considerably impressed with Fester's work and with the contacts he had with him outside the photon laboratory.

Knowlton now began to feel that perhaps the intellectual advantages that Fester had brought to the group did not quite compensate for what he felt were evidences of a breakdown in the cooperative spirit he had seen in the group before Fester's coming. More and more of the morning meetings were skipped. Fester's opinion concerning the abilities of others of the group, with the exception of Link, was obviously low. At times during morning meetings or in smaller discussions he had been on the point of rudeness, refusing to pursue an argument when he claimed it was based on the other person's ignorance of the facts involved. His impatience of others led him to also make similar remarks to Dr. Jerrold. Knowlton inferred this from a conversation with Jerrold in which Jerrold asked whether Davenport and Oliver were going to be continued on; and his failure to mention Link, the mathematician, led Knowlton to feel that this was the result of private conversations between Fester and Jerrold.

It was not difficult for Knowlton to make a quite convincing case on whether the brillance of Fester was sufficient recompense for the beginning of this breaking up of the group. He took the opportunity to speak privately with Davenport and with Oliver and it was quite clear that both of them were uncomfortable because of Fester. Knowlton didn't press the discussion beyond the point of hearing them in one way or another say that they did feel awkward and that it was sometimes difficult for them to understand the arguments he advanced, but often embarrassing to ask him to fill in the background on which his arguments were based. Knowlton did not interview Link in this manner.

About six months after Fester's coming into the photon lab, a meeting was scheduled in which the sponsors of the research were coming in to get some idea of the work and its progress. It was customary at these meetings for project heads to present the research being conducted in their groups. The members of each group were invited to other meetings which were held later in the day and open to all, but the special meetings were usually made up only of project heads, the head of the laboratory, and the sponsors.

As the time for the special meeting approached, it seemed to Knowlton that he must avoid the presentation at all cost. His reasons for this were that he could not trust himself to present the ideas and work that Fester had advanced, because of his apprehension as to whether he could present them in sufficient detail and answer such questions about them as might be asked. On the other hand, he did not feel he could ignore these newer lines of work and present only the material that he had done or that had been started before Fester's arrival. He felt also that it would not be beyond Fester at all, in his blunt and undiplomatic way—if he were present at the meeting, that is—to make comments on his [Knowlton's] presentation and reveal Knowlton's inadequacy. It also seemed quite clear that it would not be easy to keep Fester from attending the meeting, even though he was not on the administrative level of those invited.

Knowlton found an opportunity to speak to Jerrold and raised the question. He remarked to Jerrold that, with the meetings coming up and with the interest in the work and with the contributions that Fester had been making, he would probably like to come to these meetings, but there was a question of the feelings of the others in the group if Fester alone were invited. Jerrold passed this over very lightly by saying that he didn't think the group would fail to understand Fester's rather different position and that he thought that Fester by all means should be invited. Knowlton immediately said he had thought so, too; that Fester should present the work because much of it was work he had done; and, as Knowlton put it, that this would be a nice way to recognize Fester's contributions and to reward him, as he was eager to be recognized as a productive member of the lab. Jerrold agreed, and so the matter was decided.

Fester's presentation was very successful and in some ways dominated the meeting. He attracted the interest and attention of many of those who had come, and a long discussion followed his presentation. Later in the evening—with the entire laboratory staff present—in the cocktail period before the dinner, a little circle of people formed about Fester. One of them was Jerrold himself, and a lively discussion took place concerning the application of Fester's theory. All of this disturbed Knowlton, and his reaction and behavior were characteristic. He joined the circle, praised Fester to Jerrold and to others, and remarked on the brilliance of the work.

Knowlton, without consulting anyone, began at this time to take some interest in the possibility of a job elsewhere. After a few weeks he found that a new laboratory of considerable size was being organized in a nearby city, and that the kind of training he had would enable him to get a project-head job equivalent to the one he had at the lab with slightly more money.

He immediately accepted it and notified Jerrold by a letter, which he mailed on a Friday night to Jerrold's home. The letter was quite brief, and Jerrold was stunned. The letter merely said that he had found a better position; that there were personal reasons why he didn't want to appear at the lab any more; that he would be glad to come back at a later time from where he would be, some 40 miles away, to assist if there was any mixup at all in the past work; that he felt sure that Fester could, however, supply any leadership that was required for the group; and that his decision to leave so suddenly was based on some personal problems—he hinted at problems of health in his family, his mother and father. All of this was fictitious, of course. Jerrold took it at face value but still felt that this was very strange behavior and quite unaccountable, for he had always felt his relationship with Knowlton had been warm and that Knowlton was satisfied and, as a matter of fact, quite happy and productive.

Jerrold was considerably disturbed, because he had already decided to place Fester in charge of another project that was going to be set up very soon. He had been wondering how to explain this to Knowlton, in view of the obvious help Knowlton was getting from Fester and the high regard in which he held him. Jerrold had, as a matter of fact, considered the possibility that Knowlton could add to his staff another person with the kind of background and training that had been unique in Fester and had proved so valuable.

Jerrold did not make any attempt to meet Knowlton. In a way, he felt aggrieved about the whole thing. Fester, too, was surprised at the suddenness of Knowlton's departure and when Jerrold, in talking to him, asked him whether he had reasons to prefer to stay with the photon group instead of the project for the Air Force which was being organized, he chose the Air Force project and went on to that job the following week. The photon lab was hard hit. The leadership of the lab was given to Link with the understanding that this would be temporary until someone could come in to take over.   □

CASE QUESTIONS

1. What was the major problem that faced Knowlton?
2. What ego defense mechanisms did Knowlton personally use?
3. Could Rotter's notion of locus of control be used to analyze Bob Knowlton's situation?

 # THE INDIVIDUAL-ORGANIZATIONAL FIT: ETHICS AND STYLE*

Alternating between tapping his fingertips on his desk and propping his head with them, Dr. Mike Maynard stared at the memo in his office at Energy Research Labs. He had studied it most of the previous night, after it had been pushed under his door just before leaving his office the day before. Shortly he would have to decide what position to take on it. The memo was signed by the "Committee of Concerned Researchers," who wished to meet with Maynard in his office at 9:00 A.M., which was approaching.

He studied again the list of "grievances" against his boss, Wayne Newsome, president of Energy Labs. Trying to be objective, he felt some charges were exaggerated and a few untrue. Nevertheless, he had to concede that on the whole they were well founded.

More troubling was the section titled "alternative recourses." The memo asked its readers to consider which actions they would support regarding president Newsome and the problems at Energy Labs. Three possible actions were proposed.

---

* This case was prepared by Robert Knapp and is used with his permission.

The first advocated an all-out effort to replace Newsome by perhaps "going public" with a campaign to embarrass him in the media and among other important outsiders, by going over his head and taking their grievances to the board of directors, or by taking a vote among the organization's professional employees to express "no confidence" in the president.

The second approach advocated that a committee of department heads see Newsome in private about their concerns, hoping to turn him around and salvage both the deteriorating situation at Energy Labs and Newsome's job.

The third action advocated doing nothing, partly out of fear of making a bad situation worse and of avoiding wrathful revenge from the president, and partly in the hope that things would improve naturally.

Maynard had heard all these before in many different conversations, and had, in fact, contemplated doing some of them on his own. He knew he was in a unique position at Energy Labs because of his long tenure, his personal relationship with Newsome, and his close contacts with some members of the board of directors and other outsiders. Moreover, Maynard felt he, and perhaps only he, knew the root cause of the whole bad situation.

REFLECTIONS

Maynard lay back in his chair and reflected on the course of events that had led to this unfortunate but not totally surprising crisis. The drama of events tightly linked Energy Labs, president Newsome, and himself in such a way that Maynard felt himself moving to center stage.

The company was started nine years ago as a small energy research "think tank" by three university faculty members and two corporate energy specialists. Maynard was one of the original founders still at Energy Labs, and now was head of one of its major research departments. From the beginning, there was some conflict among the organization's principals about whether it should be run more like a university research lab or a profit-seeking private corporation. In the early years, those favoring a collegial or horizontal organization prevailed over those wanting a hierarchical or vertical organization, reflecting the largely academic background of its founders.

Shared decision-making seemed to work well enough until Energy Labs began to grow. Funding of research grew faster than even the most optimistic of its founders expected. A critical point was reached five years ago when both government and private funding agencies required that Energy Labs reorganize itself more like a business, implement better management and financial control systems, and hire a professional administrator with proven managerial experience.

Everyone was delighted when Wayne Newsome was successfully recruited to become president of Energy Labs. His background seemed perfectly suited to the firm's needs. He was recruited from a billion-dollar corporation, where for three years, he had been vice president of a reputable research division many times larger than Energy Labs. Before that, Newsome had retired as a two-star Air Force general. He had worked primarily in staff and management functions in the Air Force, and after receiving his MBA, spent almost five years managing high-level military research offices. He knew personally just about every important energy expert in Washington. He had the reputation of a high-energy, take-charge person, who was also a supersalesman.

Maynard remembered how hard he worked, first to get Newsome to take the job at Energy Labs, and later to assist him in adjusting to the new job and community. Perhaps it was because of this that the two became such close friends. But Maynard always believed their friendship was based more on personal qualities and mutual respect beyond their professional association. Even their wives and children had become very good friends, sharing much more than is typical among families of professional colleagues.

Maynard was touched and flattered when Newsome embraced him as his best friend at Energy Labs and took him under his wing. A rather cloistered academic craftsman-scientist, Maynard learned a great deal from Newsome about people, the business of life, and the life of business. From his relationship with Newsome, he learned how important a mentor could be, even though only 14 years separated them.

Maynard was especially proud of his involvement with Newsome during the latter's first years of leadership. The organization prospered, growing from 40 persons before Newsome took over to almost 120 persons, mostly high-talented professionals, five years later. The number of major divisions and departments had almost tripled.

Newsome proved especially talented in developing and, as he liked to say, "seducing" major funding agency heads. In those early years, everyone at Energy Labs admired Newsome, rallied behind him, and gave their extra for him and for the organization. No one could fault Newsome, not even now, for lacking aggressiveness or for failing to increase Energy Labs' national visibility. Newsome's extremely effective efforts on the outside earned him considerable respect and support from major funding agencies, as well as a respect that bordered on fear from competitors.

Anticipating who would make which arguments at the approaching meeting, Maynard recalled the many hours he had spent discussing Energy Labs' internal problems. Such a waste of time, he thought. Yet the endless discussions seemed necessary—to comfort a subordinate who had suffered an unnecessary lash from Newsome for a minor or nonexistent misstep; to sort out with other department heads the causes and possible solutions to the growing employee disaffection; to counsel people, including some of the organization's best, who were planning to leave Energy Labs out of frustration or anger at Newsome's personal antics or at his refusal to support their recommendations without any explanation.

STAFF MEETING

Last week's meeting of the five research department heads and their senior staffs highlighted the key issues, he thought. The meeting was called to work on the budget with president Newsome, but, as was happening increasingly in recent months, Newsome's secretary informed the group that the president had to leave the office suddenly on urgent outside business and could not attend. Then, as was also happening all too often, the majority of the two-hour meeting was given to discussion and debate about Newsome's performance and Energy Labs' problems.

"Here we go again," one department head said. "We all prepare for hours for another important meeting and Newsome cancels out on us again. I needed his decision yesterday on a new equipment contract, but the supplier agreed to extend the discount period until this afternoon. I really need that equipment and I'll never get that low price again. I am just going to go ahead and order it without Newsome's approval."

"He will have you on the carpet as soon as he finds out," someone commented. "I was in the same bind two weeks ago and ordered some lab remodeling when he wasn't around to approve it. I never saw him pound his desk so hard nor curse so loudly."

All of them had experienced Newsome's fulminations in recent weeks, whenever they posed a problem or even with an innocuous comment roughed some raw nerve no one really understood. Mostly the outbursts came in response to any hint, however slight, that something was not quite right with Energy Labs or with Newsome's performance.

"This guy is so edgy and explosive, I am afraid to say 'good morning' to him," one person said.

"I think he is becoming a little unbalanced, really paranoid—he even looks ill," another added.

"Thank God he is away from the building so much; at least when he is gone, I am not worried about his temper tantrums ruining my day or that of one of my people," was another comment.

"Yeh, but the guy is gone so often things are piling up and important decisions postponed; we are like a fast-moving ship with a half-time captain," another said.

Dr. Mary Richards, one of Energy Labs' brightest, most promising young prospects, had said little on previous occasions. Now, she said: "I am new here and I have been too busy trying to figure out just what the heck is going on to say much, until now. Newsome's paranoia, outbursts, and absenteeism are bad enough. But what really gets me is his macho street-fighter behavior. He even tries to cultivate that image. Every time I see those stupid quotations around his office, I cringe."

"You mean like the Vince Lombardi line about winning is the only thing?" someone asked.

"The worst is that inane rhyme by General Patton," she responded.

They all knew she was referring to the inscription on a plaque behind Newsome's desk. He loved to quote it: "In war as in loving, you've got to keep shoving."

Newsome's locker-room talk and mannerisms had been received cheerfully and without objection in his early years. They seemed a harmless part of his affectionate way of figuratively and at times literally wrapping himself around each employee and making him or her feel loved and appreciated. Now the talk seemed crude, and the backslapping and stroking, phony.

In recent months, almost all of them had experienced being stroked verbally and sometimes physically one day only to learn that Newsome had maligned them to someone else the next day.

"The guy's personality and style fit him to run a used-car lot or a mental institution, but not a research organization," Mary Richards said.

Maynard listened to the long list of complaints, as he had many times before, without saying much. As Newsome's closest associate, but also as one who had gained the respect of Energy Labs' senior employees over many years, Maynard knew they expected him to challenge or at least temper their rising chorus of complaints.

He didn't disappoint them. Partly out of conviction

and partly to play the devil's advocate—for his own thinking as well as theirs—he spoke out.

"Isn't it possible," he suggested, "that our problems may not be all or even mostly the president's doing. Our growth rate has soared since he took over. Maybe we are suffering organizational growth pains that neither he nor we can handle through no fault of anybody. We have all become overworked and strung out, and the president most of all."

Someone commented that after Newsome returned from his last oneweek vacation, he seemed more relaxed and in control, at least for a while.

"Let's not forget," Maynard continued, "how most of the same people in this room publicly applauded the president just two years ago for the great job he was doing. Before he came, we were floundering without any leadership at all. He was our white knight savior, one of you said. He put the pieces together around here. More importantly, his personal commitment to Energy Labs, his drive, and the way he made us feel appreciated—these energized all of us to really put out. This place suddenly came alive with excitement and promise. You've got to admit he provided us great leadership, at least until recently."

Another department head added a supporting comment: "Despite my alarm about our internal problems with Newsome, I've got to admit he does a hell of a job for us on the outside. He hasn't lost *that* touch."

He continued: "Just last week I watched him put on a stellar performance when he made our proposal before the Energy Development Department in Washington. He had them eating out of his hand, and I know he arm-twisted the agency's chairman at a private party afterward. The guy is an old crony of his. I'm sure we will get the contract."

Matt Blackburn, who was at the same presentation, said: "I agree it was another virtuoso performance, but it bothered me that he wasn't quite truthful in the performance specifications he promised we could meet. And his digs at our competitors were not really fair or true. I am afraid that in time outsiders will see through the bravado and b.s., just as we have. There is no doubt he is politically slick and, so far, very effective with outsiders. He'd probably make a great politician. But we need a manager who can keep things humming internally, not just a slick outside p.r. type."

"And we sure will suffer badly if, as Matt says, our credibility becomes suspect on the outside," someone commented.

"Maybe it's not so much that Newsome has changed as that we have," another speculated, going on; "maybe Newsome was the right guy for putting this organization together and sparking its early takeoff. Maybe now we need a president with different skills, one who doesn't lead so much by his own personality and by more selling, but one who can manage what we have already got going. I admit Newsome did a great job getting us launched; maybe now we need someone different to sail the ship."

Many heads nodded in agreement. There ensued a long discussion about Energy Labs' problems and needs, followed by a discussion of whether Newsome could change his style and adapt to the new needs.

Lunch hour was approaching. Danny Martinez, one of the younger but more outspoken people, said: "We've been over these same points time and time again. After lunch we will all go back to our offices to the same pile of problems, and they are never going to be solved as long as Newsome is around."

"What do you propose doing?"

Martinez had his usual ready answer, but this time it came from his close colleague, Mary Richards. Both of them had recently left major universities to join Energy Labs. At their universities, both had also experienced faculties taking "no confidence" votes on their administrators. In one case, a dean was subsequently replaced, and in another, a university president.

Richards asked the group to consider taking a "no confidence" vote on Newsome. She and Martinez seemed to persuade the more skeptical people who had never experienced such an action, that it might make sense at Energy Labs, which they pointed out was closer in nature to a university than a factory, where such votes are unheard of.

Among the various courses of actions frequently discussed, this was becoming the most popular one, at least in recent weeks.

"I am not sure," cautioned Maynard, and he asked: "How do we know how it will turn out? How do we assure it is done honestly and completely? Who will be asked to vote? What do we do with the vote after we have it?"

Martinez began to answer: "We can . . ."

But Maynard continued: "Look, we can't decide anything definite now, and I have to run to a luncheon meeting in a few minutes. I really am not sure in my own mind what or who is really the cause of our problems. There are so many different possible explanations." He paused and chose his words carefully: "There has just got to be something else going on that can explain what's happened over the last year or so. Until we are sure of the cause, we can't choose which action is best. Doesn't anybody have any new insights or information to consider before our next discussion?''

He carefully surveyed all the faces for some hint. The looks were all tired, blank, unrevealing.

"Let's get out of here," Martinez said.

The meeting ended.

TROUBLING TRUTH

Maynard knew he had lied about his ignorance. He knew the answer to his own question and now he was confident no one else did. But this knowledge only increased his burden and sense of responsibility.

His first suspicions of Newsome's drinking problem came from comments from Newsome's wife over many months. Now, in retrospect, he realized she had been growing alarmed at her husband's declining condition and sending out appeals for understanding and help.

Then there was the night when the Newsomes dined at the Maynards' house. That day Newsome had been pounded pretty hard at the board of directors meeting. Newsome drank too much and Maynard had to drive the Newsomes home. He felt at the time it was odd for Mrs. Newsome to break down so much over one too many martinis on one night.

A more definite indication had come two months ago and strictly by accident. Maynard found out from a friend at another firm that Newsome's last vacation was probably spent at a drying-out institution in another state. The friend's wife had been at the same institution at about the same time and thought she had seen Newsome there.

After much soul-searching together, the Maynards decided to reveal their suspicion of Newsome's incipient alcoholism to Mrs. Newsome. Maynard felt he had to do this both out of concern for his friends and for what was happening at Energy Labs.

After initially denying it, Mrs. Newsome confided that their suspicions were true. But she insisted that the problem was temporary and the result of special personal and business pressures that would pass.

She said that her husband developed a similar problem midway in his military career under similar pressures, but that he licked it. After a temporary setback, he resumed and, in fact, improved his successful performance on the job and progressed rapidly. She was confident that he would do the same thing again. She asked Maynard not to reveal anything about this at Energy Labs. In response to Maynard's question about whether he should reveal his knowledge to her husband and offer his help, Mrs. Newsome said she really didn't know.

Since the confirmation by Mrs. Newsome, Maynard felt better for knowing the truth, but also more troubled by what to do. He could not decide whether Mrs. Newsome's confidence that the drinking problem would pass was based on reason or simply hope.

Moreover, Maynard wasn't sure that even if Newsome beat his drinking problem, he would still be able to perform what was needed at Energy Labs. Maybe the organization had outgrown Newsome's skills and talents. Maybe a leader who excels at selling and dealing, at stimulating people by his individual drive and personality, isn't suited to manage an organization grown large, complex, and more impersonal.

At one point weeks earlier, Maynard made up his mind to openly discuss the matter with his boss and friend, and to offer his understanding and support. He asked to have lunch with Newsome. He tried to open the matter by mentioning how concerned he was about the growing talk of unionization and other problems at Energy Labs, and also how worried he was about Newsome's well-being under such pressures.

Newsome came unglued, wildly waving his arms, cursing the union advocates as "ungrateful Judases." Nobody appreciated all he had done for Energy Labs, Newsome yelled. Nobody knew all the goddamn constituencies he had to serve. Nobody worked harder at Energy Labs than he did. The outburst lasted throughout lunch, with Maynard hardly saying another word for an hour and a half.

Afterward, Maynard wondered if his timing had been bad, and whether he should try to broach the subject another time in another way. He also wondered what was on the mind of his close friend on the board of directors. When the friend asked to meet with Maynard, ostensibly about a funding proposal, he kept probing about Newsome and internal problems at Energy Labs. Did his friend know? Did he suspect? Should Maynard tell him and seek his advice?

There was a knock on Maynard's door. He looked at his watch, saw it was 9:00, and braced himself for another tense meeting. □

CASE QUESTIONS

1. Can a drinking problem alter a person's behavior and personality as suggested in the case?
2. How should Maynard, a friend of Newsome's, handle the situation he is faced with?
3. Why would a different style of managing be needed at various points in the history of an organization?

MOTIVATION

An important determinant of individual performance is motivation. But motivation is not the only determinant. Other variables such as effort expended, ability, and previous experience also influence performance. This chapter, however, concentrates on the motivation process as it affects behavior and individual performance.

Motivation is an explanatory concept that we use to make sense out of the behaviors we observe. It is important to note that motivation is inferred. Instead of measuring it directly, we manipulate certain conditions and observe how behavior changes.[1] From the changes we observe, we improve our understanding of the underlying motivation. You assumed that your best friend had made a quick stop to eat lunch when you saw his car parked outside a fast-food restaurant. But your inference was not correct, because your friend actually was talking to the manager about a job on weekends. The lesson is clear: we must always be cautious when making motivational inferences. As more and more information is accumulated, however, our inferences become more accurate, because we can eliminate alternative explanations.

THE STARTING POINT THE INDIVIDUAL

Most managers must motivate a diverse, and, in many respects, unpredictable group of people. The diversity results in different behavioral patterns that are in some manner related to needs and goals.

Needs refer to deficiencies that an individual experiences at a particular point in time. The deficiencies may be physiological (e.g., a need for food), psychological (e.g., a need for self-esteem), or sociological (e.g., a need for social interaction). Needs are viewed as energizers or triggers of behavioral responses. The implication is that when need deficiencies are present, the individual is more susceptible to managers' motivational efforts.

The importance of *goals* in any discussion of motivation is apparent. The motivational process, as interpreted by most theorists, is goal directed. The goals, or outcomes, that an employee seeks are viewed as forces that attract the person. The accomplishment of desirable goals can result in a significant reduction in need deficiencies.

As illustrated in Figure 4–1, people seek to reduce various need deficiencies. Need deficiencies trigger a search process for ways to reduce the tension

---

[1] Herbert Petri, *Motivation: Theory and Research* (Belmont, CA: Wadsworth, 1979), p. 4.

FIGURE 4—1

**The Motivational
Process: An Initial
Model**

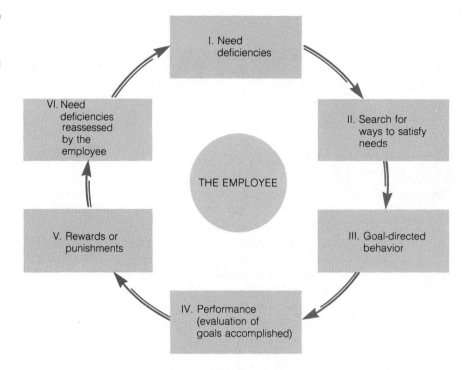

caused by the deficiencies. A course of action is selected, and goal-directed (outcome-directed) behavior occurs. After a period of time, managers assess that behavior. The performance evaluation results in some type of reward or punishment. Such outcomes are weighed by the person, and the need deficiencies are reassessed. This, in turn, triggers the process, and the circular pattern is started again.

MOTIVATION THEORIES: A CLASSIFICATION SYSTEM

Each person is attracted to some set of goals. If a manager is to predict behavior with any accuracy, he or she must know something about an employee's goals and about the actions that the employee will take to achieve them. There is no shortage of motivation theories and research findings that attempt to provide explanations of the behavior-outcome relationship. Two categories can be used to classify theories of motivation.[2] The *content theories* focus on the factors *within* the person that energize, direct, sustain, and stop behavior. They attempt to determine the specific needs that motivate people. The second category includes what are called the *process theories*. These theories provide a description and analysis of *how* behavior is energized, directed, sustained, and stopped. Both categories have important implications for managers, who are—by the nature of their jobs—involved with the motiva-

---

[2] John P. Campbell, Marvin D. Dunnette, Edward E. Lawler III, and Karl E. Weick, *Managerial Behavior, Performance, and Effectiveness* (New York: McGraw-Hill, 1970), pp. 340–56.

tional process. Three important content theories of motivation are: (1) Maslow's need hierarchy; (2) Herzberg's two-factor theory; and (3) McClelland's learned needs theory. Each of these three theories has had an impact on managerial practices and will be considered in the paragraphs that follow. Later in the chapter we shall examine some of the important process approaches.

MASLOW'S NEED HIERARCHY

The crux of Maslow's theory is that needs are arranged in a hierarchy.[3] The lowest-level needs are the physiological needs, and the highest-level needs are the self-actualization needs. These needs are defined to mean the following:

1. **Physiological:** The need for food, drink, shelter, and relief from pain.
2. **Safety and security:** The need for freedom from threat, that is, the security from threatening events or surroundings.
3. **Belongingness, social and love:** The need for friendship, affiliation, interaction, and love.
4. **Esteem:** The need for self-esteem and for esteem from others.
5. **Self-actualization:** The need to fulfill oneself by making maximum use of abilities, skills, and potential.

Maslow's theory assumes that a person attempts to satisfy the more basic needs (physiological) before directing behavior toward satisfying upper-level needs. Several other crucial points in Maslow's thinking are important to understanding the need-hierarchy approach:

1. A satisfied need ceases to motivate. For example, when a person decides that he or she is earning enough pay for contributing to the organization, money loses its power to motivate.
2. Unsatisfied needs can cause frustration, conflict, and stress. From a managerial perspective, unsatisfied needs are dangerous because they may lead to undesirable performance outcomes.
3. Maslow assumes that people have a need to grow and develop, and consequently, will strive constantly to move up the hierarchy in terms of need satisfaction. This assumption may be true for some employees, but not others.

A number of research studies have attempted to test the need-hierarchy theory. The first reported field research that tested a modified version of Maslow's need hierarchy was performed by Porter.[4] At the time of the initial studies, Porter assumed that physiological needs were being adequately satisfied for managers, so he substituted a higher-order need called autonomy,

---

[3]A. H. Maslow, "A Theory of Human Motivation," *Psychological Review,* July 1943, pp. 370–96; and A. H. Maslow, *Motivation and Personality* (New York: Harper & Row, 1954).

[4]Lyman W. Porter, "A Study of Perceived Need Satisfaction in Bottom and Middle Management Jobs," *Journal of Applied Psychology,* February 1961, pp. 1–10.

defined as the person's satisfaction with opportunities to make independent decisions, set goals, and work without close supervision.

Since the early Porter studies, other studies have reported:

1. Managers higher in the organization chain of command place greater emphasis on self-actualization and autonomy.[5]
2. Managers at lower organizational levels in small firms (less than 500 employees) are more satisfied than their counterpart managers in large firms (more than 5,000 employees); however, managers at upper levels in large companies are more satisfied than their counterparts in small companies.[6]
3. American managers overseas are more satisfied with autonomy opportunities than are their counterparts working in the United States.[7]

Despite these findings, a number of issues remain regarding the need-hierarchy theory. First, data from managers in two different companies provided little support that a hierarchy of needs exists.[8] The data suggested that only two levels of needs exist: one is the physiological level, and the other is a level which includes all other needs. Further evidence also disputes the hierarchy notions.[9] Researchers have found that as managers advance in an organization, their needs for security decrease, with a corresponding increase in their needs for social interaction, achievement, and self-actualization.

HERZBERG'S TWO-FACTOR THEORY

Herzberg developed a content theory known as the two-factor theory of motivation.[10] The two factors are called the dissatisfiers-satisfiers or the hygiene-motivators or the extrinsic-intrinsic factors, depending on the discussant of the theory. The original research which led to the theory gave rise to two specific conclusions. First, there is a set of **extrinsic** conditions, the job context, which result in *dissatisfaction* among employees when the conditions are not present. If these conditions are present, this does not necessarily motivate employees. These conditions are the *dissatisfiers* or *hygiene* factors, since they are needed to maintain at least a level of "no dissatisfaction."

---

[5] Lyman W. Porter, *Organizational Patterns of Managerial Job Attitudes* (New York: American Foundation for Management Research, 1964).

[6] Lyman W. Porter, "Job Attitudes in Management: Perceived Deficiencies in Need Fulfillment as a Function of Size of the Company," *Journal of Applied Psychology,* December 1963, pp. 386–97.

[7] John M. Ivancevich, "Perceived Need Satisfaction of Domestic versus Overseas Managers," *Journal of Applied Psychology,* August 1969, pp. 274–78.

[8] Edward E. Lawler III and J. L. Suttle, "A Causal Correlation Test of the Need Hierarchy Concept," *Organizational Behavior and Human Performance,* April 1972, pp. 265–87.

[9] Douglas T. Hall and K. E. Nougaim, "An Examination of Maslow's Need Hierarchy in an Organizational Setting," *Organizational Behavior and Human Performance,* February 1968, pp. 12–35.

[10] Frederick Herzberg, B. Mausner, and B. Synderman, *The Motivation to Work,* (New York: John Wiley & Sons, 1959).

They include:

1. Salary.
2. Job security.
3. Working conditions.
4. Status.
5. Company procedures.
6. Quality of technical supervision.
7. Quality of interpersonal relations among peers, with superiors, and with subordinates.

Second, a set of **intrinsic** conditions, the job content—when present in the job—builds strong levels of motivation that can result in good job performance. If these conditions are not present, they do not prove highly dissatisfying. The factors in this set are called the *satisfiers* or *motivators.* They include:

1. Achievement.
2. Recognition.
3. Responsibility.
4. Advancement.
5. The work itself.
6. The possibility of growth.

Herzberg's model basically assumes that job satisfaction is not a unidimensional concept. His research leads to the conclusion that two continua are needed to correctly interpret job satisfaction. Figure 4–2 presents two different views of job satisfaction. Prior to Herzberg's work, those studying motivation viewed job satisfaction as a unidimensional concept; that is, they placed job satisfaction at one end of a continuum and job dissatisfaction at the other end of the same continuum. This meant that if a job condition caused job satisfaction, removing it would cause job dissatisfaction. Similarly, if a job condition caused job dissatisfaction, removing it would cause job satisfaction.

FIGURE 4–2

Traditional versus Herzberg View of Job Satisfaction

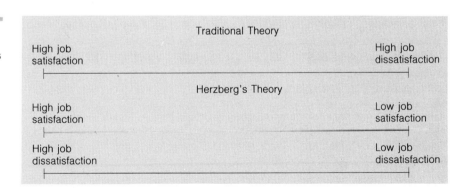

One appealing aspect of Herzberg's explanation of motivation is that the terminology is work-oriented. There is no need to translate psychological terminology into everyday language. Despite this important feature, Herzberg's work has been criticized for a number of reasons. For example, some researchers believe that Herzberg's work oversimplifies the nature of job satisfaction.[11] Other critics focus on Herzberg's methodology, which requires people to look at themselves retrospectively.[12] Still other critics charge that Herzberg has directed little attention toward testing the motivational and performance consequences of the theory.[13] In his original study, only self reports of performance were used and, in most cases, the respondents described job activities that had occurred over a long period of time.

Although the list of criticisms for Herzberg's model is long, the impact of the theory on practicing managers should not be underestimated. Many managers feel very comfortable about many of the things Herzberg includes in his two-factor discussion. From a scientific vantage point, this satisfaction presents some dangers of misuse, but from a very important, organizational-world perspective, it is appealing to managers. Consider, for example, the following OBM Encounter. It details an attempt to restructure a job to increase the number of satisfiers, and consequently enhance motivation.

INCREASING SATISFIERS ENHANCES PERFORMANCE

In the treasury department of American Telephone and Telegraph Company, educated and intelligent women handled correspondence with stockholders. They worked in a highly structured environment under close supervision in order to assure a suitable quality of correspondence. Under these conditions, quality of work was low and turnover was high.

Using a control group and a test group, the jobs of the test group were enriched as follows: (1) the women were permitted to sign their own names to the letters they prepared; (2) the women were held responsible for the quality of their work; (3) they were encouraged to become experts in the kinds of problems which appealed to them; and (4) subject-matter experts were provided for consultation regarding problems.

The control group remained unchanged after six months, but the test group improved by all measurements used. These measurements included turnover, productivity, absences, promotions from the group, and costs. The quality-measurement index climbed from the thirties to the nineties!

American Telephone and Telegraph Company also has achieved excellent results in other job-enrichment efforts. In the directory-compilation function, name omissions dropped from 2 to 1 percent. In frame wiring, errors declined from 13 to 0.5 percent, and the number of frames wired increased from 700 to over 1,200.   ☐

Source: Robert Ford, *Motivation Through the Work Itself* (New York: American Management Association, 1969).

---

[11] Marvin Dunnette, John Campbell, and M. Hakel, "Factors Contributing to Job Dissatisfaction in Six Occupational Groups," *Organizational Behavior and Human Performance*, May 1967, p. 147.

[12] Abraham K. Korman, *Industrial and Organizational Psychology* (Englewood Cliffs, N.J.: Prentice-Hall, 1971), pp. 148–50.

[13] Edward E. Lawler III, *Motivation in Work Organizations* (Monterey, Calif.: Brooks/Cole Publishing, 1973), p. 72.

McCLELLAND'S LEARNED NEEDS THEORY

McClelland has proposed a theory of motivation that is closely associated with learning concepts. He believes that many needs are acquired from the culture.[14] Three of these *learned needs* are the need for achievement (n Ach), the need for affiliation (n Aff), and the need for power (n Pow).

McClelland contends that when a need is strong in a person, its effect is to motivate the person to use behavior that leads to its satisfaction. For example, having a high n Ach encourages an individual to set challenging goals, to work hard to achieve the goals, and to use the skills and abilities needed to achieve them.

Based on research results, McClelland developed a descriptive set of factors which reflect a high need for achievement. These are:

1. The person likes to take responsibility for solving problems.
2. The person tends to set moderate achievement goals and is inclined to take calculated risks.
3. The person desires feedback on performance.

The need for affiliation reflects a desire to interact socially with people. A person with a high need for affiliation is concerned about the quality of important personal relationships, and thus, social relationships take precedent over task accomplishment. A person with a high need for power, meanwhile, concentrates on obtaining and exercising power and authority. He or she is concerned with influencing others and winning arguments. Power has two possible orientations according to McClelland. It can be negative in that the person exercising it emphasizes dominance and submission. Or power can be positive in that it reflects persuasive and inspirational behavior.

The main theme of McClelland's theory is that these needs are learned through coping with one's environment. Since needs are learned, behavior which is rewarded tends to recur at a higher frequency. Managers who are rewarded for achievement behavior learn to take moderate risks and to achieve goals. Similarly, a high need for affiliation or power can be traced to a history of receiving rewards for sociable, dominant, or inspirational behavior. As a result of the learning process, individuals develop unique configurations of needs that affect their behavior and performance. A high need for achievement, for example, may lead to entrepreneurial behavior, as is suggested in the following OBM Encounter (page 114).

There are a number of criticisms of McClelland's theory. Not the least of these criticisms is that most of the evidence available which supports the theory has been provided by McClelland or his associates. McClelland's use of projective psychological personality tests has been questioned as being unscientific. Furthermore, McClelland's claim that n Ach can be learned runs counter to a large body of literature that argues that the acquisition of motives normally occurs in childhood and is very difficult to alter in adulthood. Finally, McClelland's theory is questioned on grounds of whether or not the needs are permanently acquired. Research is needed to determine whether

---

[14] David C. McClelland, "Business Drive and National Achievement," *Harvard Business Review*, July–August 1962, pp. 99–112.

HIGH nAch AND ENTREPRENEURSHIP

What do the following individuals have in common?

- Frederick Smith
- Nolan Bushnell
- Steven Jobs

The answer: they are all extraordinarily successful entrepreneurs.

Frederick Smith founded the Federal Express Corporation to deliver packages that "absolutely, positively have to be there overnight." In the first four years, Smith's company grossed $600 million and today is a leader in the overnight delivery business.

Nolan Bushnell invented Pony, the world's first video game, and founded Atari Corporation to market the game. He subsequently sold Atari to Warner Communications in 1976 for a profit of $28 million.

Steven Jobs—at the ripe old age of 21—

developed the first successful home computer in his garage, with friend Stephen Wozniak. After six years, Jobs' company, Apple Computers, Inc., had sales of $600 million and Jobs' net worth was approximately $150 million.

Another characteristic these three gentlemen have in common is a high need to achieve. Individuals with high need achievement have a strong desire to take risks and accomplish important goals. Frequently, striking out on one's own offers greater opportunities for doing this than does staying within a corporate setting and reporting to someone else. Researchers John Welsh and Jerry White suggest that entrepreneurs tend to exhibit a high degree of self-confidence, vision, and a need to be in charge, all of which are compatible with a high achievement need. Perhaps the lesson organizations should take from this is that companies should provide their high-need-achievement employees with a reasonable chance to experience success—or run the risk that these same individuals will set up shop on their own and run their former employers out of business.   □

Source: Based in part on the article, "Striking It Rich," *Time,* February 15, 1982, pp. 38–45.

acquired needs last over a period of time. Can something learned in a training-and-development program be sustained on the job?[15] This is an issue that McClelland and others have not been able to clarify.

A SYNOPSIS OF THE THREE CONTENT THEORIES

Each of the three content theories just discussed attempts to explain behavior from a slightly different perspective. None of the theories has been accepted as the sole basis for explaining motivation. Although some critics are skeptical, it appears that people have innate and learned needs and that various job factors result in a degree of satisfaction. Thus, each of the theories provides the manager with some understanding of behavior and performance.

The three theories are compared in Figure 4–3. McClelland has proposed no lower-order needs. However, the needs for achievement and power he has identified are not identical with Herzberg's motivators or Maslow's higher order needs, but there are some similarities. A major difference between

[15] Paul R. Lawrence and Jay W. Lorsch, *Developing Organizations: Diagnosis and Action* (Reading, Mass.: Addison-Wesley Publishing, 1969).

FIGURE 4–3

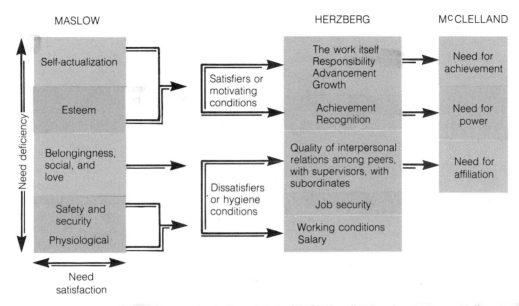

the three content theories is McClelland's emphasis on socially acquired needs. The Maslow theory offers a need classification system, and Herzberg discusses intrinsic and extrinsic job factors.

PROCESS THEORIES

The content theories we have examined focus mainly on the needs and incentives that cause behavior. The *process* theories of motivation are concerned with answering the question of *how* individual behavior is energized, directed, maintained, and stopped. This section examines three process theories: expectancy theory, equity theory, and goal setting theory.

EXPECTANCY THEORY

One of the more popular explanations of motivation was developed by Victor Vroom.[16] More than 50 studies have been done to test the accuracy of Vroom's expectancy theory in predicting employee behavior.[17] Vroom defines *motivation* as a process governing choices among alternative forms

---

[16] Victor H. Vroom, *Work and Motivation* (New York: John Wiley & Sons, 1964). For earlier work, see Kurt Lewin, *The Conceptual Representation and the Measurement of Psychological Forces* (Durham, N.C.: Duke University Press, 1938); and E. C. Tolman, *Purposive Behavior in Animals and Men* (New York: Appleton-Century-Crofts, 1932).

[17] David A. Nadler and Edward E. Lawler III, "Motivation: A Diagnostic Approach," in *Perspectives on Behavior in Organizations,* ed. J. R. Hackman, E. E. Lawler III, and L. W. Porter (New York: McGraw-Hill, 1977), pp. 26–38. Also see Edwin A. Locke, "Personnel Attitudes and Motivation," *Annual Review of Psychology* (1973), pp. 457–80; and Abraham K. Korman, Jeffrey H. Greenhaus, and Irwin J. Badin, "Personnel Attitudes and Motivation," *Annual Review of Psychology* (1977), pp. 175–96.

of voluntary activity. In his view, most behaviors are considered to be under the voluntary control of the person and consequently are motivated.

To understand expectancy theory, it is first necessary to define the important terms in the theory and explain how they operate. *First-level outcomes* resulting from behavior are those associated with doing the job itself. These outcomes include productivity, absenteeism, turnover, and quality of productivity. The *second-level outcomes* are those events (rewards or punishments) that the first-level outcomes are likely to produce, such as a merit pay increase, group acceptance or rejection, and promotion. *Instrumentality* refers to the strength of a person's belief that a particular action will lead to a particular outcome. That is, it is the perception by an individual that first-level outcomes will be associated with second-level outcomes. *Valence* refers to the preferences for outcomes as seen by the individual. For example, a person may prefer a nine percent merit increase over a transfer to a new department, or the transfer over a relocation to a new facility. An outcome is *positively* valent when it is preferred and *negatively* valent when it is not preferred or is avoided. An outcome has a valence of zero when the individual is indifferent to attaining or not attaining it. The valence concept applies to first- and second-level outcomes. For example, a person may prefer to be a high-performing (first-level outcome) employee because he or she believes that this will lead to a merit increase in pay (second-level outcome).

Expectancy refers to the individual's belief concerning the likelihood or subjective probability that a particular behavior will be followed by a particular outcome. That is, it refers to the assigned chance of something occurring because of the behavior. Expectancy has a value ranging from 0, indicating no chance that an outcome will occur after the behavior or act, to +1, indicating certainty that a particular outcome will follow an act or a behavior. Expectancy is considered in terms of probability.

In the work setting, an effort-performance expectancy is held by individuals. This expectancy represents the individual's perception of how hard it will be to achieve a particular behavior (say, completing the budget on time) and the probability of achieving that behavior. There is also a performance-outcome expectancy. In the individual's mind, every behavior is associated with outcomes (rewards or punishments). For example, an individual may have an expectancy that if the budget is completed on time, he or she will receive a day off next week. Figure 4–4 presents the general expectancy model and includes the two expectancy points (E→P and P→O).

RESEARCH ON EXPECTANCY

The empirical research to test expectancy theory continues each year. A few studies have used students in laboratory experiments. However, most of the research has been conducted in field settings. For example, one interesting study examined performance-outcome instrumentality in a temporary organization.[18] The experiment used either an hourly rate of pay (low instru-

---

[18] R. D. Pritchard and P. J. DeLeo, "Experimental Test of the Valence-Instrumentality Relationships in Job Performance," *Journal of Applied Psychology*, April 1973, pp. 264–79.

FIGURE 4—4

Expectancy Theory

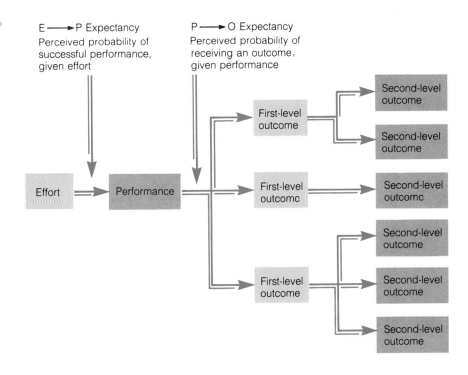

E ——▶ P Expectancy
Perceived probability of successful performance, given effort

P ——▶ O Expectancy
Perceived probability of receiving an outcome, given performance

mentality) or a piece rate (high instrumentality). After individuals had worked for three four-hour days under one pay system, they were shifted to the other system and worked three more days. Immediately following the shift in pay systems, and for all three subsequent days, the performance of the subjects who were shifted to the high-instrumentality system was higher than their own performance under the low-instrumentality system and higher than the performance of the subjects who were shifted to the low-instrumentality system.

Another area that has been researched focuses on the valence and behavior portion of the expectancy theory model. The results have been mixed. However, it appears that three conditions must hold for the valence of outcomes to be related to effort. Performance-outcome instrumentalities must be greater than zero; effort-performance expectancies must be greater than zero; and there must be some variability in the valence of outcomes.[19]

A number of difficulties are associated with expectancy theory. Many of the problems are highlighted by critiques designed to review the model.[20] One of the major problems seems to be testing the entire model using representative work groups. This problem is stressed by Lawler and Suttle when

[19] J. P. Campbell and R. D. Pritchard, "Motivation Theory in Industrial and Organizational Psychology," in *Handbook of Industrial and Organizational Psychology*, ed. M. D. Dunnette (Skokie, Ill.: Rand McNally, 1976), pp. 84–95.

[20] Robert J. House, H. Jack Shapiro, and Mahmoud A. Wahba, "Expectancy Theory as a Predictor of Work Behavior and Attitude: A Reevaluation of Empirical Evidence," *Decision Sciences*, July 1974, pp. 481–506.

they state that expectancy theory "has become so complex that it has exceeded the measures which exist to test it."[21] The measurements used typically are survey questionnaires that have not always been scientifically validated. Thus, expectancy theory is interesting, but two very crucial questions remain unanswered: (1) Can behavioral scientists completely test it? and, (2) Can managers use their findings? With respect to the second question, Nadler and Lawler have some definite opinions regarding managerial applications. Later in the chapter, in the readings selection titled "Motivation: A Diagnostic Approach," these authors identify a number of specific implications that expectancy theory has for organizations in general, and managers specifically.

EQUITY THEORY   The essence of **equity** theory is that employees compare their efforts and rewards with those of others in similar work situations. This theory of motivation is based on the assumption that individuals are motivated by a desire to be equitably treated at work. The individual works in exchange for rewards from the organization.

Four important terms in this theory are:

1. **Person:** The individual for whom equity or inequity is perceived.
2. **Comparison other:** Any group or persons used by Person as a referent regarding the ratio of inputs and outcomes.
3. **Inputs:** The individual characteristics brought by Person to the job. These may be achieved (e.g., skills, experience, learning) or ascribed (e.g., age, sex, race).
4. **Outcomes:** What Person received from the job (e.g., recognition, fringe benefits, pay).

Equity exists when employees perceive that the ratios of their inputs (efforts) to their outcomes (rewards) are equivalent to the ratios of other employees. Inequity exists when these ratios are not equivalent; an individual's own ratio of inputs to outcomes could be greater than, or less than, that of others.[22]

Change Procedures to Restore Equity.   Equity theory suggests a number of alternative ways that can be used to restore a feeling or sense of equity. Some examples of restoring equity are:

1. **Changing inputs.** The employee may decide that he or she will put less time or effort into the job.
2. **Changing outputs.** The employee may decide to produce more units since a piece-rate pay plan is being used.
3. **Changing attitudes.** Instead of changing inputs or outputs, the employee may simply change the attitude that he or she has. Instead of actually putting in more time at work, the employee may decide that "I put in enough time" to make a good contribution.

---

[21] Edward E. Lawler III and J. Lloyd Suttle, "Expectancy Theory and Job Behavior," *Organizational Behavior and Human Performance,* June 1973, p. 502.

[22] J. Stacy Adams, "Toward an Understanding of Equity," *Journal of Abnormal and Social Psychology,* November 1963, pp. 422–36.

4. **Changing the reference person.** The reference person can be changed by making comparisons with the input/output ratios of some other person. This change can restore equity.
5. **Changing the inputs or outputs of the reference person.** If the reference person is a co-worker, it might be possible to attempt to alter his or her inputs or outputs as a way to restore equity.

Research on Equity. Most of the research on equity theory has focused on pay as the basic outcome.[23] The failure to incorporate other relevant outcomes limits the impact of the theory in work situations. A review of the studies also reveals that the comparison person is not always clarified. A typical research procedure is to ask a person to compare his or her inputs and outcomes with those of a specific person. In most work situations, an employee selects the comparison person after working for some time in the organization. Two issues to consider are whether comparison persons are within the organization and whether comparison persons change during a person's work career.

Several individuals have questioned the extent to which inequity that results from overpayment (rewards) leads to perceived inequity. Locke argues that employees seldom are told they are overpaid. He believes that individuals are likely to adjust their idea of what constitutes an equitable payment to justify their pay.[24] Campbell and Pritchard point out that employer-employee exchange relationships are highly impersonal when compared to exchanges between friends. Perceived overpayment inequity may be more likely when friends are involved. Thus, individuals probably will react to overpayment inequity only when they believe that their actions have led to a friend's being treated unfairly. The individual receives few signals from the organization that it is being treated unfairly.[25]

Despite limitations, equity theory provides a relatively insightful model to help explain and predict employee attitudes about pay. The theory also has emphasized the importance of comparisons in the work situation. The identification of comparison persons seems to have some potential value when attempting to restructure a reward program. Equity theory also raises the issue of methods for resolving inequity. An inequitable situation can cause problems with morale, turnover, and absenteeism.

GOAL SETTING   There has been considerable and growing interest in applying goal setting to organizational problems and issues since Locke presented what is now considered a classic paper in 1968.[26] Locke proposed that **goal setting**

---

[23] Richard Cosier and Dan Dalton, "Equity Theory and Time: A Reformulation," *Academy of Management Review*, April 1983, pp. 311–319.

[24] Edwin A. Locke, "The Nature and Causes of Job Satisfaction," in *Handbook of Industrial and Organizational Psychology*, ed. M. Dunnette (Skokie, Ill.: Rand McNally, 1976), pp. 1297–1349.

[25] Campbell and Pritchard, "Motivation Theory," pp. 63–130.

[26] Edwin A. Locke, "Toward of Theory of Task Motivation and Incentives," *Organizational Behavior and Human Performance*, May 1968, pp. 157–89.

was a cognitive process of some practical utility. His view is that an individual's conscious goals and intentions are the primary determinants of behavior. It has been noted that "one of the commonly observed characteristics of intentional behavior is that it tends to keep going until it reaches completion."[27] That is, once a person starts something (e.g., a job, a new project), he or she pushes on until a goal is achieved. Intention plays a prominent role in goal-setting theory. Also, goal-setting theory places specific emphasis on the importance of conscious goals in explaining motivated behavior. Locke has used the notion of intentions and conscious goals to propose and provide research support for the thesis that harder conscious goals will result in higher levels of performance, if these goals are accepted by the individual.

Descriptions of Goal Setting. A goal is the object of an action. For example, the attempt to produce four units on a production line, or to cut direct costs by $3,000, or to decrease absenteeism in a department by 12 percent is a goal. Locke has carefully described the attributes or the mental (cognitive) processes of goal setting. The attributes he highlights are goal specificity, goal difficulty, and goal intensity.

Goal specificity is the degree of quantitative precision (clarity) of the goal. *Goal difficulty* is the degree of proficiency or the level of performance that is sought. *Goal intensity* pertains to the process of setting the goal or of determining how to reach it.[28] To date, goal intensity has not been widely studied, although a related concept, *goal commitment,* has been considered in a number of studies. Goal commitment is the amount of effort used to achieve a goal.

Figure 4–5 portrays applied goal setting from a managerial perspective and the sequence of events for such a goal-setting program. The key steps in applying goal setting are: (1) *diagnosis* for readiness (determining whether the people, the organization, and the technology are suited for goal setting; (2) *preparing* employees via increased interpersonal interaction, communication, training, and action plans for goal setting; (3) *emphasizing* the attributes of goals that should be understood by a manager and subordinates; (4) *conducting* intermediate reviews to make necessary adjustments in established goals; and (5) *performing* a final review to check the goals set, modified, and accomplished. Each of these steps needs to be carefully planned and implemented if goal setting is to be an effective motivational technique. In too many applications of goal setting, steps outlined in—or issues suggested by—Figure 4–5 are ignored.

Goal-Setting Research. Between 1968 and 1986, the amount of research on goal setting increased considerably. Locke's 1968 paper certainly contributed to the increase in laboratory and field research on goal setting. Another force behind the increase in interest and research was the demand

---

[27] Thomas A. Ryan, *Intentional Behavior* (New York: Ronald Press, 1970), p. 95.

[28] Edwin A. Locke, Karyll N. Shaw, Lise M. Saari, and Gary P. Latham, "Goal Setting and Task Performance: 1969–1980," *Psychological Bulletin,* July 1981, p. 129.

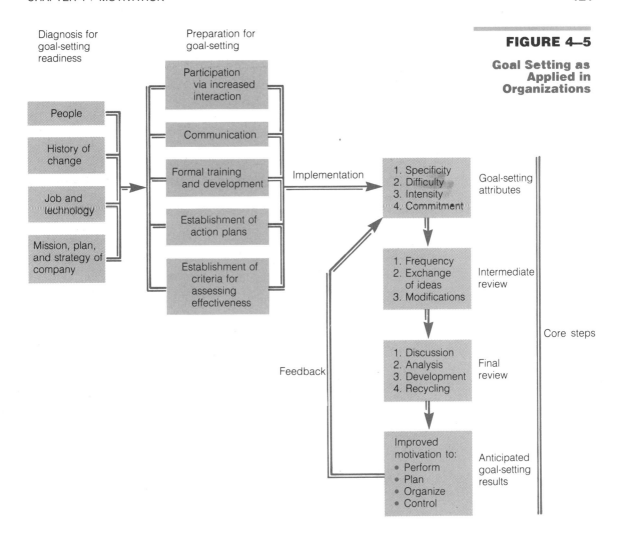

FIGURE 4—5

**Goal Setting as
Applied in
Organizations**

of managers for practical and specific techniques that they could apply in
their organizations. Goal setting offered such a technique for some managers.[29]

Empirical research findings from a variety of managerial and student samples have provided support for the theory that conscious goals regulate behavior. Yet, a number of important issues concerning goal setting still must be
examined more thoroughly. One area of debate concerns the issue of how
much subordinate participation in goal setting is optimal.[30] A field experiment
of skilled technicians compared three levels of subordinate participation: full
(the subordinates were totally involved); limited (the subordinates made some

---

[29] Edwin A. Locke, "The Ubiquity of the Technique of Goal Setting in Theories of and Approaches
to Employee Motivation," *Academy of Management Review*, July 1978, p. 600.

[30] Miriam Erez, P. Christopher Earley, and Charles Hulin, "The Impact of Participation on
Goal Acceptance and Performance: A Two-Step Model," *Academy of Management Journal*,
March 1985, pp. 50–66.

suggestions about the goals that the superior set); and none.[31] Measures of performance and satisfaction were taken over a 12-month period. The groups with full or limited participant involvement in goal-setting showed significantly more performance and satisfaction improvements than did the group that did not participate in goal setting. Interestingly, these improvements began to dissipate six to nine months after the program was started. This study suggests that there is no universally valid procedure for implementing goal setting. A contingency approach to goal setting seems to be more appropriate than prescribing a specific approach to fit all situations.

Research has found that *specific* goals lead to higher output than do vague goals such as "Do your best."[32] Field experiments using clerical workers, maintenance technicians, marketing personnel, truckers, engineering personnel, typists, and manufacturing employees have compared specific versus do-your-best goal-setting conditions.[33] The vast majority of these studies support—partly or in total—the hypothesis that specific goals lead to better performance than do vague goals. In fact, in 99 out of 100 studies reviewed by Locke and his associates, specific goals produced better results.[34]

Certain aspects of goal setting need to be subjected to scientific examination. One such area centers on individual differences and their impact on the success of goal-setting programs. Such factors as personality, career progression, training background, and personal health are important individual differences that should be considered when implementing goal-setting programs. Goal-setting programs also should be subjected to ongoing examination to monitor attitudinal and performance consequences. Some research has demonstrated that goal-setting programs tend to lose their potency over time, so there is a need to discover why this phenomenon occurs in organizations. Sound evaluation programs would assist management in identifying successes, problems, and needs.

Goal setting can be a very powerful technique for motivating employees. When used correctly, carefully monitored, and actively supported by managers, goal setting can improve performance. However, neither goal setting nor any other technique can be used to correct every problem. No applied motivational approach can be *the* technique to solve all performance problems. This, unfortunately, is what some enthusiastic advocates have turned goal setting into—a panacea for everything.

REVIEWING MOTIVATION

In this chapter, six popular theories of motivation are portrayed. The theories typically are pitted against one another in the literature. This is unfortunate since each approach can help managers better understand workplace motiva-

[31] John M. Ivancevich, "Different Goal-Setting Treatments and Their Effects on Performance and Job Satisfaction," *Academy of Management Journal,* September 1977, pp. 406–19.

[32] Locke, "Task Motivation and Incentives."

[33] For a complete analysis, see Locke et al., "Goal Setting."

[34] Ibid.

tion. Each approach attempts to organize, in a meaningful manner, major variables associated with explaining motivation in work settings.

The *content* theories are individual-oriented in that they place primary emphasis on the characteristics of people. Each of the *process* theories has a specific orientation. Expectancy theory places emphasis on individual, job, and environmental variables. It recognizes differences in needs, perceptions, and beliefs. Equity theory primarily addresses the relationship between attitudes toward inputs and outputs and reward practices. Goal-setting theory emphasizes the cognitive processes and the role of intentional behavior in motivation. A fourth process approach, organizational behavior modification (OB Mod), is discussed in the article by Fedor and Ferris, which accompanies this chapter. OB Mod focuses on reinforcing desirable organizational behavior and not reinforcing undesirable behavior. In the article, the authors provide suggestions for blending an OB Mod approach with other, more traditional, approaches to motivation.

If anything, this chapter suggests that instead of ignoring motivation, managers must take an active role in motivating their employees. Four specific conclusions are offered here:

1. Managers can influence the motivation state of employees. If performance needs to be improved, then managers must intervene and help create an atmosphere that encourages, supports, and sustains improvement.
2. Managers should be sensitive to variations in employees' needs, abilities, and goals. Managers also must consider differences in preferences (valences) for rewards.
3. Continual monitoring of needs, abilities, goals, and preferences of employees is each individual manager's responsibility and is not the domain of personnel/human resources managers only.
4. Managers need to work on providing employees with jobs that offer task challenge, diversity, and a variety of opportunities for need satisfaction.

For an example of motivation that probably does not meet these four conclusions, see the OBM Encounter which follows.

ENCOUNTER

APPLYING THE CANARY THEORY OF MOTIVATION

One of the more successful technology companies during the 1970s and 1980s has been Texas Instruments. Nonetheless, in spite of its rapid growth—or perhaps because of it— TI has had its share of problems. In trying to move ahead too quickly, TI found that its corporate resources were stretched so thin that important programs lagged behind schedule. The company, according to its president, had lost its ability to focus "on the right products, for the right growth markets, at the right time."

In an effort to address this difficulty, TI reorganized. It shook up its semiconductor group, reassigning more than a dozen top executives. Next, it assigned new executives for marketing,

Source: Based on the article by Bro Uttal, "Texas Instruments Regroups," *Fortune,* August 9, 1982, p. 40.

technology development, strategy, and consumer products. Then, a new chief financial officer was named. A company spokesman was quoted as seeing no end in sight for the restructuring.

Financial analysts who follow TI, as well as company veterans, point out that TI habitually reorganizes when problems develop, and they didn't see the latest round as any different—or any more likely to be effective. Some former TI employees refer to TI's approach as implementing the "canary theory" of motivation through anxiety. When you have 10 tons of canaries—or executives—in a 5-ton truck, you beat on the roof now and then to make sure at least half of them are up and flying. ☐

In simple terms, the theme of our discussion of motivation is that the *manager needs to be actively involved.* If motivation is to be energized, sustained, and directed, managers must know about needs, intentions, preferences, goals, and comparisons. Failure to learn and understand these types of concepts will result in many missed opportunities to help motivate employees in a positive manner.

SUMMARY OF KEYPOINTS

A. Any attempt to improve the job performance of individuals must utilize motivation theories. Motivation is concerned with behavior or, more specifically, goal-directed behavior.

B. A major reason why behaviors of employees differ is that the needs and goals of people vary. Social, cultural, hereditary, and job factors influence behaviors. In order to understand the circular nature of motivation, the manager must learn about the needs of subordinates.

C. The theories of motivation can be classified as being either content or process. Each theory in both categories emphasizes a particular orientation. Some are more explicit than others, but each illustrates that employees desire some goal(s) in performing their jobs. The manager should try to determine the various goals desired by subordinates.

D. The Maslow theory assumes that people have a need to grow and develop. The implication is that motivational programs will have a higher probability of success if the upper-level need deficiencies are reduced. Although Maslow's need hierarchy has not met most of the standards of scientific testing, it appears that an adequately fulfilled need does not provide a good target for managers in building motivators that can influence performance.

E. Herzberg's two-factor theory of motivation identifies two types of factors in the workplace: satisfiers and dissatisfiers. One apparent weakness of the theory is that its findings have not been replicated by other researchers. Despite this and other shortcomings, Herzberg's theory does focus on job-related factors in managerial terminology.

F. McClelland has proposed a theory of learned needs. The behavior associated with the needs for achievement, affiliation, and power is instrumental in the job performance of an individual. A manager should attempt to acquire an understanding of these needs.

G. The expectancy theory of motivation is concerned with the expectations of a person and how they influence behavior. One value of this theory is that it can provide the manager with a means for pinpointing desirable and undesirable outcomes associated with task performance.

H. Equity theory focuses on comparisons, tension, and tension reduction. To date, most of the research work on equity theory has involved pay. Equity theory is a more straightforward and understandable explanation of employee attitudes about pay than is expectancy theory. The manager should be aware of the fact that people compare their rewards, punishments, job tasks, and other job-related dimensions to those of others.

I. Locke's goal-setting theory proposes that an individual's goals and intentions are the primary determinants of behavior. Despite an impressive number of supportive studies, goal setting has been criticized as working primarily for easy jobs, encouraging game playing, and operating as another control check on employees.

REVIEW AND DISCUSSION QUESTIONS

1. From a managerial perspective, do you think the content approach or the process approach to motivation is the most useful?

2. What implications does Maslow's need hierarchy have for the design of organizational reward systems? Is it easier or harder to design rewards for individuals operating at upper levels of the hierarchy rather than at lower levels?

3. Many factors other than motivation influence productivity. What are some of these other factors and how can a manager know which factors, including motivation, to focus on to improve productivity?

4. As a manager, would you rather the people for whom you are responsible be extrinsically or intrinsically motivated? Explain.

5. Do you think organizations want all employees to be self-actualized? What sort of problems would managers face in that sort of organization?

6. An important key to motivation is knowledge of employee needs. What are some ways a manager might learn more about employee needs?

7. According to McClelland, some very important needs can be acquired. Do organizations have the responsibility or even the right to help instill these needs in employees? Why or why not?

8. One of the criticisms of goal setting is that it can turn into nothing more than game playing. Is this a potentially valid criticism? What can managers do to decrease the likelihood of this happening?

9. Why are the variables relevant to equity theory so difficult to measure? How important a role does perception play in determining whether an employee is receiving equitable treatment?

10. Which of the approaches to motivation discussed in this chapter seems to you to be the most useful? Explain.

R1 MOTIVATION: A DIAGNOSTIC APPROACH

DAVID A. NADLER AND
EDWARD E. LAWLER III

- What makes some people work hard while others do as little as possible?
- How can I, as a manager, influence the performance of people who work for me?
- Why do people turn over, show up late to work, and miss work entirely?

These important questions about employees' behavior can only be answered by managers who have a grasp of what motivates people. Specifically, a good understanding of motivation can serve

Source: J. R. Hackman and E. E. Lawler, *Perspectives on Behavior in Organizations*. New York: McGraw-Hill, 1977.

as a valuable tool for *understanding* the causes of behavior in organizations, for *predicting* the effects of any managerial action, and for *directing* behavior so that organizational and individual goals can be achieved.

EXISTING APPROACHES

During the past twenty years, managers have been bombarded with a number of different approaches to motivation. The terms associated with these approaches are well known—"human relations," "scientific management," "job enrichment," "need hierarchy," "self-actualization," etc. Each of these approaches has something to offer. On the other hand, each of these different approaches also has its problems in both theory and practice. Running through almost all of the approaches with which managers are familiar are a series of implicit but clearly erroneous assumptions.

Assumption 1: All employees are alike. Different theories present different ways of looking at people, but each of them assumes that all employees are basically similar in their makeup: Employees all want economic gains, or all want a pleasant climate, or all aspire to be self-actualizing, etc.

Assumption 2: All situations are alike. Most theories assume that all managerial situations are alike, and that the managerial course of action for motivation (for example, participation, job enlargement, etc.) is applicable in all situations.

Assumption 3: One best way. Out of the other two assumptions there emerges a basic principle that there is "one best way" to motivate employees.

When these "one best way" approaches are tried in the "correct" situation they will work. However, all of them are bound to fail in some situations. They are therefore not adequate managerial tools.

A NEW APPROACH

During the past ten years, a great deal of research has been done on a new approach to looking at motivation. This approach, frequently called "expectancy theory," still needs further testing, refining, and extending. However, enough is known that many behavioral scientists have concluded that it represents the most comprehensive, valid, and useful approach to understanding motivation. Further, it is apparent that it is a very useful tool for understanding motivation in organizations.

The theory is based on a number of specific assumptions about the causes of behavior in organizations.

Assumption 1: Behavior is determined by a combination of forces in the individual and forces in the environment. Neither the individual nor the environment alone determines behavior. Individuals come into organizations with certain "psychological baggage." They have past experiences and a developmental history which has given them unique sets of needs, ways of looking at the world, and expectations about how organizations will treat them. These all influence how individuals respond to their work environment. The work environment provides structures (such as a pay system or a supervisor) which influence the behavior of people. Different environments tend to produce different behavior in similar people just as dissimilar people tend to behave differently in similar environments.

LEARNING CHECKPOINT

Does Maslow's need hierarchy discuss environmental forces?

Assumption 2: People make decisions about their own behavior in organizations. While there are many constraints on the behavior of individuals in organizations, most of the behavior that is observed is the result of individuals' conscious decisions. These decisions usually fall into two categories. First, individuals make decisions about *membership behavior*—coming to work, staying at work, and in other ways being a member of the organization. Second, individuals make decisions about the amount of *effort* they will direct *towards performing their jobs.* This includes decisions about how hard to work, how much to produce, at what quality, etc.

Assumption 3: Different people have different types of needs, desires, and goals. Individuals differ on what kinds of outcomes (or rewards) they desire. These differences are not random; they can be examined systematically by an understanding of the differences in the strength of individuals' needs.

Assumption 4: People make decisions among alternative plans of behavior based on their perceptions (expectancies) of the degree to which a given behavior will lead to desired outcomes. In simple terms, people tend to do those things which they see as leading to outcomes (which can also be called "rewards") they desire and avoid doing those things they see as leading to outcomes that are not desired.

In general, the approach used here views people as having their

own needs and mental maps of what the world is like. They use these maps to make decisions about how they will behave, behaving in those ways which their mental maps indicate will lead to outcomes that will satisfy their needs. Therefore, they are inherently neither motivated nor unmotivated; motivation depends on the situation they are in, and how it fits their needs.

THE THEORY

Based on these general assumptions, expectancy theory states a number of propositions about the process by which people make decisions about their own behavior in organizational settings. While the theory is complex at first view, it is in fact made of a series of fairly straightforward observations about behavior. (The theory is presented in more technical terms in Appendix A.) Three concepts serve as the key building blocks of the theory:

Performance-outcome expectancy. Every behavior has associated with it, in an individual's mind, certain outcomes (rewards or punishments). In other words, the individual believes or expects that if he or she behaves in a certain way, he or she will get certain things.

Examples of expectancies can easily be described. An individual may have an expectancy that if he produces ten units he will receive his normal hourly rate while if he produces fifteen units he will receive his hourly pay rate plus a bonus. Similarly an individual may believe that certain levels of performance will lead to approval or disapproval from members of her work group or from her supervisor. Each performance can be seen as leading to a number of different kinds of outcomes and outcomes can differ in their types.

LEARNING CHECKPOINT

Suppose that you are a manager who is responsible for a 6-employee work team. How would you determine the performance outcome expectancy attitudes among your team?

Valence. Each outcome has a "valence" (value, worth, attractiveness) to a specific individual. Outcomes have different valences for different individuals. This comes about because valences result from individual needs and perceptions, which differ because they in turn reflect other factors in the individual's life.

For example, some individuals may value an opportunity for promotion or advancement because of their needs for achievement or power, while others may not want to be promoted and leave their current work group because of needs for affiliation with others. Similarly, a fringe benefit such as a pension plan may have great valence for an older worker but little valence for a young employee on his first job.

Effort-performance expectancy. Each behavior also has associated with it in the individual's mind a certain expectancy or probability of success. This expectancy represents the individual's perception of how hard it will be to achieve such behavior and the probability of his or her successful achievement of that behavior.

For example, you may have a strong expectancy that if you put forth the effort, you can produce ten units an hour, but that you have only a fifty-fifty chance of producing fifteen units an hour if you try.

Putting these concepts together, it is possible to make a basic statement about motivation. In general, the motivation to attempt to behave in a certain way is greatest when:

a. The individual believes that the behavior will lead to outcomes (performance-outcome expectancy).
b. The individual believes that these outcomes have positive value for him or her (valence).
c. The individual believes that he or she is able to perform at the desired level (effort-performance expectancy).

Given a number of alternative levels of behavior (ten, fifteen, and twenty units of production per hour, for example) the individual will choose that level of performance which has the greatest motivational force associated with it, as indicated by the expectancies, outcomes, and valences.

In other words, when faced with choices about behavior, the individual goes through a process of considering questions such as, "Can I perform at that level if I try?" "If I perform at that level, what will happen?" "How do I feel about those things that will happen?" The individual then decides to behave in that way which seems to have the best chance of producing positive, desired outcomes.

A General Model

On the basis of these concepts, it is possible to construct a general model of behavior in organizational settings (see Figure 1). Working from left to right in the model, motivation is seen as the force on the individual to expend effort. Motivation leads to an observed level of effort by the individual. Effort,

---

FIGURE 1

The Basic Motivation-Behavior Sequence

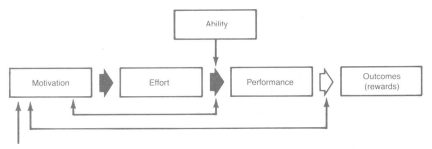

A person's motivation is a function of:
 a. Effort-to-performance expectancies
 b. Performance-to-outcome expectancies
 c. Perceived valence of outcomes

alone, however, is not enough. Performance results from a combination of the effort that an individual puts forth *and* the level of ability which he or she has (reflecting skills, training, information, etc.). Effort thus combines with ability to produce a given level of performance. As a result of performance, the individual attains certain outcomes. The model indicates this relationship in a dotted line, reflecting the fact that sometimes people perform but do not get desired outcomes. As this process of performance-reward occurs, time after time, the actual events serve to provide information which influences the individual's perceptions (particularly expectancies) and thus influences motivation in the future.

Outcomes, or rewards, fall into two major categories. First, the individual obtains outcomes from the environment. When an individual performs at a given level he or she can receive positive or negative outcomes from supervisors, co-workers, the organization's rewards systems, or other sources. These environmental rewards are thus one source of outcomes for the individual. A second source of outcomes is the individual. These include outcomes which occur purely from the performance of the task itself (feelings of accomplishment, personal worth, achievement, etc.). In a sense, the individual gives these rewards to himself or herself. The environment cannot give them or take them away directly; it can only make them possible.

Supporting Evidence

Over fifty studies have been done to test the validity of the expectancy-theory approach to predicting employee behavior.[1] Almost without exception, the studies have confirmed the predictions of the theory. As the theory predicts, the best performers in organizations tend to see a strong relationship between performing their jobs well and receiving rewards they value. In addition they have clear performance goals and feel they can perform well. Similarly, studies using the expectancy theory to predict how people choose jobs also show that individuals tend to interview for and actually take those jobs which they feel will provide the rewards they value. One study, for example, was able to correctly predict for 80 percent of the people studied which of several jobs they would take.[2] Finally, the theory correctly predicts that beliefs about the outcomes associated with performance (expectancies) will be better predictors of performance than will feelings of job satisfaction since expectancies are the critical causes of performance and satisfaction is not.

Questions about the Model

Although the results so far have been encouraging, they also indicate some problems with the model. These problems do not critically affect the managerial implications of the model, but they should be noted. The model is based on the assumption that individuals make very rational decisions after a thorough exploration of all the available alternatives and on weighing the possible outcomes of all these alternatives. When we talk to or observe individuals, however, we find that their decision processes are frequently less thorough. People often stop considering alternative behavior plans when they find one that is at least moderately satisfying, even though more rewarding plans remain to be examined.

People are also limited in the amount of information they can handle at one time, and therefore the model may indicate a process that is much more complex than the one that actually takes place. On the other hand, the model does provide enough information and is consistent enough with reality to present some clear implications for managers who are concerned with the question of how to motivate the people who work for them.

Implications for Managers

The first set of implications is directed toward the individual manager who has a group of people working for him or her and is concerned with how to motivate good performance. Since behavior is a result of forces both in the person and in the environment, you as manager need to look at and diagnose both the person and the environment. Specifically, you need to do the following:

Figure out what outcomes each employee values. As a first step, it is important to determine what kinds of outcomes or rewards have valence for your employees. For each employee you need to determine "what turns him or her on." There are various ways of finding this out, including (a) finding out employees' desires through some structured method of data collection, such as a questionnaire, (b) observing the employees' reactions to different situations or rewards, or (c) the fairly simple act of asking them what kinds of rewards they want, what kind of career goals they have, or "what's in it for them." It is important to stress here that it is very difficult to change what people want, but fairly easy to find out what they want. Thus, the skillful manager emphasizes diagnosis of needs, not changing the individuals themselves.

Determine what kinds of behavior you desire. Managers frequently talk about "good performance" without really defining what good performance is. An important step in motivating is for you yourself to figure out what kinds of performances are required and what are adequate measures or indicators of performance (quantity, quality, etc.). There is also a need to be able to define those performances in fairly specific terms so that observable and measurable behavior can be defined and subordinates can understand what is desired of them (e.g., produce ten products of a certain quality standard— rather than only produce at a high rate).

Make sure desired levels of performance are reachable. The model states that motivation is determined not only by the performance-to-outcome expectancy, but also by the effort-to-performance expectancy. The implication of this is that the levels of performance which are set as the points at which individuals receive desired outcomes must be reachable or attainable by these individuals. If the employees feel that the level of performance required to get a reward is higher than they can reasonably achieve, then their motivation to perform well will be relatively low.

Link desired outcomes to desired performances. The next step is to directly, clearly, and explicitly link those outcomes desired by employees to the specific performances desired by you. If your employee values external rewards, then the emphasis should be on the rewards systems concerned with promotion, pay, and approval. While the linking of these rewards can be initiated through your making statements to your employees,

it is extremely important that employees see a clear example of the reward process working in a fairly short period of time if the motivating "expectancies" are to be created in the employees' minds. The linking must be done by some concrete public acts, in addition to statements of intent.

If your employee values internal rewards (e.g., achievement), then you should concentrate on changing the nature of the person's job, for he or she is likely to respond well to such things as increased autonomy, feedback, and challenge, because these things will lead to a situation where good job performance is inherently rewarding. The best way to check on the adequacy of the internal and external reward system is to ask people what their perceptions of the situation are. Remember it is the perceptions of people that determine their motivation, not reality. It doesn't matter for example whether you feel a subordinate's pay is related to his or her motivation. Motivation will be present only if the subordinate sees the relationship. Many managers are misled about the behavior of their subordinates because they rely on their own perceptions of the situation and forget to find out what their subordinates feel. There is only one way to do this: ask. Questionnaires can be used here, as can personal interviews. (See Appendix B for a short version of a motivation questionnaire.)

Analyze the total situation for conflicting expectancies. Having set up positive expectancies for employees, you then need to look at the entire situation to see if other factors (informal work groups, other managers, the organization's reward systems) have set up conflicting expectancies in the minds of the employees. Motivation will

only be high when people see a number of rewards associated with good performance and few negative outcomes. Again, you can often gather this kind of information by asking your subordinates. If there are major conflicts, you need to make adjustments, either in your own performance and reward structure, or in the other sources of rewards or punishments in the environment.

Make sure changes in outcomes are large enough. In examining the motivational system, it is important to make sure that changes in outcomes or rewards are large enough to motivate significant behavior. Trivial rewards will result in trivial amounts of effort and thus trivial improvements in performance. Rewards must be large enough to motivate individuals to put forth the effort required to bring about significant changes in performance.

Check the system for its equity. The model is based on the idea that individuals are different and therefore different rewards will need to be used to motivate different individuals. On the other hand, for a motivational system to work it must be a fair one—one that has equity (not equality). Good performers should see that they get more desired rewards than do poor performers, and others in the system should see that also. Equity should not be confused with a system of equality where all are rewarded equally, with no regard to their performance. A system of equality is guaranteed to produce low motivation.

Implications for Organizations

Expectancy theory has some clear messages for those who run large organizations. It suggests how organizational structures can be designed so that they increase rather than decrease levels of motivation of organization members. While there are many different implications, a few of the major ones are as follows:

Implication 1: The design of pay and reward systems. Organizations usually get what they reward, not what they want. This can be seen in many situations, and pay systems are a good example.[3] Frequently, organizations reward people for membership (through pay tied to seniority, for example) rather than for performance. Little wonder that what the organization gets is behavior oriented towards "safe," secure employment rather than effort directed at performing well. In addition, even where organizations do pay for performance as a motivational device, they frequently negate the motivational value of the system by keeping pay secret, therefore preventing people from observing the pay-to-performance relationship that would serve to create positive, clear, and strong performance-to-reward expectancies. The implication is that organizations should put more effort into rewarding people (through pay, promotion, better job opportunities, etc.) for the performances which are desired, and that to keep these rewards secret is clearly self-defeating. In addition, it underscores the importance of the frequently ignored performance evaluation or appraisal process and the need to evaluate people based on how they perform clearly defined specific behaviors, rather than on how they score on ratings of general traits such as "honesty," "cleanliness," and other, similar terms which frequently appear as part of the performance appraisal form.

Implication 2: The design of tasks, jobs, and roles. One source of desired outcomes is the work itself. The expectancy-theory model supports much of the job enrichment literature, in saying that by designing jobs which enable people to get their needs fulfilled, organizations can bring about higher levels of motivation.[4] The major difference between the traditional approaches to job enlargement or enrichment and the expectancy-theory approach is the recognition by expectancy theory that different people have different needs and, therefore, some people may not want enlarged or enriched jobs. Thus, while the design of tasks that have more autonomy, variety, feedback, meaningfulness, etc., will lead to higher motivation in some, the organization needs to build in the opportunity for individuals to make choices about the kind of work they will do so that not everyone is forced to experience job enrichment.

Implication 3: The importance of group structures. Groups, both formal and informal, are powerful and potent sources of desired outcomes for individuals. Groups can provide or withhold acceptance, approval, affection, skill training, needed information, assistance, etc. They are a powerful force in the total motivational environment of individuals. Several implications emerge from the importance of groups. First, organizations should consider the structuring of at least a portion of rewards around group performance rather than individual performance. This is particularly important where group members have to cooperate with each other to produce a group product or service, and where the individual's contribution is often hard to determine. Second, the organization

needs to train managers to be aware of how groups can influence individual behavior and to be sensitive to the kinds of expectancies which informal groups set up and their conflict or consistency with the expectancies that the organization attempts to create.

Implication 4: The supervisor's role. The immediate supervisor has an important role in creating, monitoring, and maintaining the expectancies and reward structures which will lead to good performance. The supervisor's role in the motivation process becomes one of defining clear goals, setting clear reward expectancies, and providing the right rewards for different people (which could include both organizational rewards and personal rewards such as recognition, approval, or support from the supervisor). Thus, organizations need to provide supervisors with an awareness of the nature of motivation as well as the tools (control over organizational rewards, skill in administering those rewards) to create positive motivation.

Implication 5: Measuring motivation. If things like expectancies, the nature of the job, supervisor-controlled outcomes, satisfaction, etc., are important in understanding how well people are being motivated, then organizations need to monitor employee perceptions along these lines. One relatively cheap and reliable method of doing this is through standardized employee questionnaires. A number of organizations already use such techniques, surveying employees' perceptions and attitudes at regular intervals (ranging from once a month to once every year-and-a-half) using either standardized surveys or surveys developed specifically for the organization. Such information is useful both to the individual manager and to top management in assessing the state of human resources and the effectiveness of the organization's motivational systems.[5] (Again, see Appendix B for excerpts from a standardized survey.)

LEARNING CHECKPOINT

If motivation is an internal process why would a manager attempt to assess it by use of a standardized survey?

Implication 6: Individualizing organizations. Expectancy theory leads to a final general implication about a possible future direction for the design of organizations. Because different people have different needs and therefore have different valences, effective motivation must come through the recognition that not all employees are alike and that organizations need to be flexible in order to accommodate individual differences. This implies the "building in" of choice for employees in many areas, such as reward systems, fringe benefits,

job assignments, etc., where employees previously have had little say. A successful example of the building in of such choice can be seen in the experiments at TRW and the Educational Testing Service with "cafeteria fringe-benefits plans" which allow employees to choose the fringe benefits they want, rather than taking the expensive and often unwanted benefits which the company frequently provides to everyone.[6]

SUMMARY

Expectancy theory provides a more complex model of man for managers to work with. At the same time, it is a model which holds promise for the more effective motivation of individuals and the more effective design of organizational systems. It implies, however, the need for more exacting and thorough diagnosis by the manager to determine (a) the relevant forces in the individual, and (b) the relevant forces in the environment, both of which combine to motivate different kinds of behavior. Following diagnosis, the model implies a need to act—to develop a system of pay, promotion, job assignments, group structures, supervision, etc.—to

bring about effective motivation by providing different outcomes for different individuals.

Performance of individuals is a critical issue in making organizations work effectively. If a manager is to influence work behavior and performance, he or she must have an understanding of motivation and the factors which influence an individual's motivation to come to work, to work hard, and to work well. While simple models offer easy answers, it is the more complex models which seem to offer more promise. Managers can use models (like expectancy theory) to understand the nature of behavior and build more effective organizations.

APPENDIX A: THE EXPECTANCY THEORY MODEL IN MORE TECHNICAL TERMS

A person's motivation to exert effort towards a specific level of performance is based on his or her perceptions of associations between actions and outcomes. The critical perceptions which contribute to motivation are graphically presented in Figure 2. These perceptions can be defined as follows:

FIGURE 2

Major Terms in Expectancy Theory

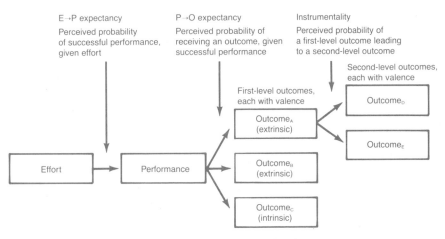

Motivation is expressed as follows: $M \cdot [E \rightarrow P] \times \geq [(P \rightarrow O) (V)]$

a. The effort-to-performance expectancy (E→P): This refers to the person's subjective probability about the likelihood that he or she can perform at a given level, or that effort on his or her part will lead to successful performance. This term can be thought of as varying from 0 to 1. In general, the less likely a person feels that he or she can perform at a given level, the less likely he or she will be to try to perform at that level. A person's E→P probabilities are also strongly influenced by each situation and by previous experience in that and similar situations.

b. The performance-to-outcomes expectancy (P→O) and valence (V): This refers to a combination of a number of beliefs about what the outcomes of successful performance will be and the value or attractiveness of these outcomes to the individual. Valence is considered to vary from +1 (very desirable) to −1 (very undesirable) and the performance-to-outcomes probabilities vary from +1 (performance sure to lead to outcome) to 0 (performance not related to outcome). In general, the more likely a person feels that performance will lead to valent outcomes, the more likely he or she will be to try to perform at the required level.

c. Instrumentality: As Figure 2 indicates, a single level of performance can be associated with a number of different outcomes, each having a certain degree of valence. Some outcomes are valent because they have direct value or attractiveness. Some outcomes, however, have valence because they are seen as leading to (or being "instrumental" for) the attainment of other "second level" outcomes which have direct value or attractiveness.

d. Intrinsic and extrinsic outcomes: Some outcomes are seen as occurring directly as a result of performing the task itself and are outcomes which the individual thus gives to himself (i.e., feelings of accomplishment, creativity, etc.). These are called "intrinsic" outcomes. Other outcomes that are associated with performance are provided or mediated by external factors (the organization, the supervisor, the work group, etc.). These outcomes are called "extrinsic" outcomes.

Along with the graphic representation of these terms presented in Figure 2, there is a simplified formula for combining these perceptions to arrive at a term expressing the relative level of motivation to exert effort towards performance at a given level. The formula expresses these relationships:

a. The person's motivation to perform is determined by the P→O expectancy multiplied by the valence (V) of the outcome. The valence of the first order outcome subsumes the instrumentalities and valences of second order outcomes. The relationship is multiplicative since there is no motivation to perform if either of the terms is zero.

b. Since a level of performance has multiple outcomes associated with it, the products of all probability-times-valence combinations are added together for all the outcomes that are seen as related to the specific performance.

c. This term (the summed P→O expectancies times valences) is then multiplied by the E→P expectancy. Again the multiplicative relationship indicates that if either term is zero, motivation is zero.

d. In summary, the strength of a person's motivation to perform effectively is influenced by (1) the person's belief that effort can be converted into performance, and (2) the net attractiveness of the events that are perceived to stem from good performance.

So far, all the terms have referred to the individual's perceptions which result in motivation and thus an intention to behave in a certain way. Figure 3 is a simplified representation of the total model, showing how these intentions get translated into actual behavior.[7] The model envisions the following sequence of events:

a. First, the strength of a person's motivation to perform correctly is most directly reflected in his or her effort—how hard he or she works. This effort expenditure may or may not result in good performance, since at least two factors must be right if effort is to be converted into performance. First, the person must possess the necessary abilities in order to perform the job well. Unless both ability and effort are high, there cannot be good performance. A second factor is the person's perception of how his or her effort can best be converted into performance. It is assumed that this perception is learned by the individual on the basis of previous experience in similar situations. This "how to do it" perception can obviously vary widely in accuracy, and—where erroneous perceptions exist—performance is low even though effort or motivation may be high.

b. Second, when performance occurs, certain amounts of outcomes are obtained by the individual. Intrinsic outcomes, not being mediated by outside forces, tend to occur regularly as a result of performance, while extrinsic outcomes may or may not accrue to the individual (indicated by the wavy line in the model).

c. Third, as a result of the obtaining of outcomes and the per-

FIGURE 3

Simplified Expectancy-Theory Model of Behavior

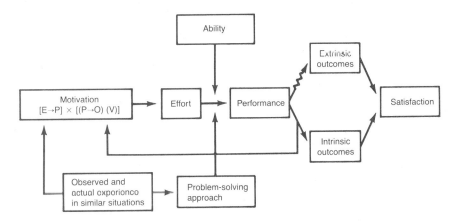

ceptions of the relative value of the outcomes obtained, the individual has a positive or negative affective response (a level of satisfaction or dissatisfaction).

d. Fourth, the model indicates that events which occur influence future behavior by altering the E→P, P→O, and V perceptions. This process is represented by the feedback loops running from actual behavior back to motivation.

APPENDIX B: MEASURING MOTIVATION USING EXPECTANCY THEORY

Expectancy theory suggests that it is useful to measure the attitudes individuals have in order to diagnose motivational problems. Such measurement helps the manager to understand why employees are motivated or not, what the strength of motivation is in different parts of the organization, and how effective different rewards are for motivating performance. A short version of a questionnaire used to measure motivation in organizations is included here.[8] Basically, three different questions need to be asked (see Tables 1, 2, and 3).

TABLE 1

Question 1: Here are some things that could happen to people if they do their jobs *especially well*. How likely is it that each of these things would happen if you performed your job *especially well*?

	Not at all likely		Somewhat likely		Quite likely		Extremely likely
a. You will get a bonus or pay increase	(1)	(2)	(3)	(4)	(5)	(6)	(7)
b. You will feel better about yourself as a person ..	(1)	(2)	(3)	(4)	(5)	(6)	(7)
c. You will have an opportunity to develop your skills and abilities	(1)	(2)	(3)	(4)	(5)	(6)	(7)
d. You will have better job security	(1)	(2)	(3)	(4)	(5)	(6)	(7)
e. You will be given chances to learn new things	(1)	(2)	(3)	(4)	(5)	(6)	(7)
f. You will be promoted or get a better job	(1)	(2)	(3)	(4)	(5)	(6)	(7)
g. You will get a feeling that you've accomplished something worthwhile	(1)	(2)	(3)	(4)	(5)	(6)	(7)
h. You will have more freedom on your job	(1)	(2)	(3)	(4)	(5)	(6)	(7)
i. You will be respected by the people you work with	(1)	(2)	(3)	(4)	(5)	(6)	(7)
j. Your supervisor will praise you	(1)	(2)	(3)	(4)	(5)	(6)	(7)
k. The people you work with will be friendly with you	(1)	(2)	(3)	(4)	(5)	(6)	(7)

TABLE 2

Question 2: Different people want different things from their work. Here is a list of things a person could have on his or her job. How *important* is each of the following to you?

	Moderately important or less			Quite important			Extremely important
How Important Is . . . ?							
a. The amount of pay you get	(1)	(2)	(3)	(4)	(5)	(6)	(7)
b. The chances you have to do something that makes you feel good about yourself as a person	(1)	(2)	(3)	(4)	(5)	(6)	(7)
c. The opportunity to develop your skills and abilities	(1)	(2)	(3)	(4)	(5)	(6)	(7)
d. The amount of job security you have	(1)	(2)	(3)	(4)	(5)	(6)	(7)
How Important Is . . . ?							
e. The chances you have to learn new things ...	(1)	(2)	(3)	(4)	(5)	(6)	(7)
f. Your chances for getting a promotion or getting a better job	(1)	(2)	(3)	(4)	(5)	(6)	(7)
g. The chances you have to accomplish something worthwhile	(1)	(2)	(3)	(4)	(5)	(6)	(7)
h. The amount of freedom you have on your job	(1)	(2)	(3)	(4)	(5)	(6)	(7)
How Important Is . . . ?							
i. The respect you receive from the people you work with	(1)	(2)	(3)	(4)	(5)	(6)	(7)
j. The praise you get from your supervisor	(1)	(2)	(3)	(4)	(5)	(6)	(7)
k. The friendliness of the people you work with ...	(1)	(2)	(3)	(4)	(5)	(6)	(7)

TABLE 3

Question 3: Below you will see a number of pairs of factors that look like this:

Warm weather → sweating   (1)   (2)   (3)   (4)   (5)   (6)   (7)

You are to indicate by checking the appropriate number to the right of each pair how often it is true for *you* personally that the first factor leads to the second on *your job*. Remember, for each pair, indicate how often it is true by checking the box under the response which seems most accurate.

	Never		Sometimes		Often		Almost always
a. Working hard → high productivity	(1)	(2)	(3)	(4)	(5)	(6)	(7)
b. Working hard → doing my job well	(1)	(2)	(3)	(4)	(5)	(6)	(7)
c. Working hard → good job performance	(1)	(2)	(3)	(4)	(5)	(6)	(7)

Using the Questionnaire Results

The results from this questionnaire can be used to calculate a *work-motivation score*. A score can be calculated for each individual and scores can be combined for groups of individuals. The procedure for obtaining a work-motivation score is as follows:

a. For each of the possible positive outcomes listed in questions 1 and 2, multiply the score for the outcome on question 1 (P→O expectancies) by the corresponding score on question 2 (valences of outcomes). Thus, score 1a would be multiplied by score 2a, score 1b by score 2b, etc.

b. All of the 1 times 2 products should be added together to get a total of all expectancies times valences

c. The total should be divided by the number of pairs (in this case, eleven) to get an average expectancy-times-valence score

d. The scores from question 3 (E→P expectancies) should be added together and then divided by three to get an average effort-to-performance expectancy score

e. Multiply the score obtained in step c (the average expectancy times valence) by the score obtained in step d (the average E→P expectancy score) to obtain a total work-motivation score

Additional Comments on the Work-Motivation Score

A number of important points should be kept in mind when using the questionnaire to get a work-motivation score. First, the questions presented here are just a short version of a larger and more comprehensive questionnaire. For more detail, the articles and publications referred to here and in the text should be consulted. Second, this is a general questionnaire. Since it is hard to anticipate in a general questionnaire what may be valent outcomes in each situation, the individual manager may want to add additional outcomes to questions 1 and 2. Third, it is important to remember that questionnaire results can be influenced by the feelings people have when they fill out the questionnaire. The use of the questionnaire as outlined above assumes a certain level of trust between manager and subordinates. People filling out questionnaires need to know what is going to be done with their answers and usually need to be assured of the confidentiality of their responses. Finally, the research indicates that, in many cases, the score obtained by simply averaging all the responses to question 1 (the P→O expectancies) will be as useful as the fully calculated work-motivation score. In each situation, the manager should experiment and find out whether the additional information in questions 2 and 3 aid in motivational diagnosis. □

REFERENCES

1. For reviews of the expectancy theory research see Mitchell, T. R. Expectancy models of job satisfaction, occupational preference and effort: A theoretical methodological, and empirical appraisal. *Psychological Bulletin,* 1974, 81, 1053–1077. For a more general discussion of expectancy theory and other approaches to motivation see Lawler, E. E. *Motivation in work organizations,* Belmont Calif.: Brooks/Cole, 1973.

2. Lawler, E. E., Kuleck, W. J., Rhode, J. G., & Sorenson, J. F. Job choice and post-decision dissonance. *Organizational Behavior and Human Performance,* 1975, 13, 133–145.

3. For a detailed discussion of the implications of expectancy theory for pay and reward systems, *see* Lawler, E. E. *Pay and organizational effectiveness: A psychological view.* New York: McGraw-Hill, 1971.

4. A good discussion of job design with an expectancy theory perspective is in Hackman, J. R., Oldham, G. R., Janson, R., & Purdy, K. A new strategy for job enrichment. *California Management Review,* Summer, 1975, p. 57.

5. The use of questionnaires for understanding and changing organizational behavior is discussed in Nadler, D. A. *Feedback and organizational development: Using data-based methods.* Reading, Mass.: Addison-Wesley, 1977.

6. The whole issue of individualizing organizations is examined in Lawler, E. E. The individualized organization: Problems and promise. *California Management Review,* 1974, 17(2), 31–39.

7. For a more detailed statement of the model see Lawler, E. E. Job attitudes and employee motivation: Theory, research and practice. *Personnel Psychology,* 1970, 23, 223–237.

8. For a complete version of the questionnaire and supporting documentation see Nadler, D. A., Cammann, C., Jenkins, G. D., & Lawler, E. E. (Eds.) *The Michigan organizational assessment package* (Progress Report II). Ann Arbor: Survey Research Center, 1975.

R² INTEGRATING OB MOD WITH COGNITIVE APPROACHES TO MOTIVATION

DONALD B. FEDOR AND
GERALD R. FERRIS

In efforts to explain behavior in organizations, behavioral scientists traditionally have conceptualized motivational processes and phenomena in either cognitive or behaviorist frameworks. While such attempts to maintain the differentiation of perspectives are regarded as advancing our understanding of behavioral outcomes, it appears that a related purpose is to set off the more widely accepted cognitive theories from the less popular behaviorist approaches. Such differentiation, regardless of intent, has served to deprive us of a potentially richer understanding of motivation and organizational behavior. Particularly for the practitioner who attempts to translate organization theories into useful prescriptions, confusion abounds. With this in mind, our purpose with this paper is to take an eclectic approach, providing specific suggestions for blending the divergent perspectives that offer prescriptive methods for maximizing worker motivation. Our focus is on bringing this blending of perspectives to bear on the legitimization and utility of what has come to be known as organizational behavior modification (OB Mod), in an attempt to address the controversy that has recently emerged in this area [Grey, 1979; Locke, 1977, 1979; Parmerlee & Schwenk, 1979].

Source: Donald B. Fedor and Gerald R. Ferris, *Academy of Management Review*, 1981, Vol. 6, No. 1, pp. 115–125.

UNDERLYING ASSUMPTIONS

The principal cognitive motivation theories in the organization literature are need-satisfaction models [Maslow, 1965], expectancy/valence theory [Vroom, 1964], and goal-setting theory [Locke, 1968]. Clearly, the cognitive component, focusing on rational behavior, is the common thread linking all three theories. Needs have been equated with the concept of "drive," a purely behavioral, noncognitive notion in the experimental psychology literature [e.g., Hull, 1943]; the organizational literature extends the need concept to cognitive elements such as self-actualization. The notion that individuals exhibit needs for growth and development traditionally has enjoyed considerable acceptance by practitioners, presumably owing to the intuitive appeal and face validity of the arguments.

LEARNING CHECKPOINT

In the chapter, needs are interpreted as being dynamic. Do the cognitive motivation theories take into consideration the fact that needs can change over time?

The assumption that individuals are composed of complex internal mechanisms that determine their behavior is perpetuated in the expectancy/valence theory of motivation [Vroom, 1964]. This theory and subsequent elaborations [e.g., Porter & Lawler, 1968] assume that individuals formulate subjective probability estimates of the ex-

tent to which a given level of effort leads to work performance (expectancies), and the extent to which a given performance level leads to certain valued outcomes (instrumentalities). Presumably, the greater the certainty in these two links, the stronger the predictability of work motivation or effort expected.

The work-design literature [e.g., Hackman & Oldham, 1980] perhaps represents a blend of the need-satisfaction and expectancy/valence theories of motivation. The approach is explicit in specifying that work itself should be designed to maximize the rewarding properties and facilitate the psychological growth of the individual.

The other work-motivation theory reflecting a cognitive orientation is the goal-setting formulation [Locke, 1968]. Sharing the idea, with expectancy/valence theory, that behavior is intentional or purposive [Tolman, 1932], this theory makes the assumption that motivation and performance are functions of goal accomplishment. While sharing certain ideas, goal setting differs from expectancy/valence theory in contextual prediction. That is, motivation is believed to be highest, in the expectancy/valence framework, when effort-to-performance and performance-to-outcome links are well defined and certain, leading to more informed subjective probability estimates structuring behavior. Alternatively, in the goal-setting framework, motivation is believed to be highest when the goals set are difficult. The inconsistency between prediction using expectancy/valance and goal-setting theories is evident.

Goals perceived as difficult would be translated into low effort-to-performance probabilities, which would result in lower motivation according to expectancy/valence theory.

The alternative perspective concerning motivation in work organizations is behavioristic in nature, and is exemplified by OB Mod. OB Mod is based on the assumption that individual behavior is a function of its consequences [e.g., Luthans & Kreitner, 1975]. By definition, the antecedents of behavior are found in the environment, not embodied in an internal state, such as personality or mind. This view differs from the cognitive one of individuals actively seeking their destiny through independent, self-determined action, and instead represents a view of behavior as a function of past and present reinforcement contingencies. This view, of course, has its roots in principles of operant conditioning, which has existed in the experimental literature for quite some time [Skinner, 1953]. Much of the present antagonism toward the application of operant conditioning principles to explaining behavior in organizations derives from reactions against the issues of determinism and control, perhaps first exemplified in a popular novel on behavioral control in society [Skinner, 1948]. This also has resulted in charges of manipulative control and Machiavellianism, which have contributed to the less-than-favorable image of OB Mod, since many are reluctant to accept the belief that behavior is determined totally by the environment.

To date, no truly eclectic approach has emerged to functionally integrate aspects of OB Mod with the cognitive orientation of widely espoused management philosophies. Thus the practitioner has

been dependent on intuitive guidance to make implementation choices.

Nord [1969] took the first step toward merging these different orientations by examining the frameworks of behaviorism and Theory X and Y assumptions detailed by McGregor [1960]. He believed that "the importance of environmental factors in determining behavior is the crucial and dominant similarity between Skinner and McGregor" [p. 377]. In this integrative attempt, Nord demonstrated, theoretically, not only the strong congruence between these supposedly competing approaches, but also the manner in which concepts of reinforcement contingency contribute to organizational effectiveness, even under the guise of a more cognitive framework. Additionally, he noted that factors of the job can be analyzed as reinforcers, whether they are considered to be intrinsic or extrinsic.

Luthans and Kreitner [1975] took the next step by demonstrating how an understanding of OB Mod techniques can facilitate the design of job enrichment, management-by-objectives programs, and organizational development interventions. These authors argue that job enrichment could profit by contingently enriching the worker's task, based on performance. Therefore, the more enriching job components would serve as naturally occurring rewards for good performance. This would be expected to eliminate the problems of reinforcing poor performance (i.e., enriching the job of the below-standards worker) or changing the job against the worker's will. Management-by-objectives is also a popular management technique that should profit from OB Mod principles. Luthans and Kreitner propose that many management-

by-objectives programs are failing because employees are not adequately reinforced for achieving performance objectives. Finally, they believe that OB Mod can legitimately play a role in organizational development interventions, because theoretically these programs are intended to facilitate or stimulate reward processes in organizations. The techniques employed typically focus on interpersonal relationships while disregarding environmental factors. Although their suggestions are appealing, there has been a virtual absence of empirical investigations directed toward testing these ideas.

Proceeding further in reducing the distance between these divergent orientations necessitates identifying specific opportunities where framework boundaries have created an absence of *concrete* data. Overlapping studies must be used to assess the relative merits of the different management approaches. The attempts to integrate and differentiate these motivational schemes to date have focused on paradigm or rightful domain implications [Grey, 1979; Locke, 1979; Parmerlee & Schwenk, 1979]. This confrontation over primarily theoretical issues is not serving the development of a motivational system that will contribute to individual and organizational effectiveness. We hope to cast this conflict in a somewhat different light, proposing new areas of investigation that will benefit the practitioner.

We will borrow from the eclectic approach recommended by Peters [1960], who argued that no single theory of motivation could explain all behavior. In essence, he proposed combining portions of a number of contributing approaches to account for all relevant factors within a construct as complex as human motivation. This advice seems particularly appropriate in that management must be concerned with both worker performance and satisfaction, neither of which has been reduced to a simple cause/effect relationship. According to some theory and research, performance and satisfaction are dependent on different variables [e.g., Lawler, 1973]. Even within the performance area, both cognitive and behavioral aspects appear relevant. Campbell and Stanley [1966] claimed that when competent researchers are strongly split over an issue, both sides are likely to be examining a different but valid portion of the complete answer.

Perhaps one of the most notable and effective attempts at integrating the cognitive and behavioral perspectives with respect to motivation is social learning theory [Bandura, 1977]. Social learning theory purportedly overemphasizes neither internal forces nor environmental factors in explaining behavior. Rather, individual functioning is seen as a continuous interaction among cognitive, behavioral, and environmental factors. Social learning theory has received attention primarily in experimental and clinical settings, but recently a concerted attempt has been made to apply it directly to explaining behavior in organizations [Davis & Luthans, 1980]. This effort focuses attention on observable behavior in "organization member-behavior-environment interaction" [p. 287].

Additionally, principles of social learning theory have been incorporated in training and development techniques. Goldstein and Sorcher [1974] incorporated the principles of social learning in their behavior modeling program for supervisors, intended to instill functional work-related behaviors. Extending this idea, it has been demonstrated that

social learning theory can explain the development of supervisory styles [Weiss, 1977] and the adoption of work values in organizations [Weiss, 1978]. Most recently, Latham and Saari [1979] applied principles of the theory in another training program for supervisors through behavior modeling.

An extensive review of OB Mod applications in business organizations revealed that research of this sort has assumed a narrow and perhaps defensive position, owing perhaps to its somewhat controversial nature. Integration of this area with others must be preceded by systematic research that begins to address some of the questions regarding the behavioral perspective. A principle question of our paper is whether the results of field studies using OB Mod methods in work organizations are providing the necessary data for effective application and integration. We have identified a number of artificial boundaries being perpetuated in research designs that are counter-productive to the potential contributions of OB Mod.

Field studies in business organizations have taken a very myopic view of the factors considered as dependent variables. Most of the current OB Mod research is conducted and interpreted as if it were an isolated discipline [Petrock & Bamboa, 1976]. Advocates of OB Mod seek to demonstrate that the method works as predicted. Luthans and Kreitner [1975] argue that changing research environments does not alter rules for behavior control. Support for the operant approach in organizational settings has been provided by several studies [At Emery Air Freight, 1973; McCarthy, 1978; Nord, 1970; Pedalino & Gamboa, 1974; Runnion, Johnson, & McWhorten, 1978; Runnion, Watson, & Mc-

Whorten, 1978]. However, despite the semblance of success, the research being conducted is not adequately addressing fundamental issues that will continue to plague OB Mod regardless of the level of sophistication in either statistical analysis or the environmental control of variables. Previous analyses of field studies by Kazdin [1973] and Andrasik [1979] are primarily concerned with whether behavior change can be attributed to the intervention as it is designed and reported. Although some commentary is valuable, this alone will not earn OB Mod a place of respect. A broadening of the research scope, as discussed later, must address the multifaceted criticisms raised by cognitively oriented behavioral scientists such as Fry [1974], Argyris [1971], and Hackman [1979]. Before detailing the areas for future investigation, we will discuss the potential benefits and costs of utilizing OB Mod.

POTENTIAL BENEFITS AND COSTS OF OB MOD

OB Mod is behavior- or performance-oriented. Unlike the case with need- and expectancy-based theories, managers focus on performance-related behaviors of workers, not on underlying psychological states as a means of achieving performance goals. Thus, the manager is not forced into the position of playing the role of clinician. Management based on worker needs or expectancies necessitates a considerable degree of subjective evaluation and, perhaps, periodic professional assessment. With OB Mod, however, it is incumbent upon management to determine and communicate specific performance objectives and definitive plans of action. The reduction in management's flexibility and room for arbitrary action could be cause for resisting the use of such a system. Despite this requirement, Cummings and Molloy in their discussion of OB Mod conclude that "one of its major contributions . . . is to show how qualitative aspects of performance can be quantified" [1977, p. 185].

Luthans and Kreitner [1975] emphasize that managers using OB Mod do not directly manage the individual. Instead, an environment is created that reinforces desired behavior. The implication is that the operant approach turns control of supervision over to workers, since supervisory behavior is directly contingent on subordinate actions. In the typical OB Mod intervention utilizing positive verbal reinforcement, the manager is trained to wait for the appropriate response from the worker. So while the worker's reinforcement is contingent on his own behavior, the manager's behavior becomes directly dependent on it. Interestingly, this appears to be a refinement of what naturally occurs between subordinates and their superiors. There is some empirical support in the leadership literature for the claim that subordinate performance causes leader behavior [e.g., Barrows, 1976; Lowin & Craig, 1968]. An additional perspective on this issue is presented by Luthans and Davis [1979]. They discuss how the individual can use structuring of the environment and planning of consequences to enhance behavioral self-control.

In conjunction with a performance orientation, OB Mod strongly de-emphasizes the use of punishment in organizational settings. Laboratory research results support the belief that desirable behavior should be reinforced and that undesirable behavior should be allowed to extinguish through the withholding of reinforcement.

Lack of punishment in work settings can be important for employee relations and the general working climate. One reason is that the worker may associate the punishment with the supervision instead of the punished act. An additional cost of punishment is increased employee stress, which can result in retaliation or withdrawal from work [Gupta & Beehr, 1979]. It may be worthwhile to consider the predominance of punitive control in light of the current pervasiveness of worker alienation [Walton, 1980].

Reese [1966] believes that punishment may be the dominant method of behavior control because of its innate capacity to immediately halt undesired behavior. Presumably, an immediate halt would convey to management a feeling of greater accomplishment and control. However, punishment does not ensure or even direct proper performance, as OB Mod purports to do. The benefit of using punishment is that its effects require less diligence and patience than operant techniques. So while positive reinforcement can be viewed as beneficial to human relations and employee training, it does appear to necessitate additional time and effort that must be absorbed by management during the initial conditioning phases.

It should be noted that management is expected to fully analyze the tasks assigned to its workers. The implementation of an OB Mod program is typically preceded by a "performance audit." Management cannot justifiably base recommendations for performance improvement intervention solely on work-group attitude. In our own experience in supervisor training, we have observed that different behavioral components become aggregated along with the inferences

concerning individual attitudes. The charge against the worker then is escalated from mere poor performance to an assumed personality flaw as well. Typically there is little attempt to separate the components of performance, to zero-in on those aspects in need of improvement. The supervisor's reaction to the worker will then be based on the image held of that individual as a poor worker, troublemaker, and so forth, virtually ignoring observable behaviors in many cases. In contrast, the performance audit provides a systematic framework within which to make such behavioral determinations. It sets a base line that can be compared to the objective the organization has established. In some cases, the audit identifies unforeseen discrepancies [At Emery Air Freight, 1973].

OB Mod's measurement bias reflects its behaviorist heritage. It is a scientifically based theory that allows managers and supervisors to accurately assess program progress. Changes in quantifiable variables are recorded and used instead of attitudinal measures. The inclusion of psychological states currently confounds the motivation issue for practitioners. Therefore, the ability of management to generate and analyze its own data, after appropriate training, adjusts the intervention to the practitioner's level of sophistication. As Nord states, "the Skinnerian approach leads to rational planning in order to control outcomes previously viewed as spontaneous consequences. This approach could expand the area of planning and rational action in administration" [1969, p. 401].

Most applications of behavior modification in work organizations include positive verbal feedback or objective feedback as a reinforcer to effect performance changes. The belief that feedback is a major factor in the OB Mod intervention is not at all unusual. Feedback is a core dimension of contemporary measures of job characteristics [Hackman & Oldham, 1975; Sims, Szilagyi, & Keller, 1976] and is consistent with performance appraisal systems objectives to let workers know where they stand [Haynes, 1980], and with the philosophy implicit in the quality of working life movements. OB Mod takes a substantially different approach by formalizing both the types and the timing of reinforcement, regardless of whether the focus is on feedback, pay, or other valued rewards. Although the question of whether rewards must be immediately contingent on behavior/performance will likely remain a debatable issue for some time, OB Mod utilizes a schedule of reinforcement stressing timing as an issue in the development of a supportive environment that will elicit and reinforce desired behavior. Such a prescriptive strategy may offend practitioners and theorists who emphasize individual needs and differences, but it does ensure that the worker will be provided with feedback concerning correct behavior. This is essential for practical application where the prescription "more feedback" is found lacking in specificity.

OB Mod interventions often begin with a great deal of verbal reinforcement and then gradually lessen the frequency of this external feedback. The expectation is that the direct performance feedback from the task will naturally take over the reinforcer role. So, over the course of an OB Mod program, there is a shift in emphasis from supervision to aspects of the job itself. For individuals beginning a new job, the OB Mod prescription is consistent with results presented by Katz [1978]. He found that during the initial stages of an individual's job, task feedback is strongly desired. Following the usual OB Mod schedule of reinforcement, early frequent feedback tapers off to later permit greater autonomy.

In summary, OB Mod provides a definitive framework from which to implement and test an intervention by taking into account the types and timing of reinforcement that supports or punishes job behaviors. It is obvious that we have a positive view of OB Mod; we believe that this approach has an orientation and associated techniques that are useful and complementary to popular motivation schemes. The next step is to begin collecting organizational data that will test the fit between OB Mod and other orientations. This necessitates expanding the parameters considered appropriate by behaviorist researchers. The following topics represent a partial list of issues OB Mod researchers need to consider more directly.

THE ROLE OF PARTICIPATION

Participation in decision making has become a popular issue during this decade, owing largely to its convergence with individual growth, job involvement, and job enrichment. OB Mod, on the other hand, has been viewed typically as a top-down approach that is applied to the employee with virtually no concern for individual development [Hackman, 1979]. In theory, these orientations are in clear opposition. The role of participation in operant conditioning can be viewed in a number of ways. Since people presumably react to their environment based on reinforcement history, feelings of involvement and individual growth could be considered irrelevant. Participation might be perceived as a confounding factor in the intervention if it causes changes in the experimental design or in the reinforcers. Conversely, getting the participants to assist in developing the OB Mod program, such as determining the proper reinforcers, designating the "best" behaviors to accomplish the stated objectives, and discovering the reinforcers utilized by the informal organization could eliminate some of the problems. The feeling of involvement itself may be an effective reinforcer.

Komaki, Waddell, and Pearce [1977] were forced to use a participative approach in order to secure the cooperation of the participants in conducting their experiment. Although this was mentioned, it was not cited as a relevant factor in interpreting the reported success of the experiment. Nord [1970] suggests using worker ideas about the type of program and rewards as valuable input with which to modify and refine the OB Mod project. In this way, the positive verbal reinforcement is seen as a way to enhance communication between managers and workers.

In each of these cases, as in most OB Mod interventions, there is a conspicuous attempt to account for those factors that cannot be controlled directly. It is interesting that researchers concerned with the generalizability of their experimental designs feel justified in ignoring the facilitative function of a cognitive factor as potentially persuasive as participation. Unfortunately, no research reviewed to date has compared the efficacy of OB Mod interventions for groups with and without participant involvement. A comparative research design would address the question of the extent to which these theoretically divergent orientations are, in fact, complementary.

OB MOD AND GOAL SETTING

We believe that OB Mod and goal setting are complementary techniques originating from divergent perspectives. Both orientations focus on goal attainment, but traditionally have selected different factors for experimentation. For this reason, the distinction between OB Mod and goal setting can be blurred in an applied setting. As previously noted, the objective of most OB Mod interventions is to have the standards and feedback from the task eventually take over the reinforcement role [At Emery Air Freight, 1973]. The individual presumably is performing at a higher level, owing to greater goal difficulty [Locke, 1968]. Many of the goal-setting investigations have been concerned with the effect of incentives on performance and the extent to which they affect performance through goal level [Locke, 1968; Pritchard & Curtis, 1973; Terborg, 1976]. The overlap of these two orientations is apparent, but it is virtually always ignored. None of the organization-based OB Mod studies we reviewed discussed differential target levels of performance. The relevant factors for behaviorists doing field research seem to be the following: to determine the correct or desirable behavior, to select the appropriate reinforcement(s) and the schedule of application, and to test the level of goal attainment within an appropriate experimental design. Our argument is that OB Mod and goal set-

LEARNING CHECKPOINT

Why haven't applied organizational goal setting researchers as displayed in Figure 4–5 tested the complementarity of goal setting and OB Mod?

ting focus on different aspects of the same issue. The information concerning differential goal setting should be tested in conjunction with OB Mod.

We find it interesting that the goal-setting literature [e.g., Latham & Yukl, 1975, 1976] has focused on the relationship between assigned goals and those set participatively. Operant conditioning techniques traditionally have relied on unilaterally set target behaviors and standards of performance. This adds further support to the belief that OB Mod ignores individual perceptions and expectations. The gain or loss caused by assigning objectives also has not been explored adequately to date.

WORKER AND MANAGER RESPONSES TO BEHAVIOR MODIFICATION

OB Mod has been criticized severely for being dehumanizing and ignoring individual cognitive processes [e.g., Fry, 1974]. Even though findings from current research do not support the belief that satisfaction is consistently related to productivity [Locke, 1976], worker responses to their jobs can have an impact on labor relations, absenteeism, tardiness, and turnover—areas of particular concern to management. Typically, OB Mod field experiments measure the effects of an intervention on, for example, absenteeism, with the issue of morale addressed only briefly in the conclusion. Cummings and Molloy [1977] cite the lack of attitudinal references in their review of OB Mod research. Only Adams [1975] has examined the relationship between positive reinforcement and attitudes about product quality. His results, however, were inconclusive.

A related issue has to do with management's reaction to workers when positive verbal reinforcement is used as part of an OB Mod program. Adams noted that one supervisor adopted a less autocratic style of management as a result of the forced interaction with subordinates. Nord [1970] suggested using the increased level of supervisory response as a method for involving the individual in the job. In addition, the negative sanctions used by management (i.e., punishment) are greatly reduced, because managers are forced to relate to their subordinates on a positive basis. Presumably, this experience should precipitate some attitudinal change in managers, but such potential benefits have not been evaluated to date. So, although the application of operant conditioning techniques is less Machiavellian than the underlying theory might suggest, research has not shown any sustained interest in dispelling this negative image. Regardless of the behaviorist bias against attitudinal measures, the worker's response to any intervention is an important factor for managers. Therefore, assessing these attitudes should be equally relevant to the research and should be incorporated in future OB Mod designs.

OB MOD AND WORK DESIGN

When viewing work design within a systems framework, one must account for the worker, the work itself, and the work context (pay, co-workers, supervision, etc.). Corresponding to the above factors and their interaction, a number of salient issues arise for practitioners interested in a pragmatic approach to work design. These issues can be classified under three headings: individual differences, locus of control, and tradeoffs between different design alternatives.

Traditional work design theorists deal with both individual differences and the work context by measuring growth-need strength (GNS) and satisfaction with specific contextual variables (see Hackman & Oldman [1980] for a review). Essentially, if the focal individual has a sufficient level of GNS and demonstrates satisfaction with the job context, then the work design process is intended to create an enriching task [Oldham, Hackman, & Pearce, 1976]. This entails designing the task to provide such things as increased skill variety, autonomy, and feedback. The implication is that the locus of control should reside with the individual worker. Factors typically of concern in traditional work design research are those intrinsic to the task. These factors occur through the process of performing the task, and are therefore mediated by the worker and not by other organizational agents or mechanisms external to the individual. This orientation suggests that work design fits neatly into a managerial framework where the worker is granted greater latitude within which to function. Deci's [1975] research on internal motivation indicates that for tasks which are intrinsically enriched, extrinsic variables, which supposedly alter the locus of control from internal to external, cause a decrease in internal motivation. As a result, at the managerial end of the job spectrum, where tasks exhibit more design flexibility, the traditional job design method seems appropriate and possible to implement.

OB Mod again poses a divergent orientation. Individual differences are literally ignored and the notion of determining individual satisfaction with compensation and work context, as advocated by Oldham, Hackman, and Pearce [1976] and equity theory research [Adams, 1965], does not fit its behaviorist framework. The reinforcers, in an OB Mod intervention, generally are mediated externally—despite Nord's [1969] argument that, owing to the contingent nature of the reinforcement, the individual retains ultimate control. For tasks that cannot be sufficiently enriched, OB Mod offers an attractive alternative. This may be one reason why this motivational technique has been predominantly applied to blue-collar positions. Presumably it is better to provide external feedback when the task itself does not than to simply ignore the deficiency.

From the above approaches to work design, it is easy to conceptualize a number of potential alternatives available to the organization designer when tasks fall somewhere between the extremes of "impossible" and "easily enriched." For example, an organization could expend its resources to redesign a task, building in greater skill variety, or use the same resources to provide the job holder with a greater variety of reinforcers external to the task. Cummings and Molloy [1977] identify such alternatives as the choice within the organization. In situations where different action levels represent realistic alternatives, the incongruity between these orientations becomes extremely confusing. Despite Nord's [1969] belief that reinforcers are the common denominators, there are different costs and benefits to these available choices. Perceptual differences may not directly affect motivation or performance, but these factors could be important to other organizational elements, such as the climate and the attractiveness of the organization.

An additional consideration is that jobs are sometimes designed or redesigned to correct for anticipated problems in worker motivation or satisfaction. Management may desire to act before predicted behavioral changes take place. Therefore, the responses workers have to different job components are sometimes used as behavioral predictors. For example, if the research suggesting that absenteeism is not an effective indicator of future turnover is correct, there may be no behavioral antecedents to identify a worker's propensity to leave the organization. In other words, if "behavioral units" of job tenure cannot be identified, then it may not be possible to determine the efficacy of current reinforcement until it fails to produce the desired results. In this case, valued employees could be lost before the necessity for a design change would be realized. So despite the inexact and unstable nature of internal states [Salancik & Pfeffer, 1977], assessing worker attitudes may, in some instances, be the only available indicator of future difficulties.

The focal problem here is a paucity of comparative studies between behaviorist and nonbehaviorist methods. Apparently, only Cummings and Molloy [1977] have reviewed and compared different orientations within the framework of the quality of working life and productivity to determine the different action levers relied on and the types of outcomes achieved in research interventions. More detailed studies are necessary to determine the immediate outcomes and the more indirect implications of selecting different approaches. To date, there are no available data on whether the choice of an intervention should be influenced by the individual(s) being targeted, the type of task, or the climate of the organization. Work design theorists sensitive to the locus-of-control issue presumably would argue that substituting OB Mod techniques for intrinsic components will never be a satisfying tradeoff for the worker. Nord [1969], Luthans and Kreitner [1975], and others would likely counter with the argument that if reinforcement is designed properly, there should be no qualitative differences. At this point consultants and practitioners must rely on their own intuition in the absence of concrete evidence.

COMPLEXITY AND CREATIVITY

As previously noted, most of the jobs used to generate test data for OB Mod could be classified as blue-collar positions. The environment is usually stable and the worker's function can be dissected into reinforceable behavioral events. Two related issues emerge from these factors, concerning complexity and creativity. One question is: How is OB Mod adapted to *complex managerial positions* that do not have clearly defined tasks? In spite of the case cited by Luthans and Kreitner [1975] suggesting that complex behaviors, such as initiative, can be effectively reinforced, OB Mod may, in fact, be more applicable to lower-level organizational positions. From anecdotal accounts such as those presented by Kerr [1975], it is evident that we must not merely reinforce the components of the job that are quantifiable. If the entire job is not reinforced, employee responses will center on activities that consistently gain positive feedback. The remaining functions of the job will be allowed to extinguish along with the inappropriate behaviors.

To our knowledge, no comparative studies exist demonstrating the efficiency of OB Mod in relation to other motivational techniques. Andrasik confirms this conclusion in stating that "none of the [interventions reviewed] consisted of comparisons with alternative, non-behavioral approaches" [1979, p. 99]. In the absence of quantifiable data, how is the manager in charge of the OB Mod intervention to deal with qualitative information? Needless to say, behavioral researchers must begin to report and analyze interventions involving all levels of the organizational hierarchy.

The more important question, however, deals with *creativity*. If the individual's job is broken down into behavioral units, will this not drastically reduce worker flexibility in making behavioral (qualitative) adjustments? The incentive to search for more efficient work patterns would be greatly decreased unless reinforcement for creativity were built into the program. Unfortunately, this idea was not tested in any of the experiments reviewed. This potential problem coincides with the discussion concerning participation. Involving employees in project design and maintenance may circumvent the problems of selecting the most effective behavior, determining appropriate reinforcement for creative activities, or encouraging feedback with which to change ineffective or inappropriate elements of the OB Mod program. However, with no evidence available at present, such a hypothesis awaits empirical examination.

CONCLUSION

OB Mod is a behavior- or performance-oriented management technique. Quantitative output data are used to design a reinforcing environment for appropriate work behavior. This offers management a straightforward method for analyzing the effect of supervision and other reinforcers, such as pay, on worker conduct. As a perspective divergent from more intuitively appealing and generally accepted cognitive motivation theories, OB Mod has been cast as a separate discipline and forced to justify its existence and defend its viability. Possibly because of this ostracism, OB Mod proponents have narrowed their research focus to charting behavioral changes while ignoring implications of their interventions, such as the participants' attitudinal responses resulting from the intervention.

We have sought to illuminate the differences between the two orientations on the issue of employee motivation. Our emphasis has been on suggesting further research that may necessitate a reconceptualization of the purpose of OB Mod assessments in business organizations. Instead of escalating this conflict over paradigm definition and justification as others have done [e.g., Parmerlee & Schwenk, 1979], we have tried to take a pragmatic view of the linkages between these now competing perspectives.

We hope this paper will encourage the functional incorporation of effective motivational techniques, whether currently labeled cognitive or behaviorist. The current state of the art is generating considerable confusion for those interested in applying social science research findings to real problems of creating work environments that are motivating and satisfying. □

LEARNING CHECKPOINT

Are cognitive motivation theories of any more practical value to managers than OB Mod approaches? Why?

REFERENCES

Adams, E. E. Behavior modification in quality control. *Academy of Management Journal*, 1975, *18*, 662–679.

Adams, J. S. Inequity in social exchange. In L. Berkowitz (Ed.), *Advances in experimental social psychology*. New York: Academic Press, 1965.

Andrasik, F. Organizational behavior modification in business settings: A methodological and content review. *Journal of Organizational Behavior Management*, 1979, *2*, 85–102.

Argyris, C. Beyond freedom and dignity by B. F. Skinner: A review essay. *Harvard Educational Review*, 1971, *41*, 550–567.

At Emery Air Freight: Positive reinforcement boosts performance. *Organizational Dynamics*, 1973, *1*, 41–50.

Bandura, A. *Social learning theory*. Englewood Cliffs, N.J.: Prentice-Hall, 1977.

Barrows, J. C. Worker performance and task complexity as causal determinants of leader behavior style and flexibility. *Journal of Applied Psychology*, 1976, *61*, 443–440.

Campbell, D. T.; & Stanley, J. C. *Experimental and quasi-experimental designs for research*. Chicago: Rand-McNally, 1966.

Cummings, T. C.; & Molloy, E. S. *Improving productivity and the quality of work life*. New York: Praeger, 1977.

Davis, T. R. V.; & Luthans, F. A social learning approach to organizational behavior. *Academy of Management Review*, 1980, *5*, 281–290.

Deci, E. L. *Intrinsic motivation*. New York: Plenum, 1975.

Fry, F. L. Operant conditioning in organizational settings: Of mice or men? *Personnel*, 1974, *51*, 17–24.

Goldstein, A. P.; & Sorcher, M. *Changing supervisor behavior*. New York: Pergamon, 1974.

Grey, J. L. The myths of the myths about behavior modification in organizations: A reply to Locke's criticism of behavior modification. *Academy of Management Review*, 1979, *1*, 121–129.

Gupta, N.; & Beehr, T. A. Job stress and employee behaviors. *Organizational Behavior & Human Performance*, 1979, *23*, 373–387.

Hackman, J. R. Informal speech given at the Friday Forum, University of Illinois, Urbana-Champaign, September 21, 1979.

Hackman, J. R.; & Oldham, G. R. *Work redesign*. Reading, Mass.: Addison-Wesley, 1980.

Hackman, J. R.; & Oldham, G. R. Development of the job diagnostic survey. *Journal of Applied Psychology*, 1975, *60*, 159–170.

Haynes, M. G. Developing an appraisal program. In K. M. Rowland, M. London, G. R. Ferris, & J. L. Sherman (Eds.), *Current issues in personnel management*. Boston: Allyn & Bacon, 1980.

Hull, C. L. *Principles of behavior*. New York: Appleton-Century-Crofts, 1943.

Katz, R. Job longevity as a situational factor in job satisfaction. *Administrative Science Quarterly*, 1978, *28*, 204–222.

Kazdin, A. E. Methodological and assessment considerations in evaluating reinforcement programs in applied settings. *Journal of Applied Behavioral Analysis*, 1973, *6*, 517–521.

Kerr, S. On the folly of rewarding A while hoping for B. *Academy of Management Journal*, 1975, *18*, 769–783.

Komaki, J.; Waddell, W. M.; & Pearce, G. M. The applied behavior analysis approach and individual employee: Improving performance in two small businesses. *Organizational Behavior & Human Performance*, 1977, *19*, 337–352.

Latham, G. P.; & Saari, L. M. Application of social learning theory to training supervisors through behavioral modeling. *Journal of Applied Psychology*, 1979, *64*, 239–246.

Latham, G. P.; & Yukl, G. A. Assigned versus participative goal setting with educated and uneducated woods workers. *Journal of Applied Psychology*, 1975, *60*, 299–302.

Latham, G. P.; & Yukl, G. A. Effects of assigned and participative goal setting on performance and job satisfaction. *Journal of Applied Psychology*, 1976, *51*, 166–171.

Lawler, E. E. *Motivation in work organizations*. Monterey, Calif.: Brooks/Cole, 1973.

Locke, E. A. Toward a theory of task motivation and incentives. *Organizational Behavior & Human Performance*, 1968, *3*, 157–189.

Locke, E. A. The nature and causes of job satisfaction. In M. D. Dunnette (Ed.), *Handbook of industrial and organizational psychology*. Chicago: Rand-McNally, 1976.

Locke, E. A. The myths of behavior mod. in organizations. *Academy of Management Review*, 1977, *2*, 543–553.

Locke, E. A. Myths in "The myths of the myths about behavior mod. in organizations." *Academy of Management Review*, 1979, *1*, 131–136.

Lowin, A.; & Craig, J. R. The influence of level of performance on managerial style: An experimental object-lesson in the ambiguity of correlational data. *Organizational Behavior & Human Performance*, 1968, *3*, 449–458.

Luthans, F.; & Davis, T. R. V. Behavioral self-management: The missing link in managerial effectiveness. *Organizational Dynamics*, Summer 1979, 42–60.

Luthans, F.; & Kreitner, R. *Organizational behavior modification*. Glenview, Ill.: Scott, Foresman, 1975.

Maslow, A. H. *Eupsychian management*. Homewood, Ill.: Irwin-Dorsey, 1965.

McCarthy, M. Decreasing the incidence of "high bobbins" in a textile spinning department through a group feedback procedure. *Journal of Organizational Behavior Management*, 1978, *1*, 150–154.

McGregor, D. *The human side of enterprise*. New York: McGraw-Hill, 1960.

Nord, W. R. Beyond the teaching machine: The neglected area of operant conditioning in the theory and practice of management. *Organizational Behavior & Human Performance*, 1969, *5*, 375–401.

Nord, W. R. Improving attendance through rewards. *Personnel Administration*, 1970, *33*, 37–41.

Oldham, G. R.; Hackman, J. R.; & Pearce, J. L. Conditions under which employees respond positively to enriched work. *Journal of Applied Psychology,* 1976, *61,* 395–403.

Parmerlee, M.; & Schwenk, C. Radical behaviorism in organizations: Misconceptions in the Locke-Grey debate. *Academy of Management Review,* 1979, *4,* 601–607.

Pedalino, E.; & Gamboa, V. V. Behavior modification and absenteeism: Intervention in one industrial setting. *Journal of Applied Psychology,* 1974, *59,* 694–698.

Peters, R. S. *The concept of motivation.* New York: Humanities Press, 1960.

Petrock, F.; & Gamboa, V. V. Expectancy theory and operant conditioning: A conceptual comparison. In W. R. Nord (Ed.), *Concepts and controversy in organizational behavior* (2nd ed.). Santa Monica, Calif.: Goodyear, 1976.

Porter, L. W.; & Lawler, E. E. *Managerial attitudes and performance.* Homewood, Ill.: Irwin-Dorsey, 1968.

Pritchard, R. D.; & Curtis, M. I. The influence of goal setting and financial incentives on task performance. *Organizational Behavior & Human Performance,* 1973, *10,* 175–183.

Reese, E. P. *The analysis of human operant behavior.* Dubuque, Iowa: William C. Brown, 1966.

Runnion, A.; Johnson, T.; & McWhorten, J. The effects of feedback and reinforcement on truck turnaround time in materials transportation. *Journal of Organizational Behavior Management,* 1978, *1,* 110–117.

Runnion, A.; Watson, J. O.; & McWhorten, J. Energy savings in interstate transportation through feedback and reinforcement. *Journal of Organizational Behavior Management,* 1978, *1,* 180–191.

Salancik, G. R.; & Pfeffer, J. An examination of the need-satisfaction model of job attitudes. *Administrative Science Quarterly,* 1977, *22,* 427–456.

Sims, H. P.; Szilagyi, A. D.; & Keller, R. T. The measurement of job characteristics. *Academy of Management Journal,* 1976, *19,* 195–224.

Skinner, B. F. *Science and human behavior.* New York: Free Press, 1953.

Skinner, B. F. *Walden two.* New York: MacMillan, 1948.

Terborg, J. R. The motivational components of goal setting. *Journal of Applied Psychology,* 1976, *61,* 613–621.

Tolman, E. C. *Purposive behavior in animals and men.* New York: Century, 1932.

Vroom, V. H. *Work and motivation.* New York: Wiley, 1964.

Walton, R. E. How to counter alienation in the plant. In K. M. Rowland, M. London, G. R. Ferris, & J. L. Sherman (Eds.), *Current issues in personnel management.* Boston: Allyn & Bacon, 1980.

▷1 YOUR MOTIVATION TO MANAGE

How motivated are you to manage? It is your motivation to manage that will provide some indication of how likely you are to be satisfied with a management position. There is no ideal formula for having a desire to manage, but one indication can be obtained by answering a few questions.

The "Motivation to Manage" (MTM) scale is a subjective assessment and you may have some error, but at least it will sensitize you to the key variables and encourage you to think about these issues.

Activities that are preferred and enjoyed are very different for the person with a high versus a low Motivation to Manage. Jobs with given characteristics are better and less well suited to each managerial type. The table below indicates those job characteristics that are best matched with people with high MTM and low MTM.

Source: "Motivation to Manage" is an exercise developed by Dennis P. Slevin, *Executive Survival Manual.* Innodyne, Inc., P.O. Box 11386, Pittsburgh, PA 15238.

MOTIVATION 1

MOTIVATION TO MANAGE AUDIT

How motivated to manage are you?

Complete this instrument by circling the number for each item that represents your best estimate of your current level.

	Well Below Average	Average	Well Above Average
1. Favorable attitude toward authority		0 1 2 3 4 5 6 7 8 9 10	
2. Desire to compete		0 1 2 3 4 5 6 7 8 9 10	
3. Assertive motivation		0 1 2 3 4 5 6 7 8 9 10	
4. Desire to exercise power		0 1 2 3 4 5 6 7 8 9 10	
5. Desire for a distinctive position		0 1 2 3 4 5 6 7 8 9 10	
6. A sense of responsibility		0 1 2 3 4 5 6 7 8 9 10	

TOTAL MOTIVATION TO MANAGE = _____

Now place a check mark next to the number for each item that represents your best estimate of where you would *like to be*. The difference between your *desired* and *actual* score for each item is your Motivation to Manage deficit on that factor. It will be used in completing your Motivation to Manage Action Plan (Motivation 2).

TABLE 1

Job Characteristics Associated with Motivation to Manage (MTM)

Low MTM	High MTM
Relatively small span of control	Large span of control
Small number of subordinates	Large number of subordinates
High technical/engineering component	High people/budgetary component
Maintain "hands-on" expertise	Surround oneself with technical experts
Limited number of activities per day	As many as 200 activities per day
Few interruptions	Many interruptions
Time for reading, analyzing	Time for interactions
Serve as facilitator to staff	Serve as "boss" to staff
Career progression = increase in technical expertise	Career progression = managerial advancement
Little exercise of power is required	Much intervention in lives of others
Lower stress position	Higher stress position

MTM/Job Fit

In order for you to be satisfied and successful in an organizational role, you must first attempt to match your basic motivation to the job. Does your job fit your Motivation to Manage? Different jobs require different levels of MTM. Look at Table 1 and try to determine if you are in a high or low MTM job. Suppose that you have just concluded that you have low Motivation to Manage? What should you do?

You have two alternatives:

1. Select jobs that are more appropriate to your MTM
2. Attempt to change your MTM

In order for you to be happy, fulfilled, and successful in your job, you must fit the job requirements. There must be a match between your motivation and the characteristics of the job, the activities you like to do and those demanded by the job. Thorough and accurate self-assessment regarding your Motivation to Manage is very important information as you make career choices.

Changing Your Motivation to Manage

It is generally accepted in psychology that a certain amount of motivation is learned. McClelland has claimed the ability to teach people to increase their need for achievement. He has also concluded that successful managers have a higher need for power than their need for affiliation. This seems compatible with the MTM in that one must be prepared to exercise power over others in order to succeed as a manager.

Is it possible to increase a person's Motivation to Manage? Perhaps. Little research has been done in this area. There are no figures to cite. However, look at the six components of Motivation to Manage. They are *learned* motives. Therefore, one should be able to change them. Is it possible to change your Motivation to Change? Definitely. If you want to.

Do you *want* to change your Motivation to Manage? If yes, you will need to formulate an action plan for changing each of the components of managerial motivation.

Go back to the Motivation to Manage Audit (Motivation 1). Look at your desired level for each of the factors in the Motivation to Manage in your present position. The difference between the desired level and your actual level provides a *managerial motivation* deficit for each factor. Specify on the Motivation to Manage Action Plan (Motivation 2) the specific steps that you might take to increase your MTM on each factor to remove the deficit.

MOTIVATION 2

MOTIVATION TO MANAGE ACTION PLAN

Record your Motivation to Manage deficit (desired–actual) for each factor below. Then specify appropriate action steps you might take to increase your Motivation to Manage on each factor and remove the deficit.

1. Favorable Attitude Toward Authority   Deficit: _____

    Action Plan: _____

    _____

    _____

    _____ Probability of Success: _____

2. Desire to Compete   Deficit: _____

    Action Plan: _____

    _____

    _____

    _____ Probability of Success: _____

3. Assertive Motivation   Deficit: _____

    Action Plan: _____

    _____

    _____

    _____ Probability of Success: _____

4. Desire to Exercise Power   Deficit: _____

    Action Plan: _____

    _____

    _____

    _____ Probability of Success: _____

5. Desire for Distinctive Position   Deficit: _____

    Action Plan: _____

    _____

    _____

    _____ Probability of Success: _____

6. A Sense of Responsibility   Deficit: _____

    Action Plan: _____

    _____

    _____

    _____ Probability of Success: _____

You have now had an opportunity to assess in a personal way your Motivation to Manage. The logical steps in this assessment are portrayed in the flow chart shown in Figure 1. Try to accomplish this in as perceptive a way as possible. It's fun to consider your own personal motivational structures and to talk to others about career, job, and personal needs. If you can better understand where you are concerning your motivation to manage, you will be in a better position to perform your job at peak efficiency. If your Motiva-

tion to Manage is insufficient for your current or future job prospects, then you must seriously consider changing these needs or changing your career. Millions of people get matched to millions of jobs through ad hoc and almost accidental sequences of events. In this exercise you are provided with a framework for consciously and analytically attempting to assess the match between your motivation structure and the manager's job.

FIGURE 1

Motivating Yourself and Others

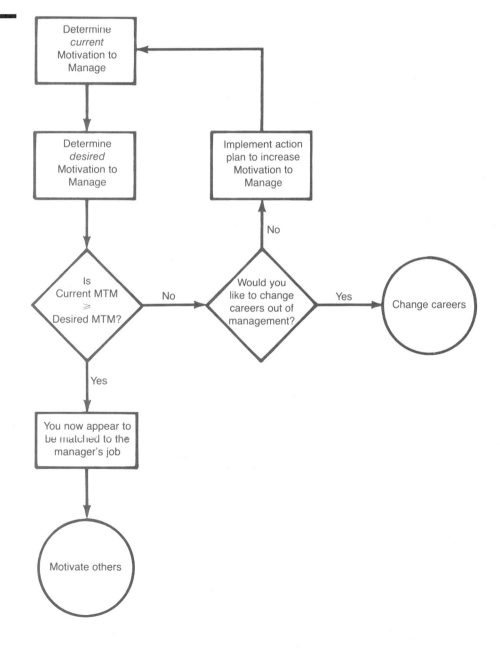

2 GOAL SETTING— HOW TO DO IT

Each person is to work alone for at least 30 minutes with this exercise. After sufficient time has elapsed for each person to work through the exercise, the instructor will go over each goal and ask for comments from the class or group. The discussion should display the understanding of goals that each participant has and what will be needed to improve his or her goal-writing skills.

Writing and evaluating goals seem simple, but they are often not done well in organizations. The press of time, previous habits, and little concern about the attributes of a goal statement are reasons why goals are often poorly constructed. Actually, a number of guidelines should be followed in preparing goals.

1. A well-presented goal statement contains four elements:
    a.   An action or accomplishment verb.
    b.   A single and measurable result.
    c.   A date of completion.
    d.   A cost in terms of effort, resources, or money or some combination of these factors.
2. A well-presented goal statement is short; it is not a paragraph. It should be presented in a sentence.
3. A well-presented goal statement specifies only what and when and doesn't get into how or why.
4. A well-presented goal statement is challenging and attainable. It should cause the person to stretch his or her skills, abilities, and efforts.
5. A well-presented goal statement is meaningful and important. It should be a priority item.
6. A well-presented goal statement must be acceptable to you so that you will try hard to accomplish the goal.

The goal statement model should be:

To (action or accomplishment verb) (single result) by (a date—keep it realistic) at (effort, use of what resource, cost).

An example for a production operation:

To reduce the production cost per unit of Mint toothpaste by at least 3 percent by March 1, at a changeover of equipment expense not to exceed $45,000.

Examine the next four statements that are presented as goal statements. Below each goal write a critique of the statement. Is it a good goal statement? Why? Discuss your viewpoints in the class group discussion.

To reduce my blood pressure to an acceptable level.

_____

_____

_____

_____

_____

_____

_____

_____

To make financial investments with a guaranteed minimum return of at least 16 percent.

_____
_____
_____
_____
_____
_____
_____

To spend a minimum of 45 minutes a day on a doctor-approved exercise plan, starting Monday, lasting for six months, at no expense.

_____
_____
_____
_____
_____
_____
_____

To spend more time reading non-work-related novels and books during the next year.

_____
_____
_____
_____
_____
_____
_____

APPLYING MOTIVATION THEORY EXERCISE

OBJECTIVES

1. To evaluate the merits of different motivation theories.

2. To emphasize the decisions that must be made by managers in motivating people.

3. To apply motivation principles.

STARTING THE EXERCISE

Set up groups of five to eight students to read the facts and the situation facing Margo Williams.

In the chapter, a number of popular content theories were discussed. Some of the major points raised were the following:

Maslow: Motivation involves satisfying needs in a hierarchical order.

Herzberg: Some job factors are intrinsically satisfying and motivate individuals.

McClelland: Motives are acquired from a person's culture.

With these three theories in mind, review the work situation that is currently facing Margo Williams.

Margo Williams is a project engineer director in a large construction company. She is responsible for scheduling projects, meeting customers, reporting progress on projects, controlling costs, and developing subordinates. A total of 20 men and 8 women report to Margo. All of them are college graduates and have had at least eight years of job experience. Margo is a Ph.D. engineer, but she has only had four years of project engineering experience.

The biggest problems facing Margo involve the lack of respect and response that she receives from her subordinates. Margo's supervisor has considered these problems and assumes that her moderate record of success could be improved if she could correct the situation. Margo is now considering a course of action that could motivate her subordinates to show more respect and respond more favorably to her requests.

EXERCISE PROCEDURES

1. Set up small discussion groups of five to eight students to develop a motivation plan for Margo. The group should work on developing a plan that uses the motivation principles discussed in this chapter.

2. After the group has worked together for about 30 minutes, a group leader should present the plan to the class.

3. Discuss each group's plan for the remainder of the class period.

THE NEED HIERARCHY*

OBJECTIVES

1. To experience firsthand the concepts of one of the work-motivation theories—in this case, the popular Maslow hierarchy of needs.

2. To get personal feedback on your opinions of the use of motivational techniques in human resources management.

3. To compare your need levels with class colleagues.

STARTING THE EXERCISE

The following questions have seven possible responses:

1. Please mark one of the seven responses by circling the number that corresponds to the response that fits your opinion. For example,

if you "strongly agree," circle the number "+3."

2. Complete every item. You have about ten minutes to do so.

		Strongly agree	Agree	Slightly agree	Don't know	Slightly disagree	Disagree	Strongly disagree
		+3	+2	+1	0	−1	−2	−3
1.	Special wage increases should be given to employees who do their jobs very well.	+3	+2	+1	0	−1	−2	−3
2.	Better job descriptions would be helpful so that employees will know exactly what is expected of them.	+3	+2	+1	0	−1	−2	−3
3.	Employees need to be reminded that their jobs are dependent on the company's ability to compete effectively.	+3	+2	+1	0	−1	−2	−3
4.	Supervisors should give a good deal of attention to the physical working conditions of their employees.	+3	+2	+1	0	−1	−2	−3
5.	Supervisors ought to work hard to develop a friendly working atmosphere among their people.	+3	+2	+1	0	−1	−2	−3
6.	Individual recognition for above-standard performance means a lot to employees.	+3	+2	+1	0	−1	−2	−3
7.	Indifferent supervision can often bruise feelings.	+3	+2	+1	0	−1	−2	−3
8.	Employees want to feel that their real skills and capacities are put to use on their jobs.	+3	+2	+1	0	−1	−2	−3
9.	The company retirement benefits and stock programs are important factors in keeping employees on their jobs.	+3	+2	+1	0	−1	−2	−3

* Source: John E. Jones and J. William Pfeiffer (Eds.), *The Annual Handbook for Group Facilitators.* San Diego: University Associates, 1973, pp. 43–45.

	Strongly agree	Agree	Slightly agree	Don't know	Slightly disagree	Disagree	Strongly disagree
	+3	+2	+1	0	−1	−2	−3
10. Almost every job can be made more stimulating and challenging.	+3	+2	+1	0	−1	−2	−3
11. Many employees want to give their best in everything they do.	+3	+2	+1	0	−1	−2	−3
12. Management could show more interest in the employees by sponsoring social events after hours.	+3	+2	+1	0	−1	−2	−3
13. Pride in one's work is actually an important reward.	+3	+2	+1	0	−1	−2	−3
14. Employees want to be able to think of themselves as "the best" at their own jobs.	+3	+2	+1	0	−1	−2	−3
15. The quality of the relationships in the informal work group is quite important.	+3	+2	+1	0	−1	−2	−3
16. Individual incentive bonuses would improve the performance of employees.	+3	+2	+1	0	−1	−2	−3
17. Visibility with upper management is important to employees.	+3	+2	+1	0	−1	−2	−3
18. Employees generally like to schedule their own work and to make job-related decisions with a minimum of supervision.	+3	+2	+1	0	−1	−2	−3
19. Job security is important to employees.	+3	+2	+1	0	−1	−2	−3
20. Having good equipment to work with is important to employees.	+3	+2	+1	0	−1	−2	−3

3. Transfer the numbers you circled in the questionnaire to the appropriate places in the spaces below.

Self-actualization needs		Esteem needs		Belongingness needs	
Statement No.	Score	Statement No.	Score	Statement No.	Score
10	____	6	____	5	____
11	____	8	____	7	____
13	____	14	____	12	____
18	____	17	____	15	____
Total	____	Total	____	Total	____

	Safety needs			Basic needs	
	Statement No.	Score		Statement No.	Score
	2	____		1	____
	3	____		4	____
	9	____		16	____
	19	____		20	____
	Total	____		Total	____

4. Record your total scores in the following chart by marking an "X" in each row next to the number of your total score for that area of needs motivation.

	−12	−10	−8	−6	−4	−2	0	+2	+4	+6	+8	+10	+12
Self-actualization													
Esteem													
Belonging													
Safety													
Basic													

Low   High
use   use

By examining the chart you can see the relative strength you attach to each of the needs in Maslow's hierarchy. There are no right answers here, but most work-motivation theorists imply that most people are concerned mainly with the upper-level needs (that is, belongingness, esteem, and self-actualization).

5. The instructor will form groups of 4 to 6 to discuss the need hierarchy findings.

1 STEINBERG AND ROSS*

Tom Boyd's footsteps rang loudly off the raw cement floor and echoed against the still unfinished walls of the office tower. He was inspecting the new office facility for Steinberg & Ross, an accounting firm. Steinberg & Ross was also new, having been created only recently by the merger of two established firms. As administrative partner, Tom oversaw all phases of the move to the new quarters. In conjunction with the move, all existing office practices and procedures were being evaluated, revised, or replaced. One area that had long been a source of friction and difficulty for both of the predecessor firms was the organization of the administrative staff and its relationship to the professional staff. Tom's regular responsibilities would include the management of this administrative staff once the move was completed. He was determined to prevent the troubles that had beset this area in the past and to organize the administrative staff in a manner that would best serve the needs of the firm. Tom's concerns were shared by the other partners in the firm. As he gazed around the vast, empty space before him, Tom thought again of the clean-slate mandate he had requested and received at the last partners' meeting: he was to use any combination of functions, employees, and organizational arrangements he thought necessary, as long as it worked and he stayed within budget.

COMPANY BACKGROUND

Steinberg & Ross was created in the fall of 1978 by the merger of two established, mid-size accounting firms, Steinberg, Newman & Company and Ross, Easley & Grey. At the time, it also became affiliated with a large, national accounting firm, although not one of the "big eight." This affiliation provided Steinberg & Ross with a special ancillary services, a Washington, D.C. tax office, a New York City office that monitored the activities of the Securities and Exchange Commission, and a national management consulting practice, specializing in health care and electronic data processing (EDP) consulting. The merged firm represented the tenth largest firm in its market (and the largest local firm) and was positioned to offer its clients the full range of accounting and related services associated with a "big eight" firm, while still providing a local character, personalized service, and reasonable fees. The partners believed that this strategy would enable the firm to grow rapidly, primarily by attracting smaller clients from local firms with the promise of more professional service.

ORGANIZATION

The firm was formally organized as a partnership, an arrangement typical of accounting, consulting, legal, and other service firms. Exhibit 1 presents an organizational chart. The firm was run by the twenty-six partners, who also owned the business. They met at least monthly to set policy, discuss business developments, and monitor profits and profit-sharing. Sterling Grey, the partner-in-charge, played a coordinator's role and occasionally was called upon to represent the firm as a legal signatory or spokesman. He did not, however, have any direct, formal authority over the other partners. Indeed, the partners individually experienced very little control over their daily activities. Except for the monthly meetings and the fairly common practice of informally consulting with each other over practice development (attracting new business) or a particularly thorny accounting problem, the partners operated autonomously, building and maintaining their practices as they saw fit.

The differences in their management style were noteworthy. One partner, for example, was secretly referred to as "five-o'clock Phil" for his irritating habit of leaving everything until the last minute. By contrast, Don Landsdowne, the newest partner, who had joined the firm after reaching the level of manager in a "big eight" firm, was a model of organization and planning whose work always seemed on schedule and under control. The widespread differences in management style was exacerbated by Steinberg & Ross's history; different partners had developed different styles in the two predecessor firms. Although Tom Boyd was not pleased with this state of affairs, he seriously doubted that any improvement was likely in the near future. Eventually, he thought, the old or premerger partners would retire, to be replaced by new partners, trained in a consistent Steinberg & Ross management style. Until then, however, the partners' idiosyncrasies were a fact of life with which he and the administrative staff would have to cope.

Beneath the partners was arrayed the *professional staff*. These 148 individuals were the accountants who

---

* Source: David A. Nadler, Michael L. Tushman, and Nina G. Hatvany, *Managing Operations*. Boston: Little Brown and Co., 1982, pp. 512–520.

produced the firm's services. They were grouped according to an explicit hierarchy reflecting seniority, authority, and pay. They ranged in age and responsibility from managers, in their late forties, who were candidates for partnership (hence ownership of the business), to staff accountants in their early twenties, who had yet to even complete the CPA licensing exam.

Their work environment was characterized by a pressured, grueling pace—especially during "the season," the January to April 15 period of year-end audits and tax return preparation when a six- or seven-day workweek was the norm. In addition, their career development was characterized by an "up or out" philosophy. The accountants were subject to a performance evaluation after each assignment. These evaluations were shared with the individuals involved and then maintained in personnel files by Tom Boyd. Shortly after the close of the season, the partners would meet to review these performance records and decide promotions and terminations, a process reputed to be highly subjective. Attrition was high; out of an entering "class" of a dozen staff accountants, only one would be likely to reach the level of manager. The combination of these factors tended to produce an atmosphere of stress and urgency in the office.

Before the merger, the *administrative staff* in both predecessor firms had been organized in a rather adhoc, patchwork manner. Some aspects of the organization arrangements followed conventional office practices, such as the assignment of one executive secretary to each partner. Other aspects, particularly in the area of annual report production, had developed erratically, reflecting the unsystematic adoption of new technologies in reproduction or word processing. Indeed, most of the problems between the administrative and professional staffs centered in the area of report production.

All administrative staff were hourly wage earners. Normally, they worked a 35 hour week. During the season, however, the normal week became 37½ hours, with overtime pay (time and a half) paid after forty hours. Administrative staff were evaluated once a year by the immediate supervisor, or by Mildred Teicher, the office manager, when there was no direct supervisor. Evaluation was on the basis of overall performance. Bonuses and salary increases also reflected each employee's overall performance. These bonuses and salary increases were awarded by dividing up a fixed pool of dollars among the administrative staff, a task which was Tom Boyd's responsibility. The pool was determined each year by the partners, who generally set aside a fixed percentage of the firm's total

profit. The exact profit figure was known only to the partners themselves, but in recent years the pool Tom was given to allocate had averaged about $60,000.00 (to be divided among approximately seventy administrative staff), an amount that Tom estimated to be about 2.5 percent of profits.

Profits were determined as follows: For each engagement, the client was charged a fee, based solely on the number of hours worked by each level of accountant (a staff accountant billed at about $40/hr, a partner might bill at $150/hr) plus out-of-pocket expenses such as travel or report production costs. When the fee was received, 10 percent was immediately deducted and paid to the partner in charge of the engagement as a new or continuing finder's fee. The remainder was pooled with like sums from other engagements, from which regular business expenses such as salaries, wages, and rent, were paid. Any remaining amount was profit. Some of this was retained as working capital, some distributed to the administrative staff bonus pool, and the rest was allocated among the partners on the basis of their proportional share of the business—that is, the dollar value of their individual clients as a percentage of the firm's total fees. It was thus in the individual partner's financial interest to maximize his or her own practice, developing it and serving it, even at the expense of a fellow partner's client service.

NATURE OF THE WORK— PROFESSIONAL STAFF

The professional accounting services offered by Steinberg & Ross fell roughly into two categories: audit work and tax work. The former constituted the bulk of the work and involved the auditing of a client's financial records and the certification of the financial statements in the client's annual report. Typically, the work was carried out in teams composed of a partner (who maintained client contact, reviewed final reports, and signed off on the report with a legally binding signature of the firm); a manager (who had overall responsibility for the scheduling of the audit work, especially the field work at the client's, the writing of the report in the office, and so on; the supervisor (who oversaw the on-site work on a daily basis and reviewed/authored the report in the office); and several senior and staff accountants (who verified records in the field, completed and checked calculations and figures, and composed initial report drafts). These teams varied in size and composition according to the size and needs of the client. Staff accountants were usually

EXHIBIT 1

**Organization Chart
of Steinberg & Ross**

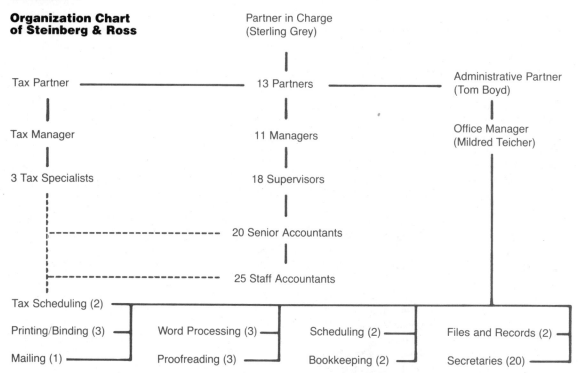

assigned sequentially, to one assignment (or engagement, in the accounting parlance) at a time. All others, however, commonly juggled multiple assignments. There was a formal system, administered by the scheduling department, for assigning available accountants to a team. (See Exhibit 1.) However most managers preferred to build a team by recruiting individuals with whom they had worked in the past and/or who offered a special expertise relevant to the engagement.

Despite an elaborate and rigorous planning system, engagements frequently fell behind schedule. In addition, last-minute negotiations with clients often resulted in changes in the figures or footnotes on the annual report. Thus accountants often found themselves pulled off one job to meet some crisis on another. Furthermore, partners, indeed all the accountants, were often absent from the office. Their absences were necessitated by their personal involvement in maintaining client contact or developing new business. As a result, the manager, and often the supervisor as well, needed to be kept fully informed of the status of an audit in order to respond to client questions and complaints and to effect necessary rescheduling

or personnel redeployment. Although much of the field work could normally be done in the fall, the final audit could not conclude, and the audit report could not be written, until the client had actually closed the books for the year. Although frequent efforts had been made to convince clients to change their fiscal year, most preferred to end it on the traditional December 31, a situation that exacerbated the pressures of the season in conjunction with tax return work.

Tax work, unlike audit work, tended to be more individualized. While corporate tax returns presented complex problems and were a lucrative practice area, individual tax returns were not. Many of the larger accounting firms had phased out this latter practice area, except for those returns prepared as a professional courtesy for officers of important corporate clients. Steinberg & Ross, however, still maintained a practice in this area, viewing it as a part of their personalized service much valued by many of their clients. Individual tax returns were not that complex or difficult to prepare; they were simply numerous and required a corresponding time commitment, usually from staff or senior accountants, before being passed to the firm's tax specialists. The demands of this work served chiefly to add to the pressure and office tensions.

NATURE OF THE WORK— ADMINISTRATIVE STAFF

The administrative staff support performed a number of functions necessary for the effective operation of the office. This support staff included secretaries (individual for the partners, shared for the managers), bookkeepers, file clerks (who kept track of the myriad records required for accounting work), and those employees involved in the production of audit reports. Tom had broken down the key functions of this latter group as follows.

Word Processing

Transfers the accountant's handwritten pencil copy into printed format suitable for mass reproduction.

Proofreading

In accounting work, accuracy was paramount. In-process reports needed to be checked for both computational and grammatical errors.

Report Review

This was a critical function, performed by Sidney Weiss. Although a manager-level accountant, Sidney had long ago realized that he would never make partner and had accepted this post as a kind of sinecure rather than face the likely termination. His task was to review and edit each report to ensure that it was in compliance with the latest edicts and standards set by the several regulatory groups that affected the accounting profession. Failure to conduct such reviews could leave the firm and the relevant partner dangerously liable to legal action. Sidney had developed a formidable expertise in this area; there had been no instances of successful legal actions brought against the firm or its partners since he had taken over this area. He was the one person in the firm who could overrule a partner on when to release a report. A thin and frail-looking chain-smoker, he was as overworked as he was accurate. At present, there was no back-up person for this work.

Corrections

Both proofreading and report review routinely discovered errors. In view of Sidney's work load, Tom felt that all computational and grammatical errors should be corrected before the report review stage. However, Sidney often inserted long, precisely worded paragraphs into the reports. Tom was unsure whether these inserts should be checked by proofreading or by Sidney himself.

Partner Sign-off

The partner in charge of each engagement was the only person who could legally sign the firm's name on the report. Ostensibly, partners thoroughly reviewed each report before signing, but except for Don Landsdowne, no partner had noticed a mistake within memory. The major difficulty here, Tom thought, was that partners were frequently out of the office. A report could sit unsigned for days while its delivery date drew closer and closer.

Printing

Steinberg & Ross had recently purchased a high speed offset press and photographic plate-maker. Unfortunately, the press required extensive setup time, and the high speed could only be utilized through long production runs. Bob Berens, the current pressman, also looked after the ordering of paper stocks. The print shop also housed a high-speed [photocopying] machine, run by a technician, and a low-speed machine for "casual" operators.

Binding

Ideally, binding could take place twelve or more hours after a report was printed, to allow for drying of the ink. In practice, reports were often bound "hot off the press," a practice that inevitably lead to blurred or smeared reports and on occasion to complaints from clients, complaints that the partners never hesitated to pass on to Tom.

Mailing

When time permitted or distance demanded, reports were mailed to clients. Often partners would hand deliver the reports to the client, or express and courier services would be used.

The administrative staff employee complement for each of these key functions is shown in Exhibit 1. Tom felt that the current staffing levels were sufficient to handle the current and anticipated work load. He had reviewed the individual personnel and concluded that they were sufficiently hard-working and competent (several even had advanced degrees); they were capable of doing a number of different jobs and were also nonunion and thus not contractually restricted to one function. There were, however, some restrictions. In the short run, there was limited flexibility of staff across functions. Word processing required extensive training, effectively excluding the use of other administrative staff in this area. Similarly, printing required specialized skills and knowledge to run the press, although not to do the binding (a technology which could be taught in half a day). Proofreading's functions were equally divided between correcting for "grammar"—a catchword for a number of sophisticated editing skills—and correcting for calculations—a far more routine rechecking of the accountants' math. Up until now, there had been no way to determine the capacity of the whole staff working together because their income was largely dependent on overtime pay earned during the season, a situation which discouraged cooperation among them. Tom knew that, if he should decide additional staff were needed, he could spend approximately $100,000, if he could justify it. It was in the partners' (and thus his own) interest, however, to spend less, or none. The administrative staff employees fell into four rough "salary and fringe" categories, as follows:

Level	Position Type	Cost
I	Professional (for instance, Sidney in report review)	$60,000
II	Managerial (for instance, M. Teicher)	$20,000
III	Clerical (skilled/trained)	$12,000
IV	Clerical (unskilled)	$ 8,000

Nevertheless, Tom felt that he probably possessed sufficient employee strength in each function and that his major task was to organize them into an effective arrangement.

In order to facilitate this arrangement, Tom had devised a tentative work-flow chart (see Exhibits 2 and 3) that laid out the tasks to be performed in the report production process. He was not fully satisfied with his attempt; it seemed to raise more questions than it answered:

- Although he felt he had captured all of the required tasks, Tom was interested in additional, "optional" tasks. In particular, he wondered how the reports might best be transferred from one task to the next (the black arrows). Currently, it was done by the individual who had performed the preceding task, but was that the best way?

- Tom was also far from confident that his sequence of the tasks was optimal. Perhaps the task order could be more effectively arranged.

- Although the work-flow chart made the system look very rational and planned, Tom knew that the chart misrepresented the daily chaos. He knew that the generation of a client review copy of the report and the partner's ensuing discussions with the client initiated a continuing demand on the system (the "hollow" arrow) for corrections, revisions, schedule changes, and the like. How could the system be organized to respond effectively to this demand?

- There were five major decision points in the process. Were these opportunities for quality control activities and for recording report progress, or were they merely unnecessary roadblocks?

- Was there really only one system? Could there actually be a number of smaller, simpler, parallel systems?

CURRENT PROBLEMS

In considering his assignment, Tom had spoken at length with a number of the employees. Bob Berens, the pressman, seemed particularly irritated:

I guess I just don't know what they want. All the reports I get in here all say the same thing—date due: ASAP [as soon as possible]. They just don't understand how the press works. I run three stock sizes: covers, spread sheets, and regular pages. It takes me about twenty minutes to change from one format to another. If I can run all covers, then all spread sheets, then all regular pages I can get twelve reports out every day; but if I have to do each report separately—covers, spreads, regulars, covers, spreads, regulars—I'll be lucky to get four out. Even then, sometimes I can't tell which report to run first. I've had scenes where I had two partners right down in the shop, arguing with me and each other over which of their reports to run first. Two guys each making over a hundred grand a year, partners, ready to stick each other in the back over a lousy half an hour. They agree on one thing, though. If I tell 'em I'll run both reports at the same time—you know, take a little longer on both instead of one on time and one real late—they both say, "No, me first!"

Don Landsdowne saw things a little differently:

The situation here is absurd. All the way through an engagement, I bust my hump, and everybody else's for that matter, to make sure things are on time. Then the thing goes into report production, and it disappears! If I've got a worried client on the phone, can I put him

EXHIBIT 2

Tentative Work Flow

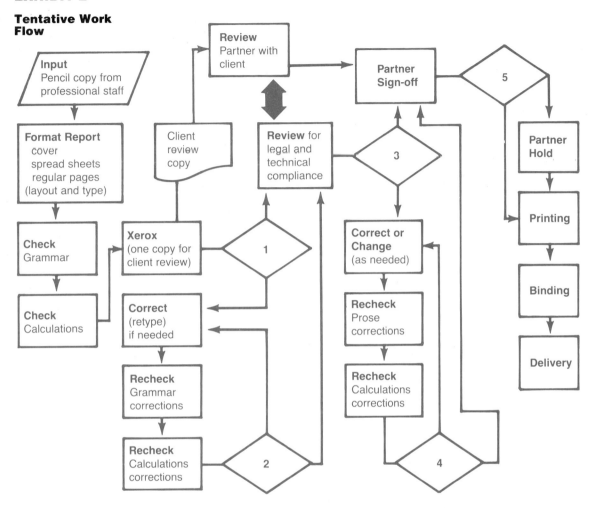

EXHIBIT 3

Decision Points in Tentative Work Flow

1. If report is OK, send to REVIEW. If corrections are needed, send on to CORRECT.
2. If report is OK, send to REVIEW. If corrections still needed, send back to CORRECT.
3. If report passes REVIEW, send on to PARTNER for signature. If modifications/changes have been made, send on to CORRECT or CHANGE.
4. If review modifications have been correctly made, send on to PARTNER for signature. Otherwise, send back to CORRECT or CHANGE.
5. Sometimes, partners will hold a report until a client is ready to release it. (Sometimes, partners hold reports accidentally, for instance, five-o'clock Phil.) The choice here is to hold or send on to printing.

on hold, make a quick call and find out when his report will be ready? No way! There's no use in even telling him I'll call him back with the answer. When I go looking for it no one can tell me. No one knows where the report is. I have to chase it down step by step. Even when I find where it is, each person there can only tell me when they'll be through with it, not when it will be completely done. The way it stands now, my best bet is to tell the client a date I think we can live with and then go kick Sidney's, Bob's, and everybody else's butt to get the thing done by that date. It's a waste of my time, but so far it's the only way. Sometimes I even think they do five-o'clock Phil's stuff faster, just to get rid of him and his constant hassles.

Bernice Segal, who ran a word processing machine spoke of a different problem:

> A big problem for word processing is how we divide up the work. People bring us reports all the time and say, "Here, do this." Lately, Mildred [Teicher] has tried to regulate what we get and divide it equally among us. But she's busy being the office manager, so it's kind of hit or miss. You can't really divide up a report to work on because you don't know the advance page numbers until the beginning pages have been typed. So it's one report for you, one report for me, except that some reports are thirty pages long and some are eight. The overtime is nice to get, but not when they're yelling at you all day for the report.

Carolyn Miller, the youngest and only female manager, had her own view of the situation:

> When a partner is out of the office, it's up to me to make sure the report gets out. Half the time, I hear the same thing, "Sidney's got it and won't release it." It's really frustrating; there's nothing you can do but wait for it to hit the fan. Sidney wants to clear things with the partner, but the partner's not here, and Sidney won't

clear it with me. The other managers have the same trouble. Once, on a report we were just dying for, I stole the thing out of Sidney's office during his lunch hour and had Bob start running it even though it hadn't been cleared. Later, when Sidney was finished with it, we did have to rerun a few pages, but overall we'd saved a bundle of time. Bob was real nice about it, but it was definitely a one-time thing. He has enough problems with clients making last-minute changes, never mind us.

As Tom paced about the new office, he reviewed the demands his new organization would have to meet:

Quality	Demand
Speed	Clients
Accuracy	Regulatory Agencies
Responsiveness	
Flexibility	Partners' styles
"Reportability"	Need to know report progress
Differentiation	Workers' skills, identity, and rewards
Balanced work flow	Efficiency, employee morale

Tom laughed silently. All it has to be is all things to all people, he thought. He glanced around the office once more. Completion was expected in three weeks. □

CASE QUESTIONS

1. Does Bob Berens have a motivation problem?
2. Should Tom attempt to discover what others view as the most pressing problems at Steinberg and Ross? Why?
3. How can the merger of two firms create a work culture that causes motivation problems?

2 STATE EMPLOY-MENT AGENCY*

Frank Duncan, the commissioner of the State Employment Agency in a state along the Eastern Seaboard, was reviewing the agency's system for evaluating the results of its efforts. He gave the casewriter some background on state employment agencies in general and

on the changes made in the review system in his agency over the past year.

State employment agencies were set up during the Depression years to administer unemployment benefits to workers unfortunate enough to lose their jobs. The agencies are largely federally funded but state-administered, and a large proportion of their federal funding is tied to the state unemployment level. Since their foundings and in particular in the Great

---

* Source: David A. Nadler, Michael L. Tushman, and Nina G. Hatvany, *Managing Operations*. Boston: Little Brown and Co., 1982, pp. 520–525.

EXHIBIT 1

State Employment Agency: Organizational Chart*

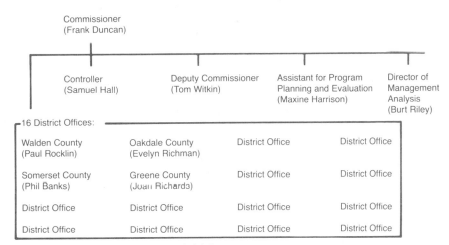

*Names of persons mentioned in the case are included.

Society years of Lyndon Johnson, the role of these agencies expanded to cover helping people assess their own training needs and helping them to find jobs. The typical agency has several district offices within the state and is staffed by employment counselors. These counselors hold a series of interviews with clients in an attempt to assess their skills and the jobs for which they would be best suited. Suitable candidates are referred to local employers with vacancies. Those clients who remain unemployed because they are not offered jobs continue to receive unemployment benefits.

In general, the job of an employment counselor is a routine one, involving standardized interview formats and detailed bureaucratic routines for referrals and placements. The duties of counselors are as follows: They receive requests for workers over the phone. The order forms on which job openings are described are filed in a common pool in each office. Most of the officials' time is spent interviewing applicants for jobs. After ascertaining the client's qualifications, the interviewer searches the office files for suitable vacancies. If an acceptable job is found, he or she refers the client to it and later phones the employer to learn whether the client has been hired. The bulk of an employment counselor's time, aside from interviewing, is spent filling out the forms necessary for completion of each stage of the successful processing of a client.

A district office of the State Employment Agency was located in each of the sixteen counties of the state (see Exhibit 1). These offices varied greatly in terms of the population and degree of industrialization of the area in which they were located and hence in terms of the number of unemployed persons and the number of available jobs. However, the overall mission of the agency was clear: to serve workers seeking employment and employers seeking workers throughout the state. Operations within each of the district offices were also performed in a similar fashion. Most of the counselors employed by the agency viewed themselves as professionals, but this orientation was strongest in the Walden County office. While employees in the other districts had been assigned, and had received their training, at different times, the majority of those in Walden County received their training together after the Vietnam War at a time when intensive counseling had been stressed, since many returning veterans needed occupational advice. In this situation, the group developed a common professional code, which discouraged speedy placement as constituting defective employment service. Quality, rather than quantity, was stressed in this office. In addition, counselors in this office were not particularly concerned with performance because almost all of them were veterans, whose employment could not be terminated except for cause. At the same time, while a system of merit pay existed, it offered little motivation as bonuses were small in comparison to base pay, which depended solely on number of years in service. Overall, external motivation was small—salary increases were automatic and career paths were limited. There was nowhere to go from counselor as the opportunities for promotion were relatively scarce.

A year previously, on being appointed, Frank Duncan had reviewed the management control practices in the agency and had noted that the number of interviews held per month was the only operation that was statistically counted for each district office. Duncan recognized the obvious limitations of such an evaluation method. An individual district office could look good relative to other district offices if employment counselors concentrated on maximizing the number of interviews they conducted. There was no guarantee that this approach to performance of the agency's mission would result in effective matching of jobs and clients. Consequently, Duncan resolved to give high priority to the development of an alternative management control system.

Duncan stated:

I requested Burt Riley, director of management analysis, and Maxine Harrison, assistant to the commissioner for program planning and evaluation, to develop a system for measuring overall performance of each district office. It was my general plan that Riley and Harrison would draw up a list of objectives that they thought every district office should meet if performance is to be considered satisfactory. After checking these with me for approval, they would go out to the districts and get the approval of the district managers around the state. My thought here was that if the district managers would agree in advance to a set of objective criteria there would be no personal ugliness attached when, at the end of the year, one of the standards is not met. It would simply be a matter of saying, "Well, we agreed at the beginning that the annual ratio of placements to interviews should be 60 percent. If it turns out to be 50 percent, that's that." It is an objective fact to be dealt with, not a personal blame put on the districts by my staff.

After two months of project work, including discussions with several district office directors, Riley and Harrison recommended a system of fifteen controls (Exhibit 2) for all district offices. The controls were about equally divided between budgetary items relating to the outputs of the agency. As Burt Riley explained,

The advantage of such a system of controls is that the top management of the agency can very quickly look across one page of the computer output to detect there is trouble in a district. On that output, the sixteen districts are listed across the top. Down the left is the quantitative level expected for that item. Under each district's column is listed the actual performance of that district. Performances rated satisfactory or above are listed in the ordinary way, and those below satisfactory are starred. Scanning down a column, one can get a complete and quick picture of what went wrong in that district. Or, if one scans across columns, he can see instantly which district is performing below satisfactory and which above. This kind of document enables us to manage by exception. We do not have to have our minds filled with thousands of details and figures. The factors for success are already there. The figures are all there. The exceptions are highlighted. We can evaluate the whole agency in a few hours and can have letters of inquiry going out within a day, asking why something went wrong. This is a real help to us and to the district offices.

During the process of setting standards, Maxine Harrison proposed one standard that dealt with the total district office expenditures (item 15 in Exhibit 2). Burt Riley suggested that this one expense standard was insufficient and added to various expense breakdowns shown as items 9 and 14 in Exhibit 2. Harrison objected to this level of detail, and so the two staff managers presented the issue to Duncan. Riley explained, "If we only get a lump sum expenditure figure, it will be practically useless to top management. All we could say is 'Your expenditures are exceeding

EXHIBIT 2

Areas of Measurement

1. The number of interviews held
2. The number of clients referred to a job
3. The number of placements made (referred client was hired)
4. The proportion of interviews resulting in referrals
5. The proportion of referrals resulting in placements
6. The proportion of interviews resulting in placements
7. The number of notifications sent to the insurance office
8. The number of application forms made out
9. Employment interview expense
10. Unemployment claim expense
11. Overhead expense
12. Supervisory and management overhead expense
13. New program expense
14. Hours of unallocated personnel time
15. Total office expenditures

budget.' We ought to include at least the additional six breakdowns.''

After Harrison and Riley finished debating the issue, Duncan responded, ''Well, it seems that you two cannot agree on this matter. My own inclination is that we in headquarters must be informed. I believe we should include these additional items.'' Maxine Harrison's comment on the discussion was, ''That settled that.''

Duncan had one additional suggestion to make at this meeting.

> It appears that most of the standards you've set are technically correct. That is, they represent reasonable expectations regarding what the average district office should achieve. But there is another aspect of standards you have overlooked. I'm referring to the need to capture the attention and imagination of people who must carry out these standards. No person will exceed an easy goal. Have you set these standards in relation to an individual's extra effort—the kind one has to stretch to achieve?

Riley and Harrison agreed that they had set the standards as if personnel were working at a normal pace. ''Just what 'normal' is,'' Riley said, ''is not too clear. But I think it means a person working with average energy at a job the person hopes to accomplish. If you set individual standards too high, then competition among counselors will be encouraged. We don't want counselors hiding job openings from one another.''

Duncan said that eventually he got Riley and Harrison to agree to raising the achievement levels on a number of items.

> I told them that achievement didn't occur without challenge. I offered to take some time out to review all of the fifteen standards working out challenging levels item by item. We ended, for example, by raising the level of performance on the ratio of referrals to interviews from 75 percent to 80 percent. The acceptable unemployment claim expense figure was decreased by 5 percent. Similar changes were made on most standards.
>
> Later, at a meeting of all district office directors, I explained that forces beyond our control are continuously setting demanding standards for the agency—the state of the overall economy, new unemployment legislation at the federal and state levels, geographical differences in employment demand, the changing mix of occupational skills, and other such factors make it essential that we properly control agency activities. There was a certain amount of reaction against both the standards we put into the list and the level we specified for each standard. However, in the end I told them that they could change the levels of the standards if they really wanted to. At

that point, they all seemed to see both the necessity for checkpoints by headquarters and for challenging performance levels.

Mr. Duncan described the first year of operation under the new control system.

> We've been operating under the new management control system for one year. Overall, I'm quite pleased with the system. I'm confident that it's been a major factor in our overall improvement over the previous fiscal year when the comparable figure was 55 percent. Of course, no system is perfect. I will give you some examples of the issues we're concerned about. We all are interested in learning from this first year of experience and implementing any necessary revisions.
>
> At the end of the first year (we review the performance of each district office on an annual basis only), Samuel Hall, the agency controller, sent out a routine inquiry to Paul Rocklin, director of the district office in Walden County. Under the procedures, the whole results tabulation is sent in multiple copies to Hall, Riley, Harrison, myself, and Tom Witkin, my deputy commissioner. Each of us concentrates on particular items. Hall pays special attention to budgetary controls. As he scanned the control report, he noted that unemployment claim expense for the Walden County District Office was 6 percent above the standard. It was one of the few starred figures in the row for unemployment claim expense. Most districts were in the black. So Hall sent out the letter to Rocklin listing this exception. Riley also sent Rocklin a letter for an exception in the number of clients referred to jobs.

> Rocklin exploded when he received the letters of inquiry. He called me on the telephone and said that the system was grossly unfair. Boy, was he steamed. Since his total district office expenditures were under the targeted figure, he wanted to know why my staff people were pestering him about details. He also said, ''In the expense area, the real need is to have low total expenditures. I performed according to the spirit of that need by compensating for some unexpected turnover in the unemployment claims section. We were short-handed most of the year and had to spend some time training the new personnel we did hire. My supervisors and I worked overtime to help. In addition, we made concerted efforts to become more efficient in all other sections of the office.''

> I assured Rocklin that we appreciated his extra efforts and ingenuity in compensating for the turnover problem. That didn't seem to do a lot of good. He said that as the headquarters people like Riley and Hall scan the reports they form impressions without knowing the facts. That under the guise of ''management by exception'' or ''management by objective'' they look for the starred figures in a report, send out their letters of inquiry, and

get a negative picture of his operating abilities. Of course, I assured him that the letter was one of inquiry.

Rocklin suggested that the way to correct this situation is simply to remove the detailed expenditure standards [items 9–14] and to leave only the total district office expenditure standard [item 15]. Actually, I will have to give this some more thought. That would defeat the original arguments we settled when we included them. This is one alternative for overcoming this, but I'm hoping I can achieve both Rocklin's and Riley's objectives.

Another problem is actually in Rocklin's favor. On that total expenditure measure, his district was one of only four districts that achieved the standard. All the others were in the red. We circulated the whole evaluation report to all district managers, and I got seven suggestions from different districts that this target was too demanding. I must admit that I don't like to see a horizontal row of figures all starred. It looks as if something is wrong with the agency. And the seven district managers complained that it looks as if there's something wrong with them. On the other hand, my "stretch" theory worked with Rocklin. His back was against the wall, and he devoted a lot of creativity and energy to obtaining efficiencies in other areas, so that he would make a good showing on his total cost. Maybe the other district managers ought to do that.

While Rocklin is certainly the most vocal critic of our new control system, I learned of some other problems during a meeting last week with district directors in the southern part of the state. The purpose of the meeting was to discuss some regional unemployment problems specific to that area. After we completed the major business discussion, the conversation turned to the new management control system. Phil Banks, director of the Somerset County district, began the conversation.

"Frank, I'm afraid there are some consequences of implementing this system that we didn't completely anticipate. In particular, I'm referring to the relationship between the quantitative figures reported in the control system and the annual performance review for an individual interviewer. Several of my interviewers are completely alienated by the new system. One interviewer came to see me complaining about the rating she received from her supervisor. Before the new system had been introduced, the supervisor gave her a low rating because her production wasn't high enough.

After the new system was introduced, the interviewer was high on the various performance indices. However,

her rating was low again. As a result of this, the interviewer and her coworkers believe that some supervisors will use statistics to confirm their subjective judgments. As they see it, 'Figures can't lie, but liars can figure.' "

Joan Richards, director of the Greene County office, spoke next: "I'm also disturbed about the new system. Apparently, some of my interviewers have resorted to some ingenious means for outgaming the system by maximizing their performance indices.

"For example, occasionally a client who has been temporarily laid off expects to return to the former job within the next few days. After confirming this with the employer, the interviewer makes out a job order and 'refers' the client to his own job. In this way the interviewer improves his or her number of referrals and placements (and the corresponding proportional indices) without having accomplished the objective that these indices were designed to measure, that is, without having found a job for a client."

The next manager to speak was Evelyn Richman of the Oakdale County office: "The worst thing about these records is that they create unhealthy competition between interviewers. The records lead to competition and outright falsification. I don't say they all do that, but it happens. . . . You can't expect anything else. If you make production so important, some people will feel that they have to increase their figures by any means. The only way you can stop it is by discontinuing the control reports."

I [Frank Duncan] interrupted at this point and indicated my dismay at their reports. I indicated that it was essential to determine if these negative practices were widespread in the agency.

More significantly, these comments along with Rocklin's complaints have convinced me that we should review the control system to see if changes are needed. □

CASE QUESTIONS

1. What is the major motivational problem associated with the control system?
2. Would there have been any value at the beginning of the development of the control system for Burt Riley and Maxine Harrison to include some of the counselors in the work of creating a system?
3. What intrinsic motivational factors, if any, are part of the 15 areas being measured (Exhibit 2)?

REWARDING AND PUNISHING INDIVIDUAL BEHAVIOR

Organizations use a variety of rewards to attract and retain people and to motivate them to achieve their personal and organizational goals.[1] The manner and timing of distributing rewards are important issues that managers must address almost daily. Managers distribute such rewards as pay, transfers, promotions, praise, and recognition. They also can help create the climate that results in more challenging and satisfying jobs. Unfortunately, managers sometimes are faced with the task of eliminating undesirable behavior and performance. Although punishment and discipline are controversial topics, they also are discussed in this chapter. Failure to do so would deny the reality of what occurs in organizational settings.

The use of rewards and punishments in organizations represents an attempt to influence the behavior of organizational members. That is, it is an attempt to *reinforce* the continuation or elimination of certain action. The basic assumption is that behavior is influenced by its consequences and that it is possible to affect behavior by controlling such consequences. The idea that consequences of behavior are critical in determining future behavior has significant implications for managing people in organizational settings. Consequently, we begin our discussion of rewarding and punishing individual behavior by examining the topic of reinforcement.

REINFORCEMENT THEORY

Attempts to influence behavior through the use of rewards and punishments that are consequences of the behavior is called *operant conditioning*. Operants are behaviors that can be controlled by altering the consequences that follow them. Most workplace behaviors are operants. Examples of operant behaviors are performing job-related tasks, reading a budget report, or coming to work on time. A number of important principles of operant conditioning can aid the manager in attempting to influence behavior.

Reinforcement. Reinforcement is an extremely important principle of conditioning. Managers often use *positive* reinforcers to influence behavior. A positive reinforcer is a stimulus which, when added to the situation, strength-

---

[1] Kae H. Chung and Leon G. Megginson, *Organizational Behavior* (New York: Harper & Row, 1981), p. 363.

ens the probability of a behavioral response. Thus, if the positive reinforcer has value to the person, it can be used to improve performance. (It should be noted, however, that a positive reinforcer which has value to one person may not have value to another person.) Sometimes, *negative* reinforcers may be used. Negative reinforcement refers to an increase in the frequency of a response following removal of the negative reinforcer immediately after the response. As an example, exerting high degrees of effort to complete a job may be negatively reinforced by not having to listen to the "nagging" boss. That is, completing the job through increased effort (behavior) minimizes the likelihood of having to listen to a nagging stream of unwanted advice (negative reinforcer) from a superior.

Punishment.   Punishment is defined as presenting an uncomfortable or unwanted consequence for a particular behavioral response.[2] While punishment can suppress behavior if used effectively, it is a controversial method of behavior modification in organizations. Some work-related factors that can be considered punishments include a superior's criticism, being fired, being suspended, receiving an undesirable transfer or assignment, or being demoted.

Reinforcement Schedules.   It is extremely important to properly time the rewards or punishments used in an organization. The timing of these outcomes is called *reinforcement scheduling.* In the simplest schedule, the response is reinforced each time it occurs. This is called *continuous reinforcement.* If reinforcement occurs only after some instances of a response and not after each response, an *intermittent reinforcement* schedule is being used. From a practical viewpoint, it is virtually impossible to reinforce continually every desirable behavior. Consequently, in organizational settings, almost all reinforcement is intermittent in nature.

An intermittent schedule means that reinforcement does not occur after every acceptable behavior. The assumption is that learning is more permanent when correct behavior is rewarded only part of the time.[3] Ferster and Skinner have presented four types of intermittent reinforcement schedules.[4] Briefly, the four are:

1. *Fixed interval.* A reinforcer is applied only when the desired behavior occurs after the passage of a certain period of time since the last reinforcer was applied. An example would be to only praise positive performance once a week and not at other times. The fixed interval is one week.

---

[2] W. E. Craighead, A. E. Kazdin, and M. J. Mahoney, *Behavior Modification* (Boston: Houghton Mifflin, 1976), pp. 112–20.

[3] Lise M. Saari and Gary P. Latham, "Employee Reactions to Continuous and Variable Ratio Reinforcement Schedules Involving a Monetary Incentive," *Journal of Applied Psychology,* August 1982, pp. 506–508.

[4] C. B. Ferster and B. F. Skinner, *Schedules of Reinforcement* (New York: Appleton-Century-Crofts, 1957).

2. *Variable interval.* A reinforcer is applied at some variable interval of time. A promotion is an example.
3. *Fixed ratio.* A reinforcer is applied only if a fixed number of desired responses has occurred. An example would be paying a lathe operator a $10 bonus when the operator has produced 50 consecutive pieces which pass quality control inspection.
4. *Variable ratio.* A reinforcer is applied only after a number of desired responses, with the number of desired responses changing from situation to situation, around an average. For a classic example of a variable ratio schedule, consider the following OBM Encounter:

REINFORCEMENT THEORY AND THE CASINO BOTTOM LINE

Reinforcement theory is alive and well among casino owners in Atlantic City, New Jersey, and Las Vegas, Nevada. These owners know how people react to reinforcement.

Most players of slot machines assume that jackpots occur according to some random reinforcement schedule. If the casino owners set the machines to pay off on a fixed-ratio schedule, then counting the number of pulls between each jackpot would be a successful technique. If the slots were on a fixed-interval schedule, then the player simply would have to watch the clock and time the occurrence of jackpots. The casino owners know that players are more likely to stay with the machine and feed in coins if there is a random-reinforcement schedule. Then the players have no idea when they will strike it rich. They must keep playing to win, even once or twice. Thus, what we find in Atlantic City and Las Vegas is a program of random reinforcement.

The casino owners also know the value of atmosphere in keeping players at the machine. An atmosphere of excitement is created because people all around seem to be winning. The owners have accomplished this excitement by connecting each slot machine to a central control. Why? So that when any single slot machine hits a jackpot, sirens wail, lights flash, bells sound off, and screams of joy and displays of pleasure are heard and seen by everyone. The sights and sounds inform everyone that it pays to keep playing.

Does it work? Absolutely. Above all else, casino owners are business people. Their objective is to make a profit. They have learned that what keeps the slot machine player coming back more effectively than anything else is a variable ratio schedule of reinforcement. □

Research has shown that higher rates of response usually are achieved with ratio rather than interval schedules. This finding is understandable since high response rates do not necessarily speed up the delivery of a reinforcer in an interval schedule, as they do with ratio schedules.

Now that you have been introduced to some basic principles of reinforcement, we shall turn to a consideration of reinforcing, through the use of rewards and punishments, behaviors desired by managers.

A MODEL OF INDIVIDUAL REWARDS

A model that illustrates how rewards fit into the overall policies and programs of an organization can prove useful to managers. The main objectives of reward programs are: (1) to attract qualified people to *join* the organization, (2) to *keep* employees coming to work, and (3) to *motivate* employees to achieve high levels of performance. Figure 5–1 presents a model that attempts to integrate satisfaction, motivation, performance, and rewards. Reading Figure 5–1 from left to right suggests that the motivation to exert effort is not enough to cause acceptable performance. Performance results from a combination of the effort of an individual and the individual's level of ability, skill, and experience. The performance results of the individual are evaluated either formally or informally by management. As a result of the evaluation, two types of rewards can be distributed: intrinsic or extrinsic. The rewards are evaluated by the individual. To the extent that the rewards are satisfactory and equitable, the individual achieves a level of satisfaction.

FIGURE 5–1

The Reward Process

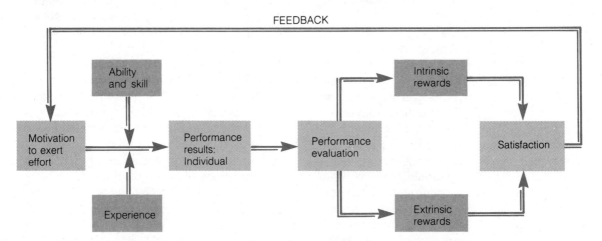

A significant amount of research has been done on what determines whether individuals will be satisfied with rewards. Lawler has summarized five conclusions based on the behavioral science research literature. They are:

1. *Satisfaction with a reward is a function both of how much is received and of how much the individual feels should be received.*
2. *An individual's feelings of satisfaction are influenced by comparisons with what happens to others.* (Recall the discussion of equity theory in Chapter 4.)
3. *Satisfaction is influenced by how satisfied employees are with both intrinsic and extrinsic rewards.*
4. *People differ in the rewards they desire and in how important different rewards are to them.*
5. *Some extrinsic rewards are satisfying because they lead to other rewards.*

For example, money is a reward that leads to other things such as prestige, security, and shelter.[5]

The relationship between rewards and satisfaction is not perfectly understood, nor is it static in nature. The relationship changes because people and the environment change. There are, however, some important considerations that managers could use to develop and distribute rewards. Any reward package should: (1) be sufficient to satisfy basic needs (e.g., food, shelter); (2) be considered equitable; and (3) be individually oriented.[6] To these could be added the very important point made by Steven Kerr in his article accompanying this chapter. For rewards to have their desired effect, they must reward the behavior that management wishes to encourage. Too often, as Kerr points out, what actually get rewarded are behaviors which the manager is trying to *discourage*.

INTRINSIC AND EXTRINSIC REWARDS

The rewards shown in Figure 5–1 are classified into two broad categories, *extrinsic* and *intrinsic*. Whether rewards are extrinsic or intrinsic, it is important to first consider the rewards *valued* by the person. An individual will put forth little effort unless the reward has value. Both extrinsic and intrinsic rewards can have value.[7]

EXTRINSIC REWARDS

Financial Rewards: Salary and Wages.   Money is a major extrinsic reward. It has been said that "although it is generally agreed that money is the major mechanism for rewarding and modifying behavior in industry . . . very little is known about how it works."[8] To really understand how money modifies behavior, the perceptions and preferences of the person being rewarded must be understood. Of course, this is a challenging task for a manager to complete successfully. Unless employees can see a connection between performance and merit increases, money will not be a powerful motivator.

Many organizations utilize some type of incentive pay play to motivate employees. Lawler presents the most comprehensive summary of the various pay plans and their effectiveness as motivators.[9] Each plan is evaluated on the basis of the following questions:

1.   How effective is it in creating the perception that pay is related to performance?

---

[5] Edward E. Lawler III, "Reward Systems," in *Improving Life at Work*, eds. J. Richard Hackman and J. Lloyd Suttle (Santa Monica, Calif.: Goodyear Publishing, 1977), pp. 163–226.

[6] Ibid., p. 168.

[7] Richard A. Guzzo, "Types of Rewards, Cognitions, and Work Motivation," *Academy of Management Review*, January 1979, pp. 75–86.

[8] R. L. Opsahl and M. D. Dunnette, "The Role of Financial Compensation in Industrial Motivation," *Psychological Bulletin*, August 1966, p. 114.

[9] Edward E. Lawler III, *Pay and Organizational Effectiveness* (New York: McGraw-Hill, 1971), pp. 164–70.

TABLE 5-1

Evaluation of Pay-
Incentive Plans in
Organizations

Type of Pay Plan	Performance Criteria	Perceived Pay-Per-formance Linkage	Minimization of Negative Consequences	Perceived Relationship between Other Rewards and Performance
Salary plan				
For individuals	Productivity	Good	Neutral	Neutral
	Cost effectiveness	Fair	Neutral	Neutral
	Superiors' rating	Fair	Neutral	Fair
For group	Productivity	Fair	Neutral	Fair
	Cost effectiveness	Fair	Neutral	Fair
	Superiors' rating	Fair	Neutral	Fair
For total organization	Productivity	Fair	Neutral	Fair
	Cost effectiveness	Fair	Neutral	Fair
	Profits	Neutral	Neutral	Fair
Bonus plan				
For individuals	Productivity	Excellent	Poor	Neutral
	Cost effectiveness	Good	Poor	Neutral
	Superiors' rating	Good	Poor	Fair
For group	Productivity	Good	Neutral	Fair
	Cost effectiveness	Good	Neutral	Fair
	Superiors' rating	Good	Neutral	Fair
For total organization	Productivity	Good	Neutral	Fair
	Cost effectiveness	Good	Neutral	Fair
	Profits	Fair	Neutral	Fair

Source: Adapted from Edward E. Lawler III, *Pay and Organizational Effectiveness* (New York: McGraw-Hill, 1971), table 9–3, p. 165.

2. How well does it minimize the perceived negative consequences of good performance?
3. How well does it contribute to the perception that important rewards other than pay (e.g., praise and interest shown in the employee by a respected superior) result in good performance? A summary of Lawler's ideas is presented in Table 5–1.

While the idea of tying financial rewards to performance certainly is not a new one, interest in this approach has increased significantly in recent years as organizations attempt to improve productivity. The following OBM Encounter describes what some companies are doing:

 ENCOUNTER

BASING WORKERS' REWARDS ON THEIR PERFORMANCE

According to the compensation consulting firms surveyed by *The Wall Street Journal,* basing employee rewards—specifically pay—on per-

formance is one of the hottest management and labor trends around. Under such plans, lower-level and middle-level workers increasingly are being compensated for their productivity, while automatic cost-of-living adjust-

Source: Based on the article by Carrie Dolan, "Back to Piecework," *The Wall Street Journal,* November 15, 1985, pp. 1, 10.

ments are going out the window. A survey by Hay Management Consultants of 600 companies found that, while 11 percent of companies currently are using pay-for-performance systems throughout the organization, three times as many are gearing up to go to that kind of system.

Companies oriented in the pay-for-performance direction tend to be those in the most competitive businesses. BankAmerica Corporation, for example, didn't get interested in pay-for-performance until its earnings and market share dropped significantly in the face of lean and mean competitors such as Citicorp and Wells Fargo. Under BankAmerica's system, the corporation rates the performance of its 86,000 employees, placing approximately equal numbers in each of five performance levels. Employees in the top level receive raises at least 40 percent better than the bottom group gets, and the bottom group has a limited amount

of time to either get out of the lowest level or get out of the company.

General Motors is the largest company to convert to a pay-for-performance system. It placed all 110,000 of its North American salaried staff on pay-for-performance, abandoning automatic cost-of-living adjustments. In doing so, GM joins BankAmerica, TRW Inc., Honeywell, and Hewlett-Packard in using an entirely merit-based pay plan.

The plans are not without their problems. Some employees do not like them, some managers are uncomfortable in evaluating employees for differential pay increases, and union opposition is strong. As Edward Lawler, a management professor at the University of Southern California, says: "There's no question that pay-for-performance is coming back to center stage. But the chances for abuse are enormous. It's very arbitrary to define what 'top' performance is." ☐

Financial Rewards: Fringe Benefits.   In most cases, fringe benefits are primarily financial. There are some fringe benefits, however, such as IBM's recreation program for employees and General Mills' picnic grounds, that are not entirely financial. The major financial fringe benefit in most organizations is the pension plan. For most employees, the opportunity to participate in the pension plan is a valued reward. Fringe benefits such as pension plans, hospitalization, and vacations usually are not contingent on the performance of employees. In most cases, fringe benefit plans are based on seniority or attendance.

Interpersonal Rewards.   The manager has some power to distribute such interpersonal rewards as status and recognition. By assigning individuals to prestigious jobs, the manager can attempt to improve or remove the status a person possesses. However, if co-workers do not believe that a person merits a particular job, it is likely that status will not be enhanced. By reviewing performance, managers can, in some situations, grant what they consider to be job changes that improve status. The manager and co-workers both play a role in granting job status.

Promotions.   For many employees, promotion does not happen often; some employees never experience it in their careers. The manager making a promotion reward decision attempts to match the right person with the job. Criteria often used to reach promotion decisions are performance and seniority. Performance, if it can be accurately assessed, is often given significant weight in promotion reward allocations.

INTRINSIC REWARDS

Completion. The ability to start and finish a project or job is important to some individuals. These people value what is called *task completion*. The effect that completing a task has on a person is a form of self-reward. Some people have a need to complete tasks. Opportunities that allow such people to complete tasks can have a powerful motivating effect.

Achievement. Achievement is a self-administered reward that is derived when a person reaches a challenging goal. McClelland has found that there are individual differences in striving for achievement.[10] Some individuals seek challenging goals, while others tend to seek moderate or low goals. In goal-setting programs, it has been proposed that difficult goals result in a higher level of individual performance than do moderate goals. However, even in such programs, individual differences must be considered before reaching conclusions about the importance of achievement rewards.

Autonomy. There are some people who want jobs that provide them with the right and privilege to make decisions and operate without being closely supervised. A feeling of autonomy could result from the freedom to do what the employee considers best in a particular situation. In jobs that are highly structured and controlled by management, it is difficult to create tasks that lead to a feeling of autonomy.

Personal Growth. The personal growth of any individual is a unique experience. An individual who is experiencing such growth senses his or her development and can see how his or her capabilities are being expanded. By expanding capabilities, a person is able to maximize or at least satisfy skill potential. Some people often become dissatisfied with their jobs and organizations if they are not allowed or encouraged to develop their skills.

ADMINISTERING REWARDS

Managers are faced with the decision of how to administer rewards. Three major theoretical approaches to reward administration are: (1) positive reinforcement; (2) modeling and social imitation; and (3) expectancy.[11]

Positive Reinforcement. In administering a positive reinforcement program, the emphasis is on the desired behavior that leads to job performance, rather than performance alone. The basic foundation of administering rewards through positive reinforcement is the relationship between behavior and its consequences. This relationship was discussed earlier in the chapter. While positive reinforcement can be a useful method of shaping desired behavior, other considerations concerning the type of reward schedule to use are also important. This relates to the discussion of continuous and intermittent schedules presented earlier. Suffice it to say that management

---

[10] David C. McClelland, *The Achieving Society* (New York: D. Van Nostrand, 1961).

[11] Lyman W. Porter, "Turning Work into Nonwork: The Rewarding Environment," in *Work and Nonwork in the Year 2001,* ed. M. D. Dunnette (Belmont, CA: Wadsworth, 1973), p. 122, suggests three approaches. Porter introduces operant conditioning. We believe that when rewards are being discussed, positive reinforcement should be used.

should explore the possible consequences of different types of reward schedules for individuals. It is important to know how employees respond to continuous, fixed interval, and fixed ratio ratio schedules.

Modeling and Social Imitation.   There is little doubt that many human skills and behaviors are acquired by observational learning, or simply, imitation. Observational learning equips a person to duplicate a response, but whether the response actually is imitated depends on whether the model person was rewarded or punished for particular behaviors. If a person is to be motivated, he or she must observe models receiving reinforcements that are valued. In order to use modeling to administer rewards, managers must determine who responds to this approach. In addition, selecting appropriate models is a necessary step. Finally, the context in which modeling occurs needs to be considered. That is, if high performance is the goal and it is almost impossible to achieve that goal because of limited resources, the manager should conclude that modeling is not appropriate.[12]

Expectancy Theory.   The expectancy approach, like the other two methods of administering rewards, requires managerial action. Managers must determine the kinds of rewards employees desire and do whatever is possible to distribute those rewards. Or, they must create conditions so that what is available in the form of rewards can be applied. In some situations, it simply is not possible to provide the rewards that are valued and preferred. Therefore, managers often have to increase the desirability of other rewards.

A manager can, and often will, use principles from each of the three methods of administering rewards—positive reinforcement, modeling, and expectancy. Each of these methods indicates that job performance of employees is a result of the application of effort. To generate the effort to perform, managers can use positive reinforcers, modeling, and expectations.

REWARDS AND TURNOVER AND ABSENTEEISM

Some managers assume that low turnover is a mark of an effective organization. This view is somewhat controversial, because a high quit rate means more expense for an organization. However, some organizations would benefit if disruptive and low performers quit.[13] Thus, the issue of turnover needs to focus on the *frequency* and on *who* is leaving.

Ideally, if managers could develop reward systems that retained the best performers and caused poor performers to leave, the overall effectiveness of an organization would improve.[14] To approach this ideal state, an equitable

---

[12] The discussion of Porter, "Turning Work Into Nonwork," was used in the development of this section.

[13] Dan R. Dalton, David M. Krackhardt, and Lyman W. Porter, "Functional Turnover: An Empirical Assessment," *Journal of Applied Psychology*, December 1982, pp. 716–21.

[14] Dan R. Dalton and William D. Tudor, "Turnover: A Lucrative Hard Dollar Phenomenon," *Academy of Management Review*, April 1982, p. 212.

and favorably compared reward system must exist. The feeling of *equity* and *favorable comparison* has an external orientation. That is, the equity of rewards and favorableness involves comparisons with external parties. This orientation is used because quitting most often means that a person leaves one organization for an alternative elsewhere.

There is no perfect means for retaining high performers. It appears that a reward system based on **merit** should encourage most of the better performers to remain with the organization. There also has to be some differential in the reward system that discriminates between high and low performers, the point being that the high performers must receive significantly more extrinsic and intrinsic rewards than the low performers.

Absenteeism, no matter for what reason, is a costly and disruptive problem facing managers.[15] It is costly because it reduces output and disruptive because it requires that schedules and programs be modified. It is estimated that absenteeism in the United States results in the loss of more than 400 million workdays per year, or about 5.1 days per employee.[16] Employees go to work because they are motivated to do so. The level of motivation will remain high if an individual feels that attendance will lead to more valued rewards and fewer negative consequences than alternative behaviors.

Managers appear to have some influence over attendance behavior. They have the ability to punish, establish bonus systems, and allow employee participation in developing plans. Whether these or other approaches will reduce absenteeism is determined by the value of the rewards perceived by employees, the amount of the rewards, and whether employees perceive a relationship between attendance and rewards. These same characteristics appear every time we analyze the effects of rewards on organizational behavior.

REWARDS AND JOB PERFORMANCE

There is agreement among behaviorists and managers that extrinsic and intrinsic rewards can be used to motivate job performance. It is also clear that certain conditions must exist if rewards are to motivate good job performance: the rewards must be *valued* by the person, and they must be related to the level of job performance that is to be motivated.[17]

In Chapter 4, expectancy motivation theory was presented. It was stated that, according to the theory, every behavior has associated with it (in a person's mind) certain outcomes or rewards or punishments. In other words, an assembly-line worker may believe that by behaving in a certain way, he or she will get certain things. This is a description of the *performance-outcome*

[15] Gary Johns and Nigel Nicholson, "The Meanings of Absence: New Strategies for Theory and Research," in *Research in Organizational Behavior*, eds. B. M. Staw and L. L. Cummings (Greenwich, CT: JAI Press, 1982), pp. 127–72.

[16] Richard M. Steers and Susan R. Rhodes, "A New Look at Absenteeism," *Personnel*, November-December 1980, pp. 60–65.

[17] Michael W. Spicer, "A Public Choice Approach to Motivating People in Bureaucratic Organizations," *Academy of Management Review*, July 1985, pp. 518–526.

expectancy. The worker may expect that a steady performance of 10 units a day eventually will result in a transfer to a more challenging job. On the other hand, the worker may expect that a steady performance of 10 units a day will result in being considered a rate-buster by co-workers.

Each outcome has a *valence* or value to the person. Outcomes such as pay, promotion, a reprimand, or a better job have different values for different people. This occurs because each person has different needs and perceptions. Thus, in considering which rewards to use, a manager has to be astute at considering individual differences. If valued rewards are used to motivate, they can result in the exertion of effort to achieve high levels of performance.

REWARDS AND ORGANIZATIONAL COMMITMENT

There is little research on the relationship between rewards and organizational commitment. **Commitment** to an organization involves three attitudes: (1) a sense of identification with the organization's goals, (2) a feeling of involvement in organizational duties, and (3) a feeling of loyalty for the organization.[18] Research evidence indicates that the absence of commitment can reduce organizational effectiveness.[19] People who are committed are less likely to quit and accept other jobs. Thus, the costs of high turnover are not incurred. In addition, committed and highly skilled employees require less supervision. Close supervision and a rigid monitoring control process are time-consuming and costly. Furthermore, a committed employee perceives the value and importance of integrating individual and organizational goals. The employee thinks of his or her goals and the organization's goals in personal terms.

Intrinsic rewards are especially important for the development of organizational commitment. Organizations able to meet employee needs by providing achievement opportunities and by recognizing achievement when it occurs have a significant impact on commitment. Thus, managers need to develop intrinsic reward systems that focus on personal importance or self-esteem, to integrate individual and organizational goals, and to design challenging jobs.

INNOVATIVE REWARD SYSTEMS

The typical list of rewards that managers can and do distribute in organizations has been discussed above. Pay, fringe benefits, and opportunities to achieve challenging goals are considered rewards by most people. It also is generally accepted that rewards are administered by managers through such processes as reinforcement, modeling, and expectancies. What are some of the newer and innovative, yet largely untested, reward programs with which some managers have been experimenting? Three different approaches to rewards are

---

[18] Arnon E. Reichers, "A Review and Reconceptualization of Organizational Commitment," *Academy of Management Review,* July 1985, pp. 465–476.

[19] R. T. Mowday, L. W. Porter, and R. M. Steers, *Employee-Organization Linkages* (New York: Academic Press, 1982).

cafeteria-style fringe benefits, banking time-off, and paying all employees a salary.

Cafeteria-style Fringe Benefits.   In a cafeteria-style plan, management places an upper limit on how much the organization is willing to spend on fringe benefits. The employee then is asked to decide how he or she would like to receive the total fringe benefit amount. The employee is able to develop a personally attractive fringe benefit package. Some employees take all of the fringes in cash or purchase special medical protection plans. The cafeteria plan provides individuals with the benefits they prefer rather than the benefits that someone else establishes for them.

Banking Time Off.   A time-off feature is attractive to most people. In essence, most companies have a time-off system built into their vacation programs. Employees receive different amounts of time off based on the number of years they have worked for the organization. An extension of such a time-off reward could be granted for certain levels of performance. That is, a bank of time-off credits could be built up contingent on performance achievements. In some instances, time off is tied directly—and immediately— to performance, as the following OBM Encounter illustrates.

ENCOUNTER
WHEN YOU'RE FINISHED WITH YOUR WORK, YOU CAN GO HOME

From an organization's perspective, there is a drawback to the typical time-off-for-performance program: the company loses its best people. Since only the top performers are rewarded, the average or poor performer stays on the job, while the best workers are enjoying their reward of not working. A large manufacturing facility in California has gotten around that problem, however. Here is the story:

A group of assemblers at the plant asked their supervisor if they could go home once they had met their daily assembly quota. At the time the query was made, the supervisor was trying to deal with a significant quality-control problem in the final assembled product (medical equipment). Seeing a way to address his quality control concerns and the workers' interest in going home once the quota was reached, the supervisor hit upon a plan. Assemblers would assume responsibility for doing their own inspection, and they could leave whenever the day's quota and inspections were done. A spot-checker randomly examined each day's output, and if there were quality problems, the assembler had to redo the entire batch on his own time.

Within three months, quality control had improved significantly; in fact, it was better than it had ever been under the previous system of using separate inspectors. While a small group of assemblers had to redo their work occasionally, more than 90 percent of them were finished with their work by lunchtime on a typical day, freeing their supervisor to devote his attention to other areas of the plant. ☐

Source: Based on the article by W. C. Hamner and E. P. Hamner, "Behavior Modification on the Bottom Line," *Organizational Dynamics,* Fall 1976, pp. 3–21.

The All-Salaried Team.   In most organizations, managers are paid salaries and nonmanagers receive hourly wages. The practice of paying all employees a salary is supposed to improve loyalty, commitment, and self-esteem. The notion of being a part of a team is projected by the salary-for-everyone practice. One benefit of the all-salary practice considered important by nonmanagers is that it eliminates punching a time clock. To date, rigorous investigations of the influence, if any, of the all-salary practice are not available. It does seem to have promise, however, when applied to some employees.

The strengths and weaknesses of these three approaches are summarized in Table 5–2.

TABLE 5–2

Three Innovative Reward Approaches: A Summary and Comparison

Reward Approach	Major Strengths	Major Weaknesses	Research Support
Cafeteria-style fringe benefits	Since employees have different desires and needs, a program can be tailored that fits the individual.	The administration can become complex and costly. The more employees involved, the more difficult it is to efficiently operate the approach	Limited since only a few programs have been scientifically examined
Banking time-off	Can be integrated with performance in that time-off credits can be made contingent on performance achievements	Requires that an organization have a valid, reliable, and equitable performance appraisal program.	Extremely limited
All-salaried team	Eliminates treating some employees as insiders and some as outsiders. Everyone is paid a salary and is a member of the team.	Assumes that everyone wants to be a team member and paid a salary. Some individuals value being nonmanagers and nonsalaried.	None available

PUNISHMENT AND DISCIPLINE

In organizational behavior and management, the analysis and discussion of job motivation focus primarily on eliciting desired behavior and performance. However, managers occasionally are faced with eliminating undesired behavior and inadequate performance. Despite their unpleasant connotations, punishment and disciplinary measures are used in organizations to eliminate undesired behavior and poor performance.[20] Examples of behaviors that

---

[20] Richard D. Arvey and John M. Ivancevich, "Punishment in Organizations: A Review, Proposal, and Research Suggestions," *Academy of Management Journal,* January 1980, pp. 123–32.

have been punished in organizations include absenteeism, tardiness, leaving the work station, fighting, violating safety rules, abusing customers, theft, work slowdown, profane language, and drug use.

Punishment is the presentation of an aversive event or the removal of a positive event following a response that decreases the frequency of the response.[21] A relationship or contingency exists between a defined response and an aversive consequence or stimulus (e.g., a pay reduction for being absent or a publicized memo informing you of poor performance). The resistance of some to the use of punishment is based on moral grounds, the moral position being that pain is bad and should always be avoided. *Discipline* is the use of some form of punishment or sanction when employees deviate from the rules. Not all disciplinary measures are a form of punishment.[22] For example, suppose that frequent absence results in a three-day suspension from work. If the person suspended does not like his job and prefers to stay home, he will not regard the suspension as aversive. In such a situation, the disciplined person has not been punished.

Instead of discussing discipline programs, we prefer to discuss punishment. The punishment literature contains the theoretical framework and basis for organizational progressive discipline programs (whereby a sequence of penalties for violations is administered, each one slightly more severe than the previous one). It should be noted that managers prefer to acknowledge that their firms have discipline programs as opposed to admitting that punishment is used.

PUNISHMENT AND BEHAVIOR

The earliest theoretical explanation of punishment was advanced by Thorndike.[23] Thorndike proposed that punishment exerted its effect on behavior by weakening the connection between a stimulus and a response. According to this theory, the proverbial child caught with a hand in the cookie jar and immediately punished would, on subsequent occasions, no longer be under the influence of the cookie jar or the cookies in it. The jar and the cookies would have lost their power to control the behavior of reaching into the jar. Later, Thorndike decided that punishment really had no weakening effect on behavior.[24] Thorndike's reevaluation of punishment was arrived at by his questioning of his original position. He argued that wherever punishment appears to weaken a response, it is an indirect effect. Punishment may or may not weaken a response, but it clearly cannot be the mirror image of the action of reward. For example, if an employee's response is

---

[21] Richard D. Arvey, Gregory Davis, and Sherry Nelson, "Use of Discipline in an Organization: A Field Study," *Journal of Applied Psychology,* August 1984, pp. 448–460.

[22] Ira G. Asherman, "The Corrective Discipline Process," *Personnel Journal,* July 1982, p. 528.

[23] E. L. Thorndike, *Educational Psychology,* vol. 2H: *The Psychology of Learning* (New York: Columbia University Teachers College Bureau of Publications, 1913).

[24] E. L. Thorndike, *Reward and Punishment in Animal Learning,* Contemporary Psychological Monograph, 1983, 8, no. 39.

rewarded, it is apparent that repetition of this response may also be rewarding; but if an employees' response is punished, it is not clear to the person which of the other available responses will be rewarded. In effect, Thorndike suggested that punishment does an exemplary job of telling a person what not to do but by itself carries no information that tells an individual which particular alternative course of behavior should be followed.

ARGUMENTS AGAINST USING PUNISHMENT

Besides the moral reasons cited against the use of punishment, other reasons for using it have been advanced. First, the purpose of punishment presumably is to reduce the occurrence of the specific behavior being punished. However, if the punishment is severe enough and is applied over sufficient time, it may also suppress the occurrence of socially desirable behaviors.

Second, some critics contend that the use of punishment will result in undesirable side effects (e.g., anxiety, aggressiveness). In addition, those being punished may attempt to escape or avoid (e.g., absenteeism, turnover) or show hostility toward (e.g., sabotage) management. It should be noted, however, that research support concerning the undesirable emotional side effects of punishment is not particularly strong.

Third, punishment effects are only temporary, and once the threat of punishment is removed, the undesirable response will return full force. Thus, the threat of punishment must always be there or be used. The fact is that punishment does work, and this may produce positive reinforcement for the managers to continue its use.

Fourth, through observational learning, punishment may result in negative responses from peers of the punished person. For example, individuals observing a manager punishing a colleague may imitate this behavior among themselves or toward management. In effect, the manager would be teaching employees aggressive, impersonal behavior, which is exactly what punishment is designed to eliminate.

CONDITIONS OF PUNISHMENT

Although there are logical arguments against the use of punishment in organizations, certain conditions can make its use feasible and more effective. These conditions include timing, intensity, and scheduling.

Timing. The time at which the punishment is administered is important.[25] Research suggests that the effectiveness of punishment is enhanced when the aversive event is delivered close in time to the punished response.

Intensity. Punishment achieves greater effectiveness when the aversive stimulus is relatively intense. The implication of this condition is that in order to be effective, punishment should get the immediate attention of the person being punished.[26]

---

[25] A. Trenholme and A. Baron, "Immediate and Delayed Punishment of Human Behavior by Loss of Reinforcement," *Learning and Motivation*, February 1975, pp. 62–79.

[26] J. M. Johnson, "Punishment of Human Behavior," *American Psychologist*, November 1972, pp. 1033–54.

Scheduling.   The effects of punishment depend on the schedule. Punishment can occur after *every* response (continuous schedule), a variable or fixed period of time after the undesired behavior occurred (variable or fixed-interval schedules), or after a variable or fixed number of responses have occurred (variable or fixed-ratio schedules). Some research suggests that punishment is most effective if administered on a continuous schedule.

Clarifying the Reasons.   Cognition plays an important role in punishment.[27] Providing clear, unambiguous reasons why the punishment occurred—and notice of future consequences if the response recurs—has been shown to be particularly effective. Providing reasons emphasizes to the person which specific response is responsible for the manager's action. It essentially informs the person exactly what not to do.

Impersonal.   Punishment should focus on a specific response, not on the person or general patterns of behavior.[28] The more impersonal the punishment, the less likely will the person being punished experience undesirable emotional side effects and permanent strains in the relationship with the manager.

For a more detailed discussion of these conditions influencing the effectiveness of punishment in organizations, see the second reading selection in the chapter by Arvey and Ivancevich. In addition to a discussion of the conditions, this article offers propositions regarding when and how punishment procedures will be effective.

What we have attempted to do in this section is to clarify the issue of punishment in organizations. Certainly, we prefer the predominant use of positive reinforcement. However, when a manager is faced with stopping a persistently undesirable response, positive reinforcement, negative reinforcement, or extinction alone may not be enough. These and other suggested alternatives may all be ineffective or costly. In such cases, punishment is used and undoubtedly will continue to be used. Although punishment is a complex and controversial process, continuing to ignore its use is not likely to enhance management's understanding of its application.

---

[27] Dennis W. Organ and W. Clay Hamner, *Organizational Behavior* (Plano, Tex.: Business Publications, 1982), pp. 97–98.

[28] Michael Domjan and Barbara Burkhard, *The Principles of Learning and Behavior* (Monterey, Calif.: Brooks/Cole Publishing, 1982), p. 264.

SUMMARY OF KEYPOINTS

A. Reinforcement theory relies on applying the principles of operant conditioning to motivate people. A major assumption is that behavior is influenced by its consequences.

B. The nature of reward or punishments and how they are employed influences behavior. Thus, reinforcement scheduling is an important feature of rewards and punishments.

C. It is general knowledge that certain reward process issues should be addressed if any objectives are to be accomplished. Namely, there must be enough rewards to satisfy basic needs, people make comparisons between what rewards they receive and what others receive, and individual differences in reward preferences are important issues for consideration.

D. Management can and must distribute both extrinsic and intrinsic rewards. *Extrinsic* rewards are those that are external to the job, such as promotions, fringe benefits, and pay. *Intrinsic* rewards are associated with doing the job. They include responsibility, challenge, and meaningful work.

E. Managers have many means for administering extrinsic and intrinsic rewards. Three of the most popular methods are positive reinforcement, modeling, and the application of expectancy theory principles.

F. Rewards, if used effectively, can affect such organizational behaviors as membership, turnover, absenteeism, and commitment. The research evidence showing how rewards influence these behaviors is still rather limited.

G. Some innovative reward strategies used by managers include cafeteria-style fringe benefits, banking time-off, and an all-salaried work force. These strategies have not been thoroughly examined by researchers.

H. Punishment is the presentation of an aversive event or the removal of a positive event following a response that decreases the frequency of the response.

I. Arguments against the use of punishment under any circumstance include suppression effects, undesirable emotional side effects, its temporary influence, and its influence on peers of the punished individual.

J. The use of punishment in an organization requires the consideration of timing, intensity, scheduling, clarification of reasons, and impersonality.

REVIEW AND DISCUSSION QUESTIONS

1. Why is it impractical to provide continuous reinforcement in organizations? Even if it were practical, why might it not necessarily be desirable?

2. Which type of intermittent reinforcement schedule appeals to you the most? Which one appeals to you the least? Explain.

3. What facts influence how satisfied you are with the rewards you receive? Are intrinsic or extrinsic rewards more important to you? Why?

4. What are some of the difficulties involved with administering a merit pay plan in an organization? How would you go about overcoming these difficulties?

5. Give an example of each of the three major approaches to administering rewards: positive reinforcement; modeling; and expectancy. As a manager, which would you prefer?

6. Do you think rewards are more important in attracting people to an organization or in developing commitment to the organization? Explain.

7. Cafeteria fringe benefits, banking time off and the all-salaried team are three examples of innovative reward systems. What other innovative approaches might an organization use to disperse rewards? Identify potential problems with the ideas you develop and try to find ways to overcome the problems.

8. Military organization historically have used punishment to a greater extent than business organizations. Why do you think this is the case? What do you think would happen if businesses used punishment to the same extent as the military? What if the military used it to the same extent as business organizations?

9. Punishment, like rewards, can be administered on either a continuous or intermittent schedule. Are the same schedules that are most effective for rewards the most effective ones for punishment as well? Why or why not?

10. It might seem that the ultimate form of punishment in organizations is termination. Can you think of situations where some other punishment might be viewed as more severe?

R1 ON THE FOLLY OF REWARDING A, WHILE HOPING FOR B*

STEVEN KERR

Whether dealing with monkeys, rats, or human beings, it is hardly controversial to state that most organisms seek information concerning what activities are rewarded, and then seek to do (or at least pretend to do) those things, often to the virtual exclusion of activities not rewarded. The extent to which this occurs of course will depend on the perceived attractiveness of the rewards offered, but neither operant nor expectancy theorists would quarrel with the essence of this notion.

Nevertheless, numerous examples exist of reward systems that are fouled up in that behaviors which are rewarded are those which the rewarder is trying to *discourage*, while the behavior he desires is not being rewarded at all.

In an effort to understand and explain this phenomenon, this paper presents examples from society, from organizations in general, and from profit-making firms in particular. Data from a manufacturing company and information from an insurance firm are examined to demonstrate the consequences of such reward systems for the organizations involved, and possible reasons why such reward systems continue to exist are considered.

SOCIETAL EXAMPLES
Politics

Official goals are "purposely vague and general and do not indicate . . . the host of decisions that must

* Source: Reprinted with permission from *Academy of Management Journal*, December 1975, pp. 769–783.

be made among alternative ways of achieving official goals and the priority of multiple goals . . ." (8, p. 66). They usually may be relied on to offend absolutely no one, and in this sense can be considered high-acceptance, low-quality goals. An example might be "build better schools." Operative goals are higher in quality but lower in acceptance, since they specify where the money will come from, what alternative goals will be ignored, etc.

The American citizenry supposedly wants its candidates for public office to set forth operative goals, making their proposed programs "perfectly clear," specifying sources and uses of funds, etc. However, since operative goals are lower in acceptance, and since aspirants to public office need acceptance (from at least 50.1 percent of the people), most politicians prefer to speak only of official goals, at least until after the election. They of course would agree to speak at the operative level if "punished" for not doing so. The electorate could do this by refusing to support candidates who do not speak at the operative level.

Instead, however, the American voter typically punishes (withholds support from) candidates who frankly discuss where the money will come from, rewards politicians who speak only of official goals, but hopes that candidates (despite the reward system) will discuss the issues operatively. It is academic whether it was moral for Nixon, for example, to refuse to discuss his 1968 "secret plan" to end the Vietnam war, his 1972 operative goals concerning the lifting of price controls, the reshuffling of his cabinet, etc. The point is that the reward

system made such refusal rational.

It seems worth mentioning that no manuscript can adequately define what is "moral" and what is not. However, examination of costs and benefits, combined with knowledge of what motivates a particular individual, often will suffice to determine what for him is "rational."[1] If the reward system is so designed that it is irrational to be moral, this does not necessarily mean that immorality will result. But is this not asking for trouble?

War

If some oversimplification may be permitted, let it be assumed that the primary goal of the organization (Pentagon, Luftwaffe, or whatever) is to win. Let it be assumed further that the primary goal of most individuals on the front lines is to get home alive. Then there appears to be an important conflict in goals— personally rational behavior by those at the bottom will endanger goal attainment by those at the top.

But not necessarily! It depends on how the reward system is set up. The Vietnam war was indeed a study of disobedience and rebellion, with terms such as "fragging" (killing one's own commanding officer) and "search and evade" becoming part of the military vocabulary. The difference in subordinates' acceptance of authority between World War II and Vietnam is reported to be considerable, and veterans of the Second

[1] In Simon's (10, pp. 76–77) terms, a decision is "subjectively rational" if it maximizes an individual's valued outcomes so far as his knowledge permits. A decision is "personally rational" if it is oriented toward the individual's goal.

World War often have been quoted as being outraged at the mutinous actions of many American soldiers in Vietnam.

Consider, however, some critical differences in the reward system in use during the two conflicts. What did the GI in World War II want? To go home. And when did he get to go home? When the war was won! If he disobeyed the orders to clean out the trenches and take the hills, the war would not be won and he would not go home. Furthermore, what were his chances of attaining his goal (getting home alive) if he obeyed the orders compared to his chances if he did not? What is being suggested is that the rational soldier in World War II, *whether patriotic or not,* probably found it expedient to obey.

Consider the reward system in use in Vietnam. What did the man at the bottom want? To go home. And when did he get to go home? When his tour of duty was over! This was the case *whether or not* the war was won. Furthermore, concerning the relative chance of getting home alive by obeying orders compared to the chance if they were disobeyed, it is worth noting that a mutineer in Vietnam was far more likely to be assigned rest and rehabilitation (on the assumption that fatigue was the cause) than he was to suffer any negative consequence.

In his description of the "zone of indifference," Barnard stated that "a person can and will accept a communication as authoritative only when . . . at the time of his decision, he believes it to be compatible with his personal interests as a whole" (1, p. 165). In light of the reward system used in Vietnam, would it not have been personally irrational for some orders to have been obeyed? Was not the military implementing a system

which *rewarded* disobedience, while *hoping* that soldiers (despite the reward system) would obey orders?

Medicine

Theoretically, a physician can make either of two types of error, and intuitively one seems as bad as the other. A doctor can pronounce a patient sick when he is actually well, thus causing him needless anxiety and expense, curtailment of enjoyable foods and activities, and even physical danger by subjecting him to needless medication and surgery. Alternately, a doctor can label a sick person well, and thus avoid treating what may be a serious, even fatal ailment. It might be natural to conclude that physicians seek to minimize both types of error.

Such a conclusion would be wrong.[2] It is estimated that numerous Americans are presently afflicted with iatrogenic (physician *caused*) illnesses (9). This occurs when the doctor is approached by someone complaining of a few stray symptoms. The doctor classifies and organizes these symptoms, gives them a name, and obligingly tells the patient what further symptoms may be expected. This information often acts as a self-fulfilling prophecy, with the result that from that day on the patient for all practical purposes is sick.

Why does this happen? Why are physicians so reluctant to sustain a type 2 error (pronouncing a sick person well) that they will tolerate many type 1 errors? Again, a look at the reward system is needed. The punishments for a type 2 error

[2] In one study (4) of 14,867 films for signs of tuberculosis, 1,216 positive readings turned out to be clinically negative; only 24 negative readings proved clinically active, a ratio of 50 to 1.

are real: guilt, embarrassment, and the threat of lawsuit and scandal. On the other hand, a type 1 error (labeling a well person sick) "is sometimes seen as sound clinical practice, indicating a healthy conservative approach to medicine" (9, p. 69). Type 1 errors also are likely to generate increased income and a stream of steady customers who, being well in a limited physiological sense, will not embarrass the doctor by dying abruptly.

 **LEARNING CHECKPOINT**

There seems to be no public initiated check for physicians who purposefully make Type I errors. Is it reasonable to assume that fellow physicians, through their own professional sanction systems, could or should punish blatant offenders of the Type I error? Explain.

Fellow physicians and the general public therefore are really *rewarding* Type I errors and at the same time *hoping* fervently that doctors will try not to make them.

GENERAL ORGANIZATIONAL EXAMPLES

Rehabilitation Centers and Orphanages

In terms of the prime beneficiary classification (2, p. 42) organizations such as these are supposed to exist for the "public-in-contact," that is, clients. The orphanage therefore theoretically is interested in placing as many children as possible in good homes. However, often orphanages surround themselves with so many rules concerning adoption that it is nearly impossible to pry a child out of the place. Orphanages may deny adoption unless the applicants are a married couple, both of the same religion as the child, without history of emotional or vocational instability, with a specified minimum income and a private room for the child, etc.

If the primary goal is to place children in good homes, then the rules ought to constitute means toward that goal. Goal displacement results when these "means become ends-in-themselves that displace the original goals" (2, p. 229).

To some extent these rules are required by law. But the influence of the reward system on the orphanage's management should not be ignored. Consider, for example, that the:

1. Number of children enrolled often is the most important determinant of the size of the allocated budget.
2. Number of children under the director's care also will affect the size of his staff.
3. Total organizational size will determine largely the director's prestige at the annual conventions, in the community, etc.

Therefore, to the extent that staff size, total budget, and personal prestige are valued by the orphanage's executive personnel, it becomes rational for them to make it difficult for children to be adopted. After all, who wants to be the director of the smallest orphanage in the state?

If the reward system errs in the opposite direction, paying off only for placements, extensive goal displacement again is likely to result. A common example of vocational rehabilitation in many states, for example, consists of placing someone in a job for which he has little interest and few qualifications, for two months or so, and then "rehabilitating" him again in another position. Such behavior is quite consis-

tent with the prevailing reward system, which pays off for the number of individuals placed in any position for 60 days or more. Rehabilitation counselors also confess to competing with one another to place relatively skilled clients, sometimes ignoring persons with few skills who would be harder to place. Extensively disabled clients find that counselors often prefer to work with those whose disabilities are less severe.[3]

Universities

Society *hopes* that teachers will not neglect their teaching responsibilities but *rewards* them almost entirely for research and publications. This is most true at the large and prestigious universities. Clichés such as "good research and good teaching go together" notwithstanding, professors often find that they must choose between teaching and research-oriented activities when allocating their time. Rewards for good teaching usually are limited to outstanding teacher awards, which are given to only a small percentage of good teachers and which usually bestow little money and fleeting prestige. Punishments for poor teaching also are rare.

 **LEARNING CHECKPOINT**

Suppose that punishment for teaching was a viable strategy to use to change behavior. What role could the timing, intensity, and impersonality of the punishment discussed in the chapter play in improving a teacher's classroom performance?

Rewards for research and publications, on the other hand, and punishments for failure to accom-

[3] Personal interviews conducted during 1972–73.

plish these, are commonly administered by universities at which teachers are employed. Furthermore, publication-oriented resumés usually will be well received at other universities, whereas teaching credentials, harder to document and quantify, are much less transferable. Consequently it is rational for university teachers to concentrate on research, even if to the detriment of teaching and at the expense of their students.

By the same token, it is rational for students to act based upon the goal displacement which has occurred within universities concerning what they are rewarded for. If it is assumed that a primary goal of a university is to transfer knowledge from teacher to student, then grades become identifiable as a means toward that goal, serving as motivational, control, and feedback devices to expedite the knowledge transfer. Instead, however, the grades themselves have become much more important for entrance to graduate school, successful employment, tuition refunds, parental respect, etc., than the knowledge or lack of knowledge they are supposed to signify.

It therefore should come as no surprise that information has surfaced in recent years concerning fraternity files for examinations, term-paper writing services, organized cheating at the service academies, and the like. Such activities constitute a personally rational response to a reward system which pays off for grades rather than knowledge.

BUSINESS-RELATED EXAMPLES

Ecology

Assume that the president of XYZ Corporation is confronted with the following alternatives:

1. Spend $11 million for antipollution equipment to keep from poisoning fish in the river adjacent to the plant; or
2. Do nothing, in violation of the law, and assume a one in ten chance of being caught, with a resultant $1 million fine plus the necessity of buying the equipment.

Under this not unrealistic set of choices it requires no linear program to determine that XYZ Corporation can maximize its probabilities by flouting the law. Add the fact that XYZ's president is probably being rewarded (by creditors, stockholders, and other salient parts of his task environment) according to criteria totally unrelated to the number of fish poisoned, and his probable course of action becomes clear.

Evaluation of Training

It is axiomatic that those who care about a firm's well-being should insist that the organization get fair value for its expenditures. Yet it is commonly known that firms seldom bother to evaluate a new GRID, MBO, job enrichment program, or whatever, to see if the company is getting its money's worth. Why? Certainly it is not because people have not pointed out that this situation exists; numerous practitioner-oriented articles are written each year to just this point.

The individuals (whether in personnel, manpower planning, or wherever) who normally would be responsible for conducting such evaluations are the same ones often charged with introducing the change effort in the first place. Having convinced top management to spend the money, they usually are quite animated afterwards in collecting arigorous vignettes and anecdotes about how successful the program was. The last thing many

desire is a formal, systematic, and revealing evaluation. Although members of top management may actually *hope* for such systematic evaluation, their reward systems continue to *reward* ignorance in this area. And if the personnel department abdicates its responsibility, who is to step into the breach? The change agent himself? Hardly! He is likely to be too busy collecting anecdotal "evidence" of his own, for use with his next client.

LEARNING CHECKPOINT

Would it be possible to establish a pay the trainer system based on results? That is, only pay trainers and implementers of MBO, job enrichment and other similar program in full when rigorous evaluations indicate that positive changes have occurred.

Miscellaneous

Many additional examples could be cited of systems which in fact are rewarding behaviors other than those supposedly desired by the rewarder. A few of these are described briefly below.

Most coaches disdain to discuss individual accomplishments, preferring to speak of teamwork, proper attitude, and a one-for-all spirit. Usually, however, rewards are distributed according to individual performance. The college basketball player who feeds his teammates instead of shooting will not compile impressive scoring statistics and is less likely to be drafted by the pros. The ballplayer who hits to right field to advance the runners will win neither the batting nor home run titles, and will be offered smaller raises. It therefore is rational for players to think of themselves first, and the team second.

In business organizations where rewards are dispensed for unit per-

formance or for individual goals achieved, without regard for overall effectiveness, similar attitudes often are observed. Under most Management by Objectives (MBO) systems, goals in areas where quantification is difficult often go unspecified. The organization therefore often is in a position where it *hopes* for employee effort in the areas of team building, interpersonal relations, creativity, etc., but it formally *rewards* none of these. In cases where promotions and raises are formally tied to MBO, the system itself contains a paradox in that it "asks employees to set challenging, risky goals, only to face smaller paychecks and possibly damaged careers if these goals are not accomplished" (5, p. 40).

It is *hoped* that administrators will pay attention to long-run costs and opportunities and will institute programs which will bear fruit later on. However, many organizational reward systems pay off for short-run sales and earnings only. Under such circumstances it is personally rational for officials to sacrifice long-term growth and profit (by selling off equipment and property, or by stifling research and development) for short-term advantages. This probably is most pertinent in the public sector, with the result that many public officials are unwilling to implement programs which will not show benefits by election time.

As a final, clear-cut example of a fouled-up reward system, consider the cost-plus contract or its next of kin, the allocation of next year's budget as a direct function of this year's expenditures. It probably is conceivable that those who award such budgets and contracts really hope for economy and prudence in spending. It is obvious, however, that adopting the proverb "to him who spends shall more be given," rewards not economy, but spending itself.

TWO COMPANIES' EXPERIENCES

A Manufacturing Organization

A midwest manufacturer of industrial goods had been troubled for some time by aspects of its organizational climate it believed dysfunctional. For research purposes, interviews were conducted with many employees and a questionnaire was administered on a company-wide basis, including plants and offices in several American and Canadian locations. The company strongly encouraged employee participation in the survey, and made available time and space during the workday for completion of the instrument. All employees in attendance during the day of the survey completed the questionnaire. All instruments were collected directly by the researcher, who personally administered each session. Since no one employed by the firm handled the questionnaires, and since respondent names were not asked for, it seems likely that the pledge of anonymity given was believed.

A modified version of the Expect Approval scale (7) was included as part of the questionnaire. The instrument asked respondents to indicate the degree of approval or disapproval they could expect if they performed each of the described actions. A seven-point Likert scale was used, with 1 indicating that the action would probably bring strong disapproval and 7 signifying likely strong approval.

Although normative data for this scale from studies of other organizations are unavailable, it is possible to examine fruitfully the data obtained from this survey in several ways. First, it may be worth noting that the questionnaire data corresponded closely to information gathered through interviews. Furthermore, as can be seen from the results summarized in Table A, sizable differences between various work units, and between employees at different job levels within the same work unit, were obtained. This suggests that response bias effects (social desirability in particular loomed as a potential concern) are not likely to be severe.

Most importantly, comparisons between scores obtained on the Expect Approval scale and a statement of problems which were the reason for the survey revealed that the same behaviors which managers in each division thought dysfunctional were those which lower level employees claimed were rewarded. As compared to job levels 1 to 8 in Division B (see Table A, those in Division A claimed a much higher acceptance by management of "conforming" activities. Between 31 and 37 percent of Division A employees at levels 1–8 stated that going along with the majority, agreeing with the boss, and staying on everyone's good side brought approval; only once (level 5–8 responses to one of the three items) did a majority suggest that such actions would generate disapproval.

Furthermore, responses from Division A workers at levels 1–4 indicate that behaviors geared toward risk avoidance were as likely to be rewarded as to be punished. Only at job levels 9 and above was it apparent that the reward system was positively reinforcing behaviors desired by top management. Overall, the same "tendencies toward conservatism and apple-polishing at the lower levels" which divisional management had complained about during the interviews were those claimed by subordinates to be the most rational course of action in light of the existing reward system. Management apparently was not getting the behaviors it was *hoping* for, but it certainly was getting the behaviors it was perceived by subordinates to be *rewarding*.

An Insurance Firm

The Group Health Claims Division of a large eastern insurance company provides another rich illustration of a reward system which reinforces behaviors not desired by top management.

Attempting to measure and reward accuracy in paying surgical claims, the firm systematically keeps track of the number of returned checks and letters of complaint received from policyholders. However, underpayments are likely to provoke cries of outrage from the insured, while overpayments often are accepted in courteous silence. Since it often is impossible to tell from the physician's statement which of two surgical procedures, with different allowable benefits, was performed, and since writing for clarifications will interfere with other standards used by the firm concerning "percentage of claims paid within two days of receipt," the new hire in more than one claims section is soon acquainted with the informal norm: "When in doubt, pay it out!"

The situation would be even worse were it not for the fact that other features of the firm's reward system tend to neutralize those described. For example, annual "merit" increases are given to all employees, in one of the following three amounts:

1. If the worker is "outstanding" (a select category, into which no more than two employees per section may be placed): 5 percent
2. If the worker is "above average" (normally all workers not "outstanding" are so rated): 4 percent
3. If the worker commits gross acts of negligence and irre-

TABLE A

Summary of Two Divisions' Data Relevant to Conforming and Risk-Avoidance Behaviors (Extent to Which Subjects Expect Approval)

Dimension	Item	Division and Sample	Total Responses	Percentage of Workers Responding		
				1, 2, or 3 (Disapproval)	4	5, 6, or 7 (Approval)
Risk avoidance	Making a risky decision based on the best information available at the time, but which turns out wrong.	A, levels 1–4 (lowest)	127	61	25	14
		A, levels 5–8	172	46	31	23
		A, levels 9 and above	17	41	30	30
		B, levels 1–4 (lowest)	31	58	26	16
		B, levels 5–8	19	42	42	16
		B, levels 9 and above	10	50	20	30
Risk	Setting extremely high and challenging standards and goals, and then narrowly failing to make them.	A, levels 1–4	122	47	28	25
		A, levels 5–8	168	33	26	41
		A, levels 9+	17	24	6	70
		B, levels 1–4	31	48	23	29
		B, levels 5–8	18	17	33	50
		B, levels 9+	10	30	0	70
	Setting goals which are extremely easy to make and then making them.	A, levels 1–4	124	35	30	35
		A, levels 5–8	171	47	27	26
		A, levels 9+	17	70	24	6
		B, levels 1–4	31	58	26	16
		B, levels 5–8	19	63	16	21
		B, levels 9+	10	80	0	20
	Being a "yes man" and always agreeing with the boss.	A, levels 1–4	126	46	17	37
		A, levels 5–8	180	54	14	31
		A, levels 9+	17	88	12	0
		B, levels 1–4	32	53	28	19
		B, levels 5–8	19	68	21	11
		B, levels 9+	10	80	10	10
	Always going along with the majority.	A, levels 1–4	125	40	25	35
		A, levels 5–8	173	47	21	32
		A, levels 9+	17	70	12	18
		B, levels 1–4	31	61	23	16
		B, levels 5–8	19	68	11	21
		B, levels 9+	10	80	10	10
	Being careful to stay on the good side of everyone, so that everyone agrees that you are a great guy.	A, levels 1–4	124	45	18	37
		A, levels 5–8	173	45	22	33
		A, levels 9+	17	64	6	30
		B, levels 1–4	31	54	23	23
		B, levels 5–8	19	73	11	16
		B, levels 9+	10	80	10	10

sponsibility for which he might be discharged in many other companies: 3 percent.

Now, since (a) the difference between the 5 percent theoretically attainable through hard work and the 4 percent attainable merely by living until the review data is small and (b) since insurance firms seldom dispense much of a salary increase in cash (rather, the worker's insurance benefits increase, causing him to be further overinsured), many employees are rather indifferent to the possibility of obtaining the extra one percent reward and therefore tend to ignore the norm concerning indiscriminant payments.

However, most employees are not indifferent to the rule which states that, should absences or latenesses total three or more in any six-month period, the entire 4 or 5 percent due at the next "merit" review must be forfeited. In this sense the firm may be described as *hoping* for performance, while *rewarding* attendance. What it gets, of course, is attendance. (If the absence-lateness rule appears to the reader to be stringent, it really is not. The company counts "times" rather than "days" absent, and a ten-day absence therefore counts the same as one lasting two days. A worker in danger of accumulating a third absence within six months merely has to remain ill (away from work) during his second absence until his first absence is more than six months old. The limiting factor is that at some point his salary ceases, and his sickness benefits take over. This usually is sufficient to get the younger workers to return, but for those with 20 or more years' service, the company provides sickness benefits of 90 percent of normal salary, tax-free! Therefore. . . .

Causes

Extremely diverse instances of systems which reward behavior A although the rewarder apparently hopes for behavior B have been given. These are useful to illustrate the breadth and magnitude of the phenomenon, but the diversity increases the difficulty of determining commonalities and establishing causes. However, four general factors may be pertinent to an explanation of why fouled-up reward systems seem to be so prevalent.

Fascination with an "Objective" Criterion

It has been mentioned elsewhere that:

> Most "objective" measures of productivity are objective only in that their subjective elements are (a) determined in advance, rather than coming into play at the time of the formal evaluation, and (b) well concealed on the rating instrument itself. Thus industrial firms seeking to devise objective rating systems first decide, in an arbitrary manner, what dimensions are to be rated, . . . usually including some items having little to do with organizational effectiveness while excluding others that do. Only then does Personnel Division churn out official-looking documents on which all dimensions chosen to be rated are assigned point values, categories, or whatever (6, p. 92).

Nonetheless, many individuals seek to establish simple, quantifiable standards against which to measure and reward performance. Such efforts may be successful in highly predictable areas within an organization, but are likely to cause goal displacement when applied anywhere else. Overconcern with attendance and lateness in the insurance firm and with number of people placed in the vocational re-

habilitation division may have been largely responsible for the problems described in those organizations.

Overemphasis on Highly Visible Behaviors

Difficulties often stem from the fact that some parts of the task are highly visible while other parts are not. For example, publications are easier to demonstrate than teaching, and scoring baskets and hitting home runs are more readily observable than feeding teammates and advancing base runners. Similarly, the adverse consequences of pronouncing a sick person well are more visible than those sustained by labeling a well person sick. Team-building and creativity are other examples of behaviors which may not be rewarded simply because they are hard to observe.

Hypocrisy

In some of the instances described the rewarder may have been getting the desired behavior, notwithstanding claims that the behavior was not desired. This may be true, for example, for management's attitude toward apple-polishing in the manufacturing firm (a behavior which subordinates felt was rewarded, despite management's avowed dislike of the practice). This also may explain politicians' unwillingness to revise the penalties for disobedience of ecology laws, and the failure of top management to devise reward systems which would cause systematic evaluation of training and development programs.

Emphasis on Morality or Equity Rather than Efficiency

Some consideration of other factors prevents the establishment of a system which rewards behaviors desired by the rewarder. The felt obligation of many Americans to vote for one candidate or another, for example, may impair their ability to withhold support from politicians who refuse to discuss the issues. Similarly, the concern for spreading the risks and costs of wartime military service may outweigh the advantage to be obtained by commiting personnel to combat until the war is over.

It should be noted that only with respect to the first two causes are reward systems really paying off for other than desired behaviors. In the case of the third and fourth causes the system is rewarding behaviors desired by the rewarder, and the systems are fouled up only from the standpoints of those who believe the rewarder's public statements (cause 3), or those who seek to maximize efficiency rather than other outcomes (cause 4).

CONCLUSIONS

Modern organization theory requires a recognition that the members of organizations and society possess divergent goals and motives. It therefore is unlikely that managers and their subordinates will seek the same outcomes. Three possible remedies for this potential problem are suggested.

Selection

It is theoretically possible for organizations to employ only those individuals whose goals and motives are wholly consonant with those of management. In such cases the same behaviors judged by subordinates to be rational would be perceived by management as desirable. State-of-the-art reviews of selection techniques, however, provide scant grounds for hope that such an approach would be successful (for example, see 12).

Training

Another theoretical alternative is for the organization to admit those employees whose goals are not consonant with those of management and then, through training, socialization, or whatever, alter employee goals to make them consonant. However, research on the effectiveness of such training programs, though limited, provides further grounds for pessimism (for example, see 3).

Altering the Reward System

What would have been the result if:

1. Nixon had been assured by his advisors that he could not win reelection except by discussing the issues in detail?
2. Physicians' conduct was subjected to regular examination by review boards for type 1 errors (calling healthy people ill) and to penalties (fines, censure, etc.) for errors of either type?
3. The President of XYZ Corporation had to choose between (a) spending $11 million for antipollution equipment, and (b) incurring a 50–50 chance of going to jail for five years?

Managers who complain that their workers are not motivated might do well to consider the possibility that they have installed reward systems which are paying off for behaviors other than those they are seeking. This, in part, is what happened in Vietnam, and this is what regularly frustrates societal efforts to bring about honest politicians, civic-minded managers, etc. This certainly is what happened in both the manufacturing and the insurance companies.

A first step for such managers might be to find out what behaviors currently are being rewarded. Perhaps an instrument similar to that used in the manufacturing firm could be useful for this purpose. Chances are excellent that these managers will be surprised by what they find—that their firms are not rewarding what they assume they are. In fact, such undesirable behavior by organizational members as they have observed may be explained largely by the reward systems in use.

This is not to say that all organizational behavior is determined by formal rewards and punishments. Certainly it is true that in the absence of formal reinforcement some soldiers will be patriotic, some presidents will be ecology-minded, and some orphanage directors will care about children. The point, however, is that in such cases the rewarder is not *causing* the behaviors desired but is only a fortunate bystander. For an organization to *act* upon its members, the formal reward system should positively reinforce desired behaviors, not constitute an obstacle to be overcome.

It might be wise to underscore the obvious fact that there is nothing really new in what has been said. In both theory and practice these matters have been mentioned before. Thus in many states Good Samaritan laws have been installed to protect doctors who stop to assist a stricken motorist. In states without such laws it is commonplace for doctors to refuse to stop, for fear of involvement in a subsequent lawsuit. In college basketball additional penalties have been instituted against players who foul their opponents deliberately. It has long been argued by Milton Friedman and others that penalties should be altered so as to make it irrational to disobey the ecology laws, and so on.

By altering the reward system the organization escapes the necessity of selecting only desirable people or of trying to alter undesirable ones. In Skinnerian terms (as described in 11, p. 704), "As for responsibility and goodness—as commonly defined—no one . . . would want or need them. They refer to a man's behaving well despite the absence of positive reinforcement that is obviously sufficient to explain it. Where such reinforcement exists, 'no one needs goodness.'"   □

REFERENCES

1. Barnard, Chester I. *The functions of the executive.* Cambridge, Mass.: Harvard University Press, 1964.

2. Blau, Peter M., & Scott, W. Richard, *Formal organizations.* San Francisco: Chandler, 1962.

3. Fiedler, Fred E. Predicting the effects of leadership training and experience from the contingency model. *Journal of Applied Psychology,* 1972, *56,* 114–119.

4. Garland, L. H. Studies of the accuracy of diagnostic procedures. *American Journal Roentgenological, Radium Therapy Nuclear Medicine,* 1959, *82,* 25–38.

5. Kerr, Steven. Some modifications in MBO as an OD strategy. *Academy of Management Proceedings,* 1973, pp. 39–42.

6. Kerr, Steven. What price objectivity? *American Sociologist,* 1973, *8,* 92–93.

7. Litwin, G. H., & Stringer, R. A., Jr. *Motivation and organizational climate.* Boston: Harvard University Press, 1968.

8. Perrow, Charles. The analysis of goals in complex organizations. In A. Etzioni (Ed.), *Readings on Modern Organizations.* Englewood Cliffs, N.J.: Prentice-Hall, 1969.

9. Scheff, Thomas J. Decision rules, types of error, and their consequences in medical diagnosis. In F. Massarik & P. Ratoosh (Eds.), *Mathematical Explorations in Behavioral Science.* Homewood, Ill.: Irwin, 1965.

10. Simon, Herbert A. *Administrative behavior.* New York: Free Press, 1957.

11. Swanson, G. E. Review symposium: Beyond freedom and dignity. *American Journal of Sociology,* 1972, *78,* 702–705.

12. Webster, E. *Decision making in the employment interview.* Montreal: Industrial Relations Center, McGill University, 1964.

R² PUNISHMENT IN ORGANIZATIONS: A REVIEW, PROPOSITIONS, AND RESEARCH SUGGESTIONS*

RICHARD D. ARVEY AND
JOHN M. IVANCEVICH

Despite its unpleasant connotations, the use of punishment or threat of punishment is a relatively common phenomenon in organizational and industrial settings. The topic of punishment, however, has received essentially no attention from organizational researchers. Although research in other applied settings has revealed that punishment is effective in reducing or eliminating undesirable behavior, organizational researchers and behavioralists have focused entirely

* Source: *Academy of Management Review,* January 1980, pp. 123–132. © 1980 by the Academy of Management.

on "positive" reward systems for modifying and changing employee behavior [Komaki, Barwick, & Scott, 1978; Pedalino & Gamboa, 1974; Stephens & Burroughs, 1978]. Although there are a number of procedures that can have the effect of decreasing the frequency of undesirable behavior (e.g., extinction, satiation, and physical restraint), Johnston states that there is "no indication from any data that any of these procedures provides an effect which is as immediate, enduring, or generally effective as that produced by the proper use of punishment" [1972, pp. 1050–1051].

We shall review some of what is known about punishment in laboratory and applied settings, and apply this knowledge to managerial practices in organizational settings. Specifically, we shall (1) define punishment and trace some of its historical treatments; (2) review and discuss some issues and questions concerning objections to punishment; (3) review the research literature to delimit certain variables that influence the effectiveness of punishment; (4) generate a number of propositions and hypotheses about when and how punishment procedures will be effective in organizational settings, and (5) discuss a variety of research issues associated with the study of punishment within organizational contexts.

DEFINITION OF PUNISHMENT

Although there are differences among psychologists concerning a definition of punishment, we will adopt Kazdin's concise definition, which captures the concept effectively: "Punishment is the presentation of an aversive event or the removal of a positive event following a response which decreases the frequency of that response" [1975, pp. 33–34]. There is a key point embedded within this definition. A relationship or contingency exists between some defined response and some aversive consequences or stimuli (e.g., a leader's sarcastic remarks for poor performance, or an organizational fine for tardiness). That is, the random or noncontingent administration of adversive stimuli on behavior does not represent punishment. (However, we make no strong claim that punishment operates only through strict behavioristic principles. Instead, we feel that there may be important cognitive elements that operate to directly influence or mediate the punishment process. For more discussion and criticism of behavior modification principles applied to organizations, see Locke (1977) and Babb and Kopp (1978).

 **LEARNING CHECKPOINT**

The chapter presents a number of punishable behaviors such as absenteeism, theft, work slowdowns, and use of profane language. Before any behavior is punished, management must be able to observe it at work. How could a work slowdown be observed and verified?

Punishment can occur under two kinds of circumstances. The first involves the presentation of an aversive event after a response. Psychologists often define a primary aversive event as a stimulus that is inherently aversive (e.g., electric shock, loud noises), whereas a conditioned or secondary aversive event involves a stimulus that becomes aversive through repeated pairing with an already aversive event. Many of the aversive events in organizational contexts are of this second type (e.g., reprimands, nods, gestures). A conditioned aversive stimulus may serve two distinct purposes. First, the stimulus may punish or decrease the response that led to it. Second, it may warn of or forecast some impending aversive consequence if a response is performed. Punishment involving some kind of *response cost* (e.g., paying a fine, repairing damages) is another example of an aversive event after

A second punishment circumstance involves the *removal* of positive outcomes or reinforcers after a response has been made. For example, punishment may take the form of the withdrawal of privileges, being ignored, or not being considered for promotion.

HISTORICAL PERSPECTIVES

Solomon [1964] has documented the controversies surrounding the punishment concept. Some of these controversies were first initiated by Skinner in 1938, and his position was further articulated in his book *Walden Two* [1948], in which he declared punishment to be ineffective or only temporary, and to produce undesirable side effects. Skinner's arguments were quite persuasive for most psychologists. Solomon claimed, however, that "the scientific base for the conclusions therein were shabby, because, even in 1938, there [were] conflicting data which demonstrated the great effectiveness of punishment in controlling instru-

mental behavior" [1964, p. 248]. It was not until the 1960s that punishment was recognized by researchers as an effective but extremely complex method for suppressing or eliminating behavior. In a literature review of laboratory findings, Church [1963] focused on a variety of variables that appeared to influence the effectiveness of punishment in laboratory settings. Azrin and Holz [1966] provided another review of the effect of punishment in laboratory settings. Researchers also began to study punishment as a procedure to suppress or eliminate predominantly deviant or pathological behaviors among human subjects. Punishment has been used effectively to modify such conditions as homosexuality [Feldman & MacCulloch, 1965], self-mutilating behaviors [Bucher & Lovaas, 1968; Harris & Ersner-Hersfield, 1978], alcoholism [Balke, 1965], and other behaviors. Summaries of the effectiveness of punishment on human behavior are provided by Johnston [1972], and Rimm and Masters [1974]. Parke [1972] has reviewed the effects of punishment on children's behavior. Kazdin [1975] provides an excellent review of the use of punishment in applied settings in his book on behavior modification.

Notably lacking in all of these literature reviews and interpretations are references on the use of punishment in organizational settings. Typically, discussions of punishment applied in organizations focus on what is wrong with using this method of behavioral control. Most of these discussions are laced with moral overtones and opinions concerning the use of punishment, and lack scientifically based research results.

One effort to scientifically study organizationally applied punishment is offered by Wheeler [1976]. He analyzed over 300 arbitration cases from the standpoint of the particular punitive philosophy involved in disciplinary actions (i.e., corrective, authoritarian, or humanitarian) and made an effort to integrate punishment theory with the disciplinary practices used within organizations. Moreover, he provided several suggestions for future research concerning punishment in organizational contexts. Hamner and Organ [1978] include a chapter on punishment in their recent organizational behavior book. They present arguments for and against the use of punishment and some of the factors that determine when punishment is effective. However, their presentation is based entirely on research carried out in non-organizational contexts.

Thus, it is quite clear that punishment techniques have been studied and applied effectively in clinical, laboratory, and school settings, but the study of the phenomenon in organizational contexts has remained essentially dormant. The primary theme found in the organizational behavior and management literature is that punishment is not a high priority choice for managerial application. The presumed negative consequences of its use are usually presented so convincingly that intelligent persons would not include the approach in their repertoires. This literature base is, however, non-empirical in that only a miniscule number of studies of the success or failure of punishment in organizational settings have been conducted. It is worthwhile to speculate about why this is so, particularly in view of the fact that most practicing managers have extensive experience with punishment and that most organizations incorporate punishment as an enforcer in their behavior control policies (e.g., absence-control systems).

BELIEFS ABOUT THE EFFECTS OF PUNISHMENT

In general, punishment has not been viewed favorably by organizational psychologists for several reasons. *First,* it is thought that the use of punishment by an employer will result in *undesirable emotional side effects* (e.g., anxiety, aggressive acts or feelings toward the punishing agent, or passivity or withdrawal). In addition, employees might attempt to escape or avoid (e.g., turnover, absenteeism) or show aggression toward (e.g., sabotage) the punishing agent.

The empirical evidence concerning these presumed effects is particularly weak. Johnson [1972] reports that of the numerous studies he reviewed, only one [Powell & Azrin, 1968] demonstrated these problems. Instead, his review revealed that there were indications of unexpected *improvement* in subject behavior as a result of punishment instead of withdrawal or passive responses. Kazdin's [1975] review likewise does not support the hypothesis of emotional side effects or resulting acts of aggression.

Parke [1972] suggests that undesirable side effects of punishment might occur mainly in situations where the punishing agents are indiscriminately punitive. In addition, acts of aggression may occur when the aversive event is particularly harsh and no alternative behavior is available. However, the evidence collected in non-organizational settings simply does not support the contention of significant undesirable side effects. Before any definitive conclusions about undesirable side effects of punishment in organizations are reached, evidence must be gathered within work settings to support or refute these notions.

Second, the use of punishment is thought to be *unethical* and *non-humanitarian*. Some people argue that punishment in organizations is old-fashioned and reflects a "tribal mentality" and reverts to the retributive justice theme of "an eye for an eye." This thinking confuses the notion of punishing to achieve justice ("paying back") in contrast to punishing to change or modify behavior. The first perspective views punishment as "past oriented" whereas the second perspective views punishment as having "future oriented" effects. Clearly, punishment has different connotations under the two perspectives. Retribution punishment may indeed be unethical, whereas punishment that is intended to be corrective and ultimately operate to the advantage of the person punished may not be considered unethical.

Punishment, however, does involve the systematic administration of aversive or undesirable stimuli. As Rimm and Masters [1974] have indicated, we must consider carefully the potential harm that might accompany some aversive stimuli. It is also clear that one must also consider the potential harm that can occur if *nothing* is done. As an extreme example, Rimm and Masters [1974] suggest that it is more humane to use punishment techniques to modify self-destructive behavior than to do nothing or "extinguish" these behaviors. Thus, punishment must be viewed carefully in the context in which it appears. Is it more humane for a supervisor to ignore a disruptive employee, hoping that the behavior will extinguish, than to administer immediate and consistent punishment of the disruptive responses in order to effect an immediate behavior change?

Moreover, as Bandura [1969], and Hamner and Organ [1978] succinctly point out, punishment is a frequent and naturally occurring event in all our lives that shapes a large part of our behavior. The use of aversive stimuli has always occurred in organizational settings and probably always will. Perhaps it is more ethical to study this process and apply it correctly and with a touch of humanity than to ignore or deny its value. As Skinner argues in *Beyond Freedom and Dignity* [1971], the environment plays an important role in controlling behavior. Therefore, it makes sense for us to understand and arrange environmental circumstances to achieve some kind of managed systematic control.

Third, punishment is said to *never really eliminate* undesirable responses. The effects of punishment are said to be only temporary, the undesirable response returning full force when the threat of punishment is removed [Hamner and Organ, 1978]. A rebuttal to this claim is that the recovery rate of the punished response is potentially under the control of the punishing agent. "Actually, it [recovery] is potentially just as controllable as the 'recovery' of an experimenter-reinforced response to base-line levels when extinction is begun" [Johnston, 1972, p. 1047]. That is, the kinds of punishment schedules used (e.g., intermittent or continuous), the kinds of discriminative stimuli or cues in the punishment setting that are available, and the alternative kinds of positive reinforcement contingencies for new behaviors (or no behaviors) that take the place of punished responses will influence the recovery rate. It is apparent from the reviews of Johnston [1972] and Kazdin [1975] that the effects of punishment need not always be temporary and that the recovery rate of the punished response depends on various parameters of punishment often under the control of a punish-

ing agent (managers or organizations).

VARIABLES THAT INFLUENCE THE EFFECTIVENESS OF PUNISHMENT

What, then, are some of the variables that influence the effectiveness of punishment? Moreover, how might specific variables influence the effectiveness of punishment in organizational contexts? Our intent here is to present those variables that seem to be the most salient in influencing punishment rather than attempt to be totally comprehensive.

Timing of Punishment

An aversive stimulus can be introduced at different times during the applications of punishment. It can be introduced *while* the punished response is being emitted, immediately *after* the punished response, or sometime after the response. Trenholme and Baron [1975] and reviews by Johnston [1972], Parke [1972], and Church [1963] indicate that, in general, the effectiveness of punishment is enhanced when the aversive event is delivered close in time to the punished response. Punishment of the response while it is in progress is also effective but care should be exercised that the aversive stimulus does not last longer than the punished response, otherwise the behavior emitted just before the termination of the aversive stimuli will be reinforced and strengthened. (This process is called negative reinforcement.)

In organizational settings, the implications of attempting to deliver punishment promptly are obvious. Managers or employers should apply the aversive event(s) as soon as the undesirable behavior occurs. Supervisors who wait a week or so before taking punitive action

may not be as effective in eliminating the undesirable response as those who act immediately. Despite the importance of punishing deviant behavior when it occurs, one cannot always do so.

Proposition 1: Punishment is more effective in organizational contexts if the aversive stimuli or events are delivered immediately after the undesirable response occurs than if the delivery is delayed.

Intensity

Laboratory experiments and research with children have consistently shown that punishment achieves greater effectiveness when the aversive stimulus is relatively intense [Axrin & Holz, 1966; Parke & Walters, 1967; Johnston, 1972]. The implication of these findings is that in order for punishment to be effective in organizations, it should start out at a relatively high level. Under conditions where the aversive stimulus is relatively weak, subjects may adapt to the stimulus level and continue to emit the punished behavior [Weinstein, 1969]. Hamner and Organ point out, however, that in many organizations, disciplinary procedures are set up so that punishment may begin at a very mild level and increase in intensity. "This may be much less effective (and ultimately less humanitarian) than moderately severe punishment of early instances of the offense" [1978, p. 78].

Taking the opposite view, Parke [1972] has called attention to the notion that high-intensity punishment may create a level of anxiety and impose a situation where adaptive learning (e.g., learning to discriminate between a correct and incorrect response) will not occur. In an organizational context, this might occur where an employee learning to perform a complex task (e.g., shutting down a computer) anticipates a high-intensity punishment if a response is incorrect (e.g., destroying internal computer tapes). The anxiety created by this situation may inhibit the learning process.

In addition, while aversive stimuli of high intensity levels may be the most effective in suppressing undesirable behavior, these aversive stimuli may also have the effect of suppressing other *desirable* responses. The available research appears to suggest that perhaps moderate intensity levels may be the most functional in organizational settings. Defining what are low, moderate, and high intensity levels of aversive stimuli may be difficult in organizational contexts. However, for purposes of research, these stimuli should be scaleable.

Proposition 2: Moderate levels of punishment are more effective than low or high intensity levels.

Relationships with Punishing Agents

Should the person administering punishment have a relatively close and warm relationship with the person being punished, or should the relationship be cold and distant? Research on children indicates that parents who are warm and affectionate in their relationships with their children achieve greater effectiveness when they apply punishment procedures [Parke, 1978]. The effect could be partially due to their concomitant withdrawal of affection with the administration of an aversive stimulus in the punishment situation.

The implication for organizational settings is that punishment may be most effective where supervisors have established close relationships with respect from and for employees. Hamner and Organ

[1978] suggest that punishment might be most effective when it is dispensed in an impersonal manner where the focus is on the act and not the person. Field research is needed, however, to determine whether punishment is effective because of the withdrawal of managerial affection or attention, or because of the specific aversive stimulus presented.

Proposition 3: Punishment procedures are more effective where the agent administering the punishment has relatively close and friendly relationships with the employee being punished.

Schedule of Punishment

The effects of punishment depend also on the schedule of punishment. The schedule of punishment is as important in correcting deviant behavior as the nature of the aversive event. Punishment could occur after *every* response (continuous schedule), after a variable or fixed period of time since the undesired behavior occurred (variable or fixed interval schedules), or after a variable or fixed number of responses have occurred (variable or fixed ratio schedules). Thus, some managers may be consistent in punishing employees after each undesirable behavior, whereas other managers may be inconsistent by punishing employees only after several infractions of a rule or policy have occurred. The laboratory-based research is fairly consistent in showing that punishment is most effective if administered on a continuous schedule—that is, after each response [Johnston, 1972; Parke, 1972; Azrin & Holz, 1966]. Some support is offered for this relationship in organizations by Gary [1971]. In this study, employees who were disciplined consistently for absenteeism demonstrated less absenteeism than employees who

received discipline haphazardly or not at all.

The notion of consistency may be viewed from several perspectives. Are managers consistent in punishing the same undesired behavior *over time?* Also, are supervisors consistent in punishing undesirable behavior *across employees?* Rosen and Jerdee [1974] have demonstrated that individuals are highly inconsistent in applying punishment across employees. Managers are apt to vary their enforcement of punishment of the same response depending on the tenure and skill levels of the employee.

LEARNING CHECKPOINT

Why would managers be apt to vary their enforcement of punishment because of tenure and skill levels of the employee involved?

Finally, we need to ask whether *different* managers are consistent in their applications of punishment across employees. Obviously, differential enforcement of punishment and differential intensities (penalties) will influence subordinates' perceptions of equity and fairness. It seems intuitively correct to us that an effective supervisor is not necessarily one who doesn't punish, but instead one who punishes *fairly* and *equitably.* These terms demand further clarification; however, it is beyond the scope of this paper to present a discussion of distributive justice, equity theory, and the like. The reader is referred to Walster and Walster [1975] and Deutsch [1975] for further discussion.

Another consideration that may influence a manager's consistency in administering punishment is his or her attributions concerning the cause of the specific behavior being punished [Jones & Davis, 1965]. A manager who perceives the behavior as being externally caused and beyond the control of the employee may choose *not* to administer punishment. However, employees may have little or no knowledge concerning the cause of the behavior, and therefore view the manager as inconsistent in the administration of punishment. Attribution theory has important implications in the study of punishment.

There are also situations in which particular schedules of punishment may *not* have the desired effects. For example, an aversive event can become a signal or cue for other later events—that is, it may become a discriminative stimulus. The punishing stimulus may become a sign that *no* punishment will occur for a period of time or signal that a positive reward will occur if the response occurs. Under these circumstances, we would expect an *increase* in the punished response. For example, employees may realize that once one of them is fined for being tardy, there will be no further fines for at least a week and subsequently increase the number of occasions they arrive late for work. Alternatively, the aversive stimulus could signal that no rewards are forthcoming, or that additional punishment will occur if the widespread behavior occurs. Under these situations, we would expect a *decrease* in the punished response. As Johnston states:

> The important thing to remember is that the punishing stimulus itself always occurs in the presence of and is always followed by other stimuli. To the extent that these patterns occur regularly, the punishing stimulus can come to reliably signal the presence or absence of these other stimulus conditions. The exact nature of these other stimuli (punish-

ing, reinforcing, etc.) can have considerable impact on the actual effects of the punishing stimulus [1972, p. 1043].

As one example of this phenomenon, Schmidt [1969] punished responses on a task according to either a variable interval or fixed interval schedule. Once subjects learned that punishment would be administered only after a fixed period of time, they continued to respond on the task until close to when they would be punished and then stopped. On the other hand, punishment administered on a variable schedule was more effective in suppressing the punished response, especially when the punishment (loss of money) was greater.

Based on what is already known about the importance of schedules of punishment, the following propositions seem warranted:

Proposition 4: Punishment of undesired behavior is more effective within organizations if:
a) Punishment consistently occurs after *every* undesirable response.
b) Punishment is administered consistently across different employees by the same manager.
c) Different managers are consistent in their applications of punishment for the same undesirable response.

Provision of Rationale

The administration of punishment could be more effective when a clear rationale is provided for the punishment process. Parke [1972] has noted the important role played by cognitive variables in the operation of punishment. Providing clear, unambiguous reasons concerning why the punishment occurred, and notice of future consequences if the response recurs has

been shown to be particularly effective in enhancing the effects of punishment in research with children [Parke, 1972]. Cognitive structure also appears to mediate some of the previously discussed variables influencing punishment. For example, Aronfreed [1965] found that the addition of reasoning to late-timed punishment increased its effectiveness. Moreover, Parke [1972] showed that when a rationale for punishment was provided, low-intensity punishment was just as effective as intense punishment in influencing behavior.

Proposition 5: Punishment is more effective when clear reasons are communicated to employees concerning why the punishment occurred, what the contingency is, and what the consequences of the behavior are in the future.

Alternative Responses Available

It appears that the effect of punishment is greatly enhanced if subjects have an alternative desirable response available. Moreover, if employees receive positive reinforcement for performing this alternative response, punishment is even more effective. This effect is due to two factors: (1) the employee does *not* perform the punished response (avoidance), and (2) another response is rewarded. Thus, punishment procedures that build-in explanations of alternative correct responses and reinforcement of these responses should have greater effectiveness than punishment processes that do not include alternative response options.

Proposition 6: To the extent that alternative desirable responses are available to employees and these responses are reinforced, punishment is enhanced.

HOW TO STUDY PUNISHMENT IN ORGANIZATIONS

The six propositions just stated have been offered to suggest that punishment may be effective in eliminating or suppressing deviant behavior in organizational settings. As indicated above, there is a paucity of research concerning punishment in organizational settings, possibly owing to a lack of knowledge concerning *how* to study punishment in the context of organizations. What seems to be needed are some guidelines and suggestions concerning variables and research methods that might be utilized to test the propositions.

Dependent Variables

What should be used as the dependent variables in studying punishment in organizational settings? The most obvious dependent variable is the measurement of the behavior being punished. That is, researchers should specify, record, and measure the precise behavior that is punished. If punishment is effective, a decrease in frequency or rate of that particular behavior should result. One mistake managers make is to assume that punishment will drastically alter a large range of employee behaviors. That is, they rely too much on the possibility of generalization of punishment to other behaviors. As Johnston states, "it is inappropriate simply to expect or hope for punishing effects to occur with . . . other responses in the same situation" [1972, p. 1048].

What kinds of behaviors might be candidates for study as dependent variables in organizational settings? Wheeler [1976] reviewed 339 cases appearing in the *Labor Arbitration Report* between 1970 and 1974 and classified the cases relating to discharge and discipline

according to the type of offense or undesirable behavior. The categories and frequencies that emerged were as follows:

1. Absenteeism, tardiness, leaving early (30 cases).
2. Dishonesty, theft, falsification of records (43 cases).
3. Incompetence, negligence, poor workmanship, violation of safety rules (37 cases).
4. Illegal strikes, strike violence, deliberate restriction of production (31 cases).
5. Intoxication, bringing intoxicants into the plant (18 cases).
6. Fighting, horseplay, trouble-making (34 cases).
7. Insubordination, refusal of job assignment, refusal to work overtime, fights or altercations with supervisor (98 cases).
8. Miscellaneous rule violations (48 cases).

Although additional variables might be studied, these variables outlined by Wheeler [1976] seem to be likely candidates. We should not, however, neglect the possible use of performance and satisfaction as dependent variables. It could be that punishment has organizationally undesirable effects if it is administered in a manner that violates a number of the propositions presented above. That is, if aversive events are administered noncontingently, are delayed, and given with no explanation, we would expect not only little change in the specific response presumably being punished, but also possible *decreases* in satisfaction and performance. Moreover, increases in other undesirable behaviors (sabotage, work stoppage) might be observed.

Measurement of these dependent variables may be difficult in organizational settings. However, many organizations keep records of rule infractions (when they are

observed) that may be one information source in detecting the frequency or rate of response occurrence. More use of unobtrusive observers may also be a method for obtaining accurate measurement of deviant behaviors. For example, Komaki, Barwick, and Scott [1978] used trained observers to determine the frequency of safe and unsafe behaviors. These observers were present 4 days a week for 55 minutes during each observational period. No complaints were noted about the presence of these observers. Possibly a similar measurement process could be used to determine the rates of particular undesirable job behaviors. (It would, however, have to be made clear to employees that the observers would not inform the management about who was exhibiting undesirable behavior.)

Managerial, peer, and self ratings may be additional measurement tools. For example, managers might be asked to evaluate their employees in terms of their "disruptiveness," "insubordination," and so forth, on psychometrically developed graphic rating scales. Rating scales might also be used to measure employee satisfaction and performance.

Independent Variables

Several problems confront the researcher attempting to study punishment in organizations. One of the most salient problems is determining what constitutes an aversive event or stimulus to employees. Managers have control over numerous potential punishing stimuli that range from overt and formal actions such as discharge and financial penalties to less overt behavior such as assignment of employees to undesirable tasks, subtle verbal statements, and ridicule.

Organizational   psychologists

have developed a reasonably well-defined taxonomic system of positive reinforcers that are available and used in organizational systems (e.g., recognition, praise, bonuses). What is needed is the development of a taxonomy of aversive stimuli in organizational settings. That is, what supervisory actions result in aversive situations for employees? One strategy for developing a taxonomy is to ask employees to relate situations where they felt punished in organizational settings and indicate the role their supervisors or managers played in the situation. A critical-incident method might be employed. The resulting incidents might be sorted and categorized in an effort to develop some sort of classification system. An important issue here would be the generality of the punishers. In order to serve as an effective behavior control mechanism in organizations, punishers should reduce the frequency of many kinds of behaviors across many organizations. Of course, a limitation of this critical-incident method is that it is basically retrospective. Even with this limitation, it is a start in the development of a taxonomic system.

A number of interesting side issues are worth considering here. For example, what is aversive to one employee may not be aversive to another. Moreover, what a manager perceives as a reward may actually be perceived as a punishment by an employee. A manager might assign a *challenging* task to an employee as a reward for a job well done. However, the employee may not desire a more challenging task, find it too demanding of time and effort [Tornow, 1971], and feel punished. In contrast, a manager may perceive that he or she is punishing an employee (e.g., ignoring the employee), whereas the employee may not feel that the event

is aversive. In short, there may be wide discrepancies among managers' and employees' perceptions concerning when and what aversive stimuli are delivered. Furthermore, occupational and gender differences concerning the interpretation and perceptions of aversive stimuli would be useful information to managers.

Once basic aversive events have been identified in organizational contexts, it would be desirable to measure the "dimensions" of the stimuli. That is, researchers should attempt to record and quantify such properties as the timing of stimuli, the intensity, and the schedule of presentation. In addition, efforts should be made to quantify the degree of reasoning used in the punishment situation, the kind of relationship between the employee and punishing agent, and the alternative responses available. These measures could be used as independent variables in research studies.

Precise measurement of these dimensions may be impossible. Several strategies for providing valid measures may be available, however:

1. Just as observers have been carefully trained to observe, record, and evalute specific behaviors in work-sampling procedures [Campion, 1972], so might observers be trained to *observe and record behaviors* along the dimensions specified above. That is, observers might be able to identify the length of time between the response and aversive stimulus, the schedule of punishment, the intensity of the punishment, and so forth.

2. Employees might be given a *case study* where a specific rule infraction is portrayed and then be asked to evaluate how their own managers might react to the given

infractions along the various dimensions. Thus, a "standard" response is given and the employees are asked to indicate how their managers react or punish the response. The amount of agreement among employees who share the same supervisor could be calculated as one estimate of reliability.

3. *Rating methods* might be also used, which would entail employees describing their manager's punishment behavior on a variety of rating dimensions.

Thus, there appears to be a variety of possible measurement strategies available to researchers.

RESEARCH DESIGNS

At first blush, it appears as if planned experiments dealing with punishment might be out of the question because of ethical considerations. However, there seem to be several situations where an experimental method might be appropriate. Many organizations sponsor training workshops for managers that focus on how to discipline employees. It would be possible to incorporate an experimental design into these workshops by forming experimental and comparison groups of managers. The experimental group could be introduced to some of the principles of punishment presented above and pre- and post-measures of employee behavior would be collected (for both experimental and comparison groups). Manipulation checks might be obtained through employee questionnaires. For example, Bauum and Youngblood [1975] report the results of a study in college classrooms where two kinds of attendance policies (compulsory, noncompulsory) were manipulated. Results showed that significantly higher attendance and higher performance levels as measured by examination scores were achieved by students in the compulsory-attendance classrooms. No differences in satisfaction between the treatment groups were observed. This kind of experimentation could be implemented in organizational settings without too much difficulty.

Field studies of punishment are a must if managers are to receive an accurate picture of the effects of punishment. Regression analyses could be used to assess the relationship between the punished response and such independent variables as timing, schedule, and intensity. Organizations might be identified, in the same or different industries, that clearly differ in their punishments policies and procedures and efforts made to assess corresponding differences in the frequency and rates of undesirable behaviors.

 **LEARNING CHECKPOINT**

Are any of the arguments against the use of punishment presented in the chapter significant enough to conclude that field studies will probably not be permitted because managers will not be using punishment in the future?

A FINAL WORD

The application of punishment within organizational settings is generally a neglected area of inquiry in the field of management. Punishment has such a negative connotation that most researchers would not recommend its application. However, public denial is not sufficient reason to dismiss punishment as a potential management approach for modifying and controlling behavior.

There is agreement among some researchers that punishment may be a very effective procedure in accomplishing behavior change. Although punishment is a complex process influenced by a number of variables, continuing to ignore punishment as a practical managerial strategy will not enhance our understanding of the procedure. Only rigorous research and an open dialogue will provide the insight needed to understand the effectiveness of punishment in organizational settings. The question is not so much whether punishment is good or bad. It exists and is found quite frequently in organizational settings. The question should be: How may punishment best be used to accomplish behavior change? □

REFERENCES

Aronfreed, J. *Punishment learning and internalization: Some parameters of reinforcement and cognition.* Paper read at biennial meeting of Society for Research in Child Development, Minneapolis, 1965.

Azrin, N. N., & Holz, W. C. Punishment. In W. K. Honig (Ed.). *Operant behavior: Areas of research and application.* New York: Appleton-Century-Crofts, 1966, pp. 380–447.

Babb, H. W., & Kopp, D. G. Application of behavior modification in organizations: A review and critique. *Academy of Management Review,* 1978, *3,* 281–293.

Bandura, A. *Principles of behavior modification.* New York: Holt, Rinehart, & Winston, 1969.

Bauum, J. F., & Youngblood, S. A. Impact of an organizational control policy on absenteeism, performance, and satisfaction. *Journal of Applied Psychology,* 1975, *60,* 688–694.

Balke, B. G. The application of behavior therapy to the treatment of alcoholism. *Behavior Research and Therapy,* 1965, *3,* 75–85.

Bucher, B., & Lovaas, O. I. Use of aversive stimulations in *behavior modification. In M. R. Jones (Ed.),*

Miami symposium on the prediction of behavior, 1967: Aversive stimulation. Coral Gables, Fla.: University of Miami Press, 1968.

Campion, J. E. Work sampling for personnel selection. *Journal of Applied Psychology,* 1972, *56,* 40–44.

Church, R. M. The varied effects of punishment on behavior. *Psychological Review,* 1963, *70,* 369–402.

Deutsch, M. Equity, equality, and need: What determines which value will be used as the basis of distributive justice? *The Journal of Social Issues,* 1975, *31,* 137–150.

Feldman, M. P., & MacCulloch, M. J. The application of anticipatory avoidance learning to the treatment of homosexuality: I. Theory, technique and preliminary results. *Behavior Research and Therapy,* 1965, *2,* 165–183.

Frakes, F. V. Acquisition of disliking for persons associated with punishment. *Perceptual and Motor Skills,* 1971, *33,* 251–255.

Gary, A. L. Industrial absenteeism: An evaluation of three methods of treatment. *Personnel Journal,* 1971, *50,* 352–353.

Hamner, W. C., & Organ, D. W. *Organizational behavior: An applied psychological approach.* Dallas, Tex.: Business Publications, 1978.

Harris, S., & Ersner-Hershfield, R. Behavioral suppression of seriously disruptive behavior in psychotic and retarded patients: A review of punishment and altercations. *Psychological Bulletin,* 1978, *85,* 1352–1375.

Johnston, J. M. Punishment of human behavior. *American Psychologist,* 1972, *27,* 1033–1054.

Jones, E. E., & Davis, R. E. From acts to dispositions. In L. Berkowitz (Ed.), *Advances in experimental social psychology.*

Kazadin, A. E. *Behavior modification in applied settings.* Homewood, Ill.: Dorsey, 1975.

Komaki, J., Barwick, K. D., & Scott, L. R. A behavioral approach to occupational safety: Pinpointing and reinforcing safe performance in a food manufacturing plant. *Journal of Applied Psychology,* 1978, *63,* 434–445.

Locke, E. A. The myths of behavior mod in organizations. *The Academy of Management Review,* 1977, *2,* 543–553.

Parke, R. D., & Walters, R. H. Some factors determining the efficacy of punishment inducing response inhibition. *Monographs of the Society for Research in Child Development,* 1967, *32* (Serial No. 109).

Parke, R. D. Some effects of punishment on children's behavior. In W. W. Hartup (Ed.), *The young child: Reviews of research* (Vol. 2). Washington, D.C.: National Association for the Education of Young Children, 1972.

Pedalino, E., & Gamboa, V. U. Behavior modification and absenteeism: Intervention in one industrial setting. *Journal of Applied Psychology,* 1974, *59,* 694–698.

Powell, J., & Azrin, N. The effects of shock as a punisher for cigarette smoking. *Journal of Applied Behav-ior Analysis,* 1968, *1,* 63–71.

Rimm, D. C., & Masters, J. C. *Behavior therapy: Technique and empirical findings.* New York: Academic Press, 1974.

Rosen, B., & Jerdee, T. H. Factors influencing disciplinary judgments. *Journal of Applied Psychology,* 1974, *59,* 327–331.

Schmitt, D. R. Punitive supervision and productivity: Anental analog. *Journal of Applied Psychology,* 1969, *53,* 118–123.

Skinner, B. R. *The behavior of organisms.* New York: Appleton-Century-Crofts, 1938.

Skinner, B. F. *Beyond freedom and dignity.* New York: Knopf, 1971.

Skinner, B. F. *Walden two.* New York: Macmillan, 1948.

Solomon, R. L. Punishment. *American Psychologist,* 1964, *19,* 239–253.

Stephens, T. A., & Burroughs, W. A. An application of operant condition-ing to absenteeism in a hospital setting. *Journal of Applied Psychology,* 1978, *63,* 518–521.

Tornow, W. W. The development and application of an input/outcome moderator test on the perception and reduction of inequity. *Organizational Behavior and Human Performance,* 1971, *6,* 614–638.

Trenholme, I. A., & Baron, A. Immediate and delayed punishment of human behavior by loss of reinforcement. *Learning and Motivation,* 1975, *6,* 62–79.

Walster, E., & Walster, G. W. Equity and social justice. *Journal of Social Issues,* 1975, *31,* 21–44.

Weinstein, L. Decreased sensitivity to punishment. *Psychonomic Science,* 1969, *14,* 264.

Wheeler, H. N. Punishment theory and industrial discipline. *Industrial Relations,* 1976, *15,* 235–243.

☐1 ASSESSING ALCOHOLISM

The following 20 questions were developed by medical researchers at the Johns Hopkins University Hospital and are used by them as a test in the diagnosis of the sickness of alcoholism. Complete the scale and then think about whether this self-report scale should be used as an educational-self-awareness technique for employees.

		Yes	*No*
1.	Have you lost time from work due to drinking?	___	___
2.	Has drinking made your home life unhappy?	___	___
3.	Do you drink because you are shy with people?	___	___
4.	Has drinking affected your reputation?	___	___
5.	Have you gotten into financial difficulties because of your drinking?	___	___
6.	Do you turn to lower companions and an inferior environment when drinking?	___	___
7.	Does your drinking make you careless of your family's welfare?	___	___
8.	Has your drinking decreased your ambition?	___	___
9.	Do you want a drink "the morning after"?	___	___
10.	Does your drinking cause you to have difficulty sleeping?	___	___
11.	Has your efficiency decreased since drinking?	___	___
12.	Has drinking ever jeopardized your job or business?	___	___
13.	Do you drink to escape from worries or troubles?	___	___
14.	Do you drink alone?	___	___

15. Have you ever had a complete loss of memory as a result of drinking?   — —

16. Has your physician ever treated you for drinking?   — —

17. Do you drink to build up self-confidence?   — —

18. Have you ever been in an institution or hospital on account of drinking?   — —

19. Have you ever felt remorse after drinking?   — —

20. Do you crave a drink at a definite time daily?   — —

Johns Hopkins University says one "yes" answer indicates that a drinking problem may exist and two "yes" answers indicate a probable condition. If three questions are answered "yes," it is reasonably certain that alcohol has become, or is becoming, a major problem for the patient.

D2 MY PERSONAL CHOICE SURVEY

Listed are a few questions that attempt to determine what kind of things you like and respond to in everyday life. After completing the questions read pages 169–173 in Chapter 5 and ask yourself if you are more intrinsically or extrinsically driven.

1. When I have free time I usually will _____.

2. My favorite hobby is _____.

3. My life would be more rewarding if _____.

4. My job (or school work) would be more rewarding if _____.

5. If I had $100 extra to buy something, I would _____.

6. I would work harder if _____.

7. I put in extra hours of work and effort doing my job (school work) if _____.

8. A person I respect and admire is _____.

9. The occupation that I prefer is _____.

10. A country or place that I would love to vacation in is _____.

Reread your responses and ask yourself, "what do they tell me about myself?"

MAKING CHOICES ABOUT REWARDS

OBJECTIVES

1. To illustrate individual differences in reward preferences.

2. To emphasize how both extrinsic and intrinsic rewards are considered important.

3. To enable people to explore the reasons for the reward preferences of others.

STARTING THE EXERCISE

Initially individuals will work alone establishing their own list of reward preferences after reviewing Exhibit A. Then the instructor will set up groups of four to six students to examine individual preferences and complete the exercise.

The Facts

It is possible to develop an endless list of on-the-job rewards. Presented in a random fashion in Exhibit A are some of the rewards that could be available to employees.

Exercise Procedures

Phase I: 25 minutes

1. Each individual should set up from Exhibit A a list of extrinsic and intrinsic rewards.
2. Each person should then rank-order from most important to least important the two lists.
3. From the two lists, rank the *eight* most important rewards. How many are extrinsic, and how many are intrinsic?

Phase II: 30 minutes

1. The instructor will set up groups of four to six individuals.
2. The two lists in which the extrinsic and intrinsic categories were developed should be discussed.
3. The final rank orders of the eight most important rewards should be placed on a board or chart at the front of the room.
4. The rankings should be discussed within the groups. What major differences are displayed?

EXHIBIT A

Some Possible Rewards for Employees

Company picnics
Watches
Trophies
Piped-in music
Job challenge
Achievement opportunity
Time-off for performance
Vacation
Autonomy
Pay increase

Recognition
Smile from manager
Feedback on performance
Feedback on career progress
Larger office
Club privileges
More prestigious job
More job involvement
Use of company recreation
  facilities

Participation in decisions
Stock options
Vacation trips for
  performance
Manager asking for advice
Informal leader asking for
  advice
Office with a window
The privilege of completing a
  job from start to finish

2 REWARD OR PUNISHMENT: THE LAY OFF DECISION

OBJECTIVES

1. To acquire an understanding of how difficult it is to make a lay off decision.

2. To examine how you weigh various personal and job-related behaviors to make a lay off decision.

STARTING THE EXERCISE

Read the employee descriptions and develop your own sequence of laying employees off. Number 1 would be the first laid off, Number 2 would be the second laid off and so forth. There is no perfect answer, but you should be able to defend your lay off sequence array. Is being the last person laid off a reward? For what?

After you have arrayed the employees in order of lay off the class will be divided into groups of five to eight students each to share and compare choices and reasons.

J. M. Miller, Inc. is a small job shop that manufactures parts for electronic equipment. The firm is a major supplier to a number of large equipment manufacturers. As a result of recent orders and demand, Miller's management has met on two occasions to consider cutting costs and even laying off some workers. Miller is a nonunion firm that is located in Mesquite, a suburb of Dallas, Texas. The company has prided itself on being a fair employer that has rewarded employees with bonuses and jobs without ever having to lay employees off. However, for today's meeting, the president has asked you to rank order from first to seventh the employees in the production bay that will experience the first involuntary cutbacks in the firm's history.

A description of the employees are as follows:

- **Don Dombroski**—White male; age 34; married, three children. Has worked at Miller's for six years; generally good performer who has had some incidents of absence and tardiness in the last 12 months.

- **Lu Wong Chen**—Oriental male; age 35; married, one child. Has only been at Miller's for 18 months, but is considered the top technician in the shop. Has a tendency to stay by himself and stay away from co-workers.

- **Nancy Carlatta**—White female; age 42; husband recently disabled. Has two college age children she is helping through school. Volunteers for everything, says that she must work. Does acceptable work and has been at Miller's for seven years.

- **Tito Guereba**—Hispanic male; age 24; worked at Miller's for three years; is single. Does above average work and was being considered for training courses to improve skills.

- **Mitchell Green**—Black male; age 33; married with two children. Wife was recently laid off. Has a good, steady performance record. Has been talking about attempting to unionize Miller. Worked for five years in the company.

- **Jack Aremian**—White male; age 49; married with five children. Has been at Miller's since it opened 11 years ago. Is a chronic complainer and has an alcohol problem that causes him to be excessively absent. When he is sober, his work is steady and is considered good.

- **Mary Lou Cisneros**—Hispanic female; age 30; divorced, single parent with two children. Has four years of tenure. Is considered a good performer. Because of difficulties raising a handicapped child, is considered to be quite moody. Flies off the handle when asked to do some jobs.

BOB COLLINS

Bob Collins was employed by the Mansen Company, a division of Sanford, Barnes Inc., a diversified company engaged mainly in the manufacture and sale of men's and women's apparel. The Miami plant of the Mansen Company is the largest of the nineteen manufacturing locations and has, in its organization, an industrial engineering unit.

As department head of industrial engineering in the Miami plant, Jim Douglas also has the responsibility for all industrial engineering functions in the Florida Region. This includes three smaller plants within a 275-mile radius of Miami. Jim reports to the Miami plant manager, Mr. Scott, for local projects and to the Florida regional manager, Mr. Glenn, for projects of a regional nature. Mr. Glenn had been regional manager for many years, but only for the previous twenty-three months had this been his sole responsibility. Prior to this time, he was also the manager of the Miami plant, and he was still a dominant personality in the plant, partially because of Mr. Scott's indecisiveness.

EXHIBIT 1

Partial Organization Chart. The Mansen Company.

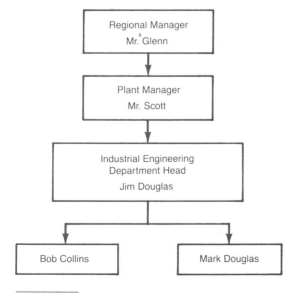

Used with permission of the authors, Richard E. Dutton and Rodney C. Sherman, University of South Florida.

Assisting Jim in Miami are two other industrial engineers, Bob Collins and Mark Douglas. Mark was hired in September, 198-, soon after his release from the army, and had been with Mansen about twenty-seven months. Bob had been with the company for about twenty-one months since leaving his last position because of a conflict there regarding a heavy workload and a schedule requiring some night work. Bob had freely given this information during his pre-employment interview, but no effort had been made to uncover the past employer's version of the situation.

Jim holds an associate degree in industrial engineering from a two-year technical school while both Bob and Mark have bachelor's degrees, in history and business respectively. All three men are army veterans. Jim and Mark had served as enlisted men for nine and two years respectively, Jim becoming a staff sergeant and Mark a sergeant. Bob served as an officer for four years reaching the rank of Captain. Bob had displayed a talent for creative and imaginative thinking in regards to mechanical development and was assigned a majority of the projects that delved into the creation, installation, and improvement of mechanical innovations and devices. In addition, he and the local head of mechanical development, Ned Larson, worked together on many of their own original ideas, both in the planning and development.

CURRENT SITUATION

One day, Bob came upon an inter-office memo, in Jim's incoming mail box, containing a question from Mr. Glenn about a mechanical project on which Bob was working. Feeling that he could save time for Jim, he picked up the memo, read it, and proceeded to Mr. Glenn's office to answer the question. When he returned, he simply put the memo back in Jim's mail box and went on with other work.

Later in the day Jim returned to the office to answer his mail, and came upon Mr. Glenn's memo. Jim sought out Bob and the following conversation ensued:

Jim: Bob, I've got a short note here from Mr. Glenn asking about the status of the cuff machine project I gave you. Where do we stand on that now?

Bob: Well, as I mentioned before, all we have to build is the automatic stacking device and then we should have the machine about ready to go. Some of the parts won't be in until the first of next week, but it should only take about a day after that to finish.

Jim: Okay, that's good. How about answering this memo to Mr. Glenn and we'll have him up-to-date on this thing?

Bob: I already have. I saw the memo earlier and went on in and brought him up on how the project stands.

Jim: Did you get a copy of this too?

Bob: No, I saw yours and decided to save you time so I went ahead and answered his question.

Jim: You mean you got this out of my box?

Bob: Yeah, I saw it as I was coming to my desk and decided to go ahead and get it out of the way.

Jim: Oh, well I'll just hold on to this for awhile then.

Several days later, Jim and Bob were discussing one of Bob's new ideas and the discussion became very heated when Jim rejected the idea as too expensive, in both time and money.

Jim: And another thing, Bob, I don't want you going through my mail box again. What's in there is none of your business unless I assign it to you.

Bob: I was just trying to do you a favor and get the memo answered. If you don't want me to do that, then I won't.

Jim: You would have answered eventually, but I don't want you to do these things unless I tell you to. I'm in charge of the department and I have to know what's going on. That reminds me of another thing. From now on, you tell me about all of the projects you're working on. I don't want any more secret projects being worked on without my knowing it. I feel pretty stupid when Mr. Scott or Mr. Glenn asks me a question about something I've never even heard of. From now on, you tell me about your ideas, and if we can work it into the schedule we will; otherwise it will have to wait until we can get to it. This also means not going to Mr. Glenn with your ideas first, and then telling me that he thinks it's a good idea and should be developed. I'll approve the ideas first, and then we'll check with him if necessary.

Bob: I know you're talking about the new sleeve hemming stacker and I just happened to mention it to Mr. Glenn this morning at coffee break and he wanted to know more about it. I had to tell him about it when he asked.

Jim: That's right. In that case you couldn't have done anything else, but from now on make sure you've cleared these ideas with me before going to him.

Mark came into the office and the discussion was ended.

The following day, Bob and Mark were leaving the office together and Bob told Mark about his discussion with Jim.

Bob: Mark, I'm so mad at Jim I'd like to quit and walk out of here right now. I know darn well I could make more money somewhere else and wouldn't have to put up with Jim. You know what really gets me down is the thousands of dollars that I can prove I've saved the company, and I can't get a decent raise. I know Jim is making about $26,000 and I feel I'm worth as much as he is, but I do realize that they have to pay him more because he's a department head. However, he's not worth the amount of difference in our salaries. I feel I should be able to get at least $1,000 a year more than I'm getting now, but the "Book" won't allow that much of a raise at one time. And besides that, I'd feel more like putting out more for the company. As it is, I want to do my best, but it's hard to feel that way when you aren't fairly paid for your work.

Mark: You know what chance you've got of getting *that* kind of a raise! What started all of this anyway?

Bob: Well, I was telling Jim about my idea for the fronts presser and he turned it down, just like he's done most of my ideas.

Mark: Did he tell you *why* he turned it down?

Bob: 'Said it would be too expensive and would take too much time. Mark, it would save us a penny a dozen which would be about $5,000 a year; they're just time studies to try and satisfy some operator who doesn't really want to work.

Mark: I know. My projects are like that too, and he turned down my idea for revamping the boxing department. You know what a bottleneck that had been. My first estimate, which was conservative, was savings of $50,000 a year plus being able to get out our weekly production. We're not anywhere near the now and spending twice the amount of money we need to. This would also allow the warehouse to have half of the present boxing area. But, Jim says it can't be done because there would have to be too much coordination between departments, and that it would take someone with more authority than we have to make it work. I told him if we were to work up the proposal and send it to Mr. Scott, he couldn't pass up those savings on a system that's workable. Of course, you know how Scott hates to make decisions, but if Mr. Glenn knew about it, it would be our main project until it was installed. You know how he likes those dollar signs.

Bob: Yeah, I know. Jim doesn't seem to understand that these little projects don't save us any money and yet he turns down ideas that will save us thousands of dollars a year. You know he doesn't know anything about mechanical development. And besides that, when you try to explain something to him and he doesn't understand it, he says it won't work. But I know that he takes some of these ideas and mentions them to Mr. Scott and Mr. Glenn, and takes credit for them. I don't like that one little bit and I'm going to tell him so one of these days. Then, after telling me my idea for the fronts presser wasn't any good, he chewed me out for going through his mail box. That happened a couple of days ago. When I tried to do him a favor by answering a question Mr. Glenn had asked in a memo and he got all upset. He didn't know anything about it anyway, so what's the difference?

Mark: Well, do you think it was right to go through his mail?

Bob: Well, I just happened to see the subject of the memo and knew it was concerned with my project so I went ahead and answered the question. I didn't go through his mail; the memo was right on top and I just happened to see it on my way to my desk.

Mark: Yes, but you *did* get into his personal mail box, and went ahead without him knowing about it. Do you see what I mean, Bob? I mean he *is* the head of the department and he needs to know what goes on within the department.

Bob: But he doesn't have to know *everything* I'm working on. It's none of his business. Most of the things Ned and I do are our own ideas and he doesn't have a thing to do with them, he doesn't even understand them. Anyway, he told me he didn't want me working on any "secret" projects, that I was to tell him about all of my ideas before I did anything with them. Well, I'll tell you, I'm going ahead and do the projects he assigns me,

but I'm *still* going to work on my own ideas whenever I get a chance. Here comes Mr. Scott, I'll see you later.

After closing hours that night and after Bob had left, Jim and Mark were still in the office.

Jim: Mark, did Bob tell you about our little discussion yesterday afternoon?

Mark: He said you had a few words.

Jim: Bob's just getting too big for his own britches. If he doesn't like something I say or do he acts like a little child. Goes around pouting and gloomy for two or three days. He's just going to have to learn that he's not running the department, although I'm sure he feels he could do a better job than I'm doing. But the thing is that he can't take any criticism. Some of his ideas are good, but others are just too far out and we don't have the time for them. He's going to have to realize that we have other things to do besides mechanical development. I know a lot of our projects cost us more to carry out than can be saved in terms of dollars, but, if we can show an operator what is being done is right—or if it's wrong—admit the error and correct the situation, then that can be worth as much as saving several thousands of dollars a year. Although we are becoming increasingly automated, we have to remember that people are still our main source of production and that without their cooperation, we're out of business. Besides, mechanical development isn't even his job, but because he has had some good ideas I've let him work with Ned on them. I know he's sensitive, and that he is worth a lot to the company because some of his ideas are worthwhile, but if he doesn't change his ways, I'm going to have to talk to Mr. Glenn about letting him go. I've got to run this department and we can't do our best when he acts up like he does. ☐

CASE QUESTIONS

1. Should Bob be disciplined or punished for going through Jim's mail? Why?
2. Suppose that Jim decides to punish Bob for going through his personal mail. What approach should be used to make the punishment effective?
3. What role could Mr. Glenn have played when Bob came directly to him to respond to the memo?

⊇ HOW HIGH THE DOC?*

Lorraine Barret was head nurse of the operating room at Mountain View Hospital. She was experiencing some difficulties in scheduling scrub technicians and circulating registered nurses to certain surgery rooms. People who had been doing fine during one surgery had come to the nursing station during clearance of the operating room to ask to be relieved of their next surgery. They complained of feeling dizzy or just in need of a break. This often put the R.N. at the desk on the spot as she had difficulty replacing personnel in the middle of the day. Requests were always granted and the employees would break for fifteen minutes to an hour, and then ask to be reassigned.

After about two weeks of this, the problem was brought to Ms. Barret's attention, and she told the nurses to send all relief requests to her personally. Gary Roberts, a certified operating room technician who had been with the hospital for two years, was the first to come to her with a request.

Barret: Gary, what seems to be the problem?

Gary: Well, Ms. Barret, I just don't feel very good and I'd just like to lie down for a while.

Barret: If you don't feel good you'd better take the rest of the day off.

Gary: I don't think I need to do that.

Barret: Gary, can you tell me what's going on around here?

EXHIBIT 1

Organization Chart, Mountain View Hospital (185 activated beds)

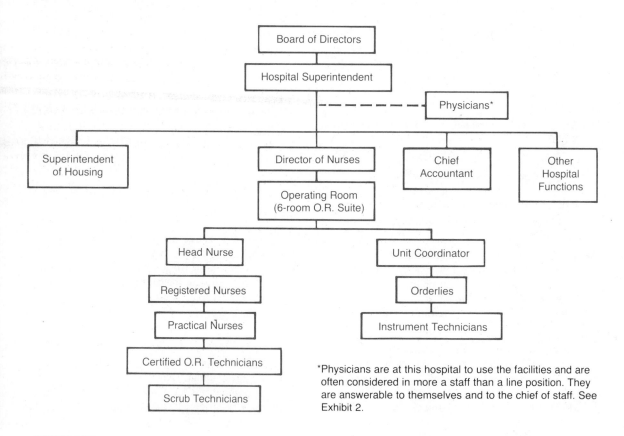

*Physicians are at this hospital to use the facilities and are often considered in more a staff than a line position. They are answerable to themselves and to the chief of staff. See Exhibit 2.

---

* This case was prepared by Professor Richard B. Chase of the College of Business Administration, University of Southern California.

EXHIBIT 2

**Organizational
Structure for
Physicians at
Mountain View
Hospital**

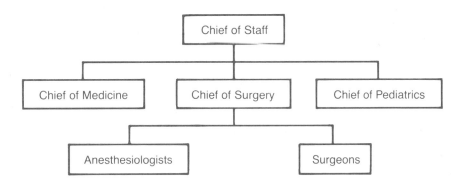

Gary: Well, most people just don't like to work for Dr. Collins. He's pretty slow and seems to be out of it most of the time.

Barret: Have you talked to Ms. Johnston, the circulating R.N., about this?

Gary: I've talked to her and Dr. Martin. Ms. Johnston gave me a hard time as usual. She says I am getting too big for my britches and if I don't like the situation I can ask for a transfer. Dr. Martin says that he's with Dr. Collins most of the time, and he looks fine to him.

Barret: Thank you, Gary, this will be kept confidential.

Ms. Barret went to ask Theresa Johnston to come in to see her. After four days without seeing her, Ms. Barret went to find her.

Barret: Theresa, I'd like to ask you some questions. I asked to see you four days ago.

Johnston: I have been trying to find time to see you.

Barret: I have some questions to ask you about Dr. Collins. Do you feel he's competent in surgery?

Johnston: As far as I know.

Barret: Have you ever seen him overly tired or not feeling well?

Johnston: Well, he did come in last week hung over, but that was an emergency. He was on call and had just been to a cocktail party the night before. That's what those techs are complaining about, isn't it?

Barret: How many times has this happened?

Johnston: Well, I don't know. But if Dr. Collins has any problems, Dr. Martin is always there to take over. I always circulate for him and I know my business. The techs are complaining because they don't like to be told what to do. They just can't take orders, and Dr. Collins gives it to them when they don't. They think just because they have been through a few cholecystectomies they can start questioning the doctors' and R.N.s' orders.

Barret: Thank you. Those are all the questions I have.

Two days later Gary Roberts gave his notice; he quit working three weeks later. Relief requests stopped coming in, but two other O.R. techs gave their notice. Absenteeism rose.

Ms. Barrett scheduled Ms. Johnston to work under another doctor and assigned Diane McEvers to circulate for Dr. Collins. Later that day, Ms. Barret went to visit the operating room where Dr. Collins was working. There she found Dr. Collins, head anesthesiologist Dr. Martin assisting, and Ms. Johnston circulating as usual. She asked where Ms. McEvers was, because she was scheduled for this surgery. She was informed by Dr. Martin that this operation could involve complications, and they needed an experienced circulator.

Barret: Dr. Martin, you have every right to request certain circulators. I would appreciate some notice before you tamper with room scheduling.

Martin: I am giving you notice that I would like to have Ms. Johnston circulate for me and Dr. Collins.

Barret: Due to some difficulties in scheduling, Ms. McEvers will circulate for you for the rest of the week. After that, if I have your request in writing, I will have no choice but to assign Ms. Johnston to you, scheduling problems or not.

Ms. McEvers worked out the week under the two doctors, and at the end of the week Ms. Barret asked to see her in her office to inquire into Dr. Collins' competence.

McEvers: I refuse to make waves here so I want this confidential. Dr. Collins often looks hung over in the morning when he does his patients pre-op. I wouldn't stand up in court and swear he had been drinking, but he sometimes smells of alcohol.

Barret: Have you ever inquired into his behavior?

McEvers: I asked Dr. Martin about it. He always has some story of Dr. Collins just being called in or not feeling up to par.

Later that week, Ms. Barret confronted Dr. Martin with this information.

Martin: Those are pretty serious charges you're leveling at Dr. Collins.

Barret: No one is accusing anybody of anything at this point.

Martin: What you're saying could have serious repercussions around here. If anyone got wind of this, it could look very bad, not only for us but for the profession and the hospital.

Barret: I am concerned here with the patients' safety.

Martin: No one is in danger. Ms. Johnston and I are always with him.

Barret: That isn't the point.

Martin: Take it to the chief of staff then, but let me give you some advice. You need some hard facts to make anything stick. You need the testimony of at least four nurses, and under the circumstances that might be hard to get. You might like to know Dr. Collins is retiring next year. ☐

CASE QUESTIONS

1. What is the problem?
2. What should Barret do to solve the problem?
3. Did Lorraine Barret act quickly enough to get to the problem in this case?

OCCUPATIONAL STRESS: AN INDIVIDUAL VIEW

LEARNING OBJECTIVES

DEFINE the terms stress and stressor.

DESCRIBE several of the more significant moderators and the role they play in the stress response.

DISCUSS a variety of individual approaches to managing stress.

COMPARE clinical with organizational approaches to stress management programs.

IDENTIFY several stressors associated with the physical environment and the individual, group, and organizational levels.

Interest in occupational stress has become widespread in recent years. However, the experience of stress is not new. Our cave-dwelling ancestors faced stress every time they left their caves and encountered their enemy, the saber-toothed tigers. The tigers of yesteryear are gone, but they have been replaced by other predators—work overload, a nagging boss, time deadlines, excessive inflation, poorly designed jobs, marital disharmony, the drive to keep up with the Joneses. These work and nonwork predators interact and create stress for individuals on and off the job.

This chapter focuses primarily on the individual at work in organizations and on the stress created in this setting. Much of the stress experienced by people in our industrialized society originates in organizations; much of the stress that originates elsewhere affects our behavior and performance in these same organizations.

In their article, "The Stress Concept in the Life Sciences," which accompanies this chapter, Richard Lazarus and Susan Folkman point out that interest in the stress concept has evolved from the 17th century to the present day. One of the issues Lazarus and Folkman address is the fact that stress has been defined in a multitude of ways. We begin this chapter with our definition of stress.

WHAT IS STRESS?

Stress means different things to many different people. The businessperson thinks of stress as frustration or emotional tension; the air traffic controller thinks of it as a problem of alertness and concentration; the biochemist thinks of it as a purely chemical event. In an uncomplicated way, it is best to consider stress as something that involves the interaction of the individual with the environment.[1] We define stress as:

> an adaptive response, mediated by individual differences and/or psychological processes, that is, a consequence of any external (environmental) action, situation, or event that places excessive psychological and/or physical demands on a person. This external action, event, or situation is known as a *stressor*.

The above working definition allows us to focus attention on specific environmental conditions that are potential sources of stress. Whether stress is felt or experienced by a particular individual will depend on that individual's

---

[1] John M. Ivancevich and Michael T. Matteson, *Stress at Work: A Managerial Perspective* (Glenview, Ill.: Scott, Foresman, 1980), p. 6.

unique characteristics. Furthermore, the definition emphasizes an *adaptive response*. The vast majority of our responses to stimuli in the work environment do not require adaptation and thus are not really potential sources of stress.

An important point to keep in mind is that a variety of dissimilar situations—work effort, fatigue, uncertainty, fear, emotional arousal—are capable of producing stress. Therefore, it is extremely difficult to isolate a single factor as the sole cause.[2]

THE GENERAL ADAPTATION SYNDROME

Stress includes both psychological and physiological components. Dr. Hans Selye, the pioneer of stress research, was the first to conceptualize the psychophysiological responses to stress.[3] Selye considered stress a nonspecific response to any demand made upon an organism. He labeled the three phases of the defense reaction that a person establishes when stressed as the **General Adaptation Syndrome (GAS).** Selye called the defense reaction *general* because stressors had effects on several areas of the body. *Adaptation* refers to a stimulation of defenses designed to help the body adjust to or deal with the stressors. And *syndrome* indicates that individual pieces of the reaction occur more or less together. The three distinct phases are called *alarm, resistance,* and *exhaustion.*

The *alarm stage* is the initial mobilization by which the body meets the challenge posed by the stressor. When a stressor is recognized, the brain sends forth a biochemical message to all of the body's systems. Respiration increases, blood pressure rises, pupils dilate, muscles tense up, and so forth.

If the stressor continues, the GAS proceeds to the *resistance stage.* Signs of being in the resistance stage include fatigue, anxiety, and tension. The person is now fighting the stressor. While resistance to a particular stressor may be. high during this stage, resistance to other stressors may be low. A person has only finite sources of energy, concentration, and ability to resist stressors. Individuals often are more illness-prone during periods of stress than at other times.[4]

The final GAS stage is *exhaustion.* Prolonged and continual exposure to the same stressor may eventually use up the adaptive energy available, and the system fighting the stressor becomes exhausted.

It is important to keep in mind that the activation of the GAS places extraordinary demands on the body. Clearly, the more frequently the GAS is activated and the longer it remains in operation, the more wear and tear there is on the psychophysiological mechanisms. The body and mind have limits. The more frequently a person is alarmed, resists, and becomes exhausted by work, nonwork, or the interaction of these activities, the more susceptible he or she becomes to fatigue, disease, aging and other negative consequences.

---

[2] Rita E. Numerof, *Managing Stress* (Rockville, Md.: Aspen Publications, 1983), p. 7.

[3] Hans Selye, *The Stress of Life* (New York: McGraw-Hill, 1976); and Hans Selye, *Stress without Distress* (Philadelphia, Pa.: J. B. Lippincott, 1974).

[4] Selye, *Stress without Distress,* p. 5.

STRESS AND WORK: A MODEL

For most employed individuals, work and work-related activities and preparation time represent more than a 40-hour-a-week commitment. Work is a major part of our lives, and work and nonwork activities are strongly interdependent. The distinction between stress at work and stress at home is an artificial one at best. Nonetheless, our main concern here is with stressors at work.

To better illustrate the link between stressors, stress, and consequences, we have developed an integrative model of stress and work. A managerial perspective is used to develop the parts of the model shown in Figure 6–1. The model divides stressors at work into four categories: physical, individual, group, and organizational. The model also presents five potential categories of the effects of stress. In this book, we are concerned primarily with the effects that influence job performance.

FIGURE 6–1

Stress and Work: A Working Model

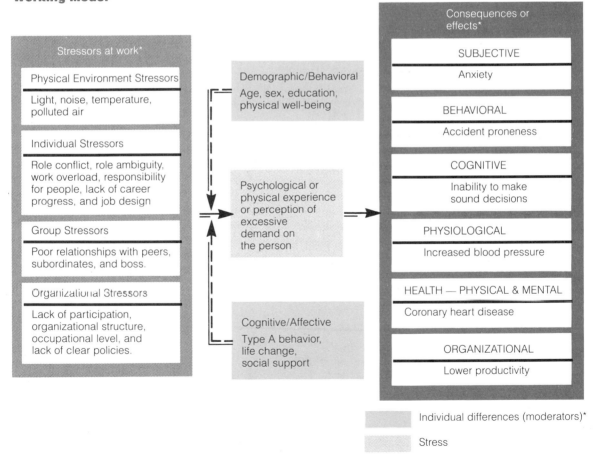

* Only some of these variables are discussed in this chapter. For a more complete discussion of these stressors and moderators, see John M. Ivancevich and Michael T. Matteson, *Stress and Work: A Managerial Perspective* (Glenview, Ill.: Scott, Foresman, 1980).

The model introduces *moderators*.[5] The moderator variables that have been investigated by occupational stress researchers include age, sex, work addiction, self-esteem, and community involvement. We have elected to discuss three moderators that have received the most research attention: Type A behavior pattern, social support, and life-change events. These are defined and explored later in this chapter.

CONSEQUENCES OF STRESS

The mobilization of the body's defense mechanisms are not the only potential consequences of contact with stressors. The effects of stress are many and varied. Some effects, of course, are positive, such as self-motivation, stimulation to work harder, and increased inspiration to live a better life. However, many effects of stress are disruptive and potentially dangerous. Cox has identified five potential consequences of the effects of stress.[6] His categories include:

Subjective Effects. Anxiety, aggression, apathy, boredom, depression, fatigue, frustration, loss of temper, low self-esteem, nervousness, feeling alone.

Behavioral effects. Accident proneness, alcoholism, drug abuse, emotional outbursts, excessive eating, excessive smoking, impulsive behavior, nervous laughter.

Cognitive effects. Inability to make sound decisions, poor concentration, short attention span, hypersensitivity to criticism, mental blocks.

Physiological effects. Increased blood glucose levels, increased heart rate and blood pressure, dryness of the mouth, sweating, dilation of pupils, hot and cold flashes.

Organizational effects. Absenteeism, turnover, low productivity, alienation from co-workers, job dissatisfaction, reduced organizational commitment and loyalty.

These five types are not all-inclusive, nor are they limited to effects on which there is universal agreement and for which there is clear scientific evidence. They merely represent some of the potential effects that frequently are associated with stress. It should not be inferred, however, that stress always causes the effects listed above.

Each of the five categories of stress effects shown in Figure 6–1 is important from a managerial perspective. In both human and monetary terms, the costs of stress are great and growing. Based on a variety of estimates and projections from government, industry, and health groups, we place the costs of stress at approximately $100 billion annually. This estimate, which probably is conservative, attempts to take into account the dollar effects of

---

[5] Robert R. Holt, "Occupational Stress," in *Handbook of Stress,* ed. L. Goldberger and S. Breznitz (New York: Free Press, 1982), pp. 419–44.

[6] T. Cox, *Stress* (Baltimore: University Park Press, 1978), p. 92.

reductions in operating effectiveness resulting from stress. These effects include poorer decision making and decreases in creativity. The huge figure also reflects the costs associated with mental and physical health problems arising from stress conditions, including hospital and medical costs, lost work time, turnover, sabotage, and a host of other variables that may contribute to stress costs.

PHYSICAL AND MENTAL HEALTH

Among the potential consequences of stress, those classified as physiological are perhaps the most controversial and organizationally dysfunctional. Those who hypothesize a link between stress and physical health problems are, in effect, suggesting that an emotional response is responsible for producing a physical change in an individual.[7] In fact, most medical textbooks attribute between 50 and 75 percent of illness to stress-related origins.[8]

Perhaps the most significant of the potential stress and physical illness relationships is that of coronary heart disease (CHD). Although virtually unknown in the industrialized world 60 years ago, CHD now accounts for half of all deaths in the United States. The disease is so pervasive that American males who are now between the ages of 45 and 55 have one chance in four of dying from a heart attack in the next 10 years.

Traditional risk factors such as obesity, smoking, heredity, high cholesterol, and high blood pressure can account for no more than about 25 percent of the incidence of coronary heart disease. There is growing medical opinion that job and life stress may be a major contributor in the remaining 75 percent.[9] For some individuals, the relationship between stress and CHD may be stronger than it is for others. The second article accompanying this chapter, ''The Hot Reactors,'' by Eliot and Breo, develops the notion of hot reactors and cold reactors and outlines an extremely interesting line of research. The research suggests that 20 percent of their sample respond to stress with *extreme* cardiovascular reactions.

Closely allied with the health consequences of stress are the mental health effects. Kornhauser studied extensively the mental health of industrial workers.[10] He did not find a relationship between mental health and such factors as salary, job security, and working conditions. Instead, clear associations between mental health and job satisfaction emerged. Poor mental health was associated with frustration growing out of not having a satisfying job.

In addition to frustration, the anxiety and depression that may be experienced by individuals under a great deal of stress may manifest itself in the form of alcoholism (about 5 percent of the adult population are problem drinkers), drug dependency (more than 150 million tranquilizer prescriptions are written in the United States annually), hospitalization (more than 25

---

[7] P. Astrand and K. Rodahl, *Textbook of Work Physiology* (New York: McGraw-Hill, 1970).

[8] M. H. Brenner, ''The Stressful Price of Prosperity,'' *Science News*, March 18, 1978, p. 166.

[9] David C. Glass, *Behavior Patterns, Stress, and Coronary Disease* (Hillsdale, N.J.: Erlbaum Associates, 1977), pp. 5–6.

[10] A. Kornhauser, *Mental Health of the Industrialized Worker* (New York: John Wiley & Sons, 1965).

percent of occupied hospital beds have people with psychological problems), and, in extreme cases, suicide.[11] Even the relatively minor mental disruptions produced by stress, such as the inability to concentrate or reduced problem-solving capabilities, may prove very costly to an organization.

Before we examine parts of the stress and work model in more detail, several caveats are in order. This model, or any model attempting to integrate stress and work phenomena, is not totally complete. There are so many important variables that a complete treatment would require much more space. Furthermore, the variables we discuss are offered only as ones that provide managerial perspectives on stress. They certainly are not the only appropriate variables to consider. Finally, accurate and reliable measurement is extremely important. Management-initiated programs to manage stress at optimal levels will depend on how well these and other variables are measured.[12]

PHYSICAL ENVIRONMENTAL STRESSORS

Physical environment stressors often are termed *blue-collar stressors* because they are more a problem in blue-collar occupations.[13] More than 14,000 workers die annually in industrial accidents (nearly 55 a day, or 7 people every working hour); more than 100,000 workers are permanently disabled every year; and employees report more than 5 million occupational injuries annually.[14] New estimates of the toll of workplace chemicals, radiation, heat stress, pesticides, and other toxic materials has led the National Institute of Occupational Safety and Health (NIOSH) to estimate that about 100,000 workers may die annually from industry-related diseases that could have been prevented.

Many blue-collar workers are nervous and stressed by the alleged health consequences of working in their present jobs. Since the passage in 1970 of the Occupational Safety and Health Act (OSHA), some of the stress experienced by individuals has been reduced. Gains can be traced to employers' increased acceptance of OSHA regulations. In addition, many unions enthusiastically support the act. Problems still exist, and management now is being held responsible by the courts for stress that is related to the physical and general work environment. The number of jury compensation awards is growing, and the court's role can be expected to become even more significant in the future.[15] The following OBM Encounter illustrates the increasing role being played both by courts and by workers' compensation boards in job stress cases.

---

[11] Herbert Peyser, "Stress and Alcohol," in *Handbook of Stress,* ed. L. Goldberger and S. Breznitz (New York: Free Press, 1982), p. 586.

[12] Roy Payne, Todd D. Jick, and Ronald J. Burke, "Whither Stress Research? An Agenda for the 1980s," *Journal of Occupational Behavior,* January 1982, pp. 131–45.

[13] Arthur B. Shostak, *Blue-Collar Stress* (Reading, Mass.: Addison-Wesley, 1980).

[14] Ibid., p. 19.

[15] John M. Ivancevich, Michael T. Matteson, and Edward Richards III, "Who's Liable for Stress on the Job?" *Harvard Business Review,* March-April 1985, pp. 60–72.

WHO'S LIABLE FOR STRESS ON THE JOB?

A law firm specializing in job-stress litigation recently has undertaken an advertising campaign which opens with this question: "Does your job make you sick?" Increasingly, employees are looking to workers' compensation boards or the civil courts to provide remuneration for alleged work-related stress and a variety of physical and mental health problems attributed to stressful job conditions. Consider the following cases in which employees won compensation:

1. A department store employee shot himself. His secretary went into a state of depression after finding him lying in a pool of blood. One year and $20,000 worth of psychiatrist bills later, she recovered. Insurance and workers' compensation refused to pay; civil court ruled in her favor.
2. A Raytheon Co. employee experienced a nervous breakdown when she learned she would be transferred to another department. A state supreme court ruled she was entitled to compensation, saying her breakdown was a "personal injury arising out of and in the course of . . . employment."
3. A Maine state trooper's duties involved cruising around a quiet, rural area. He became very depressed, however, because he was on call 24 hours a day. He claimed that because he never knew when the phone would ring, his sex life deteriorated. The state supreme court approved the officer's claim for total, permanent disability, but when the attorney general asked the court to reconsider, the trooper settled for $5,000.
4. A white sanitation supervisor in Louisville blamed his emotional problems on the stress associated with being forced to work with blacks. The state workers' compensation board awarded him maximum benefits and ordered the city to return him to an all-white job setting. □

Source: Based upon Joann Lublin, "On-The-Job Stress Leads Many Workers to File—And Win—Compensation Awards," *The Wall Street Journal,* September 17, 1980; and "Stress Claims Are Making Business Jumpy," *Business Week,* October 14, 1985.

INDIVIDUAL STRESSORS

Stressors at the individual level have been studied more than any other category presented in Figure 6–1. Role conflict is perhaps the most widely examined *individual stressor.*[16] *Role conflict* is present whenever compliance by an individual to one set of expectations about the job is in conflict with compliance to another set of expectations. Facets of role conflict include being torn by conflicting demands from a supervisor about the job, and being pressured to get along well with people with whom you are not compatible. Regardless of whether role conflict results from organizational policies or from other persons, it can be a significant stressor for some individuals. For example, a study at Goddard Space Flight Center determined that about 67 percent of employees reported some role conflict. The study further found that workers who suffered more role conflict had lower job satisfaction and higher job-related tension.[17] It is interesting to note that the researchers also

[16] Terry Beehr and Rabi Bhagat, *Human Stress and Cognitions in Organizations* (New York: John Wiley & Sons, 1985).

[17] R. L. Kahn, D. M. Wolfe, R. P. Quinn, J. D. Snoek, and R. A. Rosenthal, *Organizational Stress: Studies in Role Conflict and Ambiguity* (New York: John Wiley & Sons, 1964), p. 94.

found that the greater the power or authority of the people sending the conflicting role messages, the greater was the job dissatisfaction produced by role conflict.

In order to perform their jobs well, employees need certain information regarding what they are expected to do and not to do. Employees need to know their rights, privileges, and obligations. **Role ambiguity** is a lack of understanding about the rights, privileges, and obligations that a person has for doing the job. In the study at Goddard Space Flight Center, administrators, engineers, and scientists completed a role ambiguity stress scale. It was found that role ambiguity was significantly related to low job satisfaction and to feelings of job-related threat to one's mental and physical well-being. Furthermore, the more ambiguity a person reported, the lower was the person's utilization of intellectual skills, knowledge, and leadership skills.

Everyone has experienced *work overload* at one time or another. Overload may be of two different types: quantitative or qualitative. Having too many things to do or insufficient time to complete a job is *quantitative* overload. *Qualitative* overload, on the other hand, occurs when individuals feel that they lack the ability needed to complete their jobs or that performance standards are too high.

From a health standpoint, studies as far back as 1958 established that quantitative overload might cause biochemical changes, specifically, elevations in blood cholesterol levels.[18] One study examined the relationship of overload, underload, and stress among 1,540 executives of a major corporation. Those executives in the low and high ends of the stress ranges reported and had more significant medical problems. This study suggests that the relationship between stressors, stress, and disease may be curvilinear. That is, those who are underloaded and those who are overloaded represent two ends of a continuum, each with a significantly elevated number of medical problems.[19] The underload/overload continuum is presented in Figure 6–2. The optimal stress level provides the best balance of challenge, responsibility, and reward.

Any type of *responsibility* can be a burden for some people. Different types of responsibility apparently function differently as stressors. One way of categorizing this variable is in terms of responsibility for people versus responsibility for things. The intensive care unit nurse, the neurosurgeon, and the air traffic controller each have a high responsibility for people. One study found support for the hypothesis that responsibility for people contributes to job-related stress.[20] The more responsibility for people reported, the more likely the employee was to smoke heavily, have high blood pressure, and show elevated cholesterol levels. Conversely, the more responsibility for things the employee reported, the lower were these indicators.

---

[18] B. L. Margolis, W. M. Kroes, and R. P. Quinn, "Job Stress: An Untested Occupational Hazard," *Journal of Occupational Medicine,* October 1974, pp. 659–61.

[19] Clinton Weiman, "A Study of Occupational Stressors and the Incidence of Disease/Risk," *Journal of Occupational Medicine,* February 1977, pp. 119–22.

[20] John R. P. French and Robert D. Caplan, "Psychosocial Factors in Coronary Heart Disease," *Industrial Medicine,* September 1970, pp. 383–97.

FIGURE 6–2

**The Underload/
Overload
Continuum**

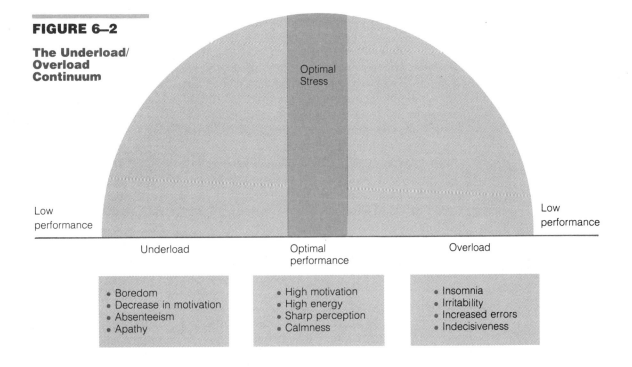

GROUP
STRESSORS

The effectiveness of any organization is influenced by the nature of the relations among groups. Many group characteristics can be powerful stressors for some individuals. A number of behavioral scientists have suggested that good relationships among the members of a work group are a central factor in individual well-being.[21] Poor relations include low trust, low supportiveness, and low interest in listening to and trying to deal with the problems that confront an employee.[22] Studies in this area have reached the same conclusion: mistrust of the persons one works with is positively related to high role ambiguity, which leads to inadequate communications among people and low job satisfaction.

ORGANIZATIONAL
STRESSORS

A problem in the study of organizational stressors is identifying which are the most important ones. Participation in decision making is considered an important part of working within organizations for some individuals. *Participation* refers to the extent that a person's knowledge, opinions, and ideas are included in the decision process. Participation can contribute to stress. Some people may be frustrated by the delays often associated with participative decision making. Others may view shared decision making as a threat to the traditional right of a supervisor or manager to have the final say.

---

[21] Chris Argyris, *Integrating the Individual and the Organization* (New York: John Wiley & Sons, 1964); and Cary L. Cooper, *Group Training and Organizational Development* (Basel, Switzerland: Karger, 1973).

[22] French and Caplan, "Psychosocial Factors."

Organizational structure is another stressor that rarely has been studied. One available study of trade salespersons examined the effects of tall (bureaucratically structured), medium, and flat (less rigidly structured) arrangements on job satisfaction, stress, and performance. It was determined that salespersons in the least bureaucratically structured arrangement experienced less stress and more job satisfaction and performed more effectively than did salespersons in the medium and tall structures.[23]

A number of studies have examined the relationship of organizational level to health effects. The majority of these studies suggest the notion that the risk of contracting such health problems as coronary heart disease increases with organizational level.[24] Not all researchers, however, support the notion that the higher one is in an organization hierarchy, the greater is the health risk. A study of Du Pont employees found that the incidence of heart disease was inversely related to salary level.[25]

The nature of the classifications used in these studies has contributed to the confusion of the results.[26] The trend now is to look in more detail at significant job components, as a way of explaining the effects of stress. Several studies, for example, have tried to assess whether inactivity or increased intellectual and emotional job demands contribute most to the increased risk of coronary heart disease. One early study contributed to this form of analysis in that it found that downtown bus drivers (sedentary jobs) and conductors (active jobs) had higher coronary heart disease than did their suburban counterparts.[27] More research is needed to determine whether emotional job demands are more powerful than inactivity in explaining the incidence of health problems.

We have considered only a very small sample of the tremendous amount of behavioral and medical research that is available on stressor, stress, and effects linkages. The information available, like other organizational research, is contradictory in some cases. However, what is available implies a number of important points. These points are:

1. There is a relationship between stressors at work and physical, psychological, and emotional changes in individuals.
2. The adaptive responses to stressors at work have been measured by self-rating, performance appraisals, and biochemical tests. Much more work must be done in properly measuring stress at work.

---

[23] John M. Ivancevich and James H. Donnelly, "Relation of Organizational Structure to Job Satisfaction, Anxiety-Stress, and Performance," *Administrative Science Quarterly*, June 1975, pp. 272–80.

[24] R. V. Marks, "Social Stress and Cardiovascular Disease," *Milbank Memorial Fund Quarterly*, April 1976, pp. 51–107.

[25] S. Pell and C. A. D'Alonzo, "Myocardial Infarction in a One-Year Industrial Study," *Journal of the American Medical Association*, June 1958, pp. 332–37.

[26] Cary L. Cooper and Judi Marshall, "Occupational Sources of Stress: A Review of the Literature Relating to Coronary Heart Disease and Mental Ill Health," *Journal of Occupational Psychology*, March 1976, pp. 11–28.

[27] J. N. Morris et al., "Coronary Heart Disease and Physical Activity at Work: Coronary Heart Disease in Different Occupations," *Lancet*, October 1953, pp. 1053–57.

3. There is no universally acceptable list of stressors. Each organization has its own unique set that should be examined.

4. Individual differences explain why the same stressor that is disruptive and unsettling to one person is challenging to another person.

MODERATORS

Stressors evoke different responses from different people. Some individuals are better able to cope with a stressor than others. They can adapt their behavior in such a way as to meet the stressor head-on. On the other hand, some individuals are predisposed to stress; that is, they are not able to adapt to the stressor.

The model presented in Figure 6–1 suggests that various factors moderate the relationship between stressors and stress. A moderator is a condition, behavior, or characteristic that qualifies the relationship between two variables. The effect may be to intensify or weaken the relationship. The relationship between the number of gallons of gasoline used and total miles driven, for example, is affected by the variable speed (a moderator). Likewise, an individual's personality may moderate or affect the extent to which that individual experiences stress as a consequence of being in contact with a particular stressor. We will briefly examine three of many possible moderators: (1) Type A Behavior Pattern (TABP); (2) Social Support; and (3) life-change events.

TYPE A BEHAVIOR PATTERN (TABP)

Cardiovascular disease is the leading cause of death in the United States. Nearly 1 million Americans die of cardiovascular disease each year, and more than 40 million Americans are afflicted with some form of the disease.[28]

In the 1950s, two medical cardiologists and researchers, Meyer Friedman and Ray Rosenman, discovered what they called the **Type A Behavior Pattern** (TABP).[29] They searched the medical literature and found that traditional coronary risk factors such as dietary cholesterol, blood pressure, and heredity could not totally explain or predict coronary heart disease (CHD). Coronary heart disease is the term given to cardiovascular diseases that are characterized by an inadequate supply of oxygen to the heart. Other factors seemed to the two researchers to be playing a major role in CHD. Through interviews with, and observation of patients, they began to uncover a pattern of behavior or traits. They eventually called this the Type A Behavior Pattern (TABP).

The person with TABP has these characteristics:

• Chronically struggles to get as many things done as possible in the shortest time period.

• Is aggressive, ambitious, competitive, and forceful.

---

[28] Virginia A. Price, *Type A Behavior Pattern* (New York: Academic Press, 1982), p. 3.

[29] Meyer Friedman and Diane Ulmer, *Treating Type A Behavior and Your Heart* (New York: Alfred A. Knopf, 1984).

- Speaks explosively, rushes others to finish what they are saying.
- Is impatient, hates to wait, considers waiting a waste of precious time.
- Is preoccupied with deadlines and is work-oriented.
- Is always in a struggle with people, things, events.

The converse, Type B individual mainly is free of the TABP characteristics and generally feels no pressing conflict with either time or persons. The Type B may have considerable drive, wants to accomplish things, and works hard. The Type B has a confident style that allows him or her to work at a steady pace and not to race against the clock. The Type A has been likened to a racehorse, the Type B to a turtle.

Since the early work of Friedman and Rosenman on TABP, a number of studies have found it to be a significant predictor of premature CHD.[30] In fact, recent literature reviews and studies suggest strongly that Type A individuals have approximately twice the risk of developing CHD as Type B individuals.[31] Furthermore, this doubled CHD risk factor for Type A persons is independent of the influence of the traditional coronary risk factors. The verdict is not unanimous, however; a recent study failed to find significant differences between Type As and Bs.[32]

Susceptible Type A Individuals.   Research is being conducted to determine which individual differences are associated with Type A tendencies. There are some indications that TABP is associated with age. In one study of males and females, it was found that the older half of the sample had lower mean Type A scores.[33] In a similar study, the 36-to 55-year-old group had the strongest Type A tendencies.[34]

Some research has found that TABP is more prevalent in males than in females.[35] However, as more women enter the work force and move into nontraditional roles for females (e.g., top-level management, project directors, research engineers, legal counsel), it is expected that TABP will become increasingly common among women. Even today, studies show that there

---

[30] For a thorough review and appraisal, see Karen A. Matthews, "Psychological Perspectives on the Type A Behavior Pattern," *Psychological Bulletin,* March 1982, pp. 293–323; and Michael T. Matteson and John M. Ivancevich, "The Coronary-Prone Behavior Pattern: A Review and Appraisal," *Social Science and Medicine,* July 1980, pp. 337–51.

[31] Ibid., p. 343.

[32] Robert Case and the Multicenter Post-Infarction Research Group, "Type A Behavior and Survival after Acute Myocardial Infarction," *New England Journal of Medicine,* March 21, 1985.

[33] M. A. Chesney and R. H. Rosenman, "Type A Behavior in the Work Setting," in *Current Concerns in Occupational Stress,* ed. C. Cooper and R. Payne (New York: John Wiley & Sons, 1980), pp. 187–212.

[34] J. H. Howard, D. A. Cunningham, and P. A. Rechnitzer, "Work Patterns Associated with Type A Behavior: A Managerial Population," *Human Relations,* September 1977, pp. 825–36.

[35] I. Waldron, "The Coronary-Prone Behavior Pattern, Blood Pressure, and Socio-Economic Studies in Women," *Journal of Psychosomatic Research,* March 1978, pp. 79–87.

is a strong association between TABP in women and the onset of coronary heart disease.[36]

The accumulated evidence at this point suggests strongly that managers attempting to manage stress should include TABP in their assessments. Failure to include TABP would ignore some of the better interdisciplinary research (behavioral and medical) that has been conducted over the past 25 years. Of all the moderators that could or should be included in a stress model, TABP seems to be one of the most promising for additional consideration.

Some evidence suggests that a Type A individual can "unlearn" Type A behaviors. This is of potential importance if the unlearning is accompanied by a reduction in CHD risk. The following OBM Encounter summarizes what has been done in this area.

 ENCOUNTER

ONCE A TYPE A, ALWAYS A TYPE A?

Does a Type A individual necessarily have to remain always a Type A? Not according to Dr. Meyer Friedman, one of the discoverers of the TABP and director of the Recurrent Coronary Prevention Project (RCPP) at the Harold Brunn Institute of Mount Zion Hospital and Medical Center in San Francisco. Dr. Friedman recruited more than a thousand men and women—each of whom had suffered at least one heart attack—to participate in the RCPP. The study was aimed at answering two questions: Can the TABP be modified, and if so, would such modification offer protection against another heart attack? Based on project results, the answer to both questions is yes. Not only did most participants who received counseling succeed in changing their behavior pattern, but they also cut their heart attack rate by 50 percent.

The RCPP program to modify Type A behavior is extensive and involves rigid adherence to a number of daily drills which the participant engages in to bring about behavior change in three major categories: (1) alleviating a sense of time urgency; (2) getting rid of free-floating hostility; (3) and disposing of self-destruct tendencies. Taken together, the purpose of the drills essentially is to reorient how one views and participates in life. Attempting such major behavioral changes is very difficult, but presumably, the motivation to do so is the strongest and most basic of all: survival.

While the RCPP is a very large, longitudinal project, it is important that the results obtained be replicated by other investigators in other settings before firm conclusions can be drawn regarding the modification of TABP. In the meantime, however, these results are very encouraging. ☐

Source: Based, in part, upon the book by Meyer Friedman and Diane Ulmer, *Treating Type A Behavior and Your Heart.* New York: Alfred A. Knopf, 1984.

[36] Chesney and Rosenman, "Type A Behavior."

**SOCIAL
SUPPORT**

Numerous literature reviews link social support with many aspects of health, illness, and quality of life.[37] The literature offers a number of definitions of social support. Some of these definitions focus on the exchange of information or material, the availability of a confidant, and gratification of basic social needs. **Social support** is defined as the comfort, assistance, or information that one receives through formal or informal contacts with individuals or groups.[38] This definition would apply to a co-worker listening to a friend who failed to receive a desired promotion, a group of recently laid-off workers helping each other find new employment, or an experienced employee helping a new hiree learn a job.

Social support has been operationalized as the number of people one interacts with, the frequency of contact with other individuals, or the individual's perceptions about the adequacy of interpersonal contact. The limited amount of research using these factors suggests that social support protects or buffers individuals from the negative consequences of stressors. One study showed significant interactions of social support and work stress for factory workers. The support of co-workers moderated the relationship between role conflict and health complaints.[39] The higher the level of social support reported, the fewer were the health complaints reported.

The best evidence to date on the importance of social support derives from the literature on rehabilitation, recovery, and adaptation to illness.[40] For example, better outcomes have been found in alcohol treatment programs when the alcoholic's family is supportive and cohesive.[41] Managerial use of social support research in reducing stress will be expanded as more organizationally based research is conducted.[42]

**LIFE-CHANGE
EVENTS**

Common sense holds that when individuals undergo extremely stressful changes in their lives, their personal health likely will suffer at some point. Research work on this intriguing proposition was initiated by Holmes and Rahe.[43] Their work led to the development of the Schedule of Recent Life Events, of which a later version was titled the Social Readjustment Rating Scale (SRRS). Through research and analysis, Holmes and Rahe weighted

---

[37] R. D. Caplan, "Patient, Provider, and Organization: Hypothesized Determinants of Adherence," *New Directions in Patient Compliance*, ed. S. J. Cohen (Lexington, Mass.: D. C. Heath, 1979); and W. B. Carveth and B. H. Gottleib, "The Measurement of Social Support and Its Relation to Stress," *Canadian Journal of Behavioral Science*, July 1979, pp. 179–88.

[38] Barbara S. Wallston, Sheryle W. Alagna, Brenda M. DeVellis, and Robert F. DeVellis, "Social Support and Physical Health," *Health Psychology*, Fall 1983, pp. 367–91.

[39] J. M. LaRocco, J. S. House, and J. R. P. French, "Social Support, Occupational Stress, and Health," *Journal of Health and Social Behavior,* June 1980, pp. 202–18.

[40] R. E. Mitchell, A. G. Billings, and R. H. Moos, "Social Support and Well Being: Implications for Prevention Programs," *Journal of Primary Prevention,* February 1982, pp. 77–98; and E. L. Cowen, "Help is Where You Find It: Four Informal Helping Groups," *American Psychologist,* April 1982, pp. 385–95.

[41] Benjamin H. Gottlieb, *Social Support Strategies* (Beverly Hills, Calif.: Sage Publications, 1983).

[42] James J. House, *Work Stress and Social Support* (Reading, Mass.: Addison-Wesley, 1981).

[43] T. H. Holmes and R. H. Rahe, "Social Readjustment Scale," *Journal of Psychosomatic Research*, 1967, pp. 213–18.

the SRRS. An individual is asked to indicate which of the listed events has happened to him or her in the past 12 months. The SRRS appears in this chapter as 6D-4.

Holmes and Rahe found that individuals reporting **life change units** totaling 150 points or less generally had good health the following year. However, those reporting life change units totaling between 150 and 300 points had about a 50 percent chance of developing a serious illness the following year. And, among individuals scoring 300 or more points, there was at least a 70 percent chance of contracting a major illness the following year.

The relationships found between life-change event scores and personal health problems have not been overwhelming.[44] The correlations in most studies between the total score and major health problems the following year have been relatively low.[45] Of course, many individuals who are exposed to many life changes show absolutely no subsequent health problems. That is, they are hardy enough to withstand the consequences of life changes.

Kobasa proposed that individuals who experienced high life-change unit scores without becoming ill might differ, in terms of personality, from individuals who had subsequent health problems.[46] She refers to the personality characteristic as "hardiness." The individuals with the hardiness personality seem to possess three important characteristics. First, they believe that they can control the events they encounter. Second, they are extremely committed to the activities in their lives. Third, they treat change in their lives as a challenge.

In a longitudinal study to test the three-characteristic theory of hardiness, managers were studied over a two-year period. It was determined that the more managers possessed hardiness characteristics, the smaller was the negative impact of life change units on their personal health.[47] Hardiness appeared to buffer the negative impact of life changes.

Some investigators feel that while major life-change events may be important, the small, ordinary kinds of events which we are more likely to experience on a day-to-day basis are perhaps of even greater significance. The following OBM Encounter details one such approach.

ENCOUNTER

HASSLES AND UPLIFTS

Frequently, the major source of stress in people's lives is the combination of somewhat triv-

ial daily "hassles" rather than a major event, according to Richard Lazarus. Lazarus contends there is evidence that little hassles which plague people every day may be more injurious to mental and physical health than major, trau-

---

[44] Scott M. Monroe, "Major and Minor Life Events as Predictors of Psychological Distress: Further Issues and Findings," *Journal of Behavioral Medicine,* June 1983, pp. 189–205.

[45] David V. Perkins, "The Assessment of Stress Using Life Events Scales," in *Handbook of Stress,* eds. L. Goldberger and S. Breznitz (New York: Free Press, 1982), pp. 320–31.

[46] S. C. Kobasa, "Stressful Life Events, Personality, and Health: An Inquiry into Hardiness," *Journal of Personality and Social Psychology,* January 1979, pp. 1–11.

[47] S. C. Kobasa, S. R. Maddi, and S. Kahn, "Hardiness and Health: A Prospective Study," *Journal of Personality and Social Psychology,* January 1982, pp. 168–77.

matic events. In fact, it is the small troubles at home that carry over and create stress at work. The assertions by Lazarus are based on a study in which middle-class, middle-aged men and women kept track of their "hassles" and "uplifts"—small positive events which might offset hassles—over a one-year period. The top 10 in descending order of frequencies were as follows:

Hassles
1. Concern about weight
2. Health of a family member
3. Rising prices
4. Home maintenance
5. Too many things to do
6. Misplacing or losing things
7. Yard work
8. Property, investment or taxes
9. Crime
10. Physical appearance

Uplifts
1. Relating well with spouse or lover
2. Relating well with friends
3. Completing a task
4. Feeling healthy
5. Getting enough sleep
6. Eating out
7. Meeting responsibilities
8. Visiting, phoning or writing someone
9. Spending time with family
10. Home pleasing to you

Source: Based on the article by Richard Lazarus, "Little Hassles Can be Hazardous to Your Health," *Psychology Today*, July 1981, pp. 58–62.

ORGANIZATIONAL PROGRAMS TO MANAGE STRESS

An astute manager never ignores a turnover or absenteeism problem, workplace drug abuse, a decline in performance, reduced quality in production, or any other sign that the organization's performance goals are not being met. The effective manager, in fact, views these occurrences as symptoms and looks beyond them to identify and correct the underlying causes. Yet most managers today likely will search for traditional causes such as poor training, defective equipment, or inadequate instructions on what needs to be done. In all likelihood, stress is not on the list of possible problems. Thus, the very first step in any program to manage stress so that it remains within tolerable limits is recognition that it exists. Any intervention program to manage stress first must determine whether stress exists and what is contributing to its existence.

Some programs indicate the specific problem on which they are focused: alcohol or drug abuse program, job relocation program, career counseling program, and so forth. Others are more general: the Emotional Health Program of Equitable Life, the Employee Assistance Center at B. F. Goodrich, the Illinois Bell Health Evaluation Program, and the Caterpillar Tractor Special Health Services.[48]

Originally, labels such as mental health were used. However, to get away from the connotation of serious psychiatric disease, companies have changed

---

[48] Andrew J. J. Brenna, "Worksite Health Promotion Can Be Cost Effective," *Personnel Administrator*, April 1983, pp. 39–42.

the names of their programs. Today, a popular name is stress management, and two prototypes of stress-management programs appear to be in use: clinical and organizational. The former is initiated by the firm and focuses on individual problems. The latter deals with units or groups in the work force and focuses on problems of the group or the total organization.

Clinical Programs. These programs are based on the traditional medical approach to treatment. Some of the elements in the programs include:

Diagnosis. Person with problem asks for help. Person or people in employee health unit attempt to diagnose problem.

Treatment. Counseling or supportive therapy is provided. If staff within company can't help, employee is referred to professionals in community.

Screening. Periodic examination of individuals in highly stressful jobs is provided to detect early indications of problems.

Prevention. Education and persuasion are used to convince employees at high risk that something must be done to help them cope with stress.

Clinical programs must be staffed by competent personnel if they are to provide benefits. The trust and respect of users must be earned. This is possible only if a qualified staff exists to provide diagnosis, treatment, screening, and prevention.

Organizational Programs. Organizational programs are aimed more broadly at an entire employee population. They are sometimes extensions of the clinical program. Often they are stimulated by problems identified in a group or a unit or by some impending change such as the relocation of a plant, the closing of a plant, or the installation of new equipment. Such programs are found in IBM, Dow Chemical, Control Data, and Equitable Life.

A variety of programs can be used to manage work stress. Included in a list of such organizational programs would be management by objectives, organizational development programs, job enrichment, redesigning the structure of the organization, establishing autonomous work groups, establishing variable work schedules, and providing employee health facilities. For example, such companies as Xerox, Rockwell International, Weyerhaeuser, and Pepsi-Cola are spending thousands of dollars for gyms equipped with treadmills, exercise bicycles, jogging tracks, and full-time physical education and health care staffs. One of the more impressive programs is found at Kimberly-Clark, where $2.5 million has been invested in a 7,000-square-foot health testing facility and a 32,000-square-foot physical fitness facility staffed by 15 full-time health care personnel.[49]

---

[49] Ivancevich and Matteson, *Stress at Work*, p. 215.

INDIVIDUAL APPROACHES TO STRESS

There are also many individual approaches to managing stress. To see this, all you have to do is visit any bookstore and look at the self-improvement section. It will be stocked with numerous "how to do it" books for reducing stress. We have selected only a few of the more popularly cited methods for individually managing stress. They have been selected because (1) some research is available on their impact, (2) they are widely cited in both the scientific literature and the popular press, and (3) scientifically sound evaluations of their effectiveness are under way.

RELAXATION

Just as stress is an adaptive response of the body, there is also an adaptive antistress response, "a relaxation response."[50] Benson reports that, in this response, muscle tension decreases, heart rate and blood pressure decrease, and breathing slows.[51] The stimuli necessary to produce relaxation include *(a)* a quiet environment, *(b)* closed eyes, *(c)* a comfortable position, and *(d)* a repetitive mental device.

MEDITATION

Transcendental meditation, or TM, is a form of meditation that has attracted many individuals. Its originator, Maharishi Mahesh Yogi, defines TM as turning the attention toward the subtler levels of thought until the mind transcends the experience of the subtlest state of thought and arrives at the source of thought.[52]

The basic procedure used in TM is simple, but the effects claimed for it are extensive. One simply sits comfortably with closed eyes and engages in the repetition of a special sound (a mantra) for about 20 minutes twice a day. Studies available indicate that TM practices are associated with reduced heart rate, lowered oxygen consumption, and decreased blood pressure.[53]

BIOFEEDBACK

Individuals can be taught to control a variety of internal body processes by using a technique called biofeedback. In biofeedback, small changes occurring in the body or brain are detected, amplified, and displayed to the person. Sophisticated recording and computer technology makes it possible for a person to attend to subtle changes in heart rate, blood pressure, temperature, and brain-wave patterns that normally would be unobservable.[54] Most of these processes are affected by stress.

The ongoing biological processes are made available to the individual by the feedback that he or she receives. The person is able to monitor what is biologically occurring. The ability to gain insight and eventual control over one's bodily processes can lead to significant changes.

---

[50] Herbert Benson, *The Relaxation Response* (New York: William Morrow, 1975).

[51] Herbert Benson and Robert L. Allen, "How Much Stress is Too Much?" *Harvard Business Review,* September-October 1980, p. 88.

[52] P. Carrington, *Freedom in Meditation* (New York: Anchor Press, 1978).

[53] D. Kuna, "Meditation and Work," *Vocational Guidance Quarterly,* June 1975, pp. 342–46.

[54] Philip G. Zimbardo, *Psychology and Life* (Glenview, Ill.: Scott, Foresman, 1979), p. 551.

Despite the results of some generally well-designed research studies, individuals using biofeedback devices must remain cautious. It is unlikely that the average employee could alter any biological process without proper training.

SUMMARY OF KEYPOINTS

A. As individuals, we establish a defense reaction to stress. This reaction is termed the General Adaptation Syndrome (GAS). The three phases of GAS are alarm, resistance, and exhaustion.

B. The consequences of stress are numerous and can be classified as subjective, behavioral, cognitive, physiological, health, and organizational.

C. Stressors are external actions, events or situations that are potentially, but not necessarily, harmful to individuals. One way to classify stressors at work is on the basis of the physical environment, at the individual level, group level, and organizational level.

D. Stressors at work evoke different responses from different people. Figure 6–1 shows a number of moderators of the stressor-stress and stress-effects relationships.

E. Three publicized and scientifically studied moderators are the Type A Behavior Pattern (TABP), social support, and life-change events.

F. Considerable research based on medical and behavioral science suggests that TABP is associated with coronary heart disease. There are, however, some nonsupportive findings, as well.

G. Numerous programs initiated and sponsored by organizations are available for managing work-related stress. Most of these programs may be characterized as being either clinical or organizational in nature.

H. Individual intervention programs for managing stress are numerous. The more promising programs of this kind include relaxation, meditation, and biofeedback.

REVIEW AND DISCUSSION QUESTIONS

1. It has been suggested that "stress is in the eyes of the beholder." What does this mean? Do you agree with it?

2. The issue of who should be responsible for dealing with work stress—the individual or the organization—is an important one. What do you think? What are the arguments for and against each position?

3. What is the relationship between work stress and work motivation? If we could eliminate all stress, what effect would this have on motivation? Explain.

4. Figure 6–1 suggests that there are several levels of work stressors. The same figure indicates a number of different consequences. Are certain stressors more or less associated with certain consequences? Explain.

5. Other than for humanitarian reasons, why should organizations be concerned about the physical and mental health consequences of work stress?

6. While there are a few exceptions, unions for the most part have not been receptive to, or supportive of, stress management programs. Why do you think this is the case? As a manager, how would you go about obtaining a union's cooperation in an organizationally sponsored stress management program?

7. Work underload may be every bit as dysfunctional as work overload. Can you think of other work variables where "too little" may be as counterproductive as "too much"?

8. Chapter 3 examined several personality characteristics or traits. How might those act as moderators of the stress-stressor relationship? What other aspects of personality might serve as moderators?

9. Many different aspects of one's life may contribute to the formation and maintenance of Type A behavior. Discuss how each of the following might contribute: the work environment; school; television; home life as a child.

10. Of the individual approaches to managing stress discussed in this chapter, which one appeals to you the most? Which one the least? Explain.

R 1 THE STRESS CONCEPT IN THE LIFE SCIENCES

RICHARD S. LAZARUS AND SUSAN FOLKMAN

It is virtually impossible today to read extensively in any of the biological or social sciences without running into the term *stress*. The concept is even more extensively discussed in the health care fields, and it is found as well in economics, political science, business, and education. At the popular level, we are flooded with messages about how stress can be prevented, managed, and even eliminated.

No one can say for sure why interest in stress has gained such widespread public attention. It is fashionable to attribute this to rapid social change (e.g., Toffler, 1970), to growing anomie in an industrial society in which we have lost some of our sense of identity and our traditional anchors and meaning (Tuchman, 1978), or to growing affluence, which frees many people from concerns about survival and allows them to turn to a search for a higher quality of life.

The issues encompassed by the concept of stress are certainly not new. Cofer and Appley (1964) wisely pointed out some years ago that the term stress ". . . has all but preempted a field previously shared by a number of other concepts. . ." (p. 441), including anxiety, conflict, frustration, emotional disturbance, trauma, alienation, and anomie. Cofer and Appley went on to say, "It is as though, when the word stress came into

vogue, each investigator, who had been working with a concept he felt was closely related, substituted the word stress . . . and continued in his same line of investigation" (p. 449).

As with many words, the term *stress* antedates its systematic or scientific use. It was used as early as the 14th century to mean hardship, straits, adversity, or affliction (cf. Lumsden, 1981). In the late 17th century Hooke (cited in Hinkle, 1973, 1977) used stress in the context of the physical sciences, although this usage was not made systematic until the early 19th century. "Load" was defined as an external force; "stress" was the ratio of the internal force (created by load) to the area over which the force acted; and "strain" was the deformation or distortion of the object (Hinkle, 1977).

The concepts of stress and strain survived, and in 19th century medicine they were conceived as a basis of ill health. As an example, Hinkle (1977) cites Sir William Osler's comments on the Jewish businessman:

> Living an intense life, absorbed in his work, devoted to his pleasures, passionately devoted to his home, the nervous energy of the Jew is taxed to the uttermost, and his system is subjected to that stress and strain which seems to be a basic factor in so many cases of angina pectoris. (p. 30)

Here, in effect, is an old version of the current concept of the Type A personality—hardly limited, incidentally, to any ethnic group—with a special vulnerability to cardiovascular disease. Some years later, Walter Cannon (1932), who gave

much research vitality to the physiology of emotion, considered stress a disturbance of homeostasis under conditions of cold, lack of oxygen, low blood sugar, and so on. Although he used the term somewhat casually, he spoke of his subjects as "under stress" and implied that the degree of stress could be measured.

By 1936, Hans Selye was using the term stress in a very special, technical sense to mean an orchestrated set of bodily defenses against any form of noxious stimulus (including psychological threats), a reaction that he called the General Adaptation Syndrome. Stress was, in effect, not an environmental demand (which Selye called a "stressor"), but a universal physiological set of reactions and processes created by such a demand. In the early 1950s Selye published an *Annual Report of Stress* (1950, 1951–1956) on his research. This work was pulled together in 1956 in a major book called *The Stress of Life*. By that time, the literature on the physiology of stress had already amounted to nearly six thousand publications a year (Appley & Trumbull, 1967). An invited address by Selye to the American Psychological Association in 1955 also helped spread interest in the concept from physiology to psychology and other behavioral sciences. Although the enormous volume of work on hormonal stress secretions that stemmed from Selye's work had obvious implications at the sociological and psychological levels of analysis, it did not actually clarify the latter processes. Nonetheless, Selye's work and its spinoffs have played a dominant role in the recent expansion of interest in stress.

Source: From Richard S. Lazarus and Susan Folkman, *Stress, Appraisal, and Coping* (New York: Springer Publishing Co., 1985), pp. 1–10.

LEARNING CHECKPOINT

What are the three stages in Selye's General Adaptation Syndrome?

Hinkle (1977) also accords an important role in the evolution of the stress concept in medicine to Harold G. Wolff, who wrote about life stress and disease in the 1940s and 1950s (e.g., Wolff, 1953). Like Selye and Cannon, who conceived of stress as a reaction of an organism besieged by environmental demands and noxious agents, Wolff appears to have regarded stress as a state of the body, although he never tried to define it systematically, as Selye did. He wrote (as cited in Hinkle, 1973, p. 31):

> I have used the word [stress] in biology to indicate that state within a living creature which results from the interaction of the organism with noxious stimuli or circumstances, i.e., it is a dynamic state within the organism; it is not a stimulus, assault, load, symbol, burden, or any aspect of environment, internal, external, social or otherwise.

This emphasis by Wolff on a "dynamic state" involving adaptation to demands, and by Selye on an orchestrated physiological response pattern, is important for several reasons. First, the term stress as used in the physical sciences refers to an inactive or passive body that is deformed (strained) by environmental loads. However, in the biological usage, stress is an active process of "fighting back"; the living body engages in adaptational efforts crucial to the maintenance or restoration of equilibrium, a concept derived from the French physiologist Claude Bernard (1815–1878) and based on his discovery of the sugar-storing

functions of the liver. Second, stress as a biological process of defense offers an interesting analogy to the psychological process we shall later call "coping," in which a person struggles to manage psychological stress. Third, the concept of a dynamic state points us toward important aspects of stress processes that might otherwise be missed, such as the resources available for coping, their costs, including disease and distress, and their benefits, including growth of competence and the joy of triumph against adversity. Finally, when one views stress as a dynamic state, attention is turned toward the ongoing relationship between the organism and the environment, and interplay and feedback. With a dynamic formulation we are less likely to settle for incomplete and inadequate definitions of stress that are based solely on what is happening within the organism.

We should also be aware of what was occurring during this period in relation to stress in sociology and psychology. Sociologists Marx, Weber, and Durkheim wrote extensively about "alienation." Durkheim (1893) viewed alienation as a condition of anomie that arises when people experience the lack or loss of acceptable norms to guide their efforts to achieve socially prescribed goals. To speak of powerlessness, meaninglessness, normlessness, isolation, and self-estrangement, which Seeman (1959, 1971) regards as the five variants of the concept of alienation (see also Kanungo, 1979; McClosky & Schaar, 1965), is clearly to place alienation under the general rubric of stress.

More contemporary sociologists have tended to prefer the term strain rather than stress, using it to mean forms of social disruption or disorganization analogous to Wolff's view of stress in an individ-

ual as a disturbed state of the body. Riots, panics, and other social disturbances such as increased incidence of suicide, crime, and mental illness are consequences of stress (strain) at the social level; they refer to group phenomena rather than to phenomena at the individual psychological level. There is often an overlap, however, between stress in sociology and psychology that is well illustrated by Smelser's (1963) sociological analysis of collective behavior (panic, riot, etc.) and the research literature on natural disaster (Baker & Chapman, 1962; Grosser, Wechsler, & Greenblatt, 1964). Other examples include Lucas's (1969) study of a coal mine disaster, Mechanic's (1978) studies of students facing examination stress, Radloff and Helmreich's (1968) study of the group stress effects of working and living under water, and studies of organizational stress (Kahn, Wolfe, Quinn, Snoek, & Rosenthal, 1964). The borderline between sociological and psychological thought becomes exceedingly difficult to draw in these instances. In addition, the terminology used is chaotic, with stress (or strain) sometimes the agent and sometimes the response. Whatever language is employed, such research surely falls within the field of stress and is part of its recent history.

On the strictly individual psychological side, stress was, for a long time, implicit as an organizing framework for thinking about psychopathology, especially in the theorizing of Freud and later psychodynamically oriented writers. However, **anxiety** was used rather than stress. The word stress did not appear in the index of *Psychological Abstracts* until 1944. Freud gave anxiety a central role in psychopathology. Blockage or delay of instinctual discharge of gratification resulted in symptoms; in later Freudian formulations, conflict-induced anxiety served as a cue or signal of danger and triggered defense mechanisms, unsatisfactory modes of coping that produced symptom patterns whose characteristics depended on the type of defense. A similar formulation, dominant in American psychology for many decades, was the reinforcement-learning theory of Hull (1943) and Spence (1956). Anxiety was viewed as a classically conditioned response that led to unserviceable (pathological) habits of anxiety-reduction (cf. Dollard & Miller, 1950). In most of the first half of the 20th century, this concept of anxiety was a major influence in psychological research and thought. The existential writings about anxiety by Kierkegaard and others were popularized in the United States by Rollo May (1950, 1958). If one recognizes that there is a heavy overlap between the concepts of anxiety and stress, and does not feel it necessary to quibble about which term is used, it could be said that the dominant view of psychopathology thus formulated was that it was a product of stress.

Empirical research on anxiety got a boost in the early 1950s with the publication of a scale for the measurement of anxiety as a trait (Taylor, 1953). The scale generated a huge amount of research on the role of anxiety in learning, memory, perception, and skilled performance, mostly from the standpoint of anxiety serving either as a drive (see Spence & Spence, 1966) or as a source of interference in cognitive activity. Much of this research was reviewed in a book edited by Spielberger (1966). Books continue to appear with the term anxiety rather than stress in the title, or using both terms, reflecting the fascination with anxiety

and anxiety as stress (e.g., Sarason & Spielberger; and Spielberger & Sarason, 1975; Spielberger, 1966, 1972).

World War II had a mobilizing effect on stress theory and research. Indeed, one of the earliest psychological applications of the term stress is found in a landmark book about the war by Grinker and Spiegel (1945) entitled *Men Under Stress*. The military was concerned with the effect of stress on functioning during combat; it could increase soldiers' vulnerability to injury or death and weaken a combat group's potential for effective action. For instance, soldiers became immobilized or panicked during critical moments under fire or on bombing missions, and a tour of duty under these conditions often led to neurotic- or psychotic-like breakdowns (see Grinker & Spiegel).

With the advent of the Korean War, many new studies were directed at the effects of stress on adrenal-cortical hormones and on skilled performance. Some of the latter were done with a view to developing principles for selecting less vulnerable combat personnel, and others to developing interventions to produce more effective functioning under stress. The war in Vietnam also had its share of research on combat stress and its psychological and physiological consequences (cf. Bourne, 1969), much of it influenced by Selye. Also concerned with stresses of war were books on the impact of bombings on civilian morale and functioning (e.g., Freud & Burlingham, 1943; Janis, 1951), manipulation of military prisoners (e.g., Biderman & Zimmer, 1961), wartime survival (e.g., von Greyerz, 1962), and the concentration camp (e.g., Bettelheim, 1960; Cohen, 1953; Dimsdale, 1980).

A major landmark in the popularization of the term stress, and of theory and research on stress, was the publication by Janis (1958) of an intensive study of surgical threat in a patient under psychoanalytic treatment. This was followed by an increasing number of books also devoted to the systematization of stress theory and methodology, and an increase in concern with the social sources of stress in the environment. Examples are books by McGrath (1970) and Levine and Scotch (1970).

Since the 1960s there has been growing recognition that while stress is an inevitable aspect of the human condition, it is coping that makes the big difference in adaptational outcome. In *Psychological Stress and the Coping Process* (Lazarus, 1966) the emphasis began to shift somewhat from stress per se to coping. Aside from popular accounts, however, there are still relatively few treatises devoted extensively to coping, but more are beginning to appear. Examples include Coelho, Hamburg, and Adams (1974), Haan (1977), Horowitz (1976), Menninger (1963), Vaillant (1977), Levinson, Darrow, Klein, Levinson, and McKee (1978), Lazarus and Launier (1978), Murphy and Moriarty (1976), Pearlin and Schooler (1978), Folkman and Lazarus (1980), Lazarus and Folkman (1984), and some anthologies on coping with diverse forms of life stress (cf. Monat & Lazarus, 1977; Moos, 1977).

MODERN DEVELOPMENTS

Five relatively recent developments have also stimulated interest in stress and coping: the concern with individual differences, the resurgence of interest in psychosomatics, the development of behavior therapy aimed at the treatment and prevention of disease or life styles that increase the risk of illness, the rise of a life course developmental perspective, and a mounting concern with the role of the environment in human affairs. Let us examine each of these briefly.

Interest in **individual differences** grew out of the research on the effects of stress on performance that was stimulated by World War II and the Korean War. This problem, which was obviously relevant to people in nonmilitary settings as well, led to hundreds of laboratory and field experiments during the 1950s (see Lazarus, 1966, for a list of reviews). The dominant view had been quite simplistic: stress or anxiety resulted in the impairment of skilled performance either by excessively heightening drive tension or by creating interference or distraction. Psychologists who were involved in this research often cited a universal law propounded by Yerkes and Dodson (1908), the so-called inverted U-shaped curve in which increments of arousal or drive tension improved task performance up to a certain level, beyond which increasing disorganization and performance impairment resulted.

 **LEARNING CHECKPOINT**

What are some of the individual differences displayed in Figure 6–2?

It became increasingly apparent, however, that there were important individual differences in response to stress; performance was not uniformly impaired or facilitated. Lazarus and Eriksen (1952), for example, found a marked increase in variance instead of an average increase or decrease in performance effectiveness under failure induced stress. Performances were made more variable by stress, some experimental subjects doing much better and others doing much worse. This and other studies made it clear that one could not predict performance simply by reference to stressful stimuli, and that to predict performance outcomes required attention to the psychological processes that created individual differences in reaction. For example, people could differ in their optimal level of arousal, or in the ways they appraised the encounter or coped with its demands.

The growing realization of the importance of person factors such as motivation and coping (cf. Lazarus, Deese, & Osler, 1952) led to changes in the formulation of the problem of stress and skilled performance. For example, many researches (e.g., Sarason, 1960, 1972, 1975) began to look at the possible effects of mediating or moderator variables and their interactions. As the definition of the problem shifted toward person factors and the processes intervening between the stressful demands of the environment and the short-term emotional and performance outcomes, studies of skilled performance under stress were largely preempted by studies of stress-related processes (e.g., cognitive appraisal and coping) that could account for individual differences in reaction.

Yet the original problem, the effects of stress on performance, has not been totally abandoned. For example, in an analytic review of current research on stress and fatigue in human performance, Schönpflug (1983) and his colleagues bring us back to familiar concepts and variables such as time pressure and the effects of noise on fatigue and the efficiency of problem solving, but with a new twist: cognitive, motivational, and coping concepts have been grafted onto the earlier concern with performance effectiveness. This keeps alive the important issues of stress and performance, yet in a way that encourages the investigation of individual differences.

Psychosomatic medicine burgeoned about 50 years ago (Lipowski, 1977) but subsequently underwent a dramatic decline until quite recently. The reasons for the decline are complex but include a poor data base for the oversimple idea that various types of disorders such as ulcers and colitis could be explained on the basis of special kinds of psychodynamic processes. Unsuccessful attempts were made to use psychodynamic formulations to identify an ''ulcer personality'' (Alexander, 1950), a ''colitis personality,'' a ''migraine personality,'' and so on. Over the past 20 years, traditional psychoanalytic concepts have lost favor, and there has been more interest in environmental factors in illness. As a result, psychosomatic medicine, which had been heavily committed to an intrapsychic emphasis, suffered a crisis of confidence.

Revival of current interest has been prompted by a number of recent changes in outlook concerning stress and illness. A major contributor is Selye's work, which gives strong support to the general conviction that social and psychological factors are, indeed, important in health and illness. Psychophysiology and medicine, for instance, have moved away from the view that disease is strictly a product of environmental agents such as bacteria, viruses, and damaging accidents and toward acceptance of the idea that vulnerability to disease or ''host resistance'' is also important.

Advanced research on stress and hormone effects on the tissues (Mason, 1971, 1974, 1975a, b, c; Mason et al., 1976) has made the concept of vulnerability acceptable to many of those suspicious of traditional psychodynamic formulations. Current psychosomatic thought is thus heavily embedded in stress theory and research and seems to have taken on a new vitality promoted, in part, by this broader, more interdisciplinary approach. A number of books on psychosomatic or behavioral medicine, including those by Weiner (1977), Weiss, Herd, and Fox (1979), and Norton (1982), attest to this resurgence of interest, as do Ader's (1981) book on the comparatively new field of psychoimmunology, and Stone, Cohen, and Adler's (1979) volume on health psychology.

We might note in passing that interest in the immune response as a factor in all kinds of illness is by no means new, but it has gathered great momentum in recent years. Broadening the concept of psychosomatics from a specific set of ailments such as ulcers and hypertension to the general concept that all illness could have psychosocial etiology in a multicausal system (cf. Weiss, 1977) has stimulated the examination of the immune response as a possible factor even in cancer, a disorder far removed from the original meaning of psychosomatic. We should expect increased multidisciplinary research activity on the immune process, and the psychological and social factors affecting it, in coming years.

More evidence of the growing commitment to the consideration of psychological factors in health comes from the decision of the American Psychological Association to form the Division of Health Psychology (Division 38), and from the publication of journals including *Health Psychology, The Journal of Behavioral Medicine, Psychophysiology, The Journal of Human Stress, The British Journal of Medical Psychology, Psychological Medicine, The Journal of Psychosomatic Research,* and the *Journal of Health and Social Behavior,* in addition to the longstanding journal *Psychosomatic Medicine.* A number of more specialized journals (e.g., dealing with biofeedback or treatment) contain related research, and more broadly based journals (e.g., *The Journal of Personality and Social Psychology, The British Journal of Clinical Psychology*) have also begun to publish studies that center on psychosomatic or health-related topics.

Behavior therapy has also emerged in recent years as an alternative to traditional psychodynamic therapy. At first its outlook was preciously scientific, positivist, and narrow, focused around classical and operant conditioning, and militantly dissociated from psychoanalytic thought. Later it began developing greater flexibility and spawned within it the cognitive behavior therapy movement (e.g., Ellis, 1962; Ellis & Grieger, 1977), which takes into account, as central factors in psychopathology and successful coping, how a person construes adaptational encounters, and focuses on interventions to change thought as well as feeling and action. Growing numbers of cognitive behavior therapists see their work as the basis of rapprochement between behavioral and psychodynamic approaches (e.g., Goldfried, 1979; A. Lazarus, 1971; Lazarus, 1980; Mahoney, 1980; Wachtel, 1980). This has led them into the realm of stress and coping, as can be seen in Meichenbaum's (1977) cognitive coping interventions, Meichenbaum and Novaco's (1978) use of the concept of "stress inoculation," in which people are trained to cope with upcoming stressful situations, and Beck's (1976) treatment of depression.

LEARNING CHECKPOINT

Would "stress inoculation" be considered an individual or an organizational approach to managing stress?

A major realignment of interest in **developmental psychology** is a fourth factor facilitating interest in stress, coping, and adaptation. The psychology of development had traditionally been focused on infancy, childhood, and adolescence. In the 1960s, stimulated in part by the marked increased in the numbers of people reaching old age, there was a growing concern with adulthood and its problems. The writings of Erikson (1963) helped turn psychology from a Freudian focus on the early years of life and the resolution of the oedipal struggle in adolescence to the realization that major psychological transformations also took place in young adulthood and even later. Developmental psychology became a field devoted to change over the life course.

At the popular level, interest in adult transitions was given impetus by Gail Sheehy's (1976) book *Passages,* which borrowed from the more scholarly and systematic work by Levinson and his colleagues (e.g., Levinson et al., 1978) on midlife transitions and crises. Writings by Neugarten (1968 a, b), Lowenthal (1977; Lowenthal, Thurnher, & Chiriboga, 1975), and Vaillant (1977) also reflected and contributed to the growing interest in adult development. At the same time, the political and social repercussions of an aging population resulted in the establishment of the National Institute on Aging and a shift of research funds toward the study of the problems of aging.

One of the central themes expressed in this new literature concerns the stress of transitions and social change and how they are coped with. There is great interest, for example, in the empty nest, midlife crises, widowhood, and retirement. At the same time, there has never been more interest than at present in the emotional development of infants and children and the ways a child comes to understand the personal significance of social relationships and interactions. Whether the focus is on development in adults or in children, issues are frequently organized around stress, coping, and adaptation.

A final factor in the increased interest in stress and coping is the emergence of a strong **environmental or social ecological focus** in behavioral science research. Clinical psychology and psychiatry had already begun to move away from a strictly intrapsychic emphasis, in which the processes thought to underlie psychopathology resided primarily within the person, and toward an environmental focus. Psychological thought in general has shifted in the same direction, toward a greater interest in the environments within which humans live. Environmental psychology (or social ecology) itself has been facilitated by the rise of ethology as a naturalistic science. As they witnessed the impact of ethological studies, social scientists became aware of their lack of understanding of the natural habitats of humans. Stress depends, in part, on the social and

physical demands of the environment (Altman & Wohlwill, 1977; Proshansky, Ittelson, & Rivlin, 1970; Stokols, 1977). Environmental constraints and environmental resources (Klausner, 1971) on which the possibilities for coping depend are also important factors. Therefore, the advent of a science of environment brought stress theory and research an extended perspective as well as new converts.

REFERENCES

Ader, R. (1981). Animal models in the study of brain, behavior and bodily disease. In H. Weiner, M. A, Hofer, & A. J. Stunkard (Eds.), *Brain, behavior, and bodily disease.* New York: Raven.

Alexander, F. (1950). *Psychosomatic medicine.* New York: Norton.

Altman, I., & Wohlwill, J. G. (Eds.). (1977). *Human behavior and environment: Advances in theory and research.* New York: Plenum.

Appley, M. H., & Trumbull, R. (1967). *Psychological stress: Issues in research.* New York: Appleton-Century-Crofts.

Baker, G. W., & Chapman, D. W. (Eds.). (1962). *Man and society in disaster.* New York: Basic Books.

Beck, A. T. (1976). *Cognitive therapy and the emotional disorders.* New York: International Universities Press.

Bettelheim, B. (1960). *The informed heart.* New York: Free Press.

Biderman, A. D., & Zimmer, H. (Eds.). (1961). *The manipulation of human behavior.* New York: Wiley.

Bourne, P. G. (Ed.). (1969). *The psychology and physiology of stress: With reference to special studies of the Vietnam war.* New York: Academic Press.

Cannon, W. B. (1932). *The wisdom of the body.* New York: Norton.

Coelho, G. V., Hamburg, D. A., & Adams, J. E. (Eds.). (1974). *Coping and adaptation.* New York: Basic Books.

Cofer, C. N., & Appley, M. H. (1964). *Motivation: Theory and research.* New York: Wiley.

Cohen, E. A. (1953). *Human behavior in the concentration camp.* New York: Norton.

Dimsdale, J. E. (Ed.). (1980). *Survivors, victims, and perpetrators: Essays on the Nazi Holocaust.* Washington, D.C.: Hemisphere.

Dollard, J., & Miller, N. W. (1950). *Personality and psychotherapy.* New York: McGraw-Hill.

Durkheim, E. (1893). *De la division du travail social.* Paris: F. Alcan. (cited in Kanungo, 1979).

Ellis, A. (1962). *Reason and emotion in psychotherapy.* New York: Lyle Stuart.

Ellis, A., & Grieger, R. (Eds.). (1977). *Handbook of rational-emotive therapy.* New York: Springer.

Erikson, E. H. (1963). *Childhood and society* (2nd ed.). New York: Norton.

Folkman, S., & Lazarus, R. S. (1980). An analysis of coping in a middle-aged community sample. *Journal of Health and Social Behavior, 21,* 219–239.

Freud, A., & Burlingham, D. (1943). *War and children.* New York: Medical War Books.

Goldfried, M. R. (1979). Anxiety reduction through cognitive-behavioral intervention. In P. C. Kendall & S. D. Hollon (Eds.), *Cognitive-behavioral interventions: Theory, research, and procedures.* New York: Academic Press.

Grinker, R. R., & Speigel, J. P. (1945). *Men under stress.* New York: McGraw-Hill.

Grosser, G. H., Wechsler, H., & Greenblatt, M. (Eds.) (1964). *The threat of impending disaster.* Cambridge, MA: The MIT Press.

Haan, N. (1977). *Coping and defending: Processes of self-environment organization.* New York: Academic Press.

Hinkle, L. E., Jr. (1973). The concept of "stress" in the biological and social sciences. *Science, Medicine & Man, 1,* 31–48.

Hinkle, L. E., Jr. (1977). The concept of "stress" in the biological and social sciences. In Z. J. Lipowski, D. R. Lipsitt, & P. C. Whybrow (Eds.), *Psychosomatic medicine: Current trends and clinical implications.* New York: Oxford University Press.

Horowitz, M. J. (1976). *Stress response syndromes*. New York: Jason Aronson.

Hull, C. L. (1943). *Principles of behavior*. New York: Appleton-Century-Crofts.

Janis, I. L. (1951). *Air war and emotional stress*. New York: McGraw-Hill.

Janis, I. L. (1958). *Psychological stress: Psychoanalytic and behavioral studies of surgical patients*. New York: Wiley.

Kahn, R. L., Wolfe, D. M., Quinn, R. P., Snoek, J. D., & Rosenthal, R. A. (1964). *Organizational stress: Studies in role conflict and ambiguity*. New York: Wiley.

Kanungo, R. N. (1979). The concepts of alienation and involvement revisited. *Psychological Bulletin, 86,* 119–138.

Klausner, S. Z. (1971). *On man and his environment*. San Francisco: Jossey-Bass.

Lazarus, A. A. (1971). *Behavior therapy and beyond*. New York: McGraw-Hill.

Lazarus, R. S. (1966). *Psychological stress and the coping process*. New York: McGraw-Hill.

Lazarus, R. S. (1980). Cognitive behavior therapy as psychodynamics revisited. In J. Mahoney (Ed.), *Psychotherapy process: Current issues and future directions*. New York: Plenum.

Lazarus, R. S., Deese, J., & Osler, S. F. (1952). The effects of psychological stress upon performance. *Psychological Bulletin, 49,* 293–317.

Lazarus, R. S., & Erikson, C. W. (1952). Effects of failure stress upon skilled performance. *Journal of Experimental Psychology, 43,* 100–105.

Lazarus, R. S., & Folkman, S. (1984). Coping and adaptation. In W. D. Gentry (Ed.), *The handbook of behavioral medicine* (pp. 282–325). New York: Guilford.

Lazarus, R. S., & Launier, R. (1978). Stress-related transactions between person and environment. In L. A. Pervin & M. Lewis (Eds.), *Perspective in international psychology*. New York: Plenum.

Levine, S., & Scotch, N. A. (1970). *Social stress*. Chicago: Aldine.

Levinson, D. J., Darrow, C. N., Klein, E. B., Levinson, M. H., & McKee, B. (1978). *The seasons of a man's life*. New York: Knopf.

Lipowski, Z. J. (1977). Psychosomatic medicine in the seventies: An overview. *American Journal of Psychiatry, 134,* 233–244.

Lowenthal, M. F. (1977). Toward a sociopsychological theory of change in adulthood and old age. In J. E. Birren & K. W. Schaie (Eds.), *Handbook of the psychology of aging*. New York: Van Nostrand Reinhold.

Lowenthal, M. F., Thurnher, M., & Chiriboga, D. (1975). *Four stages of life*. San Francisco: Jossey-Bass.

Lucas, R. A. (1969). *Men in crisis*. New York: Basic Books.

Lumsden, D. P. (1981). Is the concept of "stress" of any use anymore? In D. Randall (Ed.), *Contributions to primary prevention in mental health: Working papers*. Toronto: Toronto National Office of the Canadian Mental Health Association.

Mahoney, M. J. (Ed.). (1980). *Psychotherapy process: Current issues and future directions*. New York: Plenum.

Mason, J. W. (1971). A re-evaluation of the concept of "non-specificity" in stress theory. *Journal of Psychiatric Research, 8,* 323–333.

Mason, J. W. (1974). Specificity in the organization of neuroendocrine response profiles. In P. Seeman & G. Brown (Eds.), *Frontiers in neurology and neuroscience research*. Toronto: University of Toronto.

Mason, J. W. (1975a). Emotion as reflected in patterns of endocrine intergration. In L. Levi (Ed.), *Emotions: Their parameters and measurement*. New York: Raven.

Mason, J. W. (1975b). A historical view of the stress field: Part I. *Journal of Human Stress, 1,* 6–12.

Mason, J. W. (1975c). A historical view of the stress field: Part II. *Journal of Human Stress, 1,* 22–36.

Mason, J. W., Maher, J. T., Hartley, L. H., Mougey, E., Perlow, M. J., & Jones, L. G. (1976). Selectivity of corticosteroid and catecholamine response to various natural stimuli. In G. Serban (Ed.), *Psychopathology of human adaptation*. New York: Plenum.

May, R. (1950). *The meaning of anxiety*. New York: Ronald Press.

May, R. (1958). Contributions of existential psychotherapy. In R. May, E. Angel, & H. F. Ellenberger (Eds.), *Existence: A new dimension in psychiatry and psychology*. New York: Basic Books.

McClosky, H., & Schaar, J. H. (1965). Psychological dimensions of anomie. *American Sociological Review, 30,* 14–40. *Psychosomatic Medicine, 11,* 30–44.

McGrath, J. E. (1970). *Social and psychological factors in stress*. New York: Holt, Rinehart & Winston.

Mechanic, D. (1978). *Medical sociology* (2nd ed.). New York: Free Press.

Meichenbaum, D. (1977). *Cognitive-behavior modification: An integrative approach*. New York: Plenum.

Meichenbaum, D., & Novaco, R. (1978). Stress inoculation: A preventive approach. In C. D. Spielberger & I. G. Sarason (Eds.), *Stress and anxiety* (Vol. 5). New York: Halstead.

Menninger, K. (1963). *The vital balance: The life process in mental health and illness*. New York: Viking.

Monat, A., & Lazarus, R. S. (1977). *Stress and coping: An anthology*. New York: Columbia University Press.

Moos, R. H. (Ed.). (1977). *Coping with physical illness*. New York: Plenum.

Murphy, L. B., & Moriarty, A. E. (1976). *Vulnerability, coping, and growth: From infancy to adolescence*. New Haven: Yale University Press.

Neugarten, B. L. (1968a). Adult personality: Toward a psychology of the life cycle. In B. L. Neugarten (Ed.), *Middle age and aging: A reader in social psychology*. Chicago: University of Chicago Press.

Neugarten, B. L. (1968b). *Middle age and aging: A reader in social psychology*. Chicago: University of Chicago Press.

Norton, J. G. (1982). *Introduction to medical psychology*. New York: Free Press.

Pearlin, L. I., & Schooler, C. (1978). The structure of coping. *Journal of Health and Social Behavior, 19,* 2–21.

Proshansky, H. M., Ittleson, W. H., & Rivlin, L. G. (1970). *Environmental psychology: Man and his physical set-*

ting. New York: Holt, Rinehart & Winston.

Radloff, F., & Helmreich, R. (1968). *Groups under stress: Psychological research in SEALAB II.* New York: Appleton-Century-Crofts.

Sarason, I. G. (1960). Empirical findings and theoretical problems in the use of anxiety scales. *Psychological Bulletin, 57,* 403–415.

Sarason, I. G. (1972). Experimental approaches to test anxiety: Attention and the uses of information. In C. D. Spielberger (Ed.), *Anxiety: Current trends in theory and research* (Vol. 2). New York: Academic Press.

Sarason, I. G. (1975). Test anxiety, attention, and the general problem of anxiety. In C. D. Spielberger & I. G. Sarason (Eds.), *Stress and anxiety* (Vol. 1). Washington, D.C.: Hemisphere.

Sarason, I. G., & Spielberger, C. D.; and Spielberger, C. D., & Sarason, I. G. (Eds.). (1975). *Stress and anxiety* (Vols. 1–8). New York: Wiley. (ongoing series)

Schonpflug, W. (1983). Coping efficiency and situational demands. In G. R. J. Hockey (Ed.), *Stress and fatigue in human performance.* New York: Wiley.

Seeman, M. (1959). On the meaning of alienation. *American Sociological Review, 24,* 783–791.

Seeman, M. (1971). The urban alienations: Some dubious theses from Marx to Marcuse. *Journal of Person-*

ality and Social Psychology, 19, 135–143.

Selye, H. (1950). *The physiology and pathology of exposure to stress.* Montreal: Acta.

Selye, H. (1951–1956). *Annual report of stress.* Montreal: Acta.

Selye, H. (1956). *The stress of life.* New York: McGraw-Hill.

Sheehy, G. (1976). *Passages: Predictable crises of adult life.* New York: Dutton.

Smelser, N. J. (1963). *Theory of collective behavior.* New York: Free Press.

Spence, J. T., & Spence, K. W. (1966). The motivational components of manifest anxiety: Drive and drive stimuli. In C. D. Spielberger (Ed.), *Anxiety and behavior.* New York: Academic Press.

Spence, K. W. (1956). *Behavior theory and conditioning.* New Haven: Yale University Press.

Spielberger, C. D. (Ed.). (1966). *Anxiety and behavior.* New York: Academic Press.

Spielberger, C. D. (Ed.). (1972). *Anxiety: Current trends in theory and research* (Vols. 1 and 2). New York: Academic Press.

Stokols, D. (Ed.). (1977). *Perspectives on environment and behavior: Theory, research and applications.* New York: Plenum.

Stone, G. C., Cohen, F., & Adler, N. E. (Eds.). (1979). *Health psychology: A handbook.* San Francisco: Jossey-Bass.

Taylor, J. A. (1953). A personality scale of manifest anxiety. *Journal of Abnormal and Social Psychology, 48,* 285–290.

Toffler, A. (1970). *Future shock.* New York: Random House.

Tuchman, B. W. (1978). *A distant mirror: The calamitous 14th century.* New York: Knopf.

Vaillant, G. E. (1977). *Adaptation to life.* Boston: Little, Brown.

von Greyerz, W. (1962). *Psychology of survival.* Amsterdam: Elsevier.

Wachtel, P. L. (198). Investigation and its discontents: Some constraints on progress in psychological research. *American Psychologist, 35,* 399–408.

Weiner, H. (1977). *Psychobiology and human disease.* New York: Elsevier.

Weiss, J. H. (1977). The current state of the concept of a psychosomatic disorder. In Z. J. Lipowski, D. R. Lipsitt, & P. C. Whybrow (Eds.), *Psychosomatic medicine: Current trends and clinical applications.* New York: Oxford University Press.

Weiss, S. M., Herd, J. A., & Fox, B. H. (1981). *Perspectives on behavioral medicine.* New York: Academic Press.

Wolff, H. G. (1953). *Stress and disease.* Springfield, IL: Thomas.

Yerkes, R. M., & Dodson, J. D. (1908). The relation of strength of stimulus to rapidity of habit-formation. *Journal of Comparative Neurology and Psychology, 18,* 459–482.

THE HOT REACTORS

DR. ROBERT S. ELIOT AND DENNIS L. BREO

Hans Selye popularized the word "stress" and brought it to the attention of a wide public in 1956 in his book *The Stress of Life.* He

Source: Dr. Robert S. Eliot and Dennis L. Breo, *Is It Worth Dying For?* (New York: Bantam Books, 1984), pp. 35–54.

was not the first to use this concept, however. In the 1920s Walter Cannon described the "fight or flight" response, and beginning in the 1930s, Wilhelm Raab, one of the most advanced medical thinkers in stress research, demonstrated the risks of excess adrenaline and cortisol. Then Selye proved that stress contributed to illness and death in animals and proposed that the same effects occurred in humans.

Selye's main contribution was demonstrating that the body pays a price for the way it responds to stress.

After Selye's seminal work, the next crucial step was taken by Drs. Meyer Friedman and Ray Rosenman. In trailblazing research begun over twenty-five years ago, and described for the public in 1974 in *Type A Behavior and Your Heart,* they established that behavior is linked specifically to coronary heart disease in humans. Previously, scientists had known that traditional risk factors like smoking and obesity involved behavior—people chose to smoke and eat too much. But Friedman and Rosenman defined a new risk factor that did not involve consuming something affecting the body's organs. Their risk factor was more general: a way of responding to life. They called it "Type A" behavior.

Type A behavior, as Friedman and Rosenman defined it, is a designation given to a whole set of specific behaviors observed in a structured interview conducted by a trained researcher. The researcher looks for verbal and nonverbal signs of impatience and hostility, including fidgeting, eye-blinking, grimaces, rapid or explosive speech, sitting on the edge of the seat, interrupting others, and filling in incomplete sentences during a pause. People who do a number of these things in the interview are described as showing Type A behavior.

The person who shows Type B behavior, on the other hand, acts very differently, appearing more relaxed, sitting back in the chair, rarely if ever interrupting, and listening much more.

Type A behavior occurs with or without stress. Under stress, however, the Type A person has more opportunities to act in a typically impatient, irritable, and competitive fashion.

Friedman and Rosenman found that 15 percent of Type A's had heart attacks, compared to 7 percent of Type B's. This research has since been borne out by others. In 1980, a panel convened by the National Institutes of Health published its conclusions that Type A behavior is a risk factor equal to or greater than other risk factors in coronary heart disease.

Like all risk factors, the Type A designation describes a risk, but it can't tell us whether a specific individual will or will not get cardiovascular disease. In America, depending on how it's figured, about 70 percent of men and 50 percent of women are said to be Type A's. When more than half the population is at risk but a much smaller fraction becomes ill, it is hard to predict what will happen for any one Type A person, especially since some Type B individuals will also have heart trouble. Plenty of old and crabby Type A's have seen their younger Type B friends and colleagues die of heart attacks. However, statistically the risk is greater for Type A's.

ARE YOU A TYPE A?

If you have many of the following common Type A characteristics, you may be among those who run a higher risk of developing a narrowing of the heart's arteries that can lead to heart attack. Here is a run-down of the Friedman-Rosenman criteria by *New York Times* health columnist Jane Brody:

- Scheduling more and more activities into less and less time.
- Failing to notice or be interested in your environment or things of beauty.
- Hurrying the speech of others.
- Becoming unduly irritated when forced to wait in line or when driving behind a car you think is moving too slowly.
- Gesticulating when you talk.
- Frequent knee-jiggling or rapid tapping of your fingers.
- Explosive speech patterns or frequent use of obscenities.
- Making a fetish of always being on time.

- Having difficulty sitting and doing nothing.
- Playing nearly every game to win, even when playing with children.
- Measuring your own and others' success in terms of numbers (e.g., number of patients seen, articles written, etc.).
- Lip-clicking, head-nodding, fist-clenching, table-pounding, and sucking in air when speaking.
- Becoming impatient when watching others do things you can do better or faster.
- Rapid eye-blinking or ticlike eyebrow-lifting.

The Type A designation has been invaluable in establishing a statistical link between behavior and coronary heart disease. Friedman, Rosenman, and other researchers have further contributed in identifying anger, impatience, and competitiveness as the Type A characteristics that appear to be most closely linked with the risk of heart attack. Current research is focusing on how this behavior gets translated into physical illness.

In our clinic we also are interested in the links between feelings, behavior, and heart disease, but we have concentrated on looking at the stress profile from *inside* the body. As a cardiologist whose behavior under stress was almost fatal, I wanted to determine specifically which of my patients were most at risk, so I could help them before they had heart attacks, or keep them from having second ones. That required an objective diagnostic tool more selective and specific than Type A behavior. In developing a system to measure the body's responses to the stress of standard mental tasks, our clinic developed the concept of the "hot reactor."

 **LEARNING CHECKPOINT**

Please complete 6D-1, The Behavior Activity Profile. What did you score on each part? The total? What does this tell you about your Type A tendencies?

WHAT IS A HOT REACTOR?

Our basic hypothesis is that "hot reacting"—extreme cardiovascular reactions to standardized stress tests—indicates how people handle stress physiologically in everyday life. It's only logical to suppose that those whose cardiovascular systems react most strongly are at the greatest risk of developing stress-related cardiovascular disease.

It will take years to establish all the dimensions of this new concept. Preliminary studies, however, already show a greater risk of cardiovascular disease for those with extreme reactions to standardized stress tests. Right now we're dealing with risk statistically, in terms of groups, but we have a tool—the measurement of "hot reacting"— that shows promise of detecting and predicting *individual* risk much more precisely.

You'll recall the alarm and vigilance reactions described in the last chapter. Some people experience alarm and vigilance so strongly that when they are under stress their bodies produce large amounts of stress chemicals, which in turn cause great changes in the cardiovascular system, including remarkable rises in blood pressure. These people are the "hot reactors." Their blood pressure may be normal when they are not under stress—say, in a doctor's office, where blood pressure is usually taken. What is unusual about them is that their blood pressure rises like mad when they respond to everyday stresses.

For our research we have approximated such stresses in the Stress Lab by having healthy men, aged 25 to 65, do quick mental arithmetic and then try for a high score on a video game. Electrodes taped to their bodies measured cardiovascular performance, and computers processed hundreds of thousands of pieces of information about each man to produce a printout showing how his cardiovascular system responded.

We found that fully 17 percent of the men in this study reacted to the stress with a sudden, dramatic rise in blood pressure. In each case, the reading was in excess of 160/95—without question, a hypertensive level. Furthermore, among our patients at the Stress Clinic, 20 percent (mostly men) are hot reactors whose blood pressures soar under stress.

Most people, of course, come to our clinic precisely because they are concerned about stress and their health. And to some extent, our cut-off point of 160/95 is an arbitrary one—blood pressure is a continuum, and there's no set point at which it becomes a problem for everyone. At 160/95, however, concern is definitely warranted.

Judging from the evidence our testing has produced, we can estimate that *approximately one out of every five healthy persons who feels under stress is a hot reactor.* And what's worse, these people *do not suspect* that their bodies are paying a high price for overreacting to stress.

 **LEARNING CHECKPOINT**

Could a manager, by observation, determine whether an employee is a hot reactor? Explain.

Are Hot Reactors Always Type A's?

No. Sometimes they are and sometimes they're not. Among the people we've studied, and with the tests we use, Type A behavior occurs in cold reactors as often as it does in hot reactors.

Type A behavior and hot reacting are two very different things. To put it simply, hot reacting is an extreme cardiovascular response to stressful tasks, while Type A behavior is a particular style of interacting with an interviewer. We identify Type A behavior by watching verbal and physical reactions when an interviewer acts in a provoking or challenging way. On the other hand, we identify hot reacting by measuring the level of cardiovascular response to a set of mildly challenging mental and physical tasks that simulate daily life experience (the type of test I've just described).

Type A behavior and hot reacting both reflect feelings, but one shows up in external behavior, while the other operates at the hidden (but scientifically observable) level of physiology and metabolism. Some people may react at one level, others at the other level, and some at both. At the moment, the reason why the body selects either or both remains a mystery for research to solve.

Who Are the Hot Reactors?

These are people who overreact to stress with extreme blood pressure and chemical changes. Such people endanger themselves by expending enormous energy. They burn a dollar's worth of energy for a dime's worth of stress. They overwork their cardiovascular systems until, ultimately, their hearts may give out.

It's like drag racing with the family car. With years of that kind of treatment, the standard engine wears out. In fact, the three ways that hot reactors raise their blood pressure can be compared to three styles of dangerous driving.

Output hot reactors work their hearts hard by increasing their output of blood when they're under stress. Either they pump blood faster than normal or they pump more blood per beat. They're like drivers who speed without knowing it. When you're going eighty miles an hour and think you're doing fifty-five, your chances of hitting something—hard—are pretty high.

Output hot reactors are usually young men or women who are otherwise perfectly healthy. Often, only their blood pressure under stress identifies them as people with a potential health problem. Usually the blood pressure of output hot reactors jumps because they are burning far more energy than is required for simple mental tasks. Fortunately, young people usually have healthy hearts and their cardiovascular systems can—for a while—handle the intensified demands.

Combined hot reactors not only pump more blood, but do it against more resistance, because their blood vessels constrict in response to stress. They're like drag racers who speed at eighty miles an hour—but with the brakes on.

Combined hot reactors are often middle-aged people who started out as output reactors. Their blood pressure jumps mainly because their blood vessels are tightening up under mental stress and resisting the blood flow. Fortunately, though, their hearts can—usually—still pump harder to meet the increased resistance.

Vasoconstrictive (vessel-constricting) hot reactors raise their blood pressure mainly because their blood vessels se-verely constrict under stress. Most dangerously, their weakened hearts are no longer able to pump extra hard. These people are like drag racers who have been speeding with the brakes on for a long time, and the engine is beginning to sputter and give out.

Vasoconstrictive hot reactors are at highest risk. Their vessels are always constricted, and the heart is beginning to wear out. These people may have started as youthful output reactors and progressed through combined reacting. Now their hearts are having trouble working against the constant high resistance. If a sudden stress clamps the small vessels tight, their hearts may be unable to pump harder to keep up, and they may suffer a sudden heart attack.

Let me share some case histories with you.

Scott—an Output Hot Reactor

It was Christmas vacation and Scott was on his first trip home from an out-of-state college where he was taking premed courses. He wanted to become a doctor and his friends knew him as a "straight arrow." He had just made the dean's list for high grades. He loved sports and in his high school he was a local star basketball player. Walking through the Omaha airport, he appeared the picture of good health—tall, blond and slim. On impulse, he stopped at a blood-pressure machine, strapped the cuff on his arm, and put in the coins. The electronic figures were unblinking, but Scott did a double-take:

170 over 110. That was the reading, although the chart on the machine said that "normal" was 120 over 80.

It must be the machine, he figured. You can't trust these things. He was only nineteen years old. There was no way he could have high blood pressure.

Scott was the son of a colleague of mine. That night I got a call from his father, and minutes later, Scott was in my doorway. In ski jacket and winter boots, he looked more like a member of the U.S. Olympic team than someone with a health problem.

We went into the den where I keep a blood pressure cuff and stethoscope. I placed the stethoscope on his arm and inflated the cuff. His blood pressure was 180 over 110. Since Scott was worried, it had jumped a little higher than the reading at the airport. We were sitting in the den having a simple conversation and his heart was laboring at a level that would take most people his age about thirty minutes of hard running to reach.

"Scott, what's wrong? What's going on in your life?"

He started slowly, but the words soon tumbled out. He was determined to become a doctor, but the effort was taking a toll. He was having trouble adjusting from high school to life in a college dorm in another state. He never seemed to have time for sports or relaxation or friends. He was determined to help pay his way through college, and he was working several odd jobs. He was taking a correspondence course at night to help him with his daytime classes. He was highly motivated and intelligent, but medical school is extremely difficult to get into. He had made the dean's list, but some had done better. He was doing well, but he didn't feel good about himself.

He had high blood pressure, the "silent killer." People as young as Scott can have it and not have the slightest idea that they do. They do not feel ill. Meanwhile, the disease quietly works its damage throughout the body.

My hunch was that he had high blood pressure because he was a hot reactor. When a person's blood pressure shoots up to 180/110 while he's carrying on a conversation—as Scott's did in my home—he's displaying a powerful cardiovascular response to a mild stress.

I asked Scott to come down to my office at the medical center the next morning. Our team gave him a thorough medical examination, including having him walk on a treadmill. There was no organic cause for his high blood pressure. He appeared to be in perfect condition. He had adjusted to a number of life changes recently, but a healthy 19-year-old should have been able to handle them. Furthermore, Scott was not a Type A personality who acted intensely competitive, impatient, and hostile. He was a well-mannered, soft-spoken young man.

Our laboratory stress tests showed that Scott's blood pressure was high because his heart rate and output of blood increased dramatically under stress. His total systemic resistance—the constriction of his blood vessels—was normal. His problem was due to constantly being in the combat state—the stress reactions of alarm and vigilance—for simple mental tasks.

Scott was an output hot reactor. He was typical of many highly motivated young people who burn high-energy chemicals for low-energy needs and who are undetected early hypertensives. At Scott's age, adrenaline and cortisol have not been bombarding the arteries long enough to do serious damage; it is the heart's intensified pumping that causes the blood pressure to rise. One purpose of our laboratory evaluation is to provide an early warning system that can catch this condition before there are fixed body changes and the high blood pressure becomes chronic.

Hot Reacting Versus Hypertension

Doctors refer to fixed high blood pressure as hypertension and to people who have this chronic high blood pressure as hypertensives. Hot reacting—showing a strong increase in blood pressure under stress—is a separate phenomenon from having fixed high blood pressure at rest.

Many people develop high blood pressure for reasons unrelated to hot reacting—old age, too much weight, too much salt in the diet, and genetic predisposition, to name a few. And some hot reactors, due to compensating factors in the body, never develop fixed high blood pressure. However, hot reacting to daily stress may well precede fixed high blood pressure, because after repeated rises the body tends to adjust upward and tolerate a higher resting blood pressure.

This is a serious matter. Fixed high blood pressure can lead to a stroke or heart failure. The problem is especially serious for people who are both hot reactors and hypertensives at rest. Hot reactors may raise their blood pressure 30 to 40 times a day in response to stress—it's as though, without knowing it, they're fighting saber-toothed tigers internally over and over. The effect is to push their blood pressure higher for a longer time; and the higher the pressure is and the longer it remains high, the greater the risk of chronic hypertension and heart disease. Moreover, sudden blood pressure changes in people with weakened cardiovascular systems can set off a heart attack.

In Scott's case, the problem probably started out as occasional hot reacting to stress, alternating with periods when his blood pressure remained normal. After two or three years of hot reacting, Scott had developed established high blood pressure. But there was still time to reverse it.

Therapy for Scott involved not only medication but motivation. That meant talk, a lot of talk.

At first, Scott took medicines to reduce his high blood pressure. Then, over a period of months, he learned to recognize the stress cues that set off his blood pressure. He learned how to "feel" when his blood pressure was rising and to avoid hot reacting. Three years after starting our program, Scott was accepted to medical school. He is now a cool reactor who controls his own blood pressure without medication.

Bill—a Combined Hot Reactor

Bill is middle-aged and at risk of heart failure. Already he has had surgery to bypass clogged coronary arteries.

Most days he runs a blue-chip corporation. Today he'll just operate a simple electronic television game, the kind you might find in a bar or amusement arcade. But this game is programmed according to house rules. Our hard-driving exec must really be a pro to beat the machine. The game will get tougher as Bill gets closer to winning.

In the Stress Lab, Bill enters a soundproof room. His bare chest is festooned with sophisticated electrodes that monitor every heartbeat. From outside the room, we observe him on closed-circuit television.

As he sits down, Bill's baseline blood pressure is 134/89—the high end of the normal range. He keeps it from going higher by medication.

The game begins. The first three battles with the video game are easy, and Bill is winning.

But the computer printout shows that Bill's body is reacting with changes similar to those a long-distance runner might go through. His systolic blood pressure jumps to 207, his diastolic pressure falls to 66, his heart rate jumps 30 beats a minute, his heart's output of blood doubles, and the total resistance (constriction) of his blood vessels drops in half. In other words, his heart is pumping harder and his blood vessels are widening to accommodate the increased blood. Remarkably, after only a few seconds of playing a video game, Bill's cardiovascular system is working at a rate that took him several minutes to reach while walking uphill on a treadmill. Though Bill's heart and blood vessel reactions are following a normal pattern for a person who is excited and involved in what he is doing, the degree of this response to mental stress is nevertheless extreme.

I call for a rest period and step in to chat. Bill is eager for more.

"I'm going to lick this game yet, if it's the death of me."

"Well, pay attention. Things are going to get more difficult."

The game resumes. Suddenly the little blips on the screen are getting smaller and moving faster. Bill is losing.

And not just the game. His blood pressure has abruptly started to reverse direction—displaying a potentially fatal pattern. Within minutes, the vessels constrict, causing their resistance to the blood flow to triple, while the heart's pumping pressure drops. The heart is overtaxed and starts to falter against the dramatically increased resistance. Quickly, we stop the game.

I go into the testing room and sit down to talk to him. Bill is very angry that we have stopped. He has no idea of the price his body is paying in his effort to win at all costs.

"I'm just starting to get the hang of it. Give me a few more minutes and I'll beat this machine."

"You'll probably never beat the computer. And even if you did, would it be worth dying for?"

Bill sighs. He still wants to win the game.

Bill is a "combined" hot reactor. His blood pressure rises because both his heart's output and his blood vessels' resistance increase under mild mental stress. After years of hot reacting, Bill still burns as much energy in a business meeting as another man might while playing basketball.

Chances are that decades ago Bill was a lot like Scott, an output hot reactor with the beginnings of high blood pressure. A lifetime of headstrong competitive living has put Bill in the second stage of the hot reacting spectrum. Unfortunately, he didn't take an airport blood pressure test early enough. His arteries are resisting pretty hard fairly regularly now. His heart is still able to meet the added stress, but if he keeps the brakes on long enough, the engine is bound to fail.

For Bill, I prescribe medicines to relax the muscles of his arterial walls (opening the vessels to increased blood flow), to reduce the extreme swings in contraction and relaxation of the arteries, and to moderate his heart's extreme reaction to stress.

I also try some common sense. "Bill, don't you think it's time you learned to take things a little less seriously? Why do you give everything in your life the same high priority and attack it with an all-out effort?"

I wish I could say that he listened. But Bill has a mind of his own. It has catapulted him to the top of a Fortune 500 firm.

And if it catapults his heart into failure? "I'll take the risk," he says. "And the medication, thank you."

Believe it or not, there are a lot of people like Bill. To them, the exhilaration of winning seems worth dying for. Of course, they don't really believe it will happen. But it does.

Henry—a Vasoconstrictive Hot Reactor

Henry was tall and shuffling, with sandy hair and blue eyes. He always had something nice to say about everybody. His friends thought nothing bad would ever happen to him. Of course, they knew he had high blood pressure, but it was controlled by medication. And he had a bit of a paunch—in fact, he was clearly overweight—but then, Henry had always been "hefty." A cigarette was always drooping from the corner of his mouth, and he liked his martinis, but how could you object when these were about the only pleasures he had in life?

Henry was a public relations executive for a major East Coast insurance firm, and he knew his best days were behind him. At fifty-five, he had stayed on too long. His friend and mentor had died, and the new boss was contemptuous of Henry. The boss gave him less and less real work to do and more and more insults to swallow. After a while, Henry found himself in a smaller office without a window. When the staff went to Hawaii for a convention, Henry was left behind to tend the phones. At raise time, he was given the minimum. The boss always executed the put-downs with a big smile and a gracious, "I wish it didn't have to be this way, but. . . ."

Henry was made to feel he was lucky to have a job. And he did need the job. He was still putting four sons through college. He had two years to go to earn the pension he thought he needed to assure his happy retirement. So he took the boss's smiles and lies and tongue-lashings and tried to hang on. But there was little or no real work left for him to do. He felt purposeless.

What he ended up doing was a lot of scut-work. The boss had him editing letters, making hotel reservations, ordering coffee and Danish for staff meetings, and writing long memos about things nobody cared about and nobody would read.

Henry would start his mornings by shaving and cussing out "that tyrant who runs our office." Every night he'd down a couple of martinis to blur the memory of the day's humiliations. At work, though, he seemed calm, almost phlegmatic. The younger members of the staff thought he must like his "soft" job.

A stress specialist might have guessed that Henry was constantly in a state of vigilance. While Scott and Bill responded to stress with the alarm reaction, the arousal to performance brought on by the challenge to control, Henry's feeling that he had lost control of his life and his fear of expressing his true feelings openly made him try to survive by stifling himself, by deadening his emotions. But vigilance raised his blood pressure as much as alarm raised Scott's and Bill's.

Came a hot Monday in June: Henry was one year away from being vested in his company's pension plan. Three sons had graduated from college and the fourth was a junior. Henry had been interviewing for another job with a related organization, a job he could begin after earning his pension. It was much less money, but his wife was begging him to take it. Then the boss called Henry from a nearby hotel: a convention was in session and he insisted that Henry carry over two boxes of newspapers containing an article the boss had written.

It was only a two-block walk from the company to the hotel; the boxes were not all that heavy. So it came as a shock to everybody when Henry, riding up the hotel escalator, abruptly collapsed facedownward onto the cardboard boxes and died—the victim of a sudden heart attack.

Henry was killed by one of the leading causes of death in this country. Sudden cardiac death strikes up to 450,000 Americans a year. But as with Henry, these deaths are not really "sudden." They are the end of a long process of weakening. Henry's blood vessels had constricted so often as part of his alarm and vigilance reactions that eventually the pattern became fixed. His heart fought against this increased resistance, but after years of being overtaxed—including heavy drinking that weakened the heart muscle and plenty of nicotine and carbon monoxide from cigarettes to tighten his blood vessels even more—the heart gradually lost its ability to pump as hard as it once did. Henry's output of blood fell. When the sudden mental stress—his outrage at still another insult—hit, his cardiovascular system just couldn't adjust to the increased demand for blood. He collapsed and died.

What might have saved Henry? Drugs would have helped, but behavioral management would have been the name of the game. A crucial question someone might have asked him was, "Why do you feel such intense stress at this point in your life?"

Almost certainly he would have described a life of joyless struggle. His answer would have been, "I'm in a losing situation. I hate this job, but I can't afford to say what I think and lose this job."

In fact, Henry could not afford *not* to say what he was feeling. I would have recommended that he accept immediate intensive help, both medical and behavioral. If he would not do that, I would have suggested that he leave his job. I would have told him:

"Quit, immediately. Transfer elsewhere in the company, if you feel you must have the pension. If that is not possible, leave anyway. I know it's important and you've got years of your life invested. But is it worth dying for?"

Scott, Bill, and Henry were all hot reactors. But as you probably surmised, they were not all Type A's. Bill's behavior tested out as Type A on questionnaires and in interviews. Scott and Henry, however, looked like models of calm and tested out as Type B's, despite their being hot reactors internally.

Then there was Jeff, a classic Type A. He traveled on the fast track and wanted to stay there. If he had to break a few rules and upset a few people along the way, he was willing to do it. Yet Jeff wasn't what you might think. Let me introduce you to a cold reactor.

Jeff—Hot Head, Cool Heart

Jeff was a thirty-five-year-old reporter for a major national publication.

Intensely driven, he hurried all

over the country and occasionally the world to report breaking stories. He liked the adrenaline rush, the obstacles swept away. He loved getting the story, writing it, basking in the byline, framing the photos of celebrities he had written about, displaying the writing awards he had won. His office was a shrine to his travels and his stories.

But he worried about stress. There were a lot of deadlines. His job provided more glamour than money, and he wasn't getting any younger. He spent a great deal of time rushing for planes and drinking when the flights were delayed. Booze, in fact, was a constant companion. Someday, he wanted to find a woman he could marry—again. The first one left when he started traveling—at least he thought that was why she left. And he worked for a highly political organization. He was a hero on the road, but he would often return to find that his situation had been undercut by people in the home office.

No one ever said he couldn't write, but he had a lot of battles—over expense accounts, foreign travel, the accusations that he was a mercenary out for himself and cooperation be damned. He had to fight his own editors for photo and story placement. Sometimes he would even argue over the headlines they chose.

Could all this be harming his health? he asked.

Jeff came to Omaha for our SHAPE (Stress, Health, and Physical Evaluation) program. I found that he was in normal health. He had an unremarkable family history, and he had no trouble on the treadmill. Although he had long ago abandoned tennis and most of the other sports he enjoyed in order to stalk his stories, Jeff was in excellent physical condition.

On our psychologist's questionnaire, however, Jeff revealed that he was subject to a heart disease risk factor: he was a flaming Type A.

He got even hotter in the personal interview. Would he run a yellow light?—Always. If the car in front of him was going too slow, would he honk?—He would either get around that car or lean on the horn all day. If a person were speaking too slowly, would he hurry them along?—He would yank the words out of their throats. Jeff fidgeted in his chair, burned energy as he sat, constantly interrupted, and talked loudly and explosively. He had a number of grimaces, scowls, bursting smiles, and other facial expressions that came and went in the blinking of an eye, and he blinked more than normal, too. His voice rose and fell and he shifted back and forth in the chair, occasionally rising to pace about the room. His behavior was both frantic and hostile.

The conversation with the psychologist was taped and analyzed for what are called stylistics of speech. In loudness, explosiveness, and interrupting, Jeff was off the high end of the Type A behavior chart.

Yet, astonishingly, in the stress lab Jeff's baseline blood pressure was 105/63, or ideal. Under repeated and continuous stress testing—mental arithmetic, American history quiz, video games, plunging the hand in ice water up to the wrist—it rose no higher than 110/70. Jeff was a cold reactor. His surface behavior might be manic—he said he often appeared to be "an organism in distress"—but his heart's reactions were rock stable and cold.

On a hunch, I sent in a female interviewer to engage Jeff in a question-and-answer game. Jeff's psychological profile stamped him not only as a Type A but as a man who viewed career women as "interlopers." I thought he might rise to the competitive ploy, since the woman was supposed to win this game. But it was not to be. In checking the blood pressure of both parties playing this game, we discovered that Jeff, a trained interviewer himself, had managed to shoot the female interviewer's blood pressure up to 188/110.

During our final appraisal interview, Jeff expressed satisfaction in learning that his hectic lifestyle was not affecting his heart. But he admitted that the quality of his life was not exactly wonderful, despite his physiological calm in response to stress.

I advised him to take some time and try to even out the bumps in his roller-coaster way of life. His heart was good, but the effect of stress on the body is much like the effect of piling a load of bricks on a wooden platform. The weakest board breaks first. Jeff's cardiovascular system was healthy, but he did have a lot of headaches. Lately, he was getting a little fatigued, losing some of the joy in his work. He was drinking too much and wasting a lot of time worrying about things he couldn't change. He would do his work in manic bursts of energy and then throw away vast amounts of time. He was not well organized and, in fact, resisted organization as being "beneath a creative mind." He had exaggerated fears about his health—in fact, he was an Olympic-class hypochondriac—and he ruined a lot of personal relationships, particularly with women, by psychologically (not physiologically) overreacting to stress. Beneath the bluster, Jeff was extraordinarily sensitive, and all the turmoil was hurting him. His body was paying a price somewhere, though not in his heart and blood vessels.

I advised Jeff to establish different patterns of thinking about his life. His central problem was that his feelings were wildly exaggerated. Every time Jeff had a headache, he thought a blood vessel was going to pop in his head; every time his chest tightened, he checked his pulse to make sure his heart was still beating; every time he entered a dark bar and couldn't immediately adjust to the lack of light, he began to wonder if he were blacking out from too much booze.

A lot of people are like Jeff. They're insecure. They're sure they're going to call down something terrible on themselves and they want to be prepared, so they anticipate the worst. (I call this "horribilizing.") I convinced Jeff that he didn't need self-destructive thinking to remain creative and productive. That he could lead a balanced life. That he was better off shooting for results, not perfection.

I also taught him the most lifesaving word in the English language: No. Jeff had been taking on writing assignments without regard to his overall work load. His ego overrode his common sense. A free-lance article here, a book there, another article elsewhere. And, then, out of guilt, he would redouble his efforts on his salaried job "to make sure they know I'm still around."

We taught Jeff to accept his accomplishments and his success, to stop trying to conquer the world continually, and to cool his reactions in those situations where he could neither control nor change things.

Sometimes it's better to yield gracefully than to bang your head against a brick wall. Give yourself a break, I told Jeff. Skip a few fights. Stay home a few nights. Miss a few stories. Take time for yourself and to be with others.

Years later, Jeff is happily married and still traveling about the country. He doesn't worry as much, is less of a workaholic, and enjoys his life more.

Jeff is a cool reactor and a reformed Type A.

LEARNING CHECKPOINT

Would the hot reactor factor be considered a stressor or moderator in the stress and work model presented in Figure 6–2?

Jeff was a living demonstration of the difference between Type A behavior and hot reacting. He was *psychologically intense* most of the time, but he was not *physiologically intense*. His blood pressure rose a little under mental stress, as everyone's does, but it did not rise very much.

Jeff was like a person driving without a muffler—the car may make plenty of noise, but that has nothing to do with how the engine is working. It could be in great shape or it could be burning up; you can't tell from the revved-up sound. At the same time, driving without a muffler isn't a good idea—the noise is a strain on everybody else, if not on the engine. Extreme Type A behavior is worth modifying for that reason alone. Jeff's psychological overreactions kept him in enough hot water to harm the overall quality of his life.

The ideal way to go through life is to maintain both physiological and emotional balance. People who take life in stride instead of struggling against it can respond to a true crisis with reserves that are—to use the Rolls-Royce understatement about horsepower—adequate. ☐

BEHAVIOR ACTIVITY PROFILE—
A TYPE A MEASURE

Each of us displays certain kinds of behaviors, thought patterns of personal characteristics. For each of the 21 sets of descriptions below, circle the number which you feel best describes where you are between each pair. The best answer for each set of descriptions is the response that most nearly describes the way you feel, behave, or think. Answer these in terms of your regular or typical behavior, thoughts, or characteristics.

1. I'm always on time for appointments   7 6 5 4 3 2 1   I'm never quite on time

2. When someone is talking to me, chances are I'll anticipate what they are going to say, by nodding, interrupting or finishing sentences for them   7 6 5 4 3 2 1   listen quietly without showing any impatience

3. I frequently try to do several things at once   7 6 5 4 3 2 1   tend to take things one at a time

4. When it comes to waiting in line (at banks, theaters, etc.) I really get impatient and frustrated   7 6 5 4 3 2 1   it simply doesn't bother me

5. I always feel rushed   7 6 5 4 3 2 1   I never feel rushed

6. When it comes to my temper I find it hard to control at times   7 6 5 4 3 2 1   I just don't seem to have one

TOTAL SCORE
1–7 _____ = S

7. I tend to do most things like eating, walking and talking rapidly   7 6 5 4 3 2 1   slowly

8. Quite honestly, the things I enjoy most are job related activities   7 6 5 4 3 2 1   leisure time activities

9. At the end of a typical work day, I usually feel like I needed to get more done than I did   7 6 5 4 3 2 1   I accomplished everything I needed to

10. Someone who knows me very well would say that I would rather work than play   7 6 5 4 3 2 1   rather play than work

11. When it comes to getting ahead at work nothing is more important   7 6 5 4 3 2 1   many things are more important

12. My primary source of satisfaction comes from my job   <u>7 6 5 4 3 2 1</u>   I regularly find satisfaction in non-job pursuits, such as hobbies, friends, and family

13. Most of my friends and social acquaintances are people I know from work   <u>7 6 5 4 3 2 1</u>   not connected with my work

TOTAL SCORE
8–14 _____ **= J**

14. I'd rather stay at work than take a vacation   <u>7 6 5 4 3 2 1</u>   Nothing at work is important enough to interfere with my vacation

15. People who know me well would describe me as hard driving and competitive   <u>7 6 5 4 3 2 1</u>   relaxed and easygoing

16. In general, my behavior is governed by a desire for recognition and achievement   <u>7 6 5 4 3 2 1</u>   what I want to do—not by trying to satisfy others

17. In trying to complete a project or solve a problem I tend to wear myself out before I'll give up on it   <u>7 6 5 4 3 2 1</u>   I tend to take a break or quit if I'm feeling fatigued

18. When I play a game (tennis, cards, etc.) my enjoyment comes from winning   <u>7 6 5 4 3 2 1</u>   the social interaction

19. I like to associate with people who are dedicated to getting ahead   <u>7 6 5 4 3 2 1</u>   easygoing and take life as it comes

20. I'm not happy unless I'm always doing something   <u>7 6 5 4 3 2 1</u>   Frequently "doing nothing" can be quite enjoyable

TOTAL SCORE
15–21 _____ **= H**

21. What I enjoy doing most are competitive activities   <u>7 6 5 4 3 2 1</u>   noncompetitive pursuits

Impatience (S)	Job Involve-ment (J)	Hard Driving and Competitive (H)	Total Score (A) = S + J + H

The Behavior Activity Profile attempts to assess the three Type A coronary-prone behavior patterns, as well as provide a total score. The three a priori types of Type A coronary-prone behavior patterns are shown:

Items	Behavior Pattern		Characteristics
1–7	Impatience	(S)	anxious to interrupt fails to listen attentively frustrated by waiting (e.g., in line, for others to complete a job)
8–14	Job Involvement	(J)	focal point of attention is the job lives for the job relishes being on the job immersed by job activities
15–21	Hard driving/ Competitive	(H)	hardworking, highly competitive competitive in most aspects of life, sports, work etc. racing against the clock
1–21	Total Score	(A)	total of S + J + H represents your global Type A behavior

Score ranges for total score are:

Score	Behavior Type
122 and above	hard-core Type A
99–121	moderate Type A
90–98	low Type A
80–89	Type X
70–79	low Type B
50–69	moderate Type B
40 and below	hard core Type B

Percentile Scores

Now you can compare your score to a sample of over 1,200 respondents.

Percentile Score % of Individuals Scoring Lower	Raw Score Males	Females
99%	140	132
95%	135	126
90%	130	120
85%	124	112
80%	118	106
75%	113	101
70%	108	95
65%	102	90
60%	97	85
55%	92	80
50%	87	74
45%	81	69
40%	75	63
35%	70	58
30%	63	53
25%	58	48
20%	51	42
15%	45	36
10%	38	31
5%	29	26
1%	21	21

D 2 HEALTH RISK APPRAISAL

The Health Risk Appraisal form was developed by the Department of Health and Welfare of the Canadian government. Their initial testing program indicated that approximately one person out of every three who completed the form would modify some unhealthy aspects of lifestyle for at least a while. Figuring the potential payoff was worth it, the government mailed out over 3 million copies of the questionnaire to Canadians who were on social security. Subsequent check-ing indicated that their initial projections of the number of recipients altering their behavior was correct. Perhaps you will be among the one-third.

Choose from the three answers for each question the one answer which most nearly applies to you. The plus and minus signs next to some numbers indicate more than (+) and less than (−). Note that a few items have only two alternatives.

Exercise

_____ 1. Physical effort expended during the workday: mostly?
a) heavy labor, walking, or housework; b) —; c) deskwork

_____ 2. Participation in physical activities—skiing, golf, swimming, etc., or lawn mowing, gardening, etc.?
a) daily; b) weekly; c) seldom

_____ 3. Participation in vigorous exercise program?
a) three times weekly; b) weekly; c) seldom

_____ 4. Average miles walked or jogged per day?
a) one or more; b) less than one; c) none

_____ 5. Flights of stairs climbed per day?
a) 10 +; b) 10 −; c) —

Nutrition

_____ 6. Are you overweight?
a) no; b) 5 to 19 lbs.; c) 20 + lbs.

_____ 7. Do you eat a wide variety of foods, something from each of the following five food groups: (1) meat, fish, poultry, dried legumes, eggs, or nuts; (2) milk or milk products; (3) bread or cereals; (4) fruits; (5) vegetables?
a) each day; b) three times weekly; c) —

Alcohol

_____ 8. Average number of bottles (12 oz.) of beer per week?
a) 0 to 7; b) 8 to 15; c) 16 +

_____ 9. Average number of hard liquor (1½ oz.) drinks per week?
a) 0 to 7; b) 8 to 15; c) 16 +

_____ 10. Average number of glasses (5 oz.) of wine or cider per week?
a) 0 to 7; b) 8 to 15; c) 16 +

_____ 11. Total number of drinks per week including beer, liquor or wine?
a) 0 to 7; b) 8 to 15; c) 16 +

Drugs

_____ 12. Do you take drugs illegally?
a) no; b) —; c) yes

_____ 13. Do you consume alcoholic beverages together with certain drugs (tranquilizers, barbiturates, illegal drugs)?
a) no; b) —; c) yes

_____ 14. Do you use pain-killers improperly or excessively?
a) no; b) —; c) yes

Tobacco

_____ 15. Cigarettes smoked per day?
a) none; b) 10 −; c) 10 +

_____ 16. Cigars smoked per day?
a) none; b) 5 −; c) 5 +

_____ 17. Pipe tobacco pouches per week?
a) none; b) 2 −; c) 2 +

Personal Health

_____ 18. Do you experience periods of depression?
a) seldom; b) occasionally c) frequently

19. Does anxiety interfere with your daily activities?
    a) no; b) occasionally c) frequently
20. Do you get enough satisfying sleep?
    a) yes; b) no; c) —
21. Are you aware of the causes and dangers of VD?
    a) yes; b) no; c) —
22. Breast self-examination? (if not applicable, do not score)
    a) monthly; b) occasionally; c) —

Road and Water Safety

23. Mileage per year as driver or passenger?
    a) 10,000 −; b) 10,000 +; c) —
24. Do you often exceed the speed limit?
    a) no; b) by 10 mph +; c) by 20 mph +
25. Do you wear a seat belt?
    a) always; b) occasionally; c) never
26. Do you drive a motorcycle, moped, or snowmobile?
    a) no; b) yes; c) —
27. If yes to the above, do you always wear a regulation safety helmet?
    a) yes b) —; c) no

28. Do you ever drive under the influence of alcohol?
    a) never; b) —; c) occasionally
29. Do you ever drive when your ability may be affected by drugs?
    a) never; b —; c) occasionally
30. Are you aware of water safety rules?
    a) yes; b) no; c) —
31. If you participate in water sports or boating, do you wear a life jacket?
    a) yes; b) no; c) —

General

32. Average time watching TV per day (in hours)?
    a) 0 to 1; b) 1 to 4; c) 4 +
33. Are you familiar with first-aid procedures?
    a) yes; b) no; c) —
34. Do you ever smoke in bed?
    a) no; b) occasionally; c) regularly
35. Do you always make use of equipment provided for your safety at work?
    a) yes; b) occasionally; c) no

To score: Give yourself 1 point for each *a* answer; 3 points for each *b* answer; 5 points for each *c* answer. *Total Score:* _____

- A *total score of 35–45 is excellent.* You have a commendable lifestyle based on sensible habits and a lively awareness of personal health.
- A total score of 45–55 is *good.* With some minor change, you can develop an excellent lifestyle.
- A total score of 56–65 is *risky.* You are taking unnecessary risks with your health. Several of your habits should be changed if potential health problems are to be avoided.
- A total score of 66 and over is *hazardous.* Either you have little personal awareness of good health habits or you are choosing to ignore them. This is a danger zone.

1 MR. DANA'S COPING MECHANISM

OBJECTIVES

1. To emphasize that negative coping mechanisms are used by individuals.

2. To enable individuals to compare their interpretation of coping effectiveness with others.

STARTING THE EXERCISE

There is no one set way to prevent work stress or guarantee effective coping in stressful situations. Listed below is a personal history of how one individual copes with the stresses of work. After reading the history list some of the cognitive, emotional, and physical responses experienced by Mr. Dana. How effective is he in coping with the situation? After you individually consider the issue of effectiveness, the instructor will form small groups to discuss why or why not Mr. Dana is effective in coping with stress.

Once the group has read the personal history, evaluate the effectiveness of Mr. Dana's coping and also discuss why Mr. Dana is experiencing the amounts and types of stress portrayed in the incident.

Mr. Dana is a 49-year-old store manager. He expresses to anyone that will listen that he is stressed by the job. As he puts it: "A lot of managers haven't made it, but I've been here for 19 years." He feels that his difficult job should earn him respect off the job. He has constant arguments with his wife because she doesn't seem sympathetic about how tough his work is.

His marriage of 23 years is going through a transition because his wife has returned to school and is "growing more independent." The Dana's have two teenage children. The children expect to receive some financial help from their parents when they begin college in the near future.

Mr. Dana runs an excellent business, but he feels that he hasn't progressed well in the company. He has been offered the managerial position in larger stores, but has turned down offers because he did not want to move his family. He seems to always lament the fact that he didn't become a dentist like his father encouraged him to become as a child.

Mr. Dana behaves as if every incident on the job is a major issue. He believes that a store manager should make no errors. Making an error is the same as being unworthy or unreliable. He always questions his worth and ability and tests it against the errors he makes. He refers to himself as always being on guard against making stupid mistakes. This striving for perfection irritates a lot of his subordinates because many believe that making mistakes is a part of life that can't be avoided.

A lot of things that top management does bothers Mr. Dana. For example, he was told on Friday that he had to begin training two assistant managers next week. He is particularly upset at the timing of the directive and not being asked his opinion about the assistant's schedule of training. At this time, Mr. Dana was overloaded with other commitments and found the training assignment to be ill timed. When the assistants arrived on Monday, they were introduced to a tense, irritated store manager who didn't hide his feelings. That evening Mr. Dana unloaded his frustrations on his son who didn't move fast enough to clean up his room. A twenty-minute shouting and screaming match occurred that eventually involved the entire family. After things settled down, Mr. Dana was unhappy with himself for losing control. He became withdrawn and depressed for the next week at home and on the job.

② COMPANY STRESS REACTION CHARTS*

OBJECTIVES

1. To gain insight into our reactions and thresholds regarding stress.

2. To consider what coping mechanisms you use to deal with stress.

STARTING THE EXERCISE

1. Each of us has a unique ability to tolerate stress, specific points when stress turns from a positive to negative impact, and unique abilities to cope with stress. Figures a through e are examples of possible reactions. Individually review each of the Figures a-e and decide which one is most similar to your own. If none is similar, draw your own diagram.

2. Groups of four-six participants will form to discuss Figures A-E and the individually constructed figures.

3. Individuals in each group will exchange ideas on what coping procedures are used to reduce stress.

Bert Eltry, a successful salesperson, was noted for his ability to get along with everyone. One day he was promoted to sales manager. His new responsibilities included pushing the salespersons to work harder and listening to all their gripes. He tried to cope with the stresses of his new job by working harder and being especially patient with everyone. After about six months he got fed up and became irritable. Both sales and morale dropped during the next half year. Bert asked to be transferred back to sales and was soon his old self again.

FIGURE A

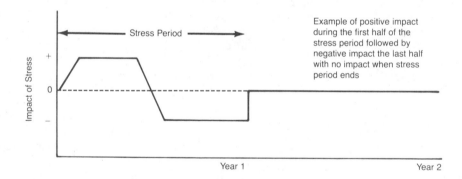

Example of positive impact during the first half of the stress period followed by negative impact the last half with no impact when stress period ends

Karl Kell, a loner, was the top analyst in the Wymar computer center. When the manager of the center quit, Karl was offered the job. Because he needed the money Karl accepted the job even though he did not feel confident about his management skills. Under the stress of the job Karl withdrew from his responsibilities and his assistant had to run the center. After one year of observing Karl flounder, top management reassigned him to his old job where he became effective once again.

Source: Adapted from Peter P. Dawson, *Fundamentals of Organizational Behavior* (Englewood Cliffs, NJ: Prentice-Hall, 1985), pp. 343–345, 393.

FIGURE B

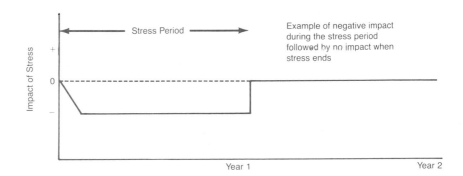

Bill Dawn enlisted in the Army during wartime and under the stress of combat performed in an outstanding manner. After a year overseas he was assigned as an instructor at Fort Ord, California. All went well for about six months, then Bill Dawn started having severe nightmares about combat, became overcautious on the practice firing range, and began drinking heavily. His performance slumped and he was given a medical discharge.

FIGURE C

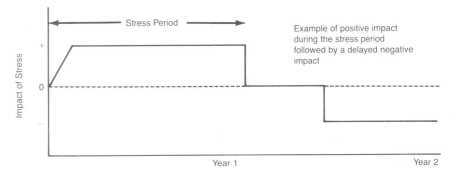

Betty Elliott did so well as manager of the Moderne Art Shop in Los Angeles that her boss offered her the project of opening a new outlet in San Diego. Under the stress of being watched by top management Betty worked day and night until the new outlet was successfully in operation. When she returned to her old job in Los Angeles she found what she had learned in San Diego made her more efficient with less effort.

FIGURE D

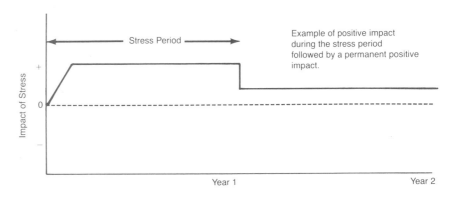

Della Ladner, a high school drop out, got a job working on an assembly line in a factory, but found the work exceedingly boring. The stress of boredom became so bad that after one year she quit and went to live with her parents. Thereafter, she never looked for another job. For twenty years she spent her time helping around the house and watching television. At age forty Della died from diseases related to obesity and alcoholism.

FIGURE E

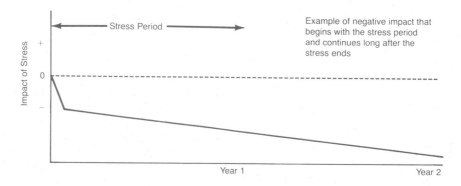

1 TIME PRESSURES, DELEGATION PROBLEMS OR CHAOS?*

It was 7:30 A.M. Tuesday, when Chet Craig, VP of Norris Oil Co., swung his car out of the driveway of his suburban home and headed to the bulk plant in Midvale. The trip took about 20 minutes which gave Chet an opportunity to think about business problems without interruption.

Norris Oil Co. is a 30 year old medium size petroleum jobbership serving an area comprised of three counties. There are 20 employees consisting of Chet's father (President and founder), a bookkeeper, an office manager/receptionist, two transport drivers, two tank-wagon drivers, a station supervisor, a warehouseman/deliveryman, ten service station employees and Chet. Chet functions as the General Manager handling the day-to-day operations. (Chet's dad makes the big, longer-range decisions and generally leaves the routine operations to Chet. Dad also spends a great deal of his time, these days, traveling and playing golf. He suffered some major health problems several years ago and decided to slow down.)

After attending college, Chet joined his father full-time in the business five years ago. (He worked during summers full time and each winter filled-in on home heating oil deliveries.) Chet has attended Phillips courses in retailing, lubricants and TBA as well as seminars on the petroleum industry, by the Oil Marketers Association. He is actively involved with the Chamber of Commerce, Rotary Club and Lion Club. Chet is married and has a 5 year old son and a 4 month old daughter.

Chet was in good spirits this morning. Various thoughts occurred to him as he said to himself, "This is going to be the day to really get things done." He thought of the day's work, first one project, then another, trying to establish priorities. He decided that the bulk lubricants implementation program was probably the most important; certainly the most urgent since competition had recently taken two of his larger, more profitable accounts by utilizing their bulk programs. He recalled discussing the program with his

*Case was prepared by John M. Ivancevich and Ralph Gurganus.

dad on Friday, and finally, after numerous discussions received the go-ahead on the concept. He had been meaning to pin his dad down on this for over three months, but something else always seemed to crop up.

"I haven't had time to really work it out," he said to himself. "I'd better get going and begin today." He then began to break down the objectives, procedures, and installation steps of the project. It gave him a feeling of satisfaction as he calculated the anticipated profits and cost savings. "It's high time," he told himself. "I should have done this a long time ago."

Chet had first wanted to get in the business almost two years after attending a seminar on bulk lube sales at the oil jobbers convention. He talked it over with Charlie Brown, his Phillips marketing representative, and both agreed that it was a good idea and worth developing. The idea was "temporarily" shelved, when Chet's dad became ill, about two years ago.

His thoughts returned to other projects, he was *determined* to get done today. He started to think about the transport truck problems they have been having—whether to repair the truck, replace it or sell it and go to common carrier hauling. He thought of the notes on his desk: the inventory analysis he needed to identify and eliminate some of the slow-moving stock items; the new station they are building in Riverpark; the new programs now offered by Phillips on appearance, credit cards, contracts, TBA, etc. He also decided this was the day to contact a back-up supplier of heating oil because last winter their only supplier had terminal problems and Chet had a tough time scrounging enough stone oil to get through the outage. There were a few other projects he could not recall offhand, but he felt sure that he could get to them sometime during the day. Again, he said to himself, "This is the day to really get rolling."

When he entered the office, Chet was met by Mary Davis, bookkeeper, who appeared troubled. "A great morning, Mary," said Chet, cheerfully.

"Well, I don't know, Chet; the bank called on the Smith Company to advise that their check for $5,000 was NSF." said Mary.

"How much do they owe" Chet asked.

"$12,000 with $8,000 45 days past due."

"Have you contacted Smith, yet?" Chet questioned.

"No" said Mary.

Chet replied, "I guess I better go over there right now and talk with Bill."

After talking with Bill at the Smith Company and receiving assurances that the $5,000 check would be good by day's end—Chet returned to the office.

He greeted a long-time customer on the loading dock who was picking up several cases of oil and some grease. The customer showed Chet a picture of his new grandson and then asked about the oil requirements of a new piece of equipment he had just purchased. When Chet was saying goodbye to the customer his office manager, Bess Parks, interrupted to say that Bob Jacobs, station supervisor, needed to talk with him—NOW!

Chet picked up the phone—only after he noticed a stack of at least ten phone messages on his desk it seems that the manager of the gas pumper and C store which Norris Oil owns and operates, called in sick and as a result Jacobs had to take over and run the station. Bob advised Chet that he had made arrangements for help to come in at 12:30 P.M. Bob asked Chet if he could pick up the bank deposits from their other two salaried stations and make the bank deposits. Chet said, "I'll take care of it."

Chet'd dad came in to talk about a complaint he had received from an old time customer involving a dealer operated station. Dad didn't want the station supervisor, Bob Jacobs, to handle the complaint, even though he admitted Bob could, because he wanted his son to give it his personal touch. Chet was feeling the pressure of the busy day but he said he would go by the station on the way home and talk with the dealer.

The warehouseman, George Pulaski, stuck his head in Chet's office to remind Chet about the truckload of lubricants arriving in the morning and asked, "Did you arrange for the part-time help to unload?" Chet had forgotten to make the arrangements and immediately called the local employment agency. He realized that he had an appointment in the morning he would have to cancel since he made it a practice to always be around when a lube shipment arrived.

Chet checked with Bess Parks, bookkeeper, to get a report on deliveries for today and tomorrow. Everything appeared okay. He had heard earlier in the day about possible delays at the terminal loading rack and, as a result, decided to call the terminal—no problems but he had to "shoot the breeze" with the manager which killed a lot of time.

Chet looked at his watch, took a deep breath, and was surprised to find that it was 3:30 P.M. and the marketing representative, Charlie Brown, was due at 4:00 P.M. This gave Chet time to contact the local equipment contractor and ask for a quote on installing two new dispensers at Jim's Service Station. After discussing and agreeing to the installation, Chet returned a call to the Oil Marketers Association. It seems that his input regarding new proposed state legislation by the state on underground tanks is required. A meeting is scheduled at the state capital, 200 miles north, Tuesday at 8:00 A.M. Chet agreed and made the necessary reservations.

Charlie Brown arrived and went over their new contract volumes on gasoline and distillates. To Chet's surprise, there did not appear to be sufficient volume to handle all the new business they have picked up recently. After a consultation with the bookkeeper regarding sales—Chet agreed to furnish Charlie with a month-by-month breakdown of required volumes for the next 12 months. Charlie also went over the list of station inspections required under the Phillips Image appearance program and established times so Chet could accompany him on the inspections. Brown wanted to go over the format for the dealer meeting planned next month but was interrupted by the phone—the transport had broken down outside of town. Chet apologized to Brown and jumped in his car to check on the transport.

On his way to the breakdown location, he remembered his thoughts this morning regarding his planned study of the transport. It turned out that the rear axle bearings were burned out. Chet called and arranged for the truck to be repaired. . . . at "after hours rates"!

It was now 6:00 P.M. and on his way back to the office, he visited with the dealer at Jim's Service Station on the customer complaint.

As he drove home Chet reviewed the day he had just completed. "Busy?" he asked himself, "Too much so—but did I accomplish anything?" The answer seemed to be "Yes, and no—there was the usual routine, the same as any other day. The Jobbership kept going and it was a good production day. Any creative or special work done?" Chet winced. "I guess not."

With a feeling of guilt Chet asked himself, "Am I an executive? I'm paid like one, and I have a responsible assignment, and the authority to carry it out. My dad thinks I'm a good manager. Yet one of the greatest returns a company gets from an executive is his innovative thinking and accomplishments. What have I done about that? Today was just like other days, and I didn't do any creative work. The projects that I was so eager to work on this morning are no further ahead than they were yesterday. What's more, I can't say that tomorrow night or the next night they'll be any closer to completion. This is a real problem, and there must be some answer to it."

Night work? Yes, sometimes. This is understood. But I've been doing too much night work lately. My wife and family deserve some of my time. After all, they are the people for whom I'm really working. If I spend much more time away from them, I'm not meeting my own personal objectives. I spend a lot of time on Chamber of Commerce work. Should I eliminate that? I feel I owe that as an obligation. Besides, I feel I'm making a worthwhile contribution in this work. Maybe I can squeeze a little time from my fraternal activities. But where does recreation fit in?"

Chet groped for the solution. "Maybe I'm just rationalizing because I schedule my own work poorly. But I don't think so. I've studied my work habits and I think I plan intelligently and delegate authority. Do I need an assistant? Possible, but that's a long-time project and I don't believe I could justify the additional overhead expense. Anyway, I doubt whether it would solve the problem."

By this time Chet had turned off the highway into the side street leading to his home. "I guess I really don't know the answer," he said to himself as he pulled into his driveway. "This morning everything seemed so simple, but now . . ." □

CASE QUESTIONS

1. What are the major stressors in Chet's life at the present time?
2. What symptoms is Chet displaying that indicate that he is under stress?
3. What type of program should Chet initiate to cope with his present stress?

② NO RESPONSE FROM MONITOR TWENTY-THREE*

Loudspeaker: IGNITION MINUS FORTY-FIVE MINUTES . . .

Paul Keller tripped the sequence switches at control monitor 23 in accordance with the countdown instruction book just to his left. All hydraulic systems were functioning normally in the second stage of the space-craft booster at checkpoint I minus forty-five. Keller automatically snapped his master control switch to GREEN and knew that his electronic impulse along with hundreds of others from similar consoles within the Cape Kennedy complex signalled continuation of the countdown.

Free momentarily from data input, Keller leaned back in his chair, stretched his arms above his head and then rubbed the back of his neck. The monitor lights on console 23 glowed routinely.

It used to be an incredible challenge, fantastically interesting work at the very fringe of man's knowledge about himself and his universe. Keller recalled his first day in Brevard County, Florida, with his wife and young daughter. How happy they were that day. Here was the future, the good life . . . forever. And Keller was going to be part of that fantastic, utopian future . . .

Loudspeaker: IGNITION MINUS THIRTY-FIVE MINUTES . . .

Keller panicked! His mind had wandered momentarily and he lost his place in the countdown instructions. Seconds later he found the correct place and tripped the proper sequence of switches for checkpoint I minus thirty-five. No problem. Keller snapped master control to GREEN and wiped his brow. He knew he was late reporting and would hear about it later.

Damn!, he thought, I used to know countdown cold for seven systems monitors without countdown instructions. But now . . . you're slipping Keller . . . you're slipping, he thought. Shaking his head, Keller reassured himself that he was overly tired today . . . just tired.

Loudspeaker: IGNITION MINUS THIRTY MINUTES . . .

Keller completed the reporting sequence for checkpoint I minus thirty, took one long last drag on his cigarette, and squashed it out in the crowded ashtray.

Utopia? Hell! It was one big rat-race and getting bigger all the time. Keller recalled how he once naively felt that his problems with Naomi would disappear after they left Minneapolis and came to the Cape with the space program. Now, ten thousand arguments later, Keller knew there was no escape . . .

"Only one can of beer left, Naomi? One stinking lousy can of beer, cold lunchmeat and potato salad? Is that all a man gets after twelve hours of mental exhaustion?"

"Oh, shut up, Paul! I'm so sick of you playing Mr. Important. You get leftovers because I never know when you're coming home . . . your daughter hardly knows you . . . and you treat us like nobodies . . . incidental to your great personal contribution to the Space Age."

"Don't knock it, Naomi. That job is plenty important to me, to the Team, and it gets you everything you've ever wanted . . . more! Between this house and the boat, we're up to our ears in debt."

"Now don't try to pin our money problems on me, Paul Keller. You're the one who has to have all the same goodies as the scientists earning twice your salary. Face it, Paul. You're just a button-pushing technician regardless of how fancy a title they give you. You can be replaced Paul. You can be replaced by any S.O.B. who can read and punch buttons!"

Loudspeaker: IGNITION MINUS TWENTY-FIVE MINUTES . . .

A red light blinked ominously indicating a potential hydraulic fluid leak in subsystem seven of stage two. Keller felt his heartbeat and pulse rate increase. Rule 1 . . . report malfunction immediately and stop the count. Keller punched POTENTIAL ABORT on the master control.

Loudspeaker: THE COUNT IS STOPPED AT IGNITION MINUS TWENTY-FOUR MINUTES SEVENTEEN SECONDS.

Keller fumbled with the countdown instructions. Any POTENTIAL ABORT required a cross check to separate an actual malfunction from sporadic signal

---

*Source: Robert D. Joyce, *Encounters in Organizational Behavior* (New York: Pergamon Press, 1972), pp. 168–172.

error. Keller began to perspire nervously as he initiated standard cross check procedures.

"Monitor 23, this is Control. Have you got an actual abort, Paul?" The voice in the headset was cool, but impatient. "Decision required in thirty seconds."

"I know, I know," Keller mumbled. "I'm cross checking right now."

Keller felt the silence closing in around him. Cross check one proved inconclusive. Keller automatically followed detailed instructions for cross check two.

"Do you need help, Keller?" asked the voice in the headset.

"No, I'm O.K."

Keller continued cross check two.

"Decision required," demanded the voice in the headset. "Dependent systems must be deactivated in fifteen seconds."

Keller read and re-read the console data. It looked like a sporadic error signal . . . the system appeared to be in order . . .

"Decision required," demanded the voice in the headset.

"Continue count," blurted Keller at last. "Subsystem seven fully operational." Keller slumped back in his chair.

Loudspeaker: THE COUNT IS RESUMED AT IGNITION MINUS TWENTY-FOUR MINUTES SEVENTEEN SECONDS.

Keller knew that within an hour after lift off, Barksdale would call him in for a personal conference. "What's wrong lately, Paul?" he would say. "Is there anything I can help with? You seem so tense lately." But he wouldn't really want to listen. Barksdale was the kind of person who read weakness into any personal problems and demanded that they be purged from the mind the moment his men checked out their consoles.

More likely Barksdale would demand that Keller make endless practice runs on cross check procedures while he stood nearby . . . watching and noting any errors . . . while the pressure grew and grew . . .

Today's performance was surely the kiss of death for any wage increase too. That was another of Barksdale's methods of obtaining flawless performance . . . which would surely lead to another scene with Naomi . . . and another sleepless night . . .
and more of those nagging stomach pains . . .
and yet another imperfect performance for Barksdale . . .

Loudspeaker: IGNITION MINUS TWENTY MINUTES . . .

The monitor lights at console twenty-three blinked routinely.

"Keller," said the voice in the earphone. "Report, please."

"Control, this is Wallace at monitor twenty-four. I don't believe Keller is feeling well. Better send someone to cover fast!"

Loudspeaker: THE COUNT IS STOPPED AT NINETEEN MINUTES THIRTY-THREE SECONDS.

"This is Control, Wallace. Assistance has been dispatched and the count is on temporary hold. What seems to be wrong with Keller?"

"Control, this is Wallace. I don't know. His eyes are open and fixed on the monitor but he won't respond to my questions. It could be a seizure or . . . a stroke."   □

CASE QUESTIONS

1. Is there any way of avoiding the more serious manifestations (as with Paul Keller) of pressure on the job? Explain.
2. Are there any early warning signs given by employees under stress? If so, what are they?
3. What is the proper role of the supervisor here? Should he attempt counseling?

INTERPERSONAL INFLUENCE AND GROUP BEHAVIOR

GROUP BEHAVIOR

This chapter examines groups in organizations. While the existence of groups in organizations probably does not alter the individual's motivation or needs, the group does influence the behavior of individuals in an organizational setting. Organizational behavior is more than simply the logical composite of the behavior of individuals. It is not their sum or product but rather a much more complex phenomenon, a very important part of which is the group. This chapter provides a model for understanding the nature of groups in organizations. The chapter explores the various types of groups, the reasons for their formation, the characteristics of groups, and some end results of group membership. What will become obvious is that groups must be understood by managers if goals are to be efficiently met.

THE NATURE OF GROUPS

No generally accepted definition of a group exists. Instead, a range of available views can be presented, and from these a comprehensive definition of a group can be developed. Although a comprehensive definition is provided there will be overlap among the interpretations offered. It should be noted that the originators of the various definitions worked in different disciplines or held diverse perspectives. Ultimately, the group in a work setting provided the focus for attempting to clarify and interpret group behavior.

A GROUP IN TERMS OF PERCEPTION

Many behavioral scientists believe that to be considered a group, the members of a group must perceive their relationships to others. For example:

> A small group is defined as any number of persons engaged in interaction with one another in a single face-to-face meeting or series of such meetings, in which each member receives some impression or perception of each other member distinct enough so that he can, either at the time or in later questioning, give some reaction to each of the others as an individual person, even though it may be only to recall that the other was present.[1]

This view points out that the members of a group must perceive the existence of each member as well as the existence of the group.

---

[1] R. F. Bales, *Interaction Process Analysis: A Method for the Study of Small Groups* (Reading, Mass.: Addison-Wesley, 1950), p. 33.

A GROUP IN TERMS OF ORGANIZATION

Sociologists view the group primarily in terms of organizational characteristics. For example, according to a sociological definition, a group is:

> an organized system of two or more individuals who are interrelated so that the system performs some function, has a standard set of role relationships among its members, and has a set of norms that regulate the function of the group and each of its members.[2]

This view emphasizes some of the important characteristics of groups, such as roles and norms, which are discussed later in this chapter.

A GROUP IN TERMS OF MOTIVATION

A group that fails to help its members satisfy their needs will have difficulty remaining viable. Employees who are not satisfying their needs in a particular group will search for other groups to aid in important need satisfactions. This view defines a group as:

> a collection of individuals whose existence as a collection is rewarding to the individuals.[3]

As pointed out in an earlier chapter, it is difficult to ascertain clearly what facets of the work organization are rewarding to individuals. The problem of identifying individual needs is a shortcoming of defining a group solely in terms of motivation.

A GROUP IN TERMS OF INTERACTION

Some theorists assume that interaction in the form of interdependence is the core of "groupness." A view that stresses interpersonal interactions is the following:

> We mean by a group a number of persons who communicate with one another often over a span of time, and who are few enough so that each person is able to communicate with all the others, not at secondhand, through other people, but face-to-face.[4]

All of these four views are important, since they each point to key features of groups. Furthermore, it can be stated that if a group exists in an organization, its members:

1. Are motivated to join.
2. Perceive the group as a unified unit of interacting people.
3. Contribute in various amounts to the group processes (i.e., some people contribute more time or energy to the group).
4. Reach agreements and have disagreements through various forms of interaction.

---

[2] J. W. McDavid and M. Harari, *Social Psychology: Individuals, Groups, Societies* (New York: Harper & Row, 1968), p. 237.

[3] Bernard M. Bass, *Leadership Psychology and Organizational Behavior* (New York: Harper & Row, 1960), p. 39.

[4] G. C. Homans, *The Human Group* (New York: Harcourt Brace Jovanovich, 1950), p. 1.

In this textbook, a **group** is defined as:

> two or more employees who interact with each other in such a manner that the behavior and/or performance of a member is influenced by the behavior and/or performance of other members.[5]

TYPES OF GROUPS

An organization has technical requirements that arise from its stated goals. The accomplishment of these goals requires that certain tasks be performed and that employees be assigned to perform these tasks. As a result, most employees will be members of a group based on their position in the organization. These are **formal groups.** On the other hand, whenever individuals associate on a fairly continuous basis, there is a tendency for groups to form whose activities may be different from those required by the organization. These are **informal groups.** Both formal groups and informal groups, it will be shown, exhibit the same general characteristics.

FORMAL GROUPS

The demands and processes of the organization lead to the formation of different types of groups. Specifically, two types of formal groups exist: command and task.

Command Group.   The command group is specified by the organization chart. The group is made up of the subordinates who report directly to a given supervisor. The authority relationship between a department manager and the supervisors, or between a senior nurse and her subordinates, is an example of a command group.

Task Group.   A task group comprises the employees who work together to complete a particular task or project. For example, the activities of clerks in an insurance company when an accident claim is filed are required tasks. These activities create a situation in which several clerks must communicate and coordinate with one another if the claim is to be handled properly. These required tasks and interactions facilitate the formation of a task group. The nurses assigned to duty in the emergency room of a hospital usually constitute a task group, since certain activities are required when a patient is treated.

INFORMAL GROUPS

Informal groups are natural groupings of people in the work situation in response to social needs. In other words, informal groups do not arise as a result of deliberate design. They evolve naturally. Two specific types of informal groups exist: interest and friendship.

---

[5] See M. E. Shaw, *Group Dynamics: The Psychology of Small Group Behavior,* 2nd ed. (New York: McGraw-Hill, 1976).

Interest Groups. Individuals who may not be members of the same command or task group may affiliate to achieve some mutual objective. Examples of interest groups include employees grouping together to present a unified front to management for more benefits and waitresses "pooling" their tips. Note that the objectives of such groups are not related to those of the organization but are specific to each group.

Friendship Groups. Many groups form because the members have something in common, such as age, political beliefs, or ethnic background. These friendship groups often extend their interaction and communication to off-the-job activities.

If employees' affiliation patterns were documented, it would become readily apparent that they belong to numerous and often overlapping groups. Why so many such groups exist is the question to which we turn next.

WHY PEOPLE FORM GROUPS

Formal and informal groups form for various reasons. Some of the reasons involve needs, proximity, attraction, goals, and economics.

THE SATISFACTION OF NEEDS

One of the most compelling reasons why people join groups is because they believe membership in a particular group will help them satisfy one or more important needs.[6] Typical employee needs which can be satisfied to a degree by their affiliation with groups include security, social, and esteem needs.

Security needs may be partially met, for example, by membership in an employee group which acts as a buffer between employees and the organizational system. Without such a group, an individual may feel alone in facing management and organizational demands. This "aloneness" leads to a degree of insecurity which can be offset by group membership. *Social needs* can be satisfied through groups, because the group provides a vehicle for an individual to interact with others. Indeed, it is difficult to imagine being able to fulfill general social needs without participating in at least some groups. *Esteem needs* may be partially met by belonging to a high-status or prestige group, membership in which is difficult to obtain or is based on some noteworthy achievement. An example would be the million-dollar round table in the life insurance business. For people with high esteem needs, membership in such a group can provide much needed satisfaction.[7]

---

[6] For a discussion of the group as an instrument for satisfaction of individual needs, see C. Gratton Kemp, *Perspectives on Group Processes* (Boston: Houghton Mifflin, 1970), pp. 26–29. Also see Linda N. Jewell and H. Joseph Reitz, *Group Effectiveness in Organizations* (Glenview, Ill.: Scott, Foresman, 1981). This is an excellent, comprehensive work devoted entirely to the subject of groups in organizational settings.

[7] See K. W. Mossholder, A. G. Bedian, and A. A. Armenakis, "Group Process-Work Outcome Relationships: A Note on the Moderating Effects of Self-Esteem," *Academy of Management Journal*, September 1982, pp. 575–85.

PROXIMITY AND ATTRACTION

Interpersonal interaction can result in group formation. Two important facets of interpersonal interaction are proximity and attraction. **Proximity** involves the physical distance between employees performing a job. **Attraction** designates the attraction of people to each other because of perceptual, attitudinal, performance, or motivational similarity.

Individuals who work in close proximity have numerous opportunities to exchange ideas, thoughts, and attitudes about various on- and off-the-job activities. These exchanges often result in some type of group formation. This proximity also makes it possible for individuals to learn about the characteristics of other people. To sustain the interaction and interest, a group often is formed. Facilitating the exposure to one another of people who work in close proximity may be a deliberate strategy by management, as illustrated in the following OBM Encounter.

ENCOUNTER
REMOVING THE PHYSICAL BARRIERS

Hewlett-Packard has long been well known for its strong belief that people are the heart and soul of any organization. This is more than a statement found in a policy manual; it is operationalized in myriad ways every day in Hewlett-Packard (HP) offices and plants. Part of this credo involves encouraging the development and maintenance of group spirit. An example is HP's site in Waltham, Mass.

The Waltham plant is a huge bullpen with only four-foot-high dividers splitting up the floor space. The idea is that by minimizing physical barriers that may separate personnel, closer cooperation and a sense of common purpose can be achieved among workers, supervisors, and managers. An HP division manager's office ($100-million unit) is a tiny, wall-less space on the factory floor, shared with a secretary. This type of close physical proximity helps also in getting different specialists to work together, such as product design people and manufacturing types. In short, everyone is accessible to everyone else. HP clearly believes this type of promoting of group effort pays dividends in terms of increased performance and loyalty.

Source: Based, in part, on an article by Gene Bylinski, "America's Best-Managed Factories," *Fortune,* May 28, 1984, p. 19.

GROUP GOALS

A group's goals, if clearly understood, can be reasons why an individual is attracted to it. For example, an individual may join a group that meets after work to become familiar with a new personal computer system. Assume that this system is to be implemented in the work organization over the next two years. The person who voluntarily joins the after-hours group believes that learning the new system is a necessary and important goal for employees.

It is not always possible to identify group goals. The assumption that formal organizational groups have clear goals must be tempered by the understanding that perception, attitudes, personality, and learning can distort goals. For example, a new employee may never be formally told the goals of the unit that he or she has joined. By observing the behavior and attitudes of others, individuals may conclude what they believe the goals to be. These perceptions may or may not be accurate. The same can be said about the goals of informal groups.

ECONOMIC REASONS

In many cases, groups form because individuals believe that they can derive greater economic benefits from their jobs if they organize. For example, individuals working at different points on an assembly line may be paid on a group-incentive basis where the production of the group determines the wages of each member. By working and cooperating as a group, the individuals may obtain higher economic benefits.

In numerous other instances, economic motives lead to group formation: workers in nonunion organizations form a group to exert pressure on top management for more benefits; top executives in a corporation form a group to review executive compensation. Whatever the circumstances, the group members have a common interest—increased economic benefits—that leads to group affiliation.

STAGES OF GROUP DEVELOPMENT

Groups learn, just as individuals do. The performance of a group depends both on individual learning and on how well the members learn to work with one another. For example, a new product committee formed for the purpose of developing a response to a competitor may evolve into a very effective team, with the interests of the company being most important. However, it may also be very ineffective if its members are more concerned about their individual departmental goals than about developing a response to a competitor. This section describes some general stages through which groups develop and points out that some kind of sequential developmental process is involved. The model we will use assumes that groups proceed through four stages of development: (1) mutual acceptance, (2) communication and decision making, (3) motivation and productivity, and (4) control and organization.[8]

MUTUAL ACCEPTANCE

In the early stages of group formation, members generally are reluctant to communicate with one another. Typically, they are not willing to express opinions, attitudes, and beliefs. This is similar to the situation facing a faculty member at the start of a new semester. Until the class members accept and trust one another, very little interaction and class discussion are likely to occur.

COMMUNICATION AND DECISION MAKING

After a group reaches the point of mutual acceptance, its members begin to communicate openly with one another. This communication results in increased confidence and even more interaction within the group. The discus-

---

[8] Bernard M. Bass, *Organizational Psychology* (Boston: Allyn & Bacon, 1965), pp. 197–98; and J. M. Ivancevich and J. T. McMahon, "Group Development, Trainer Style, and Carry-Over Job Satisfaction and Performance," *Academy of Management Journal,* September 1976, pp. 395–412. For an opposing viewpoint, see J. A. Seeger, "No Innate Phases in Group Problem Solving," *Academy of Management Review,* October 1983, pp. 683–89.

sions begin to focus more specifically on problem-solving tasks and on the development of alternative strategies to accomplish the tasks.[9]

MOTIVATION AND PRODUCTIVITY

This is the stage of development in which effort is expended to accomplish the group's goals. The group is working as a cooperative unit and not as a competitive unit.

CONTROL AND ORGANIZATION

At this point, group affiliation is valued and members are regulated by group norms. The group goals take precedence over individual goals, and the norms are compiled with, or sanctions are exercised. The ultimate sanction is ostracism for not complying with the group goals or norms. Other forms of control include temporary isolation from the group or harassment by the other members.

CHARACTERISTICS OF GROUPS

As groups evolve through their various stages of development, they begin to exhibit certain characteristics. To understand group behavior, you must be aware of these general characteristics. They are: structure, status hierarchy, roles, norms, leadership, cohesiveness, and conflict.

STRUCTURE

Within any group, some type of structure evolves over a period of time. The group members are differentiated on the basis of such factors as expertise, aggressiveness, power, and status. Each member occupies a *position* in the group. The pattern of relationships among the positions constitutes a *group structure*. In most cases, there is some type of status differences among positions such that the group structure is hierarchical. Status in formal groups usually is based on the position in the formal organization, while in informal groups, status can be based on anything relevant to the group (e.g., golf scores, ability to communicate with management).

STATUS HIERARCHY

Status and position are so similar that the terms often are used interchangeably. The status *assigned* to a particular position is typically a consequence of certain characteristics that differentiate one position from other positions. In some cases, a person is given status because of such factors as job seniority, age, or assignment. For example, the oldest worker may be perceived as being more technically proficient and is attributed status by a group of technicians. Thus, assigned status may have nothing to do with the formal status hierarchy.[10]

The status hierarchy, and particularly the deference paid to those at the top of the hierarchy, may sometimes have unintended—and undesirable— effects on performance, as the following OBM Encounter illustrates.

---

[9] See Ralph Katz, "The Effects of Group Longevity on Project Communication and Performance," *Administrative Science Quarterly,* March 1982, pp. 81–104.

[10] For a recent relevant study, see L. A. Nikolai and J. D. Bazley, "An Analysis of the Organizational Interaction of Accounting Departments," *Academy of Management Journal,* December 1977, pp. 608–21.

ENCOUNTER

STATUS HIERARCHY AND AN AIRLINE DISASTER

It was a typically cold winter day in Portland, Oregon, in December, 1978, when a McDonnell Douglas DC8 flight from New York and Denver crash-landed short of the runway by several miles. The crash, however, had nothing to do with the weather; rather, the airliner simply ran out of fuel.

Ten of the 189 persons on board were killed, so the crash did not receive the continued national media attention usually focused on airline disasters where far greater numbers of passengers perish. Yet, among commercial airline pilots, the incident is frequently cited and discussed. The plane ran out of fuel while flight crew members were preoccupied with a landing gear problem that had forced them to circle Portland for some time.

How could a variable as critical as reading the remaining fuel have gone unnoticed? Excerpts from the air transportation safety board's report show that it did not. Both the co-pilot and the flight engineer knew the fuel situation was becoming critical, but they did not do enough to warn the captain. A study of the transcript of the cockpit conversation that took place prior to the crash confirms that warnings were made, but were subtle, gentle, and extremely deferential to the senior captain. They either went unheard or unrespected. ☐

Source: Adapted from Douglas B. Feaver, "Pilots Learn to Handle Crises—and Themselves," *Washington Post,* September 12, 1982, p. A6.

ROLES   Each position in the group structure has an associated role that consists of the behaviors expected of the occupant of that position. For example, the director of nursing services in a hospital is expected to organize and control the department of nursing. The director is also expected to assist in preparing and administering the budget for the department. A nursing supervisor, on the other hand, is expected to supervise the activities of nursing personnel engaged in specific nursing services, such as obstetrics, pediatrics, and surgery. These expected behaviors generally are agreed on not only by the occupants, the director of nursing and the nursing supervisor, but by other members of the nursing group and other hospital personnel.[11]

An *expected role* is only one type of role. There are also a "perceived role" and an "enacted role." The *perceived role* is the set of behaviors that a person in a position believes he or she should enact. In some cases, the perceived role may correspond to the expected role. As discussed in Chapter 3, perception can, in some instances, be distorted or inaccurate. The *enacted role,* on the other hand, is the behavior that a person actually carries out. Thus, three possible role behaviors can result. Conflict and frustration may arise from differences in these three role types. In fairly stable or permanent groups, there typically is good agreement between expected and perceived roles. When the enacted role deviates too much from the expected role, the person either can become more like the expected role or leave the group.

---

[11] For example, see C. E. Schneier and P. W. Beatty, "The Influence of Role Prescriptions on the Performance Appraisal Process," *Academy of Management Journal,* March 1978, pp. 129–34.

Sometimes there is a conflict between different roles played by the same person. Through membership in different groups, individuals perform multiple roles. First-line supervisors are members of the management team but also are members of the group of workers they supervise. These multiple roles result in a number of expected role behaviors. In many instances, the behaviors specified by the different roles are compatible. When they are not, however, the individual experiences role conflict. There are several types of role conflict and some important consequences. Role conflict is discussed later in this chapter.

NORMS   **Norms** are the standards shared by the members of a group. Norms have certain characteristics that are important to group members. First, norms are formed only with respect to things that have significance for the group. They may be written, but very often they can be verbally communicated to members. In many cases, they may never be formally stated but somehow are known by group members. If production is important, then a norm will evolve. If helping other group members complete a task is important, then a norm will develop.[12] Second, norms are accepted in various degrees by group members. Some norms are completely accepted by all members, while other norms are only partially accepted. And third, norms may apply to every group member, or they may apply to only some group members. For example, every member may be expected to comply with the production norm, while only group leaders may be permitted to disagree verbally with a management directive.

Norm Conformity.   An issue of concern to managers is why employees conform to group norms.[13] This issue is especially important when a person with skill and capability is performing significantly below his or her capacity so that group norms are not violated. A number of variables may influence conformity to group norms. The *personal characteristics* of the individual play a role. For example, research indicates that persons of high intelligence are less likely to conform than less intelligent individuals, and authoritarian-personality types conform more than do non-authoritarians.[14] *Situational factors* such as group size and structure may influence conformity. For example, conformity may become more difficult in larger groups or in those whose members are geographically separated. *Intergroup relationships,* which include such factors as the kind of pressure the group exerts and the degree to which the member identifies with the group, are another potentially important variable.

[12] For examples, see R. J. Burke, T. Weir, and G. Duncan, "Informal Helping Relationships in Work Organizations," *Academy of Management Journal,* September 1976, pp. 370–77.

[13] Daniel C. Feldman, "The Development and Enforcement of Group Norms," *Academy of Management Review,* January 1984, pp. 47–53.

[14] Salvatore R. Maddi, *Personality Theories: A Comparative Analysis* (Homewood, Ill.: Dorsey Press, 1980), chap. 7.

Potential Consequences of Conforming to Group Norms. The research on conformity distinctly implies that conformity is a requirement of sustained group membership. The member who does not conform to important norms often is punished by a group. One form of punishment is to isolate or ignore the presence of the nonconformist. There are some potential negative and positive consequences of conformity. Conformity can result in a loss of individuality and the establishment of only moderate levels of performance. This type of behavior can be costly to an organization that needs above-average levels of performance to remain competitive. Also, potential positive consequences can occur from conformity to group norms. If no conformity existed, a manager would have a difficult, if not impossible, time in predicting a group's behavior patterns. This inability to estimate behavior could result in unsuccessful managerial attempts to channel the group's efforts toward the accomplishment of organizational goals.

In the first article accompanying this chapter, "The Development and Enforcement of Group Norms," Daniel Feldman examines in some detail how group norms develop and why they are enforced. In this article, note particularly the four conditions under which norms are most likely to be enforced.

LEADERSHIP

The leadership role is an extremely crucial characteristic of groups. The leader of a group exerts some influence over the other members of the group. In the formal group, the leader can exercise legitimately sanctioned power. That is, the leader can reward or punish members who do not comply with the directives, orders, or rules.

The leadership role also is a significant factor in an informal group. The person who becomes an informal group leader generally is viewed as a respected and high-status member who embodies the values of the group, aids the group in accomplishing its goals, and enables members to satisfy needs. Additionally, the leader is the choice of group members to represent their viewpoint outside the group, and usually is concerned with maintaining the group as a functioning unit.

COHESIVENESS

Formal and informal groups seem to possess a closeness or commonness of attitude, behavior, and performance. This closeness has been referred to as *cohesiveness*. Cohesiveness typically is regarded as a force. It acts on the members to remain in a group and is greater than the forces pulling the members away from the group. A cohesive group, then, involves individuals who are attracted to one another. A group that is low in cohesiveness does not possess interpersonal attractiveness for the members.

Since highly cohesive groups are composed of individuals who are motivated to be together, there is a tendency on the part of management to expect effective group performance. This logic is not supported conclusively by research evidence. In general, as the cohesiveness of a work group increases, the level of conformity to group norms also increases. But these norms may be inconsistent with those of the organization. The group pressures to conform are more intense in the cohesive group. The question of whether managers should encourage or discourage group cohesiveness is examined later in this chapter.

Cohesiveness and Performance.　　The concept of cohesiveness is important for understanding groups in organizations, as is the recognition of the impact of groups on performance.[15] The degree of cohesiveness in a group can have positive or negative effects, depending on how group goals match up with those of the formal organization.[16] In fact, four distinct possibilities exist, as illustrated in Figure 7–1.

FIGURE 7–1

The Relationship between Group Cohesiveness and Agreement with Organizational Goals

		Agreement with Organizational Goals	
		Low	High
Degree of Group Cohesiveness	Low	Performance oriented away from organizational goals.	Performance probably oriented toward achievement of organizational goals.
	High	Performance probably oriented away from organizational goals.	Performance oriented toward achievement of organizational goals.

Figure 7–1 indicates that if cohesiveness is high and the group accepts and agrees with formal organizational goals, then group behavior probably will be positive from the formal organization's standpoint. However, if the group is highly cohesive but has goals that are not congruent with those of the formal organization, then group behavior probably will be negative from the formal organization's standpoint.

Figure 7–1 also indicates that if a group is low in cohesiveness and the members have goals that are not in agreement with those of management, then the results probably will be negative from the standpoint of the organization. Behavior will be more on an individual basis than on a group basis, because of the low cohesiveness. On the other hand, it is possible to have a group low in cohesiveness where the members' goals agree with those of the formal organization. Here, the results probably will be positive, although again more on an individual basis than on a group basis.

When the goals of a cohesive group conflict with those of management, some form of intervention by management usually is necessary. Intervention techniques are discussed in detail in the next chapter.

[15] Karen Brown, "Explaining Group Poor Performance: An Attributional Analysis," *Academy of Management Review,* January 1984, pp. 54–63.

[16] It should be noted, of course, that cohesiveness is not the only factor which may influence performance. For just one example, see Wendy Wood, Darlene Polek, and Cheryl Aiken, "Sex Differences in Group Task Performance," *Journal of Personality and Social Psychology,* January 1985, pp. 63–71.

Groupthink. Highly cohesive groups are very important forces in organizational behavior. In other words, it is a good idea to place people with many similarities in an isolated setting, give them a common goal, and reward them for performance. On the surface, this may look like a good idea. One author has provided a very provocative account about highly cohesive groups.[17] In his book, Irving Janis has analyzed foreign policy decisions made by a number of presidential administrations and concluded that these groups were highly cohesive and close-knit. He has labeled their decision-making process **"groupthink."** Janis defines groupthink as the "deterioration of mental efficiency, reality testing, and moral judgement" in the interest of group solidarity.[18] According to Janis, groups suffering from groupthink tend to display a number of characteristics:

1.   An illusion of invulnerability.
2.   A tendency to moralize about the "goodness" of their position.
3.   A feeling of unaniminity concerning group positions and decisions.
4.   Pressure, from the group or individual members, to conform, thus silencing divergent views.
5.   Dismissal of opposing ideas from outside individuals and other groups.

Certainly, some level of group cohesiveness is necessary for a group to tackle a problem. If seven individuals from seven different organizational units are assigned a task, the task may never be completed effectively. The point, however, is that more cohesiveness may not necessarily be better. While members of task groups may redefine solving a problem to mean reaching agreement rather than making the best decision, members of cohesive groups may redefine it to mean preserving relations among group members and preserving the image of the group. Some research suggests that even among highly cohesive groups, groupthink is not a factor if the group is comprised of highly dominant individuals.[19]

INTERGROUP CONFLICT

An important characteristic of groups is that they frequently conflict with other groups in an organization. There are many reasons why groups conflict with one another, and the consequences of this conflict can be good for the organization, or it can be extremely negative.

This chapter is concerned mainly with what happens *within* groups: the types and characteristics of groups as they develop. What happens *between* groups (intergroup behavior) is the subject of the next chapter.

---

[17] Irving Janis, *Victims of Groupthink: A Psychological Study of Foreign Policy Decisions and Fiascos* (Boston: Houghton Mifflin, 1983).

[18] Ibid., p. 9.

[19] Michael Callaway, Richad Marriott, and James Esser, "Effects of Dominance on Group Decision Making: Toward a Stress-Reduction Explanation of Groupthink," *Journal of Personality and Social Psychology,* October 1985, pp. 949–52.

THE CONCEPT OF ROLE

The concept of **role** is very important to the understanding of organizational behavior. Role refers to the expected behavior patterns attributed to a particular position in an organization.

The roles of wife and husband are familiar to everyone. Those roles are culturally defined expectations associated with particular positions. A role may include attitudes and values as well as specific kinds of behavior. It is what an individual must do in order to validate his or her occupancy of a particular position. In other words, what kind of a husband or wife an individual is depends a great deal on how he or she performs the culturally defined role associated with the position.

Certain activities are expected of every position in the formal organization. These activities constitute the role for that position from the standpoint of the organization. The organization develops job descriptions that define the activities of a particular position and how it relates to other positions in the organization. However, roles may not be set forth explicitly and yet be clearly understood by group members. This is true both for formal and informal groups. Thus, whether they are formally or informally established, status hierarchies and accompanying roles are integral parts of every organization.

MULTIPLE ROLES AND ROLE SETS

Most of us play many roles simultaneously. This is because we occupy many different positions in a variety of organizations—home, work, church, civic, and so forth. Within each of these organizations, we occupy and perform certain roles. Most individuals perform **multiple roles.** We may simultaneously be playing the role of parent, mate, supervisor, and subordinate. For each position, there may be different role relationships. For example, the position of college professor involves not only the role of teacher in relation to students but also numerous other roles relating the position to administrators, peers, the community, and alumni. Each group may expect different things. For example, students may expect good classroom performance; administrators may expect classroom performance, research, and publication; the college community may expect community service; and alumni may expect help in recruiting students and athletes. This we term the **role set.** A role set refers to those individuals who have expectations for the behavior of the individual in the particular role. The more expectations, the more complex is the role set.

Multiple roles refer to different roles, while role set refers to the different expectations associated with one role. Therefore, an individual involved in many different roles, each with a complex role set, faces the ultimate in complexity of individual behavior. The concepts of multiple roles and role sets are important because there may be complications that make it extremely difficult to define specific roles, especially in organizational settings.[20] This

---

[20] An important work in this field is R. L. Kahn, D. M. Wolfe, R. P. Quinn, and J. D. Snoek, *Organizational Stress: Studies in Role Conflict and Ambiguity* (New York: John Wiley & Sons, 1964), pp. 12–26.

can often result in *role conflict* for the individual. As we saw in Chapter 6, role conflict is a major cause of individual stress in organizations.

ROLE PERCEPTION

You can understand how different individuals have different perceptions of the behavior associated with a given role. In an organizational setting, accuracy in role perception can have a definite impact on performance.[21] This matter is further complicated in an organization because there may be three different perceptions of the same role: that of the formal organization, that of the group, and that of the individual. For example, a college dean has perceptions of the role of professors, as do students and the professors themselves. As we saw in our discussion of role sets above, student perceptions of the role of a professor may be very different from those of the college administrators. This increases even further the possibility of role conflict.

ROLE CONFLICT

Because of the multiplicity of roles and role sets, it is possible for an individual to face a situation where there is simultaneous occurrence of two or more role requirements and the performance of one precludes the performance of the others. When this occurs, the individual faces a situation known as **role conflict.** Several forms of role conflict can occur in organizations.

Person-Role Conflict. Person-role conflict occurs when role requirements violate the basic values, attitudes, and needs of the individual occupying the position. A supervisor who finds it difficult to dismiss a subordinate with a family and an executive who resigns rather than engage in some unethical activity are examples of individuals experiencing this type of role conflict.[22]

Intrarole Conflict. Intrarole conflict occurs when different individuals define a role according to different sets of expectations, making it impossible for the person occupying the role to satisfy all of them. This is more likely to occur when a given role has a complex role set (many different role relationships). The supervisor in an industrial situation has a rather complex role set and thus may face intrarole conflict. On one hand, top management has a set of expectations that stresses the supervisor's role in the management hierarchy. However, the supervisor may have close friendship ties with members of the command group who may be former working peers. This is why supervisors often are described as being "in the middle."[23]

---

[21] For a relevant study, see A. D. Szilagyi, "An Empirical Test of Causal Inference between Role Perceptions, Satisfaction with Work, and Organizational Level," *Personnel Psychology,* Autumn 1977, pp. 375–88.

[22] For example, see N. Keeley, "Subjective Performance Evaluation and Person-Role Conflict under Conditions of Uncertainty," *Academy of Management Journal,* June 1977, pp. 301–14. For an analysis of some of the organizational implications of this type of conflict, see L. Roos and F. Starke, "Roles in Organizations," in *Handbook of Organizational Design,* ed. W. Starbuck and P. Nystrom (Oxford, England: Oxford University Press, 1980).

[23] For classic discussions of the conflict-laden position of foremen, see F. J. Roethlisberger, "The Foreman: Master and Victim of Double Talk," *Harvard Business Review,* September-October 1965, pp. 23 ff; and F. C. Mann and J. K. Dent, "The Supervisor: Member of Two Organizational Families," *Harvard Business Review,* November-December 1954, pp. 103–12.

Interrole Conflict. Interrole conflict can result from facing multiple roles. It occurs because individuals simultaneously perform many roles, some of which have conflicting expectations. A scientist in a chemical plant who also is a member of a management group might experience role conflict of this kind. In such a situation, the scientist may be expected to behave in accordance with the expectations of management as well as the expectations of professional chemists. A physician placed in the role of hospital administrator also may experience this type of role conflict. Sometimes, the conflict is between the individual's role as a group member on the one hand, and a member of the larger organization on the other. The following OBM Encounter is a case in point. In the next chapter, you will see that interrole conflict often is also the cause of conflict between groups in many organizations.

THE RESULTS OF ROLE CONFLICT

Behavioral scientists agree that an individual confronted with role conflict will experience psychological stress that may result in emotional problems and indecision. These problems were outlined in detail in Chapter 6. While there are certain kinds of role conflict that managers can do little to avoid, many role conflicts can be minimized. For example, some types of role conflict (especially intrarole conflict) can be the result of violations of the classical principles of chain of command and unity of command. The rationale of the early management writers for these two principles was that violation probably would cause conflicting pressures on the individual. In other words, when individuals are faced with conflicting expectations or demands from two or more sources, the likely result will be a decline in performance.

 ENCOUNTER

WHEN EMPLOYEES ARE ASKED TO TELL ON EACH OTHER

Emporium-Capwell, a California department store, is offering a bounty to employees who snitch on other employees. Recently, when employees opened their pay envelopes, they found a second check in the amount of $300. A close inspection revealed the check to be non-negotiable. An attached note from management, however, promised to reward employees for reporting co-workers who shoplift or commit other dishonest acts.

"Would you like to have this check?" read the note. "If so, simply provide the loss prevention department with information which leads to the termination of a dishonest employee. All information is treated with strict confidence and thoroughly investigated before any action is taken."

Many Emporium employees said they resented the move and would not cooperate. "I've worked here 18 years and this is the lousiest thing I've ever seen," said one. "Everybody was mad. On the one hand, they want you to work as a team and respect your co-workers. On the other, they want you to stab them in the back. I just think it's lousy."

Richard Hedges, president of the union which represents numerous Emporium-Capwell employees, agrees. He has received calls from several dozen employees concerning the plan. Hedges was quoted as saying, "It's one thing to say, 'If you have knowledge that someone is violating the law, contact us.' It's another to put out a bounty and encourage people to call with their suspicions. I think this may backfire. It will create ill will and paranoia." □

Source: From an article in the *San Francisco Examiner,* appearing in the *Houston Chronicle,* November 9, 1985, sec. 1, p. 4.

In addition, interrole conflict can be generated by conflicting expectations of formal or informal groups, with results similar to those of intrarole conflict. Thus, a highly cohesive group with goals not consistent with those of the formal organization can cause a great deal of interrole conflict for the group's members.

One final point must be made concerning role conflict. Research has shown that role conflict does occur frequently and with negative effects on performance over a wide spectrum of occupations.[24]

AN INTEGRATED MODEL OF GROUP FORMATION AND DEVELOPMENT

Figure 7–2 summarizes what has been discussed to this point. It indicates all of the potential end results of group behavior: individual performances, group performances, and overall organizational effectiveness and perfor-

FIGURE 7–2

A Model of Group Formation and Development

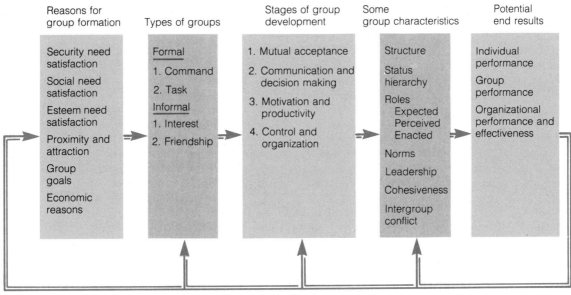

[24] R. G. Corwin, "The Professional Employee: A Study of Conflict in Nursing Roles," *American Journal of Sociology,* May 1961, pp. 604–15; J. M. Ivancevich and J. H. Donnelly, Jr., "A Study of Role Clarity and Need for Clarity for Three Occupational Groups," *Academy of Management Journal,* March 1974, pp. 28–36; R. H. Miles, "A Comparison of the Relative Impacts of Role Perceptions of Ambiguity and Conflict by Role," *Academy of Management Journal,* March 1976, pp. 25–34; L. Chonko, "The Relationship of Span of Control to Sales Representatives' Experienced Role Conflict and Role Ambuguity," *Academy of Management Journal,* June 1982, pp. 452–56; and P. J. Nicholson, Jr., and S. C. Goh, "The Relationship of Organization Structure and Interpersonal Attitudes to Role Conflict and Ambiguity in Different Work Environments," *Academy of Management Journal,* March 1983, pp. 148–56.

mance. The model also includes feedback from the potential behavioral consequences and each of the other elements in the model. Note that each segment can influence each of the other segments.

The potential end results shown in the model strongly suggest that groups are important and should be recognized as such. This idea, in fact, is the theme of Harold Leavitt's article, "Suppose We Took Groups Seriously," which accompanies this chapter. Leavitt argues that groups are—and should be so considered by management—the building blocks of organizations. In addition to the points made thus far in this chapter, Leavitt identifies several reasons groups may significantly effect organizational functioning.

SUMMARY OF KEYPOINTS

A. A group can be viewed in terms of perception, organization, motivation, or interaction. You should consider a group as employees who interact in such a manner that the behavior or performance of one group member is influenced by the behavior or performance of other group members.

B. By being aware of group characteristics and behaviors, managers can be prepared for the potential positive and negative results of group activities. In a proactive sense, a manager can intervene to modify the perceptions, attitudes, and motivations that precede the results.

C. People are attracted to groups because of their potential for satisfying needs, their physical proximity and attraction, and the appeal of group goals and activities. In essence, people are attracted to one another; this is a natural process.

D. Groups develop at different rates and with unique patterns that depend on the task, the setting, the members' individual characteristics and behavioral patterns, and the manager's style of managing.

E. Some characteristics of groups are:

1. Structure.
2. Status hierarchy.
3. Roles.
4. Norms.
5. Leadership.
6. Cohesiveness.
7. Intergroup conflict.

These characteristics pervade all groups. In an informal group these characteristics emerge from within the unit, while in a formal group they are established by the managerial process. The characteristics provide a degree of predictability for the members that is important to the group and to outsiders (e.g., management, other groups). A group that is unstable or unpredictable is a problem for its members and for others who interact with it.

F. Each group possesses some degree of cohesiveness. This attractiveness of the group can be a powerful force in influencing individual behavior and performance.

G. Research studies indicate that cohesive groups can formulate goals and norms that may or may not agree with those of management. When these goals and norms are incongruent, some form of managerial intervention is necessary.

H. The concept of role is vital to an understanding of group behavior. A role is the expected behavior patterns attributed to a particular position. Most individuals perform multiple roles, each with its own role set (expectations of others for the role). An individual involved in many different roles, each having a complex role set, faces the ultimate in complexity of individual behavior.

I. When an individual faces the simultaneous occurrence of two or more role requirements for which the performance of one precludes the performance of the others, he or she experiences role conflict. Three different types of role conflict—person-role conflict, intrarole conflict, and interrole conflict—can occur in organizational settings. Research has shown that the consequences of role conflict to the individual include increased psychological stress and other emotional reactions. Management can minimize certain types of role conflicts and should be continually aware that the consequences to the organization can include ineffective performance by individuals and groups.

REVIEW AND DISCUSSION QUESTIONS

1. Think of a formal group to which you belong. Describe the group in terms of the characteristics of groups discussed in this chapter.

2. Repeat the process above, this time for an informal group to which you belong.

3. Is it possible for the membership of a formal and informal group to be identical? Can you think of an example where this might be the case?

4. Under what circumstances might an organization encourage the formation of informal employee groups? Why might they discourage such groups?

5. Have you ever experienced role conflict? Which type of role conflict was it? What did you do to resolve the conflict? What effect did the conflict have on your behavior?

6. What is the relationship between cohesiveness of a group and its performance?

7. Why is groupthink something to be avoided? How might a manager attempt to insure that groupthink doesn't occur in his or her group?

8. Are the factors that influence group behavior the same or different from those that influence individual behavior? Explain.

9. "The informal group is potentially the most potent shaper of behavior in organizations." Do you agree or disagree with that statement? Discuss your reasons.

10. Think of some groups you have voluntarily joined. Why did you join them? Think of some groups you have stopped participating in. Why did you stop? Does joining or leaving informal groups at work have implications for management?

R¹ THE DEVELOPMENT AND ENFORCEMENT OF GROUP NORMS*

DANIEL C. FELDMAN

Group norms are the informal rules that groups adopt to regulate and regularize group members' behavior. Although these norms are infrequently written down or openly discussed, they often have a powerful, and consistent, influence on group members' behavior (Hackman, 1976).

Most of the theoretical work on group norms has focused on identifying the types of group norms (March, 1954) or on describing their structural characteristics

* Source: Reprinted from "The Development of and Enforcement of Group Norms," by Daniel C. Feldman, published in ACADEMY OF MANAGEMENT REVIEW, Vol. 9, No. 1 (January 1984), pp. 47–53 by permission of the ACADEMY OF MANAGEMENT REVIEW.

(Jackson, 1966). Empirically, most of the focus has been on examining the impact that norms have on other social phenomena. For example, Seashore (1954) and Schachter, Ellertson, McBride, and Gregory (1951) use the concept of group norms to discuss group cohesiveness; Trist and Bamforth (1951) and Whyte (1955a) use norms to examine production restriction; Janis (1972) and Longley and Pruitt (1980) use norms to illuminate group decision making; and Asch (1951) and Sherif (1936) use norms to examine conformity.

This paper focuses on two frequently overlooked aspects of the group norms literature. First, it examines *why* group norms are enforced. Why do groups desire conformity to these informal rules? Second, it examines *how* group norms develop. Why do some norms develop in one group but

not in another? Much of what is known about group norms comes from post hoc examination of their impact on outcome variables; much less has been written about how these norms actually develop and why they regulate behavior so strongly.

Understanding how group norms develop and why they are enforced is important for two reasons. First, group norms can play a large role in determining whether the group will be productive or not. If the work group feels that management is supportive, groups norms will develop that facilitate—in fact, enhance—group productivity. In contrast, if the work group feels that management is antagonistic, group norms that inhibit and impair group performance are much more likely to develop. Second, managers can play a major role in setting and changing group norms. They can use their influence to set task-facilitative norms; they can monitor whether the group's norms are functional; they can explicitly address counterproductive norms with subordinates. By understanding how norms develop and why norms are enforced, managers can better diagnose the underlying tensions and problems their groups are facing, and they can help the group develop more effective behavior patterns.

WHY NORMS ARE ENFORCED

As Shaw (1981) suggests, a group does not establish or enforce norms about every conceivable situation. Norms are formed and enforced only with respect to behaviors that have some significance for the group. The frequent distinction between task maintenance duties and social maintenance duties helps explain why groups bring selected behaviors under normative control.

Groups, like individuals, try to operate in such a way that they maximize their chances for task success and minimize their chances of task failure. First of all, a group will enforce norms that facilitate its very survival. It will try to protect itself from interference from groups external to the organization or harassment from groups internal to the organization. Second, the group will want to increase the predictability of group members' behaviors. Norms provide a basis for predicting the behavior of others, thus enabling group members to anticipate each other's actions and to prepare quick and appropriate responses (Shaw, 1981; Kiesler & Kiesler, 1970).

In addition, groups want to ensure the satisfaction of their members and prevent as much interpersonal discomfort as possible. Thus, groups also will enforce norms that

help the group avoid embarrassing interpersonal problems. Certain topics of conversation might be sanctioned, and certain types of social interaction might be openly discouraged. Moreover, norms serve an expressive function for groups (Katz & Kahn, 1978). Enforcing group norms gives group members a chance to express what their central values are, and to clarify what is distinctive about the group and central to its identity (Hackman, 1976).

 **LEARNING CHECKPOINT**

What other reasons explain why groups form in organizations?

Each of these four conditions under which group norms are most likely to be enforced is discussed in more detail below.

1. Norms are likely to be enforced if they facilitate group survival. A group will enforce norms that protect it from interference or harassment by members of other groups. For instance, a group might develop a norm not to discuss its salaries with members of other groups in the organization, so that attention will not be brought to pay inequities in its favor. Groups might also have norms about not discussing internal problems with members of other units. Such discussions might boomerang at a later date if other groups use the information to develop a better competitive strategy against the group.

Enforcing group norms also makes clear what the "boundaries" of the group are. As a result of observation of deviant behavior and the consequences that ensue, other group members are reminded of

the *range* of behavior that is acceptable to the group (Dentler & Erikson, 1959). The norms about productivity that frequently develop among piecerate workers are illustrative here. By observing a series of incidents (a person produces 50 widgets and is praised; a person produces 60 widgets and receives sharp teasing; a person produces 70 widgets and is ostracized), group members learn the limits of the group's patience: "This far, and no further." The group is less likely to be "successful" (i.e., continue to sustain the low productivity expectations of management) if it allows its jobs to be reevaluated.

The literature on conformity and deviance is consistent with this observation. The group is more likely to reject the person who violates group norms when the deviant has not been a "good" group member previously (Hollander, 1958, 1964). Individuals can generate "idiosyncrasy credits" with other group members by contributing effectively to the attainment of group goals. Individuals expend these credits when they perform poorly or dysfunctionally at work. When a group member no longer has a positive "balance" of credits to draw on when he or she deviates, the group is much more likely to reject that deviant (Hollander, 1961).

Moreover, the group is more likely to reject the deviant when the group is failing in meeting its goals successfully. When the group is successful, it can afford to be charitable or tolerant towards deviant behavior. The group may disapprove, but it has some margin for error. When the group is faced with failure, the deviance is much more sharply punished. Any behavior that negatively influences the success of the group becomes much more salient and threatening to group members (Alvarez, 1968; Wiggins, Dill, & Schwartz, 1965)

2. Norms are likely to be enforced if they simplify, or make predictable, what behavior is expected of group members. If each member of the group had to decide individually how to behave in each interaction, much time would be lost performing routine activities. Moreover, individuals would have more trouble predicting the behaviors of others and responding correctly. Norms enable group members to anticipate each other's actions and to prepare the most appropriate response in the most timely manner (Hackman, 1976; Shaw, 1981).

For instance, when attending group meetings in which proposals are presented and suggestions are requested, do the presenters really want feedback or are they simply going through the motions? Groups may develop norms that reduce this uncertainty and provide a clearer course of action, for example, make suggestions in small, informal meetings but not in large, formal meetings.

Another example comes from norms that regulate social behavior. For instance, when colleagues go out for lunch together, there can be some awkwardness about how to split the bill at the end of the meal. A group may develop a norm that gives some highly predictable or simple way of behaving, for example, split evenly, take turns picking up the tab, or pay for what each ordered.

Norms also may reinforce specific individual members' roles. A number of different roles might emerge in groups. These roles are simply expectations that are shared by group members regarding who is to carry out what types of activities under what circumstances

(Bales & Slater, 1955). Although groups obviously create pressure toward uniformity among members, there also is a tendency for groups to create and maintain *diversity* among members (Hackman, 1976). For instance, a group might have one person whom others expect to break the tension when tempers become too hot. Another group member might be expected to keep track of what is going on in other parts of the organization. A third member might be expected to take care of the "creature" needs of the group—making the coffee, making dinner reservations, and so on. A fourth member might be expected by others to take notes, keep minutes, or maintain files.

None of these roles are *formal* duties, but they are activities that the group needs accomplished and has somehow parcelled out among members. If the role expectations are not met, some important jobs might not get done, or other group members might have to take on additional responsibilities. Moreover, such role assignments reduce individual members' ambiguities about what is expected specifically of them. It is important to note, though, that who takes what role in a group also is highly influenced by individuals' personal needs. The person with a high need for structure often wants to be in the note-taking role to control the structuring activity in the group; the person who breaks the tension might dislike conflict and uses the role to circumvent it.

3. Norms are likely to be enforced if they help the group avoid embarrassing interpersonal problems. Goffman's work on "facework" gives some insight on this point. Goffman (1955) argues that each

person in a group has a "face" he or she presents to other members of a group. This "face" is analogous to what one would call "self-image," the person's perceptions of himself or herself and how he or she would like to be seen by others. Groups want to insure that no one's self-image is damaged, called into question, or embarrassed. Consequently, the group will establish norms that discourage topics of conversation or situations in which face is too likely to be inadvertently broken. For instance, groups might develop norms about not discussing romantic involvements (so that differences in moral values do not become salient) or about not getting together socially in people's homes (so that differences in taste or income do not become salient).

A good illustration of Goffman's facework occurs in the classroom. There is always palpable tension in a room when either a class is totally unprepared to discuss a case or a professor is totally unprepared to lecture or lead the discussion. One part of the awkwardness stems from the inability of the other partner in the interaction to behave as he or she is prepared to or would like to behave. The professor cannot teach if the students are not prepared, and the students cannot learn if the professors are not teaching. Another part of the awkwardness, though, stems from self-images being called into question. Although faculty are aware that not all students are serious scholars, the situation is difficult to handle if the class as a group does not even show a pretense of wanting to learn. Although students are aware that many faculty are mainly interested in research and consulting, there is a problem if the professor does not even show a pretense of caring to teach. Norms almost always develop between professor and students about what level of preparation and interest is expected by the other because both parties want to avoid awkward confrontations.

4. Norms are likely to be enforced if they express the central values of the group and clarify what is distinctive about the group's identity. Norms can provide the social justification for group activities to its members (Katz & Kahn, 1978). When the production group labels rate-busting deviant, it says: "We care more about maximizing group security than about individual profits." Group norms also convey what is distinctive about the group to outsiders. When an advertising agency labels unstylish clothes deviant, it says: "We think of ourselves, personally and professionally, as trend-setters, and being fashionably dressed conveys that to our clients and our public."

One of the key expressive functions of group norms is to define and legitimate the power of the group itself over individual members (Katz & Kahn, 1978). When groups punish norm infraction, they reinforce in the minds of group members the authority of the group. Here, too, the literature on group deviance sheds some light on the issue at hand.

It has been noted frequently that the amount of deviance in a group is rather small (Erikson, 1966; Schur, 1965). The group uses norm enforcement to show the *strength* of the group. However, if a behavior becomes so widespread that it becomes impossible to control, then the labeling of the widespread behavior as deviance becomes problematic. It simply reminds members of the *weakness* of the group. At this point, the group will redefine what is deviant more narrowly, or it will define its

job as that of keeping deviants *within bounds* rather than that of obliterating it altogether. For example, though drug use is and always has been illegal, the widespread use of drugs has led to changes in law enforcement over time. A greater distinction now is made between "hard" drugs and other controlled substances; less penalty is given to those apprehended with small amounts than large amounts; greater attention is focused on capturing large scale smugglers and traffickers than the occasional user. A group, unconsciously if not consciously, learns how much behavior it is capable of labeling deviant *and* punishing effectively.

Finally, this expressive function of group norms can be seen nicely in circumstances in which there is an inconsistency between what group members *say* is the group norm and how people actually *behave*. For instance, sometimes groups will engage in a lot of rhetoric about how much independence its managers are allowed and how much it values entrepreneurial effort; yet the harder data suggest that the more conservative, deferring, or dependent managers get rewarded. Such an inconsistency can reflect conflicts among the group's expressed values. First, the group can be ambivalent about independence; the group knows it needs to encourage more entrepreneurial efforts to flourish, but such efforts create competition and threaten the status quo. Second, the inconsistency can reveal major subgroup differences. Some people may value and encourage entrepreneurial behavior, but others do not—and the latter may control the group's rewards. Third, the inconsistency can reveal a source of the group's self-consciousness, a dichotomy between what the group is really like and how it would like

to be perceived. The group may realize that it is too conservative, yet be unable or too frightened to address its problem. The expressed group norm allows the group members a chance to present a "face" to each other and to outsiders that is more socially desirable than reality.

 **LEARNING CHECKPOINT**

Compare these reasons for group norm enforcement with those discussed in the chapter.

HOW GROUP NORMS DEVELOP

Norms usually develop gradually and informally as group members learn what behaviors are necessary for the group to function more effectively. However, it also is possible for the norm development process to be short-cut by a critical event in the group or by conscious group decision (Hackman, 1976).

Most norms develop in one or more of the following four ways: explicit statements by supervisors or co-workers; critical events in the group's history; primacy; and carryover behaviors from past situations.

1. Explicit statements by supervisors or co-workers. Norms that facilitate group survival or task success often are set by the leader of the group or powerful members (Whyte, 1955b). For instance, a group leader might explicitly set norms about not drinking at lunch because subordinates who have been drinking are more likely to have problems dealing competently with clients and top management or they are more likely to have accidents at work. The group leader might also set norms about lateness, personal phone calls, and long coffee breaks if too much productivity is lost as a result of time away from the work place.

Explicit statements by supervisors also can increase the predictability of group members' behavior. For instance, supervisors might have particular preferences for a way of analyzing problems or presenting reports. Strong norms will be set to ensure compliance with these preferences. Consequently, supervisors will have increased certainty about receiving work in the format requested, so they can plan accordingly; workers will have increased certainty about what is expected, so they will not have to outguess their boss or redo their projects.

Managers or important group members also can define the specific role expectations of individual group members. For instance, a supervisor or a co-worker might go up to a new recruit after a meeting to give the proverbial advice: "New recruits should be seen and not heard." The senior group member might be trying to prevent the new recruit from appearing brash or incompetent or from embarrassing other group members. Such interventions set specific role expectations for the new group member.

Norms that cater to supervisor preferences also are frequently established even if they are not objectively necessary to task accomplishment. For example, although organizational norms may be very democratic in terms of everybody calling each other by their first names, some managers have strong preferences about being called Mr., Ms., or Mrs. Although the form of address used in the work group does not influence group effectiveness, complying with the norm bears little cost to the group member, whereas noncompliance could cause daily friction with the supervisor. Such norms help group members avoid embarrassing interpersonal interactions with their managers.

Fourth, norms set explicitly by the supervisor frequently express the central values of the group. For instance, a dean can set very strong norms about faculty keeping office hours and being on campus daily. Such norms reaffirm to members of the academic community their teaching and service obligations, and they send signals to individuals outside the college about what is valued in faculty behavior or distinctive about the school. A dean also could set norms that allow faculty to consult or do executive development two or three days a week. Such norms, too, legitimate other types of faculty behavior and send signals to both insiders and outsiders about some central values of the college.

 **LEARNING CHECKPOINT**

What functions do group leaders perform in addition to the enforcement of group norms?

2. Critical events in the group's history. At times there is a critical event in the group's history that established an important precedent. For instance, a group member might have discussed hiring plans with members of other units in the organization, and as a result new positions were lost or there was increased competition for good applicants. Such indiscretion can substantially hinder the survival and task success of the group; very likely the offender will be either formally censured or informally rebuked. As a result of such an incident, norms about secrecy might develop that will protect the group in similar situations in the future.

An example from Janis's *Victims of Groupthink* (1972) also illustrates this point nicely. One of President Kennedy's closest advisors, Arthur Schlesinger, Jr., had serious reservations about the Bay of Pigs invasion and presented his strong objections to the Bay of Pigs plan in a memorandum to Kennedy and Secretary of State Dean Rusk. However, Schlesinger was pressured by the President's brother, Attorney General Robert Kennedy, to keep his objections to himself. Remarked Robert Kennedy to Schlesinger: "You may be right or you may be wrong, but the President has made his mind up. Don't push it any further. Now is the time for everyone to help him all they can." Such critical events led group members to silence their views and set up group norms about the bounds of disagreeing with the president.

Sometimes group norms can be set by a conscious decision of a group after a particularly good or bad experience the group has had. To illustrate, a group might have had a particularly constructive meeting and be very pleased with how much it accomplished. Several people might say, "I think the reason we got so much accomplished today is that we met really early in the morning before the rest of the staff showed up and the phone started ringing. Let's try to continue to meet at 7:30 A.M." Others might agree, and the norm is set. On the other hand, if a group notices it accomplished way too little in a meeting, it might openly discuss setting norms to cut down on ineffective behavior (e.g., having an agenda, not interrupting others while they are talking). Such norms develop to facilitate task success and to reduce uncertainty about what is expected from each individual in the group.

Critical events also can identify awkward interpersonal situations that need to be avoided in the future. For instance, a divorce between two people working in the same group might have caused a lot of acrimony and hard feeling in a unit, not only between the husband and wife but also among various other group members who got involved in the marital problems. After the unpleasant divorce, a group might develop a norm about not hiring spouses to avoid having to deal with such interpersonal problems in the future.

Finally, critical events also can give rise to norms that express the central, or distinctive, values of the group. When a peer review panel finds a physician or lawyer guilty of malpractice or malfeasance, first it establishes (or reaffirms) the rights of professionals to evaluate and criticize the professional behavior of their colleagues. Moreover, it clarifies what behaviors are inconsistent with the group's self-image or its values. When a faculty committee votes on a candidate's tenure, it, too, asserts the legitimacy of influence of senior faculty over junior faculty. In addition, it sends (hopefully) clear messages to junior faculty about its values in terms of quality of research, teaching, and service. There are important "announcement effects" of peer reviews; internal group members carefully reexamine the group's values, and outsiders draw inferences about the character of the group from such critical decisions.

3. Primacy. The first behavior pattern that emerges in a group often sets group expectations. If the first group meeting is marked by very formal interaction between supervisors and subordinates, then the group often expects future meetings to be conducted in the same way. Where people sit in meetings or rooms frequently is developed through primacy. People generally continue to sit in the same seats they sat in at their first meeting, even though those original seats are not assigned and people could change where they sit at every meeting. Most friendship groups of students develop their own "turf" in a lecture hall and are surprised/dismayed when an interloper takes "their" seats.

Norms that develop through primacy often do so to simplify, or make predictable, what behavior is expected of group members. There may be very little task impact from where people sit in meetings or how formal interactions are. However, norms develop about such behaviors to make life much more routine and predictable. Every time a group member enters a room, he or she does not have to "decide" where to sit or how formally to behave. Moreover, he or she also is much more certain about how other group members will behave.

4. Carry-over behaviors from past situations. Many group norms in organizations emerge because individual group members bring set expectations with them from other work groups in other organizations. Lawyers expect to behave towards clients in Organization I (e.g., confidentiality, setting fees) as they behaved towards those in Organization II. Doctors expect to behave toward patients in Hospital I (e.g., "bedside manner," professional distance) as they behaved in Hospital II. Accountants expect to behave towards colleagues at Firm I (e.g., dress code, adherence to statutes) as they behaved towards those at Firm II. In fact, much of what goes on in professional schools is giving new members of the profession the same standards and norms of behavior that practitioners in the field hold.

Such carry-over of individual behaviors from past situations can increase the predictability of group members' behaviors in new settings and facilitate task accomplishment. For instance, students and professors bring with them fairly constant sets of expectations from class to class. As a result, students do not have to relearn continually their roles from class to class; they know, for instance, if they come in late to take a seat quietly at the back of the room without being told. Professors also do not have to relearn continually their roles; they know, for instance, no to mumble, scribble in small print on the blackboard, or be vague when making course assignments. In addition, presumably the most task-successful norms will be the ones carried over from organization to organization.

Moreover, such carry-over norms help avoid embarrassing interpersonal situations. Individuals are more likely to know which conversations and actions provoke annoyance, irritation, or embarrassment to their colleagues. Finally, when groups carry over norms from one organization to another, they also clarify what is distinctive about the occupational or professional role. When lawyers maintain strict rules of confidentiality, when doctors maintain a consistent professional distance with patients, when accountants present a very formal physical appearance, they all assert: "These are the standards we sustain *independent* of what we could 'get away with' in this organization. This is *our* self-concept."

LEARNING CHECKPOINT

Discuss how the enforcement of group norms can lead to "groupthink."

SUMMARY

Norms generally are enforced only for behaviors that are viewed as important by most group members. Groups do not have the time or energy to regulate each and every action of individual members. Only those behaviors that ensure group survival, facilitate task accomplishment, contribute to group morale, or express the group's central values are likely to be brought under normative control. Norms that reflect these group needs will develop through explicit statements of supervisors, critical events in the group's history, primacy, or carry-over behaviors from past situations.

Empirical research on norm development and enforcement has substantially lagged descriptive and theoretical work. In large part, this may be due to the methodological problems of measuring norms and getting enough data points either across time or across groups. Until such time as empirical work progresses, however, the usefulness of group norms as a predictive concept, rather than as a post hoc explanatory device, will be severely limited. Moreover, until it is known more concretely why norms develop and why they are strongly enforced, attempts to *change* group norms will remain haphazard and difficult to accomplish. ☐

REFERENCES

Alvarez, R. Informal reactions to deviance in simulated work organizations: A laboratory experiment. *American Sociological Review*, 1968, 33, 895–912.

Asch, S. Effects of group pressure upon the modification and distortion of judgment. In M. H. Guetzkow (Ed.), *Groups, leadership, and men.* Pittsburgh: Carnegie, 1951, 117–190.

Bales, R. F., & Slater, P. E. Role differentiation in small groups. In T. Parsons, R. F. Bales, J. Olds, M. Zelditch, & P. E. Slater (Eds.), *Family, socialization, and interaction process.* Glencoe, Ill.: Free Press, 1955, 35–131.

Dentler, R. A., & Erikson, K. T. The functions of deviance in groups. *Social Problems*, 1959, 7, 98–107.

Erikson, K. T. *Wayward Puritans.* New York: Wiley, 1966.

Goffman, E. On face-work: An analysis of ritual elements in social interaction. *Psychiatry*, 1955, 18, 213–231.

Hackman, J. R. Group influences on individuals. In M. Dunnette (Ed.), *Handbook of industrial and organizational psychology.* Chicago: Rand McNally, 1976, 1455–1525.

Hollander, E. P. Conformity, status, and idiosyncrasy credit. *Psychological Review*, 1958, 65, 117–127.

Hollander, E. P. Some effects of perceived status on responses to innovative behavior. *Journal of Abnormal and Social Psychology*, 1961, 63, 247–250.

Hollander, E. P. *Leaders, groups, and influence.* New York: Oxford University Press, 1964.

Jackson, J. A conceptual and measurement model for norms and roles. *Pacific Sociological Review*, 1966, 9, 35–47.

Janis, I. *Victims of groupthink: A psychological study of foreign-policy decisions and fiascos.* New York: Houghton-Mifflin, 1972.

Katz, D., & Kahn, R. L. *The social psychology of organizations.* 2nd ed. New York: Wiley, 1978.

Kiesler, C. A., & Kiesler, S. B. *Conformity.* Reading, Mass.: Addison-Wesley, 1970.

Longley, J., & Pruitt, D. C. Groupthink: A critique of Janis' theory. In Ladd Wheeler. (Ed.), *Review of personality and social psychology.* Beverly Hills: Sage, 1980, 74–93.

March, J. Group norms and the active minority. *American Sociological Review*, 1954, 19, 733–741.

Schachter, S., Ellertson, N., McBride, D., & Gregory, D. An experimental study of cohesiveness and productivity. *Human Relations*, 1951, 4, 229–238.

Schur, E. M. *Crimes without victims.* Englewood Cliffs, N.J.: Prentice-Hall, 1965.

Seashore, S. *Group cohesiveness in the industrial work group.* Ann Arbor: Institute for Social Research, University of Michigan, 1954.

Shaw, M. *Group dynamics.* 3rd ed. New York: Harper, 1936.

Trist, E. L., & Bamforth, K. W. Some social and psychological consequences of the longwall method of coal-getting. *Human Relations*, 1951, 4, 1–38.

Whyte, W. F. *Money and motivation.* New York: Harper, 1955a.

Whyte, W. F. *Street corner society.* Chicago: University of Chicago Press, 1955b.

Wiggins, J. A., Dill, F., & Schwartz, R. D. On status-liability. *Sociometry*, 1965, 28, 197–209.

R² SUPPOSE WE TOOK GROUPS SERIOUSLY . . .*

HAROLD J. LEAVITT

INTRODUCTION

This chapter is mostly a fantasy, but not a utopian fantasy. As the title suggests, it tries to spin out some of the things that might happen if we really took small groups seriously; if, that is, we really used groups, rather than individuals, as the basic building blocks for an organization.

This seems an appropriate forum for such a fantasy. It was 50 years ago, at Hawthorne, that the informal face-to-face work group was discovered. Since then groups have been studied inside and out; they have been experimented with, observed, built, and taken apart. Small groups have become the major tool of the applied behavioral scientist. Organizational development methods are group methods. Almost all of what is called participative management is essentially based on group techniques.

So the idea of using groups as organizational mechanisms is by no means new or fantastic. The fantasy comes in proposing to start with groups, not add them in; to design organizations from scratch around small groups, rather than around individuals.

But right from the start, talk like that appears to violate a deep and important value, individualism. But this fantasy will not really turn out

* Source: Reprinted from MAN AND WORK IN SOCIETY, Eugene Louis Cass and Frederick G. Zimmer, (eds.), New York: Van Nostrand Reinhold, 1975, pp 67–77. © 1975 by Western Electric Company, Inc. Reprinted by permission of Van Nostrand Reinhold Company.

to be anti-individualistic in the end.

The rest of this reading will briefly address the following questions: (1) Is it fair to say that groups have not been taken very seriously in organizational design? (2) Why are groups even worth thinking about as organizational building materials? What are the characteristics of groups that might make them interesting enough to be worth serious attention? (3) What would it mean "to take groups seriously?" Just what kinds of things would have to be done differently? (4) What compensatory changes would probably be needed in other aspects of the organization to have groups as the basic unit? And finally, (5) is the idea of designing the organization around small face-to-face groups a very radical idea, or is it just an extension of a direction in which we are already going?

Haven't groups been taken seriously enough already? The argument that groups have not been taken "seriously" doesn't seem a hard one to make. The contemporary ideas about groups didn't really come along until the 30s and 40s. By that time a logical, rationalistic tradition for the construction of organizations already existed. That tradition was very heavily based on the notion that the individual was the construction unit. The logic moved from the projected task backward. Determine the task, the goal, then find an appropriate structure and technology, and last of all fit individual human beings into predefined man-sized pieces of the action. That was, for instance, what industrial psychology was all about during its development between the two world wars. It was con-

cerned almost entirely with individual differences and worked in the service of structuralists, fitting square human pegs to predesigned square holes. The role of the psychologist was thus ancillary to the role of the designers of the whole organization. It was a back-up, supportive role that followed more than it led design.

It was not just the logic of classical organizational theory that concentrated on the individual. The whole entrepreneurial tradition of American society supported it. Individuals, at least male individuals, were taught achievement motivation. They were taught to see individual evaluation, to compete, to see the world, organizational or otherwise, as a place in which to strive for individual accomplishment and satisfaction.

In those respects the classical design of organizations was consonant with the then existent cultural landscape. Individualized organizational structures blended with the environment of individualism. All the accessories fell into place: individual incentive schemes for hourly workers, individual merit rating and assessment schemes, tests for selection of individuals.

The unique characteristic of the organization was that it was not simply a race track within which individuals could compete, but a system in which somehow the competitive behavior of individuals could be coordinated, harnessed, and controlled in the interest of the common tasks. Of course one residual of all that was a continuing tension between individual and organization, with the organization seeking to control and coordinate the individual's activities at the same time that it tried to motivate him; while the competitive individual insisted on reaching well beyond the constraints imposed upon him by the organization. One product of this tension became the informal organization discovered here at Western; typically an informal coalition designed to fight the system.

Then it was discovered that groups could be exploited for what management saw as positive purposes, *toward* productivity instead of away from it. There followed the era of experimentation with small face-to-face groups. We learned to patch them on to existing organizations as bandaids to relieve tensions between individual and organization. We promoted coordination through group methods. We learned that groups were useful to discipline and control recalcitrant individuals.

 **LEARNING CHECKPOINT**

How is the concept of group cohesion useful for understanding how to manage groups?

Groups were fitted onto organizations. The group skills of individual members improved so that they could coordinate their efforts more effectively, control deviants more effectively, and gain more commitment from subordinate individuals. But groups were seen primarily as tools to be tacked on and utilized in the preexisting individualized organizational system. With a few notable exceptions, like Rensis Likert (1961), most did not design organizations around groups. On the contrary, as some of the ideas about small groups began to be tacked onto existing organizational models, they generated new tensions and conflicts of their own. Manag-

ers complained not only that groups were slow, but they were diffused responsibility, vitiated the power of the hierarchy because they were too "democratic and created small in-group empires which were very hard for others to penetrate." There was the period, for example, of the great gap between T-group training (which had to be conducted on "cultural islands") and the organization back home. The T-groupers therefore talked a lot about the "reentry problem," which meant in part the problem of movement from a new culture (the T-group culture) designed around groups back into the organizational culture designed around individuals.

But of course groups didn't die despite their difficulties. How could they die? They had always been there, though not always in the service of the organization. They turned out to be useful, indeed necessary, though often unrecognized tools. For organizations were growing, and professionalizing, and the need for better coordination grew even as the humanistic expectations of individuals also grew. So "acknowledged" groups (as distinct from "natural," informal groups) became fairly firmly attached even to conservative organizations, but largely as compensating addenda very often reluctantly backed into by organizational managers.

Groups have never been given a chance. It is as though someone had insisted that automobiles be designed to fit the existing terrain rather than build roads to adapt to automobiles.

Are groups worth considering as fundamental building blocks? Why would groups be more interesting than individuals as basic design units around which to build organizations? What are

the prominent characteristics of small groups? Why are they interesting? Here are several answers:

First, small groups seem to be good for people. They can satisfy important membership needs. They can provide a moderately wide range of activities for individual members. They can provide support in times of stress and crisis. They are settings in which people can learn not only cognitively but empirically to be reasonably trusting and helpful to one another. Second, groups seem to be good problem-finding tools. They seem to be useful in promoting innovation and creativity. Third, in a wide variety of decision situations, they make better decisions than individuals do. Fourth, they are great tools for implementation. They gain commitment from their members so that group decisions are like to be willingly carried out. Fifth, they can control and discipline individual members in ways that are often extremely difficult through more impersonal quasi-legal disciplinary systems. Sixth, as organizations grow large, small groups appear to be useful mechanisms for fending off many of the negative effects of large size. They help to prevent communication lines from growing too long, the hierarchy from growing too steep, and the individual from getting lost in the crowd.

There is a seventh, but altogether different kind of, argument for taking groups seriously. Thus far the designer of organizations seemed to have a choice. He could build an individualized *or* a groupy organization. A groupy organization will, de facto, have to deal with individuals; but what was learned here so long ago is that individualized organizations, must de facto, deal with groups. Groups are natural phenomena and facts of organizational life. They can be created but their spontaneous development cannot be prevented. The problem is not shall groups exist or not, but shall groups be planned or not? If not, the individualized organizational garden will sprout groupy weeds all over the place. By defining them as weeds instead of flowers, they shall continue, as in earlier days, to be treated as pests, forever fouling up the beauty of rationally designed individualized organizations, forever forming informally (and irrationally) to harrass and outgame the planners.

It is likely that the reverse could also be true, that if groups are defined as the flowers and individuals as the weeds, new problems will crop up. Surely they will, but that discussion can be delayed for at least a little while.

Who uses groups best? So groups look like interesting organizational building blocks. But before going on to consider the implications of designing organizations around groups, one useful heuristic might be to look around the existing world at those places in which groups seem to have been treated somewhat more seriously.

One place groups have become big is in Japanese organizations (Johnson and Ouchi, 1974). The Japanese seem to be very groupy and much less concerned than Americans about issues like individual accountability. Japanese organizations, of course, are thus consonant with Japanese culture, where notions of individual aggressiveness and competitiveness are de-emphasized in favor of self-effacement and group loyalty. But Japanese organizations seem to get a lot done, despite the relative suppression of the individual in favor of the group. It also appears that the advantages of the groupy Japanese style have really come to the fore in large technologically complex organizations.

LEARNING CHECKPOINT

Do you believe that the ability to manage groups is the key to Japanese business and industrial success? Explain.

Another place to look is at American conglomerates. They go to the opposite extreme, dealing with very large units. They buy large organizational units and sell units. They evaluate units. In effect they promote units by offering them extra resources as rewards for good performance. In that sense conglomerates, one might argue, are designed around groups, but the groups in question are often themselves large organizational chunks.

Groups in an individualistic culture. An architect can design a beautiful building which either blends smoothly with its environment or contrasts starkly with it. But organization designers may not have the same choice. If we design an organization which is structurally dissonant with its environment, it is conceivable that the environment will change to adjust to the organization. It seems much more likely, however, that the environment will reject the organization. If designing organizations around groups represents a sharp counterpoint to environmental trends maybe we should abort the idea.

Our environment, one can argue, is certainly highly individualized. But one can also make a less solid argument in the other direction; an argument that American society is going groupy rather than individual this year. Or at least that it is going groupy as well as individual. The evidence is sloppy at best. One can reinterpret the student revolution and the growth of antiestablishment feelings at least in part

as a reaction to the decline of those institutions that most satisfied social membership needs. One can argue that the decline of the Church, of the village, and of the extended family is leaving behind a vacuum of unsatisfied membership and belongingness motives. Certainly popular critics of American society have laid a great deal of emphasis on the loneliness and anomie that seem to have resulted not only from materialism but from the emphasis on individualism. It seems possible to argue that, insofar as there has been any significant change in the work ethic in America, the change has been toward a desire for work which is socially as well as egoistically fulfilling, and which satisfies human needs for belongingness and affiliation as well as needs for achievement.

In effect, the usual interpretation of Abraham Maslow's need hierarchy may be wrong. Usually the esteem and self-actualization levels of motivation are emphasized. Perhaps the level that is becoming operant most rapidly is neither of those, but the social-love-membership level.

The rising role of women in American society also has implications for the groupiness of organizations. There is a moderate amount of evidence that American women have been socialized more strongly into affiliative and relational sorts of attitudes than men. They probably can, in general, more comfortably work in direct achievement roles in group settings, where there are strong relational bonds among members, than in competitive, individualistic settings. Moreover it is reasonable to assume that as women take a more important place in American society some of their values and attitudes will spill over to the male side.

Although the notion of designing organizations around groups in

America in 1974 may be a little premature, it is consonant with cultural trends that may make the idea much more appropriate ten years from now.

But groups are becoming more relevant for organizational as well as cultural reasons. Groups seem to be particularly useful as coordinating and integrating mechanisms for dealing with complex tasks that require the inputs of many kinds of specialized knowledge. In fact the development of matrix-type organizations in high technology industry is perhaps one effort to modify individually designed organizations toward a more group direction; not for humanistic reasons but as a consequence of tremendous increases in the informational complexity of the jobs that need to be done.

What might a seriously groupy organization look like? Just what does it mean to design organizations around groups? Operationally how is that different from designing organizations around individuals? One approach to an answer is simply to take the things organizations do with individuals and try them out with groups. The idea is to raise the level from the atom to the molecule and *select* groups rather than individuals, *train* groups rather than individuals, *pay* groups rather than individuals, *promote* groups rather than individuals, *design jobs* for groups rather than for individuals, *fire* groups rather than individuals, and so on down the list of activities which organizations have traditionally carried on in order to use human beings in their organizations.

Some of the items on that list seem easy to handle at the group level. For example, it doesn't seem terribly hard to design jobs for groups. In effect that is what top management already does for itself to a great extent. It gives specific jobs to committees and often runs itself as a group. The problem seems to be a manageable one: designing job sets which are both big enough to require a small number of persons and also small enough to require only a small number of persons. Big enough in this context means not only jobs that would occupy the hands of group members but that would provide opportunities for learning and expansion.

Ideas like evaluating, promoting, and paying groups raise many more difficult but interesting problems. Maybe the best that can be said for such ideas is that they provide opportunities for thinking creatively about pay and evaluation. Suppose, for example, that as a reward for good work the group gets a larger salary budget than it got last year. Suppose the allocation for increases within the group is left to the group members. Certainly one can think up all sorts of difficulties that might arise. But are the potential problems necessarily any more difficult than those now generated by individual merit raises? Is there any company in America that is satisfied with its existing individual performance appraisal and salary allocation schemes? At least the issues of distributive justice within small groups would presumably be open to internal discussion and debate. One might even permit the group to allocate payments to individuals differentially at different times, in accordance with some criteria of current contribution that they might establish.

As far as performance evaluation is concerned, it is probably easier for people up the hierarchy to assess the performance of total groups than it is to assess the performance of individual members well down the hierarchy. Top managers of decentralized organizations do it all the time, except that they usually reward the former leader of the decentralized unit rather than the whole unit.

The notion of promoting groups raises another variety of difficulties. One thinks of physically transferring a whole group, for example, and of the costs associated with training a whole group to do a new job, especially if there are no bridging individuals. But there may be large advantages too. If a group moves, its members already know how to work with one another. Families may be less disrupted by movement if several move at the same time.

There is the problem of selection. Does it make sense to select groups? Initially, why not? Can't means be found for selecting not only for appropriate knowledge and skill but also for potential ability to work together? There is plenty of groundwork in the literature already.

After the initial phase, there will of course be problems of adding or subtracting individuals from existing groups. We already know a good deal about how to help new members get integrated into old groups. Incidentally, I was told recently by a plant manager in the midwest about an oddity he had encountered; the phenomenon of groups applying for work. Groups of three or four people have been coming to his plant seeking employment together. They wanted to work together and stay together.

Costs and danger points. To play this game of designing organizations around groups, what might be some important danger points? In general, a group-type organization is somewhat more like a free market than present organizations. More decisions would have to be worked out ad hoc in a continually changing way. So one would need to schedule more negotiation time both within and between groups.

One would encounter more issues of justice, for the individual vis-à-vis the group and for groups vis-à-vis one another. More and better arbitration mechanisms would probably be needed along with highly flexible and rapidly adaptive recordkeeping. But modern recordkeeping technology is, potentially, both highly flexible and rapidly adaptive.

Another specific issue is the provision of escape hatches for individuals. Groups have been known to be cruel and unjust to their deviant members. One existing escape route for the individual would of course continue to exist: departure from the organization. Another might be easy means of transfer to another group.

Another related danger of a strong group emphasis might be a tendency to drive away highly individualistic nongroup people. But the tight organizational constraints now imposed do the same thing. Indeed might not groups protect their individualists better than the impersonal rules of present-day large organizations?

Another obvious problem: If groups are emphasized by rewarding them, paying them, promoting them, and so on, groups may begin to perceive themselves as power centers, in competitive conflict with other groups. Intergroup hostilities are likely to be exacerbated unless we can design some new coping mechanisms into the organization. Likert's proposal for solving that sort of problem (and others) is the linking pin concept. The notion is that individuals serve as members of more than one group, both up and down the hierarchy and horizontally. But Likert's scheme seems to me to assume fundamentally individualized organizations in the sense that it is still individuals who

are paid, promoted and so on. In a more groupy organization, the linking pin concept has to be modified so that an individual might be a part-time member of more than one group, but still a real member. That is, for example, a portion of an individual's pay might come from each group in accordance with that group's perception of his contribution.

Certainly much more talk, both within and between groups, would be a necessary accompaniment of group emphasis, though we might argue about whether more talk should be classified as a cost or a benefit. In any case careful design of escape hatches for individuals and connections among groups would be as important in this kind of organization as would stairways between floors in the design of a private home.

There is also a danger of overdesigning groups. All groups in the organization need not look alike. Quite to the contrary. Task and technology should have significant effects on the shapes and sizes of different subgroups within the large organization. Just as individuals end up adjusting the edges of their jobs to themselves and themselves to their jobs, we should expect flexibility within groups, allowing them to adapt and modify themselves to whatever the task and technology demand.

Another initially scary problem associated with groups is the potential loss of clear formal individual leadership. Without formal leaders how will we motivate people? Without leaders how will we control and discipline people? Without leaders how will we pinpoint responsibility? Even as I write those questions I cannot help but feel that they are archaic. They are questions which are themselves a product of the basic individual building block design of old organizations. The problem

is not leaders so much as the performance of leadership functions. Surely groups will find leaders, but they will emerge from the bottom up. Given a fairly clear job description, some groups, in some settings, will set up more or less permanent leadership roles. Others may let leadership vary as the situation demands or as a function of the power that individuals within any group may possess relative to the group's needs at that time. A reasonable amount of process time can be built in to enable groups to work on the leadership problem, but the problem will have to be resolved within each group. On the advantage side of the ledger, this may even get rid of a few hierarchical levels. There should be far less need for individuals who are chiefly supervisors of other individuals' work. Groups can serve as hierarchical leaders of other groups.

 **LEARNING CHECKPOINT**

Do these costs of group-oriented management exceed the potential benefits? Explain.

Two other potential costs: With an organization of groups, there may be a great deal of infighting, and power and conflict issues will come even more to the fore than they do now. Organizations of groups may become highly political, with coalitions lining up against one another on various issues. If so, the rest of the organizational system will have to take those political problems into account, both by setting up sensible systems of intercommunications among groups, and by allocating larger amounts of time and expertise to problems of conflict resolution.

But this is not a new problem unique to groupy organizations. Conflict among groups is prevalant in large organizations which are political systems now. But because these issues have not often been foreseen and planned for, the mechanisms for dealing with them are largely ad hoc. As a result, conflict is often dealt with in extremely irrational ways.

But there is another kind of intergroup power problem that may become extremely important and difficult in groupy organizations. There is a real danger that relatively autonomous and cohesive groups may be closed, not only to other groups but more importantly to staff advice or to new technological inputs.

These problems exist at present, of course, but they may be exacerbated by group structure. I cannot see any perfect way to handle those problems. One possibility may be to make individual members of staff groups part time members of line groups. Another is to work harder to educate line groups to potential staff contributions. Of course the reward system, the old market system, will probably be the strongest force for keeping groups from staying old-fashioned in a world of new technologies and ideas.

But the nature and degree of many of the second order spin-off effects are not fully knowable at the design stage. We need to build more complete working models and pilot plants. In any case it does not seem obvious that slowdowns, either at the work face or in decision-making processes, would necessarily accompany group based organizational designs.

Some possible advantages to the organization. Finally, from an organizational perspective, what are the potential advantages to be gained from a group based organization? The first might be a sharp reduction in the number of units that need to be controlled. Control would not have

to be carried all the way down to the individual level. If the average group size is five, the number of blocks that management has to worry about is cut to 20 percent of what it was. Such a design would also probably cut the number of operational levels in the organization. In effect, levels which are now primarily supervisory would be incorporated into the groups that they supervise.

By this means many of the advantages of the small individualized organization could be brought back. These advantages would occur within groups simply because there would be a small number of blocks, albeit larger blocks, with which to build and rebuild the organization.

But most of all, and this is still uncertain, despite the extent to which we behavioral scientists have been enamoured of groups, there would be increased human advantages of cohesiveness, motivation, and commitment, and via that route, both increased productivity, stronger social glue within the organization, and a wider interaction between organization and environment.

SUMMARY

Far and away the most powerful and beloved tool of applied behavioral scientists is the small face-to-face group. Since the Western Electric researches, behavioral scientists have been learning to understand, exploit, and love groups. Groups attracted interest initially as devices for improving the implementation of decisions and to increase human commitment and motivation. They are now loved because they are also creative and innovative, they often make better quality decisions than individuals, and because they make organizational life more livable for people. One can't hire an applied behavioral scientist into an

organization who within ten minutes will not want to call a group meeting and talk things over. The group meeting is his primary technology, his primary tool.

But groups in organizations are not an invention of behavioral types. They are a natural phenomenon of organizations. Organizations develop informal groups, like it or not. It is both possible and sensible to describe most large organizations as collections of groups in interaction with one another; bargaining with one another, forming coalitions with one another, cooperating and competing with one another. It is possible and sensible too to treat the decisions that emerge from large organizations as a resultant of the interplay of forces among groups within the organization, and not just the resultant of rational analysis.

On the down side, small face-to-face groups are great tools for disciplining and controlling their members. Contemporary China, for example, has just a fraction of the number of lawyers in the United States. Partially this is a result of the lesser complexity of Chinese society and lower levels of education. But a large part of it, surprisingly enough, seems to derive from the fact that modern China is designed around small groups. Since small groups take responsibility for the discipline and control of their members, many deviant acts which would be considered illegal in the United States never enter the formal legal system in China. The law controls individual deviation less, the group controls it more (Li, 1971).

Control of individual behavior is also a major problem of large complex western organizations. This problem has driven many organizations into elaborate bureaucratic quasi-legal sets of rules, ranging from job evaluation schemes to performance evaluations to incentive systems; all individually based, all terribly complex, all creating problems of distributive justice. Any organizational design that might eliminate much of that legalistic superstructure therefore begins to look highly desirable.

Management should consider building organizations using a material now understood very well and with properties that look very promising, the small group. Until recently, at least, the human group has primarily been used for patching and mending organizations that were originally built of other materials.

The major unanswered questions in my mind are not in the understanding of groups, nor in the potential utility of the group as a building block. The more difficult answered question is whether or not the approaching era is one in which Americans would willingly work in such apparently contraindividualistic units. I think we are. □

REFERENCES

Johnson, Richard T. and Ouchi, William G. Made in America (under Japanese management). *Harvard Business Review,* September–October 1974.

Li, Victor. The development of the Chinese legal system, in John Lindbeck (ed.), *China: The management of a revolutionary society.* Seattle: University of Washington Press, 1971.

Likert, Rensis. *New patterns of management.* New York: McGraw-Hill, 1961.

D¹ GROUP EFFECTIVENESS CHECKLIST

The following 20 items serve as a checklist for you to use in describing the effectiveness of a group or groups you belong to. Complete the checklist for each such group. The larger the number of statements answered yes, the more likely the group is productive and the members are satisfied.

		Mostly Yes	Mostly No
1.	The atmosphere is relaxed and comfortable.	_____	_____
2.	Group discussion is frequent, and it is usually pertinent to the task at hand.	_____	_____
3.	Group members understand what they are trying to accomplish.	_____	_____
4.	People listen to each others' suggestions and ideas.	_____	_____
5.	Disagreements are tolerated and an attempt is made to resolve them.	_____	_____
6.	There is general agreement on most courses of action taken.	_____	_____
7.	The group welcomes frank criticism from inside and outside sources.	_____	_____
8.	When the group takes action, clear assignments are made and accepted.	_____	_____
9.	There is a well-established, relaxed working relationship among the members.	_____	_____
10.	There is a high degree of trust and confidence among the leader and subordinates.	_____	_____
11.	The group members strive hard to help the group achieve its goal.	_____	_____
12.	Suggestions and criticisms are offered and received with a helpful spirit.	_____	_____
13.	There is a cooperative rather than a competitive relationship among group members.	_____	_____
14.	The group goals are set high but not so high as to create anxieties or fear of failure.	_____	_____
15.	The leaders and members hold a high opinion of the group's capabilities.	_____	_____

* Source: Andrew J. DuBrin, CONTEMPORARY APPLIED MANAGEMENT. Plano: Business Publications, Inc., 1985, p. 169–70. Used by permission.

16. Creativity is stimulated within the group.   _____   _____
17. There is ample communication within the group of topics relevant to getting the work accomplished.   _____   _____
18. Group members feel confident in making decisions.   _____   _____
19. People are kept busy but not overloaded.   _____   _____
20. The leader of the group is well suited for the job.   _____   _____

D 2 GROUP CLIMATE ASSESSMENT

The following items allow you to describe the climate of particular groups that you belong to. Complete the questionnaire, while thinking of one group. Upon completion of the questionnaire you can score the group climate along the four dimensions of genuineness (column 1), understanding (column 2), valuing (column 3), and acceptance (column 4). The total score for each of the four columns is added to give the score for the dimension. Items 3, 6, 9, 12, and 16 are reversed in the scoring which means you must SUBTRACT 5 from the rating you give to each of these 5 items before adding up the scores in the four columns.

In the parentheses in front of the items below place the number corresponding to your perceptions of the group as a whole, using the following scale.

5 They can <u>always</u> be counted on to behave this way.
4 <u>Typically</u> I would expect them to behave this way.
3 I would <u>usually</u> expect them to behave this way.
2 They would <u>seldom</u> behave this way.
1 They would <u>rarely</u> behave this way.
0 I would <u>never</u> expect them to behave this way.

I would expect my fellow group members to

1. (___)_____ level with me.
2. ___(___)_____ get the drift of what I am trying to say.
3. _____(___)___ interrupt or ignore my comments.
4. _____(___) accept me for what I am.
5. (___)_____ feel free to let me know when I "bug" them.
6. ___(___)_____ misconstrue things I say or do.
7. _____(___)___ be interested in me.
8. _____(___) provide an atmosphere where I can be myself.
9. (___)_____ keep things to themselves to spare my feelings.
10. ___(___)_____ perceive what kind of person I really am.
11. _____(___)___ include me in what's going on.
12. _____(___) act "judgmental" with me.
13. (___)_____ be completely frank with me.
14. ___(___)_____ recognize readily when something is bothering me.
15. _____(___)___ respect me as a person, apart from my skills or status.
16. _____(___) ridicule me or disapprove if I show my peculiarities.

* Source: J. William Pfeiffer and John E. Jones, STRUCTURED EXPERIENCES FOR HUMAN RELATIONS TRAINING. Iowa City, Iowa: University Associates Press, 1971, pp. 29–30.

1 CONSENSUS-SEEKING: A GROUP RANKING TASK*

OBJECTIVES

1. To compare the results of individual decision-making with decisions made by a group.

2. To generate data to discuss decision-making patterns in task groups.

STARTING THE EXERCISE

1. Each participant is given a copy of the worksheet and is told that he has *seven* minutes to complete the task. He must work *independently* during this phase.

2. After seven minutes, the facilitator interrupts to announce that a ranking must be made by the total group, using the method of *group consensus*. The ranking of each occupation must be agreed upon by each member before it becomes a part of the group's decision. Members should try to make each ranking one with which *all* members agree at least partially. Two ground rules: no averaging, and no "majority rule" votes. The group has thirty minutes to complete its task.

3. After thirty minutes of group work (or when the group has finished, if less than thirty minutes), the facilitator should announce the "correct" ranking. Individual group members should "score" their worksheets by adding up the differences between their ranks and the key, regardless of sign. That is, make all differences positive and sum them. Low scores, of course, are better than high ones. Someone should score the group ranking also.

4. The group should compute the average score of the individual members, compare this with the group's score, and discuss the implications of the experience. This processing might be focused on leadership, compromise, decision-making strategies, the feeling content of the exercise, roles members played, or other aspects of group life.

OCCUPATIONAL PRESTIGE RANKING WORKSHEET

Instructions: Rank the following occupations according to the prestige which is attached to them in the United States. Place a "1" in front of the occupation which you feel to be most prestigious, etc., all the way to "15," least prestigious.

_____ Author of novels

_____ Newspaper columnist

_____ Policeman

_____ Banker

_____ U.S. Supreme Court Justice

_____ Lawyer

_____ Undertaker

_____ State governor

_____ Sociologist

_____ Scientist

_____ Public school teacher

_____ Dentist

_____ Psychologist

_____ College Professor

_____ Physician

---

* Source: J. William Pfeiffer and John E. Jones, STRUCTURED EXPERIENCES FOR HUMAN RELATIONS TRAINING. Iowa City, Iowa: University Associates Press, 1972, pp. 23–26. Used by permission.

PARTICIPATING IN AND OBSERVATIONS OF GROUP PROCESSES*

OBJECTIVES

1. To provide experience in partic-ipating in and observing groups un-dertaking a specific task.
2. To generate data that can be the focus of class discussion and analysis.

STARTING THE EXERCISE

The Situation

You are appointed to a personnel committee in charge of selecting a manager for the department that provides administrative services to other departments. Before you be-gin interviewing candidates, you are asked to develop a list of the personal and professional qualifica-tions the manager needs. This list will be used as the selection criteria.

The Procedure

1. Select five to seven members to serve on the committee.
2. Ask the committee to rank the items in the following list in their order of importance in selecting the department head.
3. The students not on the com-mittee should observe the group process. Some should observe the whole group, and others individual members. The observers can use observation guides A and B.
4. The observers should provide feedback to the participants.
5. The class should discuss how the committee might improve its performance.

Selection Criteria

_____ Strong institutional loy-alty

_____ Ability to give clear in-structions

_____ Ability to discipline sub-ordinates

_____ Ability to make decisions under pressure

_____ Ability to communicate

_____ Stable personality

_____ High intelligence

_____ Ability to grasp the over-all picture

_____ Ability to get along well with people

_____ Familiarity with office procedures

_____ Professional achieve-ment

_____ Ability to develop subor-dinates

A. Group Process Observation Guide

Instructions: Observe the group behavior in the following dimensions. Prepare notes for feedback.

Group Behaviors	Description	Impact
Group Goal: Are group goals clearly defined?		
Decision Procedure: Is the de-cision procedure clearly defined?		
Communication Network: What kind of communication net-work is used? Is it appropriate?		
Decision Making: What kind of decision process is used? Is it appro-priate?		

* Source: Kae H. Chung and Leon C. Megginson, ORGANIZATIONAL BEHAVIOR. New York: Harper and Row, Publishers, 1981, pp. 241–44. Used by permission.

Group Norm: Observe the degrees of cohesiveness, compatibility, and conformity.		
Group Composition: What kind of group is it?		
Other Behavior: Is there any behavior that influences the group process?		

B. Individual Role Observation Guide

Instructions: Observe one committee member. Tabulate (or note) behaviors that he or she exhibits as the group works.

Initiating Ideas: Initiates or clarifies ideas and issues.	**Confusing Issues:** Confuses others by bringing up irrelevant issues or by jumping to other issues.
Managing Conflicts: Explores, clarifies, and resolves conflicts and differences.	**Mismanaging Conflicts:** Avoids or suppresses conflicts, or creates "win-or-lose" situations.
Influencing Others: Appeases, reasons with, or persuades others.	**Forcing Others:** Gives orders or forces others to agree.
Supporting Others: Reinforces or helps others to express their opinions.	**Rejecting Others:** Deflates or antagonizes others.

Listening Attentively: Listens and responds to others' ideas and opinions.	**Showing Indifference:** Does not listen or brushes off others.
Showing Empathy: Shows the ability to see things from other people's viewpoint.	**Self-Serving Behavior:** Exhibits behavior that is self-serving.
Exhibiting Positive Nonverbal Behaviors: Pays attention to others, maintains eye contact, composure, and other signs.	**Exhibiting Negative Nonverbal Behaviors:** Tense facial expression, yawning, little eye contact, and other behaviors.

THE MUSHROOM FACTORY

The following case is an in-depth look at the events in the Accessories Department of the Esco Company, a Midwest manufacturer, during a period of rapid change.

OVERVIEW

The Accessories Department of the Esco Company produces specialty industrial items which complement the company's high volume standard products. The department was originally structured on a product basis, with Accessories having complete control and responsibility over its products from their inception through production, including customer service and customer relations. During 1972 this arrangement was changed and two groups were formed—product engineering, and manufacturing engineering. The product engineering group maintained responsibility for product inception, production of prototypes, and production start-up. They also handled customer service and relations. The manufacturing group handled the products during the production stage.

To complicate problems further, in 1973 the company purchased three small manufacturing plants and began phasing the manufacturing process out of the home plant. The manufacturing group had responsibility for transferring operations to the newly acquired factories, essentially phasing themselves out of their jobs. During this period a great deal of damage was done to the morale and working efficiency of the original parties involved. In 1974, approximately one year later, the original decision was reversed and the Accessories Department was put back on a product-oriented basis. Unfortunately, before events had a chance to smooth out or operations return to normal, the Esco Company was merged with another division of the parent company and the frequently encountered "housecleaning" of middle- and upper-management positions began.

These changes, the conflicts they caused, and the chosen methods of dealing with those conflicts will be examined below.

A CLOSER LOOK

Before the first change from product to functional orientation, the Accessories Department was divided into three product teams. (The organizational structure

Source: Theodore T. Herbert, *Organizational Behavior*. New York: MacMillan Publishing Co., 1976, pp. 293–300. Used with permission.

FIGURE 1

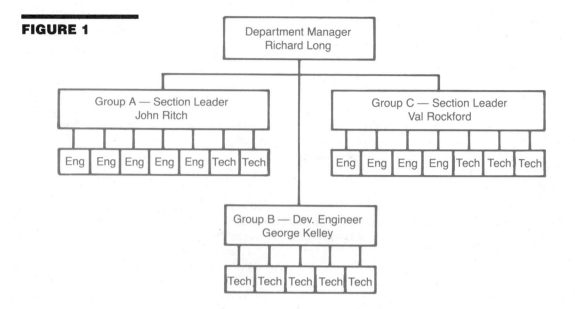

is diagrammed in Figure 1.) Two of the teams, A and C, were composed of a section leader and a combination of technicians and engineers. The third team, B, was headed by an engineer, but all of his subordinates were technicians. The department manager was Richard Long, who possessed impeccable technical credentials as a manager, although he was less successful than might be wished. Suffering from shyness, he had great difficulty communicating with his subordinates, and consequently never achieved the kind of rapport that might allow him to avoid his natural tendency to attempt to overcontrol the situation. A high achiever, Long could not delegate authority, especially to men he barely knew; at the same time, his own social inadequacies prevented him from exercising that authority on his own. In this situation, many routine company functions went undone, while the section leaders filled in the gaps on their own without adequate authority, and in some cases, without adequate information.

Jobs were assigned to the groups, based on technical specialization and existing work load. Work requests originating outside the department were specified by the department manager and then communicated (sometimes quite badly) to the assigned group head. In addition, group leaders were encouraged to develop their own ideas for accessory products, and bonus checks were distributed each year to the group that originated the most productive new ideas. In the past five years, Group A had won the bonus four times, while Group C had won it only once.

Section A

Section A was headed by John Ritch. A graduate of a top-rated engineering school, John was a pleasant, likable man who got along well with the other members of his team. An excellent engineer, John was the object of little hostility or jealousy from his team because it was obvious that he had earned his position through his technical competence. Although clearly the best engineer in the group, John did not assume that he would always have the best or only answer to a question, and generally gave all members of the team an opportunity to voice opinions and share ideas. He was especially evenhanded in dealing with the technicians, often relegated to second-class status by the engineers because of their lack of formal education. John knew, however, that on questions of production and operation, the technicians often had more experience and sometimes a more practical approach to solving problems than the engineers. Although the group generally ate lunch together and had one or two parties for special occasions each year, John did not socialize much with the other members of the group; he told them quite frankly that he got enough of the Accessories Department at work and liked to talk of other things during his free time.

Section C

Group C was headed by a young man named Valentino Rockford. The standing joke was that his mother had named him after Rudolph Valentino and he had been trying to live up to the image ever since. Val was, in fact, actually quite close to being a true "playboy." He drove a sports car, dated some of the prettiest girls most of the men had ever seen, skied like John Claude Kiley, and dressed like he had a rich uncle. The other men on the team waited eagerly every Monday morning to hear the tales of the preceding weekend. Val was not *that* good an engineer, but everybody on his team liked him and they were willing to tolerate his occasional errors in judgment and cover up for him when he came in too hung-over on Mondays to get the work out. Besides, whenever he got in too far over his head, John was always willing to take an hour and help bail him out. The team was closely knit in a locker-room sort of way, eating together, bowling together, partying together, and often going out drinking on Friday nights after work.

There had been occasions when new members of the group would complain because Team C did not get the "plum" projects, or because their bonuses were always lower than those of Team A, whose output was always far superior to their own. Whenever there were such complaints from new or existing group members, the other members of the group would make it clear that they didn't think the complaints were reasonable. Most members of the group felt that the fringe benefits of being in Group C far outweighed the disadvantages. Besides, whenever they were feeling like low man on the totem pole, they could always look at Group B and know how lucky they really were.

Section B

Group B was headed by George Kelley, an older man with engineering skills which some claimed were grossly out of date. Group B was not structured like the other groups; it had only one engineer, the section head, and was otherwise composed entirely of technicians. George, who had been with the company for many years, personally believed that he should be the department manager instead of Richard Long; he considered it a personal insult to head Section B instead of one of the larger groups composed of engineers and technicians. Because of its lack of technical depth, Group B never got any of the more interesting assignments (most of which went to John Ritch's group) and never came up with the original ideas which won merit prizes and brought one's name before management in a favorable way. George dreamed of nothing but getting the department manager's job, or being promoted out of the Accessories Department.

George didn't trust his technicians with most important matters. He felt that he had been seriously hampered in his team and often complained that he had to do everything himself because he had no competent help. In fact, over the years, George had been assigned many engineers for his group, but they had never stayed; the company, finally tired of losing good engineers, stopped putting them in Group B for George to run off. George detailed the daily assignments in minute detail for his technicians and insisted that any problems that arose be brought directly to him. In actuality the technicians had little respect for George or his technical competence, and usually took their more complex problems to John Ritch during the lunch hour.

Although the situation in the Accessories Department was not good, the work was getting done, and at least Group A was providing a serious effort toward product development. Group B was cranking out acceptable, if unimaginative, work in small but steadily dependable quantities; Group C, unlikely to do anything to endanger their team's structure, adhered within reason to company goals and objectives.

PROFITABILITY PLAN

Basically, that was the situation when management decided to move to improve the profitability of the Esco Division. For some time the top management of the parent company, in conjunction with the Esco top management, had been toying with the idea of moving the manufacturing operations to the South to increase their profit margin. Many areas in the southern states were not highly industrialized and were eager to attract manufacturing. They offered attractive tax structures and incentives such as free water and bargain prices on land. In addition, labor was plentiful, and unions had not yet taken strong hold. The company knew there would be strong resistance and decided to take slow, measured steps toward implementing the plan, allowing each reshuffling to settle down before beginning a new one.

Moreover, the company was afraid they would lose many of their good engineers if the information got out. Although they planned to retain everyone who wanted to stay on the new production engineering staff, and transfer only those who wanted to go, they were afraid the engineers might become worried about transfers and start looking for other jobs. The sites for the new manufacturing plants were somewhat less than ideal, and some of the engineers from the East already complained that Esco's Midwest location was "out in the boondocks."

With all of this in mind, it was decided to first change over to a functional orientation, establishing a product development group and a product manufacturing group. Then, when the transfer of manufacturing operations was ready to begin, one group would be deeply into the manufacturing, and ideally suited to carry it out; the group would be able to continue product development activities without interruption. Then, after the transfer of manufacturing operations, the two groups would be recombined and would again handle product development through the stage of setting up the manufacturing process which would then be transferred to the out-of-town plants.

The top management decided to share the decision with the company executives down to the department manager level; consequently Richard Long, manager of the accessories department, was informed of the impending change. It was suggested to the department managers, by one of the vice-presidents, that they leak just enough information to their departments to avoid excess, *undirected* speculation. It was suggested that they say something to the effect that they knew about the change, they couldn't discuss it, but no jobs were in danger, and the disruption was temporary. Richard Long went back to the Accessories Department and gave this message to George Kelley on the assumption that Kelley was the oldest employee of the company and, therefore, most likely to know all the other members of the department and get the word around. Kelley, of course, told no one.

THE CHANGE

When the orders came down they caught everyone but Kelley by surprise. Assignments had already been made; no one was consulted about which division he preferred to work in. Naturally John Ritch was assigned to Product Development, and most of his engineers and technicians were assigned there with him. Val Rockford was assigned to the manufacturing group, mostly because management felt that with his personality, he would make a good liaison man with the new plant when the time came. George Kelley was also assigned to manufacturing as the head of the manufacturing group.

The technicians and engineers who had worked in Groups B and C were divided up according to experience and education, the better ones generally going to Product Development. Not only was a division created in the new titles, but the product development

people were physically moved out of the Accessories Department; a manufacturing group from another department was moved in to take their space. Product Development was moved in with a small group of Research and Development people from the main product line. The Research and Development quarters were much nicer, with piped-in music and carpeting in the offices, which made the people transferred feel almost as if they had received a promotion.

The people who went with John Ritch to the new quarters were reassembled into a working team in a reasonably short time. There were one or two engineers from Val Rockford's old group who didn't like Ritch's style at first; after a while, though, they began enjoying the more demanding work, and they could still get together with Val and the old bunch after work for a couple of beers.

The members of the old group C did, in fact, maintain contact for a while, meeting for lunch and engaging in other social activities together. Some of the members who had gone with Product Development eventually dropped out, but the group managed to pick up new recruits from George Kelley's technicians. Those from the old Group B who did not fit in well with Val's group found themselves without any association at all; although they hadn't been very close before, the presence of Val's closely knit "fun" group made them feel for the first time that they were being somehow deprived. The only person who really seemed happy in the manufacturing group was George Kelley. He finally considered his position as reasonably commensurate with his abilities and what he had earned by staying with the company for fifteen years. He knew the situation might be only temporary, but he had no intention of spoiling the situation by telling anyone else.

Richard Long found that he had even less to do than before. With Product Development moved into a new section, he often handed requests for new products directly over to John Ritch, and he involved himself in overseeing the manufacturing operation, much more to his liking and talents. He was also relieved of much of the necessity for interpersonal contact, dealing almost exclusively with George Kelley who was, if anything, less gregarious than Long.

The situation in the manufacturing group was not good. There were, first, the dissident technicians who were outsiders to Val Rockford's group. Second, through contacts with the old Group C members who had been transferred to Product Development, Val and the other Group C members left in manufacturing learned of how much nicer things were in Research and Development. Jealousy and hostility quickly surfaced. To make matters worse, they had no real control over the manufacturing. If there were a manufacturing problem with the product as designed, they couldn't fix it. They were required to take it back to Product Development and let them handle the problem. Rockford did not work well under George Kelley; production began to suffer as he and his friends began to attack Kelley by refusing to do the work assigned.

PHASE II

It was at this point that management decided to move into Phase II. A small manufacturing company, which had three small plants, had been located. The company was ideal; buying instead of building moved the entire timetable up two years. The company was bought, and the announcement was made that manufacturing operations would be phased out of the home plant and moved to the South. The situation regarding product control was not changed, and the manufacturing group found itself with even less of a role then before. They didn't design it, they couldn't touch it, and now they weren't even going to manufacture it! Morale reached an all-time low in manufacturing.

SAVING PHASE

Some of the engineers began to petition the department head for relief from the situation. Richard Long, unable to communicate with these men, became unwilling even to hear their complaints. He would merely repeat that it was "company policy," that there was nothing he could do, that they should just shut up and do things by the book. As each avenue of satisfaction disappeared, morale got lower and soon "accidents" began to happen, equipment was destroyed, pilferage grew, absenteeism and turnover began to increase.

As things collapsed below him, George Kelley realized that being head of the kind of department he wanted would do him more harm than good if he didn't do something about the current situation. He tried to control the men and force them into behaving in more acceptable ways. He threatened to fire them, refused to give them raises, assigned them to heinous duties, anything he could think of to whip them into line. Nothing worked. Finally, George decided his best bet was to take a transfer to one of the new manufacturing plants. Under the circumstances, it appeared to be the best solution to the problem, relieving him of responsibility for the mess at the home plant, and

promising to make him a relatively large fish in a small pond. He put in for the transfer and got it, and Val Rockford was made the head of the manufacturing division. Morale improved but, strangely, production did not. In fact, production slumped even lower as absenteeism increased, lunch hours got longer, and partying on the job became a way of life.

Faced with the total breakdown of production, and accompanied by problems from the distant manufacturing plants where competent technical help was almost impossible to find, management decided that it was time to reorganize the department back the way it was. The merger with another division which followed closely after that reorganization back to a product orientation, saw middle and upper managers of Esco Company lose their jobs; this was largely due to poor records over the two years covering the events of this case. It was the feeling of the parent division's management that good managers would never have allowed the situation to degenerate to the point where they found it after the merger. □

CASE QUESTIONS

1. Compare the group leadership styles of John Ritch and Richard Long. Who is the more effective leader? Explain.

2. What are the group factors that explain why one section is better able to tolerate change than another section? Does management have any control over these factors? Explain.

3. Evaluate management's decision to reverse the decision to change and to reorganize the department back to the way it was.

2 EXECUTIVE RETREAT: A CASE OF GROUP FAILURE

John Matthews was a young executive at the divisional level of a large corporation. John, like a number of other young men in business throughout the United States, had been selected by higher-ups in his firm to attend a two-and-one-half-week executive development retreat.

The retreat was held at a remote camp in northern Minnesota. Although all of the necessary facilities for an enjoyable vacation were present, the structure and demands of the retreat left little time for relaxing and enjoying the surroundings. John was among sixty executives who were registered to attend the retreat. They would spend fifteen days living, working, and competing with one another.

ORGANIZATION AND ACTIVITIES

The sixty participants were broken down into five groups of twelve. Each group was provided with a group leader. This leader was a senior corporate executive who had previously attended the retreat. For fifteen days, the men were involved in a variety of academic and athletic activities.

Selected sessions of the retreat were designated for "educational activities." The men participated in seminar sessions designed to deepen their understanding of central management decision making. These sessions involved a limited amount of lecture by either the group leader or a visitor. However, the majority of time devoted to academic pursuits was spent in case studies and a business game. Athletically, a good deal of the men's time was spent in physical fitness training and athletic competition. Finally, a few sessions were conducted along the lines of sensitivity training.

Although a considerable amount of time was spent in intra-group activities, inter-group competition was also fostered. In particular, groups competed athletically and through the business game.

The remaining portions of this case represent the reflections of John Matthews on his experiences at the executive retreat.

FIRST IMPRESSIONS

It is hard to express the emotions or thoughts that were going through my mind, let alone the minds of others, when I first met the members of my group. Until now, I had been working with business acquaintances in my company's San Francisco office. When I learned of my selection for the retreat and the manner in which it would be conducted, I wondered what my new associates would be like. Would we all remain for the full two and one-half weeks of the retreat? Would I be able to take the criticisms of others? How would our group do athletically and academically? And would the other members of my group resent the fact that I could not participate in the sporting events due to an old knee injury? Subconsciously, I had been establishing the criteria by which I would accept others and they would accept me.

During the first group meeting, I tried to learn the backgrounds of others who were with me. I went through the following processes. I tried to find out where the others were from, what their education was, and the kind of experience they had accumulated. I discovered that the level at which one had worked within a firm together with whether or not he had held down a "home office" job were important because they created identification and solidarity between individuals; i.e., financial officers interacted with other financial officers, production managers with production managers, marketing people with others from marketing departments, and so forth. Our group leader made sure that he allowed enough time for all of us to meet each other before he walked in the door.

The group leader was the faculty member who had over-all responsibility for administrative functions in the group. He also graded papers and presentations, conducted all of our counseling sessions and was the all-around nursemaid for the group. Our leader, Mark, was a top-level corporate executive out of New York. This posed an immediate threat to some in the group when they first met him. After a few minutes of informal chitchat, Mark called everyone into a seminar room.

Mark made a low-key introduction of himself and the retreat. He emphasized that to be a success individually at "the camp," everyone had to cooperate and function as a group. He explained that no group always dominated intellectually or athletically. He related that his last group was not especially great in academics or athletics yet their cumulative scores both in tests and games enabled them to become the top group at the retreat. This allowed certain privileges over other groups. The point Mark kept trying to make was that the men could no longer think of themselves as individuals. "The school theme" he said, "is 'Think—Communicate—Cooperate' and I suggest that you too adopt it as your guiding principle while you are here."

GROUP MEMBERS

The following are my recollections of the other members in our group.

Wally was an older member of the group and became the group student leader. He was a middle-level manager in a large company and had no formal technical training. This may have made him reluctant to assume a leadership role in the group. He appeared to be afraid of hurting other people's feelings even though his actions usually were justified.

Dave also did not have formal technical training; however, he was one of the few who had had experience as a corporate president. He was an average student and speaker and above average in his writing ability. He appeared to be obsessed with sex. He called his wife every night, "studied" *The Art of Sensual Response,* and occasionally sniffed some musk oil which he had bought for his wife.

Jim was a financial analyst. He was one of two bachelors and was considered to be the playboy of the group. His goal was just to finish the retreat and get back to his home office.

Bob was a manager of production and operations for a leading producer of men's apparel. He, too, was a bachelor and considered himself to be a "lady-killer." To most of us he appeared to be conceited and boisterous. He claimed to be an authority on most subjects. He was also suspected of cheating in the 25-Mile Jogging Club (cheating on anything was strictly forbidden).

Larry was a director of public relations for a major steel producer. He had a liberal arts background and turned out to be our only distinguished graduate. Although he participated in everything, he never really assumed a leadership role and his contribution to the section was minimal. He was the only one (with the exception of me) who was not able to run a mile

and a half in twelve minutes. He was a good speaker but a below average writer.

Rich was an internal financial consultant. He attended Harvard Business School and was later to be considered as one of the better executive prospects at the retreat. He was a good speaker and writer. Although he was very outspoken, he did make a lot of sense. He assumed the leader's role in two major exercises; however, he never did maintain his hold as leader over the group.

Wayne was a personnel director. He was an average student, writer, and speaker. He never did assume a leader's role, possibly because he was the most naive member of the group.

Ollie was a marketing manager and was considered the "country boy" of the group. He was an average student, good speaker, and good writer. He performed many odd jobs for us and was successful in leading us to two victories in athletics.

Gary was an executive vice-president for a pipeline supplier whom I thought, at the beginning, would emerge as the leader of the group. He was poor academically, an average writer, and a good speaker. His additional duty was that of athletic chairman. Although he encouraged everyone to run 25 miles (25-Mile Club) during this period, he himself failed to achieve this goal.

Burrell was a personnel and public relations manager. He also was considered to be among the more promising men at the retreat. He was a fair speaker and an average writer. His additional duties were academic chairman and basketball coach. He was the type of guy that, if something were to go wrong, he would be in the middle of it.

Paul was manager for engineering for an electronics manufacturer. He had to spend three days of the first week of the retreat in the infirmary with a virus. This may have been one of the reasons why he was always trying to promote group functions when he got back. One thing I remember in particular about Paul is that he was always complaining about the "developmental rotation" program in his company. The program placed technically trained managers in functional areas other than their own for up to six months to provide them with career broadening. He saw the program as a threat to his own career but failed to see it as a threat to "general managers with no technical expertise." Over-all, Paul was an average speaker, writer, and student.

I, **John** did not have formal technical education for my job as division director of industrial relations. I was an average student and writer and above average speaker. I considered myself to be a harmonizer of the group. I was the only member who was excused from sports because of an injury. Although I disagreed many times with decisions that were made, I usually went along with the group in the end.

The group members lived in three locations during the school. Living in Cabin I were Dave, Wally, Jim, Bob, John, and Larry. Wayne, Burrell, and Paul lived in Cabin II, while Ollie, Rich, and Gary lived in Cabin III. Bob and John generally walked to seminar sessions together as did Wally and Larry, Wayne, Burrell, and Paul and Ollie, Rich, and Gary. Dave and Jim walked separately to the sessions. Rich and Burrell studied together regularly. Larry, Rich, and Paul generally studied together.

GROUP ORGANIZATION AND ACTIVITIES

For convenience, Mark arranged the seating alphabetically around the table (see Exhibit I). There was only one exception; Wally, the designated leader by virtue of age and experience sat near the front. Following some brief introductions and a few administrative actions, goals of the group were established.

After much haggling about the goals, which ranged from totally idealistic to extremely pragmatic, the group decided on the following goals:

1. Everyone in the group would strive to complete the program and would seek to assure that our group was ranked first among various competing groups.
2. We would strive to be the best in sports.
3. Everyone would run at least 25 miles.
4. We would strive to maintain a harmonious atmosphere in the group.

Of immediate importance to the group was developing athletically rather than academically. (In final group ratings, athletics ranked a very close second to academics in total possible points that could be scored.) In fact, it wasn't until the latter part of the school that the section would come together in academics.

EXHIBIT 1

Seating arrangement, first day.

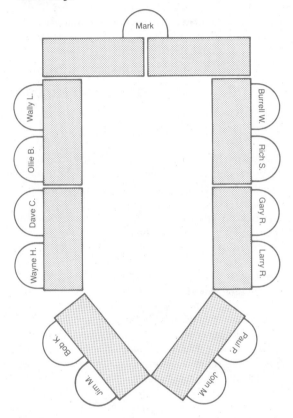

A couple of incidents that occurred during the retreat illustrated the extent of the group's success.

Toward the end of the first week, an entire afternoon was set aside for self-evaluation. The session resembled a T-group session. Most groups had lunch followed with a little beer drinking to "loosen things up." After our loosening up we started our discussion. Several comments were made that should have provoked a fiery discussion, but for some reason they never did.

I don't believe we were open that afternoon. We looked at our leadership in academics, but none of us was willing to tell Burrell that he had a weak academic program. None of us would tell Gary that our athletics program was bad and that our group looked worse than most other groups with whom we competed. We all knew these things, but were unwilling to place the blame on anyone. Our group leader must have been totally frustrated at the end of the day. How could a group, which had such high goals and such mediocre results, have allowed such an opportunity to pass by?

A few days later another group project was scheduled. An obstacle course, intriguingly called "Project X," consisted of a series of tasks to be performed by six people at a time. It was supposed to test the group's ability to recognize the problem, decide on a solution, and carry it out in a fifteen-minute period. During the break, we tallied our score, 0 for 5. Mark seemed very upset. It was the first time he got upset with the entire group. Larry commented on the episode:

> We didn't see "Project X" or even the rest of the retreat as a life or death situation. In a retreat where no one fails to graduate, it can hardly be considered as a threat to anyone's career if these group goals go unaccomplished.

Personally, I saw us as a group of individuals in search of a real leader. We were all strong in our own individual specialities in our own organizations, but couldn't muster up the same vitality and enthusiasm to carry forth this synthetically designed group toward goal achievement. Although we wouldn't openly admit it, we were not committed to our goals. Yet, even though we lacked this commitment, we still maintained the goals. Going back to the afternoon encounter session, someone suggested that we revise our goals in light of our successes and failures to date. Even though it was impossible to achieve the original goals set, they still were unchanged!

The seating as depicted in Exhibit 2 was the arrangement for the last few days.

GROUP PERFORMANCE

Our group finished the two-and-one-half-week session having accomplished the following: Out of twelve individuals, one finished as a distinguished graduate and a total of three finished in the top third of the class. Ollie made the observation, "Lacking strong leadership in education, we each went our separate ways in trying to wade through all the material."

Our second goal also shared defeat. At the beginning of the program it was felt that our group had a chance to do well in sports. During practice sessions, we appeared to be relatively good. However, practice sessions reflected one characteristic of the group. Generally, we were disorganized, and there was always a lot of joking going on. I believed this carried over

EXHIBIT 2

Seating arrangement, last few days.

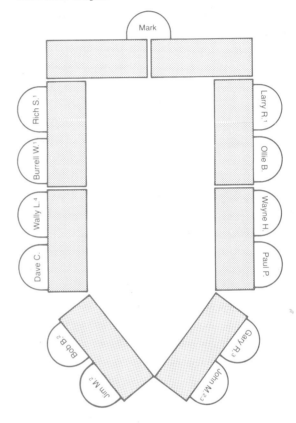

1. These individuals finished in top third of class.
2. These individuals never changed their seats.
3. Gary and John sat next to each other during the last seven days.
4. Wally never did assume the leader's position at the end of the table except when he led the two seminars.

to the games and resulted in less than full commitment to winning. Gary would get frustrated and try to motivate the team at times, but his sudden surge of spirit usually was short-lived.

The third goal also fell short of being successfully accomplished. Only six of the members of our group actually finished the 25 miles. Another important factor regarding the 25-Mile Club centered on the ethics of one individual. Bob had been suspected of not running all the miles that he logged. At first Wally and Larry had suspected this, as later all the group members living around Bob did. One member noted, "We all felt that Wally should have confronted him with our suspicions." However, because the evidence against Bob was circumstantial, Wally didn't formally say anything to Bob about the incident. One change that did develop out of the episode was that the entire group ceased to listen to or trust Bob once they suspected his cheating.

The group came closest to achieving the final goals that involved the maintenance of harmonious relationships between one another. An example of this was our mutual respect for each other's territory. As one member stated it, "When Paul went to the hospital, his seat remained vacant even though we didn't have permanently assigned seats. When he returned, everyone made a special effort to make him feel a part of the group. Even when we suspected Bob of not really completing his running, we tried not to make too big a deal out of it."

Personally, I think I got a lot out of the retreat. I learned a lot in the academic sessions and even discovered some things about myself that I hadn't realized before. But, truthfully, I never figured out our group. Sometimes I think it was a near disaster.   □

CASE QUESTIONS

1. What were the fundamental causes of the failure of the group to achieve its purposes?
2. Were there any evident group developmental processes that you can identify in the discussion of the group behaviors? What are they?
3. What could have been done at the beginning of the executive retreat to improve the chances that the groups would achieve their objectives?

INTERGROUP BEHAVIOR AND CONFLICT

LEARNING OBJECTIVES

DEFINE the term interdependence and the three special types of interdependence.

DESCRIBE the relationship between intergroup conflict and organizational performance.

DISCUSS the differences between resolution and stimulation as approaches to managing conflict.

COMPARE functional effects of conflict with dysfunctional effects.

IDENTIFY the reasons why intergroup conflict occurs.

For any organization to perform effectively, interdependent individuals and groups must establish working relationships across organizational boundaries, between individuals, and among groups. Individuals or groups may depend on one another for information, assistance, or coordinated action. But the fact is that they are interdependent. Such interdependence may foster cooperation or conflict.

For example, the production and marketing executives of a firm may meet to discuss ways to deal with foreign competition. Such a meeting may be reasonably free of conflict. Decisions get made, strategies are developed, and the executives return to work. Thus, there is intergroup cooperation to achieve a goal. However, this may not be the case if sales decline because the firm is not offering enough variety in its product line. The marketing department desires broad product lines to offer more variety to customers, while the production department desires narrow product lines to keep production costs at a manageable level and to increase productivity. Conflict is likely to occur at this point because each function has its own goals which, in this case, conflict. Thus, groups may cooperate on one point and conflict on another.

The focus of this chapter is on conflict that occurs between groups in organizations.[1] Intergroup problems are not the only type of conflict that can exist in organizations. Conflict between individuals, however, usually can be more easily resolved through existing mechanisms. Troublesome employees can be fired, transferred, or given new work schedules.

This chapter begins with an examination of attitudes toward conflict. Reasons for the existence of intergroup conflict and its consequences also are presented. Finally, we outline various techniques that have been used successfully to manage intergroup conflict.

A REALISTIC VIEW OF INTERGROUP CONFLICT

Conflict is inevitable in organizations. Intergroup conflict, however, can be both a positive and a negative force, so management should *not* strive to eliminate all conflict, only conflict that will have disruptive effects on the organization's efforts to achieve goals. Some type or degree of conflict may prove beneficial if it is used as an instrument for change or innovation. In

---

[1] See Clayton Alderfer and Ken K. Smith, "Studying Intergroup Relations Embedded in Organizations," *Administrative Science Quarterly,* March 1982, pp. 35–64.

Chapter 6, you saw that individuals have differing abilities to withstand stress. Thus, it appears that the critical issue is not conflict itself but how conflict is managed. Using this approach, we can define conflict in terms of the *effect* it has on the organization. In this respect, we shall discuss both *functional* and *dysfunctional* conflict.[2]

FUNCTIONAL CONFLICT

A **functional conflict** is a confrontation between groups that enhances and benefits the organization's performance. For example, two departments in a hospital may be in conflict over the most efficient and adaptive method of delivering health care to low-income rural families. The two departments agree on the goal but not on the means to achieve it. Whatever the outcome, low-income rural families probably will end up with better medical care once the conflict is settled. Without this type of conflict in organizations, there would be little commitment to change, and most groups likely would become stagnant. Even some inter*organizational* conflict can be functional, as the following OBM Encounter shows. Thus, functional conflict can be thought of as a type of "creative tension."

ENCOUNTER

COMPANY ATHLETIC TEAMS CAN BE A PLUS

Corporate sport is becoming serious business as companies increasingly field athletic teams to compete against other companies.

For example, American Telephone & Telegraph Co. was so determined to win the Corporate Cup track meet that it spent $25,000 to fly 80 employees to Los Angeles from work sites all over the country. As a result, AT&T won, besting 37 rivals, including defending champion GE, which spent less than $20,000 on its team.

Rebecca Parkinson, AT&T manager for employee health promotion, contends that the contests have non-health-related corporate benefits: They build "team spirit that helps the company evolve as a business." Hal Leavitt, organizational behavior professor at Stanford, agrees. "The best way to solidify your corporate culture is to have your own team competing against others," he says. "The more clearly defined a corporation's adversaries are, the better and stronger the corporation is."

FMC, another of the regular corporate competitors, also sees positive benefits. FMC, which won its fourth victory in four years at the annual National Battle of Corporate Stars, had its teams practicing two evenings a week and on Saturdays for five months before the competition. A company spokesman says the team "improves morale and gives members and the company a great deal of pride."

Most would agree that conflict on the athletic field is better than conflict in the executive suite or on the shop floor any day.   □

Source: Adapted from Delia Flores, "Dog Eat Dog: Companies Field Athletic Teams," *The Wall Street Journal,* December 3, 1985, p. 31.

---

[2] This view reflects current thinking among management theorists and a growing number of practitioners. It has been labeled the *interactionist* view. For a major work devoted entirely to the subject of organizational conflict that discusses this and other views, see Stephen P. Robbins, *Managing Organizational Conflict* (Englewood Cliffs, N.J.: Prentice-Hall, 1974). Also see K. W. Thomas, "Organizational Conflict," in *Organizational Behavior,* ed. S. Kerr (Columbus, Ohio: Grid, 1979), pp. 151–81.

DYSFUNCTIONAL CONFLICT

A **dysfunctional conflict** is any confrontation or interaction between groups that harms the organization or hinders the achievement of organizational goals. Management *must* seek to eliminate dysfunctional conflicts. Beneficial conflict often can turn into bad conflicts. In most cases, the point at which functional conflict becomes dysfunctional is impossible to identify precisely. Certain levels of stress and conflict may help create a healthy and positive movement toward goals in one group. Those same levels, however, may prove extremely disruptive and dysfunctional in another group (or at a different time for the former group). A group's tolerance for stress and conflict can also depend on the *type* of organization it serves. Automobile manufacturers, professional sports teams, and crisis organizations such as police and fire departments would have different points where functional conflict become dysfunctional than would organizations such as universities, research and development firms, and motion picture production firms.

CONFLICT AND ORGANIZATIONAL PERFORMANCE

Conflict may have either a positive or negative impact on organizational performance, depending on the nature of the conflict and how it is managed. For every organization, there is an optimal level of conflict that can be considered highly functional: it helps generate positive performance. When the conflict level is *too low,* performance can suffer. Innovation and change are difficult, and the organization may have difficulty adapting to change in its environment. If this low conflict level continues, the very survival of the organization can be threatened. On the other hand, if the conflict level becomes *too high,* the resulting chaos also can threaten the organization's survival. An example is the popular press coverage of the results of "dissension" in labor unions and its impact on performance. If fighting between rival factions in the union becomes too great, it can render the union less effective in pursuing its mission of furthering its members' interests. The proposed relationship between level of intergroup conflict and organizational performance is presented in Figure 8–1 and explained for three hypothetical situations.

VIEWS TOWARD INTERGROUP CONFLICT IN PRACTICE

Some organizational researchers contend that dysfunctional conflict should be eliminated and functional conflict encouraged. However, this is not what actually happens in most organizations.[3] In practice, most managers attempt to eliminate all types of conflict, whether dysfunctional or functional. Why is this the case? Some reasons are:

1. Anticonflict values historically have been reinforced in the home, school, and church. Traditionally, conflict between children or between children and parents has, for the most part, been discouraged. In school systems, conflict has been discouraged. Teachers had all the answers, and both teachers and children were rewarded for orderly classrooms. Finally, most religious doctrines stress peace, tranquillity, and acceptance without questioning.

---

[3] K. W. Thomas and W. H. Schmidt, "A Survey of Managerial Interests with Respect to Conflict," *Academy of Management Journal,* June 1976, pp. 315–18.

FIGURE 8–1

Proposed
Relationship
between
Intergroup
Conflict and
Organizational
Performance

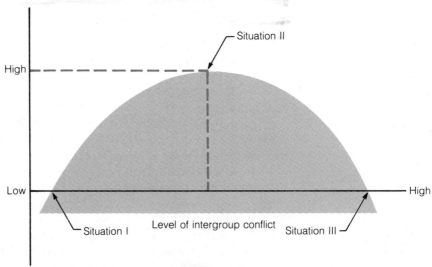

	Level of Intergroup Conflict	Probable Impact on Organization	Organization Characterized by	Level of Organizational Performance
Situation I	Low or none	Dysfunctional	Slow adaptation to environmental changes Few changes Little stimulation of ideas Apathy Stagnation	Low
Situation II	Optimal	Functional	Positive movement toward goals Innovation and change Search for problem solutions Creativity and quick adaptation to environmental changes	High
Situation III	High	Dysfunctional	Disruption Interference with activities Coordination difficult Chaos	Low

2. Managers often are evaluated and rewarded for the lack of conflict in their areas of responsibility. Anticonflict values, in fact, become part of the "culture" of the organization. Harmony and satisfaction are viewed positively, while conflicts and dissatisfaction are viewed negatively. Under such conditions, managers seek to avoid conflicts—functional or dysfunctional—that could disturb the status quo.[4]

WHY INTERGROUP CONFLICT OCCURS

Every group comes into at least partial conflict with every other group with which it interacts. This tendency is known as "the law of interorganizational conflict."[5] In this section, we examine four factors that contribute to group conflict: work interdependence, differences in goals, differences in perceptions, and the increased demand for specialists.

**INTERDEPEND-
ENCE**

Work interdependence occurs when two or more organizational groups must depend on one another to complete their tasks. The conflict potential in such situations is high. Three distinct types of interdependence among groups have been identified.[6]

Pooled Interdependence. **Pooled interdependence** requires no interaction among groups because each group, in effect, performs separately. However, the pooled performances of all the groups determine how successful the organization is. For example, the staff of an IBM sales office in one region may have no interaction with their peers in another region. Similarly, two bank branches will have little or no interaction. In both cases, however, the groups are interdependent because the performance of each must be adequate if the total organization is to thrive. The conflict potential in pooled interdependence is relatively low, and management can rely on standard rules and procedures developed at the main office for coordination.

Sequential Interdependence. **Sequential interdependence** requires one group to complete its task before another group can complete its task. Tasks are performed in a sequential fashion. In a manufacturing plant, for example, the product must be assembled before it can be painted. Thus, the assembling department must complete its task before the painting department can begin painting.

Under these circumstances, since the output of one group serves as the input for another, conflict between the groups is more likely to occur. Coordinating this type of interdependence involves effective use of the management function of planning.

---

[4] This section is based on Robbins, *Managing Organizational Conflict.*

[5] See Anthony Downs, *Inside Bureaucracy* (Boston: Little, Brown, 1968).

[6] J. Thompson, *Organizations in Action* (New York: McGraw-Hill, 1967).

Reciprocal Interdependence.   **Reciprocal interdependence** requires the output of each group to serve as input to other groups in the organization. Consider the relationships that exist between the anesthesiology staff, nursing staff, technician staff, and surgeons in a hospital operating room. This relationship creates a high degree of reciprocal interdependence. The same interdependence exists among groups involved in space launchings. Another example is the interdependence among airport control towers, flight crews, ground operations, and maintenance crews. Clearly, the potential for conflict is great in any of these situations. Effective coordination involves management's skillful use of the organizational processes of communication and decision making.[7]

All organizations have pooled interdependence among groups. Complex organizations also have sequential interdependence. The most complicated organizations experience pooled, sequential, and reciprocal interdependence among groups. The more complex the organization, the greater are the potentials for conflict and the more difficult is the task facing management.

DIFFERENCES IN GOALS

As the subunits of an organization become specialized, they often develop dissimilar goals. A goal of a production unit may include low production costs and few defective products. A goal of the research and development unit may be innovative ideas that can be converted into commercially successful new products. These different goals can lead to different expectations among the members of each unit. Because of their goal, production engineers may expect close supervision, while research scientists may expect a great deal of participation in decision making. Because of the different goals of these two groups, conflict can result when they interact. Finally, marketing departments usually have a goal of maximum gross income. On the other hand, credit departments seek to minimize credit losses. Depending on which department prevails, different customers might be selected. Here again, conflict can occur because each department has a different goal. There are certain conditions that foster intergroup conflict because of differences in goals.

Limited Resources.   When resources are limited and must be allocated, mutual dependences increase and any differences in group goals become more apparent. If money, space, the labor force, and materials were unlimited, each group could pursue, at least to a relative degree, its own goals. But in virtually all cases, resources must be allocated or shared. What often occurs in limited-resource situations is a win-lose competition that easily can result in dysfunctional conflict.

Reward Structures.   Intergroup conflict is more likely to occur when the reward system is related to individual group performance rather than to overall organizational performance. When rewards are related to individual

---

[7] For some recent research, see D. S. Cochran and D. D. White, "Intraorganizational Conflict in the Hospital Purchasing Decision," *Academy of Management Journal,* June 1981, pp. 324–32.

group performance, performance is, in fact, viewed as an independent variable, although the performance of the group is in reality very interdependent. For example, in the situation described above, suppose that the marketing group is rewarded for sales produced and that the credit group is rewarded for minimizing credit losses. In such a situation, competition will be directly reinforced and dysfunctional conflict will, inadvertently, be rewarded.

Intergroup conflict arising from differences in goals can be dysfunctional to the organization as a whole. The following OBM Encounter illustrates an all-too-common example of conflict arising out of differences in goals. Depending on the type of organization, intergroup conflicts also can be dysfunctional to third-party groups—usually the clients the organization serves. An example of this is controversy in many teaching hospitals over the conflict between meeting the goals of quality health care for patients and meeting the teaching needs of future physicians.

DIFFERENCES IN PERCEPTIONS The differences in goals can be accompanied by differing perceptions of reality, and disagreements over what constitutes reality can lead to conflict. For instance, a problem in a hospital may be viewed in one way by the administrative staff and in another way by the medical staff. Alumni and faculty may have different perceptions concerning the importance of a winning football program. Many factors cause groups in organizations to form differing perceptions of reality. The major factors include different goals, different time horizons, status incongruency, and inaccurate perceptions.

 ENCOUNTER

LABOR VS. MANAGEMENT

The battle lines at Cannon Mills are clearly drawn. On one side is Chairman and Chief Executive David Murdock, who took Cannon private a few years ago. Under his leadership, Cannon has become the nation's leading towel maker and the fourth-largest sheet producer. Unfortunately, however, the company is losing money. In an effort to stem the losses, Murdock has closed mills, laid off workers, and increased production requirements to the extent that mill workers, who are paid by the piece, have seen their pay decrease by $50 to $100 a week.

These cost-cutting measures have created an environment where the Amalgamated Clothing & Textile Workers Union feels that it has a chance to organize the more than 10,000 Cannon employees. If the union is successful, the effort will represent a major victory in a state (North Carolina) which is largely non-union. The two sides have what appears on the surface, at least, clearly different goals. The union is concerned about issues of job security, pay, and quality of work life. Murdock, who wants to rid himself of all—or at least a substantial part—of his investment in Cannon, sees a successful union drive as a major impediment to his goal of selling out.

Even if the union is unsuccessful in the first election, there may well be subsequent attempts. It took the same union 17 years and three elections to organize J. P. Stevens & Company, its last major victory. As long as there is a perceived difference in goals, where the goals are seen as mutually exclusive, the conflict will exist.   ☐

Source: Based, in part, on the article by Pete Engardio, "Why David Murdock is So Afraid of a Union," *Business Week*, October 14, 1985, p. 43.

Different Goals. Differences in group goals are an obvious contributor to differing perceptions. For instance, if the goal of marketing is to maximize sales, that department's personnel will certainly view a major breakdown in production differently than will the staff of the production department, whose goal is to minimize costs.

Different Time Horizons. Time perspectives influence how a group perceives reality. Deadlines influence the priorities and importance that groups assign to their various activities. Research scientists working for a chemical manufacturer may have a time perspective of several years, while the same firm's manufacturing engineers may work within time frames of less than a year. A bank president might focus on 5- and 10-year time spans, while middle managers might concentrate on much shorter spans. With such differences in time horizons, problems and issues deemed critical by one group may be dismissed as not important by another, and conflicts may erupt.

Status Incongruency. Conflicts concerning the relative status of different groups are common and influence perceptions. Usually, many different status standards are found in an organization, rather than an absolute one. The result is many status hierarchies. For example, status conflicts often are created by work patterns—which group initiates the work and which group responds. A production department, for instance, may perceive a change as an affront to its status because it must accept a salesperson's initiation of work. This status conflict may be aggravated deliberately by the salesperson. Academic snobbery is certainly a fact of campus life at many colleges and universities. Members of a particular academic discipline perceive themselves, for one reason or another, as having a higher status than others.

Inaccurate Perceptions. Inaccurate perceptions often cause one group to develop stereotypes about other groups. While the differences between groups may actually be small, each group will tend to exaggerate them. Thus, you will hear that "all women executives are aggressive" or "all bank trust officers behave alike." When the differences between the groups are emphasized, the stereotypes are reinforced, relations deteriorate, and conflict develops.

THE INCREASED DEMAND FOR SPECIALISTS

Conflicts between staff specialists and line generalists are probably the most common type of intergroup conflict. With the growing necessity for technical expertise in all areas of organizations, staff roles can be expected to expand and line and staff conflicts can be expected to increase. Line and staff persons simply view one another and their roles in the organization from different perspectives.[8] Table 8–1 summarizes some additional causes of conflict between staff specialists and line generalists.[9] With the growth of sophistication,

---

[8] For a classic discussion, see L. A. Allen, "The Line-Staff Relationship," *Management Record,* September 1955, pp. 346–49.

[9] See M. Dalton, "Conflicts between Staff and Line Managerial Officers," *American Sociological Review,* June 1950, pp. 342–51; A. W. Gouldner, "Cosmopolitans and Locals: Toward an

TABLE 8–1

Perceived Diminution of Line Authority. Line managers fear that specialists will encroach on their jobs and thereby diminish their authority and power. As a result, specialists often complain that line executives do not make proper use of staff specialists and do not give staff members sufficient authority.

Social and Physical Differences. Often, major differences exist between line managers and staff specialists with respect to age, education, dress, and attitudes. In many cases, staff specialists are younger than line managers and have higher educational levels or training in a specialized field.

Line Dependence on Staff Knowledge. Since line generalists often do not have the technical knowledge necessary to manage their departments, they are dependent on the specialist. The resulting gap between knowledge and authority may be even greater when the staff specialist is lower in the organizational hierarchy than the manager, which is often the case. As a result, staff members often complain that line managers resist new ideas.

Different Loyalties. Divided loyalties frequently exist between line managers and staff specialists. The staff specialist may be loyal to a discipline, while the line manager may be loyal to the organization. The member of the product development group may be a chemist first and a member of the organization second. The production manager's first loyalty, however, may be to the organization. When loyalties to a particular function or discipline are greater than loyalties to the overall organization, conflict is likely to occur.

specialization, and complexity in most organizations, line/staff conflicts will continue to be a major concern in the management of organizational behavior.

THE CONSEQUENCES OF DYSFUNCTIONAL INTERGROUP CONFLICT

Behavioral scientists have spent more than three decades researching and analyzing how dysfunctional intergroup conflict affects those who experience it.[10] They have found that groups placed in a conflict situation tend to react in fairly predictable ways. We shall now examine a number of the changes that occur *within groups* and *between groups* as a result of dysfunctional intergroup conflict.

Analysis of Latent Social Roles," *Administrative Science Quarterly,* December 1957, pp. 281–306; A. Etzioni, ed., *Complex Organizations* (New York: Holt, Rinehard & Winston, 1961); A. Etzioni, *Modern Organization* (Englewood Cliffs, N.J.: Prentice-Hall, 1964); R. W. Scott, "Professionals in Bureaucracies: Areas of Conflict," in *Professionals,* ed. H. M. Vollmer and D. L. Mills (Englewood Cliffs, N.J.: Prentice-Hall, 1966); P. R. Lawrence and J. W. Lorsch, *Organization and Environment: Managing Differentiation and Intergration* (Boston: Graduate School of Business Administration, Harvard University, 1967); J. A. Balasco and J. A. Alutto, "Line and Staff Conflicts: Some Empirical Insights," *Academy of Management Journal,* March 1969, pp. 469–77: E. Rhenman, *Conflict and Cooperation in Business* (New York: John Wiley & Sons, 1970); P. K. Berger and A. J. Grimes, "Cosmopolitan-Local: A Factor Analysis of the Construct," *Administrative Science Quarterly,* June 1973, pp. 223–35; and J. E. Sorensen and T. L. Sorensen, "The Conflict of Professionals in Bureaucratic Organizations," *Administrative Science Quarterly,* March 1974, pp. 98–106.

[10] The classic work is M. Sherif and C. Sherif, *Groups in Harmony and Tension* (New York: Harper & Row, 1953). Their study was conducted among groups in a boys' camp. They stimulated conflict between the groups and observed the changes that occurred in group behavior. Also see their "Experiments in Group Conflict," *Scientific American,* March 1956, pp. 54–58.

CHANGES WITHIN GROUPS

Many changes are likely to occur within groups involved in intergroup conflict. Unfortunately, these changes generally result in either a continuance or an escalation of the conflict.

Increased Group Cohesiveness.   Competition, conflict, or external threat usually result in group members putting aside individual differences and closing ranks. Members become more loyal to the group, and group membership becomes more attractive.

Rise in Autocratic Leadership.   In extreme conflict situations where threats are perceived, democratic methods of leadership are likely to become less popular. The members want strong leadership. Thus, the leaders are likely to become more autocratic. In the National Football League players' strike in 1982 and the PATCO strike discussed in the next chapter, the heads of each union had tremendous authority.

Focus on Activity.   When a group is in conflict, its members usually emphasize doing what the group does and doing it very well. The group becomes more task-oriented. Tolerance for members who "goof off" is low and there is less concern for individual member satisfaction. The emphasis is on accomplishing the group's task and defeating the "enemy" (the other group in the conflict).

Emphasis on Loyalty.   Conformity to group norms tends to become more important in conflict situations. Group goals take precedence over individual satisfaction as members are expected to demonstrate their loyalty. In major conflict situations, interaction with members of "the other group" may be outlawed.

CHANGES BETWEEN GROUPS

During conflicts, certain changes will probably occur *between* the groups involved.

Distorted Perceptions.   During conflicts, the perceptions of each group's members become distorted. Group members develop stronger opinions of the importance of their units. Each group sees itself as superior in performance to the other and as more important to the survival of the organization than other groups. In a conflict situation, nurses may conclude that they are more important to a patient than physicians, while physicians may consider themselves more important than hospital administrators. The marketing group in a business organization may think, "Without us selling the product, there would be no money to pay anyone else's salary." The production group meanwhile will say, "If we don't make the product, there is nothing to sell." Ultimately, none of these groups is more important, but conflict can cause their members to develop gross misperceptions of reality.

Negative Stereotyping.   As conflict increases and perceptions become more distorted, all of the negative stereotypes that may have ever existed are reinforced. A management representative may say, "I've always said these union guys are just plain greedy. Now they've proved it." The head of a local teacher's union may say, "Now we know that what all politicians are interested in is getting reelected, not the quality of education." When negative stereotyping is a factor in a conflict, the members of each group see less differences *within* their unit than actually exist and greater differences *between* the groups than actually exist.

Decreased Communication. Communications between the groups in conflict usually break down. This can be extremely dysfunctional, especially where sequential interdependence or reciprocal interdependence relationships exist between groups. The decision-making process can be disrupted, and the customers or others whom the organization serves can be affected. Consider the possible consequences to patients, for instance, if a conflict between hospital technicians and nurses continues until it lowers the quality of health care.

While these are not the only dysfunctional consequences of intergroup conflict, they are the most common and they have been well documented in the research literature.[11] Other consequences, such as violence and aggression, are less common but also occur. When intergroup conflicts take place, some form of managerial intervention is usually necessary. How managers can deal with these situations is the subject of the next section.

MANAGING INTERGROUP CONFLICT THROUGH RESOLUTION

Since managers must live with intergroup conflict, they must confront the problem of managing it.[12] In this section, you will examine techniques that have been used successfully in resolving intergroup conflicts that have reached levels dysfunctional to the organization.[13] Most of these techniques involve some type of exchange between the conflicting parties. This suggests that resolution may be facilitated by constructive negotiation. Gerard Nierenberg outlines the fundamentals of negotiating in his article which accompanies this chapter. As Nierenberg points out, in successful negotiations everyone wins, and successful negotiating is a key element in many of the following techniques.

---

[11] For additional discussion, see J. Litterer, "Conflict in Organizations: A Re-Examination," *Academy of Management Journal,* September 1966, pp. 178–86; J. W. Lorsch and J. J. Morse, *Organizations and Their Members: A Contingency Approach* (New York: Harper & Row, 1974); and E. Schein, "Intergroup Problems in Organizations," in *Organization Development: Theory, Practice, and Research,* 2d. ed. W. French, C. Bell, and R. Zawacki (Plano, Tex.: Business Publications, 1983), pp. 106–10.

[12] See David M. Herold, "Improving the Performance Effectiveness of Groups through a Task-Contingent Selection of Intervention Strategies," *Academy of Management Review,* April 1978, pp. 315–51; and R. A. Cosier and T. L. Ruble, "Research on Conflict-Handling Behavior: An Experimental Approach," *Academy of Management Journal,* December 1981, pp. 816–31.

[13] Based on Robbins, *Managing Organizational Conflict,* pp. 67–77.

**PROBLEM
SOLVING**

The confrontation method of problem solving seeks to reduce tensions through face-to-face meetings of the conflicting groups. The purpose of the meetings is to identify conflicts and resolve them. The conflicting groups openly debate various issues and bring together all relevent information until a decision has been reached. For conflicts resulting from misunderstandings or language barriers, the confrontation method has proved effective. For solving more complex problems (e.g., conflict where groups have different value systems), the method has been less successful. The following OBM Encounter provides some insights into how President Carter handled a very famous set of problem-solving sessions.

THE CAMP DAVID MEETINGS

The series of meetings between the Egyptian and Israeli leaders Sadat and Begin, which took place at Camp David and was hosted by Jimmy Carter, can, in many respects, be viewed as conflict-management sessions. In the following excerpt, renown psychologist Carl Rogers comments on Carter's conflict management approach.

I have no way of knowing whether President Carter had any psychological advice, but the Camp David sessions had many of the qualities of an intensive group experience . . . and many of its outcomes were similar. In the first place, it was informal. There was no protocol, no standing on ceremony, no formal attire. The leaders espe-

cially, and their staff members to some extent, met simply as persons. Secondly, there were many facilitative efforts. In one tense and angry meeting near the beginning, Carter simply listened to Sadat and Begin, then at the conclusion of the meeting, he summarized, much as a facilitator might have done, the issues which had been raised by each leader. The difference was that he was able to state and clarify these issues in a calm and understanding way, where they had been expressed in highly emotional ways. On another occasion, when the hostility between Sadat and Begin ran too high, Carter acted as a facilitative intermediary, carrying messages back and forth until they were willing to meet again.

☐

Source: Carl R. Rogers, "Nuclear War: A Personal Response," *APA Monitor,* August 1982, pp. 6–7.

**SUPER-
ORDINATE
GOALS**

In the resolution of conflicts between groups, the **superordinate goals** technique involves developing a common set of goals and objectives. These goals and objectives cannot be attained without the cooperation of the groups involved. In fact, they are unattainable by one group singly and supersede all other goals of any of the individual groups involved in the conflict.[14] For

---

[14] See M. Sherif and C. Sherif, *Social Psychology* (New York: Harper & Row, 1969), pp. 228–62, for a detailed discussion of this method. Sherif and Sherif conducted a number of sociopsychological experiments designed to determine effective ways of resolving conflict. Based on this research, they developed the concept of superordinate goals. Also see J. D. Hunger and L. W. Stern, "An Assessment of the Functionality of the Superordinate Goal in Reducing Conflict," *Academy of Management Journal,* December 1976, pp. 591–605.

example, several unions in the automobile and airline industries have, in recent years, agreed to forgo increases and in some cases to accept pay reductions because the survival of their firm or industry was threatened. When the crisis is over, demands for higher wages undoubtedly will return, as they have at once-struggling Chrysler Corporation.

EXPANSION OF RESOURCES

As noted earlier, a major cause of intergroup conflict is limited resources. Whatever one group succeeds in obtaining is gained at the expense of another group. The scarce resource may be a particular position (e.g., the presidency of the firm), money, space, and so forth. For example, one major publishing firm decided to expand by establishing a subsidiary firm. Most observers believed that the major reason for the expansion was to allow the firm to become involved in other segments of the market. While this was partially correct, a stronger reason was to enable the firm to stem the exit of valued personnel. By establishing the subsidiary, the firm was able to double its executive positions, since the subsidiary needed a president, various vice presidents, and other executives. Expanding resources is a very successful technique for solving conflicts in many cases, since this technique may enable almost everyone to be satisfied. In reality, however, resources usually are not easily expanded.

AVOIDANCE

Frequently, some way can be found to avoid conflict. While avoidance may not bring any long-run benefits, it certainly can work as a short-run solution. Avoiding a conflict neither effectively resolves it nor eliminates it. Eventually, the conflict will have to be faced. But, in some circumstances, avoidance may be the best temporary alternative.

SMOOTHING

The technique known as *smoothing* emphasizes the common interests of the conflicting groups and de-emphasizes their differences. The basic belief behind smoothing is that stressing shared viewpoints on certain issues facilitates movement toward a common goal. If the differences between the groups are serious, smoothing—like avoidance—is a short-run solution at best. Smoothing also may contribute to low-quality decisions whose full implications are not realized.[15]

COMPROMISE

Compromise is a traditional method for resolving intergroup conflicts.[16] With compromise, there is no distinct winner or loser, and the decision reached probably is not ideal for either group. Compromise can be used very effectively when the goal sought (for example, money) can be divided equitably. If this is not possible, one group must give up something of value as a concession.

---

[15] Dean Tjosvold, "Implications of Controversy Research for Management," *Journal of Management,* Fall/Winter 1985, pp. 21–37.

[16] For a discussion of the problems associated with compromise, see W. Notz and F. Starke, "Final Offer vs. Conventional Arbitration as Means of Conflict Management," *Administrative Science Quarterly,* June 1978, pp. 189–203.

Compromise also may involve third-party interventions, as well as total group or representative negotiating and voting.[17]

AUTHORITATIVE COMMAND

The use of authority may be the oldest and most frequently employed method for resolving intergroup conflict. Using this method, management simply resolves the conflict as it sees fit and communicates its desires to the groups involved. Subordinates usually will abide by a superior's decision, whether or not they agree with it. Thus, authoritative command usually works in the short run. As with avoidance, smoothing, and compromise, however, authoritative command does not focus on the cause of the conflict but rather on the results of it. If the causes of the conflict are still present, the conflict probably will recur.

ALTERING THE HUMAN VARIABLE

Altering the human variable involves trying to change the behavior of the members of the groups involved. This method focuses on the cause or causes of the conflict and on the attitudes of the people involved. While the method is certainly difficult, it does center on the cause of the conflict. Chapter 15 of this book focuses specifically on changing behavior. In the chapter, we shall see that while altering the human variable is slower than other methods and often costly, the results can be significant in the long run.

ALTERING THE STRUCTURAL VARIABLES

Another way to resolve intergroup disputes is to alter the structural variables. This involves changing the formal structure of the organization. Structure refers to the fixed relationships among the jobs of the organization and includes the design of jobs and departments. Altering the structure of the organization to resolve intergroup conflict involves such things as transferring, exchanging, or rotating members of the groups or having someone serve as a coordinator, liaison, or go-between who keeps groups communicating with one another.

IDENTIFYING A COMMON ENEMY

In some respects, identifying a common enemy is the negative side of superordinate goals. Groups in conflict may temporarily resolve their differences and unite to combat a common enemy. The common enemy may be a competitor that has just introduced a clearly superior product. Conflicting groups in a bank suddenly may work in close harmony when government bank examiners make a visit. The common-enemy phenomenon is very evident in domestic conflicts. Most police officers prefer not to become involved in heated domestic conflicts because, in far too many cases, the combatants close ranks and turn on the police officer.

Whatever the techniques utilized to deal with intergroup conflict (and there are undoubtedly others), the important point is that you must learn how to recognize both the existence and the causes of intergroup conflict. You must also develop skills to deal with it.

---

[17] For research on a different but related problem, see J. Sullivan, R. Peterson, N. Kameda, and J. Shimada, "The Relationship between Conflict Resolution Approaches and Trust—A Cross Cultural Study," *Academy of Management Journal,* December 1981, pp. 803–15.

FIGURE 8–2

An Overview of
Intergroup
Conflict

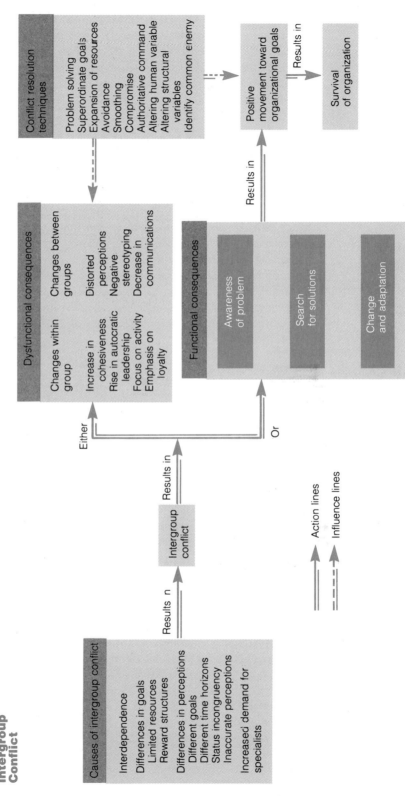

The most commonly used methods for managing intergroup conflict each have strengths and weaknesses and are effective or ineffective under different conditions and situations. What this chapter has said thus far about intergroup conflict is summarized in Figure 8–2. The figure illustrates the relationship between causes and types of intergroup conflict, the consequences of intergroup conflict, and techniques for resolution.

MANAGING INTERGROUP CONFLICT THROUGH STIMULATION

Throughout this chapter, we have stressed that some conflict is beneficial. This point is noted again in Figure 8–2, which focuses on some of the functional consequences of intergroup conflict. The figure indicates that change can develop out of conflict, from an awareness of problems, and from creative search for alternative solutions. We have already examined a situation where conflict is dysfunctional because it is too high and requires resolution. It is also possible, however, that intergroup conflict may be too low and require stimulation to generate action. The next section examines techniques that have been used successfully to stimulate conflict to a functional level, where it is contributing positively to organizational performance.[18]

COMMUNICATION

By intelligent use of the organization's communication channels, a manager can stimulate beneficial conflict. Information can be placed carefully into formal channels to create ambiguity, reevaluation, or confrontation. Information that is threatening (e.g., a proposed budget cut) can stimulate functional conflict in a department and improved performance. Carefully planted rumors also can serve a useful purpose. For example, a hospital administrator may start a rumor about a proposed reorganization of the hospital. His purpose is twofold: (1) to stimulate new ideas on how to more effectively carry out the mission of the hospital, and (2), to reduce apathy among the staff.

BRINGING OUTSIDE INDIVIDUALS INTO THE GROUP

A technique widely used to "bring back to life" a stagnant organization or subunit of an organization is to hire or transfer in individuals whose attitudes, values, and backgrounds differ from those of the group's present members. Many college faculties consciously seek new members with different backgrounds and often discourage the hiring of graduates of their own programs. This is to ensure a diversity of viewpoints on the faculty. The technique of bringing in outsiders is also used widely in government and business. Recently, a bank president decided not to promote from within for a newly created position of marketing vice president. Instead, he hired a highly successful executive from the very competitive consumer products field. The bank president felt that while the outsider knew little about marketing financial services, her approach to, and knowledge of, marketing was what the bank needed to become a strong competitor.

---

[18] See Robbins, *Managing Organizational Conflict*, chap. 9.

ALTERING THE ORGANIZATION'S STRUCTURE

Changing the structure of the organization can not only help resolve intergroup conflict; it is also excellent for *creating* conflict. For example, a school of business typically has several departments. One, named the Department of Business Administration, includes all of the faculty members who teach courses in management, marketing, finance, production management, and so forth. Accordingly, the department is rather large, with 32 members under one department chairman, who reports to the dean. A new dean recently has been hired, and he is considering dividing the business administration unit into several separate departments (e.g., departments of marketing, finance, management), each with five or six members and a chairperson. The reasoning is that reorganizing in this manner will create competition among the groups for resources, students, faculty, and so forth, where none existed before because there was only one group. Whether this change will improve performance remains to be seen.

STIMULATING COMPETITION

Many managers utilize various techniques to stimulate competition among groups. The use of a variety of incentives, such as awards and bonuses for outstanding performance, often stimulates competition. If properly utilized, such incentives can help maintain a healthy atmosphere of competition that may result in a functional level of conflict. Incentives can be given for least defective parts, highest sales, best teacher, greatest number of new customers, or in any area where increased conflict is likely to lead to more effective performance.

In these last two sections we have examined a number of approaches to managing intergroup conflict. In the second readings article accompanying this chapter, C. Brooklyn Derr discusses three specific strategies for managing conflict: collaboration, bargaining, and the use of power. The article evaluates the role of each and draws conclusions regarding their possible costs and benefits.

SUMMARY OF KEYPOINTS

A. Conflict between groups is inevitable in organizations. This conflict may be positive or negative, depending on its impact on the organization's goal achievement.

B. Functional conflict represents a confrontation between groups that enhances and benefits the organization's performance.

C. Dysfunctional conflict results from a confrontation or interaction between groups that hinders the achievement of organizational goals.

D. While most managers try to eliminate conflict, evidence indicates that for most organizations an optimal level of conflict can positively influence organizational performance.

E. Intergroup conflict results from such factors as work interdependence, differences in goals, differences in perceptions, and the increasing demand for specialists.

F. Dysfunctional conflict causes changes to take place within and between the groups involved. Within the group, there may be an increase in group cohesiveness, a rise in autocratic leadership, a focus on the task, and an emphasis on loyalty. Changes occurring between the groups include distorted perceptions, negative stereotyping, and a decrease in communication.

G. One of the difficult tasks that a manager must confront is diagnosing and managing intergroup conflict. Some useful techniques for resolving intergroup conflict include problem solving, superordinate goals, expansion of resources, avoidance, smoothing, compromise, authority, and changing either the people or the organization's structure. Each of these techniques is useful in specific situations and circumstances.

H. Conflict management techniques also exist for situations where the manager diagnoses a level of conflict that is dysfunctional because it is too low. Conflict stimulation techniques include using the communication channels, hiring or transferring in outside individuals, and changing the organization's structure. The important point is that effective conflict management involves both resolution and stimulation.

REVIEW AND DISCUSSION QUESTIONS

1. What is the difference between managing conflict and preventing it? Is one or the other a sounder approach? Explain.

2. Are there circumstances when a manager might deliberately introduce conflict into a group?

3. Identify examples of pooled, sequential, and reciprocal interdependence in the following organizations: a university, a bank, the IRS, a professional football team.

4. "There can be no progress without conflict." Discuss what this statement means with respect to organizations.

5. As organizations grow in size and complexity, interdependence increases, goal differences grow, and work and people become more specialized. Does this suggest conflict in organizations must increase? Does knowledge of these changes help us prepare for them? How?

6. When intergroup conflict occurs, changes take place within and between the conflicting groups. What are these changes? Which changes generally are positive? Which negative?

7. What are the major differences between resolution and stimulation in managing conflict? Could both be appropriate with the same groups at the same time? Explain.

8. How might you apply some of the conflict management strategies from this chapter to improving union-management relations during contract negotiations?

9. In our system of government, conflict between the two major political parties is ever present. In what ways is this conflict dysfunctional? In what ways is it functional?

10. How important are individual differences such as abilities, personality, and attitudes in causing or resolving conflict? Why is it important for a manager to be aware of these differences in dealing with conflict?

R1 FUNDAMENTALS OF NEGOTIATING*

GERARD NIERENBERG

Negotiating today is one of the least understood arts in human affairs.

Many people, due to their lack of awareness of any structured ap-

* Source: Gerard Nierenberg, *Art of Negotiating* (Hawthorne Books, Division of Elsevier-Dutton Publishing Co., 1968).

proach to the negotiating process, are forced to reuse self-taught methods that have merely appeared to work in the past—methods that were acquired, like diseases, from social contact. There is, however, an important and useful difference between merely knowing a few cunning homemade techniques and understanding the full cooperative human process of negotiation. In a successful negotiation everyone wins. Various skills and strategies are required to implement these negotiations on a moment-to-moment, day-to-day and year-to-year basis, and when these are consistent with a basic philosophy, each adds to the overall strength of the other.

The idea that everyone wins in a successful negotiation is not being

presented here solely on ethical grounds. In actuality it is considered simply good business. It is a matter of securing long-range objectives instead of short-term advantages. Negotiated solutions are likely to be longer-lasting when each party has gained and has a stake in maintaining the conclusion. The negotiator who has acquired the skills and techniques presented here will be able to negotiate successful conclusions that will satisfy all parties—replacing the outdated win-lose attitude with genuinely creative negotiating.

LEARNING CHECKPOINT

What is the view of conflict as stated in the chapter? Is this view consistent with this author's view of the importance of negotiating skills? Why?

Nothing could be simpler in definition or broader in scope than negotiation. Every desire that demands satisfaction—and every need to be met—is at least potentially an occasion for people to initiate the negotiating process. Whenever people exchange ideas with the intention of changing relationships, whenever they confer for agreement, they are negotiating.

Negotiation depends on communication. It occurs between individuals acting either for themselves or as representatives of organized groups. Therefore negotiation can be considered an element of human behavior. Aspects of it have been dealt with by both the traditional and the new behavioral sciences, from history, jurisprudence, economics, sociology, and psychology to cybernetics, general semantics, game and decision-making theory, and general systems.

Yet the full scope of negotiation is too broad to be confined to one or even a group of the existing behavioral sciences.

Every day, *The New York Times* reports hundreds of negotiations. At the United Nations and in capitals around the world attempts are made to settle the "small" wars. Government agencies negotiate with the United States Congress for appropriations. A utility company confers with a regulatory agency on rates. A strike is settled. Two companies agree to merge but must obtain the consent of the Justice Department. A small but valuable piece of real estate changes hands. These are the types of negotiations that the *Times* might describe any day of the week. Occasionally there may be a spectacular agreement, such as the nuclear test ban treaty, to attract worldwide attention. But even more important, at least to the people that participated in them, are the countless negotiations that are not mentioned in the *Times* or in any other newspaper.

Up to the present time, no general theories were available to guide an individual in his day-to-day negotiating activities. All too frequently we have had to learn to negotiate the same way we learned such things as sex—by trial and error. The man who claimed to have thirty years experience in negotiation might simply be making the same mistakes every year for thirty years.

LABOR-MANAGEMENT NEGOTIATIONS

Collective bargaining has evolved as a tool for settling labor-management disputes. Recognizing this technique as a subdivision of negotiation, both sides have initiated courses and studies in labor negoti-

ation. As a result, highly trained negotiators have dominated both sides of the bargaining table.

In the words of Professor Leon M. Labes, "Few who have had firsthand experience in the field of labor-management relations will deny that decisions reached by collective bargaining are the only ones that are completely satisfactory. Everything that can be done to encourage and foster such negotiations must be done, and many new techniques have properly been developed." In the United States these industrial negotiations are carried on under at least two ominous threats, one from each side of the bargaining table: labor's power to strike, and management's power to close, relocate, or lock out. All labor-management negotiators are constantly aware that in the event of their failure to achieve a settlement, one or both of these threats will be implemented.

In spite of the tremendous strides labor has made as a result of collective bargaining, it has generally been content with limited methods of negotiating. On one occasion, an attempt to go beyond what were seen to be restrictive methods led to the firing of the innovator. The issue, however, was not his new negotiating techniques, but his neglect of public relations. David J. McDonald failed to win reelection as president of the United Steel Workers of America in 1965 after he had attempted to bring about settlement of minor incidents and disputes before they became points of disagreement.

McDonald worked closely with his brilliant general counsel, Arthur J. Goldberg, to put an end to the long and costly strikes that had plagued the industry since World War II. Their cooperation resulted in the establishment of a human relations committee.

The committee, composed of four top representatives of the industry and of the union, met throughout the year to discuss problems and make mutually beneficial suggestions, all of this without the necessity of working under contract deadlines. This would appear to be an ideal method, one that would lead to ideal solutions. In fact it worked so well that the steel industry began to be pointed to as a model of what could be accomplished with industrial relations.

Then something went wrong. McDonald lost the union presidency to I. W. Abel, who campaigned under the slogan "Give the union back to the membership." In devising a better collective bargaining system, McDonald, Goldberg's student, had neglected one essential aspect of negotiating, namely *communication*. He failed to keep the membership closely acquainted with exactly what was happening. Complete secrecy was permitted for the new human relations committee, in order to allow its members freedom to discuss problems without fear of the industry and membership reaction. Although the end was desirable, the means permitted an insurgent group to take advantage of McDonald's failure to inform and communicate with the membership.

NOT A GAME

Negotiating has often been compared to a game. A game has definite rules and a known set of values. Each player is limited in the moves he can make, the things he can do and cannot do. True, some games have a greater element of chance than others, but in every game a set of rules governs the behavior of the players and enumerates their gains and losses. In games the rules show the risks and rewards. However, rules of this sort are not available in the unbounded life process of negotiation. In negotiating, *any* risks that are known have been learned from broad experience, not from a rule book. In a life situation the negotiator ordinarily has little or no control over the complex variables, the innumerable strategies, that the opposer may bring into the struggle. Even more difficult is to know the value structure upon which the opposer bases his strategy.

To look upon negotiations as a game to be played is to enter into the bargaining in a purely competitive spirit. With this attitude, the negotiator strives against other individuals for a goal which *he alone* hopes to attain. Even if he could persuade an opposer to "play" such a negotiating game, he would run the risk of being the absolute loser rather than the winner. In post-World War II Japan, some businessmen required that their employees study military strategy and tactics as a guide to successful business operations. How many of these employers realized that comparing business with war was only a metaphor? How many saw that the goal of a successful business deal is *not* a dead competitor?

The objective should be to achieve *agreement*, not total victory. Both parties must feel that they have gained something. Even if one side had had to give up a great deal, the overall picture is one of gain.

 **LEARNING CHECKPOINT**

Select one of the causes of intergroup conflict discussed in the chapter. How could negotiation be used to manage this particular source of conflict?

NEWSPAPERS FOLDED

Negotiation, then, is *not* a game—and it is not war. Its goal is *not* a dead competitor. A negotiator ignores this point at his own peril.

A classic example is the recent history of the newspaper business in New York City. Bertram Powers, head of the printers' union, became nationally known as a man who "drives a hard bargain." With the aid of a couple of paralyzing strikes, the printers in New York achieved what seemed to be remarkable contracts. Not only did they obtain higher wages, but the newspapers were forbidden to institute such money-saving practices as the automated setting of market tables.

The printers won their points at the negotiating table—because they held out to the end. But the newspapers were forced into an economic straitjacket. Three major newspapers merged and finally, after another long strike, folded, leaving New York with one evening and two morning papers—and leaving thousands of newspaper people with no place to work. The negotiation was "successful," but the patient died.

"COOPERATIVE EGOTISM"

Think of negotiation as a *cooperative enterprise*. If both parties enter the situation on a cooperative basis, there is a strong likelihood that they will be persuaded to strive for goals that can be shared equally. This does not mean that *every* goal will be of the same value to the participants. But it does mean that there is greater possibility for each participant to reach successful cooperative goals.

However, the competitive attitude need not be abandoned. It serves as an integrating process, a rivalry that coordinates the activities of individuals. A single side of a scissors by itself cannot cut. Competition that permits each man to measure his competence or means against the other's—and to be rewarded proportionally—is really a cooperative achievement.

A great impetus to reaching an accord is the search for common interest levels. Franklin D. Roosevelt stated: "It has always seemed to me that the best symbol of common sense was a bridge." However, let us add what Robert Benchley said: "It seems to me that the most difficult part of building a bridge would be the start."

Always be on the alert to convert divergent interests into channels of common desires. In exploring these channels, both parties to the negotiation may be stimulated by the idea of sharing common goals. These goals are reached by finding mutual interests and needs, by emphasizing the matters that can be agreed upon, and by not dwelling on points of difference.

Many negotiations conducted in a highly competitive manner have ended in what seemed to be a complete victory for one side. The alleged winner was in possession of everything he wanted and the loser had suffered a humiliating defeat. However, such a "settlement" will rarely stay settled. Unless the terms arrived at have been advantageous in some way to the "loser," he will soon seek means of changing the settlement. Unlike a game, there is no "end" to a life negotiation situation. Many times clients of mine are convinced that they have scored a complete victory over their opponents and have forced the losing side to accept absolute defeat. I attempt to explain that there are numerous continuing elements and side effects that may well affect the "final" consummation of the deal.

Even if my client has been able to overcome all objections from his opponent's attorney and accountant, the one-sided, forced settlement is not final, it will not stick. Often a wife, as final adviser, will upset the prior agreements. Husbands do have a habit of discussing their business affairs with their wives, and a wife will not hesitate to point out that he has agreed to a bad deal and that no preliminary agreement is sacred. In other cases, after quiet reconsideration, the dissatisfied party—or even a third party—may begin a lawsuit to set aside or reorganize the unfavorable settlement. An overwhelmingly one-sided settlement breeds trouble and in the end will only prove to be a great waste of time and effort. It contains the seed of its own destruction. Yet rigidly competitively oriented people often wonder why they can never seem to conclude anything. They say they work hard, but luck or life never seems to break for them. Something always goes wrong.

This should not be surprising. We could complete few tasks without the complete cooperation and assisting efforts of others. Who could drive an automobile if he could not rely on other people to comply with traffic regulations?

Negotiating is give-and-take. However, each side is watching the opposer for any clue to his prejudices that may provide a negotiating advantage.

It is fascinating to observe two master negotiators battling it out. As a rule they can arrive at a settlement very quickly. They go directly to the heart of the problem and waste no time on extraneous matters. Each side, after an initial period of probing and feeling out the other, promptly realizes that he is dealing with a master and that a quick solution is forthcoming. Many labor strikes could actually be settled at a first or second meeting, but for political or economic reasons the agreement is not verbalized until a later date. Negotiation, like a fruit, ripens in due time.

When the bargaining is conducted with all the coolness of professional gamblers at a poker game, this is merely a surface mannerism. In actuality, experts do not play a negotiating game. They are adept at the art of compromise and accommodation. They are fully aware of the necessity for finding a common ground of interest, and they avoid the pitfalls of a competitive I-must-win-the-game attitude. At the earliest possible moment in the negotiation, each side manages to convey to the other its maximum concessions and the minimum concessions expected in return. This is not done explicitly, but subtly, by innuendo and deliberate tip-offs. Such skills and techniques, arrived at through long experience and training, enable the master negotiators to reach a satisfactory settlement.

WHEN CONTROLS BECOME UNCONTROLLABLE

Sometimes, when an opponent seems on the run, there is a temptation to push him as hard as possible. But that one extra push may be the straw that breaks the camel's back.

Simply stated, one of the first lessons the negotiator must learn is *when to stop*. Negotiation, like alcohol, does not conform to the simple mathematical principles we learned as children. It's that little extra "one for the road" that can kill you. There is a *critical point* in negotiation beyond which the reaction—like that of an atomic pile—can become uncontrolled and destructive. An example may be found in the extensive research that was conducted into the causes of unscheduled work stoppages—strikes, accidents, unavailability of supplies—occurring a few years ago in the coal mines around Manchester, England. It was found that when the group size in the individual work force *exceeded a critical number,* the stoppages occurred.

So the negotiator's aim should never been "just one more." He must sense when he is approaching the critical point—and stop short of it. *All parties to a negotiation should come out with some needs satisfied.*

This can't happen when one of the parties is demolished.

It's all too easy to lose sight of this principle. In the heat of negotiation, one can be carried away.

ISSUES AND POSITIONS

Any information upon which there is disagreement can be organized into the negotiation issues. The issues then are the things on which one side takes an affirmative position and the other a negative position. Issues should be pragmatic, for it is difficult to make a definite judgment about unrealistic issues. Instead of discussing them, people have a tendency to make accusations, which then become issues. But accusations are judgments of a situation, and a judgment, say, that the seller's price is too high may or may not be correct and is quite difficult to resolve. More realistic issues can be raised by dividing the fact of the cost into elements of cost and then determining whether any of the elements can be verified as not actual and therefore able to be cut.

Questions based on emotional reactions are also nonrealistic and should be used only for the emotional effect they may produce— e.g., "Don't you think you have a nerve asking that amount?" Such questions should not be considered issues on which decisions are made.

It is important to remember that we should try to negotiate problems rather than our demands. Our demands are only a one-solution approach to the problems. There may be other solutions. If the problems are discussed, we may see that our demands are not the only solution to these problems. In the course of our negotiation, we may want to change position. Excuses for changing position can be as follows: a mediator entering the case, a change in the other side's position, intentional misinterpretation of the other side's position as a change, or a change in available facts.

When the other side makes a commitment or, let us say, sets a limit, one way of handling it would be to ignore it or not comprehend it. Another might be to make casual conversation or a joke so that the seriousness of it may be lost. Humor can serve a vital function in negotiations.

It is said that your bargaining position should conceal as well as reveal, and it is somewhat basic theory that as negotiations continue, concessions alternate from each side. A motivating factor to cause such reactions is citing principles and precedents for the other side to work with.

Each position is the sum of all the issues involved. Some negotiations have many issues: some issues are broader than others. With the resolution of the broader, more important issues, some of the minor ones seem to disappear or be resolved. As new facts are developed in fact-finding and negotiation, the posture that one takes on an issue may change, and so will the position change. A skillful negotiator is ever alert to this particular chain of events: assumptions—facts—issues—positions—decisions. If you would like to change your opposer's decisions, first try to alter his assumptions.

NEGOTIATING AGENDA

An agenda may be presented by one side or prepared by both sides, or each side may prepare two agendas: a general agenda and a detailed agenda. The general agenda is presented to the other side, and the detailed agenda is for one's own use. In a student-administration confrontation it might be possible for the agenda to consist of nonnegotiable demands. In turmoil situations the agenda is composed of items neither side would care to discuss.

Having the other side accept your agenda has its advantages. It can put the other side on the defensive. Your agenda contains the definitions of your terms in your own way. Therefore, it contains your assumptions. You should remember, however, that your agenda reveals your positions in advance and it may permit the other side to prepare a reaction to the areas that you wish to discuss. You also are not in a position to hear out the other side before presenting your agenda positions. This too is a disadvantage, for the order of procedure, or agenda, has to depend on the strategies chosen beforehand, before you know the actual posture of the opposer. The agenda might very well be considered one of the tactics used in negotiation.

Try not to permit your agenda to be bound in an arbitrary, uncontrolled arrangement. Many a negotiation has been circumscribed by an agenda based on a printed form, a contract, a lease, a union contract, or merely a chronological listing of issues. This should not be done. Attention should instead be given to the various issues to be discussed so that strategies can be developed. The issues might be listed so that the major ones are discussed first. This will prevent time from being wasted on minor issues, leaving sufficient time to discuss the major ones. As an alternative, minor issues might be listed first so that you can begin the negotiation by making concessions, expecting that as the issues become more important you will get concessions in return. Of course, the fact that you have made concessions may be regarded by your opposer as a precedent and he may expect them to continue. However, minor issues are sometimes easier to resolve, and their resolution creates an atmosphere of goodwill. If you disclose your major issue first, the other side may attempt to suspend the discussion of the major issues temporarily by embroiling the meeting in minor issues so that they can consider what they may or may not do, or they may introduce factors to balance your major issue.

Other people arrange it differently. Rather than classification on the basis of minor and major issues, they first set up a group of conditions or issues that they feel they can agree on. Having agreed, they then ask for concessions on the issues on which they are seeking agreement. Others break the issues into those involving dollars and those not involving money and attempt to resolve the nonmonetary matters first. Remember the maxim, "It's a bad plan that can't be changed."

REVEALING POSITION

When do you reveal your minimum position? This may very well depend on your opposer. It is easier to deal with an experienced negotiator than with an inexperienced one. If you are confronted with an inexperienced negotiator and expose your minimum position immediately, he is unable to appreciate it. You must educate him to enable him to see the possibilities and yet, once shown them, he may lack the experience necessary to

believe you. You do not reveal a minimum position early if your opposer needs publicity on how hard and well he has negotiated or if he must show his boss how diligent he is. If you reveal your position too quickly, it can be interpreted by the other side as excessive eagerness. It would be a better strategy to let the other side feel that it has worked very hard to move you into your position. No union or management team would chance the consequence of immediately accepting the other's first offer. There are rare situations where you may have an eager, intelligent, reasonable, well-informed, experienced opposer who does not have to report to anyone. It is possible under these circumstances that you can reveal your minimum terms at the start of the negotiation. Even in that event, however, state your objective in the negotiation indirectly. An outstanding negotiator on the other side will then work to assist you in achieving what you need as a minimum in the negotiation, and you at the same time will work with him to try to achieve the minimum that he needs.

OPPOSER'S MAXIMUM POSITION

Sometimes you will encounter an opposer who states a position that is so unreasonable that you would be wise not to reveal any position in the hope that as the negotiation continues he will change to a more favorable position because he cannot justify his first demand. At times it may be advisable, if you feel your opposer's position is completely unreasonable, to make counterproposals merely to balance his demands. State that these counterproposals are on the table as long as the demands that you consider arbitrary and unreasonable are there. For example: If the union

wants a four-day workweek, a counterdemand might be that all paid holidays be eliminated.

SUCCESS

Negotiation is a tool of human behavior, a tool anyone can use effectively. I have tried to avoid shaping it into a specialized tool that would be suitable for use only by professionals. I have sought to give the realm of negotiation new forms that are allied to the forms of other types of human activities.

The successful negotiator must combine the alertness and speed of an expert swordsman with an artist's sensitivity. He must watch his adversary across the bargaining table with the keen eye of a fencer, ever ready to spot any loophole in the defense, any shift in strategy. He is prepared to thrust at the slightest opportunity. On the other hand, he must also be the sensitive artist perceptive of the slightest variation in the color of his opponent's mood or motivation. At the correct moment he must be able to select from his palette of many colors exactly the right combination of shades and tints that will lead to mastery. Success in negotiation, aside from adequate training, is essentially a matter of sensitivity and correct timing.

Finally, the mature negotiator will have an understanding of the cooperative pattern. He will try to achieve agreement and will remember that in a successful negotiation everyone wins.

And if this is the case, why shoot it out, when we can still talk it out?

☐

LEARNING CHECKPOINT

How do the techniques of conflict management discussed in the chapter compare with negotiation?

R² MANAGING ORGANIZATIONAL CONFLICT: COLLABORATION, BARGAINING, AND POWER APPROACHES

C. BROOKLYN DERR

Conflicts are normal and natural consequences of human interaction in organizational settings. But they are also complex. Conflicts may occur for multiple reasons; for example: internal stress coming from the person and overlapping into the work place, incompatible expectations among workers and work groups, differences over task procedures, values, orientations, and desired outcomes, increasing interdependencies and work loads, and external pressures and crises.

As an illustration of this complexity, the author is well acquainted with a large urban school district in which serious conflicts occur between two associate superintendents. One party to the dispute appears to be experiencing intrapersonal stress as a result of a pending divorce and is often overly sensitive and angry. Superintendent A desires his colleague to deliver special reports to his division on a weekly basis, but Superintendent B claims that he cannot comply because of a work overload. One of these superintendents views all problems rationally-technically from a data systems point of view. The other is incensed and continually faults him for "not thinking humanistically about the needs of the kids." Moreover, pressures from the courts for forced busing have put an enormous burden on the superintendent in charge of planning and systems. He frequently

Source: *California Management Review*, XXI, 1976, pp. 76–83 by permission of the Regents of the University of California.

arrives at 7:00 A.M. and leaves the office at 6:00 P.M. He works on the weekends. While he believes in long-range planning, he sees himself in a "reactive" mode. He resents his colleague's accusations that he could beat the problem if he were better organized.

This is an article for conflict managers who want to try a variety of methods to manage serious disputes which, like the one above, may have multiple and complex causes. A contingency approach to conflict management is suggested to provide managers with a conceptual framework for knowing what to do when.

This article may appear different from the others in this section because it emphasizes the costs and feasibility issues of successful conflict management implementation. While the other authors emphasize either the desirability of a particular mode of dispute settlement or an optimal level of conflict, this contingency approach stresses the realistic constraints and complexities that are important for practical and workable conflict management methods.

THREE CONFLICT MANAGEMENT MODES

This article will focus on three major conflict management modes from which one can draw to formulate a situational theory. These are collaboration, bargaining, and power-play. Walton has already outlined the differences between collaboration and bargaining approaches.[1] Table 1 presents a modification of his ideas, with the addition of power-play, which serves to contrast the three conflict management

approaches. Tabular schemes such as that in Table 1 inevitably fail to account for overlaps. In reality, much of what is listed as collaboration also occurs in bargaining, and power-play also overlaps with bargaining. The table does serve to highlight basic differences, however.

None of these three conflict modes is appropriate for every contingency; neither is any one used without consequence. Following is a brief description of each mode with its possible cost, benefits, and requirements.

Collaboration. Collaborative theory maintains that people should surface their differences (get them out in the open) and then work on the problems until they have attained mutually satisfactory solutions. The approach assumes that people will be motivated to expend the time and energy for such problem-solving activity. It tries to maximize the possible mutual gains of the parties in the dispute and views the conflict as a creative force pushing them to achieve an improved state of affairs to which both sides are fully committed. Information is openly and willingly exchanged.[2] When the parties stagnate because they are too close to the situation to perceive viable alternatives or are too protective of their own positions, a third-party consultant may be used to help clarify the problem, sharpen the issues, find commonalties, and, in general, help them to discover a win-win position.[3]

Essentially, the collaborationists argue that theirs is the most preferred strategy for the good of the enterprise because: (1) open and honest interaction promotes authentic interpersonal relations; (2) conflict is used as a creative force for innovation and improvement; (3) this process enhances feedback and information flow; and (4) the solving of disputes has a way of improving the climate of the organization so that there is more openness, trust, risk taking, and feelings of integrity.[4]

In my consulting experience, however, I have found that collaboration is not always useful or feasible. Collaboration seems best employed when there is a combination of factors that assures the method some reasonable degree of success. Four major conditions help to determine the practicality of the collaborative mode.

First, a moderately high degree of *required interdependence* is important to force parties to expend the time and energy necessary to work out their differences. Openly confronting the issues is hard work and not likely to occur unless there is a long-term stake in developing and preserving the relationship.

 **LEARNING CHECKPOINT**

What are the three types of interdependence discussed in the chapter?

TABLE 1

Conflict Management Characteristics: Collaboration, Bargaining, Power-Play

Characteristic	Collaboration	Bargaining	Power-Play
Overall objective	1. Seeking win-win position	1. Seeking compromise or win-lose position	1. Seeking win-lose
Strategic objective	2. Emphasis on problem solving conflicts and using energy effectively	2. Emphasis on inducing and using conflicts for better bargaining positions	2. Emphasis on coping with and using conflicts to better one's power position
View of man	3. Man is open, honest, trusting, collaborative	3. Man is united in the face of a common threat	3. Man acts primarily in his own self-interest
Type of settlement	4. Psychological contracts	4. Legal contracts	4. Informal or unstated contracts
Individual's relationship to organization	5. Overall improvement orientation for the common good	5. Purposeful in pursuing goals of the group	5. Pure self-interest with a sense of limits
Efficiency/effectiveness	6. Effective but inefficient use of conflict energy	6. Periodically ineffective and inefficient use of energy	6. Efficient but ineffective use of energy
Information use	7. Information openly shared	7. Information strategically shared	7. Secrecy or distortion
Problem-solving mechanism	8. Joint problem solving	8. Trade-offs on positions to which there is apparent commitment	8. Unilateral, reciprocal manipulations to maximize self-interests
Power relationship	9. Power parity	9. Struggle for parity	9. Power inequalities accepted
Parties' support of organizational decisions	10. Voluntary (Internal commitment)	10. Voluntary support (Legal agreement)	10. Contractual support (Free to subvert)

Second, seeking collaborative solutions to conflicts involves more than simply acting together in various roles to accomplish a task and reach an objective. It also requires feeling free enough to interact openly, including conflicting, in the collaborative relationship. A kind of *power parity* must exist which allows the parties to feel free to interact candidly and use all of their resources to further their beliefs and concerns (regardless of their superior-subordinate status).

Third, there must be potential for *mutual benefits* as a result of solving the specific dispute. The person or group in conflict should "feel" a need that leads to a desire to work on the issue. This is related to the two requisites cited above. But in addition to a compelling reason and feeling enough parity to be able to collaborate, the parties themselves must perceive some significant motivation concerning the issue at hand. Their motivation often depends on whether the mutual gains are self-evident.

When there is required interdependence, power parity, and a felt need provoking the will to engage in the process, then the fourth factor comes into play. It is the extent to which there is *organizational support* for such behavior. Considerable organizational resources are needed to effectively manage conflict using the collaborative strategy. Such a program often requires a commitment of time, money, and energy. For example, the organization (including top executives) should engage in a collaborative mode systemwide, so that the norms, rewards, and punishments of the enterprise will encourage such behavior. Most people are unaccustomed to open disagreement, especially with someone of higher organizational rank, and need assurance that such behavior

will not draw reprisals.

To confront one another effectively and emerge having resolved a problem also requires numerous personal skills. Learning how to communicate effectively, how to synchronize the process, when and how to use a third party, how to engage in effective problem solving, and how to keep the tension level moderate for optimal results requires skills that can be taught but may not have already been learned. Indeed, many organizations would view such constructive openness as deviant. The enterprise should be sufficiently committed to fund training for building skills to manage conflicts via collaboration.

Thus, it has become apparent to me that the implementation of collaboration is often either infeasible (that is, the right conditions do not exist for it to work) or too costly to be justifiable. Accordingly, it becomes important to reexamine other alternative modes from the viewpoint of their benefits, costs, and feasibilities as they are related to the desired outcomes.

Power-Play. Collaborationists often view power-play as diametrically opposed to their own values and theory. Power-play, they say, will harm both the individual and the enterprise. They argue that it: (1) unleashes aggressive behaviors and hostile feelings between those involved in the power struggle, shutting off communication and interaction; (2) promotes vicious gossip, which in turn distorts the valid information needed to manage successfully; (3) drives needed information underground, where it is not used for feedback and learning from experience; (4) sometimes subverts the corporate mission through acts of sabotage and noncompliance; and (5) dis-

places goals because much of the energy employed in the power struggle is diverted from more productive purposes—in fact, winning the struggle can become a more important end than achieving an organizational goal.[5]

Much of the fear of power-play is connected with what Rapoport calls the "cataclysmic" view of conflict—that power struggles are necessarily unmanageable, irrational, and destructive. Although some escalated power struggles fit this description, Rapoport reminds us that the use of power strategies is often "strategic"—characterized by both rational self-interest and control.[6]

Four sets of considerations suggest that power-play is an appropriate method of conflict management in many situations. First, there is a view of individuals which says that *they act first and foremost in their own self-interest* and play an active power game to protect that interest. This view is increasing in popularity, reflected in the increased frequency of books on power in both the professional and popular literature.[7] Many people perceive that they can win more by competing than by collaborating. Or, they do not feel comfortable or skilled at problem solving, while they may feel particularly good, given their social experience, at power-play. Additionally, some individuals have primary outside-the-organization interests and do not want to be highly involved in or committed to their work; hence, it is not in their interest to get highly involved in collaborating.

 **LEARNING CHECKPOINT**

Is the type of labor versus management conflict described in the OBM Encounter in the chapter a power play? Explain.

Individuals typically play one or a combination of three different power games which strive for different types of power.

- **Authority** is the power that is delegated by the organization to the holder of a certain position. Formal authority results in the ability to use rewards, punishments, and other organizational resources in order to impact on persons and to affect behavior. Much has been written about positional power or authority.[8]
- **Informal influence** is normally defined as being able to affect behavior or gain compliance without holding a position of authority. Not everyone in authority has influence. Some persons have little or no authority but much influence. Some have influence far greater than that normally associated with their official role. It is possible to become influential in the enterprise without necessarily ascending the formal hierarchy.[9]
- **Autonomy.** Unlike the other power intents described above, autonomy power derives from the need to be in control of oneself and to minimize unwanted influence by others. It is manifested in one's ability to resist formal authority (control) and informal influence (normative demands) and to have ample "space" to accomplish prescribed ends using unrestricted means. Highly trained professionals, for example, seek autonomy, are little supervised, and are accountable for the quality of their end products (such as a surgical operation, a scholarly book, an architectural plan).[10]

Individuals who strive for autonomy power may be very interested in building and protecting a piece of organizational territory. They try to become indispensable so they will be the experts, have the infor-

mation, and hold unquestioned power. Autonomy-oriented persons may also have extraorganizational interests (such as a civic or religious organization) or parallel organizational interests (such as a professional association) and wish to remain "free" from organizational commitments or constraints in order to devote more time to those activities.

Power-play, it is hypothesized, will be the dominant conflict management strategy for those who seek autonomy. It has been pointed out elsewhere that it is unpolitical in organizations to appear uncooperative and "anti-system." One must appear to act in the best interest of the enterprise.[11] Those endeavors that are most self-interest-oriented, in which the interests of the worker and the organization are least congruent, require the most covert means. To be discovered as being aloof or free from the rules could cause a very negative, career-damaging impression. Autonomy is an unpopular intent in most organizations because marginality is discouraged and total commitment is rewarded. Power-play is a secretive mode that could work in the best interests of those whose covert objective is autonomy and whose desired impression is that of being committed. In contrast, collaboration requires the open sharing of personal intents and of preferred means for achieving them in the process of finding a mutually satisfactory solution.

A second set of arguments for power-play centers on the strategic reality that collaborating can increase one's vulnerability in competitive external environments. There are significant aspects of conflict of interest between firms which transact business directly or compete for resources, just as there are aspects of conflict of interest be-

tween managers within a firm over promotion and resources. Collaboration, and even bargaining, assumes the *exchange of information* necessary to resolve a problem. This information may apprise competitors of weaknesses and give them an unfair advantage. For example, disclosing strategic information (a key power-play resource) might provide another organization with data for increasing its efficiency, and therefore its competitive advantage.

Third, in some situations power-play strategies can contribute to the *joint welfare* of two adversary parties. Under conditions of routine and certainty, for example, the self-interests of the individual and the enterprise may be incompatible to a considerable degree. To maximize its objectives, the enterprise may tend to increase its efficiency through elaborate planning and control systems. The employees may likewise attempt to improve their working conditions through inclusive union contracts. In this way, power-play is the mechanism of flexibility used by both sides to cope within the confines of the rules (which are never so tightly delineated as to disallow some manipulation). Employees can use power-play to resist machine-like control; employers can use power-play to cope with union contracts during periods of uncertainty (such as rearranging work and calling for a common response to a crisis). Under this procedure, there exists a sort of dynamic equilibrium which works to the advantage of both within the rules. It is the dynamic interaction of finding compatible self-interests which is the substance of power-play conflict management. Such a mode allows multiple motives and various methods to eventually find a satisfactory equilibrium. Some activities are temporarily blocked as the power struggles are waged. Yet these are normally periods of realignment, reform and adjustment. In the long term, they may be effective ways to manage differences for the greatest number of persons and for the enterprise.

Fourth, power-play is often best suited to decide *ideological disputes*. When values or philosophies clash, the parties are usually intransigent in their conflicting positions. They refuse to problem solve or even negotiate. The only recourse is for one to try to win at the expense of the other, and although neither may emerge victorious, both may emerge saving some face and being ''right'' for having taken their stand.

• **Bargaining.** While neither party may emerge completely satisfied and one party may be clearly dissatisfied under this mode, both will at least come to terms openly about how to best resolve the most immediate issues. Bargaining can be a more or less elaborate mode of conflict management depending on the situation (from interpersonal trading to collective negotiation). The important point is that, like collaboration, a common solution to a problem can be found. The actual act of trading and compromise highlights the assumed strength and influence of each party. In this process, the power position of each side is clearly defined in direct ratio to the information it reveals to the other, the concessions it makes, the punishment or penalties it can impose.

Bargaining, while remaining unique, contains elements that overlap with both collaboration and power.[12] It resembles the collaborative process because it is a systematic method which, in some of its forms, allows for collaboration between negotiators. Bargaining

FIGURE 1

Relationship Among Strategies

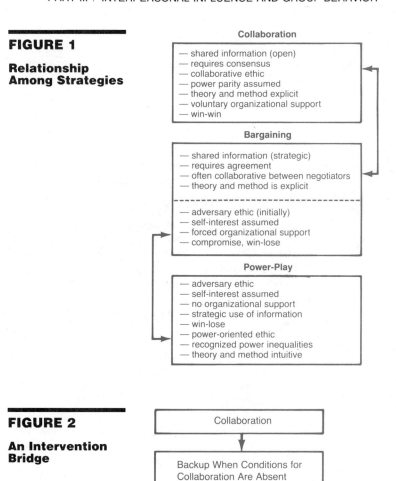

also contains many aspects of the strategic win-lose power struggles more typical in power-play. Figure 1 illustrates this point. Bargaining, therefore, can be viewed as a ''connecting bridge'' between the collaborative and power strategies of conflict management.

Bargaining employs some of the methods, values and motivational forces used in each of the other modes. Bargaining is therefore a middle-ground orientation in which

FIGURE 2

An Intervention Bridge

both power-players and collaborationists may feel somewhat comfortable. There is little hope that a power player and a collaborationist could deal effectively with one another while using their own incongruent approaches. Bargaining can serve to neutralize the values of conflict managers so that they do not impose one set of assumptions (such as collaboration) on a very different situation (such as power-play). In the Organization Development movement, for example, many instances of failure have been reported where collaborative values and methods of dispute settlement were superimposed on power settings.[13] It is proposed herein that bargaining would have better matched the intervention situation.

Bargaining might also be viewed as an intervention bridge to either elevate a stalemated power-play situation from a covert "lose-lose" condition to a situation in which both parties have at least made an explicit—albeit "hard" or power-based—agreement in their mutual interest. Or, using this bridge concept, it is a realistic alternative to fall back on when the conditions are not present for collaboration. Figure 2 illustrates this last point.

LEARNING CHECKPOINT

Would resolving conflict through what is called the use of superordinate goals fit with the notion of the bargaining conflict management mode?

Those who favor the collaborative approach would argue that bargaining is of limited value because (1) it often creates new interpersonal-organizational conflicts by virtue of the win-lose strategies employed; (2) the commitments to resolutions adopted are formal (based on having to prove that an agreement has been violated) rather than intrinsic and are, therefore, often carried out only according to the letter of the law; and (3) no more than one, perhaps neither, of the parties emerges fully satisfied.

On the other hand, bargaining seems to work well in many situations. In addition to its middleground value, it is, for example, a good way to establish *power parity*

so that more collaboration can follow. Just getting into a trading position assumes some equality, as each side recognizes that the other has something of value to offer or withhold.

Additionally, scarce resources can often be bargained according to the strategies of important interest groups, whereas they are not easily distributed using the collaborative method. Bargaining trade-offs, where some win and some lose according to a criterion of importance, seem optimally suited *to deal with conditions of scarcity*.

Some persons or groups also feel skillful at and comfortable with bargaining. It fits their *personal style*. Finally, bargaining is somewhat *economical* in that parties meet only periodically to review the old contract and to recontract.

CONCLUSIONS

It is assumed that a wide variety of organizational conflicts will occur quite naturally. Many of them will promote creative tensions which lead to system improvement. Some will serve the interests of various parties and groups without disrupting the organization itself. Others will be of such import that they must be effectively managed.

This article attempts to make the point that there is no one-best-way to manage organizational conflicts. The collaborative approach has been in vogue during the past few years but has proven inadequate on numerous occasions. This article has outlined three very different modes, one of which (power-play) is in sharp contrast with collaboration but optimal under some conditions.

In considering the use of these three modes, it is vital to separate our appreciation of organizational realities from the humanistic and sometimes utopian values that

have affected the field. Conflict modes must be tailored to the actual motives, issues, and organizational circumstances of the conflict parties. Inappropriate application of collaboration or other modes by a conflict manager, however well intentioned, is apt to be ineffective at best—and destructive to one or both parties or to the organization at worst.

The following conclusions have been drawn:

- **Collaboration** may be best employed when work relationships, which must be interdependent, would be substantially damaged by a given unresolved conflict, when the parties in conflict can openly confront their differences and state their preferences without fear of reprisal (there exists power parity in the relationship), when there is evident mutual interest in solving the dispute, and when the organization supports the open surfacing and working of disagreements.

- **Bargaining** seems to work best to establish power parity (usually between competing people or groups), as a means of distributing scarce resources, and as a somewhat efficient option of achieving a formal agreement to a common dispute. Bargaining may also be the most effective way to manage a dispute between two parties who each use one of the two other modes (collaboration, power-play) and are, therefore, unable to reach a common solution due to the disparity between them. Bargaining is often a midway or "bridge" strategy.

- **Power-play,** on the other hand, is an important way to cope with conflicts for the autonomous; advantages those who are most adept at this mode; is a means for achieving a dynamic balance of competing forces; and is often the only feasible way to resolve ideological disputes.

Of these three modes, there is perhaps the greatest need to know more about power-play. Very few empirical studies document the dynamics of power-play. One major problem has been to find an appropriate method for studying it. Since information is power and power is secretive, few will divulge their power game to researchers. Also, being "political" or "selfish" is usually a negative organizational image which requires covert rather than overt methods of power-play and an objective is to not be discovered and badly viewed. However, it is also very probable that the collaborative ethic in our field has discouraged research efforts on the uses of power-play in organizations, despite the fact that it appears to be the method most frequently used to resolve a number of kinds of differences. It is clear that more accurate descriptive theories of conflict management will require more extensive studies of the realities of power-play. ☐

REFERENCES

1. Richard E. Walton, "How to Choose Between Strategies of Conflict and Collaboration," in Warren Bennis, Kenneth Benne, and Robert Chin, eds., *Changing Organizations* (New York: Holt, Rinehart, Winston, 1969).
2. For a more detailed treatment of some of these assumptions, see C. Brooklyn Derr, "Uncovering and Working With Conflicts," in Schmuck et al., *Handbook of Organization Development in Schools* (National Press Books, 1972).
3. For a thorough treatment of third party functions in inducing collaboration, see Richard E. Walton, *Interpersonal Peacemaking: Confrontations and Third Party Consultation* (Reading, Mass.: Addison-Wesley, 1969).

4. Robert R. Blake and Jane S. Mouton, "The Fifth Achievement," *Journal of Applied Behavioral Science* (1970); Rensis Likert and Jane Gibson Likert, *New Ways of Managing Conflict* (New York: McGraw-Hill, 1976).
5. Likert and Likert, op. cit.; Alonzo McDonald, "Conflict at the Summit: A Deadly Game," *Harvard Business Review* (March-April 1972); Richard E. Walton and John M. Dutton, "The Management of Interdepartmental Conflict: A Model and Review," *Administrative Science Quarterly* (March 1969).
6. Anatol Rapoport, "Models of Conflict: Cataclysmic and Strategic," in Anthony de Reuch and Julie Knight, eds., *Conflict in Society* (Boston: Little, Brown, 1966), pp. 259–288.
7. See Robert J. Ringer, *Winning Through Intimidation* (New York: Fawcett Publications, 1974); Bloom, Coburn and Pearlman, *The New Assertive Woman* (New York: Dell, 1975); Michael Korda, *Power: How to Get It, How to Use It* (New York: Random House, 1977); and B. L. Harragan, *Games Mother Never Taught You: Corporate Gamesmanship for Women* (New York: Warner, 1977).
8. See Dalton, Barnes, and Zaleznick, *The Distribution of Authority in Formal Organizations* (Boston: Harvard Graduate School of Business, 1968); J. R. P. French, Jr., and B. Raven, "The Bases of Social Power," in D. Cartwright, *Studies in Social Power* (Ann Arbor, Mich.: Institute for Social Research, 1959); G. Gilman, "An Inquiry Into the Nature and Use of Authority," in M. Haire, *Organization Theory and Industrial Practice* (New York: Wiley, 1962).
9. Anthony Jay, *Management and Machiavelli* (New York: Holt, Rinehart and Winston, 1967); George L. Peabody, "Power, Alinsky and Other Thoughts," in H. Hornstein et al., *Social Intervention* (New York: Free Press, 1971).
10. Daniel C. Lortie, "The Balance of Control and Autonomy in Elementary School Teaching," in A. Etzioni, *The Semi-Professions and Their Organization* (New York: Free Press, 1969); William R. Scott, "Professionals in Hospi-

tals: Technology and the Organization of Work," in B. S. Georgopoulos, *Organization Research on Health Institutions* (Ann Arbor, Mich.: Institute for Social Research, 1972); and Louis R. Pondy, "Organizational Conflicts: Concepts and Models," *Administrative Science Quarterly* (September 1967).
11. Virginia E. Schein, "Individual Power and Political Behaviors in Organizations," *Academy of Management Review* (January 1977).
12. See Richard E. Walton and Robert B. McKersie, "Bargaining Dilemmas in Mixed-Motive Decision-Making," *Behavioral Science* (September 1966); and Roger Harrison, "Role Negotiation: A Tough-Minded Approach to Team Development," in W. W. Burke and H. A. Hornstein, *The Social Technology of Organizational Development* (Washington, D.C.: NTL Learning Resources, 1972).

D CONFLICT QUESTIONNAIRE*

Step 1: Questionnaire.

Complete the following questionnaire. Consider situations in which you find your wishes differing from those of another person. For each statement, think about how likely you are to respond in that way to such a situation. Check the rating that best corresponds to your response.

	Very Unlikely	Unlikely	Likely	Very Likely
1. I am usually firm in pursuing my goals.	___	___	___	___
2. I try to win my position.	___	___	___	___
3. I give up some points in exchange for others.	___	___	___	___
4. I feel that differences are not always worth worrying about.	___	___	___	___
5. I try to find a position that is intermediate between his and mine.	___	___	___	___
6. In approaching negotiations, I try to be considerate of the other person's wishes.	___	___	___	___
7. I try to show the logic and benefits of my positions.	___	___	___	___
8. I always lean toward a direct discussion of the problem.	___	___	___	___
9. I try to find a fair combination of gains and losses for both of us.	___	___	___	___
10. I attempt to immediately work through our differences.	___	___	___	___
11. I try to avoid creating unpleasantness for myself.	___	___	___	___
12. I might try to soothe the other's feelings and preserve our relationships.	___	___	___	___
13. I attempt to get all concerns and issues immediately out in the open.	___	___	___	___
14. I sometimes avoid taking positions that would create controversy.	___	___	___	___
15. I try not to hurt other's feelings.	___	___	___	___

---

* Source: Reprinted from J. W. Pfeiffer and J. E. Jones, ed., *A Handbook of Structured Experiences for Human Relations Training*, Vol. II (San Diego, California: University Associates, 1972). This exercise was developed by Arthur Shedlin and Warren H. Schmidt.

Step 2: Scoring.

Assign points to each response as follows:

   very unlikely = 1,
   unlikely = 2,
   likely = 3,
   very likely = 4.

For each mode listed, write the scores under the item number. Then add the scores on the three items for each dimension.

Competing:	Item 1	Item 2	Item 7	Total
	———	———	———	———
Collaborating:	Item 8	Item 10	Item 13	Total
	———	———	———	———
Compromising:	Item 3	Item 5	Item 9	Total
	———	———	———	———
Avoiding:	Item 4	Item 11	Item 14	Total
	———	———	———	———
Accommodating:	Item 6	Item 12	Item 15	Total
	———	———	———	———

Step 3: Discussion.

In small groups or with the class as a whole, answer the following questions.

1. What did your score pattern look like?
2. Do any patterns emerge among groups in the class?
3. Which modes have you found to be most commonly used? least commonly used?
4. Which modes have you found to be most effective? least effective?
5. In what situations has each mode been most effective?

D2 THE JOB CONFLICT QUESTIONNAIRE*

To help you develop an appreciation of the symptoms of job conflict, complete the questionnaire shown. Apply it to a place you presently work or have worked in the past. As with many other questionnaires or checklists that you complete for study or research purposes, candor is important. As before, we are not dealing with a scientifically validated instrument.

Directions: Check each of the following statements "mostly agree" or "mostly disagree" as it applies to your place of work.

	Mostly agree	Mostly disagree
1. A few of our departments do not talk to each other.	———	———
2. You frequently hear bad things said about other departments.	———	———
3. We seem to have more security guards than do most places.	———	———

---

* Source: Reprinted from Andrew J. DuBrin. *Contemporary Applied Management,* 2nd ed. (Plano, Texas: Business Publications, Inc., 1985), pp. 119–20.

4. You find a lot of graffiti about management in the restrooms.   ————   ————

5. People are fearful of making mistakes around here.   ————   ————

6. Writing nasty memos takes up a lot of our time.   ————   ————

7. A lot of people at our place of work complain about ulcers or other psychosomatic disorders.   ————   ————

8. We have considerable turnover in management.   ————   ————

9. We have considerable turnover among employees.   ————   ————

10. "Finger pointing" and blaming others happens frequently around here.   ————   ————

11. We have a lot of strong cliques.   ————   ————

12. You can almost feel the tension in some departments.   ————   ————

13. A widely used expression around here is "They are a bunch of fools."   ————   ————

14. We have had several incidents of vandalism and sabotage during the last year.   ————   ————

15. We have a lot of bickering over such matters as who should do what job.   ————   ————

16. Many people around here say, "That's not my job," when asked to do something out of the ordinary.   ————   ————

17. Some departments in the organization are practically hated.   ————   ————

18. Our organization seems more like a roller derby than a team.   ————   ————

19. People rarely help you out because they actually want you to look bad in the eyes of management.   ————   ————

20. We disagree more than we agree in our office (or factory).   ————   ————

Interpretation of Scores. Use this questionnaire primarily as a guide to sensitizing you to the presence of interpersonal and intergroup conflict in a job environment. However, as a measure of conflict, you might use this rough scoring system: if you agreed with 15 or more statements, it probably indicates that you work in a conflict-ridden environment. If you agreed with three or less items, it could mean that too little conflict exists; perhaps people in your company are in danger of becoming too complacent. Scores from 4 to 14, those outside of the extremes, probably indicate that your organization is a mixture of conflict and cooperation. Most work organizations fall into this category.

1 GROUPS AND CONFLICT RESOLUTION*

OBJECTIVE

To compare individual versus group problem solving and to examine conflict.

STARTING THE EXERCISE

1. Each individual has 15 minutes to read the story and answer the 11 questions about the story. Individuals may not refer to the story when answering the questions and may not confer with anyone else. Each person should circle T if the answer is clearly true; F if the answer is clearly false; or ? if it isn't clear from the story whether the answer is true or false.

2. Next, form small groups of four to five and make the same decisions using group consensus. No one should change his or her answers on the individual questions. The ground rules for group decisions are:

a. Group decisions should be made by consensus without reference to the story. It is illegal to vote, trade, average, flip a coin, and so forth.

b. No individual group member should give in only to reach agreement.

c. Every group member should be aware that disagreements may be resolved by facts. Conflict can lead to understanding and creativity if it does not make group members feel threatened or defensive.

3. After 20 minutes of group work, the instructor should announce the correct answers. Scoring is based on the number of correct answers out of a possible total of 11. Individuals are to score their own individual answers, and someone should score the group-decision answers. The exercise leader should then call for:

a. The group-decision score in each group

b. The average individual score in each group

c. The highest individual score in each group

4. Responses should be posted on the tally sheet. Note should be taken of those groups in which the group score was (1) higher than the average individual score and (2) higher than the best individual score. Groups should discuss the way in which individual members resolved disagreements and the effect of the ground rules on such behavior. They may consider the obstacles experienced in arriving at consensus and the possible reasons for the difference between individual and group decisions.

The Story

A businessman had just turned off the lights in the store when a man appeared and demanded money. The owner opened a cash register. The contents of the cash register were scooped up, and the man sped away. A member of the police force was notified promptly.

---

* Source: Alan Filley, *Interpersonal Conflict Resolution* (Glenview, IL: Scott, Foresman, 1975), pp. 139–142, as adopted from William H. Haney, *Communication and Organizational Behavior* (Homewood, IL: Richard D. Irwin, 1967), pp. 319–320.

Tally Sheet

Group Number	Group Score	Avg. Individual Score	Best Individual Score	Group Score Better Than Avg. Indiv?	Group Score Better Than Best Indiv?

Statements about the Story:

1. A man appeared after the owner had turned off his store lights.   T   F   ?

2. The robber was a man   T   F   ?

3. A man did not demand money.   T   F   ?

4. The man who opened the cash register was the owner.   T   F   ?

5. The store owner scooped up the contents of the cash register and ran away.   T   F   ?

6. Someone opened a cash register.   T   F   ?

7. After the man who demanded the money scooped up the contents of the cash register, he ran away.   T   F   ?

8. While the cash register contained money, the story does *not* state *how much*.   T   F   ?

9. The robber demanded money of the owner.   T   F   ?

10. The story concerns a series of events in which only three persons are referred to: the owner of the store, a man who demanded money, and a member of the police force.   T   F   ?

11. The following events in the story are true: Someone demanded money, a cash register was opened, its contents were scooped up, and a man dashed out of the store.   T   F   ?

2 WORLD BANK: AN EXERCISE IN INTERGROUP NEGOTIATION*

Step 1: The class is divided into two groups. The size of each of the groups should be no more than ten. Those not in one of the two groups are designated as observers. However, groups should not have less than six members each. The instructor will play the role of the referee/banker for the World Bank.

Step 2: Read the World Bank Instruction Sheet.

Step 3: Each group or team will have 15 minutes to organize itself and plan strategy before beginning. Before the first round each team must choose (a) two negotiators, (b) a representative, (c) a team recorder, (d) a treasurer.

Step 4: The referee/banker will signal the beginning of round one and each following round and also end the exercise in about one hour.

Step 5: Discussion. In small groups or with the entire class, answer the following questions.

1. What occurred during the exercise?
2. Was there conflict? What type?
3. What contributed to the relationships among groups?
4. Evaluate the power, leadership, motivation, and communication among groups.
5. How could the relationships have been more effective?

WORLD BANK GENERAL INSTRUCTION SHEET

This is an intergroup activity. You and your team are going to engage in a task in which money will be won or lost. *The objective is to win as much as you can.* There are two teams involved in this activity, and both teams receive identical instructions. After reading these instructions, your team has 15 minutes to organize itself and to plan its strategy.

Each team represents a country. Each country has financial dealings with the World Bank. Initially, each country contributed $100 million to the World Bank. Countries may have to pay further monies or may receive money from the World Bank in accordance with regulations and procedures described below under sections headed Finance and Payoffs.

Each team is given twenty cards. These are your *weapons*. Each card has a marked side *(X)* and an unmarked side. The marked side of the card signifies that the weapon is armed. Conversely, the blank side shows the weapon to be unarmed.

At the beginning, each team will place ten of its twenty weapons in their armed positions (marked side up) and the remaining ten in their unarmed positions (marked side down). These weapons will remain in your possession and out of sight of the other team at all times.

There will be *rounds* and *moves*. Each round consists of seven moves by each team. There will be two or more rounds in this simulation. The number of rounds depends on the time available. Payoffs are determined and recorded after each round.

1. A move consists of turning two, one, or none of the team's weapons from armed to unarmed status, or vice versa.
2. Each team has 2 minutes for each move. There are 30-second periods between moves. At the end of 2 minutes, the team must have turned two, one, or none of its weapons from armed to unarmed status, or from unarmed to armed status. If the team fails to move in the allotted time, no change can be made in weapon status until the next move.
3. The length of the 2½-minute periods between the beginning of one move and the beginning of the next is fixed and unalterable.

Each new round of the experiment begins with all weapons returned to their original positions, ten armed and ten unarmed.

Finances

The funds you have contributed to the World Bank are to be allocated in the following manner:
$60 million will be returned to each team to be used as your team's treasury during the course of the decision-making activities.
$40 million will be retained for the operation of the World Bank.

---

* Source: Adapted from John E. Jones and J. William Pfeiffer, eds. *The 1975 Annual Handbook for Group Facilitators.* (San Diego, California: University Associates, 1975).

Payoffs

1. *If there is an attack:*
   a. Each team may announce an attack on the other team by notifying the referee/banker during the 30 seconds following *any* 2-minute period used to decide upon the move (including the seventh, or final, decision period in any round). The choice of each team during the decision period just ended counts as a move. An attack may not be made during negotiations.
   b. If there is an attack (by one or both teams), two things happen: (1) the round ends, and (2) the World Bank levies a penalty of $5 million for each team.
   c. The team with the greater number of armed weapons wins $3 million for each armed weapon it has over and above the number of armed weapons of the other team. These funds are paid directly from the treasury of the losing team to the treasury of the winning team. The referee/bankers will manage this transfer of funds.
2. *If there is no attack:*
At the end of each round (seven moves), each team's treasury receives from the World Bank $2 million for each of its weapons that is at that point unarmed, and each team's treasury pays to the World Bank $2 million for each of its weapons remaining armed.

Negotiations

Between moves each team has the opportunity to communicate with the other team through its negotiators.

Either team may call for negotiations by notifying the referee/bankers during any of the 30-second periods between decisions. A team is free to accept or reject any invitation to negotiate.

Negotiators from both teams are *required* to meet after the third and sixth moves (after the 30-second period following that move, if there is no attack).

Negotiations can last no longer than 3 minutes. When the two negotiators return to their teams, the 2-minute decision period for the next move begins once again.

Negotiators are bound only by: *(a)* the 3-minute time limit for negotiations, and *(b)* their required appearance after the third and sixth moves. They are otherwise free to say whatever is necessary to benefit themselves or their teams. The teams similarly are not bound by agreements made by their negotiators, even when those agreements are made in good faith.

Special Roles

Each team has 15 minutes to organize itself to plan team strategy. During this period before the first round begins, each team must choose persons to fill the following roles. (Each team must have each of the following roles, which can be changed at any time by a decision of the team.)

- *Negotiators*—activities stated above.
- A *representative*—to communicate team decisions to the referee/bankers.
- A *recorder*—to record the moves of the team and to keep a running balance of the team's treasury.
- A *treasurer*—to execute all financial transactions with the referee/bankers.

1 INDUSTRIAL ENGINEERING AT CHEMTECH CORPORATION*

The Chemtech Corporation is a large, multiple-products chemical concern. The industrial engineering division is officially "staff" to the plant manager; the director of I.E. reports to an assistant plant manager. However, internally, I.E. is organized into areas and groups paralleling the plant manufacturing divisions and departments. An engineer in industrial engineering normally serves one or two department heads. The engineer's superior, an I.E. group leader, gives official staff support to an engineer's proposals to a production department supervisor while "working for" the superintendent of a manufacturing division.

Industrial engineering performs both measurement and methods studies. Measurement work is an elaboration of the work of the time-study person. The industrial engineer is primarily concerned with deriving figures that can be used to relate production (or other control figures) to labor use. This information may be the basis for individual and group incentive standards or for fixed-pay-labor control plans to provide data to management for evaluation purposes. The techniques have expanded from simple observation with a stop-watch to work-sampling procedures utilizing IBM card systems and various mathematical correlation techniques with electronic computers. A major part of the measurement work requires the engineer to be on the floor in the production area.

Methods work for the industrial engineering field covers a broad range from modern applications of Gilbreth's therbligs to sophisticated statistical and regression techniques utilizing modern computers. In most cases, methods study on hand motions is done before piece-rate incentive standards are set, but this type of work is of lesser interest. Layout and de-

EXHIBIT 1

Parallel Industrial Engineering and Manufacturing Organizations

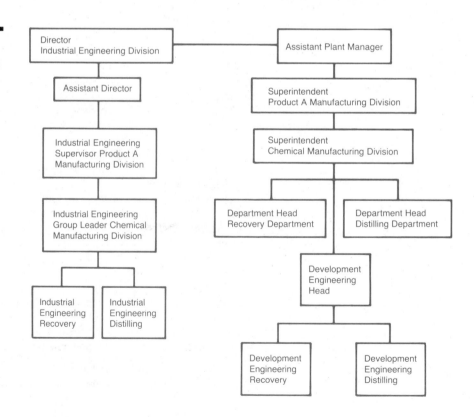

* Source: Ross A. Webber, *Management Pragmatics* (Homewood, Ill.: Richard D. Irwin, Inc., 1979), pp. 417–421.

sign have been traditional industrial engineering activities, and a substantial amount of this is done in the company. However, because of the growing field, the interest of the newer engineers is in applications of multiple-regression techniques, linear programming, and inventory control.

Industrial engineering performs both advisory and service work. The solution of recurring work-flow problems may be aided by skilled engineers who can analyze production methods. The use of piece-work systems requires that the production departments call on industrial engineering to develop incentive standards. Another service relationship involves the handling of new and revamped machine layouts and job descriptions when equipment and procedural changes are made.

The plant has a tradition of ensuring strong autonomy for the production organization at the superintendent level. In formal statements of company policy, industrial engineering is clearly subordinated to the superintendent. Industrial engineering is expected to be mainly a service or advisory staff agency, and the superintendent of the chemical manufacturing division is free to decide whether to utilize its services or not.

Service relationships are often neither comfortable nor easy to maintain. And many "advisers" do not wait to be asked. They initiate the contacts with those who are supposed to call on them. Before putting people to work on new activities and techniques, an industrial engineering manager finds it useful to have identified an existing production "problem" that needs solving. Thus, rather than waiting to be called on, industrial engineering spends substantial time in searching for problems on which it can obtain assignments.

In their work in the production department, engineers try to become intimately familiar with what appear to be difficulties. Although they may not be asked to work on these problems specifically, these problems help them to direct their thinking toward the underlying or less-apparent conditions. It is then up to the engineers to establish a case for their prospective studies, indicating their estimates of the scope of the problems and potential savings. Approval is required from both I.E. supervision and the chemical plant superintendent.

Although the ideas for assignments have originated with industrial engineers, sometimes they recognize that the nature of the jobs or the personalities of the department heads are such that chances for approval and success will be enhanced if the production people feel it was their idea. This leads to "planting" the idea with a department head. Often, both know whose

idea it is, but the fiction ensures cooperation. Actual authorization requires approval by the superintendent, and this little ruse makes it more likely that the department head will be a political ally in future discussions with the superintendent.

The industrial engineering division historically has served as a training area for the whole corporation. In academic achievement and general promise its engineers rank near the top of the firm. Employment in the industrial engineering division gives these people wide access to valuable experience and influential managers. Normal service in the department averages about three years after which the engineers generally move into a production department. The path of promotion is definitely up the line hierarchy. Few desire to stay in technical work, and many are enrolled in the local university's evening M.B.A. program.

WORK WITH CHEMICAL MANUFACTURING DIVISION SUPERINTENDENT

The superintendent of the chemical manufacturing division has a strong personality. He is in his late 40s and started in the division as a development engineer. His education as a chemical engineer and experience as a development engineer have strengthened his interest in the technical aspects of all proposals, and he exercises close supervision over innovative and capital-investment recommendations. Since most innovative ideas that are eventually adopted originate with the division's own development engineers, the superintendent encourages them to talk with him about ideas and demands it when he learns of problem areas.

In addition, the promotion ladder to chemical plant supervisory ranks is through the development engineer position. Accordingly, the superintendent is anxious to give these people as much experience as possible. He encourages (almost indoctrinates) them to work on their own without calling for advisory assistance.

To a significant extent, industrial engineering is management engineering and provides good experience for a future manager. The superintendent is aware of this and wants the development engineers to gain some of this training by performing their own work of this type.

For all these reasons, the chemical plant superintendent is opposed to any extension of industrial engineering activities beyond the relatively routine service work that they have to perform to maintain incentive plans. He discourages what he calls "idle speculation on my time and budget." His intimidation of department heads discourages them from going to him for approval of I.E. projects that they would like to see performed. The superintendent's well-maintained technical expertise subjects department heads to unpleasant grilling when they propose study programs to him.

WORK RELATIONSHIP WITH PRODUCTION DEPARTMENT SUPERVISORS

The supervisor and assistant supervisors all have come up from the ranks in the same department. Their functions consist most simply in getting people on the right jobs at the right time. The recovery department has many types of equipment and a large number of miscellaneous hand operations. All these activities are not performed simultaneously, and it is the responsibility of the supervisors to assign the workers as necessary in order to meet the schedule for each shift. The closeness and accessibility of development engineers and higher supervision relieve them of concern about technological aspects of the equipment.

There is no question that one of the most fertile sources of problem identification is the supervisors. In any discussion with them, they mention explicit problem conditions. However, the individual supervisor is not inclined to request I.E. assistance on methods problems because of a limited knowledge regarding their functions and lack of reciprocal interactions with industrial engineering. A major part of the supervisors' experience with I.E. has been as unwilling subjects of time studies for incentive pay plans (when they were still hourly paid operators).

With the exception of questions on incentive standards, supervisors seldom initiate interaction with an industrial engineer. On the other hand, virtually every completed assignment by an engineer results in some action by them. In many cases this means new forms and calculations for incentive performance of a crew. Most supervisors see little reason for having group incentive standards and intensely dislike making the necessary calculations. Except for a few initial questions, nothing in their operational job requirements makes it necessary to call in industrial engineering unless new standards are required. They try to avoid the engineer as much as possible.

Because of familiarity and physical proximity, supervisors naturally go to the development engineer or department head when they have problems or ideas. This is also related to the nature of their jobs and their production goals. For the most part, they are concerned with short-term operational matters that demand solutions relatively quickly. When it is necessary to have I.E. do service work (setting a temporary standard), this is an operational matter and they consult an engineer. However, they are not really aware of the I.E.'s availability for advisory problem solving, i.e., methods work, and even if they were, the formal procedure for requesting I.E. services of this nature discourages involvement for a short-term problem.

THE DIRECTOR'S CONCERN

Fundamentally the director of industrial engineering is dissatisfied with the relationship between engineers and production managers. In spite of an accounting procedure under which engineering service is "free" to line managers (they are not directly charged—industrial engineering is absorbed in plant overhead), production departments simply do not consult engineering on important matters as much as is thought desirable by the director and higher management. Since the company has a tradition of great autonomy for line managers, the director doubts that the plant manager would force such consultation on lower managers. Accordingly, the director is wondering how to improve industrial engineering performance so that managers would consider the engineers more helpful. □

CASE QUESTIONS

1. Analyze why the staff industrial engineers are not consulted by manufacturing management for methods work.
2. What are the possible alternative plans for improving the performance of the industrial engineering staff? What do you recommend?
3. What are the possible alternative plans for improving the relationship between industrial engineering and manufacturing management? What do you recommend?

THE NEW PRODUCT MEETING*

A product manager (PM) had arranged a meeting with representatives of manufacturing and accounting in order to present certain information and to ask them questions about a new product scheduled to go into a test market in several weeks. The meeting took place in a conference room located in the product department office area. The manufacturing and accounting personnel were already present when the PM came into the room carrying a note pad and a dummy model of the package to be used for the new product.

As he walked toward the head of the table, he tossed the package dummy onto the table and said, "Here's the box." As the package was passed around from person to person, the manufacturing and accounting managers asked about its specifications. The PM answered with precise facts and figures and told how these had been determined.

One of the manufacturing representatives asked about the brand's shelf location. The PM replied that shelf location had also been decided on, adding that an alternative location had been considered, but that: "If we go into that section of the store that is an area our competitors' salesmen visit every day, they will simply throw us into the back room."

The manufacturing man nodded. The group continued by discussing topics on the order in which the PM presented them: schedule, direct mail sample promotion, carton size, etc. In each of these areas the PM presented his plans and the reasons for them. There were no disagreements.

Things began going less smoothly, however, when the PM asked the manufacturing people about quality control. In asking the questions, the PM made reference to his superiors: "I've been asked what we are going to do to ensure the taste. This is crucial on this brand, and I've got to have something specific to say about it. How would you like to answer this?"

The manufacturing representatives replied that taste was important on all brands and that they would, of course, use the same procedures that were always used to ensure quality. A lengthy discussion followed, during which the PM asked the manufacturing representatives to write a special quality-control procedure for the new product, a step the manufacturing managers felt was unnecessary. With minor variations, the parties repeated the following statements.

PM: I'm expected to know exactly what you are going to do on this product.

Manufacturing: But we *know* how to do quality control. What's the matter, don't you trust us? We will use the same statistical techniques on this product that we do on other products having similar ingredients.

PM: I understand that this is your responsibility, but it's our concern as well. Would it be too much to ask you to send us a note saying that the quality will be what is supposed to be?

Manufacturing: You're going to have to accept that we do the job and have faith that we're going to do the same thing that we do on the other products.

PM: It's a bigger problem on this product.

Manufacturing: Well, I wish we had a little black box that we could put the product into and it would flash a light "good" or "bad." You've got to trust us.

Finally, the PM reluctantly replied: "OK, OK, so I trust you," and changed the subject by saying, "OK, what about costs?" Another lengthy discussion resulted when the PM discovered that the cost estimates for the product were now considerably higher than those the accountants had made a few months earlier. The PM expressed a feeling that perhaps the costs had been overstated, since they seemed to be based on start up, rather than full-scale production.

PM: Now, the way we're starting producing is not the real-world basis, is it? A lot can happen in six months—cartoning improvements, a lot of things. Can't we stay with the old numbers? See, I'm confronted with a situation where a pricing decision has already been made, so if contribution is less than we thought, I'm faced with having to raise

---

* Source: Case written by Dalmar Fisher, from Edgar F. Huse and James L. Bowditch, *Behavior in Organizations* (Reading, MA.: Addison-Wesley Publishing Company, 1977), pp. A40–A43.

price or reduce marketing expenditures, and I have to have an annual program on Friday on this. If people start seeing a lower contribution, I lose all we've fought for. We'll get drilled.

Accounting: If you stay with the old numbers, you'll defeat our whole structure. As we've said, right *here,* on these sheets, are the costs, and as you can see, there is a solid reason behind each of them. We are being as optimistic as we can. After all, how can you quote costs when you haven't even produced a unit of product yet?

PM: Well, that's just it. So you must be saying you're quoting the most conservative costs you can. What if we produced it at the other plant?

Accounting: Well, that would save you some money, but we can't go all the way back to the beginning on costs. You can see from these sheets how much is involved in putting these figures together.

The issue was not resolved. The PM concluded the meeting by saying that he would arrange another meeting with his superior and the controller present. The accounting managers agreed. As the participants were preparing to leave, the PM noticed his superior walking by the door. The PM went into the corridor and quickly briefed his boss on the cost problem:

PM: Look, these guys are coming in with an increase that affects the pricing structure and the marketing budget, so it's getting to be a top-management problem. They're still in there. How about coming in and letting them expose you to it?

Superior: (Frowning and taking two steps backward, away from the direction of the conference room.) What's the probability their numbers are correct?

PM: I'd say 50–50.

Superior: Now wait. Why don't you lay out the numbers on paper, and we will talk about them in the morning. Meanwhile, I'll talk to the controller and get his feel for the reliability of these numbers. See, the company has a history of coming down from these estimates. That makes them a hero. They've "saved" money.

PM: OK, I'll lay out the numbers and then see you again in the morning.

Superior: OK. See, you have to get tough with these guys. They want to make the estimates very conservative so they will look good later.

PM: Yeah.   □

CASE QUESTIONS

1. Why was agreement reached in the meeting about shelf location? Why did the cost problem remain unresolved? Was the quality-control issue resolved? How and why?
2. What did the product manager expect and want from the manufacturing and accounting representatives and from his superior? What did they expect and want from him? Why do you suppose these expectations were what they were?
3. What are the requirements for effective performance in the product manager's role? How effectively did the product manager in this case perform?

ORGANIZATIONAL POWER AND POLITICS

Power is a pervasive part of the fabric of organizational life. Managers and nonmanagers use it. They manipulate power to accomplish goals and, in many cases, to strengthen their own positions.[1] A person's success or failure in using or reacting to power is determined largely by understanding power, knowing how and when to use it, and being able to anticipate its probable effects. The purpose of this chapter is to examine power and its uses in organizations. We will look at the sources (bases) of power, how power is used, and the relationship between power and organizational politics.

POWER AND AUTHORITY

The study of power and its effects is important to understanding how organizations operate. It is possible to interpret every interaction and every social relationship in an organization as involving an exercise of power.[2] How organizational subunits and individuals are controlled is related to the issue of power. **Power** is simply defined as the ability to get things done the way one wants them to be done. The power of a manager who wants an increased amount of financial resources is his or her ability to get the desired resources. The power of a salesperson who wants his sales territory expanded is his ability to get the larger territory.

Power involves a relationship between two or more people. Robert Dahl, a political scientist, captures this important relational focus when he defines power as "A has power over B to the extent that he can get B to do something B would not otherwise do."[3] A person or group cannot have power in isolation; power has to be exercised or have the potential for being exercised in relation to some other person or group.

In organizations the use of power frequently involves the application of authority. **Authority** is the *formal* power that a person has because of the position that he or she holds in the organization. Orders from a manager in an authority position are followed because they must be followed. That is, persons in higher positions have legal authority over subordinates in lower

---

[1] Edwin Cornelius III and Frank Love, "The Power Motive and Managerial Success in a Professionally Oriented Service Industry Organization," *Journal of Applied Psychology*, February 1984, pp. 32–39.

[2] Henry Mintzberg, "Power and Organizational Life Cycles," *Academy of Management Review*, October 1984, pp. 207–24.

[3] Robert Dahl, "The Concept of Power," *Behavioral Science*, July 1957, pp. 202–03.

positions. Not following orders subjects the offender to disciplinary action just as not following society's legal directives subjects one to disciplinary action in the form of arrest and penalty. Organizational authority has the following characteristics: it is grounded in the person's *position,* rather than in the person; it is accepted by subordinates; and it is used vertically—that is, it flows from the top of the hierarchy down.

Influence is a word that one often comes across when studying power. We agree with Mintzberg and others that making a distinction between influence and power adds little to understanding.[4] Therefore, we use the terms *influence* and *power* interchangeably throughout this chapter.

POWER BASES

Salancik and Pfeffer, in their article accompanying this chapter, argue that power facilitates the organization's adaptation to its environment. The subunits (individuals, departments) able to assist in that adaptation are the ones which will hold power. Power can be derived from many sources. How power is obtained in an organization depends to a large extent on the type of power being sought. Power can be derived from interpersonal, structural, and situational bases.

INTERPERSONAL POWER

French and Raven suggested five interpersonal bases of power: legitimate, reward, coercive, expert, and referent.[5]

Legitimate Power. This signifies a person's ability to influence because of position. A person at a higher level has **legitimate power** over people below. In theory, organizational equals (e.g., all first-line supervisors) have equal, legitimate power. However, each person with legitimate power uses it with a personal flair. The terms *legitimate power* and *authority* frequently are used interchangeably.

Reward Power. This type of power is based on a person's ability to reward a follower for compliance. **Reward power** is used to back up the use of legitimate power. If followers value the rewards or potential rewards that the person can provide (recognition, a good job assignment, a pay raise, additional resources to complete a job), they may respond to orders, requests, and directions.

Coercive Power. The opposite of reward power is **coercive power,** the power to punish. Followers may comply because of fear. A manager may block a promotion or harass a subordinate for poor performance. These practices and the fear that they will be used are coercive power.

---

[4] Henry Mintzberg, *Power in and around Organizations* (Englewood Cliffs, N.J.: Prentice-Hall, 1983), p. 5.

[5] John R. P. French and Bertram Raven, "The Basis of Social Power," in *Studies in Social Power,* ed. D. Cartwright (Ann Arbor: Institute for Social Research, University of Michigan, 1959), pp. 150–67.

Expert Power. A person has **expert power** when he or she possesses special expertise that is highly valued. Experts have power even when their rank is low. An individual may possess expertise on technical, administrative, or personal matters. The more difficult it is to replace the expert, the greater is the degree of expert power that he or she possesses. Occasionally, individuals' expertise does not bestow upon them as much ability to influence as they think it does. This is vividly illustrated in the following OBM Encounter. Expert power is a personal characteristic, while legitimate, reward, and coercive power are largely prescribed by the organization.

ENCOUNTER

A CASE OF MISJUDGING POWER

What is perhaps the greatest single example in modern times of miscalculating power occurred on August 3, 1981. On that date, 11,500 members of the Professional Air Traffic Controllers Organization (PATCO) walked off the job. Conflicts between PATCO and the Federal Aviation Administration reached their peak during that summer. Despite the fact that the controllers were legally prohibited from striking, the vast majority of PATCO members took a walk. President Reagan announced that after a 48-hour "grace period," all remaining striking controllers would be fired. The same assessment of their degree of "expert power" which

had led them to strike apparently led all but a handful to remain out in the face of the President's discharge threat. Indications were that PATCO felt its members, because of their knowledge and skill and the essential role they played in aviation, held the balance of power.

It was clearly a miscalculation. The President carried out his intentions and more than 11,000 individuals lost their jobs. PATCO lost the right to represent the controllers and simply ceased to exist. In a case of legitimate power vs. expert power, the expert power side not only lost, but was totally destroyed. □

Source: Adapted from David Bowers, "What Would Make 11,500 People Quit Their Jobs?" *Organizational Dynamics,* Winter 1983, pp. 5–19.

Referent Power. Many individuals identify with and are influenced by a person because of the latter's personality or behavioral style. The charisma of the person is the basis of **referent power.** A person with charisma is admired because of his or her characteristics. The strength of a person's charisma is an indication of his or her referent power. Charisma is a term that is often used to describe politicians, entertainers, or sports figures. However, some managers are regarded as extremely charismatic by their subordinates.

The five bases of interpersonal power can be divided into two major categories: organizational and personal. Legitimate, reward, and coercive power are primarily prescribed by the organization, the position, formal groups, or specific interaction patterns. A person's legitimate power can be changed by transferring the person, rewriting the job description, or reducing the power by restructuring the organization. On the other hand, expert and referent power are very personal. They are the result of an individual's personal expertise or style, and, as such, are grounded in the person and not the organization. A contemporary example of referent power can be seen in the following OBM Encounter.

OBM ENCOUNTER

THE REFERENT POWER OF PETER V. UEBERROTH

He hasn't cured cancer, ended world poverty and hunger, or negotiated a successful nuclear disarmament treaty. But you would never know it based on the assessment by many of Peter V. Ueberroth as a miracle worker.

Peter Ueberroth is, of course, the current commissioner of baseball and the man credited for turning the 1984 Los Angeles Olympic Games from a charity event into a blue-chip investment. As baseball commissioner, he wrestled an unpopular players' strike into submission in just two days, ended an umpires' strike with seemingly little difficulty, and took a strong stand against drug abuse by professional baseball players. He has become a hero of almost mythical proportions and is viewed by some as potential presidential timber. Nearly 250,000 copies of his autobiography were ordered before the book was even released.

While not denying his considerable skills and talents, it is also true that a good deal of Ueberroth's effectiveness comes from the force of his personality—in other words, referent power. The same baseball owners who hired him also can fire him if Mr. Ueberroth takes positions they do not like. The fact is, however, he enjoys much visibility and fan support because of his popular personality and behavioral style. He has a great deal more leverage with the owners than his predecessor, Bowie Kuhn, ever had. If ever a commissioner of baseball had the power to buck the owners, it is Peter Ueberroth.

Source: Based, in part, on Hal Lancaster, "Squeeze Play," *The Wall Street Journal*, October 15, 1985, pp. I, II.

The five types of interpersonal power are not independent. On the contrary, a person can use these power bases effectively in various combinations. Also, the use of a particular power base can effect the others. Some research has suggested, for example, that when subordinates believe a manager's coercive power is increasing, they also perceive a drop in reward, referent, and legitimate power held by the manager.[6] Other research suggests that legitimate and reward power are positively related, while coercive power is inversely related to legitimate and reward power.[7]

[6] Charles N. Greene and Philip M. Podsakoff, "Effects of Withdrawal of a Performance-Contingent Reward on Supervisory Influence and Power," *Academy of Management Journal*, September 1981, pp. 527–42.

[7] Kurt Student, "Supervisory Influence and Work Group Performance," *Journal of Applied Psychology*, June 1968, pp. 188–94.

STRUCTURAL AND SITUATIONAL POWER

Pfeffer has proposed that power is primarily prescribed by structure within the organization.[8] He regards the structure of an organization as the control mechanism by which the organization is governed. In the organization's structural arrangements, decision-making discretion is allocated to various positions. Also, the structure establishes the patterns of communication and the flow of information. Thus, organizational structure creates formal power and authority (1) by specifying certain individuals to perform specific job tasks and make certain decisions; and (2) by encouraging informal power through its effect on information and communication structures within the system.[9]

We already have discussed how formal position is associated with power and authority. Certain rights, responsibilities, and privileges accrue from a person's position.[10] Other forms of structural power exist because of resources, decision making, and information.[11]

RESOURCES

Kanter argues quite convincingly that power stems from (1) access to resources, information, and support; and (2) the ability to get cooperation in doing necessary work.[12] Power occurs when a person has open channels to resources—money, human resources, technology, materials, customers, and so on. In organizations, vital resources are allocated downward along the lines of the hierarchy. The top-level manager has more power to allocate resources than do other managers further down in the managerial hierarchy. The lower level manager receives resources that are granted by top-level managers. In order to assure compliance with goals, top-level managers (e.g., presidents, vice presidents, directors) allocate resources on the basis of performance and compliance. Thus, a top-level manager usually has power over a lower-level manager because the lower level manager must receive resources from above to accomplish goals.

DECISION-MAKING POWER

The degree to which individuals or subunits (e.g., a department or a special project group) can affect decision making determines the amount of power acquired. A person or subunit with power can influence how the decision-

[8] Jeffrey Pfeffer, *Power in Organizations* (Marshfield, Mass.: Pitman Publishing, 1981), p. 117. See Pfeffer's excellent discussion in chap. 4 (pp. 99–135), on where power originates in organizational settings.

[9] Jeffrey Pfeffer, "The Micropolitics of Organizations," in *Environments and Organizations*, ed. M. W. Meyer et al. (San Francisco: Jossey-Bass, 1978), pp. 29–50.

[10] W. Graham Astley and Paramjit Sachdeva, "Structural Sources of Intraorganizational Power: A Theoretical Synthesis," *Academy of Management Review*, January 1984, pp. 104–13.

[11] The discussion of these forms of structural power is based on Pfeffer, *Power in Organizations*, pp. 104–22; and Rosabeth M. Kanter, "Power Failures in Management Circuits," *Harvard Business Review*, July-August 1979, pp. 65–75.

[12] Kanter, "Power Failures."

TABLE 9–1

Symptoms and Sources of Powerlessness

Position	Symptoms	Sources
First-line supervisors (e.g., foreman, line supervisor)	Supervise too closely Fail to train subordinates Not sufficiently oriented to the management team Inclined to do the job themselves	Routine, rule-minded jobs Limited lines of communication Limited advancement opportunities for themselves and their subordinates
Staff professionals (e.g., corporate lawyer, personnel/human resources specialist)	Create islands and set themselves up as experts Use professional standards as basis for judging work that distinguishes them from others Resist change and become conservative risk-takers	Their routine tasks are only adjuncts to real line job Blocked career advancement Replaced by outside consultants for non-routine work
Top-level managers (e.g., chief executive officer, vice president)	Short-term time horizon Top-down communication systems emphasized Reward followers to think like the manager, do not welcome bearers of bad news	Uncontrollable lines of supply Limited or blocked lines of information about lower managerial levels Diminished lines of support because of challenges to legitimacy

Source: Reprinted by permission of the Harvard Business Review. Adapted from "Power Failures in Management Circuits," by Rosabeth Moss Kanter (July–August 1979), p. 73. Copyright © 1979 by the President and Fellows of Harvard College; all rights reserved.

making process occurs, what alternatives are considered, and when a decision is made.[13] For example, when Richard Daley was mayor of Chicago, he was recognized as a power broker. He not only influenced the decision-making process, but he also had the power to decide which decision would be given priority in the city council and when decisions would be made.[14] He was a powerful politician because he was considered to be an expert at controlling each step in important decisions.

INFORMATION POWER

Having access to relevant and important information is power. Accountants generally do not have a particularly strong or apparent interpersonal power base in an organization. Rather, accountants have power because they control important information. Information is the basis for making effective decisions. Thus, those who possess information needed to make optimal decisions

---

[13] For an organizationally oriented, concise, and excellent discussion of structural and situationally oriented sources of power, see Don Hellriegel, John W. Slocum, Jr., and Richard W. Woodman, *Organizational Behavior* (St. Paul, Minn.: West Publishing, 1986), pp. 465–68.

[14] Mike Royko, *Boss: Richard J. Daley of Chicago* (New York: E. P. Dutton, 1971).

have power. The accountant's position in the organization structure may not accurately portray the amount of power that he or she wields. A true picture of a person's power is provided not only by the person's position, but also by the person's access to relevant information.

A number of organizational situations can serve as the source of either power or powerlessness (not acquiring power). The powerful manager exists because he or she allocates required resources, makes crucial decisions, and has access to important information.[15] He or she is likely to make things happen. The powerless manager, however, lacks the resources, information, and decision-making prerogatives needed to be productive. Table 9–1 presents some of the common symptoms and sources of powerlessness of first-line supervisors, staff professionals, and top-level managers.

UPWARD FLOW OF POWER

Most people think of power as being exerted in a downward direction. It is true that individuals in positions at the lower end of the power hierarchy generally have less power than do individuals in higher level positions. However, power also can be exercised up the organization.[16] In sociological terms, a person exerting power upward has personal power but no authority.

The discussion of legitimate authority suggests that individuals in higher level positions (supervisors) can exert only as much power as individuals in lower level positions (subordinates) accept. The concept of subordinate power can be linked to expertise, location, and information. Significant upward power or influence sometimes can be exerted by a relatively low-ranking secretary, computer programmer, or clerk who possesses expertise, is in a position to interact with important individuals, or has access to, and control of, important information.[17] Research has shown that expertise, location, and information control are important determinants of the power potential of employees at lower levels of the hierarchy.[18]

Two important sources of upward influence have been referred to as manipulative persuasion and manipulation.[19] **Manipulative persuasion** is a person's direct attempt to disguise the true persuasion objective. This is the hidden agenda ploy. **Manipulation** refers to the form of influence in

[15] Anthony T. Cobb, "An Episodic Model of Power: Toward an Integration of Theory and Research," *Academy of Management Review*, July 1984, pp. 482–93.

[16] Gary Yukl and Tom Taber, "The Effective Use of Managerial Power," *Personnel*, March-April 1983, pp. 37–44.

[17] L. W. Porter, R. W. Allen and H. L. Angee, "The Politics of Upward Influence in Organizations," in *Research in Organizational Behavior*, eds. L. L. Cummings and B. M. Staw (Greenwich, Conn.: JAI Press, 1981), pp. 181–216.

[18] David Mechanic, "Sources of Power in Lower Participants in Organizations," *Administrative Science Quarterly*, September 1962, pp. 349–64; and Donald C. Pelz, "Influence: A Key to Effective Leadership in the First-Line Supervisor," *Personnel*, November 1952, pp. 209–17.

[19] For an excellent discussion of upward influence, see Richard S. Blackburn, "Lower Participant Power: Toward a Conceptual Integration," *Academy of Management Review*, January 1981, pp. 127–31; and Richard T. Mowday, "The Exercise of Upward Influence in Organizations," *Administrative Science Quarterly*, March 1978, pp. 137–56.

which both the objective and the attempt are concealed. For example, instead of providing customer complaints to a manager as they are received, the clerk receiving the complaints may arrange them as he or she desires. This can be done in such a way as to place other employees or a department in a more or less favorable light. If, in this situation, the clerk has arranged the incoming complaints so that the manager in charge would reprimand a departmental supervisor whom the clerk doesn't like, the clerk's action would be considered manipulation in the upward direction.

INTERDEPARTMENTAL POWER

The primary focus to this point has been on individual power and how it is obtained. However, it is also important to consider subunit or interdepartmental power. Subunit power is the focus of the strategic contingency theory developed by Hickson. A **strategic contingency** is an event that is extremely important for accomplishing organizational goals.[20] Crozier, a French sociologist, provided insight into the idea of strategic contingencies. He studied the relationships between workers in the production and maintenance departments of French tobacco processing plants. Crozier found that the production workers enjoyed job security because of tenure, were protected against unfair disciplinary action, and were not replaced or transferred arbitrarily. The production workers were less skilled than the maintenance workers. The maintenance workers were highly skilled and were recruited and selected only after going through a rigorous screening process.

The production workers were dependent on the maintenance workers. This power differential was explained in terms of the control exercised by the maintenance workers over an important contingency. If machines were shut down, the entire plant came to a halt. Efficiently functioning machines were needed to accomplish output goals. Since the maintenance workers, at the request of the production workers, repaired machines that were down, they possessed significant power.

When machines were down, the job performance of the production workers suffered. Stoppages totally disrupted the workflow and the output of the production workers. Crozier proposed that the maintenance workers controlled a strategically contingent factor in the production process. Crozier's study provided clear evidence of subunit power differences. The study also stimulated other studies that eventually resulted in a strategic contingencies explanation of power differences.[21]

Using the work of Crozier and Hickson and his associates, it is possible

---

[20] Michel Crozier, *The Bureaucratic Phenomenon* (Chicago: University of Chicago Press, 1964).

[21] It should be noted that the strategic contingency theory was developed by D. J. Hickson and his colleagues. Other theorists and researchers have modified and discussed this approach. However, the reader is urged to use the original sources for a discussion of the complete and unmodified theory. See D. J. Hickson, C. R. Hinnings, C. A. Lee, R. E. Schneck, and J. M. Pennings, "A Strategic Contingency Theory of Intraorganizational Power," *Administrative Science Quarterly,* June 1971, pp. 216–29; and C. R. Hinnings, D. J. Hickson, J. M. Pennings, and R. E. Schneck, "Structural Conditions of Intraorganizational Power," *Administrative Science Quarterly,* March 1974, pp. 22–44.

FIGURE 9–1

**A Strategic
Contingency
Model
Of Subunit Power**

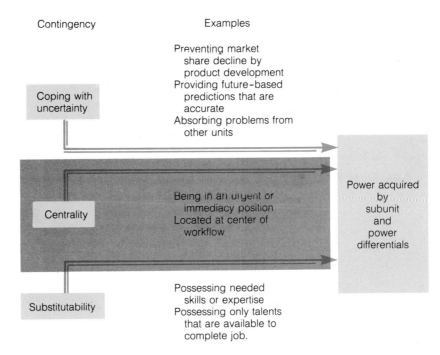

This figure is based on the detailed research work conducted by D. J. Hickson, C. R. Hinnings, C. A. Lee, R. E. Schneck, and J. M. Pennings, "A Strategic Contingency Theory of Intraorganizational Power," *Administrative Science Quarterly*, June 1971, pp. 216–29; and C. R. Hinnings, D. J. Hickson, J. M. Pennings, and R. E. Schneck, "Structural Conditions of Intraorganizational Power," *Administrative Science Quarterly*, March 1974, pp. 22–44.

to develop a concise explanation of strategic contingencies. The model presented in Figure 9–1 suggests that subunit power, the power differential between subunits, is influenced by (1) the degree of ability to cope with uncertainty; (2) the centrality of the subunit; and (3) the substitutability of the subunit.

**COPING WITH
UNCERTAINTY**

Unanticipated events can create problems for any organization or subunit. It is, therefore, the subunits most capable of coping with uncertainty that typically acquire power. There are three types of coping activities. First, there is *coping by prevention*. Here, a subunit works at reducing the probability that some difficulty will arise. One example of a coping technique is designing a new product to prevent lost sales because of new competition in the marketplace.

Second, there is *coping by information*. The use of forecasting is an example. Possessing timely forecasting information enables a subunit to deal with such events as competition, strikes, shortages of materials, and consumer demand shifts. Planning departments conducting forecasting studies acquire power when their predictions prove accurate.

Third, there is coping by *absorption*. This coping approach involves dealing with uncertainty as it impacts the subunit. For example, one subunit might take a problem employee from another subunit and attempt to retrain and redirect that employee. This is done as a favor, so that the other subunit will not have to go through the pain of terminating or continuing to put up with the employee. The subunit that takes in the problem employee gains the respect of other subunits, which results in an increase in power.

The relation of coping with uncertainty to power was expressed by Hickson as follows: "The more a subunit copes with uncertainty, the greater its power within the organization."[22]

CENTRALITY

The subunits that are most central to the flow of work in an organization typically acquire power.[23] There is no subunit that has zero centrality, since all subunits are somehow interlinked with other subunits. A measure of centrality is the degree to which the work of the subunit contributes to the final output of the organization.[24] Since a subunit is in a position to affect other subunits, it has some degree of centrality and therefore power.

Also, a subunit possesses power if its activities have a more immediate or urgent impact than that of other subunits. For example, Ben Taub is a major public hospital in Houston. The emergency and trauma treatment subunit is extremely important and crucial. It contains significant power within the hospital. Failures in this subunit could result in the death of emergency victims. On the other hand, the psychiatric subunit does important work, but not of the crucial and immediate type. Therefore, it has significantly less subunit power than the emergency and trauma treatment subunit.

SUBSTITUTABILITY

Substitutability refers to the ability of other subunits to perform the activities of a particular subunit. If an organization has or can obtain alternative sources of skill, information, and resources to perform the job done by a subunit, the subunit's power will be diminished. Training subunits lose power if training work can be done by line managers or outside consultants. On the other hand, if a subunit has unique skills and competencies (e.g., the maintenance workers in Crozier's study discussed above) that would be hard to duplicate or replace, this would tend to increase the subunit's power over other subunits.

Hickson et al. capture the importance of substitutability power when they propose that the lower the substitutability of the activities of a subunit, the greater is its power within the organization.[25]

---

[22] Hickson et al., "Strategic Contingency Theory."

[23] L. C. Freeman, D. Roeder, and R. R. Mulholland, "Centrality in Social Networks: II. Experimental Results," *Social Networks*, June 1980, pp. 119–42.

[24] Richard L. Daft, *Organization Theory and Design* (St. Paul, Minn.: West Publishing, 1983), pp. 392–98. This source contains an excellent discussion of the strategic contingency perspective in terms of managerial and organizational theory. Daft's discussion is a concise and informative presentation of the original Hickson et al. theory and research.

[25] Ibid., p. 40.

THE ILLUSION OF POWER

Admittedly, some individuals and subunits have vast amounts of power to get others to do things the way they want them done. However, there are also illusions of power. Imagine that one afternoon your supervisor asks you to step into his office. He starts the meeting: "You know we're really losing money using that Beal stamping machine. I'd like you to do a job for the company. I want you to destroy the machine and make it look like an accident." Would you comply with this request? After all, this is your supervisor, and he is in charge of everything—your pay, your promotion opportunities, your job assignments. You might ask, Does my supervisor have this much power over me?

Where a person or subunit's power starts and stops is difficult to pinpoint. You might assume that the supervisor in the hypothetical example has the specific power to get someone to do this unethical and illegal "dirty work." However, even individuals who seemingly possess only a little power can influence others. A series of studies conducted by Milgram focused on the illusion of power. In these studies, subjects who had been voluntarily recruited thought they were administering electrical shocks of varying intensity to other subjects.[26] Ostensibly, the experiment was designed to study the effects of punishment on learning. In reality the studies focused on obedience to authority.

At the experimenter's direction, 26 of 40 subjects, or 65 percent, continued to increase the intensity of the shocks they thought they were administering to another person all the way to the maximum voltage. This was in spite of the fact that the control panel indicated increasing voltage dosages as "intense," "extreme," "danger," and "severe shock." Additionally, screams could be heard coming from the booth and the subject allegedly receiving the shock begged the experimenter to stop the project. In spite of this, and even though the subjects were uncomfortable administering the shocks, they continued. Milgram stated:

> I observed a mature and initially poised businessman enter the laboratory, smiling and confident; within 20 minutes he was reduced to a twitching, stuttering wreck, who was rapidly approaching a point of nervous collapse . . . yet he continued to respond to every word of the experimenter and obeyed to the end.[27]

Why did the subjects obey the experimenter? Although the experimenter possessed no specific power over the subjects, he appeared to be a powerful person. He created an illusion of power. The experimenter dressed in a white lab coat, was addressed by others as "doctor," and was very stern. The subjects perceived the experimenter as possessing legitimacy to conduct

---

[26] S. Milgram, "Behavioral Study of Obedience," *Journal of Abnormal and Social Psychology*, October 1963, pp. 371–78; and S. Milgram, *Obedience to Authority* (New York: Harper & Row, 1974).

[27] Milgram, "Behavioral Study of Obedience," p. 377.

the study. The experimenter apparently did an excellent job of projecting the illusion of having power.

The Milgram experiments indicate that possessing power in a legitimate way is not the only way that power can be exerted. Individuals who are perceived to have power may also be able to significantly influence others. Power is often exerted by individuals who have only minimum or no actual power. The "eye of the beholder" plays an important role in the exercise of power.[28]

POLITICAL STRATEGIES AND TACTICS

Individuals and subunits continually engage in **politically oriented behavior.**[29] By politically oriented behavior we mean a number of things:

1. *Behavior* that usually is outside the legitimate, recognized power system.
2. Behavior that is designed to benefit an individual or subunit, *often* at the expense of the organization in general.[30]
3. Behavior that is intentional and is designed to acquire and maintain power.

As a result of politically oriented behaviors, the formal power that exists in an organization often is sidetracked or blocked. In the language of organizational theory, political behavior results in the displacement of power.[31]

RESEARCH ON POLITICS

A number of studies have been conducted to explore political behavior and perceptions in organizations.[32] A study of 142 purchasing agents examined their political behavior. The job objective of the purchasing agents was to negotiate and fill orders in a timely manner. However, the purchasing agents also viewed their jobs as being a crucial link with the environment— competition, price changes, market shifts.[33] Thus, the purchasing agents considered themselves information processors. This vital link of the purchasing agents with the external environment placed them in conflict with the engineer-

---

[28] S. H. Ng, *The Social Psychology of Power* (New York: Academic Press, 1980), p. 119.

[29] Manual Velasquez, Dennis J. Moberg, and Gerald F. Cavanagh, "Organizational Statesmanship and Dirty Politics: Ethical Guidelines for the Organizational Politician," *Organizational Dynamics,* Autumn 1983, p. 5.

[30] Mintzberg, *Power in and Around Organizations,* p. 172.

[31] Ibid.

[32] Dan L. Madison, Robert W. Allen, Lyman W. Porter, Patricia A. Renwick, and Bronston T. Mayes, "Organizational Politics: An Exploration of Managers' Perceptions," *Human Relations,* February 1980, pp. 79–100; Jeffrey Gantz and Victor V. Murray, "The Experience of Workplace Politics," *Academy of Management Journal,* June 1980, pp. 237–51; and Robert W. Allen, Dan L. Madison, Lyman W. Porter, Patricia A. Renwick, and Bronston T. Mayes, "Organizational Politics: Tactics and Characteristics of Its Actors," *California Management Review,* 1979, pp. 77–83.

[33] George Strauss, "Tactics of the Lateral Relationship: The Purchasing Agent," *Administrative Science Quarterly,* 1962, pp. 161–86.

TABLE 9–2

Managerial
Perceptions of
Organizational
Political Behavior

Tactic	Combined Groups	Chief Executive Officers	Staff Managers	Supervisors
Attacking or blaming others	54.0%	60.0%	50.0%	51.7%
Use of information	54.0	56.7	57.1	48.3
Image building/impression management	52.9	43.3	46.4	69.0
Developing base of support	36.8	46.7	39.3	24.1
Praising others, ingratiation	25.3	16.7	25.0	34.5
Power coalitions, strong allies	25.3	26.7	17.9	31.0
Associating with the influential	24.1	16.7	35.7	20.7
Creating obligations/reciprocity	12.6	3.3	14.3	30.7

Source: R. W. Allen, D. L. Madison, L. W. Porter, P. A. Renwick, and B. T. Mayes, "Organizational Politics: Tactics and Characteristics of Its Actors." Copyright 1979 by the Regents of the University of California. Reprinted from *California Management Review*, December 1979, p. 79 by permission of the Regents.

ing department. As a result of the conflict, attempts to influence the engineering subunit were a regular occurrence.

A variety of political tactics used by the purchasing agents were discovered in this study. They included:

1. **Rule evasion.** Evading the formal purchase procedures in the organization.
2. **Personal-political.** Using friendships to facilitate or inhibit the processing of an order.
3. **Educational.** Attempting to persuade engineering to think in purchasing terms.
4. **Organizational.** Attempting to change the formal or informal interaction patterns between engineering and purchasing.

These political tactics were used by the purchasing agents to accomplish their goals. The tactics (1) were outside the legitimate power system, (2) occasionally benefited the purchasing agent at the expense of the rest of the organization, and (3) were intentionally developed so that more power was acquired by the purchasing agent.

Another study of political behavior was conducted in the electronics industry in southern California. A total of 87 managers (30 chief executive officers, 28 higher level staff managers, and 29 supervisors) were interviewed and asked about political behavior.[34] Table 9–2 presents a summary of the eight categories of political tactics (behavior) that were mentioned most frequently by each of the three managerial groups.

The managers also were asked to describe the personal characteristics of the individuals who used political behavior effectively. Thirteen personal characteristics were identified as important. These characteristics are presented in Table 9–3.

---

[34] Allen et al., "Organizational Politics."

TABLE 9–3

Personal Characteristics of Effective Politicians

Personal Characteristics	Combined Groups	Chief Executive Officers	Staff Managers	Supervisors
Articulate	29.9%	36.7%	39.3%	12.8%
Sensitive	29.9	50.0	21.4	17.2
Socially adept	19.5	10.0	32.1	17.2
Competent	17.2	10.0	21.4	20.7
Popular	17.2	16.7	10.7	24.1
Extroverted	16.1	16.7	14.3	17.2
Self-confident	16.1	10.0	21.4	17.2
Aggressive	16.1	10.0	14.3	24.1
Ambitious	16.1	20.0	25.0	3.4
Devious	16.1	13.3	14.3	20.7
"Organization person"	12.6	20.0	3.6	13.8
Highly intelligent	11.5	20.0	10.7	3.4
Logical	10.3	3.3	21.4	6.9

Source: R. W. Allen, D. L. Madison, L. W. Porter, P. A. Renwick, and B. T. Mayes, "Organizational Politics: Tactics and Characteristics of Its Actors," Copyright 1979 by the Regents of the University of California. Reprinted from *California Management Review*, December 1979, p. 78, by permission of the Regents.

The managers in this study were aware of political behavior because it was a part of their organizational experiences. As the researchers noted, the research was not designed to praise or disparage political behavior.[35] Instead, it was intended to show that politics is a fact of organizational existence.

PLAYING POLITICS

If anything, the available (yet scanty) research indicates that politics exists in organizations and that some individuals are very adept at political behavior. Mintzberg and others describe these adept politicians as playing games.[36] The games that managers and nonmanagers engage in are intended to (1) resist authority (e.g., the insurgency game), (2) counter the resistance to authority (e.g., the counterinsurgency game), (3) build power bases (e.g., the sponsorship game and the coalition-building game), (4) defeat rivals (e.g., the line-versus-staff game), and (5) effect organizational change (e.g., the whistle-blowing game). In all, Mintzberg describes and discusses 13 types of political games. Four of these are briefly presented.

The Insurgency Game. This game is played to resist authority. For example, suppose that a plant foreman is instructed to reprimand a particular worker for violating company policies. The reprimand can be delivered according to the foreman's feelings and opinions about its worth and legitimacy. If the reprimand is delivered in a halfhearted manner, it probably will have no noticeable effect. On the other hand if it is delivered aggressively, it may be effective. Insurgency in the form of not delivering the reprimand as

---

[35] Ibid.

[36] This discussion of games relies on the presentation in Mintzberg, *Power in and Around Organizations*, chap. 13, pp. 171–271. Please refer to the source for a complete and interesting discussion of political games.

expected by a higher level authority would be difficult to detect and correct. Insurgency as a game to resist authority is practiced in organizations at all levels.

The Sponsorship Game.   This is a rather straightforward game in that a person attaches himself or herself to someone with power. The sponsor typically is the person's boss or someone else with higher power and status than those of the person. Typically, individuals attach themselves to someone who is on the move. There are a few rules involved in playing this game. First, the person must be able to show commitment and loyalty to the sponsor. Second, the person must follow each sponsor-initiated request or order. Third, the person must stay in the background and give the sponsor credit for everything. Finally, the person must be thankful and display gratitude to the sponsor. The sponsor is not only a teacher and trainer for the person, but also a power base. Some of the sponsor's power tends to rub off on the person because of his or her association with the sponsor.

The Line versus Staff Game.   The game of line manager versus staff adviser has existed for years in organizations. In essence, it is a game that pits line authority to make operating decisions against the expertise possessed by staff advisers. There are also value differences and a clash of personality. Line managers typically are more experienced, more oriented to the bottom line and more intuitive in reaching decisions. On the other hand, staff advisers tend to be younger, better educated, and more analytical decision makers.[37] These differences result in viewing the organizational world from slightly different perspectives.

Withholding information, having access to powerful authority figures, creating favorable impressions, and identifying with organizational goals are tactics used by line and staff personnel. The line versus staff clash must be controlled in organizations before it reaches the point at which organizational goals are not being achieved because of the disruption.

The Whistle-Blowing Game.   Whistle-blowing behavior is receiving increasing attention.[38] This game is played to bring about organizational change. If a person in an organization identifies a behavior that violates his or her sense of fairness, morals, ethics, or law, then he or she may blow the whistle. **Whistle-blowing** means that the person informs someone— a newspaper reporter, a government representative, a competitor—about an assumed injustice, irresponsible action, or violation of the law. The whistle-blower is attempting to correct the behavior or practice. By whistle-blowing, the person is bypassing the authority system within the organization. This is viewed in a negative light by managers who possess position power. Often,

---

[37] S. S. Hammond III, "The roles of the Manager and Management Scientist in Successful Implementation," *Sloan Management Review,* Winter 1974, pp. 1–24.

[38] J. P. Near and Marcia Miceli, "Organizational Dissonance: The Case for Whistle-Blowing," *Journal of Business Ethics,* 1985, pp. 1–16.

whistle-blowing is done secretly so that retribution by the authority system is avoided.

Whistle-blowers come from all levels in the organization.[39] For example, an Eastern Airlines pilot complained to management first and then to the public about defects in his plane's automatic pilot mechanisms. His complaints were attacked by management as being groundless. In another example, a biologist reported to the Environmental Protection Agency that his consulting firm had submitted false data to the agency on behalf of an electric utility company; he was fired. In still another publicized case, an engineer at Ford complained about the faulty design of the Pinto. Unfortunately, this whistle-blower was demoted. Many of the legal costs and settlements from Pinto crash victims might have been avoided if the whistle-blower's message had been taken more seriously.[40]

These four examples of political game playing are not offered as always being good or bad for the organization. They are games that occur in organizations with various degrees of frequency. They occur within and between subunits, and they are played by individuals representing themselves or a subunit. Certainly, political behaviors carried to an extreme can hurt individuals and subunits. However, it is unrealistic to assume that all political behavior can or should be eliminated through management intervention. Even in the most efficient, profitable, and socially responsible organizations and subunits, political behaviors and games are being acted out. As the following OBM Encounter illustrates, political behavior can even extend to the boardroom.

ENCOUNTER
POLITICS AT THE TOP

Generally, we tend to think that there is a positive relationship in organizations between performance and reward. When an individual is unusually effective in his or her job, we certainly do not assume they will be punished for it. Such is not always true, however. Consider the case of W. R. Goodwin, ex-president of Johns-Manville. When Goodwin was hired by the board of directors, Johns-Manville was a dying company, beset by innumerable difficulties. As president, Goodwin immediately began to take steps to turn the company around. He reorganized the corporation, eliminated "deadwood," and brought in young, aggressive managers, and emphasized long-range planning and return on investment.

Within five years Goodwin's actions yielded significant results: sales nearly doubled, while profits rose by 115 percent. As he flew to a board of directors meeting to proudly report that the first half of the current year had set a company earnings record, he was summarily fired.

Why? In essence, according to Herbert Mey-

---

[39] Janelle Dozier and Marcia Miceli, "Potential Predictors of Whistle-Blowing: A Prosocial Behavior Perspective," *Academy of Management Review,* October 1985, pp. 823–36.

[40] Alice L. Priest, "When Employees Think Their Company is Wrong," *Business Week,* November 24, 1980, p. 2; and Andy Pasztor, "Speaking Up Gets Biologist into Big Fight," *The Wall Street Journal,* November 26, 1980, p. 29.

ers, because Goodwin thought that his impressive performance record gave him much more power than the staid board of directors was willing to yield. For example, Goodwin had proposed that the board be expanded from 12 to 15 members, and eventually to 20. We can only guess how the original 12 felt about having their power diluted, but we do know that the board decided that, in spite of Goodwin's enviable track record, it was time for new leadership. ☐

Source: Adapted from Herber Meyers, "Shootout at the Johns-Manville Corral," *Fortune,* October 1976, pp. 146–154.

We have tried in this chapter to highlight the more important aspects of power. We have examined power sources, how power is used, and the relationship between power and politics. One other important aspect of power is the role it may play in affecting—and being affected by—the life cycle of the organization. As organizations survive and develop, there are important changes in the distribution of power around and inside them. Mintzberg discusses this aspect of power in his article "Power and Organization Life Cycles," which accompanies this chapter.

SUMMARY OF KEYPOINTS

A. Power is defined as the ability to get things done in the way that one wants them to be done.

B. Authority is a much narrower concept than power. Authority is a form of power that is made legitimate because it is accepted by subordinates or followers.

C. French and Raven introduced the notion of five interpersonal power bases—legitimate (position-based), reward, coercive (punishment-based), expert, and referent (charismatic). These five bases can be divided into two major categories: organizational and personal. Legitimate, reward, and coercive power are primarily prescribed by an organization, while expert and coercive power are based on personal qualities.

D. Structural and situational power bases also exist. An organization's structural arrangement establishes patterns of communication and information flow that play an important role in power formation and use.

E. Power and influence can flow upward, from the bottom to the top, in an organization. Lower level employees can have significant power because of expertise, location, and access and control of information. Some lower level employees acquire power through persuasion and manipulation skills.

F. Subunits within organizations acquire and use power. The strategic contingency approach addresses subunit power. A strategic contingency is an event or activity that is extremely important for accomplishing organizational goals. The strategic contingency factors that have been disclosed by research include coping with uncertainty, centrality, and substitutability.

G. Coping with uncertainty is extremely important for acquiring, retaining, and using power.

H. Individuals sometimes can exercise power because of illusion. The Milgram "obedience to authority" experiments involving faked electric shocks illustrated how the illusion of power can bring about compliance.

I. Politics is present in all organizations. Politics comprises those activities that are used to acquire, develop, and use power and other resources to obtain one's preferred outcome when there is uncertainty or disagreement about choices.

J. Mintzberg introduced the notion of political game playing. Examples of political games are the insurgency game, the sponsorship game, and the coalition-building game.

REVIEW AND DISCUSSION QUESTIONS

1. How important is the use of power in affecting daily organizational activities?

2. How might organizational members increase their own power? How might they decrease the power of others?

3. Can a manager afford to give up power to subordinates? Could turning power over to subordinates actually increase a manager's power? Explain.

4. From which interpersonal power bases do you derive power in the various groups to which you belong (work, family, social, etc.)? Do you possess any structural or situational power?

5. How might power flow upward in organizations? Have you ever been able to exercise power upwards? Discuss the situation.

6. How does coping with uncertainty increase power? Give examples of the three major types of coping activity.

7. How the illusion of power can be just as effective as actual power was clearly illustrated in the "obedience to authority" experiments of Milgram. Can you think of other examples where people have responded to the illusion of power?

8. Four of Mintzberg's political games are described in the chapter. Have you witnessed their playing in organizations of which you are a member? What other games have you seen played?

9. Sometimes "playing politics" is the most effective way of achieving objectives. Why is this the case? Should organizations be concerned about it? Why or why not?

10. "The less a manager has to rely on legitimate power as a base for influencing subordinate behavior, the more effective the manager is." Do you believe this statement is true? Explain.

R1 WHO GETS POWER—AND HOW THEY HOLD ON TO IT: A STRATEGIC CONTINGENCY MODEL OF POWER*

GERALD R. SALANCIK
JEFFREY PFEFFER

Power is held by many people to be a dirty word or, as Warren Bennis has said, "It is the organization's last dirty secret."

This article will argue that traditional "political" power, far from being a dirty business, is, in its most naked form, one of the few mechanisms available for aligning an organization with its own reality. However, institutionalized forms of

* Source: Reprinted from *Organizational Dynamics*, Winter 1977. Copyrighted by AMACON, a division of the American Management Association. All rights reserved.

power—what we prefer to call the cleaner forms of power: authority, legitimization, centralized control, regulations, and the more modern "management information systems"—tend to buffer the organization from reality and obscure the demands of its environment. Most great states and institutions declined, not because they played politics, but because they failed to accommodate to the political realities they faced. Political processes, rather than being mechanisms for unfair and unjust allocations and appointments, tend toward the realistic resolution of conflicts among interests. And power, while it eludes definition, is easy enough to recognize by its consequences—the ability of those who possess power to bring about the outcomes they desire.

The model of power we advance is an elaboration of what has been called strategic-contingency theory, a view that sees power as something that accrues to organizational subunits (individuals, departments) that cope with critical organizational problems. Power is used by subunits, indeed, used by all who have it, to enhance their own survival through control of scarce critical resources, through the placement of allies in key positions, and through the definition of organizational problems and policies. Because of the processes by which power develops and is used, organizations become both more aligned and more misaligned with their environments. This contradiction is the most interesting aspect of organizational power, and one that makes administration one of the most precarious of occupations.

WHAT IS ORGANIZATIONAL POWER?

You can walk into most organizations and ask without fear of being misunderstood, "Which are the powerful groups or people in this organization?" Although many organizational informants may be *unwilling* to tell you, it is unlikely they will be *unable* to tell you. Most people do not require explicit definitions to know what power is.

Power is simply the ability to get things done the way one wants them to be done. For a manager who wants an increased budget to launch a project that he thinks is important, his power is measured by his ability to get that budget. For an executive vice-president who wants to be chairman, his power is evidenced by his advancement toward his goal.

People in organizations not only know what you are talking about when you ask who is influential but they are likely to agree with one another to an amazing extent. Recently, we had a chance to observe this in a regional office of an insurance company. The office had 21 department managers; we asked ten of these managers to rank all 21 according to the influence each one had in the organization. Despite the fact that ranking 21 things is a difficult task, the managers sat down and began arranging the names of their colleagues and themselves in a column. Only one person bothered to ask, "What do you mean by influence?" When told "power," he responded, "Oh," and went on. We compared the rankings of all ten managers and found virtually no disagree-

ment among them in the managers ranked among the top five or the bottom five. Differences in the rankings came from department heads claiming more influence for themselves than their colleagues attributed to them.

Such agreement on those who have influence, and those who do not, was not unique to this insurance company. So far we have studied over 20 very different organizations—universities, research firms, factories, banks, retailers, to name a few. In each one we found individuals able to rate themselves and their peers on a scale of influence or power. We have done this both for specific decisions and for general impact on organizational policies. Their agreement was unusually high, which suggests that distributions of influence exist well enough in everyone's mind to be referred to with ease—and we assume with accuracy.

LEARNING CHECKPOINT

Identify and discuss the interpersonal bases of power discussed in the chapter.

WHERE DOES ORGANIZATIONAL POWER COME FROM?

Earlier we stated that power helps organizations become aligned with their realities. This hopeful prospect follows from what we have dubbed the strategic-contingencies theory of organizational power. Briefly, those subunits most able to cope with the organization's critical problems and uncertainties acquire power. In its simplest form, the strategic-contingencies theory implies that when an organization faces a number of lawsuits that threaten its existence, the legal department will gain power and influence over

organizational decisions. Somehow other organizational interest groups will recognize its critical importance and confer upon it a status and power never before enjoyed. This influence may extend beyond handling legal matters and into decisions about product design, advertising production, and so on. Such extensions undoubtedly would be accompanied by appropriate, or acceptable, verbal justifications. In time, the head of the legal department may become the head of the corporation, just as in times past the vice-president for marketing had become the president when market shares were a worrisome problem and, before him, the chief engineer, who had made the production line run as smooth as silk.

Stated in this way, the strategic-contingencies theory of power paints an appealing picture of power. To the extent that power is determined by the critical uncertainties and problems facing the organization and, in turn, influences decisions in the organization, the organization is aligned with the realities it faces. In short, power facilitates the organization's adaptation to its environment—or its problems.

We can cite many illustrations of how influence derives from a subunit's ability to deal with critical contingencies. Michel Crozier described a French cigarette factory in which the maintenance engineers had a considerable say in the plantwide operation. After some probing he discovered that the group possessed the solution to one of the major problems faced by the company, that of troubleshooting the elaborate, expensive, and irrascible automated machines that kept breaking down and dumbfounding everyone else. It was the one problem that the plant manager could in no way control.

The production workers, while

troublesome from time to time, created no insurmountable problems; the manager could reasonably predict their absenteeism or replace them when necessary. Production scheduling was something he could deal with since, by watching inventories and sales, the demand for cigarettes was known long in advance. Changes in demand could be accommodated by slowing down or speeding up the line. Supplies of tobacco and paper were also easily dealt with through stockpiles and advance orders.

The one thing that management could neither control nor accommodate to, however, was the seemingly happenstance breakdowns. And the foremen couldn't instruct the workers what to do when emergencies developed since the maintenance department kept its records of problems and solutions locked up in a cabinet or in its members' heads. The breakdowns were, in truth, a critical source of uncertainty for the organization, and the maintenance engineers were the only ones who could cope with the problem.

The engineers' strategic role in coping with breakdowns afforded them a considerable say on plant decisions. Schedules and production quotas were set in consultation with them. And the plant manager, while formally their boss, accepted their decisions about personnel in their operation. His submission was to his credit, for without their cooperation he would have had an even more difficult time in running the plant.

LEARNING CHECKPOINT

Power can be derived from many sources. What are the major sources of power in an organization as identified in the chapter?

Ignoring Critical Consequences

In this cigarette factory, sharing influence with the maintenance workers reflected the plant manager's awareness of the critical contingencies. However, when organizational members are not aware of the critical contingencies they face, and do not share influence accordingly, the failure to do so can create havoc. In one case, an insurance company's regional office was having problems with the performance of one of its departments, the coding department. From the outside, the department looked like a disaster area. The clerks who worked in it were somewhat dissatisfied; their supervisor paid little attention to them, and they resented the hard work. Several other departments were critical of this manager, claiming that she was inconsistent in meeting deadlines. The person most critical was the claims manager. He resented having to wait for work that was handled by her department, claiming that it held up his claims adjusters. Having heard the rumors about dissatisfaction among her subordinates, he attributed the situation to poor supervision. He was second in command in the office and therefore took up the issue with her immediate boss, the head of administrative services. They consulted with the personnel manager and the three of them concluded that the manager needed leadership training to improve her relations with her subordinates. The coding manager objected, saying it was a waste of time, but agreed to give more priority to the claims department's work. Within a week after the training, the results showed that her workers were happier but that the performance of her department had decreased, save for the people serving the claims department.

About this time, we began, quite independently, a study of influence in this organization. We asked the administrative services director to draw up flow charts of how the work of one department moved on to the next department. In the course of the interview, we noticed that the coding department began or interceded in the work flow of most of the other departments and casually mentioned to him, "The coding manager must be very influential." He said "No, not really. Why would you think so?" Before we could reply he recounted the story of her leadership training and the fact that things were worse. We then told him that it seemed obvious that the coding department would be influential from the fact that all the other departments depended on it. It was also clear why productivity had fallen. The coding manager took the training seriously and began spending more time raising her workers' spirits than she did worrying about the problems of all the departments that depended on her. Giving priority to the claims area only exaggerated the problem, for their work was getting done at the expense of the work of the other departments. Eventually the company hired a few more clerks to relieve the pressure in the coding department and performance returned to a more satisfactory level.

Originally we got involved with this insurance company to examine how the influence of each manager evolved from his or her department's handling of critical organizational contingencies. We reasoned that one of the most important contingencies faced by all profit-making organizations was that of generating income. Thus we expected managers would be influential to the extent to which they contributed to this function. Such was the case. The underwriting managers, who wrote the policies that committed the premiums, were the most influential; the claims managers, who kept a lid on the funds flowing out, were a close second. Least influential were the managers of functions unrelated to revenue, such as mailroom and payroll managers. And contrary to what the administrative services manager believed, the third most powerful department head (out of 21) was the woman in charge of the coding function, which consisted of rating, recording, and keeping track of the codes of all policy applications and contracts. Her peers attributed more influence to her than could have been inferred from her place on the organization chart. And it was not surprising, since they all depended on her department. The coding department's records, their accuracy and the speed with which they could be retrieved, affected virtually every other operating department in the insurance office. The underwriters depended on them in getting the contracts straight; the typing department depended on them in preparing the formal contract document; the claims department depended on them in adjusting claims; and accounting depended on them for billing. Unfortunately, the "bosses" were not aware of these dependences, for unlike the cigarette factory, there were no massive breakdowns that made them obvious, while the coding manager, who was a hard-working but quiet person, did little to announce her importance.

The cases of this plant and office illustrate nicely a basic point about the source of power in organizations. The basis for power in an organization derives from the ability of a person or subunit to take or not take actions that are desired by others. The coding manager was seen as influential by those who

depended on her department, but not by the people at the top. The engineers were influential because of their role in keeping the plant operating. The two cases differ in these respects: The coding supervisor's source of power was not as widely recognized as that of the maintenance engineers, and she did not use her source of power to influence decisions; the maintenance engineers did. Whether power is used to influence anything is a separate issue. We should not confuse this issue with the fact that power derives from a social situation in which one person has a capacity to do something and another person does not, but wants it done.

POWER SHARING IN ORGANIZATIONS

Power is shared in organizations; and it is shared out of necessity more than out of concern for principles of organizational development or participatory democracy. Power is shared because no one person controls all the desired activities in the organization. While the factory owner may hire people to operate his noisy machines, once hired they have some control over the use of the machinery. And thus they have power over him in the same way he has power over them. Who has more power over whom is a mooter point than that of recognizing the inherent nature of organizing as a sharing of power.

Let's expand on the concept that power derives from the activities desired in an organization. A major way of managing influence in organizations is through the designation of activities. In a bank we studied, we saw this principle in action. This bank was planning to install a computer system for routine credit evaluation. The bank, rather progressive-minded, was concerned that the change would have adverse effects on employees

and therefore surveyed their attitudes.

The principal opposition to the new system came, interestingly, not from the employees who performed the routine credit checks, some of whom would be relocated because of the change, but from the manager of the credit department. His reason was quite simple. The manager's primary function was to give official approval to the applications, catch any employee mistakes before giving approval, and arbitrate any difficulties the clerks had in deciding what to do. As a consequence of his role, others in the organization, including his superiors, subordinates, and colleagues, attributed considerable importance to him. He, in turn, for example, could point to the low proportion of credit approvals, compared with other financial institutions, that resulted in bad debts. Now, to his mind, a wretched machine threatened to transfer his role to a computer programmer, a man who knew nothing of finance and who, in addition, had ten years less seniority. The credit manager eventually quit for a position at a smaller firm with lower pay, but one in which he would have more influence than his redefined job would have left him with.

Because power derives from activities rather than individuals, an individual's or subgroup's power is never absolute and derives ultimately from the context of the situation. The amount of power an individual has at any one time depends, not only on the activities he or she controls, but also on the existence of other persons or means by which the activities can be achieved and on those who determine what ends are desired and, hence, on what activities are desired and critical for the organization. One's own power always depends on other people for these two reasons. Other people, or groups or organizations, can determine the definition of what is a critical contingency for the organization and can also undercut the uniqueness of the individual's personal contribution to the critical contingencies of the organization.

Perhaps one can best appreciate how situationally dependent power is by examining how it is distributed. In most societies, power organizes around scarce and critical resources. Rarely does power organize around abundant resources. In the United States, a person doesn't become powerful because he or she can drive a car. There are simply too many others who can drive with equal facility. In certain villages in Mexico, on the other hand, a person with a car is accredited with enormous social status and plays a key role in the community. In addition to scarcity, power is also limited by the need for one's capacities in a social system. While a racer's ability to drive a car around a 90· turn at 80 mph may be sparsely distributed in a society, it is not likely to lend the driver much power in the society. The ability simply does not play a central role in the activities of the society.

The fact that power revolves around scarce and critical activities, of course, makes the control and organization of those activities a major battleground in struggles for power. Even relatively abundant or trivial resources can become the bases for power if one can organize and control their allocation and the definition of what is critical. Many occupational and professional groups attempt to do just this in modern economies. Lawyers organize themselves into associations, regulate the entrance requirements for novitiates, and then get laws passed specifying situations that re-

quire the services of an attorney. Workers had little power in the conduct of industrial affairs until they organized themselves into closed and controlled systems. In recent years, women and blacks have tried to define themselves as important and critical to the social system, using law to reify their status.

In organizations there are obviously opportunities for defining certain activities as more critical than others. Indeed, the growth of managerial thinking to include defining organizational objectives and goals has done much to foster these opportunities. One sure way to liquidate the power of groups in the organization is to define the need for their services out of existence. David Halberstam presents a description of how just such a thing happened to the group of correspondents that evolved around Edward R. Murrow, the brilliant journalist, interviewer, and war correspondent of CBS News. A close friend of CBS chairman and controlling stockholder William S. Paley, Murrow, and the news department he directed, were endowed with freedom to do what they felt was right. He used it to create some of the best documentaries and commentaries ever seen on television. Unfortunately, television became too large, too powerful, and too suspect in the eyes of the federal government that licensed it. It thus became, or at least the top executives believed it had become, too dangerous to have indepth, probing commentary on the news. Crisp, dry, uneditorializing headliners were considered safer. Murrow was out and Walter Cronkite was in.

The power to define what is critical in an organization is no small power. Moreover, it is the key to understanding why organizations are either aligned with their envi-

ronments or misaligned. If an organization defines certain activities as critical when in fact they are not critical, given the flow of resources coming into the organization, it is not likely to survive, at least in its present form.

Most organizations manage to evolve a distribution of power and influence that is aligned with the critical realities they face in the environment. The environment, in turn, includes both the internal environment, the shifting situational contexts in which particular decisions get made, and the external environment that it can hope to influence but is unlikely to control.

LEARNING CHECKPOINT

Is the base of power—interpersonal, structural, or situational—likely to effect power sharing that takes place?

THE CRITICAL CONTINGENCIES

The critical contingencies facing most organizations derive from the environmental context within which they operate. This determines the available needed resources and thus determines the problems to be dealt with. That power organizes around handling these problems suggests an important mechanism by which organizations keep in tune with their external environments. The strategic-contingencies model implies that subunits that contribute to the critical resources of the organization will gain influence in the organization. Their influence presumably is then used to bend the organization's activities to the contingencies that determine its resources. This idea may strike one as obvious. But its obviousness in no way diminishes its importance. Indeed, despite its obviousness, it escapes the notice of many organizational analysts and managers, who all too frequently think of the organization in terms of a descending pyramid, in which all the departments in one tier hold equal power and status. This presumption denies the reality that departments differ in the contributions they are believed to make to the overall organization's resources, as well as to the fact that some are more equal than others.

Because of the importance of this idea to organizational effectiveness, we decided to examine it carefully in a large midwestern university. A university offers an excellent site for studying power. It is composed of departments with nominally equal power and is administered by a central executive structure much like other bureaucracies. However, at the same time it is a situation in which the departments have clearly defined identities and face diverse external environments. Each department has its own bodies of knowledge, its own institutions, its own sources of prestige and resources. Because the departments operate in different external environments, they are likely to contribute differentially to the resources of the overall organization. Thus a physics department with close ties to NASA may contribute substantially to the funds of the university; and a history department with a renowned historian in residence may contribute to the intellectual credibility or prestige of the whole university. Such variations permit one to examine how these various contributions lead to obtaining power within the university.

We analyzed the influence of 29 university departments throughout an 18-month period in their history. Our chief interest was to determine whether departments that brought more critical resources to the university would be more powerful than departments that contributed fewer or less critical resources.

To identify the critical resources each department contributed, the heads of all departments were interviewed about the importance of seven different resources to the university's success. The seven included undergraduate students (the factor determining size of the state allocations by the university), national prestige, administrative expertise, and so on. The most critical resource was found to be contract and grant monies received by a department's faculty for research or consulting services. At this university, contract and grants contributed somewhat less than 50 percent of the overall budget, with the remainder primarily coming from state appropriations. The importance attributed to contract and grant monies, and the rather minor importance of undergraduate students, was not surprising for this particular university. The university was a major center for graduate education; many of its departments ranked in the top ten of their respective fields. Grant and contract monies were the primary source of discretionary funding available for maintaining these programs of graduate education, and hence for maintaining the university's prestige. The prestige of the university itself was critical both in recruiting able students and attracting top-notch faculty.

From university records it was determined what relative contributions each of the 29 departments made to the various needs of the university (national prestige, outside grants, teaching). Thus, for instance, one department may have contributed to the university by teaching 7 percent of the instruc-tional units, bringing in 2 percent of the outside contracts and grants, and having a national ranking of 20. Another department, on the other hand, may have taught one percent of the instructional units, contributed 12 percent to the grants, and be ranked the third best department in its field within the country.

The question was: Do these different contributions determine the relative power of the departments within the university? Power was measured in several ways; but regardless of how measured, the answer was "Yes." Those three resources together accounted for about 70 percent of the variance in subunit power in the university.

But the most important predictor of departmental power was the department's contribution to the contracts and grants of the university. Sixty percent of the variance in power was due to this one factor, suggesting that the power of departments derived primarily from the dollars they provided for graduate education, the activity believed to be the most important for the organization.

THE IMPACT OF ORGANIZATIONAL POWER ON DECISION MAKING

The measure of power we used in studying this university was an analysis of the responses of the department heads we interviewed. While such perceptions of power might be of interest in their own right, they contribute little to our understanding of how the distribution of power might serve to align an organization with its critical realities. For this we must look to how power actually influences the decisions and policies of organizations.

While it is perhaps not absolutely valid, we can generally gauge the relative importance of a department of an organization by the size of the budget allocated to it relative to other departments. Clearly it is of importance to the administrators of those departments whether they get squeezed in a budget crunch or are given more funds to strike out after new opportunities. And it should also be clear that when those decisions are made and one department can go ahead and try new approaches while another must cut back on the old, then the deployment of the resources of the organization in meeting its problems is most directly affected.

Thus our study of the university led us to ask the following questions: Does power lead to influence in the organization? To answer this question, we found it useful first to ask another one, namely: Why should department heads try to influence organizational decisions to favor their own departments to the exclusion of other departments? While this second question may seem a bit naive to anyone who has witnessed the political realities of organizations, we posed it in a context of research on organizations that sees power as an illegitimate threat to the neater rational authority of modern bureaucracies. In this context, decisions are not believed to be made because of the dirty business of politics but because of the overall goals and purposes of the organization. In a university, one reasonable basis for decision making is the teaching workload of departments and the demands that follow from that workload. We would expect, therefore, that departments with heavy student demands for courses would be able to obtain funds for teaching. Another reasonable basis for decision making is quality. We would expect, for that reason, that depart-

ments with esteemed reputations would be able to obtain funds both because their quality suggests they might use such funds effectively and because such funds would allow them to maintain their quality. A rational model of bureaucracy intimates, then, that the organizational decisions taken would favor those who perform the stated purposes of the organization—teaching undergraduates and training professional and scientific talent—well.

The problem with rational models of decision making, however, is that what is rational to one person may strike another as irrational. For most departments, resources are a question of survival. While teaching undergraduates may seem to be a major goal for some members of the university, developing knowledge may seem so to others; and to still others, advising governments and other institutions about policies may seem to be the crucial business. Everyone has his own idea of the proper priorities in a just world. Thus goals rather than being clearly defined and universally agreed upon are blurred and contested throughout the organization. If such is the case, then the decisions taken on behalf of the organization as a whole are likely to reflect the goals of those who prevail in political contests, namely, those with power in the organization.

Will organizational decisions always reflect the distribution of power in the organization? Probably not. Using power for influence requires a certain expenditure of effort, time, and resources. Prudent and judicious persons are not likely to use their power needlessly or wastefully. And it is likely that power will be used to influence organizational decisions primarily under circumstances that both require and favor its use. We have exam-

ined three conditions that are likely to affect the use of power in organizations: scarcity, criticality, and uncertainty. The first suggests that subunits will try to exert influence when the resources of the organization are scarce. If there is an abundance of resources, then a particular department or a particular individual has little need to attempt influence. With little effort, he can get all he wants anyway.

The second condition, criticality, suggests that a subunit will attempt to influence decisions to obtain resources that are critical to its own survival and activities. Criticality implies that one would not waste effort, or risk being labeled obstinate, by fighting over trivial decisions affecting one's operations.

An office manager would probably balk less about a threatened cutback in copying machine usage than about a reduction in typing staff. An advertising department head would probably worry less about losing his lettering artist than his illustrator. Criticality is difficult to define because what is critical depends on people's beliefs about what is critical. Such beliefs may or may not be based on experience and knowledge and may or may not be agreed upon by all. Scarcity, for instance, may itself affect conceptions of criticality. When slack resources drop off, cutbacks have to be made—those "hard decisions," as congressmen and resplendent administrators like to call them. Managers then find themselves scrapping projects they once held dear.

The third condition that we believe affects the use of power is uncertainty: When individuals do not agree about what the organization should do or how to do it, power and other social processes will affect decisions. The reason for this is simply that, if there are no clear-cut criteria available for resolving conflicts of interest, then the only means for resolution is some form of social process, including power, status, social ties, or some arbitrary process like flipping a coin or drawing straws. Under conditions of uncertainty, the powerful manager can argue his case on any grounds and usually win it. Since there is no real consensus, other contestants are not likely to develop counter arguments or amass sufficient opposition. Moreover, because of his power and their need for access to the resources he controls, they are more likely to defer to his arguments.

Although the evidence is slight, we have found that power will influence the allocations of scarce and critical resources. In the analysis of power in the university, for instance, one of the most critical resources needed by departments is the general budget. First granted by the state legislature, the general budget is later allocated to individual departments by the university administration in response to requests from the department heads. Our analysis of the factors that contribute to a department getting more or less of this budget indicated that subunit power was the major predictor, overriding such factors as student demand for courses, national reputations of departments, or even the size of a department's faculty. Moreover, other research has shown that when the general budget has been cut back or held below previous uninflated levels, leading to monies becoming more scarce, budget allocations mirror departmental powers even more closely.

Student enrollment and faculty size, of course, do themselves relate to budget allocations, as we would expect since they determine a department's need for resources, or at least offer visible testimony of

needs. But departments are not always able to get what they need by the mere fact of needing them. In one analysis it was found that high-power departments were able to obtain budget without regard to their teaching loads and, in some cases, actually in inverse relation to their teaching loads. In contrast, low-power departments could get increases in budget only when they could justify the increases by a recent growth in teaching load, and then only when it was far in excess of norms for other departments.

General budget is only one form of resource that is allocated to departments. There are others such as special grants for student fellowships or faculty research. These are critical to departments because they affect the ability to attract other resources, such as outstanding faculty or students. We examined how power influenced the allocations of four resources department heads had described as critical and scarce.

When the four resources were arrayed from the most to the least critical and scarce, we found that departmental power best predicted the allocations of the most critical and scarce resources. In other words, the analysis of how power influences organizational allocations leads to this conclusion: Those subunits most likely to survive in times of strife are those that are more critical to the organization. Their importance to the organization gives them power to influence resource allocations that enhance their own survival.

HOW EXTERNAL ENVIRONMENT IMPACTS EXECUTIVE SELECTION

Power not only influences the survival of key groups in an organization, it also influences the selection of individuals to key leadership positions, and by such a process further aligns the organization with its environmental context.

We can illustrate this with a recent study of the selection and tenure of chief administrators in 57 hospitals in Illinois. We assumed that since the critical problems facing the organization would enhance the power of certain groups at the expense of others, then the leaders to emerge should be those most relevant to the context of the hospitals. To assess this we asked each chief administrator about his professional background and how long he had been in office. The replies were then related to the hospitals' funding, ownership, and competitive conditions for patients and staff.

One aspect of a hospital's context is the source of its budget. Some hospitals, for instance, are run much like other businesses. They sell bed space, patient care, and treatment services. They charge fees sufficient both to cover their costs and to provide capital for expansion. The main source of both their operating and capital funds is patient billings. Increasingly, patient billings are paid for, not by patients, but by private insurance companies. Insurers like Blue Cross dominate and represent a potent interest group outside a hospital's control but critical to its income. The insurance companies, in order to limit their own costs, attempt to hold down the fees allowable to hospitals, which they do effectively from their positions on state rate boards. The squeeze on hospitals that results from fees increasing slowly while costs climb rapidly more and more demands the talents of cost accountants or people trained in the technical expertise of hospital administration.

By contrast, other hospitals operate more like social service institutions, either as government healthcare units (Bellevue Hospital in New York City and Cook County Hospital in Chicago, for example) or as charitable institutions. These hospitals obtain a large proportion of their operating and capital funds, not from privately insured patients, but from government subsidies or private donations. Such institutions rather than requiring the talents of a technically efficient administrator are likely to require the savvy of someone who is well integrated into the social and political power structure of the community.

Not surprisingly, the characteristics of administrators predictably reflect the funding context of the hospitals with which they are associated. Those hospitals with larger proportions of their budget obtained from private insurance companies were most likely to have administrators with backgrounds in accounting and least likely to have administrators whose professions were business or medicine. In contrast, those hospitals with larger proportions of their budget derived from private donations and local governments were most likely to have administrators with business or professional backgrounds and least likely to have accountants. The same held for formal training in hospital management. Professional hospital administrators could easily be found in hospitals drawing their incomes from private insurance and rarely in hospitals dependent on donations or legislative appropriations.

As with the selection of administrators, the context of organizations has also been found to affect the removal of executives. The environment, as a source of organizational problems, can make it more or less difficult for executives to demonstrate their value to the organization. In the hospitals we studied, long-term administrators came from hospitals with few problems. They enjoyed amicable and stable relations with their local business and social communities and suffered little competition for funding and staff. The small city hospital director who attended civic and Elks meetings while running the only hospital within a 100-mile radius, for example, had little difficulty holding on to his job. Turnover was highest in hospitals with the most problems, a phenomenon similar to that observed in a study of industrial organizations in which turnover was highest among executives in industries with competitive environments and unstable market conditions. The interesting thing is that instability characterized the industries rather than the individual firms in them. The troublesome conditions in the individual firms were attributed, or rather misattributed, to the executives themselves.

It takes more than problems, however, to terminate a manager's leadership. The problems themselves must be relevant and critical. This is clear from the way in which an administrator's tenure is affected by the status of the hospital's operating budget. Naively we might assume that all administrators would need to show a surplus. Not necessarily so. Again, we must distinguish between those hospitals that depend on private donations for funds and those that do not. Whether an endowed budget shows a surplus or deficit is less important than the hospital's relations with benefactors. On the other hand, with a budget dependent on patient billing, a surplus is almost essential; monies for new equipment or expansion must be drawn from it, and without them quality care becomes more difficult and patients scarcer. An administrator's tenure reflected just these considerations. For those hospitals dependent upon private donations, the length of an administrator's term depended not at all on the status of the operating budget but was fairly predictable from the hospital's relations with the business community. On the other hand, in hospitals dependent on the operating budget for capital financing, the greater the deficit the shorter was the tenure of the hospital's principal administrators.

CHANGING CONTINGENCIES AND ERODING POWER BASES

The critical contingencies facing the organization may change. When they do, it is reasonable to expect that the power of individuals and subgroups will change in turn. At times the shift can be swift and shattering, as it was recently for power-holders in New York City. A few years ago it was believed that David Rockefeller was one of the ten most powerful people in the city, as tallied by *New York* magazine, which annually sniffs out power for the delectation of its readers. But that was before it was revealed that the city was in financial trouble, before Rockefeller's Chase Manhattan Bank lost some of its own financial luster, and before brother Nelson lost some of his political influence in Washington. Obviously David Rockefeller was no longer as well positioned to help bail the city out. Another loser was an attorney with considerable personal connections to the political and religious leaders of the city. His talents were no longer in much demand. The persons with more influence were the bankers and union pension fund executors who fed money to the city; community leaders who represent blacks and Spanish-Americans, in contrast, witnessed the erosion of their power bases.

One implication of the idea that power shifts with changes in organizational environments is that the dominant coalition will tend to be that group that is most appropriate for the organization's environment, as also will the leaders of an organization. One can observe this historically in the top executives of industrial firms in the United States. Up until the early 1950s, many top corporations were headed by former production line managers or engineers who gained prominence because of their abilities to cope with the problems of production. Their success, however, only spelled their demise. As production became routinized and mechanized, the problem of most firms became one of selling all those goods they so efficiently produced. Marketing executives were more frequently found in corporate boardrooms. Success outdid itself again, for keeping markets and production steady and stable requires the kind of control that can only come from acquiring competitors and suppliers or the invention of more and more appealing products—ventures that typically require enormous amounts of capital. During the 1960s, financial executives assumed the seats of power. And they, too, will give way to others. Edging over the horizon are legal experts, as regulation and antitrust suits are becoming more and more frequent in the 1970s, suits that had their beginnings in the success of the expansion generated by prior executives. The more distant future, which is likely to be dominated by multinational corporations, may see former secretaries of state and their minions increasingly serving as corporate figureheads.

THE NONADAPTIVE CONSEQUENCES OF ADAPTATION

From what we have said thus far about power aligning the organization with its own realities, an intelligent person might react with a resounding ho-hum, for it all seems too obvious: Those with the ability to get the job done are given the job to do.

However, there are two aspects of power that make it more useful for understanding organizations and their effectiveness. First, the "job" to be done has a way of expanding itself until it becomes less and less clear what the job is. Napoleon began by doing a job for France in the war with Austria and ended up Emperor, convincing many that only he could keep the peace. Hitler began by promising an end to Germany's troubling postwar depression and ended up convincing more people than is comfortable to remember that he was destined to be the savior of the world. In short, power is a capacity for influence that extends far beyond the original bases that created it. Second, power tends to take on institutionalized forms that enable it to endure well beyond its usefulness to an organization.

There is an important contradiction in what we have observed about organizational power. On the one hand we have said that power derives from the contingencies facing an organization and that when those contingencies change so do the bases for power. On the other hand we have asserted that subunits will tend to use their power to influence organizational decisions in their own favor, particularly when their own survival is threatened by the scarcity of critical resources. The first statement implies that an organization will tend to be aligned with its environment since power will tend to bring to key positions those with capabilities relevant to the context. The second implies that those in power will not give up their positions so easily; they will pursue policies that guarantee their continued domination. In short, change and stability operate through the same mechanism,

and, as a result, the organization will never be completely in phase with its environment or its needs.

The study of hospital administrators illustrates how leadership can be out of phase with reality. We argued that privately funded hospitals needed trained technical administrators more so than did hospitals funded by donations. The need as we perceived it was matched in most hospitals, but by no means in all. Some organizations did not conform with our predictions. These deviations imply that some administrators were able to maintain their positions independent of their suitability for those positions. By dividing administrators into those with long and short terms of office, one finds that the characteristics of longer-termed administrators were virtually unrelated to the hospital's context. The shorter-termed chiefs on the other hand had characteristics more appropriate for the hospital's problems. For a hospital to have a recently appointed head implies that the previous administrator had been unable to endure by institutionalizing himself.

One obvious feature of hospitals that allowed some administrators to enjoy a long tenure was a hospital's ownership. Administrators were less entrenched when their hospitals were affiliated with and dependent upon larger organizations, such as governments or churches. Private hospitals offered more secure positions for administrators. Like private corporations, they tend to have more diffused ownership, leaving the administrator unopposed as he institutionalizes his reign. Thus he endures, sometimes at the expense of the performance of the organization. Other research has demonstrated that corporations with diffuse ownership have poorer earnings than those in which the control of the manager is checked by a dominant shareholder. Firms that overload their boardrooms with more insiders than are appropriate for their context have also been found to be less profitable.

A word of caution is required about our judgment of "appropriateness." When we argue some capabilities are more appropriate for one context than another, we do so from the perspective of an outsider and on the basis of reasonable assumptions as to the problems the organization will face and the capabilities they will need. The fact that we have been able to predict the distribution of influence and the characteristics of leaders suggests that our reasoning is not incorrect. However, we do not think that all organizations follow the same pattern. The fact that we have not been able to predict outcomes with 100 percent accuracy indicates they do not.

MISTAKING CRITICAL CONTINGENCIES

One thing that allows subunits to retain their power is their ability to name their functions as critical to the organization when they may not be. Consider again our discussion of power in the university. One might wonder why the most critical tasks were defined as graduate education and scholarly research, the effect of which was to lend power to those who brought in grants and contracts. Why not something else? The reason is that the more powerful departments argued for those criteria and won their case, partly because they were more powerful.

In another analysis of this university, we found that all departments advocate self-serving criteria for budget allocation. Thus a department with large undergraduate enrollments argued that enrollments should determine budget al-

locations, a department with a strong national reputation saw prestige as the most reasonable basis for distributing funds, and so on. We further found that advocating such self-serving criteria actually benefited a department's budget allotments but, also, it paid off more for departments that were already powerful.

Organizational needs are consistent with a current distribution of power also because of a human tendency to categorize problems in familiar ways. An accountant sees problems with organizational performance as cost accountancy problems or inventory flow problems. A sales manager sees them as problems with markets, promotional strategies, or just unaggressive sales people. But what is the truth? Since it does not automatically announce itself, it is likely that those with prior credibility, or those with power, will be favored as the enlightened. This bias, while not intentionally self-serving, further concentrates power among those who already possess it, independent of changes in the organization's context.

INSTITUTIONALIZING POWER

A third reason for expecting organizational contingencies to be defined in familiar ways is that the current holders of power can structure the organization in ways that institutionalize themselves. By institutionalization we mean the establishment of relatively permanent structures and policies that favor the influence of a particular subunit. While in power, a dominant coalition has the ability to institute constitutions, rules, procedures, and information systems that limit the potential power of others while continuing their own.

The key to institutionalizing

power always is to create a device that legitimates one's own authority and diminishes the legitimacy of others. When the "Divine Right of Kings" was envisioned centuries ago it was to provide an unquestionable foundation for the supremacy of royal authority. There is generally a need to root the exercise of authority in some higher power. Modern leaders are no less affected by this need. Richard Nixon, with the aid of John Dean, reified the concept of executive privilege, which meant in effect that what the President wished not to be discussed need not be discussed.

In its simpler form, institutionalization is achieved by designating positions or roles for organizational activities. The creation of a new post legitimizes a function and forces organization members to orient to it. By designating how this new post relates to older, more established posts, moreover, one can structure an organization to enhance the importance of the function in the organization. Equally, one can diminish the importance of traditional functions. This is what happened in the end with the insurance company we mentioned that was having trouble with its coding department. As the situation unfolded, the claims director continued to feel dissatisfied about the dependency of his functions on the coding manager. Thus he instituted a reorganization that resulted in two coding departments. In so doing, of course, he placed activities that affected his department under his direct control, presumably to make the operation more effective. Similarly, consumer-product firms enhance the power of marketing by setting up a coordinating role to interface production and marketing functions and then appoint a marketing manager to fill the role.

The structures created by dominant powers sooner or later become fixed and unquestioned features of the organization. Eventually, this can be devastating. It is said that the battle of Jena in 1806 was lost by Frederick the Great, who died in 1786. Though the great Prussian leader had no direct hand in the disaster, his imprint on the army was so thorough, so embedded in its skeletal underpinnings, that the organization was inappropriate for others to lead in different times.

Another important source of institutionalized power lies in the ability to structure information systems. Setting up committees to investigate particular organizational issues and having them report only to particular individuals or groups, facilitates their awareness of problems by members of those groups while limiting the awareness of problems by the members of other groups. Obviously, those who have information are in a better position to interpret the problems of an organization, regardless of how realistically they may, in fact, do so.

Still another way to institutionalize power is to distribute rewards and resources. The dominant group may quiet competing interest groups with small favors and rewards. The credit for this artful form of cooptation belongs to Louis XIV. To avoid usurpation of his power by the nobles of France and the Fronde that had so troubled his father's reign, he built the palace at Versailles to occupy them with hunting and gossip. Awed, the courtiers basked in the reflected glories of the "Sun King" and the overwhelming setting he had created for his court.

At this point, we have not systematically studied the institutionalization of power. But we suspect it is an important condition that me-

diates between the environment of the organization and the capabilities of the organization for dealing with that environment. The more institutionalized power is within an organization, the more likely an organization will be out of phase with the realities it faces. President Richard Nixon's structuring of his White House is one of the better documented illustrations. If we go back to newspaper and magazine descriptions of how he organized his office from the beginning in 1968, most of what occurred subsequently follows almost as an afterthought. Decisions flowed through virtually only the small White House staff; rewards, small presidential favors of recognition, and perquisites were distributed by this staff to the loyal; and information from the outside world—the press, Congress, the people on the streets—was filtered by the staff and passed along only if initialed "bh." Thus it was not surprising that when Nixon met war protestors in the early dawn, the only thing he could think to talk about was the latest football game, so insulated had he become from their grief and anger.

One of the more interesting implications of institutionalized power is that executive turnover among the executives who have structured the organization is likely to be a rare event that occurs only under the most pressing crisis. If a dominant coalition is able to structure the organization and interpret the meaning of ambiguous events like declining sales and profits or lawsuits, then the "real" problems to emerge will easily be incorporated into traditional molds of thinking and acting. If opposition is designed out of the organization, the interpretations will go unquestioned. Conditions will remain stable until a crisis develops, so overwhelming

and visible that even the most adroit rhetorician would be silenced.

IMPLICATIONS FOR THE MANAGEMENT OF POWER IN ORGANIZATIONS

While we could derive numerous implications from this discussion of power, our selection would have to depend largely on whether one wanted to increase one's power, decrease the power of others, or merely maintain one's position. More important, the real implications depend on the particulars of an organizational situation. To understand power in an organization one must begin by looking outside it—into the environment—for those groups that mediate the organization's outcomes but are not themselves within its control.

Instead of ending with homilies, we will end with a reversal of where we began. Power, rather than being the dirty business it is often made out to be, is probably one of the few mechanisms for reality testing in organizations. And the cleaner forms of power, the institutional forms, rather than having the virtues they are often credited with, can lead the organization to become out of touch. The real trick to managing power in organizations is to ensure somehow that leaders cannot be unaware of the realities of their environments and cannot avoid changing to deal with those realities. That, however, would be like designing the "self-liquidating organization," an unlikely event since anyone capable of designing such an instrument would be obviously in control of the liquidations.

Management would do well to devote more attention to determining the critical contingencies of their environments. For if you conclude, as we do, that the environment sets most of the structure influencing organizational outcomes and problems, and that power derives from the organization's activities that deal with those contingencies, then it is the environment that needs managing, not power. The first step is to construct an accurate model of the environment, a process that is quite difficult for most organizations. We have recently started a project to aid administrators in systematically understanding their environments. From this experience, we have learned that the most critical blockage to perceiving an organization's reality accurately is a failure to incorporate those with the relevant expertise into the process. Most organizations have the requisite experts on hand but they are positioned so that they can be comfortably ignored.

One conclusion you can, and probably should, derive from our discussion is that power—because of the way it develops and the way it is used—will always result in the organization suboptimizing its performance. However, to this grim absolute, we add a comforting caveat: If any criteria other than power were the basis for determining an organization's decisions, the results would be even worse.

SELECTED BIBLIOGRAPHY

The literature on power is at once both voluminous and frequently empty of content. Some is philosophical musing about the concept of power, while other writing contains popularized palliatives for acquiring and exercising influence. Machiavelli's *The Prince,* if read carefully, remains the single best prescriptive treatment of power and its use. Most social scientists have approached power descriptively, attempting to understand how it is acquired, how it is used, and what

its effects are. Meyer Zald's edited collection *Power in Organizations* (Vanderbilt University Press, 1970) is one of the more useful sets of thoughts about power from a sociological perspective, while James Tedeschi's edited book, *The Social Influence Processes* (Aldine-Atherton, 1972) represents the social psychological approach to understanding power and influence. The strategic contingencies' approach, with its emphasis on the importance of uncertainty for understanding power in organizations, is described by David Hickson and his colleagues in "A Strategic Contingencies Theory of Intraorganizational Power" (*Administrative Science Quarterly,* December 1971, pp. 216–229).

Unfortunately, while many have written about power theoretically, there have been few empirical examinations of power and its use. Most of the work has taken the form of case studies. Michel Crozier's *The Bureaucratic Phenomenon* (University of Chicago Press, 1964) is important because it describes a group's source of power as control over critical activities and illustrates how power is not strictly derived from hierarchical position. J. Victor Baldridge's *Power and Conflict in the University* (John Wiley & Sons, 1971) and Andrew Pettigrew's study of computer purchase decisions in one English firm (*Politics of Organizational Decision-Making,* Tavistock, 1973) both present insights into the acquisition and use of power in specific instances. Our work has been more empirical and comparative, testing more explicitly the ideas presented in this article. The study of university decision making is reported in articles in the June 1974, pp. 135–151, and December 1974, pp. 453–473, issues of the *Administrative Science Quarterly,* the insurance firm study

in J. G. Hunt and L. L. Larson's collection, *Leadership Frontiers* (Kent State University Press, 1975), and the study of hospital administrator succession will appear in 1977 in the *Academy of Management Journal.* □

R² POWER AND ORGANIZATION LIFE CYCLES

HENRY MINTZBERG

From the earliest days of organization theory, notably in the writings of Max Weber (Gerth & Mills, 1958), the themes of ideal or pure types of organizations and of stages of organizational development have occupied an important, although never prevalent, place in the literature. The recent book by Kimberly and Miles (1980) entitled *The Organizational Life Cycle* may signal a growing interest in these themes or may, in fact, stimulate such an interest.

This interest may say more about cognition than reality, reflecting simply the need to think about complexity in order to cope with it—a point made particularly well in Allison's (1971) study of different models to interpret decision making during the Cuban missile crisis. The present author believes, however, that there is more to these themes than cognition (Miller & Mintzberg, 1983), that ideal types reflect leading tendencies in organizations, and that stages of organizational development reflect intrinsic forces that arise in organizations to change them as they develop. Studies by Woodward (1965), Burns and Stalker (1966), Lawrence and Lorsch (1967), Miles and Snow (1978), and Miller and Friesen (1978, 1980a, 1980b, 1982a), among others, have provided empirical support for the existence of clusters of attributes, or "configurations," in organizations, which would seem to resemble ideal types.

Source: Reprinted from *Academy of Management Review*, April 1984, pp. 207–224.

Theories of stages of organizational development go beyond ideal types, by postulating common sequences among them as organizations survive and develop over time. Explicit in a number of these theories is the notion of longer periods of stability interrupted by shorter ones of destructive change (Greiner, 1972). Starbuck has referred to these as "metamorphosis models," pointing out that organizations may not grow in "a smooth continuous process" so much as in one "marked by abrupt and discrete changes" in their conditions and structure (1965, p. 486). In their research on "quantum" change, Miller and Friesen (1980a, 1980b, 1982a, 1982b) have provided some strong empirical support for such models.

It is one thing, however, to produce systematic evidence to support configuration and metamorphosis in general; it is quite another to do so for specific sequences of transitions among particular types. The production of such evidence would call for the most ambitious sort of research, longitudinal in nature with a wide variety of organizations. Most related research has been narrower than this, focusing either on single transitions in specific types of organizations—for example, the shift from functional to divisionalized structure in giant American corporations, as in the research of Rumelt (1974)—or else on the sequence of transitions over the life of a single organization—as in Whyte's (1969) classic description of the development of a restaurant.

These different studies nevertheless can be pieced together to describe what seem to be common

transitions or even common sequences of transitions. Perhaps the best known sequence in the literature is that postulated for the business firm that survives and grows: creation in the form of simple, entrepreneurial structure, followed by limited growth; transition to more elaborated, bureaucratic structure, followed by extensive growth; and then diversification of strategy followed by divisionalization of structure, allowing for growth to much larger size—parts or all of which have been described by Chandler (1962); Filley and House (1969, 1976); Galbraith and Nathanson (1979); Litterer (1965); Scott (1971); and Whyte (1969). No writer claims that this sequence is inevitable. Some writers in fact show that certain kinds of organizations tend to settle in certain places and not move on, as did the "heavies" of American industry, according to Rumelt (1974), such as the steel and aluminum producers, which tended to achieve only a limited form of divisionalization. Others sometimes break the sequence by skipping stages or reverting back to earlier ones. But the assumption underlying all these writings is that the sequence described seems to be most common for the type of organization in question, and is perhaps driven by a set of unique, underlying forces in it.

Most of the research cited so far has concentrated on changes in organizational structure (and, to a lesser extent, strategy). But there has been a swing in the literature of organization theory over the last decade toward consideration of issues of power—the capacity of individuals or groups to effect, or affect, organizational outcomes

(Kanter, 1977; Russell, 1938). In the present writer's view, this swing reflects certain fundamental trends in developed societies, namely, the increasing size of organizations, and, as a result, the enhancement of their external power as systems as well as the pervasion of conflict and politics within them. Such trends clearly merit close attention by organization theorists, and they have received it in works such as Pfeffer and Salancik (1978). Because shifts in power seem to lie at the root of transitions in organization, these trends might be particularly well explained by considering stages of organizational development from the perspective of power. Such consideration may help to explain not only how organizations survive and develop, but also how they stagnate and falter, leading from the realm of stages of organizational development into that of organization life cycles.

This paper seeks to present one view of organization life cycles, described from the perspective of power—specifically, from a consideration of the changing distribution of power around and inside an organization as it survives and develops over time. To help it do so, the paper draws on selected references in a variety of disciplines—primarily management, organization theory, and sociology, but also economics, political science, and law. This description is intended to serve both general and specific purposes: in general, to stimulate thinking about issues of power, the development of organizations, and the impact of this development on society; in particular, to present one life cycle model, among the many that are possible, that may help to explain certain important trends in contemporary society. Those concerned with renewal in a society of large organizations likely will

have to consider not only how organizations arise and develop but also how they sustain themselves politically, sometimes in spite of economic forces, and how they eventually falter.

CONFIGURATIONS OF ORGANIZATIONAL POWER

Blau and Scott (1962) categorize organizations from an external perspective—in terms of whom they are supposed to serve. Etzioni (1961) does so from an internal perspective—in terms of how they achieve control over their members (and the related form of member involvement). The typology presented in this paper is developed by considering the interplay of external as well as internal systems of power.

Influences, or "stakeholders"—people who use "voice" to attain their needs through an organization (Hirschman, 1970)—may be divided into those with major time commitments to the organization (essentially the full time employees or volunteers), who will be called *internal,* and the others, who will be called *external.* The former may be described as forming an internal coalition, the latter, an external coalition. The term coalition is used, after Cyert and March (1963), to describe a set of people who vie among themselves to determine a distribution of power.

A typology of configurations of organizational power can be derived by considering the relationships among different forms of external and internal coalitions. Some possible forms of each are proposed. The external coalition may be described as *dominated* (one individual, or a group in consensus, holds the balance of power); as *divided* (a few competing groups or individuals divide power); or as

passive (no outsider seeks to exercise much power). There is some evidence (Berle & Means, 1968; Mace, 1972; Michels, 1915) as well as mathematical argumentation (Olson, 1965, 1968) that a large number of dispersed external influencers tends to produce a passive external coalition. Based on various kinds of influence or control used within the organization, five forms of the internal coalitions may be described: *personalized* (the personal controls of a leader dominate, such as the issuing of ad hoc orders); *bureaucratic* (formal standards dominate); *ideologic* (the norms of a strong internal ideology dominate); *professional* (the technical skills and knowledge of experts dominate); and *politicized* (political or conflictive forces dominate). (The situation when no one of these forms of influence dominates also will be considered.)

What relationships might be expected among these different external and internal coalitions. Four propositions are proposed to describe what may be the most common ones:

1. A dominated external coalition encourages the rise of a bureaucratic internal coalition.
2. A divided external coalition encourages the rise of a politicized internal coalition, and vice versa.
3. A personalized, ideologic, professional, or bureaucratic internal coalition encourages the rise of a passive external coalition.
4. Other combinations of the coalitions, as well as nondominant mixtures of the internal forms of influence, encourage moderate or intense levels of conflict in an organization.

Briefly, the arguments behind these propositions, which are developed at length in Mintzberg (1983), are as follows. To maintain a position of dominance yet remain in the external coalition, an influencer must bring the organization under control without actually managing it. That would seem to be most effectively accomplished by appointing the chief executive officer, specifying clear goals that can be operationalized through systems of formal control, and then holding the chief executive responsible for performance. The effect of this would be to centralize, formalize, and standardize behavior in the internal coalition, giving rise to its bureaucratic form. Studies by Heydebrand (1973), Holdaway, Newberry, Hickson, and Heron (1975), Pondy (1969), Pugh, Hickson, Hinings, and Turner (1969), Reimann (1973), and Samuel and Mannheim (1970) all support the relationship between external control of an organization and its internal centralization and/or formalization.

The second proposition is based on the assumption that conflict in one of the coalitions tends to spill over to the other. Political activity in the internal coalition encourages various internal influencers to enlist the support of different outsiders, thereby dividing the external coalition. Conflicting external influencers, by pulling parts of the internal coalition in different directions, encourage the breakdown of more legitimate forms of influence (such as authority or certified expertise) in favor of political activity.

The third proposition is based on the assumption that any focused form of influence in the internal coalition tends to discourage or pacify concerted forms of influence in the external coalition. Personalized control essentially means a strong central leader, who likely will resist outside influence (Collins & Moore,

1970). A strong internal ideology serves to knit the internal influencers into a cohesive group, which will be inclined to resist outside influence. Similarly, experts who dominate an organization seem inclined to use their expertise to pacify external influence (Thoenig & Friedberg, 1976); and a bureaucratic internal coalition, even when arising initially because of a dominated external coalition, requires a strong administrative component, and this tends to be obsessed with control of external influencers no less than inside workers (Mintzberg, 1979).

The first and third propositions suggest five combinations of the coalitions, each with power focused in one way or another. The fourth proposition extends the assumption of the second that the absence of a single focus of power breeds conflict. Whether power is divided between two forms of influence in the internal coalition (e.g., between personalized leadership and expertise) or between one focus of influ-

ence in each of the coalitions (e.g., personalized leadership inside and a dominant influencer externally), some significant level of conflict may be expected between them. In effect, the organization adopts a "hybrid" power structure, which need not, of course, be dysfunctional (as in the case of the symphony orchestra, which seems destined to combine the personalized leadership of the conductor with the expertise of the musicians, despite the tension generated).

 **LEARNING CHECKPOINT**

What form of power, interpersonal, structural, or situational, is emphasized in the four propositions?

Together these four propositions suggest six basic configurations of power, shown in Exhibit 1.

The *instrument* is an ideal type power configuration in which the

---

EXHIBIT 1

Basic Configurations of Power

External Coalition	Internal Coalition	Power Configuration
Dominated	Bureaucratic	Instrument
Passive	Bureaucratic	Closed system
Passive	Personalized	Autocracy
Passive	Ideologic	Missionary
Passive	Professional	Meritocracy
Divided	Politicized	Political arena
Dominated	Personalized	
Dominated	Ideologic	
Dominated	Professional	probably less
Dominated	Politicized	common
Passive	Politicized	and less stable,
Divided	Bureaucratic	likely to be forms of
Divided	Personalized	Political Arena
Divided	Ideologic	
Divided	Professional	

organization serves a dominant external influencer (or a number of them acting in concert). Because external control is consolidated most effectively through the use of performance standards and other formalized controls, the internal coalition emerges as bureaucratic, pursuing the operational goals that the dominant influencer imposes on it. Within the organization, personalized leadership control and strong ideology and politics are discouraged as incompatible with tight external control. Nor is a high level of internal expertise compatible with such control. This description appears to be consistent with the closely-held corporation as described by Berle and Means (1968) and Mace (1971), the prison whose external influencers form a consensus around the goal of custody as described by McCleery (1957), the "paralytic" local electricity board described by Butler, Hickson, and Wilson (1977–1978), the "coercive" organization described by Etzioni (1961), and the "appendix" organization described by Rhenman (1973).

The *closed system* also has a bureaucratic internal coalition, its internal control being based on formal standards. But it faces no focused power in its environment; its external influencers tend to be dispersed and unorganized. In other words, its external coalition is passive, either by chance or because the internal coalition actively pacified it. The administrators—notably the senior managers and the staff analysts who design the bureaucratic standards—hold the balance of power, encouraging the organization to pursue goals that serve itself as a system, notably its own growth (which in turn serves the administrators). This description resembles that of Michels (1915) for the European radical labor unions

and political parties at the turn of the century and of Berle and Means (1968) and Mace (1971) for the widely-held corporation. In the same vein, Galbraith (1967) refers to the latter as the "new industrial state"; Sampson (1973), as the "sovereign state." Note that the system is closed in one direction only—to external influence. As Galbraith describes clearly, it is hardly closed to the opposite—exercising influence over its own environment. Because the organization tends to be highly utilitarian, a strong organization ideology—characterized by belief in the pursuit of mission per se—is discouraged. So too are high levels of technical expertise, because these would enable experts to displace administrators in the power system. Even personalized controls are resisted because they weaken all of the administrators save one leader. More political activity arises in this configuration than in the closely surveyed instrument, notably between different administrators (e.g., empire building or line versus staff conflicts). But this tends to be relatively mild, contained by the pervasiveness of the bureaucratic controls.

The *autocracy* also faces a passive external coalition, but develops a different internal coalition. Here the power focuses on a single leader, who controls tightly by personal means, as Collins and Moore (1970) have described the entrepreneurial firm and Tannenbaum (1965) has described some of the utilitarian American unions. This form of control tends to preclude most politics, to discourage expertise and even bureaucratic standards, and to tolerate growth of an internal ideology only so long as it revolves around the leader. (Note that the term autocracy is meant to describe the means of

power, not its style of execution—that is, power exercised personally but not necessarily "autocratically.")

The *missionary* is an ideal type configuration dominated by a strong internal ideology, which serves to pacify the organization's external coalition. The strong system of internal beliefs, built around the organization's mission—whether that be to change society directly in some way, change it indirectly by attracting members and changing them, or merely offering members some pursuit attractive to them—serves to integrate tightly the efforts of the insiders. Indeed, once socialized and indoctrinated, the members tend to become highly loyal to the ideology, and so can share power more or less equally, trusted to act in the best interests of the organization. This normative control tends to reduce political activity sharply, and also to discourage the use of authority in the form of either personalized or bureaucratic controls. Even expertise tends to be discouraged, because it introduces status differences that can be incompatible with the egalitarian norms. Related descriptions of organization can be found in the work of Niv (1978) of American religious communes, Sills (1957) of the Foundation for Infantile Paralysis, and Rosner (1969) of the traditional Israeli kibutzim. The Chinese Cultural Revolution, as discussed, for example, by Eoyang (1972), the "organizational weapon" described by Selznick (1952), and, more generally, the "normative" organization described by Etzioni (1961) also seem to resemble the missionary.

The *meritocracy*, a term popularized by Young (1959), focuses its power on its technical expertise, on which it is dependent for survival. Hence its internal coalition is of the professional type. The presence of different types of experts can give rise to a certain level of political activity, particularly at the administrative levels, because the system of authority tends to be relatively weak in this configuration. Personal and bureaucratic controls tend to be discouraged as incompatible with a strong system of expertise. So, too, does strong organization ideology tend to be discouraged, because—to reverse a comment above—it requires an egalitarianism that can be incompatible with the status differences inherent in various forms of expertise. Moreover, as highly trained and mobile professionals, the most powerful influencers in this configuration are less inclined to express loyalty to the organization than to their own professions. Influencer pressures of various kinds frequently develop in the external coalition but, as this configuration is characterized here, internal expertise usually is able to pacify them. This description appears to be compatible with Butler et al.'s (1977–1978) description of the university they studied, with Gross's (1968) description of private American universities in general, and with Cressey's (1958) description of treatment (or rehabilitation) oriented prisons.

Finally, the ideal type called the *political arena* emerges when an organization is captured by conflict, in whole or in significant part. Some forms of the political arena have no center of power—no key influencer and no central legitimate form of influence. Instead, conflict is pervasive, the internal coalition being politicized and the external coalition divided, much as in Allison's (1971) governmental politics model. Other forms have two or more centers of power around which the conflict revolves. The po-

litical arena also may be characterized by intense conflict, which normally must be of brief duration if the organization is to survive, or by more moderate conflict, which can sometimes endure. Combining these characteristics gives rise to four basic forms of the political arena. Three are partial. The *confrontation* is characterized by brief conflict of an intense nature concentrated between two centers of power, as, for example, Perrow (1970) describes the attempt by an alliance of government and an industry cartel to control a maverick shipping firm (essentially a confrontation between a consensus-dominated external coalition and a personalized internal coalition). The *shaky alliance* also is characterized by concentrated conflict, but this is of a more moderate and hence possibly enduring nature, as in the symphony orchestra discussed earlier or perhaps in the public American universities described by Gross (1968), with government on one side and academic professionals on the other. In the *politicized organization*, the conflict is pervasive (i.e., not concentrated between any well-defined power centers) but moderate, and hence possibly enduring, a condition that seems to be emerging in what Blumberg (1971) describes as "the politicization of the corporation." The fourth is the ideal type in its purest form, called the *complete political arena*, characterized by conflict that is both pervasive and intense, and hence typically brief. (Of the four remaining combinations possible, two are left out because intense conflict is not considered likely to endure and the organization to survive, and the other two because the label political arena seems to be unwarranted for conflicts that are both moderate and brief.) The political arena can be a dysfunctional configuration of

power, wasting resources that might better be spent pursuing mission and serving clients. But it also can serve a number of functional purposes: inducing necessary but resisted changes in organization power (Mumford & Pettigrew, 1975), as when confrontation must be used to dislodge an existing but outmoded leadership; enabling certain necessary hybrids to function as shaky alliances (such as the symphony orchestra discussed earlier; and, to be discussed later, speeding up the death of spent organizations so as to help recycle their resources.

This typology maps on to another one that the author has developed, of five configurations of structure and situation—Mintzberg (1979)—as follows: autocracy corresponds to simple structure; the instrument and closed system are two forms of machine bureaucracy, one externally, the other internally controlled, with the latter sometimes taking the divisionalized form—for reasons discussed later in this paper; the meritocracy can take two forms of structural configuration, professional bureaucracy and adhocracy; and the missionary and political arena were not discussed in terms of structural configurations, although the former was alluded to at the end of the previous work.

TRANSITIONS BETWEEN THE CONFIGURATIONS

The second step in the development of the life cycle model is to consider the likely transitions between the various configurations. A total of 36 transitions are conceivable (each of the six to the other five as well as to a different form of itself, as when one leader replaces another in autocracy). Examples of all 36 can easily be found. A reading of the transitions described in the research as well as practitioner literature suggests, however, that some may be more common than others. For example, there is a good deal of evidence on the transition from the instrument to the closed system in business firms as they grow and their stockholding becomes dispersed (Berle & Means, 1968). Indeed, Moyer (1970) and Pfeffer and Salancik (1978) suggest that growth may be a strategy pursued deliberately to disperse shareholding, that is, to pacify the external coalition. Examples of the opposite transition can, of course, be found, but they seem to be less common.

A life cycle model, in the terms introduced so far in this paper, would describe and justify a sequence, or a small number of sequences, of configurations, from the establishment of organizations to their demise. In other words, it would order the transitions in some logical pattern. Such a model would rely on the most common transitions in order to maximize its explanatory power, but it would also have to justify its choices of some transitions over others.

The prime difference between the transitions that appeared to be rather common and the others seems to lie in the nature of the forces causing each. The less common transitions appear to be driven by forces *external* to the configuration itself or the organization's stage of development. For example, a new technology may cause the shifting of power in an organization from an entrenched group of administrators to some new group of experts—in other words, it drives a closed system towards a meritocracy. The most common transitions, in contrast, seem to be driven by a very different set of forces, ones *intrinsic* to the nature of the

configuration itself and the organization's particular stage of development. To be more specific, each of the power configurations appears to contain forces working to destroy it from within—each, in other words, seems to sow the seeds of its own destruction. And this destruction seems also to dictate the likely transition(s) (assuming that the organization itself, as opposed to its configuration of power, survives). For example, when repeated instances occur of autocracies faltering because of their reliance on a single leader (who dies, leaves, or loses touch as the organization grows), then centralization and precariousness would seem to be intrinsic destructive forces in this configuration. And when external influencers appear with frequency to save the organization, by taking power over it, then the transition to the instrument configuration, as a means to reduce precariousness, would seem to be at least one natural transition for the autocracy.

A wide variety of external forces can occur, inducing any conceivable transition from one configuration to another. Such transitions therefore cannot be predicted, at least not by studying the organization itself. From its perspective, such changes are idiosyncratic, and consequently cannot be used to build a life cycle model.

The intrinsic forces, in contrast, would seem to be fewer and more orderly in their effect. Specifically, in the absence of external forces, these intrinsic ones should enable us to predict transitions (or, in the presence of external forces, at least to predict transitions in populations of organizations statistically). And by combining these likely transitions over time, from the inception of organizations to their demise, one should be able to produce a

model of organization life cycles.

Of the 36 possible transitions, 9 appeared to be most common and most readily explained by intrinsic destructive forces. Another two, perhaps somewhat less common, also seemed to be driven by intrinsic forces but countered by other intrinsic forces. These are listed below (with the last two shown in parentheses), with the reasons for their choice given in the next section.

Autocracy	→ Instrument
Autocracy	→ Missionary
Autocracy	→ Meritocracy
Instrument	→ Closed system
Missionary	→ Closed system
Closed System	→ Closed system
Meritocracy	→ Meritocracy
Closed system	→ Political arena (in stable form)
Meritocracy	→ Political arena (in stable form)
(Autocracy	→ Closed system)
(Political arena	→ Autocracy)

A LIFE CYCLE MODEL

In the nine main transitions listed above, a sequence of the various configurations of organizational power is evident. As noted earlier, it is this sequence that defines the model of organization life cycles presented in this paper.

First, no configuration is shown leading to autocracy. And autocracy is the only configuration shown leading to more than one configuration different from itself. The implication is that this configuration belongs at the beginning of the life cycle model, giving rise to different paths of development. In contrast, following all the possible sequences leads eventually to a stable form of the political arena. Hence this configuration appears to belong at the end of the life cycle (assuming, of course, that the organization itself survives all the stages and negotiates all the necessary transitions). The other configurations appear to fall into intermediate stages, the instrument and missionary earlier, the closed system and the meritocracy later. Four stages thus are suggested in all. As illustrated in Figure 1, these are labeled formation (as autocracy), development (as instrument or missionary), maturity (as closed system or meritocracy), and decline (as political arena). The nine main transitions are shown as solid lines, with the two others indicated by dotted lines. Along some of these lines (as well as at the end of the model) are shown what the model hypothesizes to be transitory, unstable states of the political arena—confrontations or shaky alliances during transitions (often, in fact, inducing them). Although decline and

eventual demise are shown as the last stage of the model, the propensity of certain of the configurations to cause the demise of an organization in an earlier stage also is indicated, in the form of two parallel lines.

Before describing the model in detail, one point should be made about its tone. All theory necessarily simplifies and so distorts reality. The social world is full of nuances; in theorizing, one ignores much of this in order to comprehend what seem to be its leading tendencies. In answer to the question whether these configurations of power exist, the answer must be yes and no: no, because no organization is ever as simple as an ideal type; yes, for any configuration that reflects a leading tendency in some organizations at certain points in their development. Thus, when autocracy is described as the likely configuration at the founding of an organization,

strong leadership is simply being identified as a leading tendency in new organizations, just as the description of the political arena in a final stage is meant to suggest that spent organizations seem to experience a good deal of political activity. Autocracy and political arena are simply labels for these leading tendencies—labels, used to develop the model. Moreover, it should be emphasized that this model is just one among the many that are possible, based on one particular line of argument developed by an individual with a particular perspective. It is proposed as much to stimulate inquiry into issues believed to be important in contemporary society as to try to capture some of the reality of organizations.

Formation as Autocracy

Consider the conditions at the very outset of an organization. It presumably has a mission and some

---

FIGURE 1

A Model of Organization Life Cycles

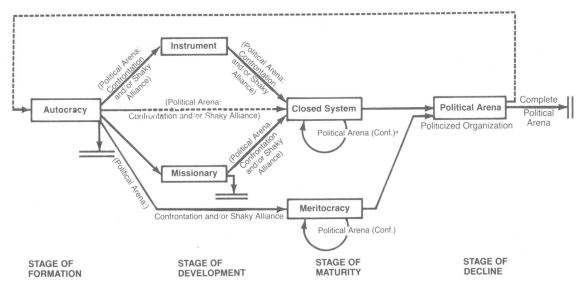

ªPossibly to autocracy temporarily
= Signifies demise of the organization

resources to draw upon, but it likely has little else—no existing structure, standards, internal ideology, or facilities. It may have a founding leader, or else someone to appoint that leader, but it is not likely to have any other full time members.

It is, in fact, typically the job of the founding leader to create the initial structure, acquire the facilities, and, above all, hire the first employees (or attract the initial volunteers). In the absence of established institutional procedures and beliefs, power tends, as a result, to focus personally on the leader. Moreover, potential external influencers may be inclined to leave the new organization alone: excessive demands at the outset, when the organization is most vulnerable, could destroy it. Hence the internal coalition of the new organization may very well be personalized and its external coalition passive, giving rise to the autocracy configuration.

This initial period of autocracy may not last long, however. The first experts hired, for example, may draw off much of the leader's personal power and so encourage a transition toward meritocracy. Or, if there is much repetition in the operations, procedures may become established after a short time, and so induce a transition towards a form of bureaucracy, as instrument or closed system.

There are factors, however, that encourage the endurance of the initial autocracy configuration. For one thing, forceful leaders often are relied on to set up new organizations, to ensure their creation on firm foundations. Concurrently, strong-willed individuals are attracted to the leadership of new organizations, in which they can have considerable latitude to act. Moreover, founding leaders have unique opportunities to build organizations to enhance their own influence—to establish procedures and norms that reinforce their personal styles of management, to hire employees loyal to themselves, and so on.

Thus, it is not uncommon for organizations to retain an autocracy configuration throughout their founding leaders' tenure in office, sometimes for decades and sometimes despite strong forces for transition to another configuration. A classic case of this appeared in the Ford Motor Company, whose founder retained his strong system of personalized (and in this case, truly "autocratic") control right up to his death and, consequently, almost destroyed the results of a lifetime of work.

 **LEARNING CHECKPOINT**

In autocracy would a strategic contingency model be of any value in explaining power and how it evolves?

Transitions to Development Stage

Organizations as autocracies tend to be precarious ones for a number of reasons. Many are young, and so not firmly established; they typically are small (because personalized control is difficult to maintain in a large organization); and, above all, they rely for management on a single individual. One heart attack can literally wipe out their prime coordinating mechanism. Or, if the leader on whom they are so reliant loses touch, there may be no one else to step in—no insider with the knowledge or will to confront the leader, no outsider active enough to care. Hence, many organizations die as autocracies, indicated in Figure 1 by the first two parallel lines. Indeed, the death of the organization may be the most natural transition for autocracy, the forces destroying it inherent in its own makeup.

Often, however, precariousness seems to kill the configuration rather than the organization. When autocracy proves unstable, the organization is driven to another configuration. Of the five that remain in the framework, it is believed that transition to three of them is most likely, because of forces intrinsic in autocracy itself, and to a fourth somewhat less so because of intrinsic forces that both promote and counter it.

The most natural transition for the autocracy configuration may be to the missionary, at least after the departure of a charismatic leader. Founding leaders of organizations often are highly charismatic individuals. When they depart, there may be a natural tendency for those who remain to consolidate and institutionalize that charisma in the form of "sagas," norms, and traditions (Clark, 1970, 1972), thereby coalescing around an ideology and so effecting a transition to the missionary. (Or, to look at this the other way, before an organization can emerge as an egalitarian missionary, it may require a period of strong, charismatic leadership in order to establish its ideology.) Left on their own, that may be inclined to happen to many autocracies after the departure of charismatic founders.

But many are not left on their own. (And many are not founded by charismatic leaders in the first place.) Being vulnerable after the departure of their founders, or even during their founders' reign, they become prime candidates for takeover and fall prey to external influences (as Perrow, 1970, describes the fate of the maverick shipping company). Some even seek the protective umbrella of an external influencer, as when an aging entrepreneur or the heir sells the company to a conglomerate firm to ensure its financial health. Of course, an external influencer who commissioned the founding of an organization in the first place, and who waited patiently through an initial stage of autocracy, will eventually move in to consolidate one's power. In all of these cases, the external influencers consolidate their power by instituting bureaucratic controls through a subservient management, thereby rendering organizations as their instruments. Thus, a second natural and probably more common transition is hypothesized: *Many autocracies tend to become instruments, usually because of their own inherent precariousness.*

The transition from autocracy to missionary is likely to be smooth so long as no external influencer interrupts it, but transition to the instrument can involve conflict. A founding leader in personal control of an organization is apt to fight an external attempt at takeover. So, too, the other insiders, on the departure of a charismatic leader, likely will resist any attempt by outsiders to render the organization their instrument, because that usually means replacing the budding ideology by bureaucratic controls. Larcon and Reitter (1978, 1979) describe the employees of an elite French furniture manufacturer who resisted attempts by the American parent to consolidate power bureaucratically and convert the firm to conventional mass production. The two sides in the conflict may battle outright until one dominates, perhaps reaching an implicit alliance for a time to avoid destroying the organization altogether (as when a conglomerate retains temporarily a firm's leader after a hos-

tile takeover). Thus, as shown in Figure 1, it is hypothesized, that *the transition from autocracy to instrument may be accompanied by an intermediate, and probably unstable and so brief, period of political arena, in the form of confrontation and/or shaky alliance.* But once the transition is complete, the organization likely will settle down to the relative calm and stability of its role as instrument, with its power firmly lodged in its external coalition.

Not all autocracies become instruments or missionaries, however. *Another possible transaction for the autocracy is to the closed system,* although this is considered less likely because of the presence of opposing intrinsic forces, and so is shown by a dotted line in Figure 1. In this case, the administrators as a group succeed the single leader as the center of power. Government dictatorships, for example, often are followed by such bureaucratic regimes, as in the Soviet Union after Stalin. The same thing often happens after an entrepreneur has personally built a large corporation, or an autocratic labor leader, a large utilitarian union (Tannenbaum, 1965; Wilensky, 1961). All of these examples suggest a prime condition under which this transition to the closed system might be expected to override a transition to the missionary or the instrument: when an organization has grown sufficiently large under personalized leadership to have an already established administrative structure. Indeed, the growth of such a structure often involves conflict before the leader departs—between personal and bureaucratic controls. And on the leader's departure, different administrators may vie for the leadership or may confront external influencers seeking to take over the organization.

Hence, it is hypothesized that *there is the probable appearance of the political arena, in the form of a shaky alliance and/or confrontation, during the transition from autocracy to the closed system.*

This transition of autocracy to the closed system configuration is considered to be less likely than transition to the missionary or instrument, however, because one force in autocracy tends to oppose it: the predominance of personalized power itself. The leader who controls an organization personally can take various steps to avoid such conflict with administrators—one can keep the organization small (so that it will have little need for administrators), leave as soon as more elaborate administration becomes necessary (and so encourage an early transition to another configuration), or simply refuse to allow the development of a strong administration despite the growth of the organization. Each of these steps would encourage an eventual transition to the instrument or the missionary rather than directly to the closed system.

One other transition is likely for autocracy, under one particular condition. It is hypothesized that *when an organization is highly dependent on technical skills and knowledge, a rather early transition to the meritocracy configuration is to be expected.* Given the need for such expertise, the period of autocracy is likely to be relatively brief, because experts often assume considerable power soon after they have settled into place in a new organization. Medical doctors, for example, bring their knowledge and skills with them to the job; thus a new hospital may be ready to function much like an older one soon after it has been established. This stands in contrast to the organization that does not depend on trained experts, and so must work out many of its own procedures, thereby prolonging its stage of formation. Again, it is hypothesized that *the transition from autocracy to meritocracy may be accomplished by a form of the political arena.* Experts intent on taking over power quickly may confront a founding leader in no rush to surrender personalized control, or the two may form a shaky alliance for a time.

Maturity as Political Arena or Meritocracy

So far, organizations have been described as forming as autocracies and typically developing as missionaries or instruments, unless growth or expertise induced direct transition to the closed system or meritocracy instead.

What should happen next to those organizations that developed as missionaries or instruments? Essentially the same thing that happened more directly to the autocracies that grew large: it is hypothesized that *assuming they survive and continue to develop, both instruments and missionaries tend to be drawn eventually to the closed system power configuration.* Another way to express this is that as organizations develop, their procedures tend to become routinized as formal standards, their administrators tend to augment their own power (even in the face of concentrated external influence), and the full time insiders in general come to think of the organization increasingly as a vehicle to serve themselves rather than serving some outsider or some noble mission.

The instrument configuration, as noted earlier, can be maintained only if the dominant external influencer is able to exercise control without having to manage the organization. But two sets of forces

make this arrangement inherently vulnerable. First are those that encourage the dispersal of external influence, including the very growth of the organization itself (Berle & Means, 1968; Michels, 1915). Second are the forces that discourage the external surveillance of internal performance. Surveillance of this kind takes energy, but external influencers are external precisely because they have only limited energy to devote to the organization. Some run out of energy, others lose interest (as in the case of heirs to business firms who do not take the trouble to exercise their legal control; Mace, 1971). Moreover, the growth and development of an organization complicates the external surveillance of it (Moyer, 1970).

The organization as instrument must, as described earlier, develop an administrative apparatus to operationalize the goals imposed on it by its dominant external influencer. This consolidates internal power in the hands of administrators, who are supposed to use it in the interests of the external influencer. But when external surveillance slackens, and as established administrators naturally seek to enhance their own power, they become increasingly inclined to exploit their direct control of decision making for their own purposes. They may even try to pacify the external coalition by dispersing the power of its dominant influencer. Moyer (1970), for example, describes how managers of corporations can use a strategy of diversification to diffuse shareholding, and Pfeffer and Salancik (1978) describe how the power of important clients and suppliers can be weakened through vertical integration as well as diversification.

Any force that enhances the power of administrators at the ex-

pense of external influencers encourages a transition to the closed system. Indeed, such a transition is facilitated because it requires no change in internal coalition. That coalition continues to be dominated by the system of bureaucratic controls; only new goals need be plugged in at the top by which the organization as a system can be better served. Classic examples of this transition are the closely-held American business corporations that became widely held (Berle & Means, 1968), and as a result came to favor the goal of growth over that of profit (Donaldson, 1963; Galbraith, 1967; Monsen, Chieu & Cooley, 1968).

Missionaries seem inclined to undergo the same transition, but because of somewhat different intrinsic forces. First, time tends to blunt strong ideology, converting enthusiasm into obligation, traditions into dogmas, norms into rules. Excitement diminishes as unrealistic expectations are not met, or realistic ones are. The forces of bureaucracy come to challenge those of ideology. Second is the rise of administrative influence as the organization develops. Every organization requires administrators. But as Selznick (1952) points out, the ideological organization must find ways to maintain discipline without emphasizing administrative authority, because that threatens its egalitarian nature. The Israeli kibbutzim, for example, rotate people in administrative positions. But the development of the organization, as pointed out in the discussion of transitions from the autocracy, naturally reinforces administrative influence. Status differences thus arise between managers and workers, hierarchy is reinforced, and a transition toward the closed system is encouraged. In his study of radical European political parties and labor unions early in this century, Michels (1915) was so convinced about the inevitability of this transition that he described it under the label "the iron law of the oligarchy."

Of course, not all missionaries survive long enough to make this transition. As both Selznick (1952) and Niv (1978) point out, every missionary sits on a knife edge between isolation and assimilation.

Isolation may be one way to protect the ideology from contamination, but it threatens the survival of the organization. According to the evidence Niv presents, many such organizations run out of resources and/or members and die as missionaries (an eventuality shown by the second two parallel lines in Figure 1). Even among those able to survive with protected ideologies, there is the danger of displacement of missionary zeal by personal needs ("prayers are cut short . . . to leave more time for square dances," Etzioni, 1964, p. 13), which amounts to an equivalent transition toward the closed system configuration. For a number of examples, see Sills (1957) and Gussfield (1957).

As for assimilation, that exposes the ideology to outside forces and the organization itself to the strong tendencies in society to bureaucratize structure—to cede to what can be called "the imperatives of administration" (Mintzberg, Otis, Shamsie, & Waters, 1983). Indeed, organizations intent on the systematic pervasive spread of their missions may have to develop elaborate administrative apparatuses to secure the necessary resources and achieve the necessary scale, although the cost, in terms of lost inspiration, may be high. Thus, just as charisma is institutionalized into ideology through the transition from autocracy to missionary, so

too ideology—normative control—can later be institutionalized into bureaucratic control through the transition from missionary to the closed system.

Despite all these natural pressures, it is hypothesized, that *the transition from both the instrument and the missionary to the closed system is likely to involve a form of the political arena.* When administrators seek power in the face of either a dominant external influencer or some members at least who remain committed to an ideology, the two sides are likely to engage each other in brief periods of confrontation or else to form a shaky alliance during a period of transition (Hirschman, 1970, p. 93).

Thus the discussion leads to the conclusion that in the absence of external forces, organizations that survive and grow are inclined to end up as closed systems when they are fully developed, unless the need for expertise draws them to the meritocracy configuration instead. But meritocracy, in fact, appears to represent a variation on the same theme as the closed system. Both configurations serve to seal the organization off in good part from external influence, and to concentrate power in the hands of insiders who, while using it to enhance the pursuit of the organization's mission, also exploit much of it to serve themselves. In one case it is the administrators who gain the power, in the other it is the experts—which group it is depends on how much technical expertise the organization requires. But the consequences are not so very different. Indeed, these two configurations appear to be the most stable of the six, presumably because of the difficulty of displacing the power of administrators or experts who are firmly entrenched.

Thus both are seen as very enduring configurations, organizations being able to sustain themselves in these states for long periods of time. That is why they are shown in parallel in Figure 1 under the stage called "maturity."

There may be one other intrinsic force that explains the duration of these two configurations—their capacity to renew themselves after they stagnate. As shown by the loops under each in Figure 1, it is hypothesized that *a common and natural transition for both the closed system and the meritocracy is to a different and renewed state of itself, through the confrontation form of political arena.*

The meritocracy typically houses various kinds of experts. As significant changes take place in its need for expertise, newer experts are able to challenge more established ones to displace them in the pecking order of power (Galbraith, 1971). The configuration remains; only the ranking of the actors changes. In like manner, power in the closed system concentrates not on a single administrator but on a group of them. Those at the center of power may get used to pursuing given strategies with standard procedures in the absence of concentrated external influence, and so lose touch with the environment when it changes. As Salancik and Pfeffner note, "The more institutionalized power is within an organization, the more likely an organization will be out of place with the realities it faces" (1977, p. 19). But the organization can renew itself when junior administrators replace senior ones. Because the closed system contains no natural means of succession, other than for the established leaders to name their own successors, politics emerges as the natural means to displace an ineffective leadership. In just such a context, Zald and Berger (1978) describe a form of "organizational coup d'état," staged by a group of young Turks. [Also see Weber, in Gerth and Mills, (1958).] These authors note that the coup d'état retains the structure—and, in effect, the power configuration—changing only those who fill its senior positions. For an extended discussion of the role of political activities among administrators and experts in changing established organizations, see Pettigrew (1973) and Mumford and Pettigrew (1975).

Sometimes radical change in strategy is necessary after such a change in leadership in order to renew the closed system. But its internal coalition, being bureaucratic, tends to resist such change. Thus, the organization may have to revert to autocracy for a brief time, suspending bureaucratic procedures to allow its new leader to exercise personal control to force in the necessary changes (Mintzberg, 1979, p. 347). The fully developed organization normally cannot tolerate such personal control for long, however, with the result that once the necessary strategic changes have been made, strong forces likely will arise for a return to a bureaucratic internal coalition and the closed system configuration (and, possibly, for another change of leadership, to rid the organization of personalized control). Miller and Friesen (1980a) provide evidence on the high frequency with which change in leadership accompanies radical change in strategy.

It is believed that the other configurations lack the same capacity for self-renewal, for different reasons. The leader of autocracy can easily lose touch as well, but the rest of the organization as well as the external coalition often is too weak to produce anyone willing or able to displace the leader (in the context of autocracy, at least). In the instrument, it is separation of control of management (power from knowledge) that can impede self-renewal, although the dominant external influencer certainly is in a position to replace the chief executive at will. As for the missionary, self-renewal is discouraged because strong ideology tends to be sacrosanct. A missionary may be predisposed to changing the world, but seldom itself. Stagnation in each of these configurations, therefore, seems more likely to lead to the demise of the organization (particularly in the autocracy and missionary) or else to a transition to another configuration. Thus, the autocracy, missionary, and instrument are likely to be shorter lived configurations, on average, than the closed system and meritocracy. In life cycle terms, the stages of the former might be described as equivalent to childhood for the autocracy and adolescence for the missionary and the instrument, compared with maturity or adulthood for the closed system and meritocracy.

Decline in the Form of Political Arena

What happens to the mature organization? Does it simply carry on, periodically renewing itself? Or does it falter eventually, and disappear? And if so, how? The discussion so far certainly has had a degree of speculation, although certain support has been available for many of the hypotheses. At this point, however, the empirical evidence on organizational demise becomes even more sparse, and the degree of speculation necessarily increases.

The first point on demise is that although the stage of maturity can be long—supported by the capacity of closed systems and meritocracies to renew themselves repeatedly—it is likely to end eventually. Every system at some point has to weaken whether because of internal inadequacies or external pressures (or, more likely, both together). The second point is that demise is unlikely to come in the form of closed system or meritocracy. An organization with one of these configurations is too established, too stable, and, especially in the case of the closed system, too powerful. [One form of meritocracy, previously referred to as operating adhocracy—Mintzberg (1979)—may be an exception because of its need to maintain a steady stream of incoming ad hoc projects.] Something therefore would be expected to drive the organization to another configuration, which in turn weakens it.

LEARNING CHECKPOINT

Would whistle-blowing be more prevalent in an organization that is in a state of decline? Why?

Continuing the line or argument, some intrinsic forces must arise in each of these configurations to sow the seeds of its own destruction and effect a transition. In both the closed system and the meritocracy, it is believed that the forces of destruction lie in their own detachment from external influence. To paraphrase Lord Acton, their absolute power tends eventually to corrupt them absolutely.

As the closed system gets larger and more powerful, there may be a natural tendency for its members to become more indulgent in their use of its power, more arrogant about their own influence. This can bring them into increasing conflict with one another—for example, over the distribution of the surpluses—and thereby begin to politicize the internal coalition. Moreover, this behavior is likely to attract the attention of external influencers, who may begin to question the legitimacy of the whole configuration of power. They may form different pressure groups to challenge the insiders—much as Ralph Nader and his associates have repeatedly challenged General Motors—which gradually would tend to divide the external coalition and create conflict between the external and internal coalitions. Hence it is hypothesized that *the eventual transition for the closed system no longer able to renew itself is likely to be to the political arena, in the form of the politicized organization* (i.e., pervasive and moderate conflict). Blumberg (1971), for example, describes the gradual politicization of the giant American corporation in much this way.

It is hypothesized further that *the same type of transition might eventually be expected from the meritocracy no longer able to renew itself.* This, too, is a power configuration predicated on the influence of an elite group of insiders who control the organization. Relatively free of the constraints of external influencers and even, to a large extent, administrative controls, the experts also can become more indulgent in the use of their power—for example, treating clients callously and ignoring the needs of the organization itself. This can easily politicize the internal coalition, which in meritocracy tends to be on the verge of that state in any event. And as the system of politics begins to displace that or expertise in the internal coalition, various external influencers, concerned about the performance of

the organization and the behavior of its experts, may become more active. The external coalition may thereby become divided, and because the internal experts are likely to resist external influence, conflict can arise between the two coalitions. Again, the result would be a transition to the political arena configuration, in the moderate, enduring form labelled here as the politicized organization.

What happens to the organization that has adopted this form of power configuration? Can it escape its pervasive politics? Does it meet an early demise? In the most common case, the inclination is to suggest a negative answer to both questions. In showing the renewal loops under both the closed system and the meritocracy earlier, it was argued in effect that both of these configurations can escape temporary states of intense politics (the form of political arena labelled confrontation). Indeed, it was argued that politics is a force that arises to renew each of these configurations. But the politicized organization form of political arena is different. Here the politics is moderate but pervasive, infiltrating both coalitions as well as the relationships between the two of them. Politics, in other words, captures the organization and its immediate environment, and it thereby becomes a way of functioning—of working out relationships and making decisions—for example, through bargaining instead of calculation or individual judgment (Thompson & Truden, 1964). And once a well developed and long established organization has been so captured—in other words, once it has attracted a variety of conflicting external influencers and allowed its internal influencers to get used to pursuing their needs through politics—it may never be able to escape. Which of

the giant and highly politicized organizations in contemporary society—in government or out—is ever likely to escape conflict? Which of their major groups of influencers—internal or external—is ever likely to leave them alone?

By the same token, given the established positions of these organizations, and the only moderate conflict pervading them, their demise is not likely to come quickly either, despite their inherent inefficiencies. Indeed, politics can very well sustain them, as they exploit the privileged positions they developed as closed systems or meritocracies to support themselves artificially, or politically—that is, through contacts and influence rather than efficient pursuit of mission, as Perrow (1970), for example, describes the behavior of Consolidated Edison of New York. As Pfeffer and Salancik note, "Large organizations, because they are interdependent with so many other organizations and with so many people, such as employees and investors, are supported by society long after they are able to satisfy demands efficiently" (1978, p. 131). The expected result is that the stage of politicized organization can be rather enduring, especially in cases in which performance is difficult to measure yet support tends to come on a self-perpetuating basis, as in the case of a regulating agency funded by government.

But to say that the state of moderate, pervasive politics tends to be enduring is not to deny the possibility—indeed the likelihood *eventually*—of organizational demise. Few organizations seem to survive several generations, and hardly any, like the Catholic Church, span different eras of history.

The demise of the politicized organization, it is believed, stems from decline of the organization's privileged position and specifically from the loss of any means of artificial support. No organization, in this writer's view, can sustain pervasive conflict without some form of these; and no organization can retain these forever. It is hypothesized that *once an organization captured by pervasive conflict loses its privileged position and/or its artificial means of support, it is most likely to make a transition to the complete form of political arena (intense and pervasive conflict), followed quickly by its demise.* That is to say, once demise becomes imminent, the pervasive conflict is likely to intensify—as influencers seek to protect their own interests and to gain a final share in the spoils—and this breaks down the organizational process completely. Thus it is believed that the complete political arena not only arises when organizational death approaches, but that it also serves to kill the organization decisively.

This argument is not meant to close the door on renewal entirely. Some organizations do manage to pull themselves out of a state of pervasive conflict and renew themselves, like the legendary Phoenix that arises from its own ashes every five hundred years to begin a new cycle. In this case, it is hypothesized that *organization renewal, where possible after a stage of politicized organization, is likely to begin with autocracy.* The main reason for this claim is that it takes very strong leadership to effect such a renewal. Much as in the case of new organizations, renewed organizations need strong leaders who can create new structures, hire new people, and rid the organization of established procedures. Such leaders tend to consolidate power around themselves personally. Moreover, as Hamblin (1958) has demonstrated under laboratory condi-

tions, autocracy seems to be the configuration best suited to the resolution of crisis, because of its tightly centralized power. And conflict almost to the point of demise certainly means crisis. In other words, a leader with near absolute power to effect change likely represents the greatest hope—if not the only hope—of renewing an organization captured by conflict. But the task is considered to be such a difficult one that the loop in Figure 1 from the political arena back to autocracy is shown as a dotted line, to suggest that the demise of the politicized organization is a more likely eventuality.

LIFE CYCLES IN A WORLD OF ORGANIZATIONS

This model is presented to suggest leading tendencies in some organizations, not definite occurrences in all of them. Reality is always more complex than its description on paper. Such description labels, and thereby oversimplifies and distorts, but that should not detract from the help it offers in comprehending the reality.

The model suggests that as organizations survive and develop, their power systems tend to become more diffuse, more complex, more ambiguous, and at some point, less functional, even though, ironically, more stable. Present in most if not all organizations are a number of tendencies—deference to leadership, support of mission, service to external constituency, protection of themselves as systems (or at least of their own members), and conflict among their different actors. But it is also believed that many organizations pass through series of power stages, each relatively stable in nature (although brought on by brief periods of instability), during which various of

these tendencies are more prominent than others. The early stages seems to be characterized by more focused forms of power, the later ones by more dispersed forms. Strong leadership seems often to be a leading tendency at the outset, enabling organizations to establish themselves (although making them precarious). Once established, many organizations seem to become more responsive to external service, either directly through the catering to an identifiable constituency or indirectly through the enthusiastic pursuit of mission. Here organizations would *seem* to be serving society most effectively. Not long after, however, many seem to turn inward. Leadership does not disappear, nor does service to external constituency or pursuit of mission, but a certain tendency to serve the organization as a system unto itself, or at least to serve its elite members (whether administrators or experts), may become prominent. This would seem to represent the beginning of a certain corruption, but it also can be a time when the organization is in fact able to serve society most broadly. Society pays a price for organizations that serve themselves and their key members, but it also extracts from them services on a scale it cannot expect from other organizations. Unfortunately, however, the process of corruption may continue, so that eventually a new tendency may become prominent—namely, conflict among a wide variety of insiders and outsiders who wish to use the organization for their own purposes. Leadership, service to external constituency or to mission, even service to the system itself, all get displaced somewhat by conflict, to the detriment of performance. The demise of the organization then is to be expected.

The implication of this model

is that once established, organizations peak in their service to society and then begin to decline. Applying the model to a population of organizations, one therefore would expect a healthy society to be one that sustains a steady level of replacement of old, spent organizations by young, energetic ones.

Unfortunately the present society seems to be one that distorts this process. It seems to be one of giant organizations, many of them sustained by artificial or political means. That is to say, it seems to be increasingly dominated by closed systems and political arenas, many of them supported by distortions in markets, by the power of mass communication, by arrangements they have established with each other, or by governments fearful of the consequences of their demise. Such organizations are sustained perhaps because people are caught in the web of the organizations' (and their own) power or perhaps in the hope that organizations will somehow be able to renew themselves. The model suggests, however, that this may be a false hope. It suggests further that, in a population of organizations, sustenance of these organizations can distort the life cycle process, creating an excess of older organizations, bunched up at the end of the process, that monopolize the resources needed to create new ones.

Yet even if renewal were possible, it is questionable whether that would be the most desirable course. The mythical Phoenix may arise in the freshness of youth; the real organization does not. Legacies remain, which influence behavior. The organization may be wiser for its experiences, but it also must be wearier.

It is an irony of contemporary society that older organizations de-signed to serve themselves as systems are so stable and those captured by conflict so protected, while younger organizations that respond to creative leadership or that exhibit strong sense of mission are inherently so vulnerable, and so unfashionable. Today it almost seems wrong to believe in what is produced, as opposed to how, or, more to the point, for whose personal benefit. Should we not be encouraging the demise of large, spent organizations, so that they can be replaced in a natural cycle of renewal by younger, smaller, less constrained and more vibrant ones? Does the society that discourages the demise of its spent organizations not risk its own demise instead? □

REFERENCES

Allison, G. T. *Essence of decision: Explaining the Cuban missile crisis.* Boston: Little, Brown, 1971.

Berle, A. A., Jr., & Means, G. C. *The modern corporation and private property.* Rev. ed. New York: Harcourt, Brace and World, 1968.

Blau, P. M., & Scott, W. R. *Formal organizations: A comparative approach.* San Francisco: Chandler, 1962.

Blumberg, P. I. The politicization of the corporation. *The Business Lawyer,* 1971, 26, 1551–1587.

Burns, T., & Stalker, G. M. *The management of innovation.* 2nd ed. London: Tavistock, 1966.

Butler, R. J., Hickson, D. J., Wilson, D. C., & Axelsson R. Organizational power, politicking and paralysis. *Organization and Administrative Sciences,* Winter 1977–78, 7, 45–59.

Chandler, A. D. *Strategy and structure.* Cambridge, Mass: M.I.T. Press, 1962.

Clark, B. R. *The distinctive college.* Chicago: Aldine, 1970.

Clark, B. R. The organizational saga in higher education. *Administrative Science Quarterly,* 1972, 17, 178–184.

Collins, O. F., & Moore, D. G. *The organization makers.* New York: Appleton, Century, Crofts, 1970.

Cressey, D. R. Achievement of an unstated organizational goal: An observation of prisons. *The Pacific Sociological Review,* Fall 1958, 1, 43–49.

Cyert, R. M., & March, J. G. *A behavioral theory of the firm.* Englewood Cliffs, N.J.: Prentice-Hall, 1963.

Donaldson, G. Financial goals: Management versus stockholders. *Harvard Business Review,* 1963, 41(3), 116–129.

Eoyang, C. K. *Differentiation and integration in communist China.* Working paper, Graduate School of Business, Stanford University, 1972.

Etzioni, A. *A comparative analysis of complex organizations.* New York: Free Press, 1961.

Etzioni, A. *Modern organizations.* Englewood Cliffs, N.J.: Prentice Hall, 1964.

Filley, A. C., & House, R. J. *Managerial process and organizational behavior.* 2nd ed. Glenview, Ill.: Scott, Foresman, 1976 (1st ed., 1969).

Galbraith, J. K. *The new industrial state.* Boston: Houghton-Mifflin, 1967.

Galbraith, J. R. Matrix organization designs. *Business Horizons,* February 1971, 14(1), 29–40.

Galbraith, J. R., & Nathanson, D. A. The role of organizational structure and process in strategy implementation. In D. E. Schendel & C. W. Hofer (Eds.) *Strategic management: A new view of business policy and planning.* Boston: Little, Brown, 1979, 249–283.

Gerth, H. H., & Mills, C. W. (Eds.), *From Max Weber: Essays in sociology.* New York: Oxford University Press, 1958.

Greiner, L. E. Evolution and revolution as organizations grow. *Harvard Business Review,* 1972, 50(4), 37–46.

Gross, E. Universities as organizations: A research approach. *American Sociological Review,* 1968, 33, 518–544.

Gussfield, J. R. The problem of generations in an organizational structure. *Social Forces,* 1957, 35, 323–330.

Hamblin, R. L. Leadership and crises. *Sociometry,* 1958, 21, 322–335.

Heydebrand, W. V. Autonomy, complexity, and non-bureaucratic coordination in professional organizations. In W. V. Heydebrand (Ed.), *Comparative organizations.* Englewood, Cliffs, N.J.: Prentice-Hall, 1973, 158–189.

Hirschman, A. O. *Exit, voice, and loyalty: Responses to decline in firms, organizations and states.* Cambridge, Mass.: Harvard University Press, 1970.

Holdaway, E. A., Newberry, J. F., Hickson, D. J., & Heron, R. P. Dimensions of organizations in complex societies: The educational sector. *Administrative Science Quarterly,* 1975, 20, 37–58.

Kanter, R. M. *Men and women of the corporation.* New York: Basic Books, 1977.

Kimberly, J. R., & Miles, R. H. *The organizational life cycle.* San Francisco: Jossey-Bass, 1980.

Larçon, J. P., & Reitter, R. Corporate identity and societal strategy. Paper presented to seminar on Societal Strategy and the Business Firm, European Institute for Advanced Studies in Management, Brussels, 1978.

Larçon, J. P., & Reitter, R. *Structures de pouvoir et identité de l'entreprise.* Millau, France: Les Editions Fernand Nathan, 1979.

Lawrence, P. R., & Lorsch, J. W. *Organization and environment.* Homewood, Ill.: Irwin, 1967.

Litterer, J. A. *The analysis of organizations.* New York: Wiley, 1965.

Mace, M. L. *Directors: Myth and reality.* Cambridge, Mass.: Division of Research, Graduate School of Business Administration, Harvard University, 1971.

McCleery, R. H. *Policy change in prison management.* East Lansing, Michigan: Michigan State University, 1957.

Michels, R. *Political parties, a sociological study of the oligarchical tendencies of modern democracy.* New York: Free Press, 1915 (translated from the Italian).

Miles, R., & Snow, C. *Organizational strategy, structure and process.* New York: McGraw-Hill, 1978.

Miller, D., & Friesen, P. Archetypes of strategy formulation. *Management Science,* 1978, 24, 921–933.

Miller, D., & Friesen, P. Momentum and revolution in organizational adaptation. *Academy of Management Journal,* 1980a, 23, 591–614.

Miller, D., & Friesen, P. Archetypes of organizational transition. *Administrative Science Quarterly,* 1980b, 25, 269–299.

Miller, D., & Friesen, P. Structural change and performance: Quantum versus piecemeal-incremental approaches. *Academy of Management Journal.* 1982a, 25, 867–892.

Miller, D., & Friesen, P. The longitudinal analysis of organizations: A methodological perspective. *Management Science,* 1982b, 28, 1013–1034.

Miller, D., & Mintzberg, H. The case for configuration. In G. Morgan (Ed.), *Beyond method: Strategies for social research,* Beverly Hills, Cal.: Sage, 1983, 57–73.

Mintzberg, H. *The structuring of organizations: A synthesis of the research.* Englewood Cliffs, N.J.: Prentice-Hall, 1979.

Mintzberg, H. *Power in and around organizations.* Englewood Cliffs, N.J.: Prentice-Hall, 1983.

Mintzberg, H., Otis, S., Shamsie J., & Waters, J. A. Strategy of design: A study of "architects in co-partnership." Paper presented at Significant Developments in Strategic Management Conference, University of Texas at Arlington, 1983.

Monsen, R. J., Chiu, J. S., & Cooley, O. E.: The effect of separation of ownership and control on the performance of the large firm. *Quarterly Journal of Economics,* 1968, 82, 435–451.

Moyer, R. C. Berle and Means revisited: The conglomerate merger. *Business and Society,* 1970, 10(2), 20–29.

Mumford, E., & Pettigrew, A. *Implementing strategic decisions.* New York: Longman, 1975.

Niv, A. *Survival of social innovation: The case of communes.* Working paper, the Jerusalem Institute of Management, Tel Aviv, 1978.

Olson, M., Jr. *The logic of collective action: Public goods and the theory of groups.* Cambridge, Mass.: Harvard University Press, 1965.

Olson, M., Jr. A theory of groups and organizations. In B. M. Russett (Ed.), *Economic theories of international politics.* Chicago: Markham, 1968, 139–147.

Perrow, C. *Organizational analysis: A sociological view.* New York: Wadsworth, 1970.

Pettigrew, A. M. *The politics of organizational decision-making.* London: Tavistock, 1973.

Pfeffer, J., & Salancik, G. R. *The external control of organizations: A resource dependence perspective.* New York: Harper and Row, 1978.

Pondy, L. R. Effects of size, complexity and ownership on administrative intensity. *Administrative Science Quarterly,* 1969, 14, 47–60.

Pugh, D. S., Hickson, D. J., Hinings, C. R., & Turner, C. The context of organization structures. *Administrative Science Quarterly,* 1969, 14, 97–114.

Reimann, B. C. On the dimensions of bureaucratic structure: An empirical reappraisal. *Administrative Science Quarterly,* 1973, 18, 462–476.

Rhenman, E. *Organization theory for long-range planning.* New York: Wiley, 1973.

Rosner, M. *Principal types and problems of direct democracy in the Kibbutz.* Givat Haviva, Israel: Working paper, Social Research Center on the Kibbutz, 1969.

Rumelt, R. P. *Strategy, structure, and economic performance.* Boston: Division of Research, Graduate School of Business Administration, Harvard University, 1974.

Russell, B. *Power: A new social analysis.* London: George Allen and Unwin, 1938.

Salancik, G. R., & Pfeffer, J. Who gets power—And how they hold on to it: A strategic-contingency model of power. *Organizational Dynamics.* 1977, 5(3), 3–21.

Sampson, A. *The sovereign state of ITT.* New York: Stein and Day, 1973.

Samuel, Y., & Mannheim, B. F. A multidimensional approach toward a typology of bureaucracy. *Administrative Science Quarterly,* 1970, 15, 216–228.

Scott, B. R. *Stages of corporate development, Part I.* Working paper, Harvard Business School, 14-371-294;

BP993, 1971.

Selznick, P. *The organizational weapon: A study of Bolshevik strategy and tactics.* New York: McGraw-Hill, 1952.

Sills, D. L. *The volunteers.* New York: Free Press, 1957.

Starbuck, W. H., Organizational growth and development. In J. G. March (Ed.), *Handbook of organizations.* Chicago: Rand-McNally, 1965, 451–533.

Tannenbaum, A. S. Unions. In J. G. March (Ed.), *Handbook of organizations.* Chicago: Rand-McNally, 1965, 710–763.

Thoenig, J. C. & Friedberg, E. The power of the field staff: The case of the ministry of public works, urban affairs and housing in France. In A. F. Leemans (Ed.), *The management of change in government.* The Hague: Martinus Nijoff, 1976, 314–337.

Thompson, J. D., & Truden A. Strategies, structures, and processes of organizational decisions. In H. J. Leavitt & L. R. Pondy (Eds.), *Readings in managerial psychology.* Chicago: University of Chicago Press, 1964, 496–515.

Whyte, W. F. *Organizational behavior: Theory and application.* Homewood, Ill.: Irwin-Dorsey, 1969.

Wilensky, H. L. The trade union as bureaucracy. In A. Etzioni (Ed.), *Complex organizations: A sociological reader.* New York: Holt, Rinehart and Winston, 1961, 221–234.

Woodward, J. *Industrial organization: Theory and practice.* London: Oxford University Press, 1965.

Young, M. *The rise of the meritocracy: 1870–2023.* New York: Random House, 1959.

Zald, M. N., & Berger, M. A. Social movements in organizations: Coup d'État, insurgency, and mass movements. *American Journal of Sociology*, 1978, 83, 823–861.

D1 POLITICAL ORIENTATION QUESTIONNAIRE*

	Mostly Agree	Mostly Disagree

Answer each question according to whether you mostly agree or mostly disagree, even if it is difficult for you to decide which alternative best describes your opinion.

1. Only a fool would correct a boss's mistakes.   _____   _____

2. If I have certain confidential information, I release it to my advantage.   _____   _____

3. I would be careful not to hire a subordinate who had more formal education than I.   _____   _____

4. If I do somebody a favor, I remember to cash in on it.   _____   _____

5. Given the opportunity, I would cultivate friendships with powerful people.   _____   _____

6. I like the idea of saying nice things about a rival in order to get that person transferred from my department.   _____   _____

7. Why not take credit for other people's work? They would do the same to me.   _____   _____

8. Given the chance, I would offer to help my boss build some shelves at home.   _____   _____

9. I laugh heartily at my boss's jokes, even when they are not funny.   _____   _____

---

* Source: Reprinted from Andrew DuBrin, *Human Relations: A Job Oriented Approach* (Reston, Virginia: Reston Publishing Co., 1978), Chapter 14.

10. I would be sure to attend a company picnic even if I had the chance to do something I enjoyed more that day.   _____   _____

11. If I knew an executive in my company was stealing money, I would use it against him or her in asking for favors.   _____   _____

12. I would first find out my boss's political preferences before discussing politics with him or her.   _____   _____

13. I think using memos to zap people for their mistakes is a good idea (especially when I want to show that person up).   _____   _____

14. If I wanted something done by a co-worker, I would be willing to say "If you don't get this done, our boss might be very unhappy."   _____   _____

15. I would invite my boss to a party at my house, even if I did not like him or her.   _____   _____

16. If I were in a position to, I would have lunch with the "right people" at least twice a week.   _____   _____

17. Richard M. Nixon's bugging the democratic headquarters would have been a clever idea if he had not been caught.   _____   _____

18. Power for its own sake is one of life's most precious commodities.   _____   _____

19. Having a high school named after me would be an incredible thrill.   _____   _____

20. Reading about job politics is as much fun as reading an adventure story.   _____   _____

Interpretation of Scores

Each statement you checked "Mostly Agree" is worth 1 point toward your political orientation score. A score of 16 or over suggests that you have a strong inclination toward playing politics. A high score of this nature also suggests that you have strong needs for power. Scores of 5 or less suggest that you are not inclined toward political maneuvering and that you are not strongly power driven.

This questionnaire is designed primarily for research purposes and to encourage you to think about the topic under study. The Political Orientation Questionnaire lacks the scientific properties of a validated personality or interest test.

▌② THE ROLE OF POLITICS IN ORGANIZATIONAL DECISIONS*

Rank the following organizational decisions in the order in which you believe politics would play a part. The most political should be ranked 1 and the least political should be ranked 11.

		Ranking
1.	Promotions and Transfers	_____
2.	Hiring	_____
3.	Pay	_____
4.	Budget Allocation	_____
5.	Facilities, Equipment Allocation	_____
6.	Delegation of Authority	_____
7.	Interdepartmental Coordination	_____
8.	Personnel Policies	_____
9.	Disciplinary Penalties	_____
10.	Work Appraisals	_____
11.	Grievances and Complaints	_____

▌① OCCUPATIONAL POWER: DIFFERENCES AND TACTICS

OBJECTIVES

1. To examine the power bases of various occupations.
2. To illustrate the difference in opinion about power bases.

STARTING THE EXERCISE

Step 1: 5 minutes

Individually rank the following occupations according to the overall power that they would generally possess in their organizations. Place a 1 in front of the occupation that you feel to be the most powerful in its particular organization, a 15 in front of the occupation that you feel to be the least powerful in its particular organization, and numbers 2 through 14 in front of the remaining occupations.

_____ Nurse in a hospital

_____ President of major university

_____ Chief executive officer of major firm

_____ Medical technologist in hospital

_____ Counselor in personnel unit of major firm

_____ College professor in major university

_____ Machinist in major firm

_____ Accountant in hospital

_____ District sales manager in major firm

_____ Research and Development Scientist in High-Technology Firm

_____ Police officer

_____ Navy ensign

_____ Homemaker (full time)

_____ Secretary (president's) in major firm

_____ U.S. senator

---

* Source: Adapted from Jeffrey Gandz and Robert J. Litschert, "The Experience of Workplace Politics," *Academy of Management Journal*, June 1980, pp. 237–251.

Step 2: 15 minutes
Decide which of the occupations listed would have the strongest legitimate reward, and coercive power bases. Write a 50-word report describing why you selected each of the occupations as the most powerful in each of the three categories of interpersonal power.

Step 3: 10 minutes
Select the least powerful occupation from your ranking, and develop a brief list of power and political tactics that could be used to enhance the power of this occupation.

Step 4: 15 minutes
The instructor will form small groups of four, six, or eight students to discuss the rankings, the brief reports on power bases, and the lists of power and political tactics.

Step 5: 5–10 minutes
The instructor will wrap up the session by discussing briefly the findings of the small groups.

2 POWER, POLITICS, AND MANAGERIAL SUCCESS*

OBJECTIVES

1. To confront the organizational realities of power.
2. To develop a personal perspective on the implications of power and politics for managerial success.

STARTING THE EXERCISE

1. Form into groups as directed by your instructor.
2. Read the following statement:**
3. Decide whether you agree or disagree with this statement and why. Discuss your viewpoint with others in your work group.
4. Have a spokesperson prepare to share the results of the discussion within the group with the class.
5. The instructor will request group reports and lead follow-up discussion on power, politics, and managerial success.

Most successful managers are successful because they understand how the system works and are willing and able to manipulate rules, regulations, and procedures to mobilize support and overcome opposition so that their ideas are accepted and their needs are met. Thus, power should not be construed as something negative but merely as a means of getting things done in a way that may or may not reflect purely rational decision making and a totally objective consideration of all the facts.

---

* Source: John R. Schermerhorn, Jr., James G. Hunt, and Richard N. Osborn, *Managing Organizational Behavior*, 2nd Ed. (New York: John Wiley & Sons, 1985), p. 577.
** This statement is from Keith Provan, "Power and Politics in Organizations," *The Owen Manager*, Spring/Summer 1983, p. 11.

DUMAS PUBLIC LIBRARY*

PART 1

It came as a surprise when Jeff Mallet learned of the conflict between Debra Dickenson and Helen Hendricks because he knew them both personally and regarded them both as competent administrators. Debra Dickenson, 38, was the youngest mayor in the state when she was elected three years ago, and was the first female mayor in Kimball's history. She was widely recognized for her high levels of energy and dedication. Helen Hendricks, 62, had been the head librarian at Dumas Public Library for 15 years and was widely acknowledged among Kimball citizens as being primarily responsible for the high quality of the library services to the community.

Dumas Public Library serves the citizens of Kimball, New Mexico, a town of 20,000 people in rural eastern New Mexico. Kimball is dominated by the 16,000-student state university located there and this university presence creates a rather unique clientele for the public library. The library has enjoyed a history of solid citizen support and has until recently benefited from cordial relations between the library staff and the city's administration.

The library is housed in a modern, air-conditioned structure with carpeted floors and attractive furnishings. Approximately 35,000 volumes are on the shelves. The 1978 budget, including payroll, acquisition of new books, and building maintenance, was $195,000.

The library has no formal organization. Helen Hendricks has reporting to her five full-time employees, three of whom are professional librarians. Completing the staff are 10 half-time permanent employees, 10 to 12 unpaid volunteers, and an occasional intern from the university.

The city is governed by an elected city council and mayor. Day-to-day administration is the responsibility of Ralph Riesen, the city supervisor, who is a permanent employee of the city.

Jeff Mallet, professor of management, first learned about the existence of strained relationships between the library and the city administration from Linda Turner, adult services librarian. According to Linda, feelings of distrust and animosity toward City Hall had been growing recently among the library staff. Linda was concerned about the unhealthy climate that this hostility was creating at the library.

Several weeks later Jeff had an opportunity to talk with Debra Dickenson and Ralph Riesen. Jeff said he had heard that relations between City Hall and the library were not good. Debra and Ralph confirmed that relations between the two groups had reached an intolerably low level, and they agreed something would have to be done about it. Debra and Ralph expressed bewilderment about what could be done to improve the situation. "If you have any ideas or suggestions, I'd certainly like to hear them," Debra said.

Jeff suggested that it might prove helpful to have an outsider interview members of both groups to provide some independent perspective. He volunteered his services for this purpose. Debra and Ralph readily agreed to Jeff's offer.

The next day Jeff was talking to Paul Everest, a fellow business faculty member and consultant, about the situation at the library. Jeff invited Paul to join him on the case and Paul accepted.

Next week Jeff made a series of personal visits and phone calls to the key staff members from City Hall and the library. An agreement was reached to have Jeff and Paul interview both groups and make recommendations. Appointments were made for an interview with Debra Dickenson and Ralph Riesen at City Hall, followed by one with Helen Hendricks, Linda Turner, and Maude Richardson (children's librarian) at the library.

PART 2

The View from City Hall As Told to Jeff Mallet and Paul Everest

Debra: I'm really concerned about the way things have developed between us here at City Hall and the library staff. There is animosity between these two groups, and the situation has been worse over the past few months. There's not nearly the level of cooperation that there should be.

I'll be eager to consider any suggestions that you [professors] might have for how to improve the situation. I know that something has to be done,

---

* This case was written by Mark Hammer, Professor of Management, Washington State University and Gary G. Whitney, Associate Professor of Management, University of San Diego.

and I'm willing to devote some time and effort to working on it.

The problem at the library is that I no longer have administrative control over their operations. In the past, the library has reported to the mayor through the city supervisor and that has worked reasonably well. Recently however, we discovered that legislation passed back in the 1930s makes it very clear that the library board of trustees has the legal authority for the conduct of the day-to-day operations of the library.

My concern is that since the library is a part of the city administration, the city is legally responsible for its operations. I'm talking specifically about legal liability for such things as personnel selection, equal employment opportunity regulations, purchasing guidelines, and budgeting procedures set down by the state. In the case of lawsuits and budget overruns, it seems clear to me that the city will be liable and hence we need to have administrative control over these matters. Also, it just makes good common sense for us to coordinate certain administrative functions from City Hall, such as personnel selection and budgeting. Basically the library staff agrees with us on this, and we have been doing many of these functions at City Hall.

One of the things that irks me most about Helen Hendricks [head librarian] and her staff is that they continue to insist on politicizing the budget making process, even when they know or should know that this is an extremely disruptive and unfair practice. I have made it pretty clear to all the department heads within the city that the budget making process should be one where budget requests are submitted to the city administration and to the City Council along with the implications of funding increases or decreases. Based on that input, the City Council then decides on the services that it wants in a nonemotional manner. The City Council represents the citizens and that is a perfectly democratic procedure.

Prior to the recent budget preparation period, the City Council gave budget directives to all city departments. The library board chose to ignore these directives and submitted their own budget. Subsequently, the library staff started a big political campaign to pack the council chambers at all the budget hearings with patrons of the library and other citizens who supported the library's request for more funding.

I have tried to point out to Helen how disruptive and unfair this is. The fact is that almost every city department serves some constituency and could, if they were so inclined, rally citizen support from among their clients or constituents to bring political pressure to bear on the City Council and other members of the city administration to fund their individual projects. It seems obvious to me that this is a chaotic way to try to prepare a city budget. Special interest politics has no place in the preparation of the city budget which is fair to all parties concerned. Only people who have looked at the entire city budget and have considered the total revenues available to the city and the cost and benefit tradeoffs made by each one of the city departments are in any position to judge whether any particular department is reasonably funded or not. The fact is that there are prime financial needs in all of the city departments and the library is not alone.

I support the library wholeheartedly; we all do. I'm just not one bit impressed when the librarians campaign to have a flock of citizens pack the council chambers to stand there and tell us that they support the library. That is not a helpful input to the budget making process. Everybody supports the library.

Following one occurrence of inappropriate political lobbying last fall, I expressed my annoyance to Walter Roy [chairperson of the library board of trustees]. Subsequently, Helen was told by the board to cease her lobbying activities. I think she got the message, but I know the lobbying did not stop. That tells me that the trustees do not have control over the library staff.

Don't get me wrong. Helen Hendricks has done a marvelous job down there at the library, but things just haven't been the same since her husband died unexpectedly two years ago. She seems to have retreated into a womb or something. I think she uses the library staff as a personal support group. I don't know who is running the library anymore, but it certainly isn't Helen. I think the staff is running the library to tell you the truth.

Ralph: I too have noticed the worsening relations between us and the library staff. Part of the problem may be the physical isolation of the library and the fact that they don't interact much with other city personnel. [The library is three blocks from City Hall.]

If you ask me I think there is a case of paranoia down there at the library. Some of them seem to believe that I'm out to get them. In fact, I have a definite feeling that several of the library staff members think that I'm some sort of an ogre.

I think many of the problems that the library staff think they have are more imaginary than real. I remember once I talked to Helen and she was complaining about some things. I asked her to make a list of grievances that they had, ways in which they had less money or things that weren't satisfactory. Do you know, I've never gotten any list from Helen. I really don't think they have any substantial problems that aren't of their own making.

Debra: I get the impression that the library staff feels that they are picked on and mistreated. The fact is that the library has the best working conditions of almost any other department in the city. Not only are their working conditions congenial and agreeable, but the clientele they serve are all happy and supportive of the library. It's a totally positive environment. That's quite a bit different from the city engineer's department where they have to talk to irate contractors and home owners, or the police who have to deal with drug offenders and unhappy traffic violators.

I'm still very confused about the proper roles of the library administration, the library board of trustees, and the city administration.

Ralph: Lynn King [the city Finance Director] is another player in this scenario. Lynn probably has more interaction with the library staff on a day-to-day basis than anybody else here in City Hall. She deals with them on matters of auditing, purchasing procedures, and employee selection procedures. There have been disagreements and friction generated over a number of these issues. Lynn really distrusts Helen as an administrator.

Debra: I really would like to hear from the library staff on their perceptions of what our problems are. I don't really know what they think.

One of the areas that Helen and I have had disagreements on has been that of Helen's classification within the city administrative system. Helen seems to think that she should be classified as a department director. The trouble is that Helen's responsibilities are simply not equivalent to those of other department directors within the city. Each of the other directors has at least two major administrative functions reporting to him or her. For example, the director of public safety has both police and fire reporting to him.

When we reorganized the city administration recently, we changed it so that Helen was reporting to the mayor through the director of public services, Jack Feldner. Helen got all bent out of shape that she wasn't reporting directly to the mayor and that she had to report through someone else. She made such a fuss about it that we finally agreed to her request and Ralph issued a memo of understanding to Helen to the effect that she still had direct access to us here at City Hall and that we would interact with her on a direct basis.

One of the City Council members introduced a proposal to classify Helen as a department head recently, but this proposal was withdrawn at my request. I'm afraid that as a result some people are getting the impression that I am not really supportive of the library. I really am, but my concern in this matter is with equity—all the other department directors have considerably more administrative responsibility than Helen does and they wouldn't consider it fair to have Helen classified as a department director.

Ralph: Helen keeps raising the issue of her salary level. I'm convinced that Helen is fairly paid in relation to other city employees. The trouble is that all city employees are underpaid compared to university salaries and we're *never* going to catch up. Dissatisfaction with pay is just one of those things that we have to accept and live with.

Despite what Helen says, I don't think salary is that big a problem. I remember from the supervision class that you [Jeff] taught that according to Herzberg, pay is a hygiene factor. I don't think that we're going to solve any big problems down at the library by working on hygiene factors.

Debra: An incident that happened recently will illustrate what I consider to be totally unprofessional conduct on the part of the library staff. As you know, I recently refused to reappoint Cecil Hockman to the library board of trustees after his first term expired. Now as the mayor, I have the duty and obligation to the citizens of Kimball to appoint people to boards that I think are best qualified to do the jobs. I had my reasons for not reappointing Cecil, reasons which I consider to be good. Because we are making agreements with the trustees about the administration of the library, I want trustees who will work with us to try to reach a compromise. Cecil has never agreed to any compromise action and would stop library cooperative efforts.

What happened was that somebody down at the library called a reporter and told them about my refusal to reappoint Cecil Hockman. They apparently said that I had a vendetta going against Cecil and that a reporter should look into this. The reporter did check with Mr. Hockman and got a bunch of quotes from him concerning my nonsupport for library programs. Then the reporter called me and asked me if I wanted to respond to the charges. I *was furious.* I told her, "No, I do not want to respond." I did explain my duties and responsibilities as mayor to the reporter and she subsequently decided that there was no story.

Sometimes I feel like calling Helen up here on the carpet and telling her to shape up her act or get out. It becomes clearer to me all the time that whatever else she is, Helen is not a competent administrator.

If the problems we're having with administration at the library can't be solved we are going to be forced to look at the issue of regionalization of this library; that is, of having the city library join the county system along with the library in Morton. However, it is apparent to me that the idea of regionalization is extremely threatening to everybody down at the library. This showed up recently when the Capital Expenditures Committee recommended, among other things in its report to City Council, that the feasibility of regionalization of the city's library, cemetery, and health care facilities be studied. You wouldn't believe how upset the librarians became over that recommendation. They got a City Council member to make a motion that the recommendation be deleted from the committee's report, and unfortunately it passed. The librarians clearly didn't even want the issue studied!

PART 3

The View from the Library as Told to Jeff Mallet and Paul Everest

Helen: I'm surprised and delighted to hear you [*professors*] report that Debra Dickenson and Ralph Riesen are really interested in improving relations with us here at the library. I feel that we have been wasting a lot of time down here because of the poor relations we have with City Hall, and I wasn't at all sure how concerned they felt about it up there.

One of the main problems that I see between us and the city administration is their general resentment toward anything involving political pressure.

I sense that Debra and Ralph get upset when the community voices opinions which are contrary to their views. I sometimes get the feeling that they would like to run the city without interference from citizens. However, that's the very nature of the political process. The mayor's job is inherently a political one. You shouldn't be in that position and expect to be immune from public pressure. So, I don't think it's appropriate that Debra gets upset when the citizens rally to support a program that they want.

During the recent budget hearings we have had lots of good people come to our defense. The library board of trustees have been very supportive. The AAUW [*American Association of University Women*] has several members who have been strong supporters. These friends have been instrumental in helping us make the case to the mayor and the City Council that the community really supports a quality program here at the library.

Linda: *We* don't seem to have any problems of misunderstanding or nonsupport from either the library board of trustees or the City Council. I feel good about our relations with both of these groups. When we have gone to the City Council with our recommendations and proposals, they have been sympathetic and supportive. In the budget hearings both the library board and the City Council supported our proposed budget over the objections of Debra and Ralph. In effect, we bypassed the city administration and we came out better than if we had gone to them first, as they apparently wanted us to do.

One example of a way in which we have felt "under attack" by City Hall has been the way they have acted in regard to the appointment of members of the library board of trustees.

Helen: That's right. You probably heard that just recently Debra refused to reappoint Cecil Hockman to the board for a second term. Now Cecil has been a strong, energetic supporter of the library. He has given a great deal of his time and dedication to public service on the library board. Mr. Hockman's first term on the board has just recently expired, and for no apparent reason Debra has declined to reappoint him, even though it has been customary in the past that members serve for two terms. So, Cecil Hockman is not only eligible for reappointment, but he has demonstrated in his first term that he is a dedicated and concerned public citizen.

It seems apparent to us that Debra resents anyone who supports the library as strongly as Cecil Hockman did. You see Cecil initiated some legal research which determined that the library board of trustees has the ultimate legislative authority for the administration of the library. Furthermore, Cecil Hockman took the initiative to argue our budget proposals before the City Council. Debra did not appreciate either of these, I am sure, and now it seems that she is out to get him.

In the past, I have always participated with the mayor when selecting candidates for the library board. The mayor has always been glad to have my input and opinion on which citizens would be good for the library board. None of that consultation has gone on between Debra and me recently; I just find out about her board appointments by reading the newspaper.

Linda: Another way that we have felt attacked by the city administration has been the way we were treated in the recent reorganization of the city administrative hierarchy.

Helen: What they did was to demote the library by changing the reporting patterns so that instead of reporting directly to the city supervisor, I was directed to report through Jack Feldner, the director of public services.

This reassignment of the library was a serious downgrading of our status within the city. I was really upset when I learned that they expected me to report *through* Jack Feldner. Why, I have more education than Jack does, I have longer service to the City of Kimball than he does, and I supervise a *lot* of people here at the library. The very idea that the library with its staff of professionals should be considered subordinate to someone whose main concern is parks and recreation was an appalling idea to us over here. You see, that demotes us from one of the major functional units within the city administration to merely one of the concerns of the Parks and Recreation Department. I don't have anything against Jack Feldner, but I don't think it's right to have the city library subordinate to him and his department.

I was told that in the reorganization of the city administration I was not considered an administrator [department director level] because I supervise so few people. However, Lynn King [finance director] only supervises a few people, and she doesn't have the education I do either.

Maude: I don't think that they regard us as professionals over here, but we *are* professionals. Each one of us has had five years of college plus additional professional training, and yet we continually get treated as if we were mere clerks.

Linda: An incident which illustrates the library's diminished status was City Hall's insistance that Helen could not retain the title of "library director." The title library director is common among librarians having similar jobs to Helen's. Among the staff here at the library, it seems the logical choice of position titles. And yet the city administration insisted that Helen could not be called a "director." So they suggested that we call her the "library supervisor." Of course, "supervisor" denotes someone just above the clerical level; someone who is supervising a bunch of clerks. That seems natural to them, but the idea is appalling over here. We hassled back and forth over different possible titles for Helen's position and finally settled on "city librarian." This title is less descriptive than "library director" and reflects Helen's lowered status in the city.

Maude: I don't think Helen is regarded as an administrator by the city administration. I don't think they really know how many people she has reporting to her, or how much leadership it takes to coordinate all the volunteer help we have. Helen has a substantial administrative job to keep this library running smoothly.

Helen: Going along with that is their resistance to paying me a salary reflecting my abilities and contribution. My salary is simply not in line with the requirements of this job, my education, and the experience I have with the City of Kimball. I know that I'm paid less than many other people in the city who have less education and less experience than I do. The city administration simply refuses to recognize the importance of my job.

Jeff: How would your salary compare, Helen, to other library directors having similar jobs around the state?

Helen: Well, I would have to say that my salary today reflects some very significant adjustments upward which were made during the 1960s. At that time the university was under heavy pressure to equalize the salaries of its female professionals, and the City of Kimball also upgraded their women's salaries at the same time. So I shared with some other women in some impressive gains during the 1960s.

If you looked just at the figures, my salary wouldn't look that far off relative to other city librarians. However, the figures don't reflect the quality of education I have received, the length of my service to the City of Kimball, and the contributions that I have made to the development of this library today.

Jeff: Could you give us an example or two of specific ways that the library's effectiveness has been impaired by the actions of members of the city administration?

Helen: Certainly. One good example would be the copier incident. That's a long story. Sometime ago we experienced an equipment failure with the copier which we had for patrons to use. Therefore, I asked permission from the board of trustees to allocate Kimball Fund [donated] money to purchase a new copier, and they approved. I went ahead with procedures to order a new copier. The next thing that I learned was that Debra had disallowed the purchase. She said that I should have checked with her first.

I was flabbergasted. I had never felt that I had to check with the mayor on decisions like that. Furthermore, I was angry because she had ruled on the decision without checking into what the reasons for it were. I felt "zapped" by Debra, like I have in several other situations.

It seems to me that I did the right thing by checking with my board of trustees on the decision I made. As you know, by legislation they have the responsibility for the administrative functions of the library. When they have approved a decision like this, what basis does the mayor have for interfering in our decision?

Another way that Debra has demonstrated her lack of support for the library is by advancing the idea that the library should be regionalized to become a part of the county system. Anybody who knows anything about the library regards this as a preposterous idea.

In the first place, to seriously consider the idea of regionalization you would have to undertake a rather comprehensive study of the consequences. That in itself would be a major, expensive undertaking, which I don't think Debra is ready to shoulder. It is clear to me if such a study were done, the result would overwhelmingly favor the present organizational arrangement. We have very little in common with the Morton Library, and nothing at all to be gained by being put in the county system. Kimball is a unique community with citizens who have very different expectations from those in the remainder of the county, which is largely rural. The whole idea of regionalization is so preposterous that it seems to me to be irresponsible to even advance the idea.

I get the feeling that Debra is accumulating a checklist against me. I have had a fear for sometime now that Debra could at any time try to have me fired. I get the feeling in talking to them that I'm not getting straight messages from them.

At least there's one thing to be grateful for—I just passed my 62nd birthday and can't be deprived of my pension if I am fired or forced to resign. I would like to stay on until I am 65, but the way things are going between Debra and me I never know.

I get to feeling sad and hopeless and despairing when I think about the way I'm regarded at City Hall. I think it's tragic when someone like me has given many dedicated years of service and has made major contributions to building a strong program, and then finds themselves spending their last few years in an atmosphere of distrust and unappreciation. I think I deserve better.

Linda: The distrust in our relationship shows itself practically every time we have an interaction. Recently I have taken on the duties of adult services librarian and have been out visiting members of other city departments discussing ways that the library could be of service to them. I have had really warm and friendly receptions from everybody I have visited, with the exception of Ralph Riesen. When I talked to him in the same way that I had the other people, I felt like I got a cold shoulder. He seemed very uninterested. What I would most like would be to talk straight to Debra and Ralph and get straight answers in return.

Helen: We shouldn't overlook the fact that there have been some positive developments recently. For example, the new personnel officer, Joyce Gardner, came down and visited us last week. She was very understanding and very sympathetic about our problems. I am rather optimistic that many of our problems concerning selection, advertising, and interviewing will be better now that Joyce is here.

Linda: The recent hiring of two part-time people with Joyce's advice and help is an example of how well things can be done and how we and the city administration can work together. We should find more ways to use our separate expertise cooperatively!

Helen: Also, I am encouraged by the cooperation I have been getting from Jack Feldner. He recently responded favorably to my request for a crew to come over here and help with moving books away from an area where we had a leaking roof. I haven't always felt that I've had Jack's complete support and cooperation, but lately I've been feeling better about that.

One example of an item I'll bet is on Debra's checklist against me is the fact that the library is over its budget this year. Now the reason for this is that since the budgeting processes have been centralized in City Hall, I simply haven't had access to the kind of information I need to keep track of the budget. I'm afraid that I'm going to be unjustifiably blamed for this situation. This is an example of the kind of information I should not have to ask for—they should automatically give it to me.

Linda: I *am* concerned about the way that these crises with the city affect our morale and productivity. I have observed these when these crises come up we of the staff cease to care about our work as much, we spend *much* time rehashing incidents to reassure ourselves, and we do not do as good a job because we do not feel secure or appreciated. I am amazed to see myself doing this, as I like my job, but I do find myself lowering the quality of my work when I feel threatened, and I see others doing it too. So, continued bad feelings are counterproductive and inefficient.

Maude: One indicator of the kind of relationship which Debra has with us down here in the library is the reaction she gets when she comes down here. I remember a time when she was down here recently. We were all very nervous and very alert. It was like we all suspected that she was up to no good being down here, and we had to watch her every step.

PART 4

Meetings 1 and 2

After reviewing what they had learned in the meetings with City Hall and the library staff, Jeff and Paul decided to recommend a series of four two-hour meetings. They formulated tentative meeting agendas and sent copies to each of the five prospective participants. After informal checks had established the agreement of each of the five to the proposed meetings, the consultants sent a confirming memo to each, announcing the time and place for each of the four meetings.

Meeting 1: March 19

The agenda presented by the consultants for the first meeting included a brief introduction by the consultants, an expectations check, a sharing appreciation exercise, and a closing process check.

Following the introduction, the participants were asked to participate in an expectations check. For the first half of this exercise each person was asked to write on two separate sheets of paper (1) their hopes, and (2) their fears for the upcoming series of meetings. In the second half of the exercise these hopes and fears were shared, posted on newsprint, and discussed. This exercise activity took about 40 minutes.

The "sharing appreciations" exercise contained four steps. In the first step each of the participants was given three-by-five-inch cards and asked to write appreciation messages to the other participants. Each message was to be addressed to another person on a separate card and was to be unsigned. A format suggested was: "I appreciate _____ about you." Each person was asked to write at least one such message to each of the other four participants present.

In step two of the appreciations exercise the cards were collected and sorted and then read by one facilitator while the other wrote the appreciations on newsprint. The result was one large newsprint sheet of appreciation messages for each of the five participants.

In step three each person was instructed to add to their individual sheets other things for which they would like to be appreciated, or for which they felt they deserved appreciation.

Step four consisted of a series of one-on-one conferences where each participant met individually with each of the other four participants for five minutes. During these conferences each member of the pair was asked to *acknowledge* to the other person the appreciations which had been contributed by other participants, and further to acknowledge the appreciations which he or she had contributed or agreed with. The sharing appreciations exercise took about 30 minutes.

The final activity for Meeting 1 was a process check, where participants were invited to share their feelings about the activities of the first meeting and about the upcoming meetings.

The expectations check generated a list of hopes and fears which was posted on two large sheets of newsprint. The main themes reflected in the "hopes" list included desires to improve working relations and communications between the library and the city, to clarify reporting patterns, to know others as individuals, to develop a more relaxed atmosphere among group members, to confront differences, to reduce felt threats, and to restore library staff confidence.

The list of fears included the following: that the library would become even more committed to single-issue political activity; that the meetings would result in "unpleasant repercussions" for some; that information shared in the meetings would get out and be damaging or embarrassing; that the meetings would be a waste of time; that the library would move further away from the rest of the city and become more entrenched; and that Debra and Ralph would become too busy to attend one or more of the meetings.

The general mood during the meeting was one of caution. Jeff and Paul noted that the appreciations shared were quite general and that some uneasiness was sensed during the appreciation sharing exercise. The process check at the end of the meeting revealed mildly positive reactions. Ralph seemed cool and reserved; he said that there were no dramatic gains but that he was willing to continue. Linda seconded Ralph's sentiment. Debra and Maude seemed to be more positive and appeared to feel reassured. Helen appeared to have very positive feelings about the meeting; she expressed reduced apprehensions about the meetings and increased comfort with the other participants.

Meeting 2: March 21

The meeting began with a brief introduction to the planned activities by Paul. He also apologized for having to leave early that day. Instructions were then given for the first phase of an "image exchange" exercise. Participants were told that each group was to meet in a separate room and prepare two lists. The first list was to summarize their own group's images of the other group, including thoughts, attitudes, feelings, perceptions, and behavior. The second list was to predict what the other group's images recorded in their first list would be.

After approximately 30 minutes of list preparation time, the two groups were reconvened to share the lists. During the list-sharing period a ground rule was enforced which disallowed debate and discussion but which allowed questions for clarification.

The librarians were invited to share their list of images of the city administration first. As they did so, Jeff (Paul had gone) summarized the entries on newsprint. Next the city administration's images of the library were shared and posted. Time was allowed for clarification questions after each list had been aired.

Next the two groups shared their predictions of the other group's list with the librarians again going first. The time required for the sharing of the four lists was approximately 40 minutes. These four lists are reproduced in Exhibit 1.

Following the image exchange periods the groups were again sent to separate rooms. This time each group was instructed to create a prioritized list of issues needing resolution. Twenty minutes was allocated for this activity.

The final activity of Meeting 2 was the sharing of the two lists of priority issues. Exhibit 2 shows the priority issues which were generated in this activity. This sharing and posting used up the remainder of the meeting time available.

At the conclusion of the meeting, Jeff's impression was that there was a general sense of tension relief that this long-repressed animosity was finally out in the open. Debra appeared to feel particularly good about the meeting when she left. Jeff was impressed by the casualness and informality with which Ralph engaged in musing conversation concerning the meeting with the three librarians for 15 minutes after the meeting. This was the first time that Jeff could remember Ralph's being relaxed and at ease in any of the meetings concerning the library. Jeff guessed that Ralph might have felt good that some real progress had been made during this meeting.

Two days after this meeting, Linda reported to Jeff that the librarians left the meeting feeling quite discouraged.

Consultants' Meeting: March 22

Jeff Mallet and Paul Everest met at Paul's house to compare notes on the progress of the meetings so far, and to discuss strategy for the upcoming meetings.

When Paul saw the two priority lists of issues for resolution which had been generated by the two groups, he had an immediate reaction. Paul noted that the items listed by the librarians appeared to reflect a willingness to compromise, collaborate, or negotiate; whereas, those items listed by Debra and Ralph appeared to reflect the expectation that it was the library which should do the changing. Jeff and Paul wondered if this was a pattern. They recalled other times when

EXHIBIT 1

Image Exchange Data From Second Meeting of City Hall and Library Administration

A. Library Administration views of City Hall
1. They are suspicious of the library.
2. They are well-intentioned but inept.
3. They are uninterested in the library program.
4. They are protective of their own power.
5. They are unfriendly.
6. They want the library to accept administrative changes from City Hall, but are unwilling to accept administrative changes made by the Library Board.
7. They don't really want public input.
8. They are very willing to put Library Staff (especially Helen) between power play of City Hall and the Library Board.
9. They are personally against Helen.

B. City Hall views of Library Administration
1. They have limited or no respect for the administrative abilities of City Hall.
2. "Massive paranoia" exists among the Library Staff.
3. The librarians have been operating a propaganda organ:
    a. Internally with Library Staff.
    b. Externally with City Council and the public.
4. The Library Staff has used the Library Board as a separate political support group.
5. There has been a concerted program by the librarians to establish a separate political base and become invulnerable.
6. Library personnel operate a tight "clique."
7. Library personnel distrust (and dislike and despise . . .) City Hall.

8. Library personnel wish to do their own thing without coordination.
9. Library personnel don't readily accept administrative assistance.

C. Library Administration's predictions of City Hall views of Library Administration
1. They think we are paranoid.
2. They think we are snobbish and isolated.
3. They think we are spreading our views of the problem among staff and public.
4. They think we are overprotective of the library.
5. They think we are inappropriately political.
6. They think we are encouraging the Library Board to move away from City Hall.

D. City Hall's predictions of Library views of City Hall
1. They think that we believe the library is not a critical service, it is dispensable, or first to go in a crunch.
2. They think we are nonsupportive of the library.
3. They think we discriminate against the library.
4. They think we impose unreasonable guidelines.
5. They think we have a vendetta against the library.
6. They think we are uncaring and unhelpful.
7. They think that the library gets the short end of resource allocations.
8. They think that we are fast to control and restrict, but seldom volunteer assistance.

EXHIBIT 2

Priority Issues for Resolution Second Meeting, City Hall and Library Administration

A. Priorities of Library Staff
1. Clarify the role of the Library Board of Trustees:
    a. Statewide.
    b. Citywide.
    c. Vis-á-vis the library staff.
2. Clarify the roles of the library's staff, library administration, and City Hall.
3. Reach agreement regarding appropriate political activity for the library.
4. Develop mutual respect for one anothers' administrative abilities.

B. Priorities of City Hall
1. (Debra) Inappropriate political activity.
2. (Ralph) Resolve the perception that City Hall is doing something "bad" to Helen, i.e., perceived vendetta.
3. Library's impression that City Hall is uninterested in the library program
4. Library's impression that members of City Hall are being protective of their own power.

they had vague feelings that perhaps Debra or Ralph or both regarded the meetings as an opportunity to get the library to shape up. Following the meeting, Jeff had the feeling that the three librarians had seemed to take the instructions and the sessions more seriously than did Debra and Ralph. Jeff had hoped that the period for sharing the four lists would leave everyone in an introspective mood. This seemed to take place for the librarians, but not for Debra and Ralph.

After reflecting on the outcomes from Meeting 2, Jeff reported feeling overwhelmed by the pervasiveness of the issue concerning appropriate political activity. His review had led him to the conclusion that this issue was so fundamental to all the problems being experienced between the library and City Hall that it was likely to be futile to work on any specific issues before addressing this major one.

As Jeff saw it, there were two major questions which needed to be resolved. First, what is the relationship of the library board of trustees to City Hall? And second, how are the diametrically opposed views expressed by the library and City Hall concerning appropriate political activity going to be resolved? It seemed to Jeff that neither of these issues could be settled by the group which had been meeting with Jeff and Paul. Instead, it seemed more plausible that these issues needed to be referred to either the library board or to the City Council.

Paul agreed that there were no instant solutions in sight, and that the appropriate strategy for where to go with the present group was not at all apparent.

After some discussion, Paul and Jeff agreed on the prognosis that until the overriding issue of political activity was dealt with, administrative issues would probably be resistant to solution. They further agreed that it seemed unlikely that solutions to the political activity question could be generated from within the present group, and that action strategies to address this issue probably would have to come from the City Council or the Library Board.

Concerning strategy for Meeting 3, Paul and Jeff agreed to begin it by reviewing for the participants the consultants' interpretations of the outcome of Meeting 2 and to invite them to join in a problem-solving session concerning appropriate action strategies. Paul and Jeff could think of two strategies which might prove fruitful:

1.   Refer the issue of appropriateness of political activity to the City Council with a request for a definitive guideline on what activities are appropriate.

2.   Have Debra and Helen get together, with or without a process consultant, to work out an agreement concerning political activity.

Jeff and Paul discussed whether the issue of the newspaper reporter being called should be brought up and dealt with at the next meeting. They agreed that Debra had stored up much resentment over this issue, and that if it came out it could be a "heavy" confrontation. Jeff and Paul were very uncertain about whether the issue could be constructively dealt with in one meeting. The uncertainties concerning the outcome of such a confrontation led Paul and Jeff to agree that they should probably try to avoid confronting this issue at the next meeting.

PART 5: MEETINGS 3 AND 4

Meeting 3: March 26

As Jeff and Paul arrived at the Savings Bank Community Room for Meeting 3, they exchanged the sentiment, "God knows what's going to happen today!"

As participants entered the meeting room, they were given a three-page handout summarizing the previous meetings' outcomes. This handout contained the data generated in Meeting 2 from the image exchange exercise and the priority issues for resolution list (Exhibits 2 and 3).

Jeff began by sharing some of his and Paul's reflections concerning the pervasiveness of the political issue. He raised the question about whether administrative concerns could be addressed while the political issue remained unsolved. He further voiced some skepticism concerning whether the present group was the appropriate one to settle the political issue, or whether it could.

At this time, Jeff spent some time reflecting on the nature of the conflict over political activities. He tried to summarize the position of each of the two parties to the conflict. In doing this Jeff emphasized his understanding that each of the parties had a position which was logically defensible, internally consistent, and supportable by others.

Jeff concluded by inviting the group members to comment on the consultants' diagnosis of the problem, and to join in a problem-solving session to identify reasonable options which could be taken. The remainder of the meeting time was used for unstructured discussion, with the exception of a brief process check at the end of the meeting.

EXHIBIT 3

City Hall and Library Administration Action List

Issue	Action
Calling reporter anonymously.	Announcement at staff meeting. (Helen will do. OK to break confidentiality.)
Offer by Debra to spend time in library.	Helen will schedule with staff and Debra.
Reporting relations.	Helen will draft memo to library board by May 2 asking them for direction or clarification on the following issues: Legal liability; errors and omissions. Property. Maintenance. Reporting relations. Political activity. Debra and Ralph will review memo. Ralph and Helen will attend May 2 meeting of Library Board.
Maintaining good relations.	Debra, Ralph, Helen, Linda, and Maude will meet for brown bag luncheons. First luncheon: Tuesday, April 24, 12:00 to 1:00 in Ralph's office; Linda will facilitate. Participants to begin with "check-in" concerning problem issues and good news. Facilitator and location will rotate for subsequent luncheons. Brown bag discussion item: exchanging of staff people.
Perception that City Hall is going to do something bad to Helen.	Brown bag luncheon "check-in" item.
Perception that City Hall is "inept." Perception that library staff is "incompetent."	All such evaluative stereotypes were declared inoperative by Jeff, who banned their use in thought and speech.

Paul served in a process observation role during this meeting. During the time that Jeff was giving an overview of the problem situation, Paul noted the reactions of the five participants. Linda, Helen, and Ralph all seemed quite attentive. Debra and Maude were observed to be staring intently at their handouts for long periods of time. This was particularly true for Maude, who hardly shifted her gaze from her handout for almost 20 minutes. Paul noted that Maude looked dejected, and that she was avoiding eye contact with others present. Because the meeting room was chilly, Maude (along with most of the others) was feeling physically cold. Maude had also mentioned that she was coming down with a cold.

After Jeff had finished his introductory remarks, Debra abruptly initiated a discussion of political activity on the part of the library staff. Debra's remarks may be paraphrased as follows:

Politics is a fact of life now. The library staff has started something that will be very hard to stop. They have politicized the budgeting process and it will be very hard to go back to a nonpolitical procedure. What I need to know from the library staff is whether these activities are going to continue. If they are, there are going to be unpleasant repercussions which the library staff should understand.

There are two things that are really bothering me; first, the fact that someone from the library called a newspaper reporter to ask that my "vendetta" against Cecil Hockman and the library be investigated. When I got that telephone call from the reporter, I felt "angry, betrayed, and nonplussed." Second is the issue of political activity by library staff members aimed at packing the City Council chambers with citizens supporting the library. That represents a clear violation of instructions from the library board, and leads me to wonder, "Who's running the library, anyway?"

When Debra made the point that the library staff had disregarded instructions concerning political activity, Helen pointed out that the library staff did not perceive that they had received any such instructions. Following Helen's point, discussion proceeded in another direction, with no overt evidence that Helen's comment was heard or understood.

Following Debra's expression of her feelings about the telephone call, Helen and Linda expressed consternation that the telephone call had been made. Both made it very clear that they thought such a telephone call was inappropriate. Linda said, "I didn't realize we had sunk to that low a level," and Helen seconded Linda's sentiment. During this conversation Maude was noticeably quiet, and was avoiding eye contact.

Ralph said, "When I come in the library, I feel hostility all around me." When Ralph had said this, Paul intervened and asked Ralph to focus on his personal feelings when he was in this situation. Ralph's responses generally depicted his impressions of library staff members' attitudes. Paul pursued the issue by asking Ralph two more times to focus on and report his own feelings in this situation. After Ralph's responses again did not describe his own feelings, Jeff probed him by asking if he might have been feeling hurt, or disliked, or disrespected. In response to this prompting Ralph acknowledged that some of these guesses were accurate.

At this point Paul intervened with a few observations designed to set the stage for the librarians to air some of their feelings. With a few minor exceptions, the librarians did not divulge their feelings on issues.

At one point in the conversation Debra offered "to spend a week working in the library," if that would help to resolve some of the problems. Helen responded to this offer with apparent guardedness, citing the difficulties of time scheduling and the requirements of attending the human understanding workshops currently being conducted for all city employees. Debra seemed annoyed that Helen's reaction to her offer was not totally positive. At this point Maude made a pointed observation to Debra: "I have to tell you that

there are some people in the library who will be pretty hostile toward you."

The question of whether the library should regionalize by joining the Morton County system was raised. Debra expressed dismay that the library staff, the library board of trustees, and several others had reacted so vehemently to the proposal that regionalization should be studied. The librarians responded to Debra's sentiment by assertively pointing out that the proposal (which had been part of a report to the City Council by the Capital Expenditures Committee) did not call for a study but called for *implementation* which was to occur by January 1, 1980. Both Debra and Ralph replied that they were sure that the wording of the Capital Expenditures Committee report was that the January 1, 1980, date was the deadline for *completion of a study*. The librarians were equally certain that their interpretation of the report was correct. Members of both groups vowed to get a copy of the committee report to bring to the next meeting.

Discussion of the regionalization issue continued. Helen referred to a previous study concerning regionalization which had been conducted by the League of Women Voters. This study had gathered some utilization data. Helen felt that the study supported her opinion that regionalization would be most unwise. Debra said that she had not seen or heard of the league's study, and was very interested: "That's the kind of information I need to know."

At this point one of the librarians volunteered that they had prepared a "fact sheet" concerning the regionalization issue. Debra expressed surprise at hearing about the fact sheet. Paul noted that Debra seemed annoyed about learning about the fact sheet, and that Ralph gave the librarians a dirty look during this time. The librarians at this point explained that the fact sheet was prepared in response to a request by an individual City Council member.

Lively discussion of substantive issues was continuing when Jeff interrupted at a few minutes before the end of the meeting time to ask for a process check. During this check the general sentiment expressed was, "Whew! we really got into it today!" Linda said that she thought a lot had been accomplished, and nods of agreement from other participants were noted. Ralph acknowledged some real accomplishment for the first time. Paul and Jeff shared both surprise and relief that the issue concerning the reporter had been successfully dealt with and largely defused. In fact, they expressed the view that the whole issue of political activity had been defused at least somewhat.

Meeting 4: March 25

The meeting began with Paul and Jeff suggesting a review of the "Priority Issues for Resolution" list generated in Meeting 2. The consultants suggested that the group make an "action/no action" decision for each of the priority issues. This was to provide some closure for this last of four scheduled meetings.

During the last half of the meeting Paul started an action list on newsprint, and he and Jeff pressed the participants for specific action commitments as the discussion approached agreement. The last ten minutes of the meeting was spent reviewing the list of hopes and fears generated at the beginning of Meeting 1.

The action list that Paul constructed on newsprint during the last half of the meeting is shown in Exhibit 3. The last issue on the action list, i.e., the perceptions of "ineptness" and "incompetence," still had not been discussed as the end of the meeting time approached. Jeff called attention to the issue, and shared the perception of the consultants that the range of specific behaviors which each group found upsetting in the other group seemed quite small, too small to support the "inept" or "incompetent" generalizations. He pointed out that feedback on specific behaviors had been constructively shared during the four meetings, but that feedback on broad evaluative generalizations was hard to respond to constructively. Jeff urged each participant to consciously avoid lapsing into the use of such evaluative stereotypes, and instead to concentrate on specific behaviors.

During the review of the hopes and fears lists the general feeling was that most of the hopes had been either partially or fully realized, and that most of the fears had dissipated. Concerning the fear that the meetings might prove to be a waste of time, Ralph said, "that remains to be seen." Concerning the hope that better working relations would be developed, all participants seemed to agree that this had been accomplished.

**PART 6:
FOLLOW-UP**

A survey instrument called the Intergroup Profile was used by the consultants to measure the climate existing between City Hall and the library staff. This instrument has eight Likert-type questions concerning the climate

perceived by group members, and can demonstrate differences in the perceptions of group members existing between two groups. Measurements were taken in March before the first intergroup meeting, and in May, six weeks after the last meeting. Parallel measurements were obtained from nine separate control organizations.[1]

Data analysis revealed that the library/City Hall climate prior to the meetings was considerably worse than that existing in any of the nine control organizations ($p < .0001$). Following the meeting the library/City Hall climate scores had improved substantially ($p < .001$), but were still lower than the scores of any control organization.

In early August, four months after meeting 4, a two-page written evaluation form was filled out by each of the five meeting participants. Their responses reflected general agreement that, as a result of the meetings, the climate between City Hall and the library had improved, but not dramatically.

Ralph Risen commented, "We achieved a better understanding of positions, but no real resolution of conflicts. The conflicts that exist are political rather than personal."

Debra Dickenson noted that the meetings had provided ". . . a good chance to share concerns," and that they resulted in ". . . better feelings for the individuals involved." She continued:

> There is a period of transition that is required—just plain time to see how we all deal with the next 'challenge to authority'. Political changes have an effect. I don't feel the library personnel understand the scope of city demands and needs any better than before. In my opinion they just feel we are being nicer to them. Their anxieties are relieved a bit so the climate is improved. There is a value to that without a doubt.

Helen Hendricks noted three specific changes which had resulted from the meetings:

1. The librarian is aware that her personal situation cannot improve but she is not threatened by further deterioration of her position.
2. The administrative reporting pattern between library administration, library board, and city supervisor has improved.
3. The library staff is more united and supportive than ever.

---

[1] Copies of the instrument and data analysis available from the case authors.

Additional comments made by Helen included the following:

> I believe the library's fears and concerns were substantiated by the meetings but it was good to bring them into the open. The librarian's and city supervisor's personal contacts are slightly improved.
>
> The problems at the library stemmed from the city administration decision to regroup the city program with the resultant downgrading of the library service and personal demotion of the Librarian—the view of the library. The city administration did not recognize this as the cause.

Linda Turner reported that the meetings ". . . relieved the mayor's mind by allowing her a chance to 'let off steam'. Coming from the library, I [now] feel more relaxed in talking with the mayor and city supervisor—though not totally relaxed. The city librarian and city supervisor can now talk to each other—this is by far the most important result."

Maude Richardson concurred with Linda and Helen that the relationship between the city librarian and the city supervisor was much more comfortable. She also observed that "foul-ups at City Hall are no longer seen as personally directed at the library."

☐

CASE QUESTIONS

1. In your opinion, how do situations such as this develop? Why are they allowed to reach an "intolerably low level"?
2. Evaluate Paul and Jeff's approach to bringing about a resolution of the problems between City Hall and the Library.
3. What would you recommend to reduce the possibility of similar problems happening in the future between City Hall and other city departments?

2 THE POWER CENTER AT GEICO CORPORATION

John J. Byrne is chairperson of Geico Corporation, the Washington, D.C., auto insurer. He took over in 1976, when the firm was on the verge of bankruptcy. Within a few years, he succeeded in building a culture at Geico that was based on consensus management and inflexible operator rules. He found, however, that one of his inflexible rules stood in the way of Geico's sales growth. Byrne could have used his authority as chief executive to change the rule, but instead he chose to muddle. That way it took four years to bring about a change that he could have commanded from his position of power with a one-page memo.

Byrnes' career began at Lincoln National Life as a roving reinsurance actuary. In 1967, he moved to the Traveler's Insurance. In six years, he was promoted to executive vice president. He describes himself as a pusher, a driver who sometimes pushes his ideas too hard.

During his first few months at Geico, Byrne was putting out fires and not really concerned about building a productive work culture. He was going strictly by the books and relying on his position power to do the job. That is, he was influencing others by the use of legitimate, reward, and coercive power bases, the position power that is prescribed by the organization. He hired and fired and put together his own Geico management team.

Byrne describes his muddling style as a blend of management by objectives and consensus management. He believes that top management should not make policy decisions by itself. Instead, it should create a company culture and style in which power is shared and subordinates are trusted to perform well.

Byrne is considered a politician by some managers. He has tailored Geico's culture to fit his personality. He will yield and bend to group decisions, but he

Based on Stratford P. Sherman, "Muddling to Victory at Geico," *Fortune*, September 5, 1983, pp. 66–80.

stays in control of the decision-making process. Long before any major issue is put to the group, Byrne will be moving from office to office, gently nudging group members, listening, and getting to know what group members are thinking and feeling. He is jockeying for advice, coaxing, and letting others know what he thinks.

Byrne uses "challenge sessions" as a tool to stimulate and prod other managers. This is how they work. Each manager circulates copies of his or her proposed budget and goals for the year to a group of other managers. Each manager must sit alone at the front of the room presenting his or her proposals. The other managers then attack the proposals from every direction. It is not acceptable to simply "rubber-stamp" another manager's proposals. Managers are expected to sell their proposals to others. The challenge sessions last 12 to 16 hours a day, five days a week, for three weeks.

At the end of the challenge sessions, each manager has accepted responsibility for a one-year corporate operating plan. Byrne is firm about not rewarding with a bonus any manager who fails to meet his or her goals. If managers hold back and try to set lower goals at the challenge sessions, Byrne has a knack for spotting this and letting the manager know it. He wants his managers to perform and pushes them to set realistic, challenging objectives. His philosophy is that results are the key to success at Geico. He states

that as long as the employee gets results, "I don't care if he shines his shoes with a brick."

Indoctrinated in Byrne's style of managing, Geico managers are cost cutters and realistic goal setters, and they perform their jobs with zeal. Byrne has pushed, led by example, subtly coerced, and motivated the Geico management team. In addition, he listens and shares power through the muddling process. Byrne is patient, and he will wait for managers to finally see the light.

Byrne prides himself on creating a corporate culture that permits power to be shared. The sharing has facilitated trust, internal communication, and realistic targets. Instead of relying on power, fear, and coercion, Byrne has taken another route. When he perceives a need for major changes, he waits for the lieutenants to see the need before issuing orders. □

CASE QUESTIONS

1. Some critics of Byrne's style claim that it can work in insurance but that if it were tried in a more volatile and unpredictable industry, competition would simply pass you by. What is your opinion?
2. What types of power bases does Byrne actually rely on to perform his job as chairperson at Geico?
3. How does Byrne combine power and politics to perform his job?

LEADERSHIP

LEARNING OBJECTIVES

DEFINE the term *leadership.*

DESCRIBE how leadership research has evolved from trait approaches, through personal-behavior approaches, to situational or contingency approaches.

DISCUSS the similarities and differences among the various situational approaches.

COMPARE the decision styles in the Vroom-Yetton model with the leadership styles in the path-goal approach.

IDENTIFY the factors which determine the favorableness of the situation in the Fiedler model.

In all of the groups to which you have belonged—family, sports team, social club, study group, work unit—there typically was a person who was more influential than the others. The most influential person in these groups probably was called a leader. Leaders are extremely important in a variety of organizational settings. Indeed, organizations would be less efficient without leaders, and, in extreme cases, they would be unable to accomplish purposeful goals. For these and similar reasons, leadership has been the center of attention of theorists, researchers, and practitioners.

Although leadership is important and has been studied by behavioral scientists for decades, it is still somewhat of a mystery.[1] Even after thousands of studies, there is still a lack of consensus among the experts on exactly what leadership is and how it should be analyzed. This issue is addressed in detail in the first readings selection accompanying this chapter, "The Ambiguity of Leadership," by Jeffrey Pfeffer. Further reflecting this ambiguity, this chapter examines a number of somewhat distinct perspectives of leadership.

LEADERSHIP DEFINED

The five bases of interpersonal power discussed in Chapter 9 suggest that power can be defined as the ability to influence another person's behavior. Where one individual attempts to affect the behavior of a group without using the coercive form of power, we describe the effort as leadership. More specifically, **"Leadership** is an attempt at influencing the activities of followers through the communication process and toward the attainment of some goal or goals."[2] This definition implies that leadership involves the use of influence and that all relationships can involve leadership. A second element in the definition involves the importance of the communication process. The clarity and accuracy of communication affect the behavior and performance of followers.

Another element of the definition focuses on the accomplishment of goals. The effective leader may have to deal with individual, group, and organizational goals. Leader effectiveness typically is considered in terms of the degree of accomplishment of one or a combination of these goals.

---

[1] Bernard M. Bass, *Stogdill's Handbook of Leadership* (New York: Free Press, 1982).

[2] Edwin A. Fleishman, "Twenty Years of Consideration and Structure," in *Current Developments in the Study of Leadership,* eds. Edwin A. Fleishman and James G. Hunt (Carbondale: Southern Illinois University Press, 1973), p. 3.

FIGURE 10–1

**A Leadership
Model: Sources,
Moderators,
Outcomes**

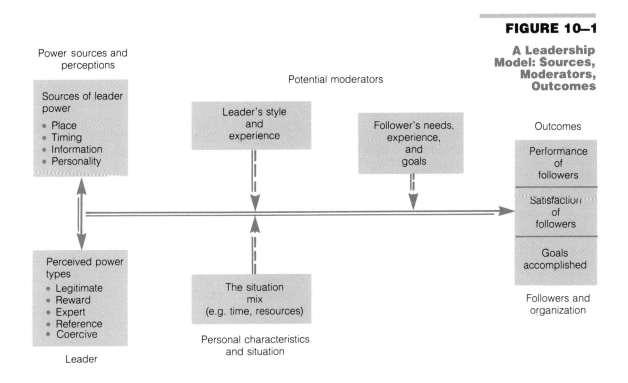

Power sources and
perceptions

Sources of leader
power

- Place
- Timing
- Information
- Personality

Perceived power
types

- Legitimate
- Reward
- Expert
- Reference
- Coercive

Leader

Potential moderators

Leader's style
and
experience

Follower's needs,
experience,
and
goals

The situation
mix
(e.g. time, resources)

Personal characteristics
and situation

Outcomes

Performance
of
followers

Satisfaction
of
followers

Goals
accomplished

Followers and
organization

Figure 10–1 represents a model of leadership based upon the above definition. The model summarizes the key sources and perceived bases of interpersonal power. It also presents some of the possible moderating factors between the sources and perceived bases of power and outcomes (goals). The model suggests that (1) a successful leader is one who is aware of sources of power and the importance of perceived power; (2) the leader does not rely on coercive power; (3) the sources of a leader's power include place, time, and information and personality characteristics; and (4) the accomplishment of goals depends not only on power sources and perceptions but also on follower needs, the situation, and the experience of the leader.[3] The relationship outlined in the model between power sources and outcomes is another issue discussed by Pfeffer in his article.

TRAIT THEORIES

Much of the early work on leadership focused on identifying the traits of effective leaders. This approach was based on the assumption that a finite number of individual traits of effective leaders could be found. Thus, most research was designed to identify intellectual, personality, and physical traits of successful leaders.

---

[3] See Arthur G. Jago, "Leadership: Perspectives in Theory and Research," *Management Science,* March 1982, pp. 315–36.

INTELLECTUAL TRAITS

Dimensions of intelligence that have been associated with leadership effectiveness include decisiveness, judgmental ability, knowledge, and verbal abilities. In a review of 35 studies, Stogdill found a general trend indicating that leaders were somewhat more intelligent than their followers, but not exceedingly more so.[4] Extreme intelligence differences tended to be dysfunctional.

PERSONALITY TRAITS

Some research suggests that personality traits such as alertness, originality, personal integrity, and self-confidence are associated with effective leadership.[5] Still other investigators identify creativity, emotional balance, nonconformity, and diplomacy.[6] A major difficulty in attempts to relate personality and leadership has been finding valid ways to measure personality traits. Progress, however, although slow, is being made.[7]

PHYSICAL TRAITS

Studies of the relationship between effective leadership and physical characteristics such as age, height, weight, and appearance provide contradictory results. Being taller and heavier than the average of a group certainly is not advantageous for achieving a leader position.[8] However, many organizations believe that a physically large person is required to secure compliance from followers. This notion relies heavily on the coercive or fear basis of power. On the other hand, Truman, Gandhi, Napoleon, and Stalin are examples of individuals of small stature who rose to positions of leadership.

Although traits such as these have, in some studies, differentiated effective from ineffective leaders, many contradictory findings still exist. Consequently, after years of speculation and research, we are not even close to identifying a specific set of leadership traits. Thus, the trait approach, while interesting and intuitively appealing, does not seem to be very efficient for identifying and predicting leadership potential. Nonetheless, as the following OBM Encounter illustrates, describing leaders on the basis of traits remains a common practice.

OBM ENCOUNTER

TRAITS OF THE SUPERLEADER

What is it that makes an individual exert a good deal of effort for one leader, but do just enough to slide by for another? According to the results of interviews with 90 outstanding leaders, including CEOs of some of the nation's largest corporations, university presidents, and coaches of consistently winning athletic teams, the answer is that the truly outstanding leader—

---

[4] Ralph M. Stogdill, *Handbook of Leadership* (New York: Free Press, 1974), pp. 43–44.

[5] For example, see Chris Argyris, "Some Characteristics of Successful Executives," *Personnel Journal,* June 1955, pp. 50–63; and J. A. Hornaday and C. J. Bunker, "The Nature of the Entrepreneur," *Personnel Psychology,* Spring 1970, pp. 47–54.

[6] Barnard M. Bass, *Stogdill's Handbook of Leadership,* pp. 75–76.

[7] For example, see James Conley, "Longitudinal Stability of Personality Traits: A Multiact-Multimethod-Multioccasion Analysis," *Journal of Personality and Social Psychology,* November 1985, pp. 1266–82.

[8] Ralph M. Stogdill, "Personal Factors Associated with Leadership," *Journal of Applied Psychology,* January 1948, pp. 35–71.

a superleader—can imbue his or her followers with a sense of mission.

"People would rather dedicate their lives to a cause they believe in than lead lives of pampered idleness," says Warren Bennis, who conducted the interviews. Bennis identified five traits his superleaders had in common:

- **Vision:** The capacity to create a compelling picture of the desired state of affairs that inspires performance.
- **Communication:** The ability to portray the vision clearly and in a way which enlists the support of followers.
- **Persistence:** The ability to continue plow-

ing ahead regardless of obstacles.

- **Empowerment:** The ability to create a structure that effectively uses others' talents to achieve the objectives.
- **Organizational Ability:** The capacity to monitor followers, learn from mistakes and, consequently, improve performance.

Bennis also concluded that superleaders are not necessarily superpersons. "Socially, a lot of these people are absolute misfits. Very few of them seem to be capable of small talk. For them, nothing is done without a purpose, and when they're not on that purpose, they're boring."   □

Source: Adapted from an article by Stephen Fox, Associated Press, Los Angeles, November 21, 1982.

PERSONAL-BEHAVIORAL THEORIES

In the late 1940s, researchers began to explore the notion that how a person acts determines that person's leadership effectiveness. Instead of searching for traits, these researchers examined behaviors and their impact on the performance and satisfaction of followers. Today, there are a number of well-known personal-behavioral theories of leadership. We examine two of the more prominent ones in this chapter.

THE UNIVERSITY OF MICHIGAN STUDIES

In 1947 Likert began studying how best to manage the efforts of individuals to achieve desired performance and satisfaction objectives.[9] The purpose of most of the leadership research of the Likert-inspired team at the University of Michigan has been to discover the principles and methods of effective leadership. Through interviewing leaders and followers, the researchers identified two distinct styles of leadership, referred to as *job-centered* and *employee-centered*. The job-centered leader practices close supervision so that subordinates perform their tasks using specified procedures. This type of leader relies on coercion, reward, and legitimate power to influence the behavior and performance of followers. The concern for people is viewed as important but as a luxury that a leader cannot always afford.

The *employee-centered* leader believes in delegating decision making and aiding followers in satisfying their needs by creating a supportive work environment. The employee-centered leader is concerned with followers' personal advancement, growth, and achievement. These actions are assumed to be conducive to the support of group formation and development.

[9] For a review of this work, see Rensis Likert, *New Patterns of Management* (New York: McGraw-Hill, 1961); and Rensis Likert, *The Human Organization* (New York: McGraw-Hill, 1967).

The Michigan series of studies does not clearly show that one particular style of leadership is always the most effective. Moreover, it only examines two aspects of leadership—task and people behavior.

THE OHIO STATE STUDIES

Among the several large research programs on leadership that developed after World War II, one of the most significant was headed by Fleishman and his associates at Ohio State University. This program resulted in a two-factor theory of leadership.[10] The studies isolated two leadership factors, referred to as *initiating structure* and *consideration*. The definitions of these factors are as follows: **initiating structure** involves behavior in which the leader organizes and defines the relationships in the group, tends to establish well-defined patterns and channels of communication, and spells out ways of getting the job done. **Consideration** involves behavior indicating friendship, mutual trust, respect, warmth, and rapport between the leader and the followers.

Since the original research, there have been numerous studies of the relationship between these two leadership dimensions and various effectiveness criteria. Many of the early results stimulated the generalization that leaders above average in both consideration and initiating structure were more effective. In a study at International Harvester, however, the researchers began to find some more complicated interpretations of the two dimensions. In a study of supervisors, it was found that those scoring higher on initiating structure had higher proficiency ratings (ratings received from superiors) but also had more employee grievances. The higher consideration score was related to lower proficiency ratings and lower absences.[11]

The Michigan and Ohio State theories each attempt to isolate broad dimensions of leadership behavior. In so doing, they have provided practitioners with information on what behaviors leaders should possess. This knowledge has resulted in the establishment of training programs for individuals who perform leadership tasks. Each of the approaches also is associated with highly respected theorists, researchers, or consultants, and each has been studied in different organizational settings. Yet the linkage between leadership and such important performance indicators as production, efficiency, and satisfaction has not been conclusively resolved by either of the two personal-behavioral theories.[12]

---

[10] For a review of the studies, see Stogdill, *Handbook of Leadership,* chap. 11. Also see Edwin A. Fleishman, "The Measurement of Leadership Attitudes in Industry," *Journal of Applied Psychology,* June 1953, pp. 153–58; C. L. Shartle, *Executive Performance and Leadership* (Englewood Cliffs, N.J.: Prentice-Hall, 1956); Edwin A. Fleishman, E. F. Harris, and H. E. Burtt, *Leadership and Supervision in Industry* (Columbus: Bureau of Educational Research, Ohio State University, 1955); and Fleishman, "Twenty Years of Consideration and Structure."

[11] Fleishman, Harris, and Burtt, *Leadership and Supervision.*

[12] For a discussion of the relationship between leadership and performance see, for example, Jonathan Smith, Kenneth Carron, and Ralph Alexander, "Leadership: It Can Make a Difference," *Academy of Management Journal,* December 1984, pp. 765–76.

SITUATIONAL THEORIES

The search for the "best" set of traits or behavior has failed to discover an effective leadership mix and style for all situations. What has evolved are situation-leadership theories that suggest that leadership effectiveness depends on the fit between personality, task, power, attitudes, and perceptions.[13] As the importance of situational factors and leader assessment of forces became more recognized, leadership research became more systematic, and contingency models of leadership began to appear in the organizational behavior and management literature. There are several publicized and researched situation-oriented leadership approaches. The most prominent of these are the Fiedler contingency model, the Vroom Yetton normative model; and path-goal theory. Each model has its advocates, and each attempts to identify the leader behaviors most appropriate for a series of leadership situations. Also, each model attempts to identify the leader-situation patterns that are important for effective leadership.

THE CONTINGENCY LEADERSHIP MODEL

The contingency model of leadership effectiveness was developed by Fiedler.[14] The model postulates that the performance of groups is dependent on the interaction between leadership style and situational favorableness. Leadership style is measured by the *Least-Preferred Co-Worker Scale* (LPC), an instrument developed by Fiedler which assesses the degree of positive or negative feelings held by a person toward someone with whom he or she least prefers to work. Low scores on the LPC are thought to reflect a *task-oriented,* or controlling, structuring leadership style. High scores are associated with a *relationship-oriented,* or passive, considerate leadership style.

Fiedler proposes three factors which determine how favorable the leadership environment is, or the degree of situational favorableness. *Leader-member relations* refers to the degree of confidence, trust, and respect that the followers have in their leader. This is the most important factor. *Task structure* is the second most important factor and refers to the extent to which the tasks the followers are engaged in are structured. That is, is it clearly specified and known what followers are supposed to do, how they are to do it, when and in what sequence it is to be done, and what decision options they have (high structure)? Or, are these factors unclear, ambiguous, unspecifiable (low structure)? *Position power* is the final factor and refers to the power inherent in the leadership position. Generally, greater authority equals greater position power.

Together, these three factors determine how favorable the situation is for the leader. Good leader-member relations, high task structure, and strong

---

[13] Fleishman, "Twenty Years of Consideration and Structure."

[14] Fred E. Fiedler, *A Theory of Leadership Effectiveness* (New York: McGraw-Hill, 1967).

position power constitute the most favorable situation. Poor relations, low degree of structure, and weak position power represent the least favorable situation. The varying degrees of favorableness and the corresponding appropriate leadership style are shown in Figure 10–2.

FIGURE 10–2

Summary of Fiedler's Situational Variables and Their Preferred Leadership Styles

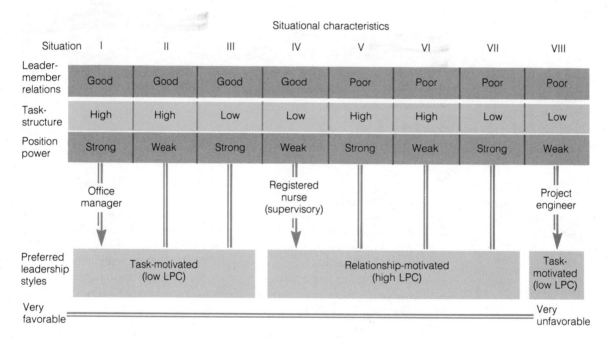

Fiedler contends that a permissive, more lenient (relationship-oriented) style is best when the situation is moderately favorable or moderately unfavorable. Thus, if a leader is moderately liked and possesses some power, and the job tasks for subordinates are somewhat vague, the leadership style needed to achieve the best results are relationship-oriented. In contrast, when the situation is highly favorable or highly unfavorable, a task-oriented approach generally produces the desired performance. Fiedler bases his conclusion regarding the relationship between leadership style and situational favorableness on more than two decades of research in business, educational, and military settings.[15]

Fiedler is not particularly optimistic that leaders successfully can be trained to change their preferred leadership style. Consequently, he sees changing the favorableness of the situation as a better alternative. In doing this, a first step recommended by Fiedler is to determine whether leaders are task-

---

[15] Fred E. Fiedler, "How Do You Make Leaders More Effective? New Answers to an Old Puzzle," *Organizational Dynamics,* Autumn 1972, pp. 3–8.

or relationship-oriented. Next, the organization needs to diagnose and classify the situational favorableness of its leadership positions. Finally, the organization must select the best strategy to bring about improved effectiveness. If leadership training is selected as an option, then it should devote special attention to teaching participants how to modify their environments and their jobs to fit their styles of leadership. That is, leaders should be trained to change their leadership situations. Fiedler's recent work indicates that when leaders can recognize the situations in which they are most successful, they can then begin to modify their own situations.[16] The following OBM Encounter details some specific ways leaders might attempt to change various aspects of their situations.

ENCOUNTER

GUIDELINES FOR MODIFYING SITUATIONAL FAVORABLENESS

Modifying Leader-Member Relations

1. Spend more—or less—informal time with your subordinates (lunch, leisure activities, etc.).
2. Request particular people for work in your group.
3. Volunteer to direct difficult or troublesome subordinates.
4. Suggest or effect transfers of particular subordinates into or out of your unit.
5. Raise morale by obtaining positive outcomes for subordinates (e.g., special bonuses, time-off, attractive jobs).

Modifying Task Structure

If you wish to work with less structured tasks, you can:

1. Ask your boss, whenever possible, to give you the new or unusual problems and let you figure out how to get them done.
2. Bring the problems and tasks to your group members, and invite them to work with you on the planning and decision-making phases of the tasks.

If you wish to work with more highly structured tasks, you can:

1. Ask your superior to give you, whenever possible, the tasks that are more structured or to give you more detailed instructions.
2. Break the job down into smaller subtasks that can be more highly structured.

Modifying Position Power

To raise your position power, you can:

1. Show your subordinates "who's boss" by exercising fully the powers that the organization provides.
2. Make sure that information to your group gets channeled through you.

To lower your position power, you can:

1. Call on members of your group to participate in planning and decision-making functions.
2. Let your assistants exercise relatively more power.   ☐

---

[16] Fred E. Fiedler, "The Leadership Game: Matching the Man to the Situation," *Organizational Dynamics,* Winter 1976, pp. 6–16.

A CRITIQUE OF THE CONTINGENCY MODEL

Fiedler's model and research have elicited a number of pointed criticisms and concerns. First, Graen and others present evidence that research support for the model is not strong, especially if studies conducted by researchers not associated with Fiedler are examined.[17] The earlier support and enthusiasm for the model came from Fiedler and his students, who conducted numerous studies of leaders. Second, a number of researchers have called attention to the questionable measurement of the LPC. These researchers claim that the reliability and validity of the LPC questionnaire measure are low.[18] Third, the meaning of the variables presented by Fiedler is not clear. For example, what is the point at which a "structured" task becomes an "unstructured" task?

Despite these criticisms, Fiedler's contingency model has made significant contributions to the study and application of leadership. His view of leadership has stimulated numerous research studies and much-needed debate about the dynamics of leader behavior. Fiedler has pointed the way in situational approaches and made others uncomfortably aware of the complexities of the leadership process.

THE VROOM-YETTON MODEL OF LEADERSHIP

Vroom and Yetton have developed a leadership decision-making model that indicates the kinds of situations in which various degrees of participative decision making would be appropriate.[19] In contrast to Fiedler, Vroom and Yetton attempt to provide a *normative model* that a leader can use in making decisions. Their approach assumes that no single leadership style is appropriate for every situation. Unlike Fiedler, Vroom and Yetton assume that leaders must be flexible enough to change their leadership styles to fit situations.

Selection of the appropriate decision-making process involves considering two criteria of decision effectiveness: quality and acceptance. *Decision quality* refers to the extent to which the decision impacts job performance. For example, deciding what type of cafeteria furniture to buy requires low decision quality because it has little impact on job performance, while a decision on production goals requires high decision quality. *Decision acceptance* refers to how important it is that subordinates be committed to or accept the decision in order that it may be successfully implemented. Buying cafeteria furniture does not really require group acceptance to be successfully implemented, while setting production goals does. Rules used to predict both quality and acceptance concerns are defined in Table 10–1.

---

[17] G. Graen, J. B. Orris, and K. M. Alvares, "Contingency Model of Leadership Effectiveness: Some Experimental Results," *Journal of Applied Psychology*, June 1971, pp. 196–201.

[18] C. A. Schriesheim, B. D. Bannister, and W. H. Money, "Psychometric Properties of the LPC Scale: An Extension of Rice's Review," *Academy of Management Review*, April 1979, pp. 287–90.

[19] Victor H. Vroom and Philip Yetton, *Leadership and Decision Making* (Pittsburgh: University of Pittsburgh Press, 1973).

TABLE 10–1

Decision Styles for Leadership: Individuals and Groups

Individual Level	Group Level
AI. You solve the problem or make the decision yourself, using information available to you at that time.	**AI.** You solve the problem or make the decision yourself, using information available to you at that time.
AII. You obtain any necessary information from the subordinate, then decide on the solution to the problem yourself. You may or may not tell the subordinate what the problem is in getting the information from him. The role played by your subordinate in making the decision is clearly one of providing specific information that you request, rather than generating or evaluating alternative solutions.	**AII.** You obtain any necessary information from subordinates, then decide on the solution to the problem yourself. You may or may not tell the subordinates what the problem is in getting the information from them. The role played by your subordinates in making the decision is clearly one of providing specific information that you request, rather than generating or evaluating solutions.
CI. You share the problem with the relevant subordinate, getting ideas and suggestions. Then *you* make the decision. This decision may or may not reflect your subordinate's influence.	**CI.** You share the problem with the relevant subordinates individually, getting their ideas and suggestions without bringing them together as a group. Then *you* make the decision. This decision may or may not reflect your subordinates' influence.
GI. You share the problem with one of your subordinates, and together you analyze the problem and arrive at a mutually satisfactory solution in an atmosphere of free and open exchange of information and ideas. You both contribute to the resolution of the problem, with the relative contribution of each being dependent on knowledge rather than formal authority.	**CII.** You share the problem with your subordinates in a group meeting. In this meeting, you obtain their ideas and suggestions. Then *you* make the decision, which may or may not reflect your subordinates' influence.
DI. You delegate the problem to one of your subordinates, providing him or her with any relevant information that you possess, but giving him or her responsibility for solving the problem alone. Any solution that the person reaches will receive your support.	**GII.** You share the problem with your subordinates as a group. Together, you generate and evaluate alternatives and attempt to reach agreement (consensus) on a solution. Your role is much like that of chairman, coordinating the discussion, keeping it focused on the problem, and making sure that the critical issues are discussed. You do not try to influence the group to adopt "your" solution, and you are willing to accept and implement any solution that has the support of the entire group.

The Vroom-Yetton model makes a distinction between two types of decision situations facing leaders: those whose solutions affect only one of the leader's followers (individual) and those where several followers are affected (group). Five different leadership decision styles that fit individual and group situations are available. These are defined in Table 10–2. In the table, A stands for autocratic, C for consultative, G for group, and D for delegative.

Vroom and Yetton suggest that leaders perform a diagnosis of the decision situation by applying the rules shown in Table 10–1. The application of these seven rules can be illustrated by use of a decision tree chart such as the one shown in Figure 10–3. The chart is read from left to right. Begin by considering the situation and asking question A. If the answer to A is

TABLE 10–2

Rules Underlying
the Vroom-Yetton
Model

RULES TO PROTECT THE QUALITY OF THE DECISION

1. **The leader information rule.** If the quality of the decision is important and the leader does not possess enough information or expertise to solve the problem by himself, then AI is eliminated from the feasible set.

2. **The goal congruence rule.** If the quality of the decision is important and subordinates are not likely to pursue the organization goals in their efforts to solve the problem, then GII is eliminated from the feasible set.

3. **The unstructured problem rule.** In decisions in which the quality of the decision is important, if the leader lacks the necessary information or expertise to solve the problem by himself and if the problem is unstructured, the method of solving the problem should provide for interaction among subordinates likely to possess relevant information. Accordingly, AI, AII, and CI are eliminated from the feasible set.

RULES TO PROTECT THE ACCEPTANCE OF THE DECISION

4. **The acceptance rule.** If the acceptance of the decision by subordinates is critical to effective implementation and if it is not certain that an autocratic decision will be accepted, AI and AII are eliminated from the feasible set.

5. **The conflict rule.** If the acceptance of the decision is critical, an autocratic decision is not certain to be accepted, and disagreement among subordinates in methods of attaining the organizational goal is likely, the methods used in solving the problem should enable those in disagreement to resolve their differences with full knowledge of the problem. Accordingly, under these conditions, AI, AII, and CI, which permit no interaction among subordinates and therefore provide no opportunity for those in conflict to resolve their differences, are eliminated from the feasible set. Their use runs the risk of leaving some of the subordinates with less than the needed commitment to the final decision.

6. **The fairness rule.** If the quality of the decision is unimportant but acceptance of the decision is critical and not certain to result from an autocratic decision, it is important that the decision process used generate the needed acceptance. The decision process used should permit the subordinates to interact with one another and negotiate over the fair method of resolving any differences, with full responsibility on them for determining what is fair and equitable. Accordingly, under these circumstances, AI, AII, CI, and CII are eliminated from the feasible set.

7. **The acceptance priority rule.** If acceptance is critical and not certain to result from an autocratic decision, and if subordinates are motivated to pursue the organizational goals represented in the problem, then methods that provide equal partnership in the decision-making process can provide greater acceptance without risking decision quality. Accordingly, AI, AII, CI, and CII are eliminated from the feasible set.

Source: "On the Validity of the Vroom-Yetton Model" by V. H. Vroom and A. G. Jago, *Journal of Applied Psychology*, April 1978, 151–62. Copyright © 1978 by the American Psychological Association. Reprinted by permission of the publisher and authors.

no, question D is then asked, but if the answer to A is yes, ask question B. The leader would proceed from left to right until a terminal or end point is reached. For example, the feasible solutions at point 1 are AI, AII, CI, CII, and GII. On the other hand, the feasible solution suggested at point 11 is GII. Each of the styles suggested is likely to lead to a high-quality decision acceptable to subordinates. Since this is the case, most leaders and managers believe that it is wisest to choose the most autocratic of the styles. The leader can save time by doing so without risking decision quality or acceptance. The specific style of leadership attempted would be based on the time needed to make a decision, the leader's preference, and the ability, knowledge, and experience of subordinates. Vroom and Yetton have developed a time-efficient Model A version of the decision tree,[20] which would lead to the selection of the least time consuming leadership style. The decision tree used in Figure 10–3 is the Model B or group development version. It maximizes the development of subordinates through increased participation in decision making when possible.

FIGURE 10–3

Decision Process Flowchart (Feasible Set)

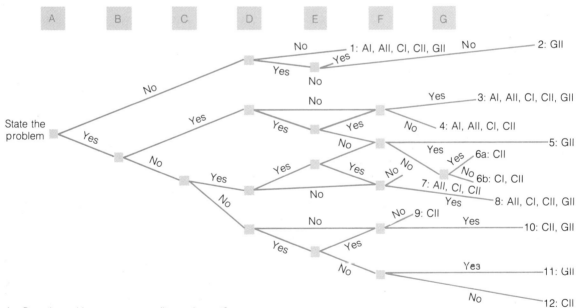

A. Does the problem possess a quality requirement?
B. Do I have sufficient information to make a high-quality decision?
C. Is the problem structured?
D. Is acceptance of the decision by subordinates important for effective implementation?
E. If I were to make the decision by myself, am I reasonably certain that it would be accepted by my subordinates?
F. Do subordinates share the organizational goals to be attained in solving the problem?
G. Is conflict among subordinates likely in preferred solutions?

---

[20] Victor H. Vroom, "Can Leaders Learn to Lead?" *Organizational Dynamics*, Winter 1976, pp. 17–28.

A CRITIQUE OF THE VROOM-YETTON MODEL

The Vroom-Yetton model has been specifically criticized on a number of issues.[21] First, the reliance on self-report data is considered a major threat to the validity of the model. Leaders (managers) are asked to list the details of one successful and one unsuccessful decision-making situation that they personally faced. The experience reporting occurs after the manager has studied the five decision styles and rational problem solving and practiced choosing a decision process for each of 30 decision scenarios.

Second, the methods just described to determine a leader's view of successful and unsuccessful behavior are also subject to experimenter and social desirability effects. Since managers previously have studied rational problem solving, there may be an experimenter influence on the results. Furthermore, there may be a tendency to want to appear more participative than one actually is in decision-making situations. It is socially desirable to permit followers or subordinates to participate.

Despite the criticisms, the Vroom-Yetton approach to leadership is an important contribution. The model was developed after thorough experimentation with similar models. In addition, tests of the model are at least as rigorous and, in most cases, seem more carefully planned and executed than tests of other leadership approaches.[22] Also, one important organizational implication of the model involves training. If current and future research support the validity of the model, more effective leadership will result if leaders are trained or instructed to use the model.[23] Training would enable leaders to choose the appropriate level of follower/subordinate participation.

PATH-GOAL MODEL

Like the other situational or contingency leadership approaches, the **path-goal model** attempts to predict leadership effectiveness in different situations. According to this model, leaders are effective because of their positive impact on followers' motivation, ability to perform, and satisfaction. The theory is designated path-goal because it focuses on how the leader influences the followers' perceptions of work goals, self-development goals, and paths to goal attainment.[24]

The foundation of path-goal theory is the expectancy motivation theory, discussed in Chapter 4. Some early work on the path-goal theory asserts that leaders will be effective by making rewards available to subordinates and by making those rewards contingent on the subordinates' accomplishment

---

[21] R. H. George Field, "A Critique of the Vroom-Yetton Contingency Model of Leadership Behavior," *Academy of Management Review*, April 1979, pp. 249–57.

[22] See, for example, Madeline Heilman, Harvey Hornstein, Jack Cage, and Judith Herschlag, "Reactions to Prescribed Behavior as a Function of Role Perspective: The Case of the Vroom-Yetton Model," *Journal of Applied Psychology*, February 1984, pp. 50–60.

[23] Arthur G. Jago, "Leadership Perspectives in Theory and Research," draft paper in College of Business Working Paper Series, University of Houston, 1979, p. 31.

[24] Robert J. House, "A Path-Goal Theory of Leadership Effectiveness," *Administrative Science Quarterly*, September 1971, pp. 32–39. Also see Robert J. House and Terence R. Mitchell, "Path-Goal Theory of Leadership," *Journal of Contemporary Business*, Autumn 1974, pp. 81–98, which is the basis for the discussion.

of specific goals.[25] It is argued that an important part of the leader's job is to clarify for subordinates the kind of behavior that is most likely to result in goal accomplishment. This activity is referred to as *path clarification.*

The early path-goal work led to the development of a complex theory involving four specific styles of leader behavior (directive, supportive, participative, and achievement) and three types of subordinate attitudes (job satisfaction, acceptance of the leader, and expectations about effort-performance-reward relationships.)[26] The *directive leader* tends to let subordinates know what is expected of them. The *supportive leader* treats subordinates as equals. The *participative leader* consults with subordinates and uses their suggestions and ideas before reaching a decision. The *achievement-oriented* leader sets challenging goals, expects subordinates to perform at the highest level, and continually seeks improvement in performance.

Two types of situational or contingency variables are considered in the path-goal theory. These variables are the *personal characteristics of subordinates* and the *environmental pressures and demands* with which subordinates must cope in order to accomplish work goals and derive satisfaction.

Two important personal characteristics are subordinates' perceptions of their own ability and relevant experience. The higher the degree of perceived ability and/or relevant experience relative to the task demands, the less likely the subordinates are to accept a directive leadership style. The environmental variables include factors that are not within the control of subordinates but nonetheless are important to satisfaction or the ability to perform effectively.[27] These include the tasks, the organization's authority system, and the work group itself. Any of these environmental factors can motivate or constrain the subordinates.

The path-goal theory proposes that leader behavior will be motivational to the extent that it helps subordinates cope with environmental uncertainties. A leader who is able to reduce the uncertainties of the job is considered to be a motivator because he or she increases the subordinates' expectations that their efforts will lead to desirable rewards.

A CRITIQUE OF THE PATH-GOAL MODEL

The path-goal model, like the Vroom-Yetton model, warrants further study. Some question remains about the predictive power of the path-goal model. One researcher suggested that subordinate performance might be the cause of changes in leader behavior instead of, as predicted by the model, the other way around.[28] A review of the path-goal approach suggested that the model has resulted in the development of only a few hypotheses. These

---

[25] Martin G. Evans, "The Effects of Supervisory Behavior on the Path-Goal Relationship," *Organizational Behavior and Human Performance,* May 1970, pp. 277–98. Also see Martin G. Evans, "Effects of Supervisory Behavior: Extensions of Path-Goal Theory of Motivation," *Journal of Applied Psychology,* April 1974, pp. 172–78.

[26] Robert J. House and Gary Dessler, "The Path-Goal Theory of Leadership: Some Post Hoc and A Priori Tests," in *Contingency Approaches to Leadership,* ed. James G. Hunt (Carbondale: Southern Illinois University Press, 1974).

[27] House and Mitchell, "Path-Goal Theory of Leadership," p. 87.

[28] C. Greene, "Questions of Causation in the Path-Goal Theory of Leadership," *Academy of Management Journal,* March 1979, pp. 22–41.

reviewers also point to the record of inconsistent research results associated with the model. Additionally, much of the research to date has involved only partial tests of the model.[29]

On the positive side, however, the path-goal model is an improvement over the trait and personal-behavioral theories. It attempts to indicate which factors affect the motivation to perform. In addition, the path-goal approach introduces both situational factors and individual differences when examining leader behavior and outcomes such as satisfaction and performance. The path-goal approach makes an effort to explain why a particular style of leadership works best in a given situation. As more research accumulates, this type of explanation will have practical utility for those interested in the leadership process in work settings.

COMPARISON OF THE SITUATIONAL APPROACHES

Three current models for examining leadership have been presented. These models have similarities and differences. They are similar in that they (1) focus on the dynamics of leadership, (2) have stimulated research on leadership, and (3) remain controversial because of measurement problems, limited research testing, or contradictory research results.

The themes of each model are summarized in Table 10–3. Fiedler's model has been the most tested and perhaps the most controversial. His view of

TABLE 10–3

A Comparison of Three Situational Approaches to Leadership

Approach	Leader Behavior/Style	Situational Factors	Outcome Criteria
Fiedler's contingency model	Task-oriented (low LPC) Relationship-oriented (high LPC)	Task-structure Leader-member relations Position power	Group's effectiveness
Vroom-Yetton	Autocratic Consultative Group	Quality of decision Information requirement Problem structure Followers' acceptance of decision Mutuality of follower and organizational goals Level of follower conflict	Quality of decision Acceptance of decision by followers Time to make decisions
Path-goal	Directive Supportive Participative Achievement-oriented	Follower characteristics Environmental factors	Satisfaction Performance

Source: Adapted from Edwin P. Hollander, *Leadership Dynamics* (New York: Free Press, 1978).

[29] J. Faulk and E. Wendler, "Dimensionality of Leader-Subordinate Interactions: A Path-Goal Approach," *Organizational Behavioral Human Performance*, 1982, pp. 241–64.

leader behavior centers on task- and relationship-oriented tendencies and how these tendencies interact with task and position power. Vroom and Yetton view leader behavior in terms of autocratic, consultative, or group styles. Finally, the path-goal approach emphasizes the instrumental actions of leaders and four styles for conducting these actions—directive, supportive, participative, and achievement-oriented.

The situational variables discussed in each approach differ somewhat. There is also a different view of outcome criteria for assessing how successful the leader behavior has been. Fiedler discusses leader effectiveness; Vroom and Yetton discuss the quality of a decision, follower acceptance, and the timeliness of the decision; the path-goal approach focuses on satisfaction and performance.

The second article accompanying this chapter, "Leadership: Good, Better, Best" by Bernard Boss, also discusses leadership from a situational perspective. This article analyzes what the author refers to as transactional leadership and transformational leadership. In making a case for the latter, Boss stresses the importance of leader *charisma,* a source of power discussed in Chapter 9.

SOME REMAINING ISSUES REGARDING LEADERSHIP

The trait, personal-behavioral, and situational theories have advanced the understanding of leadership and have stimulated important research studies. However, a number of gaps still remain in the current understanding of the process and outcomes of leadership in work organizations. Two particularly interesting leadership issues are: (1) Does leadership cause—or is it more significantly affected by—follower satisfaction and performance? and (2), are these substitutes for leadership that affect satisfaction and performance?

IS LEADER BEHAVIOR A CAUSE OR AN EFFECT?

We have implied that leader behavior has an effect on the follower's performance and job satisfaction. There is, however, a sound basis from which one can argue that follower performance and satisfaction cause the leader to vary his or her leadership style. It has been argued that a person will develop positive attitudes toward objects that are instrumental to the satisfaction of his or her needs.[30] This argument can be extended to leader-follower relationships. For example, organizations reward leaders (managers) based on the performance of followers (subordinates). If this is the case, leaders might be expected to develop positive attitudes toward high-performing followers. Let us say that an employee, Joe, because of outstanding performance, enables his boss, Mary, to receive the supervisory excellence award, a bonus of $1,000. The expectation then is that Mary would think highly of Joe and reward him with a better work schedule or job assignment. In this case, Joe's behavior leads to Mary's being rewarded, and she in turn rewards Joe.

---

[30] D. Katz and E. Stotland, "A Preliminary Statement to a Theory of Attitude Structure and Change," in *Psychology: A Study of Science,* ed. S. Koch (New York: McGraw-Hill, 1959).

In a field study, data were collected from first-line managers and from two of each manager's first-line supervisors. The purpose of this research was to assess the direction of causal influence in relationships between leader and follower variables. The results strongly suggested that (1) leader consideration behavior caused subordinate satisfaction and (2), follower performance caused changes in the leader's emphasis on both consideration and the structuring of behavior-performance relationships.[31]

The research available on the cause-effect issue is still quite limited. It is premature to conclude that all leader behavior, or even a significant portion of such behavior, is a response to follower behavior. However, there is a need to examine the leader-follower relationship in terms of *reciprocal causation*. That is, leader behavior causes follower behavior and follower behavior causes leader behavior.

SUBSTITUTES FOR LEADERSHIP

A wide variety of individual, task, environmental, and organizational characteristics have been identified as factors that influence relationships between leader behavior and follower satisfaction and performance. Some of these variables (e.g., follower expectations of leader behavior) appear to influence which leadership style will enable the leader to motivate and direct followers. Others function, however, as *substitutes for leadership*. Substitute variables tend to negate the leader's ability either to increase or decrease follower satisfaction or performance.[32]

It is claimed that substitutes for leadership are prominent in many organizational settings. As the following OBM Encounter illustrates, leadership substitutes may be quite prevalent in certain settings. However, the dominant leadership approaches fail to include substitutes for leadership in discussing the leader behavior-follower satisfaction and performance relationship.

ENCOUNTER

WHEN LEADERS ARE NOT NEEDED

While we may not fully understand the role leadership substitutes play in various organizational settings, there is little doubt that a variety of different factors can operate to reduce the need for leadership and consequently, the need for people in formal leadership positions. Consider the following case:

SMC Hendrick, Inc., a Massachusetts management consulting firm which specializes in computerized analysis of how businesses are operated, found that almost one-third of middle management in 11 major banks could be eliminated with no significant harmful consequences and no negative impact on the quality of services provided. The study found that, rather than providing "leadership," managers spend half of their time engaging in activities that readily could be done by technicians, clerks, and others in nonleadership positions. Using managers to perform these operations adds millions of dollars to bank overhead annually.

---

[31] Charles N. Greene, "The Reciprocal Nature of Influence between Leader and Subordinate," *Journal of Applied Psychology*, April 1975, pp. 187–93.

[32] Steven Kerr and John M. Jermier, "Substitutes for Leadership: Their Meaning and Measurement," *Organizational Behavior and Human Performance*, December 1978, pp. 376–403.

Moro than 48,000 bank managers and workers were surveyed in the study, which failed to uncover any significant positive reasons for maintaining such large cadres of management personnel. On average, the study found managers oversaw only four employees, although in the better organized banks, this number grew to seven.

From the standpoint of overall organizational effectiveness and efficiency, perhaps too much "leadership" is as counterproductive as too little. ☐

Source: Based, in part, from the article, "A Consultant's View: Managers Manage Too Few, Too Much," *New England Business,* May 17, 1982, pp. 30–32.

Table 10–4, based on previously conducted research, provides substitutes for only two of the more popular leader behavior styles—relationship-oriented and task-oriented. For each of these leader behavior styles, Kerr and Jermier present which substitutes (characteristics of the subordinate, the task, or the organization) will serve to neutralize the style.[33] For example, an experienced, well-trained, and knowledgeable employee does not need a leader to structure the task (e.g., a task-oriented leader). Likewise, a job (task) that provides its own feedback does not need a task-oriented leader to inform

TABLE 10–4

Substitutes for Leadership

Characteristic	Will Tend to Neutralize	
	Relationship-Oriented	Task-Oriented
Of the subordinate:		
1. Ability, experience, training, knowledge		X
2. Need for independence	X	X
3. "Professional" orientation	X	X
4. Indifference toward organizational rewards	X	X
Of the task:		
5. Unambiguous and routine		X
6. Methodologically invariant		X
7. Provides its own feedback concerning accomplishment		X
8. Intrinsically satisfying	X	
Of the organization:		
9. Formalization (explicit plans, goals, and areas of responsibility)		X
10. Inflexibility (rigid, unbending rules and procedures)		X
11. Highly specified and active advisory and staff functions		X
12. Close-knit, cohesive work groups	X	X
13. Organizational rewards not within the leader's control	X	X
14. Spatial distance between superior and subordinates	X	X

Source: Adapted from Steven Kerr and John M. Jermier, "Substitutes for Leadership: Their Meaning and Measurement," *Organizational Behavior and Human Performance,* December 1978, p. 378.

---

[33] Ibid.

the employee how he or she is doing. Also, an employee in a close-knit, cohesive group does not need a supportive, relationship-oriented leader. The group is a substitute for this type of leader.

Admittedly, we do not fully understand the leader-follower relationship in organizational settings. The need to continue searching for guidelines and principles is apparent. Such searching now seems to be centered on more careful analysis of a situational perspective of leadership and on issues such as the cause-effect question, the constraints on leader behavior, and substitutes for leadership. We feel that it is better to study leaders and substitutes for leaders than to use catchy descriptions to identify leaders. This type of study and analysis can result in the development of programs to train, prepare, and develop employees for leadership roles.

This chapter has presented the idea that a single, universally accepted theory of leadership is not available. Each of the perspectives covered in the chapter provides insight into leadership. The fact is that various traits of leaders (e.g., intelligence, personality) influence how they behave with followers. Also, situational variables and follower characteristics (e.g., needs, abilities, experience) affect a leader's behavior. Therefore, traits, personal-behavioral, and situational characteristics must be considered when attempting to understand leadership in organizational settings.

SUMMARY OF KEYPOINTS

A. Leadership is an ability to influence followers that involves the use of power and the acceptance of the leader by the followers. This ability to influence followers is related to the followers' need satisfaction.

B. The trait approach has resulted in attempts to predict leadership effectiveness from physical, sociological, and psychological traits. The search for traits has led to studies involving effectiveness and such factors as height, weight, intelligence, and personality.

C. A great deal of semantic confusion and overlap continues regarding the definition of leadership behavior. Such terms as *employee-centered, job-centered, initiating structure,* and *consideration* are classified as personal-behavioral descriptions of what the leader does.

D. The personal-behavioral approaches suggest that situational variables such as the follower's expectations, skills, role clarity, and previous experiences should be seriously considered by leaders. Leaders can do little to improve effectiveness unless they can properly modify these variables or change their style of leadership.

E. The *situational approach* emphasizes the importance of forces within the leader, the subordinates, and the organization. These forces interact and must be properly diagnosed if effectiveness is to be achieved.

F. The *contingency model* proposes that the performance of groups is dependent on the interaction of leadership style and situational favorableness. The three crucial situational factors are leader-member relations, task structure, and position power.

G. Vroom and Yetton have developed a leadership model that can be used to select the amount of group decision-making participation needed in a variety of problem situations. The model suggests that the amount of subordinate participation depends on the leader's skill and knowledge, whether a quality decision is needed, the extent to which the problem is structured, and whether acceptance by subordinates is needed to implement the decision.

H. The leader's role in the *path-goal theory* is (1) to increase the number and kinds of personal payoffs to subordinates and (2) to provide guidance and counsel for clarifying paths and reducing problems when seeking various outcomes.

I. Some evidence raises the question of whether leader behavior causes follower satisfaction or performance, or vice versa. Followers may have a significant impact on leader behavior or style.

J. Subordinates can be influenced by substitutes for leader behavior. Task, subordinate, and organizational substitutes exist. These substitutes include ability, experience, the routineness of the task, and group cohesiveness.

REVIEW AND DISCUSSION QUESTIONS

1. Do organizations do a good job in selecting people for leadership positions? Are there ways in which they could do a better job?

2. "Great leaders are born, not made." Is this statement generally true? Is it ever true? What implications does it have for organizations?

3. Organizations annually spend a great deal of money on leadership training. Is this a wise investment? Are there other, less costly ways of improving leadership?

4. How much control does a leader have over situational favorableness? How might a leader improve favorableness?

5. The seven decision rules underlying the Vroom-Yetton model are very important in determining appropriate leader behavior. Summarize these rules in the form of questions which should be asked.

6. According to the path-goal approach, a number of factors are thought to influence outcomes in the form of satisfaction and performance. What are these factors?

7. Several of the situational approaches require the leader to behave differently in different situations. Is there a risk that this type of behavior flexibility could be perceived by subordinates as inconsistency and unpredictability? Discuss.

8. Which of the situational approaches is most attractive to you? Why?

9. It has been suggested that good leadership is knowing when to take charge and when to delegate. How consistent is this with the various situational approaches discussed in the chapter.

10. The trait approach to leadership has not proven to be particularly helpful to use in understanding leadership. Why is this, do you think? Does it mean that there are no traits associated with leadership effectiveness?

THE AMBIGUITY OF LEADERSHIP

JEFFREY PFEFFER

Leadership has for some time been a major topic in social and organizational psychology. Underlying much of this research has been the assumption that leadership is causally related to organizational performance. Through an analysis of leadership styles, behaviors, or characteristics (depending on the theoretical perspective chosen), the argument has been made that more effective leaders can be selected or trained or, alternatively, the situation can be configured to provide for enhanced leader and organizational effectiveness.

Three problems with emphasis on leadership as a concept can be posed: (a) ambiguity in definition and measurement of the concept

Reprinted, by permission of the *Academy of Management Review* (January 1977).

itself; (b) the question of whether leadership has discernible effects on organizational outcomes; and (c) the selection process in succession to leadership positions, which frequently uses organizationally irrelevant criteria and which has implications for normative theories of leadership. The argument here is that leadership is of interest primarily as a phenomenological construct. Leaders serve as symbols for representing personal causation of social events. How and why are such attributions of personal effects made? Instead of focusing on leadership and its effects, how do people make inferences about and react to phenomena labelled as leadership (5)?

THE AMBIGUITY OF THE CONCEPT

While there have been many studies of leadership, the dimensions

and definition of the concept remain unclear. To treat leadership as a separate concept, it must be distinguished from other social influence phenomena. Hollander and Julian (24) and Bavelas (2) did not draw distinctions between leadership and other processes of social influence. A major point of the Hollander and Julian review was that leadership research might develop more rapidly if more general theories of social influence were incorporated. Calder (5) also argued that there is no unique content to the construct of leadership that is not subsumed under other, more general models of behavior.

LEARNING CHECKPOINT

Does the definition of leadership in the chapter suffer from ambiguity?

Kochan, Schmidt, and DeCotiis (33) attempted to distinguish leadership from related concepts of authority and social power. In leadership, influence rights are voluntarily conferred. Power does not require goal compatability—merely dependence—but leadership implies some congruence between the objectives of the leader and the led. These distinctions depend on the ability to distinguish voluntary from involuntary compliance and to assess goal compatibility. Goal statements may be retrospective inferences from action (46, 53) and problems of distinguishing voluntary from involuntary compliance also exist (32). Apparently there are few meaningful distinctions between leadership and other concepts of social influence. Thus, an understanding of the phenomena subsumed under the rubric of leadership may not require the construct of leadership (5).

While there is some agreement that leadership is related to social influence, more disagreement concerns the basic dimensions of leader behavior. Some have argued that there are two tasks to be accomplished in groups—maintenance of the group and performance of some task or activity—and thus leader behavior might be described along these two dimensions (1, 6, 8, 25). The dimensions emerging from the Ohio State leadership studies—consideration and initiating structure—may be seen as similar to the two components of group maintenance and task accomplishment (18).

Other dimensions of leadership behavior have also been proposed (4). Day and Hamblin (10) analyzed leadership in terms of the closeness and punitiveness of the supervision. Several authors have conceptualized leadership behavior in terms of the authority and discre-

tion subordinates are permitted (23, 36, 51). Fiedler (14) analyzed leadership in terms of the least-preferred-co-worker scale (LPC), but the meaning and behavioral attributes of this dimension of leadership behavior remain controversial.

The proliferation of dimensions is partly a function of research strategies frequently employed. Factor analysis on a large number of items describing behavior has frequently been used. This procedure tends to produce as many factors as the analyst decides to find, and permits the development of a large number of possible factor structures. The resultant factors must be named and further imprecision is introduced. Deciding on a summative concept to represent a factor is inevitably a partly subjective process.

Literature assessing the effects of leadership tends to be equivocal. Sales (45) summarized leadership literature employing the authoritarian-democratic typology and concluded that effects on performance were small and inconsistent. Reviewing the literature on consideration and initiating structure dimensions, Korman (34) reported relatively small and inconsistent results, and Kerr and Schriesheim (30) reported more consistent effects of the two dimensions. Better results apparently emerge when moderating factors are taken into account, including subordinate personalities (50), and situational characteristics (23, 51). Kerr, et al. (31) list many moderating effects grouped under the headings of subordinate considerations, supervisor considerations, and task considerations. Even if each set of considerations consisted of only one factor (which it does not), an attempt to account for the effects of leader behavior would necessitate considering four-way interactions. While social reality is complex and

contingent, it seems desirable to attempt to find more parsimonious explanations for the phenomena under study.

THE EFFECTS OF LEADERS

Hall asked a basic question about leadership: is there any evidence on the magnitude of the effects of leadership (17, p. 248)? Surprisingly, he could find little evidence. Given the resources that have been spent studying, selecting, and training leaders, one might expect that the question of whether or not leaders matter would have been addressed earlier (12).

There are at least three reasons why it might be argued that the observed effects of leaders on organizational outcomes would be small. First, those obtaining leadership positions are selected, and perhaps only certain, limited styles of behavior may be chosen. Second, once in the leadership position, the discretion and behavior of the leader are constrained. And third, leaders can typically affect only a few of the variables that may impact organizational performance.

Homogeneity of Leaders

Persons are selected to leadership positions. As a consequence of this selection process, the range of behaviors or characteristics exhibited by leaders is reduced, making it more problematic to empirically discover an effect of leadership. There are many types of constraints on the selection process. The attraction literature suggests that there is a tendency for persons to like those they perceive as similar (3). In critical decisions such as the selections of persons for leadership positions, compatible styles of behavior probably will be chosen.

Selection of persons is also constrained by the internal system of influence in the organization. As Zald (56) noted, succession is a critical decision, affected by political influence and by environmental contingencies faced by the organization. As Thompson (49) noted, leaders may be selected for their capacity to deal with various organizational contingencies. In a study of characteristics of hospital administrators, Pfeffer and Salancik (42) found a relationship between the hospital's context and the characteristics and tenure of the administrators. To the extent that the contingencies and power distribution within the organization remain stable, the abilities and behaviors of those selected into leadership positions will also remain stable.

Finally, the selection of persons to leadership positions is affected by a self-selection process. Organizations and roles have images, providing information about their character. Persons are likely to select themselves into organizations and roles based upon their preferences for the dimensions of the organizational and role characteristics as perceived through these images. The self-selection of persons would tend to work along with organizational selection to limit the range of abilities and behaviors in a given organizational role.

Such selection processes would tend to increase homogeneity more within a single organization than across organizations. Yet many studies of leadership effect at the work group level have compared groups within a single organization. If there comes to be a widely shared, socially constructed definition of leadership behaviors or characteristics which guides the selection process, then leadership activity may come to be defined similarly in various organizations,

leading to the selection of only those who match the constructed image of a leader.

Constraints on Leader Behavior

Analyses of leadership have frequently presumed that leadership style or leader behavior was an independent variable that could be selected or trained at will to conform to what research would find to be optimal. Even theorists who took a more contingent view of appropriate leadership behavior generally assumed that with proper training, appropriate behavior could be produced (51). Fiedler (13), noting how hard it was to change behavior, suggested changing the situational characteristics rather than the person, but this was an unusual suggestion in the context of prevailing literature which suggested that leadership style was something to be strategically selected according to the variables of the particular leadership theory.

But the leader is embedded in a social system, which constrains behavior. The leader has a role set (27), in which members have expectations for appropriate behavior and persons make efforts to modify the leader's behavior. Pressures to conform to the expectations of peers, subordinates, and superiors are all relevant in determining actual behavior.

Leaders, even in high-level positions, have unilateral control over fewer resources and fewer policies than might be expected. Investment decisions may require approval of others, while hiring and promotion decisions may be accomplished by committees. Leader behavior is constrained by both the demands of others in the role set and by organizationally prescribed limitations on the sphere of activity and influence.

External Factors

Many factors that may affect organizational performance are outside a leader's control, even if he or she were to have complete discretion over major areas of organizational decisions. For example, consider the executive in a construction firm. Costs are largely determined by operation of commodities and labor markets; and demand is largely affected by interest rates, availability of mortgage money, and economic conditions which are affected by governmental policies over which the executive has little control. School superintendents have little control over birth rates and community economic development, both of which profoundly affect school system budgets. While the leader may react to contingencies as they arise, or may be a better or worse forecaster, in accounting for variation in organizational outcomes, he or she may account for relatively little compared to external factors.

Second, the leader's success or failure may be partly due to circumstances unique to the organization but still outside his or her control. Leader positions in organizations vary in terms of the strength and position of the organization. The choice of a new executive does not fundamentally alter a market and financial position that has developed over years and affects the leader's ability to make strategic changes and the likelihood that the organization will do well or poorly. Organizations have relatively enduring strengths and weaknesses. The choice of a particular leader for a particular position has limited impact on these capabilities.

Empirical Evidence

Two studies have assessed the effects of leadership changes in major positions in organizations. Lieberson and O'Connor (35) examined 167 business firms in 13 industries over a 20 year period, allocating variance in sales, profits, and profit margins to one of four sources: year (general economic conditions), industry, company effects, and effects of changes in the top executive position. They concluded that compared to other factors, administration had a limited effect on organizational outcomes.

Using a similar analytical procedure, Salancik and Pfeffer (44) examined the effects of mayors on city budgets for 30 U.S. cities. Data on expenditures by budget category were collected for 1951–1968. Variance in amount and proportion of expenditures was apportioned to the year, the city, or the mayor. The mayoral effect was relatively small, with the city accounting for most of the variance, although the mayor effect was larger for expenditure categories that were not as directly connected to important interest groups. Salancik and Pfeffer argued that the effects of the mayor were limited both by absence of power to control many of the expenditures and tax sources, and by construction of policies in response to demands from interests in the environment.

If leadership is defined as a strictly interpersonal phenomenon, the relevance of these two studies for the issue of leadership effects becomes problematic. But such a conceptualization seems unduly restrictive, and is certainly inconsistent with Selznick's (47) conceptualization of leadership as strategic management and decision making. If one cannot observe differences when leaders change, then what does it matter who occupies the positions or how they behave?

Pfeffer and Salancik (41) investigated the extent to which behaviors selected by first-line supervisors were constrained by expectations of others in their role set. Variance in task and social behaviors could be accounted for by role-set expectations, with adherence to various demands made by role-set participants a function of similarity and relative power. Lowin and Craig (37) experimentally demonstrated that leader behavior was determined by the subordinate's own behavior. Both studies illustrate that leader behaviors are responses to the demands of the social context.

The effect of leadership may vary depending upon level in the organizational hierarchy, while the appropriate activities and behaviors may also vary with organizational level (26, 40). For the most part, empirical studies of leadership have dealt with first-line supervisors or leaders with relatively low organizational status (17). If leadership has any impact, it should be more evident at higher organizational levels or where there is more discretion in decisions and activities.

LEARNING CHECKPOINT

The leadership model in Figure 10–1 indicates that leaders can influence outcomes. Which outcome listed in the model would higher-level organizational managers/leaders (chief executive officers) have the most influence over?

THE PROCESS OF SELECTING LEADERS

Along with the suggestion that leadership may not account for much variance in organizational outcomes, it can be argued that merit or ability may not account for much variation in hiring and advance-

ment of organizational personnel. These two ideas are related. If competence is hard to judge, or if leadership competence does not greatly affect organizational outcomes, then other, person-dependent criteria may be sufficient. Effective leadership styles may not predict career success when other variables such as social background are controlled.

Belief in the importance of leadership is frequently accompanied by belief that persons occupying leadership positions are selected and trained according to how well they can enhance the organization's performance. Belief in a leadership effect leads to development of a set of activities oriented toward enhancing leadership effectiveness. Simultaneously, persons managing their own careers are likely to place emphasis on activities and developing behaviors that will enhance their own leadership skills, assuming that such a strategy will facilitate advancement.

Research on the bases for hiring and promotion has been concentrated on examination of academic positions (e.g., 7, 19, 20). This is possibly the result of availability of relatively precise and unambiguous measures of performance, such as number of publications or citations. Evidence on criteria used in selecting and advancing personnel in industry is more indirect.

Studies have attempted to predict either the compensation or the attainment of general management positions of MBA students, using personality and other background information (21, 22, 54). There is some evidence that managerial success can be predicted by indicators of ability and motivation such as test scores and grades, but the amount of variance explained is typically quite small.

A second line of research has

investigated characteristics and backgrounds of persons attaining leadership positions in major organizations in society. Domhoff (11), Mills (38), and Warner and Abbeglin (52) found a strong preponderance of persons with upper-class backgrounds occupying leadership positions. The implication of these findings is that studies of graduate success, including the success of MBA's, would explain more variance if the family background of the person were included.

A third line of inquiry uses a tracking model. The dynamic model developed is one in which access to elite universities is affected by social status (28) and, in turn, social status and attendance at elite universities affect later career outcomes (9, 43, 48, 55).

Unless one is willing to make the argument that attendance at elite universities or coming from an upper-class background is perfectly correlated with merit, the evidence suggests that succession to leadership positions is not strictly based on meritocratic criteria. Such a conclusion is consistent with the inability of studies attempting to predict the success of MBA graduates to account for much variance, even when a variety of personality and ability factors are used.

Beliefs about the bases for social mobility are important for social stability. As long as persons believe that positions are allocated on meritocratic grounds, they are more likely to be satisfied with the social order and with their position in it. This satisfaction derives from the belief that occupational position results from application of fair and reasonable criteria, and that the opportunity exists for mobility if the person improves skills and performance.

If succession to leadership positions is determined by person-based criteria such as social origins or social connections (16), then efforts to enhance managerial effectiveness with the expectation that this will lead to career success divert attention from the processes of stratification actually operating within organizations. Leadership literature has been implicitly aimed at two audiences. Organizations were told how to become more effective, and persons were told what behaviors to acquire in order to become effective, and hence, advance in their careers. The possibility that neither organizational outcomes nor career success are related to leadership behaviors leaves leadership research facing issues of relevance and importance.

THE ATTRIBUTION OF LEADERSHIP

Kelley conceptualized the layman as:

> an applied scientist, that is, as a person concerned about applying his knowledge of causal relationships in order to *exercise control* of his world (29, p. 2).

Reviewing a series of studies dealing with the attributional process, he concluded that persons were not only interested in understanding their world correctly, but also in controlling it.

> The view here proposed is that attribution processes are to be understood not only as a means of providing the individual with a veridical view of his world, but as a means of encouraging and maintaining his effective exercise of control in that world (29, p. 22).

Controllable factors will have high salience as candidates for causal explanation, while a bias toward the more important causes may shift the attributional emphasis toward causes that are not controllable (29, p. 23). The study of attribution is a study of naive psychology—an examination of how persons make sense out of the events taking place around them.

If Kelley is correct that individuals will tend to develop attributions that give them a feeling of control, then emphasis on leadership may derive partially from a desire to believe in the effectiveness and importance of individual action, since individual action is more controllable than contextual variables. Lieberson and O'Connor (35) made essentially the same point in introducing their paper on the effects of top management changes on organizational performance. Given the desire for control and a feeling of personal effectiveness, organizational outcomes are more likely to be attributed to individual actions, regardless of their actual causes.

Leadership is attributed by observers. Social action has meaning only through a phenomenological process (46). The identification of certain organizational roles as leadership positions guides the construction of meaning in the direction of attributing effects to the actions of those positions. While Bavelas (2) argued that the functions of leadership, such as task accomplishment and group maintenance, are shared throughout the group, this fact provides no simply and potentially controllable focus for attributing causality. Rather, the identification of leadership positions provides a simpler and more readily changeable model of reality. When causality is lodged in one or a few persons rather than being a function of a complex set of interactions among all group members, changes can be made by replacing or influencing the occupant of the leadership position. Causes of organizational actions are readily identified in this simple causal structure.

Even if, empirically, leadership has little effect, and even if succession to leadership positions is not predicated on ability or performance, the belief in leadership effects and meritocratic succession provides a simple causal framework and a justification for the structure of the social collectivity. More importantly, the beliefs interpret social actions in terms that indicate potential for effective individual intervention or control. The personification of social causality serves too many uses to be easily overcome. Whether or not leader behavior actually influences performance or effectiveness, it is important because people believe it does.

LEARNING CHECKPOINT

Assume that there is some merit in the path-goal explanation of leadership. Why would subordinates reach a conclusion that their leader was effective in helping them attain job related goals (e.g., higher-quality output)?

One consequence of the attribution of causality to leaders and leadership is that leaders come to be symbols. Mintzberg (39), in his discussion of the roles of managers, wrote of the symbolic role, but more in terms of attendance at formal events and formally representing the organization. The symbolic role of leadership is more important than implied in such a description. The leader as a symbol provides a target for action when difficulties occur, serving as a scapegoat when things go wrong. Gamson and Scotch (15) noted that in baseball,

the firing of the manager served a scapegoating purpose. One cannot fire the whole team, yet when performance is poor, something must be done. The firing of the manager conveys to the world and to the actors involved that success is the result of personal actions, and that steps can and will be taken to enhance organizational performance.

The attribution of causality to leadership may be reinforced by organizational actions, such as the inauguration process, the choice process, and providing the leader with symbols and ceremony. If leaders are chosen by using a random number table, persons are less likely to believe in their effects than if there is an elaborate search or selection process followed by an elaborate ceremony signifying the changing of control, and if the leader then has a variety of perquisites and symbols that distinguish him or her from the rest of the organization. Construction of the importance of leadership in a given social context is the outcome of various social processes, which can be empirically examined.

Since belief in the leadership effect provides a feeling of personal control, one might argue that efforts to increase the attribution of causality to leaders would occur more when it is more necessary and more problematic to attribute causality to controllable factors. Such an argument would lead to the hypothesis that the more the *context* actually effects organizational outcomes, the more efforts will be made to ensure attribution to *leadership*. When leaders really do have effects, it is less necessary to engage in rituals indicating their effects. Such rituals are more likely when there is uncertainty and unpredictability associated with the organization's operations. This results both from the desire to feel control in

uncertain situations and from the fact that in ambiguous contexts, it is easier to attribute consequences to leadership without facing possible disconfirmation.

The leader is, in part, an actor. Through statements and actions, the leader attempts to reinforce the operation of an attribution process which tends to vest causality in that position in the social structure. Successful leaders, as perceived by members of the social system, are those who can separate themselves from organizational failures and associate themselves with organizational successes. Since the meaning of action is socially constructed, this involves manipulation of symbols to reinforce the desired process of attribution. For instance, if a manager knows that business in his or her division is about to improve because of the economic cycle, the leader may, nevertheless, write recommendations and undertake actions and changes that are highly visible and that will tend to identify his or her behavior closely with the division. A manager who perceives impending failure will attempt to associate the division and its policies and decisions with others, particularly persons in higher organizational positions, and to disassociate himself or herself from the division's performance, occasionally even transferring or moving to another organization.

CONCLUSION

The theme of this article has been that analysis of leadership and leadership processes must be contingent on the intent of the researcher. If the interest is in understanding the causality of social phenomena as reliably and accurately as possible, then the concept of leadership may be a poor place to begin. The issue of the effects of leadership is open to question. But examination of situational variables that accompany more or less leadership effect is a worthwhile task.

The more phenomenological analysis of leadership directs attention to the process by which social causality is attributed, and focuses on the distinction between causality as perceived by group members and causality as assessed by an outside observer. Leadership is associated with a set of myths reinforcing a social construction of meaning which legitimates leadership role occupants, provides belief in potential mobility for those not in leadership roles, and attributes social causality to leadership roles, thereby providing a belief in the effectiveness of individual control. In analyzing leadership, this mythology and the process by which such mythology is created and supported should be separated from analysis of leadership as a social influence process, operating within constraints. □

REFERENCES

1. Bales, R. F. *Interaction Process Analysis: A Method for the Study of Small Groups* (Reading, Mass.: Addison-Wesley, 1950).

2. Bavelas, Alex. "Leadership: Man and Function," *Administrative Science Quarterly,* Vol. 4 (1960), 491–498.

3. Berscheid, Ellen, and Elaine Walster. *Interpersonal Attraction* (Reading, Mass.: Addison-Wesley, 1969).

4. Bowers, David G., and Stanley E. Seashore. "Predicting Organizational Effectiveness with a Four-Factor Theory of Leadership." *Administrative Science Quarterly,* Vol. 11 (1966), 238–263.

5. Calder, Bobby J. "An Attribution Theory of Leadership," in B. Staw and G. Salancik (Eds.), *New Directions in Organizational Behavior* (Chicago: St. Clair Press, 1976), in press.

6. Cartwright, Dorwin C., and Alvin Zander. *Group Dynamics: Research and Theory,* 3rd ed. (Evanston, Ill.: Row, Peterson, 1960).

7. Cole, Jonathan R., and Stephen Cole. *Social Stratification in Science* (Chicago: University of Chicago Press, 1973).

8. Collins, Barry E., and Harold Guetzkow. *A Social Psychology of Group Processes for Decision-Making* (New York: Wiley, 1964).

9. Collins, Randall. "Functional and Conflict Theories of Stratification," *American Sociological Review,* Vol. 36 (1971), 1002–1019.

10. Day, R. C., and R. L. Hamblin. "Some Effects of Close and Punitive Styles of Supervision," *American Journal of Sociology,* Vol. 69 (1964), 499–510.

11. Domhoff, G. William. *Who Rules America?* (Englewood Cliffs, N.J.: Prentice-Hall, 1967).

12. Dubin, Robert. "Supervision and Productivity: Empirical Findings and Theoretical Considerations," in R. Dubin, G. C. Homans, F. C. Mann, and D. C. Miller (Eds.), *Leadership and Productivity* (San Francisco: Chandler Publishing Co., 1965), pp. 1–50.

13. Fiedler, Fred E. "Engineering the Job to Fit the Manager," *Harvard Business Review,* Vol. 43 (1965), 115–122.

14. Fiedler, Fred E. *A Theory of Leadership Effectiveness* (New York: McGraw-Hill, 1967).

15. Gamson, William A., and Norman A. Scotch. "Scapegoating in Baseball," *American Journal of Sociology,* Vol. 70 (1964), 69–72.

16. Granovetter, Mark. *Getting a Job* (Cambridge, Mass.: Harvard University Press, 1974).

17. Hall, Richard H. *Organizations: Structure and Process* (Englewood Cliffs, N.J.: Prentice-Hall, 1972).

18. Halpin, A. W., and J. Winer. "A Factorial Study of the Leader Behavior Description Questionnaire," in R. M. Stogdill and A. E. Coons (Eds.), *Leader Behavior: Its Description and Measurement* (Columbus, Ohio: Bureau of Business Research, Ohio State University, 1957), pp. 39–51.

19. Hargens, L. L. "Patterns of Mobility of New Ph.D.'s Among American Academic Institutions," *Sociology of Education,* Vol. 42 (1969), 18–37.

20. Hargens, L. L., and W. O. Hagstrom. "Sponsored and Contest Mobility of American Academic Scientists," *Sociology of Education,* Vol. 40 (1967), 24–38.

21. Harrell, Thomas W. "High Earning MBA's," *Personnel Psychology,* Vol. 25 (1972), 523–530.

22. Harrell, Thomas W., and Margaret S. Harrell. "Predictors of Management Success." *Stanford University Graduate School of Business, Technical Report No. 3 to the Office of Naval Research.*

23. Heller, Frank, and Gary Yukl. "Participation, Managerial Decision-Making, and Situational Variables," *Organizational Behavior and Human Performance,* Vol. 4 (1969), 227–241.

24. Hollander, Edwin P., and James W. Julian. "Contemporary Trends in the Analysis of Leadership Processes," *Psychological Bulletin,* Vol. 71 (1969), 387–397.

25. House, Robert J. "A Path Goal Theory of Leader Effectiveness," *Administrative Science Quarterly,* Vol. 16 (1971), 321–338.

26. Hunt, J. G. "Leadership Style Effects at Two Managerial Levels in a Simulated Organization," *Administrative Science Quarterly,* Vol. 16 (1971), 476–485.

27. Kahn, R. L., D. M. Wolfe, R. P. Quinn, and J. D. Snoek. *Organizational Stress: Studies in Role Conflict and Ambiguity* (New York: Wiley, 1964).

28. Karabel, J., and A. W. Astin. "Social Class, Academic Ability, and College 'Quality'," *Social Forces,* Vol. 53 (1975), 381–398.

29. Kelley, Harold H. *Attribution in Social Interaction* (Morristown, N.J.: General Learning Press, 1971).

30. Kerr, Steven, and Chester Schriesheim. "Consideration, Initiating Structure and Organizational Criteria—An Update of Korman's 1966 Review," *Personnel Psychology,* Vol. 27 (1974), 555–568.

31. Kerr, S., C. Schriesheim, C. J. Murphy, and R. M. Stogdill, "Toward A Contingency Theory of Leadership Based Upon the Consideration and Initiating Structure Literature," *Organizational Behavior and Human Performance,* Vol. 12 (1974), 62–82.

32. Kiesler, C., and S. Kiesler. *Conformity* (Reading, Mass.: Addison-Wesley, 1969).

33. Kochan, T. A., S. M. Schmidt, and T. A. DeCotiis. "Superior-Subordinate Relations: Leadership and Headship," *Human Relations,* Vol. 28 (1975), 279–294.

34. Korman, A. K. "Consideration, Initiating Structure, and Organizational Criteria—A Review," *Personnel Psychology,* Vol. 19 (1966), 349–362.

35. Lieberson, Stanley, and James F. O'Connor. "Leadership and Organizational Performance: A Study of Large Corporations," *American Sociological Review,* Vol. 37 (1972), 117–130.

36. Lippitt, Ronald. "An Experimental Study of the Effect of Democratic and Authoritarian Group Atmospheres," *University of Iowa Studies in Child Welfare,* Vol. 16 (1940), 43–195.

37. Lowin, A., and J. R. Craig. "The Influence of Level of Performance on Managerial Style: An Experimental Object-Lesson in the Ambiguity of Correlational Data," *Organizational Behavior and Human Performance,* Vol. 3 (1968), 440–458.

38. Mills, C. Wright. "The American Business Elite: A Collective Portrait," in C. W. Mills, *Power, Politics, and People* (New York: Oxford University Press, 1963), pp. 110–139.

39. Mintzberg, Henry. *The Nature of Managerial Work* (New York: Harper and Row, 1973).

40. Nealey, Stanley M., and Milton R. Blood. "Leadership Performance of Nursing Supervisors at Two Organizational Levels," *Journal of Applied Psychology,* Vol. 52 (1968), 414–442.

41. Pfeffer, Jeffrey, and Gerald R. Salancik. "Determinants of Supervisory Behavior: A Role Set Analysis," *Human Relations,* Vol. 28 (1975), 139–154.

42. Pfeffer, Jeffrey, and Gerald R. Salancik. "Organizational Context and the Characteristics and Tenure of Hospital Administrators," *Academy of Management Journal,* Vol. 20 (1977), in press.

43. Reed, R. H., and H. P. Miller. "Some Determinants of the Variation in Earnings for College Men," *Journal of Human Resources,* Vol. 5 (1970), 117–190.

44. Salancik, Gerald R., and Jeffrey Pfeffer. "Constraints on Administrator Discretion: The Limited Influence of Mayors on City Budgets," *Urban Affairs Quarterly,* in press.

45. Sales, Stephen M. "Supervisory Style and Productivity: Review and Theory," *Personnel Psychology,* Vol. 19 (1966), 275–286.

46. Schutz, Alfred. *The Phenomenology of the Social World* (Evanston, Ill.: Northwestern University Press, 1967).

47. Selznick, P. *Leadership in Administration* (Evanston, Ill.: Row, Peterson, 1957).

48. Spaeth, J. L., and A. M. Greeley. *Recent Alumni and Higher Education* (New York: McGraw-Hill, 1970).

49. Thompson, James D. *Organizations in Action* (New York: McGraw-Hill, 1967).

50. Vroom, Victor H. "Some Personality Determinants of the Effects of Participation," *Journal of Abnormal and Social Psychology,* Vol. 59 (1959), 322–327.

51. Vroom, Victor H., and Philip W. Yetton. *Leadership and Decision-Making* (Pittsburgh: University of Pittsburgh Press, 1973).

52. Warner, W. L., and J. C. Abbeglin. *Big Business Leaders in America* (New York: Harper and Brothers, 1955).

53. Weick, Karl E. *The Social Psychology of Organizing* (Reading, Mass.: Addison-Wesley, 1969).

54. Weinstein, Alan G., and V. Srinivasan. "Predicting Managerial Success of Master of Business Administration (MBA) Graduates," *Journal of Applied Psychology,* Vol. 59 (1974), 207–212.

55. Wolfle, Dael. *The Uses of Talent* (Princeton: Princeton University Press, 1971).

56. Zald, Mayer N. "Who Shall Rule? A Political Analysis of Succession in a Large Welfare Organization," *Pacific Sociological Review,* Vol. 8 (1965), 52–60.

R² LEADERSHIP: GOOD, BETTER, BEST

BERNARD M. BASS

What does Lee Iacocca have that many other executives lack? Charisma. What would have happened to Chrysler without him? It probably would have gone bankrupt.

Here are two more questions: How much does business and industry encourage the emergence of leaders like Iacocca? And how much effort has organizational psychology put into research on charismatic leadership? The answers are that business and industry have usually discouraged charismatic leadership and that, for the most part, organizational psychology has ignored the subject. It has been customary to see leadership as a

method of getting subordinates to meet job requirements by handing out rewards or punishments.

Take a look at Barry Bargainer. Barry considers himself to be a good leader. He meets with subordinates to clarify expectations—what is required of them and what they can expect in return. As long as they meet his expectations, Barry doesn't bother them.

Cynthia Changer is a different kind of leader. When facing a crisis,

Cynthia inspires her team's involvement and participation in a "mission." She solidifies it with simple words and images and keeps reminding her staff about it. She has frequent one-to-one chats with each of her employees at his or her work station. She is consultant, coach, teacher, and mother figure.

Barry Bargainer, a transactional leader, may inspire a reasonable degree of involvement, loyalty, commitment, and performance from his subordinates. But Cynthia Changer, using a transformational approach, can do much more.

LEARNING CHECKPOINT

What leadership traits would be used to describe Barry Bargainer and Cynthia Changer?

The first part of this article contrasts transactional and transformational leadership styles and the results that are obtained when managers select each approach. The second section reports on surveys of personnel in the military and in industry and examines factors in both approaches to leadership, as they emerged from the survey results. Transformational leadership is presented as a way to augment transactional approaches to management, since it is often more effective in achieving higher levels of improvement and change among employees.

A NEW PARADIGM

For half a century, leadership research has been devoted to studying the effects of democratic and autocratic approaches. Much investigative time has gone into the question of who should decide—

the leader or the led. Equally important to research has been the distinction between task orientation and relations orientation. Still another issue has been the need of the leader to "initiate structure" for subordinates and to be considerate of them. At the same time, increasing attention has been paid to the ability to promote change in individuals, groups, and organizations.

The need to promote change and deal with resistance to it has, in turn, put an emphasis on democratic, participative, relations-oriented, and considerate leadership. Contingent rewards have been stressed in training and research with somewhat limited results.

In the past, we have mostly considered how to marginally improve and maintain the quantity or quality of performance, how to substitute one goal for another, how to shift attention from one action to another, how to reduce resistance to particular actions, or how to implement decisions. But higher-order changes are also possible. Increases in effort and the rate at which a group's speed and accuracy improve can sometimes be accelerated. Such higher-order changes also may involve larger shifts in attitudes, beliefs, values, and needs. Quantum leaps in performance may result when a group is roused out of its despair by a leader with innovative or revolutionary ideas and a vision of future possibilities. Leaders may help bring about a radical shift in attention. The context may be changed by leaders. They may change what the followers see as figure and what they see as ground or raise the level of maturity of their needs and wants. For example, followers' concerns may be elevated from their need for safety and security to their need for recognition and achievement.

The lower order of improve-

ment—changes in degree or marginal improvement—can be seen as the result of leadership that is an exchange process: a *transaction* in which followers' needs are met if their performance measures up to their explicit or implicit contracts with their leader. But higher-order improvement calls for *transformational* leadership. There is a great deal of difference between the two types of leadership.

TRANSACTIONAL LEADERSHIP IN ACTION

Transactional leaders like Barry Bargainer recognize what actions subordinates must take to achieve outcomes. Transactional leaders clarify these role and task requirements for their subordinates so that they are confident in exerting necessary efforts. Transactional leaders also recognize subordinates' needs and wants and clarify how they will be satisfied if necessary efforts are made. (See Exhibit 1 on the following page.) This approach is currently stressed in leadership training, and it is good as far as it goes; however, the transactional approach has numerous shortcomings.

First, even after training, managers do not fully utilize transactional leadership. Time pressures, poor appraisal methods, doubts about the efficacy of positive reinforcement, leader and subordinate discomfort with the method, and lack of management skills are all partly responsible. How reinforcements are scheduled, how timely they are, and how variable or consistent they are all mediate the degree of their influence.

Some leaders, practicing management by exception, intervene only when things go wrong. In this instance, the manager's discomfort about giving negative feedback is even more self-defeating. When

EXHIBIT 1

Transactional Leadership (L = Leader; F = Follower)

supervisors attribute poor performance to lack of ability, they tend to "pull their punches" by distorting feedback so that it is more positive than it should be.

Another common problem occurs when supervisors say and actually believe they are giving feedback to their subordinates, who feel they are not receiving it. For example, Barry Bargainer may meet with his group of subordinates to complain that things are not going well. Barry thinks he is giving negative feedback while his subordinates only hear Barry grumbling about conditions. Barry may give Henry a pat on the back for a job he thinks has been well done. Henry may feel that he knows he did a good job, and it was condescending for Barry to mention it.

People differ considerably in their preference for external reinforcement or self-reinforcement. Task-oriented and experienced subordinates generally are likely to be self-reinforcing. They may say: "If I have done something well, I know it without other people telling me so," and "As long as I think that I have done something well, I am not too concerned about what other people think I have done."

Subordinates and supervisors attach differing importance to various kinds of feedback. Many subordinates attach more importance than do supervisors to their own success or failure with particular tasks, and to their own comparisons with the work of others. Subordinates are also likely to attach more importance than do supervisors to co-workers' comments about their work. Supervisors tend to put the most weight on their own comments to their subordinates, and to recommendations for rewards they, as supervisors, can make, such as raises, promotions, and more interesting assignmets.

Transactional leadership often fails because the leaders lack the reputation for being able to deliver rewards. Transactional leaders who fulfill the self-interested expectations of their subordinates gain and maintain the reputation for being able to deliver pay, promotions, and recognition. Those that fail to deliver lose their reputation and are not considered to be effective leaders.

Transactional leadership may be abandoned by managers when noncontingent rewards (employees are treated well, regardless of performance) will work just as well to boost performance. For example, in a large, nonprofit organization, a study by Phillip Podsakoff et al. showed that contingent rewards (those given only if performance warrants them) did contribute to employee performance, but noncontingent rewards were correlated almost as strongly with performance as contingent rewards.

Noncontingent rewards may provide a secure situation in which employees' self-reinforcement serves as a consequence for good performance (for example, IBM's straight salaries for all employees). An employee's feeling of obligation to the organization for providing noncontingent rewards fuels his or her effort to perform at least adequately. The Japanese experience is exemplary; in the top third of such Japanese firms as Toyota, Sony, and Mitsubishi, employees and the companies feel a mutual sense of lifetime obligation. Being a good family member does not bring immediate pay raises and promotions, but overall family success will bring year-end bonuses. Ultimately, opportunities to advance to a higher level and salary will depend on overall meritorious performance.

When the contingent reinforcement used is aversive (reinforcement that recipients prefer to avoid), the success of the transactional leader usually plummets. In the same not-for-profit organization studied by Podsakoff et al., neither contingent reprimand, disapproval, nor punishment had any effect on performance or overall employee satisfaction. The same results have been observed in other organizations. Contingent approval and disapproval by results-oriented leaders did improve subordinates' understanding of what was expected of them but failed to have much effect on motivation or performance. In general, reprimand may be useful in highlighting what not to do, but usually it does not contribute to positive motivation, particularly when subordinates are expected to be innovative and creative.

Even when it is based solely on rewards, transactional leadership can have unintended consequences. When expounding on the principles of leadership, Vice Admiral James B. Stockdale argued that people do not like to be programmed:

> . . . . You cannot persuade [people] to act in their own self-interest all of the time. A good leader appreciates contrariness.

> . . . . some men all of the time and all men some of the time knowingly will do what is clearly to their disadvantage if only because they do not like to be suffocated by carrot-and-stick coercion. I will not be a piano key; I will not bow to the tyranny of reason.

In working subtly against transactional leadership, employees may take shortcuts to complete the exchange of reward for compliance. For instance, quality may suffer if the leader does not monitor it as closely as he or she does the quantity of output. The employee may begin to react defensively rather than adequately; in some cases, reaction formation, withdrawal, hostility, or "game playing" may result.

THE ALTERNATIVE: ADD TRANSFORMATIONAL LEADERSHIP TO THE MANAGER-EMPLOYEE RELATIONSHIP

James McGregor Burns, the biographer of Franklin D. Roosevelt and of John F. Kennedy, was the first to contrast transactional with transformational leadership. The transformational leader motivates us to do more than we originally expected to do. Such a transformation can be achieved in the following ways:

1. Raising our level of consciousness about the importance and value of designated outcomes and ways of reaching these outcomes.
2. Getting us to transcend our own self-interests for the sake of the team, organization, or larger polity.
3. Raising our need level on Abraham Maslow's hierarchy from, say, the need for security to the need for recognition, or expanding our portfolio of needs by, for example, adding the need for self-actualization to the need for recognition.

Cynthia Changer is a transformational leader; Barry Bargainer is not. Exhibit 2 is a model of transformational leadership that starts with a current level of effort based on a follower's current level of confidence and desire for designated outcomes. A transactional leader contributes to such confidence and desire by clarifying what performance is required and how needs will be satisfied as a consequence. The transformational leader induces additional effort by directly increasing the follower's confidence as well as by elevating the value of outcomes through expanding his or her transcendental interests and level or breadth of needs in Maslow's hierarchy.

The need for more transformational leaders in business and industry was illustrated in an in-depth interview survey of a representative national sample of 845 working Americans. The survey found that while most employees liked and respected their managers, they felt their managers really didn't know how to motivate employees to do their best. Although 70% endorsed the work ethic, only 23% said they were working as hard as they could in their jobs. Only 9% agreed that their performance was motivated by transaction; most reported that there actually was little connection between how much they earned and the level of effort they put into the job.

REPORT ON A STUDY OF TRANSFORMATIONAL LEADERSHIP

I set out to find evidence of transformational leadership and its effects at various levels in industrial and military organizations, *not just at the top.*

I defined transformational leadership for 70 senior executives. Then, I asked them to describe in detail a transformational leader whom they had encountered at any time during their career. All respondents claimed to have known at least one such person. Most cited a former immediate supervisor or higher-level manager in the organization. A few mentioned family members, consultants, or counselors.

This transformational leader induced respondents to work ridiculous hours *and to do more than they ever expected to do.* Respondents reported that they aimed to satisfy the transformational leader's expectations and to give the leader all the support asked of them. They wanted to emulate the leader. The transformational leader increased their awareness of and promoted a higher quality of performance and greater innovativeness. Such a leader convinced followers to extend themselves and to develop themselves further. Total commitment to and belief in the organization emerged as consequences of belief in the leader and heightened self-confidence.

Many respondents (all were male) indicated that the transformational leader they could identify in their own careers was like a benevolent father who remained friendly and treated the respondent as an equal despite the leader's greater knowledge and experience. The leader provided a model of integrity and fairness and also set clear and high standards of perfor-

mance. He encouraged followers with advice, help, support, recognition, and openness. He gave followers a sense of confidence in his intellect, yet was a good listener. He gave followers autonomy and encouraged their self-development. He was willing to share his greater knowledge and expertise with them. Yet he could be formal and firm and would reprimand followers when necessary. Most respondents, however, were inclined to see the transforming leader as informal and accessible. Such a leader could be counted on to stand up for his subordinates. Along with the heightened and changed motivation and awareness, frequent reactions of followers to the transforming leader included trust, strong liking, admiration, loyalty, and respect.

In conducting a second survey, I used the descriptions from the first to create a questionnaire of 73 behavioral items. Responses to each item were on a five-point frequency scale. A total of 176 senior U.S. Army officers completed the questionnaire describing the behavior of their immediate superiors. Five factors emerged from a statistical factor analysis of the data. Two dealt with transactional leadership, the exchange relationship between superior and subordinate: contingent reward, by which subordinates earned benefits for compliance with the leader's clarification of the paths toward goals, and management by exception, by which the leader gave negative feedback for failure to meet agreed-upon standards. Three of the factors dealt with transformational leadership—the

EXHIBIT 2

Transformational Leadership
(L = Leader; F = Follower)

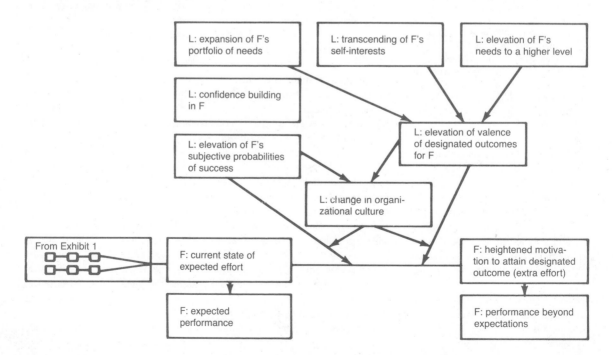

broadening and elevating of goals and of subordinates' confidence in their ability to go beyond expectations. These factors were (1) charismatic leadership (leaders aroused enthusiasm, faith, loyalty, and pride and trust in themselves and their aims); (2) individualized consideration (leaders maintained a developmental and individualistic orientation toward subordinates); and (3) intellectual stimulation (leaders enhanced the problem-solving capabilities of their associates). An interesting sidelight was that more transformational leadership was observed (by respondents) in combat units than in support units.

As expected, the three transformational factors were more highly correlated with perceived unit effectiveness than were the two transactional factors. Parallel results were obtained for subordinates' satisfaction with their leader. Charismatic, considerate, and intellectually stimulating leaders were far more satisfying to work for than were those who merely practiced the transactions of contingent reinforcement. I obtained similar results from a survey of 256 business managers, 23 educational administrators, and 45 professionals. Moreover, in these latter samples, respondents reported that they made greater efforts when leaders were charismatic, individualizing, and intellectually stimulating. Contingent reward was also fairly predictive of extra effort, but management by exception was counterproductive. Further analysis of the data by my colleague, David Waldman, supported the model shown in Exhibit 2. The analysis demonstrated that when a leader displayed transformational abilities and engaged in transactional relationships, extra effort made by subordinates was above and beyond what could be attributed to transactional factors alone.

TRANSACTIONAL FACTORS: CONTINGENT REINFORCEMENT AND MANAGEMENT-BY-EXCEPTION

According to our questionnaire surveys, positive and aversive contingent reinforcement are the two ways managers in organized settings engage in transactional leadership to influence employee performance. Ordinarily, contingent reward takes two forms: praise for work well done and recommendations for pay increases, bonuses, and promotion. In addition, this kind of reward can take the form of commendations for effort or public recognition and honors for outstanding service.

Contingent punishment can take several forms as a reaction to a deviation from norms—when, for example, production falls below agreed-upon standards or quality falls below acceptable levels. The manager may merely call attention to the deviation. Being told of one's failure to meet standards may be sufficient punishment to change behavior. Being told why one has failed can be helpful, particularly to the inexperienced or inexpert subordinate, especially if the negative feedback is coupled with further clarification about what kind of performance is expected. While other penalties—such as fines, suspensions without pay, loss of leader support, or discharge—may be imposed, these are less frequently used and are less likely to promote effectiveness.

When the manager, for one reason or another, chooses to intervene only when failures, breakdowns, and deviations occur, he or she is practicing management by exception. The rationale of those who use this practice is, "If it ain't broke, don't fix it!" The research studies I have completed with military officers, business executives, professionals, and educational administrators generally indicate that as a steady diet, management by exception can be counterproductive. But contingent rewards yield a fairly good return in terms of subordinate effort and performance. Nevertheless, in the aggregate, there will be additional payoff when the transformational factors appear in a leader's portfolio.

Charismatic and Inspirational Leadership

Charisma is not exclusively the province of world-class leaders or a few generals or admirals. It is to be found to some degree in industrial and military leaders throughout organizations. Furthermore, charisma is the most important component in the larger concept of transformational leadership. In my study I found that many followers described their military or industrial leader as someone who made everyone enthusiastic about assignments, who inspired loyalty to the organization, who commanded respect from everyone, who had a special gift of seeing what was really important, and who had a sense of mission that excited responses. Followers had complete faith in the leaders with charisma, felt proud to be associated with them, and trusted their capacity to overcome any obstacle. Charismatic leaders served as symbols of success and accomplishment for their followers.

Charisma is one of the elements separating the ordinary manager from the true leader in organizational settings. The leader attracts intense feelings of love (and sometimes hatred) from his or her subordinates. They want to identify with the leader. Although feelings about ordinary managers are bland, relations are smoother and steadier. Like most intimate relationships, the relations between the charismatic leader and his or her followers tend to be more turbulent.

There may be a scarcity of charismatic leaders in business and industry because managers lack the necessary skills. On the other hand, managers who have the skills may not recognize opportunity or may be unwilling to risk what is required to stand out so visibly among their peers. More charismatic leaders potentially exist in organizational settings; furthermore, they may be necessary to an organization's success.

The ability to inspire—arouse emotions, animate, enliven, or even exalt—is an important aspect of charisma. Inspirational leadership involves the arousal and heightening of motivation among followers. Followers can be inspired by a cold, calculating, intellectual discourse, the brilliance of a breakthrough, or the beauty of an argument. Yet it is the followers' emotions that ultimately have been aroused. Followers may hold an intellectual genius in awe and reverence, but the inspirational influence on them is emotional.

Consider the specific leadership behaviors Gary Yukl used to illustrate what he meant by inspirational leadership:

> My supervisor held a meeting to talk about how vital the new contract is for the company and said he was confident we could handle it if we all did our part. My boss told us we were the best design group he had ever worked with and he was sure that this new product was going to break every sales record in the company.

The inspiring supervisor was not dispassionate. The supervisor talked about how *vital* the new contract was to the company. He said he was *confident* in his people. He told them they were the *best* group he had *ever* worked with. He was sure the product would *break every record*.

In summary, as a consequence of his or her self-confidence, absence of inner conflict, self-determination, and requisite abilities, a leader will be held in high esteem by followers, particularly in times of trouble. He or she can generally inspire them by emotional support and appeals that will transform their level of motivation beyond original expectations. Such a leader can sometimes also inspire followers by means of intellectual stimulation. The charismatic leader can do one or the other, or both.

 **LEARNING CHECKPOINT**

Look back at the Vroom-Yetton explanation of leadership. Is there any discussion of or reference to what is referred to as charisma? Explain.

Individualized Consideration

The transformational leader has a developmental orientation toward followers. He evaluates followers' potential both to perform their present job and to hold future positions of greater responsibility. The leader sets examples and assigns tasks on an individual basis to followers to help significantly alter their abilities and motivations as well as to satisfy immediate organizational needs.

Delegating challenging work and increasing subordinate responsibilities are particularly useful approaches to individualized development. As General Omar Bradley pointed out, there is no better way to develop leadership than to give an individual a job involving responsibility and let him work it out. A survey of 208 chief executives and senior officers by Charles Margerison reported that important career influences on them before age 35 included being "stretched" by immediate bosses and being given leadership experience, overall responsibility for important tasks, and wide experience in many functions.

The transformational leader will consciously or unconsciously serve as a role model for subordinates. For example, in the Margerison survey, the executives attributed their own successful development as managers to having had early on in their careers managers who were models.

Managerial training supports the idea that managers profit from role models. What may be different in what I propose, however, is that the transformational leader emphasizes *individualism*. Personal influence and the one-to-one superior-subordinate relationship is of primary importance to the development of leaders. An organizational culture of individualism, even of elitism, should be encouraged; an organization should focus attention on identifying prospective leaders among subordinates.

Individualized attention is viewed as especially important by the new military commander of a unit. The commander is expected to learn the names of all those in the units at least two levels below his and to become familiar with their jobs. *Military leaders need to avoid treating all subordinates alike.* They must discover what best motivates each individual soldier or sailor and how to employ him most effectively. They must be generous in the use of their time. But as General Eugene Meyer notes, the leaders' interest must be genuine.

Individualized consideration implies that seniors maintain face-to-face contact or at least frequent telephone contact with juniors. The Intel Corporation accepted the fact that recently graduated engineers are more up to date on the latest advances in technology than are experienced executives of greater power and status in the firm. Therefore, the firm has consciously encouraged frequent contact and open communication between the recent college graduates and the senior executives through leveling arrangements. Senior executives and junior professionals are all housed in small, unpretentious, accessible offices that share common facilities. The organization stresses that influence is based on knowledge rather than power. In other well-managed firms, "walk-around management" promotes individual contact and communication between those low and high in the hierarchy.

In another study of a high-tech company, Rudi Klauss and Bernard Bass found that project engineers were most influenced by and gained most of their information relevant to decision making from informal contact and individual discussion rather than from written documentation. This company did not believe that the aggregated data from management information systems were the most important inputs for decision making. Rather, two-thirds to three-quarters of the total work time of managers was spent in oral communication. It was the immediate, timely tidbits of gossip, speculation, opinion, and relevant facts that was most influential, not generalized reports reviewing conditions over a recent period of time. Individualized attention of superior to subordinate provided this opportunity for inputs of current and timely information.

Managers are most likely to make face-to-face contact with col-leagues at their same organizational level (or by telephone for such colleagues at a distance physically). For superiors and subordinates, written memos are more frequently used. Yet regular, face-to-face debriefing sessions to disseminate important information from superior to subordinate will provide a better basis for organizational decision making and make the superior better equipped to deal with the erratic flow of work and demands on his or her time and the speed that decision making often requires. Unfortunately, unless personal contact becomes a matter of policy (such as walk-around management), communications from superior to subordinate are more likely to be on paper—or now, no doubt, increasingly on computer—rather than face-to-face.

Individualized consideration is reflected when a manager keeps each employee fully informed about what is happening and why—preferably in a two-way conversation rather than a written memo. Employees come to feel that they are on the inside of developments and do not remain bystanders. Sudden changes of plan are less likely to surprise them. If the interaction is two-way, employees have the opportunity to ask questions to clarify understanding. At the same time, managers learn first-hand their subordinates' concerns.

Individualized consideration is also demonstrated when the senior executive or professional takes time to serve as mentor for the junior executive or professional. A mentor is a trusted counselor who accepts a guiding role in the development of a younger or less experienced member of the organization. The mentor uses his or her greater knowledge, experience, and status to help develop his or her protégé and not simply to pull the protégé up the organization ladder on the mentor's coattails. This relationship is different from one in which a manager is supportive or provides advice when asked for it. Compared with the formal, distant relationship most often seen between a high-level executive and a junior somewhere down the line, the mentor is paternalistic or maternalistic and perhaps is a role model for the junior person.

A follow-up of 122 recently promoted people in business indicated that two-thirds had had mentors. This popularity of mentoring in business, government, and industry reflects the current interest on the part of both individuals and organizations in the career development of the individual employee.

Intellectual Stimulation

The statement, "These ideas have forced me to rethink some of my own ideas, which I had never questioned before," sums up the kind of intellectual stimulation that a transformational leader can provide. Intellectual stimulation can lead to other comments like, "She enables me to think about old problems in new ways," or "He provides me with new ways of looking at things that used to be a puzzle for me."

Intellectual stimulation arouses in followers the awareness of problems and how they may be solved. It promotes the hygiene of logic that is compelling and convincing. It stirs the imagination and generates thoughts and insights. It is not the call to immediate action aroused by emotional stimulation. This intellectual stimulation is seen in a discrete leap in the followers' conceptualization, comprehension, and discernment of the nature of the problems they face and their solutions.

Executives should and can play a role as transforming leaders to the degree that they articulate what they discern, comprehend, visualize, and conceptualize to their colleagues and followers. They should articulate what they see as the opportunities and threats facing their organization (or unit within it) and the organization's strengths, weaknesses, and comparative advantages. Leadership in complex organizations must include the ability to manage the problem-solving process in such a way that important problems are identified and solutions of high quality are found and carried out with the full commitment of organization members.

The intellectual component may be obscured by surface considerations. Accused of making snap decisions, General George Patton commented: "I've been studying the art of war for 40-odd years . . . [A] surgeon who decides in the course of an operation to change its objective is not making a snap decision but one based on knowledge, experience, and training. So am I."

The importance of a leader's technical expertise and intellectual power, particularly in high-performing systems, often is ignored in comparison with the attention paid to his or her interpersonal competence. Where would Polaroid be without Edwin Land? What kind of corporation would Occidental Petroleum be without Armand Hammer?

In this intellectual sphere, we see systematic differences between transformational and transactional leaders. The transformational leader may be less willing to accept the status quo and more likely to seek new ways of doing things while taking maximum advantage of opportunities. Transactional managers will focus on what can

clearly work, will keep time constraints in mind, and will do what seems to be most efficient and free of risk.

What may intellectually separate the two kinds of leaders is that transformational leaders are likely to be more proactive than reactive in their thinking, more creative, novel, and innovative in their ideas, and less inhibited in their ideational search for solutions. Transactional leaders may be equally bright, but their focus is on how best to keep running the system for which they are responsible; they react to problems generated by observed deviances and modify conditions as needed while remaining ever mindful of organizational constraints.

TRANSFORMATIONAL LEADERSHIP: BENEVOLENT OR MALEVOLENT?

Charismatic leadership, individualized consideration, and intellectual stimulation have been clearly seen in the moving and shaking that took place between 1982 and 1984 in a number of firms, such as General Electric, Campbell Soup, and Coca Cola. In each instance, the transformation could be attributed to a newly appointed chief. These transformational leaders were responsible for iconoclastic changes of image, increased organizational flexibility, and an upsurge of new products and new approaches. In each case, the transformational leadership of John F. Welch, Jr. of General Electric, Gordon McGovern of Campbell Soup, and Roberto Goizueta of Coca Cola paid off in invigoration and revitalization of their firms and an acceleration in business success.

Clearly, heads may be broken, feelings hurt, and anxieties raised with the advent of transformational leaders such as Welch, McGovern,

or Goizueta. "Business as usual" is no longer tolerated. Such transformations may be moral or immoral.

For James Burns, transformational leadership is moral if it deals with true needs and is based on informed choice. The moral transformational leader is one who is guided by such universal ethical principles as respect for human dignity and equal rights. The leadership mobilizes and directs support for "more general and comprehensive values that express followers' more fundamental and enduring needs" (*Leadership,* Harper, 1978). Moral leadership helps followers to see the real conflict between competing values, the inconsistencies between espoused values and behavior, the need for realignments in values, and the need for changes in behavior or transformations of institutions. Burns argued that if the need levels elevated by transformational leaders were not authentic, then the leadership was immoral.

LEARNING CHECKPOINT

Now that you have a good understanding of transformational and transactional leadership think about the point raised in the chapter about cause and effect. Are these types of leadership causes or effects? Explain.

The well-being of organizational life will be better served in the long run by moral leadership. That is, transformations that result in the fulfillment of real needs will prove to be more beneficial to the organization than transformations that deal with manufactured needs and group delusions. Organizational leaders should subscribe to a code of ethics that is accepted by their society and their profession.

The ethical transformational leader aims toward and succeeds in promoting changes in a firm—changes that strengthen firm viability, increase satisfaction of owners, managers, employees, and customers, and increase the value of the firm's products. But transformational leaders can be immoral if they create changes based on false images that cater to the fantasies of constituencies. Firms can be driven into the ground by such leaders. A transformational leader can lull employees and shareholders alike with false hopes and expectations while he or she is preparing to depart in a golden parachute after selling out the company's interests.

Whether transformational or transactional leadership will take hold within an organization will depend to some extent on what is happening or has happened outside of it. Welch, McGovern, and Goizueta all came into power to transform firms that were in danger of failing to keep pace with changes in the marketplace. Transformational leadership is more likely to emerge in times of distress and rapid change.

The personalities of followers will affect a leader's ability to be transformational. Charisma is a two-way process. A leader is seen as charismatic if he or she has followers who imbue him or her with extraordinary value and personal power. This is more easily done when subordinates have highly dependent personalities. On the other hand, subordinates who pride themselves on their own rationality, skepticism, independence, and concern for rules of law and precedent are less likely to be influenced by a charismatic leader or the leader who tries to use emotional

inspiration. Subordinates who are egalitarian, self-confident, highly educated, self-reinforcing, and high in status are likely to resist charismatic leaders.

WHICH KIND OF LEADERSHIP SHOULD MANAGERS USE?

Managers need to appreciate what kind of leadership is expected of them. Current leadership training and management development emphasize transactional leadership, which is good as far as it goes, but clearly has its limits. Transactional leaders will let their subordinates know what is expected of them and what they can hope to receive in exchange for fulfilling expectations. Clarification makes subordinates confident that they can fulfill expectations and achieve mutually valued outcomes. But subordinates' confidence and the value they place on potential outcomes can be further increased, through transformational leadership. Leadership, in other words, can become an inspiration to make extraordinary efforts.

Charismatic leadership is central to the transformational leadership process. Charismatic leaders have great referent power and influence. Followers want to identify with them and to emulate them. Followers develop intense feelings about them, and above all have trust and confidence in them. Transformational leaders may arouse their followers emotionally and inspire them to extra effort and greater accomplishment. As subordinates become competent with the mainly transformational leader's encouragement and support, contingent reinforcement may be abandoned in favor of self-reinforcement.

Clearly, there are situations in which the transformational approach may not be appropriate. At

the same time, organizations need to draw more on the resources of charismatic leaders, who often can induce followers to aspire to and maintain much higher levels of productivity than they would have reached if they had been operating only through the transactional process. □

REFERENCES

For more of the limitations of transactional leadership, reliance on contingent reinforcement, and the extent to which manipulative leadership is counterproductive, see "Management Styles Associated with Organizational, Task, Personal and Interpersonal Contingencies," by Bernard Bass, Enzo Valenzi, Dana Farrow, and Robert Solomon (*Journal of Applied Psychology*, December 1975); "Dimensionality of Leader-Subordinate Interactions: A Path-Goal Investigation," by Janet Fulk and Eric Wendler (*Organizational Behavior and Human Performance*, October 1982); "Evaluation of Feedback Sources as a Function of Role and Organizational Development," by Martin Greller (*Journal of Applied Psychology*, February 1980); "Performance Attributional Effects on Feedback from Supervisors," by Daniel Ilgen and William Knowlton (*Organizational Behavior and Human Performance*, June 1980); "Applied Behavior Analysis," by Judi Komacki (*The Industrial Psychologist*, February 1981); "Effect of Leader Contingent and Non-Contingent Reward and Punishment Behaviors on Subordinate Performance and Satisfaction," by Phillip Podsakoff, William Todor, and Richard Skov (*Academy of Management Journal*, December 1982); and "A Role Set Analysis of Managerial Reputation," by Ann Tsui (*Proceedings of the Academy of Management*, August 1982).

Admiral Stockdale's quotation can be found in "The Principles of Leadership" (*American Educator*, April 1981). General Patton's comment is in *Before the Colors Fade: Portrait* of a Soldier: George S. Patton (Houghton-Mifflin, 1964), by Frederick Ayer, Jr. General Meyer's comment is in "Leadership: A Return to Basics," by Edward Meyer (*Military Review*, July 1980).

For the seminal discussion on transformational leadership, see *Leadership* by James Burns (Harper & Row, 1978). For more on the impact or potential impact of transformational leadership, see *In Search of Excellence*, by Thomas Peters and Robert Waterman (Harper & Row, 1982); *Leadership in Organizations*, by Gary Yukl (Prentice-Hall, 1981); "Managers and Leaders: Are They Different?" by Abraham Zaleznik (*Harvard Business Review*, May/June 1977); and "Leadership Transforms Vision

into Action," by Warren Bennis (*Industry Week*, May 31, 1982).

For more on communications between executives and employees, see *The Nature of Managerial Work*, by Henry Mintzberg (Harper & Row, 1973) and *Interpersonal Communication in Organizations*, by Rudi Klauss and Bernard Bass (Academic Press, 1982). A discussion of the Intel Corporation appears in Klauss and Bass' book.

Information on mentoring and managerial development may be found in *Problem Solving and the Executive Mind, Symposium: Functioning of the Executive Mind* by David Kolb (Case Western Reserve University, April 1982); *The Seasons of a Man's Life*, by Daniel Levinson, Charlotte Darrow, Edward Klein, Maria Levin-

son, and Braxton McKee (Knopf, 1978); *How Chief Executives Succeed*, by Charles Margerison (MCB Publications, Bradford, England, 1980); "A Theory of Human Motivation," by Abraham Maslow (*Psychological Review*, July 1943); and "Moving Up: Role Models, Mentors and the Patron System," by Eileen Shapiro, Florence Haseltine, and Mary Row (*Sloan Management Review*, Spring 1978).

Details about the impact of John F. Welch, Gordon McGovern, and Roberto Goizueta had on their companies can be found in the September 17, 1984 issue of the *Wall Street Journal*.

D1 APPLYING CONTINGENCY LEADERSHIP*

1. Do the following before coming to class:
   a. Review Fiedler's contingency theory as discussed in this chapter.
   b. Complete and score the following least preferred co-worker (LPC) scale before coming to class. This provides Fiedler's perspective on your leadership style. Think about how closely his perspective corresponds to your view of *your* leadership style.
   c. Think of a current or recent assignment in which you are functioning or have functioned as a leader.
   d. Rate the situation selected in part 1 (c) on the following chart.

Leader-member relations	good	poor
Task structure	high	low
Position power	strong	weak

   e. Now rate the degree of control this situation offers a leader.

Situational control	high	moderate	low

   f. Think about how well your leadership style (measured by the LPC scale) matches the demands of this situation, both in terms of Fiedler's model and in terms of your actual experience in the situation.
   g. Bring the results of (a) through (f) with you to class.
2. Form groups in class as assigned by your instructor.
3. Share and discuss your situational control summaries and LPC scores.
4. Develop a summary of each individual's case example and its implications in terms of the type of leadership style needed.
5. Have a spokesperson prepared to report to the class on the summary in part 4 in terms of
   a. Differences and similarities in the situational control found in each case.
   b. How well each person's LPC scores seem to agree with that person's intuitive feelings about his or her leadership style.
   c. The degree of match or mismatch between

---

* Source: Adapted from John R. Schermerhorn, Jr., James G. Hunt, and Richard N. Osborn, *Managing Organizational Behavior* (New York: John Wiley, 1985), pp. 615–617; and Fred E. Fiedler, Martin M. Chemers, and Linda Mahar, *Improving Leadership Effectiveness* (New York: John Wiley, 1976), pp. 5–7. Used with permission.

leadership style and situational control in the cases presented by group members.

    d. Some steps that might be taken to address any mismatches in the various cases.

6. Reconvene as a total class to hear reports and discuss implications of the exercise.

Least Preferred Co-Workers (LPC) Scale

Throughout your life you will have worked in many groups with a wide variety of different people—on your job, in social groups, in church organizations, in volunteer groups, on athletic teams, and in many other situations. Some of your co-workers may have been very easy to work with in attaining the group's goals, while others were less so.

Think of all the people with whom you have ever worked, and then think of the person with whom you could work *least well.* He or she may be someone with whom you work now or with whom you have worked in the past. This does not have to be the person you liked least well, but should be the person with whom you could work *least well.*

Describe this person on the scale that follows by placing an "X" in the appropriate space.

Look at the words at both ends of the line before your mark your "X." *There are no right or wrong answers.* Work rapidly; your first answer is likely to be the best. Do not omit any items, and mark each item only once.

Now describe the person with whom you can work least well.

Scoring

	8	7	6	5	4	3	2	1		
Pleasant	8	7	6	5	4	3	2	1	Unpleasant	_____
Friendly	8	7	6	5	4	3	2	1	Unfriendly	_____
Rejecting	1	2	3	4	5	6	7	8	Accepting	_____
Tense	1	2	3	4	5	6	7	8	Relaxed	_____
Distant	1	2	3	4	5	6	7	8	Close	_____
Cold	1	2	3	4	5	6	7	8	Warm	_____
Supportive	8	7	6	5	4	3	2	1	Hostile	_____
Boring	1	2	3	4	5	6	7	8	Interesting	_____
Quarrelsome	1	2	3	4	5	6	7	8	Harmonious	_____
Gloomy	1	2	3	4	5	6	7	8	Cheerful	_____
Open	8	7	6	5	4	3	2	1	Guarded	_____
Backbiting	1	2	3	4	5	6	7	8	Loyal	_____
Untrustworthy	1	2	3	4	5	6	7	8	Trustworthy	_____
Considerate	8	7	6	5	4	3	2	1	Inconsiderate	_____
Nasty	1	2	3	4	5	6	7	8	Nice	_____
Agreeable	8	7	6	5	4	3	2	1	Disagreeable	_____
Insincere	1	2	3	4	5	6	7	8	Sincere	_____
Kind	8	7	6	5	4	3	2	1	Unkind	

SCORING

Determine your LPC score and its implied leadership style by adding the numbers recorded in the right-hand column. Mark this total in the space provided.

If your score is 64 or higher, Fiedler considers you to be a high-LPC person. The high-LPC person essentially says of his or her least preferred co-worker, "Even if I can't work with you, you may still be an okay person." Because of this sensitivity for relationships with others, the high LPC person is considered to be "relationship motivated" as a leader.

If your score is 57 or lower, you are a low-LPC leader. A low-LPC person describes the least preferred co-worker in very negative terms. Essentially he or she says, "Work is extremely important to me; there-

fore, if you are a poor co-worker and prevent me in my efforts to get things done, than I can't accept you in other respects either." This low-LPC individual is termed "task-motivated" as a leader.

A score of 58 to 63 indicates a possible mix of motivations and goals. If you fall in this range, Fiedler argues that you will need to decide for yourself where you fit between task and relationship motivations.

As indicated in the chapter Fiedler proposes that in order to determine how favorable a situation is, three dimensions need to be assessed—leader-member relations, task structure, and position power. Below are the three scales used to assess the dimensions. If you are currently working, complete these scales

LEADER-MEMBER RELATIONS SCALE

Circle the number which best represents your response to each item.

	Strongly agree	Agree	Neither agree nor disagree	Disagree	Strongly disagree
1. The people I supervise have trouble getting along with each other.	1	2	3	4	5
2. My subordinates are reliable and trustworthy.	5	4	3	2	1
3. There seems to be a friendly atmosphere among the people I supervise.	5	4	3	2	1
4. My subordinates always cooperate with me in getting the job done.	5	4	3	2	1
5. There is friction between my subordinates and myself.	1	2	3	4	5
6. My subordinates give me a good deal of help and support in getting the job done.	5	4	3	2	1
7. The people I supervise work well together in getting the job done.	5	4	3	2	1
8. I have good relations with the people I supervise.	5	4	3	2	1

Total Score [ ]

SCORING

Simply add the circled numbers for each item above and write in the total. The highest possible score is 40. A score of 25 or above indicates good leader-

member relations, a score of 20–25 indicates moderate leader-member relations, and a score below 20 indicates poor leader-member relations.

TASK STRUCTURE RATING SCALE—PART 1

Circle the number in the appropriate column.	**Usually true**	**Sometimes true**	**Seldom true**
Is the goal clearly stated or known?			
1. Is there a blueprint, picture, model, or detailed description available of the finished product or service?	2	1	0
2. Is there a person available to advise and give a description of the finished product or service, or how the job should be done?	2	1	0
Is there only one way to accomplish the task?			
3. Is there a step-by-step procedure, or a standard operating procedure which indicates in detail the process which is to be followed?	2	1	0
4. Is there a specific way to subdivide the task into separate parts or steps?	2	1	0
5. Are there some ways which are clearly recognized as better than others for performing this task?	2	1	0
Is there only one correct answer or solution?			
6. Is it obvious when the task is finished and the correct solution has been found?	2	1	0
7. Is there a book, manual, or job description which indicates the best solution or the best outcome for the task?	2	1	0
Is it easy to check whether the job was done right?			
8. Is there a generally agreed understanding about the standards the particular product or service has to meet to be considered acceptable?	2	1	0
9. Is the evaluation of this task generally made on some quantitative basis?	2	1	0
10. Can the leader and the group find out how well the task has been accomplished in enough time to improve future performance?	2	1	0

SCORING

Add lines (a) and (b) of the training and experience adjustment, then *subtract* this from the subtotal given in Part 1. *Note:* Do not adjust jobs with Part 1 task structure scores of 6 or below.

Total Score ☐

TASK STRUCTURE RATING SCALE—PART 2
Training and Experience Adjustment

a) Compared to others in this or similar positions, how much *training* has the leader had?

3	2	1	9
No training at all	Very little training	A moderate amount of training	A great deal of training

b) Compared to others in this or similar positions, how much experience has the leader had?

6	4	2	0
No experience at all	Very little experience	A moderate amount of experience	A great deal of experience

Subtotal from Part 1 □

Subtract training and experience adjustment □

Total Task Structure Score □

SCORING

Simply add the circled numbers for each item in Part 1 and write in the subtotal. Then subtract the training and experience adjustment (if any) from Part 2 to provide a total task structure score. The total possible score is 20, half as much as the leader-member relations scale. A score of 14 or above is high in task structure, a score of 7–13 is medium in structure, and a score below 7 is low in structure.

POSITION POWER RATING SCALE

Circle the number which best represents your answer.

1. Can the leader directly or by recommendation administer rewards and punishments to his subordinates?

2	1	0
Can act directly or can recommend with high effectiveness	Can recommend but with mixed results	No

2. Can the leader directly or by recommendation affect the promotion, demotion, hiring, or firing of his subordinates?

2	1	0
Can act directly or can recommend with high effectiveness	Can recommend but with mixed results	No

3. Does the leader have the knowledge necessary to assign tasks to subordinates and instruct them in task completion?

2	1	0
Yes	Sometimes or in some aspects	No

SCORING

Simply add the circled numbers for each item above and write in the total, which can range from 0 to 10, half as much as the task structure score. A score of 7–10 indicates high position power, 4–6 indicates moderate position power, and 3 or below indicates low position power.

4. Is it the leader's job to evaluate the performance of his subordinates?

2	1	0
Yes	Sometimes or in some aspects	No

5. Has the leader been given some official title of authority by the organization (e.g., foreman, department head, platoon leader)?

2	0
Yes	No

Total Score [ ]

SCORING

If your total score is from 10–30, you have described a low-control situation calling for a task-motivated (LPC score of 57 and below) leadership style. If it is from 31–50, you have described a moderate-control situation calling for a relationship-motivated (64 and above) style. If your score is from 51–70, you have described a high-control situation which again calls for a task-motivated style of leadership.

Situational Control Summary

Write in below your score for each of the diagnostic instruments.

LPC score	___
Leader-member relations total	___
Task structure total	___
Position power total	___
Grand total for leader-member relations, task structure, and position power	___

Source: Adapted with permission from F. E. Fiedler, M. M. Chemers, and L. Mahar, *Improving Leadership Effectiveness* (New York: Wiley, 1976), p. 77. Copyright John Wiley & Sons, Inc. Publishers, 1976.

D2 LEADERSHIP STYLE AND PHILOSOPHY

All of us have an image in our heads of how a leader should act which makes up our leadership philosophy. For the purpose of helping you think more clearly about certain elements of your own philosophy, twenty topic areas of management are presented below. Each has three alternatives. You are first to read all three alternatives so you will have a general understanding of their content. You are then to select the alternative that most nearly corresponds with your own views and assign it a 1; select the one that least corresponds with your views and give it a 3; and finally, assign a 2 to the remaining alternative. Your answer should appear like the following. No two alternatives should receive the same number, and each must be rated.

Example. Personal relationships with employees:

16.   3
17.   1
18.   2

For the purpose of completing this exercise, assume you are in a manager's job, just above the first line of supervision, and that you have five to seven units reporting to you. The supervisors of these units would make up your immediate team. The ratings you assign below indicate how you feel management functions, processes, and what policies should be conducted with your team and throughout the organization generally.

Write your responses in the "Your Answer" column

Your Answer

I. Leading operating activities:

For the most part I lead by using staff and committee meetings for reviewing progress reports which are thoroughly developed according to our division's regulations.

1. ____

I see myself primarily as a facilitator providing guidance and support for team members in achieving programs we have agreed upon.

2. ____

I determine how my team wants to direct activities, and I usually go along with them.

3. ____

II. Control over operating activities:

I work out with my subordinates the framework for operations and reporting and then provide for maximum self-direction within the confines set up.

4. ____

There is no real substitute for a manager running a "tight ship." It is a manager's responsibility to stay on

Your Answer

top of the major operations and the people running them.

5. ____

Control can be best achieved by following a system of policies, procedures, and requirements so that everyone has the basic framework of guidance as to what is expected.

6. ____

III. Meetings:

I hold a short staff meeting two mornings each week for open discussion and coffee. The real value comes from the feelings of being on the same cooperative team.

7. ____

Meetings and committees are valuable for many organizational purposes, but they must be conducted with agendas and procedures to save time.

8. ____

I find I can keep track of what each person is doing by having frequent individual meetings with each person reporting to me. This almost eliminates the need for group meetings.

9. ____

Your Answer

Your Answer

IV. Concerning status symbols, privileges, and perquisites for managers, my position is:

We all want status. These are part of the reward for demonstrated competence and aggressiveness. To openly and candidly make this known within the organization is an aid in motivating managers.

10. ____

Creating a supportive atmosphere with informality and a minimal use of status-type indicators can contribute to the morale of the employees.

11. ____

Too much emphasis upon status indicators can unfavorably influence communication and the way people interact. More can be gained by stressing what we are trying to achieve together.

12. ____

V. In regard to women wanting equal opportunities for management positions, I believe:

All individuals should be given the opportunity for developing their full potential for management positions regardless of sex.

13. ____

I would give them full consideration, but the fact that women historically have not achieved leadership positions shows the probability of their becoming equal to men in assuming managerial responsibility is questionable.

14. ____

This is best handled by organizational policies which assure systematic review of all women candidates for promotion on a continuing basis.

15. ____

VI. Personal relationships with employees:

We have arrived at a time when warm friendships on the job are just as appropriate as any other type of friendship.

16. ____

Maintain good personal relationships on the job but avoid socializing of the job.

17. ____

You have to maintain your position with a certain amount of distance both on and off the job.

18. ____

VII. A frequent complaint from organizations concerns people who have been employed for many years and seem no longer to be fully productive. Organizational effectiveness can be served by:

Facing up to the situation and realistically finding some way to get rid of the "deadwood."

19. ____

Recognizing that humane treatment is foremost, both from the ethical point of view and the effect any company action might have on the other employees.

20. ____

Finding different jobs for these people which might spur their interest and use their capabilities.

21. ____

VIII. Employees are continuously concerned about fair treatment. I believe:

I follow the company policies as much as possible, because they have been written specifically for the purpose of assuring that employees receive fair treatment in many activity areas.

22. ____

The manager is in the position of a judge in determining what is fair, but he always has to be responsive to the problem of how his actions will be perceived by the employees.

23. ____

When deciding what is fair, the main thing is to make sure the people working for you know you really care about them.

24. ____

Your Answer   Your Answer

IX. There are many views on keeping up productivity in a business office situation. I believe that:

If a relaxed atmosphere is created in an office, the employees will generate their own pressure.

25. ____

Whenever possible, methods should be found of setting up work schedules so that pressure comes from the assignment system and work load rather than from the supervisor.

26. ____

Keeping people under a certain amount of pressure from the supervisor results in work being turned out at a good rate.

27. ____

X. Formal organizational life breeds informal organizations and cliques. I believe:

A well-managed, well-controlled organization minimizes the opportunity for these to become a problem. When informal organizations or cliques do become active, measures can be found to neutralize them.

28. ____

The boss who is known to fight for his people is not likely to have trouble in this regard, since he will probably have the informal organization on his side.

29. ____

The team approach with open communications and a problem-solving orientation can integrate informal groups into work activities.

30. ____

XI. How to motivate people to work:

A manager can motivate people by showing drive, enthusiasm, and high commitment for what he is doing. Being an appropriate example is all-important.

31. ____

A manager has to stress results and high standards but should arrange

the work in such a way that everyone has the maximum opportunity for self-management.

32. ____

There are two factors that are foremost: first, there is still no substitute for simply being considerate of people, and secondly, they will work hard if they feel they are accepted as a member of the group.

33. ____

XII. When I am looking for leadership talent among my employees, I operate on the assumption that:

The majority of the people have some potential for developing leadership capabilities.

34. ____

It is something you either have or don't have, and the task is to find those who have it.

35. ____

It is most important to make sure that the individuals you select for future leaders will be able to fit into the style and character of the organization.

36. ____

XIII. Delegation is a matter of:

Assigning whatever responsibility you assume the individual will have to shoulder if he is going to make an effective manager.

37. ____

Letting the individual decide when he believes he is ready to assume more responsibility.

38. ____

Gradually releasing responsibility as you observe the individual is ready for it.

39. ____

XIV. In my company, I support a promotion policy that selects:

Tactful, reasonable leaders who keep the people satisfied while attaining reasonably good production.

40. ____

Your Answer

Your Answer

Leaders whose results records show they have high standards and are getting high commitment from people.   41. ____

Leaders who go all out for the people, since they are what makes the company go.   42. ____

XV. Concerning communication problems with subordinates:

If the employees know the boss is open to feedback, they will usually take the initiative to clear up communication problems when they arise.   43. ____

You probably won't have communication problems if you concentrate on getting all the information out to people so they know what you want them to do to complete their work.   44. ____

The manager has to develop communication skills to persuade, sell, and even negotiate to get the job accomplished.   45. ____

XVI. When conflict arises between employees, I believe:

If a manager creates the climate where everyone feels he is part of the family, disagreements can often be overcome by emphasizing the positive and what we have going for us.   46. ____

Often a manager facing conflict is in a similar role to that developed by labor: he has to examine the issues involved, look for answers acceptable to both sides, and find middle-ground solutions when necessary.   47. ____

Conflict can destroy effectiveness. It must be dealt with firmly so people will know it will not be permitted.   48. ____

XVII. Participative management (letting employees participate in the decision-making processes):

The main advantage comes from having employees serve on committees and special task forces where their ideas can be used.   49. ____

When people have taken part in a decision, they are more apt to be committed to carry it out.   50. ____

It is needed to give people a sense of personal worth and importance.   51. ____

XVIII. Managing competition between different working elements of an organization:

Stressing common goals among the units or competing against your own record is the most meaningful approach.   52. ____

It's natural to want to be on a winning team, which means you want your part of the organization to do better than the others.   53. ____

It always exists so the main thing is to make sure your people don't become too obvious about it or let it get out of hand.   54. ____

XIX. When employees start expressing their concerns and feelings, I would:

Encourage people to say what they are feeling so management can be responsive to their needs.   55. ____

Stress what is logical and rational and tell people to keep feelings and emotions out of our work relationships.   56. ____

Keep a low profile, that is, play things in low key so feelings do not get ruffled; make compromises necessary to maintain this atmosphere.   57. ____

XX. Completing the annual performance evaluation on employees:

Performance evaluation can be an effective means of developing influence over people; if they know what behavior you are rewarding and correcting, they can better measure up to your expectations.   58. _____

The major value of the annual report is that it provides the opportunity to recognize the employee for what he is doing well.   59. _____

Performance evaluation can be made meaningful by the superior and the subordinate agreeing upon what goals are to be accomplished and how the expected results are to be evaluated.   60. _____

Complete the answer sheet to examine your style and philosophy of leadership.

Answer Sheet for Leadership Styles Questionnaire

Copy your answers from the questionnaire on Leadership Style and Philosophy. Total your scores where indicated.

No. of Item	Your Answer	No. of Item	Your Answer	No. of Item	Your Answer	No. of Item	Your Answer
		1.	_____	3.	_____	2.	_____
5.	_____	6.	_____			4.	_____
9.	_____	8.	_____	7.	_____		
10.	_____			11.	_____	12.	_____
14.	_____	15.	_____			13.	_____
18.	_____	17.	_____	16.	_____		
19.	_____			20.	_____	21.	_____
		22.	_____	24.	_____	23.	_____
27.	_____	26.	_____	25.	_____		
28.	_____			29.	_____	30.	_____
		31.	_____	33.	_____	32.	_____
35.	_____	36.	_____			34.	_____
37.	_____			38.	_____	39.	_____
		40.	_____	42.	_____	41.	_____
44.	_____	45.	_____			43.	_____
48.	_____	47.	_____	46.	_____		
		49.	_____	51.	_____	50.	_____
53.	_____	54.	_____			52.	_____
56.	_____	57.	_____	55.	_____		
58.	_____			59.	_____	60.	_____
Total Box A	[ ]	Total Box B	[ ]	Total Box C	[ ]	Total Box D	[ ] = 120

After you have totaled boxes A through D, mark an X on the corresponding scales on the lower half of the form at a point corresponding to the number appearing in the box; if Box A is 20, for example, the scale on A should be marked at 20. When all four scales have been completed, draw a connecting line between the Xs. This represents your profile for four different leadership styles. Bring your results to class for discussion.

Put an X on the scales below to represent your numerical scores for the boxes above.

_____	[A] 15	20	25	30	35	40	45
_____	[B] 15	20	25	30	35	40	45
_____	[C] 15	20	25	30	35	40	45
_____	[D] 15	20	25	30	35	40	45

LEADERSHIP STYLE ANALYSIS

OBJECTIVES

1. To learn how to diagnose different leadership situations.

2. To learn how to apply a systematic procedure for analyzing situations.

3. To improve understanding of how to reach a decision.

STARTING THE EXERCISE

Review the "Decision Process Flowchart" in Figure 10–3. The instructor will then form groups of four to five people to analyze each of the following three cases. Try to reach a group consensus on which decision style is best for the particular case. You are to select the best style based on use of the Vroom-Yetton model, available decision styles, and decision rules. Each case should take a group between 30 and 45 minutes to analyze.

EXERCISE PROCEDURES

Phase I: 10–15 minutes
Individually read case and select proper decision style, using Vroom-Yetton model.

Phase II: 30–45 minutes
Join group appointed by instructor, and reach group consensus.

Phase III: 20 minutes
Each group spokesperson presents group's response and rationale to other groups.

These phases should be used for each of the cases.

Case I

Setting: Corporate Headquarters
Your Position: Vice President

As marketing vice president, you frequently receive nonroutine requests from customers. One such request, from a relatively new customer, is for extended terms on a large purchase ($2.5 million) involving several of your product lines. The request is for extremely favorable terms that you would not consider except for the high inventory level of most product lines at the present time due to the unanticipated slack period that the company has experienced over the last six months.

You realize that the request is probably a starting point for negotiations, and you have proved your abilities to negotiate the most favorable arrangements in the past. As preparation for these negotiations, you have familiarized yourself with the financial situation of the customer, using various investment reports that you receive regularly.

Reporting to you are four sales managers, each of whom has responsibility for a single product line. They know of the order, and like you, they believe that it is important to negotiate terms with minimum risk and maximum returns to the company. They are likely to differ on what constitutes an acceptable level of risk. The two younger managers have developed a reputation of being "risk takers," whereas the two more senior managers are substantially more conservative.

Case II

Setting: Toy Manufacturer
Your Position: Vice President, Engineering and Design

You are a vice president in a large toy manufacturing company, and your responsibilities include the design of new products that will meet the changing demand in this uncertain and very competitive industry. Your design teams, each under the supervision of a department head, are therefore under constant pressure to produce novel, marketable ideas.

At the opposite end of the manufacturing process is the quality control department, which is under the authority of the vice president, production. When quality control has encountered a serious problem that may be due to design features, its staff has consulted with one or more of your department heads to obtain their recommendations for any changes in the production process. In the wake of consumer concern over the safety of children's toys, however, the responsibilities of quality control have recently been expanded to ensure not only the quality but also the safety of your products. The first major problem in this area has arisen. A preliminary consumer report has "blacklisted" one of your new products without giving any specific reason or justification. This has upset you and others in the organization since it was believed that this product would be one of the most profitable items in the coming Christmas season.

The consumer group has provided your company with an opportunity to respond to the report before it is made public. The head of quality control has therefore consulted with your design people, but you have been told that they became somewhat defensive and dismissed the report as "overreactive fanatic nonsense." Your people told quality control that, while freak accidents were always possible, the product was certainly safe as designed. They argued that the report should simply be ignored.

Since the issue is far from routine, you have decided to give it your personal attention. Because your design teams have been intimately involved in all aspects of the development of the item, you suspect that their response was extreme and was perhaps governed more by their emotional reaction to the report than by the facts. You are not convinced that the consumer group is totally irresponsible, and you are anxious to explore the problem in detail and to recommend to quality control any changes that may be required from a design standpoint. The firm's image as a producer of high-quality toys could suffer a serious blow if the report were made public and public confidence were lost as a result.

You will have to depend heavily on the background and experience of your design teams to help you in analyzing the problem. Even though quality control will be responsible for the decision to implement any changes that you may ultimately recommend, your own subordinates have the background of design experience that could enable you to set standards for what is "safe" and to suggest any design modifications that would meet these standards.

Case III

Setting: Corporate Headquarters
Your Position: Vice President

The sales executives in your home office spent a great deal of time visiting regional sales offices. As marketing vice president, you are concerned that the expenses incurred on these trips are excessive—especially now, when the economic outlook seems bleak and general belt-tightening measures are being carried out in every department.

Having recently been promoted from the ranks of your subordinates, you are keenly aware of some cost-saving measures that could be introduced. You have, in fact, asked the accounting department to review a sample of past expense reports, and it has agreed with your conclusion that several highly favored travel "luxuries" could be curtailed. For example, your sales executives, could restrict first-class air travel to only those occasions when economy class is unavailable, and airport limousine service to hotels could be used instead of taxis where possible. Even more savings could be made if your personnel carefully planned trips such that multiple purposes could be achieved where possible.

The success of any cost-saving measures, however, depends on the commitment of your subordinates. You do not have the time (or the desire) to closely review the expense reports of these sales executives. You suspect, though, that they do not share your concerns over the matter. Having once been in their position, you know that they feel themselves to be deserving of travel amenities.

The problem is to determine which changes, if any, are to be made in current travel and expense account practices in light of the new economic conditions.

② TASK AND PEOPLE ORIENTATIONS

OBJECTIVES
1. To evaluate oneself in terms of the leadership dimensions of task orientation and people orientation.
2. To compare your leadership orientation with others.

STARTING THE EXERCISE
1. Without prior discussion, fill out the Leadership Questionnaire below. Do not read the rest of this until you have completed the test. In order to locate yourself on the Leadership Style Profile Sheet, you will score your own questionnaire on the dimensions of task orientation (T) and people orientation (P).

EXERCISE PROCEDURES
1. The scoring is as follows:
a. Circle the item number for items 8, 12, 17, 18, 19, 30, 34, and 35.
b. Write the number 1 in front of a *circled item number* if you responded S (seldom) or N (never) to that item.
c. Also write a number 1 in front of *item numbers not circled* if you responded A (always) or F (frequently).
d. Circle the number 1's which you have written in front of the following items: 3, 5, 8, 10, 15, 18, 19, 22, 24, 26, 28, 30, 32, 34, and 35.
e. *Count the circled number 1's.* This is your score for the level of your concern for people. Record the score in the blank following the letter P at the end of the questionnaire.

f. *Count the uncircled number 1's.* This is your score for your concern for the task. Record this number in the blank following the letter T.
2. Next look at the Leadership Style Profile Sheet on p. 462 and follow the directions.
3. Participants can predict how they will appear on the profile prior to scoring the questionnaire.
4. Paired participants already acquainted can predict each other's scores. If they are not acquainted, they can discuss their reactions to the questionnaire items to find some bases for this prediction.

LEADERSHIP QUESTIONNAIRE
Directions: The following items describe aspects of leadership behavior. Respond to each item according to the way you would most likely act if you were the leader of a work group. Circle whether you would most likely behave in the described way: always (A), frequently (F), occasionally (O), seldom (S), or never (N). Once the test is completed, go back to #2 and #3 under exercise procedures.

A F O S N   **1.** I would most likely act as the spokesperson of the group.
A F O S N   **2.** I would encourage overtime work.
A F O S N   **3.** I would allow members complete freedom in their work.
A F O S N   **4.** I would encourage the use of uniform procedures.
A F O S N   **5.** I would permit the members to use their own judgment in solving problems.
A F O S N   **6.** I would stress being ahead of competing groups.
A F O S N   **7.** I would speak as a representative of the group.
A F O S N   **8.** I would needle members for greater effort.
A F O S N   **9.** I would try out my ideas in the group.
A F O S N   **10.** I would let the members do their work they way they think best.
A F O S N   **11.** I would be working hard for a promotion.
A F O S N   **12.** I would tolerate postponement and uncertainty.
A F O S N   **13.** I would speak for the group if there were visitors present.
A F O S N   **14.** I would keep the work moving at a rapid pace.
A F O S N   **15.** I would turn the members loose on a job and let them go to it.
A F O S N   **16.** I would settle conflicts when they occur in the group.
A F O S N   **17.** I would get swamped by details.
A F O S N   **18.** I would represent the group at outside meetings.
A F O S N   **19.** I would be reluctant to allow the members any freedom of action.

Source: J. William Pfeiffer and John E. Jones (Eds.), *Structured Experiences for Human Relations Training* (San Diego: University Associates Press, 1974). Originally adapted from Sergiovanni, Metzeus, and Burden's revision of the "Leadership Behavior Description Questionnaire," *American Educational Research Journal*, Vol. 6, 1969, pp. 62–79.

A F O S N	**20.**	I would decide what should be done and how it should be done.
A F O S N	**21.**	I would push for increased production.
A F O S N	**22.**	I would let some members have authority which I could keep.
A F O S N	**23.**	Things would usually turn out as I had predicted.
A F O S N	**24.**	I would allow the group a high degree of initiative.
A F O S N	**25.**	I would assign group members to particular tasks.
A F O S N	**26.**	I would be willing to make changes.
A F O S N	**27.**	I would ask the members to work harder.
A F O S N	**28.**	I would trust the group members to exercise good judgment.
A F O S N	**29.**	I would schedule the work to be done.
A F O S N	**30.**	I would refuse to explain my actions.
A F O S N	**31.**	I would persuade others that my ideas are to their advantage.
A F O S N	**32.**	I would permit the group to set its own pace.
A F O S N	**33.**	I would urge the group to beat its previous record.
A F O S N	**34.**	I would act without consulting the group.
A F O S N	**35.**	I would ask that group members follow standard rules and regulations.

T _____   P _____

T-P LEADERSHIP STYLE PROFILE SHEET

Directions: To determine your style of leadership, mark your score on the concern for task dimension (T) on the left-hand arrow below. Next, move to the right-hand arrow and mark your score on the concern for people dimension (P). Draw a straight line that intersects the P and T scores. The point at which that line crosses the shared leadership arrow indicates your score on that dimension.

1 L. J. SUMMERS COMPANY

Jon Reese couldn't think of a time in the history of L. J. Summers Company when there had been as much anti-company sentiment among the workers as had emerged in the past few weeks. He knew that Mr. Summers would place the blame on him for the problems with the production workers because Jon was supposed to be helping Mr. Summer's son, Blaine, to become oriented to his new position. Blaine had only recently taken over as production manager of the company (see Exhibit 1, page 464). Blaine was unpopular with most of the workers, but the events of the past weeks had caused him to be resented even more. This resentment had increased to the point that several of the male workers had quit and all the women in the assembly department had refused to work.

The programs that had caused the resentment among the workers were instituted by Blaine to reduce waste and lower production costs, but they had produced completely opposite results. Jon knew that on Monday morning he would have to explain to Mr. Summers why the workers had reacted as they did and that he would have to present a plan to resolve the employee problems, reduce waste, and decrease production costs.

COMPANY HISTORY

L. J. Summers Company manufactured large sliding doors made of many narrow aluminum panels held together by thick rubber strips, which allowed the door to collapse as it was opened. Some of the doors were as high as eighteen feet and were used in buildings to section off large areas. The company had grown rapidly in its early years due mainly to the expansion of the building program of the firm's major customer, which accounted for nearly 90 percent of Summers' business.

When L. J. Summers began the business, his was the only firm that manufactured the large sliding doors. Recently, however, several other firms had begun to market similar doors. One firm in particular had been bidding to obtain business from Summers' major customer. Fearing that the competitor might be able to underbid his company, Mr. Summers began urging his assistant, Jon, to increase efficiency and cut production costs.

CONDITIONS BEFORE THE COST REDUCTION PROGRAMS

A family-type atmosphere had existed at Summers before the cost reduction programs were instituted. There was little direct supervision of the workers from the front office, and no pressure was put on them to meet production standards. Several of the employees worked overtime regularly without supervision. The foremen and workers often played cards together during lunchtime, and company parties after work were common and popular. Mr. Summers was generally on friendly terms with all the employees, although he was known to get angry if something displeased him. He also participated freely in the daily operations of the company.

As Mr. Summers's assistant, Jon was responsible for seeing to it that the company achieved the goals established by Mr. Summers. Jon was considered hard-working and persuasive by most of the employees and had a reputation of not giving in easily to employee complaints.

Blaine Summers had only recently become the production manager of Summers. He was in his early twenties, married, and had a good build. Several of the workers commented that Blaine liked to show off his strength in front of others. He was known to be very meticulous about keeping the shop orderly and neat, even to the point of making sure that packing crates were stacked "his way." It was often commented among the other employees how Blaine seemed to be trying to impress his father. Many workers voiced the opinion that the only reason Blaine was production manager was that his father owned the company. They also resented his using company employees and materials to build a swing set for his children and to repair his camper.

Blaine, commenting to Jon one day that the major problem with production was the workers, added that people of such caliber as the Summers' employees

Source: Reprinted by permission from *Organization and People* (2nd Edition), by J. B. Ritchie and Paul Thompson; Copyright 1976, 1980, 1984, by West Publishing Company. All rights reserved. PP. 358–362.

did not understand how important cost reduction was and that they would rather sit around and talk all day than work. Blaine rarely spoke to the workers but left most of the reprimanding and firing up to his assistant, Evelyn Brown.

Summers employed about seventy people to perform the warehousing, assembly, and door-jamb building, as well as the packing and shipping operations done on the doors. Each operation was supervised by a foreman, and crews ranged from three men in warehousing to twenty-five women in the assembly department. The foremen were usually employees with the most seniority and were responsible for quality and on-time production output. Most of the foremen had good relationships with the workers.

The majority of the work done at Summers consisted of repetitive assembly tasks requiring very little skill or training; for example, in the pinning department the workers operated a punch press, which made holes in the panels. The job consisted of punching the hole and then inserting a metal pin into it. Workers commented that it was very tiring and boring to stand at the press during the whole shift without frequent breaks.

Wages at Summers were considered to be low for the area. The workers griped about the low pay but said that they tried to compensate by taking frequent breaks, working overtime, and "taking small items home at night." Most of the workers who worked overtime were in the door-jamb department, the operation requiring the most skill. Several of these workers either worked very little or slept during overtime hours they reportedly worked.

The majority of the male employees were in their mid-twenties; about half of them were unmarried. There was a great turnover among the unmarried male workers. The female employees were either young and single or older married women. The twenty-five women who worked in production were all in the assembly department under Lela Pims.

THE COST REDUCTION PROGRAMS

Shortly after Mr. Summers began stressing the need to reduce waste and increase production, Blaine called the foremen together and told them that they would be responsible for stricter discipline among the employees. Unless each forman could reduce waste and improve production in his department, he would either be replaced or receive no pay increases.

EXHIBIT 1

**L. J. Summers Company
Organization Chart**

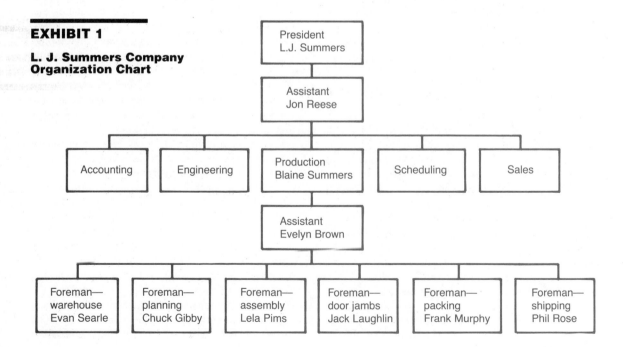

The efforts of the foremen to make the workers eliminate wasteful activities and increase output brought immediate resistance and resentment. The employees' reactions were typified by the following comment: "What has gotten into Chuck lately? He's been chewing us out for the same old things we've always done. All he thinks about now is increasing production." Several of the foremen commented that they didn't like the front office making them the "bad guys" in the eyes of the workers. The workers didn't change their work habits as a result of the pressure put on them by the foremen, but a growing spirit of antagonism between the workers and the foremen was apparent.

After several weeks of no apparent improvement in production, Jon called a meeting with the workers to announce that the plant would go on a four-day, ten-hour-a-day work week in order to reduce operating costs. He stressed that the workers would enjoy having a three-day weekend. This was greeted with enthusiasm by some of the younger employees, but several of the older women complained that the schedule would be too tiring for them and that they would rather work five days a week. The proposal was voted on and passed by a two-to-one margin. Next Jon stated that there would be no more unsupervised overtime and that all overtime had to be approved in advance by Blaine. Overtime would be allowed only if some specific job had to be finished. Those who had been working overtime protested vigorously, saying that this would only result in lagging behind schedule, but Jon remained firm on this new rule.

Shortly after the meeting, several workers in the door-jamb department made plans to stage a work slowdown so that the department would fall behind schedule and they would have to work overtime to catch up. One of the workers, who had previously been the hardest working in the department said, "We will tell them that we are working as fast as possible and that we just can't do as much as we used to in a five-day week. The only thing they could do would be to fire us, and they would never do that." Similar tactics were devised by workers in other departments. Some workers said that if they couldn't have overtime they would find a better paying job elsewhere.

Blaine, observing what was going on, told Jon, "They think I can't tell that they are staging a slowdown. Well, I simply won't approve any overtime, and after Jack's department gets way behind I'll let him have it for fouling up scheduling."

After a few weeks of continued slowdown, Blaine drew up a set of specific rules, which were posted on the company bulletin board early one Monday morning (see Exhibit 2). This brought immediate criticism from the workers. During the next week they continued to deliberately violate the posted rules. On Friday two of the male employees quit because they were penalized for arriving late to work and for "lounging around" during working hours. As they left they said they would be waiting for their foreman after work to get even with him for turning them in.

That same day the entire assembly department (all women) staged a work stoppage to protest an action taken against Myrtle King, an employee of the company since the beginning. The action resulted from a run-in she had with Lela Pims, foreman of the assembly department. Myrtle was about 60 years old and had been turned in by Lela for resting too much. She became furious, saying she couldn't work ten hours a day. Several of her friends had organized the work stoppage after Myrtle had been sent home without pay credit for the day. The stoppage was also inspired by some talk among the workers of forming a union. The women seemed to favor this idea more than the men.

When Blaine found out about the incident he tried joking with the women and in jest threatened to fire them if they did not begin working again. When he saw he was getting nowhere he returned to the front office. One of the workers commented, "He thinks he can send us home and push us around and then all he has to do is tell us to go back to work and we will. Well, this place can't operate without us."

Jon soon appeared and called Lela into his office and began talking with her. Later he persuaded the women to go back to work and told them that there would be a meeting with all the female employees on Monday morning.

EXHIBIT 2

Production Shop Regulations

---

1. Anyone reporting late to work will lose one half hour's pay for each five minutes of lateness. The same applies to punching in after lunch.
2. No one is to leave the machine or post without the permission of the supervisor.
3. Anyone observed not working will be noted and if sufficient occurrences are counted the employee will be dismissed.

Jon wondered what steps he should take to solve the problems at L. J. Summers Company. The efforts of management to increase efficiency and reduce production costs had definitely caused resentment among the workers. Even more disappointing was the fact that the company accountant had just announced that waste and costs had increased since the new programs had been instituted, and the company scheduler reported that Summers was farther behind on shipments than ever before.   □

CASE QUESTIONS

1. Describe the cause of the problem that led to the production slowdown by employees at the Summers Company.
2. How might management's concern about production costs and waste have been handled in a way that would have avoided the problems that occurred?
3. What kind of leadership procedures are now needed to resolve the problems management now faces?

THE CASE OF THE CHANGING CAGE*

PART I

The voucher-check filing unit was a work unit in the home office of the Atlantic Insurance Company. The assigned task of the unit was to file checks and vouchers written by the company as they were cashed and returned. This filing was the necessary foundation for the main function of the unit: locating any particular check for examination upon demand. There were usually eight to ten requests for specific checks from as many different departments during the day. One of the most frequent reasons checks were requested from the unit was to determine whether checks in payment of claims against the company had been cashed. Thus efficiency in the unit directly affected customer satisfaction with the company. Complaints or inquiries about payments could not be answered with the accuracy and speed conducive to client satisfaction unless the unit could supply the necessary document immediately.

Toward the end of the year nine workers manned this unit. There was an assistant (a position equivalent to a foreman in a factory) named Miss Dunn, five other full-time employees, and three part-time workers.

The work area of the unit was well-defined. Walls bounded the unit on three sides. The one exterior wall was pierced by light-admitting north windows. The west interior partition was blank. A door opening into a corridor pierced the south interior partition. The east side of the work area was enclosed by a steel mesh reaching from wall to wall and floor to ceiling. This open metal barrier gave rise to the customary name of the unit—"The Voucher Cage." A sliding door through this mesh gave access from the unit's territory to the work area of the rest of the company's agency audit division, of which it was a part, located on the same floor.

The unit's territory was kept inviolate by locks on both doors, fastened at all times. No one not working within the cage was permitted inside unless his name appeared on a special list in the custody of Miss Dunn. The door through the steel mesh was used generally for departmental business. Messengers and runners from other departments usually came to the corridor door and pressed a buzzer for service.

The steel mesh front was reinforced by a rank of metal filing cases where checks were filed. Lined up just inside the barrier, they hid the unit's workers from the view of workers outside their territory, including the section head responsible for overall supervision of this unit according to the company's formal plan of operation.

CASE QUESTION

1. What type of power does Miss Dunn possess?

* Source: Adapted from "Topography and Culture: The Case of the Changing Cage," by Cara E. Richards and Henry F. Dobyns; reproduced by permission of the Society for Applied Anthropology from *Human Organization,* Vol. 16, No. 1, 1957.

PART II

On top of the cabinets which were backed against the steel mesh, one of the male employees in the unit neatly stacked pasteboard boxes in which checks were transported to the cage. They were later reused to hold older checks sent into storage. His intention was less getting these boxes out of the way than increasing the effective height of the sight barrier so the section head could not see into the cage "even when he stood up."

The girls stood at the door of the cage that led into the corridor and talked to the messenger boys. The workers also slipped out this door unnoticed to bring in their customary afternoon snack. Inside the cage, the workers sometimes engaged in a good-natured game of rubber band "sniping."

Workers in the cage possessed good capacity to work together consistently and workers outside the cage often expressed envy of those in it because of the "nice people" and friendly atmosphere there. The unit had no apparent difficulty keeping up with its work load.

CASE QUESTION

1. Is there an unwritten boundary that employees in the cage want to preserve?

PART III

For some time prior to that year the controller's department of the company had not been able to meet its own standards of efficient service to clients. Company officials felt the primary cause to be spatial. Various divisions of the controller's department were scattered over the entire twenty-two-story company building. Communication between them required phone calls, messengers, or personal visits, all costing time. The spatial separation had not seemed very important when the company's business volume was smaller prior to World War II. But business had grown tremendously since then, and spatial separation appeared increasingly inefficient.

Finally in November company officials began to consolidate the controller's department by relocating two divisions together on one floor. One was the agency audit division, which included the voucher-check filing unit. As soon as the decision to move was made, lower-level supervisors were called in to help with planning. Line workers were not consulted, but were kept informed by the assistants of planning

progress. Company officials were concerned about the problem of transporting many tons of equipment and some 200 workers from two locations to another single location without disrupting work flow. So the move was planned to occur over a single weekend, using the most efficient resources available. Assistants were kept busy planning positions for files and desks in the new location.

Desks, files, chairs, and even wastebaskets were numbered prior to the move, and relocated according to a master chart checked on the spot by the assistant. Employees were briefed as to where the new location was and which elevators they should take to reach it. The company successfully transported the paraphernalia of the voucher check filing unit from one floor to another over one weekend. Workers in the cage quit Friday afternoon at the old stand, reported back Monday at the new.

The exterior boundaries of the new cage were still three building walls and the steel mesh, but the new cage possessed only one door—the sliding door through the steel mesh into the work area of the rest of the agency audit division. The territory of the cage had also been reduced in size. An entire bank of filing cabinets had to be left behind in the old location to be taken over by the unit moving there. The new cage was arranged so that there was no longer a row of metal filing cabinets lined up inside the steel mesh obstructing the view into the cage.

PART IV

When the workers in the cage inquired about the removal of the filing cabinets from along the steel mesh fencing, they found that Mr. Burke had insisted that these cabinets be rearranged so his view into the cage would not be obstructed by them. Miss Dunn had tried to retain the cabinets in their prior position, but her efforts had been overridden.

Mr. Burke disapproved of conversation. Since he could see workers conversing in the new cage, he "requested" Miss Dunn to put a stop to all unnecessary talk. Attempts by female clerks to talk to messenger boys brought the wrath of her superior down on Miss Dunn, who was then forced to reprimand the girls.

Mr. Burke also disapproved of an untidy work area, and any boxes or papers which were in sight were a source of annoyance to him. He did not exert supervision directly, but would "request" Miss Dunn to "do something about those boxes." In the new cage, desks had to be completely cleared at the end of the day, in contrast to the work-in-progress files left out in the old cage. Boxes could not accumulate on top of filing cases.

The custom of afternoon snacking also ran into trouble. Lacking a corridor door, the food-bringers had to venture forth and pack back their snack tray through the work area of the rest of their section, bringing a hitherto unique custom to the attention of workers outside the cage. The latter promptly recognized the desirability of afternoon snacks and began agitation for the same privilege. This annoyed the section head, who forbade workers in the cage from continuing this custom.

CASE QUESTION

1.   What should Miss Dunn do about Burke's directives and requests?

PART V

Mr. Burke later made a rule which permitted one worker to leave the new cage at a set time every afternoon to bring up food for the rest. This rigidity irked cage personnel, accustomed to snack when the mood struck, or none at all. Having made his concession to the cage force, Mr. Burke was unable to prevent workers outside the cage from doing the same thing. What had once been unique to the workers in the cage was now common practice in the section.

Although Miss Dunn never outwardly expressed anything but compliance and approval of superior directives, she exhibited definite signs of anxiety. All the cage workers reacted against Burke's increased domination. When he imposed his decisions upon the voucher-check filing unit, he became "Old Grandma" to its personnel. The cage workers sneered at him and ridiculed him behind his back. Workers who formerly had obeyed company policy as a matter of course began to find reasons for loafing and obstructing work in the new cage. One of the changes that took place in the behavior of the workers had to do with their game of rubber band sniping. All knew Mr. Burke would disapprove of this game. It became highly clandestine and fraught with dangers. Yet shooting rubber bands *increased.*

Newly-arrived checks were put out of sight as soon as possible, filed or not. Workers hid unfiled checks, generally stuffing them into desk drawers or unused file drawers. Since boxes were forbidden, there were fewer unused file drawers than there had been in the old cage. So the day's work was sometimes undone when several clerks hastily shoved vouchers and checks indiscriminately into the same file drawer at the end of the day.

Before a worker in the cage filed incoming checks, she measured with her ruler the thickness in inches of each bundle she filed. At the end of each day she totaled her input and reported to Miss Dunn. All incoming checks were measured upon arrival. Thus Miss Dunn had a rough estimate of unit intake compared with file input. Theoretically she was able to tell at any time how much unfiled material she had on hand and how well the unit was keeping up with its task. Despite this running check, when the annual inventory of unfiled checks on hand in the cage was taken at the beginning of the calendar year, a seriously large backlog of unfiled checks was found. To the surprise and dismay of Miss Dunn, the inventory showed the unit to be far behind schedule, filing more slowly than before the relocation of the cage.   □

CASE QUESTION

1.   Is Miss Dunn exhibiting any specific and relevant leadership characteristics?

11 ORGANIZATIONAL STRUCTURE AND DESIGN

Organizational structure and design are important factors influencing the behavior of the individuals and groups that comprise the organization. The importance of structure as a source of influence on behavior is so widely accepted that some experts define the concept in the following terms: Organizational structure relates to "those features of the organization that serve to *control* or distinguish its parts."[1] Our common experience enables us to recognize the validity of this statement. Most of us know from having worked that behavior in an organization was "controlled" in the sense that we were unable to make absolutely free choices in what we did and how we did it. The basis for much of this control can be found in the structure of the organization, that is, the way in which organizational activities are patterned and grouped together. Thus, when we discuss structure in the following pages we are referring to a *relatively stable framework of jobs and departments that influences the behavior of individuals and groups toward organizational goals.*

Organizations are purposive and goal-oriented, so it follows that the structure of organizations also is purposive and goal-directed. Our concept of organizational structure takes into account the existence of purposes and goals, and our attitude is that management should think of structure in terms of its contribution to organizational effectiveness, even though the exact nature of the relationship between structure and effectiveness is inherently difficult to know.[2] Structure alone, however, is only one part of the organization. As William Scott points out in his article accompanying this chapter, the only meaningful way to study the organization is to study it as a system. That is what Scott does, in the article entitled "Organization Theory: An Overview and an Appraisal." Likewise, that is the orientation of this chapter as we examine structural and design variables in the context of a total organization system.

DESIGNING AN ORGANIZATIONAL STRUCTURE

Managers who set out to design an organizational structure face difficult decisions. They must choose among a myriad of alternative frameworks of

---

[1] Robert H. Miles, *Macro Organizational Behavior* (Santa Monica, Calif.: Goodyear Publishing, 1980), p. 18.

[2] Judith Alexander and W. Alan Randolph, "The Fit between Technology and Structure as a Predictor of Performance in Nursing Subunits," *Academy of Management Journal,* December 1985, pp. 844–59.

jobs and departments. The process by which they make these choices is termed *organizational design,* which means quite simply the decisions and actions that result in an organizational structure.[3] The outcome of organizational design decisions is a system of jobs and work groups, including the processes that link them. Regardless of how or by whom these design decisions are made, the content of the decisions is always the same. The first two decisions identified below focus on individual jobs. The third and fourth focus on departments, or groups of jobs.

1.   Managers decide how to divide the overall tasks into successively smaller jobs. They divide the total activities of the task into smaller sets of related activities. Although jobs have many characteristics, the most important one is their degree of *specialization.*
2.   Managers distribute authority among jobs. Authority is the right to make decisions without approval by a higher manager and to exact obedience from designated other people. All jobs contain the right to make decisions within prescribed limits. But not all jobs contain the right to exact obedience from others.

The outcomes of these two decisions are jobs that management assigns to individuals. The jobs have two distinct attributes: *activities* and *authority.* The next two decisions affect the manner in which the jobs are grouped into departments.

3.   Managers decide the bases on which individual jobs are to be grouped together. This decision can result in groups containing jobs that are relatively homogeneous or heterogeneous.
4.   Finally, managers decide the appropriate size of the group reporting to each superior. This is a decision relating to span of control.

Thus, organizational structures vary depending on the choices that managers make. If we consider each of the four design decisions to be a continuum of possible choices, the alternative structures can be depicted as follows:

	Specialization	
Division of Labor:		
	High	Low
	Delegation	
Authority		
	High	Low
	Basis	
Departmentalization:		
	Homogeneous	Heterogeneous
	Number	
Span of control:		
	Few	Many

---

[3] Hugh C. Willmott, "The Structuring of Organizational Structures: A Note," *Administrative Science Quarterly,* September 1981, pp. 470–74.

Generally speaking, organizational structures tend toward one extreme or the other along each continuum. Structures tending to the left are characterized by a number of terms, including classical, formalistic, structured, bureaucratic, System 1, and mechanistic. Structures tending to the right are termed neoclassical, informalistic, unstructured, nonbureaucratic, System 4, and organic. These terms are in no way precise or universally understood, and this imprecision provides evidence of the relative immaturity of the state of knowledge about organizational design.

DIVISION OF LABOR

Division of labor concerns the extent to which jobs are specialized. Managers divide the total task of the organization into specific jobs having specified *activities*. The activities define what the person performing a particular job is to do and to get done. For example the activities of the job "accounting clerk" can be defined in terms of the *methods* and *procedures* required to process a certain quantity of transactions during a specified period of time. Various accounting clerks could use the same methods and procedures to process *different types* of transactions. One accounting clerk could be processing accounts receivable; the others could be processing accounts payable. Thus, *jobs can be specialized both by method and by application of the method*.

The economic advantages of dividing work into specialized jobs are the principal historical reasons for the creation of organizations. As societies became more and more industrialized and urbanized, craft production gave away to mass production. Mass production depends on the ability to obtain the economic benefits of specialized labor, and organizations are the most effective means for obtaining specialized labor. Although managers are concerned with more than the economic implications of jobs, they seldom lose sight of specialization as the rationale for dividing work among jobs.

DELEGATION OF AUTHORITY

Managers decide how much authority is to be delegated to each job and each jobholder. As we have noted, authority refers to the right of individuals to make decisions without approval by higher management and to exact obedience from others. A sales manager can be delegated the right to hire salespersons (a decision) and the right to assign them to specific territories (obedience). Another sales manager may not have the right to hire but may have the right to assign territories. Thus, the degree of delegated authority can be relatively high or relatively low with respect to both aspects of authority. And for any particular job, there is a range of alternative configurations of authority delegation. Managers must balance the relative gains and losses of alternatives. Let us evaluate some of these.

First, relatively high delegation of authority encourages the development of professional managers. As decision-making authority is pushed down (delegated) in the organization, managers have opportunities to make significant decisions and to gain skills that enable them to cope with problems of higher management and to advance in the company. The advancement of managers on the basis of demonstrated performance can eliminate favoritism and result in improved promotion decisions.

Second, high delegation of authority can lead to a competitive climate within the organization. Managers are motivated to contribute in this competitive atmosphere, since they are compared with their peers on various performance measures. A competitive environment in which managers compete on how well they achieve sales, cost reduction, and employee development targets can be a positive factor in overall organizational performance.

Finally, high delegation of authority enables managers to exercise more autonomy, and thus satisfy their desires to participate in problem solving. This autonomy can lead to managerial creativity and ingenuity that contribute to the adaptiveness and development of the organization and managers. As we have seen in earlier chapters, opportunities to participate in setting goals can be positive motivators. But a necessary condition for goal setting is the authority to make decisions.

These are only three of the benefits associated with delegated authority. As is usually the case, benefits are not totally free of costs. Costs of delegated authority include the expense associated with training managers to make the decisions that go along with their authority, and the fact that many managers become accustomed to making decisions and consequently resist delegating authority to subordinates. There are, of course, other costs. Like most managerial decisions, whether authority should be delegated in high or low degrees is not necessarily a simple issue to resolve. The following OBM Encounter examines one possible byproduct of delegating authority: lean corporate staffs.

ENCOUNTER

DELEGATION AND THE RULE OF 100

Thomas Peters and Robert Waterman, in their book *In Search of Excellence,* make the point that simple organizational structures resulting in a high degree of autonomy (which comes about as a result of delegated authority) tend to be the rule among many of the most effectively run organizations. An indication of how much delegation exists can be found in the size of corporate staffs: smaller staffs suggest more delegation. Peters and Waterman have come up with what they call the "rule of 100." With very few exceptions, there is seldom a need for more than 100 people in the corporate headquarters. Among the examples they cite:

- Emerson Electric, with 54,000 employees, has fewer than 100 at corporate headquarters.
- Dana, with 35,000 employees, has cut its staff from 500 to approximately 100.
- Schlumberger, a diversified international oil service company, has a corporate staff of 90.

Other examples of successful organizations with lean corporate staffs abound: Johnson & Johnson, McDonalds, Ore-Ida, ROLM, and

Source: Based upon Thomas J. Peters and Robert H. Waterman, Jr., *In Search of Excellence* (New York: Harper & Row, 1982).

Wal-Mart. In many instances, the lean staff policy is a reflection of a long-standing corporate policy. The late Ray Kroc, founder of McDonalds, always believed that less is more when it came to corporate management. Similarly, Sam Walton, founder of the Wal-Mart chain of discount outlets, believes in the empty headquarters rule. The key, he says, is to get into the stores and listen. While a high degree of delegated authority is not for everyone, clearly it is working for these highly successful companies. ☐

DEPARTMENTALIZATION

The process of defining the activities and authority of jobs is analytical. The total task of the organization is broken down into successively smaller ones. Then management must combine the divided tasks into groups or departments.

The rationale for grouping jobs rests on the necessity for coordinating them. The specialized jobs are separate, interrelated parts of the total task, whose accomplishment requires the completion of each of the jobs. But the jobs must be performed in the specific manner and sequence intended by management when they were defined. As the number of specialized jobs in an organization increases, there comes a point when the jobs can no longer be coordinated effectively by a single manager. Thus, to create manageable numbers of jobs, they are combined into smaller groups and a new job is defined, that of manager of the group. The crucial managerial consideration when creating departments is determining the *bases* for grouping jobs. These bases are termed *departmentalization* bases, and some of the more widely used ones are described in the following sections.

FUNCTIONAL DEPARTMEN- TALIZATION

Managers can combine jobs according to the *functions* of the organization. Every organization must undertake certain activities in order to do its work. These necessary activities are the organization's functions. The functions of a hospital include surgery, psychiatry, housekeeping, pharmacy, and personnel. The functions of a manufacturing firm include production, marketing, finance, accounting, and personnel.

The Oldsmobile Division of General Motors is structured on a functional basis, as depicted in Figure 11–1. The functions are engineering, manufacturing, reliability, distribution, finance, personnel, public relations, and purchasing. The management of General Motors decided that these eight functions should be the bases for combining the jobs of the Oldsmobile Division. Other divisions of General Motors use different functional bases, depending on the decisions of management.

The principal advantage of functional departmentalization is its efficiency. It seems logical to have a department that consists of experts in a particular field such as production or accounting. By having departments of specialists, management creates highly efficient units. An accountant generally is more efficient when working with accountants and other individuals who have similar backgrounds and interests. They can share expertise to get the work done.

FIGURE 11–1

Organizational
Structure of
Oldsmobile Division

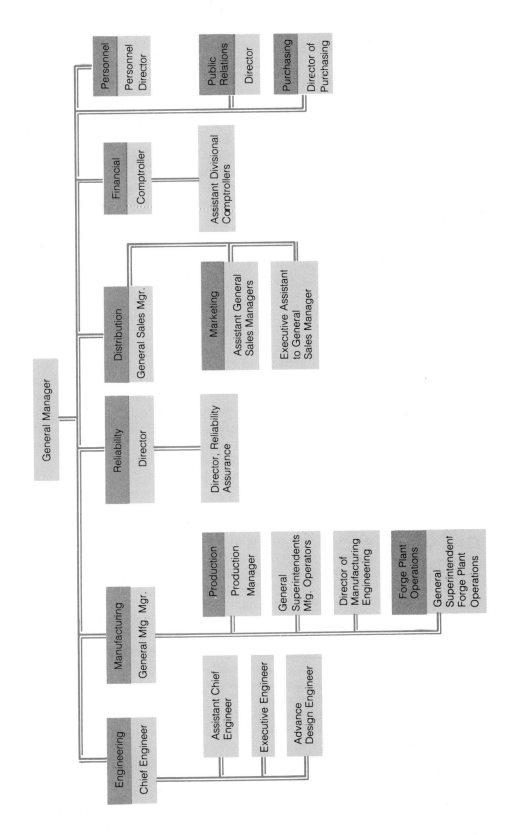

A major disadvantage of this departmental basis, however, is that because specialists are working with and encouraging one another in their area of expertise and interest, the organizational goals may be sacrificed in favor of departmental goals. Accountants may see only their problems and not those of production or marketing or the total organization. In other words, identification with the department and its culture often is stronger than identification with the organization and its culture.

TERRITORIAL DEPARTMEN-TALIZATION

Another commonly adopted method for departmentalizing is to establish groups on the basis of geographic area. The rationale for this method is that all activities in a given region should be assigned to a manager. This individual will be in charge of all operations in that geographic area.

In large organizations, territorial arrangements are advantageous because the physical dispersion of activities makes centralized coordination difficult. It is extremely difficult for a sales manager in New York, for example, to manage salespersons in Kansas City.

R. H. Macy & Co., Inc. is an organization structured along territorial lines. The divisions of the department store reflect the locations of Macy stores in the several states in which they operate. The managers of individual stores in a specific city report to a regional president. Thus, the manager of Macy's in Sacramento reports to the president of Macy's California; the manager of Macy's in Joplin, Missouri, and Wichita, Kansas, both report to the president of Macy's Missouri-Kansas.

Territorial departmentalization provides a training ground for managerial personnel. The company is able to place managers in territories, then assess their progress in that geographic region. The experience that managers acquire in a territory away from headquarters provides valuable insights about how products and services are accepted in the field.

PRODUCT DEPARTMEN-TALIZATION

Managers of many large, diversified companies group jobs on the basis of product. All of the jobs associated with producing and selling a product or product line are placed under the direction of one manager. Product becomes the preferred basis as a firm grows by increasing the number of products it markets. As a firm grows, it becomes difficult to coordinate the various functional departments and establishing product units becomes advantageous. This form of organization allows personnel to develop total expertise in researching, manufacturing, and distributing a product line. Concentration of the authority, responsibility, and accountability in a specific product department allows top management to coordinate actions.

The Consumer Products Division of Kimberly-Clark reflects product departmentalization. The specific product groups shown in Figure 11–2 include feminine hygiene, household, and commercial products. Within each of these units, we find production and marketing personnel. Since the managers of product divisions coordinate the sales, manufacturing, and distribution of a product, they become the overseers of a profit center. In this manner, profit responsibility is implemented in product-based organizations. Managers often are asked to establish profit goals at the beginning of a time period and then to compare actual profit with planned profit.

FIGURE 11–2

**Organizational Structure
of Consumer Products Division,
Kimberly-Clark Corporation**

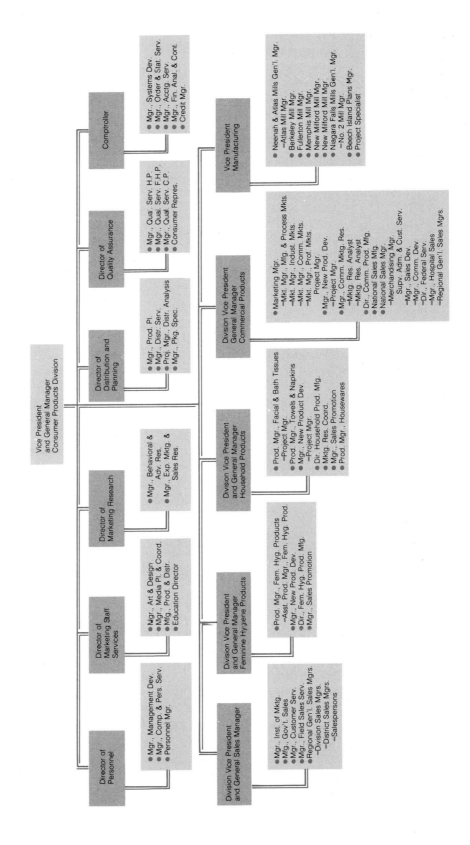

CUSTOMER DEPARTMEN-TALIZATION

Customers and clients can be a basis for grouping jobs. Examples of customer-oriented departments are the organizational structures of educational institutions. Some institutions have regular (day and night) courses and extension divisions. In some instances, a professor will be affiliated solely with the regular division or the extension division. In fact, the title of some faculty positions often specifically mentions the extension division.

Another form of customer departmentalization is the loan department in a commercial bank. Loan officers often are associated with industrial, commercial, or agricultural loans. The customer will be served by one of these three loan officers.

Some department stores are departmentalized to some degree on a customer basis. They have such groupings as university shops, men's clothing, and boys' clothing. They have bargain floors that carry a lower quality of university, men's, and boys' clothing.

MIXED AND CHANGING DEPARTMEN-TALIZATION

The bases for departments do not remain unchanged in organizations. Because of the importance of departments, managers change the bases as conditions warrant. An organization chart should be viewed as much like a snapshot of a moving object. The action is "frozen" for a moment, but the viewer understands that the object continued in motion. Over time, organizations will use a mix of bases. Sometimes they will use function. At other times, they will use product, territory, and customer. Moreover, within the same organization, there will be different bases at different levels of management. For example, the departmental basis at the corporate level of General Motors is product type—compact and full-size cars—with an executive vice president heading up each division. The general managers of the Chevrolet and Pontiac divisions report to the compact car vice president; the general managers of the Buick, Oldsmobile, and Cadillac divisions report to the full-size car vice president. But below the general managers, function is at the departmental basis, as we noted in Figure 11–1. The following OBM Encounter provides an example of changing structure to meet changing situations.

ENCOUNTER
CHANGING STRUCTURE AT MONSANTO

As discussed in the text, changes in an organization's environment may suggest that changes in organizational arrangements are either desirable or necessary. Frequently, we tend to think that the larger the organization, the more engrained is its structure and, consequently, the more unlikely it is to change. While

this may be true in some situations, such was not the case at Monsanto.

Howard Schneiderman, Monsanto's senior vice president for research and development, explains that the huge corporation is working to develop products which come from human ingenuity and innovation as opposed to those which come from huge amounts of capital investment. To facilitate this move from its traditional business to the development and marketing of patented products, Monsanto is

Source: Based, in part, on D. P. Garino, "Monsanto Slowly But Deliberately Shifts Emphasis to Research, Patented Products," *The Wall Street Journal*, January 13, 1983, p. 33.

restructuring. The new structure groups together areas of emphasis, including a nutrition-chemicals division, an agricultural products company, and an industrial chemical unit.

The new structure is designed to facilitate the shift in capital spending from expanding existing plants to building new research facilities. An important point here is that this change in structure was not implemented overnight. It has taken John Hanley, the chief executive officer at Monsanto, more than ten years to shift the company's emphasis from the commodity chemical business toward the manufacture of patented products. The new structure reduces the number of operating companies and significantly redistributes executive responsibilities. Changes of such magnitude must be done carefully, following more of an evolutionary time frame than a revolutionary one. □

Departmentalization is a critical variable in effective coordination of activities. The degree of coordination that management achieves depends greatly on having appropriate department bases at each level in the organization. An equally important variable is the determination of each manager's span of control.

SPAN OF CONTROL

The determination of appropriate bases for departmentalization establishes the kinds of jobs that will be grouped together. But it does not establish the *number* of jobs to be included in a specific group. That determination is the issue of **span of control.** Generally, the issue comes down to the decision of how many people a manager can oversee. Will the organization be more effective if the span of control is relatively wide or narrow? This question basically is concerned with determining the volume of interpersonal relationships that the department's manager is able to handle. The number of *potential* interpersonal relationships between a manager and subordinates can be calculated as follows:

$$R = N \left(\frac{2^N}{2} + N - 1 \right)$$

where R designates the number of relationships and N is the number of subordinates assigned to the manager's command group. This formula is simply a method for counting the number of potential relationships that can exist. Table 11–1 shows the results of using the formula to calculate the potential relationships between 1 manager and 1 through 9 and 18

TABLE 11–1

Potential Relationships

Number of Subordinates	Number of Relationships
1	1
2	6
3	18
4	44
5	100
6	222
7	490
8	1,080
9	2,376
18	2,359,602

subordinates. Note that the rate of change in potential relationships increases *geometrically* as the number of subordinates increases *arithmetically.*

The critical consideration in determining the manager's span of control is not the number of *potential* relationships, however. Rather, it is the frequency and intensity of the *actual* relationships that are important. Not all relationships will occur, and those that do will vary in importance. If we shift our attention from potential to actual relationships as the basis for determining optimum span of control, at least three factors appear to be important:

1. **Required Contact.** In research and development, medical, and production work, there is a need for frequent contact and a high degree of coordination between a superior and subordinates. For example, the research and development team leader may have to consult frequently with team members so that a project is completed within a time period that will allow the organization to place a product on the market by a certain date. Thus, instead of relying on memos and reports, it is in the best interest of the organization to have as many in-depth contacts with the team as possible. A large span of control would preclude contacting subordinates so frequently, and this could delay the completion of the project. In general, the greater the inherent ambiguity that exists in an individual's job, the greater is the need for supervision to avoid conflict and stress.[4]

2. **Degree of Specialization.** The degree of specialization among employees is a critical consideration in establishing the span of control at all levels of management. It is generally accepted that a manager at a lower organizational level can oversee more subordinates because work at the lower level is more specialized and less complicated than work at higher levels of management. Management can combine highly specialized and similar jobs into relatively large departments, because the employees who do those jobs may not need close supervision.

3. **Ability to Communicate.** Instructions, guidelines, and policies must be communicated verbally to subordinates in most work situations. The need to discuss job-related factors influences the span of control. An individual who can clearly and concisely communicate with subordinates is able to manage more people than one who cannot do so.

Depending on the situation, one or another of these factors may play a greater or lesser role in determining optimal control spans. In short, our knowledge of span of control is incomplete, and the search for a full answer to the question of optimal control span continues.[5]

---

[4] Lawrence B. Chonko, "The Relationship of Span of Control to Sales Representatives' Experienced Role Conflict and Role Ambiguity," *Academy of Management Journal,* June 1982, pp. 452–56.

[5] Robert D. Dewar and Donald P. Simet, "A Level-Specific Prediction of Spans of Control Examining the Effects of Size, Technology, and Specialization," *Academy of Management Journal,* March 1981, pp. 5–24.

DIMENSIONS OF STRUCTURE

The four design decisions (division of labor, delegation of authority, departmentalization, and span of control) result in a structure of organizations. Researchers and practitioners of management have attempted to develop their understanding of relationships between structures and performance, attitudes, satisfaction, and other variables thought to be important. The development of understanding has been hampered not only by the complexity of the relationships themselves, but also by the difficulty of defining and measuring the concept of organizational structure.

Although universal agreement on a common set of dimensions that measure differences in structure is neither possible nor desirable, some suggestions can be made. At present, three dimensions often are used in research and practice to describe structure. They are *formalization, centralization,* and *complexity.*[6]

FORMALIZA-TION

The dimension of **formalization** refers to the extent to which expectations regarding the means and ends of work are specified and written. An organizational structure that is described as highly formalized is one in which rules and procedures are available to prescribe what each individual should be doing. Organizations with such structures would have written standard operating procedures, specified directives, and explicit policies. In terms of the four design decisions, formalization is the result of high specialization of labor, high delegation of authority, the use of functional departments, and wide spans of control.[7]

Although formalization is defined in terms of the existence of written rules and procedures, it is important to understand how these are viewed by the employees. In organizations with all the appearances of formalization—complete with thick manuals of rules, procedures, and policies—employees may not perceive the manuals as affecting their behavior. Thus, even though rules and procedures exist, they must be enforced if they are to affect behavior.[8]

CENTRALIZA-TION

Centralization refers to the location of decision-making authority in the hierarchy of the organization. More specifically, the concept refers to the delegation of authority among the jobs in the organization. Typically, researchers and practitioners think of centralization in terms of (1) decision making and (2) control. Despite the apparent simplicity of the concept, it can be complex.

---

[6] Richard S. Blackburn, "Dimensions of Structure: A Review and Reappraisal," *Academy of Management Review,* January 1982, pp. 59–66.

[7] See Peter H. Grinyear and Masoud Yasai-Ardekani, "Dimensions of Organizational Structure: A Critical Replication," *Academy of Management Journal,* September 1980, pp. 405–21, for discussion of formalization in relation to centralization.

[8] Eric J. Walton, "The Comparison of Measures of Organization Structure," *Academy of Management Review,* January 1981, pp. 155–60.

The complexity of centralization derives from three sources. First, people at the same level can have different decision-making authority. Second, not all decisions are of equal importance in organizations. For example, a typical management practice is to delegate authority to make routine operating decisions (i.e., decentralization) but to retain authority to make strategic decisions (i.e. centralization). Third, individuals may not perceive that they really have authority, even though their job descriptions include it. Thus, objectively they have authority, but subjectively they do not.[9]

COMPLEXITY

Complexity is the direct outgrowth of dividing work and creating departments. Specifically, the concept refers to the number of distinctly different job titles, or occupational groupings, and the number of distinctly different units, or departments. The fundamental idea is that organizations with a great many different kinds and types of jobs and units create more complicated managerial and organizational problems than do those with fewer jobs and departments.

Complexity, then, relates to *differences* among jobs and units. It is not surprising, therefore, that *differentiation* is often used synonymously with complexity. Moreover, it has become standard practice to use the term *horizontal differentiation* to refer to the number of different units at the same level;[10] *vertical differentiation* refers to the number of levels in the organization.

Figure 11–3 displays the relationship between the three dimensions of organizational structure and the four design decisions. Note that the figure shows only the causes of *high* formalization, centralization, and complexity. However, the relationships are symmetrical: the causes of *low* formalization, centralization, and complexity are the opposite of those shown in Figure 11–3.

FIGURE 11–3

Organizational Dimensions and Organizational Decisions

High formalization:	Results from:	1. High specialization 2. Delegated authority 3. Functional departments 4. Wide spans of control
High centralization:	Results from:	1. High specialization 2. Centralized authority 3. Functional departments 4. Wide spans of control
High complexity:	Results from:	1. High specialization 2. Delegated authority 3. Territorial, customer, and product departments 4. Narrow spans of control

---

[9] Jeffrey D. Ford, "Institutional versus Questionnaire Measures of Organizational Structure," *Academy of Management Journal,* September 1979, pp. 601–10.

[10] Richard L. Daft and Patricia J. Bradshaw, "The Process of Horizontal Differentiation: Two Models," *Administrative Science Quarterly,* September 1980, pp. 441–56.

ORGANIZATIONAL DESIGN MODELS

As we have seen, organizational design refers to managerial decision making aimed at determining the structure and processes that coordinate and control the jobs of the organization. The outcome of organizational design decisions is the framework or structure of the organization. Earlier in this chapter, we examined a number of factors and dimensions that influence the structure which ultimately emerges. In this section, we briefly examine two general organizational design models that have had significant impact on management theory and practice. While there is little uniformity in the terms used to designate the models, we refer to them as *mechanistic* and *organic*.[11] In the chapter's final section, we review an emerging organizational design: the matrix.

THE MECHANISTIC MODEL

During the early part of the 20th century, a body of literature emerged that considered the problem of designing the structure of an organization as but one of a number of managerial tasks, including planning and controlling. The objective of the contributors to that body of literature was to define *principles* that could guide managers in the performance of their tasks. Numerous theorists and management practitioners made contributions to this literature, including names such as Fayol, Follet, and Weber. While each contributor made a unique contribution, they all had a common thread. They each described the same type of organization, one that functioned in a machine-like manner to accomplish the organization's goals in a highly efficient manner. Thus, the term *mechanistic* aptly describes such organizations. Mechanistic organizations emphasize the importance of achieving high levels of production and efficiency through the use of extensive rules and procedures, centralized authority, and high specialization:

1. Activities are specialized into clearly defined jobs and tasks.
2. Persons of higher rank typically have greater knowledge of the problems facing the organization than those at lower levels. Unresolved problems are thus passed up the hierarchy. . . .
3. Standardized policies, procedures, and rules guide much of the decision making in the organization.
4. Rewards are chiefly obtained through obedience to instructions from supervisors.[12]

The mechanistic model achieves high levels of efficiency due to its structural characteristics. It is highly complex because of its emphasis on specialization of labor; it is highly centralized because of its emphasis on authority and accountability; and it is highly formalized because of its emphasis on function as the primary basis of departmentalization.

---

[11] Tom Burns and G. M. Stalker, *The Management of Innovation* (London: Tavistock Publications, 1961). Burns and Stalker are largely responsible for the terms *mechanistic* and *organic*.

[12] C. R. Gullet, "Mechanistic vs. Organic Organizations: What Does the Future Hold?" *Personnel Administrator,* 1975, p. 17.

**THE ORGANIC
MODEL**

The **organic model** of organizational design stands in sharp contrast to the mechanistic model. The organizational characteristics and practices that underlie the organic model are distinctly different from those that underlie the mechanistic model. The most distinct differences between the two models results from the different effectiveness criteria that each seeks to maximize. While the mechanistic model seeks to maximize efficiency and production, the organic model seeks to maximize flexibility and adaptability:

1. There is a de-emphasis on job descriptions and specialization. Persons become involved in problem solving when they have the knowledge or skill that will help solve the problem.
2. It is not assumed that persons holding higher positions are necessarily better informed than at lower levels.
3. Horizontal and lateral organizational relationships are given as much or more attention as vertical relationships.
4. Status and rank differences are de-emphasized.
5. The formal structure of the organization is less permanent and more changeable.[13]

The organic organization is flexible and adaptable to changing environmental demands because its design encourages greater utilization of the human potential. Managers are encouraged to adopt practices that tap the full range of human motivations through job design which stresses personal growth and responsibility. Decision making, control, and goal-setting processes are decentralized and are shared at all levels of the organization. Communications flow throughout the organization, not simply down the chain of command. These practices are intended to implement a basic assumption of the organic model, which states that an organization will be effective to the extent that its structure is "such as to ensure a maximum probability that in all interactions and in all relationships with the organization, each member, in the light of his background, values, desires, and expectations, will view the experience as supportive and one which builds and maintains a sense of personal worth and importance."[14]

An organizational design that provides individuals with this sense of personal worth and motivation and that facilitates flexibility and adaptability would have the following characteristics:

1. It would be relatively simple because of its deemphasis on specialization and its emphasis on increasing job range.
2. It would be relatively decentralized because of its emphasis on delegation of authority and increasing job depth.
3. And it would be relatively informalized because of its emphasis on product and customer as bases for departmentation.

---

[13] Ibid.

[14] Rensis Likert, *New Patterns of Management* (New York: McGraw-Hill, 1961); and Rensis Likert, *The Human Organization* (New York: McGraw-Hill, 1967).

Which of the two models is the best? The answer, as you might suspect, is neither. Both models have their proponents and, more importantly, both have strengths and weaknesses. That is one reason for the emergence of the matrix design.

MATRIX ORGANIZATIONAL DESIGN

A matrix design attempts to maximize the strengths and minimize the weaknesses of both the mechanistic and organic designs. In practical terms, the matrix design combines functional and product departmental bases.[15] Among the many companies that use matrix organization are American Cyanamid, Avco, Carborundum, Caterpillar Tractor, Hughes Aircraft, ITT, Monsanto Chemical, National Cash Register, Prudential Insurance, TWR, and Texas Instruments. Public sector users include public health and social service agencies.[16] Although the exact meaning of matrix organization is not well established, the most typical meaning defines it as a balanced compromise between functional and product organization, between departmentalization by process and by purpose.[17]

The matrix organizational design achieves the desired balance by superimposing, or overlaying, a horizontal structure of authority, influence, and communication on the vertical structure. The arrangement can be described as in Figure 11–4; personnel assigned in each cell belong not only to the functional department but also to a particular product or project. For example, manufacturing, marketing, engineering, and finance specialists will be assigned to work on one or more projects or products A, B, C, D, and E. As a consequence, personnel will report to two managers, one in their functional department and one in the project or product unit. The existence of a *dual authority* system is a distinguishing characteristic of matrix organization.

FIGURE 11–4

Matrix Organizations

Projects, Products	Functions			
	Manufacturing	Marketing	Engineering	Finance
Project or product A				
Project or product B				
Project or product C				
Project or product D				
Project or product E				

---

[15] Richard L. Daft, *Organization Theory and Design* (St. Paul: West Publishing, 1983), p. 237.

[16] Kenneth Knight, "Matrix Organization: A Review," *Journal of Management Studies*, May 1976, p. 111.

[17] Ibid., p. 114.

Matrix structures are found in organizations (1) that require responses to rapid change in two or more environments, such as technology and markets; (2) that face uncertainties generating high information-processing requirements; and (3) that must deal with financial and human resources constraints.[18] Managers confronting these circumstances must obtain certain advantages that are most likely to be realized with matrix organizations.[19]

ADVANTAGES OF MATRIX ORGANIZATION

A number of advantages can be associated with the matrix design. Some of the more important ones are as follows:

Efficient Use of Resources. Matrix organization facilitates the utilization of highly specialized staff and equipment. Each project or product unit can share the specialized resource with other units, rather than duplicating it to provide independent coverage for each. This is particularly advantageous when projects require less than the full-time efforts of the specialist. For example, a project may require only half of a computer scientist's time. Rather than having underutilized computer scientists assigned to each of several projects, the organization can keep fewer computer scientists fully utilized by shifting them from project to project.

Flexibility in Conditions of Change and Uncertainty. Timely response to change requires information and communication channels that efficiently get the necessary information to the right people at the right time. Matrix structures encourage constant interaction among project unit and functional department members. Information is channeled vertically and horizontally as people exchange technical knowledge. The result is quicker response to competitive conditions, technological breakthroughs, and other environmental conditions.

Technical Excellence. Technical specialists interact with other specialists while assigned to a project. Such interaction encourages cross-fertilization of ideas, as when a computer scientist must discuss the pros and cons of electronic data processing with a financial accounting expert. Each specialist must be able to listen to, understand, and respond to the views of the other. At the same time, specialists maintain ongoing contact with members of their own discipline because they are also members of a functional department.

Freeing Top Management for Long-Range Planning. An initial stimulus for the development of matrix organizations is that top management becomes increasingly involved with day-to-day operations. Environmental changes tend to create problems that cross functional and product departments and that cannot be resolved by the lower level managers. For example,

---

[18] Paul R. Lawrence, Harvey F. Kolodny, and Stanley M. Davis, "The Human Side of the Matrix," *Organizational Dynamics,* September 1977, p. 47.

[19] The following discussion is based on Knight, "Matrix Organization."

when competitive conditions create the need to develop new products at faster rates, the existing procedures become bogged down. Top management then is called on to settle conflicts among the functional managers. Matrix organization makes it possible for top management to delegate ongoing decision making, thus providing more time for long-range planning.

Providing Opportunities for Personal Development. Members of matrix organizations are given considerable opportunity to develop their skills and knowledge. They are placed in groups consisting of individuals representing diverse parts of the organization. They must, therefore, come to appreciate the different points of view expressed by these individuals; each group member becomes more aware of the total organization. Moreover, members of matrix organizations have opportunities to learn something of other specialties. Engineers develop knowledge of financial issues; accountants learn about marketing. The experience broadens each specialist's knowledge, not only of the organization, but of other scientific and technical disciplines.

Although matrix designs offer a number of potential advantages as outlined above, it is not a universally embraced form of structure. The following OBM Encounter suggests why.

ENCOUNTER
MATRIX DESIGNS ARE NOT FOR EVERYONE

Not all organizations are enthusiastic about matrix designs, and not all matrix designs which have been implemented have been successful. A case in point was the Applied Devices Center (ADC) of Northern Electric Company. ADC was built from the ground floor up as a matrix organization, based on the very latest behavioral science research and theory. Cited as one of the most impressive examples of matrix design, ADC wrestled continually with its implementation. The nature of the matrix design demanded new behaviors both from technical specialists and managers alike—behaviors which took time to learn. Various economic and marketing problems arose before the learning process was complete, and some eight years after it began, ADC was terminated, a victim, in part, of the complexity surrounding the introduction of a matrix design.

ADC is not alone. Huge, Dutch-based Philips has given up on its matrix design because of concern that it was having negative effects on entrepreneurship within the company. While Chase Manhattan Bank recently has decided to implement a matrix design, its close competitor, Citibank, has backed away from its elaborate matrix structure. Thomas J. Peters suggests that the root cause of these defections may be found in the complexity of matrix designs and the effects of that complexity on behavior, particularly strategic behavior.

In spite of these examples, however, matrix designs are flourishing. The TRW Systems Group started its matrix structure in the late 1950s and is still going strong. So is NASA, which has had a matrix organization for more than 25 years. The key to success is in recognition of the fact that implementing a matrix takes a great deal of time, and, as Harvey Kolodny suggests, a matrix ultimately is more a change in behavior of organizational members than it is a new structural design. ☐

Source: Adapted from Harvey F. Kolodny, "Managing in a Matrix," Indiana University, 1981; and Thomas J. Peters, "Beyond the Matrix Organization," *Business Horizons,* October 1979, pp. 15–27.

DIFFERENT FORMS OF MATRIX ORGANIZATION

Matrix organization forms can be depicted as existing in the middle of a continuum that has mechanistic organizations at one extreme and organic organizations at the other. Organizations can move from mechanistic to matrix forms or from organic to matrix forms. Ordinarily, the process of moving to matrix organization is evolutionary. That is, as the present structure proves incapable of dealing with rapid technological and market changes, management attempts to cope by establishing procedures and positions that are outside the normal routine.

Galbraith describes this evolutionary process as follows:

Task Force.   When a competitor develops a new product that quickly captures the market, a rapid response is necessary. In a mechanistic organization, however, new product development often is too time-consuming because of the need to coordinate the various units that must be involved. A convenient approach is to create a task force of individuals from each functional department and to charge it with the responsibility for expediting the process. The task force achieves its objective and dissolves, and members return to their primary assignment.

Teams.   If product or technological breakthrough generates a family of products that move through successive stages of new and improved products, the temporary task force concept is ineffective. A typical next step is to create permanent teams that consist of representatives from each functional department. The teams meet regularly to resolve interdepartmental issues and to achieve coordination. When not involved with issues associated with new product development, the team members work on their regular assignments.

Product Managers.   If the persistence of the technological breakthrough makes new product development a way of life, top management will create the roles of product managers. In a sense, product managers chair the teams, but they are not permanent positions. Ordinarily, they report to top management, but they have no formal authority over the team members. They must rely on their expertise and interpersonal skills to influence the team members. Companies such as General Foods, DuPont, and IBM make considerable use of the product management concept.

Product Management Departments.   The final step in the evolution to matrix organization is the creation of product management departments with subproduct managers for each product line. In some instances, the subproduct managers are selected from specific functional departments and continue to report directly to their functional managers. There is considerable diversity in the application of matrix organization, yet the essential feature is the creation of overlapping authority and the existence of dual authority.

A FINAL WORD

Managers must consider many complex factors and variables to design an optimal organizational structure. We have discussed several of the more important ones in this chapter. As we have seen, the key design decisions are division of labor, departmentalization, spans of control, and delegation of authority. These decisions, which reflect environmental and managerial interactions, are complex. Matching the appropriate structure to these factors is not an easy task.

The overall structure of tasks and authority that results from the key decisions is a specific *design*. The specific design chosen can play an important role in effecting organizational performance levels. John Pearce and Fred David, in their article, "A Social Network Approach to Organizational Design-Performance," which accompanies this chapter, argue that design influences performance through its impact on group structural variables. The alternative designs range along a continuum, with mechanistic design at one extreme and organic design at the other. Both, according to Pearce and David, affect performance favorably, but for different reasons. The matrix design, at the midpoint, represents a balance between the two extremes.

Organizational structures differ on many dimensions. Regardless of the specific configuration of the parts, however, the overriding purpose of structure and design is to channel the behavior of individuals and groups into patterns which contribute to organizational effectiveness and efficiency. An extremely critical factor in effective organizational performance is the specific nature of the tasks organizational members are called upon to perform. This topic of job design and its effects on the overall quality of work life are explored in the final chapter in this section.

SUMMARY OF KEYPOINTS

A. The structure of an organization consists of relatively fixed and stable relationships among jobs and groups of jobs. The primary purpose of organizational structure is to influence the *behavior* of individuals and groups so as to achieve effective performance.

B. Four key managerial decisions determine organization structures. These decisions are dividing work, delegating authority, departmentalizing jobs into groups, and determining spans of control.

C. The four key decisions are interrelated and interdependent, although each has certain specific problems that can be considered apart from the others.

D. Dividing the overall task into smaller related tasks, jobs, depends initially on the technical and economic advantages of specialization of labor.

E. Delegating authority enables an individual to make decisions and exact obedience without approval by higher management. Like other organizing issues, delegated authority is a relative, not absolute, concept. All individuals in an organization, whether managers or nonmanagers, have some authority. The question is whether they have enough to do their jobs.

E. The grouping of jobs into departments requires the selection of common bases such as function, territory, product, or customer. Each basis has advantages and disadvantages that must be evaluated in terms of overall effectiveness.

F. The optimal span of control is no one specific number of subordinates. Although the number of *potential* relationships increases geometrically as the number of subordinates increases arithmetically, the important considerations are the frequency and intensity of the actual relationships.

G. Organizational structures differ as a consequence of the four management decisions. In order to measure these differences, it is necessary to identify measurable attributes, or dimensions, of structure. Three often-used dimensions are complexity, centralization, and formalization.

H. Complexity refers to the extent to which the jobs in the organization are relatively specialized; centralization refers to the extent to which authority is retained in the jobs of top management; and formalization refers to the extent to which policies, rules, and procedures exist in written form.

I. The task and authority relationships among jobs and groups of jobs must be defined and structured according to rational bases. Two specific, yet contradictory, models are *mechanistic* and *organic*. Mechanistic design is characterized by highly specialized jobs, ho-

mogeneous departments, narrow spans of control, and relatively centralized authority.

J. An alternative organic design proposes that the more effective organizations have relatively despecialized jobs, heterogeneous departments, wide spans of controls, and decentralized authority.

K. An emerging design, termed the *matrix organization,* attempts to maximize the strengths and minimize the weaknesses of both the mechanistic and organic models in a design which combines functional and product department bases and relies on a dual authority system.

REVIEW AND DISCUSSION QUESTIONS

1. The larger the span of control, the fewer the number of managers. Is this good or bad from an organization's perspective? Comment.

2. What is the difference between organizational *structure* and *design?*

3. What type of departmentalization exists in a university? Can you recommend an alternative type?

4. If you were starting a new company, what would you want to consider before deciding how it should be structured?

5. Can you think of a particular company or type of industry that tends toward a mechanistic design? What advantages and disadvantages could you see if that organization or industry adopted a more organic design form?

6. Think of a company or industry that favors an

organic design. What might be the pluses and negatives of moving toward the mechanistic end of the continuum?

7. How are the three dimensions of formalization, complexity, and centralization used to measure differences in structures?

8. What cues might a manager have that suggest there is a problem with the design of an organization? Is changing an existing decision a different kind of task from designing a brand new structure? Explain.

9. Changes in organizational size affect structure. In what ways might growth (increasing size) affect an organization's structure? In what ways might consolidation (decreasing size) affect structure?

10. Matrix designs have been hailed as providing an alternative to purely mechanistic or organic structure. Do you think the use of matrix designs will grow? Why or why not? What are some of the potential problems of the dual authority concept of matrix designs?

R¹ ORGANIZATION THEORY: AN OVERVIEW AND AN APPRAISAL*

WILLIAM G. SCOTT

Man is intent on drawing himself into a web of collectivized patterns.

* Source: William G. Scott, "Organization Theory: An Overview and an Appraisal," *Academy of Management Journal,* April 1961, pp. 7–26. Reprinted by permission.

"Modern man has learned to accommodate himself to a world increasingly organized. The trend toward ever more explicit and consciously drawn relationships is profound and sweeping; it is marked by depth no less than by extension."[1] This comment by Seidenberg nicely summarizes the pervasive influence of organization

in many forms of human activity.

Some of the reasons for intense organizational activity are found in the fundamental transitions which revolutionized our society, changing it from a rural culture, to a culture based on technology, industry, and the city. From these changes, a way of life emerged characterized by the *proximity* and *dependency* of people on each other. Proximity and dependency, as conditions of social life, harbor the threats of human conflict, capricious antisocial behavior, instability of human relationships, and uncertainty about the nature of the social structure with its concomitant roles.

Of course, these threats to social integrity are present to some degree in all societies, ranging from the primitive to the modern. But, these threats become dangerous when the harmonious functioning of a society rests on the maintenance of a highly intricate, delicately balanced form of human collaboration. The civilization we have created depends on the preservation of a precarious balance. Hence, disrupting forces impinging on this shaky form of collaboration must be eliminated or minimized.

Traditionally, organization is viewed as a vehicle for accomplishing goals and objectives. While this approach is useful, it tends to obscure the inner workings and internal purposes of organization itself. Another fruitful way of treating organization is as a mechanism having the ultimate purpose of offsetting those forces which undermine human collaboration. In this sense, organization tends to minimize conflict, and to lessen the significance of individual behavior which deviates from values that the organization has established as worthwhile. Further, organization increases stability in human relationships by reducing uncertainty regarding the nature of the system's structure and the human roles which are inherent to it. Corollary to this point, organization enhances the predictability of human action, because it limits the number of behavioral alternatives available to an individual. As Presthus points out:

Organization is defined as a system

of structural interpersonal relations . . . individuals are differentiated in terms of authority, status, and role with the result that personal interaction is prescribed . . . Anticipated reactions tend to occur, while ambiguity and spontaneity are decreased.[2]

In addition to all of this, organization has built-in safeguards. Besides prescribing acceptable forms of behavior for those who elect to submit to it, organization is also able to counterbalance the influence of human action which transcends its established patterns.[3]

Few segments of society have engaged in organizing more intensively than business.[4] The reason is clear. Business depends on what organization offers. Business needs a system of relationships among functions; it needs stability, continuity, and predictability in its internal activities and external contacts. Business also appears to need harmonious relationships among the people and processes which make it up. Put another way, a business organization has to be free, relatively, from destructive tendencies which may be caused by divergent interests.

As a foundation for meeting these needs rests administrative science. A major element of this science is organization theory, which provides the grounds for management activities in a number of significant areas of business endeavor. Organization theory, however, is not a homogeneous science based on generally accepted principles. Various theories of organization have been, and are being evolved. For example, something called "modern organization theory" has recently emerged, raising the wrath of some traditionalists, but also capturing the imagination of a rather elite *avant-garde.*

The thesis of this paper is that

modern organization theory, when stripped of its irrelevancies, redundancies, and "speech defects," is a logical and vital evolution in management thought. In order for this thesis to be supported, the reader must endure a review and appraisal of more traditional forms of organization theory which may seem elementary to him.

In any event, three theories of organization are having considerable influence on management thought and practice. They are arbitrarily labeled in this paper as the classical, the neoclassical, and the modern. Each of these is fairly distinct; but they are not unrelated. Also, these theories are on-going, being actively supported by several schools of management thought.

THE CLASSICAL DOCTRINE

For lack of a better method of identification, it will be said that the classical doctrine deals almost exclusively with the *anatomy of formal organization.* This doctrine can be traced back to Frederick W. Taylor's interest in functional foremanship and planning staffs. But most students of management thought would agree that in the United States, the first systematic approach to organization, and the first comprehensive attempt to find organizational universals, is dated 1931 when Mooney and Reiley published *Onward Industry.*[5] Subsequently, numerous books, following the classical vein, have appeared. Two of the more recent are Brech's, *Organization*[6] and Allen's, *Management and Organization.*[7]

Classical organization theory is built around four key pillars. They are the division of labor, the scalar and functional processes, structure, and span of control. Given these major elements just about all of classical organization theory can be derived.

(1) *The division of labor* is without doubt the cornerstone among the four elements.[8] From it the other elements flow as corollaries. For example, *scalar* and *functional* growth requires specialization and departmentalization of functions. Organization *structure* is naturally dependent upon the direction which specialization of activities travels in company development. Finally, *span of control* problems result from the number of specialized functions under the jurisdiction of a manager.

(2) *The scalar and functional processes* deal with the vertical and horizontal growth of the organization, respectively.[9] The scalar process refers to the growth of the chain of command, the delegation of authority and responsibility, unity of command, and the obligation to report.

The division of the organization into specialized parts and the regrouping of the parts into compatible units are matters pertaining to the functional process. This process focuses on the horizontal evolution of the line and staff in a formal organization.

(3) *Structure* is the logical relationships of functions in an organization, arranged to accomplish the objectives of the company efficiently. Structure implies system and pattern. Classical organization theory usually works with two basic structures, the line and the staff. However, such activities as committee and liaison functions fall quite readily into the purview of structural considerations. Again, structure is the vehicle for introducing logical and consistent relation-

ships among the diverse functions which comprise the organization.[10]

(4) *The span of control* concept relates to the number of subordinates a manager can effectively supervise. Graicunas has been credited with first elaborating the point that there are numerical limitations to the subordinates one man can control.[11] In a recent statement on the subject, Brech points out, "span" refers to" . . . the number of persons, themselves carrying managerial and supervisory responsibilities, for whom the senior manager retains his over-embracing responsibility of direction and planning, co-ordination, motivation, and control."[12] Regardless of interpretation, span of control has significance, in part, for the shape of the organization which evolves through growth. Wide span yields a flat structure; short span results in a tall structure. Further, the span concept directs attention to the complexity of human and functional interrelationships in an organization.

It would not be fair to say that the classical school is unaware of the day-to-day administrative problems of the organization. Paramount among these problems are those stemming from human interactions. But the interplay of individual personality, informal groups, intraorganizational conflict, and the decision-making processes in the formal structure appears largely to be neglected by classical organization theory. Additionally, the classical theory overlooks the contributions of the behavioral sciences by failing to incorporate them in its doctrine in any systematic way. In summary, classical organization theory has relevant insights into the nature of organization, but the value of this theory is limited by

its narrow concentration on the formal anatomy of organization.

LEARNING CHECKPOINT

Why were the Classicists interested in these four key pillars of organizational theory?

NEOCLASSICAL THEORY OF ORGANIZATION

The neoclassical theory of organization embarked on the task of compensating for some of the deficiencies in classical doctrine. The neoclassical school is commonly identified with the human relations movement. Generally, the neoclassical approach takes the postulates of the classical school, regarding the pillars of organization as givens. But these postulates are regarded as modified by people, acting independently or within the context of the informal organization.

One of the main contributions of the neoclassical school is the introduction of behavioral sciences in an integrated fashion into the theory of organization. Through the use of these sciences, the human relationists demonstrate how the pillars of the classical doctrine are affected by the impact of human actions. Further, the neoclassical approach includes a systematic treatment of the informal organization, showing its influence on the formal structure.

Thus, the neoclassical approach to organization theory gives evidence of accepting classical doctrine, but superimposing on it modifications resulting from individual behavior, and the influence of the informal group. The inspiration of the neoclassical school were the Hawthorne studies.[13] Current examples of the neoclassical approach are found in human relations books like Gardner and Moore, *Human Relations in Industry,*[14] and Davis, *Human Relations in Business.*[15] To a more limited extent, work in industrial sociology also reflects a neoclassical point of view.[16]

It would be useful to look briefly at some of the contributions made to organization theory by the neoclassicists. First to be considered are modifications of the pillars of classical doctrine; second is the informal organization.

Examples of the Neoclassical Approach to the Pillars of Formal Organization Theory

(1) The *division of labor* has been a long standing subject of comment in the field of human relations. Very early in the history of industrial psychology study was made of industrial fatigue and monotony caused by the specialization of the work.[17] Later, attention shifted to the isolation of the worker, and his feeling of anonymity resulting from insignificant jobs which contributed negligibly to the final product.[18]

Also, specialization influences the work of management. As an organization expands, the need concomitantly arises for managerial motivation and coordination of the activities of others. Both motivation and coordination in turn relate to executive leadership. Thus, in part, stemming from the growth of industrial specialization, the neoclassical school has developed a large body of theory relating to motivation, coordination, and leadership. Much of this theory is derived from the social sciences.

(2) Two aspects of the *scalar and functional* processes which have been treated with some degree of intensity by the neoclassical school are the delegation of authority and responsibility, and gaps in

or overlapping of functional jurisdictions. The classical theory assumes something of perfection in the delegation and functionalization processes. The neoclassical school points out that human problems are caused by imperfections in the way these processes are handled.

For example, too much or insufficient delegation may render an executive incapable of action. The failure to delegate authority and responsibility equally may result in frustration for the delegatee. Overlapping of authorities often causes clashes in personality. Gaps in authority cause failures in getting jobs done, with one party blaming the other for shortcomings in performance.[19]

The neoclassical school says that the scalar and functional processes are theoretically valid, but tend to deteriorate in practice. The ways in which they break down are described, and some of the human causes are pointed out. In addition the neoclassicists make recommendations, suggesting various "human tools" which will facilitate the operation of these processes.

(3) *Structure* provides endless avenues of analysis for the neoclassical theory of organization. The theme is that human behavior disrupts the best laid organizational plans, and thwarts the cleanness of the logical relationships founded in the structure. The neoclassical critique of structure centers on frictions which appear internally among people performing different functions.

Line and staff relations is a problem area, much discussed, in this respect. Many companies seem to have difficulty keeping the line and staff working together harmoniously. Both Dalton[20] and Juran[21] have engaged in research to discover the causes of friction, and

to suggest remedies.

Of course, line-staff relations represent only one of the many problems of structural frictions described by the neoclassicists. As often as not, the neoclassicists will offer prescriptions for the elimination of conflict in structure. Among the more important harmony-rendering formulae are participation, junior boards, bottom-up management, joint committees, recognition of human dignity, and "better" communication.

(4) An executive's *span of control* is a function of human determinants, and the reduction of span to a precise, universally applicable ratio is silly, according to the neoclassicists. Some of the determinants of span are individual differences in managerial abilities, the type of people and functions supervised, and the extent of communication effectiveness.

Coupled with the span of control question are the human implications of the type of structure which emerges. That is, is a tall structure with a short span or a flat structure with a wide span more conducive to good human relations and high morale? The answer is situational. Short span results in tight supervision; wide span requires a good deal of delegation with looser controls. Because of individual and organizational differences, sometimes one is better than the other. There is a tendency to favor the looser form of organization, however, for the reason that tall structures breed autocratic leadership, which is often pointed out as a cause of low morale.[22]

LEARNING CHECKPOINT

Explain the basis for the argument that the Neoclassicists believed that there is "one-best way" to organize.

The Neoclassical View of the Informal Organization

Nothing more than the barest mention of the informal organization is given even in the most recent classical treatises on organization theory.[23] Systematic discussion of this form of organization has been left to the neoclassicists. The informal organization refers to people in group associations at work, but these associations are not specified in the "blueprint" of the formal organization. The informal organization means natural groupings of people in the work situation.

In a general way, the informal organization appears in response to the social need—the need of people to associate with others. However, for analytical purposes, this explanation is not particularly satisfying. Research has produced the following, more specific determinants underlying the appearance of informal organizations.

(1) The *location* determinant simply states that in order to form into groups of any lasting nature, people have to have frequent face-to-face contact. Thus, the geography of physical location in a plant or office is an important factor in predicting who will be in what group.[24]

(2) *Occupation* is key factor determining the rise and composition of informal groups. There is a tendency for people performing similar jobs to group together.[25]

(3) *Interests* are another determinant for informal group formation. Even though people might be in the same location, performing similar jobs, differences of interest among them explain why several small, instead of one large, informal organizations emerge.

(4) *Special issues* often result in the formation of informal groups, but this determinant is set apart from the three previously mentioned. In this case, people who do not necessarily have similar interests, occupations, or locations may join together for a common cause. Once the issue is resolved, then the tendency is to revert to the more "natural" group forms.[26] Thus, special issues give rise to a rather impermanent informal association; groups based on the other three determinants tend to be more lasting.

When informal organizations come into being they assume certain characteristics. Since understanding these characteristics is important for management practice, they are noted below:

(1) Informal organizations act as agencies of *social control*. They generate a culture based on certain norms of conduct which, in turn, demands conformity from group members. These standards may be at odds with the values set by the formal organization. So an individual may very well find himself in a situation of conflicting demands.

(2) The form of human interrelationships in the informal organization requires *techniques of analysis* different from those used to plot the relationships of people in a formal organization. The method used for determining the structure of the informal group is called *sociometric analysis*. Sociometry reveals the complex structure of interpersonal relations which is based on premises fundamentally unlike the logic of the formal organization.

(3) Informal organizations have *status and communication* systems peculiar to themselves, not necessarily derived from the formal systems. For example, the grapevine is the subject of much neoclassical study.

(4) Survival of the informal organization requires stable continuing relationships among the people in them. Thus, it has been observed that the informal organization *resists change*.[27] Considerable attention is given by the neoclassicists to overcoming informal resistance to change.

(5) The last aspect of analysis which appears to be central to the neoclassical view of the informal organization is the study of the *informal leader*. Discussion revolves around who the informal leader is, how he assumes this role, what characteristics are peculiar to him, and how he can help the manager accomplish his objectives in the formal organization.[28]

This brief sketch of some of the major facets of informal organization theory has neglected, so far, one important topic treated by the neoclassical school. It is the way in which the formal and informal organizations interact.

A conventional way of looking at the interaction of the two is the "live and let live" point of view. Management should recognize that the informal organization exists, nothing can destroy it, and so the executive might just as well work with it. Working with the informal organization involves not threatening its existence unnecessarily, listening to opinions expressed for the group by the leader, allowing group participation in decision-making situations, and controlling the grapevine by prompt release of accurate information.[29]

While this approach is management centered, it is not unreasonable to expect that informal group standards and norms could make themselves felt on formal organizational policy. An honestly conceived effort by managers to establish a working relationship with the informal organization could result in an association where both formal and informal views would be reciprocally modified. The danger which at all costs should be avoided is that "working with the informal organization" does not degenerate into a shallow disguise for human manipulation.

Some neoclassical writing in organization theory, especially that coming from the management-oriented segment of this school, gives the impression that the formal and informal organizations are distinct, and at times, quite irreconcilable factors in a company. The interaction which takes place between the two is something akin to the interaction between the company and a labor union, or a government agency, or another company.

The concept of the social system is another approach to the interactional climate. While this concept can be properly classified as neoclassical, it borders on the modern theories of organization. The phrase "social system" means that an organization is a complex of mutually interdependent, but variable, factors.

These factors include individuals and their attitudes and motives, jobs, the physical work setting, the formal organization, and the informal organizations. These factors, and many others, are woven into an overall pattern of interdependency. From this point of view, the formal and informal organizations lose their distinctiveness, but find real meaning, in terms of human behavior, in the operation of the system as a whole. Thus, the study of organization turns away from descriptions of its component parts, and is refocused on the system of interrelationships among the parts.

One of the major contributions of the Hawthorne studies was the integration of Pareto's idea of the social system into a meaningful method of analysis for the study of behavior in human organizations.[30] This concept is still vitally im-

portant. But unfortunately some work in the field of human relations undertaken by the neoclassicists has overlooked, or perhaps discounted, the significance of this consideration.[31]

The fundamental insight regarding the social system, developed and applied to the industrial scene by Hawthorne researchers, did not find much extension in subsequent work in the neoclassical vein. Indeed, the neoclassical school after the Hawthorne studies generally seemed content to engage in descriptive generalizations, or particularized empirical research studies which did not have much meaning outside their own context.

The neoclassical school of organization theory has been called bankrupt. Criticisms range from "human relations is a tool for cynical puppeteering of people," to "human relations is nothing more than a trifling body of empirical and descriptive information." There is a good deal of truth in both criticisms, but another appraisal of the neoclassical school of organization theory is offered here. The neoclassical approach has provided valuable contributions to the lore of organization. But, like the classical theory, the neoclassical doctrine suffers from incompleteness, a shortsighted perspective, and lack of integration among the many facets of human behavior studied by it. Modern organization theory has made a move to cover the shortcomings of the current body of theoretical knowledge.

MODERN ORGANIZATION THEORY

The distinctive qualities of modern organization theory are its conceptual-analytical base, its reliance on empirical research data and, above all, its integrating nature. These

qualities are framed in a philosophy which accepts the premise that the only meaningful way to study organization is to study it as a system. As Henderson put it, the study of a system must rely on a method of analysis, ". . . involving the simultaneous variations of mutually dependent variables."[32] Human systems, of course, contain a huge number of dependent variables which defy the most complex simultaneous equations to solve.

Nevertheless, system analysis has its own peculiar point of view which aims to study organization in the way Henderson suggests. It treats organization as a system of mutually dependent variables. As a result, modern organization theory, which accepts system analysis, shifts the conceptual level of organization study above the classical and neoclassical theories. Modern organization theory asks a range of interrelated questions which are not seriously considered by the two other theories.

Key among these questions are: (1) What are the strategic parts of the system? (2) What is the nature of their mutual dependency? (3) What are the main processes in the system which link the parts together, and facilitate their adjustment to each other? (4) What are the goals sought by systems?[33]

Modern organization theory is in no way a unified body of thought. Each writer and researcher has his special emphasis when he considers the system. Perhaps the most evident unifying thread in the study of systems is the effort to look at the organization in its totality. Representative books in this field are March and Simon, *Organizations*,[34] and Haire's anthology, *Modern Organization Theory*.[35]

Instead of attempting a review of different writers' contributions to modern organization theory, it will be more useful to discuss the various ingredients involved in system analysis. They are the parts, the interactions, the processes, and the goals of systems.

The Parts of the System and Their Interdependency

The first basic part of the system is the *individual,* and the personality structure he brings to the organization. Elementary to an individual's personality are motives and attitudes which condition the range of expectancies he hopes to satisfy by participating in the system.

The second part of the system is the formal arrangement of functions, usually called the *formal organization.* The formal organization is the interrelated pattern of jobs which make up the structure of a system. Certain writers, like Argyris, see a fundamental conflict resulting from the demands made by the system, and the structure of the mature, normal personality. In any event, the individual has expectancies regarding the job he is to perform; and, conversely, the job makes demands on, or has expectancies relating to, the performance of the individual. Considerable attention has been given by writers in modern organization theory to incongruencies resulting from the interaction of organizational and individual demands.[36]

The third part in the organization system is the *informal organization.* Enough has been said already about the nature of this organization. But it must be noted that an interactional pattern exists between the individual and the informal group. This interactional arrangement can be conveniently discussed as the mutual modification of expectancies. The informal organization has demands which it makes on members in terms of anticipated forms of behavior, and the individual has expectancies of satisfaction he hopes to derive from association with people on the job. Both these sets of expectancies interact, resulting in the individual modifying his behavior to accord with the demands of the group, and the group, perhaps, modifying what it expects from an individual because of the impact of his personality on group norms.[37]

Much of what has been said about the various expectancy systems in an organization can also be treated using status and role concepts. Part of modern organization theory rests on research finds in social-psychology relative to reciprocal patterns of behavior stemming from role demands generated by both the formal and informal organizations, and role perceptions peculiar to the individual. Bakke's *fusion process* is largely concerned with the modification of role expectancies. The fusion process is a force, according to Bakke, which acts to weld divergent elements together for the preservation of organizational integrity.[38]

The fifth part of system analysis is the *physical setting* in which the job is performed. Although this element of the system may be implicit in what has been said already about the formal organization and its functions, it is well to separate it. In the physical surroundings of work, interactions are present in complex man-machine systems. The human "engineer" cannot approach the problems posed by such interrelationships in a purely technical, engineering fashion. As Haire says, these problems lie in the domain of the social theorist.[39] Attention must be centered on responses demanded from a logically ordered production function, often with the view of minimizing the error in the system. From this standpoint, work cannot be effectively organized unless the psychological, social, and physiological characteristics of people participating in the work environment are considered. Machines and processes should be designed to fit certain generally observed psychological and physiological properties of men, rather than hiring men to fit machines.

In summary, the parts of the system which appear to be of strategic importance are the individual, the formal structure, the informal organization, status and role patterns, and the physical environment of work. Again, these parts are woven into a configuration called the organizational system. The process which link the parts are taken up next.

The Linking Processes

One can say, with a good deal of glibness, that all the parts mentioned above are interrelated. Although this observation is quite correct, it does not mean too much in terms of system theory unless some attempt is made to analyze the processes by which the interaction is achieved. Role theory is devoted to certain types of interactional processes. In addition, modern organization theorists point to three other linking activities which appear to be universal to human systems of organized behavior. These processes are communication, balance, and decision making.

(1) Communication is mentioned often in neoclassical theory, but the emphasis is on description of forms of communication activity, *i.e.,* formal-informal, vertical-horizontal, line-staff. Communication, as a mechanism which links the segments of the system together, is overlooked by way of much considered analysis.

One aspect of modern organization theory is study of the communication network in the system. Communication is viewed as the method by which action is evoked from the parts of the system. Communication acts not only as stimuli resulting in action, but also as a control and coordination mechanism linking the decision centers in the system into a synchronized pattern. Deutsch points out that organizations are composed of parts which communicate with each other, receive messages from the outside world, and store information. Taken together, these communication functions of the parts comprise a configuration representing the total system.[40] More is to be said about communication later in the discussion of the cybernetic model.

(2) The concept of *balance* as a linking process involves a series of some rather complex ideas. Balance refers to an equilibrating mechanism whereby the various parts of the system are maintained in a harmoniously structured relationship to each other.

The necessity for the balance concept logically flows from the nature of systems themselves. It is impossible to conceive of an ordered relationship among the parts of a system without also introducing the idea of a stabilizing or an adapting mechanism.

Balance appears in two varieties—quasi-automatic and innovative. Both forms of balance act to insure system integrity in face of changing conditions, either internal or external to the system. The first form of balance, quasi-automatic, refers to what some think are "homeostatic" properties of systems. That is, systems seem to exhibit built-in propensities to maintain steady states.

If human organizations are open, self-maintaining systems, then control and regulatory processes are necessary. The issue hinges on the degree to which stabilizing processes in systems, when adapting to change, are automatic. March and Simon have an interesting answer to this problem, which in part is based on the type of change and the adjustment necessary to adapt to the change. Systems have programs of action which are put into effect when a change is perceived. If the change is relatively minor, and if the change comes within the purview of established programs of action, then it might be fairly confidently predicted that the adaptation made by the system will be quasi-automatic.[41]

The role of innovative, creative balancing efforts now needs to be examined. The need for innovation arises when adaptation to a change is outside the scope of existing programs designed for the purpose of keeping the system in balance. New programs have to be evolved in order for the system to maintain internal harmony.

New programs are created by trial and error search for feasible action alternatives to cope with a given change. But innovation is subject to the limitations and possibilities inherent in the quantity and variety of information present in a system at a particular time. New combinations of alternatives for innovative purposes depend on:

(a) the possible range of output of the system, or the capacity of the system to supply information.

(b) the range of available information in the memory of the system.

(c) the operating rules (program) governing the analysis and flow of information within the system.

(d) the ability of the system to "forget" previously learned solutions to change problems.[42] A system with too good a memory might narrow its behavioral choices to such an extent as to stifle innovation. In simpler language, old learned programs might be used to adapt to change, when newly innovated programs are necessary.[43]

Much of what has been said about communication and balance brings to mind a cybernetic model in which both these processes have vital roles. Cybernetics has to do with feedback and control in all kinds of systems. Its purpose is to maintain systems stability in the face of change. Cybernetics cannot be studied without considering communication networks, information flow, and some kind of balancing process aimed at preserving the integrity of the system.

Cybernetics directs attention to key questions regarding the system. These questions are: How are communication centers connected, and how are they maintained? Corollary to this question: what is the structure of the feedback system? Next, what information is stored in the organization, and at what points? And as a corollary: how accessible is this information to decision-making centers? Third, how conscious is the organization of the operation of its own parts? That is, to what extent do the policy centers receive control information with sufficient frequency and relevancy to create a real awareness of the operation of the segments of the system? Finally, what are the learning (innovating) capabilities of the system?[44]

Answers to the question posed by cybernetics are crucial to understanding both the balancing and communication processes in systems.[45] Although cybernetics has been applied largely to technical-engineering problems of automation, the model of feedback, control, and regulation in all systems has a good deal of generality. Cybernetics is a fruitful area which can be used to synthesize the processes of communication and balance.

(3) A wide spectrum of topics dealing with types of decisions in human systems makes up the core of analysis of another important process in organizations. Decision analysis is one of the major contributions of March and Simon in their book *Organizations*. The two major classes of decisions they discuss are decisions to produce and decisions to participate in the system.[46]

Decisions to produce are largely a result of an interaction between individual attitudes and the demands of organization. Motivation analysis becomes central to studying the nature and results of the interaction. Individual decisions to participate in the organization reflect on such issues as the relationship between organizational rewards versus the demands made by the organization. Participation decisions also focus attention on the reasons why individuals remain in or leave organizations.

March and Simon treat decisions as internal variables in an organization which depend on jobs, individual expectations and motivations, and organizational structure. Marschak[47] looks on the decision process as an independent variable upon which the survival of the organization is based. In this case, the organization is viewed as having, inherent to its structure, the ability to maximize survival requisites through its established decision processes.

The Goals of Organization

Organization has three goals which

may be either intermeshed or independent ends in themselves. They are growth, stability, and interaction. The last goal refers to organizations which exist primarily to provide a medium for association of its members with others. Interestingly enough these goals seem to apply to different forms of organization at varying levels of complexity, ranging from simple clockwork mechanisms to social systems.

These similarities in organizational purposes have been observed by a number of people, and a field of thought and research called general system theory has developed, dedicated to the task of discovering organizational universals. The dream of general system theory is to create a science of organizational universals, or if you will, a universal science using common organizational elements found in all systems as a starting point.

Modern organization theory is on the periphery of general system theory. Both general system theory and modern organization theory studies:

(1) the parts (individuals) in aggregates, and the movement of individuals into and out of the system.

(2) the interaction of individuals with the environment found in the system.

(3) the interactions among individuals in the system.

(4) general growth and stability problems of systems.[48]

Modern organization theory and general system theory are similar in that they look at organization as an integrated whole. They differ, however, in terms of their generality. General system theory is concerned with every level of system,

whereas modern organizational theory focuses primarily on human organization.

The question might be asked, what can the science of administration gain by the study of system levels other than human? Before attempting an answer, note should be made of what these other levels are. Boulding presents a convenient method of classification:

(1) The static structure—a level of framework, the anatomy of a system; for example, the structure of the universe.

(2) The simple dynamic system—the level of clockworks, predetermined necessary motions.

(3) The cybernetic system—the level of the thermostat, the system moves to maintain a given equilibrium through a process of self-regulation.

(4) The open system—level of self-maintaining systems, moves toward and includes living organisms.

(5) The genetic-societal system—level of cell society, characterized by a division of labor among cells.

(6) Animal systems—level of mobility, evidence of goal-directed behavior.

(7) Human systems—level of symbol interpretation and idea communication.

(8) Social system—level of human organization.

(9) Transcendental systems—level of ultimates and absolutes which exhibit systematic structure but are unknowable in essence.[49]

This approach to the study of systems by finding universals common at all levels of organization offers intriguing possibilities for administrative organization theory. A good deal of light could be thrown on social systems if structurally analogous elements could be found in the simpler types of systems. For example, cybernetic systems have characteristics which seem to be similar to feedback, regulation, and control phenomena in human organization. Considerable danger, however, lies in poorly founded analogies. Superficial similarities between simpler system forms and social systems are apparent everywhere. Instinctually based ant societies, for example, do not yield particularly instructive lessons for understanding rationally conceived human organizations. Thus, care should be taken that analogies used to bridge system levels are not mere devices for literary enrichment. For analogies to have usefulness and validity, they must exhibit inherent structural similarities or implicitly identical operational principles.[50]

Modern organization theory leads, as it has been shown, almost inevitably into a discussion of general system theory. A science of organizational universals has some strong advocates, particularly among biologists.[51] Organization theorists in administrative science cannot afford to overlook the contributions of general system theory. Indeed, modern organization concepts could offer a great deal to those working with general system theory. But the ideas dealt with in the general theory are exceedingly exclusive.

Speaking of the concept of equilibrium as a unifying element in all systems, Easton says, "It (equilibrium) leaves the impression that we have a useful general theory when in fact, lacking measurability, it is a mere pretense for knowledge."[52] The inability to qualify and measure universal organization elements undermines the success of pragmatic tests to which general system theory might be put.

Organization Theory: Quo Vadis?

Most sciences have a vision of the universe to which they are applied, and administrative science is not an exception. This universe is composed of parts. One purpose of science is to synthesize the parts into an organized conception of its field of study. As a science matures, its theorems about the configuration of its universe change. The direction of change in three sciences, physics, economics, and sociology, are noted briefly for comparison with the development of an administrative view of human organization.

The first comprehensive and empirically verifiable outlook of the physical universe was presented by Newton in his *Principia*. Classical physics, founded on Newton's work, constitutes a grand scheme in which a wide range of physical phenomena could be organized and predicted. Newtonian physics may rightfully be regarded as "macro" in nature, because its system of organization was concerned largely with gross events of which the movement of celestial bodies, waves, energy forms, and strain are examples. For years classical physics was supreme, being applied continuously to smaller and smaller classes of phenomena in the physical universe. Physicists at one time adopted the view that everything in their realm could be discovered by simply subdividing problems. Physics thus moved into the "micro" order.

But in the nineteenth century a revolution took place motivated largely because events were being noted which could not be explained adequately by the conceptual framework supplied by the classical school. The consequences of this revolution are brilliantly described by Eddington:

> From the point of view of philosophy of science the conception associated with entropy must I think be ranked as the great contribution of the nineteenth century to scientific thought. It marked a reaction from the view that everything to which science need pay attention is discovered by microscopic dissection of objects. It provided an alternative standpoint in which the centre of interest is shifted from the entities reached by the customary analysis (atoms, electric potentials, etc.) to qualities possessed by the system as a whole, which cannot be split up and located—a little bit here, and a little bit there. . . .
>
> We often think that when we have completed our study of *one* we know all about *two*, because "two" is "one and one." We forget that we have still to make a study of "and." Secondary physics is the study of "and"—that is to say, of organization.[53]

Although modern physics often deals in minute quantities and oscillations, the conception of the physicist is on the "macro" scale. He is concerned with the "and," or the organization of the world in which the events occur. These developments did not invalidate classical physics as to its usefulness for explaining a certain range of phenomena. But classical physics is no longer the undisputed law of the universe. It is a special case.

Early economic theory, and Adam Smith's *Wealth of Nations* comes to mind, examined economic problems in the macro order. The *Wealth of Nations* is mainly concerned with matters of national income and welfare. Later, the economics of the firm, microeconomics, dominated the theoretical scene in this science. And, finally, with Keynes' *The General Theory of Employment Interest and Money,* a systematic approach to the economic universe was re-introduced on the macro level.

The first era of the developing science of sociology was occupied by the great social "system build-ers." Comte, the so-called father of sociology, had a macro view of society in that his chief works are devoted to social reorganization. Comte was concerned with the in-terrelationships among social, polit-ical, religious, and educational insti-tutions. As sociology progressed, the science of society compressed. Emphasis shifted from the macro approach of the pioneers to de-tailed, empirical study of small so-cial units. The compression of soci-ological analysis was accompanied by study of social pathology or disorganization.

In general, physics, economics, and sociology appear to have two things in common. First, they of-fered a macro point of view as their initial systematic comprehension of their area of study. Second, as the science developed, attention frag-mented into analysis of the parts of the organization, rather than at-tending to the system as a whole. This is the micro phase.

In physics and economics, dis-content was evidenced by some scientists at the continual atomiza-tion of the universe. The reaction to the micro approach was a new theory or theories dealing with the total system, on the macro level again. This third phase of scientific development seems to be more ev-ident in physics and economics than in sociology.

The reason for the "macro-mi-cro-macro" order of scientific prog-ress lies, perhaps, in the hypothesis that usually the things which strike man first are of great magnitude. The scientist attempts to discover

order in the vastness. But after ma-cro laws or models of systems are postulated, variations appear which demand analysis, not so much in terms of the entire system, but more in terms of the specific parts which make it up. Then, intense study of microcosm may result in new general laws, replacing the old models of organization. Or, the old and the new models may stand to-gether, each explaining a different class of phenomenon. Or, the old and the new concepts of organiza-tion may be welded to produce a single creative synthesis.

Now, what does all this have to do with the problem of organiza-tion in administrative science? Or-ganization concepts seem to have gone through the same order of development in this field as in the three just mentioned. It is evident that the classical theory of organiza-tion, particularly as in the work of Mooney and Reiley, is concerned with principles common to all orga-nizations. It is a macro-organiza-tional view. The classical approach to organization, however, dealt with the gross anatomical parts and processes of the formal organiza-tion. Like classical physics, the clas-sical theory of organization is a spe-cial case. Neither are especially well equipped to account for variation from their established framework.

Many variations in the classical administrative model result from human behavior. The only way these variations could be under-stood was by a microscopic exami-nation of particularized, situational aspects of human behavior. The mission of the neoclassical school thus is "micro-analysis."

It was observed earlier, that somewhere along the line the con-cept of the social system, which is the key to understanding the Haw-thorne studies, faded into the back-ground. Maybe the idea is so obvi-

ous that it was lost to the view of researchers and writers in human relations. In any event, the press of research in the micro-cosmic universes of the informal organiza-tion, morale and productivity, lead-ership, participation, and the like forced the notion of the social sys-tem into limbo. Now, with the ad-vent of modern organization the-ory, the social system has been resurrected.

Modern organization theory ap-pears to be concerned with Edding-ton's "and." This school claims that its operational hypothesis is based on a macro point of view; that is, the study of organization as a whole. This nobility of purpose should not obscure, however, cer-tain difficulties faced by this field as it is presently constituted. Mod-ern organization theory raises two questions which should be ex-plored further. First, would it not be more accurate to speak of mod-ern organization theories? Second, just how much of modern organiza-tion theory is modern?

The first question can be an-swered with a quick affirmative. Aside from the notion of the sys-tem, there are few, if any, other ideas of a unifying nature. Except for several important exceptions,[54] modern organization theorists tend to pursue their pet points of view,[55] suggesting they are part of system theory, but not troubling to show by what mystical means they arrive at this conclusion.

The irony of it all is that a field dealing with systems has, indeed, little system. Modern organization theory needs a framework, and it needs an integration of issues into a common conception of organiza-tion. Admittedly, this is a large or-der. But it is curious not to find serious analytical treatment of sub-jects like cybernetics or general sys-tem theory in Haire's, *Modern Or-*

ganizational Theory which claims to be a representative example of work in this field. Beer has ample evidence in his book *Cybernetics and Management* that cybernetics, if imaginatively approached, provides a valuable conceptual base for the study of systems.

The second question suggests an ambiguous answer. Modern organization theory is in part a product of the past; system analysis is not a new idea. Further, modern organization theory relies for supporting data on microcosmic research studies, generally drawn from the journals of the last ten years. The newness of modern organization theory, perhaps, is its effort to synthesize recent research contributions of many fields into a system theory characterized by a reoriented conception of organization.

One might ask, but what is the modern theorist reorienting? A clue is found in the almost snobbish disdain assumed by some authors of the neo-classical human relations school, and particularly, the classical school. Re-evaluation of the classical school of organization is overdue. However, this does not mean that its contributions to organization theory are irrelevant and should be overlooked in the rush to get on the "behavioral science bandwagon."

Haire announces that the papers appearing in *Modern Organization Theory* constitute, "the ragged leading edge of a wave of theoretical development."[56] Ragged, yes; but leading no! The papers appearing in this book do not represent a theoretical breakthrough in the concept of organization. Haire's collection is an interesting potpourri with several contributions of considerable significance. But readers should beware that they will not find vastly

new insights into organizational behavior in this book, if they have kept up with the literature of the social sciences, and have dabbled to some extent in the esoteria of biological theories of growth, information theory, and mathematical model building. For those who have not maintained the pace, *Modern Organization Theory* serves the admirable purpose of bringing them up-to-date on a rather diversified number of subjects.

Some work in modern organization theory is pioneering, making its appraisal difficult and future uncertain. While the direction of this endeavor is unclear, one thing is patently true. Human behavior in organizations, and indeed, organization itself, cannot be adequately understood within the ground rules of classical and neoclassical doctrines. Appreciation of human organization requires a *creative* synthesis of massive amounts of empirical data, a high order of deductive reasoning, imaginative research studies, and a taste for individual and social values. Accomplishment of all these objectives, and the inclusion of them into a framework of the concept of the system, appears to be the goal of modern organization theory. The vitality of administrative science rests on the advances modern theorists make along this line.

 **LEARNING CHECKPOINT**

Could you have predicted in 1960 the emergence of contingency theory as the emerging point of view during the 1980's? Explain.

Modern organization theory, 1960 style, is an amorphous aggre-

gation of synthesizers and restaters, with a few extending leadership on the frontier. For the sake of these few, it is well to admonish that pouring old wine into new bottles may make the spirits cloudy. Unfortunately, modern organization theory has almost succeeded in achieving the status of a fad. Popularization and exploitation contributed to the disrepute into which human relations has fallen. It would be a great waste if modern organization theory yields to the same fate, particularly since both modern organization theory and human relations draw from the same promising source of inspiration—system analysis.

Modern organization theory needs tools of analysis and a conceptual framework uniquely its own, but it must also allow for the incorporation of relevant contributions of many fields. It may be that the framework will come from general system theory. New areas of research such as decision theory, information theory, and cybernetics also offer reasonable expectations of analytical and conceptual tools. Modern organization theory represents a frontier of research which has great significance for management. The potential is great, because it offers the opportunity for uniting what is valuable in classical theory with the social and natural sciences into a systematic and integrated conception of human organization. □

REFERENCES

1. Roderick Seidenburg, *Post Historic Man* (Boston: Beacon Press, 1951), p. 1.
2. Robert V. Presthus, "Toward a Theory of Organizational Behavior," *Administrative Science Quarterly,* June, 1958, p. 50.
3. Regulation and predictability of human behavior are matters of degree

varying with different organizations on something of a continuum. At one extreme are bureaucratic type organizations with tight bonds of regulation. At the other extreme, are voluntary associations, and informal organizations with relatively loose bonds of regulation.

This point has an interesting sidelight. A bureaucracy with tight controls and a high degree of predictability of human action appears to be unable to distinguish between destructive and creative deviations from established values. Thus the only thing which is safeguarded is the *status quo*.

4. The monolithic institutions of the military and government are other cases of organizational preoccupation.

5. James D. Mooney and Alan C. Reiley, *Onward Industry* (New York: Harper and Brothers, 1931). Later published by James D. Mooney under the title *Principles of Organization*.

6. E. F. L. Brech, *Organization* (London: Longmans, Green and Company, 1957).

7. Louis A. Allen, *Management and Organization* (New York: McGraw-Hill Book Company, 1958).

8. Usually the division of labor is treated under a topical heading of departmentation, see for example: Harold Koontz and Cyril O'Donnell, *Principles of Management* (New York: McGraw-Hill Book Company, 1959), Chapter 7.

9. These processes are discussed at length in Ralph Currier Davis, *The Fundamentals of Top Management* (New York: Harper and Brothers, 1951), Chapter 7.

10. For a discussion of structure see: William H. Newman, *Administrative Action* (Englewood Cliffs: Prentice-Hall, Incorporated, 1951), Chapter 16.

11. V. A. Graicunas, "Relationships in Organization," *Papers on the Science of Administration* (New York: Columbia University, 1937).

12. Brech, *op. cit.*, p. 78.

13. See: F. J. Roethlisberger and William J. Dickson, *Management and the Worker* (Cambridge: Harvard University Press, 1939).

14. Burleigh B. Gardner and David G. Moore, *Human Relations in Industry*

(Homewood: Richard D. Irwin, 1955).

15. Keith Davis, *Human Relations in Business* (New York: McGraw-Hill Book Company, 1957).

16. For example see: Delbert C. Miller and William H. Form, *Industrial Sociology* (New York: Harper and Brothers, 1951).

17. See: Hugo Munsterberg, *Psychology and Industrial Efficiency* (Boston: Houghton Mifflin Company, 1913).

18. Probably the classic work is Elton Mayo, *The Human Problems of an Industrial Civilization* (Cambridge: Harvard University, 1946, first printed 1933).

19. For further discussion of the human relations implications of the scalar and functional processes see: Keith Davis, *op. cit.*, pp. 60–66.

20. Melville Dalton, "Conflicts between Staff and Line Managerial Officers," *American Sociological Review,* June, 1950, pp. 342–351.

21. J. M. Juran, "Improving the Relationship between Staff and Line," *Personnel,* May, 1956, pp. 515–524.

22. *Gardner and Moore., op. cit,* pp. 237–243.

23. For example: Brech, *op. cit.,* pp. 27–29; and Allen, *op. cit.,* pp. 61–62.

24. See: Leon Festinger, Stanley Schachter, and Kurt Back, *Social Pressures in Informal Groups* (New York: Harper and Brothers, 1950), pp. 153–163.

25. For example see: W. Fred Cottrell, *The Railroader,* (Palo Alto: The Stanford University Press, 1940), Chapter 3.

26. Except in cases where the existence of an organization is necessary for the continued maintenance of employee interest. Under these conditions the previously informal association may emerge as a formal group, such as a union.

27. Probably the classic study of resistance to change is: Lester Coch and John R. P. French, Jr., "Overcoming Resistance to Change," in Schuvier Dean Hoslett (editor) *Human Factors in Management* (New York: Harper and Brothers, 1951) pp. 242–268.

28. For example see: Robert Saltonstall, *Human Relations in Administration* (New York: McGraw-Hill Book

Company, 1959), pp. 330–331; and Keith Davis, *op. cit,* pp. 99–101.

29. For an example of this approach see: John T. Doutt, "Management Must Manage the Informal Group, Too," *Advanced Management,* May, 1959, pp. 26–28.

30. See: Roethlisberger and Dickson, *op. cit.,* Chapter 24.

31. A check of management human relations texts, the organization and human relations chapters of principles of management texts, and texts on conventional organization theory for management courses reveals little or no treatment of the concept of the social system.

32. Lawrence J. Henderson, *Pareto's General Sociology* (Cambridge: Harvard University Press, 1935), p. 13.

33. There is another question which cannot be treated in the scope of this paper. It asks, what research tools should be used for the study of the system?

34. James G. March and Herbert A. Simon, *Organizations* (New York: John Wiley and Sons, 1958).

35. Mason Haire, (editor) *Modern Organization Theory* (New York: John Wiley and Sons, 1959).

36. See Chris Argyris, *Personality and Organization* (New York: Harper and Brothers, 1957), esp. Chapters 2, 3, 7.

37. For a larger treatment of this subject see: George C. Homans, *The Human Group* (New York: Harcourt, Brace and Company, 1950), Chapter 5.

38. E. Wight Bakke, "Concept of the Social Organization," in *Modern Organization Theory,* Mason Haire, (editor) (New York: John Wiley and Sons, 1959), pp. 60–61.

39. Mason Haire, "Psychology and the Study of Business: Joint Behavioral Sciences," in *Social Science Research on Business: Product and Potential* (New York: Columbia University Press, 1959), pp. 53–59.

40. Karl W. Deutsch "On Communication Models in the Social Sciences," *Public Opinion Quarterly,* 16 (1952), pp. 356–380.

41. March and Simon, *op. cit.,* pp. 139–140.

42. Mervyn L. Cadwallader, "The Cybernetic Analysis of Change in Complex Social Organization," *The American Journal of Sociology,* September, 1959, p. 156.

43. It is conceivable for innovative behavior to be programmed into the system.

44. These are questions adapted from Deutsch, *op. cit.,* 368–370.

45. Answers to these questions would require a comprehensive volume. One of the best approaches currently available is Stafford Beer, *Cybernetics and Management* (New York: John Wiley and Sons, 1959).

46. March and Simon, *op. cit.,* Chapters 3 and 4.

47. Jacob Marschak, "Efficient and Viable Organizational Forms" in *Modern Organization Theory,* Mason Haire, editor, (New York: John Wiley and Sons, 1959), pp. 307–320.

48. Kenneth E. Boulding, "General System Theory—The Skelton of a Science," *Management Science,* April, 1956, pp. 200–202.

49. *Ibid.,* pp. 202–205.

50. Seidenberg, *op. cit.,* p. 136. The fruitful use of the type of analogies spoken of by Seidenberg is evident in the application of thermodynamic principles, particularly the entropy concept, to communication theory. See: Claude E. Shannon and Warren Weaver, *The Mathematical Theory of Communication,* (Urbana: The University of Illinois Press, 1949). Further, the existence of a complete analogy between the operational behavior of the thermodynamic systems, electrical communications systems, and biological systems has been noted by: Y. S. Touloukian, *The Concept of Entropy in Communication, Living Organisms, and Thermodynamics,* Research Bulletin 130, Purdue Engineering Experiment Station.

51. For example see: Ludwig von Bertalanffy, *Problem of Life* (London: Watts and Company, 1952).

52. David Easton, "Limits of the Equilibrium Model in Social Research," in *Profits and Problems of Homeostatic Models in the Behavioral Sciences,* Publication 1, Chicago Behavioral Sciences, 1953, p. 39.

53. Sir Arthur Eddington, *The Nature of the Physical World* (Ann Arbor: The University of Michigan Press, 1958), pp. 103–104.

54. For example: E. Wight Bakke, *op. cit.,* pp. 18–75.

55. There is a large selection including decision theory, individual-organization interaction, motivation, vitality, stability, growth, and graph theory, to mention a few.

56. Mason Haire, "General Issues," in Mason Haire (editor), *Modern Organization Theory* (New York: John Wiley and Sons, 1959), p. 2.

R² SOCIAL NETWORK APPROACH TO ORGANIZATIONAL DESIGN-PERFORMANCE*

JOHN A. PEARCE AND
FRED R. DAVID

Organizational theories have long been concerned with the impact of organizational design on performance (Dalton, Todor, Spendolini, Fielding, & Porter, 1980; Lawrence & Lorsch, 1969; Pennings, 1975). Although it is now clear that variations in design do affect performance (Dalton et al., 1980; Ivancevich & Donnelly, 1975; Van de Ven, Delbecq, & Koenig, 1976),

* Source: From John A. Pearce and Fred R. David, "A Social Network Approach to Organization Design-Performance", *Academy of Management Review* (July 1983), pp. 436–44. Reprinted by permission.

there is a continued reason for interest. Specifically, the nature of the relationship between the two variables has yet to be defined.

The two traditional approaches to studying the design-performance relationship in organizations have been neo-Weberian research and contingency research. Neo-Weberian research has studied the relationship between individual performance and organizational size, complexity, formalization, and centralization. Contingency research has examined the relationship between individual performance and organizational environment and technology. Unfortunately, neither of these approaches has yielded substantive results or provided a framework for organizational design decision making. The neo-Weberian approach to organiza-

tional analysis appears to have faltered because it neither focused on explicating structure nor realized that evolving structures capture organizational learning and experience (Lodahl & Williams, 1978; Tichy & Fombrun, 1979). The shortcoming of the contingency approach seemingly resulted from an inability to resolve the problem of multiple contingencies when they are simultaneously present (Burack & Negandhi, 1977). Differences and inadequacies related to operational definitions and criterion measures also complicated the resolution of these problems.

The discouraging long term prognoses for the neo-Weberian and contingency approaches recently have directed researchers' attentions to an interesting alternative. Specifically, as suggested by

Tichy, Tushman, and Fombrun (1979), macro level organizational design characteristics do not directly influence group performance but, instead, their influence on performance is moderated by group level characteristics. As Tichy et al. suggest, organizational design may impact group performance principally because of its effects on communication (i.e., information) flow. Such effects may either augment or retard the information processing capability of the organization and ultimately impact the performance of individual groups (MacCrimmon, 1974; Mears, 1974; Pelz & Andrews, 1966). Thus, though organizational design may indeed influence group performance, its impact may be mediated by group structural properties that mask the underlying significance of the design-performance relationship.

In an effort to advance the study of this perspective, this paper presents a conceptualization of organizational design-performance based on group structural properties as key moderating variables in the design-performance relationship. That is, macro level characteristics are proposed to affect group structural properties, and these group defined characteristics, in turn, are

posited to have a direct impact on performance. This conceptualization of a double link relationship is depicted in Figure 1.

LEARNING CHECKPOINT

Explain the important differences between mechanistic and organic organizational designs.

SOCIAL NETWORK RESEARCH

An organization can be conceived of as a bounded social system in which there is a relatively stable network of interpersonal linkages through which messages flow and which affect the productivity and maintenance of the system (Schuler, 1975). From this perspective, one way to study organizational phenomena is to examine the formal and informal ties that connect groups and individuals within a firm. Social network analysis takes such an approach by addressing the causes, natures, and consequences of alternative interaction patterns over time. It principally involves the study of both information exchange and influence

relationships. It involves the comparison of prescribed group structures (such as work teams, departments, or divisions) and emergent group structures (such as informal cliques and friendships). Finally, it facilitates the characterization of groups in terms of the number and types of individual role players (stars, liaisons, and isolates) and the frequency, direction, and compatibility of intragroup communications.

The potential contribution of social network analysis thus is as a means to address important unanswered questions regarding the design-performance relationship in organizations because it explicitly focuses on interpersonal processes and is capable of linking macro and group level approaches to the study of organizations (Crozier, 1972; Fombrun, 1982; Tichy & Fombrun, 1979; Tichy et al., 1979). It does so by serving as the genesis for the study of group structural properties that define the communication flows in organizations. These properties are the structural characteristics of an emergent network that describe alternative interactions patterns among individuals in a group.

The group structural properties

FIGURE 1

A Conceptualization of the Design Performance Relationship

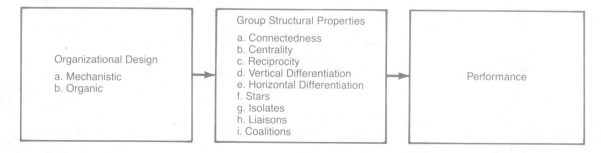

that have been studied most frequently in prior research can be categorized as descriptive of the group or descriptive of individuals within a group. Properties that are descriptive of the group include:

1. Connectedness—the extent to which group members identify with the goals of other members of their groups; it is a measure of group cohesiveness (O'Reilly & Roberts, 1977).
2. Centrality—the degree to which relations are guided by the formal hierarchy (Tichy et al., 1979).
3. Reciprocity—the degree to which there is two-way communication in a workgroup (Newcomb, 1979).
4. Vertical differentiation—the degree to which different organizational hierarchy levels are represented in a given work group network (O'Reilly & Roberts, 1979).
5. Horizontal differentiation—the degree to which different job areas are represented in a given work group network (Mohr, 1979).
6. Coalitions—perceived linkages among several individuals who believe that their ability to dominate organizational relationships is greater as a group than as individuals (Thibaut & Kelley, 1959). Coalitions also can be used as individual descriptors when the analysis focuses on a person's membership or nonmembership in specific emergent groups.

Group structural properties that are descriptive of individuals who serve specific communications functions for a group include:

7. Stars—individuals who are seen as having a great deal of influence on the jobs of most group members and who are the focus of most communication within the group (Tichy & Fombrun, 1979).
8. Isolates—individuals who are seen as involved in almost no communication within the group and as being encoupled from the network (Tichy et al., 1979).
9. Liaisons—individuals who serve as intermediaries among various emergent work groups within a department (Schwartz & Jacobson, 1977).

PRIOR NETWORK RESEARCH ON DESIGN-PERFORMANCE

A summary of the research that has used a social network approach to study either link of the herein conceptualized double link relationship among organizational design, group structural properties, and group performance is provided in Table 1 and Table 3, respectively.

The sociometric based research efforts summarized in Table 1 focus on the first link—between organizational design and group structural properties. For the purposes of this analysis, organizational design is defined on the mechanistic-organic continuum. In general, mechanistic designs are characterized by highly specific and delimiting job descriptors, highly formalized procedures, and centralization. Organic designs are defined as characterized by the direct opposites (Leifer & Huber, 1977).

As indicated in Table 1, mechanistic and organic organizations appear to be differentially associated with various structural properties. Specifically, prior research has found that organic structures tend to exhibit greater connectedness, greater reciprocity, and fewer isolates; mechanistic organizations are characterized by lower centrality, lower density, and a larger number of clusters (Payne & Pheysey, 1971; Tichy & Fombrun, 1979; Tichy et al., 1979; Tushman, 1979). Thus, the findings suggest that type of organizational design may directly affect the emergence of group structural variables. That is, given one mechanistic and one organic organization, different patterns of relationships are likely to prevail (Tichy et al., 1979). Network analysis offers the ability to identify these differences.

One caveat that is important to note at this juncture, however, is that focusing solely on organic and mechanistic organizational designs, without discussion of the inherent differences in their attributes, contributes to an empirically attractive parsimony but detracts from an understanding of the multidimensional nature of the design-type continuum. This viewpoint has been appreciated by most researchers with design-performance interest and has been particularly well addressed by Burns and Stalker (1961). As shown in Table 2, they identified 11 factors on which organizations can be assessed, with the bipolar opposites of each scaled factor labelled mechanistic and organic. Appropriately, then, one measure of the maturity of design-performance research is the incorporation of such factor comparisons.

The second link in developing a conceptualization of organizational design and performance concerns the relationship between group structural properties and group performance. As indicated in Table 3, stars, liaisons, reciprocity, and connectedness appear to be positively related to measures of performance (Katz & Tushman, 1979; Killworth & Bernard, 1974; O'Reilly & Roberts, 1977;

TABLE 1

Social Network Research That Has Investigated the Relationship Between Organizational Design and Group Structural Properties

Date	Sample	Author	Structural Properties Investigated	Principal Findings
1971	Three manufacturing firms	Roy L. Payne Diana C. Pheysey	Vertical interaction Vertical influence Horizontal interaction Horizontal influence	A taller hierarchy increases the possibility for vertical interaction and influence processes. The potential for horizontal interaction and influence is greater in organic than in mechanistic structures.
1977	Three naval aviation units	Charles O'Reilly Karlene Roberts	Vertical differentiation Connectedness Reciprocity Horizontal differentiation	Groups with greater vertical differentiation, connectedness, and reciprocity are characterized by greater information accuracy. Groups with greater horizontal differentiation and connectedness have more open communication.
1979	An R&D laboratory of a large U.S. corporation	Michael Tushman	Reciprocity Task interdependence[a] Task environment[a] Task characteristics[a]	Reciprocity is highest in (matrix design) departments of an organization.
1979	Two manufacturing firms	Noel Tichy Michael Tushman Charles Fombrun	Bridges Coalitions Reciprocity Centrality Clustering Density Openness Connectedness Multiplexity[a] Stars[a] Liaisons[a] Isolates[a] Gatekeepers[a] Reachability[a] Stability[a]	Mechanistic organizations exhibit a greater number of bridges and coalitions. Organic organizations exhibit greater reciprocity, centrality, density, openness, and connectedness.
1979	Three manufacturing firms	Noel Tichy Charles Fombrun	Centrality Fit Clustering Connectedness Bridges Coalitions and cliques Mean visibility[a] Deviation in visibility[a] Interrank membership[a] Openness[a] Stars[a] Liaisons[a] Isolates[a]	Centrality is greater in organic than in mechanistic organizations. This implies a close fit between the prescribed and emergent networks. Connectedness is greater in mechanistic than in organic organizations. Mechanistic organizations exhibit a greater number of bridges and coalitions.

[a] No conclusive statement can be made about the relationship between this variable and organizational design as a result of the research.

TABLE 2

Characterizations of Mechanistic and Organic Structures[a]

Mechanistic Structure	Factor	Organic Structure
A mechanistic management system is appropriate to stable conditions. It is characterized by:		The organic form is appropriate to changing conditions, which give rise constantly to fresh problems and unforeseen requirements for action which cannot be broken down or distributed automatically arising from the functional roles defined within a hierarchical structure. It is characterized by:
(a) the specialized differentiation of functional task into which the problems and tasks facing the concern as a whole are broken down;	differentiation and integration	(a) the contributive nature of special knowledge and experience to the common task of the concern;
(b) the abstract nature of each individual task, which is pursued with techniques and purposes more or less distinct from those of the concern as a whole;	work focus	(b) the "realistic" nature of the individual task, which is seen as set by the total situation of the concern;
(c) the reconciliation, for each level in the hierarchy, of these distinct performances by the immediate superiors, who are also, in turn, responsible for seeing that each is relevant in his own special part of the main task;	task definition	(c) the adjustment and continual redefinition of individual tasks through interaction with others;
(d) the precise definition of rights and obligations and technical methods attached to each functional role;	role definition	(d) the shedding of "responsibility" as a limited field of rights, obligations and methods;
(e) the translation of rights and obligations and methods into the responsibilities of a functional position;	responsibility	(e) the spread of commitment to the concern beyond any technical definition;
(f) hierarchic structure of control, authority and communication;	structure	(f) a network structure of control, authority, and communication;
(g) a reinforcement of the hierarchic structure by the location of knowledge of actualities exclusively at the top of the hierarchy;	locus of authority	(g) omniscience no longer imputed to the head of the concern; knowledge about the technical or commercial nature of the here and now task may be located anywhere in the network; this location becoming the ad hoc centre of control authority and communication;
(h) the tendency for interaction between members of the concern to be vertical;	communication flow	(h) a lateral rather than a vertical direction of communication, communication between people of different rank;
(i) a tendency for operations and working behavior to be governed by the instructions and decisions issued by superiors;	communication context	(i) a content of communication which consists of information and advice rather than instructions and decisions;
(j) insistence on loyalty to the concern and obedience to superiors as a condition of membership;	loyalty	(j) commitment to the concern's task and to the "technological ethos" of material progress and expansion is more highly valued than loyalty and obedience;
(k) a greater importance and prestige attaching to internal (local) than to general (cosmopolitan) knowledge, experience, and skill.	prestige	(k) importance and prestige attach to affiliations and expertise valid in the industrial and technical and commercial milieux external to the firm.

[a] Source: Burns & Stalker, 1961, pp. 119–125.

Schwartz & Jacobson, 1977; Tushman, 1977). Although these results from social network research are extremely encouraging, the findings to date are far from conclusive. Studies have varied in the properties that they have investigated, and those studies using comparable variables have produced somewhat mixed results. For example, O'Reilly and Roberts (1977) reported that reciprocity in groups is positively related to group productivity, but Newcomb (1979) reported that the two are unrelated.

Tushman (1977) reported that stars and liaisons exert more influence on group behavior than others. But Tichy and Fombrun (1979) could not report that these role occupants significantly affected group performance or behavior. Thus, it would seem that although group structural properties may be related to group performance, there have been too few studies (six) to be certain. In addition, the issue of performance has been insufficiently addressed, as seen both by the small number of studies and by the diversity of

the research settings. So, once again, the absence of collaborative studies tempers what otherwise might be an enthusiastic response to the empirically based findings that have linked group structure to performance.

 **LEARNING CHECKPOINT**

Why should a manager be interested in the relationship between organizational design and group characteristics?

TABLE 3

Social Network Research That Has Investigated the Relationship Between Group Structural Properties and Performance

Date	Sample	Author	Structural Properties Investigated	Principal Findings
1974	Inmates of a female prison	Peter Killworth Russell Bernard	Stars Liaisons Cliques[a] Isolates[a]	Of the group variables investigated, stars and liaisons have the most influence on organization members.
1977	Three naval aviation units	Charles O'Reilly Karlene Roberts	Reciprocity Vertical differentiation[a] Horizontal differentiation[a] Connectedness[a]	The correlation between reciprocity and group effectiveness is positive and significant.
1977	University faculty and administrators	Donald Schwartz Eugene Jacobson	Liaisons Isolates[a] Reciprocity[a]	Liaisons tend to exhibit higher job performance than do nonliaisons.
1977	An R&D laboratory of a large U.S. corporation	Michael Tushman	Stars Liaisons Gatekeepers[a]	Stars and liaisons tend to exhibit higher job performance than do nonstars and nonliaisons when level of communication and influence are used as indirect measures of job performance.
1979	A group of 17 individuals	Theodore Newcomb	Reciprocity	Reciprocity is not significantly related to group performance.
1979	An industrial R&D laboratory	Ralph Katz Michael Tushman	Connectedness Role Specialization[a] Reciprocity[a]	A significant positive relationship exists between connectedness and group performance for technical service projects.

[a] No conclusive statement can be made about the relationship between this variable and performance as a result of the research.

FIGURE 2

Details of the Design-Performance Model

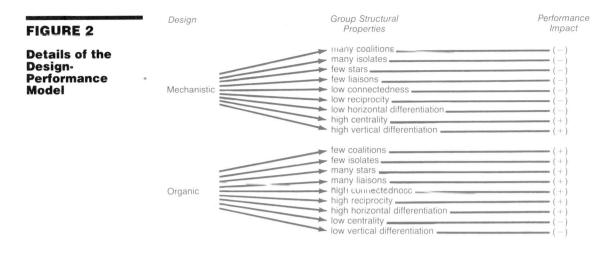

The small number and methodological limitations of prior studies notwithstanding, published research provides considerable convergent support for the "design→group structure→performance" model. In fact, 10 of the 11 social network-based studies reviewed in Tables 1 and 3 found at least one significant relationship between group structural properties and either organizational design or group performance. Additionally, there were no instances of opposing findings (i.e., positive/negative) in any pair of the research results. Finally, some significant findings may have been concealed by the sometimes confusing array of terms that are used in social network research to describe similar concepts.

HYPOTHESES FOR INVESTIGATION

The details of the design-performance conceptualization can now be more fully explicated. Figure 2 proposes the net impact on group performance of each of the nine group structural properties, given either a mechanistic or an organic design. As suggested by the figure,

mechanistic designs are hypothesized to affect employee performance positively because of the designs' favorable impact in developing centrality and vertical differentiation within emergent groups. Organic designs are hypothesized to affect employee performance positively because of their favorable impact both in minimizing coalition and isolate formation and in augmenting the development of stars, liaisons, connectedness, reciprocity, and horizontal differentiation.

The overview model shown as Figure 2 is in fact a composite of 18 hypotheses developed from the literature review and associated conceptualizations, which it is hoped will advance empirical exploration of the evolving design-performance theory.

The first set of these hypotheses, as summarized in section 1 of Table 4, focuses on the relationship between organizational design and group structural variables—the first link in the design-performance conceptualization. These hypotheses, which contrast organic and mechanistic designs, and accompanying abbreviated rationales are as follows:

H1: *Coalitions will be more prevalent in mechanistic than in organic designs.* Rationale: In mechanistic settings, coalitions are more likely to develop to provide individuals with a basic support and affiliation group (Tichy & Fombrun, 1979).

H2: *Stars will be more prevalent in organic than in mechanistic designs.* Rationale: The more organic the organization, the fewer the interaction isolates, the greater the number of bridge roles, and the higher the level of interaction among network members, all of which contribute to star formation (Tichy & Fombrun, 1979; Tushman, 1977).

H3: *Isolates will be more prevalent in mechanistic designs.* Rationale: Organic structures exhibit fewer interaction isolates (Schwartz & Jacobson, 1977; Tichy & Fombrun, 1979; Tichy et al., 1979).

H4: *Liaisons will be more prevalent in organic designs.* Rationale: The more organic the organization, the higher the level of interaction among the network members and the higher the degree of participation in influence exchanges (Schwartz & Jacobson, 1977; Tichy & Fombrun, 1979; Tushman, 1977).

TABLE 4

**Hypotheses
for Future Research**

I. Hypotheses concerning the relationship between organizational design and group structural properties

		Mechanistic Design	Organic Design
1.	Prevalence of coalitions	Many	Few
2.	Prevalence of stars	Few	Many
3.	Prevalence of isolates	Many	Few
4.	Prevalence of liaisons	Few	Many
5.	Group connectedness	Low	High
6.	Group reciprocity	Low	High
7.	Group centrality	High	Low
8.	Group vertical differentiation	High	Low
9.	Group horizontal differentiation	Low	High

II. Hypotheses concerning the relationship between group structural properties and performance

		Effect on Performance
10.	Coalition membership	−
11.	Star role	+
12.	Isolate role	−
13.	Liaison role	+
14.	High group connectedness	+
15.	High group reciprocity	+
16.	High group centrality	+
17.	High group vertical differentiation	+
18.	High group horizontal differentiation	+

H5: *Group connectedness will be characteristic of organic designs.* Rationale: Highly interactive clusters typically are encountered in organic structures (Tichy & Fombrun, 1979; Tichy et al., 1979).

H6: *Reciprocity will be more characteristic of organic designs.* Rationale: Organic designs exhibit relatively more numerous reciprocated influence nominations (Tichy & Fombrun, 1979; Tichy et al., 1979).

H7: *Centrality will be more characteristic of mechanistic designs.* Rationale: Prescribed networks of influence have been found to differ less substantially from emergent networks in mechanistic structures (Tichy & Fombrun, 1979; Tichy et al., 1979).

H8: *Horizontal differentiation will be more characteristic of organic designs.* Rationale: Organic structures often exhibit the flatter hierarchies known for lateral interaction and influence (Payne & Pheysey, 1971).

H9: *Vertical differentiation will be more characteristic of mechanistic designs.* Rationale: Prescribed multilevel groups, which more frequently appear in mechanistic structures, are more likely to be reflected in emergent networks (Tichy & Fombrun, 1979).

The hypotheses summarized in section II of Table 4 refer to the second link in the design-performance conceptualization—the re-

lationship between group structural properties and employee performance. These nine hypotheses, and a condensed rationale for each, are as follows:

H10: *Coalition membership will be negatively associated with employee performance.* Rationale: Coalitions form to increase control over task and social units that rarely include high performers (Tichy & Fombrun, 1979).

H11: *Stars will exhibit higher performance than nonstars.* Rationale: Stars have significantly more communication than do nonstars with professional, technical, and operational areas inside and outside the organization, which provides a communications/productivity advantage (Tushman, 1977).

H12: *Isolates will exhibit lower performance than nonisolates.* Rationale: Isolates have significantly less communication than do nonisolates with professional, technical, and operational areas inside and outside the organization, which serves as a communication/productivity disadvantage (Schwartz & Jacobson, 1977; Tichy et al., 1979; Tushman, 1977).

H13: *Liaisons will exhibit higher performance than nonliaisons.* Rationale: Liaisons exhibit higher levels of competence and trustworthiness than do nonliaison members of the organization, which partially defines productivity (Schwartz & Jacobson, 1977).

H14: *Groups characterized by high connectedness will exhibit high performance.* Rationale: Cohesiveness typically is associated with accurate communication, high satisfaction, and low absenteeism and turnover (Terborg, Castore, & DeNinno, 1976).

H15: *Groups demonstrating high levels of reciprocity will exhibit high performance.* Rationale: Reciprocity has been positively and significantly related to group effectiveness (Negandhi & Reimann, 1973).

H16: *Groups that display a high degree of centrality will exhibit high performance.* Rationale: Centrality reflects consistency between emergent groups and the perceived optimal design of the prescribed networks (Tichy & Fombrun, 1979).

H17: *Groups that display high degrees of horizontal differentiation will exhibit high performance.* Rationale: Horizontally integrated groups are characterized by communication openness, which has been shown to be positively related to group effectiveness (O'Reilly & Roberts, 1977).

H18: *Groups that display high degrees of vertical differentiation will exhibit high performance.* Rationale: Vertically integrated groups are characterized by information accuracy, which has been shown to be positively related to group effectiveness (O'Reilly & Roberts, 1977).

As an example of how the hypotheses can be paired to produce the rationale for a double link design-performance relationship, consider the case of a mechanistic design, its effect on the development of vertical differentiation, and the resultant performance impact. As for the first link, mechanistic structures, which are characterized by differentiation and superiors' responsibility for reconciliation between levels in a reinforced hierarchical structure (see Table 2, items a, c, and g), are likely to facilitate communication flows between organizational levels, thereby encouraging vertical differentiation (H9). In some respects, such firms mandate vertical linkages through prescribed multilevel groups as a means of legitimizing their hierarchical designs. As for the second link, because vertical differentiation has been shown to be positively related to group effectiveness as a consequence of high accuracy in communications, groups that are characterized by a high degree of vertical differentiation are likely to exhibit high performance (H18). It could be concluded that performance of organizations with a mechanistic design should be enhanced as a consequence of a high degree of vertical differentiation within their units and work groups.

DISCUSSION

The results of the present work support the premise and appropriateness of subsequent empirical research. First, the conceptualization developed herein provides an extensive rationale for the study of group structural properties as a potential link between organizational design variables and group performance. As disclosed by the literature reviewed, the inability to make this link with a construct that incorporates both group level and macro level components historically has been a vexing problem for organizational researchers.

 **LEARNING CHECKPOINT**

What variables other than group properties intervene between structure and performance?

Second, the results of previous research provide support for the use of social network analysis in the study of organizational relationships. Although it has long been recognized that informal groups emerge in organizations, the social network approach allows those groups to be identified and defined by a number of specific characteristics. It therefore can be proposed that future research more extensively utilize network analysis to study organizational design-performance relationships.

In summary, this review suggests that organizational design influences group performance through its impact on group structural variables. Empirical verification of this conceptualization could progress through three phases. Phase 1 would involve controlled experimentation to investigate the internal validity of the hypotheses summarized in Table 4. This initial phase is especially critical because prior research that has examined the relationship between group structural variables and both organizational design and employee performance is limited and inconclusive. Complicating the execution of phase 1 are the few contingency factors that prior research has taken into consideration. Does the size of a prescribed group influence the numbers and sizes of associated emergent groups? Is the "design→group structure→performance" model equally applicable at alternative levels or in distinctive divisions of an organization? Is the model equally valid for heterogeneous as well as homogeneous groups of employees? Is the model accommodating of various production technologies, reward systems, and leadership styles? Or, on another empirical front, is the model complete? For example, do group structural properties impact performance independently, or are there interactive effects between and among properties that result in differential effects on worker efficiency and effectiveness?

Phase 2 would focus on cross-sectional and longitudinal field surveys in order to establish the external validity and stability of the phase 1 findings. Several computer algorithms currently are available to assist in this phase. The algorithms facilitate the process of organizing and analyzing social network data at various organizationally defined levels. These empirical models are grounded in the manipulation of proximity measures, in which proximity is an index that reflects the social distance between individuals. BLOCKER (Breiger, Boorman, & Arabie, 1975), COMPLT (Alba & Gutmann, 1974a), and SOCK (Alba & Gutmann, 1974b) use product moment correlations between column vectors of nominations received by pairs of individuals as their index of social proximity. CATIJ (Killworth & Bernard, 1974) and CONCOR (Breiger, Boorman, and Arabie, 1975) employ canonical correlations and factor analysis, re-

spectively. The output of these program packages is sets of graphs or sociograms that display the network of relationships among the studied individuals and groups, thereby providing the structural definitions needed for hypothesis testing.

Phase 3 would involve field experimentation to determine the practical and theoretical implications of managing group structural variables. In this final phase, organizations would develop and test methods to encourage and discourage, as appropriate, specific group structural properties as a means to enhance the strength of the organizational design-performance relationship.

Success with this research stream could serve to revitalize neo-Weberian and contingency research. There already is evidence to suggest that these two approaches have been stifled by the failure to consider group structural variables in their design-performance equations. Thus, if the "design→group structure→performance" model is empirically validated, a wide spectrum of past research will deserve reconsideration, and innovative empirical opportunities could expand manyfold. □

REFERENCES

Alba, R., & Gutmann, M. P. *COMPLT.* Unpublished manuscript, Columbia University Bureau of Applied Social Research, 1974a.

Alba, R., & Gutman, M. P. *SOCK: A sociometric analysis system.* Bureau of Applied Social Research, Columbia University, 1974.

Breiger, R., Boorman, S., & Arabie, P. An algorithm for clustering relational data with applications to social network analysis and comparison with multidimensional scaling. *Journal of Mathematical Psychology,* 1975, 12, 328–383.

Burack, E. H., & Negandhi, A. R. *Organization design: Theoretical perspectives and empirical findings.* Kent, Ohio: The Kent State University Press, 1977.

Burns, T., & Stalker, G. M. *The management of innovation.* London: Tavistock, 1961.

Crozier, M. Relationships between micro and macro sociology. *Human Relations,* 1972, 25, 239–251.

Dalton, D. R., Todor, W. D., Spendolini, M. F., Fielding, G. J., & Porter, L. W. Organization structure and performance: A critical review. *Academy of Management Review,* 1980, 5, 49–64.

Fombrun, G. J. Strategies for network research in organizations. *Academy of Management Review,* 1982, 7, 280–291.

Ivancevich, F. M., & Donnelly, F. H. Relation of organizational structure to job satisfaction, anxiety-stress, and performance. *Administrative Science Quarterly,* 1975, 20, 272–280.

Katz, R., & Tushman, M. Communication patterns, project performance, and task characteristics: An empirical evaluation and integration in an R & D setting. *Organizational Behavior and Human Performance,* 1979, 23, 139–162.

Killworth, P., & Bernard, H. R. CATIJ: A new sociometric and its application to a prison living unit. *Human Organization,* 1974, 33, 335–350.

Lawrence, P., & Lorsch, J. *Organization and environment.* Homewood, Ill.: Irwin, 1969.

Leifer, R., & Huber, G. P. Relations among perceived environmental uncertainty, organization structure, and boundary spanning. *Administrative Science Quarterly,* 1977, 22, 235–247.

Lodahl, T., & Williams, L. *Office automation.* Unpublished manuscript, Cornell University, 1978.

MacCrimmon, K. Descriptive aspects of team theory: Observation, communication and decision heuristics in information systems. *Management Science,* 1974, 20, 1323–1334.

Mears, P. Structuring communication in a working group. *Journal of Communication,* 1974, 24, 71–79.

Mohr, L. B. Organizational technology and organizational structure. *Administrative Science Quarterly,* 1979, 16, 444–459.

Negandhi, A. R., & Reimann, B. C. Task environment, decentralization, and organization effectiveness. *Human Relations,* 1973, 26, 203–214.

Newcomb, T. M. Reciprocity of interpersonal attraction: A nonconfirmation of a plausible hypothesis. *Social Psychology Quarterly,* 1979, 42, 299–306.

O'Reilly, C., & Roberts, K. Task group structure, communication and effectiveness in three organizations. *Journal of Applied Psychology,* 1977, 62, 674–681.

Payne, R., & Pheysey, D. Organization structure and sociometric nominations among line managers in three contrasted organizations. *European Journal of Social Psychology,* 1971, 1, 261–284.

Pelz, D., & Andrews, F. *Scientists in organizations.* New York: Wiley, 1966.

Pennings, J. The relevance of the structural-contingency model for organizational effectiveness. *Administrative Science Quarterly,* 1975, 20, 393–410.

Schuler, R. S. Role perceptions, satisfaction, and performance: A partial reconciliation. *Journal of Applied Psychology,* 1975, 60, 683–687.

Schwartz, D., & Jacobson, E. Organizational communication network analysis: The liaison communication role. *Organizational Behavior and Human Performance,* 1977, 18, 158–174.

Terborg, J. R., Castore, C., & DeNinno, J. A. A longitudinal field investigation of the impact of group composition on group performance and cohesion. *Journal of Personality and Social Psychology,* 1976, 34, 782–790.

Thibaut, J., & Kelley, H. *The social psychology of groups.* New York: Wiley, 1959.

Tichy, N. M., & Fombrun, C. Network analysis in organizational settings. *Human Relations,* 1979, 32, 923–965.

Tichy, N. M., Tushman, M., & Fombrun, C. Social network analysis in organizational settings. *Academy of Management Review,* 1979, 4, 507–519.

Tushman, M. L. Special boundary roles of the innovation process. *Administrative Science Quarterly,* 1977, 22, 587–605.

Tushman, M. L. Work characteristics and subunit communication structure: A contingency analysis. *Administrative Science Quarterly,* 1979, 24, 82–97.

Van de Ven, A., Delbecq, A., & Koenig, R. Determinants of coordination modes within organizations. *American Sociological Review,* 1976, 41, 322–338.

D1 ASSESSING ORGANIZATIONAL DIMENSIONS—MECHANISTIC/ORGANIC

The following assessment allows you to identify the extent to which an organization has organic-mechanistic characteristics. Think of an organization that you work or have worked for and describe it using the following 10 items. You can then use the scoring key to locate the organization on the organic-mechanistic continuum.

Instructions: Describe the extent to which each of the following 10 statements is true of or accurately characterizes the organization in question.

	To a very great extent	To a considerable extent	To a moderate extent	To a slight extent	To almost no extent
1. This organization has clear rules and regulations that everyone is expected to follow closely.	☐	☐	☐	☐	☐
2. Policies in this organization are reviewed by the people they affect before being implemented.	☐	☐	☐	☐	☐

Source: Marshall Sashkin and William C. Morris, *Organizational Behavior* (Reston, VA: Reston Publishing Co., 1984), pp. 360–361.

3. In this organization a major concern is that everyone be allowed to develop their talents and abilities.

☐ ☐ ☐ ☐ ☐

4. Everyone in this organization knows who their immediate supervisor is; reporting relationships are clearly defined.

☐ ☐ ☐ ☐ ☐

5. Jobs in this organization are clearly defined; everyone knows exactly what is expected of a person in any specific job position.

☐ ☐ ☐ ☐ ☐

6. Work groups are typically temporary and change often in this organization.

☐ ☐ ☐ ☐ ☐

7. All decisions in this organization must be reviewed and approved by upper level management.

☐ ☐ ☐ ☐ ☐

8. In this organization the emphasis is on adapting effectively to constant environmental change.

☐ ☐ ☐ ☐ ☐

9. Jobs in this organization are usually broken down into highly specialized, smaller tasks.

☐ ☐ ☐ ☐ ☐

10. Standard activities in this organization are always covered by clearly outlined procedures that define the sequence of actions that everyone is expected to follow.

☐ ☐ ☐ ☐ ☐

Scoring

On the scoring grid, circle the numbers that correspond to your response to each of the 10 questions. Enter the numbers in the boxes, then add up all the numbers in boxes. This is your ORG MECH Score.

	Q1	Q2	Q3	Q4	Q5	Q6	Q7	Q8	Q9	Q10
Great	5	5	1	5	5	1	5	1	5	5
Considerable	4	4	2	4	4	2	4	2	4	4
Moderate	3	3	3	3	3	3	3	3	3	3
Slight	2	2	4	2	2	4	2	4	2	2
No	1	1	5	1	1	5	1	5	1	1
	☐	☐	☐	☐	☐	☐	☐	☐	☐	☐

Total Score: ☐

Interpretation

High scores indicate high degrees of mechanistic/bureaucratic organizational characteristics. Low scores are associated with adaptive/organic organizational characteristics.

10	20	30	40	50
Highly Organic		Mixed		Highly Mechanistic

D₂ ASSESSING ORGANIZATIONAL FORMALITY

The formality of an organization is a key determinant of the job behavior of its employees and clients acting in relation to the organization. The following 15 items enable you to rate the degree of formalism that exists in organizations that you have worked for or otherwise been a member of. Answer each question by checking the appropriate column. The scoring key is as follows:

Definitely true   1
More true than false   2

More false than true   3
Definitely false   4

Calculate the total score by converting your responses to the equivalent values (the range will be from 15 to 60), the higher the score the more formal is the organization.

	Definitely true	More true than false	More false than true	Definitely false
1. First, I feel that I am my own boss in most matters.	——	——	——	——
2. A person can make his own decisions here without checking with anybody else.	——	——	——	——
3. How things are done around here is left pretty much up to the person doing the work.	——	——	——	——
4. People here are allowed to do almost as they please.	——	——	——	——
5. Most people here make their own rules on the job.	——	——	——	——
6. The employees are constantly being checked on for rule violations.	——	——	——	——
7. People here feel as though they are constantly being watched to see that they obey all the rules.	——	——	——	——
8. There is no rules manual.	——	——	——	——
9. There is a complete written job description for my job.	——	——	——	——
10. Whatever situation arises, we have procedures to follow in dealing with it.	——	——	——	——
11. Everyone has a specific job to do.	——	——	——	——
12. Going through the proper channels is constantly stressed.	——	——	——	——
13. The organization keeps a written record of everyone's job performance.	——	——	——	——
14. We are to follow strict operating procedures at all times.	——	——	——	——
15. Whenever we have a problem, we are supposed to go to the same person for an answer.	——	——	——	——

Source: Jerald Hage and Michael Aiken, "Routine Technology, Social Structure, and Organizational Goals," ADMINISTRATIVE SCIENCE QUARTERLY, (September 1969), pp. 366–76.

DESIGNING THE NEW ORGANIZATION

OBJECTIVES

1. To become aware of the difficulty of finding a best design.
2. To illustrate the role that environmental forces play in design decisions.

STARTING THE EXERCISE

I. A few years ago, George Ballas got so frustrated trying to keep his lawn neatly trimmed around the roots of oak trees that he developed what is now called the Weed Eater. The original Weed Eater was made from a popcorn can which had holes in it and was threaded with nylon fishing line. Weed Eater sales in 1972 totaled $568,000, but by 1978, sales were in excess of $100 million. There are now 20 or so similar devices on the market.

Two brothers from Pittsburgh, George and Jim Gammons, are starting a new venture called Lawn Trimmers, Inc. They are attempting to develop an organization that makes a profit by selling Lawn Trimmers which do not wear out for over 2,000 trimming applications. The Weed Eaters and similar products often have breaks in the nylon lines which require the user to turn off the trimmer and readjust the line. The Gammons have developed a new type of cutting fabric that is not physically harmful and cuts for over 2,000 applications.

In order to sell the Lawn Trimmers, the Gammons brothers will have to market their products through retail establishments. They will make the products in their shop in Pittsburgh and ship them to the retail establishments. The profits will come entirely from the sales of the Lawn Trimmers to retail establishments. The price of the product is already set, and it appears that there will be sufficient market demand to sell at least 6,000 Lawn Trimmers annually.

II. The instructor will set up teams of five to eight students to serve as organizational design experts who will provide the Gammons brothers with the best structure for their new venture. The groups should meet and establish a design that would be feasible for the Gammons at this stage in their venture.
III. Each group should select a spokesperson to make a short presentation of the group's organizational design for the Gammons.
IV. The class should compare the various designs and discuss why there are similarities and differences in what is presented.

A learning note: This exercise will show that organizational design necessitates making assumptions about the market, competition, labor resources, scheduling, and profit margins, to name just a few areas. There is no one best design that should be regarded as a final answer.

PAPER PLANE CORPORATION

OBJECTIVES

1. To illustrate how division of labor can be efficiently structured.
2. To illustrate how a competitive atmosphere can be created among groups.

STARTING THE EXERCISE

Unlimited groups of six participants each are used in this exercise. These groups may be directed simultaneously in the same room. Approximately a full class period is needed to complete the exercise. Each person should have assembly instructions and a summary sheet, which are shown on the following pages, and ample stacks of paper (8-½ by 11 inches). The physical setting should be a room large enough so that the individual groups of six can work without interference from the other groups. A working space should be provided for each group.

Source: Louis Potheni in Fred Luthans, *Organizational Behavior* (New York: McGraw-Hill, 1985), p. 655.

- The participants are doing an exercise in production methodology.
- Each group must work independently of the other groups.
- Each group will choose a manager and an inspector, and the remaining participants will be employees.

- The objective is to make paper airplanes in the most profitable manner possible.
- The facilitator will give the signal to start. This is a 10-minute, timed event utilizing competition among the groups.
- After the first round, everyone should report their production and profits to the entire group. They also should note the effect, if any, of the manager in terms of the performance of the group.
- This same procedure is followed for as many rounds as there is time.

PAPER PLANE CORPORATION: DATA SHEET

Your group is the complete work force for Paper Plane Corporation. Established in 1943, Paper Plane has led the market in paper plane production. Presently under new management, the company is contracting to make aircraft for the U.S. Air Force. You must establish an efficient production plant to produce these aircraft. You must make your contract with the Air Force under the following conditions:

1. The Air Force will pay $20,000 per airplane.
2. The aircraft must pass a strict inspection made by the facilitator.
3. A penalty of $25,000 per airplane will be subtracted for failure to meet the production requirements.
4. Labor and other overhead will be computed at $300,000.
5. Cost of materials will be $3,000 per bid plane. If you bid for 10 but only make 8, you must pay the cost of materials for those you failed to make or which did not pass inspection.

Summary sheet

Round 1:
Bid: _____ Aircraft @ $20,000.00 per aircraft = _____

Results: _____ Aircraft @ $20,000.00 per aircraft = _____

Less: $300,000.00 overhead _____ × $3,000 cost of raw materials

_____ × $25,000 penalty

Profit: _____

Round 2:
Bid: _____ Aircraft @ $20,000.00 per aircraft = _____

Results: _____ Aircraft @ $20,000.00 per aircraft = _____

Less: $300,000.00 overhead _____ × $3,000 cost of raw materials

_____ × $25,000 penalty

Profit: _____

Round 3:
Bid: _____ Aircraft @ $20,000.00 per aircraft = _____

Results: _____ Aircraft @ $20,000.00 per aircraft = _____

Less: $300,000.00 overhead _____ × $30,000 cost of raw materials

_____ × $25,000 penalty

Profit: _____

Instructions for aircraft assembly

Step 1: Take a sheet of paper and fold it in half, then open it back up.

Step 2: Fold upper corners to the middle.

Step 3: Fold the corners to the middle again.

Step 4: Fold in half.

Step 5: Fold both wings down.

Step 6: Fold tail fins up.

 Completed aircraft

1 EAGLE AIRLINES*

Eagle Airlines was a medium-sized regional airline serving the southwest quarter of the United States. The company had been growing rapidly in the last 15 years, partially as a result of dynamic company activity but also as a result of the rapid economic growth of the area which it served.

The most outstanding of the areas was Bartlett City. Bartlett City's growth since the middle 1940s had rested on two primary developments. One was the very rapid growth of manufacturing and research establishments concerned with defense work. Some firms located here at the urging of government agencies to build new defense plants and laboratories away from coastal areas. Others moved to this location because of the attractive climate and scenery, which was considered an advantage in attracting technicians, engineers, and scientists for work on advanced military projects. Once some plants and research laboratories were developed, smaller, independent firms sprang up in the community for the purpose of servicing and supplying those which were established first. These developments encouraged the rapid growth of local construction and the opening of numerous attractive housing developments. The second basis for growth was the completion, also in the 1940s, of a major irrigation project that opened a large area for intensive cultivation.

While the economy of Bartlett City had grown rapidly, it was in many ways tied to coastal areas, where parent firms or home offices of many of the local establishments existed. Also, since many of its industries serviced the national defense effort, they consequently had to be closely connected with matters decided on in Washington or other places distant from Bartlett City. Finally, it had many strong financial and business ties with major coastal cities, such as San Francisco and Los Angeles. As a result, executives, engineers, and scientists in Bartlett City industries were frequently in contact with the major business, political, and scientific centers of the country, particularly those on the West Coast. In making a trip, for example, to Los Angeles from Bartlett City, one was faced with using one of three alternative modes of travel: auto, private corporate jet, or commercial jet flight. Eagle Airlines had the sole route between Bartlett City and Los Angeles, which was found to be a most lucrative run and to which it gave a great deal of attention.

COMPANY MANAGEMENT

The rapid growth of Eagle Airlines was held by many to be in no small degree a result of the skill of its management. It should be pointed out that its top management had been particularly skillful in obtaining and defending its route structure and had been particularly successful in financing, at advantageous terms, the acquisition of modern aircraft, particularly jet-powered airplanes. Top management emphasized "decentralization," in which the lower members of management were given as much freedom as possible to fulfill their responsibilities in whatever way they thought best. This policy was thought to have built a dynamic, aggressive, and extremely able group of middle- and lower-level executives who had been particularly imaginative in finding ways to expand and improve the operation of the firm. This decentralization had always been accompanied by the understanding that the individual manager must "deliver." This policy, or actually philosophy, was conveyed and reinforced through letters, personal conversations, and example. Executives who increased sales or reduced costs, or in some manner made their operations more efficient, were rewarded in a number of ways. Praise, both public and private, was given to executives who improved their unit's performance. Bonuses for increased sales or cost reduction were both generous and frequent, and promotions came rapidly to those who managed outstanding units. The chairman of the board, who was also chief executive officer during this period of growth, frequently used words that were only half-jokingly claimed by other executives to be the company motto. "This company's success rests upon expansion and efficiency."

THE LOCAL UNIT

Eagle Airlines was organized as shown in Figure 1. The three major divisions were Operations, which was involved in scheduling and operating the planes over the entire route system; Sales, which was concerned

---

* Source: Prepared by Joseph A. Litterer. Used by permission.

FIGURE 1

Partial Organization Chart of Eagle Airlines.

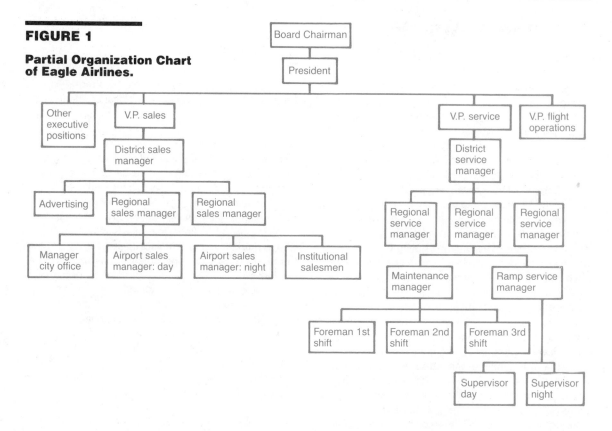

with advertising all phases of airline service, maintaining ticket offices in all cities and airports, and also selling to institutional customers such as companies and government agencies; and Service, which was concerned with activities at the airport, maintenance, handling baggage, loading passengers, and similar functions.

For all practical purposes, operations had no local offices in that it had to operate the entire system. Sales and service had both district and local or regional offices. The sales manager in Bartlett City, for example, was responsible for the ticket sales at the airport and in maintaining a downtown ticket office, as well as for institutional sales to the local companies and agencies. Service was usually broken into a number of subdivisions at the local level, so that at Bartlett City there was a ramp service manager who was responsible for handling everything pertaining to the airplane while it was on the ground, but not while it was under maintenance. The manager would, therefore, be responsible for the loading and unloading of all baggage, mail, and passengers. That individual was also responsible for cleaning the planes between flights, having

food put on board, getting baggage to the customers and picking up from them, guiding passengers on and off the aircraft, and checking their tickets when they arrived at the terminal.

Consistent with company policy of decentralization and individual accountability, each of these local people had an individual budget and standards of performance. A sales manager, for example, was given complete authority to hire, train, and fire whatever salespeople or any other personnel he or she thought necessary. The sales manager knew what his or her budget was and was expected to stick within it and reduce it if possible. Furthermore, the sales manager knew what the standards of performance relevant to sales volume were. The company placed great emphasis on an increase in sales rather than in absolute volume of sales. Hence, the sales manager at Bartlett City, as at all other local units, knew that individual performance would be evaluated, not on matching past sales volume, but by increasing it a certain percentage. The percentage would vary from one location to another depending upon the number of conditions: market potential, absolute volume, and similar terms.

Although the percentage increase might vary, it was always there and was known by the company as the "ratchet." The regional service manager had no actual sales figure to be held accountable for, but that manager did have costs that were expected to be controlled and, if at all possible, reduced. While there was no similar "ratchet," such as a percentage reduction of costs expected each year, there was continual pressure on the local ramp manager in the form of exhortation, suggestions, and illustrations of managers who had successfully found ways to reduce costs.

PLAN OF THE SALES MANAGER

Carl Dodds, sales manager in Bartlett City, had been with Eagle Airlines seven years, during which time he had had three promotions. Upon graduation from a Western state university, he had started working for Eagle Airlines in the San Francisco office as a ticket clerk at the local airport. Within a year he had been made accounts sales representative, selling airline service to local companies and institutions. Within two years he had become a local sales manager at San Jose, the smallest of the company's sales offices. Six months ago he had received his promotion to Bartlett City, the second largest sales office and, until recently, the one growing most rapidly. Dodd's superior looked at him as a particularly dynamic, inventive salesperson and sales manager. He seemed gifted at finding spectacular ways of substantially increasing sales. In previous positions he had developed a number of attention-getting promotion packages that met with spectacular results. Higher management looked to him to again increase sales at Bartlett City, which had leveled out about a year ago with the decline in the economy. It was not known how long the decline would continue.

Some of Dodd's previous associates in the other parts of the company agreed that he had been imaginative in developing some spectacular promotion schemes but also felt that success had always been of the short-run variety—he had made sudden bursts at the expense of long-term growth. They further claimed that he had been fortunate in always being promoted out of a position before the consequences of his activity caught up with him.

Since coming to Bartlett City, Dodds had been intensively studying the local market situation, making contacts with the various companies and big business executives, hiring some new salespeople, and training them after having, as he called it, weeded out some deadwood. He had also increased advertising and redecorated the downtown sales office. In spite of

this activity, in his own mind, he had been largely getting ready for his major effort.

Dodds defined his sales situation this way. The airline had done well attracting customers who wanted speed and convenience. However, a considerable number of business executives drove or used a company plane. He adopted and embellished a popular local image of the Bartlett City executive as a dynamic, imaginative, administrator-scientist who represented a new type of business tycoon. In Dodd's mind, what he had to do was sell this young dynamic, new type of tycoon the comfort and gracious service that, apparently, such a person thought should come to him or her in this new role. His new plan then was to do everything possible to give the "new tycoons" this sort of service. He therefore developed a plan to set up *Tycoon Specials* on certain of the flights carrying the greatest number of these business executives. This plan was to begin with the flight between Bartlett City and Los Angeles.

In this plan the customer-executive upon arriving at the ticket-checking counter for the *Tycoon Special* flight would be asked to select his or her own seat. This then would be reserved in the customer's name. Upon arriving at the ramp for boarding, the customer would be greeted by name by the gate attendant, usually dressed plainly but neatly in a white top, blue cap, and slacks, but now in a gold coat and a simulated turban. Stretching between the gate and the aircraft was to be a wide, rich-red carpet. Upon arrival, the customer's name would be announced through a special intercom to the plane. As the individual walked down the red carpet, the customer-executive would note that the flight hostess would appear smiling at the door, ready to greet him or her by name before being ushered to the appropriate seat, identified by a card with the executive's name, indicating, "This seat is reserved for Tycoon _____."

Once in flight this deluxe service would continue, with the hostesses changing into more comfortable and feminine-looking lounge dresses and serving a choice of champagne, wine, and cocktails along with exotic and varied hors d'oeuvres. There were other details to the plan, but this will give you some idea of its general nature. In this way, Dodds thought surely that he would be able to not only match but exceed the services and comfort some executives thought they obtained by alternative means of transportation.

Dodds's great problem was in getting the plan operational. Almost all the service had to be provided by people who did not report to him. This would be supplied by the local ramp service manager, to whom the gate clerk reported, and who would have to provide the red carpet, the additional gold uniforms, turbans, and the other paraphenalia necessary to create the impression that Dodds had in mind. The local ramp service manager, Chris Edwards, had been particularly abrupt in rejecting this proposal, insisting that it did not make sense and that he was going to have absolutely nothing to do with it. Dodds had in several meetings attempted to "sell," persuade, pressure, and finally threaten Edwards into accepting the plan. Edwards refusal had become more adamant and pointed at every step. Relationships between the two, never close or cordial, had deteriorated until there was nothing but the most unrestrained hostility expressed between them.

REACTION OF THE SERVICE MANAGER

Chris Edwards was a graduate engineer who had worked for the company for about 10 years. He had first started in the maintenance department of the firm and had gradually risen through several supervisory positions before being given this position as service manager with Eagle. It was the first position he had had in which he had an independent budget and was held individually accountable. After three years in this capacity, he personally felt and had been led to believe by several higher executives in the company that he had acquired as much experience in this position as was necessary. He was, therefore, looking forward to a new assignment, which probably involved a promotion in the very near future. He realized that this promotion would probably be based upon his earlier proven technical competence and his more recent experience in his present position, where he had run a particularly efficient operation. This was evidenced by several reductions in his operating expenses, due to efficiencies he had installed, and by other measures of performance, such as reduction in the time necessary to service, fuel, and load aircraft.

After having met with increasingly adamant refusals by Edwards, Dodds had gone to his superior, pointing out that he was being hampered by Edwards in his effort to increase sales and advance the company. Dodds's supervisor had made a point of seeing his counterpart, in the service area, asking if something could not be done by the service people at Bartlett City to support the sales effort. Upon inquiry, Edwards's superior learned the details of the request from Edwards and the reasons for his refusal. Dodds kept insistent pressure on his superior, asking to have something done about the local service manager's obstinacy. Eventually, word of the continued arguments between Dodds and Edwards went up the chain of command to the vice president of sales and later to the vice president in charge of service. One day while discussing this issue, their conversation was overheard by the president. Upon hearing the story, he made the comment that these personality clashes would either have to be straightened out or one or both of the men either transferred or, for that matter, fired. He emphatically insisted that the company could not operate efficiently with an unnecessary expenditure of energy going into personal disputes. □

CASE QUESTIONS

1. Evaluate the firm's organization design in terms of the important contingency factors which are relevant in this instance.
2. What changes would you recommend be made in the present organization design?
3. What do you believe will be the most important sources of resistance to changing the organization structure?

 **SUPRA OIL COMPANY**

John Nichols, a university research worker, had a talk with Mr. Bennet about the headquarters sales organization of the Supra Oil Company, one of the larger integrated oil companies in the country. Excerpts from the conversation follow:

Nichols: You mentioned that you're planning to make some organizational changes here at headquarters. I wonder if you could tell me something about that.

Bennett: Well, sure I will. I don't want to take too much credit for this thing, but it sort of got started because in the last couple of years I've been doing some beefing around here about the fact that I was being kept terribly busy with a lot of the operating details of the sales organization. You can see what I mean by looking at the organization chart we have been working under. [Mr. Bennett produced a chart from his desk drawer and indicated all the people that were currently reporting to him.] [See Exhibit 1 for a copy of this chart.]

You can see that with all these people looking to me for leadership I am not in a position to give them the right kind of guidance that I think they should have on their jobs. I just couldn't take the time. It didn't work too badly some time ago, but since I've been made a member of the board of directors, those activities have taken more of my time. What with being on additional committees and things of that kind, I just couldn't give 17 headquarters' division managers the amount of help and attention that they really need. I think one of the things that they miss is that they're not in close enough touch with me or anybody else higher up the line so that we can be in a good position to appraise their work. We hear about it from some of the field people when they are doing a lousy job, but we don't hear much about it if they're doing a good job. Occasionally, a field man will report that he is getting a lot of help from some staff outfit here, but that's rather rare. So we don't have a very good basis for appraising the good things that they do. So we started talking about what might be done to straighten this out.

Our plans are taking pretty definite shape now. Let me show you what we have in mind. [Mr. Bennett sketched on a pad of paper a diagram to indicate the planned organizational changes.] [See Exhibit 2.] You see, we will have two regional managers instead of three. We'll be making one of the present regional managers the manager of the headquarters sales divisions. Those are the divisions that specialize in promoting and selling our different specialty products. Then we'll set up a new job for Wingate, who has been acting as an administrative assistant here at headquarters. He'll take charge of a good number of headquarters sales staff divisions that were reporting directly to me. Those are staff divisions like price analysis and advertising. We will also give each of the two remaining regional managers an assistant manager. Those will be new positions too.

Nichols: How did you get these plans started?

Bennett: I raised it with Shepard [vice president of sales] quite a while back.

EXHIBIT 1

Partial organization chart of the sales department

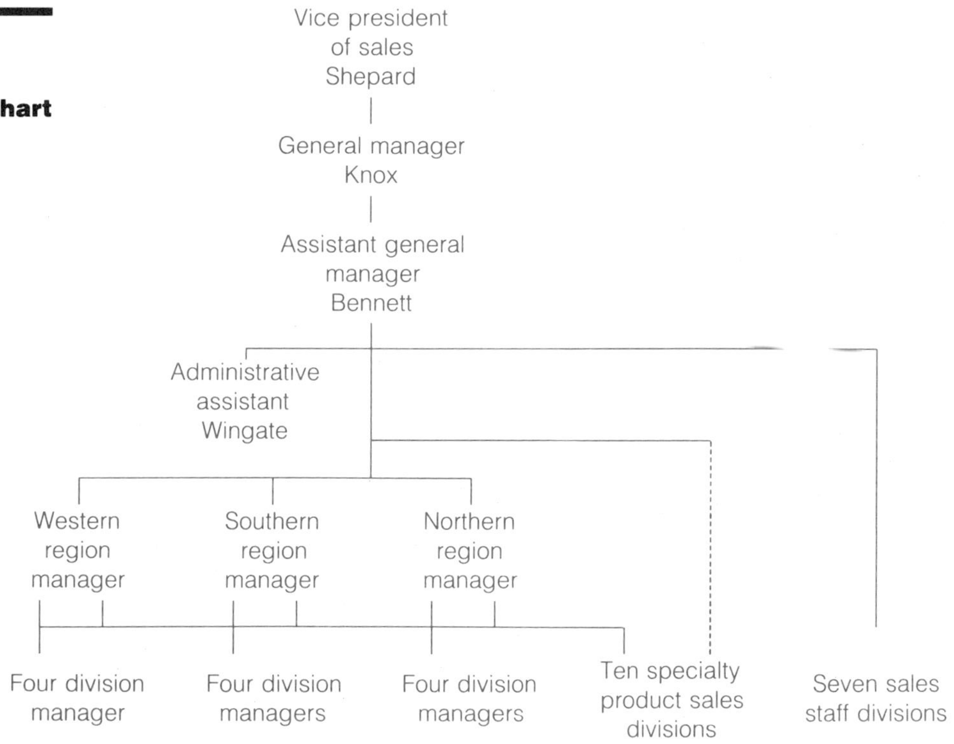

EXHIBIT 2

Proposed organization chart of the sales department

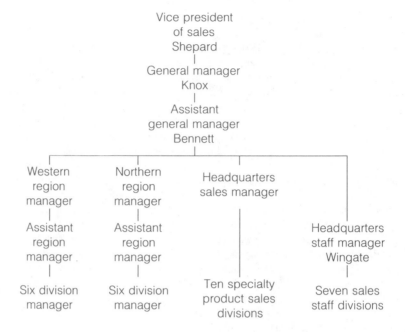

Nichols: Would you say that was maybe six months ago?

Bennett: I think it probably was six months ago. Shepard's first reaction was unfavorable. You see, I expected him to feel that way because he was the one that had the most to do with setting up our current organizational plan. But I approached him on it two or three times and complained a little bit and kept raising the question, and finally he said, "Well, I'm going to be leaving here pretty soon. You people have got to live with the organization. If you think it would work better some other way, I certainly won't object to your changing it." Well, that sort of thing gave me the green light, so then I went ahead and raised the question with Mr. Weld [president]. That is, Mr. Knox [general sales manager] and I did. The first time we went to him we talked about it in general terms. He said he thought it sounded like a pretty good idea and asked that we come back with two or three alternative ways of doing the thing in very specific terms. We talked to him once since then and, as a matter of fact, I'm going to see him this afternoon to see if he'll give us a final OK to go ahead with these plans.

Nichols: If you get his approval, what would you predict—that it might be another month before the change actually takes place?

Bennett: Well, I would say so. I think if we've got this thing going in a month that we will be doing pretty well. I'm going to want to talk to my regional managers and then the headquarters divisional managers about this, but they should buy it all right. I think it will be a fairly simple job to sell it to them. You see, they will in effect be getting more chance to have access to their boss. I think it will work out much better, and they will see the point to it.

Nichols: You say that you are making one less region and making the third regional manager the head of—I guess you are calling him the headquarters sales manager. Are all three of those jobs going to continue to be on an equal level?

Bennett: Yes, they will, but actually this job of headquarters sales manager will be sort of a training position for somebody to step into my job here as assistant general sales manager. That's what we have in mind. I think it will be a good assignment for training for my job. Then too, we're going to be able to open up a couple of new positions here, the assistant regional managers. I think that is going to be very useful from a management development standpoint. You see, one of our problems is that a number of the top executives here are all about the same age. You see, Knox and myself and the three regional managers are all about the same age, and then the heads of a lot of our headquarters divisions here are men of about our age who—well, they won't retire immediately, but they don't have a terribly long time to go. So we can't look to too many of those people to be our successors here at headquarters. We want to bring in some people from the field who will step in here as assistant regional managers in training for the job of regional managers.

Nichols: I take it then that you will be picking the people for those jobs from your field division men on the basis of talent and ability rather than on the basis of seniority.

Bennett: Yes, that's right, we're going to pay very little attention to seniority in picking them. As a matter of fact, the two people we have in mind are two of our newest division managers, but they are both very able people. We think this will give us a chance to give them a good training for future development here.

This change that we are proposing, however, will not drastically change anybody's status here at headquarters, and I don't think it is going to cause as much trouble to put it in. You see, nobody will be jumped over the head of anybody else ahead of them in the management line. We think it's going to help a lot to have an assistant regional manager in here because that means that both he and the regional manager will be able to spend more time out with the field organization. One will be able to cover matters here at headquarters while the other is gone.

Nichols: Does that mean that your field people will be getting more top-level supervision as a result of this change?

Bennett: Well, in a sense that's true of course, but it won't be taking any authority or responsibility from the field people. We just feel that they will be in closer personal contact with the people here at headquarters. We think it is very necessary that we do more of that. You see, if our regional managers and assistant managers can get out in the field and meet with the people, they will have a better basis for appraising different people that come along, and they can make sure we get the best people in the jobs that open up. Sometimes it's pretty hard to tell here at headquarters just who some of the best people are out in the field. You see, some division may have a job open up, and they will have a candidate for that job whom they

will recommend highly for the promotion. That may be all well and good, but we want to know whether or not there may be a better man in some other division whom we aren't hearing about who might be shifted over for that promotion. You can't blame the division people for that sort of thing because they will have their favorite candidate and will of course be recommending him. We've made a few mistakes along the way because of this sort of thing, and if we have more personal contact we will be able to do a better job of it.

Nichols: Will this mean that you will be able to spend more time in the field?

Bennett: Yes, I do hope that it will mean that. I want to do that very much. I think I ought to get out in the field more to keep in touch with what's going on in the market. It's really pretty hard to keep in touch with things while you are spending your time here at headquarters. You know, I want to get out and talk to people and see what they are talking about and see what kind of problems they are up against.

Nichols: I've heard several comments on this business of getting a feel for the market by getting out in the field. I take it that this is quite a different process from keeping in touch with the market on what you might call a statistical basis?

Bennett: Well, yes, it is. You see, I can look at the reports here in the office, and I may see that some district or some division is not doing too well at all on the basis of the figures in comparison with the competition. But I don't know just what the story is behind those figures. On a personal basis I could probably begin to get some answers to it. It could be any one of a number of things. I might go out there and find that it's a temporary situation because the competition is in effect going out and buying the business away from us, or I might find out that our people are not being very smart or aggressive about promoting our products, or I might find out that they do not know some of the facilities we have available that would help them compete for the business. You see, one way we can compete for the business is the fact that this company has available some pretty good capital resources; and if we don't have good outlets in a given district, we're often in a position to offer to put up some capital to get some better outlets. That way we can do a better job of competing for the business, and sometimes the local people don't know that these possibilities exist, or perhaps they're a little reticent about putting up proposals. Or even if they do put up proposals, if we haven't been out in the field to see for ourselves what's going on, we probably don't do as good a job of appraising the proposals they do put up.

Nichols: In other words, the figures tell you that maybe something ought to be checked into, but you've got to go out and talk to people to find out what is really going on?

Bennett: Yes, that's right. You have to take a personal look. You can find out a lot faster than you can by correspondence just what is going on and what can be done about it.

Nichols: Won't this reorganization mean that some of the people both here and in the field will have new bosses now?

Bennett: Yes, that's right, but it's not too drastic a change. You see, we used to have only two regional managers some time ago. I guess we shifted off that system some four or five years ago. When I was out in the field as manager of a division, I was reporting in to the northern regional manager, who was Mr. Shepard at that time. Then I was brought in here as his assistant for the whole region. It was about that time that we set up this business of having three regions and I was named one of the regional managers, and at that time Mr. Shepard became general manager.

Nichols: Well, it sounds as if that previous move might have been motivated somewhat by a desire to develop people and perhaps give you a chance to take over a regional managership before you might otherwise have had a chance to.

Bennett: Yes, I think that's right. At that time, that move was the way we could open things up for further management development, and now we are sort of doing it the other way around. Everybody knows that the arrangement we are now proposing may well be changed again in a few more years.

We like to change the organization around a little bit like this from time to time just to let people know that we are not going to be static about things. Of course, we want to do it in a way so that some of our senior people do not get bypassed or jumped over by some of the younger ones, because that not only bothers the individual but it also hurts morale further down in the organization. You see, when some of the people further down

see some of that sort of thing happening, they are apt to conclude that it might happen to them some day, and it's pretty discouraging to them. The way we are doing it now we can bring up some younger people without jumping over anybody's head who is senior.

I think an organization change of this kind is also useful in that it indicates to some of our younger people that they need not feel discouraged if they are in a position where someone is above them in line who shows no signs of being promoted on up. This situation might make a person feel that he is being blocked from future promotion by his boss. But he is encouraged when he sees an occasional organizational shift of this kind because it makes him realize that things can happen in the future that might shift the organization around to a point where he can be sprung loose for a move on up even though his boss may not be promotable.

Nichols: Then I take it that one of the predominant thoughts in this whole reorganization was one of management development?

Bennett: Oh, that's certainly true. That was one of the prime reasons we're proposing this, because we think it will help us develop our managers and this gives us a way of doing it without upsetting the organization too much.

That afternoon Mr. Bennett kept the appointment with Mr. Weld that was mentioned in the conversation above. Upon entering Mr. Weld's office, Mr. Bennett handed Mr. Weld a copy of the revised sales organization chart.

Bennett: Here's a final version of our reorganizational plans. Do you think it is all right to go ahead on this?   □

CASE QUESTIONS

1. What are the bases for the departments of Supra Oil before and after the change? What other differences can you identify in organization structure after the change?

2. What will be the probable effects of the change on organizational behavior variables such as motivation and group development?

3. What is your opinion about the attitude that organization structures should be changed just for the sake of change?

 **JOB DESIGN**

The building blocks of organizational structures are the jobs that people perform. There are many causes of individual, group, and organizational effectiveness. A major cause is the job performance of employees. Job design refers to the process by which managers decide individual job tasks and authority. Apart from the very practical issues associated with job design, that is, issues that relate to effectiveness in economic, political, and monetary terms, we can appreciate its importance in social and psychological terms. As noted in earlier chapters, jobs can be sources of psychological stress and even mental and physical impairment. On a more positive note, jobs can provide income, meaningful life experiences, self-esteem, esteem from others, regulation of our lives, and association with others.[1] Thus, the well-being of organizations and people depends on how well management is able to design jobs.

JOB DESIGN AND QUALITY OF WORK LIFE

In recent years, the issue of designing jobs has gone beyond the determination of the most efficient way to perform tasks. The concept of quality of work life is now widely used to refer to "the degree to which members of work organizations are able to satisfy important personal needs through their experiences in organizations."[2] The emphasis on satisfaction of personal needs does not imply de-emphasis of organizational needs. Instead, contemporary managers are finding that when the personal needs of employees are satisfied, the performance of the organization itself is enhanced.

As America moves into the 1990s, the challenge to managers is to provide for both quality of work-life and improved production and efficiency through reindustrialization. At present, the trade-offs between the gains in human terms from improved quality of work-life and the gains in economic terms from reindustrialization are not fully known. Some believe that it will be necessary to defer quality of work-life efforts if we are to make the American economy more productive and efficient.[3] Others observe that reindustrialization can present opportunities to combine quality of work-life with reindustrialization efforts.[4]

---

[1] David F. Smith, "The Functions of Work," *Omega,* 1975, pp. 383–93.

[2] J. Richard Hackman and J. Lloyd Suttle, eds., *Improving Life at Work* (Santa Monica, Calif.: Goodyear Publishing, 1977), p. 4.

[3] Amitai Etzioni, "Choose America Must—Between 'Reindustrialization and Quality of Life'," *Across the Board,* October 1980, pp. 43–49.

[4] D. J. Skrovan, ed., *Quality of Work Life* (Reading, Mass.: Addison-Wesley Publishing, 1983).

Another consideration affecting job design and quality of work life issues is the changing nature of business activity. We are witnessing the birth of an information-based economy in which the management of information plays a dominant role. New jobs, and even newer electronic technology available for performing these jobs, create special job design challenges. It is this particular challenge addressed by Calvin Pava's article which forms a part of this chapter.

Job design and redesign techniques attempt (1) to identify the most important needs of employees and the organization and (2) to remove obstacles in the workplace that frustrate those needs. Managers hope that the results are jobs that fulfill important individual needs and contribute to individual, group, and organizational effectiveness. There is no question that managers are, in fact, redesigning jobs and job settings. But whether the outcomes of those managerial actions are positive is debatable. Obviously, designing and redesigning jobs is complex. The remainder of this chapter reviews the important theories, research, and practices of job design. As will be seen, contemporary management has at its disposal a wide range of techniques that facilitate the achievement of personal and organizational performance.

A CONCEPTUAL MODEL OF JOB DESIGN

The conceptual model depicted in Figure 12–1 is based on the extensive research literature that has appeared in the last 20 years. The model includes the various terms and concepts that appear in the current literature. When linked together, these concepts describe the important determinants of job performance and organizational effectiveness. The model takes into account a number of sources of complexity. It recognizes that individuals react differently to jobs. While one person may derive positive satisfaction from a job, another may not. The model also recognizes the difficult trade-offs between organizational and individual needs. For example, the technology of manufacturing (an environmental difference) may dictate that management adopt assembly-line mass-production methods and low-skilled jobs to achieve optimal efficiency. Such jobs, however, may result in great unrest and worker discontent. Perhaps these costs could be avoided by a more careful balancing of organizational and individual needs.

FIGURE 12–1

Job Design and
Job Performance

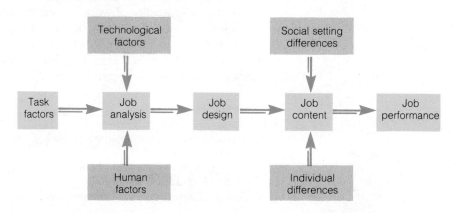

The ideas reflected in Figure 12–1 are the bases for this chapter. We present each important factor that is the cause or the effect of job design, beginning with job analysis.

JOB ANALYSIS

Job analysis is the process of decision making that translates task, human, and technological factors into job designs. Either managers or personnel specialists undertake the process, and a number of approaches exist to assist them. Two of the more widely used approaches are functional job analysis (FJA) and the position analysis questionnaire (PAQ).

FUNCTIONAL JOB ANALYSIS

Functional job analysis focuses attention on task and technological factors. FJA directs attention to the following four aspects of each job or class of jobs:

1. What the worker *does* in relation to data, people, and jobs.
2. What *methods* and *techniques* the worker uses.
3. What *machines, tools,* and *equipment* the worker uses.
4. What *materials, products, subject matter,* or *services* the worker produces.

The first three aspects relate to job *activities*. The fourth aspect relates to job *performance*. FJA provides descriptions of jobs that can be the bases for classifying jobs according to any one of the four dimensions. In addition to defining what activities, methods, and machines make up the job, FJA also defines what the individual doing the job should produce. FJA can, therefore, be the basis for defining standards of performance.

FJA is the most popular and widely used of the job analysis methods.[5] In addition, it is the basis for the most extensive available list of occupational titles.[6]

POSITION ANALYSIS QUESTIONNAIRE

The **position analysis questionnaire** takes into account human as well as task and technological factors. PAQ has been the object of considerable attention by researchers and practitioners who believe that accurate job analysis must take human factors into account.[7] PAQ analysis attempts to identify the following six job aspects:

1. Information sources critical to job performance.
2. Information processing and decision making critical to job performance.
3. Physical activity and dexterity required of the job.
4. Interpersonal relationships required of the job.

---

[5] Marc J. Wallace, Jr., N. Fredric Crandall, and Charles H. Fay, *Administering Human Resources* (New York: Random House, 1982), p. 196.

[6] U.S. Department of Labor, *Dictionary of Occupational Titles,* 4th ed. (Washington, DC: U.S. Government Printing Office, 1977).

[7] E. J. McCormick, P. R. Jeanneret, and R. C. Mecham, "A Study of Job Characteristics and Job Dimensions as Based on the Position Analysis Questionnaire (PAQ)," *Journal of Applied Psychology,* August 1972, pp. 347–68.

5.   Physical working conditions and the reactions of individuals to those conditions.
6.   Other job characteristics such as work schedule and work responsibilities.

It is important to note that FJA and PAQ overlap considerably. Each attempts to identify job activities that are necessary, given the task to be done and the technology with which to do it. But PAQ also considers the individual's psychological responses to the job and its environment. Thus, PAQ acknowledges that job designs should combine the effects of all three factors.

Numerous methods exist to perform job analysis. PAQ and FJA appear to be two of the most popular ones. A recent survey of the opinions of expert job analysts bear out the popularity of PAQ and FJA. But the survey also suggests that different methods make different contributions to organizational purposes.[8]

JOB DESIGNS

Job designs are the results of job analysis. They specify three characteristics of jobs: range, depth, and relationships.

RANGE AND DEPTH

The **range** of a job refers to the number of tasks that a jobholder performs. The person who performs eight tasks to complete a job has a wider job range than does the person who performs four tasks. In most instances, the greater the number of tasks performed, the longer it takes to complete the job.

A second job characteristic is **depth,** the amount of discretion that an individual has to decide job activities and job outcomes. In many instances, job range relates to personal influence as well as delegated authority. Thus, an employee with the same job title and at the same organizational level as another employee may possess more, less, or the same amount of job depth because of personal influence.

Job range and depth distinguish one job from another not only within the same organization but also among different organizations. To illustrate how jobs differ in range and depth, Figure 12–2 depicts the differences for selected jobs of business firms, hospitals, and universities. For example, business research scientists, hospital chiefs of surgery, and university presidents generally have high job range and significant job depth. Research scientists perform a large number of tasks and usually are not closely supervised. Chiefs of surgery have significant job range in that they oversee and counsel on many diverse surgical matters. In addition, they are not supervised closely

---

[8] Edward L. Levine, Ronald A. Ash, Hardy Hall, and Frank Sistrunk, "Evaluation of Job Analysis Methods by Experienced Job Analysis," *Academy of Management Journal,* June 1983, pp. 339–48.

FIGURE 12–2

Job Depth and Range

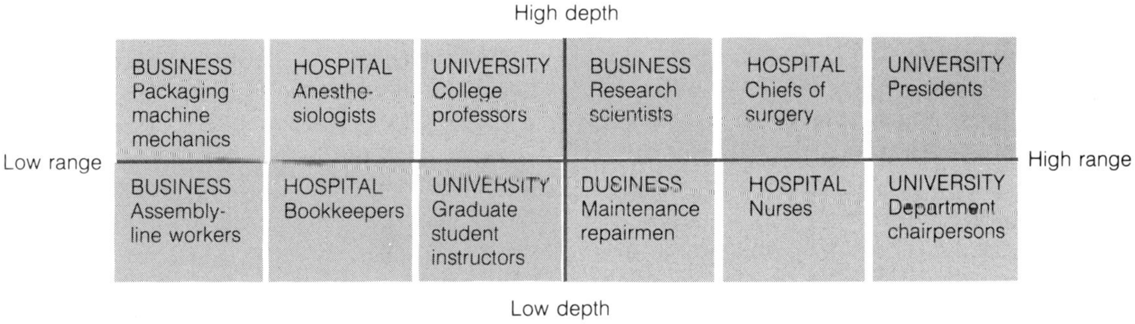

High depth

BUSINESS Packaging machine mechanics	HOSPITAL Anesthe- siologists	UNIVERSITY College professors	BUSINESS Research scientists	HOSPITAL Chiefs of surgery	UNIVERSITY Presidents
BUSINESS Assembly- line workers	HOSPITAL Bookkeepers	UNIVERSITY Graduate student instructors	BUSINESS Maintenance repairmen	HOSPITAL Nurses	UNIVERSITY Department chairpersons

Low range / High range

Low depth

and they have the authority to influence hospital surgery policies and proce-dures.

University presidents have a large number of tasks to perform. They speak to alumni groups, politicians, community representatives, and students. They develop, in consultation with others, policies on admissions, fund raising, and adult education. They can alter the faculty recruitment philosophy and thus alter the course of the entire institution. For example, a university presi-dent may want to build an institution that is noted for high-quality classroom instruction and for the excellent services that it provides to the community. This thrust may lead to recruiting and selecting professors who want to concentrate on these two specific goals. In contrast, another president may want to foster outstanding research and high-quality classroom instruction. Of course, still another president may attempt to develop an institution that is noted for instruction, research, and service. The critical point is that university presidents have sufficient job depth to alter the course of a university's direc-tion.

Highly specialized jobs are those that have few tasks to accomplish and use prescribed means to accomplish them. Such jobs are quite routine; they also tend to be controlled by specific rules and procedures (low depth). A highly despecialized job (high range) has many tasks to accomplish and discretion regarding means and ends (high depth). Within an organization, there typically are great differences among jobs in both range and depth. Although there are no precise equations that managers can use to decide job range and depth, they can follow this guideline: Given the economic and technical requirements of the organization's mission, goals, and objectives, what is the optimal point along the continuum of range and depth for each job?

Taken together, range and depth may affect how stimulating or boring a particular job is perceived as being. The following OBM Encounter addresses the issue of jobs and boredom.

JOBS AND BOREDOM

Whether or not a job is considered boring is a function of a number of things: aspects of the job, aspects of the individual doing the job, and even aspects of the environment in which the job is done. Clearly, however, job range and job depth are important factors in determining boredom. Consider, for example, the following jobs, all of which are rated as some of the most boring in industry. All would rank very low in both range and depth: copying machine operator, forklift-truck driver, elevator operator, highway toll collector, car washer, bank guard, and assembly line worker.

While most people would agree that these may be boring jobs, there is less agreement on whether or not this is a problem. The University of Michigan Institute for Social Research, based on interviews with more than 2,000 workers, concluded that boring jobs may attract workers who are temperamentally suited to them. In other words, certain types of workers are able to better adjust to boring jobs than others. Another study, conducted over a six-year period at a General Motors plant, noted that employees tended to stay in jobs because of the job security and fringe benefits offered, and never mentioned boredom as a factor in determining their satisfaction. ☐

Source: Taken from "Those Boring Jobs—Not All That Dull," *U.S. News and World Report,* December 1, 1975, pp. 64–65; and Kenneth Jenkins, "Do We Really Need Job Enrichment?" *Management World,* January 1981, p. 39.

JOB RELATIONSHIPS

Job relationships are determined by managers' decisions regarding departmentalization bases and spans of control. It becomes the manager's responsibility to coordinate the resulting groups toward organizational purposes. The decisions regarding departmentalization bases and spans of control determine the nature and extent of jobholders' interpersonal relationships, individually and within groups. As we have seen already in the discussion of groups in organizations, group performance is effected in part by group cohesiveness. And the degree of group cohesiveness depends on the quality and kinds of interpersonal relationships established by jobholders assigned to a task or command group.

The wider the span of control, the larger is the group and consequently the more difficult it is to establish friendship and interest relationships. People in larger groups are less likely to communicate (and interact sufficiently to form interpersonal ties) than people in smaller groups. Without the opportunity to communicate, people will be unable to establish cohesive work groups. Thus, an important source of satisfaction may be lost for individuals who seek to fulfill social and esteem needs through relationships with co-workers.

The basis for departmentalization that management selects also has important implications for job relationships. The functional basis places jobs with similar depth and range in the same groups, while the product, territory, and customer bases place jobs with dissimilar depth and range in the same groups. Thus, people in functional departments will have much the same specialty. Product, territory, and customer departments, however, comprise heterogeneous jobs. Individuals who work in heterogeneous departments experience feelings of dissatisfaction, stress, and involvement more intensely than do individuals who work in homogeneous, functional departments. People with homogeneous backgrounds, skills, and training have more common interests than do people whose backgrounds, skills, and training are heterogeneous. Thus, it is easier for them to establish satisfying social relationships with less stress, but also with less involvement in the department's activities.

Job designs describe the *objective* characteristics of jobs. That is, through job analysis techniques such as FJA and PAQ, managers can describe jobs in terms of the activities required to produce a specified outcome. But before we can understand the relationship between jobs and performance, we must consider yet another factor—job content

JOB CONTENT   Taylor proposed that the way to improve work, that is, to make it more efficient, is to determine (1) the "best way" to do a task (motion study) and (2) the standard time for completion of the task (time study). Motion study determines preferred work activities in relation to raw materials, product design, order of work, tools, equipment, and work-place layout. Time study determines the preferred time for performing each job activity. Through motion and time study, practitioners of scientific management design jobs solely in terms of technical data.

The belief that the design of a job can be based solely on technical data ignores the very large role played by the individual who performs the job. In this section, the issue of **job content** is examined. As you will see, the manner in which individuals react to their jobs depends on their unique characteristics.

Job content refers to the aspects of a job that define its general nature as *perceived by the jobholder as influenced by the social setting.* It is important to distinguish between the *objective* properties of jobs and the *subjective* properties of jobs as reflected in the perceptions of the people who perform them.[9] Managers cannot understand the causes of job performance without considering such individual differences as personality, needs, and span of attention.[10] According to Figure 12–1, job content precedes job performance. Thus, if managers desire to increase job performance by changing job content, they can change job design, individual perceptions, or social settings—all of which are causes of job content.

If management is to understand perceived job content, some method for measuring it must exist.[11] In response to this need, organizational behavior researchers have attempted to measure job content in a variety of work

---

[9] Kenneth R. Brousseau, "Toward a Dynamic Model of Job-Person Relationships: Findings, Research Questions, and Implications for Work System Design," *Academy of Management Review*, January 1983, pp. 33–45.

[10] Donald P. Schwab and L. L. Cummings, "A Theoretical Analysis of the Impact of Task Scope on Employee Performance," *Academy of Management Review*, April 1976, pp. 31–32.

[11] Thomas W. Ferratt, Randall B. Dunham, and Jon L. Pierce, "Self-Report Measures of Job Characteristics and Affective Responses: An Examination of Discriminant Validity," *Academy of Management Journal*, December 1981, pp. 780–94.

settings. The methods that researchers use rely on questionnaires, completed by jobholders. These questionnaires measure the jobholder's perceptions of certain job *characteristics.*

JOB CHARACTER- ISTICS

The pioneering effort to measure job content through employee responses to a questionnaire resulted in the identification of six characteristics: variety, autonomy, required interaction, knowledge and skill required, and responsibility.[12] The index of these six characteristics is termed the Requisite Task Attribute Index (RTAI). The original RTAI has been extensively reviewed and analyzed. One important development was the review by Hackman and Lawler, who revised the index to include the six characteristics shown in Table 12–1.[13] Other researchers have identified similar characteristics.[14]

TABLE 12–1

Selected Job Characteristics

Variety. The degree to which a job requires employees to perform a wide range of operations in their work and/or the degree to which employees must use a variety of equipment and procedures in their work.

Autonomy. The extent to which employees have a major say in scheduling their work, selecting the equipment they will use, and deciding on procedures to be followed.

Task identity. The extent to which employees do an entire or whole piece of work and can clearly identify with the results of their efforts.

Feedback. The degree to which employees, as they are working, receive information that reveals how well they are performing on the job.

Dealing with others. The degree to which a job requires employees to deal with other people to complete their work.

Friendship opportunities. The degree to which a job allows employees to talk with one another on the job and to establish informal relationships with other employees at work.

Source: Henry P. Sims, Jr., Andrew D. Szilagyi, and Robert T. Keller, "The Measurement of Job Characteristics," *Academy of Management Journal,* June 1976, p. 197.

Variety, task identity, and *feedback* are perceptions of job range; *autonomy* is the perception of job depth; and *dealing with others* and *friendship opportunities* reflect perceptions of job relationships. Employees sharing similar perceptions, job designs, and social settings should report similar job characteristics. Employees whose perceptions are different, however, report different job characteristics of the *same* job. For example, an individual with a high

---

[12] Arthur N. Turner and Paul R. Lawrence, *Industrial Jobs and the Worker: An Investigation of Response to Task Attributes* (Cambridge, Mass.: Harvard University Press, 1965).

[13] J. Richard Hackman and Edward E. Lawler III, "Employee Reactions to Job Characteristics," *Journal of Applied Psychology,* June 1971, pp. 259–86; and J. Richard Hackman and Greg R. Oldham, "Development of the Job Diagnostic Survey," *Journal of Applied Psychology,* April 1975, pp. 159–70.

[14] Michael A. Campion and Paul Thayer, "Development and Field Evaluation of an Interdisciplinary Measure of Job Design," *Journal of Applied Psychology,* February 1985, pp. 29–43.

need for social belonging would perceive "friendship opportunities" differently than would another individual with a low need for social belonging.

Individual differences in the strength of needs, particularly the strength of growth needs, have been shown to influence the perception of task variety. Employees with relatively weak higher order needs are less concerned with performing a variety of tasks than are employees with relatively strong growth needs. Thus, managers expecting higher performance to result from increased task variety would be disappointed if the jobholders did not have strong growth needs. Even individuals with strong growth needs cannot respond continuously to the opportunity to perform more and more tasks. At some point, performance turns down as these individuals reach the limits imposed by their abilities and time. For such individuals, the relationship between performance and task variety is likely to be curvilinear.[15]

Differences in the social settings of work also affect perceptions of job content. Examples of such differences include leadership style[16] and what other people say about the job.[17] More than one research study has pointed out that how one perceives a job is greatly affected by what other people say about it. If your friends state that their jobs are boring, you are likely to state that your job is also boring. If an individual perceives a job as boring, job performance no doubt will suffer. Job content, then, results from the interaction of many factors in the work situation.

JOB PERFORMANCE

Job performance includes a number of outcomes. In this section, we discuss performance outcomes that have value to the organization and to the individual.

OBJECTIVE OUTCOMES

Quantity and quality of output, absenteeism, tardiness, and turnover are objective outcomes that can be measured in quantitative terms. For each job, implicit or explicit standards exist for each of these objective outcomes. Industrial engineering studies establish standards for daily quantity, and quality control specialists establish tolerance limits for acceptable quality. These aspects of job performance account for characteristics of the product, client, or service for which the jobholder is responsible. But job performance include other outcomes.

---

[15] Joseph E. Champoux, "A Three Sample Test of Some Extensions to the Job Characteristics Model of Work Motivation," *Academy of Management Journal,* September 1980, pp. 466–78.

[16] Ricky W. Griffin, "Supervisory Behavior as a Source of Perceived Task Scope," *Journal of Occupational Psychology,* September 1981, pp. 175–82.

[17] Joe Thomas and Ricky W. Griffin, "The Social Information Processing Model of Task Design: A Review of the Literature," *Academy of Management Review,* October 1983, pp. 672–82; Ricky W. Griffin, "Objective and Subjective Sources of Information in Task Redesign: A Field Experiment," *Administrative Science Quarterly,* June 1983, pp. 184–200; and Jeffrey Pfeffer, "A Partial Test of the Social Information-Processing Model of Job Attitudes," *Human Relations,* July 1980, pp. 457–76.

PERSONAL BEHAVIOR OUTCOMES

The jobholder reacts to the work itself either by attending regularly or being absent, by staying with the job, or by quitting. Moreover, physiological and health-related problems can be consequences of job performance. Stress related to job performance can contribute to physical and mental impairment. Accidents and occupationally related disease also can result from job performance.

INTRINSIC AND EXTRINSIC OUTCOMES

Job outcomes may be intrinsic or extrinsic. The distinction between intrinsic and extrinsic outcomes is important for understanding the reactions of people to their jobs.[18] In a general sense, intrinsic outcomes are objects or events that follow from the worker's own efforts and do not require the involvement of any other person. More simply, they are outcomes that clearly are related to action on the worker's part. Such outcomes typically are thought to be solely in the province of professional and technical jobs; yet all jobs potentially have opportunities for intrinsic outcomes. Intrinsic outcomes involve feelings of responsibility, challenge, and recognition and result from such job characteristics as variety, autonomy, identity, and significance.

Extrinsic outcomes, however, are objects or events that follow from the worker's own efforts in conjunction with other factors that are not directly involved in the job itself. Pay, working conditions, co-workers, and even supervision are characteristics of the workplace that potentially are job outcomes but are not a fundamental part of the work itself. Dealing with others and friendship interactions are sources of extrinsic outcomes.

JOB SATISFACTION OUTCOME

Job satisfaction depends on the levels of intrinsic and extrinsic outcomes and on how the jobholder views them. These outcomes have different values for different people. For some people, responsible and challenging work may have neutral or even negative value. For other people, such work outcomes may have high positive value. People differ in the importance that they attach to job outcomes. That difference alone would account for different levels of job satisfaction for essentially the same job tasks.

Another important individual difference is job involvement.[19] People differ in the extent to which (1) work is a central life interest, (2) they actively participate in work, (3) they perceive work as central to self-esteem, and (4) they perceive work as consistent with their self-concept. Persons who are not involved in their work cannot be expected to realize the same satisfaction as those who are. This variable accounts for the fact that two workers could report different levels of satisfaction for the same performance levels.

A final individual difference is the perceived equity of the outcome in terms of what the jobholder considers a fair reward. If the rewards are perceived to be unfair in relation to those of others in similar jobs requiring similar effort, the jobholder will experience dissatisfaction and will seek means

---

[18] Arthur P. Brief and Ramon J. Aldag, "The Intrinsic-Extrinsic Dichotomy: Toward Conceptual Clarity," *Academy of Management Review*, July 1977, pp. 496–500.

[19] S. D. Saleh and James Hosek, "Job Involvement: Concepts and Measurements," *Academy of Management Journal*, June 1976, pp. 213–24.

to restore the equity, either by seeking greater rewards (primarily extrinsic) or by reducing effort.

Thus, we see that job performance includes many potential outcomes. Some are of primary value to the organization—the objective outcomes, for example. Others are of primary importance to the individual—for example, job satisfaction. Job performance is, without doubt, a complex variable that depends on the interplay of numerous factors. Managers can make some sense of the issue by understanding the motivational implications of jobs.

MOTIVATIONAL PROPERTIES OF JOBS AND JOB PERFORMANCE

The interest of organizational behavior researchers and managers in the motivational properties of jobs is based on the understanding that job performance depends on more than the ability of the jobholder. Specifically, job performance is determined by the interaction of ability and motivation as expressed by the equation:

$$\text{Job performance} = \text{Ability} \times \text{Motivation}$$

The equation reflects the fact that one person's job performance can be greater than that of another person because of greater ability, greater motivation, or both. It also reflects the possibility that job performance could be zero even if the jobholder has ability; in such instances, motivation would have to be zero. Thus, it is imperative that management consider the potential impact of the motivational properties of jobs.

The field of organizational behavior has advanced a number of suggestions for improving the motivational properties of jobs. Invariably, the suggestions, termed *job redesign strategies,* attempt to improve job performance through changes in job range and depth. In the next section, the more significant job redesign strategies are reviewed.

REDESIGNING JOB RANGE: JOB ROTATION AND JOB ENLARGEMENT

The earliest attempts to redesign jobs date to the scientific management era. The efforts at that time emphasized efficiency criteria. As a result, the individual tasks that a job comprised were made limited, uniform, and repetitive. This practice led to narrow job range and, consequently, to reported high levels of job discontent, turnover, absenteeism, and dissatisfaction. Accordingly, strategies were devised that widened job range by increasing the requisite activities of jobs. Two of these new strategies were *job rotation* and *job enlargement.*

JOB ROTATION The managers of such organizations as Western Electric, Ford, Bethelehem Steel, and TRW Systems have utilized different forms of the **job rotation** strategy. This strategy involves rotating an individual from one job to another. Thus, the individual is expected to complete more job activities since each job includes different tasks. Job rotation involves increasing the range of jobs and the perception of variety in the job content. Increasing task variety should, according to expectancy theory, increase the valence associated with job satisfaction. However, the practice of job rotation does not change the basic characteristics of the assigned jobs. Critics state that this approach involves nothing more than having people perform several boring and monotonous jobs rather than one. An alternative strategy is job enlargement.

JOB ENLARGEMENT

The pioneering study by Walker and Guest was concerned with the social and psychological problems associated with mass-production jobs in automobile assembly plants.[20] Walker and Guest found that many workers were dissatisfied with their highly specialized jobs. In particular, they disliked mechanical pacing, the repetitiveness of operations, and the lack of a sense of accomplishment.

Walker and Guest also found a positive relationship between job range and job satisfaction. The findings of their study gave early support for those motivation theories which predicted that increases in job range would increase job satisfaction and other objective job outcomes. **Job enlargement** strategies focus on the opposite of dividing work—they are a form of despecialization, or increasing the number of tasks that an employee performs. For example, a job is designed so that the individual performs six tasks instead of three.

Although, in many instances, an enlarged job requires a longer training period, it usually increases job satisfaction because boredom is reduced. The implication, of course, is that this will lead to improvement in other performance outcomes.

The concept and practice of job enlargement have become considerably more sophisticated. In recent years, effective job enlargement has involved more than simply increasing task variety. In addition, it has been necessary to redesign certain other aspects of job range. For example, machine-paced control has been replaced by worker-paced control.[21] Each of the changes that have been made has involved balancing the gains and losses of varying degrees of division of labor.

Some employees cannot cope with enlarged jobs because they cannot comprehend complexity; moreover, their attention span may be so short that they cannot stay with and complete an enlarged set of tasks. However, if employees are known to be amenable to job enlargement and if they have the requisite ability, then job enlargement should increase satisfaction and product quality and decrease absenteeism and turnover. These gains are not without costs, including the likelihood that employees will demand larger salaries in exchange for their performance of enlarged jobs. Yet these

---

[20] Charles R. Walker and Robert H. Guest, *The Man on the Assembly Line* (Cambridge, Mass.: Harvard University Press, 1952).

[21] Kae H. Chung and Monica F. Ross, "Differences in Motivational Properties between Job Enlargement and Job Enrichment," *Academy of Management Review*, January 1977, pp. 114–15.

costs must be borne if management desires to implement *job enrichment,* the redesign strategy that enlarges job depth. Job enlargement is a necessary precondition for job enrichment.

REDESIGNING JOB DEPTH: JOB ENRICHMENT

The impetus for redesigning job depth was provided by Herzberg's two-factor theory of motivation.[22] The basis of this theory is that the factors that meet individuals' need for psychological growth, especially responsibility, job challenge, and achievement, must be characteristic of their jobs. The application of Herzberg's theory is termed **job enrichment.**

The implementation of job enrichment is realized through direct changes in job depth. Managers can provide employees with greater opportunities to exercise discretion by making the following changes:

1. *Direct feedback.* The evaluation of performance should be timely and direct.
2. *New learning.* A good job enables people to feel that they are growing. All jobs should provide opportunities to learn.
3. *Scheduling.* People should be able to schedule some part of their own work.
4. *Uniqueness.* Each job should have some unique qualities or features.
5. *Control over resources.* Individuals should have some control over job related resources.
6. *Personal accountability.* People should be provided with an opportunity to be accountable for the job.

As the theory and practice of job enrichment have evolved, managers have become aware that successful applications require numerous changes in the way work is done. Some of the more important changes include delegating greater authority to workers to participate in decisions, to set their own goals, and to evaluate their (and their work groups') performance. Job enrichment also involves changing the nature and style of managers' behavior. Managers must be willing and able to delegate authority. Given the ability of employees to carry out enriched jobs and the willingness of managers to delegate authority, gains in performance can be expected. These positive outcomes are the result of increasing employees' expectancies that efforts will lead to performance, that performance will lead to intrinsic and extrinsic rewards, and that these rewards will have the power to satisfy needs.[23]

An application of job enrichment in a service organization is illustrated in the following OBM Encounter.

---

[22] Frederick Herzberg, "The Wise Old Turk," *Harvard Business Review,* September-October 1974, pp. 70–80.

[23] Kae H. Chung, *Motivational Theories and Practices* (Columbus, Ohio: Grid, 1977), p. 204.

ENCOUNTER

OBM

JOB ENRICHMENT AT CITIBANK

Citibank recently undertook an extensive change in the ways its employees did their work. According to George E. Seegers, a bank vice president, a customer survey indicated that the bank scored very low on "customer service." Upon examining the causes of the problem, the bank management concluded that the reason was that its employees didn't "feel like somebody." They were dissatisfied with their rather mundane jobs, created in part by the decision of the bank some time ago to introduce automatic teller machines. Building on the idea that everybody wants to feel like somebody, the bank undertook extensive changes designed to recognize the individuality of employees, as well as customers.

Among the many changes implemented were the following:

- Encouraging communications between the functional departments: operations, marketing, and servicing.

- Decentralizing operations so that one person could handle an entire transaction from the time it came into the bank until the time it left.
- Putting the employees who did the job in direct contact with the customers and the computers.
- Asking the people who did the job what was boring or troublesome *before* the bank automated.
- Undertaking considerable training and education for the entire work force.

These changes in job design were made over a two-year period. The changes were accompanied by training sessions that taught the new skills. It was also necessary to develop new attitudes among the management personnel, including the attitude that employee opinions were valuable and desirable inputs into decisions.   □

Source: Roy W. Walters, "The Citibank Project: Improving Productivity through Work Design," in *The Innovative Organization,* ed. Robert Zager and Michael P. Rosow (Elmsford, N.Y.: Pergamon Press, 1982).

REDESIGNING JOB RANGE AND DEPTH: COMBINED APPROACH

Job enrichment and job enlargement are not competing strategies. Job enlargement, but not job enrichment, may be compatible with the needs, values, and abilities of some individuals. Yet job enrichment, when appropriate, necessarily involves job enlargement. A promising new approach to job redesign is one that attempts to integrate the two approaches: the job characteristic model. Hackman, Oldham, Janson, and Purdy devised the approach and based it on the Job Diagnostic Survey, cited in an earlier section.[24] While we will briefly summarize a portion of the approach here, the entire model is presented in their article, "A New Strategy for Job Enrichment" which accompanies this chapter.

The model attempts to account for the interrelationships among (1) certain

---

[24] J. Richard Hackman, Greg Oldham, Robert Janson, and Kenneth Purdy, "New Strategy for Job Enrichment," *California Management Review,* Summer 1975, pp. 57–71; and Hackman and Oldham, "Development of the Job Diagnostic Survey."

FIGURE 12–3

The Job Characteristics Model

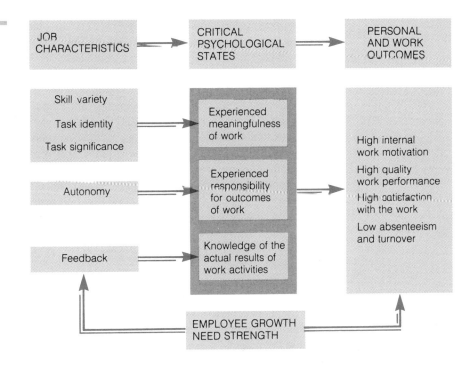

Source: J. Richard Hackman and Greg R. Oldham, "Development of the Job Diagnostic Survey," *Journal of Applied Psychology* 60(1975): 159–170.

job characteristics; (2) psychological states associated with motivation, satisfaction, and performance; (3) job outcomes; and (4) growth-need strength. Figure 12–3 describes the relationships among these variables. The core dimensions of the job consist of characteristics first described by Turner and Lawrence.[25] According to this model, although variety, identity, significance, autonomy, and feedback do not completely describe job content, they sufficiently describe those aspects of job content that management can manipulate to bring about gains in productivity.

The steps management can take to increase the core dimensions of the job include combining task elements, assigning whole pieces of work (i.e., work modules), allowing discretion in the selection of work methods, and permitting self-paced control. These actions increase task variety, identity, and significance. Consequently, they increase the "experienced meaningfulness of work." Permitting employee participation and self-evaluation and creating autonomous work groups increases the feedback and autonomy dimensions along with the psychological states "experienced responsibility" and "knowledge of actual results."

The positive benefits of these redesign efforts are moderated by individual differences in the strength of employees' growth needs. That is, employees with strong need for accomplishment, learning, and challenge will respond

---

[25] Turner and Lawrence, *Industrial Jobs.*

more positively than employees with relatively weak growth needs. In other, more familiar, terms, employees who have high need for self-esteem and self-actualization are the more likely candidates for job redesign. If employees who lack either the need strength or the ability to perform redesigned jobs are forced to participate in job redesign programs, they may experience stress, anxiety, adjustment problems, erratic performance, turnover, and absenteeism.

The available research is meager on the interrelationships among individual differences, job content, and performance. It is apparent, however, that managers must cope with significant problems in matching employee needs and differences with organizational needs.[26] The difficulty of doing this is indicated by the finding of one study that, of the 125 firms surveyed, only five had made any efforts to redesign jobs.[27]

REDESIGNING WORK SCHEDULES

What a person does in a particular job and *how* the job gets done are not the only aspects of jobs that have received interest. *When* the job is done, or the *work schedule,* also has drawn the attention of managers and organizational researchers. In recent years, two related innovations in work scheduling have been applied in organizations. First, there has been a move to shorten the workweek (i.e., fewer days per week and/or fewer hours per day). Called the *modified workweek,* the most common variation is four 10-hour days, often designated as the 4/40.

The second is discretionary working time or staggered or flexible working hours. *Flexitime,* also known as gliding time, is extremely popular.[28] It allows employees to choose when they come to work and leave work, within constraints set by management. Flexitime schedules attempt to shift some control over working time to the employee. These schedules give some autonomy, self-management, and decision making to employees, thus increasing job depth.

In the following few paragraphs, we will focus on one of these work scheduling variations, the modified workweek, briefly describing it and offering a critique of its advantages and disadvantages.

DESCRIPTION OF THE MODIFIED WORKWEEK

The 4/40 (there are also the 3/36 and the 4/32) is a regular full-time workweek of 40 hours that are worked in four 10-hour days instead of five 8-hour days. Four-day and other compressed workweeks began to be used in the United States around 1970.

[26] William E. Zierden, "Congruence in the Work Situation: Effects of Growth Needs, Management Style, and Job Structure on Job-Related Satisfactions," *Journal of Occupational Behavior,* October 1980, pp. 297–310.

[27] Fred Luthans and W. E. Reif, "Job Enrichment: Long on Theory, Short on Practice," *Organizational Dynamics,* Fall 1974, pp. 30–43.

[28] David Ralston, William Anthony, and David Gustafson, "Employees May Love Flextime, But What Does It Do to the Organization's Productivity?" *Journal of Applied Psychology,* May 1985, pp. 272–79.

The 4/40 plan provides the employee with long weekends throughout the year. The incentive for the 4/40 is the belief that the system will lead to increased productivity. The employee will benefit from increased leisure time and from more freedom to pursue personal business, a family life, and educational objectives.

Modified workweeks are suitable for some situations. They can help businesses that have costly start-ups and shutdowns, unutilized capital equipment, and long travel time to job sites. For example, police departments could use three 10-hour shifts per day to get 6 hours of double staffing during high-crime night hours. Road construction crews could go out for four days for 10 hours at a time to cut down the number of trips made to work sites. Computer operators could use two 12-hour shifts, each working three consecutive days, to get round-the-clock utilization on Monday through Saturday.

A BRIEF CRITIQUE OF THE MODIFIED WORKWEEK

For workers, the four-day workweek yields two clear advantages: a three-day weekend and one less commuting trip per week. There are problems in providing customer service and covering necessary duties on the fifth day that limit 4/40 applications to only some jobs. There are also problems associated with a longer day—fatigue, higher accident-proneness, less time for evening meetings during the week.

The results of research on the modified workweek are mixed. There seem to be short-run improvements in need satisfaction and absenteeism. Even such short-run improvements, of course, are welcomed by any organization. However, are these enough to change a system from a 5/40 to a 4/40? Each organization must answer this question for itself.

Despite the mixed research results on the 4/40, a renewed energy crunch or a stronger move to energy conservation could make the modified workweek more popular during the remainder of the 1980s and into the 1990s. In addition, if laws eventually are passed that do not force an employer to pay employees an overtime premium for all hours worked beyond eight in a day, the 4/40 may be used in more organizations.

The following OBM Encounter summarizes an application of the modified workweek.

ENCOUNTER

THE MODIFIED WORKWEEK AT MEREDITH CORPORATION

At the Meredith Corporation's printing plant in Des Moines, Iowa, four-day weekends are no longer a fantasy, but a reality. Under the terms of a collective agreement reached between labor and management, printing plant employees work three 12-hour days for a 36-hour week. Several factors entered into the decision to give the 3/36 a try. One was the need to keep printing presses operating as continuously as possible. High-speed presses require high capital expenditures and, consequently, five-day workweeks could not be justified.

To meet these needs, a fourth crew was assigned where there previously had been only three. The company also created two 12-hour shifts to allow continuous press operation six days a week. One crew works each shift Monday through Thursday, while the other two

Source: Based on an item appearing in *Management Review,* January 1981, p. 31.

crews work the Thursday-through-Saturday shifts. When necessary, Sunday work is divided between the shifts. Personnel policies have been adjusted so that earnings and benefits are not affected by the shorter workweek.

The 3/36 arrangement has had a positive effect on recruitment. The new system also has eliminated excessive overtime demands and yielded an increase in productivity. Based on the results in the printing plant area, the company intends to extend the system to other capital-intensive operations where there is sufficient volume to support it.

Since a primary source of organizational effectiveness is job performance, managers should design jobs according to the best-available knowledge. At present, the strategies for designing and redesigning jobs and modifying work schedules have evolved from scientific management approaches to programs that emphasize issues related to quality of work life. Job enlargement and job enrichment are important, but often incomplete, strategies. The same may be said for work rescheduling plans. Strategies that take into account individual differences probably have the greatest probability of success, assuming compatible environmental, situational, and management conditions. Managers who are proficient in diagnosing their own people and organizations to determine the applicability of specific approaches will find the greatest degree of success.

SUMMARY OF KEYPOINTS

A. Job design involves managerial decisions and actions that specify objective job depth, range, and relationships to satisfy organizational requirements as well as the social and personal requirements of jobholders.

B. Contemporary managers must consider the issue of quality of work life when designing jobs. This issue reflects society's concern for work experiences that contribute to the personal growth and development of employees.

C. Strategies for increasing the potential of jobs to satisfy the social and personal requirements of jobholders have gone through an evolutionary process. The initial efforts were directed toward job rotation and job enlargement. These strategies produced some gains in job satisfaction but did not change primary motivators such as responsibility, achievement, and autonomy.

D. During the 1960s, job enrichment became a widely recognized strategy for improving quality of work-life factors. This strategy, based on Herzberg's motivation theory, involves increasing the *depth* of jobs through greater delegation of authority to jobholders. Despite some major successes, job enrichment is not universally applicable because it does not consider individual differences.

E. Individual differences now are recognized as crucial variables to consider when designing jobs. Experience, cognitive complexity, needs, values, and perceptions of equity are some of the individual differences that influence the reactions of jobholders to the scope and relationships of their jobs. When individual differences are combined with environmental, situational, and managerial differences, job design decisions become increasingly complex.

F. The most recently developed strategy of job design emphasizes the importance of core job characteristics as perceived by jobholders. Although measurements of individual differences remain a problem, managers should be encouraged to examine ways to increase positive perceptions of variety, identity, significance, autonomy, and feedback. Doing so increases the potential for high-quality work performance and high job satisfaction, given that jobholders possess relatively high growth need strength.

G. Alternative work schedules represent a new approach to improve quality of work life, and consequently, the motivational properties of jobs. Two approaches to work scheduling which have met with some success are the modified work week and flexitime.

REVIEW AND DISCUSSION QUESTIONS

1. Why is job analysis such an important part of any job design or redesign activity?

2. Do you think it is becoming easier or more difficult to design jobs in a way that enhances the quality of work life? Explain.

3. How does functional job analysis differ from the use of the Position Analysis Questionnaire? Which one provides the most information?

4. How might the range and depth of the following jobs be increased: automobile assembly worker, letter carrier, school bus driver, grocery store cashier?

5. Consider the course in which you are using this text as a "job." How would you describe this job in terms of the job characteristics in Table 12–1?

6. Is job enlargement or enrichment a good idea for all jobs? Why or why not?

7. In what ways might the modified workweek be used to satisfy the needs discussed in Chapter 4?

8. Are job rotation, enlargement, and enrichment strategies more compatible with mechanistic or organic designs? Explain.

9. "Job redesign is simply an attempt by management to get more out of an employee under the guise of improving the quality of work life." Do you agree or disagree with this statement? Explain.

10. From an organization's perspective, are some job performance outcomes more or less important than others? Is the same true from an individual employee's perspective?

R1 A NEW STRATEGY FOR JOB ENRICHMENT

J. RICHARD HACKMAN, GREG OLDHAN, ROBERT JANSON, AND KENNETH PURDY

. . . We present here a new strategy for going about the redesign of work. The strategy is based on three years of collaborative work and cross-fertilization among the authors—two of whom are academic researchers and two of whom are active practitioners in job enrichment. Our approach is new, but it has been tested in many organizations. It draws on the contributions of both management practice and psychological theory, but it is firmly in the middle ground between them. It builds on and complements previous work by Herzberg and others, but provides for

Source: *California Management Review,* Summer 1975, pp. 57–71.

the first time a set of tools for *diagnosing* existing jobs—and a map for translating the diagnostic results into specific action steps for change.

What we have, then, is the following:

1. A theory that specifies when people will get personally "turned on" to their work. The theory shows what kinds of jobs are most likely to generate excitement and commitment about work, and what kinds of employees it works best for.

2. A set of action steps for job enrichment based on the theory, which prescribe in concrete terms what to do to make jobs more motivating for the people who do them.

3. Evidence that the theory holds water and that it can be used to bring about measurable—and sometimes dramatic—improvements in employee work

behavior, in job satisfaction, and in the financial performance of the organizational unit involved.

THE THEORY BEHIND THE STRATEGY

What makes people get turned on to their work?

For workers who are really prospering in their jobs, work is likely to be a lot like play. Consider, for example, a golfer at a driving range, practicing to get rid of a hook. His activity is *meaningful* to him; he has chosen to do it because he gets a "kick" from testing his skills by playing the game. He knows that he alone is *responsible* for what happens when he hits the ball. And he has *knowledge of the results* within a few seconds.

Behavioral scientists have found that the three "psychological states" experienced by the golfer

FIGURE 1

Relationships Among Core Job Dimensions, Critical Psychological States, and On-The-Job Outcomes

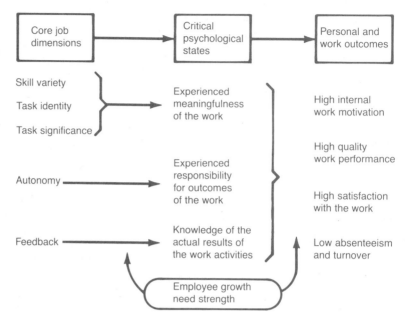

in the above example also are critical in determining a person's motivation and satisfaction on the job.

Experienced meaningfulness. The individual must perceive his work as worthwhile or important by some system of values he accepts.

Experienced responsibility. He must believe that he personally is accountable for the outcomes of his efforts.

Knowledge of results. He must be able to determine, on some fairly regular basis, whether or not the outcomes of his work are satisfactory.

When these three conditions are present, a person tends to feel very good about himself when he performs well. And those good feelings will prompt him to try to continue to do well—so he can continue to earn the positive feelings in the future. That is what is meant by "internal motivation"—being turned on to one's work because of the

positive internal feelings that are generated by doing well, rather than being dependent on external factors (such as incentive pay or compliments from the boss) for the motivation to work effectively.

What if one of the three psychological states is missing? Motivation drops markedly. Suppose, for example, that our golfer has settled in at the driving range to practice for a couple of hours. Suddenly a fog drifts in over the range. He can no longer see if the ball starts to tail off to the left a hundred yards out. The satisfaction he got from hitting straight down the middle—and the motivation to try to correct something whenever he didn't—are both gone. If the fog stays, it's likely that he soon will be packing up his clubs.

The relationship between the three psychological states and on-the-job outcomes is illustrated in Figure 1. When all three are high, then internal work motivation, job satisfaction, and work quality are high, and absenteeism and turnover are low.

What job characteristics make it happen?

Recent research has identified five "core" characteristics of jobs that elicit the psychological states described above.[1-3] These five core job dimensions provide the key to objectively measuring jobs and to changing them so that they have high potential for motivating people who do them.

Toward meaningful work.
Three of the five core dimensions

[1] A. N. Turner and P. R. Lawrence. *Industrial Jobs and the Worker* (Cambridge, Mass.: Harvard Graduate School of Business Administration, 1965).

[2] J. R. Hackman and E. E. Lawler, "Employee Reactions to Job Characteristics," *Journal of Applied Psychology Monograph,* 1971, pp. 259–286.

[3] J. R. Hackman and G. R. Oldham. *Motivation Through the Design of Work: Test of a Theory,* Technical Report No. 6. (New Haven, Conn.; Department of Administrative Sciences, Yale University, 1974).

contribute to a job's meaningfulness for the worker:

1. **Skill variety.** The degree to which a job requires the worker to perform activities that challenge his skills and abilities. When even a single skill is involved, there is at least a seed of potential meaningfulness. When several are involved, the job has the potential of appealing to more of the whole person, and also of avoiding the monotony of performing the same task repeatedly, no matter how much skill it may require.

2. **Task identity.** The degree to which the job requires completion of a "whole" and identifiable piece of work—doing a job from beginning to end with a visible outcome. For example, it is clearly more meaningful to an employee to build complete toasters than to attach electrical cord after electrical cord, especially if he never sees a completed toaster. (Note that the whole job, in this example, probably would involve greater skill variety as well as task identity.)

3. **Task significance.** The degree to which the job has a substantial and perceivable impact on the lives of other people, whether in the immediate organization or the world at large. The worker who tightens nuts on aircraft brake assemblies is more likely to perceive his work as significant than the worker who fills small boxes with paper clips—even though the skill levels involved may be comparable.

Each of these three jobs dimensions represents an important route to experienced meaningfulness. If the job is high in all three, the worker is quite likely to experience his job as very meaningful. It is not necessary, however, for a job to be very high in all three dimensions. If the job is low in any one of them, there will be a drop in overall experienced meaningfulness. But even when two dimensions are low the worker may find the job meaningful if the third is high enough.

Toward personal responsibility. A fourth core dimension leads a worker to experience increased responsibility in his job. This is *autonomy,* the degree to which the job gives the worker freedom, independence, and discretion in scheduling work and determining how he will carry it out. People in highly autonomous jobs know that they are personally responsible for successes and failures. To the extent that their autonomy is high, then, how the work goes will be felt to depend more on the individual's own efforts and initiatives—rather than on detailed instructions from the boss or from a manual of job procedures.

Toward knowledge of results. The fifth and last core dimension is *feedback.* This is the degree to which a worker, in carrying out the work activities required by the job, gets information about the effectiveness of his efforts. Feedback is most powerful when it comes directly from the work itself—for example, when a worker has the responsibility for gauging and otherwise checking a component he has just finished, and learns in the process that he has lowered his reject rate by meeting specifications more consistently.

The overall "motivating potential" of a job. Figure 1 shows how the five core dimensions combine to affect the psychological states that are critical in determining whether or not an employee will be internally moti-

vated to work effectively. Indeed, when using an instrument to be described later, it is possible to compute a "motivating potential score" (MPS) for any job. The MPS provides a single summary index of the degree to which the objective characteristics of the job will prompt high internal work motivation. Following the theory outlined above, a job high in motivating potential must be high in at least one (and hopefully more) of the three dimensions that lead to experienced meaningfulness and high in both autonomy and feedback as well. The MPS provides a quantitative index of the degree to which this is in fact the case (see Appendix for detailed formula). As will be seen later, the MPS can be very useful in diagnosing jobs and in assessing the effectiveness of job-enrichment activities.

Does the theory work for everybody?

Unfortunately not. Not everyone is able to become internally motivated in his work, even when the motivating potential of a job is very high indeed.

Research has shown that the *psychological needs* of people are very important in determining who can (and who cannot) become internally motivated at work. Some people have strong needs for personal accomplishment, for learning and developing themselves beyond where they are now, for being stimulated and challenged, and so on. These people are high in "growth-need strength."

Figure 2 shows diagrammatically the proposition that individual growth needs have the power to moderate the relationship between the characteristics of jobs and work outcomes. Many workers with high growth needs will turn on eagerly when they have jobs that are high

FIGURE 2

The Moderating Effect of Employee Growth-Need Strength.

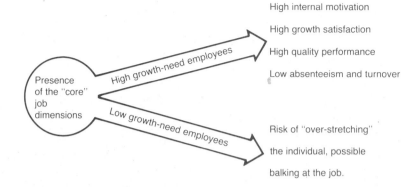

Presence of the "core" job dimensions

High growth-need employees
→ High internal motivation
High growth satisfaction
High quality performance
Low absenteeism and turnover

Low growth-need employees
→ Risk of "over-stretching" the individual, possible balking at the job.

in the core dimensions. Workers whose growth needs are not so strong may respond less eagerly—or, at first, even balk at being "pushed" or "stretched" too far.

Psychologists who emphasize human potential argue that everyone has within him at least a spark of the need to grow and develop personally. Steadily accumulating evidence shows, however, that unless that spark is pretty strong, chances are it will get snuffed out by one's experiences in typical organizations. So, a person who has worked for 20 years in stulifying jobs may find it difficult or impossible to become internally motivated overnight when given the opportunity.

We should be cautious, however, about creating rigid categories of people based on their measured growth-need strength at any particular time. It is true that we can predict from these measures who is likely to become internally motivated on a job and who will be less willing or able to do so. But what we do not know yet is whether or not the growth-need "spark" can be rekindled for those individuals who have had their growth needs dampened, by years of growth-depressing experience in their organizations.

Since it is often the organization that is responsible for currently low

levels of growth desires, we believe that the organization also should provide the individual with the chance to reverse that trend whenever possible, even if that means putting a person in a job where he may be "stretched" more than he wants to be. He can always move back later to the old job—and in the meantime the embers of his growth needs just might burst back into flame, to his surprise and pleasure, and for the good of the organization.

LEARNING CHECKPOINT

Compare this theory of motivation to work to Herzberg's theory of motivation to work. What are the similarities? differences?

FROM THEORY TO PRACTICE: A TECHNOLOGY FOR JOB ENRICHMENT

When job enrichment fails, it often fails because of inadequate *diagnosis* of the target job and employees' reactions to it. Often, for example, job enrichment is assumed by management to be a solution to "people problems" on the job and is implemented even though there has been no diagnostic activity to indicate that the root of the problem is in fact how the work is designed.

At other times, some diagnosis is made—but it provides no concrete guidance about what specific aspects of the job require change. In either case, the success of job enrichment may wind up depending more on the quality of the intuition of the change agent—or his luck—than on a solid base of data about the people and the work.

In the paragraphs to follow, we outline a new technology for use in job enrichment which explicitly addresses the diagnostic as well as the action components of the change process. The technology has two parts: (1) a set of diagnostic tools that are useful in evaluating jobs and people's reactions to them prior to change—and in pinpointing exactly what aspects of specific jobs are most critical to a successful change attempt: and (2) a set of "implementing concepts" that provide concrete guidance for action steps in job enrichment. The implementing concepts are tied directly to the diagnostic tools; the output of the diagnostic activity specifies which action steps are likely to have the most impact in a particular situation.

The diagnostic tools

Central to the diagnostic procedure we propose is a package of instruments to be used by employees, supervisors, and outside observers in assessing the target job and employees' reactions to it [4] These instruments gauge the following:

1. The objective characteristics of the jobs themselves, including both an overall indication of the "motivating potential" of the job as it exists (that is, the MPS score) and the score of the job on each of the five core dimensions described previously. Because knowing the strengths and weaknesses of the job is critical to any work-redesign effort, assessments of the job are made by supervisors and outside observers as well as the employees themselves—and the final assessment of a job uses data from all three sources.

2. The current levels of motivation, satisfaction, and work performance of employees on the job. In addition to satisfaction with the work itself, measures are taken of how people feel about other aspects of the work setting, such as pay, supervision, and relationships with co-workers.

3. The level of growth-need strength of the employees. As indicated earlier, employees who have strong growth needs are more likely to be more responsive to job enrichment than employees with weak growth needs. Therefore, it is important to know at the outset just what kinds of satisfactions the people who do the job are (and are not) motivated to obtain from their work. This will make it possible to identify which persons are best to start

changes with, and which may need help in adapting to the newly enriched job.

What, then, might be the actual steps one would take in carrying out a job diagnosis using these tools? Although the approach to any particular diagnosis depends upon the specifics of the particular work situation involved, the sequence of questions listed below is fairly typical.

Step 1. Are motivation and satisfaction central to the problem?

Sometimes organizations undertake job enrichment to improve the work motivation and satisfaction of employees when in fact the real problem with work performance lies elsewhere—for example, in a poorly designed production system, in an error-prone computer, and so on. The first step is to examine the scores of employees on the motivation and satisfaction portions of the diagnostic instrument. (The questionnaire taken by employees is called the Job Diagnostic Survey and will be referred to hereafter as the JDS.) If motivation and satisfaction are problematic, the change agent would continue to Step 2; if not, he would look to other aspects of the work situation to identify the real problem.

Step 2. Is the job low in motivating potential?

To answer this question, one would examine the motivating potential score of the target job and compare it to the MPS's of other jobs to determine whether or not *the job itself* is a probable cause of the motivational problems documented in Step 1. If the job turns out to be low on the MPS, one would continue to Step 3; if it scores high,

attention should be given to other possible reasons for the motivational difficulties (such as the pay system, the nature of supervision, and so on).

Step 3. What specific aspects of the job are causing the difficulty?

This step involves examining the job on each of the five core dimensions to pinpoint the specific strengths and weaknesses of the job as it is currently structured. It is useful at this stage to construct a "profile" of the target job, to make visually apparent where improvements need to be made. An illustrative profile for two jobs (one "good" job and one job needing improvement) is shown in Figure 3.

Job A is an engineering maintenance job and is high on all of the core dimensions; the MPS of this job is a very high 260. (MPS scores can range from 1 to about 350; an "average" score would be about 125.) Job enrichment would not be recommended for this job; if employees working on the job were unproductive and unhappy, the reasons are likely to have little to do with the nature or design of the work itself.

Job B, on the other hand, has many problems. This job involves the routine and repetitive processing of checks in the "back room" of a bank. The MPS is 30, which is quite low—and indeed, would be even lower if it were not for the moderately high task significance of the job. (Task significance is moderately high because the people are handling large amounts of other people's money, and therefore the quality of their efforts potentially has important consequences for their unseen clients.) The job provides the individuals with very little direct feedback

[4] J. R. Hackman and G. R. Oldham, "Development of the Job Diagnostic Survey," *Journal of Applied Psychology,* 1975, pp. 159–70.

FIGURE 3

The JDS Diagnostic Profile for a "Good" and a "Bad" Job

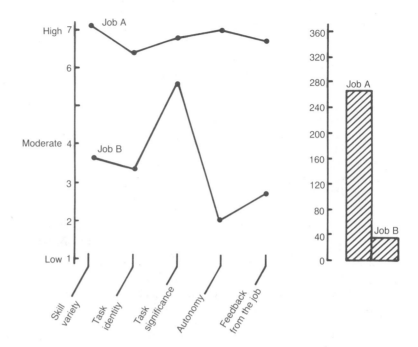

about how effectively they are doing it; the employees have little autonomy in how they go about doing the job; and the job is moderately low in both skill variety and task identity.

For Job B, then, there is plenty of room for improvement—and many avenues to examine in planning job changes. For still other jobs, the avenues for change often turn out to be considerably more specific: for example, feedback and autonomy may be reasonably high, but one or more of the core dimensions that contribute to the experienced meaningfulness of the job (skill variety, task identity, and task significance) may be low. In such a case, attention would turn to ways to increase the standing of the job on these latter three dimensions.

Step 4. How "ready" are the employees for change?

Once it has been documented that there is need for improvement in the job—and the particularly trou-

blesome aspects of the job have been identified then it is time to begin to think about the specific action steps which will be taken to enrich the job. An important factor in such planning is the level of growth needs of the employees, since employees high on growth needs usually respond more readily to job enrichment than do employees with little need for growth. The JDS provides a direct measure of the growth-need strength of the employees. This measure can be very helpful in planning how to introduce the changes to the people (for instance, cautiously versus dramatically), and in deciding who should be among the first group of employees to have their jobs changed.

In actual use of the diagnostic package, additional information is generated which supplements and expands the basic diagnostic questions outlined above. The point of the above discussion is merely to indicate the kinds of questions which we believe to be most impor-

tant in diagnosing a job prior to changing it. We now turn to how the diagnostic conclusions are translated into specific job changes.

The Implementing Concepts

Five "implementing concepts" for job enrichment are identified and discussed below.[5] Each one is a specific action step aimed at improving both the quality of the working experience for the individual and his work productivity. They are: (1) forming natural work units; (2) combining tasks; (3) establishing client relationships; (4) vertical loading; (5) opening feedback channels.

The links between the implementing concepts and the core dimensions are shown in Figure 4—which illustrates our theory of job

[5] R. W. Walters and Associates. *Job Enrichment for Results* (Cambridge, Mass.: Addison-Wesley Publishing Co., Inc., 1975).

FIGURE 4

The Full Model: How Use of the Implementing Concepts Can Lead to Positive Outcomes

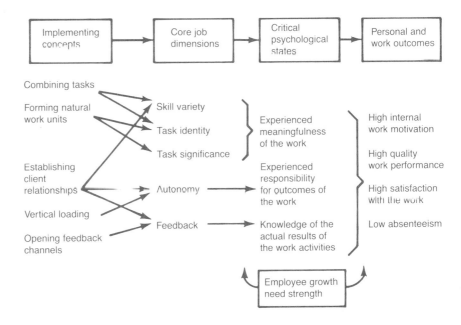

enrichment, ranging from the concrete action steps through the core dimensions and the psychological states to the actual personal and work outcomes.

After completing the diagnosis of a job, a change agent would know which of the core dimensions were most in need of remedial attention. He could then turn to Figure 4 and select those implementing concepts that specifically deal with the most troublesome parts of the existing job. How this would take place in practice will be seen below.

Forming natural work units.
The notion of distributing work in some logical way may seem to be an obvious part of the design of any job. In many cases, however, the logic is one imposed by just about any consideration except jobholder satisfaction and motivation. Such considerations include technological dictates, level of worker training or experience, "efficiency" as defined by industrial engineering, and current workload. In many cases the cluster of tasks a worker faces during a typical day

or week is natural to anyone *but* the worker.

For example, suppose that a typing pool (consisting of one supervisor and ten typists) handles all work for one division of a company. Jobs are delivered in rough draft or dictated form to the supervisor, who distributes them as evenly as possible among the typists. In such circumstances the individual letters, reports, and other tasks performed by a given typist in one day or week are randomly assigned. There is no basis for identifying with the work or the person or department for whom it is performed, or for placing any personal value upon it.

The principle underlying natural units of work, by contrast, is "ownership"—a worker's sense of continuing responsibility for an identifiable body of work. Two steps are involved in creating natural work units. The first is to identify the basic work items. In the typing pool, for example, the items might be "pages to be typed." The second step is to group the items in natural categories. For example, each typ-

ist might be assigned continuing responsibility for all jobs requested by one or several specific departments. The assignments should be made, of course, in such a way that workloads are about equal in the long run. (For example, one typist might end up with all the work from one busy department, while another handles jobs from several smaller units.)

At this point we can begin to see specifically how the job-design principles relate to the core dimensions (cf., Figure 4). The ownership fostered by natural units of work can make the difference between a feeling that work is meaningful and rewarding and the feeling that it is irrelevant and boring. As the diagram shows, natural units of work are directly related to two of the core dimensions: task identity and task significance.

A typist whose work is assigned naturally rather than randomly—say, by departments—has a much greater chance of performing a whole job to completion. Instead of typing one section of a large report, the individual is likely to type the whole thing, with knowledge of exactly what the product of the work is (task identity). Furthermore, over time the typist will develop a growing sense of how the work affects co-workers in the department serviced (task significance).

Combining tasks. The very existence of a pool made up entirely of persons whose sole function is typing reflects a fractionalization of jobs that has been a basic precept of "scientific management." Most obvious in assembly-line work, fractionalization has been applied to nonmanufacturing jobs as well. It is typically justified by efficiency, which is usually defined in terms of either low costs or some time-and-motion type of criteria.

It is hard to find fault with measuring efficiency ultimately in terms of cost-effectiveness. In doing so, however, a manager should be sure to consider *all* the costs involved. It is possible, for example, for highly fractionalized jobs to meet all the time-and-motion criteria of efficiency, but if the resulting job is so unrewarding that performing it day after day leads to high turnover, absenteeism, drugs and alcohol, and strikes, then productivity is really lower (and costs higher) than data on efficiency might indicate.

The principle of combining tasks, then, suggests that whenever possible existing and fractionalized tasks should be put together to form new and larger modules of work. At the Medfield, Massachusetts plant of Corning Glass Works the assembly of a laboratory hot plate has been redesigned along the lines suggested here. Each hot plate now is assembled from start to finish by one operator, instead of going through several separate operations that are performed by different people.

Some tasks, if combined into a meaningfully large module of work, would be more than an individual could do by himself. In such cases, it is often useful to consider assigning the new larger task to a small *team* of workers—who are given great autonomy for its completion. At the Racine, Wisconsin plant of Emerson Electric, the assembly process for trash disposal appliances was restructured this way. Instead of a sequence of moving the appliance from station to station, the assembly now is done from start to finish by one team. Such teams include both men and women to permit switching off the heavier and more delicate aspects of the work. The team responsible is identified on the appliance. In case of customer complaints, the team often drafts the reply.

As a job-design principle, task combination, like natural units of work, expands the task identity of the job. For example, the hot-plate assembler can see and identify with a finished product ready for shipment, rather than a nearly invisible junction of solder. Moreover, the more tasks that are combined into a single worker's job, the greater the variety of skills he must call on in performing the job. So task combination also leads directly to greater skill variety—the third core dimension that contributes to the overall experienced meaningfulness of the work.

LEARNING CHECKPOINT

Explain how combining jobs into natural work units, or teams, applies some of the ideas of group development.

Establishing client relationships. One consequence of fractionalization is that the typical worker has little or no contact with (or even awareness of) the ultimate user of his product or service. By encouraging and enabling employees to establish direct relationships with the clients of their work, improvements often can be realized simultaneously on three of the core dimensions. Feedback increases, because of additional opportunities for the individual to receive praise or criticism of his work outputs directly. Skill variety often increases, because of the necessity to develop and exercise one's interpersonal skills in maintaining the client relationship. And autonomy can increase because the individual often is given personal responsibility for deciding how to manage his relationships with the clients of his work.

Creating client relationships is a three-step process. First, the client must be identified. Second, the most direct contact possible between the worker and the client must be established. Third, criteria must be set up by which the client can judge the quality of the product or service he receives. And whenever possible, the client should have a means of relaying his judgments directly back to the worker.

The contact between worker and client should be as great as possible and as frequent as necessary. Face-to-face contact is highly desirable, at least occasionally. Where that is impossible or impractical, telephone and mail can suffice. In any case, it is important that the performance criteria by which the worker will be rated by the client must be mutually understood and agreed upon.

Vertical loading. Typically the split between the "doing" of a job and the "planning" and "controlling" of the work has evolved along with horizontal fractionalization. Its rationale, once again, has been "efficiency through specialization." And once again, the excess of specialization that has emerged has resulted in unexpected but significant costs in motivation, morale, and work quality. In vertical loading, the intent is to partially close the gap between the doing and the controlling parts of the job—and thereby reap some important motivational advantages.

Of all the job-design principles, vertical loading may be the single most crucial one. In some cases, where it has been impossible to implement any other changes, vertical loading alone has had significant motivational effects.

When a job is vertically loaded, responsibilities and controls that formerly were reserved for high levels of management are added to the job. There are many ways to accomplish this:

- Return to the job holder greater discretion in setting schedules, deciding on work methods, checking on quality, and advising or helping to train less experienced workers.
- Grant additional authority. The objective should be to advance workers from a position of no authority or highly restricted authority to positions of reviewed, and eventually, near-total authority for his own work.
- Time management. The job holder should have the greatest possible freedom to decide when to start and stop work, when to break, and how to assign priorities.
- Troubleshooting and crisis decisions. Workers should be encouraged to seek problem solutions on their own, rather than calling immediately for the supervisor.
- Financial controls. Some degree of knowledge and control over budgets and other financial aspects of a job can often be highly motivating. However, access to

this information frequently tends to be restricted. Workers can benefit from knowing something about the costs of their jobs, the potential effect upon profit, and various financial and budgetary alternatives.

When a job is vertically loaded it will inevitably increase in *autonomy*. And as shown in Figure 4, this increase in objective personal control over the work will also lead to an increased feeling of personal responsibility for the work, and ultimately to higher internal work motivation.

- Opening feedback channels. In virtually all jobs there are ways to open channels of feedback to individuals or teams to help them learn whether their performance is improving, deteriorating, or remaining at a constant level. While there are numerous channels through which information about performance can be provided, it generally is better for a worker to learn about his performance *directly as he does his job*—rather than from management on an occasional basis.

Job-provided feedback usually is more immediate and private than supervisor-supplied feedback, and it increases the worker's feelings of personal control over his work in the bargain. Moreover, it avoids many of the potentially disruptive interpersonal problems that can develop when the only way a worker has to find out how he is doing is through direct messages or subtle cues from the boss.

Exactly what should be done to open channels for job-provided feedback will vary from job to job and organization to organization. Yet in many cases the changes involve simply removing existing blocks that isolate the worker from

naturally occurring data about performance—rather than generating entirely new feedback mechanisms. For example:

- Establishing direct client relationships often removes blocks between the worker and natural external sources of data about his work.
- Quality-control efforts in many organizations often eliminate a natural source of feedback. The quality check on a product or service is done by persons other than those responsible for the work. Feedback to the workers—if there is any—is belated and diluted. It often fosters a tendency to think of quality as "someone else's concern." By placing quality control close to the worker (perhaps even in his own hands), the quantity and quality of data about performance available to him can dramatically increase.
- Tradition and established procedure in many organizations dictate that records about performance be kept by a supervisor and transmitted up (not down) in the organizational hierarchy. Sometimes supervisors even check the work and correct any errors themselves. The worker who made the error never knows it occurred—and is denied the very information that could enhance both his internal work motivation and the technical adequacy of his performance. In many cases it is possible to provide standard summaries of performance records directly to the worker (as well as to his superior), thereby giving him personally and regularly the data he needs to improve his performance.
- Computers and other automated operations sometimes can be used to provide the indi-

vidual with data now blocked from him. Many clerical operations, for example, are now performed on computer consoles. These consoles often can be programmed to provide the clerk with immediate feedback in the form of a CRT display or a printout indicating that an error has been made. Some systems even have been programmed to provide the operator with a positive feedback message when a period of error-free performance has been sustained.

Many organizations simply have not recognized the importance of feedback as a motivator. Data on quality and other aspects of performance are viewed as being of interest only to management. Worse still, the *standards* for acceptable performance often are kept from workers as well. As a result, workers who would be interested in following the daily or weekly ups and downs of their performance, and in trying accordingly to improve, are deprived of the very guidelines they need to do so. They are like the golfer we mentioned earlier, whose efforts to correct his hook are stopped dead by fog over the driving range.

THE STRATEGY IN ACTION: HOW WELL DOES IT WORK?

So far we have examined a basic theory of how people get turned on to their work; a set of core dimensions of jobs that create the conditions for such internal work motivation to develop on the job; and a set of five implementing concepts that are the action steps recommended to boost a job on the core dimensions and thereby increase employee motivation, satisfaction, and productivity.

The remaining question is straightforward and important: *Does it work?* In reality, that question is twofold. First, does the theory itself hold water, or are we barking up the wrong conceptual tree? And second, does the change strategy really lead to measurable differences when it is applied in an actual organizational setting?

This section summarizes the findings we have generated to date on these questions.

Is the job-enrichment theory correct?

In general, the answer seems to be yes. The JDS instrument has been taken by more than 1,000 employees working on about 100 diverse jobs in more than a dozen organizations over the last two years. These data have been analyzed to test the basic motivational theory—and especially the impact of the core job dimensions on worker motivation, satisfaction, and behavior on the job. An illustrative overview of some of the findings is given below.[6]

1. People who work on jobs high on the core dimensions are more motivated and satisfied than are people who work on jobs that score low on the dimensions. Employees with jobs high on the core dimensions (MPS scores greater than 240) were compared to those who held unmotivating jobs (MPS scores less than 40). As shown in Figure 5, employees with high MPS jobs were higher on (a) the three psychological states, (b) internal work motivation, (c) general satisfaction, and (d) "growth" satisfaction.

2. Figure 6 shows that the same is true for measures of actual behavior at work—absenteeism and performance effectiveness—although less strongly so for the performance measure.

3. Responses to jobs high in motivating potential are more positive for people who have strong growth needs than for people with weak needs for growth. In Figure 7 the linear relationship between the motivating potential of a job and employees' level of internal work motivation is shown, separately for people with high versus low growth needs as measured by the JDS. While both groups of employees show increases in internal motivation as MPS increases, the *rate* of increase is significantly greater for the group of employees who have strong needs for growth.

How does the change strategy work in practice?

The results summarized above suggest that both the theory and the diagnostic instrument work when used with real people in real organizations. In this section, we summarize a job-enrichment project conducted at The Travelers Insurance Companies, which illustrates how the change procedures themselves work in practice.

The Travelers project was designed with two purposes in mind. One was to achieve improvements in morale, productivity, and other indicators of employee well-being. The other was to test the general effectiveness of the strategy for job enrichment we have summarized in this article.

The work group chosen was a keypunching operation. The group's function was to transfer in-

[6] Hackman and Oldham, *Motivation.*

FIGURE 5

Employee Reactions to Jobs High and Low in Motivating Potential for Two Banks and a Steel Firm

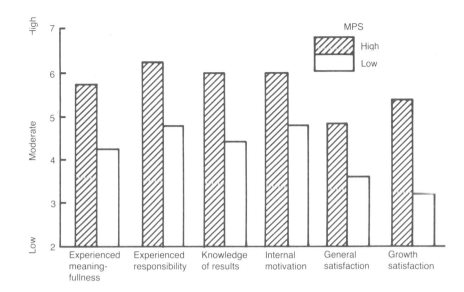

FIGURE 6

Absenteeism and Job Performance for Employees with Jobs High and Low in Motivating Potential

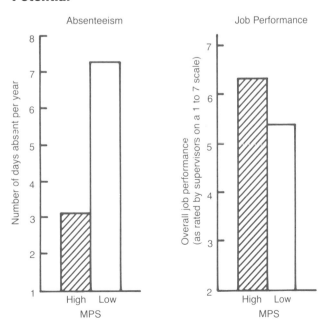

formation from printed or written documents onto punched cards for computer input. The work group consisted of 98 keypunch operators and verifiers (both in the same job classification), plus seven assignment clerks. All reported to a supervisor who, in turn, reported to the assistant manager and manager of the data-input division.

The size of individual punching orders varied considerably, from a few cards to as many as 2,500. Some work came to the work group with a specified delivery date, while other orders were to be given routine service on a predetermined schedule.

Assignment clerks received the jobs from the user departments. After reviewing the work for obvious errors, omissions, and legibility problems, the assignment clerk parceled out the work in batches expected to take about one hour. If the clerk found the work not suitable for punching it went to the supervisor, who either returned the work to the user department or cleared up problems by phone. When work went to operators for punching, it was with the instruc-

FIGURE 7

Relationship Between the Motivating Potential of a Job and the Internal Work Motivation of Employees (shown separately for employees with strong versus weak growth-need strength.)

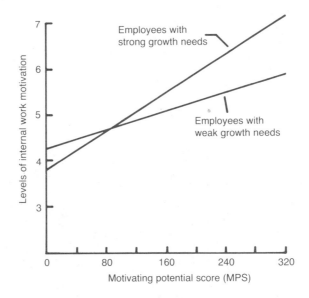

tion, "Punch only what you see. Don't correct errors, no matter how obvious they look."

Because of the high cost of computer time, keypunched work was 100 percent verified—a task that consumed nearly as many man-hours as the punching itself. Then the cards went to the supervisor, who screened the jobs for due dates before sending them to the computer. Errors detected in verification were assigned to various operators at random to be corrected.

The computer output from the cards was sent to the originating department, accompanied by a printout of errors. Eventually the printout went back to the supervisor for final correction.

A great many phenomena indicated that the problems being experienced in the work group might be the result of poor motivation. As the only person performing supervisory functions of any kind, the supervisor spent most of his time responding to crisis situations, which recurred continually. He also had to deal almost daily with employees' salary grievances or other complaints. Employees frequently

showed apathy or outright hostility toward their jobs.

Rates of work output, by accepted work-measurement standards, were inadequate. Error rates were high. Due dates and schedules frequently were missed. Absenteeism was higher than average, especially before and after weekends and holidays.

The single, rather unusual exception was turnover. It was lower than the company-wide average for similar jobs. The company has attributed this fact to a poor job market in the base period just before the project began, and to an older, relatively more settled work force—made up, incidentally, entirely of women.

The diagnosis

Using some of the tools and techniques we have outlined, a consulting team from the Management Services Department and from Roy W. Walters & Associates concluded that the keypunch-operator's job exhibited the following serious weaknesses in terms of the core dimensions.

Skill variety. There was

none. Only a single skill was involved—the ability to punch adequately the data on the batch of documents.

Task identity. Virtually nonexistent. Batches were assembled to provide an even workload, but not whole identifiable jobs.

Task significance. Not apparent. The keypunching operation was a necessary step in providing service to the company's customers. The individual operator was isolated by an assignment clerk and a supervisor from any knowledge of what the operation meant to the using department, let alone its meaning to the ultimate customer.

Autonomy. None. The operators had no freedom to arrange their daily tasks to meet schedules, to resolve problems with the using department, or even to correct, in punching, information that was obviously wrong.

Feedback. None. Once a batch was out of the operator's hands, she had no assured chance of seeing evidence of its quality or inadequacy.

Design of the experimental trial

Since the diagnosis indicated that the motivating potential of the job was extremely low, it was decided to attempt to improve the motivation and productivity of the work group through job enrichment. Moreover, it was possible to design an experimental test of the effects of the changes to be introduced: the results of changes made in the target work group were to be compared with trends in a control work group of similar size and demographic make-up. Since the control group was located more than a mile away, there appeared to be little risk of communication between members of the two groups.

A base period was defined before the start of the experimental trial period, and appropriate data were gathered on the productivity, absenteeism, and work attitudes of members of both groups. Data also were available on turnover; but since turnover was already below average in the target group, prospective changes in this measure were deemed insignificant.

An educational session was conducted with supervisors, at which they were given the theory and implementing concepts and actually helped to design the job changes themselves. Out of this session came an active plan consisting of about 25 change items that would significantly affect the design of the target jobs.

The implementing concepts and the changes

Because the job as it existed was rather uniformly low on the core job dimensions, all five of the implementing concepts were used in enriching it.

Natural units of work. The random batch assignment of work was replaced by assigning to each operator continuing responsibility for certain accounts—either particular departments or particular recurring jobs. Any work for those accounts now always goes to the same operator.

Task combination. Some planning and controlling functions were combined with the central task of keypunching. In this case, however, these additions can be more suitably discussed under the remaining three implementing concepts.

Client relationships. Each operator was given several channels of direct contact with clients. The operators, not their assignment clerks, now inspect their documents for correctness and legibility. When problems arise, the operator, not the supervisor, takes them up with the client.

Feedback. In addition to feedback from client contact, the operators were provided with a number of additional sources of data about their performance. The computer department now returns incorrect cards to the operators who punched them, and operators correct their own errors. Each operator also keeps her own file of copies of her errors. These can be reviewed to determine trends in error frequency and types of errors. Each operator receives weekly a computer printout of her errors and productivity, which is sent to her directly, rather than given to her by the supervisor.

Vertical loading. Besides consulting directly with clients about work questions, operators now have the authority to correct obvious coding errors on their own. Operators may set their own schedules and plan their daily work, as long as they meet schedules. Some competent operators have been given the option of not verifying their work and making their own program changes.

Results of the trial

The results were dramatic. The number of operators declined from 90 to 60. This occurred partly through attrition and partly through transfer to other departments. Some of the operators were promoted to higher-paying jobs in departments whose cards they had been handling—something that had never occurred before. Some details of the results are given below.

Quantity of work. The control group, with no job changes made, showed an increase in productivity of 8.1 percent during the trial period. The experimental group showed an increase of 39.6 percent.

Error rates. To assess work quality, error rates were recorded for about 40 operators in the experimental group. All were experienced, and all had been in their jobs before the job-enrichment program began. For two months before the study, these operators had a collective error rate of 1.53 percent. For two months toward the end of the study, the collective error rate was 0.99 percent. By the end of the study the number of operators with poor performance had dropped from 11.1 percent to 5.5 percent.

Absenteeism. The experimental group registered a 24.1 percent decline in absences. The control group, by contrast, showed a 29 percent *increase*.

Attitudes toward the job. An attitude survey given at the start of the project showed that the two groups scored about average, and nearly identically, in nine different areas of work satisfaction. At the end of the project the survey was repeated. The control group showed an insignificant 0.5 percent improvement, while the experimental group's overall satisfaction score rose 16.5 percent.

Selective elimination of controls. Demonstrated improvements in operator proficiency permitted them to work with fewer controls. Travelers estimates that the reduction of controls had the same effect as adding seven operators—a saving even beyond the effects of improved productivity and lowered absenteeism.

Role of the supervisor.
One of the most significant findings in the Travelers experiment was the effect of the changes on the supervisor's job, and thus on the rest of the organization. The operators took on many responsibilities that had been reserved at least to the unit leaders and sometimes to the supervisor. The unit leaders, in turn, assumed some of the day-to-day supervisory functions that had plagued the supervisor. Instead of spending his days supervising the behavior of subordinates and dealing with crises, he was able to devote time to developing feedback systems, setting up work modules and spearheading the enrichment effort—in other words, managing. It should be noted, however, that helping supervisors change their own work activities when their subordinates' jobs have been enriched is itself a challenging task. And if appropriate attention and help are not given to supervisors in such cases, they rapidly can become disaffected—and a job-enrichment "backlash" can result.[7]

[7] E. E. Lawler III; J. R. Hackman, and S. Kaufman, "Effects of Job Redesign: A Field Experiment." *Journal of Applied Social Psychology*, (1973), pp. 49–62.

LEARNING CHECKPOINT

What leadership theory is most applicable to situations in which job redesign is applied? Are changes in leadership behavior required in all instances of job redesign efforts?

SUMMARY

By applying work-measurement standards to the changes wrought by job enrichment—attitude and quality, absenteeism, and selective administration of controls—Travelers was able to estimate the total dollar impact of the project. Actual savings in salaries and machine rental charges during the first year totaled $64,305. Potential savings by further application of the changes were put at $91,937 annually. Thus, by almost any measure used—from the work attitudes of individual employees to dollar savings for the company as a whole—The Travelers test of the job-enrichment strategy proveda success.

CONCLUSIONS

In this article we have presented a new strategy for the redesign of work in general and for job enrichment in particular. The approach has four main characteristics:

1. It is grounded in a basic psychological theory of what motivates people in their work.
2. It emphasizes that planning for job changes should be done on the basis of *data* about the jobs and the people who do them—and a set of diagnostic instruments is provided to collect such data.
3. It provides a set of specific implementing concepts to guide actual job changes, as well as a set of theory-based rules for selecting *which* action steps are likely to be most beneficial in a given situation.

4. The strategy is buttressed by a set of findings showing that the theory holds water, that the diagnostic procedures are practical and informative, and that the implementing concepts can lead to changes that are beneficial both to organizations and to the people who work in them.

We believe that job enrichment is moving beyond the stage where it can be considered "yet another management fad." Instead, it represents a potentially powerful strategy for change that can help organizations achieve their goals for higher quality work—and at the same time further the equally legitimate needs of contemporary employees for a more meaningful work experience. Yet there are pressing questions about job enrichment and its use that remain to be answered.

Prominent among these is the question of employee participation in planning and implementing work redesign. The diagnostic tools and implementing concepts we have presented are neither designed nor intended for use only by management. Rather, our belief is that the effectiveness of job enrichment is likely to be enhanced when the tasks of diagnosing and changing jobs are undertaken *collaboratively* by management and by the employees whose work will be affected.

Moreover, the effects of work redesign on the broader organization remain generally uncharted. Evidence now is accumulating that when jobs are changed, turbulence can appear in the surrounding organization—for example, in supervisory-subordinate relationships, in pay and benefit plans, and so on. Such turbulence can be viewed by management either as a problem with job enrichment, or as an opportunity for further and broader organizational development by teams of managers and employees. To the degree that management takes the latter view, we believe, the oft-espoused goal of achieving basic organizational change through the redesign of work may come increasingly within reach.

The diagnostic tools and implementing concepts we have presented are useful in deciding on and designing basic changes in the jobs themselves. They do not address the broader issues of who plans the changes, how they are carried out, and how they are followed up. The way these broader questions are dealt with, we believe, may determine whether job enrichment will grow up—or whether it will die an early and unfortunate death, like so many other fledgling behavioral-science approaches to organizational change.

APPENDIX

For the algebraically inclined, the Motivating Potential Score is computed as follows:

$$MPS = \left[\frac{\text{Skill variety} + \text{Task identity} + \text{Task significance}}{3}\right] \times \text{Autonomy} \times \text{Feedback}$$

It should be noted that in some cases the MPS score can be *too* high for positive job satisfaction and effective performance—in effect overstimulating the person who holds the job. This paper focuses on jobs which are toward the low end of the scale—and which potentially can be improved through job enrichment.

Acknowledgements. The authors acknowledge with great appreciation the editorial assistance of John Hickey in the preparation of this paper, and the help of Kenneth Brousseau, Daniel Feldman, and Linda Frank in collecting the data that are summarized here. The research activities reported were supported in part by the Organizational Effectiveness Research Program of the Office of Naval Research, and the Manpower Administration of the U.S. Department of Labor, both through contracts to Yale University. □

R² DESIGNING MANAGERIAL AND PROFESSIONAL WORK FOR HIGH PERFORMANCE: A SOCIOTECHNICAL APPROACH*

CALVIN H. P. PAVA

Improving the performance of managers and professionals is emerging as a cardinal concern for the eighties. Yet ideas about how to improve the performance of "knowledge work" are scanty, and there are few systematic methods by which to analyze or redesign the way managerial and professional work is organized. Against this paucity stands a rich heritage of work-design methods developed in the factory. Foremost among these is sociotechnical design, which, since its inception in the 1950s, has become a powerful means for designing high-performance organizations.[1]

This article formulates a new approach to the design of managerial and professional work. It is based upon the fundamental postulates of sociotechnical design but represents a significant departure from the traditional analytic techniques used in the factory. The result is a method by which managers and professionals can redesign their own unit for a higher level of performance. This technique renders organizations more productive for knowledge work and can guide the selection and deployment of new office technology.

AN EMERGING CHALLENGE

The changing structure of our economy is creating a new priority on the agenda of organizational leaders. Approaching the turn of this century, we see the emergence of an "information economy" in which the creation and management of information is becoming the dominant sector of activity. This transformation is reflected in labor-force statistics, which show the proportion of U.S. workers employed in white-collar jobs as rising from 20 percent in 1978 to a projected 40 percent in 1988.[2] At the same time, existing data suggest that

* Source: Reprinted by permission from *National Productivity Review* © 1983 *Executive Enterprises Publications Co.*, New York, NY.

[1] E. L. Trist, "The Evolution of Socio-Technical Systems," (Toronto, Ont: Quality of Working Life Centre, occasional paper #2, 1981).

[2] R. P. Uhlig, D. J. Farber, and J. H. Bair, *The Office of the Future* (Amsterdam: North Holland, 1979).

productivity improvement has remained virtually flat in the information sector. For example, analysis of data from 1972 to 1977 indicates that the rate of productivity for U.S. blue-collar workers rose 2 percent annually, while that for white-collar workers rose 0.4 percent annually.[3] A different analysis estimated that between 1960 and 1970, blue-collar productivity grew 83 percent, whereas white-collar productivity increased only 4 percent.[4] None of these studies is precise, but overall they indicate a major opportunity for faster improvement in the productivity of white-collar work. A major item of management's priorities through the 1980s will therefore be to build more productive office organizations.

Not all white-collar work affects the bottom line equally. Professional and managerial employees draw the greatest dollar volume of salary. In 1979, total compensation for U.S. secretarial, typist, and clerical personnel totaled $125 billion. At the same time, total compensation for professional, managerial, and administrative personnel totaled $400 billion.[5] From the standpoint of a cost-benefit ratio, enhancing the productivity of these latter workers offers exceptional opportunities for adding value.

Yet attempts to rationalize such labor as if it were a set of factory operations usually fail. To enhance the performance of such work, management will need to draw

[3] Diebold Group, *People Impacts of Office Technology* (New York: Automated Office Program Document 019, 1982).

[4] A. Purchase and C. F. Glover, "Office of the Future," SRI Long Range Planning Service, No. 1001.

[5] "Multiclient Study of Managerial/Professional Productivity," New York: Booz, Allen, and Hamilton, Inc., 1979.

upon new concepts and methods that suit the texture of managerial and professional endeavors rather than prevailing models drawn from industrial factory work.

The emergence of new office technology further complicates the enhancement of managerial and professional work. The declining costs of microelectronics and accumulating experience with information-systems design are creating a pervasive shift in office tools. A proliferation of new office equipment is coming to market: smart typewriters, word processors, desk top work stations, smart public branch phone exchanges, integrated voice-data switches, local area networks, facsimile transmitters, cellular radio, and numerous software products. Foreseeable developments through the 1980s promise yet further remarkable offerings that include greater networking capabilities, limited voice input/output, and rudimentary inferential (artificial intelligence) software.

Advertising by equipment vendors aside, this flood of new technology will have mixed effects that both encourage and complicate the improvement of productivity for the manager and professional. New information technology will allow unprecedented augmentation of the capabilities of knowledge workers, but performance will not improve magically by simply installing new equipment. New operator skills, procedural developments, structural transformation, and cultural metamorphosis will all be essential for the harvesting of real operational advantages from exotic new office technology.

In the past, new operator skills and procedural changes have been the primary domain for learning and change, with specialist staffs and vendors providing key impetus and support. More advanced office

equipment, with still higher functionality and greater capacity for interconnection, makes changes in organizational structure and culture more important than before. These are realms that cannot be entrusted to staff specialists or vendors alone. Management must take an active role to shape how new technology reshapes the structure, ethos, and mission of knowledge work. Only inside this context of management prerogative can new equipment be selected with any real organizational validity.

An emerging information economy and a changing office tool stock thus present a double-edged challenge in the decade ahead. Extracting genuine operational improvements amidst a changing work force and enhanced technology requires that managers find new ways to organize work in the office.

THE HERITAGE OF SOCIOTECHNICAL DESIGN

Sociotechnical design is a way of designing high-performance organizations. It consists of both theory and procedure. Sociotechnical theory is general; it establishes a novel way of viewing work and its organization. Sociotechnical procedure is analytic; based upon the theory, it provides one means of searching for a way to organize work better. The analytic method is not imposed unilaterally by an outside expert. Rather, it entails self-design, whereby people can analyze their own operation and how to improve it.

Originated in England at the Tavistock Institute during the 1950s, a sociotechnical theory was the first approach that viewed work as a system of technical and social components. The technical subsystem is the tools and procedures used to create desired outputs, and the social subsystem is the division of labor and methods of coordination by which tools and procedures are managed.

The social and the technical represent dissimilar elements; each is a distinct realm that operates according to different laws. The technical subsystem is subject to the physical constraints that govern transformation of raw materials into finished products and to the procedural arrangements for structuring the orderly progression of labor. The social subsystem of work is shaped by psychological and social conditions that affect the patterns of interaction through which people operate the technical subsystem.

Sociotechnical theory maintains that high performance is obtained by coupling these dissimilar realms in mutually enhancing ways. Hence, the sociotechnical approach stresses finding a "best match" between social and technical subsystems. This emphasis goes beyond job enrichment for its own sake by insisting that better quality work be harnessed to the improvement of the technical production flow.

Beyond Taylorist Principles

This emphasis upon "best match" runs counter to prevailing tradition. Since the 1920s, American enterprise has applied principles based upon Frederick W. Taylor's "scientific management" to determine the organization of work. This approach led to emphasizing simplification of jobs and reliance upon mechanization as ways to organize work for better results. Job simplification is a tendency to divide work into the smallest possible units. The idea is that narrow, repetitive tasks maximize efficiency and minimize

replacement costs. Reliance upon mechanization is an inclination to maximize the level of automation, thereby minimizing human toil and error. These postulates seemed helpful through the 1950s as America's production line became the quintessential model of efficient organization.

But times have changed since the principles of job simplification and maximum automation were developed. Our more affluent and better educated labor force brings a different set of expectations to the work place. High wages in exchange for simplistic work managed by unilateral decree is no longer sufficient to evoke high levels of performance. Meanwhile, the evolution of technology has changed the very texture of work itself. With the growing prevalence of integrated, automatic systems, narrow responsibility requiring less real initiative does not any longer yield a competitive edge. Rather, there is a need for workers to exercise broadly responsible initiative on a continuing basis if outstanding performance is to be achieved.

In the U.S., breakdown of the traditional approach to work design has been evident in some of our most essential industries. The auto industry is a case in point. Labor strife in 1972 at General Motors' Lordstown plant dramatically underscored the need for a fundamental transformation in how work is organized. At the time, Lordstown housed America's most technologically advanced automotive assembly line. In accord with the Taylorist principles of efficiency, automation was maximized and worker roles greatly simplified. Workers went on strike to protest the low quality of their jobs in this supposedly optimal system. Overoptimization of technology by itself and subpar development of the

plant's social system led to a deterioration in the overall performance of the facility. The Lordstown episode marked a watershed in American management of human resources. It signified the need to obtain superior performance in ways that depart from traditional reliance upon simple work and purely technological optimization.

With an emphasis upon striking a best match between social and technical subsystems, sociotechnical design represents a genuine alternative to outmoded Taylorist principles. But sociotechnical design consists of more than general theory. It also entails specific analytic procedures by which people can design a better match between the social and technical aspects of work. This analytic method was for the most part developed in factory settings.

 **LEARNING CHECKPOINT**

Are Taylor's principles of scientific management irrelevant to the vast majority of jobs in the professional work sector of the economy?

The method of sociotechnical analysis examines the technical subsystem, the social subsystem, and their overall mission. The technical subsystem is analyzed as a sequence of operations that converts inputs to outputs. Particular attention is given to variations, or errors, that can arise in any step of the conversion process and to the systematic interdependencies that run between upstream and downstream errors. The social subsystem is scrutinized in terms of each organizational role in order to examine the motivational factors for each job along with patterns of information and responsibility that designate how people manage the technical conversion process. In addition, the overall mission of the unit is revalidated by analyzing its environment, history, and purpose.

This analysis reveals information that permits alternative types of organization to be considered. Often, a sociotechnical analysis leads people to establish a work-group form of organization. In work-group organizations, a cluster of steps in the overall conversion process is assigned to a group of workers. The group is responsible for an interim product that results from these steps. Ideally, the group manages day-to-day operations itself. Individual workers are responsible for being effective group contributors, which often entails learning a variety of production, maintenance, and management skills. Supervision becomes less detailed and less authoritarian as coaching tends to replace decree, and there is greater worker involvement in long-range issues.

Designed through sociotechnical analysis, work-group organization can achieve better performance than can traditional forms of organization. This advantage has been demonstrated in a variety of industries such as refining, chemical processing, automotive fabrication and assembly, food production, semiconductor wafer fabrication, and light industrial production. Today, a number of major firms depend upon the sociotechnical approach to systematically gain higher productivity and employee commitment.

Application of sociotechnical design to white-collar work has been limited. Most attempts have involved clerical or support-staff work in word processing, records management, and claims processing. Until recently there have been few attempts to design managerial

and professional work from a sociotechnical perspective. But prior results indicate that sociotechnical design offers considerable promise for performance improvement. This history of success against the moving background of new information technology and a new economic order makes translation of sociotechnical design from the factory to the office a realm of substantial opportunity.

APPLYING SOCIOTECHNICAL DESIGN TO OFFICE WORK

The term "office" is actually a misnomer. Office work denotes a wide assortment of operations that includes everything from ticket processing to strategic planning. People who work in offices do many different things. They hold different jobs, run different sorts of operations, and draw upon a variety of skills and equipment. Many forms of office work may have the same basic activities, such as filing, telephoning, and writing. But merely improving each of these component activities is not equivalent to substantive improvement in the guts of a particular office operation.

One useful way to categorize this variety of office work is in terms of routine and nonroutine tasks.[6] The relative balance of each type of work is different for various sorts of office jobs. Routine work primarily involves completing a structured problem. The tasks are characterized by accuracy of detail, short-term horizon, predominantly internal information, and narrow scope. The work usually proceeds through

[6] C. Pava, "Microelectronics and The Design of Organization," Working Paper 82–67, Harvard Business School Division of Research, 1982.

some kind of linear and sequential conversion process, a series of particular steps that yields a predefined output. Office jobs with a predominance of routine work have typically been the province of nonexempt clerical and staff-support workers (usually female) and to exempt staff administering fixed, repetitive procedures.

Nonroutine office work primarily involves managing unstructured or semistructured problems. Professional and managerial jobs are in this category. These jobs are characterized by plausible but general information inputs, variable detail, extended and unfixed time horizons, internal and external data, and diffuse or general scope. Such work rarely proceeds through a sequential conversion process. Instead, the less structured nature of problems may frequently require abandoning stepwise progression. Often, multiple objectives must be balanced through time, which further undermines strictly linear progression by diffusing the clarity of both initial problem and desired outcome. For example, changing the strategic posture of a firm almost never proceeds through explicitly orderly "corporate planning." Instead of advancing through discrete linear steps, the executive must orchestrate a disjointed, nonsequential, consensus-building process. Progression is nonlinear, with the start and finish of the process never totally clear.

Admittedly, this is a rough set of categories, but virtually any office job can be located along this routine-nonroutine continuum in relative proximity to other jobs.

The people who undertake routine and nonroutine office work are characteristically different in background and expectation. Most general managers and professionals are highly trained. Their education focuses upon individual practice, and by definition they expect to wield a degree of unilateral expertise and authority. Expectations about work activities, career advancement, and reward emphasize individual performance and ability. In contrast, those employed in routine office activities, where highly specialized training is less prevalent, are more likely to develop a group identification. Furthermore, managers and professionals cannot easily learn each others' skills, which is a usual requisite for work-group organization with its task rotation.

This range of work in an office requires modifications in the sociotechnical approach for white-collar settings. The existing form of analysis and design appears best suited to routine office work, which more closely resembles the factory settings where the initial analytic procedure was developed. Because of the sequential progression of activity in routine office work, the classic form of technical analysis, in terms of processing steps and their variances, remains applicable. The stability of work engenders clearly defined niches that are amenable to the standard form of social analysis with its emphasis upon work-quality factors for each specific role. Because they are less likely to emphasize individual performance, people engaged in routine office work may consider work groups as a viable alternative to current organizational patterns. Given the boredom that inherently creeps into routine office tasks, work-group organization may appear as a particularly welcome and enriching option that adds complexity to tasks.

Nonroutine office work appears less amenable to the conventional form of sociotechnical analysis. A strictly sequential chain of steps either simply does not exist or fails to capture the essence of such work. Also, the constellation of individuals needed to run nonroutine work is always shifting, depending upon changing circumstance, while social analysis emphasizes stable, discrete roles and their accumulation of satisfying features. Finally, work-group design runs against the more individualistic orientation of managers and professionals, making it a less viable alternative for nonroutine office work. Since the complexity of such work often is already overwhelming, work-group alternatives may actually generate excessive task variety in an indiscriminate fashion. Furthermore, the highly specialized training required for nonroutine work precludes the genuine rotation of skills and duties that is normally found in work-group organizations.

A SOCIOTECHNICAL APPROACH FOR NONROUTINE WORK

For improving performance in the domain of nonroutine office work, the sociotechnical design approach—analysis of technical and social subsystems to design a best match between subsystems—still applies overall. But the specific units of analysis must be transformed, thereby rendering a new procedure for the analysis and design of high performance work.

One alternative method derived from recent work is based upon a revised concept of social and technical subsystems that applies to nonroutine office endeavors. This new approach discards notions of sequential conversion processes and fixed-role analysis that characterize the more traditional form of analysis. Instead, the technical and social aspects of office work are seen respectively in terms of *deliberations* and *discretionary coalitions*.

Deliberations concerning a topic can be seen to occur in various forums. These forums are arenas in which a topic is deliberated either with one's self (tracing alternative projections on the back of an envelope) or with others (holding a meeting where the topic is discussed). Forums may be structured, semi-structured, or unstructured. Often, important topics are deliberated through more than one forum. For instance, the redirection of a division's strategy is a highly complex affair. As a topic it may be pursued through multiple forums, including ad hoc discussions, occasional individual reflection, special retreat meetings, key allocation or promotional processes, and formal strategic planning sessions.

In the traditional sociotechnical method, technical analysis hinges upon sequential operations and their variances, but in nonroutine office work, with the prevalence of multiple and nonlinear conversion processes, the technical analysis is better conducted in terms of deliberations with topics and forums. Apparently disordered and disarrayed, deliberations constitute the actual gist of "information work" for nonroutine tasks in the office.

As an uncommon category of analysis, deliberations are easily mistaken for limited but more familiar terms. For instance, deliberations are not decisions. Decisions are discrete choices where one alternative is pursued at the expense of others. Deliberations are a more continuous affair than decisions, but decisions may occasionally be rendered from deliberations. Deliberations are the context and subtext of decisions, rather than the act of decision making itself. Also, deliberations are not just meetings. Meetings are sessions where people gather. They can be one vital forum in a deliberation, but they are not the deliberation itself. Nor will more meetings necessarily improve the conduct of deliberation. Often the inverse is true. The concept of deliberations points to forums of encounter, exchange, and reflection other than meetings that also can help to resolve an ambiguous topic.

A new analytic concept of the social subsystem is also required, one that corresponds to the concept of deliberations in the technical subsystem. Discretionary coalitions provide one way to view the social subsystem of nonroutine office work. Discretionary coalitions are alliances struck of necessity in which intelligent trade-offs are made for the sake of general objectives.

Discretionary coalitions arise because of the continuing equivocality of nonroutine office issues. Since a definitive solution is unobtainable, a process of continuing trade-off becomes essential. In product design specification, for example, every function and specialty will tend to seek optimization of its own narrow subunit agenda. Research and development will want the most exotic design possible; manufacturing will insist on a design that is easily produced; and marketing may require total compatibility with earlier products, perhaps at the cost of higher functionality or lower production costs. But commercial viability requires that no one function or speciality triumph completely. All sides are reciprocally interdependent; inherently they are divergent and yet necessary to each other. Under these circumstances, high performance becomes the ability to balance contention with informed trade-offs.

Discretionary coalitions are networks of people who must jointly render a continuing series of informed trade-offs on some equivocal topic of deliberation. A coali-

tion's composition is driven by both parsimony (excluding extraneous persons) and necessity (including required persons); the chain of command is short-circuited, and to the coalition belong all the necessary players regardless of their formal rank or assignment.

Deliberations and discretionary coalitions together provide a new analytic framework for the redesign of nonroutine office work. High performance for truly knotty nonroutine office work requires building effective discretionary coalitions around key topics of deliberation.

Typically a dysfunctional arrangement takes hold. Deliberations become obscurely defined, losing their clear focus and priority. In their place administrative procedures, long since ossified, become an obsession for their own sake. A maze of red tape obscures the genuine realities of an enterprise. Coalitions go unacknowledged. By default there emerge narrow allegiances and uninformative, ceremonial patterns of involvement. The wrong patterns of people go chasing after the wrong issues. Everyone may appear busy, but effectiveness declines. This decline cannot be cured by pep talks, relations training, or a veneer of exotic new office technology. What is required is a fundamental reformation to bring viable coalitions into alignment with deliberations of genuine importance.

 **LEARNING CHECKPOINT**

What core dimensions of jobs are being changed in the redesign strategy for nonroutine work?

Reformulating Deliberations and Discretionary Coalitions

A new form of sociotechnical analysis is needed to reformulate deliber-

ations and their attendant coalitions. A specific method outlined by the author enables members of a unit to better match the technical and social aspects of their work in terms of key deliberations and discretionary coalitions.[7] More effective organizations can thereby be designed for nonroutine office work on a systematic basis. Improved deliberations can be developed selectively, with explicit charters. Discretionary coalitions can be designated for each deliberation. Responsibilities should be specified for every party involved. Policies should be established for compensation, promotion, assignment, and symbolic parity that create within the coalition a balance of influence among the various informed perspectives represented.

This alternative form of sociotechnical design leads to a new format of organization—reticular organization—different from the work-group configuration that often results from the more traditional method. Reticular organization is characterized by constantly shifting networks of information and authority. There is very little of the cross-training or job switching that normally characterizes work-group organizations. Instead, the axis of reference and identification alters ceaselessly within an ever-changing complex of deliberation-coalition configurations. Within that complex, an ongoing balance among divergent interests is maintained across a set of deliberations in a fluid way that complements the purely formal chain of command. Coalitions become acknowledged, legitimate, and adapt-

[7] C. Pava, *Managing New Office Technology: An Organizational Strategy* (New York: The Free Press, 1983).

able. Previously underground phenomena come to the surface. Emphasis is upon harnessing contention to engender understanding among various parties and intelligent trade-offs.

In and of itself, reticular organization may not alter the formal chart of organization as explicitly as a work-group design. Instead, the transformation is more subtle, it runs "between the lines." Everyday sequences of communication change. Ongoing dialogue between disparate functions grows more dynamic, and issues get taken full circle with greater care and frequency. Relations between managers may "click" as rigid lines of traditional demarcation become less absolute and confining. The result is improved performance as nonroutine tasks are undertaken with better deliberations and more effective coalitions.

CASE STUDY: A STRATEGIC PLANNING GROUP

An alternative sociotechnical design method for nonroutine office work, based upon new concepts like deliberations and coalitions, is exemplified by the Strategic Planning Group in a rapidly growing $180-million firm. A new integrated information system was proposed to help the group function better. Based on prior experience, the executive in charge of the unit suspected that enhanced technology alone would prove insufficient. Rather, the unit's overall function and specific operations needed thorough renewal.

An organization design project was therefore undertaken before design purchase or installation of the new computer system. Individuals representing the variety of people in the planning unit were asked to join a design team. Meet-

ing weekly, the design team analyzed current operations and proposed a new organization design. Major staff and line executives became members of a steering committee. To guide the entire project and to help the design team and the steering committee, an outside consultant was retained.

Early steps of the analysis required the design team to research and identify major trends in the planning group, the company, and the company's environment. Some major developments became apparent. First, the company's major source of competitive advantage was shifting from cost to advanced technology and project features. Second, the firm's most promising opportunities lay in second- or third-generation projects rather than first-generation offerings obtained from acquisitions. Third, the nature of the planning function was changing from acquisitions development to internal coordination between functions and to adaptation to growing competition. The design team capped this phase of analysis with the formulation of a mission statement that emphasized the planning unit's role as corporate "glue" amid rising complexity. This statement was ratified, with some revision, by the steering committee.

Next, the design team analyzed the technical subsystem of work in the planning unit. Because of the highly ambiguous and nonlinear nature of the unit's work, the analysis was couched in terms of deliberation topics. The following were selected: elicit identification of recent market and competitor trends, evoke new product category designations, appraise and match dispersed development resources, broker new product applications, and collate joint agreement opportunities that may exist in-house. This portrait of the unit's work was

counterintuitive. It revealed that the planning unit mostly addressed interactive processes rather than confining itself to just abstract analysis. The design team recognized that the unit's analytical prowess yielded advantage only if it led to the edification of other groups in the firm. Technical analysis proceeded, with the design team specifying key deliberations and the forums through which they were conducted.

Following the interim report to the steering committee, the design team proceeded to analyze the planning department's subsystem in terms of the discretionary coalitions needed to maintain the key deliberations of the unit. A coalition was traced for each deliberation, noting the parties involved, information required, characteristic bias, and relative status. The analysis permitted the design team to check for proper alignment between the micropolitical landscape of their unit and the major topics of deliberation, to see if there were any mismatches between the two. For example, it was discovered that R&D lacked a good channel through which to inquire about recent market trends, and that diametrically opposed biases caused all sides to leave this gap unacknowledged and unsolved.

LEARNING CHECKPOINT

What other types of jobs lend themselves to the kind of analysis that was applied to strategic planners? What are the underlying dimensions of these types of jobs?

Alternative Organization Outline

Finally, the design team proceeded to outline an alternative organization for the planning unit. This proved to be a difficult task, since the new design did not simply leap out of the data collected thus far. Rather than defining every detail, the design team outlined a number of minimum critical specifications for a more effective planning organization. Among these were:

1. Mission. A reason for the unit's existence in terms of greater coordination and liaison with a more complex environment.
2. Philosophy. An ethos for the way people should be managed in the planning unit, emphasizing clear understanding of goals, autonomy of methods, and more work in small teams.
3. Social System Changes. A set of proposals for changes in the unit's social subsystem, including:
    a. Charters for deliberations including topics, desired outcomes, concerned parties, and respective contributions;
    b. Greater recognition of direct involvement with parties outside the unit in planning processes;
    c. Less complex job ratings with fewer levels and more flexible job descriptions; and
    d. New recruitment strategies to attract a better mix of appropriate talent.
4. Technical System Changes. A set of proposals for changes in the unit's technical subsystem, including:
    a. Establishment of new forums for deliberations— including reports, meetings, and reviews—elimination of many outmoded

forums, and consolidation of splintered forums;
    b. Changes in physical layout and distribution of resources, such as planning unit conference rooms in other areas of the firm; and
    c. Proposals for enhanced information systems (data and telecommunications) that genuinely augment key deliberations with a blend of functions overlooked in the initial proposal for a new computer installation.

Together, these changes would shift the basic pattern of organization away from an overly formal structure. The design proposed movement toward a reticular organization in which a changing network of information exchange and authority arrangements grows to complement the rigid scaffold of a purely hierarchical structure.[8]

The proposed changes eventually won consent and were implemented with extensive consultation from the steering committee and a great measure of interaction with others in the unit and the firm. Preliminary indications show that the redesigned planning organization sustains a much greater level of contribution to the firm's conduct and that future planning needs will be met with a leaner staff. Meanwhile, turnover has declined and more planners are being accepted into line positions. Beyond any of these initial results, the process of sociotechnical design also created a group experienced in organizational analysis that is both able and willing to improve other aspects of the firm's operation with the same method.

CONCLUSION

The conventional method of sociotechnical design and the new variation suggested here together comprise a spectrum of analytic methods for the design of high-performance office organizations. Units with mostly routine tasks are best suited for the established analytic procedure and for the work-group format that may result. Managerial and professional units that do highly nonroutine information work are better served by the alternative method stressing deliberations, coalitions, and reticular organization. Between these lies a vast range of middle-ground applications for units doing mixed routine and nonroutine work. These operations should adopt a hybrid approach in which aspects of the two divergent methods of analysis are selectively blended.[9]

Overall, this spectrum of methods (routine, nonroutine, and hybrid) permits a contingency framework that gives sociotechnical design sufficient variety for widespread application in the office. The general principles at the core of a sociotechnical approach remain valid throughout all ranges of the spectrum. But these postulates are implemented through different kinds of analysis, contingent upon the level of routinization involved.

Sufficient cumulative experience with sociotechnical design makes it possible to speak today of a high-performance factory: a work-group facility designed to make people and technology enhance each other. Major firms now routinely depend upon this approach to gain superior commitment and performance in their operations. The realm of knowledge work has not yet attained such a

[8] C. Pava, "Microelectronics and The Design of Organization."

[9] C. Pava, *Managing New Office Technology*.

consistent vision. The high-performance office as a general guide for exceptional performance of knowledge work remains embryonic. More experience with sociotechnical design in the office is needed before clear patterns emerge. With time, a general profile will appear that provides an outline of the high-performance office. Early exploration of this frontier today will afford substantial advantage later for those who seek to organize information-based work more effectively. □

₁ JOB INNOVATION*

The following questionnaire items will enable you to assess your motivation to engage in innovative behavior on the job. The reference point can be the job you presently hold or if not now employed, a job you most recently held. Answer each of the six questions and determine the total score by adding the numbers in the parentheses adjacent to each response. The higher the score, the greater the motivation to find innovative ways to do the job.

1. In your kind of work, if a person tries to change his usual way of doing things, how does it generally turn out?

    (1) _____ Usually turns out worse; the tried and true methods work best in my work

    (3) _____ Usually doesn't make much difference

    (5) _____ Usually turns out better; our methods need improvement

2. Some people prefer doing a job in pretty much the same way because this way they can count on always doing a good job. Others like to go out of their way in order to think up new ways of doing things. How is it with you on your job?

    (1) _____ I always prefer doing things pretty much in the same way

    (2) _____ I mostly prefer doing things pretty much in the same way

    (4) _____ I mostly prefer doing things in new and different ways

    (5) _____ I always prefer doing things in new and different ways

3. How often do you try out, on your own, a better or faster way of doing something on the job?

    (5) _____ Once a week or more often

    (4) _____ Two or three times a month

    (3) _____ About once a month

    (2) _____ Every few months

    (1) _____ Rarely or never

4. How often do you get chances to try out your own ideas on your job, either before or after checking with your supervisor?

    (5) _____ Several times a week or more

    (4) _____ About once a week

    (3) _____ Several times a month

    (2) _____ About once a month

    (1) _____ Less than once a month

---

* Source: Martin Patchen, SOME QUESTIONNAIRE MEASURES OF EMPLOYEE MOTIVATION AND MORALE. Ann Arbor, Mich.: Survey Research Center, University of Michigan, 1965, pp. 1–25.

5. In my kind of job, it's usually better to let your supervisor worry about new or better ways of doing things.

   (1) ＿＿ Strongly agree
   (2) ＿＿ Mostly agree
   (4) ＿＿ Mostly disagree
   (5) ＿＿ Strongly disagree

6. How many times in the past year have you suggested to your supervisor a different or better way of doing something on the job?

   (1) ＿＿ Never had occasion to do this during the past year
   (2) ＿＿ Once or twice
   (3) ＿＿ About three times
   (4) ＿＿ About five times
   (5) ＿＿ Six to ten times
   (6) ＿＿ More than ten times had occasion to do this during the past year

D² JOB INVOLVEMENT

The following 20 items will enable you to describe the extent of your involvement on the job you presently have. If you are not now working think of the job you most recently held. Answer the items according to whether you: strongly agree (1), agree (2), disagree (3), or strongly disagree (4). When you complete the entire questionnaire, add the scores on the individual items to obtain your job involvement score:

＿＿ 1. I'll stay overtime to finish a job, even if I'm not paid for it.
＿＿ 2. You can measure a person pretty well by how good a job he does.
＿＿ 3. The major satisfaction in my life comes from my job.
＿＿ 4. For me, mornings at work really fly by.
＿＿ 5. I usually show up for work a little early, to get things ready.
＿＿ 6. The most important things that happen to me involve my work.
＿＿ 7. Sometimes I lie awake at night thinking ahead to the next day's work.
＿＿ 8. I'm really a perfectionist about my work.
＿＿ 9. I feel depressed when I fail at something connected with my job.
＿＿ 10. I have other activities more important than my work.
＿＿ 11. I live, eat, and breathe my job.
＿＿ 12. I would probably keep working even if I didn't need the money.
＿＿ 13. Quite often I feel like staying home from work instead of coming in.
＿＿ 14. To me, my work is only a small part of who I am.

Source: Thomas M. Lodahl and Mathilde Kejner, "The Definition and Measurement of Job Involvement," JOURNAL OF APPLIED PSYCHOLOGY, February, 1965, pp. 24–23.

_____ 15. I am very much involved personally in my work.

_____ 16. I avoid taking on extra duties and responsibilities in my work.

_____ 17. I used to be more ambitious about my work than I am now.

_____ 18. Most things in life are more important than work.

_____ 19. I used to care more about my work, but now other things are more important to me.

_____ 20. Sometimes I'd like to kick myself for the mistakes I make in my work.

JOB DESIGN PREFERENCES

OBJECTIVES

1. To illustrate individual differences in preferences about various job design characteristics.

2. To illustrate how your preferences may differ from those of others.

3. To examine the most important and least important job design characteristics and how managers would cope with them.

STARTING THE EXERCISE

First you will respond to a questionnaire asking about your job design preferences and how you view the preferences of others. After working through the questionnaire *individually*, small groups will be formed. In the groups discussion will focus on the individual differences in preferences expressed by group members.

Job design is concerned with a number of attributes of a job. Among these attributes are the job itself, the requirements of the job, the interpersonal interaction opportunities on the job, and performance outcomes. There are certain attributes that are preferred by individuals. Some prefer job autonomy, while others prefer to be chal-

lenged by different tasks. It is obvious that individual differences in preferences would be an important consideration for managers. An exciting job for one person may be a demeaning and boring job for another individual. Managers could use this type of information in attempting to create job design conditions that allow organizational goals and individual goals and preferences to be matched.

The Job Preference form is presented below. Please read it carefully and complete it after considering each characteristic listed. Due to space limitations not all job design characteristics are included for your consideration. Use only those that are included on the form.

Phase I: 15 minutes
1. Individually complete the A and B portions of the Job Design Preference form.

Phase II: 45 minutes
1. The instructor will form groups of four to six students.
2. Discuss the differences in the rankings individuals made on the A and B parts of the form.
3. Present each of the A rank orders of group members on a flip

chart or the blackboard. Analyze the areas of agreement and disagreement.
4. Discuss what implications the A and B rankings would have to a *manager* who would have to supervise a group such as the group you are in. That is, what could a manager do to cope with the individual differences displayed in steps 1, 2, and 3 above.

JOB DESIGN PREFERENCES

A. Your Job Design Preferences

Decide which of the following is most important to you. Place a *1* in front of the most important characteristic. Then decide which is the second most important characteristic to you and place a *2* in front of it. Continue numbering the items in order of importance until the least important is ranked *10*. There are no right answers since individuals differ in their job design preferences. Do not discuss your individual rankings until the instructor forms groups.

_____ Variety in tasks

_____ Feedback on performance from doing the job

_____ Autonomy

_____ Working as a team

_____ Responsibility

_____ Developing friendships on the job

_____ Task identity

_____ Task significance

_____ Having the resources to perform well

_____ Feedback on performance from others (e.g., the manager, co-workers)

B. Others Job Design Preferences

In the A section you have provided your preferences, now number the items as you think others would rank them. Consider others who are in your course, class, or program. That is, those who are also completing this exercise. Rank the factors from 1 (most important) to 10 (least important).

_____ Variety in tasks

_____ Feedback on performance from doing the job

_____ Autonomy

_____ Working as a team

_____ Responsibility

_____ Developing friendships on the job

_____ Task identity

_____ Task significance

_____ Having the resources to perform well

_____ Feedback on performance from others (e.g., the manager, co-workers)

 JOB DESIGN PROFILE

OBJECTIVES

1. To understand how jobs are designed.

2. To understand how people feel about their jobs.

STARTING THE EXERCISE

Find a work group in your community that will allow you to observe people at work and talk to them about their jobs. It may be in an office, a factory, school, or the like. Using the guidelines below, come up with a profile of the jobs within one of the work groups of the organization you visit. You should attempt to measure the jobs through observation of the employees' performance such that you can complete the job profile. If different jobs exist in the group, pick one or two which seem to be more specialized.

JOB PROFILE

Job Title _____   Organization _____

Circle the most appropriate number

Number of motions performed	Large number of motions	7 6 5 4 3 2 1	Small number repeated often
Number of operations performed	Large number of different operations	7 6 5 4 3 2 1	Small number repeated often
Number of different tools used to do the job	Large number	7 6 5 4 3 2 1	Small number
Human interaction	High	7 6 5 4 3 2 1	Low
Freedom and control	High	7 6 5 4 3 2 1	Low—machine paced
Responsibility, autonomy	High	7 6 5 4 3 2 1	Low
Degree of physical exertion	High	7 6 5 4 3 2 1	Low
Environment	Pleasant	7 6 5 4 3 2 1	Unpleasant
Numbers of places work performed	Single location	7 6 5 4 3 2 1	Many locations
Location of work	Inside	7 6 5 4 3 2 1	Outside
Timing of work	Continuous, intense	7 6 5 4 3 2 1	Intermittent

After completing the job profile, ask several of the employees how they feel about their jobs—if they are satisfied or would like to see their jobs changed in some way.

Ideally, you should ask if you can come back to talk to the employees after you do some further analysis, explained below. If that is not possible, after you have observed the work group for some time, ask the employees how they feel about their jobs. For example, you could ask:

Do you like your job?

Do you think your job is routine/dull/monotonous/repetitious?

Do you find ways to add variety to your job? What are they?

If your job were to be enriched or enlarged, how would you like that? (Give examples of additional functions workers might be able to perform.)

If your job were changed in this way, would you expect to be paid more?

Again, ideally, this should be done on a second visit, if possible. Before that visit, find a job profile (if you have observed more than one kind of job) that appears to be very narrow in scope (more specialized, fewer motions, repetitive, few operations, few tools, machine paced). Develop a job redesign strategy to enlarge that person's job and reorganize the work of the work group you studied. Then make the second visit with this redesign strategy to find out employee reactions to it as outlined above. If that is not possible, you should still create a design strategy of enlargement or enrichment based on the information from your first visit.

Bring your job profiles, redesign strategy, and employee reactions (to current design and proposed redesign) to class for discussion.

Source: William F. Glueck and Lawrence R. Jauch, *The Managerial Experience* (Hinsdale, IL: The Dryden Press, 1982), pp. 173–74.

1 HAUSSER FOOD PRODUCTS COMPANY

Brenda Cooper, the southeastern regional sales manager for the Hausser Food Products Company (HFP) expressed her concern to a researcher from a well-known eastern business school:

> I think during the past year I've begun to make some progress here, but the situation is a lot more difficult than I thought when I first arrived. Our current methods of selling products just are not adequate, and the people in the field don't seem interested in coming up with new ideas or approaches to selling.

BACKGROUND

Hausser Food Products Company is a leading producer and marketer of baby foods in the United States. The company manufactures and markets a whole line of foods for the baby market including strained meats, vegetables, fruits, and combination dishes. The product line includes foods that are completely strained, for infants, as well as foods that are partially strained or chopped, for children six months and older. HFP has traditionally been the leader in this field. The company has no other major product lines. Its products are known for their high quality and the Hausser name is well known to most consumers.

HFP owns its production and warehousing facilities. Its well-developed distribution network provides direct delivery of products to the warehouses and stores of most major food chains. The smallest segment of its market is composed of a limited number of institutions for children, which purchase HFP products in bulk.

HFP has a long history in the baby food business. Traditionally the market leader, it has over the years maintained a market share of approximately 60 percent. During the 1960s the firm experienced rapid expansion and growth. The number of different types of baby food products increased tremendously to keep up with increasing demand for more foods and a greater variety of products. During the period from the middle 1960s through the mid 1970s, growth in sales approached 15 percent compounded yearly.

During the past few years, HFP has faced a greatly changing market for infant foods. The sudden decrease in the birth rate brought about major changes in the infant food business, and projections of sales had to be altered drastically. In addition, the new concern about food additives, including flavorings, dyes, and preservatives, also had its impact on the baby food market. Many consumer advocates argued that it would be safer for parents to make their own baby foods than to purchase the commercially prepared products such as those manufactured by HFP. Finally, competition in the baby food market also increased. Private names competed on the basis of price against the nationally advertised brand names.

These changing conditions have been viewed with great alarm by the top management of HFP. The drop in growth of sales (to 3 percent in the most recent year) was accompanied by an even greater drop in earnings as management found itself with unused plant and warehouse capacity. Management is currently concerned with looking for new ways of stimulating demand for HFP products as well as the longer-range problem of finding new complementary products to develop and market.

THE MARKETING ORGANIZATION

In 1975 a researcher from a major business school became involved in studying the marketing organization of HFP as part of a larger-scale research project. His inquiries led him to look closely at the sales department and to investigate some of the problems that were being experienced there.

The marketing function at HFP is directed by a vice-president for marketing who reports directly to the president of HFP (see a partial organizational chart in Exhibit 1). The vice-president for marketing has five functional directors reporting to him. Each of these directors is responsible for one of the major areas of marketing activity, including market research, market planning, sales promotion, advertising, and sales. The sales department, which has been the focus of much recent concern, is headed by the director of sales, who directs selling activities for the entire United States. The country is broken up into seven regions, each of which has a regional sales manager. Regions are further broken up into districts (each of which may include a range of area from several states to part of a city, depending upon the particular location). The district manager heads up the HFP "sales team" for

Source: David A. Nadler, Michael L. Tushman, and Nina G. Hatvany, *Managing Organizations* (Boston: Little, Brown and Co., 1982), pp. 483–88.

EXHIBIT 1

Partial Chart of Formal Organization Structure of Hausser Food Products

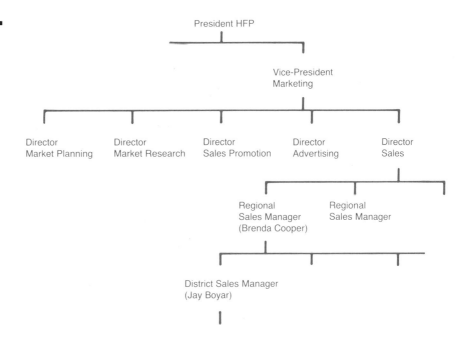

each district. It is this sales team that has the ultimate job of selling HFP products to customers, offering promotions, maintaining contact with the customers, assuring adequate shelf space, and so on.

A key element in the marketing organization is the regional sales manager. This has been an entry position to HFP for many bright, aggressive, and well-trained young people who subsequently have risen to high-level jobs within the company. The current president of the company, the vice-president for marketing, and three of the five marketing directors all began their careers at HFP as regional sales managers.

Brenda Cooper, the southeast regional sales manager, is fairly typical of the kind of person who is placed in that position. Brenda entered an MBA program immediately following graduation from one of the best women's colleges in the country. Majoring in marketing, she did extremely well in business school and graduated near the top of her class. Upon graduation she received many job offers and took a position as an assistant product manager in a large nonfood consumer products company. During four years at that firm she performed extremely well both in the management of existing products and in the launching of new products. By the end of her fourth year, however, she was becoming restless, and seeing no opportunities for quick advancement, decided to accept an offer to become a regional sales manager at HFP. The salary was attractive, plus she would receive a potentially large bonus based on the profit perfor-

mance of the entire company. Brenda was also attracted by the possibility of advancement within the company. She had heard that many of the senior staff had started as regional managers. At the end of her first year Brenda is still very concerned about doing well in her job; in particular she is adjusting to her role as manager with six district managers reporting to her.

THE SALES PLAN

Much of the activity of the regional managers centers around the yearly sales plan. The sales plan is essentially a budget that includes projections of sales, expenses, and profit. It serves as the basic yardstick against which the performance of regional managers is measured.

Each year the sales plan is developed through the following multistage process:

1. The director of market planning comes up with a projection of sales for the coming year. At the same time, the director of sales asks regional managers for their projections of sales for the next year. These projections are usually extrapolations of the previous year's figures with adjustments for major changes in the market year (if any).

2. The two directors (market planning and sales) and their staffs go through a negotiation process to resolve the difference that usually exists between their two projections (market planning always tending to

be higher). Out of these negotiations emerges the sales plan for the coming year. This plan includes budgeted expenditures for promotions, advertising, expenses, and the like, as well as projected sales volume and profit.

3. The sales director allocates portions of the sales plan to regional managers, who are responsible for "meeting plan" within their own regions. Regional managers in turn allocate parts of the plan to each of their district sales managers and teams.

4. The district managers receive the plan in the form of sales targets and expense budgets for the coming year. The district manager typically receives a relatively low base salary combined with a relatively large yearly bonus, which is based entirely on the performance, as measured against the sales plan, of the sales team. At the end of the year, the district manager is also given a pool of bonus dollars, also based on team performance against plan, to be distributed to the individual salespeople. Salespeople also receive relatively low base salaries and look to their yearly bonuses as a major source of income.

THE PROBLEM OF THE REGIONAL SALES MANAGERS

As part of his investigation, the researcher visited Brenda Cooper in her Atlanta office. After describing the operations of her region, Brenda began to talk about some of the problems she was facing:

> We in HFP are currently wrestling with the problem of a very mature product line. Top management has begun to see the critical need to diversify, in other words to hedge our bets with some other lines of products which are not dependent upon a steadily increasing birth rate. They have been talking about some interesting and exciting things, but any new product is still a few years away from being introduced. . . . In the meantime, it is the job of us out here in the field to come up with new ideas to help keep up sales of our existing product line. I think there must be better ways of selling our product, and I am sure that there are new things that we can do to get much more performance out of the line than we are seeing now. The problem is that the best ideas usually come in from the field, from the salesmen themselves, and we really have had very little from our sales teams. They seem content to continue to let the products sell themselves and just keep the shelves stocked, as they have for years. I just don't get any new ideas or approaches from my sales teams.

Brenda and the researcher then spent some time going over the figures for sales in her region, and in particular the sales performance of the different regions. As they were going over the figures, Brenda noted:

> Look here at Jay Boyar and his group in Florida. This is a prime example of the kind of problem I am facing. While we have been facing decreasing growth in sales, and actual drop off of sales some places, Jay's group consistently comes in at 10 percent above the sales plan. I've been down there and met with them and I've talked with Jay numerous times, but I can't figure out how they do it. They must be doing something that could be used in other places; but every time I ask how they do it, I get very vague answers like, "Well, we work very hard down here," or "We work together as a group; that's how we are able to do well." I'm sure it must be more than that, but I can't seem to get them to open up.

A VISIT TO THE FLORIDA SALES TEAM

Intrigued with the Florida figures, the researcher arranged an extended visit (during January and February) with the Florida sales team. The researcher was given a letter of introduction from the vice-president for marketing. This letter explained that he was collecting background information for a major research project that would help the company, that any information collected would be confidential, and that the sales team should provide him with any assistance that he needed.

At first Jay Boyar and his group made no attempt to hide their suspicion of the researcher. Slowly, however, as the researcher spent numerous days in the field, riding around the Florida roads with each of the salespeople, they began to trust him and open up about how they felt about their jobs and the company. (See Exhibit 2 for a listing of the staff of the Florida sales team.)

David Berz, the unofficial assistant team manager, talked at length about why he liked his job:

> What I really like is the freedom. I'm really my own boss most of the time. I don't have to be sitting in an office for the whole day, with some supervisor hanging over my shoulder and looking at all my work. I get to be outside, here in the car, doing what I like to be doing—being out in the world, talking to people, and making the sale.

Neil Portnow, who had been with the company longer than any of the other team members, commented on the group:

EXHIBIT 2

Listing of Staff of Florida Sales Team

Name	Position	Age	Years w/HFP	Education
Jay Boyar	District sales manager	52	30	high school
David Berz	Salesman (assistant manager)	50	30	high school
Neil Portnow	Salesman	56	36	high school
Alby Sicgol	Salesman	49	18	½ year college
Mike Wolly	Salesman	35	12	2 years college
John Cassis	Salesman	28	4	B.A.
Fred Hopengarten	Salesman	30	3	B.A.

This is really a great bunch of guys to work with. I've been with a couple of different groups, but this is the best. I've been together with Dave and Jay for about fifteen years now, and I wouldn't trade it for anything. Jay is really one of us; he knows that we know how to do our jobs, and he doesn't try to put a lot of controls on us. We go about doing the job the way we know is best, and that is OK with Jay.

The guys are also good because they help you out. When I was sick last year, they all pitched in to cover my territory so that we could make our plan plus 10 percent without reporting my illness to the company. They can also be hard on someone who doesn't realize how things work here. A few years back, when one of the young guys, Fred, came with us, he was all fired up. He was gonna sell baby food to half the mothers in Florida, personally! He didn't realize that you have to take your time and not waste your effort for the company. The other guys gave him a little bit of a hard time at first—he found his orders getting lost and shipments being changed—but when he finally came to his senses, they treated him great and showed him the ropes.

Following up on the references to the company, the researcher asked Neil to talk more about HFP as a place to work:

It's all pretty simple; the company is out to screw the salesperson. Up in Atlanta and New York, all they are concerned about is the numbers; meet the plan, no matter what. The worst thing is if you work hard, meet the plan, and then keep going so you can earn some decent money. Then they go and change the plan next year. They increase the sales quota so that you have to work harder just to earn the same money! It just doesn't pay to bust your ass. . . .

The people in Atlanta also want all kinds of paperwork; sales reports, call reports, all kinds of reports. If you filled out all of the things that they want you to fill out, you'd spend all your time doing paperwork and no time out selling, looking for new accounts, making cold calls, or any of the things that a salesman really is supposed to do if he's gonna keep on top of his area.

As he talked with the other salesmen, the researcher found general agreement with Neil's views on the company. Alby Siegel added:

The biggest joke they got going is the suggestion plan. They want us to come up with new ideas about how the company should make more money. The joke of it is, if you come up with an idea that, for instance, makes the company a couple of hundred thousand in profit across the country, they are generous enough to give you $500. That's the top figure; $500 for your idea. That amount of money is an insult. . . .

One thing you have to remember is that in one way or another, we're all in this for the money. Despite what they say, it's not the greatest life being out on the road all of the time, staying in motels, fighting the competition. But it's worth it because I can earn more money doing this job than anything else I could do. I can live better than most professional men with all their college degrees. . . . Jay is pretty good about the money thing, too. He makes sure that we get our bonus, year in and year out, and he keeps the people in Atlanta from taking our bonus checks away from us. He's not management—he's one of us. You can really tell it during the team meetings. Once every two months we all meet in Tampa and spend a day going over the accounts and talking about ideas for selling. We spend the whole day in this hotel room, working, and then we go out and spend the whole night on the town, usually drinking. Jay is one of us . . . many is the night that I've helped carry him back to the hotel.

After about four weeks with the team, the researcher got a chance to participate in one of the bimonthly team meetings. During lunch, Jay came over to him and began to talk:

Listen, I need to talk over something with you before we start the afternoon meeting. We trust you so we're going to let you in on our little discovery. You may have noticed that we aren't doing so badly, and you're right. The reason is a little finding made by Alby about three years ago. He was out in one of the stores and he noticed that a lot of people buying our products were not mothers of young children, but old people! We started looking around, and we began to notice that a lot of older people were buying HFP jars. We talked with some of them, and it turns out that they like our stuff, particularly those people who have all kinds of teeth problems.

Since then we've developed a very lucrative trade with a number of old folks' homes, and we've been able to sell to them through some of the supermarkets that are located in areas where there is a larger older population. It's a great new piece of the market; it takes the pressure off of us to make plan, and we don't even have to push it very hard to keep making plan and about 10 percent.

We've also been pretty successful in keeping Atlanta from finding out. If they knew, they'd up our plan, leaving us no time to sell, no time to develop new customers, no time to make cold calls, or anything. This way we use this new area as a little cushion, and it helps us to stay on top of our territory. I had to tell you because we'll be talking about the old people this afternoon. The boys seem to think you are OK, so I'm trusting you with it. I hope I'm not making a mistake telling you this.

BACK IN ATLANTA

Soon after the Tampa meeting, the researcher left the Florida sales team and headed back for New York. On the way back he stopped off for a final brief visit with Brenda Cooper. He found her even more concerned about her problems:

I'm getting all kinds of pressure from New York to jack up my sales in the region. They are pushing me to increase plan for the next year. I really am beginning to feel that my job is on the line on this one. If I can't come up with something that is good in the coming year, the future for me at HFP looks bleak.

At the same time I'm getting flak from my district managers. They all say that they're running flat out as is and they can't squeeze any more sales out of the district than they already are. Even Jay Boyar is complaining that he may not make plan if we have another increase next year. At the same time, he always seems to pull out his 10 percent extra by the end of the year. I wonder what they're really doing down there.   □

CASE QUESTIONS

1. Why did the Florida sales group withhold information from the home office?
2. Do you believe that withholding information is a common practice among personnel in the field? Explain.
3. How could field personnel jobs be designed so as to encourage open communication with home office personnel?

LORDSTOWN PLANT OF GENERAL MOTORS

INTRODUCTION

In December 1971, the management of the Lordstown Plant was very much concerned with an unusually high rate of defective Vegas coming off the assembly line. For the previous several weeks, the lot with a capacity of 2,000 cars had been filled with Vegas which were waiting for rework before they could be shipped out to the dealers around the country.

The management was particularly disturbed by the fact that many of the defects were not the kinds of quality deficiency normally expected in an assembly production of automobiles.[1] There was a countless number of Vegas with their windshields broken, upholstery slashed, ignition keys broken, signal levers bent, rear-view mirrors broken, or carburetors clogged with washers. There were cases in which, as the Plant Manager put it, "the whole engine blocks passed by 40 men without any work done on them."

Since then, the incident in the Lordstown Plant has been much publicized in news media, drawing public interest. It has also been frequently discussed in the classroom and in the academic circles. While some people viewed the event as "young worker revolt," others reacted to it as a simple "labor problem." Some viewed it as "worker sabotage," and others called it "industrial Woodstock."

This case describes some background and important incidents leading to this much publicized and discussed industrial event.

The General Motors Corporation is the nation's largest manufacturer. The Company is a leading example among many industrial organizations which have achieved organizational growth and success through decentralization. The philosophy of decentralization has been one of the most valued traditions in General Motors from the days of Alfred Sloan in the 1930's through Charles Wilson and Harlow Curtice in the 1950's and up to recent years.

Under decentralized management, each of the company's car divisions, Cadillac, Buick, Oldsmobile, Pontiac and Chevrolet, was given a maximum autonomy in the management of its manufacturing and marketing operations. The assembly operations were no exception, each division managing its own assembly work. The car bodies built by Fisher Body were assembled in various locations under maximum control and coordination between the Fisher Body and each car division.

In the mid-1960's, however, the decentralization in divisional assembly operations was subject to a critical review. At the divisional level, the company was experiencing serious problems of worker absenteeism and increasing cost with declines in quality and productivity. They were reflected in the overall profit margins which were declining from 10% to 7% in the late 1960's. The autonomy in the divided management in body manufacturing and assembly operations, in separate locations in many cases, became questionable under the declining profit situation.

In light of these developments, General Motors began to consolidate in some instances the divided management of body and chassis assembly operations into a single management under the already existing General Motors Assembly Division (GMAD) in order to better coordinate the two operations. The GMAD was given an overall responsibility to integrate the two operations in these instances and see that the numerous parts and components going into car assembly get to the right places in the right amounts at the right times.[2]

---

[1] The normal defect rate requiring rework was fluctuating between 1–2% at the time.

[2] A typical assembly plant has five major assembly lines—hard trim, soft trim, body, paint, and final—supported by sub-assembly lines which feed to the main lines such components as engines, transmissions, wheels and tires, radiators, gas tanks, front and sheet metal, and scores of other items. The average vehicle on assembly lines has more than 5,500 items with quality checks numbering 5 million in a typical GMAD assembly plant in a 16-hour a day operation.

Source: This case was prepared by Hak-Chong Lee, State University of New York at Albany, and is used here with his permission. This case was developed for instructional purposes from published sources and interviews with the General Motors Assembly Division officials in Warren, Michigan, and Lordstown, Ohio. The case was read and minor corrections were made by the Public Relations Office of the GMAD. However, the author is solely responsible for the content of the case. The author appreciates the cooperation of General Motors. He also appreciates the suggestions of Professor Anthony Athos of Harvard and Mr. John Grix of General Motors which improved this case.

THE GENERAL MOTORS ASSEMBLY DIVISION (GMAD)

The GMAD was originally established in the mid 1930's, when the company needed an additional assembly plant to meet the increasing demands for Buick, Oldsmobile, and Pontiac automobiles. The demands for these cars were growing so much beyond the available capacity at the time that the company began, for the first time, to build an assembly plant on the west coast which could turn out all three lines of cars rather than an individual line. As this novel approach became successful, similar plants turning out a multiple line of cars were built in seven other locations in the east, south and midwest. In the 1960's the demand for Chevrolet production also increased, and some Buick-Oldsmobile-Pontiac plants began to assemble Chevrolet products. Accordingly, the name of the division was changed to GMAD in 1965.

In order to improve the quality and productivity, the GMAD increased its control over the operations of body manufacturing and assembly. It reorganized jobs, launched programs to improve efficiency, and reduced the causes of defects which required repairs and rework. With many positive results attained under the GMAD management, the company extended the single management concept to six more assembly locations in 1968 which had been run by the Fisher Body and Chevrolet Divisions. In 1971, the GM further extended the concept to four additional Chevrolet-Fisher Body assembly facilities, consolidating the separate management under which the body and chassis assembly had been operating. One of these plants was the Lordstown Plant.

The series of consolidation brought to eighteen the number of assembly plants operated by the GMAD. In terms of total production, they were producing about 75% of all cars and 67% of trucks built by the GM. Also in 1971, one of the plants under the GMAD administration began building certain Cadillac models, thus involving GMAD in production of automobiles for each of the GM's five domestic car divisions as well as trucks for both Chevrolet and GMC Truck and Coach Division.

THE LORDSTOWN COMPLEX

The Lordstown complex is located in Trumbull County in Ohio, about 15 miles west of Youngstown and 30 miles east of Akron. It consists of the Vega assembly plant, the van-truck assembly plant, and Fisher Body metal fabricating plant, occupying about 1,000 acres of land. GMAD which operates the Vega and van-truck assembly plants is also located in the Lordstown complex. The three plants are in the heart of the heavy industrial triangle of Youngstown, Akron and Cleveland. With Youngstown as a center of steel production. Akron the home of rubber industries, and Cleveland as a major center for heavy manufacturing, the Lordstown complex commands a good strategic and logistic location for automobile assembly.

The original assembly plant was originally built in 1964–1966 to assemble Impalas. But in 1970 it was converted into Vega assembly with extensive arrangements. The van-truck assembly plant was constructed in 1969, and the Fisher Body metal fabricating plant was further added in 1970 to carry out stamping operations to produce sheet metal components used in Vega and van assemblies. In October 1971, the Chevrolet Vega and van-assembly plants and Fisher Body Vega assembly plants which had been operating under separate management were merged into a single jurisdiction of the GMAD.

WORK FORCE AT THE LORDSTOWN PLANT

There are over 11,400 employees working in the Lordstown Plant (as of 1973). Approximately 6,000 people, of whom 5,500 are on hourly payroll, work in the Vega assembly plant. About 2,600 workers, 2,100 of them paid hourly, work in van-truck assembly. As members of the United Auto Workers Union, Local 1112, the workers command good wages and benefits. They start out on the line at about $5.00 an hour, get a 10¢ an hour increase within 30 days, and another 10¢ after 90 days. Benefits come to $2.50 an hour.[3] The supplemental unemployment benefits virtually guarantee the worker's wages throughout the year. If the worker is laid off, he gets more than 90% of his wages for 52 weeks. He is also eligible for up to six days for holidays, excused absence or bereavement, and up to four weeks vacation.

The work force at the plant is almost entirely made up of local people with 92% coming from the immediate area of a 20-mile radius. Lordstown itself is a small rural town of about 500 residents. A sizable city closest to the plant is Warren, 5 miles away, which together with Youngstown supplies about two-thirds of the work force. The majority of the workers (57.5%)

---

[3] In GM, the average worker on the line earns $12,500 a year with fringe benefits of $3,000.

are married, 7.6% are home owners, and 20.2% are buying their homes. Of those who do not own their own homes (72%), over one-half are still living with their parents. The rest live in rented houses or apartments.

The workers in the plant are generally young. Although various news media reported the average worker age as 24 years old, and in some parts of the plant as 22 years, the company records show that the overall average worker age was somewhat above 29 years as of 1971–72. The national average is 42. The work force at Lordstown is the second youngest among GM's 25 assembly plants around the country. The fact that the Lordstown plant is the GM's newest assembly plant may partly explain the relatively young work force.

The educational profile of the Lordstown workers indicates that only 22.2% have less than a high school education. Nearly two-thirds or 62% are high school graduates, and 16% are either college graduates or have attended college. Another 26% have attended trade school. The average education of 13.2 years makes the Lordstown workers among the best educated in GM's assembly plants.

THE VEGA ASSEMBLY LINE

Conceived as a major competitive product against the increasing influx of foreign cars which were being produced at as low as one-fourth the labor rate in this country, the Vega was specifically designed with a maximum production efficiency and economy in mind. From the initial stages of planning, the Vega was designed by a special task team with most sophisticated techniques, using computers in designing the outer skin of the car and making the tapes that form the dies. Computers were also used to match up parts, measure the stack tolerances, measure safety performance under head-on collision, and make all necessary corrections before the first 1971 model car was ever built. The 2300-cubic-centimeter all-aluminum, 4-cylinder engine, was designed to give gas economy comparable to the foreign imports.

The Vega was also designed with the plant and the people in mind. As the GM's newest plant, the Vega assembly plant was known as the "super plant" with the most modern and sophisticated designs to maximize efficiency. It featured the newest engineering techniques and a variety of new power tools and automatic devices to eliminate much of the heavy lifting and physical labor. The line gave the workers an easier access to the car body, reducing the amount of bending and crawling in and out, as in other plants around the country. The unitized body in large components like pre-fab housing made the assembly easier and lighter with greater body integrity. Most difficult and tedious tasks were eliminated or simplified, on-line variations of the job were minimized, and the most modern tooling and mechanization was used to the highest possible degree of reliability.

It was also the fastest moving assembly line in the industry. The average time per assembly job was 36 seconds with a maximum of 100 cars rolling off the assembly line per hour for a daily production of 1,600 cars from two shift operations. The time cycle per job in other assembly plants averaged about 55 seconds. Although the high speed of the line did not necessarily imply greater work load or job requirement, it was a part of the GM's attempt to maximize economy in Vega assembly. The fact that the Vega was designed to have 43% fewer parts than a full-size car also helped the high-speed line and economy.

IMPACT OF GMAD AND REORGANIZATION IN THE LORDSTOWN PLANT

As stated previously, the assembly operations at Lordstown had originally been run by Fisher Body and Chevrolet as two plants. There were two organizations, two plant managers, two unions, and two service organizations. The consolidation of the two organizations into a single operating system under the GMAD in October 1971 required a difficult task of reorganization and dealing with the consequences of manpower reduction such as work slowdown, worker discipline, grievances, etc.

As duplicating units such as production, maintenance, inspection, and personnel were consolidated, there was a problem of selecting the personnel to manage the new organization. There were chief inspectors, personnel directors and production superintendents as well as production and service workers to be displaced or reassigned. Unions which had been representing their respective plants also had to go through reorganization. Union elections were held to merge the separate union committees at Fisher Body and Chevrolet in a single union bargaining committee. This eliminated one full local union shop committee.

At the same time, GMAD launched an effort to improve production efficiency more in line with that in other assembly plants. It included increasing job efficiency through reorganization and better coordination between the body and chassis assembly, and improving controls over product quality and worker absenteeism. This effort coincided with the plant's early operational stage at the time which required adjustments in line balance and work methods. Like other assembly plants, the Vega assembly plant was going through an initial period of diseconomy caused by suboptimal operations, imbalance in the assembly line, and somewhat redundant work force. According to management, line adjustment and work changes were a normal process in accelerating the assembly operation to the peak performance the plant had been designed for after the initial break-in and start-up period.

As for job efficiency, the GMAD initiated changes in those work sequences and work methods which were not well coordinated under the divided managements of body and chassis assembly. For example, previous to the GMAD, Fisher Body had been delivering the car body complete with interior trim to the final assembly lines, where oftentimes the workers soiled the front seats as they did further assembly operations. GMAD changed this practice so that the seats were installed as one of the last operations in building the car. Fisher Body also had been delivering the car body with complete panel instrument frame which made it extremely difficult for the assembly workers to reach behind the frame in installing the instrument panels. The GMAD improved the job method so that the box containing the entire instrument panels was installed on the assembly line. Such improvements in job sequences and job methods resulted in savings in time and the number of workers required. Consequently, there were some jobs where the assembly time was cut down and/or the number of workers was reduced.

GMAD also put more strict control over worker absenteeism and the causes for defect work; the reduction in absenteeism was expected to require less relief men, and the improvement in quality and less repair work were to require less repairmen. In implementing these changes, the GMAD instituted a strong policy of dealing with worker slowdowns via strict disciplinary measures including dismissal. It was rumored that the inspectors and foremen passing defective cars would be fired on the spot.

Many workers were laid off as a result of the reorganization and job changes. The union was claiming that as many as 700 workers were laid off. Management, on the other hand, put the layoff figure at 375 to which the union later conceded.[4] Although manage-

ment claimed that the changes in job sequence and method in some assembly work did not bring a substantial change in the overall speed or pace of the assembly line, the workers perceived the job change as "tightening" the assembly line. The union charged that the GMAD brought a return of an old-fashioned line speedup and a "sweatshop style" of management reminiscent of the 1930's, making the men do more work at the same pay. The workers were blaming the "tightened" assembly line for the drastic increase in quality defects. As one worker commented, "That's the fastest line in the world. We have about 40 seconds to do our job. The company adds one more thing and it can kill us. We can't get the stuff done on time and a car goes by. The company then blames us for sabotage and shoddy work."

The number of worker grievances also increased drastically. Before GMAD took over, there were about 100 grievances in the plant. Since then, grievances increased to 5,000, 1,000 of which were related to the charge that too much work had been added to the job. The worker resentment was particularly great in "towveyor" assembly and seat sub-assembly areas. The "towveyor" is the area where engines and transmissions are assembled. Like seat sub-assembly there is a great concentration of workers working together in close proximity. Also, these jobs are typically for beginning assemblers who tend to make the work crew in these areas younger and better educated.

The workers in the plant were particularly resentful of the company's strict policy in implementing the changes. They stated that the tougher the company became, the more they would stiffen their resistance even though other jobs were scarce in the market. One worker said, "In some of the other plants where the GMAD did the same thing, the workers were older and they took this. But, I've got 25 years ahead of me in this plant." Another worker commented, "I saw a woman running to keep pace with the fast line. I'm not going to run for anybody. There ain't anyone in that plant that is going to tell me to run." One foreman said, "The problem with the workers here is not so much that they don't want to work, but that they just don't want to take orders. They don't believe in any kind of authority."

While the workers were resisting management orders, there were some indications that the first-line supervisors had not been adequately trained to perform satisfactory supervisory roles. The average super-

---

[4] All of the workers who had been laid off were later reinstated as the plant needed additional workers to perform assembly jobs for optional features to Vega, i.e., vinyl top, etc., which were later introduced. In addition, some workers were put to work at the van-assembly plant.

EXHIBIT 1

Flowchart of major assembly operations.

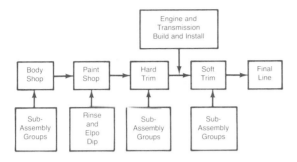

visor at the time had less than 3 years of experience, and 20% of the supervisors had less than 1 year's experience. Typically, they were young, somewhat lacking in knowledge of the provisions of the union contract and other supervisory duties, and less than adequately trained to handle the workers in the threatening and hostile environment which was developing.

Another significant fact was that the strong reactions of the workers were not entirely from the organizational and job changes brought about by the GMAD alone. Management noted that there was a significant amount of worker reactions in the areas where the company hadn't changed anything at all. Management felt that the intense resentment was particularly due to the nature of the work force in Lordstown. The plant was not only made up of young people, but also the work force reflected the characteristics of "tough labor" in steel, coal and rubber industries in the surrounding communities. Many of the workers in fact came from families who made their living working in these industries. Management also noted that the worker resistance had been much greater in the Lordstown Plant than in other plants where similar changes had been made.

A good part of the young workers' resentment also seemed to be related to the unskilled and repetitive nature of the assembly work. One management official admitted that the company was facing a difficult task in getting workers to "take pride" in the product they were assembling. Many of them were benefiting from the company's tuition assistance plan which was supporting their college education in the evening. With this educated background, obviously assembly work was not fulfilling their high work expectations. Also, the job market was tight at the time, and they could neither find any meaningful jobs elsewhere nor, even

if found, could they afford to give up the good money and fringe benefits they were earning on their assembly-line jobs. This made them frustrated, according to company officials.

Many industrial engineers were questioning whether the direction of management toward assembly line work could continue. As the jobs became easier, simpler, and repetitive, requiring less physical effort, there were less and less traces of skill and increased monotony. The worker unrest indicated that they not only wanted to go back to the work pace prior to the "speedup" (pre-October pace), but also wanted the company to do something about the boring and meaningless assembly work. One worker commented, "The company has got to do something to change the job so that a guy can take an interest in the job. A guy can't do the same thing 8 hours a day year after year. And it's got to be more than the company just saying to a guy, 'Okay, instead of 6 spots on the weld, you'll do 5 spots.'"

As the worker resentment mounted, the UAW Local 1112 decided in early January 1972 to consider possible authorization for a strike against the Lordstown Plant in a fight against the job changes. In the meantime, the union and management bargaining teams worked hard on worker grievances; they reduced the number of grievances from 5,000 to a few hundred; management even indicated that it would restore some of the eliminated jobs. However, the bargaining failed to produce accord on the issues of seniority rights and shift preference, which were related to wider issues of job changes and layoff.

A vote was held in early February 1972. Nearly 90% of the workers came out to vote which was the heaviest turnout in the history of the Local. With 97% of the votes supporting, the workers went out on strike in early March.

In March 1972, with the strike in effect, the management of the Lordstown Plant was assessing the impact of the GMAD and the resultant strike in the Plant. It was estimated that the work disruption because of the worker resentment and slowdown had already cost the company 12,000 Vegas and 4,000 trucks amounting to $45 million. There had been repeated closedowns of assembly lines since December 1971, because of the worker slowdowns and the cars passing down the line without all necessary operations performed on them. The car lot was full with 2,000 cars waiting for repair work.

There had also been an amazing number of complaints from Chevrolet dealers, 6,000 complaints in November alone, about the quality of the Vegas shipped to them. This was more than the combined complaints from the other assembly plants.

The strike in the Lordstown Plant was expected to affect other plants. The plants at Tonawanda, New York and Buffalo, New York were supplying parts for Vega. Despite the costly impact of the worker resistance and the strike, the management felt that the job changes and cost reductions were essential if the Vega were to return a profit to the company. The plant had to be operating at about 90% capacity to break even. Not only had the plant with highly automated features cost twice as much as estimated, but also the Vega itself ended up weighing 10% more than had been planned.

While the company had to do something to increase the production efficiency in the Lordstown Plant, the management was wondering whether it couldn't have planned and implemented the organizational and job changes differently in view of the costly disruption of the operations and the organizational stress the Plant had been experiencing.   ☐

CASE QUESTIONS

1. Evaluate whether the job redesign efforts at the Lordstown plant were successful.
2. What are the important lessons to be learned from the Lordstown Experience regarding job redesign as a way to improve productivity?
3. What other job redesign approaches could have been used at the Lordstown plant? What advantages would they have offered in comparison to the one that was used?

PART V

ORGANIZATIONAL PROCESSES

DECISION MAKING

LEARNING OBJECTIVES

DEFINE the terms Delphi technique and nominal group technique.

DESCRIBE the differences between individual and group decision making.

DISCUSS behavioral factors which influence the decision-making process.

COMPARE programmed and nonprogrammed decisions.

IDENTIFY the specific steps in the decision-making process.

The focus of this chapter is on decision making. The quality of the decisions that managers reach is the yardstick of their effectiveness. Indeed, it has been suggested that management *is* decision making, and because it is, the very essence of the entire managerial process is to be found in its study. Increasingly, however, important decisions are being made in organizations by nonmanagers. Thus, while decision making is an important management process, it is fundamentally a *people* process. This chapter, therefore, describes and analyzes decision making in terms that reflect the ways in which people make decisions based upon their understanding of individual, group, and organizational goals and objectives.

TYPES OF DECISIONS

Managers in various kinds of organizations may be separated by background, lifestyle, and distance, but sooner or later, they must all make decisions. Even when the decision process is highly participative in nature, with full involvement by subordinates, it is the manager who ultimately is responsible for the outcomes of a decision. In this section, our purpose is to present a classification system into which various kinds of decisions can be placed, regardless of whether the manager makes the decision unilaterally or in consultation with, or delegation to, subordinates.

Specialists in the field of decision making have developed several ways of classifying different types of decisions. For the most part, these classification systems are similar, differing mainly in terminology. We use the widely adopted distinction suggested by Herbert Simon.[1] Simon distinguishes between two types of decisions:

1. *Programmed decisions.* If a particular situation occurs often, a routine procedure usually will be worked out for solving it. Thus, decisions are **programmed** to the extent that they are repetitive and routine and a definite procedure has been developed for handling them.

2. *Nonprogrammed decisions.* Decisions are **nonprogrammed** when they are novel and unstructured. Thus, there is no established procedure for handling the problem, either because it has not arisen in exactly the same manner before or because it is complex or extremely important. Such decisions deserve special treatment.

---

[1] Herbert A. Simon, *The New Science of Management Decision* (New York: Harper & Row, 1960), pp. 5–6.

TABLE 13–1

Types of Decisions

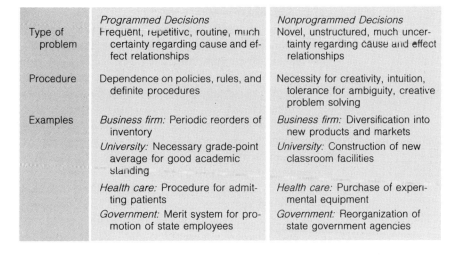

	Programmed Decisions	Nonprogrammed Decisions
Type of problem	Frequent, repetitive, routine, much certainty regarding cause and effect relationships	Novel, unstructured, much uncertainty regarding cause and effect relationships
Procedure	Dependence on policies, rules, and definite procedures	Necessity for creativity, intuition, tolerance for ambiguity, creative problem solving
Examples	*Business firm:* Periodic reorders of inventory	*Business firm:* Diversification into new products and markets
	University: Necessary grade-point average for good academic standing	*University:* Construction of new classroom facilities
	Health care: Procedure for admitting patients	*Health care:* Purchase of experimental equipment
	Government: Merit system for promotion of state employees	*Government:* Reorganization of state government agencies

While the two classifications are broad, they point out the importance of differentiating between programmed and nonprogrammed decisions. The managements of most organizations face great numbers of programmed decisions in their daily operations. Such decisions should be treated without expending unnecessary organizational resources on them. On the other hand, the nonprogrammed decision must be properly identified as such since it is this type of decision that forms the basis for allocating billions of dollars worth of resources in our economy every year. Unfortunately, it is the human process involving this type of decision that we know the least about.[2] Table 13–1 presents a breakdown of the different types of decisions, with examples of each type in different kinds of organizations. The table illustrates that programmed and nonprogrammed decisions require different kinds of procedures and apply to distinctly different types of problems.

Traditionally, programmed decisions have been handled through rules, standard operating procedures, and the structure of the organization that develops specific procedures for handling them. More recently, operations researchers—through the development of mathematical models—have facilitated the handling of these types of decisions.

On the other hand, nonprogrammed decisions usually have been handled by general problem-solving processes, judgment, intuition, and creativity. Unfortunately, the advances that modern management techniques have made in improving nonprogrammed decision making have not been nearly as great as the advances they have made in improving programmed decision making.[3]

---

[2] Stephen A. Stumpf, Dale E. Zand, and Richard D. Freedman, "Designing Groups for Judgmental Decisions," *Academy of Management Review,* October 1979, pp. 589–600.

[3] See Herbert A. Simon, *The Shape of Automation* (New York: Harper & Row, 1965); and I. L. Janis and L. Mann, *Decision Making: A Psychological Analysis of Conflict, Choice, and Commitment* (New York: Free Press, 1977).

Ideally, the main concern of top management should be nonprogrammed decisions, while first-level management should be concerned with programmed decisions. Middle managers in most organizations concentrate mostly on programmed decisions, although in some cases they will participate in nonprogrammed decisions. In other words, the nature, frequency, and degree of certainty surrounding a problem should dictate at what level of management the decision should be made.

Obviously, problems arise in those organizations where top management expends much time and effort on programmed decisions. One unfortunate result of this practice is a neglect of long-range planning. In such cases, long-range planning is subordinated to other activities, whether the organization is successful or is having problems. If the organization is successful, this justifies continuing the policies and practices that have achieved success. If the organization experiences difficulty, its current problems have first priority and occupy the time of top management. In either case, long-range planning ends up being neglected.

Finally, the neglect of long-range planning usually results in an overemphasis on short-run control. This results in a lack of delegation of authority to lower levels of management, which often has adverse effects on motivation and satisfaction.

THE DECISION-MAKING PROCESS

Decisions should be thought of as *means* rather than ends. They are the *organizational mechanisms* through which an attempt is made to achieve a desired state. They are, in effect, an *organizational response* to a problem. Every decision is the outcome of a dynamic process that is influenced by a multitude of forces. This process is diagrammed in Figure 13–1. The reader should not, however, interpret this outline to mean that decision making is a fixed procedure. It is a sequential process rather than a series of steps. This sequence diagram enables us to examine each element in the normal progression that leads to a decision.

Examination of Figure 13–1 reveals that it is more applicable to nonprogrammed decisions than to programmed decisions. Problems that occur infrequently, with a great deal of uncertainty surrounding the outcome, require that the manager utilize the entire process. For problems that occur frequently, however, it is not necessary to consider the entire process. If a policy is established to handle such problems, it will not be necessary to develop and evaluate alternatives each time a problem of this kind arises.

ESTABLISHING SPECIFIC GOALS AND OBJECTIVES AND MEASURING RESULTS

Goals and objectives are needed in each area where performance influences the effectiveness of the organization. If goals and objectives are adequately established, they will dictate what results must be achieved and what measures will indicate whether or not they have been achieved.

FIGURE 13–1

The Decision-Making Process

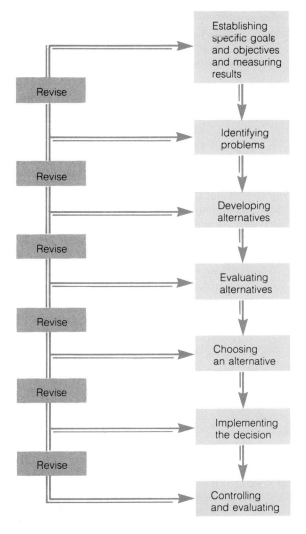

IDENTIFYING PROBLEMS

A necessary condition for a decision is a problem. That is, if problems did not exist, there would be no need for decisions.[4] This underscores the importance of establishing goals and objectives. How critical a problem is for the organization is measured by the gap between the levels of performance specified in the organization's goals and objectives and the levels of performance attained. Thus, a gap of 20 percent between a sales volume objective and the volume of sales actually achieved signifies that some problem exists.

It is easy to understand that a problem exists when a gap occurs between desired results and actual results. However, certain factors often lead to difficulties in identifying exactly what the problem is.[5] These factors are:

---

[4] Two excellent references on this and related problems are W. E. Pounds, "The Process of Problem Finding," *Industrial Management Review,* Fall 1969, pp. 1–19; and C. E. Watson, "The Problems of Problem Solving," *Business Horizons,* August 1976, pp. 88–94.

[5] See G. P. Huber, *Managerial Decision Making* (Glenview, Ill.: Scott, Foresman, 1980).

1. Perceptual Problems.   As noted in Chapter 3, individual perceptions may act in such a way as to protect or defend us from unpleasant perceptions. Thus, negative information may be selectively perceived in such a way as to distort its true meaning. It also may be totally ignored. For example, a college dean may fail to identify increasing class sizes as a problem while at the same time being sensitive to problems faced by the president of the university in raising funds for the school.

2. Defining Problems in Terms of Solutions.   This is really a form of jumping to conclusions. For example, a sales manager may say, "The decrease in profits is due to our poor product quality." The sales manager's definition of the problem suggests a particular solution: the improvement of product quality in the production department. Certainly, other solutions may be possible. Perhaps the sales force has been inadequately selected or trained. Perhaps competitors have a superior product.

3. Identifying Symptoms as Problems.   "Our problem is a 32-percent decline in orders." While it is certainly true that orders have declined, the decline in orders is really a symptom of the real problem. When the manager identifies the real problem, the cause of the decline in orders will be found.

Problems usually are of three types: opportunity, crisis, or routine.[6] **Crisis** and **routine** problems present themselves and must be attended to by the managers. **Opportunities,** on the other hand, usually must be found. They await discovery, and they often go unnoticed and eventually are lost by an inattentive manager. This is because, by their very nature, most crises and routine problems demand immediate attention. Thus, a manager may spend more time in handling problems than in pursuing important new opportunities.[7] Many well-managed organizations try to draw attention away from crises and routine problems and toward longer-range issues through planning activities and goal-setting programs.

DEVELOPING ALTERNATIVES

Before a decision is made, feasible alternatives should be developed (actually these are potential solutions to the problem), and the potential consequences of each alternative should be considered. This is really a search process in which the relevant internal and external environments of the organization are investigated to provide information that can be developed into possible alternatives. Obviously, this search is conducted within certain time and cost constraints, since only so much effort can be devoted to developing alternatives.[8]

---

[6] H. Mintzberg, D. Raisinghavi, and A. Theoret, "The Structure of 'Unstructured' Decision Processes," *Administrative Science Quarterly,* Spring 1976, pp. 246–75.

[7] James W. Fredrickson, "Effects of Decision Motive and Organizational Performance Level on Strategic Decision Processes," *Academy of Management Journal,* December 1985, pp. 821–43.

[8] For a recent example, see Howard M. Weiss, Daniel R. Ilgen, and Michael E. Sharbaugh, "Effects of Life and Job Stress on Information Search Behavior of Organizational Members," *Journal of Applied Psychology,* February 1982, pp. 60–66.

For example, a sales manager may identify an inadequately trained sales force as the cause of declining sales. The sales manager then would identify possible alternatives for solving the problem, such as (1) a sales training program conducted at the home office by management, (2) a sales training program conducted by a professional training organization at a site away from the home office, or (3) more intense on-the-job training.

EVALUATING ALTERNATIVES

Once alternatives have been developed, they must be evaluated and compared. In every decision situation, the objective in making a decision is to select the alternative that will produce the most favorable outcomes and the least unfavorable outcomes. This again points up the necessity of objectives and goals, since, in selecting from among alternatives, the decision maker should be guided by the previously established goals and objectives. The alternative-outcome relationship is based on three possible conditions:

1. *Certainty.* The decision maker has complete knowledge of the probability of the outcome of each alternative.
2. *Uncertainty.* The decision maker has absolutely no knowledge of the probability of the outcome of each alternative.
3. *Risk.* The decision maker has some probabilistic estimate of the outcomes of each alternative.

Decision making under conditions of risk is probably the most common situation. It is in evaluating alternatives under these conditions that statisticians and operations researchers have made important contributions to decision making. Their methods have proved especially useful in the analysis and ranking of alternatives. Sometimes, however, as the following OBM Encounter illustrates, less "scientific" approaches are used.

HUNCH PLAYING AND DECISION MAKING

On occasion, decision makers—when asked what led them to make a particular decision—admit that they had a "feeling" or "played a hunch." Consider the following examples:

Robert Jensen, chairman of General Cable Corporation, has had to make strategic decisions regarding diversifying, which involved more than $300 million in sell-offs and acquisitions. He states: "On each decision, the mathematical analysis only got me to the point where my intuition had to take over."

The late Ray Kroc recounted how he decided to invest $2.7 million in 1960 to purchase the McDonald name, a decision considered to be a bad deal by his lawyer. Kroc said: "I closed my office door, cussed up and down, threw things out the window, called my lawyer back and said: 'Take it.' I felt in my funny bone it was a sure thing."

Jean Paul Getty, the oil billionaire, in recalling his early days in the Texas oil fields, tells the story of how he sent his geologists to gather core samples in order to assess the likelihood of striking oil in a particular lease. The geologists performed their analyses and concluded there was no oil. Getty, however, just *felt* oil

Source: Based, in part, on an article by Roy Rowan, "Those Business Hunches are More than Blind Faith," *Fortune*, April 23, 1979, pp. 111–114.

was there and ordered drilling, anyway. The result was one of the richest fields with which Getty was ever associated.

So, while playing a hunch may pay dividends, keep in mind that planned, systematic approaches to decision making are, in the long run, going to produce the best decisions. For every story like those above, there are hundreds where a decision maker played a hunch—and lost.   □

CHOOSING AN ALTERNATIVE

The purpose in selecting an alternative is to solve a problem in order to achieve a predetermined objective. This point is an important one. It means that a decision is not an end in itself but only a means to an end. While the decision maker chooses the alternative that is expected to result in the achievement of the objective, the selection of that alternative should not be as an isolated act. If it is, the factors that led to and lead from the decision are likely to be excluded. Specifically, the steps following the decision should include implementation, control, and evaluation. The critical point is that decision making is *more* than an act of choosing; it is a dynamic process.[9]

Unfortunately for most managers, situations rarely exist in which one alternative achieves the desired objective without having some positive or negative impact on another objective. Situations often exist where two objectives cannot be optimized simultaneously. If one objective is *optimized*, the other is *suboptimized*. In a business organization, for example, if production is optimized, employee morale may be suboptimized, or vice versa. Or a hospital superintendent optimizes a short-run objective such as maintenance costs at the expense of a long-run objective such as high-quality patient care. Thus, the multiplicity of organizational objectives complicates the real world of the decision maker.[10]

A situation could also exist where attainment of an organizational objective would be at the expense of a societal objective. The reality of such situations is seen clearly in the rise of ecology groups, environmentalists, and the consumerist movement. Apparently, these groups question the priorities (organizational as against societal) of certain organizational decision makers. In any case, whether an organizational objective conflicts with another organizational objective or with a societal objective, the values of the decision maker will strongly influence the alternative chosen. Individual values were discussed earlier, and their influence on the decision-making process should be clear.

Thus, in managerial decision making, *optimal* solutions often are impossible. This is because the decision maker cannot possibly know all of the available alternatives, the consequences of each alternative, and the probability of occurrence of these consequences. Thus, rather than being an *optimizer,* the decision maker is a *satisficer,* selecting the alternative that meets an acceptable (satisfactory) standard.[11]

---

[9] This important point is discussed in detail in E. F. Harrison, *The Managerial Decision-Making Process* (Boston: Houghton Mifflin, 1975); and Huber, *Managerial Decision Making.* These are excellent comprehensive works on the subject of managerial decision making.

[10] See R. L. Daft, "System Influence on Organizational Decision Making: The Case of Resource Allocation," *Academy of Management Journal,* March 1978, pp. 6–22.

[11] For a comprehensive discussion devoted solely to this problem, *see* Janis and Mann, *Decision Making,* chap. 2.

IMPLEMENTING THE DECISION

Any decision is little more than an abstraction if it is not implemented. In other words, a decision must be effectively implemented in order to achieve the objective for which it was made. It is entirely possible for a "good" decision to be hurt by poor implementation. In this sense, implementation may be more important than the actual choice of the alternative.

Since, in most situations, implementing decisions involves people, the test of the soundness of a decision is the behavior of the people involved relative to the decision. While a decision may be technically sound, it can be undermined easily by dissatisfied subordinates. Subordinates cannot be manipulated in the same manner as other resources. Thus, a manager's job not only is to choose good solutions but also to transform such solutions into behavior in the organization. This is done by effectively communicating with the appropriate individuals and groups.[12]

CONTROL AND EVALUATION

Effective management involves periodic measurements of results. Actual results are compared with planned results (the objective), and if deviations exist, changes must be made. Here again, we see the importance of measurable objectives. If such objectives do not exist, then there is no way to judge performance. If actual results do not match planned results, changes must be made in the solution chosen, in its implementation, or in the original objective, if it is deemed unattainable. If the original objective must be revised, then the entire decision-making process will be reactivated. The important point is that once a decision is implemented, a manager cannot assume that the outcome will meet the original objective. Some system of control and evaluation is necessary to make sure the *actual results* are consistent with the *results planned for* when the decision was made.

Sometimes the result or outcome of a decision is unexpected, or is perceived differently by different people. Dealing with this possibility is an important part of the evaluation phase in the decision process. How a manager evaluates the results of a decision, along with suggestions on dealing with the outcome, is the topic of the article "Consequences," which accompanies this chapter.

BEHAVIORAL INFLUENCES ON INDIVIDUAL DECISION MAKING

Several behavioral factors influence the decision-making process. Some of these factors influence only certain aspects of the process, while others influence the entire process. However, each may have an impact and, therefore, must be understood to fully appreciate decision making as a process in organizations. Four individual behavioral factors—values, personality, propensity for risk, and potential for dissonance—are discussed in this section. Each of these factors has been shown to have a significant impact on the decision-making process.

---

[12] Teresa M. Harrison, "Communication and Participative Decision Making: An Exploratory Study," *Personnel Psychology,* Spring 1985, pp. 93–116.

VALUES   In the context of decision making, **values** can be thought of as the guidelines that a person uses when confronted with a situation in which a choice must be made. Values are acquired early in life and are a basic (often taken for granted) part of an individual's thoughts. The influence of values on the decision-making process is profound:

In *establishing objectives,* it is necessary to make value judgments regarding the selection of opportunities and the assignment of priorities.

In *developing alternatives,* it is necessary to make value judgments about the various possibilities.

In *choosing an alternative,* the values of the decision maker influence which alternative is chosen.

In *implementing* a decision, value judgments are necessary in choosing the means for implementation.

In the *evaluation and control* phase, value judgments cannot be avoided when corrective action is taken.[13]

It is clear that values pervade the decision-making process. They are reflected in the decision maker's behavior before making the decision, in making the decision, and in putting the decision into effect.

PERSONALITY   Decision makers are influenced by many psychological forces, both conscious and subconscious. One of the most important of these forces is the decision makers' personality, which is strongly reflected in the choices they make. Some studies have examined the effect of selected personality variables on the process of decision making.[14] These studies generally have focused on the following sets of variables:

1. *Personality variables.* These include the attitudes, beliefs, and needs of the individual.
2. *Situational variables.* These pertain to the external, observable situations in which individuals find themselves.
3. *Interactional variables.* These pertain to the momentary state of the individual as a result of the interaction of a specific situation with characteristics of the individual's personality.

The most important conclusions concerning the influence of personality on the decision-making process are as follows:

- It is unlikely that one person can be equally proficient in all aspects of the decision-making process. The results suggest that some people will

---

[13] Harrison, *Managerial Decision-Making Process,* p. 42.

[14] Orville C. Brun, Jr. et al., *Personality and Decision Processes* (Stanford, CA: Stanford University Press, 1962). Also see P. A. Renwick and H. Tose, "The Effects of Sex, Marital Status, and Educational Background on Selected Decisions," *Academy of Management Journal,* March 1978, pp. 93–103; and A. A. Abdel-Halim, "Effects of Task and Personality Characteristics on Subordinate Responses to Participative Decision Making," *Academy of Management Journal,* September 1983, pp. 477–84.

do better in one part of the process, while others will do better in another part.

- Such characteristics as intelligence are associated with different phases of the decision-making process.
- The relation of personality to the decision-making process may vary for different groups on the basis of such factors as sex and social status.

An important contribution of this research is that it determined that the personality traits of the decision maker combine with certain situational and interactional variables to influence the decision-making process.

PROPENSITY FOR RISK

From personal experience, you undoubtedly are aware that decision makers vary greatly in their propensity for taking risks. This one specific aspect of personality strongly influences the decision-making process. A decision maker who has a low aversion to risk will establish different objectives, evaluate alternatives differently, and select different alternatives than will another decision maker in the same situation who has a high aversion to risk. The latter will attempt to make choices where the risk or uncertainty is low or where the certainty of the outcome is high. You will see later in the chapter that many people are bolder and more innovative and advocate greater risk-taking in groups than as individuals. Apparently, such people are more willing to accept risk as members of a group.

Some organizations attempt to encourage risk-taking behavior by minimizing the penalties for making high-risk decisions that turn out to be wrong. The following OBM Encounter illustrates an example of this.

 ENCOUNTER
WHERE BAD DECISIONS ARE GOOD

Sometimes the safest decisions are not the best ones. A problem faced by organizations everywhere is how to get organizational members to be willing to take reasonable risks if the potential payoffs justify it. Many employees feel that making safe, yet suboptimal, decisions, is preferable to running the risks of failure by making decisions with greater potential rewards but lower likelihood of success.

At Heinz's highly successful frozen foods subsidiary, Ore-Ida, the company is trying to change this. Aware of the fact that the risk-taking behavior they want sometimes will result in poor decisions, the company has defined what it calls the "perfect failure" and has ar-

ranged for a cannon to be shot off in celebration every time one occurs. The cannon symbolizes that a mistake has been made, admitted, learned from, and then forgiven. Because bad decisions are openly discussed and treated positively, the risk-taking behavior is continued in decision making that the organization wants.

When the bad decision involves a substantive activity, such as a research project that is getting nowhere, the "perfect failure" program creates positive feelings toward calling a halt to the project early, rather than letting it drag on and continue to consume time, money, and other resources. ☐

Source: Thomas Peters and Robert Waterman, "How the Best-Run Companies Turn So-So Performers Into Winners," *Management Review*, November-December 1982, pp. 8–16.

POTENTIAL FOR
DISSONANCE
Much attention has been focused on the forces and influences affecting the decision maker before a decision is made, and on the decision itself. But only recently has attention been given to what happens *after* a decision has been made. Specifically, behavioral scientists have focused attention on the occurrence of postdecision anxiety.

Such anxiety is related to what Festinger calls "cognitive dissonance."[15] Festinger's **cognitive dissonance** theory states that there is often a lack of consistency or harmony among an individual's various cognitions (attitudes, beliefs, and so on) after a decision has been made. That is, there will be a conflict between what the decision maker knows and believes and what was done, and as a result the decision maker will have doubts and second thoughts about the choice that was made. In addition, there is a likelihood that the intensity of the anxiety will be greater when any of the following conditions exist:

1. The decision is an important one psychologically or financially.
2. There are a number of foregone alternatives.
3. The foregone alternatives have many favorable features.

Each of these conditions is present in many decisions in all types of organizations. You can expect, therefore, that post-decision dissonance will be present among many decision makers, especially those at higher levels in the organization.

When dissonance occurs, it can, of course, be reduced by admitting that a mistake has been made. Unfortunately, many individuals are reluctant to admit that they have made a wrong decision. These individuals will be more likely to use one or more of the following methods to reduce their dissonance:

1. Seek information that supports the wisdom of their decision.
2. Selectively perceive (distort) information in a way that supports their decision.
3. Adopt a less favorable view of the foregone alternatives.
4. Minimize the importance of the negative aspects of the decision and exaggerate the importance of the positive aspects.[16]

While each of us may resort to some of this behavior in our personal decision making, it is easy to see how a great deal of it could be extremely harmful in terms of organizational effectiveness. The potential for dissonance is influenced heavily by one's personality, specifically one's self-confidence and persuasibility. In fact, all of the behavioral influences are closely interrelated and are only isolated here for purposes of discussion. For example,

---

[15] Leon Festinger, *A Theory of Cognitive Dissonance* (New York: Harper & Row, 1957), chap. 1.

[16] W. J. McGuire, "Cognitive Consistency and Attitude Change," *Journal of Abnormal and Social Psychology*, May 1960, pp. 345–53. Also see J. S. Adams, "Reduction of Cognitive Dissonance by Seeking Consonant Information," *Journal of Abnormal and Social Psychology*, January 1961, pp. 74–78; D. S. Holmes and B. K. Houston, "Effectiveness of Situation Redefinition and Affective Isolation in Coping with Stress," *Journal of Personality and Social Psychology*, August 1974, pp. 212–18; and C. A. O'Reilly III, "Variations in Decision Makers' Use of Information Sources: The Impact of Quality and Accessibility of Information," *Academy of Management Journal*, December 1982, pp. 756–71.

what kind of a risk-taker you are and your potential for anxiety following a decision are very closely related, and both are strongly influenced by your personality, your perceptions, and your value system. Before managers can fully understand the dynamics of the decision-making process, they must appreciate the behavioral influences on themselves and other decision makers in the organization when they make decisions.

GROUP DECISION MAKING

The first parts of this chapter focused on individuals making decisions. In most organizations, however, a great deal of decision making is achieved through committees, teams, task forces, and other kinds of groups. This is because managers frequently face situations in which they must seek and combine judgments in group meetings. This is especially true for nonprogrammed problems, which are novel, with much uncertainty regarding the outcome. In most organizations, it is unusual to find decisions on such problems being made by one individual on a regular basis. The increased complexity of many of these problems requires specialized knowledge in numerous fields, usually not possessed by one person. This requirement, coupled with the reality that the decisions made eventually must be accepted and implemented by many units throughout the organization, has increased the use of the collective approach to the decision-making process. The result for many managers has been an endless amount of time spent in meetings of committees and other groups. It has been found that many managers spend as much as 80 percent of their working time in committee meetings.[17] The following OBM Encounter details one company's emphasis on group decision making.

 ENCOUNTER

GROUP DECISION MAKING AT PENNEY'S

Retailing is not an industry typically associated with being at the forefront of management techniques. Nonetheless, one of the largest retailers in the country, J.C. Penney, has for years adapted management techniques ahead of most other companies. Such is the case with group decision making.

The move toward group decision making at Penney's has a very specific underlying objective: to help develop managers who feel comfortable with the company's reoriented merchandising thrust. Many observers feel that this move toward group decision making has played a major role in Penney's recent upsurge in profitability.

Penney's relies very heavily on the use of committees. A permanent management committee, consisting of the top 14 officers, makes collective decisions concerning strategic planning, executive succession, and merchandising. Permanent subcommittees are delegated the task of handling key parts of the business, while ad hoc groups are formed to deal with specific, non-recurring issues.

One of the by-products, in addition to sounder decisions, is that both enthusiasm and morale are positively effected, because key personnel know they will have an opportunity to make inputs. ☐

Source: Adapted from "Teamwork Pays Off at Penney's," *Business Week,* April 12, 1982, p. 107.

[17] A. H. Van de Ven, *An Applied Experimental Test of Alternative Decision-Making Processes* (Kent, Ohio: Center for Business and Economic Research Press, Kent State University, 1973).

**INDIVIDUAL
VERSUS GROUP
DECISION
MAKING**

Considerable debate has occurred over the relative effectiveness of individual versus group decision making. Groups usually take more time to reach a decision than individuals do. But bringing together individual specialists and experts has its benefits, since the mutually reinforcing impact of their interaction results in better decisions. In fact, a great deal of research has shown that consensus decisions with five or more participants are superior to individual decision making, majority vote, and leader decisions.[18] Unfortunately, open discussion has been found to be negatively influenced by such behavioral factors as the pressure to conform: the influence of a dominant personality type in the group; "status incongruity," as a result of which, lower-status participants are inhibited by higher status participants and "go along" even though they believe that their own ideas are superior; and the attempt of certain participants to influence others because these participants are perceived to be expert in the problem area.[19]

Certain decisions appear to be better made by groups, while others appear better suited to individual decision making. Nonprogrammed decisions appear to be better suited to group decision making. Such decisions usually call for pooled talent in arriving at a solution; the decisions are so important that they are frequently made by top managers and, to a somewhat lesser extent, by middle managers.

In terms of the decision-making process itself, the following points concerning group processes for nonprogrammed decisions can be made:

1. In *establishing objectives,* groups probably are superior to individuals because of the greater amount of knowledge available to groups.
2. In *identifying alternatives,* the individual efforts of group members are necessary to ensure a broad search in the various functional areas of the organization.
3. In *evaluating alternatives,* the collective judgment of the group, with its wider range of viewpoints, seems superior to that of the individual decision maker.
4. In *choosing an alternative,* it has been shown that group interaction and the achievement of consensus usually result in the acceptance of more risk than would be accepted by an individual decision maker. In any event, the group decision is more likely to be accepted as a result

---

[18] For examples, see Charles Holloman and Harold Henrick, "Adequacy of Group Decisions as a Function of the Decision-Making Process," *Academy of Management Journal,* June 1972, pp. 175–84; Andrew H. Van de Ven and Andre Delbecq, "Nominal versus Interacting Group Processes for Committee Decision-Making Effectiveness," *Academy of Management Journal,* June 1972, pp. 203–12; and B. M. Staw, "The Escalation of Commitment to a Course of Action," *Academy of Management Review,* October 1981, pp. 577–88.

[19] For examples, see Soloman Asch, "Studies of Independence and Conformity," *Psychological Monographs,* 1956, pp. 68–70; Norman Dalkey and Olaf Helmer, "An Experimental Application of Delphi Method to Use of Experts," *Management Science,* April 1963, pp. 458–67; E. M. Bridges, W. J. Doyle, and D. J. Mahan, "Effects of Hierarchical Differentiation on Group Productivity, Efficiency, and Risk-Taking," *Administrative Science Quarterly,* Fall 1968, pp. 305–39; Victor Vroom, Lester Grant, and Timothy Cotten, "The Consequences of Social Interaction

FIGURE 13—2

Probable Relationship between Quality of Group Decision and Method Utilized

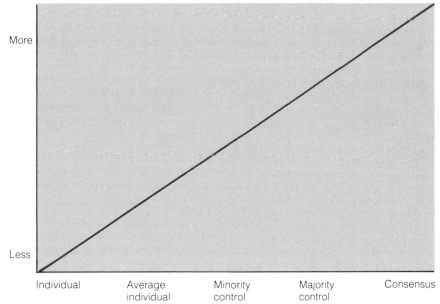

Probable quality of decision

More

Less

Individual | Average individual | Minority control | Majority control | Consensus

Method of utilization of group resources

of the participation of those affected by its consequences.

5. *Implementation* of a decision, whether or not it is made by a group, usually is accomplished by individual managers. Thus, since a group cannot be held responsible, the responsibility for implementation necessarily rests with the individual manager.

Figure 13–2 summarizes the research on group decision making. It presents the relationship between the probable quality of a decision and the method utilized to reach the decision. It indicates that as we move from "individual" to "consensus," the quality of the decision improves. Note also that each successive method involves a higher level of mutual influence by group members. Thus, for a complex problem requiring pooled knowledge, the quality of the decision is likely to be higher as the group moves toward achieving consensus.[20]

in Group Problem Solving," *Organizational Behavior and Human Performance*, February 1969, pp. 77–95; P. A. Collaras and L. R. Anderson, "Effect of Perceived Expertise upon Creativity of Members of Brainstorming Groups," *Journal of Applied Psychology*, April 1969, pp. 159–63; D. Tjosvold and R. H. G. Field, "Effects of Social Context on Consensus and Majority Vote Decision Making," *Academy of Management Journal*, September 1983, pp. 500–06; and Carrie Leana, "A Partial Test of Janis' Groupthink Model: Effects of Group Cohensiveness and Leader Behavior on Defective Decision Making," *Journal of Management*, Spring 1985, pp. 5–17.

[20] For a discussion of group decision making in complex problems, see Stuart Hart, Mark Boroush, Gordon Enk, and William Hornick, "Managing Complexity Through Consensus Mapping: Technology for the Structuring of Group Decisions," *Academy of Management Review*, July 1985, pp. 587–600.

The first readings article that is part of this chapter, "Decisions, Decisions, Decisions," by Jay Hall, focuses on group decision making. The article confirms the relationship displayed in Figure 13–2 and makes the point that the quality of group decisions can be improved significantly by following a very few, basic rules.

CREATIVITY IN GROUP DECISION MAKING

If groups are better suited to nonprogrammed decisions than individuals are, then an atmosphere fostering group creativity must be created. In this respect, group decision making may be similar to brainstorming in that discussion must be free-flowing and spontaneous. All group members must participate, and the evaluation of individual ideas must be suspended in the beginning to encourage participation. However, a decision must be reached, and this is where group decision making differs from brainstorming. Figure 13–3 presents guidelines for developing the permissive atmosphere that is important for creative decision making.

TECHNIQUES FOR STIMULATING CREATIVITY

It seems safe to say that, in many instances, group decision making is preferable to individual decision making. But we have all heard the statement, "A camel is a racehorse designed by a committee." Thus, while the necessity and the benefits of group decision making are recognized, numerous problems also are associated with it, some of which already have been noted. Practicing managers are in need of specific techniques that will enable them to increase the benefits from group decision making while reducing the problems associated with it.

We shall examine three techniques that, when properly utilized, have been found to be extremely useful in increasing the creative capability of a group in generating ideas, understanding problems, and reaching better decisions. Increasing the creative capability of a group is especially necessary when individuals from diverse sectors of the organization must pool their judgments and create a satisfactory course of action for the organization. The three techniques are known as brainstorming, the Delphi technique, and the nominal group technique.

Brainstorming. In many situations, groups are expected to produce creative or imaginative solutions to organizational problems. In such instances, **brainstorming** often has been found to enhance the creative output of the group. The technique of brainstorming includes a strict series of rules. The purpose of the rules is to promote the generation of ideas while, at the same time, avoiding the inhibitions of members that usually are caused by face-to-face groups. The basic rules are:

- No idea is too ridiculous. Group members are encouraged to state any extreme or outlandish idea.
- Each idea presented belongs to the group, not to the person stating it. In this way, it is hoped that group members will utilize and build on the ideas of others.
- No idea can be criticized. The purpose of the session is to generate, not evaluate, ideas.

FIGURE 13–3

Creative Group Decision Making

Group Structure

The group is composed of heterogeneous, generally competent personnel who bring to bear on the problem diverse frames of reference, representing channels to each relevant body of knowledge (including contact with outside resource personnel who offer expertise not encompassed by the organization), with a leader who facilitates the creative process.

Group Roles

Each individual explores with the entire group all ideas (no matter how intuitively and roughly formed) that bear on the problem.

Group Processes

The problem-solving process is characterized by:

1. Spontaneous communication between members (not focused on the leader).
2. Full participation from each member.
3. Separation of idea generation from idea evaluation.
4. Separation of problem definition from generation of solution strategies.
5. Shifting of roles, so that interaction that mediates problem solving (particularly search activities and clarification by means of constant questioning directed both to individual members and to the whole group) is not the sole responsibility of the leader.
6. Suspension of judgment and avoidance of early concern with solutions, so that the emphasis is on analysis and exploration, rather than on early commitment to solutions.

Group Style

The social-emotional tone of the group is characterized by:

1. A relaxed, nonstressful environment.
2. Ego-supportive interaction, where open give-and-take between members is at the same time courteous.
3. Behavior that is motivated by interest in the problem, rather than concern with short-run payoff.
4. Absence of penalties attached to any espoused idea or position.

Group Norms

1. Are supportive of originality and unusual ideas and allow for eccentricity.
2. Seek behavior that separates source from content in evaluating information and ideas.
3. Stress a nonauthoritarian view, with a realistic view of life and independence of judgment.
4. Support humor and undisciplined exploration of viewpoints.
5. Seek openness in communication, where mature, self-confident individuals offer "crude" ideas to the group for mutual exploration without threat to the individuals for "exposing" themselves.
6. Deliberately avoid giving credence to short-run results or short-run decisiveness.
7. Seek consensus but accept majority rule when consensus is unobtainable.

Source: Andre L. Delbecq, "The Management of Decision Making within the Firm: Three Strategies for Three Types of Decision Making," *Academy of Management Journal*, December 1967, pp. 334–35.

Brainstorming is widely used in advertising and some other fields, where it apparently is effective. In other situations, it has been less successful because there is no evaluation or ranking of the ideas generated. Thus, the group never really concludes the problem-solving process.[21]

The Delphi Technique. This technique involves the solicitation and comparison of anonymous judgments on the topic of interest through a set of sequential questionnaires that are interspersed with summarized information and feedback of opinions from earlier responses.[22]

The **Delphi process** retains the advantage of having several judges, while removing the biasing effects that might occur during face-to-face interaction. The basic approach has been to collect anonymous judgments by mail questionnaire. For example, the members independently generate their ideas to answer the first questionnaire and return it. The staff members summarize the responses as the group consensus, and feed this summary back, along with a second questionnaire for reassessment. Based on this feedback, the respondents independently evaluate their earlier responses. The underlying belief is that the consensus estimate will result in a better decision after several rounds of anonymous group judgment. While it is possible to continue the procedure for several rounds, studies have shown essentially no significant change after the second round of estimation.[23]

The Nominal Group Technique (NGT). NGT has gained increasing recognition in health, social service, education, industry, and government organizations.[24] The term **Nominal Group Technique** was adopted by earlier researchers to refer to processes that bring people together but do not allow them to communicate verbally. Thus, the collection of people is a group "nominally," or "in name only." You will see, however, that NGT in its present form combines both verbal and nonverbal stages.

Basically, NGT is a structured group meeting that proceeds as follows: A group of individuals (7 to 10) sit around a table but do not speak to one another. Rather, each person writes ideas on a pad of paper. After five minutes, a structured sharing of ideas takes place. Each person around the table presents one idea. A person designated as recorder writes the ideas on a flip chart in full view of the entire group. This continues until all of the participants indicate that they have no further ideas to share. There is still no discussion.

The output of this phase is a list of ideas (usually between 18 and 25). The next phase involves structured discussion in which each idea receives

---

[21] For a review of research on brainstorming, see T. J. Bouchard, "Whatever Happened to Brainstorming?" *Journal of Creative Behavior,* Fall 1971, pp. 182–89.

[22] Norman Dalkey, *The Delphi Method: An Experimental Study of Group Opinion* (Santa Monica, Calif.: Rand Corporation, 1969). This is a classic work on the Delphi method.

[23] Norman Dalkey, *Experiments in Group Prediction* (Santa Monica, Calif.: Rand Corporation, 1968).

[24] See Andre L. Delbecq, Andrew H. Van de Ven, and David H. Gustafson, *Group Techniques for Program Planning* (Glenview, Ill.: Scott, Foresman, 1975). The discussion here is based on this work.

attention before a vote is taken. This is achieved by asking for clarification or stating the degree of support for each idea listed on the flip chart. The next stage involves independent voting in which each participant, in private, selects priorities by ranking or voting. The group decision is the mathematically pooled outcome of the individual votes.

Both the Delphi technique and NGT are relatively new, but each has had an excellent record of successes. Basic differences between them are:

1. Delphi participants typically are anonymous to one another, while NGT participants become acquainted.
2. NGT participants meet face-to-face around a table, while Delphi participants are physically distant and never meet face-to-face.
3. In the Delphi process, all communication between participants is by way of written questionnaires and feedback from the monitoring staff. In NGT, communication is direct between participants.[25]

Practical considerations, of course, often influence which technique is used. For example, such factors as the number of working hours available, costs, and the physical proximity of participants will influence which technique is selected.

Our discussion here has not been designed to make the reader an expert in the Delphi process or NGT.[26] Our purpose throughout this section has been to indicate the frequency and importance of group decision making in every type of organization. The three techniques discussed are practical devices whose purpose is to improve the *effectiveness* of group decisions.

Decision making is a common responsibility shared by all executives, regardless of functional area or management level. Every day, managers are required to make decisions that shape the future of their organization as well as their own futures. The quality of these decisions is the yardstick of the managers' effectiveness. Some of these decisions may have a strong impact on the organization's success, while others will be important but less crucial. However, *all* of the decisions will have some effect (positive or negative, large or small) on the organization.

SUMMARY OF KEYPOINTS

A. Decision making is a fundamental process in organizations. Managers make decisions on the basis of the information (communication) that they receive through the organizational structure and the behavior of individuals and groups within it.

B. Decision making distinguishes managers from nonmanagers. The quality of the decisions that managers make determines their effectiveness as managers.

C. Decisions may be classified as programmed or nonprogrammed, depending on the type of problem. Most programmed decisions should be made at the first level in the organization, while nonprogrammed decisions should be made mostly by top management.

---

[25] Ibid., p. 18.

[26] The reader desiring to learn more about each of these techniques is encouraged to consult Delbecq, Van de Ven, and Gustafson, *Group Techniques for Program Planning;* and Frederick C. Miner, Jr., "A Comparative Analysis of Three Diverse Groups' Decision-Making Approaches, *Academy of Management Journal,* March 1979, pp. 81–93.

D. Decision making should not be thought of as an end but as a *means* to achieve organizational goals and objectives. Decisions are organizational responses to problems.

E. Decision making should be viewed as a multi-phased *process* of which the actual choice is only one phase.

F. The decision-making process is influenced by numerous environmental and behavioral factors. Different decision makers may select different alternatives in the same situation because of different values, perceptions, and personalities.

G. A great deal of nonprogrammed decision making is carried on in group situations. Much evidence exists to support the claim that, in most instances, group decisions are superior to individual decisions. Three relatively new techniques (brainstorming, the Delphi technique, and the Nominal Group Technique) have the purpose of improving the effectiveness of group decisions. The management of collective decision making must be a vital concern for future managers.

REVIEW AND DISCUSSION QUESTIONS

1. "The source of most of our problems is someone else's solution to an earlier problem." Do you agree with this statement? What implications does this statement have for organizational decision making?

2. Are most decisions in organizations of the programmed or nonprogrammed type? For which type is group decision making most appropriate? For which type is creativity most appropriate?

3. "Decisions should be thought of as means rather than ends." Explain what this statement means and what effect it should have on decision making.

4. Why is the development of alternatives a distinct and separate step from the evaluation of alternatives?

5. What role does personality play in decision making? Can you think of an example from your own experience where the personality of a decision maker clearly influenced his or her decision?

6. What are the relative advantages and disadvantages of individual versus group decision making?

7. Creativity requires nonconformity of thinking. Does that explain why so many organizational decisions are noncreative? What can be done to stimulate creative decision making in an organization?

8. Is a low propensity for risk taking a desirable or undesirable characteristic in an organizational decision maker? Explain.

9. Can individuals be trained to make better decisions? What aspects of decision making do you think could be most improved through training decision makers?

10. Think of a reasonably important nonprogrammed decision you have made recently. Did you employ an approach similar to the decision-making process outlined in Figure 13–1? How good was your decision? Could it have been improved by using the decision-making process? Explain.

R¹ DECISIONS, DECISIONS, DECISIONS*

JAY HALL

A disgruntled group member once defined a camel as a horse put together by a committee. Group decisions often are frustrating and

* Source: Reprinted from *Psychology Today*, November 1971. Copyright by Ziff Davis Publishing Company.

inadequate. All members want agreement, but they also want to make their own points heard. So they bargain, they compromise, and the final product is often a potpourri that no group member really believes in. And when group members expect their decisions to be inadequate, they usually are—a self-fulfilling prophecy.

But the group process need not be so ineffective. I have found that when a group's final decision is compared to the independent points of view that the members held before entering the group, the group's effort is almost always an improvement over its average individual resource, and often it is better than even the best individual contribution.

A decision exercise that I developed to illustrate this potential is *Lost On The Moon:* Astronauts have crashlanded on the moon, and their mission is to reach the mother ship 200 miles away. The task is to rank 15 items according to how useful each would be to the lunar mission.

I got experts at National Aeronautics and Space Administration's Crew Equipment Research Department to rank the 15 items for me, with the help of Matthew Radnofsky of NASA's Manned Spacecraft Center in Houston. So there is a correct solution to the *Lost On The Moon* task, or at least a *best* solution.

When individuals take the *Lost On The Moon* test on their own and then meet with three to seven other persons to produce a consensus on the test, the group's decision may be better—closer to NASA's expert opinion—than any of the individual decisions had been.

 **LEARNING CHECKPOINT**

What types of decisions appear to be better suited for groups? Why?

Whether or not this happens depends on the ground rules that the group operates by. I have discovered several rules for group effectiveness in studying the behavior of thousands of small groups.

MOVIE

As a social-psychological consultant to industry I have conducted many seminars on group effectiveness for management executives. A favorite exercise in these seminars, developed by Robert R. Blake and a group of his graduate students, involves the movie *12 Angry Men*, a juryroom drama that is itself an excellent study of group behavior. It is a feature-length movie, released by United Artists, with superb veteran actors, including Henry Fonda, Lee J. Cobb and E. G. Marshall, and it allows viewers to go through a unique group-decision experience of their own.

The movie opens as 12 weary jurymen receive instructions from the judge in a murder trial, then file into the juryroom. It appears that their deliberations will be brief. They are eager for a quick verdict— it's a hot day, they are tired and close to agreement. They have heard overpowering testimony that the teen-aged defendant had killed his father with a knife.

They take an informal poll, and all are willing to vote "guilty" except one man—played by Henry Fonda. They continue to deliberate, and each man explains how he feels about the case. Many try to persuade the maverick juror to go along. E. G. Marshall, as a superobjective stockbroker, tallies all the facts in the case and concludes that it is obvious the boy is guilty. Still, says Fonda, there is a reasonable doubt.

After 38 minutes of movie time they take a second vote—this time by secret ballot, with Fonda abstaining. When the foreman (played by Martin Balsam) counts the slips of paper, there are 10 votes for "guilty" and one for "not guilty."

At this point I stop the movie.

GUESS

"As you can see," I tell the audience, "one of the jurors has switched his vote to 'not guilty.' On the basis of what you have seen of the men—their occupations, their backgrounds, their apparent biases and personalities—I want you to guess which juror it was. By the end of the movie all of the jurors, one by one, have changed to 'not guilty.' Your task is to predict the order in which they will change their votes."

The viewers, already assigned to groups of five to eight members, have a seating chart of the jury to familiarize themselves with the film's characters. They rank Henry Fonda as juror number one, because he was the first to vote "not guilty." I instruct the subjects to rank each of the other jurors in the order in which he will change his vote.

The task is of course subjective and imprecise. But it is reasonable, because in the first 38 minutes of the film, scriptwriter Reginald Rose foreshadows the outcome by supplying insights into each juror. Jack Klugman, for example, reveals that he was raised in a slum environment similar to the defendant's. Ed Begley, as an overtly bigoted old garage-owner, is incredulous that anyone could fail to see guilt in the dark-skinned defendant. And Jack Warden implies that he will go along with any decision that will speed up the deliberations—he wants to go to a baseball game across town.

I tell the seminar subjects that they can have as much time as they want to make their individual rankings. They usually take 10 to 15 minutes. I then ask the subjects to make the same judgments in their small groups—they must reach agreement and produce a group decision on the sequence in which the jurors will shift their votes.

GRIST

In their small groups the subjects realize that they have developed different impressions of the 12 angry men. For example, Lee J. Cobb has revealed in the movie that his son, about the same age as the defendant, is cowardly, ungrateful and disrespectful. Some take this to mean that Cobb will therefore be one of the last to change because he is prejudiced against all young people. Others think that Cobb is brooding over his lost son and will atone for his own mistreatment of and lack of understanding for his son by giving the defendant a symbolic last chance. Still others argue, from a different perspective, that Cobb will be the last to change his vote because Hollywood filmmakers would want to save a famous star for a last dramatic holdout of the movie. These arguments are grist for the decision mill. I give the groups as much time as they need to reach a decision. Most take about an hour. When every group has reached its final ranking the subjects reassemble and see the rest of the movie.

I score the individual and group predictions for accuracy by errorpoints. For example, a subject who predicted that the baseball fan would be the ninth juror to switch would be off by two error-points, because the baseball fan was actually seventh. Another subject who said the baseball fan would be fifth would also be off by two points. The total score is the sum of all the error-points. The best possible score is zero, the worst is 60. The average individual score is about 22.

CONTINUITY

The *12 Angry Men* task is an excellent research tool for investigating the group-decision process. In one of my first experiments with this task I wanted to find whether groups assembled just for the experiment would be as effective as already-established groups in which the members knew each oth-

er's strengths and weaknesses. Martha Williams and I studied several established groups of business managers that had spent at least 50 hours together. Seven men who had worked together for several years in an office made up one group, for example, and five men who had served on a research committee made up another. We studied 20 such groups, and 20 ad-hoc groups made up of similar businessmen who had not worked together prior to the experiment.

The established and ad-hoc groups started with comparable resources—their average individual scores were about 23 error-points in each case. After discussions the ad-hoc groups improved their scores to 16.6 points, on the average, but the established groups improved significantly more, to 13.15.

There was also a clear difference in the ways the groups handled conflict. For example, one group might have members with individual scores ranging from 20 to 26, with an average of 23. Another might have the same average, with scores ranging from 10 to 40. The two groups would obviously have different levels of initial conflict.

We measured the degree of conflict within each of the 20 ad-hoc groups, and found that the 20 with the lowest internal conflict did slightly better than the 10 that had started with a wide range of opinions. In established groups, however, the amount of initial agreement was critical—the groups that started with great internal conflict did much better than groups with less conflict. A wide variety of opinions is beneficial to an established group, but disruptive to an ad-hoc group.

The reason, I believe, lies in the different ways people perceive and respond to conflict. Differences of opinion are not likely to be seen

as particularly threatening to a group that is already well-established. Disagreements are seen as natural; they indicate a need for further discussion and offer a variety of alternative solutions, but they don't imply interpersonal hostility or threaten the integrity of the group.

But in a group of semistrangers the situation is different. Here there is no group commitment, and the cohesion is tenuous and temporary. Conflict threatens the group's already flimsy interpersonal structure, thus members try to smooth conflicts over rather than resolve them. When disagreement arises, the members of an ad-hoc group make quick compromises to get along with each other, or they resort to neutral, automatic solutions, such as majority rule. It is possible, of course, for even cohesive groups to find it more important to get along than to find the best solution to a problem. When that happens, they are practicing what Irving Janis calls groupthink.

DEALING

We analyzed the group data to see whether the groups actually had different ways of dealing with conflict. We found that groups faced with high internal conflicts tended to abandon the existing resources in the group and come up with *unique solutions*—choices that none of the members had originally held. For example if individual members of a group ranked the stockbroker as number two, number nine and number eleven, the group might decide on a unique solution for the stockbroker and rank him number four. When we studied the unique solutions that our groups came up with, we found that in established groups the unique solutions tended to be good ones—on the whole better than the average individual ratings. The unique solutions that ad-hoc groups produced, however, did not improve upon the resources already available in the group. The tendency to produce wildly inaccurate solutions was most pronounced in the ad-hoc groups that had great internal conflict.

In other words, unique solutions in the established groups tended to be *creative;* while in the ad-hoc groups the unique solutions were *compromises.*

As group members experience each other more and more, they seem to develop more effective ways to deal with conflict, and the group becomes more and more effective in making decisions. Established groups do not necessarily make quicker decisions (established groups and ad-hoc groups took about the same amount of time to reach agreement and the groups that finished quickly did no better or worse than groups that took a long time) but established groups make better, more accurate decisions. Still, the established groups were not as effective as they might have been.

Knowing this, I wondered whether it would be possible to train groups to be more effective. Martha Williams and I took advantage of several two-week laboratory programs in group dynamics designed to teach people the attitudes toward group action that we had observed in established groups. The programs taught the critical elements of group life with several exercises that allowed participants to confront and solve dilemmas in actual group practice.

To see whether these programs actually produced effective group members, we studied 51 college-student trainees. After the training sessions we let some of these subjects work in the same groups they

had been in throughout training. We divided the other trainees into new ad-hoc groups just for the *12 Angry Men* task. We also tested 45 similar college students—some in established school groups and some in ad-hoc groups—who had not gone through the training programs.

To find whether our results could be generalized to other populations, we also ran identical studies on 141 management executives—ranking from foreman to company president—and on 140 neuro-psychiatric patients who had been in hospitals for periods from several months to several years.

SYNERGY

In these studies we found that the ad-hoc or established nature of a group made little difference. More important was whether group members had undergone training in group effectiveness. Trained groups did significantly better than untrained groups. And although the three populations started out at different levels on the *12 Angry Men* task (the college students did better than the businessmen, and the businessmen did better than patients), group-effectiveness training was a leveler: trained mental patients actually did better in groups than untrained business executives did.

We were especially pleased to find that many trained groups did better than even their best individual members. We called this happy event *synergy:* the ability of a group to outperform even its own best individual resource. The ad-hoc groups achieved synergy about as often as the established groups did, but the lab-training program was more important—half of the trained groups achieved synergy, but only 13 per cent of the untrained groups

did. Needless to say, we were encouraged by these results, but I wondered whether a full two-week lab program was necessary. Perhaps the lessons of the lab training could be learned more quickly.

I carefully studied several hundred groups to see whether there were typical behaviors that the most effective groups had in common and whether there were interfering strategies that characterized groups that did poorly.

I found that groups that had improved the most and scored the best consistently tried to get every member involved. They actively sought out the points of disagreement, and thus promoted conflicts, especially in the early stages. The most ineffective groups, on the other hand, tended to use simple decision techniques, such as majority rule, averaging and bargaining. They seemed to feel a strain toward convergence, as if it were more important to complete the task than to come up with a decision they could all agree on. As one subject in a particularly inept group put it, "the members seemed more committed to reaching a decision than to committing themselves to the decision they reached."

LEARNING CHECKPOINT

In terms of the decision-making process discussed in the chapter, what conclusions can you state concerning group processes for nonprogrammed decisions?

RULES

When I summarized the behaviors of the most effective groups I found I could list all of the apparent decision rules in the form of instructions for group consensus on one typewritten page essentially as follows:

GROUP-DECISION INSTRUCTIONS

Consensus is a decision process for making full use of available resources and for resolving conflicts creatively. Consensus is difficult to reach, so not every ranking will meet with everyone's complete approval. Complete unanimity is not the goal—it is rarely achieved. But each individual should be able to accept the group rankings on the basis of logic and feasibility. When all group members feel this way, you have reached consensus as defined here, and the judgment may be entered as a group decision. This means, in effect, that a single person can block the group if he thinks it necessary; at the same time, he should use this option in the best sense of reciprocity. Here are some guidelines to use in achieving consensus:

1. Avoid arguing for your own rankings. Present your position as lucidly and logically as possible, but listen to the other members' reactions and consider them carefully before you press your point.

2. Do not assume that someone must win and someone must lose when discussion reaches a stalemate. Instead, look for the next-most-acceptable alternative for all parties.

3. Do not change your mind simply to avoid conflict and to reach agreement and harmony. When agreement seems to come too quickly and easily, be suspicious. Explore the reasons and be sure everyone accepts the solution for basically similar or complementary reasons. Yield only to positions that have objective

and logically sound foundations.

4. Avoid conflict-reducing techniques such as majority vote, averages, coin-flips and bargaining. When a dissenting member finally agrees, don't feel that he must be rewarded by having his own way on some later point.

5. Differences of opinion are natural and expected. Seek them out and try to involve everyone in the decision process. Disagreements can help the group's decision because with a wide range of information and opinions, there is a greater chance that the group will hit upon more adequate solutions.

TEST

These instructions seem to encapsulate the lessons that the trainees had learned in the two-week lab programs. I wondered whether untrained persons could become effective group members by simply reading the list of rules instead of going through the full training program. Fred Watson and I answered this question, using the *Lost On The Moon* exercise with 148 upper-management personnel from several small business organizations. We separated the subjects randomly into 32 discussion groups of four to six members each. They worked on other group activities for about six hours before taking the *Lost On The Moon* test, so in terms of previous experience with each other, the groups were somewhere between the ad-hoc and established groups of our previous studies.

After all subjects had taken the test individually we had 16 of the groups go to their respective group

meeting rooms to reach the best decisions they could. We gave the remaining 16 groups the simple instruction sheet and went over it briefly before they went to their meeting rooms.

The instructions were effective. The uninstructed groups, which started with average individual resources of 47.5 error points, produced final decisions averaging about 34 points. But the instructed groups improved significantly more—from 45 points as individuals to 26 points as groups.

SUCCESS

The most important factor that determined how well a group performed was the success of its unique judgments—those instances in which the group abandoned existing resources in favor of a new solution that they created for themselves. Both types of groups produced unique judgments on 27 per cent of their decisions. But the instructed groups created qualitatively better solutions than the uninstructed groups did. Thus, the uninstructed groups responded to internal conflict with compromises, which may have eased group tensions, but did not improve the group's decisions. Instructed groups, on the other hand, used conflict to their advantage as an opportunity for creativity.

Most of the instructed groups achieved synergy—75 per cent produced group decisions that surpassed even the best individual decisions. Only 25 per cent of the uninstructed groups did this.

UP

We reached two major conclusions from these studies: (1) that groups function as their members make them function, and (2) that conflict, effectively managed, is a necessary precondition for creativity. Thus, when they follow a few brief instructions, decision-making groups can be expected to do better than even their best members, at least on multiple-judgment tasks of the sort we have studied. There is nothing in the group process that makes committees, boards and panels inherently inept.

LEARNING CHECKPOINT

What are some of the more popular techniques for stimulating creativity in group decision making?

Ludicrous, ineffective solutions to problems are the product of groups that are pessimistic about their own potential, and have imperfect ways of dealing with conflict.

The horse that is put together by a committee that understands group dynamics won't turn out to be a camel; it may be a thoroughbred filly fit for the Triple Crown.

□

R² CONSEQUENCES

MORGAN W. McCALL AND
ROBERT E. KAPLAN

Managerial decision making is a complex process: streams of information and events get recognized as problems, a complex set of factors affect what problems will get attention, and still another set of factors influence whether action will be quick and direct or long and drawn out. Once action is taken, everyone watches attentively for the consequences. The players and interested spectators look on like hunters watching to see whether the rifle shot has felled a deer. This kind of drama surrounded the press conference held by the CEO of Johnson and Johnson after poisoned Tylenol killed several people in the Chicago area. How would he handle this extremely delicate moment with a shocked nation looking on?

Source: Morgan W. McCall and Robert E. Kaplan, *Whatever It Takes: Decision Makers at Work* (Englewood Cliffs, NJ: Prentice-Hall, 1984).

Managers take action not for its own sake but to achieve results. The consequences flowing from decisions are diverse, whether the decision is a discrete, quick action or a convoluted accumulation of actions that adds up to a completed project or an enacted policy.

The decision may be no decision at all but a failed attempt to decide. One manager we interviewed evoked an almost existential despair and complained poignantly about management's inability to act:

Management team meetings are frustrating to me because we discuss things but we come out with no solutions, recommendations, nothing— just smoke. (Kaplan, Lombardo, & Mazique, 1983, p. 34)

Or if a decision is actually reached, it is not necessarily implemented. Another manager from the same organization lamented the fact that problems which management had supposedly solved remained unresolved because responsibility wasn't clearly determined.

There are cases where a problem comes up and it's dealt with, but too many come up and either we don't arrive at a solution or it isn't clear who's responsible and it comes up again and again. . . . We're horrendous on follow-up. (Kaplan et al., 1983, p. 31)

Or if the solution is implemented, it may not work, and the manager is back to the drawing board—assuming the manager doesn't become discouraged by the setback, and avoids the temptation to rationalize the failure.

Or a decision can be made and action can actually follow, but the result may not be what was intended. As one executive told us:

Sometimes you make a decision, and what you get is exactly opposite from what you anticipated. A beautiful illustration is the Germans bombing London [during World War II]. They thought they would destroy the morale and they got exactly the opposite.

Even if the action has the intended effect, it may also have unintended consequences. A corporation we are acquainted with has launched Quality-of-Worklife projects in its plants, projects with sufficient bite that workers have responded by becoming much more involved in the corporation's renewed effort to produce quality products. But as production workers have taken more responsibility and become less alienated, their foremen and supervisors have unexpectedly lost motivation. In beginning to solve the problem of worker alienation by expanding their responsibilities, management has inadvertently alienated first- and second-level supervision by, in effect, shrinking their jobs.

Finally, solutions that work and produce no special negative side effects don't endure forever. Managers solve a problem and, if the solution sticks, they turn their attention to the host of other problems clamoring for their attention. But the solution doesn't necessarily last, not because it wasn't a good solution but because times change.

Having emerged victorious as decision makers, managers can't afford to become complacent; solutions wear out and eventually need to be repaired or replaced. Actions and consequences are often thought of in terms of decision and implementation, as seen in the following comment by a general manager:

> Making decisions is easy, but getting them implemented sometimes is nearly impossible (quoted in Kotter, 1982, p. 17).

 **LEARNING CHECKPOINT**

Do you think that it would be easier to implement a nonprogrammed or a programmed decision (see Table 13–1)?

Although it is common parlance to talk of decision and implementation, we prefer to see implementation as, in many cases, itself consisting of a "plurality of subdecisions" (Mintzberg et al., 1976, p. 252), each of which has to be implemented. It is easy to overblow the importance of the decision that authorizes a capital expenditure, an acquisition, or a divestiture, and to underrate the work that follows as mere implementation. A corporate executive concurred on this point:

> Winning the battle of approval for the main action should not be confused with developing the strategy for how the battle lines will be drawn and how the battle will be fought. The action plan to follow is likely multi-phasic and requires no less careful thought than the main action itself. If somebody, having received approval of an action, just goes ahead and acts without thinking through the various steps, they're likely to stub their toes.

In managerial life, then, there is no rest for the weary. Problems flowing to the managers may get disposed of permanently but they are just as likely to take up residence. If managers get approval for a solution, then they may next have to implement the solution, or oversee the people assigned to implement it. When they try to implement a decision, the solution may fail and put them back on square one. Or the solution may work but in the process create a new set of problems that gets dropped in the manager's lap. Nor can managers expect a problem to stay solved, because solutions unravel as the problems they were designed to solve evolve over time. There is no end to problems, even for effective managers.

Given this complexity, it is no surprise that the consequences of

managerial action are not always clear victories or defeats. The world of the manager is rarely amenable to simple, unambiguous learning. Kanter (1977) has even suggested that managers operate under an "inverse law of certainty:" "The more important the management decision, the less precise the tools to deal with it . . . and the longer it will take before anyone knows it was right" (p. 53). As one manager we interviewed put it:

> In management there are few clear victories. There are so many gray areas. That interminable gray is what causes stress. The things that stay constantly unresolved are the ones that sap your strength.

While bankruptcy or a million dollar cost overrun appear to be concrete indicators of the quality of managerial decisions, the causes of such outcomes are usually quite complicated. Seldom are such things caused by a single managerial decision, nor is it obvious that a different decision would have changed the outcome.

The first thing to recognize, then, is that the consequences of managerial decisions are ambiguous and can be interpreted in different ways. In some cases it is not clear what action was taken. Other times the action is clear but the consequences are obscured. In still other cases, action and consequences may be clear, but the relationship between the two may be murky.

THE AMBIGUITY OF ACTION AND CONSEQUENCES

Just as the original recognition and definition of a problem involves the interpretation of ambiguous information and events, discovering the consequences of one's action is often a matter of interpretation. The first hitch is that the *action itself* may be seen differently by different people. Managerial decisions, particularly important ones, usually comprise a set of smaller decisions made over time. Not all participants in a decision cycle may agree that a decision has been made or what it was. A tabled project, for example, may be viewed as postponed by one manager and terminated by another. (Helping to shroud action is the tendency of some managers to sidestep clear responsibility for decisions.) As a university administrator explained it:

> People here don't like to make clear decisions because they're held accountable. They prefer to talk around things, and then act on them. If it works, fine. If not, then heads don't have to roll.

The second hitch is that the *consequences* of action, like the action itself, are subject to different interpretations by various participants. This is particularly true for tough problems where effects may take a long time (months or even years) to appear. Was it the new president's aggressive marketing stance or the improved economy that increased sales last year?

Decision making cannot be divorced from a manager's values (Taylor, 1965). Managers place different emphasis on outcomes such as return to shareholders, quality of work, and social responsibility. Shareholder returns may be measured as market share by one manager, profitability by another, and may be viewed in either the short run or the long run. Because decisions have multiple consequences, the criteria used to evaluate a decision will depend on which consequences are emphasized by whom. The development of a technologi-

cal marvel that is ahead of its time may be a success to the R&D manager but a failure to the sales manager hunting for a market.

A case in point is IBM's STRETCH computer, a machine of advanced design developed originally for atomic research in the late 1950s. For technical and marketing reasons, the program ended up losing $20 million. Thomas Watson, Jr. pronounced the computer a disaster, an assessment that certain technical people and certain high-level executives did not agree with. In fact, when it later became apparent that the innovative STRETCH technology influenced the design of subsequent, successful computers, even Watson changed his mind about the computer (Fishman, 1981). History gets rewritten with the passage of time. Years later, Watson said about the costs of developing the computer: "A better fifty million we never spent, but it took seven or eight years to find out" (Fishman, 1981, p. 120).

In another sense, too, consequences are hard to pin down. When managers choose a course of action, they pass up other alternatives and can never know what would have happened if they had taken another course. One executive made the point this way:

> I walked down this road and I don't know where the [other] road would have gone because this is the road I chose. So you never really know whether that was the right decision to make. For example, I was responsible for equalizing the vacation between exempt employees and hourly and non-exempt employees. I argued that if vacation is a time of rest and recharge, then the non-exempt and hourly need that time as much as the exempt. It did wonders for the morale of the non-exempt, and the exempt felt that we

had taken something away from them. So we changed the vacation policy, and the change worked. But the paths we looked at and didn't choose may have worked better or worse. There's no way of knowing.

Managers never know what would have happened if they had chosen what Robert Frost called "the road not taken."

A third hitch is that even when actions and consequences are known, the connection between them can still be ambiguous. This is because there is usually a time lag, often a long one, between an action and its results. It has been estimated, for example, that ". . . it takes three to five years of blood, sweat, and tears to get a company 'turned around again' after a crisis" (Smith, 1963, p. 206). One executive stated:

> I guess there are relatively few actions taken where the structure is so simple that the action is taken now and the consequences follow immediately. That isn't in the realm of management. If I punch the key on the typewriter, the consequence follows immediately after the action. But in the typical management process, an action or series of actions are taken and then in the period following are the consequences. And there are other variables so it's not just my action which affects the consequences.

During a lag, then, many things can happen other than implementation of decision, and knowing what actually "caused" the result can become problematic. Ilgen, Fisher, and Taylor (1979) provide an interesting example, noting that there are primitive tribes which are unaware of the connection between intercourse and childbearing. The reason for this is the nine-month delay between conception and birth, during which time other events occur, most of them extraneous to pregnancy. Similarly, organizational decisions have consequences which may be uninterpretable even well into the future.

An additional consequence of the lag between decisions and results is that the people who have to live with the results may not be the same people who made the decisions. To the extent that turnover in management is rapid (20–40 percent per year, according to some estimates) and lags are long, decision makers leave results behind them for the next incumbent. This has been a particular bane for U.S. presidents who face the results of their predecessors' programs. The general public tends to blame the incumbent for failure to solve problems that resulted from the decisions of others.

Conversely, managers sometimes get credit for good performance that they were not solely responsible for. They may have succeeded, for example, with the help of excellent staff support. This tendency to credit a person and overlook the person's circumstances has been called the "fundamental attribution error:" We tend "to underestimate the impact of situational determinants and to overestimate the importance of personal factors" (Ross, 1977, p. 193). But behavior is shaped by situation as well as personality. This tendency causes problems when a manager's effective performance is assumed to reside in his or her person and to be transferable anywhere. Functional managers are promoted to general management positions, and general managers are transferred from one business to an entirely different business, and they sometimes fail because of this (Kotter, 1982). Thus, because the connection between action and consequences is misread, managers are moved beyond their sphere of competence and the Peter Principle strikes again.

The connection between actions and consequences can also be muddied by the weak correspondence between the magnitude of decisions and the magnitude of their consequences. March and Olsen (1976) noted that "tiny (and essentially unpredictable) variations in events can make large differences in final outcomes" (p. 20). The "minor" decision by party functionaries to raid the opposition party's headquarters may escalate to full-scale impeachment proceedings and resignation of the President of the United States, as happened with Watergate. The converse can also happen. Major organizational interventions sometimes have little real impact on the organization or its performance (Mirvis & Berg, 1977).

In summary, a variety of forces act to blur the interpretation of action, consequences, and the relationship between the two, particularly for convoluted decisions. Determining what happened is more a matter of negotiation and impression management than an objective assessment of facts.

Meetings held to examine a decision may produce a variety of interpretations of the consequences. Those who have supported a decision tend to judge it a success, as did the executive quoted above about the decision he had made to equalize the vacation benefits of exempt and nonexempt:

> You have to live with yourself—you're pretty good at rationalizing that what you did was the right action. In fact, today I still think it was the right action. I don't feel it, I know it. I don't have any data to say it was the right action; all that comes internally.

Decision makers stick by their guns, even in the face of overwhelming evidence opposing their position. Napoleon provided a pure case of this in his disastrous Russian campaign in 1812, when he proclaimed:

> In affairs of state one must never retreat, never retrace one's steps, never admit an error—that brings disrepute. When one makes a mistake, one must stick to it. That makes it right! (de Segur, 1958, p. 127)

Decision makers may even manipulate and distort data on the decision's effects in order to support their case (Carter, 1971). The control over interpretation systems (Weick, 1979) is a powerful means to shape the evaluation of outcomes. The annual stockholders report and the company newsletter contain excellent examples of how even the most noxious events can be presented in a positive light through selective emphasis on certain aspects rather than others.

CONSEQUENCES, WHILE AMBIGUOUS, DO MATTER

Consequences, like problems, are what people make of them. One person's example of poor management is another's example of overwhelming environmental forces that no one could predict. This fundamental ambiguity hardly means that decisions do not have consequences. It is the *importance* of the *interpretations* of consequences that in fact causes such investment in figuring out what happened. (This is particularly true when there is a hint of failure; managers are much more sanguine about success.)

There are at least three types of consequences of decisions. First are the effects of decisions on the formation of precedent, both for the organization and the individual manager; second are the impacts on relationships resulting from participation in or exclusion from the decision cycle; and third, decision-making success or failure becomes a manager's track record.

Let's look at each type of consequence. Decisions accumulate; problems tend to recur. These two elements mean that, in time, satisfactory decisions set precedents for the policy, rules, and procedures guiding future action. In short, the organization moves toward making the handling of problems routine. Strategic direction is often the result of a series of decisions made over time, each of which influences the succeeding decision.

An analogous process goes on in the manager's head, as accumulated actions become cause-effect models of the world and how it works.* This is probably what is meant by experience or organizational savvy.

It would be inefficient for either organizations or managers not to routinize decision making. No one would ever have time to solve problems if every problem required a novel response. Newspapers, for example, have evolved structures and procedures to routinize the handling of unexpected, fast-breaking news events (Tuchman, 1978). The attempts to establish efficient action sequences for problems is, however, a mixed blessing. The development of formal procedures, rules, and policies affects all aspects of the decision cycle, from problem recognition to the type of solution chosen. The very efficiency of such guidelines creates a subtle pressure to define new problems as old problems, to choose priorities without thought, and to use historical solutions rather than generate novel ones. This is

particularly true when managers respond to crises; they tend to rely on proven programs, concentrate on improving efficiency, and avoid innovative solutions (Whetton, 1980).

Thus, the making of decisions creates consequences through the evolution of precedent (often formalized into procedures) and through the accumulation of decisions into strategic directions. But the decision-making process also affects relationships among the people involved. People whose advice is taken seriously are likely to have positive feelings. Those who were not involved and feel they should have been, or whose advice was solicited but ignored, are not likely to feel so good about it.

The nature of the interactions between the central decision maker and his or her peers (or others over whom the manager has no formal authority) lay the groundwork for future cooperation. In convoluted decision making, many such people may be involved and responsiveness to their concerns will affect their willingness to involve, or be involved with, the manager in future problem solving. Specifically, convoluted decision processes require a manager to consider carefully whom to involve, the degree of involvement, the timing of involvement, and whom to inform of the outcome. If there is conflict among the people involved, the manager has the additional diplomatic task of dealing with the people who "lose out."

Quick decisions also affect relationships, largely with those people who feel they should have been consulted. In this case, the manager must devote energy to unruffling feathers, or run the risk of alienating people who may be important in a future situation.

Relationships with superiors are

also affected, especially when a decision must be "sold up" to higher management. Exposure to managers at levels higher than one's boss is usually infrequent, so the impressions made can have lasting effects.

All of this is related to the track record of the manager. Put simply, a manager viewed as competent is more likely to get proposals approved than one seen as less competent (Carter, 1971; Cyert et al., 1979). A reputation for competence is formed, at least partially, on the basis of how often a manager is "right." So decisions, and particularly the perceived consequences of decisions, accumulate to separate the less successful from the more successful managers. It has even been suggested, for example, that managers seen as successful by the organization are those who dissociate from failure and associate themselves with success (Pfeffer, 1978).

Unfortunately, it is not always possible to dissociate oneself from failure. Failure is always an unwelcome guest in organizations and, if one manager adeptly avoids a given instance, it has a way of showing up on another manager's doorstep. When the Nixon administration's policy of supporting West Pakistan during the Indian-Pakistan war of 1971 became unpopular, President Nixon saw fit to disown the policy. In the public eye, it then became Secretary of State Kissinger's policy. "Nixon could not resist the temptation of letting me twist slowly, slowly in the wind" (Kissinger, 1979, p. 918). It was weeks, too, before Nixon stopped avoiding Kissinger personally.

Failure is a hot potato. Still, it is too extreme to say that if a manager makes a serious mistake, he or she is through. ("Good people are a scarce commodity, you don't throw away good people—unless it's a betrayal of trust or breaking the law.") But failure sets even good people back. Look what happened to the two individuals chiefly responsible for the development of IBM's STRETCH computer, judged at the time to be a disaster:

> At the time the program was killed, both the chief designer, Stephen Dunwell, and the executive in charge of it, Charlie de Carlo, had gone into the penalty box. Watson, recalling this, said "poor Dunwell had to crawl into a cocoon for three or four years, but I apologized publicly to him later" (Fishman, 1981, p. 120).

So it is understandable why managers put distance between themselves and failure; it hurts their reputations.

LIVING WITH THE RESULTS

We have seen that the consequences of important, complex decisions are essentially ambiguous. Like defining what a problem is, defining the results of action is an interpretive process. This means

that it is subject to certain human tendencies: People seek to reduce uncertainty, use simple models to interpret what's happening around them, and sometimes don't hear information if it is contrary to what they are expecting. One way managers cope with ambiguity is to look for numbers, such as return on investment or percent of quota, as a means of being more objective. Forecasts, for example, tend to become the criteria against which to judge the efficacy of action. Similarly, many organizations have also invested heavily in management information systems that routinely deliver large amounts of quantitative performance data.

While all of these approaches can help in assessing decisions, they can also be deceptive. There is no magic in quantification, and as was the case in recognizing problems, an over-reliance on numbers can divert attention from the rich complexity of the issues. Numbers and trends are particularly risky in fast-changing environments where what has been true historically may not be true now. For instance, what

was true for the oil companies when prices were controlled is not necessarily true under decontrol. What was historically unprofitable may not remain so, given world oil prices, depletion of supply, and inflation.

Given that consequences require interpretation even when numbers are available, what does this mean for managerial decision makers? First, they should be aware that *all* models of how the world works are simplifications of reality, and that different people may use different models to explain the same events. In a sense, the rules that guide managers in assessing decision quality are figments of their experience.

Second, perceptions of consequences *are* taken seriously. They can become policy; they do become part of the track record of the manager involved. On important problems, then, managers are well advised to negotiate perceptions of consequences—to try to reach some agreement with important people on how it went. This process may work differently for the

The Ambiguity of Knowing What Happened

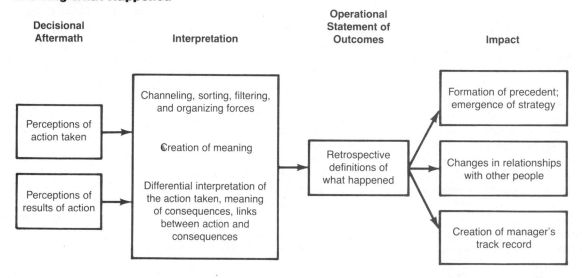

quick decision cycles than it does for the convoluted. Effective quick-cycle, action-first decision making depends on feedback. Knowing how a hip shot turned out allows a manager to take corrective action, but the very efficiency of the quick cycle disinclines managers to spend time on follow-up.

In long and convoluted decision making, involving many people over time, analysis of consequences begins during the decision process. The negotiation over what is important begins early in the problem-solving process; involving the right people at the right times can create shared responsibility and common perceptions. On the other hand, involving numerous people in diffuse processes may result in many of them never knowing how things came out or what difference their contribution made.

Put succinctly, a manager needs to consider carefully what role to take in negotiating the outcomes of action. A few ''rules of thumb'' can be summarized as follows:

1. *Recognize that evaluating decisions involves managing perceptions.* For most day-to-day problems, what others think may be irrelevant. But for certain important problems, what others think happened may be more important than what actually happened.

This means that managers need to consider both tactics and strategy when problem solving. Knowing whom to involve, when to involve them, and how to involve them is an intuitive but critical choice. In some cases it is important to keep the decision-making process visible, especially when the manager wants others to know that all reasonable efforts were made. In other cases, the manager may want to keep a low profile, staying some distance away from the problem and getting his or her act together

before letting the problem become visible.

What's important is the manager's awareness that decision making is as much the management of a process as it is the making of a choice. Assuming responsibility for a problem also implies responsibility for how the problem is solved.

2. *Pick causes carefully.* This applies not just because it serves a manager's self-interest, but also because solving problems is a question of priorities and available time. Association with certain decisions determines one's track record. The other side of the coin is that convoluted decisions (which often result from even trivial problems) consume time and energy. While managers should not shy away from sticky problems, they should be realistic about investing effort in either the trivial or the intractable.

3. *Inoculate against risk.* Making decisions is a risky business, but so is avoiding decisions:

> Unhappily, corporate difficulties are more often the result of inaction in the face of a dangerous change than of being the hopeless victim of circumstances. It's the exceptional executive who can bring himself to admit that a crisis is in the making; the unexpected report of trouble, like Banquo's ghost, just doesn't fit into the scheme of things. Even fewer are the executives with the courage to take drastic action in time. On the contrary, case histories reveal too many instances where top management procrastinated about an emergent crisis. (Smith, 1963, p. 19)

When assessing a problem, a manager should consider the consequences of failure to act as well as those of a potential action. At the same time, when contemplating a risk-filled decision, a manager should take certain precautions: anticipate as well as possible

the likely consequences, especially the negative ones; and touch base with at least some of the powerful people in the organization. An executive echoed this advice when he told us how he went about deciding whether to take on a big project:

> I'd put the thing together the best I could and spell out in considerable detail what all the costs would be and what the potential payout would be—spell it out as well as I could. Then I'd take it to a couple of the directors [members of the board] that were particularly interested. Sit down and go over it. I knew that if these two guys went along with me, they had a lot of influence with the rest of the directors and chances are, if we all decided it was the right thing to do, there wouldn't be any drastic repercussions [if it didn't work out].

To protect themselves against downside risk, astute managers imagine the worst and line up allies who agree that the risk is worth taking.

 **LEARNING CHECKPOINT**

Can group decision making avert making mistakes on such situations as producing wide-bodied planes when the market evaporates?

1. *Develop and use strong feedback systems.* Be aggressive in finding out about consequences. Experience is only a good teacher when the data one generates through action are collected and interpreted. It is hard enough to know accurately the consequences of our actions, even if we have a good network; it is virtually impossible if we have no reliable information.

Since managers are reluctant to show themselves (or their superiors) in a bad light, news about failed solutions can be extremely hard to come by. A corollary to the inverse law of uncertainty mentioned earlier in this chapter is the inverse law of feedback: The higher a manager's position in the organization, the more constricted are the feedback channels upward. This law operates with a vengeance when, as one executive put it, "executives are susceptible to a belief in their own infallibility."

5. *Accept failure (your own), if it happens.* Even the best managers make mistakes: To be human is to be fallible. Because executives so jealously guard their reputations as capable people, they may go to the extreme of never admitting mistakes. One executive said:

> There are some executive suites and corporate environments in which the executive, if he makes mistakes (which, of course, every executive does) never lets those mistakes be seen by others. That's a self-destructive course. An executive who does that becomes uptight and withdrawn from his environment and out of touch with reality (Kaplan, 1982, p. 3).

In contrast, the effective managers we interviewed took a different tack. One executive said:

> If things work out well, then I thank everybody. . . . If things didn't work out, and I was the driving force, then it's my fault.

Similarly, another executive told us:

> Everybody knows you make mistakes, so why not admit it. I make it a point to admit the blunders. Once I admit it, I feel better about it. It doesn't bother me. It's really a painful thing to keep trying to not admit some things. You have to carry that around as a burden until you get if off your chest.

In addition to admitting mistakes, it is important not to be defeated by them. An executive stated:

> You just have to have the ego strength to lose and not let it discourage you. Everytime you lose, you learn something. Everytime you lose, it's another bet or piece of information that's going to help you win next time.

Defeat teaches, if the manager is willing to learn. But the temptation is strong to shun responsibility and to withdraw from the problem. A successful manager, a gutsy manager, is one who faces up to decisions that have failed and regroups and makes them less of a failure or sometimes even a success. In defeat, the effective managers neither fold their tents nor do they necessarily persist in the same course; they stick with the problem and consider *different* solutions.

6. *Accept other people's failure.* It's no wonder, given the climate that prevails in many organizations, that people avoid failure like the plague.

> In my experience, if the corporation does something and it turns out well, then everybody had a part in the decisions. If it turns out poorly, then there's usually some guy that caused it.

Small wonder that so many managers are gun-shy about making decisions. An executive confided that he felt this squeeze in the last company he worked for:

> I ask myself, "why do I find decision making so easy now, whereas it was sometimes so difficult then?" The answer I came up with was, "Well, there was tremendous pressure from above to be right or else." There are some organizations that have little or no tolerance for people who make mistakes. Therefore people don't make mistakes.

They don't make mistakes because they play it safe. They avoid risks. Said another executive:

> The biggest problem with decision makers are the kind of guys who have to be right all the time. Those are the ones who are in deep trouble. They just have to be right every single time so therefore they're never going to take a risk.

To create a climate in which people don't have to be right every time and where they can feel free to take risks, managers can do a couple of things. First, they can encourage their people to try things on a small scale—modest experiments, which, if they fail, do no great damage (Peters & Waterman, 1982). Second, they can set a good example:

> You know, if you walk in and say, "God, did I blow that. Jesus Christ, did I screw up today" and tell a story about how badly you screwed up, they're going to be a lot more open to telling you things that they've screwed up. . . . It works so well with the people at work, and they feel very comfortable in saying to you when they've made a mistake. So you get more data, more factual data, and they don't have to figure out all the rationalizations of why what they did was right.

7. *Don't rest on your laurels.* When managers enjoy the sweet taste of victory, they must be alert to the present dangers. For one thing, they must remember to share the wealth. We have seen that it is easy to be generous with blame; it is also tempting—but counterproductive—to be stingy with praise. A university administrator advised:

> Much of what you do isn't personal; you don't do it by yourself. There are many actors. And the applause is great enough to share with everyone.

Echoed by several other managers, this advice is especially important to managers who, like the one just quoted, expect to keep collaborators and sponsors committed to a long-term project (Kanter, 1977).

The other present danger of winning is complacency. A certain mental inertia sets in and lulls the manager into extrapolating a comfortable present into the indefinite future. As president of Pan Am, Juan Trippe had become accustomed to an annual 15 percent market growth and counted on that growth continuing when he made his company the "launch customer" for the new wide-bodied planes (Newhouse, 1982):

> Talking about Trippe, the executive who was at the time Pan Am's chief of engineering said: "Trippe would not have looked at marketing analysis. There was no planning department in Pan Am. Trippe sat in his corner office, made plans, and then made them come true." (Newhouse, 1982)

Unfortunately, as soon as the airline and aircraft industries became committed to wide-bodied planes, the early-1970s recession hit and the market for the planes evaporated.

 **LEARNING CHECKPOINT**

How did Ore-Ida attempt to encourage risk taking behavior? Do you think it will work? (see Chapter Encounter).

Even with success, sustained success, managers must remain vigilant. Said one executive:

> When one's decisions turn out alright, one should resist the temptation to spend very much time basking in the glory of those right decisions. They need to be reexamined on a continuous basis to be sure that the decision that was right yesterday continues to be right today.

The manager must continually "sift through the good news looking for evidence of future problems" (Fox, 1976).

Unfortunately, handling victory is not the manager's greatest challenge, because most of what the manager does is contend with problems:

> Ninety percent of their time is spent on problems; ten percent on victory dinners, celebrations, etc. And very often the celebration for a wonderful victory coincides with the discovery of a terrible new problem. Rarely is victory unstained by a concurrent encroaching defeat (Fox, 1976).

□

REFERENCES

Carter, E. The behavioral theory of the firm and top-level corporate decisions. *Administrative Science Quarterly*, 1971, *16*(4), 413–428.

Cyert, R., DeGroot, M., & Holt, C. Capital allocation within a firm. *Behavioral Science*, 1979, *24*(5), 287–295.

de Segur, Count Philipe-Paul. *Napoleon's Russian campaign.* Translated from the French by J. David Townsend. Chicago: Time-Life Books, 1958.

Fishman, K. D. *The computer establishment.* New York: Harper & Row, 1981.

Fox, J. M. *Executive qualities.* Reading, Mass.: Addison-Wesley, 1976.

Ilgen, D., Fisher, C., & Taylor, M. Consequences of individual feedback on behavior in organizations. *Journal of Applied Psychology,* 1979, *64*(4), 349–371.

Kanter, R. *Men and women of the corporation.* New York: Basic Books, 1977.

Kaplan, R. E. An executive's reflections on executives: An interview with Roger T. Kelley. *Issues & Observations.* Greensboro, N.C.: Center for Creative Leadership, 1982 *2*(2), 1–4.

Kaplan, R. E. Lombardo, M. M., & Mazique, M. S. *A mirror for managers: Using simulation to develop management teams* (Tech. Rep. No. 23). Greensboro, N.C.: Center for Creative Leadership, 1983.

Kissinger, H. A. *White house years.* Boston: Little, Brown, 1979.

Kotter, J. P. *The general managers.* New York: The Free Press, 1982.

March, J. G., & Olsen, J. P. *Ambiguity and choice in organizations.* Bergen, Norway: Universitetsforlaget, 1976.

Mintzberg, H., Raisinghani, D., & Theoret, A. The structure of "unstructured" decision processes. *Administrative Science Quarterly*, 1976, *21*, 246–275.

Mirvis, P., & Berg, D. (Eds.). *Failures in organization development and change.* New York: Wiley, 1977.

Newhouse, J. A sporting game (Part IV). *The New Yorker*, July 5, 1982.

Peters, T. J., & Waterman, R. H., Jr. *In search of excellence.* New York: Harper & Row, 1982.

Pfeffer, J. The ambiguity of leadership. In M. W. McCall, Jr., & M. M. Lombardo (Eds.), *Leadership: Where else can we go?* Durham, N.C.: Duke University Press, 1978.

Ross, L. The intuitive psychologist and his shortcomings: Distortions in the attribution process. In L. Berkowitz, (Ed.), *Advances in experimental social psychology* (Vol. 10). New York: Academic Press, 1977.

Smith, R. *Corporations in crisis.* Garden City, N.Y.: Doubleday, 1963.

Taylor, D. Decision making and problem solving. In J. March (Ed.), *Handbook of organizations.* Chicago: Rand McNally, 1965, 48–86.

Tuchman, G. *Making news: A study in the construction of reality.* New York: Free Press, 1978.

Weick, K. *The social psychology of organizing* (2nd ed.). Reading, Mass.: Addison-Wesley, 1979.

Whetton, D. Organizational decline: A neglected topic in organizational science. *Academy of Management Review*, 1980, *5*(4), 577–588.

D⒈ PROBLEM SOLVING QUESTIONNAIRE

Part I. Circle the response that comes closest to how you usually feel or act. There are no right or wrong responses to any of these items.

1. I am more careful about
   a. people's feelings.
   b. their rights.
2. I usually get on better with
   a. imaginative people.
   b. realistic people.
3. It is a higher compliment to be called
   a. a person of real feeling.
   b. a consistently reasonable person.
4. In doing something with many other people, it appeals more to me
   a. to do it in the accepted way.
   b. to invent a way of my own.
5. I get more annoyed at
   a. fancy theories.
   b. people who do not like theories.
6. It is higher praise to call someone
   a. a person of vision.
   b. a person of common sense.
7. I more often let
   a. my heart rule my head.
   b. my head rule my heart.
8. I think it is a worse fault
   a. to show too much warmth.
   b. to be unsympathetic.
9. If I were a teacher, I would rather teach
   a. courses involving theory.
   b. fact courses.

Part II. Which word in the following pair appeals to you more? Circle a. or b.

10.	a.	compassion	b.	foresight
11.	a.	justice	b.	mercy
12.	a.	production	b.	design
13.	a.	gentle	b.	firm
14.	a.	uncritical	b.	critical
15.	a.	literal	b.	figurative
16.	a.	imaginative	b.	matter-of-fact

Scoring Key

Mark each of your responses on the following scales. Then use the point value column to arrive at your score. For example, if you answered *a* to the first question, you would check *1a* in the feeling column.

This response receives zero points when you add up the point value column. Instructions for classifying your scores are indicated below the scales.

Sensation	Point Value	Intuition	Point Value	Thinking	Point Value	Feeling	Point Value
2 b ___	1	2 a ___	2	1 b ___	1	1 a ___	0
4 a ___	1	4 b ___	1	3 b ___	2	3 a ___	1
5 a ___	1	5 b ___	1	7 b ___	1	7 a ___	1
6 b ___	1	6 a ___	0	8 a ___	0	8 b ___	1
9 b ___	2	9 a ___	2	10 b ___	2	10 a ___	1
12 a ___	1	12 b ___	0	11 a ___	2	11 b ___	1
15 a ___	1	15 b ___	1	13 b ___	1	13 a ___	1
16 b ___	2	16 a ___	0	14 b ___	0	14 a ___	1
Maximum Point Value	(10)		(7)		(9)		(7)

Source: Adapted from the Myers-Briggs Type indicator and a scale developed by Don Hellriegel, John Slocum and Richard W. Woodman, *Organizational Behavior*, 3rd ed., (St. Paul, MN: West Publishing Co., 1983 pp. 127–141.)

Classifying Total Scores

Write *intuition* if your intuition score is equal to or greater than your sensation score.

Write *sensation* if sensation score is greater than your intuition score.

Write *feeling* if your feeling score is greater than your thinking score.

Write *thinking* if your thinking score is greater than your feeling score.

D2 HOW CREATIVE ARE YOU?*

In recent years, several task-oriented tests have been developed to measure creative abilities and behavior. While certainly useful, they do not adequately tap the complex network of behaviors, the particular personality traits, attitudes, motivations, values, interests and other variables that predispose a person to think creatively.

To arrive at assessment measures that would cover a broader range of creative attributes, our organization developed an inventory type of test. A partial version of this instrument is featured below.

After each statement, indicate with a letter the degree or extent with which you agree or disagree with it:

A = strongly agree
B = agree
C = in between or don't know
D = disagree
E = strongly disagree.

Mark your answers as accurately and frankly as possible. Try not to "second guess" how a creative person might respond to each statement.

1. I always work with a great deal of certainty that I'm following the correct procedures for solving a particular problem. _____
2. It would be a waste of time for me to ask questions if I had no hope of obtaining answers. _____
3. I feel that a logical step-by-step method is best for solving problems. _____
4. I occasionally voice opinions in groups that seem to turn some people off. _____
5. I spend a great deal of time thinking about what others think of me. _____
6. I feel that I may have a special contribution to give to the world. _____
7. It is more important for me to do what I believe to be right than to try to win the approval of others. _____
8. People who seem unsure and uncertain about things lose my respect. _____
9. I am able to stick with difficult problems over extended periods of time. _____
10. On occasion I get overly enthusiastic about things. _____
11. I often get my best ideas when doing nothing in particular. _____
12. I rely on intuitive hunches and the feeling of "rightness" or "wrongness" when moving toward the solution of a problem. _____
13. When problem solving, I work faster analyzing the problem and slower when synthesizing the information I've gathered. _____
14. I like hobbies which involve collecting things. _____
15. Daydreaming has provided the impetus for many of my more important projects. _____
16. If I had to choose from two occupations other than the one I now have, I would rather be a physician than an explorer. _____

17. I can get along more easily with people if they belong to about the same social and business class as myself. _____
18. I have a high degree of aesthetic sensitivity. _____
19. Intuitive hunches are unreliable guides in problem solving. _____
20. I am much more interested in coming up with new ideas than I am in trying to sell them to others. _____
21. I tend to avoid situations in which I might feel inferior. _____
22. In evaluating information, the source of it is more important to me than the content. _____
23. I like people who follow the rule "business before pleasure." _____
24. One's own self-respect is much more important than the respect of others. _____
25. I feel that people who strive for perfection are unwise. _____
26. I like work in which I must influence others. _____
27. It is important for me to have a place for everything and everything in its place. _____
28. People who are willing to entertain "crackpot" ideas are impractical. _____
29. I rather enjoy fooling around with new ideas, even if there is no practical payoff. _____
30. When a certain approach to a problem doesn't work, I can quickly reorient my thinking. _____
31. I don't like to ask questions that show ignorance. _____
32. I am able to more easily change my interests to pursue a job or career than I can change a job to pursue my interests. _____
33. Inability to solve a problem is frequently due to asking the wrong questions. _____
34. I can frequently anticipate the solution to my problems. _____
35. It is a waste of time to analyze one's failures. _____
36. Only fuzzy thinkers resort to metaphors and analogies. _____
37. At times I have so enjoyed the ingenuity of a crook that I hoped he or she would go scotfree. _____
38. I frequently begin work on a problem which I can only dimly sense and not yet express. _____
39. I frequently tend to forget things such as names of people, streets, highways, small towns, etc. _____
40. I feel that hard work is the basic factor in success. _____
41. To be regarded as a good team member is important to me. _____
42. I know how to keep my inner impulses in check. _____
43. I am a thoroughly dependable and responsible person. _____
44. I resent things being uncertain and unpredictable. _____
45. I prefer to work with others in a team effort rather than solo. _____
46. The trouble with many people is that they take things too seriously. _____
47. I am frequently haunted by my problems and cannot let go of them. _____
48. I can easily give up immediate gain or comfort to reach the goals I have set. _____
49. If I were a college professor, I would rather teach factual courses than those involving theory. _____
50. I'm attracted to the mystery of life. _____

Scoring Instructions. To compute your percentage score, circle and add up the values assigned to each item.

	Strongly Agree A	Agree B	In-Between or Don't Know C	Disagree D	Strongly Disagree E
1.	−2	−1	0	+1	+2
2.	−2	−1	0	+1	+2
3.	−2	−1	0	+1	+2
4.	+2	+1	0	−1	−2
5.	−2	−1	0	+1	+2
6.	+2	+1	0	−1	−2
7.	+2	+1	0	−1	−2
8.	−2	−1	0	+1	+2
9.	+2	+1	0	−1	−2
10.	+2	+1	0	−1	−2
11.	+2	+1	0	−1	−2
12.	+2	+1	0	−1	−2
13.	−2	−1	0	+1	+2
14.	−2	−1	0	+1	+2
15.	+2	+1	0	−1	−2
16.	−2	−1	0	+1	+2
17.	−2	−1	0	+1	+2
18.	+2	+1	0	−1	−2
19.	−2	−1	0	+1	+2
20.	+2	+1	0	−1	−2
21.	−2	−1	0	+1	+2
22.	−2	−1	0	+1	+2
23.	−2	−1	0	+1	+2
24.	+2	+1	0	−1	−2
25.	−2	−1	0	+1	+1
26.	−2	−1	0	+1	+2
27.	−2	−1	0	+1	+2
28.	−2	−1	0	+1	+2
29.	+2	+1	0	−1	−2
30.	+2	+1	0	−1	−2
31.	−2	−1	0	+1	+2
32.	−2	−1	0	+1	+2
33.	+2	+1	0	−1	−2
34.	+2	+1	0	−1	−2
35.	−2	−1	0	+1	+2
36.	−2	−1	0	+1	+2
37.	+2	+1	0	−1	−2
38.	+2	+1	0	−1	−2
39.	+2	+1	0	−1	−2
40.	+2	+1	0	−1	−2
41.	−2	−1	0	+1	+2
42.	−2	−1	0	+1	+2
43.	−2	−1	0	+1	+2
44.	−2	−1	0	+1	+2
45.	−2	−1	0	+1	+2
46.	+2	+1	0	−1	−2
47.	+2	+1	0	−1	−2
48.	+2	+1	0	−1	−2
49.	−2	−1	0	+1	+2
50.	+2	+1	0	−1	−2

80 to 100	Very creative	20 to 39	Below average
60 to 79	Above average	−100 to 19	Noncreative
40 to 59	Average		

Further information about the test, "How Creative Are You?" is available from Princeton Creative Research, Inc., 10 Nassau St., P.O. Box 122, Princeton, NJ 08542.

LOST-AT-SEA DECISION MAKING

OBJECTIVE

To offer you the opportunity to compare individual versus group decision making.

STARTING THE EXERCISE

Suppose that you are adrift on a private yacht in the South Pacific. As a consequence of a fire of unknown origin, much of the yacht and its contents have been destroyed. The yacht is now slowly sinking. Your location is unclear because of the destruction of critical navigational equipment and because you and the crew were distracted trying to bring the fire under control. Your best estimate is that you are approximately one thousand miles south-southwest of the nearest land.

Listed are 15 items that are intact and undamaged after the fire. In addition to these articles, you have a serviceable rubber life raft with oars, large enough to carry yourself, the crew, and all the items listed here. The total contents of all survivors' pockets are a package of cigarettes, several books of matches, and five one-dollar bills.

	(1) Individual Ranking	(2) Group Ranking	(3) Ranking Key
Sextant	____	____	____
Shaving mirror	____	____	____
Five-gallon can of water	____	____	____
Mosquito netting	____	____	____
One case of U.S. Army C rations	____	____	____
Maps of the Pacific Ocean	____	____	____
Seat cushion (flotation device approved by the Coast Guard)	____	____	____
Two-gallon can of oil/gas mixture	____	____	____
Small transistor radio	____	____	____
Shark repellent	____	____	____
Twenty-square feet of opaque plastic	____	____	____
One quart of 160-proof Puerto Rican rum	____	____	____
Fifteen feet of nylon rope	____	____	____
Two boxes of chocolate bars	____	____	____
Fishing kit	____	____	____

1. Working independently and without discussing the problem or the merits of any of the items, your task is to rank the 15 items in terms of their importance to your survival. Under column 1, headed "Individual Ranking," place the number **1** by the most important item, the number **2** by the second most important, and so on through number **15,** the least important. When you are through, *do not discuss* the problem or rankings of items with anyone.
2. Your instructor will establish teams of four to six students. The task for your team is to rank the 15 items, according to the group's consensus, on order of importance to your survival. Do not vote or average team-members' rankings; try to reach agreement on each item. Base your decision on knowledge, logic, or the experiences of group members. Try to avoid basing the decision on personal preference. Enter the group's ranking in column 2, "Group Ranking." This process should take between 20 and 30 minutes, or as the instructor requires.
3. When everyone is through, your instructor will read the correct ranking, provided by officers of the U.S. Merchant Marines. Enter the correct ranks in column 3, headed "Ranking Key."

4. Compute the accuracy of your individual ranking. For each item, use the absolute value (ignore plus and minus signs) of the difference between column 1 and column 3. Add up these absolute values to get your *Individual Accuracy Index*. Enter it here: _____ .

5. Perform the same operation as in Step 4, but use columns 2 and 3 for your group ranking. Adding up the absolute values yields your *Group Accuracy Index*. Enter it here: _____ .

6. Compute the *average* of your group's Individual Accuracy Indexes. Do this by adding up each member's Individual Accuracy Index and dividing the result by the number of group members. Enter it here: _____ .

7. Identify the *lowest* Individual Accuracy Index in your group. This is the most correct ranking in your group. Enter it here: _____ .

The Learning Message

This exercise is designed to let you experience group decision-making. Think about how discussion, reflection, and the exchange of opinions influenced your final decision.

2 WHO GETS THE OVERTIME?*

OBJECTIVES

1. To examine small group decision making.

2. To use role playing as a learning method.

STARTING THE EXERCISE

Task 1:

A. The instructor will briefly discuss role playing. There are a number of ways to role play, and it is used for a variety of purposes. In this case, each member of your team will be given a role in a group decision-making problem. You will be comfortable in doing this if you follow this guidance: Remember that this is not a theatrical production. You are not being asked to take the lead in the school play. All you are being asked to do is to play yourself as you would feel if you were in the situation described in the role you will be given.

For instance, if you were a student who had worked hard, had done what you considered to be excellent work, and had received a D for the final grade in a course, how would you behave if you decided to confront your professor on this? This situation could be role played by you, with someone else playing the role of the instructor from his viewpoint, which would probably be different from yours. The roles of our exercise are similar in that you will have some idea of how you would behave if you were in the situation described.

B. Each team is to arrange itself in a circle and note that Kim is the supervisor for this specific exercise. (*Note:* All the exercises in this book are to be completed with your permanent team. If the class

* Source: Reprinted from James B. Lau, *Behavior in Organizations: An Experimental Approach* (Homewood, Ill.: Richard D. Irwin, Inc., 1975), pp. 57–59.

is not working in permanent teams, participants are to form groups of six and elect a supervisor for this exercise.) Starting clockwise from the supervisor, the role assignments are as follows:

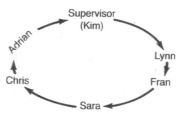

All roles except Sara's can be played by a man or a woman. Sara's role must be played by a woman. If only five members are present, eliminate the role of Chris. If only four are present in the team, the members should be assigned to other groups to fill vacancies and the remainder should be observers.

C. The instructor will read the Appendix instruction sheet aloud while the class follows it.

D. Turn to your own role assignment sheet which the instructor will provide. After you have read the role description and understand it, turn it face down and use it as a name card so your team members can identify your role name during the exercise. Do not tell others what your role instructions are. When the exercise begins, play your role naturally without referring back to your sheet. Remember, when facts or events arise that are not covered by the roles, make up things that are consistent with the way it might be in a real-life situation.

E. When Kim, the supervisor, has studied and understands her role, she will stand. When the supervisors for all groups are standing, the instructor will give the signal to begin the exercise. When Kim sits down, assume she has just entered her office and greet her with a hearty "Good Morning!" She will tell you what to do from this point on. (*Note for Kim:* If you have only five on the team, including yourself, announce to your group that Adrian called in sick and read them her role. Adrian is to be taken into consideration in arriving at the solution.)

F. Observers, if there are any, are to be assigned one to a group for the purpose of observing and, possibly, reporting to the class at the end of the session how the decision was made. Observers are *not* to enter into the process.
(Time for introduction: 10 minutes)
(Time for role playing: 20–25 minutes)

Task 2:

A. When the role playing has been completed, the instructor will ask each foreman to give the name of the person in the role play who got the overtime. The names are to be listed on the blackboard for all groups (using the chart from below), but no discussion is to take place this time. The listing provides the class with information as to which groups agree and disagree with their choice.

Group	Who Got the Overtime	How Decision Was Made	Who Was Dissatisfied
#1			
#2			
#3			

B. The instructor will now interview each group on the following questions:
1. Why did the chosen person get the overtime?
2. How was the decision made? (He will write these on the chart.)
3. What players were satisfied and dissatisfied, and why?
4. How did the foreman feel about his role?
5. How did the players feel about the way the foreman played his role?

C. After all groups have been interviewed, the instructor will pose the following questions:
1. What are the similarities and differences in the group decision process of the teams?
2. Was this a good way to decide who should have the overtime?
3. What are some situations other than overtime to which this group decision process might be applied?
4. Are there any students who have participated in group decisions in work situations? If so, they should describe these experiences.
5. Consider other issues raised by the students.
   (Time: 25 minutes)

1 NED NORMAN, COMMITTEE CHAIRMAN*

Ned Norman tried to reconstruct, in his own mind, the series of events that had culminated in that most unusual committee meeting this morning.

For example, each of the committee members had suddenly seemed to be stubbornly resisting any suggestions that did not exactly coincide with their own ideas for implementing the program under consideration. This unwillingness to budge from some preconceived position was not like the normal behavior patterns of most of the committee participants. Of course, some of the comments made in one of last week's sessions about "old-fashioned, seat-of-the-pants decision making" had ruffled a few feathers but Ned did not really think this was the reason things had suddenly bogged down today. Still, Ned thought it might be worthwhile to review in his mind what had taken place in this morning's meeting to see if some clues existed to explain the problem.

First, Ned recalled starting the session by saying that the committee had discussed, in past meetings, several of the factors connected with the proposed expanded-services program and it now seemed about time to make a decision as to which way to go. Ned remembered that Robert Roman had protested that they had barely scratched the surface of the possibilities for implementing the program. Then, both Sherman Stith and Tod Tooley, who worked in the statistics branch of Division Baker, had sided with Roman and were most insistent that additional time was needed to research in depth some of the other avenues of approach to solving the problems associated with starting the new program.

Walt West had entered the fray by stating that this seemed a little uncalled for, since previous experience had clearly indicated that expansion programs, such as this one, should be implemented through selected area district offices. This had brought forth the statement by Sherman Stith that experience was more often than not a lousy teacher, which was followed by Tod Tooley repeating his unfortunate statement about old-fashioned decision-making! And, of course, Robert Roman had not helped matters at all by saying that it was obviously far better to go a little bit slower in such matters by trying any new program in one

area first, rather than to have the committee members look "unprogressive" by just "trudging along on the same old cow paths!"

In fact, as Ned suddenly realized, if he hadn't almost intuitively exercised his prerogatives as chairman to stop the trend that was developing, he might have had a real melee on his hands right then! It was obvious that things were increasingly touchy among the members, so much so that despite his best efforts, everyone had simply refused either to participate or to support any of the ideas he (Ned) had offered to break the deadlock.

Feeling a little frustrated, early that same afternoon Ned had sought the counsel of his boss, who advised him to go talk to the division directors for whom the various committee members worked. In each area visited, Ned found that the division director was already aware of the committee problems and each one had his own ideas as to what should be done about them.

The director of Division Able stated that he was not much in sympathy with people who wanted to make a big deal out of every program that came along. He recalled the problem six years ago when the first computer had arrived in the agency and was hailed as the manager's replacement in decision making. He noted that, although the computer was still here, so was he, and that he had probably made better decisions, as a result of his broad background and knowledge, than the computer ever would! The Division Able director told Ned that he had been on several deadlocked committees but that, when he was chairman, he had simply made the decision for the committee and solved the problem. He suggested Ned do likewise.

The Division Baker director stated that he knew Ned was one of those guys who wanted to use the best information available in estimating a program's performance. He told Ned that Sherman and Tod, who worked in Division Baker, had briefed him on the problems the committee had encountered and that, in his opinion, their investigative approach was the proper one to take. After all, stated the director, it logically followed that a decision could be no better than the research effort put into it. He also told Ned

---

* Source: This case was written by Professor William D. Heier of Arizona State University.

that, although he realized research might cost a little money, he had told Sherman and Tod to go ahead and collect the data they needed to determine the best way to implement the expansion program. The director flatly stated, "These are my men and my division will be footing the bill for this research, so no one else has any gripe about the cost aspects." He expressed the opinion that almost any price would be cheap if it would awaken some of the company employees to the tremendous values of a scientific approach to decision making.

The Division Charlie director stated, quite bluntly, that he was not particularly interested in how the expansion program was decided. He said it looked to him like the easiest way to get the thing moving was to do it a piece at a time. That way, he noted, you can evaluate how it looks without committing the company to a full-scale expansion. He concluded by saying, "It doesn't take a lot of figuring to figure that one out!"

The Division Delta director stated that the aspect of "time" was against the committee's looking at all angles and that a decision should be made after looking at two or three possible solutions. He stated that he needed Quentin Quinn, his representative on Ned's committee, for another job and hoped the committee would be finished very quickly.

Ned now realized that he had more of a problem than he had suspected. In view of the approaches and opinions expressed by the division directors, it seemed highly unlikely that any of the committee members would move from their present position. Ergo, Ned is now chairman of a deadlocked committee!

In pondering his dilemma, Ned considered various ways to break the impasse. First, as chairman, he could simply exert his authority and try to force a solution. This was guaranteed to alienate most of the committee members and the division directors, who had representatives on the committee.

Second, Ned considered returning to his boss, who had formed the committee, with the recommendation that the committee be disbanded. While the reasons for this recommendation would be easy to explain, Ned's failure to prevent this problem might be much more difficult.

As a third possibility, the idea occurred to Ned that he might ask each committee member to bring to the next meeting, in writing, his recommended plan for implementing the program. Since these would surely represent the thinking of the four division directors, this information could then be presented by Ned to his boss with a request for guidance. If his boss could be persuaded to make a choice, Ned's problem would be solved. Of the three ideas he had considered, Ned liked the last one the best. Accordingly, he reached for the telephone preparatory to calling the first of his impossible committee members! □

CASE QUESTIONS

1. What does this case illustrate about the process of group decision making?
2. Discuss and evaluate the comments made by each division director.
3. What advice would you give Ned Norman?

⑫ ASPEN COUNTY HIGH SCHOOL*

The following is part of a conversation between the Superintendent of Schools and Mr. Don Mason, Aspen County High School Principal, that took place at the regular Wednesday meeting of the Aspen County School District Board of Trustees during the last week of March.

Superintendent: Don, it seems like every time you come to our meeting you've got your hand out for more money. Last month it was money for new band uniforms. Before that you were trying to tell us the athletic teams needed another $2,000 worth of equipment. Now you hit us with this across-the-board raise for your faculty. You know we're working on a very limited budget and we have other demands that must be met, too.

Don Mason: Of course, it costs money to run a school district. I can understand your problems. But remember, the only way we're going to be able to offer good instruction to this community is by having well-qualified teachers on the staff. And good teachers cost money! Besides, remember you promised us last year when we asked for a raise that we'd get it this year, and. . . .

Superintendent: Now, just a minute Don. We never promised you that you'd get a raise this year. We simply said that it was impossible to give you a raise *last* year because Western Steel had closed down as a result of the strike and the district's income was decreased substantially.

At that time we thought that Western Steel would soon be operating at full steam and that we would have the funds available for a raise *this year.* As everyone knows only too well, Western still is only operating at about one-third capacity. This means that their payroll is only about one third. Quite a few people have moved from the area to get jobs. Business income is low and some of the shops have closed their doors permanently. We just don't have the money in the General Fund and we probably couldn't pass a special bond issue at this late date anyway.

Aspen County School District was a unified district comprised of four elementary schools, two junior high schools, and one high school. The district served the entire population of the county. The major source of income for this small western community was Western Steel. Strikes and slowdowns at Western Steel often had resulted in extreme fluctuations in the population and the financial well-being of the community. As a result of these problems and others, the superintendent and the Board experienced frequent discord with the teachers and administrators on financial matters.

At 8:30 A.M. the following Monday, the thirty-seven faculty members and administrators of Aspen High School held their weekly faculty meeting. The meeting was called to order by the vice-principal of the high school, Bob Lane.

Bob Lane (Vice-Principal): We have a lot of business to cover in our meeting this morning, but first I think it is appropriate that we hear from Don. As most of you know by now, Don went to bat for the faculty against the Board for a salary increase and he wants to bring this item up first so that everyone will understand exactly how things are progressing.

Don Mason (Principal): I met with the Board last Thursday and asked about that raise they had promised us. They gave the same old excuse of no funds. It looks like we're going to have a tough battle on our hands if we expect to get an across-the-board raise this year. Since their major objection appears to be a lack of funds, the Teachers' Welfare Committee has been working over the weekend on possible ways that the funds can be obtained. They have worked up a couple of alternatives that can be presented. The most attractive one involves not receiving your three summer months' checks in one lump sum in June as some of you have been doing. Phil, why don't you explain just how that is going to work?

Phil, the chairman of the Teachers' Welfare Committee, then explained to the group that approximately one half of the teachers had been exercising the option

---

* Source: This case was written by Professor Sherman Tingey and reprinted with permission from B. J. White, J. H. Stamm, and L. W. Foster, *Cases in Organizations: Behavior, Structure, Processes,* Plano, Texas: Business Publications, Inc., 1976, pp. 184–193.

to receive their three summer checks in a lump sum at the beginning of the summer. If receipt of these checks could be postponed until after June 30, the expense would appear in the next fiscal year. This could be a permanent postponement. If only 75 percent of those now exercising this option were willing to forego this advantage, enough funds would be created to finance the desired salary increases. A hand vote of those who were willing to give up this option indicated that 16 of the 18 teachers involved would probably be able to rearrange their financial affairs to support the proposal.

Don Mason: Thanks very much for your support. I'll present this proposal to the Board this Thursday and see if we can't work something out. Bob and I were talking just yesterday and we both expressed the opinion that we have an excellent staff here at the high school and we think that you deserve a raise in the salary schedule. Besides, Bob and I are on a schedule, too, and we'd benefit from a raise the same as you would. Both "X" County and "Y" County received schedule increases this year and our county is falling behind.

The meeting was turned over to Bob who conducted the remaining business. That same afternoon a group of teachers were discussing the situation in the teachers' lounge after school.

Teacher A: I heard Bill [an English teacher] say that he was going to investigate the possibility of a position at Sacramento if it looked like we weren't going to get a raise this year. Do you think we'll get the raise?

Teacher B: Naw, we probably won't. But I wouldn't leave because of that alone. Money isn't everything. I think the kind of work environment we have here is worth something. Not very often will you find a school where both the principal and vice-principal will stand behind their teachers and support them 100 percent. I think that's one of the reasons Don and Bob are so well liked by the teachers.

Teacher C: I'll agree with that! I'll never forget that incident with Bob Lane when I first came here. You remember that he asked me to be the Lettermen's Club Advisor? None of the coaches wanted the job because it takes a lot of time and the kids are pretty rough to handle. Well, anyway, when he introduced me to the Club members, he said

that the administration would stand behind me in whatever I wanted to do as long as I thought it was for the best benefit of the Club.

Later, when I told the Club members that the initiation had to be toned down considerably because of the danger of seriously hurting someone, they stormed right into Bob Lane's office complaining. They figured that since they had to go through all that rough stuff to be initiated, it was only fair for them to "get revenge" against the new members. Boy, it really made me feel good when I found out Bob had told them, "If that's the way your advisor wants it, then that's the way its going to be." It surely made my job a lot easier from then on.

Teacher A: Do you remember that problem I had in the Boys' Cooking Class right at the first of the year?

Teacher B: No, what was that?

Teacher A: Well, it really wasn't a problem. I was nervous since this was my first teaching job. We were supposed to be making cookies. Two boys were laughing and goofing around and somehow they broke a bottle of milk. I was so upset that I sent them to the office. Really it was just an accident, but Don gave the boys a talking to anyway and told them not to goof off in class. I realized afterward that sending them to the office was too strong of a discipline measure, but I was surely glad that Don stuck up for me anyway.

Teacher D: I really think a lot of Don and Bob. Remember last fall when I was teaching that adult evening class in bookkeeping? Dayle [another teacher] and I had gone out for a little deer hunting after school one afternoon. We shot a three-point near the top of Hogback Mountain and it took us a lot longer than we expected to get that deer out. The class I was teaching was supposed to meet at 7:00 and we didn't get back to town until about 7:30. When Don phoned my home about 7:20 and found out that I was still out deer hunting, he said, "I'll tell the students to go ahead and work on their own. He's probably shot a big one and is having difficulty getting it out."

When I got to class 40 minutes late all my students were still there waiting for a deer hunting story. After class I met Don in the hall and he asked just one question: "Did you get your deer?"

The following Thursday at the Board of Trustees' meeting, Principal Don Mason presented the proposal of the Teachers' Welfare Committee in an effort to show the board members where they could get the funds for a salary increase. After considerable discussion of the proposal, the Board said they would take it into consideration but still didn't feel a salary increase would be forthcoming.

At this point in the meeting, the Board revealed to Don Mason that during the week they had decided to set his salary for the next year at $24,000. They emphasized that he would be receiving $1800 increase in addition to the regular yearly increment of $800. They also emphasized that they expected a lot more cooperation from him in the future.

Mason expressed his thanks for the raise but also expressed his opinion that the teachers should also receive a salary schedule increase. He then rose to leave. As he was leaving he heard one member of the Board whisper, "Boy, talk about ungrateful!"

At the next Board meeting, Mason had arranged for members of the Teachers' Welfare Committee to meet before the Board in an effort to convince the board members of the necessity of a salary schedule raise and that the means for the raise were accessible. After the presentation by the committee, the Board said they would consider this information and requested time to verify the data the committee was using. They also expressed their opinion that there was little hope of obtaining raises this year.

Three days later, all the teachers at the high school received notification of a special faculty meeting to be held immediately after school for the purpose of discussing recent events in the negotiations of salary increases.

As some of the teachers met in the hall on the way to the meeting, Teacher G was asked if he knew what was going on. He replied, "I don't know for sure, but Bob Lane said it was 'something big' and for everyone to be sure to attend."

Teacher H: Maybe we're going to get our raise after all!

Teacher G: Not a chance! You know as well as I do the Board isn't going to let Don tell them what they should do. Something else must be in the air.

As Bob Lane, the vice-principal, called the meeting to order, some of the teachers were commenting on the absence of Principal Don Mason.

Bob Lane: I think everyone is here now. We've called this special meeting because we think that

you should know exactly what has been going on during the past few days. Apparently Don has pushed the Board a little too hard for salary increases for the teachers. The night before last one of the board members called me at my home around 9:00 and asked me if I could come over to his house. When I arrived, three of the board members were there to greet me. They asked how I liked my job as an administrator in the high school and I told them I really enjoyed my work here. Then they asked me if I would like to be principal of the high school next year with a nice increase in salary. [Several oh's and ah's were heard in the group.] All I could think of was: What about Don? I asked them if Don had quit and they said, "No, but we aren't going to offer him a contract for next year." [Looks of astonishment and surprise appeared on many faces as a few teachers leaned over and whispered to each other.]

When I asked them why they weren't offering Don a contract, they said it was personal and they didn't want to discuss it with anyone. Well, I didn't hesitate to tell them if they didn't offer Don a contract for next year, they needn't offer me one either because I wouldn't sign it. Now I think this is information that you should know. I think Don finds himself in this position because of his efforts to help you teachers. If there is any way that you can support Don in his fight, I certainly think you should, and I know that he would welcome your help.

At this point Bob Lane left the room and Teacher P, the president of the High School Teachers' Association, took over the meeting. The room was filled with loud talk and excitement.

Teacher P: May I have your attention, please! I know that this is quite an unexpected turn of events. It surprised me as much as it did you when Bob explained the situation to me about an hour ago. But you haven't heard the whole story yet. Don met with the Board in a special meeting that was called at Don's request last evening. He specifically requested reasons for his dismissal, but the Board said they did not have to give any reasons for their actions.

Contracts will be offered on the first of May—that's about ten days away. What can we do to help Don?

Teacher D: (jumping up excitedly): Well, I'll tell you one thing! If they fire Don they can find a replacement for me too. I don't want to work for a Board that can fire someone without any reason other than disagreeing with them.

Teacher E: I have no ties here. The main reason I stay is because I like to teach under Don and Bob. If they go, I'll go too, and I'd like to see the rest of you do the same.

The faculty meeting continued for another hour. It was determined by secret ballot that approximately 90 percent of the faculty would be able and willing to support Principal Mason in the following manner: If Don Mason was not offered a contract, the teachers would not sign their contracts. It was also decided that this information should be conveyed to the Board immediately.

On May 1, the teachers received their contracts in sealed envelopes. Also in each mailbox was a mimeographed note saying Don Mason had not received a contract. All contracts were to be returned to the Board of Trustees by May 15.

During the next two weeks the following appeared in the local newspaper:

Dear Editor:

I read in *The Daily Times* this evening that Mr. Don Mason has requested four times a statement from the school board as to why his contract was not renewed as principal of the Aspen High School.

I do not know much about civil law, but I do know of a moral law that reads: "Do unto others as you wish them to do unto you." Any person who has been employed in a school system whether principal or teacher for a period of years is definitely entitled, as a matter of courtesy, to be given an explanation as to why his contract is not renewed.

I feel this very unjust to the man and the teachers as a whole. No teacher can feel secure under an administration of this caliber. I think the public should demand an explanation. Any innocent member of the school board who sits back and lets this go on is as guilty as the rest.

Sincerely,
A parent

The following letter was signed by approximately one fourth of the 650 students at Aspen High School.

Dear Editor:

What is the school board trying to do by dismissing Mr. Mason without giving any reasons? We feel that Mr. Mason has done an excellent job of building up our high school.

We have been told that better than 90 percent of our teachers have refused to sign their contracts for the coming year. This would result in drastic conditions for our school system. If this happens our school could possibly become a nonaccredited school. This could pose many problems for the seniors planning to attend college.

Parents! Are we the only ones concerned about these problems?

A citizens committee had been formed to investigate the current school "crisis." This committee had requested the investigating services of Dr. Williams, an executive from the State Education Association. A special meeting was held at which Dr. Williams reported his initial findings to the Citizens Committee. The newspaper printed the following as part of the report of that meeting:

> It was stated during the meeting that there has been a complete breakdown of the communications between teachers, administrators, and school board members, thus creating a crisis in the education system. There has been unwillingness on the part of the school board, it was said, to discuss the situations as they arise with the persons involved. In addition. . . .

> Dr. Williams stated that he had checked with attorneys on such a problem and he was now certain that a school board has the right to refuse to give new contracts to teachers without having to give an explanation of the refusal. However, to prevent the type of breakdown that now exists here, that person should be called in and an explanation given as to the cause for action.

Five days prior to May 15, the date the contracts had to be returned to the Board, the local paper printed the following in its editorial column:

> This week appears to be the week of decision, for the contracts are supposed to be returned to the school board within five days. The Board is apparently counting upon most of the good teachers signing up by the deadline.

> Thinking on the basis of the present situation and eliminating what is already "water under the bridge," there seem to be three things that could happen: (1) the school board could reverse its decision regarding the principal, or (2) the teachers could decide they want their jobs even more than they want victory in this strange fight, or (3) the board and the teachers could remain adamant and the board could attempt to recruit as many new teachers as needed.

CASE QUESTIONS

1. Evaluate and defend the decision from the point of view of the Aspen County School District Board of Trustees.
2. Evaluate and criticize the decision from the point of view of the faculty at Aspen County High School.
3. What does this case illustrate about the processes of communication and decision making?

14 COMMUNICATION

LEARNING OBJECTIVES

DEFINE the terms *encoding* and *decoding*.

DESCRIBE four different interpersonal communication styles.

DISCUSS the role that the grapevine plays in organizational communication.

COMPARE the use of feedback with that of exposure for improving interpersonal communication.

IDENTIFY the more significant barriers to effective communication.

The focus of this chapter is the process of organizational communication. Communicating, like the process of decision making discussed in the previous chapter, pervades everything that all organizational members—particularly managers—do. The managerial functions of planning, organizing, leading, and controlling all involve communicative activity. In fact, communication is an absolutely essential element in all organizational processes.

THE IMPORTANCE OF COMMUNICATION

"You said to get to it as soon as I could—how did I know you meant now?" "How did I know she was really serious about resigning?" In these and similar situations, someone usually ends up saying: "What we have here is a failure to communicate." This statement has meaning to everyone because each of us has faced situations in which the basic problem was communication. Whether on a person-to-person basis, nation-to-nation, in organizations, or in small groups, breakdowns in communication are pervasive.

It would be extremely difficult to find an aspect of a manager's job that does not involve communication. Serious problems arise when directives are misunderstood, when casual kidding in a work group leads to anger, or when informal remarks by a top-level manager are distorted. Each of these situations is a result of a breakdown somewhere in the process of communication.

Accordingly, the pertinent question is not whether managers engage in communication or not, because communication is inherent to the functioning of an organization. Rather, the pertinent question is whether managers will communicate well or poorly. In other words, communication itself is unavoidable in an organization's functioning; only *effective* communication is avoidable. *Every manager must be a communicator.* In fact, everything that a manager does communicates something in some way to somebody or some group. The only question is: "With what *effect*?" While this may appear an overstatement at this point, it will become apparent as you proceed through the chapter. Despite the tremendous advances in communication and information technology, communication among people in organizations leaves much to be desired. Communication among people does not depend on technology, but rather on forces in people and their surroundings. It is a "process" that occurs "within" people.

THE COMMUNICATION PROCESS

The general process of communication is presented in Figure 14–1. The process contains five elements—the communicator, the message, the medium, the receiver, and feedback. It can be simply summarized as: Who . . . says what . . . in what way . . . to whom . . . with what effect?[1] To appreciate each element in the process, we must examine how communication works.

FIGURE 14–1

The
Communication
Process

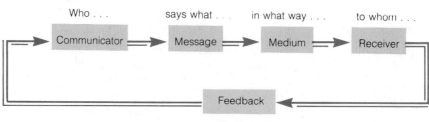

... with what effect

HOW COMMUNICATION WORKS

Communication experts tell us that effective communication is the result of a common understanding between the communicator and the receiver. In fact, the word **communication** is derived from the Latin *(communis)*, meaning "common." The communicator seeks to establish a "commonness" with a receiver. Hence, we can define communication as the *transmission of information and understanding through the use of common symbols.* The common symbols may be verbal or nonverbal. You will see later that in the context of an organizational structure, information can flow up and down (vertical), across (horizontal), and down and across (diagonal).

The most widely used contemporary model of the process of communication has evolved mainly from the work of Shannon and Weaver, and Schramm.[2] These researchers were concerned with describing the general process of communication that could be useful in all situations. The model that evolved from their work is helpful for understanding communication. The basic elements include a communicator, an encoder, a message, a medium, a decoder, a receiver, feedback, and noise. The model is presented in Figure 14–2. Each element in the model can be examined in the context of an organization.

THE ELEMENTS OF COMMUNICATION

Communicator. In an organizational framework, the communicator is an employee with ideas, intentions, information, and a purpose for communicating.

---

[1] These five questions were first suggested in H. D. Lasswell, *Power and Personality* (New York: W. W. Norton, 1948), pp. 37–51.

[2] Claude Shannon and Warren Weaver, *The Mathematical Theory of Communication* (Urbana: University of Illinois Press, 1948); and Wilbur Schramm, "How Communication Works," in *The Process and Effects of Mass Communication,* ed. Wilbur Schramm (Urbana: University of Illinois Press, 1953), pp. 3–26.

FIGURE 14–2

A Communication Model

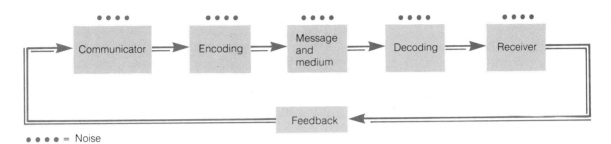

● ● ● ● = Noise

Encoding. Given the communicator, an encoding process must take place that translates the communicator's ideas into a systematic set of symbols— into a language expressing the communicator's purpose. The major form of encoding is language. For example, a manager often takes accounting information, sales reports, and computer data and translates them into one message. The function of encoding, then, is to provide a form in which ideas and purposes can be expressed as a message.

Message. The result of the encoding process is the message. The purpose of the communicator is expressed in the form of the message—either *verbal* or *nonverbal*. Managers have numerous purposes for communicating, such as to have others understand their ideas, to understand the ideas of others, to gain acceptance of themselves or their ideas, or to produce action. The message, then, is what the individual hopes to communicate to the intended receiver, and the exact form it takes depends, to a great extent, on the medium used to carry the message. Decisions relating to the two are inseparable.

Not as obvious, however, are *unintended messages* that can be sent by silence or inaction on a particular issue as well as decisions of which goals and objectives not to pursue and which methods not to utilize. For example, a decision to utilize one type of performance evaluation method rather than another may send a "message" to certain people. An instructor's decision not to give a final examination may send an unintended "message" to certain students that the course is too easy. This is what we meant earlier when we said that everything a manager does communicates.

Medium. The medium is the carrier of the message. Organizations provide information to members in a variety of ways, including face-to-face communication, telephone, group meetings, computers, memos, policy statements, reward systems, production schedules, and sales forecasts. The following OBM Encounter illustrates how some organizations are trying to improve the use of one particular medium, namely writing.

ENCOUNTER

IMPROVING WRITTEN COMMUNICATIONS

Increasingly, organizations are holding training programs developed in-house or calling upon outside consultants to teach their employees how to communicate more effectively in writing. Some companies send managerial personnel to one-day "tune-up" classes, while others sponsor workshops lasting several days. In any event, the reason is the same: Companies have come to realize that poorly written memos, letters, and reports waste time and money and can mean that important information winds up in the trash or is otherwise discarded. Poor writing also can irritate customers and lose business.

While not everyone agrees, most companies feel such courses are sound investments. About 34 percent of all companies with 50 or more employees provide some type of writing training, according to *Training Magazine*. Most of the companies that provide this training get instructors from one of two sources: companies that specialize in communications consulting, or from an increasing number of English and communications professors who moonlight or who have entered the business full time.

Furthermore, companies say that employees consistently express interest in writing training. G. D. Searle's consumer-products division, for one, spent $7,000 in 1985 to teach managers how to write better. Other companies engaged in similar activities, including Amoco, Southwestern Bell, Chevron, and Automatic Timing & Controls Company.   □

Source: Based upon Cynthia F. Mitchell, "Firms Seek Cure for Dull Memos; Find Windy Writers Hard to Curb," *The Wall Street Journal,* October 4, 1985, p. 33.

Decoding-Receiver.   For the process of communication to be completed, the message must be decoded in terms of relevance to the receiver. *Decoding* is a technical term for the receiver's thought processes. Decoding, then, involves interpretation. *Receivers* interpret (decode) the message in light of their own previous experiences and frames of reference. Thus, a salesperson is likely to decode a memo from the company president differently than a production manager will. A nursing supervisor is likely to decode a memo from the hospital administrator differently than the chief of surgery will. The closer the decoded message is to the intent desired by the communicator, the more effective is the communication. This underscores the importance of the communicator being "receiver-oriented."

Feedback.   Provision for feedback in the communication process is desirable.[3] *One-way* communication processes are those that do not allow receiver-to-communicator feedback. This may increase the potential for distortion between the intended message and the received message.[4] A feedback loop provides a channel for receiver response that enables the communicator to determine whether the message has been received and has produced

---

[3] For a theoretical discussion of feedback, see D. M. Herold and M. M. Greller, "Feedback: The Definition of a Construct," *Academy of Management Journal,* March 1977, pp. 142–47.

[4] For the classic experimental study comparing one-way and two-way communications, see Harold J. Leavitt and R. A. H. Mueller, "Some Effects of Feedback on Communications," *Human Relations,* November 1951, pp. 401–10. Also see H. J. Leavitt, *Managerial Psychology* (Chicago: University of Chicago Press, 1978).

the intended response. *Two-way* communication processes provide for this important receiver-to-communicator feedback. The communication of performance information is just one example of where feedback is an extremely important feature of the communication process.[5]

For the manager, communication feedback may come in many ways. In face-to-face situations, *direct* feedback through verbal exchanges is possible, as are such subtle means of communication as facial expressions of discontent or misunderstanding. In addition, *indirect* means of feedback (such as declines in productivity, the poor quality of production, increased absenteeism or turnover, and a lack of coordination and/or conflict between units) may indicate communication breakdowns.

Noise.   In the framework of human communication, noise can be thought of as those factors that distort the intended message. Noise may occur in each of the elements of communication. For example, a manager who is under a severe time constraint may be forced to act without communicating or may communicate hastily with incomplete information. Or a subordinate may attach a different meaning to a word or phrase than was intended by the manager. These are examples of noise in the communication process.

The elements discussed in this section are essential for communication to occur. They should not, however, be viewed as separate. They are, rather descriptive of the acts that have to be performed for any type of communication to occur. The communication may be vertical (superior-subordinate, subordinate-superior) or horizontal (peer-peer). Or it may involve one individual and a group. But the elements discussed here must be present.

NONVERBAL MESSAGES   The information sent by a communicator that is unrelated to the verbal information—that is, nonverbal messages or *nonverbal communication*—is a relatively recent area of research among behavioral scientists. The major interest has been in the *physical cues* that characterize the communicator's physical presentation. These cues include such modes of transmitting nonverbal messages as head, face, and eye movements, posture, distance, gestures, voice tone, and clothing and dress choices.[6] Nonverbal messages themselves are influenced by factors such as the gender of the communicator.[7]

Research indicates that facial expressions and eye contact and movements generally provide information about the *type* of emotion, while such physical cues as distance, posture, and gestures indicate the *intensity* of the emotion. These conclusions are important to managers. They indicate that communicators often send a great deal more information than is obtained in these

---

[5] Carol Watson and Paul Grubb, "Beliefs About Performance Feedback: An Exploration of the Job Holder's Perspective." Paper presented at the National Academy of Management Meeting, San Diego, California, August 1985.

[6] Andrew J. DuBrin, *Contemporary Applied Management* (Plano, Tex.: Business Publications, Inc., 1982), pp. 127–34.

[7] Nicole Steckler and Robert Rosenthal, "Sex Differences in Nonverbal and Verbal Communication with Bosses, Peers, and Subordinates," *Journal of Applied Psychology*, February 1985, pp. 157–63.

verbal messages. To increase the effectiveness of communication, you must be aware of the nonverbal as well as the verbal content of your messages.

COMMUNICATING WITHIN ORGANIZATIONS

The design of an organization should provide for communication in four distinct directions: downward, upward, horizontal, and diagonal. Since these directions of communication establish the framework within which communication in an organization takes place, let us briefly examine each one. This examination will enable you to better appreciate the barriers to effective organizational communication and the means to overcome these barriers.[8]

Downward Communication. This type of communication flows downward from individuals in higher levels of the hierarchy to those in lower levels. The most common forms of **downward communication** are job instructions, official memos, policy statements, procedures, manuals, and company publications. In many organizations, downward communication often is both inadequate and inaccurate. This is evidenced in the often-heard statement among organization members that "we have absolutely no idea what's happening." Such complaints indicate inadequate downward communication and the need of individuals for information relevant to their jobs. The absence of job-related information can create unnecessary stress among organization members.[9] A similar situation is faced by a student who has not been told the requirements and expectations of an instructor.

Upward Communication. An effective organization needs **upward communication** as much as it needs downward communication.[10] In such situations, the communicator is at a lower level in the organization than the receiver. We shall see later that effective upward communication is difficult to achieve, especially in larger organizations. Some of the most common upward communication flows are suggestion boxes, group meetings, and appeal or grievance procedures. In their absence, people somehow find ways to adopt nonexistent or inadequate upward communication channels. This has been evidenced by the emergence of "underground" employee publications in many large organizations.

Horizontal Communication. Often overlooked in the design of most organizations is provision for **horizontal communication.** When the chairperson of the accounting department communicates with the chairperson of the marketing department concerning the course offerings in a college of

---

[8] For a general discussion, see S. B. Bacharach and M. Aiken, "Communication in Administrative Bureaucracies," *Academy of Management Journal,* September 1977, pp. 365–77.

[9] J. M. Ivancevich and J. H. Donnelly, Jr., "A Study of Role Clarity and Need for Clarity in Three Occupational Groups," *Academy of Management Journal,* March 1974, pp. 28–36.

[10] For an example, see Warren K. Schilit and Edwin Locke, "A Study of Upward Influence in Organizations," *Administrative Science Quarterly,* January 1982, pp. 304–16.

business administration, the flow of communication is horizontal. Although vertical (upward and downward) communication flows are the primary considerations in organizational design, effective organizations also need horizontal communication. Horizontal communication—for example, communication between production and sales in a business organization and among the different departments or colleges within a university—is necessary for the coordination and integration of diverse organizational functions.

Since mechanisms for assuring horizontal communication ordinarily do not exist in an organization's design, its facilitation is left to individual managers. Peer-to-peer communication often is necessary for coordination and also can provide social need satisfaction.

Diagonal Communication.   While it is probably the least-used channel of communication in organizations, **diagonal communication** is important in situations where members cannot communicate effectively through other channels. For example, the comptroller of a large organization may wish to conduct a distribution cost analysis. One part of that task may involve having the sales force send a special report directly to the comptroller rather than going through the traditional channels in the marketing department. Thus, the flow of communication would be diagonal as opposed to vertical (upward) and horizontal. In this case, a diagonal channel would be the most efficient in terms of time and effort for the organization.

INTERPERSONAL COMMUNICATIONS

Within an organization, communication flows from individual to individual in face-to-face and group settings. Such flows are termed *interpersonal communications* and can vary from direct orders to casual expressions. Interpersonal behavior could not exist without interpersonal communication. Because of its very nature, interpersonal communication sometimes is difficult to measure.[11]

One particularly interesting aspect of interpersonal communications concerns influence attempts. These are efforts by a communicator to persuade an individual or group to act or behave in a desired manner. The communication strategy used to accomplish this is the subject of the article, "The Language of Persuasion," by Kipnis and Smith, which accompanies this chapter. While we do not deal directly with the topic of persuasion in this section on interpersonal communication, it is an important subject for managers, and the Kipnis and Smith reading deserves close attention.

The problems that arise when managers attempt to communicate with other people can be traced to *perceptual differences and interpersonal style differences*. We know from Chapter 3 that each manager perceives the world in terms of his or her background, experiences, personality, frame of reference, and attitude. The primary way in which managers relate to and learn from the environment (including the people in that environment) is through infor-

---

[11] Larry Penley and Brian Hawkins, "Studying Interpersonal Communications in Organizations: A Leadership Application," *Academy of Management Journal,* June 1985, pp. 309–26.

mation received and transmitted. And the way in which managers receive and transmit information depends, in part, on how they relate to two very important *senders* of information, *themselves* and *others*.

INTERPERSONAL STYLES

Interpersonal style refers to *the way in which an individual prefers to relate to others.* The fact that much of the relationship among people involves communication indicates the importance of interpersonal style.

We begin by recognizing that information is held by oneself and by others but that each of us does not fully have or know that information. The different combinations of knowing and not knowing relevant information are shown in Figure 14–3. The figure identifies four combinations, or regions, of information known and unknown by the self and others and is popularly referred to as the Johari Window.[12] The Johari model is explored in detail in the article "Communication Revisited," by Jay Hall, which is part of this chapter. The essentials of the model are briefly examined here.

FIGURE 14–3

The Johari Window: Interpersonal Styles and Communications

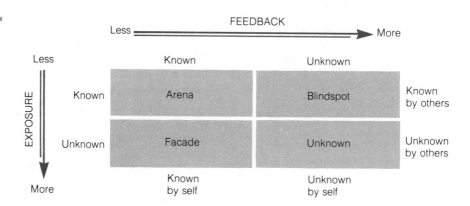

The Arena.   The region most conducive to effective interpersonal relationships and communication is termed the **Arena.** In this setting, all of the information necessary to carry on effective communication is known to both the communicator (self) and the receivers (others). For a communication attempt to be in the Arena region, the parties involved must share identical feelings, data, assumptions, and skills. Since the Arena is the area of common understanding, the larger it becomes, the more effective communication will be.

The Blindspot.   When relevant information is known to others but not to the self, a **Blindspot** area results. This constitutes a handicap for the self, since one can hardly understand the behaviors, decisions, and potentials

---

[12] Joseph Luft, "The Johari Window," *Human Relations and Training News,* January 1961, pp. 6–7. The discussion here is based on a later adaptation. See J. Hall, "Communication Revisited," *California Management Review,* Fall 1973, pp. 56–67.

of others if he or she doesn't have the information on which these are based. Others have the advantage of knowing their own reactions, feelings, perceptions, and so forth, while the self is unaware of these. Consequently, interpersonal relationships and communications suffer.

The Facade.   When information is known to the self but unknown to others, a person (self) may react to superficial communications, that is, present a "false front" or facade. Information that we perceive as potentially prejudicial to a relationship or that we keep to ourselves out of fear, desire for power, or whatever, makes up the **Facade.** This protective front, in turn, serves a defensive function for the self. Such a situation is particularly damaging when a subordinate "knows" and an immediate supervisor "does not know." The Facade, like the Blindspot, diminishes the Arena and reduces the possibility of effective communication.

The Unknown.   This region constitutes that portion of the relationship where relevant information is not known by the self or by other parties. As is often stated, "I don't understand them, and they don't understand me." It is easy to see that interpersonal communication will be poor under such circumstances. Circumstances of this kind often occur in organizations when individuals in different specialties must communicate to coordinate what they do.

Figure 14–3 indicates that an individual can improve interpersonal communications by utilizing two strategies, exposure and feedback.

Exposure.   Increasing the Arena area by reducing the Facade area requires that the individual be open and honest in sharing information with others. The process that the self uses to increase the information known to others is termed **exposure** because it sometimes leaves the self in a vulnerable position. Exposing one's true feelings by "telling it like it is" will often involve risks.

Feedback.   When the self does not know or understand, more effective communications can be developed through **feedback** from those who do know. Thus, the Blindspot can be reduced, with a corresponding increase in the Arena. Of course, whether the use of feedback is possible depends on the individual's willingness to "hear" it and on the willingness of others to give it. Thus, the individual is less able to control the provision of feedback than the provision of exposure. Obtaining feedback is dependent on the active cooperation of others, while exposure requires the active behavior of the communicator and the passive listening of others.

MANAGERIAL STYLES AND INTERPERSONAL STYLES

The day-to-day activities of managers place a high value on effective interpersonal communications. Managers provide *information* (which must be *understood*); they give *commands* and *instructions* (which must be *obeyed* and *learned*); and they make *efforts to influence* and *persuade* (which must be *accepted* and *acted on*). Thus, the way in which managers communicate, both as senders and receivers, is crucial for obtaining effective performance.

Theoretically, managers who desire to communicate effectively can use both exposure and feedback to enlarge the area of common understanding, the Arena. As a practical matter, such is not the case. Managers differ in their ability and willingness to use exposure and feedback. At least four different managerial styles can be identified.

Type A. Managers who use neither exposure nor feedback are said to have a **Type A** style. The Unknown region predominates in this style because such managers are unwilling to enlarge the area of their own knowledge or the knowledge of others. Type A managers exhibit anxiety and hostility and give the appearance of aloofness and coldness toward others. If an organization has a large number of such managers in key positions, then you would expect to find poor and ineffective interpersonal communications and a loss of individual creativity. Type A managers often display the characteristics of autocratic leaders.

Type B. Some managers desire some degree of satisfying relationships with their subordinates, but, because of their personalities and attitudes, these managers are unable to open up and express their feelings and sentiments. Consequently, they cannot use exposure and must rely on feedback. The Facade is the predominant feature of interpersonal relationships when managers overuse feedback to the exclusion of exposure. The subordinates probably will distrust such managers because they realize that these managers are holding back their own ideas and opinions. **Type B** behavior often is displayed by managers who desire to practice some form of permissive leadership.

Type C. Managers who value their own ideas and opinions, but not the ideas and opinions of others, will use exposure at the expense of feedback. The consequence of this style is the perpetuation and enlargement of the Blindspot. Subordinates will soon realize that such managers are not particularly interested in communicating, only in telling. Consequently, **Type C** managers usually have subordinates who are hostile, insecure, and resentful. Subordinates soon learn that such managers mainly are interested in maintaining their own sense of importance and prestige.

Type D. The most effective interpersonal communication style is one that uses a balance of exposure and feedback. Managers who are secure in their positions will feel free to expose their own feelings and to obtain feedback from others. To the extent that a manager practices **Type D** behavior successfully, the Arena region becomes larger and communication becomes more effective.

To summarize our discussion, we should emphasize the importance of interpersonal styles in determining the effectiveness of interpersonal communication. The primary force in determining the effectiveness of interpersonal communication is the attitude of managers toward exposure and feedback. The most effective approach is that of the Type D manager. Types A, B, and C managers resort to behaviors that are detrimental to the effectiveness of communication and to organizational performance. For a more complete discussion of the four types see the Jay Hall article which accompanies this chapter.

BARRIERS TO EFFECTIVE COMMUNICATION

A good question at this point is: "Why does communication break down?" On the surface, the answer is relatively easy. We have identified the elements of communication as the communicator, encoding, the message, the medium, decoding, the receiver, and feedback. If noise exists in these elements in any way, complete clarity of meaning and understanding will not occur. A manager has no greater responsibility than to develop effective communications. In this section we discuss several barriers to effective communication that can exist both in organizational and interpersonal communications.

FRAME OF REFERENCE

Different individuals can interpret the same communication differently, depending on their previous experiences. This results in variations in the encoding and decoding processes. Communication specialists agree that this is the most important factor that breaks down the "commonness" in communications. When the encoding and decoding processes are not alike, communication tends to break down. Thus, while the communicator actually is speaking the "same language" as the receiver, the message conflicts with the way the receiver "catalogs" the world. If a large area is shared in common, effective communication is facilitated. If a large area is not shared in common—if there has been no common experience—then communication becomes impossible or, at best, highly distorted. The important point is that communicators can encode and receivers can decode only in terms of their experiences.[13] As a result, distortion often occurs because of differing frames of reference. People in various organizational functions interpret the same situation differently. A business problem will be viewed differently by the marketing manager than by the production manager. An efficiency problem in a hospital will be viewed by the nursing staff from its frame of reference and experiences, which may result in interpretations different from those of the physician staff. Different *levels* in the organization also will have different frames of reference. Firstline supervisors have frames of reference that differ in many respects from those of vice presidents. They are in different positions in the organization structure, and this influences their frames of reference.[14] As a result, their needs, values, attitudes, and expectations will differ, and this difference often will result in unintentional distortion of communication. This

---

[13] For a recent related study, see J. D. Hatfield and R. C. Huseman, "Perceptual Congruence about Communication as Related to Satisfaction: Moderating Effects of Individual Characteristics," *Academy of Management Journal*, June 1982, pp. 349–58.

[14] See K. M. Watson, "An Analysis of Communication Patterns: A Method for Discriminating Leader and Subordinate Roles," *Academy of Management Journal*, March 1982, pp. 107–20.

is not to say that either group is wrong or right. All it means is that, in any situation, individuals will choose the part of their own past experiences that relates to the current experience and is helpful in forming conclusions and judgments.

SELECTIVE LISTENING

This is a form of selective perception in which we tend to block out new information, especially if it conflicts with what we believe. Thus, when we receive a directive from management, we notice only those things that reaffirm our beliefs. Those things that conflict with our preconceived notions we either do not note at all or we distort to confirm our preconceptions.

For example, a notice may be sent to all operating departments that costs must be reduced if the organization is to earn a profit. The communication may not achieve its desired effect, because it conflicts with the "reality" of the receivers. Thus, operating employees may ignore or be amused by such information in light of the large salaries, travel allowances, and expense accounts of some executives. Whether or not they are justified is irrelevant; what is important is that such preconceptions result in breakdowns in communication.

VALUE JUDGMENTS

In every communication situation, value judgments are made by the receiver. This basically involves assigning an overall worth to a message prior to receiving the entire communication. Value judgments may be based on the receiver's evaluation of the communicator or previous experiences with the communicator or on the message's anticipated meaning. For example, a hospital administrator may pay little attention to a memorandum from a nursing supervisor because "she's always complaining about something." A college professor may consider a merit evaluation meeting with the department chairperson as "going through the motions" because the faculty member perceives the chairperson as having little or no power in the administration of the college. A cohesive work group may form negative value judgments concerning all actions by management.

SOURCE CREDIBILITY

Source credibility is the trust, confidence, and faith that the receiver has in the words and actions of the communicator. The level of credibility that the receiver assigns to the communicator in turn directly affects how the receiver views and reacts to words, ideas, and actions of the communicator.

Thus, how subordinates view a communication from their manager is affected by their evaluation of the manager. This, of course, is heavily influenced by previous experiences with the manager. Again, we see that everything done by a manager communicates. A group of hospital medical staff who view the hospital administrator as less than honest, manipulative, and not to be trusted are apt to assign nonexistent motives to any communication from the administrator. Union leaders who view management as exploiters and managers who view union leaders as political animals are likely to engage in little real communication.

FILTERING

Filtering is a common occurrence in upward communication in organizations. It refers to the "manipulation" of information so that the receiver perceives it as positive. Subordinates "cover up" unfavorable information in messages to their superiors. The reason for such filtering should be clear; this is the direction (upward) that carries control information to management. Management makes merit evaluations, grants salary increases, and promotes individuals based on what it receives by way of the upward channel. The temptation to filter is likely to be strong at every level in the organization.

IN-GROUP LANGUAGE

Each of us undoubtedly has had associations with experts and been subjected to highly technical jargon, only to learn that the unfamiliar words or phrases described very simple procedures or very familiar objects. Many students are asked by researchers to "complete an instrument as part of an experimental treatment." The student soon learns that this involves nothing more than filling out a paper-and-pencil questionnaire.

Often, occupational, professional, and social groups develop words or phrases that have meaning only to members. Such special language can serve many useful purposes. It can provide members with feelings of belongingness, cohesiveness, and, in many cases, self-esteem. It also can facilitate effective communication *within* the group. The use of in-group language can, however, result in severe communication breakdowns when outsiders or other groups are involved. This is especially the case when groups use such language in an organization, not for the purpose of transmitting information and understanding, but rather to communicate a mystique about the group or its function. The following OBM Encounter lists some examples of in-group definitions.

ENCOUNTER
SOME EXAMPLES OF ORGANI-ZATIONAL OBFUSCATION

The following list of office definitions were collected at a Douglas Aircraft plant in Los Angeles. They humorously point out the use of words and phrases that would confuse anyone who was not a member of the in-group.

- It Is In Process—It is so wrapped up in red tape that the situation is hopeless.
- A Program—Any assignment that can't be completed with a single phone call.
- To Activate—To make copies and add more names to the memo.
- To Implement a Program—To hire more people and expand the office.
- Under Consideration—Never heard of it.

- Under Active Consideration—We're looking in the files for it.
- We Are Taking a Survey—We need more time to think of an answer.
- Note and Initial—Let's spread the responsibility for this.
- Let's Get Together on This—I'm assuming you're as confused as I am.
- Give Us the Benefit of Your Thinking—We'll listen to what you have to say, as long as it doesn't interfere with what we have already decided to do.
- We Will Advise You in Due Course—If we figure it out, we'll let you know.

Source: Adapted from Lyle Sussman and Paul Krivonos, *Communication for Supervisors and Managers* (Sherman Oaks, Calif.: Alfred Publishing Co., 1979).

STATUS DIFFERENCES

Organizations often express hierarchical rank through a variety of symbols—titles, offices, carpets, and so on. Such status differences can be perceived as threats by persons lower in the hierarchy, and this can prevent or distort communication. Rather than look incompetent, a nurse may prefer to remain quiet instead of expressing an opinion or asking a question of the nursing supervisor.

Many times, superiors, in an effort to utilize their time efficiently, make this barrier more difficult to surmount. The governmental administrator or bank vice president may be accessible only by making an advance appointment or by passing the careful quizzing of a secretary. This widens the communication gap between superiors and subordinates.

TIME PRESSURES

The pressure of time is an important barrier to communication. An obvious problem is that managers do not have the time to communicate frequently with every subordinate. However, time pressures often can lead to far more serious problems than this. *Short-circuiting* is a failure of the formally prescribed communication system that often results from time pressures. What it means simply is that someone has been left out of the formal channel of communication who normally would be included.

For example, suppose a salesperson needs a rush order for a very important customer and goes directly to the production manager with the request, since the production manager owes the salesperson a favor. Other members of the sales force get word of this and become upset over this preferential treatment and report it to the sales manager. Obviously, the sales manager would know nothing of the "deal," since the sales manager has been short-circuited. In some cases, however, going through formal channels is extremely costly or is impossible from a practical standpoint. Consider the impact on a hospital patient if a nurse had to report a critical malfunction in life support equipment to the nursing team leader, who in turn had to report it to the hospital engineer, who would instruct a staff engineer to make the repair.

COMMUNICATION OVERLOAD

One of the vital tasks performed by a manager is decision making. One of the necessary conditions for effective decisions is *information*. Because of the advances in communication technology, the difficulty is not in generating information. In fact, the last decade often has been described as the "Information Era" or the "Age of Information." Managers often feel "buried" by the deluge of information and data to which they are exposed. As a result, people cannot absorb or adequately respond to all of the messages that are directed to them. They "screen out" the majority of messages, which in effect means that these messages are never decoded. Thus, the area of organizational communication is one in which "more" is not always "better."[15]

The barriers to communication that have been discussed here, while common, are by no means the only ones. Examining each barrier indicates that they are either *within individuals* (e.g., frame of reference, value judgments) or

---

[15] See Charles A. O'Reilly III, "Individuals and Information Overload in Organizations: Is More Necessarily Better?" *Academy of Management Journal*, December 1980, pp. 684–96.

within organizations (e.g., in-group language, filtering). This point is important because attempts to improve communication must, of necessity, focus on changing people and/or changing the organization structure.[16]

IMPROVING COMMUNICATION IN ORGANIZATIONS

Managers striving to become better communicators have two separate tasks that they must accomplish. First, they must improve their *messages*—the information they wish to transmit. Second, they must seek to improve their own *understanding* of what other people are trying to communicate to them. What this means is that they must become better encoders and decoders. *They must strive not only to be understood but also to understand.* The techniques discussed here can contribute to accomplishing these two important tasks.

FOLLOWING UP   This involves assuming that you are misunderstood and, whenever possible, attempting to determine whether your intended meaning actually was received. As we have seen, meaning often is in the mind of the receiver. An accounting unit leader in a government office passes on to accounting staff members notices of openings in other agencies. While longtime employees may understand this as a friendly gesture, a new employee might interpret it as an evaluation of poor performance and a suggestion to leave.

REGULATING INFORMATION FLOW   The regulation of communication can ensure an optimum flow of information to managers, thereby eliminating the barrier of "communication overload."[17] Communication is regulated in terms of both quality and quantity. The idea is based on the *exception principle* of management, which states that only significant deviations from policies and procedures should be brought to the attention of superiors. In terms of formal communication, then, superiors should be communicated with only on matters of exception and not for the sake of communication.

UTILIZING FEEDBACK   Earlier in the chapter, feedback was identified as an important element in effective two-way communication. It provides a channel for receiver response that enables the communicator to determine whether the message has been received and has produced the intended response.

In face-to-face communication, direct feedback is possible. In downward communication, however, inaccuracies often occur because of insufficient opportunity for feedback from receivers. Thus, a memorandum addressing

---

[16] For a study on the importance of communication, see P. M. Muchinsky, "Organizational Communication: Relationships to Organizational Climate and Job Satisfaction," *Academy of Management Journal,* December 1977, pp. 592–607.

[17] This is described as the principle of "sufficiency" by William G. Scott and Terence R. Mitchell, *Organizational Theory: A Structural and Behavioral Analysis* (Homewood, Ill.: Richard D. Irwin, 1972), p. 161.

an important policy statement may be distributed to all employees, but this does not guarantee that communication has occurred. You might expect that feedback in the form of upward communication would be encouraged more in organic organizations, but the mechanisms discussed earlier that can be utilized to encourage upward communication are found in many different organizational designs.

EMPATHY

This involves being receiver-oriented rather than communicator-oriented. The form of the communication should depend largely on what is known about the receiver. Empathy requires communicators to place themselves in the shoes of the receiver in order to anticipate how the message is likely to be decoded. Empathy is the ability to put oneself in the other person's role and to assume that individual's viewpoints and emotions. Remember that the greater the gap between the experiences and background of the communicator and the receiver, the greater is the effort that must be made to find a common ground of understanding—where there are overlapping fields of experience.[18]

REPETITION

Repetition is an accepted principle of learning. Introducing repetition or redundancy into communication (especially that of a technical nature) ensures that if one part of the message is not understood, other parts will carry the same message. New employees often are provided with the same basic information in several different forms when first joining an organization. Likewise, students receive much redundant information when first entering a university. This is to ensure that registration procedures, course requirements, and new terms such as matriculation and quality points are communicated.

ENCOURAGING MUTUAL TRUST

We know that time pressures often negate the possibility that managers will be able to follow up communication and encourage feedback or upward communication every time they communicate. Under such circumstances, an atmosphere of mutual confidence and trust between managers and their subordinates can facilitate communication.[19] Managers who develop a climate of trust will find that following up on each communication is less critical and that no loss in understanding will result among subordinates from a failure to follow up on each communication. This is because they have fostered high "source credibility" among subordinates.

EFFECTIVE TIMING

Individuals are exposed to thousands of messages daily. Many of these messages are never decoded and received, because of the impossibility of taking

---

[18] A technique known as *sensitivity training* has been utilized for many purposes in organizations, one of which is to improve the ability of managers to empathize. The technique is discussed in Chapter 15.

[19] See Karlene H. Roberts and Charles A. O'Reilly III, "Failures in Upward Communication in Organizations: Three Possible Culprits," *Academy of Management Journal*, June 1974, pp. 205–15; and Leland P. Bradford, Jack R. Gibb, and Kenneth D. Benne, eds., *T-Group Theory and Laboratory Method: Innovation in Re-Education* (New York: John Wiley & Sons, 1965), pp. 285–86.

in all the messages. It is important for managers to note that while they are attempting to communicate with a receiver, other messages are being received simultaneously. Thus, the message that managers send may not be "heard." Messages are more likely to be understood when they are not competing with other messages. On an everyday basis, effective communication can be facilitated by properly timing major announcements. The barriers discussed earlier often are the result of poor timing that results in distortions and value judgments.

SIMPLIFYING LANGUAGE

Complex language has been identified as a major barrier to effective communication. Students often suffer when their teachers use technical jargon that transforms simple concepts into complex puzzles.

Universities are not the only place where this occurs, however. Government agencies also are known for their often incomprehensible communications. We already have noted instances where professional people use in-group language in attempting to communicate with individuals outside their group. Managers must remember that effective communication involves transmitting *understanding* as well as information. If the receiver does not understand, then there has been no communication. Managers must encode messages in words, appeals, and symbols that are meaningful to the receiver.

EFFECTIVE LISTENING

It has been said that to improve communication, managers must seek to be understood but also to *understand*. This involves listening. One method of encouraging someone to express true feelings, desires, and emotions is to listen. Just listening is not enough, however; you must listen with understanding. Removing distractions, putting the speaker at ease, showing the speaker you want to listen, and asking questions all contribute to good listening.[20]

Such guidelines can be useful to managers. More important than guidelines, however, is the *decision to listen*. The above guidelines are useless unless the manager makes a conscious decision to listen. The realization that effective communication involves being understood as well as understanding probably is far more important than guidelines.

USING THE GRAPEVINE

The grapevine is an important informal communication channel that exists in all organizations. It basically serves as a bypassing mechanism, and in many cases it is faster than the formal system it bypasses. The grapevine has been aptly described in the following manner: "With the rapidity of a burning train, it filters out of the woodwork, past the manager's office, through the locker room, and along the corridors."[21] Because it is flexible and usually involves face-to-face communication, the grapevine transmits information rapidly. The resignation of an executive may be common knowledge long before it is officially announced.

For management, the grapevine frequently may be an *effective* means

---

[20] Keith Davis, *Human Behavior at Work* (New York: McGraw-Hill, 1980), p. 394.
[21] Ibid., p. 267.

of communication. It is likely to have a stronger impact on receivers because it involves face-to-face exchange and allows for feedback. Because it satisfies many psychological needs, the grapevine will always exist. More than 75 percent of the information in the grapevine may be accurate. Of course, the portion that is distorted can be devastating. The point, however, is that if the grapevine is inevitable, managers should seek to utilize it or at least attempt to increase its accuracy. One way to minimize the undesirable aspects of the grapevine is to improve other forms of communication. If information exists on issues relevant to subordinates, then damaging rumors are less likely to develop.

The grapevine is, of course, just one example of informal communications in organizations. The following OBM Encounter presents some additional examples.

INFORMAL COMMUNICATIONS

In their best-selling book, *In Search of Excellence,* Thomas Peters and Robert Waterman suggest that one characteristic of truly excellent companies is that they are a network of open, informal communications. A few of the examples they cite are:

United Airlines. Getting managers out of the office is deliberately encouraged to facilitate informal exchanges. The practice is known as "MBWA"—Management by Walking About.

Hewlett-Packard. Here, MBWA also is practiced, but at HP, the "MBWA" stands for Management by Wandering Around.

Corning Glass. In its new engineering facility, management installed escalators rather than elevators to increase the opportunity for face-to-face contact.

Levi Strauss. This company is one of many that facilitate informal communication by promoting an open-door policy. At Levi Strauss, however, the policy means so much that they call it the "fifth freedom."

Walt Disney Productions. In an effort to encourage informal communication, everyone from the president down wears a tag with only his or her name on it.   □

Source: Thomas J. Peters and Robert H. Waterman, Jr., *In Search of Excellence* (New York: Harper & Row, 1982).

In conclusion, it would be hard to find an aspect of a manager's job that does not involve communication. If everyone in the organization had common points of view, communicating would be easy. Unfortunately, this is not the case. Each member comes to the organization with a distinct personality, background, experience, and frame of reference. The structure of the organization itself influences status relationships and the distance (levels) between individuals, which in turn influence the ability of individuals to communicate.

In this chapter, we have tried to convey the basic elements in the process of communication and what it takes to communicate effectively. These elements are necessary whether the communication is face-to-face or written

FIGURE 14-4

Improving
Communication
in Organizations
(Narrowing the
Communication
Gap)

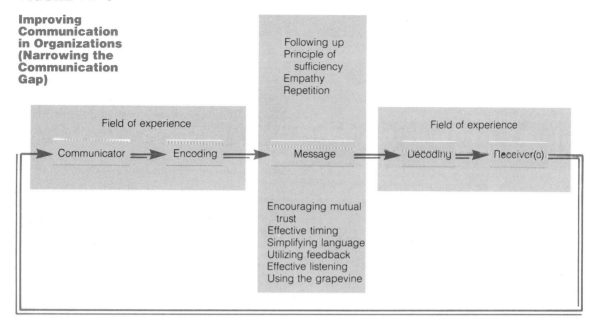

and communicated vertically, horizontally, or diagonally within an organizational structure.

Several common communication barriers and several means to improve communication were discussed. Figure 14–4 illustrates the means that can be used to facilitate more effective communication. We realize that often there is not enough time to utilize many of the techniques for improving communication, and that skills such as empathy and effective listening are not easy to develop. The figure does, however, illustrate the challenge of communicating effectively, and it suggests what is required. Figure 14–4 shows that communicating is a matter of transmitting and receiving. Managers must be effective at both. They must understand as well as be understood.

SUMMARY OF KEYPOINTS

A. Communication is one of the vital processes that breathe life into an organizational structure. Communication is unavoidable in an organization's work; only *effective* communication is avoidable.

B. The quality of managerial decisions depends in large part on the quality of information available. Communication is the transmission of information and understanding through the use of common symbols.

C. Everything that a manager does communicates.

The only question is: "With what *effect?*" Every manager is a communicator.

D. The process of communication consists of several basic elements that must always be present if effective communication is to result. These elements are the communicator, the message, the medium, the receiver, and feedback.

E. Organizational design and the communication process are inseparable. The design of an organization must provide for communication in three distinct directions: vertical, horizontal, and diagonal.

F. When the encoding and decoding processes are

homogeneous, communication is most effective. When they become heterogeneous, communication tends to break down. Numerous barriers exist that contribute to communication breakdowns. Managers must be aware of the barriers that are relevant to their situations.

G. Numerous techniques exist that aid in improving communication and can be utilized by managers. However, a prerequisite to their use is the conscious realization by the individual manager that communication involves understanding as well as being understood. An effective communicator also must be an effective receiver.

REVIEW AND DISCUSSION QUESTIONS

1. In your personal experience, what are the most frequent reasons for communication failures?

2. Can you think of a communication transaction you have been a part of when an encoding or decoding error was made? What was the cause? What could have been done to avoid it?

3. Is there a difference between communicating and exchanging information? Explain.

4. In what ways do you use nonverbal communication? Would your communication be more effective if you used it more or less? Why?

5. In organizations, what are the primary objectives of downward communications? Upward? Horizontal?

6. Which of the four interpersonal communication styles most nearly matches your own? Does your own style change depending on the nature of the communication situation you are in?

7. A number of barriers to effective communication were identified in the chapter. How many of these occur as a result of differing perceptions between communicators?

8. One study revealed that 55 percent of our communication time is spent transmitting and 45 percent is spent receiving. If true, what are the implications of this finding?

9. How does communication affect the interpersonal influence topics we discussed in Chapters 7–10?

10. "Organizations should be less concerned with improving communication than with reducing the volume of information they disseminate to employees." Do you agree with this statement? What possible negative consequences might result if organizations followed this recommendation?

ACTIVE LISTENING*

CARL B. ROGERS
RICHARD E. FARSON

THE MEANING OF ACTIVE LISTENING

One basic responsibility of the supervisor or executive is the development, adjustment, and integration of individual employees. He tries to develop employee potential, delegate responsibility, and

* Source: Reprinted by permission of the Industrial Relations Center, The University of Chicago.

achieve cooperation. To do so, he must have, among other abilities, the ability to listen intelligently and carefully to those with whom he works.

There are, however, many kinds of listening skills. The lawyer, for example, when questioning a witness, listens for contradictions, irrelevancies, errors, and weaknesses. But this is not the kind of listening skill we are concerned with. The lawyer usually is not listening in order to help the witness adjust or cooperate or produce. On the other hand, we will be concerned with listening skills which *will help* employees gain a clearer understanding of their situations, take responsibility, and cooperate with each other.

Two Examples

The kind of listening we have in mind is called "active listening." It is called "active" because the listener has a very definite responsibility. He does not passively absorb the words which are spoken to him. He actively tries to grasp the facts and the feelings in what he hears, and he tries, by his listening, to help the speaker work out his own problems.

To get a fuller picture of what is meant by active listening, let us consider two different approaches to the same work problem.

Example No. 1

Foreman: Hey, Al, I don't get this production order. We can't handle this run today. What do they think we are?

Supervisor: But that's the order. So get it out as soon as you can. We're under terrific pressure this week.

Foreman: Don't they know we're behind schedule already because of that press breakdown?

Supervisor: Look, Kelly, I don't decide what goes on upstairs. I just have to see that the work gets out, and that's what I'm gonna do.

Foreman: The guys aren't gonna like this.

Supervisor: That's something you'll have to work out with them, not me.

Example No. 2

Foreman: Hey, Ross, I don't get this production order. We can't handle this run today. What do they think we are?

Supervisor: Sounds like you are pretty sore about it, Kelly.

Foreman: I sure am. We were just about getting back to schedule after that press breakdown. Now this comes along.

Supervisor: As if you didn't have enough work to do, huh?

Foreman: Yeah. I don't know how I'm gonna tell the guys about this.

Supervisor: Hate to face 'em with it now, is that it?

Foreman: I really do. They're under a real strain today. Seems like everything we do around here is rush, rush.

Supervisor: I guess you feel like it's unfair to load anything more on them.

Foreman: Well, yeah. I know there must be plenty of pressure on everybody up the line, but—well, if that's the way it is—guess I'd better get the word to 'em.

There are obviously many differences between these two examples. The main one, however, is that Ross, the supervisor in the second example, is using the active-listening approach. He is listening and responding in a way that makes it clear that he appreciates both the meaning and the feeling behind what Kelly is saying.

Active listening does not necessarily mean long sessions spent listening to grievances, personal or otherwise. It is simply a way of approaching those problems which arise out of the usual day-to-day events of any job.

To be effective, active listening must be firmly grounded in the basic attitudes of the user. We cannot employ it as a technique if our fundamental attitudes are in conflict with its basic concepts. If we try, our behavior will be empty and sterile, and our associates will be quick to recognize this. Until we can demonstrate a spirit which genuinely respects the potential worth of the individual, which considers his sights and trusts his capacity for self-direction, we cannot begin to be effective listeners.

LEARNING CHECKPOINT

Recall a conversation you had recently with a supervisor, professor, spouse, etc. Did active listening occur? Why?

What We Achieve by Listening

Active listening is an important way to bring about changes in people. Despite the popular notion that listening is a passive approach, clinical and research evidence clearly shows that sensitive listening is a most *effective* agent for individual personality change and group development. Listening brings about changes in people's attitudes toward themselves and others; it also brings about changes in their basic values and personal philosophy. People who have been listened to in this new and special way become more emotionally mature, more open to their experiences, less defensive, more democratic, and less authoritarian.

When people are listened to sensitively, they tend to listen to themselves with more care and to make clear exactly what they are feeling and thinking. Group members tend to listen more to each other, to become less argumentative, more ready to incorporate other points of view. Because listening reduces the threat of having one's ideas criticized, the person is better able to see them for what they are and is more likely to feel that his contributions are worthwhile.

Not the least important result of listening is the change that takes place within the listener himself. Besides providing more information than any other activity, listening builds deep, positive relationships and tends to alter constructively the attitudes of the listener. Listening is a growth experience.

These, then, are some of the worthwhile results we can expect from active listening. But how do we go about this kind of listening? How do we become active listeners?

HOW TO LISTEN

Active listening aims to bring about changes in people. To achieve this end, it relies upon definite techniques—things to do and things to avoid doing. Before discussing these techniques, however, we should first understand why they are effective. To do so, we must understand how the individual personality develops.

The Growth of the Individual

Through all of our lives, from early childhood on, we have learned to think of ourselves in certain very definite ways. We have built up pictures of ourselves. Sometimes these self-pictures are pretty realistic, but at other times they are not. For example, an overage, overweight lady may fancy herself a youthful, ravishing siren, or an awkward teen-ager regard himself as a star athlete.

All of us have experiences which fit the way we need to think about ourselves. These we accept. But it much harder to accept experiences which don't fit. And sometimes, if it is very important for us to hang on to this self-picture, we don't accept or admit these experiences at all.

These self-pictures are not necessarily attractive. A man, for example, may regard himself as incompetent and worthless. He may feel that he is doing his job poorly in spite of favorable appraisals by

the company. As long as he has these feelings about himself, he must deny any experiences which would seem not to fit this self-picture—in this case any that might indicate to him that he is competent. It is so necessary for him to maintain this self-picture that he is threatened by anything which would tend to change it. Thus, when the company raises his salary, it may seem to him only additional proof that he is a fraud. He must hold onto this self-picture because, bad or good, it's the only thing he has by which he can identify himself.

This is why direct attempts to change this individual or change his self-picture are particularly threatening. He is forced to defend himself or to completely deny the experience. This denial of experience and defense of the self-picture tend to bring on rigidity of behavior and create difficulties in personal adjustment.

The active-listening approach, on the other hand, does not present a threat to the individual's self-picture. He does not have to defend it. He is able to explore it, see it for what it is, and make his own decision about how realistic it is. And he is then in a position to change.

If I want to help a man reduce his defensiveness and become more adaptive, I must try to remove the threat of myself as his potential changer. As long as the atmosphere is threatening, there can be no effective communication. So I must create a climate which is neither critical, evaluative, nor moralizing. It must be an atmosphere of equality and freedom, permissiveness and understanding, acceptance and warmth. It is in this climate and this climate only that the individual feels safe enough to incorpo-

rate new experiences and new values into his concept of himself. Let's see how active listening helps to create this climate.

What to Avoid

When we encounter a person with a problem our usual response is to try to change his way of looking at things—to get him to see his situation the way we see it or would like him to see it. We plead, reason, scold, encourage, insult, prod—anything to bring about a change in the desired direction, that is, in the direction we want him to travel. What we seldom realize, however, is that, under these circumstances, we are usually responding to *our own* needs to see the world in certain ways. It is always difficult for us to tolerate and understand actions which are different from the ways in which *we* believe *we* should act. If, however, we can free ourselves from the need to influence and direct others in our own paths, we enable ourselves to listen with understanding and thereby employ the most potent available agent of change.

One problem the listener faces is that of responding to demands for decisions, judgments, and evaluations. He is constantly called upon to agree or disagree with someone or something. Yet, as he well knows, the question or challenge frequently is a masked expression of feelings or needs which the speaker is far more anxious to communicate than he is to have the surface questions answered. Because he cannot speak these feelings openly, the speaker must disguise them to himself and to others in an acceptable form. To illustrate, let us examine some typical questions and the types of answers that might best elicit the feelings beneath them.

Employee's Question	Listener's Answer
Just whose responsibility is the toolroom?	Do you feel that someone is challenging your authority in there?
Don't you think younger able people should be promoted before senior but less able ones?	It seems to you they should, I take it.
What does the super expect us to do about those broken-down machines?	You're pretty disgusted with those machines, aren't you?
Don't you think I've improved over the last review period?	Sounds as if you feel like you've really picked up over these last few months.

These responses recognize the questions but leave the way open for the employee to say what is really bothering him. They allow the listener to participate in the problem or situation without shouldering all responsibility for decision making or actions. This is a process of thinking *with* people instead of *for* or *about* them.

Passing judgment, whether critical or favorable, makes free expression difficult. Similarly, advice and information are almost always seen as efforts to change a person and thus serve as barriers to his self-expression and the development of a creative relationship. Moreover, advice is seldom taken, and information hardly ever utilized. The eager young trainee probably will not become patient just because he is advised that "the road to success in business is a long, difficult one, and you must be patient." And it is no more helpful for him to learn that "only one out of a hundred trainees reaches a top management position."

Interestingly, it is a difficult lesson to learn that positive *evaluations* are sometimes as blocking as negative ones. It is almost as destructive to the freedom of a relationship to tell a person that he is good or capable or right, as to tell him otherwise. To evaluate him positively may make it more difficult for him to tell of the faults that distress him or the ways in which he believes he is not competent.

Encouragement also may be seen as an attempt to motivate the speaker in certain directions or hold him off, rather than as support. "I'm sure everything will work out O.K." is not a helpful response to the person who is deeply discouraged about a problem.

In other words, most of the techniques and devices common to human relationships are found to be of little use in establishing the type of relationship we are seeking here.

What to Do

Just what does active listening entail, then? Basically, it requires that we get inside the speaker, that we grasp, *from his point of view,* just what it is he is communicating to us. More than that, we must convey to the speaker that we are seeing things from his point of view. To listen actively, then means that there are several things we must do.

Listen for Total Meaning.

Any message a person tries to get across usually has two components: the *content* of the message and the *feeling* or attitude underlying this content. Both are important; both give the message *meaning*. It is this total meaning of the message that we try to understand. For example, a machinist comes to his foreman and says, "I've finished that lathe setup." This message has obvious content and perhaps calls upon the foreman for another work assignment. Suppose, on the other hand, that he says, "Well, I'm finally finished with that damned lathe setup." The content is the same, but the total meaning of the message has changed—and changed in an important way for both the foreman and the worker. Here sensitive listening can facilitate the relationship. Suppose the foreman were to respond by simply giving another work assignment. Would the employee feel that he had gotten his total message across? Would he feel free to talk to his foreman? Will he feel better about his job, more anxious to do good work on the next assignment?

Now, on the other hand, suppose the foreman were to respond with, "Glad to have it over with, huh?" or "Had a pretty rough time of it?" or "Guess you don't feel like doing anything like that again," or anything else that tells the worker that he heard and understands. It doesn't necessarily mean that the next work assignment need be changed or that he must spend an hour listening to the worker complain about the setup problems he encountered. He may do a number of things differently in the light of the new information he has from the worker—but not necessarily. It's just that *extra* sensitivity on the part of the foreman which can transform an average working climate into a good one.

Respond to Feelings.

In some instances, the content is far less important than the feeling which underlies it. To catch the full flavor or meaning of the message, one must respond particularly to the feeling component. If, for instance, our machinist had said, "I'd like to melt this lathe down and make paper clips out of it," responding to content would be obviously absurd. But to respond to his disgust or anger in trying to work with his lathe recognizes the meaning of this message. There are various shadings of these components in the meaning of any message. Each time, the listener must try to remain sensitive to the total meaning the message has to the speaker. What is he trying to tell me? What does this mean to him? How does he see this situation?

Note All Cues. Not all communication is verbal. The speaker's words alone don't tell us everything he is communicating. And hence, truly sensitive listening requires that we become aware of several kinds of communication besides verbal. The way in which a speaker hesitates in his speech can tell us much about his feelings. So, too, can the inflection of his voice. He may stress certain points loudly and clearly and may mumble others. We should also note such things as the person's facial expressions, body posture, hand movements, eye movements, and breathing. All of these help to convey his total message.

LEARNING CHECKPOINT

At what point in the communication process in Figure 14–1 (Chapter) is listening most important?

What We Communicate by Listening

The first reaction of most people when they consider listening as a possible method for dealing with human beings is that listening cannot be sufficient in itself. Because it is passive, they feel, listening does not communicate anything to the speaker. Actually, nothing could be

farther from the truth.

By consistently listening to a speaker, you are conveying the idea that: "I'm interested in you as a person, and I think that what you feel is important. I respect your thoughts, and even if I don't agree with them, I know that they are valid for you. I feel sure that you have a contribution to make. I'm not trying to change you or evaluate you. I just want to understand you. I think you're worth listening to, and I want you to know that I'm the kind of a person you can talk to."

The subtle but most important aspect of this is that it is the *demonstration* of the message that works. While it is most difficult to convince someone that you respect him by *telling* him so, you are much more likely to get this message across by really *behaving* that way—by actually *having* and *demonstrating* respect for this person. Listening does this most effectively.

Like other behavior, listening behavior is contagious. This has implications for all communication problems, whether between two people or within a large organization. To ensure good communication between associates up and down the line, one must first take the responsibility for setting a pattern of listening. Just as one learns that anger is usually met with anger, argument with argument, and deception with deception one can learn that listening can be met with listening. Every person who feels responsibility in a situation can set the tone of the interaction, and the important lesson in this is that any behavior exhibited by one person will eventually be responded to with similar behavior in the other person.

It is far more difficult to stimulate constructive behavior in another person but far more profitable. Lis-

tening is one of these constructive behaviors, but if one's attitude is to "wait out" the speaker rather than really listen to him, it will fail. The one who consistently listens with understanding, however, is the one who eventually is most likely to be listened to. If you really want to be heard and understood by another, you can develop him as a potential listener, ready for new ideas, provided you can first develop yourself in these ways and sincerely listen with understanding and respect.

Testing for Understanding

Because understanding another person is actually far more difficult than it at first seems, it is important to test constantly your ability to see the world in the way the speaker sees it. You can do this by reflecting in your own words what the speaker seems to mean by his words and actions. His response to this will tell you whether or not he feels understood. A good rule of thumb is to assume that you never really understand until you can communicate this understanding to the other's satisfaction.

Here is an experiment to test your skill in listening. The next time you become involved in a lively or controversial discussion with another person, stop for a moment and suggest that you adopt this ground rule for continued discussion: Before either participant in the discussion can make a point or express an opinion of his own, he must first restate aloud the previous point or position of the other person. This restatement must be in his own words (merely parroting the words of another does not prove that one has understood but only that he has heard the words). The restatement must be accurate enough to satisfy the speaker before the listener can be allowed to speak for himself.

This is something you could try in your own discussion group. Have someone express himself on some topic of emotional concern to the group. Then, before another member expresses his own feelings and thought, he must rephrase the *meaning* expressed by the previous speaker to that individual's satisfaction. Note the changes in the emotional climate and in the quality of the discussion when you try this.

LEARNING CHECKPOINT

Select five barriers to effective communication discussed in the chapter. How can active listening help to overcome these barriers?

PROBLEMS IN ACTIVE LISTENING

Active listening is not an easy skill to acquire. It demands practice. Perhaps more important, it may require changes in our own basic attitudes. These changes come slowly and sometimes with considerable difficulty. Let us look at some of the major problems in active listening and what can be done to overcome them.

The Personal Risk

To be effective at all in active listening, one must have a sincere interest in the speaker. We all live in glass houses as far as our attitudes are concerned. They always show through. And if we are only making a pretense of interest in the speaker, he will quickly pick this up, either consciously or unconsciously. And once he does, he will no longer express himself freely.

Active listening carries a strong element of personal risk. If we man-

age to accomplish what we are describing here—to sense deeply the feeling of another person, to understand the meaning his experiences have for him, to see the world as he sees it—we risk being changed ourselves. For example, if we permit ourselves to listen our way into the psychological life of a labor leader or agitator—to get the meaning which life has for him—we risk coming to see the world as he sees it. It is threatening to give up, even momentarily, what we believe and start thinking in someone else's terms. It takes a great deal of inner security and courage to be able to risk one's self in understanding another.

For the supervisor, the courage to take another's point of view generally means that he must see *himself* through another's eyes—he must be able to see himself as others see him. To do this may sometimes be unpleasant, but it is far more *difficult* than unpleasant. We are so accustomed to viewing ourselves in certain ways—to seeing and hearing only what we want to see and hear—that it is extremely difficult for a person to free himself from his needs to see things these ways.

Developing an attitude of sincere interest in the speaker is thus no easy task. It can be developed only by being willing to risk seeing the world from the speaker's point of view. If we have a number of such experiences, however, they will shape an attitude which will allow us to be truly genuine in our interest in the speaker.

Hostile Expressions

The listener will often hear negative, hostile expressions directed at himself. Such expressions are always hard to listen to. No one likes to hear hostile words. And it is not

easy to get to the point where one is strong enough to permit these attacks without finding it necessary to defend oneself or retaliate.

Because we all fear that people will crumble under the attack of genuine negative feelings, we tend to perpetuate an attitude of pseudo peace. It is as if we cannot tolerate conflict at all for fear of the damage it could do to us, to the situation, to the others involved. But of course the real damage is done to all these by the denial and suppression of negative feelings.

Out-of-place Expressions

There is also the problem of out-of-place expressions—expressions dealing with behavior which is not usually acceptable in our society. In the extreme forms that present themselves before psychotherapists, expressions of sexual perversity or homicidal fantasies are often found blocking to the listener because of their obvious threatening quality. At less extreme levels, we all find unnatural or inappropriate behavior difficult to handle. That is, anything from an off-color story told in mixed company to a man weeping is likely to produce a problem situation.

In any face-to-face situation, we will find instances of this type which will momentarily, if not permanently, block any communication. In business and industry, any expressions of weakness or incompetency will generally be regarded as unacceptable and therefore will block good two-way communication. For example, it is difficult to listen to a supervisor tell of his feelings of failure in being able to "take charge" of a situation in his department, because *all* administrators are supposed to be able to "take charge."

Accepting Positive Feelings

It is both interesting and perplexing to note that negative or hostile feelings or expressions are much easier to deal with in any face-to-face relationship than are truly and deeply positive feelings. This is especially true for the businessman, because the culture expects him to be independent, bold, clever, and aggressive and manifest no feelings of warmth, gentleness, and intimacy. He therefore comes to regard these feelings as soft and inappropriate. But no matter how they are regarded, they remain a human need. The denial of these feelings in himself and his associates does not get the executive out of the problem of dealing with them. They simply become veiled and confused. If recognized, they would work for the total effort; unrecognized, they work against it.

Emotional Danger Signals

The listener's own emotions are sometimes a barrier to active listening. When emotions are at their height, which is when listening is most necessary, it is most difficult to set aside one's own concerns and be understanding. Our emotions are often our own worst enemies when we try to become listeners. The more involved and invested we are in a particular situation or problem, the less we are likely to be willing or able to listen to the feelings and attitudes of others. That is, the more we find it necessary to respond to our own needs, the less we are able to respond to the needs of another. Let us look at some of the main danger signals that warn us that our emotions may be interfering with our listening.

Defensiveness. The points about which one is most vocal and dogmatic, the points which one is most anxious to impose on others—these are always the points one is trying to talk oneself into believing. So one danger signal becomes apparent when you find yourself stressing a point or trying to convince another. It is at these times that you are likely to be less secure and consequently less able to listen.

Resentment of Opposition. It is always easier to listen to an idea which is similar to one of your own than to an opposing view. Sometimes, in order to clear the air, it is helpful to pause for a moment when you feel your ideas and position being challenged, reflect on the situation, and express your concern to the speaker.

Clash of Personalities. Here again, our experience has consistently shown us that the genuine expression of feelings on the part of the listener will be more helpful in developing a sound relationship than the suppression of them. This is so whether the feelings be resentment, hostility, threat, or admiration. A basically honest relationship, whatever the nature of it, is the most productive of all. The other party becomes secure when he learns that the listener can express his feelings honestly and openly to him. We should keep this in mind when we begin to fear a clash of personalities in the listening relationship. Otherwise, fear of our own emotions will choke off full expression of feelings.

Listening to Ourselves

To listen to oneself is a prerequisite for listening to others. And it is often an effective means of dealing with the problems we have outlined above. When we are most aroused, excited, and demanding, we are least able to understand our own feelings and attitudes. Yet, in dealing with the problems of others, it becomes most important to be sure of one's own position, values, and needs.

The ability to recognize and understand the meaning which a particular episode has for you, with all the feelings which it stimulates in you, and the ability to express this meaning when you find it getting in the way of active listening will clear the air and enable you once again to be free to listen. That is, if some person or situation touches off feelings within you which tend to block your attempts to listen with understanding, begin listening to yourself. It is much more helpful in developing effective relationships to avoid suppressing these feelings. Speak them out as clearly as you can, and try to enlist the other person as a listener to your feelings. A person's listening ability is limited by his ability to listen to himself.

ACTIVE LISTENING AND COMPANY GOALS

- How can listening improve production?
- We're in business, and it's a rugged, fast, competitive affair. How are we going to find time to counsel our employees?
- We have to concern ourselves with organizational problems first.
- We can't afford to spend all day listening when there's a job to be done.
- What's morale got to do with production?
- Sometimes we have to sacrifice an individual for the good of the rest of the people in the company.

Those of us who are trying to advance the listening approach in industry hear these comments frequently. And because they are so honest and legitimate, they pose a real problem. Unfortunately, the answers are not so clear-cut as the questions.

INDIVIDUAL IMPORTANCE

One answer is based on an assumption that is central to the listening approach. That assumption is: The kind of behavior which helps the individual will eventually be the best thing that could be done for the group. Or saying it another way: The things that are best for the individual are best for the company. This is a conviction of ours, based on our experience in psychology and education. The research evidence from industry is only beginning to come in. We find that putting the group first, at the expense of the individual, besides being an uncomfortable individual experience, does *not* unify the group. In fact, it tends to make the group less a group. The members become anxious and suspicious.

We are not at all sure in just what ways the group does benefit from a concern demonstrated for an individual, but we have several strong leads. One is that the group feels more secure when an individual is being listened to and provided for with concern and sensitivity. And we assume that a secure group will ultimately be a better group. When each individual feels that he need not fear exposing himself to the group, he is likely to contribute more freely and spontaneously. When the leader of a group responds to the individual, puts the individual first, the other members of the group will follow suit and the group will come to act as a unit in recognizing and responding

to the needs of a particular member. This positive, constructive action seems to be a much more satisfying experience for a group than the experience of dispensing with a member.

LISTENING AND PRODUCTION

Whether listening or any other activity designed to better human relations in an industry actually raises production—whether morale has a definite relationship to production—is not known for sure. There are some who frankly hold that there is no relationship to be expected between morale and production—that production often depends upon the social misfit, the eccentric, or the isolate. And there are some who simply choose to work in a climate of cooperation and harmony, in a high-morale group, quite aside from the question of increased production.

A report from the Survey Research Center[1] at the University of Michigan on research conducted at the Prudential Life Insurance Company lists seven findings relating to production and morale. Firstline supervisors in high-production work groups were found to differ from those in low-production work groups in that they

1. Are under less close supervision from their own supervisors.
2. Place less direct emphasis upon production as the goal.
3. Encourage employee participation in the making of decisions.
4. Are more employee-centered.

[1] "Productivity, Supervision, and Employee Morale," *Human Relations*, Series I, Report 1. Survey Research Center, University of Michigan, Ann Arbor, Mich.

5. Spend more of their time in supervision and less in straight production work.
6. Have a greater feeling of confidence in their supervisory roles.
7. Feel that they know where they stand with the company.

After mentioning that other dimensions of morale, such as identification with the company, intrinsic job satisfaction, and satisfaction with job status, were not found significantly related to productivity, the report goes on to suggest the following psychological interpretation:

> People are more effectively motivated when they are given some degree of freedom in the way in which they do their work than when every action is prescribed in advance. They do better when some degree of decision making about their jobs is possible than when all decisions are made for them. They respond more adequately when they are treated as personalities than as cogs in a machine. In short, if the ego motivations of self-determination, of self-expression, of a sense of personal worth can be tapped, the individual can be more effectively energized. The use of external sanctions or pressuring for production may work to some degree, but not to the extent that the more internalized motives do. When the individual comes to identify himself with his job and with the work of his group, human resources are much more fully utilized in the production process.

The Survey Research Center has also conducted studies among workers in other industries. In discussing the results of these studies, Robert L. Kahn writes:

> In the studies of clerical workers, railroad workers, and workers in

heavy industry, the supervisors with the better production records gave a larger proportion of their time to supervisory functions, especially to the interpersonal aspects of their jobs. The supervisors of the lower-producing sections were more likely to spend their time in tasks which the men themselves were performing, or in the paperwork aspects of their jobs.[2]

MAXIMUM CREATIVENESS

There may never be enough research evidence to satisfy everyone on this question. But speaking from a business point of view, in terms of the problem of developing resources for production, the maximum creativeness and productive effort of the human beings in the organization are the richest untapped source of power still existing. The difference between the maximum productive capacity of people and that output which industry is now realizing is immense. We simply suggest that this maximum capacity might be closer to

[2] Robert L. Kahn, "The Human Factors Underlying Industrial Productivity," *Michigan Business Review*. November, 1952.

realization if we sought to release the motivation that already exists within people rather than try to stimulate them externally.

This releasing of the individual is made possible, first of all, by sensitive listening, with respect and understanding. Listening is a beginning toward making the individual feel himself worthy of making contributions, and this could result in a very dynamic and productive organization. Competitive business is never too rugged or too busy to take time to procure the most efficient technological advances or to develop rich raw-material resources. But these in comparison to the resources that are already within the people in the plant are paltry. This is industry's major procurement problem.

G. L. Clements, president of Jewel Tea Co., Inc., in talking about the collaborative approach to management, says:

> We feel that this type of approach recognizes that there is a secret ballot going on at all times among the people in any business. They vote for or against their supervisors. A favorable vote for the supervisor shows up in the cooperation, teamwork, understanding, and production of the group. To win this

secret ballot, each supervisor must share the problems of his group and work for them.[3]

The decision to spend time listening to his employees is a decision each supervisor or executive has to make for himself. Executives seldom have much to do with products or processes. They have to deal with people who must in turn deal with people who will deal with products or processes. The higher one goes up the line, the more one will be concerned with human relations problems, simply because people are all one has to work with. The minute we take a man from his bench and make him a foreman, he is removed from the basic production of goods and now must begin relating to individuals instead of nuts and bolts. People are different from things, and our foreman is called upon for a different line of skills completely. His new tasks call upon him to be a special kind of person. The development of himself as a listener is a first step in becoming this special person.

□

[3] G. L. Clemens, "Time for Democracy in Action at the Executive Level," address given before the AMA Personnel Conference, Feb 28, 1951.

R² THE LANGUAGE OF PERSUASION

DAVID KIPNIS AND
STUART SCHMIDT

"I had all the facts and figures ready before I made my suggestions to my boss." (Manager)

"I kept insisting that we do it my

Source: Reprinted from *Psychology Today*, April 1985, pp. 40–46.

way. She finally caved in." (Husband)

"I think it's about time that you stop thinking these negative things about yourself." (Psychotherapist)

"Send out more horses, skirr the country round. Hang those that talk of fear. Give me mine armour." (Macbeth, Act 5)

These diverse statements—rational, insistent, emotional—have one thing in common. They all show people trying to persuade others, a skill we all treasure. Books about power and influence are read by young executives eager for promotion, by politicians anxious to sway their constituents, by lonely people looking to win and hold a mate and by harried parents trying to make their children see the light.

Despite this interest in persuasion, most people are not really aware of how they go about it. They spend more time choosing their clothes than they do their influence styles. Even fewer are aware of how their styles affect others or themselves. Although shouts and demands may make people dance to our tune, we will probably lose their goodwill. Beyond that, our opinion of others may change for the worse when we use hard or abusive tactics (see "The View from the Top," *Psychology Today,* December 1984).

Popular books on influencing others give contradictory advice. Some advocate assertiveness, others stealth and still others reason and logic. Could they all be right? We decided to see for ourselves what kinds of influence people actually use in personal and work situations and why they choose the tactics they do.

We conducted studies of dating couples and business managers in which the couples described how they attempted to influence their partners and the managers told how they attempted to influence their subordinates, peers and superiors at work. We then used these descriptions as the basis for separate questionnaires in which we asked other couples and managers how frequently they employed each tactic. Using factor analysis and other statistical techniques, we found that the tactics could be classified into three basic strategies— hard, soft and rational (see the "Influence Strategies" box).

These labels describe the tactics from the standpoint of the person using them. Since influencing someone is a social act, its meaning depends upon the observer's vantage point. For example, a wife

might ask her husband, "I wonder what we should do about the newspapers in the garage?" The husband could consider this remark nagging to get him to clean up the garage. The wife might say her remark was simply a friendly suggestion that he consider the state of the garage. An outside observer might feel that the wife's remark was just conversation, not a real attempt to influence.

As the box illustrates, hard tactics involve demanding, shouting and assertiveness. With soft tactics, people act nice and flatter others to get their way. Rational tactics involve the use of logic and bargaining to demonstrate why compliance or compromise is the best solution.

Why do people shout and demand in one instance, flatter in a

second and offer to compromise in a third? One common explanation is that the choice of tactics is based upon what "feels right" in each case. A more pragmatic answer is that the choice of tactics is based strictly on what works.

Our studies show that the reasons are more complex. When we examine how people actually use influence, we find that they use many different strategies, depending on the situation and the person being influenced. We gathered information from 195 dating and married couples, and from 360 first- and second-line managers in the United States, Australia and Great Britain. We asked which influence tactics they used, how frequently and in what conditions.

The choice of strategies varied predictably for both managers (see

INFLUENCE STRATEGIES		
Strategy	**Couples**	**Managers**
Hard	I get angry and demand that he/she give in.	I simply order the person to do what I ask.
	As the first step I make him/her feel stupid and worthless.	I threaten to give an unsatisfactory performance evaluation.
	I say I'll leave him/her if my spouse does not agree.	I get higher management to back up my request.
Soft	I act warm and charming before bringing up the subject.	I act very humble while making my request.
	I am so nice that he/she cannot refuse.	I make the person feel important by saying that she/he has the brains and experience to do what I want.
Rational	I offer to compromise; I'll give up a little if she/he gives up a little.	I offer to exchange favors: You do this for me, and I'll do something for you.
	We talk, discussing our views objectively without arguments.	I explain the reason for my request.

the "Bystanders" box) and couples. It depends on their particular objectives, relative power position and expectations about the willingness of others to do what they want. These expectations are often based on individual traits and biases rather than facts.

OBJECTIVES

One of our grandmothers always advised sweetly, "Act nice if you want a favor." We found that people do, indeed, vary their tactics according to what they want.

At work, for instance, managers frequently rely on soft tactics—flattery, praise, acting humble—when they want something from a boss such as time off or better assignments. However, when managers want to persuade the boss to accept ideas, such as a new work procedure, they're more likely to use reason and logic. Occasionally, they will even try hard tactics, such as going over the boss's head, if he or she can't be moved any other way.

 **LEARNING CHECKPOINT**

How can a manager be certain that an attempt to persuade a boss is working as planned?

Couples also vary their choice of tactics depending upon what they want from each other. Personal benefits such as choosing a movie or restaurant for the night call for a soft, loving approach. When they want to change a spouse's unacceptable behavior, anger, threats and other hard tactics come into play.

POWER POSITIONS

People who control resources, emotions or finances valued by

BYSTANDERS, TACTICIANS AND SHOTGUN MANAGERS

When we analyzed data from our study of managers, three distinct types emerged:

Shotgun managers use any and all means to get their way. Compared with the others we studied, they have the least managerial experience, hold staff rather than line positions and express the greatest number of personal needs (to receive benefits) and organizational needs (to sell their ideas) that require them to exercise influence. Shotgun managers are young, ambitious and unwilling to take no for an answer.

Tacticians rely heavily on reason to influence others. They usually have considerable power in an organization, direct units that do technologically complex work and feel they influence company policy.

Bystanders are the timid souls of the sample. They seldom use their managerial power to persuade others. Bystanders usually direct units that do routine work and have been in the same job for more years, on the average, than the other managers. Our impression is that they are marking time and feel it is futile even to try to influence others.

WHY PEOPLE CHOOSE EACH STRATEGY

Hard tactics are normally used when:
- Influencer has the advantage.
- Resistance is anticipated.
- Target's behavior violates social or organizational norms.

Soft tactics are normally used when:
- Influencer is at a disadvantage.
- Resistance is anticipated.
- The goal is to get benefits for one's self.

Rational tactics are normally used when:
- Neither party has a real power advantage.
- Resistance is not anticipated.
- The goal is to get benefits for one's self and one's organization.

---

others clearly have the advantage in a relationship, whether it is commercial or personal. In our research with couples, we discovered which partner was dominant by asking who made the final decision about issues such as spending money, choosing friends and other family matters. We found that people who say they control the relationship ("I have the final say") often rely on hard tactics to get their way. Those

who share decision power ("We decide together") bargain rationally and often compromise. Partners who admit that they have little power ("My partner has the final say") usually favor soft tactics.

We found the same patterns among managers. The more one-sided the power relationship at work, the more likely managers are to demand, get angry and insist with people who work for them,

THE SHAKESPEARE CONNECTION

The best art is life condensed, with its truths shown clearly and accurately. One of us (Kipnis) decided to test what has been learned about tactics of influence by comparing this understanding with how two of William Shakespeare's most famous characters go about persuading others. Each time King Lear and Macbeth try to influence someone in the play, successfully or not, the attempt was coded as hard, soft or rational. For example:

Hard tactic
"Kent, on thy life, no more."

(*Lear*, Act I, Scene 1)

Soft tactic
"Pray do not mock me. I am a very foolish fond old man."

(*Lear*, Act IV, Scene 7)

Rational tactic
"Think upon what hath chanced; and . . . the interim having weighed it, let us speak. . . ."

(*Macbeth*, Act I, Scene 3)

Both Macbeth and Lear consistently attempt to influence others throughout the plays, more in the last act than earlier. This finding is particularly interesting in regard to Lear, since he is thought of as an increasingly feeble, dying old man. Yet, when you analyze his words, he tries to exercise influence more frequently in the fifth act than at any other time in the play.

But the methods Lear and Macbeth use change dramatically during the five acts. As the table below indicates, Lear's tactics become increasingly soft, while Macbeth's become harder and harder.

Art, then, imitates life. Both Lear and Macbeth choose their tactics in relation to their power. Since Lear has given up his major base of power (his kingdom) in Act I, he must plead and use soft words. Macbeth, who has gained a kingdom, turns increasingly to tough tactics.

Influence Tactics* in *King Lear* and *Macbeth*

Tactic	King Lear					Macbeth				
	Act I	Act II	Act III	Act IV	Act V	Act I	Act II	Act III	Act IV	Act V
Hard	64	57	13	14	0	33	36	44	75	77
Soft	16	38	25	79	100	33	36	9	19	4
Rational	20	5	63	7	0	33	27	47	6	19

* Expressed in percentages. Some columns don't add up to 100 because the figures are rounded off.

and the more likely they are to act humble and flatter when they are persuading their bosses.

The fact that people change influence tactics depending on their power over the other person is hardly surprising. What is surprising is how universal the link is between power and tactics. Our surveys and those conducted by others have found this relationship among children trying to influence younger children or older children, and among executives dealing with executives at other companies more or less powerful than their own, as well as among spouses and business managers dealing with their own subordinates and bosses.

There seems to be an "Iron Law of Power": The greater the discrepancy in clout between the influencer and the target, the greater the likelihood that hard tactics will be used. People with power don't always use hard tactics as their first choice. At first, most simply request and explain. They turn to demands and threats (the iron fist lurking under the velvet glove of reason) only when someone seems reluctant or refuses to comply with their request.

In contrast, people with little power are likely to stop trying or immediately shift to soft tactics when they encounter resistance. They feel the costs associated with the use of hard or even rational tactics are unacceptable. They are unwilling to take the chance of angering a boss, a spouse or an older child by using anything but soft methods.

EXPECTATIONS AND BIASES

We have found that people also vary their strategies according to how successful they expect to be in influencing their targets. When they believe that someone is likely to do what is asked, they make simple requests. When they anticipate resistance and have the power, they use hard tactics.

This anticipation may be realistic. Just as a robber knows that without a gun, a polite request for money is unlikely to persuade, a boss knows that a request for work on Saturday needs more than a smile to back it up. But less realistic personal and situational factors sometimes make us expect resistance where none exists. People who are low in self-esteem and self-confidence, for instance, have difficulty believing that others will comply with simple requests.

We found that lack of confidence and low self-esteem are characteristic of managers who bark orders and refuse to discuss the issues involved, of couples who constantly shout and scream at each other and of parents who rely on harsh discipline. These hard tactics result from the self-defeating assumption that others will not listen unless they are treated roughly.

LEARNING CHECKPOINT

Are there any work situations in which hard tactics are perhaps the most likely to succeed?

search, and that of others, shows that orders, shouts and threats are more likely to be used between blacks and whites or men and women. The simple perception that "these people are different than I am" leads to the idea that "they are not as reasonable as I am" and must be ordered about.

The reasons shown in the "Why People Choose" box are generalizations. They don't necessarily describe how a particular person will act in a particular situation. People may use influence tactics because of habit, lack of forethought or lack of social sensitivity. Most of us would be more effective persuaders if we analyzed why we act as we do. Simply writing a short description of a recent incident in which we tried to persuade someone can help us understand better our own tactics, why we use them and, perhaps, why a rational approach might be better.

People who know we have studied the matter sometimes ask, "Which tactics work best?" The answer is that they all work if they are used at the right time with the right person. But both hard and soft tactics involve costs to the user even when they succeed. Hard tactics often alienate the people being influenced and create a climate of hostility and resistance. Soft tactics—acting nice, being humble—may lessen self-respect and self-esteem. In contrast, we found that people who rely chiefly on logic, reason and compromise to get their way are the most satisfied both with their business lives and with their personal relationships.   □

LEARNING CHECKPOINT

Does this mean that upward communication has little chance of accomplishing anything in an organization?

Social situations and biases can also distort expectations of cooperation. Misunderstandings based on differences in attitudes, race or sex can lead to hard tactics. Our re-

D1 ARE YOU PASSIVE, ASSERTIVE, OR AGGRESSIVE?*

<table>
<tr><td></td><td></td><td>**Mostly True**</td><td>**Mostly False**</td></tr>
</table>

The following questionnaire is designed to give you tentative insight into your current tendencies toward nonassertiveness (passivity), assertiveness, or aggressiveness. As with other questionnaires presented in this book, The Assertiveness Scale is primarily a self-examination and discussion device. Answer each question Mostly true or Mostly false, as it applies to you.

		Mostly True	Mostly False
1.	It is extremely difficult for me to turn down a sales representative when that individual is a nice person.	___	___
2.	I express criticism freely.	___	___
3.	If another person were being very unfair, I would bring it to that person's attention.	___	___
4.	Work is no place to let your feelings show.	___	___
5.	No use asking for favors, people get what they deserve on the job.	___	___
6.	Business is not the place for tact; say what you think.	___	___
7.	If a person looked like he or she were in a hurry, I would let that person in front of me in a supermarket line.	___	___
8.	A weakness of mine is that I'm too nice a person.	___	___
9.	If my restaurant bill is even 25 cents more than it should be, I demand that the mistake be corrected.	___	___
10.	I have laughed out loud in public more than once.	___	___
11.	I've been described as too outspoken by several people.	___	___
12.	I am quite willing to have the store take back a piece of furniture that has a scratch.	___	___
13.	I dread having to express anger toward a co-worker.	___	___
14.	People often say that I'm too reserved and emotionally controlled.	___	___
15.	Nice guys and gals finish last in business.	___	___
16.	I fight for my rights down to the last detail.	___	___
17.	I have no misgivings about returning an overcoat to the store if it doesn't fit me properly.	___	___
18.	If I have had an argument with a person, I try to avoid him or her.	___	___
19.	I insist on my spouse (roommate, or partner) doing his or her fair share of undesirable chores.	___	___
20.	It is difficult for me to look directly at another person when the two of us are in disagreement.	___	___
21.	I have cried among friends more than once.	___	___
22.	If someone near me at a movie kept up a conversation with another person, I would ask him or her to stop.	___	___
23.	I am able to turn down social engagements with people I do not particularly care for.	___	___

* Source: Reprinted from Andrew J. DuBrin, *Contemporary Applied Management*, 2nd ed. (Plano, Texas: Business Publications, Inc., 1985), pp. 50–52.

24. It is poor taste to express what you really feel about another individual. _____ _____
25. I sometimes show my anger by swearing at or belittling another person. _____ _____
26. I am reluctant to speak up in a meeting. _____ _____
27. I find it relatively easy to ask friends for small favors such as giving me a lift to work when my car is being serviced or repaired. _____ _____
28. If another person was smoking in a restaurant and it bothered me, I would inform that person. _____ _____
29. I often finish other people's sentences for them. _____ _____
30. It is relatively easy for me to express love and affection toward another person. _____ _____

Scoring and Interpretation

Score yourself plus 1 for each of your answers that agrees with the scoring key. If your score is 10 or less, it is probable that you are currently a nonassertive individual. A score of 11 through 24 suggests that you are an assertive individual. A score of 25 or higher suggests that you are an aggressive individual. Retake this test about 30 days from now to give yourself some indication of the stability of your answers. You might also discuss your answers with a close friend to determine if that person has a similar perception of your assertiveness. Here is the scoring key.

1. Mostly false	11. Mostly true	21. Mostly true
2. Mostly true	12. Mostly true	22. Mostly true
3. Mostly true	13. Mostly false	23. Mostly true
4. Mostly false	14. Mostly false	24. Mostly false
5. Mostly false	15. Mostly true	25. Mostly true
6. Mostly true	16. Mostly true	26. Mostly false
7. Mostly false	17. Mostly true	27. Mostly true
8. Mostly false	18. Mostly false	28. Mostly true
9. Mostly true	19. Mostly true	29. Mostly true
10. Mostly true	20. Mostly false	30. Mostly true

D2 MENTAL COMMUNICATIONS

Look at the description presented in the next paragraph. The description should result in the formation of a mental image of an animal. Attempt to draw the animal based on the encyclopedia description. Is it a cow? An amardillo? A shark? Why do we form different mental images based on the same communications?

The body is stout, with arched back; the limbs are short and stout, armed with strong, blunt claws; the ears long; the tail thick at the base and tapering gradually. The elongated head is set on a short thick neck, and at the extremity of the snout is a disc in which the nostrils open. The mouth is small and tubular, furnished with a long extensil tongue. A large individual measured 6 ft., 8 in. In color it is pale sandy or yellow, the hair being scanty and allowing the skin to show.

 **UPWARD APPRAISAL***

OBJECTIVES

1. To practice the art of giving feedback to an organizational superior.
2. To observe the dynamics of status as a communication barrier.
3. To allow the instructor to practice and demonstrate the techniques of active listening and to receive constructive feedback on the course.

STARTING THE EXERCISE

1. Form work groups as assigned by your instructor.
2. The instructor will leave the room.
3. Convene in your assigned work groups for a period of 10 minutes. Create a list of comments, problems, issues, and concerns you would like to have communicated to the instructor in regard to the course experience to date.
4. Select one person from the group to act as spokesperson in communicating the group's feelings to the instructor.
5. The spokespersons should briefly convene to decide on what physical arrangement of chairs, tables, and so forth is most appropriate to conduct the feedback session. The classroom should then be rearranged to fit the desired specifications.
6. While the spokespersons convene, persons in the remaining groups should discuss how they expect the forthcoming communications event to develop. Will it be a good experience for all parties concerned? Be prepared to observe critically the actual communication process.
7. The instructor should be invited to return, and the feedback session will begin. Observers should make notes so that they may make constructive comments at the conclusion of the exercise.
8. Once the feedback session is completed, the instructor will call upon the observers for comments, ask the spokespersons for their reactions, and open the session to general discussion.

REMEMBER

Your interest in the exercise is twofold: (1) to communicate your feelings to the instructor and (2) to learn more about the process of giving and receiving feedback.

 **FRUSTRATION, CLARITY, ACCURACY**

OBJECTIVES

1. To display the features of the communication process.
2. To identify the differences between one-way and two-way communications.
3. To examine the reactions of individuals to one- and two-way communications.

STARTING THE EXERCISE

The instructor will give the same message to two separate groups. These groups will receive the private message only one time. They are not permitted to ask the instructor questions about the message.

The Facts

The instructor will serve as the initiator of a message to two separate groups of three or four students. The groups will attempt to develop a clear understanding of what the instructor said. They will then return to the main classroom, where other students will serve as communication chains for the message. Both a one-way chain and a two-way chain will be used. To complete both the one- and two-way communication versions of this exercise, a minimum of 22 students will be needed. If a class does not have 22 students, the instructor will need to make some modifications.

Exercise Procedures

Phase I: Group Communication: 10 minutes
Group 1 and Group 2, consisting of three or four students, will be selected. The groups should be isolated from each other to receive the message. The instructor will read *one time* the same message to the two groups in

---

* Source: Based on Eugene Owens, "Upward Appraisal: An Exercise in Subordinate's Critique of Superior's Performance," *Exchange: The Organizational Behavior Teaching Journal*, Vol. 3 (1978), pp. 41–42.

their separate rooms or isolated areas. Each group will discuss the message for no more than five minutes.

Phase II: One-Way Communication: 10 minutes

Four students who are not in Groups 1 or 2 will serve as the *chain* for one of the groups, and four other students will serve as the chain for the other group. A representative of Group 1 will whisper the message to the first person in the four-person chain, who, in turn, will pass on the private message to the second member, and so on. Talking between members in the chain is not permitted. Only one person, the transmitter, is permitted to speak. The last person in the chain will write the message down and hand it to the instructor. The same one-way communication process will be followed in Group 2.

Phase III: Two-Way Communication: 20 minutes

Four new students who have not participated in either Phases 1 or 2 will serve as the Group 1 chain. A representative of Group 1 will discuss the message with the first person in the chain. The representative and the first person can discuss the message privately from other members in the chain. When the discussants are ready and within the allocated time limit, the first person in the chain will then discuss the message privately with the second person in the chain. These private two-way discussions will continue until the time allotted has expired or until the last person in the chain hears the message and writes it for the instructor. The same two-way communication process will be followed in Group 2.

Phase IV: Analysis of the Exercise: 20 minutes

Each participant should evaluate the exercise. Some of the issues to consider are:

a. One-way versus two-way communication accuracy.
b. Attitudes of the different participants. Were any participants frustrated? About what?
c. What were some of the barriers to effective communication?

THE ROAD TO HELL*

John Baker, chief engineer of the Caribbean Bauxite Company Limited of Barracania in the West Indies, was making his final preparations to leave the island. His promotion to production manager of Keso Mining Corporation near Winnipeg—one of Continental Ore's fast-expanding Canadian enterprises—had been announced a month before, and now everything had been tidied up except the last vital interview with his successor, the able young Barracanian Matthew Rennalls. It was vital that this interview be a success and that Rennalls leave Baker's office uplifted and encouraged to face the challenge of his new job. A touch on the bell would have brought Rennalls walking into the room, but Baker delayed the moment and gazed thoughtfully through the window, considering just exactly what he was going to say and, more particularly, how he was going to say it.

Baker, an English expatriate, was forty-five years old and had served his twenty-three years with Continental Ore in many different places: the Far East; several countries of Africa; Europe; and, for the last two years, the West Indies. He had not cared much for his previous assignment in Hamburg and was delighted when the West Indian appointment came through. Climate was not the only attraction. Baker had always preferred working overseas in what were called the "developing countries" because he felt he had an innate knack—more than most other expatriates working for Continental Ore—of knowing just how to get on with regional staff. Twenty-four hours in Barracania, however, soon made him realize that he would need all of his innate knack if he were to deal effectively with the problems in this field that now awaited him.

At his first interview with Glenda Hutchins, the production manager, the whole problem of Rennalls and his future was discussed. There and then it was made quite clear to Baker that one of his most important tasks would be the grooming of Rennalls as his successor. Hutchins had pointed out that not only was Rennalls one of the brightest Barracanian prospects on the staff of Caribbean Bauxite—at London University he had taken first-class honors in the B.Sc. engineering degree—but, being the son of the minister

of finance and economic planning, he also had no small political pull.

Carribean Bauxite had been particularly pleased when Rennalls decided to work for it rather than for the government in which his father had such a prominent post. The company ascribed his action to the effect of its vigorous and liberal regionalization program that, since World War II, had produced eighteen Barracanians at the middle management level and given Caribbean Bauxite a good lead in this respect over all other international concerns operating in Barracania. The success of this timely regionalization policy had led to excellent relations with the government—a relationship that gained added importance when Barracania, three years later, became independent, an occasion that encouraged a critical and challenging attitude toward the role foreign interest would have to play in the new Barracania. Hutchins, therefore, had little difficulty convincing Baker that the successful career development of Rennalls was of the first importance.

The interview with Hutchins was now two years in the past, and Baker, leaning back in his office chair, reviewed just how successful he had been in the grooming of Rennalls. What aspects of the latter's character had helped, and what had hindered? What about his own personality? How had that helped or hindered? The first item to go on the credit side, without question, would be the ability of Rennalls to master the technical aspects of his job. From the start he had shown keenness and enthusiasm, and he had often impressed Baker with his ability in tackling new assignments and the constructive comments he invariably made in departmental discussions. He was popular with all ranks of Barracanian staff and had an ease of manner that stood him in good stead when dealing with his expatriate seniors.

These were all assets, but what about the debit side? First and foremost was his racial consciousness. His four years at London University had accentuated this feeling and made him sensitive to any sign of condescension on the part of expatriates. Perhaps to give expression to this sentiment, as soon as he returned home from London, he threw himself into poli-

---

* Source: Prepared by the late Gareth Evans of Shell International Petroleum Company, Ltd.

tics on behalf of the United Action Party, who were later to win the preindependence elections and provide the country with its first prime minister.

The ambitions of Rennalls—and he certainly was ambitious—did not, however, lie in politics. Staunch nationalist he was, but he saw that he could serve himself and his country best—For was not bauxite responsible for nearly half the value of Barracania's export trade?—by putting his engineering talent to the best use possible. On this account, Hutchins found that he had an unexpectedly easy task in persuading Rennalls to give up his political work before entering the production department as an assistant engineer.

It was, Baker knew, Rennall's well-repressed sense of racial consciousness that had prevented their relationship from being as close as it should have been. On the surface, nothing could have seemed more agreeable. Formality between the two was minimal. Baker was delighted to find that his assistant shared his own peculiar "shaggy dog" sense of humor, so jokes were continually being exchanged. They entertained one another at their houses and often played tennis together—and yet the barrier remained invisible, indefinable, but ever present. The existence of this screen between them was a constant source of frustration to Baker, since it indicated a weakness which he was loath to accept. If successful with people of all other nationalities, why not with Rennalls?

At least he had managed to break through to Rennalls more successfully than had any other expatriate. In fact, it was the young Barracanian's attitude—sometimes overbearing, sometimes cynical—toward other company expatriates that had been one of the subjects Baker raised last year when he discussed Rennall's staff report with him. Baker knew, too, that he would have to raise the same subject again in the forthcoming interview, because Martha Jackson, the senior draughter, had complained only yesterday about the rudeness of Rennalls. With this thought in mind, Baker leaned forward and spoke into the intercom: "Would you come in, Matt, please? I'd like a word with you." Rennalls came in, and Baker held out a box and said, "Do sit down. Have a cigarette."

He paused while he held out his lighter and then went on. "As you know, Matt, I'll be off to Canada in a few days' time, and before I go, I thought it would be useful if we could have a final chat together. It is indeed with some deference that I suggest I can be of help. You will shortly be sitting in this chair doing the job I am now doing, but I, on the other hand, am ten years older, so perhaps you can accept the idea that I may be able to give you the benefit of my longer experience."

Baker saw Rennalls stiffen slightly in his chair as he made this point, so he added in explanation, "You and I have attended enough company courses to remember those repeated requests by the personnel manager to tell people how they are getting on as often as the convenient moment arises, and not just the automatic once a year when, by regulation, staff reports have to be discussed."

Rennalls nodded his agreement, so Baker went on, "I shall always remember the last job performance discussion I had with my previous boss back in Germany. She used what she called the 'plus and minus technique.' She firmly believed that when seniors seek to improve the work performance of their staff by discussion, their prime objective should be to make sure the latter leave the interview encouraged and inspired to improve. Any criticism, therefore, must be constructive and helpful. She said that one very good way to encourage a person—and I fully agree with her—is to discuss good points, the plus factors, as well as weak ones, the minus factors. So I thought, Matt, it would be a good idea to run our discussion along these lines."

Rennalls offered no comment, so Baker continued. "Let me say, therefore, right away, that as far as your own work performance is concerned, the pluses far outweigh the minuses. I have, for instance, been most impressed with the way you have adapted your considerable theoretical knowledge to master the practical techniques of your job—that ingenious method you used to get air down to the fifth shaft level is a sufficient case in point. At departmental meetings I have invariably found your comments well taken and helpful. In fact, you will be interested to know that only last week I reported to Ms. Hutchins that, from the technical point of view, she could not wish for a more able person to succeed to the position of chief engineer."

"That's very good indeed of you, John," cut in Rennalls with a smile of thanks. "My only worry now is how to live up to such a high recommendation."

"Of that I am quite sure," returned Baker, "especially if you can overcome the minus factor which I would like now to discuss with you. It is one that I have talked about before, so I'll come straight to the point. I have noticed that you are more friendly and get on better with your fellow Barracanians than you do with Europeans. In point of fact, I had a complaint only yesterday from Ms. Jackson, who said you had been rude to her—and not for the first time, either.

"There is, Matt, I am sure, no need for me to tell you how necessary it will be for you to get on well with expatriates, because until the company has trained up sufficient men of your caliber, Europeans are bound to occupy senior positions here in Barracania. All this is vital to your future interests, so can I help you in any way?"

While Baker was speaking on this theme, Rennalls sat tensed in his chair, and it was some seconds before he replied. "It is quite extraordinary, isn't it, how one can convey an impression to others so at variance with what one intends? I can only assure you once again that my disputes with Jackson—and you may remember also Godson—have had nothing at all to do with the color of their skins. I promise you that if a Barracanian had behaved in an equally peremptory manner, I would have reacted in precisely the same way. And again, if I may say it within these four walls, I am sure I am not the only one who has found Jackson and Godson difficult. I could mention the names of several expatriates who have felt the same. However, I am really sorry to have created this impression of not being able to get on with Europeans—it is an entirely false one—and I quite realize that I must do all I can to correct it as quickly as possible. On your last point, regarding Europeans holding senior positions in the company for some time to come, I quite accept the situation. I know that Caribbean Bauxite—as it has been doing for many years now—will promote Barracanians as soon as their experience warrants it. And, finally, I would like to assure you, John—and my father thinks the same, too—that I am very happy in my work here and hope to stay with the company for many years to come."

Rennalls had spoken earnestly, and Baker, although not convinced by what he had heard, did not think he could pursue the matter further except to say, "All right, Matt, my impression may be wrong, but I would like to remind you about the truth of that old saying 'What is important is not what is true, but what is believed.' Let it rest at that."

But suddenly Baker knew that he did not want to "let it rest at that." He was disappointed once again at not being able to break through to Rennalls and at having again had to listen to his bland denial that there was any racial prejudice in his makeup.

Baker, who had intended to end the interview at this point, decided to try another tack. "To return for a moment to the plus and minus technique I was telling you about just now, there is another plus factor I forgot to mention. I would like to congratulate you

not only on the caliber of your work, but also on the ability you have shown in overcoming a challenge that I, as a European, have never had to meet.

"Continental Ore is, as you know, a typical commercial enterprise—admittedly a big one—that is a product of the economic and social environment of the United States and western Europe. My ancestors have all been brought up in this environment for the past two or three hundred years, and I have, therefore, been able to live in a world in which commerce (as we know it today) has been part and parcel of my being. It has not been something revolutionary and new that has suddenly entered my life. In your case," went on Baker, "the situation is different, because you and your forebears have only had some fifty and not two or three hundred years. Again, Matt, let me congratulate you—and people like you—on having so successfully overcome this particular hurdle. It is for this very reason that I think the outlook for Barracania—and particularly Caribbean Bauxite—is so bright."

Rennalls had listened intently, and when Baker finished, he replied, "Well, once again, John, I have to thank you for what you have said, and, for my part, I can only say that it is gratifying to know that my own personal effort has been so much appreciated. I hope that more people will soon come to think as you do."

There was a pause, and, for a moment, Baker thought hopefully that he was about to achieve his long-awaited breakthrough. But Rennalls merely smiled back. The barrier remained unbreached. There were some five minutes' cheerful conversation about the contrast between the Caribbean and Canadian climates and whether the West Indies had any hope of beating England in the Fifth Test before Baker drew the interview to a close. Although he was as far as ever from knowing the real Rennalls, he was nevertheless glad that the interview had run along in this friendly manner and, particularly, that it had ended on such a cheerful note.

This feeling, however, lasted only until the following morning. Baker had some farewells to make, so he arrived at the office considerably later than usual. He had no sooner sat down at his desk than his secretary walked into the room with a worried frown on her face. Her words came fast. "When I arrived this morning, I found Mr. Rennalls already waiting at my door. He seemed very angry and told me in quite a peremptory manner that he had a vital letter to dictate that must be sent off without any delay. He was so worked up that he couldn't keep still and kept pacing about the room, which is most unlike him. He wouldn't even wait to read what he had dictated. Just signed the page where he thought the letter would end. It has been distributed, and your copy is in your in tray."

Puzzled and feeling vaguely uneasy, Baker opened the envelope marked "Confidential" and read the following letter:

FROM:	Assistant Engineer	SUBJECT:	Assessment of Interview Between Messrs. Baker and Rennalls
TO:	The Chief Engineer, Caribbean Bauxite Limited	DATE:	14th August, 1982

It has always been my practice to respect the advice given me by seniors, so after our interview, I decided to give careful thought once again to its main points and so make sure that I had understood all that had been said. As I promised you at the time, I had every intention of putting your advice to the best effect.

It was not, therefore, until I had sat down quietly in my home yesterday evening to consider the interview objectively that its main purport became clear. Only then did the full enormity of what you said dawn on me. The more I thought about it, the more convinced I was that I had hit upon the real truth—and the more furious I became. With a facility in the English language which I—a poor Barracanian—cannot hope to match, you had the audacity to insult me (and through me every Barracanian worth his salt) by claiming that our knowledge of modern living is only a paltry fifty years old, while yours goes back two hundred to three hundred years. As if your materialistic commercial environment could possibly be compared with the spiritual values of our culture! I'll have you know that if much of what I saw in London is representative of your boasted culture, I hope fervently that it will never come to Barracania. By what right do you have the effrontery to condescend to us? At heart, all you Europeans think us barbarians, or, as you say amongst yourselves, we are "just down from the trees."

Far into the night I discussed this matter with my father, and he is as disgusted as I. He agrees with me that any company whose senior staff think as you do is no place for any Barracanian proud of his culture and race. So much for all the company claptrap and specious propaganda about regionalisation and Barracania for the Barracanians.

I feel ashamed and betrayed. Please accept this letter as my resignation, which I wish to become effective immediately.

cc: Production Manager
      Managing Director   □

CASE QUESTIONS

1. What in your opinion did Baker hope to accomplish as a result of his conversation with Rennalls? Did he succeed? Why or why not?
2. Did nonverbal communications play a part in this case? Be specific and give examples.
3. What could Baker and Rennalls have done to improve the situation described in the case?

2 A CASE OF MISUNDERSTANDING: MR. HART AND MR. BING*

In a department of a large industrial organization there were seven workers (four men and three women) engaged in testing and inspecting panels of electronic equipment. In this department one of the workers, Bing was having trouble with his immediate supervisor, Hart, who had formerly been a worker in the department. Had we been observers in this department we would have seen Bing carrying two or three panels at a time from the racks where they were stored to the bench where he inspected them together. For this activity we would have seen him charging double or triple set-up time. We would have heard him occasionally singing at work. Also we would have seen him usually leaving his work position a few minutes early to go to lunch, and noticed that other employees sometimes accompanied him. And had we been present at one specific occasion, we would have heard Hart telling Bing that he disapproved of these activities and that he wanted Bing to stop doing them. However, not being present to hear the actual verbal exchange that took place in this interaction, let us note what Bing and Hart each said to a personnel representative.

WHAT BING SAID

In talking about his practice of charging double or triple setup time for panels which he inspected all at one time, Bing said:

> This is a perfectly legal thing to do. We've always been doing it. Mr. Hart, the supervisor, has other ideas about it, though: he claims it's cheating the company. He came over to the bench a day or two ago and let me know just how he felt about the matter. Boy, did we go at it! It wasn't so much the fact that he called me down on it, but more the way in which he did it. He's a sarcastic bastard. I've never seen anyone like him. He's not content just to say in a manlike way what's on his mind, but he prefers to do it in a way that makes you want to crawl inside a crack in the floor. What a guy! I don't mind being called down by a supervisor, but I like to be treated like a man, and not humiliated like a school teacher does a naughty kid. He's been pulling this stuff ever since he's been promoted. He's lost his friendly way and seems to be having some difficulty in knowing how to manage us employees. He's a changed man over

what he used to be like when he was a worker on the bench with us several years ago.

> When he pulled this kind of stuff on me the other day, I got so damn mad I called in the union representative. I knew that the thing I was doing was permitted by the contract, but I was intent on making some trouble for Mr. Hart, just because he persists in this sarcastic way of handling me. I am about fed up with the whole damn situation. I'm trying every means I can to get myself transferred out of this group. If I don't succeed and I'm forced to stay on here, I'm going to screw him in every way I can. He's not going to pull this kind of kid stuff any longer on me. When the union representative questioned him on the case, he finally had to back down, because according to the contract an employee can use any time-saving method or device in order to speed up the process as long as the quality standards of the job are met.

> You see, he knows that I do professional singing on the outside. He hears the people talking about my career in music. I guess he figures I can be so cocky because I have another means of earning some money. Actually, the employees here enjoy having me sing while we work, but he thinks I'm disturbing them and causing them to "goof-off" from their work. Occasionally, I leave the job a few minutes early and go down to the washroom to wash up before lunch. Sometimes several others in the group will accompany me, and so Mr. Hart automatically thinks I'm the leader and usually bawls me out for the whole thing.

> So, you can see, I'm a marked man around here: He keeps watching me like a hawk. Naturally, this makes me very uncomfortable. That's why I'm sure a transfer would be the best thing. I've asked him for it, but he didn't give me any satisfaction at the time. While I remain here, I'm going to keep my nose clean, but whenever I get the chance, I'm going to slip it to him, but good.

WHAT HART SAID

Here, on the other hand, is what Hart told the personnel representative:

> Say, I think you should be in on this. My dear little friend Bing is heading himself into a show-down with me. Recently it was brought to my attention that Bing has been taking double and triple set-up time for panels which he is actually inspecting at one time. In effect,

---

* Source: Reproduced by permission of the President and Fellows of Harvard College.

that's cheating, and I've called him down on it several times before. A few days ago it was brought to my attention again, and so this time I really let him have it in no uncertain terms. He's been getting away with this for too long and I'm going to put an end to it once and for all. I know he didn't like me calling him on it because a few hours later he had the union representative breathing down my back. Well, anyway, I let them both know I'll not tolerate the practice any longer, and I let Bing know that if he continues to do this kind of thing, I'm inclined to think the guy's mentally deficient, because talking to him has actually no meaning to him whatsoever. I've tried just about every approach to jar some sense into that guy's head, and I've just about given it up as a bad deal.

I don't know what it is about the guy, but I think he's harboring some deep feelings against me. For what, I don't know, because I've tried to handle that bird with kid gloves. But his whole attitude around here on the job is one of indifference, and he certainly isn't a good influence on the rest of my group. Frankly, I think he purposely tried to agitate them against me at times, too. It seems to me he may be suffering from illusions of grandeur, because all he does all day long is sit over there and croon his fool head off. Thinks he's a Frank Sinatra! No kidding! I understand he takes singing lessons and he's working with some of the local bands in the city. All of which is OK by me; but when his outside interests start interfering with his efficiency on the job, then I've got to start paying closer attention to the situation. For this reason I've been keeping my eye on that bird and if he steps out of line any more, he and I are going to part ways.

You know there's an old saying, "You can't make a silk purse out of a sow's ear." The guy is simply unscrupulous. He feels no obligation to do a real day's work. Yet I know the guy can do a good job, because for a long time he did. But in recent months he's slipped, for some reason, and his whole attitude on the job has changed. Why, it's even getting to the point now where I think he's inducing other employees to "goof off" a few minutes before the lunch whistle and go down to the washroom and clean up on company time. I've called him on it several times, but words just don't seem to make any lasting impression on him. Well, if he keeps it up much longer, he's going to find himself on the way out. He's asked me for a transfer, so I know he wants to go. But I didn't give him an answer when he asked me, because I was storming mad at the time, and I may have told him to go somewhere else. □

CASE QUESTIONS

1. Based on the discussion of the elements of communication in the chapter, where are the breakdowns in communications occurring in this case?
2. What barriers to effective communication are present in this case?
3. What in your opinion must be done to improve communication between Mr. Hart and Mr. Bing?

ORGANIZATIONAL CHANGE AND DEVELOPMENT

LEARNING OBJECTIVES

DEFINE what is meant by the term organizational development.

DESCRIBE the steps which should be followed in managing an organizational development effort.

DISCUSS the three major categories of development methods.

COMPARE alternative behavioral methods.

IDENTIFY, by level, the depth of an intended change effort.

The process by which managers sense and respond to the necessity for change has been the focus of much research and practical attention in recent years. If managers were able to design perfect sociotechnical organizations and if the scientific, market, and technical environments were stable and predictable, there would be no pressure for change. But such is not the case. The statement that "we live in the midst of constant change" has become a well-worn but relevant cliche. Of course, the need for change affects organizations differently; those that operate in relatively certain environments need to be less concerned with change than those that operate in less certain environments.

The literature and practice that deal with the process of organizational change cannot be conveniently classified because of the yet-unsettled nature of this aspect of organizational behavior. Various conceptualizations and theories and their meanings and interpretations are subject to considerable disagreement.[1] The current trend is to use the term *organizational development* (OD) to refer to the process of preparing for and managing change. This, however, is a very broad statement which fails to address any of the specifics of OD, either in terms of technique or objectives. The following definition identifies all the significant aspects of OD:

> The term "Organizational development" . . . implies a normative, reeducation strategy intended to affect systems of beliefs, values, and attitudes within the organization so that it can adapt better to the accelerated rate of change in technology, in our industrial environment and society in general. It also includes formal organizational restructuring which is frequently initiated, facilitated and reinforced by the normative and behavioral changes.[2]

The three subobjectives of OD are "changing attitudes or values, modifying behavior, and inducing change in structure and policy."[3] However, it is con-

---

[1] For an insightful recent discussion, see James G. March, "Footnotes to Organizational Change," *Administrative Science Quarterly,* December 1981, pp. 563–77.

[2] Alexander Winn, "The Laboratory Approach to Organizational Development: A Tentative Model of Planned Change," paper read at the annual conference, British Psychological Society, Oxford, September 1968, and cited in Robert T. Golembiewski, "Organizational Development in Public Agencies: Perspective on Theory and Practice," *Public Administration Review,* July-August 1969, p. 367.

[3] Ibid., p. 367.

ceivable that the OD strategy might well emphasize one or another of these subobjectives. For example, if the structure of an organization is optimal in management's view, the OD process might attempt to educate personnel to adopt behaviors consistent with that structure. Such would be the case for leadership training in participative management in an organization that already has an organic structure. Regardless of whether one, two, or all three subobjectives are emphasized, the desired end result of virtually any OD effort is improved organizational functioning. The following OBM Encounter illustrates one way of thinking about the role OD might play.

 ENCOUNTER

ORGANIZATIONAL DEVELOPMENT AND THE ROAST PIG PROBLEM

Sometimes, well-intentioned changes in organizations do not work—or do not continue working after initial success—because of what Rosabeth Moss Kanter calls the "roast pig" problem. Out of all the events and components of a change, what is the core that really makes it work? That is, what is the essence of the change? Essentially, this is the problem of understanding *why* something works.

Kanter refers to this as the roast pig problem after Charles Lamb's classic essay, "A Dissertation on Roast Pig," a satirical tale of how the art of roasting was discovered in a Chinese village that did not cook its food. According to the tale, a child accidentally set fire to a house with a pig inside and the villagers, poking around the ruins, discovered a new delicacy.

This eventually led to a rash of house fires. The moral of the story is that when you do not understand how the pig gets cooked, you have to burn a whole house down every time you want a roast pork dinner.

The roast pig problem can plague any organization that lacks an understanding of itself or of what is essential to making a change or innovation work and what is superfluous. The consequences of this lack of understanding can be twofold. First, as a particular way of doing things gets locked into place, further experimentation may be discouraged—house burning may become so ritualistic that the search for other cooking methods may end. Second, and perhaps more important, the organization may waste a great number of houses.

Sound, effective organizational development efforts are designed to eliminate the roast pig problem.   ☐

Source: Based, in part, on a section from Rosabeth Moss Kanter, *The Change Masters: Innovation for Productivity in the American Corporation* (New York: Simon & Schuster, 1983).

Organizational development, as the term is used in contemporary management practice, has certain distinguishing characteristics:

1. *It is planned.* OD is a data-based approach to change that involves all of the ingredients that go into managerial planning. It involves goal setting, action planning, implementation, monitoring, and taking corrective action when necessary.
2. *It is problem-oriented.* OD attempts to apply theory and research from a number of disciplines, including behavioral science, to the solution of organizational problems.

3. *It reflects a systems approach.* OD is both systemic and systematic. It is a way of more closely linking the human resources and potential of an organization to its technology, structure, and management processes.

4. *It is an integral part of the management process.* OD is not something that is done to the organization by outsiders. It becomes a way of managing organizational change processes.

5. *It is not a "fix-it" strategy.* OD is a continuous and ongoing process. It is not a series of ad hoc activities designed to implement a specific change. It takes time for OD to become a way of life in the organization.

6. *It focuses on improvement.* The emphasis of OD is on improvement. It is not just for "sick" organizations or for "healthy" ones. It is something that can benefit almost any organization.

7. *It is action-oriented.* The focus of OD is on accomplishments and results. Unlike approaches to change that tend to describe how organizational change takes place, the emphasis of OD is on getting things done.

8. *It is based on sound theory and practice.* OD is not a gimmick or a fad. It is solidly based on the theory and research of a number of disciplines.[4]

Organizational development as a recognized process for managing change has a relatively short history. In the first readings article accompanying this chapter, Wendell French discusses the emergence and early history of the OD movement, which began in the 1940s. A significant influence identified by French was sensitivity training, a technique discussed later in this chapter.

A MODEL FOR MANAGING ORGANIZATIONAL DEVELOPMENT

Any organizational development effort must be designed systematically. This argues for an analytical approach that breaks the OD process into constituent steps, logically sequenced. For this purpose we propose the model shown in Figure 15–1. It identifies the key elements and decision points that managers can follow. A manager considers each of them, either explicitly or implicitly, to undertake an OD program.[5]

The model presumes that forces for change act continually on the organization. This assumption reflects the dynamic character of the modern world. At the same time, It Is the manager's responsibility to sort out the information that reflects the magnitude of change forces.[6] The information is the basis

---

[4] Newton Margulies and Anthony P. Raia, *Conceptual Foundations of Organizational Development* (New York: McGraw-Hill, 1978), p. 25.

[5] Equivalent models for managing organizational development are discussed in Eric L. Herzog, "Improving Productivity via Organizational Development," *Training and Development Journal,* April 1980, pp. 36–39; and Roland L. Warren, *Social Change and Human Purpose: Toward Understanding and Action* (Skokie, Ill.: Rand McNally, 1977).

[6] Sara Kiesler and Lee Sproull, "Managerial Response to Changing Environments: Perspectives on Problem Solving from Social Cognition," *Administrative Science Quarterly,* December 1982, pp. 548–70.

FIGURE 15–1

**A Model for the Management
of Organizational Development**

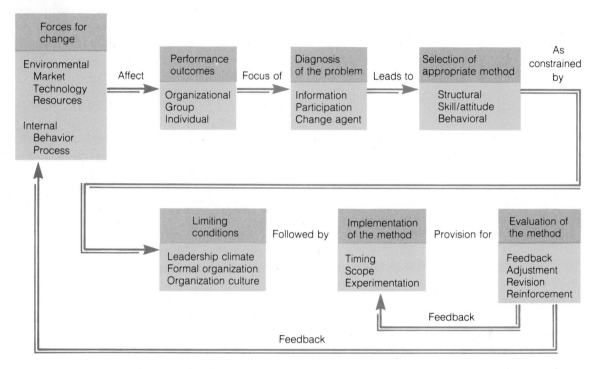

for recognizing when change is needed; it is equally desirable to recognize when change is not needed. Increasingly, however, change efforts are being utilized to solve an array of organizational problems.[7] Once managers recognize that something is malfunctioning, they must diagnose the problem and identify relevant alternative techniques. The selected technique must be appropriate to the problem, as constrained by certain limiting conditions. Finally, the manager must implement the change and monitor the change processes and results. The model includes feedback to the implementation step and to the forces-for-change step. It suggests no "final solution"; rather, it emphasizes that the manager operates in a dynamic setting wherein the only certainty is change itself.

FORCES FOR CHANGE

The forces for change can be classified conveniently into two groups. They are: (1) environmental forces and (2) internal forces. **Environmental forces** are beyond the control of management. Internal forces operate inside the firm and generally are within the control of management.

---

[7] Louis White and Kevin Wooten, "Ethical Dilemmas in Various Stages of Organizational Development," *Academy of Management Review,* October 1983, pp. 690–97.

ENVIRONMENTAL FORCES

The manager of a business firm historically has been concerned with reacting to changes in the *marketplace*. Competitors introduce new products, increase their advertising, reduce their prices, or increase their customer service. In each case, a response is required unless the manager is content to permit the erosion of profit and market share. At the same time, changes occur in customer tastes and incomes. The firm's products may no longer have customer appeal; customers may be able to purchase less expensive, higher-quality forms of the same products.

The second source of environmental change forces is *technology*. The knowledge explosion has introduced new technology for nearly every business function. Computers have made possible high-speed data processing and the solution to complex production problems. New machines and new processes have revolutionized the way in which many products are manufactured and distributed. Technological advance is a permanent fixture in the business world, and, as a force for change, it will continue to demand attention.

The third source of environmental change forces is *social* and *political* change. Business managers must be "tuned in" to the great movements over which they have no control but which, in time, influence their firm's fate. Sophisticated mass communications and international markets create great potential for business, but they also pose great threats to those managers who are unable to understand what is going on. Finally, the relationship between government and business becomes much closer as new regulations are imposed. These pressures for change reflect the increasing complexity and interdependence of modern living.

To cope effectively with external changes, an organization's boundary functions must be sensitive to these changes. These boundary functions must bridge the external environment with units of the organization.[8] *Boundary roles* such as marketing research, labor relations, personnel recruiting, purchasing, and some areas of finance must sense changes in the external environment and convey information on these changes to managers.

INTERNAL FORCES

Internal forces for change, which occur within the organization, usually can be traced to *process* and *behavioral* problems. The process problems include breakdowns in decision making and communications. Decisions are not being made, are made too late, or are of poor quality. Communications are short-circuited, redundant, or simply inadequate. Tasks are not undertaken or not completed because the person responsible did not "get the word." Because of inadequate or nonexistent communications, a customer order is not filled, a grievance is not processed, or an invoice is not filed and the supplier is not paid. Interpersonal and interdepartmental conflicts reflect breakdowns in organizational processes.

Low levels of morale and high levels of absenteeism and turnover are symptoms of behavioral problems that must be diagnosed. A wildcat strike

---

[8] For a recent related study, see David F. Caldwell and Charles A. O'Reilly III, "Boundary Spanning and Individual Performance: The Impact of Self-Monitoring," *Journal of Applied Psychology,* February 1982, pp. 124–27.

or a walkout may be the most tangible sign of a problem, yet such tactics usually are employed because they arouse management to action. A certain level of employee discontent exists in most organizations, and a great danger is to ignore employee complaints and suggestions. But the process of change includes the *recognition* phase, and it is at this point that management must decide to act or not to act.

DIAGNOSIS OF A PROBLEM

Appropriate action is necessarily preceded by diagnosis of the symptoms of the problem. Experience and judgment are critical to this phase unless the problem is readily apparent to all observers. Ordinarily, however, managers can disagree on the nature of the problem. There is no formula for accurate diagnosis, but the following questions point the manager in the right direction:

1. What is the problem as distinct from the symptoms of the problem?
2. What must be changed to resolve the problem?
3. What outcomes (objectives) are expected from the change, and how will those outcomes be measured?

The answers to these questions can come from information ordinarily found in the organization's information system. Or it may be necessary to generate ad hoc information through the creation of committees or task forces. Meetings between managers and employees provide a variety of viewpoints that can be sifted through by a smaller group. Technical operational problems may be easily diagnosed, but more subtle behavioral problems usually entail extensive analysis.

Managers must make two key decisions prior to undertaking the diagnostic phase. They must determine the degree to which subordinates will participate in the process, and they must decide whether a change agent will be used. These two decisions have implications not only for the diagnosed process but also for the eventual success of the entire program.

THE DEGREE OF SUBORDINATE PARTICIPATION

The degree to which subordinates participate in decisions that affect their activities has been the subject of much practical and theoretical discussion. Fayol, for example, spoke of the principle of centralization in terms of the extent to which subordinates contribute to decision making. The researchers at the Hawthorne plant discovered the positive impact of supervisory styles that permit employees some say in the way they do their work. In fact, the Hawthorne studies produced the first scientific evidence of the relationship between employee participation and production. Other studies followed, including the classic Coch and French[9] and Lewin[10] research, which provided evidence that participation by subordinates could lead to higher levels of

[9] Lester Coch and John R. P. French, Jr., "Overcoming Resistance to Change," *Human Relations,* August 1948, pp. 512–32.

[10] Kurt Lewin, "Frontiers in Group Dynamics," *Human Relations,* June 1947, pp. 5–41.

production, satisfaction, and efficiency. The article, ''Patterns of Organizational Change,'' by Larry Greiner, which is part of this chapter, discusses in some detail the issue of subordinate participation. Since this is such an important issue, however, we will briefly examine one aspect of it here: the extent of subordination participation.

The actual *degree* to which subordinates are actively involved in the development program is not simply an either-or decision. A continuum more aptly describes the decision, as shown in Figure 15–2. The figure identifies two extreme positions (unilateral and delegated) and a middle-of-the-road approach (shared) to change.[11]

FIGURE 15–2

Strategies for Introducing Major and/or Minor Changes

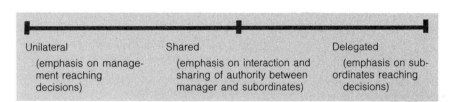

Unilateral

(emphasis on management reaching decisions)

Shared

(emphasis on interaction and sharing of authority between manager and subordinates)

Delegated

(emphasis on subordinates reaching decisions)

With the *unilateral approach,* subordinates make no contribution to the development, or change, program. The definition and solution to the problem are proposed by management. This may be accomplished by *decree,* a situation in which the superior dictates a program and subordinates are expected to accept it without question. A second unilateral approach is *replacement.* Here, certain personnel are replaced on the premise that key personnel are the crucial factors in developing the organization. Finally, the unilateral approach may focus on *structure,* wherein alterations are made to the organizational structure by administrative fiat.

At the other extreme from the unilateral approach is the *delegated approach.* In this approach, the subordinates actively participate in the development program, in one of two forms.[12] In a *discussion group,* managers and their subordinates meet, discuss the problem, and identify the appropriate development method, with the managers being very careful not to impose their own solution on the group. In the *T-group* form, the emphasis is on increasing the individual's self-awareness. The T-group is less structured than the discussion group. In this context, it is used to initiate the development program and is not the central focus. For example, the T group could identify MBO as the development method to be implemented.

The *delegated approach* focuses on having the subordinates interact with the superior and eventually work out a development approach. If used correctly, the delegated approach is a major step in creating a climate of full subordinate participation.

Finally, the *shared approach* is built on the assumption that authority is present in the organization and must be exercised after, and only after,

---

[11] Larry E. Greiner, ''Patterns of Organizational Change,'' *Harvard Business Review,* May-June 1967, pp. 119–30.

[12] Ibid., pp. 121–22.

giving careful consideration to such matters as the magnitude of the development effort, the people involved, and the time available for introducing the method. This approach also focuses on the sharing of authority to make decisions. It is employed in two slightly different formats:

1. *Group decision making.* The problem is defined by management and communicated to the subordinates. The subordinates are then free to develop alternative solutions and to select what they believe is the best method to be implemented. It is assumed that the subordinates will feel a greater commitment to the solution selected because they participated in its selection.
2. *Group problem solving.* This form stresses both the definition of the problem and the selection of a possible solution. Here, authority is shared throughout the process, from problem identification to problem solution. It is assumed that because the group is involved in the entire decision process, it will have increased insight into the development program that is finally implemented.

A survey of published cases of organizational change notes that the shared approach was relatively more successful than the unilateral or delegated approaches.[13]

THE ROLE OF CHANGE AGENTS

Because there is a tendency to seek answers in traditional solutions, the intervention of an outsider usually is necessary. The intervener, or **change agent,** brings a different perspective to the situation and serves as a challenge to the status quo.

The success of any change program rests heavily on the quality and workability of the relationship between the change agent and the key decision makers within the organization. Thus, the form of intervention is a crucial phase.

To intervene is to enter into an ongoing organization, or among persons, or between departments, for the purpose of helping them improve their effectiveness.[14] A number of forms of intervention are used in organizations. First, there is the *external* change agent who is asked to intervene and provide recommendations for bringing about change. Second, there is the *internal* change agent. This is an individual who is working for the organization and knows something about its problems. Finally, a number of organizations have used a combination *external-internal* change team to intervene and develop programs. This approach attempts to use the resources and knowledge base of both external and internal change agents.

Each of the three forms of intervention has advantages and disadvantages. The external change agent is often viewed as an outsider. When this belief

[13] Ibid., pp. 119–30.

[14] Wendell L. French and Cecil H. Bell Jr., *Organizational Development: Behavioral Science Interventions for Organizational Improvement* (Englewood Cliffs, N.J.: Prentice-Hall, 1984).

is held by employees inside the company, there is a need to establish rapport between the change agent and decision makers. The change agent's views on the problems faced by the organization often are different from the decision maker's views, and this leads to problems in establishing rapport. The differences in viewpoints often result in a mistrust of the external change agent by the policymakers or a segment of the policymakers.

The internal change agent often is viewed as being more closely associated with one unit or group of individuals than with any other. This perceived favoritism leads to resistance to change by those who are not included in the internal change agent's circle of close friends. The internal change agent, however, is familiar with the organization and its personnel, and this knowledge can be valuable in preparing for and implementing change.[15]

The third type of intervention, the combination external-internal team, is the rarest, but it seems to have an excellent chance for success. In this type of intervention, the outsider's objectivity and professional knowledge are blended with the insider's knowledge of the organization and its human resources. This blending of knowledge often results in increased trust and confidence among the parties involved. The ability of the combination external-internal team to communicate and develop a more positive rapport can reduce the resistance to any change that is forthcoming.

Regardless of the form of intervention, the role of the change agent is critical. Change agents facilitate the diagnostic phase by gathering, interpreting, and presenting data. If the diagnostic part of the process is faulty, the remainder of the OD process is significantly flawed.

ALTERNATIVE DEVELOPMENT TECHNIQUES

The choice of a particular development technique depends on the nature of the problem that management has diagnosed. Management must determine which alternative is most likely to produce the desired outcome, whether it involves improvement in skills, attitudes, behavior, or structure. As we have noted, diagnosis of the problem includes specification of the outcome that management desires from the change. Later in the chapter, we describe a number of change techniques, some of which have been discussed in previous chapters. These techniques are classified according to whether their major focus is to change skills, attitudes, behavior, or structure. This classification of techniques for organizational change in no way implies a distinct division among the areas of change. On the contrary, the interrelationships among skills, attitudes, behavior, and structure must be acknowledged and anticipated.

---

[15] Jerome Adams and John J. Sherwood, "An Evaluation of Organizational Effectiveness: An Appraisal of How Army Internal Consultants Use Survey Feedback in a Military Setting," *Group and Organization Studies*, June 1979, pp. 170–82.

RECOGNITION OF LIMITING CONDITIONS

The selection of any developmental technique should be based on diagnosis of the problem, but the choice is tempered by certain conditions that exist at the time. Scholars identify three sources of influence on the outcome of management development programs, and these can be generalized to cover the entire range of organizational development efforts, whether attitudinal, behavioral, or structural. The three sources are leadership climate, formal organization, and organizational culture.

Leadership climate refers to the nature of the work environment that results from "the leadership style and administrative practices" of superiors. Any OD program that does not have the support and commitment of management has only a slim chance of success. The **formal organization** must be compatible with the proposed change. The formal organization includes the philosophy and policies of top management, as well as legal precedent, organizational structure, and the systems of control. Finally, the **organizational culture** refers to the impact on the environment resulting from group norms, values, and informal activities. A proposed change in work methods, for example, can run counter to the expectations and attitudes of the work group, and if such is the case, the OD strategy must anticipate the resulting resistance.

Implementation of OD that does not consider the constraints imposed by prevailing conditions within the organizations may, of course, amplify the problem that triggered the developmental process. If OD is implemented in this way, the potential for subsequent problems is greater than ordinarily would be expected. Taken together, the prevailing conditions constitute the climate for change, and they can be positive or negative.

IMPLEMENTING THE METHOD

The implementation of the OD method has two dimensions—**timing** and **scope.** Timing refers to the selection of the appropriate time at which to initiate the method, and scope refers to the selection of the appropriate scale. The matter of timing depends on a number of factors, particularly the organization's operating cycle and the groundwork that has preceded the OD program. Certainly, if a program is of considerable magnitude, it is desirable that it not compete with day-to-day operations; thus, the change might well be implemented during a slack period. On the other hand, if the program is critical to the survival of the organization, then immediate implementation is in order. The scope of the program depends on the strategy. The program may be implemented throughout the organization. Or it may be phased into the organization level by level or department by department. The shared strategy makes use of a phased approach, which limits the scope but provides feedback for each subsequent implementation.

The method that finally is selected usually is not implemented on a grand scale; rather, it is implemented on a small scale in various units throughout the organization. Not even the most detailed planning can anticipate all the consequences of implementing a particular method. Thus, it may be necessary to experiment and to search for new information that can bear on the program.

EVALUATING THE PROGRAM

An OD program represents an expenditure of organizational resources in exchange for some desired result. The resources take the form of money and time that have alternative uses. The result is in the form of increased organizational effectiveness—production, efficiency, and satisfaction in the short run; adaptiveness and development in the intermediate run; survival in the long run. Accordingly, some provision must be made to evaluate the program in terms of expenditures and results.[16]

Generally, an evaluation would follow the steps of evaluative research. The steps include:

1. Determining the objectives of the program.
2. Describing the activities undertaken to achieve the objectives.
3. Measuring the effects of the program.
4. Establishing baseline points against which changes can be compared.
5. Controlling extraneous factors, preferably through the use of a control group.
6. Detecting unanticipated consequences.

The application of this model will not always be possible. For example, managers do not always specify objectives in precise terms, and control groups are difficult to establish in some instances. Nevertheless, the difficulties of evaluation should not discourage attempts to evaluate.[17]

ORGANIZATIONAL CHANGE AND DEVELOPMENT METHODS

As noted previously, effective organizational change and development requires the active involvement of managers. Managers have a variety of change and development methods to select from, depending on the objectives they hope to accomplish. One way of viewing objectives is from the perspective of the *depth* of the intended change.

Depth of intended change refers to the scope and intensity of the change efforts. A useful distinction here is between the *formal* and *informal* aspects

---

[16] W. M. Vicars and D. D. Hartke, "Evaluating OD Evaluations: A Status Report," *Group and Organizational Studies*, 1982, pp. 402–17.

[17] Wendell French, "A Checklist for Organizing and Implementing an OD Effort," in *Organization Development: Theory, Practice, Research*, ed. W. L. French, C. H. Bell Jr., and R. A. Zawacki (Plano, Tex.: Business Publications, 1983), pp. 451–59; and Richard Woodman and Sandy Wayne, "An Investigation of Positive-Findings Bias in Evaluation of Organization Development Interventions," *Academy of Management Journal*, December 1985, pp. 889–913.

of organizations. Formal organizational components are observable, rational, and oriented toward structural factors. The informal components are not observable to all people; they are affective, and oriented to process and behavioral factors. Generally speaking, as one moves from formal aspects of the organization to informal aspects, the scope and intensity increase. As scope and intensity increase, so does the depth of the change.

The relationship between source of the problem and degree of intended change is illustrated in Figure 15–3; it suggests that there are 10 levels, or targets, of an OD program. As the target moves from left to right and, consequently, deeper into the organization, the OD program becomes more person- and group-centered. It will rely more on sociopsychological knowledge and less on technical-economic knowledge. Levels I through IV involve formal components, including structure, policies, and practices of the organization. Levels V and VI involve both formal and informal components, including skills and attitudes of managerial and nonmanagerial personnel. Levels VII through X involve informal components, including the behavior of groups and individuals. For each of these levels, one or more OD *methods* can be possible solutions. These methods are the focus of the remaining discussion.

STRUCTURAL DEVELOPMENT METHODS

Structural development in the context of organizational change refers to managerial action that attempts to improve effectiveness through a change in the formal structure of task and authority relationships. The organizational structure creates the bases for relatively stable human and social relationships. These relationships can, in time, become irrelevant for organizational effectiveness. For example, the jobs that people do may become obsolete, and thus irrelevant. But to change the jobs also changes the relationships among the employees. Members of the organization may resist efforts to disrupt these relationships.

Structural changes affect some aspects of the formal task and authority definitions. As you have seen, the design of an organization involves the definition and specification of job range and depth, the grouping of jobs in departments, the determination of the size of the groups reporting to a single manager, and the delegation of authority. Two methods designed to change all or some aspect of the organizational structure are management by objectives (MBO) and System 4. These methods are appropriate when the problem is diagnosed as being Levels I through IV.

MANAGEMENT BY OBJECTIVES

Management by objectives encourages managers to participate in the establishment of objectives for themselves and their units.[18] The process also can include the participation of nonmanagers in the determination of

---

[18] Original statements of MBO may be found in Peter Drucker, *The Practice of Management* (New York: Harper & Row, 1954); George Odiorne, *Management by Objectives* (New York: Pitman Publishing, 1965); and W. J. Reddin, *Effective Management by Objectives* (New York: McGraw-Hill, 1970).

FIGURE 15–3

Model of Organizational Development Targets

STRUCTURAL TARGETS				BEHAVIORAL TARGETS					
Level I	Level II	Level III	Level IV	Level V	Level VI	Level VII	Level VIII	Level IX	Level X
Organizational structure	Operating policies and practices	Personnel policies and practices	Job performance appraisal and improvement	Management attitudes and skills	Non-management attitudes and skills	Intergroup behavior	Intragroup behavior	Individual behavior	Individual-group behavior

LOW ←———————— Depth of intended change ————————→ HIGH

Adapted from Richard J. Selfridge and Stanley L. Sokolik, "A Comprehensive View of Organizational Development," *MSU Business Topics*, Winter 1975. p. 49.

their specific objectives. Successful use of MBO depends on the ability of participants to define their objectives in terms of their contribution to the total organization and to be able to accomplish them.

The original work of Drucker[19] and subsequent writings by others[20] provide the basis for three guidelines for implementing MBO:

1. Superiors and subordinates meet and discuss objectives that contribute to overall goals.
2. Superiors and subordinates jointly establish attainable objectives for the subordinates.
3. Superior and subordinates meet at a predetermined later date to evaluate the subordinates' progress toward the objectives.

The exact procedures employed in implementing MBO vary from organization to organization and from unit to unit. However, the basic elements of objective setting, participation of subordinates in objective setting, and feedback and evaluation usually are parts of any MBO program. The intended consequences of MBO include improved contribution to the organization, improved attitudes and satisfaction of participants, and greater role clarity. MBO is highly developed and widely used in business, health care, and governmental organizations.

SYSTEM 4 ORGANIZATION

System 4 organization is an important application of the organic organizational design. Moreover, according to Likert, System 4 is an "ideal type" of organization for achieving high levels of performance and any deviation from the ideal (System 4) represents reduced levels of performance. Thus, managers should develop their organizations toward System 4 characteristics. According to Likert, an organization can be described in terms of eight characteristics.[21] They are:

1. Leadership.
2. Motivation.
3. Communication.
4. Interaction.

5. Decision making.
6. Goal setting.
7. Control.
8. Performance.

Furthermore, each of these characteristics can be measured through the use of a questionnaire, which members of the organization (usually managers)

---

[19] See Ronald G. Greenwood, "Management by Objectives: As Developed by Peter Drucker, Assisted by Harold Smiddy," *Academy of Management Review,* April 1981, pp. 225–30.

[20] For discussions of applications of MBO in a variety of settings, see *First Tango in Boston: A Seminar on Organizational Change and Development* (Washington, D.C.: National Training and Development Services, 1973); "Management by Objectives in the Federal Government," *Bureaucrat,* Winter 1974; Kevin W. Mossholder and H. Dudley Dewhirst, "The Appropriateness of Management-by-Objectives for Development and Research Personnel," *Journal of Management,* Fall 1980, pp. 145–56; and David E. Terpstra, Philip D. Olson, and Brad Lockeman, "The Effects of MBO on Levels of Performance and Satisfaction among University Faculty," *Group and Organizational Studies,* September 1982, pp. 253–66.

[21] Rensis Likert, *The Human Organization* (New York: McGraw-Hill, 1967).

complete. The 51-item questionnaire devised by Likert asks respondents to indicate their perceptions or the extent to which the characteristics that define the System 4 organization are present in their own organization. Subsequent training programs emphasize the concepts of System 4 and the application of the concepts to the present organization. According to Likert, higher performance ordinarily should result through the use of: (1) supportive, group-oriented leadership; and (2) equalization of authority to set goals, implement control, and make decisions. The improved performance derives from positive changes in employee attitudes that are induced by the changes in organizational structure.[22]

SKILL AND ATTITUDE DEVELOPMENT METHODS

The most widely used methods for developing employee productivity are training programs.[23] These programs are designed to improve participants' knowledge, skills, and attitudes toward their jobs and the organization. The training may be part of a larger effort such as MBO or System 4 programs, or it may be directed toward specific objectives. In the usual case, managerial training is directed toward the development of communication and decision-making skills, thus improving the organization's fundamental processes.

Because of the multiplicity of training programs, we will briefly describe only a very few of the more representative and widely publicized types in this section. One way of characterizing these various programs is by their *site.* That is, some programs take place at the job site (on-the-job training), while others are deliberately situated away from the work environment (off-the-job training). Advantages and disadvantages of each will be identified.

On-the-Job Training. A popular philosophy over the years has been to train employees on the job. It is assumed that if training occurs off the job, there will be a loss in performance when the trainees are transferred back to the job. It is also proposed that on-the-job training is best from an economic standpoint, since employees are producing while they undergo training.

Corning Glass Works has an extensive on-the-job training program. It begins with an assessment of the needs for training as identified by department heads. The training unit then matches the identified training needs with classroom instruction. The classroom instructor moves to the workplace, where the classroom instruction is reinforced by actual on-the-job application. As employees master each job requirement, they receive credits that become part of their performance evaluation.[24]

---

[22] Heinz Weihrich and Andre-Sean Rigny, ''Toward System-4 through Transactional Analysis,'' *Journal of Systems Management,* July 1980, pp. 67–80.

[23] Stephen R. Michael, ''Organizational Change Techniques: Their Present, Their Future,'' *Organizational Dynamics,* Summer 1982, pp. 67–80.

[24] John G. Dickey, ''Training with a Focus on the Individual,'' *Personnel Administrator,* June 1982, pp. 37–38.

On-the-job training has a number of shortcomings. First, employees may be placed in a stress-laden situation even before learning the job. This may result in accidents or poor initial attitudes about the job. Second, the areas in which employees are being trained often are congested. Finally, if a number of trainees are learning in various job locations, the trainer must move around constantly to monitor their performance.

Two specific types of on-the-job training are job-instruction training and junior executive boards. Formulated during World War II by the War Manpower Board, *job-instruction training* provides a set of guidelines for undertaking on-the-job training for white- and blue-collar employees. After trainees are introduced to the job, they receive a step-by-step review and demonstration of the job functions. When trainees are sufficiently confident that they understand the job, they demonstrate their ability to perform the job. This demonstration continues until the trainees reach a satisfactory level of performance. The objective of this approach is to bring about a positive change in performance that is reflected in high production, lower scrap costs, and so on.

Junior executive boards is a technique popularized by the McCormick Company. It concentrates on providing junior-level (middle- and lower-level) managers with top-level management problem-solving experience. The junior executive may serve on a committee or junior board that is considering some major decision concerning investments or personnel planning. The assumption in this type of training is that the trainee will acquire an appreciation for the decisions being made "upstairs" and that this can be translated into a better overall view of the organization's direction and difficulties. In addition, the ability of the junior executive to contribute to problem solving can be assessed.

Off-the-Job Training.   Traditionally, organizations have found it necessary to provide training that supplements on-the-job efforts. Some of the advantages of off-the-job training are:

1. It lets executives get away from the pressures of the job and work in a climate in which "party line" thinking is discouraged and self-analysis is stimulated.
2. It presents a challenge to executives that, in general, enhances their motivation to develop themselves.
3. It provides resource people and resource material—faculty members, fellow executives, and literature—that contribute suggestions and ideas for the executives to "try on for size" as they attempt to change, develop, and grow.

The theme of the advantages cited above is that trainees are more stimulated to learn by being away from job pressures. This is certainly debatable since it is questionable whether much of what is learned can be transferred back to the job. Attending a case problem-solving program in San Diego is quite different from facing irate customers in Detroit.

However, despite the difficulty of transferring knowledge from the classroom-type environment to the office, plant, or hospital, off-the-job training programs are still very popular and widely utilized. This can be seen from the wide variety of program topics offered. The following OBM Encounter provides some examples.

A MULTITUDE OF TRAINING PROGRAMS

Employee training programs are a multimillion-dollar industry. Aside from "in-house" programs where the training is developed by and for a particular company, thousands of training program sessions are held every year, open to employees of any organization who wish to attend—and, of course, pay the fee. Listed below are several examples of the many programs available.

The Dynamics of Personal and Organizational
   Growth
Improving Employee Relations
Effective Team Building
Assertiveness for Career Success
How to Motivate for Superior Performance
Helping Communicators Communicate
Managing Management Time

Dealing with Job Stress
Winning with Leadership Skills
Managing Behavior Change
Making Unions Unnecessary
Preparing for Tomorrow's Managerial
   Challenges
Supervising Women
Creative Problem Solving
How to Achieve Success in the New Job
What Managers Should Know about
   Behavioral Science
Effective Delegation
How to Make Better Decisions
Managing the Unsatisfactory Performer
Changing Employee Behavior
How Successful Managers Manage
What Managers Do

Two popular off-the-job training techniques are the discussion or conference approach and the case study and role-playing method. The *discussion or conference approach* provides the participants with opportunities to exchange ideas and recollections of experiences. Through the interaction in the sessions, the participants stimulate one another's thinking, broaden their outlook, and improve their communicative abilities. Because of the interaction between trainer and participants in this approach, the trainer must be highly skilled and must understand the importance of reinforcing positive behavior and feeding back clearly the contribution of each participant to the group discussion.

The *case study and role-playing method* provides trainees with a description of some events that actually occurred in an organization. The case may describe the manner in which a nursing supervisor tried to motivate subordinates or the type of wage and salary program that was implemented in a retail store. Trainees read the case, identify the problems, and reach solutions.

In role playing, trainees are asked to participate actively in the case study. That is, they act out a case as if it were a play. This form of learning is an application of experiential learning that is based on the concept of learning by doing.[25] One participant may be the supervisor, and three other participants may play the role of subordinates. The rationale is that role playing enables the participants to actually "feel" what the cases are all about.

BEHAVIORAL DEVELOPMENT METHODS

Levels VII through X require methods that delve deeply into group and individual behavior processes. Intergroup, intragroup, individual-group, and individual behavior often involve emotional and perceptual processes that interfere with effective organizational functioning. These development targets have received the greatest amount of attention from OD experts, and a considerable number of methods therefore have been devised for attacking them. Instead of cataloging all these methods, we will discuss only three of them: sensitivity training, the managerial grid, and team building.

Sensitivity Training.   This highly publicized development method focuses on individual and individual-group problems.[26] "Sensitivity" in this context means sensitivity to self and to self-other relationships. An assumption of sensitivity training is that the causes of poor task performance are the emotional problems of the people who must collectively achieve the goal. Consequently, eliminating these problems removes a major impediment to task performance. Sensitivity training stresses the *process* rather than the *content* of training and focuses on *emotional* rather than *conceptual* training. Thus, this form of training is quite different from traditional forms of training that emphasize the acquisition of a predetermined set of concepts with immediate application to the workplace.

The process of sensitivity training includes a group (a T-group) that in most cases meets at some place away from the job. The group, under the direction of a trainer, can engage in a group dialogue that has no agenda and no focus. The objective is to provide an environment that produces its own learning experiences.[27] As group members engage in the dialogue, they are encouraged to learn about themselves as they deal with others. They explore their needs and their attitudes as revealed through their behavior toward others in the group and through the behavior of others in the group toward them.

On balance, the scientific research to date has not been particularly supportive of sensitivity training as an effective organizational development method. Its popularity among managers has declined appreciably during recent years. This, in turn, has led to the development of a number of variations to the

---

[25] P. Jervis, "Analysing Decision Behavior: Learning Models and Learning Styles as Diagnostic Aids," *Personnel Review,* 1983, pp. 26–38.

[26] Kenneth N. Wexley and Gary P. Latham, *Developing and Training Human Resources in Organizations* (Glenview, Ill.: Scott, Foresman, 1981), p. 184.

[27] Elliot Aronson, "Communication in Sensitivity Training Groups," in *Organization Development,* ed. Wendell L. French, Cecil H. Bell Jr., and Robert A. Zawacki (Plano, Tex.: Business Publications, 1983), pp. 249–53.

basic approach which tend to delve less deeply into the non-work-related feelings and sentiments of the participants and instead focus only on task-relevant behavior. The variations have yet to be well evaluated.

The Managerial Grid. This OD approach is based on a theory of leadership behavior.[28] The two dimensions of leadership that the developers of the program, Blake and Mouton, identify are *concern for production* and *concern for people.* A balanced concern for production and people is the most effective leadership style, according to Blake and Mouton. The managerial grid program requires not only the development of this style *but also the development of group behavior that supports and sustains it.* The entire program consists of six sequential phases that are undertaken over a three-to-five-year period.

The six phases can be separated into two major segments. The first two phases provide the foundation for the four later phases.

1. *Laboratory-seminar training.* This is typically a one-week conference designed to introduce managers to the grid philosophy and objectives. During this period, each participant's leadership style is assessed and reviewed.
2. *Intragroup development.* In this phase, superiors and their immediate subordinates explore their managerial styles and operating practices as a group. Together with Phase I, the objective is to familiarize participants with grid concepts, improve relationships between individuals and groups, and increase managers' problem-solving capacities.
3. *Intergroup development.* This phase involves group-to-group working relationships and focuses on building effective group roles and norms that improve intergroup relationships.
4. *Organizational goal setting.* The immediate objective of this phase is to set up a model of an effective organization for the future.
5. *Goal attainment.* This phase uses some of the group and educational procedures that were used in Phase I, but the concern is on the total organization. Problems are defined and groups move toward problem solution using grid concepts and philosophy.
6. *Stabilization.* This final phase focuses on stabilizing the changes brought about in prior phases. This phase also enables management to evaluate the total program.

The longevity of the managerial grid method suggests that it is more than a fad to practicing managers. Thus, it would appear that more rigorous studies of what it can and cannot accomplish are required. Only by properly studying this approach can those interested in implementing it as a developmental method generally understand how it can change employee behavior.

Team Building. The managerial grid approach develops a group process to support and sustain a particular leadership style. It is not necessary, however,

---

[28] Robert R. Blake and Jane S. Mouton, *The Versatile Manager* (Homewood, Ill.: Richard D. Irwin, 1982).

to develop group behavior around any one leadership style. Rather, group processes can develop to perform more effectively through *team building.*[29] Whereas the managerial grid is a comprehensive technique, the focus of team building is the work group.

The purpose of team building is to enable work groups to get their work done more effectively, to improve their performance.[30] The work groups may be existing, or relatively new, command and task groups. The specific aims of the intervention include setting goals and priorities, analyzing the ways the group does its work, examining the group's norms and processes for communicating and decision making, and examining the interpersonal relationships within the group. As each of these aims is undertaken, the group is placed in the position of having to recognize explicitly the contributions, positive and negative, of each group member.[31]

The process by which these aims is achieved begins with *diagnostic* meetings. Often lasting an entire day, the meetings enable each group member to share with other members his or her perceptions of problems. Subsequently, a *plan of action* must be agreed on. The action plan should call on each of the group members, individually or as part of a subgroup, to undertake a specific action to alleviate one or more of the problems.

Team building is also effective when new groups are being formed. Problems often exist when new organizational units, project teams, or task forces are created. Typically, such groups have certain characteristics that must be overcome if the groups are to perform effectively. For example:

1. Confusion exists as to roles and relationships.
2. Members have a fairly clear understanding of short-term goals.
3. Group members have technical competence that puts them on the team.
4. Members often pay more attention to the tasks of the team than to the relationships among the team members.

To combat these tendencies, the new group could schedule team building meetings during the first few weeks of its life.

Sometimes team building efforts may not include an explicit diagnostic phase, but focus instead on simply attempting to improve the extent to which individuals function as part of an overall team effort. The following OBM Encounter illustrates an example of this.

---

[29] S. Jay Liebowitz and Kenneth P. de Meuse, "The Application of Team Building," *Human Relations,* January 1982, pp. 1–18.

[30] Richard W. Woodman and John J. Sherwood, "Effects of Team Development Intervention: A Field Experiment," *Journal of Applied Behavioral Science,* April-June 1980, pp. 211–17; and R. Wayne Boss, "Organizational Development in the Health Care Field: A Confrontational Team-Building Design," *Journal of Health and Human Resources Administration,* Summer 1983, pp. 72–91.

[31] Richard L. Hughes, William E. Rosenbach, and William H. Clover, "Team Development in an Intact, Ongoing Work Group," *Group and Organizational Studies,* June 1983, pp. 161–81.

FORD MOTOR EXECUTIVES STUDY TEAMWORK

You would think Ford's top-ranking executives know more about the automobile industry than anything else. So why has Ford begun to call them into headquarters from all over the world for instruction in, among other things, the current auto business environment?

Sure, they know their jobs. But do they know how to function as part of a well-oiled, cohesive, international Ford executive team? Ford didn't noticeably worry about such things in the past. But in a new age of fierce international competition, the company doesn't want to take team morale of its top management for granted. Ford, like GM and Chrysler, had a variety of training programs for executives. Most, however, were geared toward improving technical skills. There was little team building.

Says Nancy Badore, psychologist and program development director: "We had begun to realize over the last couple of years that it is important for the executive, as well as the manager and supervisor, to think through what their role is in the company, and to think through what the challenges are coming up, and to really have a forum to allow that to be done."

The team building course for executives is not significantly different in its intent from courses offered to assembly line workers. Increasingly, with more fierce competition and emphasis on quality, workers at all levels at Ford, GM, and Chrysler are receiving training focusing on attitudes and the need for teamwork. ☐

Source: Adapted from James V. Higgins, "Ford Execs Taking Courses, in Teamwork," *Houston Chronicle,* December 17, 1985, Sec. 3, p. 8.

Although the reports of team building indicate mixed results, the evidence suggests that group processes improve through team building efforts.[32] This record of success accounts for the increasing use of team building as an OD method.[33]

MULTIMETHOD OD PROGRAMS

In the previous sections, we have reviewed the characteristics of a number of organizational development methods. The success of OD efforts depends in part on matching the method and the depth of intervention. Thus, a manager should be wary of the claims of proponents for all-purpose methods. Each method, whether System 4, MBO, or sensitivity training, has a primary focus, or target, of change. Managers will be disappointed if they expect changes in targets that are not affected by the method. If the change required is broad-based, involving several targets, or depths of intervention, then the OD program must incorporate more than one method.

A recent review of the record of OD interventions in bringing about change concluded that multimethod approaches had had better success than single-method ones.[34] Nichols compared the effects of sensitivity training, team

[32] Kenneth P. de Meuse and S. Jay Liebowitz, "An Empirical Analysis of Team-Building Research," *Group and Organizational Studies,* September 1981, pp. 357–58.

[33] W. J. Heisler, "Patterns of OD in Practice," in *Organization Development,* ed. Daniel Robey and Steven Altman (New York: Macmillan, 1982), pp. 23–29.

[34] John M. Nicholas, "The Comparative Impact of Organization Development Interventions on Hard Criteria Measures," *Academy of Management Review,* October 1982, pp. 531–42.

building, job enrichment, and job redesign and concluded that no one method was successful in all instances (an expected conclusion, given what we have said above). But he also found that significant changes occurred when several methods were combined. One such combination includes three discrete steps that involve all levels of the organization. The three steps are: (1) all employees participate in goal-setting, decision-making, and job redesign; (2) employee collaboration is developed through team building; and (3) the organizational structure is reorganized to accommodate the new levels of participation and collaboration. The application of these three steps can go a long way toward meeting some of the arguments against specific OD methods. The overriding managerial concern is transfer of learning to the work environment. Only under these circumstances can OD methods be considered effective.

Effective organizational development requires accurate diagnosis of problems, the selection of appropriate targets for change, and the application of appropriate, usually multiple, OD methods. The valued outcome of OD is an organization whose separate parts are directed toward common purposes. Integrated, multimethod OD programs are promising means for achieving that outcome.[35]

SUMMARY OF KEYPOINTS

A. The need to consider organizational development arises from changes in the inter- and extraorganizational environment. Changes in input, output, technological, and scientific subenvironments may indicate the need to consider the feasibility of a long-term, systematically managed program for changing the structure, process, and behavior of the organization. Even in the absence of environmental changes, organizational processes and behavior may become dysfunctional for achieving organizational effectiveness.

B. In addition to serving as the bases for problem identification, the diagnostic data also establish the basis for subsequent evaluation of the organizational development effort.

C. The problem must be diagnosed, and managers can undertake the analysis by considering these questions:

1. What is the problem as distinct from its symptoms?
2. What must be changed to resolve the problem?
3. What outcomes are expected, and how will these outcomes be measured?

The managerial response to these questions should be stated in terms of criteria that reflect organizational effectiveness. Measurable outcomes such as production, efficiency, satisfaction, adaptiveness, and development must be linked to skill, attitudinal, behavioral, and structural changes that are necessitated by the problem identification.

D. The last step of the OD process is the decision to provide for an evaluation procedure. The ideal situation would be to structure the procedure in the manner of an experimental design. That is, the end results should be operationally defined and measurements should be taken, before and after, in both the organization undergoing development and in a second organization (the "control group"). Or, if the scope of the program is limited to a subunit, a second subunit could serve as a control group. The purpose of an evaluation is not only to enable management to account for its use of resources but also to provide feedback. Corrections can be taken in the implementation phase based on this feedback.

E. Analysis of the problem, identification of alternatives, and recognition of constraints lead to the selection of the most promising method and strategy. The selection is based on the principle of maximizing expected returns to the organization.

F. Although there is, by nature, considerable overlap among the levels for which a particular method is

[35] Mark Mendenhall and Gary Oddou, "The Integrative Approach to OD: McGregor Revisited," *Group and Organizational Studies*, September 1983, pp. 291–302.

appropriate, each has a primary focus. One would not expect, for example, that MBO will be effective in changing behaviors at level X, although it may have some effect on behaviors at levels VII and VIII.

G. The number of OD methods is considerable and is constantly increasing. Only a few of the more widely used ones have been discussed. Managers considering the possibility of OD should consult a more detailed description of them. Several such descriptions appear in the citations and additional references of this chapter.

REVIEW AND DISCUSSION QUESTIONS

1. Organizational development represents *planned* change. How might the fact that it is planned, as opposed to unplanned or spontaneous, affect people's receptivity to it?

2. Can you think of a time when you had to change your behavior in some way? What were your feelings about making such a change?

3. Contrast the degree of subordinate participation in unilateral, delegated, and shared approaches to change. Which would you prefer as a subordinate? As a manager?

4. What are some of the advantages and disadvantages to being a change agent? Is that a role you would like to play?

5. It is often said that "the more things change, the more they stay the same." What does this mean in the context of organizational development?

6. Do you think organizations might differ in their receptivity to organizational development efforts as a function of being in different industries? Explain.

7. Discuss the relationship between the degree of intended change and the type of organizational development method used.

8. Of the various change methods discussed in this chapter, which single one would you apply to the college you are attending to make it a better organization? Explain why and what you would hope to accomplish.

9. "Change must be introduced very carefully, because you can never go back to the way things were before you made the change." What does this statement mean? What implications does it have for organizational development?

10. Why is it important to evaluate change efforts, and why is the evaluation so difficult to do?

R1 THE EMERGENCE AND EARLY HISTORY OF ORGANIZATION DEVELOPMENT

WENDELL L. FRENCH

Systematic organization development activities have a recent history and, to use the analogy of a mangrove tree, have at least three important trunk stems. One trunk

Source: From Wendell L. French, "The Emergence and Early History of Organization Development: With Reference to Influences on and Interaction among Some of the Key Actors," GROUP AND ORGANIZATION STUDIES, September, 1982, pp. 261–278.

stem of OD consists of innovations in the application of laboratory training insights to complex organizations. A second major stem is survey research and feedback methodology. Both are intertwined with a third stem, the emergence of action research. Paralleling these stems, and to some extent linked, was the emergence of the Tavistock sociotechnical and socioclinical approaches. The key actors focused upon in this account interacted with each other and were influenced by experiences and concepts from many fields, as we will see.

This account attempts to capture some—certainly not all—of the major highlights in the history of OD up until about 1960, with a few references to events in the early and mid-1960s. A more exhaustive and lengthy history would focus on additional persons, institutions, and conceptual roots of that early period, and on a number of practitioners, theorists, and researchers whose seminal contributions were conspicuous in the 1960s, 1970s, and early 1980s.

THE LABORATORY TRAINING STEM

The T-Group

One stem of OD, laboratory training, essentially consisting of unstructured small-group situations in which participants learn from their own interactions and the evolving dynamics of the group, began to develop about 1946 from various experiments in the use of discussion groups to achieve changes in behavior in back-home situations. In particular, an Inter-Group Relations workshop held at the State Teachers College in New Britain, Connecticut, in the summer of 1946 was important in the emergence of laboratory training. This workshop was sponsored by the Connecticut Interracial Commission and the Research Center for Group Dynamics, then at MIT.

The Research Center for Group Dynamics (RCGD) had been founded in 1945 under the direction of Kurt Lewin, a prolific theorist, researcher, and practitioner in interpersonal, group, intergroup, and community relationships. Lewin had been recruited by MIT largely through the efforts of Douglas McGregor of the Sloan School of Management there. Lewin's original staff included Marian Radke, Leon Festinger, Ronald Lippitt, and Dorwin Cartwright (Benne, Bradford, Gibb, & Lippitt, 1975, pp. 1–6; Marrow, 1969, pp. 210–214). Lewin's field theory and his conceptualizing about group dynamics, change processes, and action research were of profound influence on the people who were associated with the various stems of OD.

The staff for the New Britain Workshop of 1946 consisted of Kurt Lewin, Kenneth Benne, Leland Bradford, and Ronald Lippitt. Feedback at the end of each day

to groups, group leaders, and members about their individual and group behavior stimulated great interest and appeared to produce more insight and learning than did lectures and seminars. From this experience emerged the "National Training Laboratory in Group Development," which was organized by Benne, Bradford, and Lippitt (Lewin died in early 1947), and which held a three-week session during the summer of 1947 at the Gould Academy in Bethel, Maine. The work of that summer was to evolve into the National Training Laboratory, later called the NTL Institute for Applied Behavioral Science, and into contemporary T-group training (Benne et al., 1975, pp. 1–6; Narrow, 1969, pp. 210–214). Out of the Bethel experiences and NTL grew a significant number of laboratory training centers sponsored by universities, such as the Western Training Laboratory sponsored by UCLA (Benne et al., 1975, p. 6).

In addition to Lewin and his work, influences on Bradford, Lippitt, and Benne relative to the invention of the T-group and the subsequent emergence of OD included extensive experience with role playing and Moreno's psychodrama (Smith, 1980, pp. 8–91). Further, Bradford and Benne had been influenced by John Dewey's philosophy of education, including concepts about learning and change and about the transactional nature of man and his environment (Chin & Benne, 1969, pp. 100–102). In addition, Benne had been influenced by the works of Mary Follett, an early management theorist, including her ideas about integrative solutions to problems in organizations (Chin & Benne, 1969, p. 102).

As a footnote to the emergence of the T-group, the widespread use

of flip-chart paper as a convenient way to record, retrieve, and display data in OD activities and in training sessions was invented by Ronald Lippitt and Lee Bradford during the 1946 New Britain sessions. As Lippitt reports:

> The blackboards were very inadequate, and we needed to preserve a lot of the material we produced. So I went down to the local newspaper and got a donation of the end of press runs. The paper was still on the rollers. We had a "cutting bee" of Lee, Ken, myself and several others to roll the sheets out and cut them into standard sizes that we could put up in quantity with masking tape on the blackboards and walls of the classrooms.[1]

Over the next decade, as trainers began to work with social systems of more permanency and complexity than T-groups, they began to experience considerable frustration in the transfer of laboratory behavioral skills and insights of individuals into the solution of problems in organizations. Personal skills learned in the "stranger" T-groups setting were very difficult to transfer to complex organizations. However, the training of "teams" from the same organization had emerged early at Bethel and undoubtedly was a link to the total organizational focus of Douglas McGregor, Herbert Shepard, and Robert Blake, just as it subsequently became the focus of Richard Beckhard, Chris Argyris, Jack Gibb, Warren Bennis, and others.[2] All had been T-group trainers in NTL programs.

LEARNING CHECKPOINT

Does the early use of T-Groups apply principles and values that permeate the more general approaches to organization development? Explain.

Douglas McGregor

As a professor-consultant working with Union Carbide, beginning about 1957, Douglas McGregor was one of the first behavioral scientists to begin to solve the transfer problem and to talk systematically about and help implement the application of T-group skills to complex organizations (Beckhard, Burke, & Steele, 1967; Jones, 1967). In collaboration with McGregor, John Paul Jones, who had come up through industrial relations at Union Carbide, had, with the support of a corporate executive vice-president and director, Birny Mason, Jr. (later president of the corporation), established a small internal consulting group which in large part used behavioral science knowledge in assisting line managers and their subordinates in learning how to be more effective as groups. McGregor's ideas were a dominant force in this consulting group; other behavioral scientists who had an influence on Jones's thinking were Rensis Likert and Mason Haire. Jones's organization was later called an "organization development group" (Burck, 1965; McGregor, 1967, pp. 106–110).[3]

Herbert Shepard

During the same year (1957), Herbert Shepard, through introductions by Douglas McGregor, joined the employee relations department of Esso Standard Oil (now Exxon) as a research associate. Shepard was to have a major impact on the emergence of OD. While we will focus mainly on Shepard's work at Esso, it should also be noted that Shepard was later involved in community development activities and, in 1960, at the Case Institute of Technology, founded the first Ph.D. program devoted to training OD specialists.

Before joining Esso, Shepard had completed his doctorate at MIT and had stayed for a time as a faculty member in the Industrial Relations Section. Among influences on Shepard were Roethlisberger and Dickson's *Management and the Worker* (1939) and a biography of Clarence Hicks. (As a consultant to Standard Oil, Hicks had helped to develop participative approaches to personnel management and labor relations [French, 1982, pp. 29–30].) Shepard was also influenced by Farrell Toombs, who had been a counselor at the Hawthorne plant and had trained under Carl Rogers, a leading theorist and practitioner in nondirective counseling. In addition, Shepard had been heavily influenced by the writings of Kurt Lewin. NTL influence was also an important part of Shepard's background; he attended an NTL lab in 1950 and subsequently was a staff member in many of its programs.[4]

In 1958 and 1959, Shepard launched three experiments in organization development at major Esso refineries: Bayonne, Baton Rouge, and Bayway. At Bayonne, an interview survey and diagnosis were made and discussed with top management, followed by a series of three-day laboratories for all members of management.

Buchanan and Shepard

Paul Buchanan, who had been using a somewhat similar approach in Republic Aviation, collaborated with Shepard at Bayonne and subsequently joined the Esso staff. Buchanan had previously been employed as a consulting psychologist by the Naval Ordnance Test Station at China Lake, California, where he had engaged the managers in a number of activities as early as 1952, including "retreats" in which they worked on interpersonal relations. (In 1961, Shepard was applying OD approaches to community development at China Lake, conducting one-week labs for cross-sections of the civilian and military populations toward the resolution of a number of community and intercommunity issues.)[5]

Blake and Shepard

At Baton Rouge, Robert Blake joined Shepard, and the two initiated a series of two-week laboratories attended by all members of "middle" management. At first an effort was made to combine the case method with the laboratory method, but the designs soon emphasized T-groups, organizational exercises, and lectures. One innovation in this training program was an emphasis on intergroup as well as interpersonal relations. Although working on interpersonal problems affecting work performance was clearly an organizational effort, between-group problem-solving had even more organization development implications, in that a broader and more complex segment of the organization was involved.

At Baton Rouge, efforts to involve top management failed, and as a result follow-up resources for implementing organization development were not made available. By the time the Bayway program started, two fundamental OD lessons had been learned: the requirement for active involvement in and leadership of the program by top management, and the need for on-the-job application.

At Bayway there were two significant innovations. First, Shepard, Blake, and Murray Horwitz utilized the instrumented laboratory that Blake and Jane Mouton had been developing in social psychology classes at the University of Texas and that they later developed into the Managerial Grid approach to organization development.[6] Second, at Bayway more resources were devoted to team development, consultation, intergroup conflict resolution, and so forth than were devoted to laboratory training of "cousins," that is, organization members from different departments. As Robert Blake stated: "It was learning to *reject* T-group stranger-type labs that permitted OD to come into focus," and it was intergroup projects in particular that "triggered real OD."[7]

Robert Blake

As in the case of Shepard and others, influences on Robert Blake up to that point were important in the emergence of OD. While at Berea College, majoring in psychology and philosophy, Blake had been strongly influenced by the works of Korzybski and by general semantics and found that "seeing discrete things as representative of a continuous series was much more stimulating and rewarding than just seeing two things as 'opposites.' " This thinking contributed in later years to Blake's conceptualization of the Managerial Grid with Jane Mouton and to their intergroup research on win/lose dynamics. This intergroup research and the subsequent design of their intergroup conflict management workshops were also heavily influenced by Muzafer Sherif's fundamental research on intergroup dynamics.[8] Jane Mouton's influence on Blake's thinking and on the development of the grid stemmed partly, in her words, "from my undergraduate work (at Texas) in pure mathematics and physics which emphasized the significance of measurement, experimental design, and a scientific approach to phenomena."[9]

During World War II, Blake served in the Psychological Research Unit of the Army Air Force,

where he interacted with a large number of behavioral scientists, including sociologists. This contributed to his interest in "looking at the system rather than the individuals within the system on an isolated one-by-one basis."[10] (This is one of many probable links between systems concepts or systems theory and OD.)

Another major influence on Blake had been the work of John Bowlby, a medical member of the Tavistock Clinic in London who was working in family group therapy. After completing his Ph.D. work in clinical psychology, Blake went to England for 16 months in 1948–49 to study, observe, and do research at Tavistock. As Blake tells it:

> Bowlby had the clear notion that treating the mental illness of an individual out of context was an . . . ineffective way of aiding a person. . . . As a result, John was unprepared to see patients, particularly children, in isolation from their family settings. He would see the intact family: mother, father, siblings. . . . I am sure you can see from what I have said that if you substitute the word organization for family and substitute the concept of development for therapy, the natural next step in my mind was organization development.

Among others at Tavistock who influenced Blake were Wilfred Bion, Henry Ezriel, Eric Trist, and Elliott Jaques.[11]

After returning from Tavistock and taking an appointment at Harvard, Blake joined the staff for the summer NTL programs at Bethel. His first assignment was co-responsibility for a T-group with John R. P. French. Blake was a member of the Bethel staff from 1951 to 1957 and continued after that with NTL labs for managers at Harriman House, Harriman, New York.

Among other influences on Blake were Moreno's action orientation to training, through the use of psychodrama and sociodrama, and Tolman's notions of purposiveness in man.[12]

LEARNING CHECKPOINT

How do the organization development approaches of Blake and others assure the commitment of top management?

Richard Beckhard

Richard Beckhard, another major figure in the emergence and extension of the OD field, came from a career in the theatre. In his words:

> I came out of a whole different world—the theatre—and went to NTL in 1950 as a result of some discussions with Lee Bradford and Ron Lippitt. At that time they were interested in improving the effectiveness of the communications in large meetings and I became involved as head of the general sessions program. But I also got hooked on the whole movement. I made a career change and set up the meetings organization, "Conference Counselors." My first major contact was the staging of the 1950 White House conference on children and youth. . . . I was brought in to stage the large general sessions with six thousand people. . . . At the same time I joined the NTL summer staff. . . . My mentors in the field were Lee Bradford, in the early days, and Ron Lippitt and later, Ren Likert, and very particularly, Doug McGregor, who became both mentor, friend, father figure . . . and in the later years, brother. Doug and I began appearing on similar programs. One day coming back on the train from Cincinnati to Boston, Doug asked if I was interested in joining MIT. . . . In the period

1958–63, I had worked with him (McGregor) on two or three projects. He brought me to Union Carbide, where I replaced him in working with John Paul Jones, and later, George Murray and the group. We [also] worked together at . . . Pennsylvania Bell and . . . at General Mills.[13]

Beckhard worked with McGregor at General Mills in 1959 or 1960, where McGregor was working with Dewey Balsch, vice-president of personnel and industrial relations, in an attempt to facilitate "a total organizational culture change program which today might be called quality of work life or OD." Beckhard goes on to say: "The issues that were being worked on were relationships between workers and supervision; roles of supervision and management at various levels; participative management."[14]

Beckhard developed the first major nondegree training program in OD, NTL's Program for Specialists in Organizational Training and Development (PSOTD). The first session was an intensive four-week session held in the summer of 1967 at Bethel, Maine. Core staff members the first year were Beckhard as dean, Warner Burke, and Fritz Steele. Additional resource persons the first year were Herbert Shepard, Sheldon Davis, and Chris Argyris. Beckhard was also active in the development and conducting of NTL's middle and senior management conferences and president's labs.[15]

The Term "Organization Development"

It is not entirely clear who coined the term *organization development,* but it is likely that it emerged more or less simultaneously in two or three places through the conceptualization of Robert Blake, Herbert Shepard, Jane Mouton, Douglas McGregor, and Richard Beckhard.[16] The phrase *development group* had been used earlier by Blake and Mouton in connection with human relations training at the University of Texas and appeared in their 1956 document that was distributed for use in the Baton Rouge experiment.[17] The same phrase appeared in a Mouton and Blake article first published in the journal *Group Psychotherapy* in 1957. The Baton Rouge T-groups run by Shepard and Blake were called *development groups,*[18] and this program of T-groups was called "organization development" to distinguish it from the complementary management development programs already under way.[19]

Referring to his consulting with McGregor at General Mills, Beckhard gives this account of the term's emergence there:

> At that time we wanted to put a label on the program at General Mills. . . . We clearly didn't want to call it management development because it was total organization-wide, nor was it human relations training although there was a component of that in it. We didn't want to call it organization improvement because that's a static term, so we labelled the program "Organization Development," meaning system-wide change effort.[20]

The Role of Personnel and Industrial Relations Executives

It is of considerable significance that the emergence of organization development efforts in three of the first corporations to be extensively involved—Union Carbide, Esso, and General Mills—included personnel and industrial relations people seeing themselves in new roles. At Union Carbide, Jones, in industrial relations, now saw himself in the role of behavioral science consultant to other managers (Burck, 1965, p. 149). At Esso, the headquarters human relations research division began to view itself as an internal consulting group offering services to field managers rather than as a research group developing reports for top management (Kolb, 1960).[21] At General Mills, the vice-president of personnel and industrial relations saw his role as including leadership in conceptualizing and coordinating changes in the culture of the total organization.

THE SURVEY RESEARCH AND FEEDBACK STEM[22]

Survey research and feedback, a specialized form of action research, constitutes the second major stem in the history of organization development. The history of this stem, in particular, revolves around the techniques and approach developed by staff members at the Survey Research Center of the University of Michigan over a period of years.

Rensis Likert

The SRC was founded in 1946 after Rensis Likert, director of the Division of Program Surveys of the Federal Bureau of Agricultural Economics, and other key members of the division, moved to Michigan. Likert held a Ph.D. in psychology from Columbia, and his dissertation, "A Technique for the Measurement of Attitudes," was the classic study in which the widely used five-point "Likert Scale" was developed. After a period of university teaching, Likert had been employed by the Life Insurance Agency Management Association, where he conducted research on leadership, motivation, morale, and productivity. He had then moved to the U.S. Department of

Agriculture, where his Division of Program Surveys furthered a more scientific approach to survey research in its work with various federal departments, including the Office of War Information (ISR Newsletter, 1981, p. 6). After helping to develop and direct the Survey Research Center following World War II, in 1948 Likert became the director of a new Institute for Social Research that included both the SRC and the Research Center for Group Dynamics, the latter moving to Michigan from MIT after Lewin's death.

Floyd Mann, Rensis Likert, and Others

Part of the emergence of survey research and feedback was based on the refinements made by SRC staff members in survey methodology. Another part was the evolution of the feedback methodology. As related by Likert:

> In 1947, I was able to interest the Detroit Edison Company in a company-wide study of employee perceptions, behavior, reactions and attitudes which was conducted in 1948. Floyd Mann, who had joined the SRC staff in 1947, was the study director on the project. I provided general direction. Three persons from D.E.: Blair Swartz, Sylvanus Leahy and Robert Schwab with Mann and me worked on the problem of how the company could best use the data from the survey to bring improvement in management and performance. This led to the development and use of the survey-feedback method. Floyd particularly played a key role in this development. He found that when the survey data were reported to a manager (or supervisor) and he or she failed to discuss the results with subordinates and failed to plan with them what the manager and others should do to bring improvement, little change occurred. On the other

hand, when the manager discussed the results with subordinates and planned with them what to do to bring improvement, substantial favorable changes occurred.[23]

Another aspect of the Detroit Edison Study was the process of feeding back data from an attitude survey to the participating departments in what Mann calls an "interlocking chain of conferences" (Mann, 1957). Additional insights are provided by Baumgartel, who participated in the project, and who drew the following conclusions from the Detroit Edison Study:

> The results of this experimental study lend support to the idea that an intensive, group discussion procedure for utilizing the results of an employee questionnaire survey can be an effective tool for introducing positive change in a business organization. It may be that the effectiveness of this method, in comparison to traditional training courses, is that it deals with the system of human relationships as a whole (superior and subordinate can change together) and it deals with each manager, supervisor, and employee in the context of his own job, his own problems, and his own work relationships [Baumgartel, 1959, pp. 2–6].

LINKS BETWEEN THE LABORATORY-TRAINING STEM AND THE SURVEY FEEDBACK STEM

Links between people who were later to be key figures in the laboratory-training stem of OD and people who were to be key figures in the survey feedback stem occurred as early as 1940 and continued over the years. These links were undoubtedly of significance in the evolution of both stems. Of particular interest are the links between Likert and Lewin and between Li-

kert and key figures in the laboratory-training stem of OD. As Likert states it: "I met Lewin at the APA annual meeting at State College, Pa., I believe in 1940. When he came to Washington during the War, I saw him several times and got to know him and his family quite well."[24] In 1944 Likert arranged a dinner at which Douglas McGregor and Kurt Lewin explored the feasibility of a group dynamics center at MIT (Marrow, 1969, p. 164).

Likert further refers to McGregor: "I met McGregor during the war and came to know him very well after Lewin had set up the RCGD at MIT. After the War, Doug became very interested in the research on leadership and organizations that we were doing in the Institute for Social Research. He visited us frequently and I saw him often at Antioch and at MIT after he returned." Likert goes on to refer to the first NTL lab for managers which was held at Arden House in 1956: "Douglas McGregor and I helped Lee Bradford launch it. . . . Staff members in the 1956 lab were: Beckhard, Benne, Bradford, Gordon Lippitt, Malott, Shepard and I. Argyris, Blake and McGregor joined the staff for the 1957 Arden House lab."[25]

Links between group dynamics and survey feedback people were extensive, of course, after the RCGD moved to Michigan with the encouragement of Rensis Likert and members of the SRC. Among the top people in the RCGD who moved to Michigan were Leon Festinger, Dorwin Cartwright, Ronald Lippitt, and John R. P. French, Jr. Cartwright, who was selected by the group to be the director of the RCGD, was particularly knowledgeable about survey research, since he had been on the staff of the Division of Program Surveys with Likert and others during World War II.[26]

THE ACTION RESEARCH STEM[27]

Participant action research underlies most of the interventions that have been invented in the evolution of OD. Participant action research can be briefly described as a collaborative, client/consultant inquiry consisting of preliminary diagnosis, data gathering from the client group, data feedback to the client group, data exploration and action planning by the client group, and action. Participant action research is one of four versions of action research; the other three, as described by Chein, Cook and Harding are "diagnostic," "empirical," and "experimental" (1948, pp. 43–50).

Kurt Lewin and Students

Kurt Lewin and his students conducted numerous action research projects in the mid-1940s and early 1950s (Marrow, 1964). An example of this orientation is the following statement by Lewin:

> To be effective, this fact-finding has to be linked with the action organization itself: it has to be part of a feedback system which links a reconnaissance branch of the organization with the branches which do the action [Lewin, 1947, p. 150].

Lewin introduced a program of action research at the Harwood Manufacturing Corporation, which he first visited in 1939. Alfred Marrow, a social psychologist, was an officer of the company and worked closely with Lewin and subsequent researchers from the Research Center for Group Dynamics. The studies that emerged focused on such areas as group standards, group decision making, and change

processes. The classic study by Coch and French (1948) on resistance to change was one of the projects that emerged. The ongoing relationship between the RCGD and Harwood culminated in the comprehensive action-research, OD effort that took place after Harwood acquired the Weldon Manufacturing Company in 1962 (Marrow, Bowers, & Seashore, 1967).

William Whyte and Edith Hamilton

William F. Whyte and Edith L. Hamilton used action research in their work with Chicago's Tremont Hotel in 1945 and 1946. They described their work as follows:

> What was the project? It was an action-research program for management. We developed a process for applying human relations research findings to the changing of organization behavior. The word process is important, for this was not a one-shot affair. The project involved a continuous gathering and analysis of human relations research data and the feeding of the findings into the organization in such a way as to change behavior [Whyte & Hamilton, 1964, pp. 1–2].

John Collier and Others

Like Lewin, John Collier, Commissioner of Indian Affairs from 1933 to 1945, found that action research was an important tool in the improvement of race relations:

> We had in mind research impelled from central areas of needed action. And since action is by nature not only specialized but also integrative to more than the specialties, our needed research must be of the integrative sort. Again, since the findings of the research must be carried into effect by the administrator and the layman, and must be criticized by them through their experience, the administrator and the layman must

themselves participate creatively in the research, impelled as it is from their own need [Collier, 1945, pp. 275–276].

Among others who used and wrote about action research in its early history, as described by French and Bell (1978, pp. 88–100), were Corey, Shepard, Lippitt and Radke, Jaques, and Sofer. Stephen Corey (1953) was an advocate of action research to improve school practices. Herbert Shepard (1960, pp. 33–34), discussed above, described action research interventions in the oil refineries where he was a consultant. Ronald Lippitt and Marion Radke (1964, pp. 167–176) used action research in a community relations project. Elliot Jaques (1952) used action research in his long-range work with a factory in England. Cyril Sofer (1962) used action research methods in three diverse organizations where he was a researcher-consultant. The work of these and other scholars and practitioners in the invention and utilization of action research was basic in the evolution of OD.

SOCIOTECHNICAL AND SOCIOCLINICAL PARALLELS

Somewhat parallel to the work of the RCGD, the SRC, and NTL was the work of the Tavistock Clinic in England. The clinic had been founded in 1920 as an out-patient facility to provide psychotherapy based on psychoanalytic theory and insights from the treatment of battle neurosis in World War I. A group focus emerged early in the work of Tavistock in the context of family therapy in which the child and the parent received treatment simultaneously (Dicks, 1970, pp. 1, 32). The action-research mode also emerged at Tavistock in attempts to give practical help to families, organizations, and committees.

W. R. Bion, John Rickman, and Others

The staff of the Tavistock Clinic was extensively influenced by such innovations as World War II applications of social psychology to psychiatry; the work of W. R. Bion, John Rickman, and others in group therapy; Lewin's notions about the "social field" in which a problem was occurring: and by Lewin's theory and experience with action research. Bion, Rickman, and others had been involved with the six-week "Northfield Experiment" at a military hospital near Birmingham during World War II, an experiment in which each soldier was required to join a group that both performed some task, such as handicraft or map reading, and discussed feelings, interpersonal relations, and administrative and managerial problems as well. Insights from this experiment were to carry over into Bion's theory of group behavior (Dicks, 1970, pp. 5, 7, 133, 140; DeBoard, 1978, pp. 35–43).

Eric Trist

It is of significance that Tavistock's sociotechnical approach to restructuring work grew out of Eric Trist's visit to a coal mine and his insights as to the relevance of Lewin's work on group dynamics and Bion's work on leaderless groups to mining problems. Trist was also influenced by the systems concepts of Von Bertalanffy and Andres Angyal (Sashkin, 1980). Trist's subsequent experiments in work redesign and the use of semiautonomous work teams in coal mining were the forerunners of other work redesign experiments in various industries in Europe, India, and the United States. Thus there is a clear histori-

cal link between the group dynamics field and sociotechnical approaches to assisting organizations.

Tavistock-U.S. Links

Tavistock leaders, including Trist and Bion, had frequent contact with Kurt Lewin, Rensis Likert, and others in the United States. One product of this collaboration was the decision to publish *Human Relations* as a joint publication between Tavistock and MIT's Research Center for Group Dynamics (Sashkin, 1980). Some Americans prominent in the emergence and evolution of the OD field, for example, Robert Blake, as we noted earlier, and Warren Bennis,[28] studied at Tavistock.

 **LEARNING CHECKPOINT**

Explain how the socio-technical approach to organization development can be used as the basis for job redesign strategy.

SUMMARY COMMENTS

By the early 1960s, organization development had emerged largely from the applied behavioral sciences and had three major stems: the invention of the T-group and innovations in the application of laboratory training insights to complex organizations; the invention of survey feedback technology; and the emergence of action research. Parallel and linked to these stems was the emergence of the Tavistock sociotechnical and socioclinical approaches. The key figures focused on in this essay interacted with each other and across these stems and were influenced by concepts and experiences from a wide variety of disciplines and settings. Among

these disciplines and settings were clinical and social psychology, including field theory, family group therapy, military psychology and psychiatry, the theatre, general semantics, mathematics and physics, philosophy, psychodrama, nondirective counseling, survey methodology, experimental and action research, community development, systems theory, sociotechnical approaches, personnel and industrial relations, and general management. □

NOTES

1. Correspondence with the author, November 23, 1981.
2. Correspondence with the author, August 16, 1971. According to Lippitt, as early as 1945 Bradford and Lippitt were conducting "three-level training" at Freedman's Hospital in Washington, D.C., in an effort "to induce interdependent changes in all parts of the same system" and were using "intergroup task forces to work on the solution of specific problems identified across groups." Lippitt also reports that Leland Bradford had long been acting on a basic concept of "multiple entry," i.e., simultaneously training and working with several groups in the organization.
3. According to correspondence with Rensis Likert, discussions between McGregor and John Paul Jones occurred in the summer of 1957 when Jones attended one of the annual seminars at Aspen, Colorado, organized by Hollis Peter of the Foundation for Research on Human Behavior and conducted by Douglas McGregor, Mason Haire, and Rensis Likert. Correspondence with the author, March 1, 1977.
4. This paragraph is based on interviews with Herbert Shepard by the author, August 3, 1981.
5. Much of the historical account in the above two paragraphs and the following three paragraphs is based on correspondence and interviews with Herbert Shepard, with some information added from correspondence with Robert Blake. Shepard correspondence with the author, March 1, 1971; July

18, 1971; interview with Herbert Shepard, August 3, 1981. Blake correspondence with the author, March 8, April 12, and June 10, 1971. See also Porter (1976).

6. Blake and Shepard correspondence with the author. For further reference to Murray Horwitz and Paul Buchanan, as well as comments about the innovative contributions of Michael Blansfield, see Shepard (1964, pp. 382–383). See also Sashkin (1978, pp. 401–407). Blake and Mouton credit Muzafer and Carolyn Sherif with important contributions to early intergroup experiments and give credit to the contributions of Frank Cassens of Humble Oil and Refinery in the early phases of the Esso program (Blake & Mouton, 1962; Blake & Mouton, 1976, pp. 332–336).

7. Correspondence with the author, March 8, 1981.

8. Blake correspondence with the author, November 12, 1981.

9. Correspondence with the author, February 19, 1982.

10. Correspondence, November 12, 1981.

11. Ibid.

12. Ibid.

13. Correspondence with the author, December 17, 1981.

14. Ibid.

15. Based partly on Beckhard correspondence, December 17, 1981.

16. Interpretations of Shepard interview, August 13, 1981; Shepard correspondence, March 1, 1971; Blake correspondence, March 8, April 12, 1971; Richard Beckhard correspondence, December 17, 1981; and Porter (1974).

17. Blake correspondence, April 12, 1971.

18. Ibid.

19. Interview with Herbert Shepard by the author, August 3, 1981.

20. Correspondence, December 17, 1981.

21. The phrase *organization development* is used several times in this monograph based on a 1959 meeting about the Esso programs and written by Kolb, Shepard, Blake, and others (Kolb, 1960).

22. This section is based largely on correspondence with Rensis Likert and

partially on "The Career of Rensis Likert" (*ISR Newsletter*, 1971); *A Quarter Century of Social Research* (Institute for Social Research, 1971); and "Rensis Likert: A Final Tribute" (*ISR Newsletter*, 1981).

23. Correspondence with the author, March 1, 1977.

24. Ibid.

25. Ibid.

26. Ibid.

27. I am indebted to Cecil Bell for his research contribution to this section (French & Bell, 1978, Ch. 8). See also Frohman, Sashkin, & Kavanagh (1976).

28. Warren Bennis, address, Academy of Management, San Diego, California, August 3, 1981.

REFERENCES

Baumgartel, H. Using employee questionnaire results for improving organizations: The survey feedback experiment. *Kansas Business Review,* 1959, *12,* (December), 2–6.

Beckhard, R., Burke, W. W., & Steele, F. I. The program for specialists in organization training and development. NTL Institute for Applied Behavioral Science, December 1967, p. 11 (mimeo)

Benne, K. D., Bradford, L. P., Gibb, J. R., & Lippitt, R. O. (Eds.) *The Laboratory method of changing and learning: Theory and application.* Palo Alto, CA: Science and Behavior Books, 1975.

Blake, R. R., & Mouton, J. S. The instrumented training laboratory. In I. R. Wechsler and E. H. Schein (Eds.) *Selected readings series five: Issues in training.* Washington, DC: National Training Laboratories, 1962.

Blake, R. R., & Mouton, J. S. *Diary of an OD man.* Houston: Gulf, 1976.

Blake, R. R., Shepard, H., & Mouton, J. S. *Managing intergroup conflict in industry.* Houston: Gulf, 1964.

Burck, G. Union Carbide's patient schemers. *Fortune,* 1965, *72*(6), 147–149.

Chein, I., Cook, S., & Harding, J. The field of action research. *American Psychologist,* 1948, *3*(2), 43–50.

Chin, R., & Benne, K. D., General strategies for effecting changes in hu-

man systems. In W. G. Bennis, K. D. Benne, & R. Chin (Eds.) *The planning of change* (2nd ed.) New York: Holt, Rinehart & Winston, 1969.

Coch, L. & French, J. R. P., Jr. Overcoming resistance to change. *Human Relations,* 1948, *1,* 512–532.

Collier, J. United States Indian Administration as a laboratory of ethnic relations. *Social Research,* 1945, *12,* 275–276.

Corey, S. M. *Action research to improve school practices.* New York: Teachers College, Columbia University, 1953.

DeBoard, R. *The psychoanalysis of organizations.* London: Tavistock, 1978.

Dicks, H. V. *Fifty years of the Tavistock Clinic.* London: Routledge & Kegan Paul, 1970.

French, W. L. *The personnel management process* (5th ed.). Boston: Houghton Mifflin, 1982.

French, W. L., & Bell, C. H., Jr. *Organization development: Behavioral science interventions for organization improvement* (2nd ed.). Englewood Cliffs, NJ: Prentice-Hall, 1978.

Frohman, M. A., Sashkin, M., & Kavanagh, M. J. Action research applied to organization development. *Organization and Administrative Sciences,* 1976, 7(1, 2), 129–142.

Institute for Social Research, *A quarter century of social research.* Ann Arbor, MI: Author, 1971.

ISR Newsletter. The career of Rensis Likert. Institute for Social Research, Winter 1971.

ISR Newsletter. Rensis Likert: A final tribute. Institute for Social Research, Winter, 1981.

Jaques, E. *The changing culture of a factory.* New York: Dryden Press, 1942.

Jones, J. P. What's wrong with work? In National Association of Manufacturers, *What's wrong with work?* New York: Author, 1967.

Kolb, H. D. Introduction. In Foundation for Research on Human Behavior, *An action research program for organization improvement.* Ann Arbor, MI: Author, 1960.

Lewin, K. Frontiers in human relations

II. Channels of group life, social planning and action research. *Human Relations,* 1947, *1*(2), 143–153.

Lippitt, R., & Radke, M. New trends in the investigation of prejudice. *Annals of the American Academy of Political and Social Science,* 1946, *24*(4), 167–176.

Mann, F. C. Studying and creating change: A means to understanding social organization. In C. M. Arensberg et al. (Eds.), *Research in industrial human relations.* New York: Harper & Row, 1957. (Industrial Relations Research Association Publication No. 17).

Marrow, A. J. Risks and uncertainties in action research. *Journal of Social Issues,* 1964, *20*(3), 17.

Marrow, A. J. *The practical theorist: The life and work of Kurt Lewin.* New York: Basic Books, 1969.

Marrow, A. J., Bowers, D. G., & Seashore, S. E. *Management by participation.* New York: Harper & Row, 1967.

McGregor, D. M. *The professional manager.* New York: McGraw-Hill, 1967.

Mouton, J. S. & Blake, R. R. University training in human relations skills. *Group Psychotherapy,* 1957, *10,* 342–345.

Porter, L. OD: Some questions, some answers—An interview with Beckhard and Shepard. *OD Practitioner,* 1974, *6* (Autumn), 1.

Porter, L. A conversation with Bob Tannenbaum. *OD Practitioner,* 1976, *8* (October), 1–5ff.

Roethlisberger, F. J. & Dickson, W. J. *Management and the worker.* Cambridge, MA: Harvard University Press, 1939.

Sashkin, M. Interview with Eric Trist. *Group & Organization Studies,* 1980, *5*(2), 144–155.

Sashkin, M. Interview with Robert R. Blake and Jane Srygley Mouton. *Group & Organization Studies,* 1978, *3*(4), 401–407.

Shepard, H. A. An action research model. In Foundation for Research on Human Behavior, *An action research program for organization improvement.* Ann Arbor, MI: Author, 1960.

Shepard, H. A. Exploration in observant participation. In L. P. Bradford, J. R. Gibb, & K. D. Benne, *T-Group theory and laboratory method.* New York: Wiley, 1964.

Smith, P. B. (Ed.) *Small groups and personal change.* London: Methuen, 1980.

Sofer, C. *The organization from within.* Chicago: Quadrangle Books, 1962.

Whyte, W. F., & Hamilton, E. L. *Action research for management.* Homewood, IL: Irwin-Dorsey, 1964.

R² PATTERNS OF ORGANIZATION CHANGE*

LARRY E. GREINER

Today many top managers are attempting to introduce sweeping and basic changes in the behavior and practices of the supervisors and the subordinates throughout their organizations. Whereas only a few years ago the target of organization change was limited to a small work group or a single department, especially at lower levels, the focus is now converging on the organization as a whole, reaching out to

* Source: From Larry E. Greiner, "Patterns of Organization Change," HARVARD BUSINESS REVIEW, Vol 45, No. 3 (May–June 1967), pp. 119–128. Copyright © 1967 by the President and Fellows of Harvard College. All rights reserved.

include many divisions and levels at once, and even the top managers themselves. There is a critical need at this time to understand better this complex process, especially in terms of which approaches lead to successful changes and which actions fail to achieve the desired results.

REVOLUTIONARY PROCESS

The shifting emphasis from small- to large-scale organization change represents a significant departure from past managerial thinking. For many years, change was regarded more as an evolutionary than a revolutionary process. The evolutionary assumption reflected the view that change is a product of one minor adjustment after another, fueled by time and subtle environ-

mental forces largely outside the direct control of management. This relatively passive philosophy of managing change is typically expressed in words like these:

> Our company is continuing to benefit from a dynamically expanding market. While our share of the market has remained the same, our sales have increased 15% over the past year. In order to handle this increased business, we have added a new marketing vice president and may have to double our sales force in the next two years.

Such an optimistic statement frequently belies an unbounding faith in a beneficent environment. Perhaps this philosophy was adequate in less competitive times, when small patchwork changes, such as replacing a manager here and there, were sufficient to maintain profitability. But now the environments around organizations are changing rapidly and are challenging managements to become far more alert and inventive than they ever were before.

Management Awakening

In recent years more and more top managements have begun to realize that fragmented changes are seldom effective in stemming the underlying tides of stagnation and complacency that can subtly creep into a profitable and growing organization. While rigid and uncreative attitudes are slow to develop, they are also slow to disappear, even in the face of frequent personnel changes. Most often these signs of decay can be recognized in managerial behavior that (a) is oriented more to the past than to the future, (b) recognizes the obligations of ritual more than the challenges of current problems, and (c) owes allegiance more to department goals than to overall company objectives.

Management's recent awakening to these danger signs has been stimulated largely by the rapidly changing tempo and quality of its environment. Consider:

- Computer technology has narrowed the decision time span.
- Mass communication has heightened public awareness of consumer products.
- New management knowledge and techniques have come into being.
- Technological discoveries have multiplied.
- New world markets have opened up.
- Social drives for equality have intensified.
- Governmental demands and regulations have increased.

As a result, many organizations are currently being challenged to shift, or even reverse, gears in order to survive, let alone prosper.

A number of top managements have come around to adopting a revolutionary attitude toward change, in order to bridge the gap between a dynamic environment and a stagnant organization. They feel that they can no longer sit back and condone organizational self indulgence, waiting for time to heal all wounds. So, through a number of means, revolutionary attempts are now being made to transform their organizations rapidly by altering the behavior and attitudes of their line and staff personnel at all levels of management. While each organization obviously varies in its approach, the overarching goal seems to be the same: to get everyone psychologically redirected toward solving the problems and challenges of today's business environment. Here, for example, is how one company president describes his current goal for change:

> I've got to get this organization moving, and soon. Many of our managers act as if we were still selling the products that used to be our bread and butter. We're in a different business now, and I'm not sure that they realize it. Somehow we've got to start recognizing our problems, and then become more competent in solving them. This applies to everyone here, including me and the janitor. I'm starting with a massive reorganization which I hope will get us pulling together instead of in fifty separate directions.

Striking Similarities

Although there still are not many studies of organization change, the number is growing; and a survey of them shows that it is already possible to detect some striking similarities running throughout their findings. I shall report some of these similarities, under two headings:

1. *Common approaches* being used to initiate organization change.

2. *Reported results*—what happened in a number of cases of actual organization change.

I shall begin with the approaches, and then attempt to place them within the perspective of what has happened when these approaches were applied. As we shall see, only a few of the approaches used tend to facilitate successful change, but even here we find that each is aided by unplanned forces preceding and following its use. Finally, I shall conclude with some tentative interpretations as to what I think is actually taking place when an organization change occurs.

COMMON APPROACHES

In looking at the various major approaches being used to *introduce* organization change, one is immediately struck by their position along a "power distribution" continuum. At one extreme are those which rely on *unilateral* authority. More toward the middle of the continuum are the *shared* approaches. Finally, at the opposite extreme are the *delegated* approaches.

As we shall see later, the *shared* approaches tend to be emphasized in the more successful organization changes. Just why this is so is an important question we will consider in the concluding section. For now, though, let us gain a clearer picture of the various approaches as they appear most frequently in the literature of organization change.

Unilateral Action

At this extreme on the power distribution continuum, the organization change is implemented through an emphasis on the authority of a man's hierarchial position in the company. Here, the definition and solution to the problem at hand tend to be specified by the upper echelons and directed downward through formal and impersonal control mechanisms. The use of unilateral authority to introduce organization change appears in three forms.

- *By Decree.* This is probably the most commonly used approach, having its roots in centuries of practice within military and government bureaucracies and taking its authority from the formal position of the person introducing the change. It is essentially a "one-way" announcement that is directed downward to the lower levels in the organization. The spirit of the communication reads something like "today we are this way—tomorrow we must be that way."

  In its concrete form it may appear as a memorandum, lecture, policy statement, or verbal command. The general nature of the decree approach is impersonal, formal, and task-oriented. It assumes that people are highly rational and best motivated by authoritative directions. Its expectation is that people will comply in their outward behavior and that this compliance will lead to more effective results.

- *By Replacement.* Often resorted to when the decree approach fails, this involves the replacement of key persons. It is based on the assumption that organization problems tend to reside in a few strategically located individuals, and that replacing these people will bring about sweeping and basic

changes. As in the decree form, this change is usually initiated at the top and directed downward by a high authority figure. At the same time, however, it tends to be somewhat more personal, since particular individuals are singled out for replacement. Nevertheless, it retains much of the formality and explicit concern for task accomplishment that is common to the decree approach. Similarly, it holds no false optimism about the ability of individuals to change their own behavior without clear outside direction.

- *By Structure.* This odd and familiar change approach is currently receiving much reevaluation by behavioral scientists. In its earlier form, it involved a highly rational approach to the design of formal organization and to the layout of technology. The basic assumption here was that people behaved in close agreement with the structure and technology governing them. However, it tended to have serious drawbacks, since what seemed logical on paper was not necessarily logical for human goals.

Recently attempts have been made to alter the organizational structure in line with what is becoming known about both the logics and nonlogics of human behavior, such as engineering the job to fit the man, on the one hand, or adjusting formal authority to match informal authority, on the other hand. These attempts, however, still rely heavily on mechanisms for change that tend to be relatively formal, impersonal, and located outside the individual. At the same time, however, because of greater concern for the effects of structure on people, they can probably be

characterized as more personal, subtle, and less directive than either the decree or replacement approaches.

LEARNING CHECKPOINT

What is the relationship between the use of unilateral action to implement change and the use of task-oriented leadership?

Sharing of Power

More toward the middle of the power distribution continuum, as noted earlier, are the shared approaches, where authority is still present and used, yet there is also interaction and sharing of power. This approach to change is utilized in two forms.

- *By Group Decision Making.* Here the problems still tend to be defined unilaterally from above, but lower-level groups are usually left free to develop alternative solutions and to choose among them. The main assumption tends to be that individuals develop more commitment to action when they have a voice in the decisions that affect them. The net result is that power is shared between bosses and subordinates, though there is a division of labor between those who define the problems and those who develop the solutions.

- *By Group Problem Solving.* This form emphasizes both the definition and the solution of problems within the context of group discussion. Here power is shared throughout the decision process, but, unlike group decision making, there is an added opportunity for lower-level subordinates to define the problem. The assumption underlying this approach is not only that people gain greater commitment from being exposed to a wider decision-making role, but also that they have significant knowledge to contribute to the definition of the problem.

Delegated Authority

At the other extreme from unilateral authority are found the delegated approaches, where almost complete responsibility for defining and acting on problems is turned over to the subordinates. These also appear in two forms.

- *By Case Discussion.* This method focuses more on the acquisition of knowledge and skills than on the solution of specific problems at hand. An authority figure, usually a teacher or boss, uses his power only to guide a general discussion of information describing a problem situation, such as a case or a report of research results. The "teacher" refrains from imposing his own analysis or solutions on the group. Instead, he encourages individual members to arrive at their own insights, and they are left to use them as they see fit. The implicit assumption here is that individuals, through the medium of discussion about concrete situations, will develop general problem-solving skills to aid them in carrying out subsequent individual and organization changes.
- *By T-Group Sessions.* These sessions, once conducted mainly in outside courses for representatives of many different organizations, are increasingly being used inside individual companies for effecting change. Usually, they are con-

fined to top management, with the hope that beneficial "spillover" will result for the rest of the organization. The primary emphasis of the T-group tends to be on increasing an individual's self-awareness and sensitivity to group social processes. Compared to the previously discussed approaches, the T-group places much less emphasis on the discussion and solution of task-related problems. Instead, the data for discussion are typically the interpersonal actions of individuals in the group; no specific task is assigned to the group.

The basic assumption underlying this approach is that exposure to a structureless situation will release unconscious emotional energies within individuals, which, in turn, will lead to self-analysis, insight, and behavioral change. The authority figure in the group, usually a professional trainer, avoids asserting his own authority in structuring the group. Instead, he often attempts to become an accepted and influential member of the group. Thus, in comparison to the other approaches, much more authority is turned over to the group, from which position it is expected to chart its own course of change in an atmosphere of great informality and highly personal exchanges.

REPORTED RESULTS

As we have seen, each of the major approaches, as well as the various forms within them, rests on certain assumptions about what *should* happen when it is applied to initiate change. Now let us step back and consider what actually *does* happen—before, during, and after a particular approach is introduced.

To discover whether there are certain dimensions of organization

change that might stand out against the background of characteristics unique to one company, we conducted a survey of 18 studies of organization change. Specifically, we were looking for the existence of dominant patterns of similarity and/or difference running across all of these studies. As we went along, relevant information was written down and compared with the other studies in regard to (a) the conditions leading up to an attempted change, (b) the manner in which the change was introduced, (c) the critical blocks and/or facilitators encountered during implementation, and (d) the more lasting results which appeared over a period of time.

The survey findings show some intriguing similarities and differences between those studies reporting "successful" change patterns and those disclosing "less successful" changes—*i.e.,* failure to achieve the desired results. The successful changes generally appear as those which:

- Spread throughout the organization to include and affect many people.
- Produce positive changes in line and staff attitudes.
- Prompt people to behave more efficiently in solving problems and in relating to others.
- Result in improved organization performance.

Significantly, the less successful changes fall short on all of these dimensions.

LEARNING CHECKPOINT

Compare these characteristics of successful change with dimensions of organizational effectiveness. Which of the characteristics relate to each of the short, intermediate, and long-run dimensions?

"Success" Patterns

Using the category breakdown just cited as the baseline for "success," the survey reveals some very distinct patterns on the evolution of change. In all, eight major patterns are identifiable in five studies reporting successful change, and six other success studies show quite similar characteristics, although the information contained in each is somewhat less complete. *(See the Appendix for studies included in the survey.)* Consider:

1. The organization, and especially top management, is under considerable external and internal pressure for improvement long before an explicit organization change is contemplated. Performance and/or morale are low. Top management seems to be groping for a solution to its problems.
2. A new man, known for his ability to introduce improvements, enters the organization, either as the official head of the organization, or as a consultant who deals directly with the head of the organization.
3. An initial act of the new man is to encourage a reexamination of past practices and current problems within the organization.
4. The head of the organization and his immediate subordinates assume a direct and highly involved role in conducting this reexamination.
5. The new man, with top management support, engages several levels of the organization in collaborative, fact-finding, problem-solving discussions to identify and diagnose current organization problems.
6. The new man provides others with new ideas and methods for developing solutions to problems, again at many levels of the organization.
7. The solutions and decisions are developed, tested, and found creditable for solving problems on a small scale before an attempt is made to widen the scope of change to larger problems and the entire organization.
8. The change effort spreads with each success experience, and as management support grows, it is gradually absorbed permanently into the organization's way of life.

The likely significance of these similarities becomes more apparent when we consider the patterns found in the less successful organization changes. Let us briefly make this contrast before speculating further about why the successful changes seem to unfold as they do.

"Failure" Forms

Apart from their common "failure" to achieve the desired results, the most striking overall characteristic of seven less successful change studies is a singular lack of consistency—not just between studies, but within studies. Where each of the successful changes follows a similar and highly consistent route of one step building on another, the less successful changes are much less orderly *(see Appendix for a list of these studies)*.

There are three interesting patterns of inconsistency:

1. The less successful changes begin from a variety of starting points. This is in contrast to the successful changes, which begin from a common point—i.e., strong pressure both externally and internally. Only one less successful change, for example, began with outside pressure on the organization; another originated with the hiring of a consultant; and a third started with the presence of internal pressure, but without outside pressure.
2. Another pattern of inconsistency is found in the sequence of change steps. In the successful change patterns, we observe some degree of logical consistency between steps, as each seems to make possible the next. But in the less successful changes, there are wide and seemingly illogical gaps in sequence. One study, for instance, described a big jump from the reaction to outside pressure to the installation of an unskilled newcomer who immediately attempted large-scale changes. In another case, the company lacked the presence of a newcomer to provide new methods and ideas to the organization. A third failed to achieve the cooperation and involvment of top management. And a fourth missed the step of obtaining early successes while experimenting with new change methods.
3. A final pattern of inconsistency is evident in the major approaches used to introduce change. In the successful cases, it seems fairly clear that *shared* approaches are used—i.e., authority figures seek the participation of subordinates in joint decision making. In the less successful attempts, however, the approaches used lie closer to the extreme ends of the power distribution continuum. Thus, in five less successful change studies, a *unilateral* approach (decree, replacement, structural) was used, while in two other studies a *delegated* approach (data discussion, T-group) was applied. None

of the less successful change studies reported the use of a *shared* approach.

How can we use this lack of consistency in the sequence of change steps and this absence of shared power to explain the less successful change attempts? In the next section, I shall examine in greater depth the successful changes, which, unlike the less successful ones, are marked by a high degree of consistency and the use of shared power. My intent here will be not only to develop a tentative explanation of the more successful changes, but in so doing to explain the less successful attempts within the same framework.

POWER REDISTRIBUTION

Keeping in mind that the survey evidence on which both the successful and the less successful patterns are based is quite limited, I would like to propose a tentative explanatory scheme for viewing the change process as a whole, and also for considering specific managerial action steps within this overall process. The framework for this scheme hinges on two key notions:

1. Successful change depends basically on a *redistribution of power* within the structure of an organization. (By *power,* I mean the locus of formal authority and influence which typically is top management. By *redistribution,* I mean a significant alteration in the traditional practices that the power structure uses in making decisions. I propose that this redistribution move toward the greater use of *shared* power.)
2. Power redistribution occurs through a *developmental process of change.* (This implies

that organization change is not a black to white affair occurring overnight through a single casual mechanism. Rather, as we shall see, it involves a number of phrases, each containing specific elements and multiple causes that provoke a needed *reaction* from the power structure, which, in turn, sets the stage for the next phase in the process.)

Using the survey evidence from the successful patterns, I have divided the change process into six phases, each of them broken down into the particular stimulus and reaction which appear critical for moving the power structure from one phase to another. Figure 1 represents an abstract view of these two key notions in operation.

Let us now consider how each of these phases and their specific elements make themselves evident in the patterns of successful change, as well as how their absence contributes to the less successful changes.

I. Pressure & Arousal

This initial stage indicates a need to shake the power structure at its very foundation. Until the ground under the top managers begins to shift, it seems unlikely that they will be sufficiently aroused to see the need for change, both in themselves and in the rest of the organization.

The success patterns suggest that strong pressures in areas of top management responsibility are likely to provoke the greatest concern for organization change. These pressures seem to come

FIGURE 1

Dynamics of Successful Organization Change

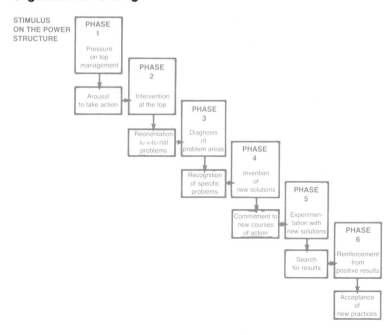

from two broad sources: (1) serious environmental factors, such as lower sales, stockholder discontent, or competitor breakthroughs; and (2) internal events, such as a union strike, low productivity, high costs, or interdepartmental conflict. These pressures fall into responsibility areas that top managers can readily see as reflecting on their own capability. An excerpt from one successful change study shows how this pressure and arousal process began:

> "Pressure" was the common expression used at all levels. Urgent telephone calls, telegrams, letters and memoranda were being received by the plant from central headquarters. . . . Faced with an increase in directives from above and cognizant of Plant Y's low performance position, the manager knew that he was, as he put it, "on the spot."[1]

As this example points out, it is probably significant when both environmental and internal pressures exist simultaneously. When only one is present, or when the two are offsetting (*e.g.,* high profits despite low morale), it is easier for top management to excuse the pressure as only temporary or inconsequential. However, when both are present at once, it is easier to see that the organization is not performing effectively.

The presence of severe pressure is not so clearly evident in the less successful changes. In one case, there was internal pressure for more effective working relations between top management and lower levels; yet the company was doing reasonably well from a profit standpoint. In another case, there was environmental pressure for a centralized purchasing system, but little pressure from within for such a change.

II. Intervention & Reorientation

While strong pressure may arouse the power structure, this does not provide automatic assurance that top management will see its problems or take the correct action to solve them. Quite likely, top management, when under severe pressure, may be inclined to rationalize its problems by blaming them on a group other than itself, such as "that lousy union" or "that meddling government."

As a result, we find a second stage in the successful change patterns—namely, intervention by an outsider. Important here seems to be the combination of the fact that the newcomer enters at the top of the organization and the fact that he is respected for his skills at improving organization practices. Being a newcomer probably allows him to make a relatively objective appraisal of the organization; entering at the top gives him ready access to those people who make decisions affecting the entire organization; and his being respected is likely to give added weight to his initial comments about the organization.

Thus we find the newcomer in an ideal position to reorient the power structure to its own internal problems. This occurs in the successful changes as the newcomer encourages the top managers to reexamine their past practices and current problems. The effect appears to be one of causing the power structure to suspend, at least temporarily, its traditional habit of presuming beforehand where the "real" problems reside. Otherwise, we would not find top management undertaking the third stage—identifying and diagnosing organization problems. We can see how an outsider was accomplishing this re-

orientation in the following comment by the plant manager in one successful change study:

> I didn't like what the consultant told me about our problems being inside the organization instead of outside. But he was an outsider, supposedly an expert at this sort of thing. So maybe he could see our problems better than we could. I asked him what we ought to do, and he said that we should begin to identify our specific problems.[2]

Three of the less successful changes missed this step. Two of the three attempted large-scale changes without the assistance of an outsider, while the third relied on an outsider who lacked the necessary expertise for reorienting top management.

III. Diagnosis & Recognition

Here, we find the power structure, from top to bottom, as well as the newcomer, joining in to assemble information and collaborate in seeking the location and causes of problems. This process begins at the top, then moves gradually down through the organizational hierarchy. Most often, this occurs in meetings attended by people from various organization levels.

A *shared* approach to power and change makes itself evident during this stage. Through consulting with subordinates on the nature of problems, the top managers are seen as indicating a willingness to involve others in the decision-making process. Discussion topics, which formerly may have been regarded as taboo, are now treated as legitimate areas for further inquiry. We see the diagnosis and recognition process taking place in this example from one successful change study:

The manager's role in the first few months, as he saw it, was to ask questions and to find out what ideas for improvement would emerge from the group as a whole. The process of information gathering took several forms, the principal one being face-to-face conversations between the manager and his subordinates, supervisors on the lower levels, hourly workers, and union representatives. Ideas were then listed for the agenda of weekly planning sessions.[3]

The significance of this step seems to go beyond the possible intellectual benefits derived from a thorough diagnosis of organization problems. This is due to the fact that in front of *every* subordinate there is evidence that (a) top management is willing to change, (b) important problems are being acknowledged and faced up to, and (c) ideas from lower levels are being valued by upper levels.

The less successful changes all seem to avoid this step. For example, on the one hand, those top managements that took a *unilateral* approach seemed to presume ahead of time that they knew what the real problems were and how to fix them. On the other hand, those that took a *delegated* approach tended to abdicate responsibility by turning over authority to lower levels in such a nondirective way that subordinates seemed to question the sincerity and real interest of top management.

IV. Invention & Commitment

Once problems are recognized, it is another matter to develop effective solutions and to obtain full commitment for implementing them. Traditional practices and solutions within an organization often maintain a hold that is difficult to shed. The temptation is always

there, especially for the power structure, to apply old solutions to new problems. Thus, a fourth phase—the invention of new and unique solutions which have high commitment from the power structure—seems to be necessary.

The successful changes disclose widespread and intensive searches for creative solutions, with the newcomer again playing an active role. In each instance the newcomer involves the entire management in learning and practicing new forms of behavior which seek to tap and release the creative resources of many people. Again, as in the previous phase, the method for obtaining solutions is based on a *shared* power concept. Here the emphasis is placed on the use of collaboration and participation in developing group solutions to the problems identified in Phase III.

The potency of this model for obtaining both quality decisions and high commitment to action has been demonstrated repeatedly in research. In three successful changes, the model was introduced as a part of the Phase III diagnosis sessions, with the newcomer either presenting it through his informal comments or subtly conveying it through his own guiding actions as the attention of the group turned to the search for a solution. In two other studies, formal training programs were used to introduce and to help implement the model. For all successful changes, the outcome is essentially the same—a large number of people collaborate to invent solutions that are of their own making and which have their own endorsement.

It is significant that none of the less successful changes reach this fourth stage. Instead, the seeds of failure, sown in the previous phases, grow into instances of serious resistance to change. As a re-

sult, top management in such cases falls back, gives up, or regroups for another effort. Because these studies conclude their reports at this stage, we are not able to determine the final outcome of the less successful change attempts.

V. Experimentation & Search

Each of the successful change studies reports a fifth stage—that of "reality testing" before large-scale changes are introduced. In this phase not only the validity of specific decisions made in Phase IV, but also the underlying model for making these decisions (*shared* power), falls under careful organization scrutiny. Instead of making only big decisions at the top, a number of small decisions are implemented at *all* levels of the organization. Further, these decisions tend to be regarded more as experiments than as final, irreversible decisions. People at all organization levels seem to be searching for supporting evidence in their environment—*e.g.*, dollar savings or higher motivation—before judging the relative merits of their actions. This concern is reflected in the comment of a consultant involved in one successful change:

As might be expected, there was something less than a smooth, unresisted, uncomplicated transition to a new pattern of leadership and organizational activity. Events as they unfolded presented a mixture of success and failures, frustrations and satisfactions. . . . With considerable apprehension, the supervisors agreed to go along with any feasible solution the employees might propose.[4]

This atmosphere of tentativeness is understandable when we think of a power structure undergoing change. On the one hand, lower-level managers are undoubtedly concerned with whether top management will support their decisions. If lower-level managers make decisions that fail, or are subsequently reversed by top levels, then their own future careers may be in jeopardy. Or, on the other hand, if higher-level managers, who are held responsible for the survival of the firm, do not see tangible improvements, then they may revert to the status quo or seek other approaches to change.

Thus, with these experimental attempts at change and the accompanying search for signs of payoff, there begins a final stage where people receive the results and react to them.

VI. Reinforcement & Acceptance

Each of the studies of successful change reports improvements in organization performance. Furthermore, there are relatively clear indications of strong support for change from all organization levels. Obviously, positive results have a strong reinforcing effect—that is, people are rewarded and encouraged to continue and even to expand the changes they are making. We see this expansion effect occurring as more and more problems are identified and a greater number of people participate in the solution of them. Consider this comment by a foreman in one study:

> I've noticed a real difference in the hourly workers. They seem a lot more willing to work, and I can't explain just why it is, but something has happened all right. I suppose it's being treated better. My boss treats me better because he gets treated better. People above me listen to me, and I hope, at least, that I listen to my people below me.[5]

The most significant effect of this phase is probably a greater and more permanent acceptance at all levels of the underlying methods used to bring about the change. In each of the successful changes, the use of *shared* power is more of an institutionalized and continuing practice than just a "one shot" method used to introduce change. With such a reorientation in the decision-making practices of the power structure, it hardly appears likely that these organizations will "slip back" to their previous behavior.

LEARNING CHECKPOINT

Explain the manner in which the shared-approach applies principles of learning and participative management.

LOOKING AHEAD

What is needed in future changes in organization is less intuition and more consideration of the evidence that is now emerging from studies in this area. While it would be unwise to take too literally each of the major patterns identified in this article (future research will undoubtedly dispel, modify, or elaborate on them), their overall import suggests that it is time to put to bed some of the common myths about organization change. As I see it, there are four positive actions called for.

1. We must revise our egocentric notions that organization change is heavily dependent on a master blueprint designed and executed in one fell swoop by an omniscient consultant or top manager.

The patterns identified here clearly indicate that change is the outgrowth of several actions, some planned and some unplanned, each related to the other and occurring over time. The successful changes begin with pressure, which is unplanned from the organization's point of view. Then the more planned stages come into focus as top management initiates a series of events designed to involve lower-level people in the problem-solving process. But, even here, there are usually unplanned events as subordinates begin to "talk back" and raise issues that top management probably does not anticipate. Moreover, there are the concluding stages of experiencing success, partly affected by conscious design but just as often due to forces outside the control of the planners.

2. We too often assume that organization change is for "those people downstairs," who are somehow perceived as less intelligent and less productive than "those upstairs."

Contrary to this assumption, the success patterns point to the importance of top management seeing itself as part of the organization's problems and becoming actively involved in finding solutions to them. Without the involvement and commitment of top management, it is doubtful that lower levels can see the need for change or, if they do, be willing to take the risks that such change entails.

3. We need to reduce our fond attachment for both unilateral and delegated approaches to change.

The *unilateral* approach, although tempting because its procedures are readily accessible to top management, generally serves only to perpetuate the myths and disadvantages of omniscience and downward thinking. On the other hand, the *delegated* approach, while appealing because of its "democratic" connotations, may remove the power structure from direct involvment in a process that calls for its strong guidance and active support.

The findings discussed in this article highlight the use of the more difficult, but perhaps more fruitful, *shared* power approach. As top managers join in to open up their power structures and their organizations to an exchange of influence between upper and lower levels, they may be unleashing new surges of energy and creativity not previously imagined.

4. There is a need for managers, consultants, skeptics, and researchers to become less parochial in their viewpoints.

For too long, each of us has acted as if cross-fertilization is unproductive. Much more constructive dialogue and joint effort are needed if we are to understand better and act wisely in terms of the complexities and stakes inherent in the difficult problems of introducing organization change. ☐

APPENDIX: SURVEY OF STUDIES

Those reporting "successful" organization changes include:

Robert R. Blake, Jane S. Mouton, Louis B. Barnes, and Larry E. Greiner, "Breakthrough in Organization Development," HBR November–December 1964, p. 133.

Robert H. Guest, *Organization Change: The Effect of Successful Leadership* (Homewood, Illinois, The Dorsey Press, Inc., 1962).

Elliott Jaques, *The Changing Culture of a Factory* (New York, The Dryden Press, Inc., 1952).

A. K. Rice, *Productivity and Social Organization: The Ahmedabad Experiment* (London, Tavistock Publications, Ltd., 1958).

S. E. Seashore and D. G. Bowers, *Changing the Structure and Functioning of an Organization* (Ann Arbor, Survey Research Center, The University of Michigan, Monograph No. 33, 1963).

Those showing similar "success" patterns, but containing somewhat less complete information:

Gene W. Dalton, Louis B. Barnes, and Abraham Zaleznik, *The Authority Structure as a Change Variable* (Paper presented at the 57th meeting of the American Sociological Association, August 1962, Washington, D.C.).

Paul R. Lawrence, *The Changing of Organization Behavior Patterns: A Case Study of Decentralization* (Boston, Division of Research, Harvard Business School, 1958).

Paul R. Lawrence, et al, "Battleship Y," *Organizational Behavior and Administration* (Homewood, Illinois, The Dorsey Press, Inc.), p. 328 (1965 edition).

Floyd C. Mann, "Studying and Creating Change: A Means to Understanding Social Organization," *Research in Industrial Human Relations,* edited by C. M. Arensberg et al (New York, Harper and Brothers, 1957).

C. Sofer, *The Organization from Within* (London, Tavistock Publications, Ltd., 1961).

William F. Whyte, *Pattern for Industrial Peace* (New York, Harper and Brothers, 1951).

Included here are studies which reveal "less successful" change patterns:

Chris Argyris, *Interpersonal Competence and Organizational Effectiveness* (Homewood, Illinois, The Dorsey Press, Inc., 1962), especially pp. 254–257.

A. Gouldner, *Patterns of Industrial Bureaucracy* (Glencoe, Illinois, The Free Press, 1964).

Paul R. Lawrence et al, "The Dashman Company" and "Flint Electric," *Organizational Behavior and Administration* (Homewood, Illinois, The Dorsey Press, Inc.), p. 16 (1965 edition) and p. 600 (1961 edition).

George Strauss, "The Set-Up Man: A Case Study of Organizational Change," *Human Organization,* Vol. 13, 1954, p. 17.

A. J. M. Sykes, "The Effects of a Super-

visory Training Course in Changing Supervisors' Perceptions and Expectations of the Role of Management," *Human Relations,* Vol. 15, 1962, p. 227.

William F. Whyte, *Money and Motivation* (New York, Harper and Brothers, 1955).

REFERENCES

1. Robert H. Guest, *Organization Change: The Effect of Successful Leadership* (Homewood, Ill.: The Dorsey Press, Inc., 1962), p. 18.

2. From my unpublished doctoral dissertation, "Organization and Development" (Harvard Business School, June 1965).

3. Guest, *op. cit.,* p. 50.

4. S. E. Seashore and D. G. Bowers, *Changing the Structure and Functioning of an Organization* (Ann Arbor, Survey Research Center, The University of Michigan, Monograph No. 33, 1963), p. 29.

5. Guest, *op. cit.,* p. 64.

D1 ACCEPTANCE OF JOB CHANGE*

The following questionnaire items will enable you to assess your acceptance of changes in your job. The reference point can be the job you presently hold or if not now employed, a job you most recently held. Answer each of the five questions and determine the total score by adding the numbers in the parentheses adjacent to each response. The higher the score, the greater the acceptance of job change.

1. Sometimes changes in the way a job is done are more trouble than they are worth because they create a lot of problems and confusion. How often do you feel that changes which have affected you and your job at (name of organization) have been like this?

    (1) _____ 50% or more of the changes have been more trouble than they're worth
    (2) _____ About 40% of the changes
    (3) _____ About 25% of the changes
    (4) _____ About 15% of the changes
    (5) _____ Only 5% or fewer of the changes have been more trouble than they're worth

2. From time to time changes in policies, procedures, and equipment are introduced by the management. How often do these changes lead to better ways of doing things?

    (1) _____ Changes of this kind never improve things
    (2) _____ They seldom do
    (3) _____ About half of the time they do
    (4) _____ Most of the time they do
    (5) _____ Changes of this kind are always an improvement

3. How well do the various people in the plant or offices who are affected by these changes accept them?

    (1) _____ Very few of the people involved accept the changes
    (2) _____ Less than half do
    (3) _____ About half of them do
    (4) _____ Most of them do
    (5) _____ Practically all of the people involved accept the changes

4. In general, how do you *now* feel about changes during the past year that affected the way your job is done?

    (1) _____ Made things somewhat worse
    (2) _____ Not improved things at all
    (3) _____ Not improved things very much
    (4) _____ Improved things somewhat
    (5) _____ Been a big improvement
        _____ There have been no changes in my job in the past year

---

* Source: Martin Patchen, SOME QUESTIONNAIRE MEASURES OF EMPLOYEE MOTIVATION AND MORALE. Ann Arbor, Mich.: Survey Research Center, University of Michigan, 1965, pp. 1–14 and 40–47.

5.   During the past year when changes were introduced that affected the way your job is done, how did you feel about them *at first*?

At first I thought the changes would:

(1) _____ Make things somewhat worse

(2) _____ Not improve things at all

(3) _____ Not improve things very much

(4) _____ Improve things somewhat

(5) _____ Be a big improvement

_____ There have been no changes in my job in the past year

②2 DO I REALLY RESIST CHANGES?

Change has been a part of everyone's life. Some are able to cope with the uncertainties, suddenness, and frequency of changes in a constructive manner. On the other hand, some have been ill-prepared, emotionally upset, and even physically disabled by the changes in their lives—moving from one location to another, being fired from a job, losing a close friend, etc. There is also the typical resistance to change response that we seem to adopt no matter how large or small the change. People resist change psychologically, physically, behaviorally, and emotionally. Using a short paragraph format, write up a description of how you resisted the following type of changes in your life. In the paragraph indicate what you can remember about how you resisted, the intensity of the resistance, and the length of time you resisted.

I.   How I resisted the situation when I graduated high school and was getting ready to attend college.

II. How I resisted receiving my first failing or poor grade on an examination in college.

III. How I resist throwing away things (clothes, pictures, memorabilia) from the past.

After preparing and rereading these paragraphs determine if there is a common pattern to your resistance of change and rate the intensity of your resistance. Also, think about whether a manager can actually do much to reduce the intensity of his or her workers' resistance to changes in the work place.

THE BEACON AIRCRAFT COMPANY*

OBJECTIVES

1. To illustrate how forces for change and for stability must be managed in organizational development programs.

2. To illustrate the effects of alternative change techniques on the relative strength of forces for change and forces for stability.

STARTING THE EXERCISE

This exercise will help show how the process model of change can help managers develop a set of strategies for organizational change. By understanding the driving and resisting forces in a change situation, managers can systematically attempt to unfreeze the status quo, introduce the necessary change, and refreeze the new status quo.

THE SITUATION

The marketing division of the Beacon Aircraft Company has gone through two reorganizations in the past two years. Initially, its structure changed from a functional to a matrix form. But the matrix structure did not satisfy some functional managers. They complained that the structure confused the authority and responsibility relationships. In reaction to these complaints, the marketing manager revised the structure back to the functional form. This new structure maintained market and project groups, which were managed by project managers with a few general staff personnel. But no functional specialists were assigned to these groups.

After the change, some problems began to surface. Project managers complained that they could not obtain adequate assistance from functional staffs. It not only took more time to obtain necessary assistance, but it also created problems in establishing stable relationships with functional staff members. Since these problems affected their services to customers, project managers demanded a change in the organizational structure—probably again toward a matrix structure. Faced with these complaints and demands from project managers, the vice-president is pondering another reorganization. He has requested an outside consultant to help him in the reorganization plan.

THE PROCEDURE

1. Divide yourselves into groups of five to seven and take the role of consultants.
2. Each group identifies the driving and resisting forces found in the firm. List these forces below.

The driving forces	The resisting forces
_____	_____
_____	_____
_____	_____
_____	_____
_____	_____
_____	_____

3. Each group develops a set of strategies for increasing the driving forces and another set for reducing the resisting forces.
4. Each group prepares a list of changes it wants to introduce.
5. The class reassembles and hears each group's recommendations.

---

* Source: Kae H. Chung and Leon C. Megginson, *Organizational Behavior* (New York: Harper & Row, 1981), pp. 498–99. Used by permission.

THE NEED FOR CHANGE

OBJECTIVES

1. To understand how different change techniques can be used to solve problems.

2. To illustrate how resistance to change can affect the outcome of change efforts.

STARTING THE EXERCISE

I. Establish groups of five or fewer students. Each group is to prepare a short consultant's report concerning the Southeast Par Telephone staffing situation. Specifically, the president wants the consultants to determine the organization's problem and to develop a solution that results in the fewest complaints.

The exercise is more informative if one group of students from the class serves as evaluators of the presentations. This group would be the panel reviewing the analysis of the other groups.

II. The Southeast Par Telephone situation is as follows:

Over the past three years, Southeast Par Telephone Co. has had a terrible record of recruiting young, qualified management trainees for positions in the accounting, operations, traffic, and maintenance departments. The company has a reputation of paying well and treating employees well, but it is also considered to be an organization with limited advancement opportunity.

The company is searching for young men and women between 21 and 35 years old, with college degrees (preferably some graduate education), who are willing to work different shifts during the two-year training cycle.

The unemployment rate in the city is 5.1 percent, which is below the national average, and the company is located eight miles west of the city. Management is puzzled about the company's inability to bring in qualified people for well-paying trainee positions.

III. Each group should develop a consultants' report which emphasizes the problem, the diagnosis that should be used, the most feasible change strategy, and the anticipated resistance consequences of any change strategy.

IV. Each group should select a spokesperson to make a short presentation emphasizing the points in III to the evaluating group.

V. The evaluating group should then select the best consultants' report and discuss with the entire class why this particular report was selected.

DAVIS REGIONAL MEDICAL CENTER*

Davis Regional Medical Center is an acute care, general hospital located in Charlesville, a community of 35,000 in the southwestern United States. The organization began in 1950 as a 35-bed facility known as Davis County Hospital. The hospital grew to a capacity of 55 beds after its first three years of operation. Economic growth in the region along with a rapid influx of people resulted in additional expansions and by 1968 the hospital had reached its present capacity of 166 beds.

The population in the region has grown steadily over the last fifteen years. (The population of Davis County was approximately 56,800 in 1960 and 86,600 in 1975.) However, the hospital size has remained unchanged. Approximately 500 people are

employed at Davis. The medical staff consists of 75 doctors and dentists. A substantial majority of the medical staff are specialists. Therefore, the hospital offers a wide range of medical services. Current estimates are that the hospital serves 10,000 inpatients and approximately 16,000 outpatients each year.

REGIONAL MEDICAL CENTER

In 1972, the board of directors of the hospital concluded that it was necessary to undertake a major expansion of the hospital's physical plant if it were to continue to adequately serve residents in and around the Charlesville area. Hospital managers and board members had received numerous complaints

* Source: From Donald D. White and H. William Vroman. ACTION IN ORGANIZATIONS. Copyright © 1977 by Holbrook Press, Inc., subsidiary of Allyn and Bacon, Inc., Boston. Reprinted with permission.

concerning overcrowded conditions in the hospital. Beds for patients often were found in the halls and waiting rooms, considerable delays were experienced by new patients registering at the hospital due to the lack of available space, and numerous offices and hallways had become storage points for inventory material and equipment. At one point, hospital administrators were informed by State Health Department officials that if equipment and cartons of supplies were not removed from various hallways, the hospital would not be licensed for the coming year and therefore could not be accredited by the Joint Commission (a national accrediting agency).

The situation had become critical by the time the final decision was made on the expansion. It was decided that a major building effort costing twelve million dollars would be undertaken. The number of beds in the medical facility were to be increased from 166 to 248, and a number of existing services were to be expanded in the new facility. Shortly after the expansion decision was made, the board also changed the name of the hospital from Davis County Hospital to Davis Regional Medical Center. The purpose of this name change was to more accurately reflect the services available and the population served by the growing medical complex. A fund raising drive in Charlesville managed to provide a base of one million dollars with which to begin the expansion. However, a feasibility study completed during the drive suggested that the performance of the hospital (based on past figures) could not financially support the total planned expansion. Therefore, a revised plan was decided upon.

ADMINISTRATIVE AND ORGANIZATIONAL BACKGROUND

Davis Regional Medical Center, like similar county hospitals in the state, is governed by a seven-member board of directors. State law provided that the board be appointed by the local county judge. As with any political system, appointments are based on a combination of individual qualifications and the political postures of board members. Historically, the board had not provided strong leadership to the hospital. However, recent appointments, together with strong leadership from a new board chairman, had greatly increased the activity and contribution of the board to the operation of the hospital.

The administrator of any county hospital is placed in a unique position of having to respond to political pressures and medical needs of the people whom he serves. In addition, he often finds himself between pressures created by his medical staff, employees, and the public. The toll which these pressures create sometimes is quite high. Such was the case at Davis Regional Medical Center. Within the ten-year period from 1965 to 1975, the hospital had four separate administrators.

EXHIBIT 1

Past Administration at DRMC

Administrator	Years	Reason for Termination
G. B.	1949–53	Under pressure to resign (personal)
B. C.	1953–55	A series of problems both financial and political; asked to resign
H. M. (R.N.)	1955–62	Considered to be a good administrator; resigned under positive circumstances; she may have felt that the job was becoming "Too Big" for her
F. H.	1962–67	Hospital showed a $250,000 loss; was asked to resign
G. E.	1967–71	Illness; under mild pressure to resign
R. W.	1971–74	Was asked to resign
C. B.	1974–present	Currently the DRMC Administrator

Three of those administrators along with the one acting administrator served in the position during the last five years.

Reasons for the turnovers were numerous. One administrator, Frederick Harold, was asked to resign after the hospital lost over $250,000 in a period of two years. His replacement, Glen Easton, was charged with the responsibility of putting the hospital back in the black. Within one year Easton had done so. However, during the end of his term as administrator, his decisions affecting patients and employees alike became more and more autocratic and seemingly unrealistic. For example, he once forced an orderly to enter the room of a critically ill patient to collect a dollar-a-day charge for TV service. He had instructed the employee to collect one dollar from each patient each day that the patient was in the room. Acts such as these received considerable attention throughout the community. Later, it was discovered that Easton had leukemia, and he retired from his position as administrator. (A number of his later decisions were attributed, in part, by those around him to his illness. His replacement was Robert Winston who had served as assistant administrator under his predecessor for a period of two years.

The board appointed Winston as administrator of the hospital in 1971. He served in that position until he was asked to resign in 1974. Persons who worked with the hospital during his tenure as administrator (outside consultants and hospital managers), described him as unimaginative and unwilling to put in the necessary work to develop and maintain a strong medical facility. In his final months as administrator, he was on the hospital premises from four to six hours a day. Although reasons for his requested resignation were never made public, personal problems which were believed to interfere with the fulfillment of his administrative responsibilities were cited by the board.

Due to the suddenness with which Winston had been asked to tender his resignation, the board had not yet begun its search for a new administrator. In the interim period of five months Donald Dale, who served as assistant administrator under Winston, was named as acting administrator. He was closely assisted by Larry Engels, the Director of Personnel. The two men worked closely as a team making day-to-day operating decisions.

Dale and Engels were aware of acute employee morale and motivation problems within the medical center. They attributed these problems to the lack of leadership under which the hospital had been operating and employee concerns about what the new ad-

ministrator would be like. Both recently had attended a seminar for hospital administrators in which the importance of employee attitudes and participation had been a major subject. In particular, they had been impressed by the discussion and illustration of a Management by Objectives (MBO) system designed for health care organizations. They were convinced that such a system would help create greater *esprit de corps* at Davis Regional Medical Center and improve the exchange of ideas and information between department heads within the hospital. Furthermore, the director of personnel believed that supervisory and department head training programs would have to be conducted in order to prepare management personnel throughout the organization for the hoped for MBO-type system.

In July, 1974, the director of personnel contacted Dr. John Connors, a university professor and management consultant. It had been Dr. Connors who earlier that year had presented the administrator seminar that Engels and Dale attended. They arranged to meet together and to discuss the present situation at Davis Regional Medical Center. During the next month, the two administrators and Dr. Connors met on numerous occasions and discussed the problems and needs of the hospital.

Both Dale and Engels were emphatic about wanting to develop a more employee-oriented administration. For example, they created a non-supervisory employee council which met once a month to discuss with the two men problems and conditions throughout the hospital. The intended purpose of this council was to provide a means by which Dale and Engels could enhance two-way communication between the hospital administration and the employees at Davis. Each department elected one person to represent them in the council. Initially, most of the communication was from the top down. However, shortly after the council had been created, a core of employees rose to take leadership of the group. They elected a spokesman and requested that they be permitted to meet once a month without either Dale or Engels present. Thereafter, the employee representatives met twice monthly, once with the administrators and once without them.

Dale and Engels also shared the view that some form of management training should be developed and conducted for department heads and hospital supervisors, whom they saw as the key to hospital effectiveness. There was some hesitancy on the part of Dr. Connors and Mr. Dale to initiate such a program prior to the selection of a new administrator. Both men believed that it might be unfair to saddle a new administrator with a program that he might not favor. The director of personnel, however, felt strongly that the program should be initiated "as soon as possible."

Such a program subsequently was designed by Dr. Connors and agreed upon by the three men. Shortly thereafter, Mr. Dale was informed that a new administrator had been selected by the Board of Directors. The new administrator was scheduled to take over his post at DRMC in approximately four weeks. Mr. Dale told Dr. Connors that his discussions with the new administrator, Mr. Benson, led him to believe that Mr. Benson would be favorable to a management development program. However, both men decided to wait until a formal meeting could be held with Mr. Benson before proceeding with the actual program.

A NEW LEADER FOR THE "TROOPS"

Arnold Benson came to Davis Hospital from a multi-facility complex in St. Louis, Missouri. He had been selected out of 70 applicants for the position of administrator at Davis County Hospital. Benson was a young man 33 years of age. He held bachelor's and master's degrees in business administration and had considerable experience working in hospital organizations. In his words, "My objective was to become a professional hospital administrator. I realized that since I did not yet have a master's degree in hospital administration I would have to go with a 'back door approach' by working my way up the ranks."

Thus, Benson's first position in a hospital was that of director of purchasing and personnel in a 118-bed facility. He next took the position of assistant administrator in a 156-bed Catholic hospital. In a period of two years, he rose from assistant administrator to associate administrator and finally to that of administrator of the hospital. Finally he became administrator of a 144-bed and a 134-bed multi-hospital complex in St. Louis, Missouri. He remained in the hospital for four years "gaining exposure, experience and expertise." Prior to his hospital experiences, Mr. Benson had worked for a year and a half on a General Motors assembly line while going to college. He also had spent four years in the Marine Corps, having enlisted when he was seventeen years old.

In the summer of 1974, Arnold Benson began looking for a new position as a hospital administrator. He believed that he had learned a great deal in his present job; however, he was anxious to relocate in a smaller community. The St. Louis Hospital of which he was administrator was located in a predominantly black, low-income, ghetto area. His hospital had been a prime target for numerous union drives (none of which were successful) and he had overseen a major expansion of the hospital facilities. He wanted to relocate in a community of less than 50,000 population somewhere in the southwestern United States. His salary requirements were rather stringent due to his experience in administration. Therefore, he was very pleased when he was selected as the new administrator at Davis Regional.

Benson was a tall athletic-looking man whose mild manners and easygoing Texas drawl tended to hide his "down-to-business" approach to administration. Soon after arriving, he realized that he would be facing many problems inside and outside of the hospital in the next few months. He knew that the most pressing of these was the hospital expansion. Moreover, it was clear to him that the first concern of certain members of the board of directors was the financial position of the hospital.

Financial concerns plagued Mr. Benson from the moment he arrived at Davis Regional Medical Center. During his first weeks on the job, the building program finances consumed almost 50 percent of his time. In addition, two particular decisions, both of which would have a direct impact on hospital employees, had to be made.

The first of these decisions concerned a 10¢ across-the-board pay increase that was due to all hospital employees in January. Mr. Benson had not been told of this promised increase until he had been at the hospital for some time. Immediately upon learning of the proposed increase, he sat down and calculated its impact on his budget. The total cost to the medical center appeared to be well in excess of $200,000. Feeling the need to hold the line on expenses, Mr. Benson decided not to put through the wage increase. In his words, "When I 'came aboard' the board charged me with the financial responsibility of the medical center. If the troops were to get their pay increase in January, it would throw the entire budget out of kilter. I have only been here three weeks, and quite frankly the '75 budget didn't get the attention it deserved." After making his decision, Mr. Benson dictated a memo announcing that while employees at Davis could expect to receive up to a 6 percent increase for the new year, the 10¢ across-the-board increase would not be given. Mr. Benson also stressed that the total financial posture of the hospital would have to be re-evaluated. The memo was posted on the employee bulletin board.

Soon after the memo was posted, a rumor circulated throughout the hospital that the board of directors was about to purchase a new automobile for Mr. Benson. Pictures of Cadillacs and Mark IV Continentals were placed on the bulletin board on an almost daily basis. His memo concerning denial of the pay increase was slashed with a knife and various comments were written on it. (The hospital-owned automobile which Benson actually used was a Ford Galaxie driven by the previous administrator.)

Recognizing the discontent over his decision, Benson met with members of the employee advisory council to discuss the pay question. Several members of the group quoted statistics showing that on the average blue-collar workers throughout the United States were being paid more than were most hospital employees. Mr. Benson replied that he thought it was unfair to quote blue-collar statistics and that he believed the most that a hospital employee at the medical center could look forward to would be to live comfortably. He then asked the members of the advisory council if they would work harder if they received 10¢ per-hour increase. According to Benson, "When all responded negatively, I told them point blank that it appeared that it would be foolish to reward people ten more cents per hour with no increase in productivity." He did go on to tell those present that he would do his best to see to it that they received some pay increases (up to 6 percent based on merit) as soon as the necessary funds became available. In addition, he told them that he hoped to put in effect a new wage and salary administration program in the near future.

The employee council also voiced complaints about

EXHIBIT 2

Managerial Personnel on Payroll When Benson Was Hired

Name	Department	Tenure with DRMC	
		Years Employed	Years as Department Head
J. C.	Physical Therapy	25	21
D. T.	Nuclear Medicine	18	6
D. D.	Assistant Administrator	11½	11½
B. G.	Housekeeping	9	2
G. H.	Radiology	8½	8½
K. F.	Nursing	7	2½
L. H.	Dietary	7	7
L. E.	Personnel	5	4
J. H.	E.M.S.	5	1
P. G.	Purchasing	4	1
L. C.	Child Care	4	3
T. M.	Pharmacy	4	2
E. B.	Laboratory	3	2½
D. B.	Medical Records	2½	2½
J. G.	Maintenance	2½	2½
L. P.	Respiratory Therapy	2	2
E. I.	Social Service	1	1
M. R.	Volunteers	1	1
M. K.	Comptroller	1	1

Explanation:
1. Two new departments, EKG and EEG, were added shortly after Benson's arrival. Previously, their functions and personnel were under Nuclear Medicine.
2. Of those department heads listed above, the following persons left DRMC within six months after Benson's arrival. K. F. (resignation requested); L. H. (resigned following demotion); L. E. (resignation requested); P. G. (resigned, but was to have been replaced); E. B. (resigned to take promotion elsewhere); L. P. (resigned to take a similar position elsewhere, was dissatisfied at DRMC).

other conditions at Davis hospital. Over a period of the next few weeks. Mr. Benson saw to it that many of the problems were dealt with to the group's satisfaction. However, when the last "demand" was met he announced that he believed that there was no longer a need for the advisory group. A question was raised by one of the employees concerning whether or not the group would be permitted to re-form if subsequent problems arose. Mr. Benson replied that it would not be permitted to do so.

Benson was confronted by a second important decision not long after the incident involving the pay increase memo. The hospital had been able to obtain the money necessary for expansion through tax exempt revenue bonds. However, the building program itself did not include much needed parking lots. Arnold Benson, therefore, found it necessary to take his request for an additional 1.3 million dollars to the local banking community. Although the bankers agreed to underwrite the project, the feasibility study on which their decision was based indicated that the parking lots would have to be income-generating entities in their own right. Prior to this time, all parking in hospital lots was provided without charge to the medical staff, employees, and visitors. Now, however, it was clear to Benson that all parties would in the future be required to pay a parking fee.

Although he expected resistance on the issue from the doctors, he was more concerned about the reactions of general employees to the decision. The fact that he had been confronted by this second decision so shortly after his refusal to grant the across-the-board pay increase further aggravated his situation. As far as Benson was concerned, the decision had been made. However, he and Dr. Connors agreed that its announcement should be temporarily postponed.

MANAGEMENT DEVELOPMENT

In early January, department heads from throughout the hospital began meeting with Dr. Connors as part of an overall management development program. Those participating met in a series of seven two-hour sessions. The total program took place over a period of approximately one month. (A similar program was conducted for supervisors during the following month.)

According to Mr. Dale, the purpose of the management programs was twofold. He believed that it was necessary to provide those hospital employees in management positions with some form of supervisory training. He also felt that the program would be a good

way to single out the department heads and supervisors for "special attention."

The sessions were recommended to the department heads and supervisors by Mr. Benson, however, participation remained voluntary. All but two department heads attended the series of sessions. (Although Mr. Benson and Mr. Dale requested that they be permitted to attend the classes, it was agreed that their presence might inhibit the participation of department heads. Both men were provided with copies of all materials distributed, but neither attended the formal sessions.)

The content of the programs included traditional subjects such as the elements and techniques of supervision. However, emphasis also was placed on achieving improved interpersonal relations between department heads and improving the exchange of information between the departments themselves. (See Exhibit 3)

One event which took place during the sessions dramatized that a certain amount of distrust and lack of cooperation existed between many department heads throughout the hospital. During one of the early sessions, the participants were asked to complete evaluation forms that were to be used in connection with an exercise known as the Johari Window. The purpose of the exercise was to help the managers see themselves more clearly as others saw them and to help others in the group in a similar manner by providing them with "image feedback" information. The theory behind the exercise together with its purpose was explained to those present. Each manager was asked to write the name of every department head (including him/herself) and to list at least one asset and one liability of that person. Dr. Connors requested that the completed forms be returned to him at the beginning of the next session. The name of the individual providing the "feedback" information was not to be placed on the sheet itself. Dr. Connors explained that he would facilitate the exchange of feedback at the next session by reading the name of a participant followed by the assets and liabilities which were identified by his/her peers.

As he had planned, Dr. Connors began the next session by asking that all feedback sheets be passed in to him. Much to his surprise only about half of the sheets were returned and most of them were insufficiently completed. After a short pause, he asked those present to explain why they had failed to complete the assignment. Following a brief discussion, it was evident that the department heads had decided in another meeting that they would not complete the

EXHIBIT 3

**Outline of Supervisory Development
Program Davis Regional Medical Center**

Session[1]	Assignments
1 Introductory Comments and an Icebreaker Supervisory Functions: Models and the Environment Preparing for our Sessions	Case Study
2 The Hospital Organization: Authority, Power and Informal Relationships	Case Study Ch. 15[2]
3 Understanding Ourselves and Others	Case Study
4 Leading and Motivating Employees	Case Study, Film Ch. 1,2
5 Improving Interpersonal and Interdepartmental Communications	Ch. 4, Nominal Grouping Exercise, Role Play
6 Setting Goals and Making Decisions	Case Study, Role Play, Ch. 6, 9
7 Evaluating and Handling Employee Conflict	Ch. 11,12, Case Study, Role Play

[1] Sessions—(1 hour and 50 minutes; last 15–20 minutes spent answering questions and dealing with problems on an individual basis.)

[2] Chapters were taken from a hospital supervisory management book selected for the program by Dr. Connors.

feedback sheet. Reasons for not wanting to complete the assignment ranged from claims that the participants did not know one another well enough (prior to the management program many of the department heads did not know one another by name, although a "get acquainted" exercise was used in the first session) to fear that the information assembled on each individual would in some way be used against him or her. One woman openly expressed concern that other department heads at the meeting might misuse the information. Another head privately suggested that some of those in attendance thought that Dr. Connors, himself, might take the information to the administrator. The discussion that followed the failure to hand in the assignment had a cathartic effect on the group. For the first time, many of those in attendance "opened up" and talked about the lack of communication and trust that existed between the department heads and between the department heads and the administrator.

Dr. Connors ended the session by again explaining that the purpose of the exercise was to "improve our understandings of ourselves as well as of those with whom we associate throughout the hospital." After another brief discussion, it was agreed by all that the feedback sheets would be completed and returned

at the following session. At that next session, the exercise was completed smoothly. Many of the managers commented afterwards that they believed that the exercise had been beneficial and had helped to open up the group. One department head did comment, however, "To tell you the truth, I think our refusal to complete the feedback sheets helped to break the ice between us. You know, it is the first time we really ever got together and agreed on something."

Subsequent sessions of the department head development program produced numerous positive comments and favorable evaluations of the overall program. Upon completion of the program, each participant received a certificate signed by Mr. Benson and Dr. Connors.

FOLLOW-UP

A few days after the department heads' program was completed, Mr. Benson asked Dr. Connors to meet with him. He began their conference by stating that he was pleased with what he had heard about the sessions and was anxious to insure that the momentum which had been created would not be lost. He asked Dr. Connors what he thought of bringing all of the department heads together for a weekend retreat at a resort area not far from Charlesville. Dr. Connors was pleased with Mr. Benson's suggestion. He told the administrator that he had seriously considered recommending that such a retreat take place, but was hesitant to do so because of the financial situation at the hospital. Mr. Benson replied that the money for the retreat could be found since he anticipated that the outcome of the retreat would have a positive impact on the operation of the facility.

The following week Mr. Benson told department heads at their weekly meeting on January 31 that the retreat had been scheduled for the weekend of February 14 and 15. He went on to explain that the department heads would gather on Friday morning at the hospital and would drive directly to the resort. All expenses would be paid by the medical center. He told them that he hoped that the meeting would permit a free exchange of ideas.

During the week before the scheduled retreat, Mr. Connors received an invitation from Mr. Benson to meet with the department heads in their meeting on Thursday. Dr. Connors agreed to do so as long as neither Mr. Benson nor Mr. Dale would be present at the meeting.

The meeting itself brought quite a surprise. It was immediately evident to Dr. Connors that the mood of the department heads was not what he had expected. As he walked into the room he heard the men and women present voicing numerous complaints to one another. When they saw Dr. Connors the group immediately quieted down. It was not clear to him whether or not they had been told he would be attending the meeting. Therefore, he explained his presence and told them that he was interested in how things had been going the two or three weeks since their last session. Much to his surprise, the grumbling began immediately. Some of the complaints were minor. However, one complaint in particular took Dr. Connors by surprise. That complaint focused on the upcoming retreat. A few department heads stated that they did not know whether or not they would go to the resort with the rest of the group. One newly married woman stated that it was Valentine's Day and her husband did not want her to leave. Two other heads said they had previous plans to attend a Valentine's Day dance at the Country Club that Friday evening. As discussion continued, it became apparent that the department heads had been told rather than consulted about the retreat. Some expressed displeasure with being "forced" into going to the retreat and using

part of their weekend without first being asked their opinion.

Dr. Connors listened carefully and explained to the managers that he himself believed that the retreat was a good idea. He told them about how he had planned on suggesting such an activity to the administrator, but how Mr. Benson had come up with the idea on his own. Moreover, he told them that he believed that they should give Mr. Benson "a chance" during the weekend to see what might come out of the retreat. There were a few supportive comments made by one or two department heads and the meeting broke up.

Dr. Connors left the meeting disturbed. He had not expected to find the level of dissatisfaction which existed among the department heads. As he walked toward the entrance of the hospital he asked himself whether or not he should try to provide any further assistance to Mr. Benson before the group left for the retreat the next morning. He decided to stop in and see the administrator before leaving the hospital.

□

CASE QUESTIONS

1. Is the idea of going on a retreat a good one? What do you think will be accomplished at the retreat?

2. Evaluate the educational component of the organizational development program.

3. Identify the steps of the change process as undertaken at Davis Regional Medical Center. Are the steps taken in the appropriate order? Explain.

² GET RID OF FRANKLIN!*

The Franklin problem apparently started about the time that Harold Newland, President of Newland Electronics Corporation, issued this memorandum:

To:　Staff　　　　　　　　　　　　　　December 2
From:　H. Newland
Subject:　Organizational Changes

As you are all well aware, growth at Newland Electronics Corporation this past year has exceeded our planned estimates. Sales of our unique microswitches and relays have risen above the 15 million dollar lovol with anticipated sales to reach 18.5 million next year. This is a credit to our entire organization.

This growth will require several organizational changes if we are to continue our success pattern. Our new organizational structure will reflect additional specialization within our existing functional groups. For some it will be a blessing, since many persons will not be required to "wear as many hats as before."

Effective immediately, I will personally intensify our efforts in long range product and market planning. Mr. Charles Murphy will become Executive Vice-President, responsible for overall plant management. Mr. Martin Brown will now devote full time to our sales effort as Vice-President—Marketing. We are now seeking a qualified person to assume the position of Vice-President—Finance.

Dr. Arnold Wilson, who has provided much of our recent technological growth as Supervisor of the New Products Group, will become Vice-President—Operations.

Additional changes at other levels will be announced by Mr. Murphy as they are effected.

H. NEWLAND

The next memorandum was released two weeks later:

To:　Staff　　　　　　　　　　　　　　December 18
From:　A. Wilson
Subject:　Changes in the Operations Department

The following promotions are announced, effective immediately:

Edward Bellman—Director of Manufacturing
Robert Maxey—Director of Engineering
Matthew Doyle—Supervisor of Product Engineering
Thomas Carlson—Supervisor of New Products
Harry Pleasant—Manufacturing Superintendent

The attached organization chart will now apply.

A. WILSON

Approved: C. MURPHY

---

* Source: Reprinted from Robert D. Joyce, ENCOUNTERS IN ORGANIZATIONAL BEHAVIOR, 1972 with permission of Pergamon Press, Ltd., Oxford, England.

It was March. Dr. Arnold Wilson had only been Vice-President—Operations, for two months, but it had seemed like a year. It was one thing to solve technical problems as he had been doing as former head of the New Products Group. Lately, however, it seemed as if all he did each day was listen to "people" problems. Now he had another problem.

Wilson was aware that there was some friction between Bill Franklin of Engineering Services and Matthew Doyle of Product Engineering. Apparently the situation had worsened because both Doyle and Bob Maxey, the new Director of Engineering, came to Wilson's office this morning and demanded that Franklin be terminated.

Maxey and Doyle brought two charges against Franklin:

1. Franklin was not cooperating with Doyle's Product Engineering Group (production engineering). Drafts and technical writing support requests were constantly ignored. Projects were falling behind schedule.

2. Franklin personally was too young and inexperienced to handle this responsibility in a growing organization. He also was lacking in technical electronics know-how and preferred drinking coffee to learning his job. He ran his group like a kindergarten—all for fun and no effort.

Their proposal was to terminate Franklin or transfer him out of the Engineering Department. Maxey did not have authority to terminate a group supervisor and had brought the problem to Wilson.

Bill Franklin was twenty-nine and an Industrial Management graduate. He had spent two years in the Army and had been at Newland for three years. He started as an engineer in Product Engineering when the supervisor there was Milt Henry. Henry had liked Franklin, and when Henry decided to leave Newland, he suggested the creation of a new Engineering Services Group to provide technical writing, drafting, and related services to both the engineering and manufacturing areas. It was to be a talent pool on call when

EXHIBIT A

Newland Electronics Corporation (after Organizational Changes)

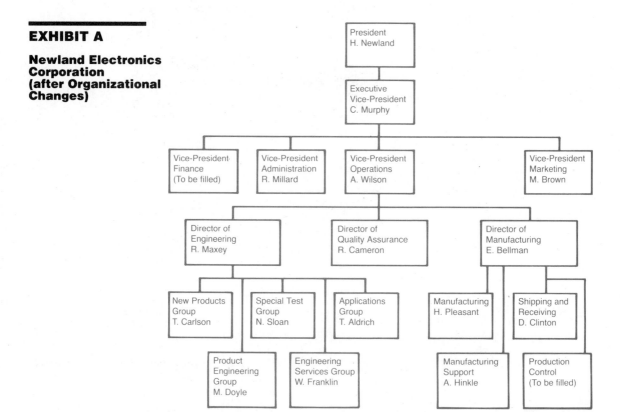

Organization Chart (January)

EXHIBIT B

Newland Electronics Corporation (before Organizational Changes)

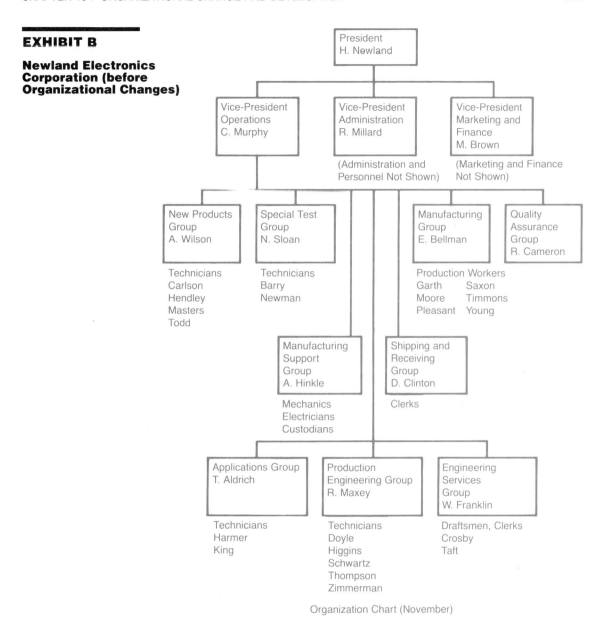

Organization Chart (November)

needed. Henry suggested young Franklin to head this new group and Franklin got the job.

Henry was not replaced from within. Instead, Charles Murphy selected Robert Maxey, a senior engineer from another small firm within the industry. Maxey was well qualified. He had a B.S. and M.S. in Electrical Engineering and twelve years experience. Maxey later brought in three engineers who had worked with him before . . . Doyle, Higgins, and Zimmerman. From almost that point on there was constant

conflict between Franklin and Product Engineering, particularly Maxey and Doyle.

When Maxey and Doyle left, Wilson called Bill Franklin to his office. Franklin was enraged, but not surprised at the charges. He said that Maxey and Doyle told him they were taking the problem to Wilson.

Franklin claimed that over 70 percent of his technical writing and drafting effort was already being supplied to Product Engineering. The remainder was spread out thinly to all other user areas. He agreed he could use more draftsmen, but felt the problem was deeper than that. In Franklin's opinion, Maxey and Doyle just had to have everything their own way. They were demanding a complete change in the drawing and specification numbering system. Franklin felt they wanted specifications systems like those used in their prior company. They were also purposely hypercritical of errors, and vastly exaggerated this as supposed incompetence. They really wanted control of drafting and specs by making it part of Product Engineering. Franklin felt this was coming and would not tolerate it.

He stressed his management ability as supervisor of the largest engineering group and felt his people were extremely loyal and hardworking, citing the facts that he had the lowest turnover and absentee rates in the entire plant.

Wilson suggested the possibility of a transfer to manufacturing but Franklin was cool to the idea. He felt it would be a demotion. Franklin offered his solution to the problem. "I'm doing my job like always. Get Maxey and Doyle off my back!"

Wilson decided to get more information from other likely sources. Ed Bellman had an opinion:

"Franklin is a bright young man. We all like him out here. I've heard he is technically weak, but he seems to be a good supervisor. I would consider him in floor supervision or for a spot in our new Production Control Group. I talked with him a few weeks ago, but he didn't seem very interested."

Wilson (to himself)—

Bellman is still miffed at being passed over for Vice-President—Operations. He is a good production man but lacks formal education. He would have difficulty managing my technical people.

Bellman (to himself)—

So, Ph.D. Wilson develops a product or two and they start grooming him for the top. I wonder how long he can work these problems out on his slide rule. The men's room scuttlebutt has it that the prima donna engineering types are looking to this Franklin decision as a test of Wilson's management ability. Good luck, Doctor Wilson.

Wilson conducted several additional discussions.
    Carlson said:

"I've had no problems with Franklin, but then you (Dr. Wilson) did most of the liaison with him before your promotion. I don't think he fully carries his share though."

Sloan said:

"My complaint is a lack of technical writing. Franklin says it's getting diverted to Product Engineering. The work quality seems all right though. Mr. Maxey and Mr. Doyle are pretty sharp guys and are real assets to our company."

Aldrich said:

"Franklin is a friendly guy, but as an Industrial Management graduate, he just doesn't have enough technical background in electronics. Perhaps night school courses would help. I think the feelings of a new Engineering Manager should be given special consideration."

Cameron said:

"Franklin works relaxed . . . perhaps too relaxed. But he has management organization and personnel ability that puts most of us to shame. Several months ago I tried to talk two of his men into a transfer to Quality Assurance. I thought they would jump at the opportunity even though no raises were involved. Neither one left."

Wilson had been trained to be a logical person and was disturbed by the emotional way almost everyone had responded when the Franklin situation was discussed. Wilson wished he had more facts to work with but felt he had to take some type of action very soon.   ☐

CASE QUESTIONS

1. What should Wilson now do?
2. What caused the organizational change? Was the change successful? Explain.
3. Should Wilson consider the need for further change or modification of the organization? Why?

EPILOGUE

We have now completed our presentation of *Organizational Behavior and Management*. As we indicated at the onset, we live in an organized society. Realistically, it is now virtually impossible to escape organizations. The vast majority of us work in organizations and will spend the remainder of our working years in organizations. Therefore, the intent of this book has been to study, examine, and review organizations and what takes place within them.

The main actors throughout our presentation have been people—specifically, the employees of organizations, the managers and non-managers. It is *people* who conduct the affairs, transactions, and productive work in organizations. It is *people* who perform well or slow down production or quit to join other organizations. It is *people* who make decisions. It is *people* who lead others, engage in political behavior, distribute rewards, and grow and develop. Thus, this book purposefully has focused on the behavior of people in organizations.

As you now know, theories of human behavior are numerous, sometimes confusing, and often contradictory. Nevertheless, theorists, researchers, and managers continue the search to become more knowledgeable about people. In fact, the field of study now called organizational behavior has evolved because managers and society want to know more about people within organizations.

PEOPLE IN ORGANIZATIONS

The concern for people performing jobs in organizations is not new. What is relatively new, however, is that we are finally becoming more scientific in our study of people within organizations. The importance and use of the scientific approach have been emphasized throughout this book.

The scientific approach to the study of people in organizations is the result of such factors as: (1) the managers' need for more than simple, intuitive opinions to make decisions and solve problems; (2) the contributions of a number of behavioral disciplines; (3) a trend away from a "one best way" philosophy and description of people toward a more contingency-based approach; and (4) shifts in the political, economic, international, and competitive environments in which organizations are attempting to survive. Although the scientific approach will not always provide the perfect answer, it does provide a useful framework for the study and analysis of people in organizations.

THE MANAGER: THEORIST, RESEARCHER, AND PRACTITIONER

As indicated throughout this book, more and more managers need to know and use theories, review relevant research findings, and apply techniques that work. Furthermore, to be successful, managers need to acquire and develop diagnostic skills. Managers in organizational settings diagnose perceptions, attitudes, group norms, intergroup conflict, power relationships, political tactics, noncompliance, low morale, and other topics covered throughout the book. As suggested, these are difficult factors to diagnose.

Managers usually perform their diagnostic tasks in settings that occasionally are turbulent, ambiguous, and unreceptive. This suggests that managers' lives are challenging but also potentially troublesome. For example, research findings indicate that managers:

- Work long hours.
- Are extremely busy.
- Perform work that is fragmented.
- Have numerous tasks to perform.
- Are primarily involved with oral communication.
- Use a lot of interpersonal contact.
- Are not the best reflective planners.
- Are not generally aware of how they use their time.

The manager's job is exciting. It is dynamic, filled with challenges and uncertainty, and involves people. This excitement is what we hope has been portrayed in the book. We admit that managing organizational behavior is difficult, but we also know that managers are extremely important in our society.

ORGANIZATIONAL BEHAVIOR: REVISITED

We pointed out early that many of the theories, research findings, and practical applications that managers review, use, and modify have evolved from the behavioral disciplines. As a result of this evolution, we now have reached a point where the field of organizational behavior is recognized as an integrative attempt to apply the behavioral sciences.

In Chapter 1, we defined organizational behavior (OB) as:

The study of human behavior, attitudes, and performance within an organizational setting; drawing on theory, methods, and principles from such disciplines as psychology, sociology, and cultural anthropology to learn about *individual* perceptions, values, learning capacities, and actions while working in *groups* and within the total *organization;* analyzing the external environment's effect on the organization and its human resources, missions, objectives, and strategies.

Each part of this definition has been covered in the book. However, as we noted in Chapter 1, it is valuable to consider OB as: (1) a way of thinking;

(2) an eclectic field of study; (3) humanistic; (4) performance-oriented; (5) concerned about how the environment affects people; and (6) scientifically based. These features spell out why OB is now considered an applied field of study.

The integration of the behavioral sciences into OB has significant value to practicing managers. It provides them with theories, research, and techniques that they can use and modify in their unique organizational context. Figure 1 presents many of the topics discussed in the chapters in the context of OB.

FIGURE 1

The Manager's Guide to Applied Organizational Behavior

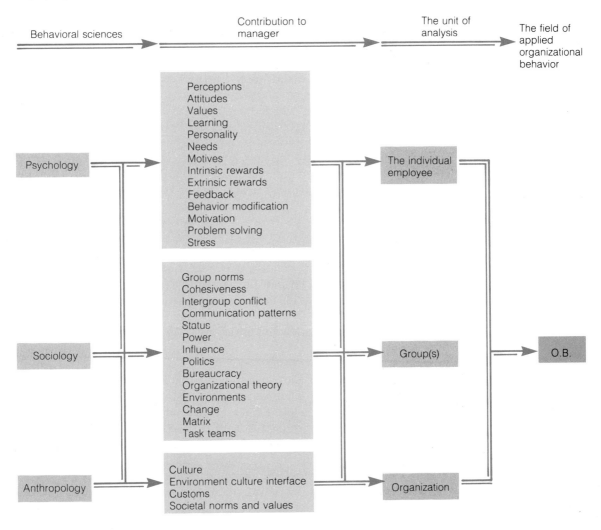

THE TREND AWAY FROM SIMPLE ANSWERS

The prominence of the contingency theme indicates that simple, universally accepted answers do not exist. There are simple explanations that can provide insight about people in organizations, but they are often incomplete, misleading, and unrealistic. For example, the trait theories of leadership are concise but are considered unrealistic and nonpredictive. In their place have emerged more complex, yet unproved theories of leadership such as the path-goal and Vroom-Yetton models.

The trend away from the simple toward the more complex is found at every level of analysis—individual, group, and organizational—and for most organizational behavior topics from individual perception to goal setting to team building to career planning. Unfortunately, many theorists and researchers have failed to explain their more complex theories and models to managers. In many cases, they have, instead, added jargon and complexity at the expense of clarity, practical utility, and meaningfulness. This is unfortunately a verdict reached by too many managers. Consequently, managers in many cases have refused to permit the testing of these theories and models in their organizations. If additional knowledge is to be gained from scientifically testing more complex theories and models, there will be a need to improve the clarity of these approaches.

Certainly, simple answers are not sufficient for most organizational problem areas. However, there is nothing sacred about a more complex approach. Each approach will have to meet three tests: (1) Is it understandable? (2) Is it better than the simpler approaches? and (3) Can it be applied to managers? Conduct your own evaluation of some of the more complex theories and models that we presented—the Vroom-Yetton model, matrix design, strategic power contingencies, superordinate goals, and the path-goal theory of leadership. Being understandable means that the approach can be explained.

THE ENVIRONMENT

In an era of inflation, disinflation, international conflict, increasing foreign competition, and growing concern about the quality of life, managers are searching for better insight into and answers to problems. These shifting environmental forces have led to the growth of interest in the kind of environmental topics covered in *Organizational Behavior and Management*. In addition, more and more organizations are scientifically monitoring environmental forces. This monitoring provides a source of information that is vitally needed to make changes within organizations.

Managers now realize that environmental forces operate on the internal functioning of an organization—the individuals, groups, and total system. There is acceptance of the thesis that the interaction of multiple forces causes people, groups, and the organization to behave. The exact nature of this causality is not yet clear. However, managers now accept the premise that environmental forces must be considered when examining the behaviors occurring within organizations. Studying how people behave within organizations without considering the environment results in unrealistic, incomplete, and misleading conclusions.

ADDITIONAL WORK TO BE DONE

Instead of offering just another set of predictions about what the future holds for managers, organizations, and society, we prefer to spell out some areas for additional theorizing, research, and application. We have tried to provide an analysis of people working in organizations. Hopefully, you can distill from the chapters, cases, exercises, readings, and actual organizational situations a sense of what organizations are and what they do. Furthermore, the book has pointed out many areas that need to be developed further. Some of these areas needing additional work are briefly identified in the paragraphs that follow.

THEORIES

Well-articulated theories relevant to managerial practice need to be developed more completely for understanding individual, group, and organizational characteristics. These theories must be coherent, use managerial language, be testable, and possess the ability to be reasonably generalized from one setting to the next. The theories will have to incorporate the changing nature of society, the labor force, and economic conditions.

For example, Maslow's need hierarchy has a commonsensical appeal, but does it apply to women, blacks, handicapped employees, overworked managers, and employees in dangerous occupations? The questionable validity of the theory should cause serious doubts. Is it possible to develop or use a more complex explanation of motivation? We believe that it is possible if more effort is made to expand the domain of a theory without increasing its jargon. Clarity of presentation should be a major criterion in the development of theories in the field of organizational behavior.

HISTORY

We propose that more attention be paid to the history of organizations. The way in which organizations operate today and will operate tomorrow is influenced significantly by past events. We need to take a closer look at the actions of key managers and leaders—at how strategic policy decisions were reached, how managers responded to various crises, and what skills seemed valuable in solving problems. There seems to be a reluctance to even consult history, and what is lost is some of the explanation of how an organization became what it is today. We need a historical branch in the field of organizational behavior as much as we need a theoretical, research, and application orientation.

MEASUREMENT

The measurement techniques for studying behavior and testing theories need to be improved. Sole reliance on self-report surveys is questionable and not highly recommended. We now have the theoretical, psychometry, and statistical capabilities to develop more valid, reliable, and practical techniques than the self-report survey. We need to work on measurement in conjunction with managers so that measuring procedures are developed that not only have psychometric power but also appeal to managers. We are not suggesting the elimination of self-report surveys, only the redirection of effort toward other techniques such as observation, interviewing, and the use of documents and records.

COSTS VERSUS BENEFITS

The economic and psychological costs versus benefits of such techniques as goal setting, leadership training, rater training, career pathing, job enrichment, and matrix organizational structures need to be seriously evaluated. Few studies even estimate the costs of such techniques. We need to begin evaluating techniques in terms of costs (economic and noneconomic) and benefits (economic and noneconomic). Accountants and economists have much to offer the field of organizational behavior in terms of methods for analyzing costs and benefits. Since managers are held accountable for their actions, it seems important to work more systematically on the issue of costs versus benefits.

Applied organizational behavior programs need to be carefully scrutinized so that their short- and long-term contributions can be pinpointed. It is to the manager's benefit to take advantage of available methods for demonstrating costs versus benefits. Top management is likely to increase requests for data and analyses on the costs versus benefits of applied organizational behavior practices.

TECHNOLOGICAL

Managing people in organizations as we approach the 1990s is not easy. At the same time that so many businesses have been failing or teetering, new industries have been born: biotechnology, fiber optics, electronics, satellite teleconferencing, and many more. What's fueling these new industries? People—people with imagination, the need to excel, and a willingness to work hard and put in long hours.

Just as crop rotation brought a revolution to the farm, and machines and engines ushered in the industrial revolution, we are in the middle of a new revolution. The center of that revolution is people. The present technological revolution is not based on acts of physical labor but on the art of thinking. The major resource is the mind. Evidence of the revolution is everywhere—in robotics, in computers, in laser technology. What will be needed are strategies, programs, and procedures to harness, control, and monitor technological wizardry and power. The management of that wizardry and power so that the human condition will improve will require the use of theories, research, and applications offered by organizational behavioralists.

Managers will need to be prepared for the utilization of the new technologies. New theories of motivation, leadership, and organizational change will be needed to take optimum advantage of the new technologies. An experimental, scientific method-oriented mind-set will be needed to properly assess, modify, and put into practice the new technologies. What is the best organizational arrangement? What kinds of people are productive in that arrangement? How should people be rewarded in such an arrangement? Who will be displaced by new organizational arrangements? What will be the social and work impact of technological and structural changes? These and similar questions will have to be explored if the full benefits of technological growth and change are to be realized. The quantitative and qualitative tools, techniques, and methods for such exploration are what organizational behavioralists can provide.

TRAINING AND DEVELOPMENT

The training of managers to recognize important contingencies and appropriate responses needs to be undertaken. Managers need to be trained in problem-solving and decision-making skills to make the most efficient use of organizational resources. Unless managers are properly trained, goal attainment will be placed in serious jeopardy, productivity will suffer, and the quality of work-life will decline. Not only must formal training occur, but there also must be scientific evaluation of its effectiveness. Are managers more successful, more responsive to contingency factors, more aware of the environment, and more thorough problem solvers after training? These questions can only be answered if the training is evaluated with valid and reliable measures.

FOREIGN MANAGEMENT PRACTICES

The economic development and growth of such nations as Japan, Canada, West Germany, and Australia are the result of many factors, including government policies, favorable trade pacts with other nations, sound planning and forecasting, and effective managerial practices. The classic view of an economic miracle is the story of Japan. "Made in Japan" was once the mark of shoddy merchandise. However, it is now a badge of quality for everything from compact automobiles to videotape recorders. Are there any lessons for those interested in people working in organizations? We believe so.

There is a need in the field of OB to learn from the experience of foreign organizations as well as domestic organizations. Study and analysis of the relationship between workers and their companies in Japan and elsewhere can provide insight into the managerial techniques being used. Why do Japanese workers have a sense that the company is the base of their lives? Can this feeling be generated for the U.S. worker? Should this feeling be generated? These and similar questions need to be studied at the individual, group, and organizational levels. We are suggesting that the application of OB can be improved by examining *what* has been used successfully and *how* it was used in other organizations around the world.

Some American companies have begun experimenting with Japanese-style management techniques. What is now needed are careful and long-term analyses of these experiments. We need to scientifically study foreign management practices so that we can separate fact from fiction. We believe that the wonders of foreign management practices have been exaggerated to the point of fantasy and fable in some cases. We must examine these practices to learn and to analyze how and why a management practice operates as it does.

There are major differences in the economic and political systems and cultures of such nations as Japan, Canada, West Germany, and the United States. Some of the managerial techniques that are successful in one nation may not be successful in other nations. We need to find out why some things work and others fail. Studies on these matters should be conducted by using the scientific approach encouraged in this book. Furthermore, inquiring into what works and what doesn't should proceed at three levels of analysis—the individual, the group, and the organization.

**WOMEN AND
MINORITIES**
Since the early 1970s, more and more women and minorities have moved into organizational careers. As a result of this development, the following kinds of questions are being asked: Do women fear success? Can blacks effectively manage white subordinates? How do Mexican-Americans feel about working for women managers? Do men and women differ in aggressiveness, risk-taking propensity, commitment, and the work ethic?

It would be foolish to deny that, at present, women and minorities working in organizations are relatively misunderstood. What is needed are sound, scientific investigations of men, women, blacks, Mexican-Americans, and others performing managerial and nonmanagerial jobs in organizational settings. We need data to examine and locate differences in style and characteristics, if they do exist. Preconceptions, tacit assumptions, and personal opinions should be replaced with comparative research that is based on sound quantitative and qualitative procedures.

These are only a few of the areas that need more dialogue, debate, theory building, research, and experimentation. Instead of suggesting an ideal model of organizational behavior as the foremost need, we have elected to call attention to a few specific areas of interest and concern. Of course, work must proceed in integrating concepts, variables, and causal linkages in the field of organizational behavior. However, just as important is the need to study and analyze more thoroughly the people working within organizations. We need theories, frameworks, and techniques to manage more effectively, but we should never lose sight of people as individuals, working in groups, and as part of the total organization.

> "Only the supremely wise and the
> abysmally ignorant do not change."
> —Confucius

APPENDIX A

QUANTITATIVE AND QUALITATIVE RESEARCH TECHNIQUES FOR STUDYING ORGANIZATIONAL BEHAVIOR AND MANAGEMENT PRACTICE

SOURCES OF KNOWLEDGE ABOUT ORGANIZATIONS

The vast majority of the research reports and writing on organizations are contained in technical papers known as journals. Some of these journals, such as the *Academy of Management Review,* are devoted entirely to topics of management and organization, while such journals as *Organizational Behavior and Human Decision Processes* are devoted largely to the results of laboratory studies. Such journals as the *Harvard Business Review,* are general business journals, while the *American Sociological Review* and the *Journal of Applied Psychology* are general behavioral science journals. These business and behavioral science journals often contain articles of interest to students of management. Table A-1 presents a selective list of journals.

The sources in Table A-1 provide information, data, and discussion about what is occurring within and among organizations. This knowledge base provides managers with available research information that could prove useful in their own organizations or situations.

HISTORY AS A WAY OF KNOWING ABOUT ORGANIZATIONS

The oldest approach to the study of organizations is through the history of organizations, societies, and institutions. Throughout human history, people have joined with others to accomplish their goals, first in families, later in tribes and other, more sophisticated political units. Ancient peoples constructed pyramids, temples, and ships; they created systems of government, farming, commerce, and warfare. For example, Greek historians tell us that it took 100,000 men to build the great pyramid of Khufu in Egypt. The project took more than 20 years to complete. It was almost as high as the Washington Monument and had a base that would cover eight football fields. Remember, these people had no construction equipment or computers. One

TABLE A–1

Selected Sources of Writing and Research on Organizations

1. Academy of Management Journal	13. Human Organization	25. Management International Review
2. Academy of Management Review	14. Human Resource Management	26. Management Review
3. Administrative Management	15. Industrial and Labor Relations Review	27. Management Science
4. Administrative Science Quarterly	16. Industrial Engineering	28. Organizational Behavior and Human Decision Processes
5. Advanced Management Journal	17. Industrial Management Review	29. Organizational Dynamics
6. American Sociological Review	18. Journal of Applied Behavioral Science	30. Personnel
7. Business Horizons	19. Journal of Applied Psychology	31. Personnel Journal
8. Business Management	20. Journal of Business	32. Personnel Psychology
9. California Management Review	21. Journal of International Business Studies	33. Public Administration Review
10. Decision Sciences	22. Journal of Management	34. Public Personnel Review
11. Fortune	23. Journal of Management Case Studies	35. Strategic Management Journal
12. Hospital and Health Services Administration	24. Journal of Management Studies	36. Training and Development Journal

thing they did have, though, was *organization*. While these "joint efforts" did not have formal names such as "XYZ Corporation," the idea of "getting organized" was quite widespread throughout early civilizations. The literature of the times refers to such managerial concepts as planning, staff assistance, division of labor, control, and leadership.[1]

The administration of the vast Roman Empire required the application of organization and management concepts. In fact, it has been said that "the real secret of the greatness of the Romans was their genius for organization."[2] This is because the Romans used certain principles of organization to coordinate the diverse activities of the empire.

If judged by age alone, the Roman Catholic Church would have to be considered the most effective organization of all time. While its success is the result of many factors, one of these factors is certainly the effectiveness of its organization and management. For example, a hierarchy of authority, a territorial organization, specialization of activities by function, and use of the staff principle were integral parts of early church organization.

Finally, it is not surprising that some important concepts and practices in modern organizations can be traced to military organizations. This is because, like the church, military organizations were faced with problems of managing

---

[1] For an excellent discussion of organizations in ancient societies, see Claude S. George., Jr., *The History of Management Thought* (Englewood Cliffs, N.J.: Prentice-Hall, 1968), pp. 3–26.

[2] James D. Mooney, *The Principles of Organization* (New York: Harper & Row, 1939), p. 63.

large, geographically dispersed groups. As did the church, military organizations adopted early the concept of staff as an advisory function for line personnel.

Knowledge of the history of organizations in earlier societies can be useful for the future manager. In fact, many of the early concepts and practices are being utilized successfully today. However, you may ask whether heavy reliance on the past is a good guide to the present and future. We shall see that time and organizational setting have much to do with what works in management.

EXPERIENCE AS A WAY OF KNOWING ABOUT ORGANIZATIONS

Some of the earliest books on management and organizations were written by successful practitioners. Most of these individuals were business executives, and their writings focused on how it was for them during their time with one or more companies. They usually put forward certain general principles or practices that had worked well for them. Although using the writings and experiences of practitioners sounds "practical," it has its drawbacks. Successful managers are susceptible to the same perceptual phenomena as each of us. Their accounts, therefore, are based on their own preconceptions and biases. No matter how objective their approaches, the accounts may not be entirely complete or accurate. In addition, the accounts also may be superficial, since they often are after-the-fact reflections of situations in which, when the situations were occurring, the managers had little time to think about how or why they were doing something. As a result, the suggestions in such accounts often are oversimplified. Finally, as with history, what worked yesterday may not work today or tomorrow.[3]

SCIENCE AS A WAY OF KNOWING ABOUT ORGANIZATIONS

We have noted that a major interest in this book was the behavioral sciences which have produced theory, research, and generalizations concerning the behavior, structure, and processes of organizations. The interest of behavioral scientists in the problems of organizations is relatively new, becoming popular in the early 1950s. At that time, an organization known as the Foundation for Research on Human Behavior was established. The objectives of this organization were to promote and support behavioral science research in business, government, and other types of organizations.

Many advocates of the scientific approach believe that practicing managers and teachers have accepted prevalent practices and principles without the benefit of scientific validation. They believe that scientific procedures should be used whenever possible to validate practice. Because of their work, many of the earlier practices and principles have been discounted or modified and others have been validated.

---

[3] Ian I. Mitroff, "Why Our Old Pictures of the World Do Not Work Anymore," in E. E. Lawler III et al. (Eds.), *Doing Research That is Useful for Theory and Research* (San Francisco: Jossey-Bass, 1985), pp. 18–44.

RESEARCH IN THE BEHAVIORAL SCIENCES

Present research in the behavioral sciences is extremely varied with respect to the scope and methods used. One common thread among the various disciplines is the study of human behavior through the use of scientific procedures. Thus, it is necessary to examine the nature of science as it is applied to human behavior. Some critics believe that a science of human behavior is unattainable and that the scientific procedures used to gain knowledge in the physical sciences cannot be adapted to the study of humans, especially humans in organizations.

The authors do not intend to become involved in these arguments. However, we believe that the scientific approach is applicable to management and organizational studies.[4] Furthermore, as we have already pointed out, there are means other than scientific procedures that have provided important knowledge concerning people in organizations.

The manager of the future will draw from the behavioral sciences just as the physician draws from the biological sciences. The manager must know what to expect from the behavioral sciences, their strengths and weaknesses, just as the physician must know what to expect from bacteriology and how it can serve as a diagnostic tool. However, the manager, like the physician, is a practitioner. He or she must make decisions in the present, whether or not science has all the answers, and certainly cannot wait until it finds them before acting.

THE SCIENTIFIC APPROACH

Most current philosophers of science define "science" in terms of what they consider to be its one universal and unique feature: *method*. The greatest advantage of the scientific approach is that it has one characteristic not found in any other method of attaining knowledge: *Self-correction*.[5] The scientific approach, is an objective, systematic, and controlled process with built-in checks all along the way to knowledge. These checks control and verify the scientist's activities and conclusions to enable the attainment of knowledge independent of the scientist's own biases and preconceptions.

Most scientists agree that there is no single scientific method. Instead, there are several methods that scientists can and do use. Thus, it probably makes more sense to say that there is a scientific approach. Table A-2 summarizes the major characteristic of this approach. While only an "ideal" science would exhibit all of them, they are nevertheless the hallmarks of the scientific approach. They exhibit the basic nature—objective, systematic, controlled—of the scientific approach, which enables others to have confidence in research results. What is important is the overall fundamental idea that the scientific approach is a controlled rational process.

---

[4] A similar debate has taken place for years over the issue of whether management is a science. For relevant discussions, the interested reader should consult R. E. Gribbons and S. D. Hunt, "Is Management a Science?" *Academy of Management Review,* January 1978, pp. 139–43; O. Behling, "Some Problems in the Philosophy of Science of Organizations," *Academy of Management Review,* April 1978, pp. 193–201; and O. Behling, "The Case for the Natural Science Model for Research in Organizational Behavior and Organization Theory," *Academy of Management Review,* October 1980, pp. 483–90.

[5] See Fred N. Kerlinger, *Foundations of Behavioral Research* (New York: Holt, Rinehart & Winston, 1973), p. 6.

TABLE A-2

Characteristics of the Scientific Approach

1. *The procedures are public.* A scientific report contains a complete description of what was done, to enable other researchers in the field to follow each step of the investigation as if they were actually present.
2. *The definitions are precise.* The procedures used, the variables measured, and how they were measured must be clearly stated. For example, if examining motivation among employees in a given plant, it would be necessary to define what is meant by motivation and how it was measured (for example, number of units produced, number of absences).
3. *The data collecting is objective.* Objectivity is a key feature of the scientific approach. Bias in collecting and interpreting data has no place in science.
4. *The findings must be replicable.* This enables another interested researcher to test the results of a study by attempting to reproduce them.
5. *The approach is systematic and cumulative.* This relates to one of the underlying purposes of science, to develop a unified body of knowledge.
6. *The purposes are explanation, understanding, and prediction.* All scientists want to know "why" and "how." If they determine "why" and "how" and are able to provide proof, they can then predict the particular conditions under which specific events (human behavior in the case of behavioral sciences) will occur. Prediction is the ultimate objective of behavioral science, as it is of all science.

Source: Bernard Berelson and Gary A. Steiner, *Human Behavior: An Inventory of Scientific Findings* (New York: Harcourt Brace Jovanovich, 1964), pp. 16–18.

METHODS OF INQUIRY USED BY BEHAVIORAL SCIENTISTS

How do behavioral scientists gain knowledge about the functioning of organizations?[6] Just as physical scientists have certain tools and methods for obtaining information, so do behavioral scientists. These usually are referred to as *research designs*. In broad terms, three basic designs are used by behavioral scientists: the case study, the field study, and the experiment.

Case Study. A case study attempts to examine numerous characteristics of one or more people, usually over an extended time period. For years, anthropologists have studied the customs and behavior of various groups by actually living among them. Some organizational researchers have done the same thing. They have worked and socialized with the groups of employees that they were studying.[7] The reports on such investigations usually are in the form of a case study. For example, a sociologist might report the key factors and incidents that led to a strike by a group of blue-collar workers.

The chief limitations of the case-study approach for gaining knowledge about the functioning of organizations are:

1. Rarely can you find two cases that can be meaningfully compared in terms of essential characteristics. In other words, in another firm of another size, the same factors might not have resulted in a strike.

[6] A cross section of papers on gaining knowledge about organizations can be found in Thomas S. Bateman and Gerald R. Ferris, *Methods and Analysis in Organizational Research* (Reston, Va.: Reston Publishing, 1984).

[7] See E. Chinoy, *The Automobile Worker and the American Dream* (Garden City, N.Y.: Doubleday Publishing, 1955); and D. Roy, "Banana Time—Job Satisfaction and Informal Interaction," *Human Organization,* 1960, pp. 158–69.

2. Rarely can case studies be repeated or their findings verified.
3. The significance of the findings is left to the subjective interpretation of the researcher. Like the practitioner, the researcher attempts to describe reality, but it is reality as perceived by one person (or a very small group). The researcher has training, biases, and preconceptions that inadvertently can distort the report. A psychologist may give an entirely different view of a group of blue-collar workers than would be given by a sociologist.
4. Since the results of a case study are based on a sample of one, the ability to generalize from them may be limited.[8]

Despite these limitations, the case study is widely used as a method of studying organizations. It is extremely valuable in answering exploratory questions.

Field Study.   In attempts to add more reality and rigor to the study of organizations, behavioral scientists have developed several systematic field research techniques such as personal interviews, observation, archival data, and questionnaire surveys. These methods are used individually or in combination. They are used to investigate current practices or events, and with these methods, unlike some other methods, the researcher does not rely entirely on what the subjects say. The researcher may personally interview other people in the organization—fellow workers, subordinates, and superiors—to gain a more balanced view before drawing conclusions.[9] In addition, archival data, records, charts, and statistics on file may be used to analyze a problem or hypothesis.

A very popular field study technique involves the use of expertly prepared questionnaires. Not only are such questionnaires less subject to unintentional distortion than personal interviews, but they also enable the researcher to greatly increase the number of individuals participating. Figure A-1 presents part of a questionnaire that is used in organizations to evaluate ratee perceptions of a performance appraisal interview program. The questionnaire enables the collection of data on particular characteristics that are of interest (for example, equity, accuracy, and clarity). The seven-point scales measure a person's perceptions of the degree to which the performance appraisal interviews possess a given characteristic.

In most cases, surveys are limited to a description of the current state of the situation. However, if researchers are aware of factors that may account

---

[8] Based in part on Robert J. House, "Scientific Investigation in Management," *Management International Review*, 1970, pp. 141–42. The interested reader should see G. Morgan and L. Smircich, "The Case for Qualitative Research," *Academy of Management Review*, October 1980, pp. 491–500; and L. R. Jauch, R. N. Osborn, and T. N. Martin, "Structured Content Analysis of Cases: A Complementary Method for Organizational Research," *Academy of Management Review*, October 1980, pp. 517–26.

[9] See G. R. Salancik, "Field Stimulations for Organizational Behavior Research," *Administrative Science Quarterly*, December 1979, pp. 638–49, for an interesting approach to field studies.

FIGURE A-1

Scale
for Assessing
GANAT Appraisal
Interviews

Part A: Appraisal Interview

The following items deal with the formal appraisal interview used in conjunction with the GANAT project program. Please circle the number that best describes your opinion of the most recent interview session.

		Very False						Very True
1.	The appraisal interview covered my entire job.	1	2	3	4	5	6	7
2.	The discussion of my performance during the appraisal interview was covered equitably.	1	2	3	4	5	6	7
3.	The appraisal interview was accurately conducted.	1	2	3	4	5	6	7
4.	I didn't have to ask for any clarification.	1	2	3	4	5	6	7
5.	The interview was fair in every respect.	1	2	3	4	5	6	7
6.	The interview really raised my anxiety level.	1	2	3	4	5	6	7
7.	The interview's purpose was simply not clear to me.	1	2	3	4	5	6	7
8.	The appraisal interview really made me think about working smarter on the job.	1	2	3	4	5	6	7
9.	The appraisal interview was encouraging to me personally.	1	2	3	4	5	6	7
10.	I dreaded the actual interview itself.	1	2	3	4	5	6	7
11.	The boss was totally aboveboard in all phases of the interview.	1	2	3	4	5	6	7
12.	The interview gave me some direction and purpose.	1	2	3	4	5	6	7
13.	The interview really pinpointed areas for improvement.	1	2	3	4	5	6	7
14.	The interview was disorganized and frustrating.	1	2	3	4	5	6	7
15.	I disliked the interview because the intent was not clear.	1	2	3	4	5	6	7
16.	The appraisal interviewer (boss) was not well trained.	1	2	3	4	5	6	7
17.	The interview has been my guide for correcting weaknesses.	1	2	3	4	5	6	7
18.	I understood the meaning of each performance area better after the interview.	1	2	3	4	5	6	7
19.	The interview time was too rushed.	1	2	3	4	5	6	7
20.	I received no advanced notice about the interview.	1	2	3	4	5	6	7
21.	During the interview, my performance was fairly analyzed.	1	2	3	4	5	6	7
22.	I was often upset because the interview data were not accurate.	1	2	3	4	5	6	7
23.	My record as it was introduced in the interview contained no errors.	1	2	3	4	5	6	7

Source: This interview appraisal form was developed by John M. Ivancevich and sponsored by research funds provided by the GANAT Company.

for survey findings, they can make conjectural statements (known as hypotheses) about the relationship between two or more factors and relate the survey data to those factors. Thus, instead of just describing perceptions of performance evaluation, the researchers could make finer distinctions (for example, distinctions regarding job tenure, salary level, or education) among groups of ratees. Comparisons and statistical tests could then be applied to determine differences, similarities, or relationships. Finally, *longitudinal* studies involving observations made over time are used to describe changes that have taken place. Thus, in the situation described here, we can become aware of changes in overall ratee perceptions of appraisal interviews over time, as well as ratee perceptions relating to individual managers.[10]

Despite their advantages over many of the other methods of gaining knowledge about organizations, field studies are not without problems. Here again, researchers have training, interests, and expectations that they bring with them.[11] Thus, a researcher inadvertently may ignore a vital technological factor when conducting a study of employee morale while concentrating only on behavioral factors. Also, the fact that a researcher is present may influence how the individual responds. This weakness of field studies has long been recognized and is noted in some of the earliest field research in organizations.

Experiment.　The experiment is potentially the most rigorous of scientific techniques. For an investigation to be considered an experiment, it must contain two elements—manipulation of some variable (independent variable) and observation or measurement of the results (dependent variable) while maintaining all other factors unchanged. Thus, in an organization, a behavioral scientist could change one organizational factor and observe the results while attempting to keep everything else unchanged.[12] There are two general types of experiments.

In a *laboratory experiment,* the environment is created by the researcher. For example, a management researcher may work with a small, voluntary group in a classroom. The group may be students or managers. They may be asked to communicate, perform tasks, or make decisions under different sets of conditions designated by the researcher. The laboratory setting permits the researcher to control closely the conditions under which observations

---

[10] The design of surveys and the development and administration of questionnaires are better left to trained individuals if valid results are to be obtained. The interested reader might consult Seymour Sudman and Norman M. Bradburn, *Asking Questions: A Practical Guide to Questionnaire Design* (San Francisco: Jossey-Bass, 1982).

[11] For an excellent article on the relationship between what researchers want to see and what they do see, consult G. Nettler, "Wanting and Knowing," *American Behavioral Scientist,* July 1973, pp. 5–26.

[12] For a volume devoted entirely to experiments in organizations, see W. M. Evan, ed., *Organizational Experiments: Laboratory and Field Research* (New York: Harper & Row, 1971). Also see J. A. Waters, P. F. Salipante, Jr., and W. W. Notz, "The Experimenting Organization: Using the Results of Behavioral Science Research," *Academy of Management Review,* July 1978, pp. 483–92.

are made. The intention is to isolate the relevant variables and to measure the response of dependent variables when the independent variable is manipulated. Laboratory experiments are useful when the conditions required to test a hypothesis are not practically or readily obtainable in natural situations and when the situation to be studied can be replicated under laboratory conditions. For such situations, many schools of business have behavioral science laboratories where such experimentation is done.

In a *field experiment,* the investigator attempts to manipulate and control variables in the natural setting rather than in a laboratory. Early experiments in organizations included manipulating physical working conditions such as rest periods, refreshments, and lighting. Today, behavioral scientists attempt to manipulate a host of additional factors.[13] For example, a training program might be introduced for one group of managers but not for another. Comparisons of performance, attitudes, and so on could be obtained later at one point or at several different points (a longitudinal study) to determine what effect, if any, the training program had on the managers' performances and attitudes.

The experiment is especially appealing to many researchers because it is the prototype of the scientific approach. It is the ideal toward which every science strives. However, while its potential is still great, the experiment has not produced a great breadth of knowledge about the functioning of organizations. Laboratory experiments suffer the risk of "artificiality." The results of such experiments often do not extend to real organizations. Teams of business administration or psychology students working on decision problems may provide a great deal of information for researchers. Unfortunately, it is questionable whether this knowledge can be extended to a group of managers or nonmanagers making decisions under severe time constraints.[14]

Field experiments also have drawbacks. First, researchers cannot "control" every possible influencing factor (even if they knew them all) as they can in a laboratory. Here again, the fact that a researcher is present may make people behave differently, especially if they are aware that they are participating in an experiment. Experimentation in the behavioral sciences, and more specifically, experimentation in organizations, is a complex matter.

In a *true experiment,* the researcher has complete control over the experiment: the who, what, when, where, and how. A *quasi-experiment,* on the other hand, is an experiment in which the researcher lacks the degree of control over conditions that is possible in a true experiment. In the vast majority of organizational studies, it is impossible to completely control everything. Thus, quasi-experiments typically are the rule when organizational behavior is studied via an experiment.

---

[13] See an account of the classic Hawthorne studies in Fritz J. Roethlisberger and W. J. Dickson, *Management and the Worker* (Boston: Division of Research, Harvard Business School, 1939). The original purpose of the studies, which were conducted at the Chicago Hawthorne Plant of Western Electric, was to investigate the relationship between productivity and physical working conditions.

[14] See K. E. Weick, "Laboratory Experimentation with Organizations: A Reappraisal," *Academy of Management Review,* January 1977, pp. 123–27, for a discussion of this problem.

Finally, with each of the methods of inquiry utilized by behavioral scientists, some type of *measurement* usually is necessary. For knowledge to be meaningful, it often must be compared with or related to something else. As a result, research questions (hypotheses) usually are stated in terms of how differences in the magnitude of some variable are related to differences in the magnitude of some other variable.

The variables studied are measured by research instruments. Those instruments may be psychological tests, such as personality or intelligence tests; questionnaires designed to obtain attitudes or other information, such as the questionnaire shown in Figure A-1; or, in some cases, electronic devices to measure eye movement or blood pressure.

It is very important that a research instrument be both *reliable* and *valid*. Reliability is the consistency of the measure. In other words, repeated measures with the same instrument should produce the same results or scores. Validity is concerned with whether the research instrument actually measures what it is supposed to be measuring. Thus, it is possible for a research instrument to be reliable but not valid. For example, a test designed to measure intelligence could yield consistent scores over a large number of people but not be measuring intelligence.

RESEARCH DESIGNS

A number of designs are used in experiments to study organizational behavior. To illustrate some of the available designs, we shall use the example of a training program being offered to a group of firstline supervisors. Suppose the task of the researcher is to design an experiment that will permit the assessment of the degree to which the program influenced the performance of the supervisors. We will use the following symbols in our discussion:

S = The subjects, the supervisors participating in the experiment.
O = The observation and measurement devices used by the researcher (that is, ratings of supervisors' performance by superiors).
X = The experimental treatment, the manipulated variable (that is, the training program).
R = The randomization process.[15]

ONE-SHOT DESIGN

If we assume that all supervisors go through the training program, it will be difficult for the researchers to evaluate it. This is because the researchers cannot compare the group with another group that did not undergo the training program. This design is called a *one-shot* design and is diagrammed as follows:

$$X \quad O$$

---

[15] R.H. Helmstader, *Research Concepts in Human Behavior* (New York: Appleton-Century-Crofts, 1970); William C. Scott and Terence R. Mitchell, *Organization Theory: A Structural and Behavioral Analysis* (Homewood, Ill.: Richard D. Irwin, 1976); and D. W. Emory, *Business Research Methods* (Homewood, Ill.: Richard D. Irwin, 1980).

The letter X stands for the experimental treatment (that is, the training program) and the letter O for the observation of performance on the job. The measure of performance could be in the form of an average score based on ratings of superiors. However, the researchers in no way can determine whether performance was influenced at all by the training program. This experimental design is rarely used because of its weaknesses.

ONE-GROUP PRETEST-POSTTEST DESIGN

The previous design can be improved upon by first gathering performance data on the supervisors, instituting the training program, then remeasuring their performance. This is diagrammed as follows:

$$O_1 \quad X \quad O_2$$

Thus, a pretest is given in time period 1, the program is administered, and a posttest is administered in time period 2. If $O_2 > O_1$, the differences can be attributed to the training program.

Numerous factors can confound the results obtained with this design. For example, suppose new equipment has been installed between O_1 and O_2. This could explain the differences in the performance scores. Thus, a *history* factor may have influenced our results. Other factors could influence our results. The most recurrent factors are listed along with their definitions in Table A-3.[16] Examination of Table A-3 indicates that results achieved in

TABLE A-3

Some Sources of Error in Experimental Studies

Factor	Definition
1. History	Events other than the experimental treatment (X) that occurred between pretest and posttest.
2. Maturation	Changes in the subject group with the passage of time that are not associated with the experimental treatment (X).
3. Testing	Changes in the performance of the subjects because measurement of their performance makes them aware that they are part of an experiment (that is, measures often alter what is being measured).
4. Instrumentation	Changes in the measures of participants' performance that are the result of changes in the measurement instruments or the conditions under which the measuring is done (for example, wear on machinery, boredom, fatigue on the part of observers).
5. Selection	When participants are assigned to experimental and control groups on any basis other than random assignment. Any selection method other than random assignment will result in systematic biases that will result in differences between groups that are unrelated to the effects of the experimental treatment (X).
6. Mortality	If some participants drop out of the experiment before it is completed, the experimental and control groups may not be comparable.
7. Interaction effects	Any of the above factors may interact with the experimental treatment, resulting in confounding effects on the results. For example, the types of individuals withdrawing from a study (mortality) may differ for the experimental group and the control group.

---

[16] Ibid.

this design also may be confounded by *maturation* (the supervisors may learn to do a better job between O_1 and O_2, which would increase their performance regardless of training), *testing* (the measure of performance in O_1 may make the supervisors aware that they are being evaluated, which may make them work harder and increase their performance), and *instrumentation* (if the performance observations are made at different times of the day, the results could be influenced by fatigue). Each of these factors offers explanations for changes in performance other than the training program. Obviously, this design can be improved upon.

STATIC-GROUP COMPARISON DESIGN

In this design, half of the supervisors would be allowed to enroll for the training. Once the enrollment reached 50 percent of the supervisors, the training program would begin. After some period of time, the group of supervisors who enrolled in the program would be compared with those who did not enroll. This design is diagrammed as follows:

$$X \quad O$$
$$O$$

Since the supervisors were not randomly assigned to each group, it is highly possible that the group that enrolled consists of the more highly motivated or more intelligent supervisors. Thus, *selection* is a major problem with this design. However, note that the addition of a *control group* (comparison group) has eliminated many of the error factors associated with the first two designs. The problem here is that the subjects were not randomly assigned to the experimental group (undergoing training) and the control group (no training). Therefore, it is possible that differences may exist between the two groups that are not related to the training.

The three designs discussed thus far (one-shot, one-group pretest-posttest, static-group comparisons) have been described as "pseudo-experimental" or "quasi-experimental" designs. When true experimentation cannot be achieved, these designs (especially the last two) are preferred over no research at all or over relying on personal opinion. The following three designs can be considered "true" experimental designs because the researcher has complete control over the situation in the sense of determining precisely who will participate in the experiment and which subjects will or will not receive the experimental treatment.

PRETEST-POSTTEST CONTROL GROUP DESIGN

This design is one of the simplest forms of true experimentation used in the study of human behavior. It is diagrammed as follows:

$$R \quad O_1 \quad X \quad O_2$$
$$R \quad O_1 \quad \quad O_2$$

Note that this design is similar to the one-group pretest-posttest design except that a control group has been added and the participants have been randomly assigned to both groups. Which group is to receive the training (experimental group) and which will not (control group) is also randomly determined. The two groups may be said to be equivalent at the time of the initial observations, and at the time the final observations are made, and different only in that one group has received training, while the other has not. In other words, if the change from O_1 to O_2 is greater in the experimental group than in the control group, we can attribute the difference to the training program rather than selection, testing, maturation, and so forth.

The major weakness of the pretest-posttest control group design is one of *interaction* (selection and treatment), where individuals are aware that they are participating in an experiment. In other words, being observed the first time makes all of the participants work more diligently, both those who are in the training group and those who are in the control group. Here, the participants in the training program will be more receptive to training because of the pretest. This problem of interaction can be overcome by using a posttest-only control group design.

POSTTEST-ONLY CONTROL GROUP DESIGN

In this design, the participants are randomly assigned to two groups, the training is administered to one group, and the scores on the posttests are compared (performance envaluated). It is diagrammed as follows:

$$R \quad X \quad O$$
$$R \qquad O$$

This eliminates the problem of the previous design by not administering a pretest. However, the dependent variable (performance) is an ultimate rather than a relative measure of achievement. Also, the researcher does not have a group that was pretested and posttested without receiving the experimental treatment (training program). Such a group can provide valuable information on the effects of history, maturation, instrumentation, and so on. However, where a pretest is difficult to obtain or where its use is likely to make the participants aware that an experiment is being carried on, this approach may be much preferred to the pretest-posttest control group design.

SOLOMON FOUR-GROUP DESIGN

This design is a combination of the previous two designs and is diagrammed as follows:

Group 1	R	O_1	X	O_2
Group 2	R	O_1		O_2
Group 3	R		X	O_2
Group 4	R			O_2

Where gain or change in behavior is the desired dependent variable, this design should be used. This design is the most desirable of all the designs examined here. While it does not control any more sources of invalid results, it does permit the estimation of the extent of the effects of some of the sources of error. In our example here, the supervisors are randomly assigned to four groups, two of which will receive the training, one with a pretest and one without. Therefore, the researcher can examine, among other things, the effects of history (Group 1 to Group 2), testing (Group 2 to Group 4), and testing-treatment interaction (Group 2 to Group 3). Clearly, this design is the most complex, utilizing more participants, and it will be more costly. The added value of the additional information will have to be compared to the additional costs.[17]

QUALITATIVE RESEARCH

Instead of using experimental designs and concentrating on measurement issues, some researchers use qualitative research procedures. The notion of applying qualitative research methods to studying behavior within organizations recently has been addressed in leading research outlets.[18] The term *qualitative methods* is used to describe an array of interpretative techniques that attempt to describe and clarify the meaning of naturally occurring phenomena. It is by design rather open-ended and interpretative. The researcher's interpretation and description are the significant data collection acts in a qualitative study. In essence, qualitative data are defined as those (1) whose meanings are subjective, (2) that are rarely quantifiable, and (3) that are difficult to use in making quantitative comparisons.

Using both quantitative and qualitative methods in the same study can, in some cases, achieve a comprehensiveness that neither approach, if used alone, could achieve.[19] Another possible advantage of the combined use of the quantitative and qualitative methods is that the use of multiple methods could help check for congruence in findings. This is extremely important, especially when prescribing management interventions on the base of research.[20]

The quantitative approach to organizational behavior research is exemplified by precise definitions, control groups, objective data collection, use of the scientific method, and replicable findings. These characteristics are presented in Table A-2. The importance of reliability, validity, and accurate measurement is always stressed. On the other hand, qualitative research is more concerned with the meaning of what is observed. Since organizations are so complex, a range of quantitative and qualitative techniques can be used side by side to learn about individual, group, and organizational behavior.[21]

Qualitative methodology uses the experience and intuition of the researcher to describe the organizational processes and structures that are being studied.

---

[17] For a complete coverage of this area, see Kerlinger, *Foundations of Behavioral Research,* pp. 300–76; Helmstader, *Research Concepts in Human Behavior,* pp. 91–121; and Emory, *Business Research Methods,* pp. 330–65.

[18] John Van Maanen, ed., *Qualitative Methodology* (Beverly Hills, Calif.: Sage Publications, 1983).

[19] Christopher Stone, "Qualitative Research: A Viable Psychological Alternative," *Psychological Reports,* Winter 1985, pp. 63–75.

[20] Laura D. Goodwin and William L. Goodwin, "Qualitative vs. Quantitative Research, or Qualitative and Quantitative Research," *Nursing Research,* November-December 1984, pp. 378–380.

[21] Richard L. Daft, "Learning the Craft of Organizational Research," *Academy of Management Review,* October 1983, pp. 539–46.

The data collected by a qualitative researcher requires him or her to become very close to the situation or problem being studied. For example, a qualitative method that is used is called by anthropologists the *ethnographic method.*[22] When this method is used, the researcher typically studies a phenomenon for long periods of time as a *participant-observer.* The researcher becomes part of the situation being studied in order to feel what it is like for the people in that situation. The researcher becomes totally immersed in other people's realities.

Participant observation usually is supplemented by a variety of quantitative data collection tools such as structured interviews and self-report questionnaires. A variety of techniques is used so that the researcher can cross-check the results obtained from observation and recorded in field notes.

In training researchers in the ethnographic method, it is a common practice to place them in unfamiliar settings. A researcher may sit with and listen to workers on a production line, drive around in a police car to observe police officers, or do cleanup work in a surgical operating room. The training is designed to improve the researcher's ability to record, categorize, and code what is being observed.

An example of qualitative research involvement is present in Van Maanen's participant-observer study of a big-city police department. He went through police academy training and then accompanied police officers on their daily rounds. He functioned with police officers in daily encounters. Thus, he was able to provide vivid descriptions of what police work was like.[23]

Other qualitative techniques include content analysis (e.g., the researcher's interpretation of field notes), informal interviewing, archival data surveys and historical analysis, and the use of unobtrusive measures (e.g., data whose collection is not influenced by a researcher's presence). An example of the last would be the wear and tear on a couch in a cardiologist's office. As reported in the discussion of the Type A Behavior Pattern in Chapter 6, the wear and tear was on the edges of the couch, which suggested anxiety and hyperactive behavior. Qualitative research appears to rely more on multiple sources of data than on any one source. The current research literature suggests a number of characteristics associated with qualitative research:[24]

1. *Analytical induction.* Qualitative research begins with the closeup, first-hand inspection of organizational life.
2. *Proximity.* Researchers desire to witness firsthand what is being studied. If the application of rewards is what is being studied, the researcher would want to observe episodes of reward distribution.
3. *Ordinary behavior.* The topics of research interest should be ordinary, normal, routine behaviors.

---

[22] Anthony F. C. Wallace, "Paradigmatic Processes in Cultural Change," *American Anthropologist,* 1972, pp. 467–78.

[23] John Van Maanen, J. M. Dobbs, Jr., and R. R. Faulkner, *Varieties of Qualitative Research* (Beverly Hills, Calif.: Sage Publications, 1982).

[24] Van Maanen, *Qualitative Methodology,* pp. 255–56.

4. *Descriptive emphasis.* Qualitative research seeks descriptions for what is occurring in any given place and time. The aim is to disclose and reveal, not merely to order data and to predict.
5. *Shrinking variance.* Qualitative research is geared toward the explanation of similarity and coherence. There is a greater emphasis on commonality and on things shared in organizational settings than on things not shared.
6. *Enlighten the consumer.* The consumer of qualitative research could be a manager. A major objective is to enlighten without confusing him or her. This is accomplished by providing commentary that is coherent and logically persuasive.

Researchers and managers do not have to choose either quantitative or qualitative research data and interpretation. There are convincing and relevant arguments that more than one method of research should be used when studying organizational behavior. Quantitative and qualitative research methods and procedures have much to offer practicing managers. Blending and integrating quantitative and qualitative research are what researchers and managers must do in the years ahead to better understand, cope with, and modify organizational behavior.

GLOSSARY OF TERMS

Ability. A trait, biological or learned, that permits a person to do something mental or physical.

Adaptiveness. A criterion of effectiveness that refers to the ability of the organization to respond to change that is induced by either internal or external stimuli. An equivalent term is *flexibility,* although adaptiveness connotes an intermediate time frame, whereas flexibility ordinarily is used in a short-run sense.

Attitudes. Mental states of readiness for need arousal.

Authority. Authority resides in the relationship between positions and in the role expectations of the position occupants. Thus, an influence attempt based on authority generally is not resisted because, when joining an organization, individuals become aware that the exercise of authority is required of supervisors and that compliance is required of subordinates. The recognition of authority is necessary for organizational effectiveness and is a cost of organizational membership.

Banking Time Off. A reward practice of allowing employees to build up time-off credits for such things as good performance or attendance. The employees then receive the time off in addition to the regular vacation time granted by the organization because of seniority.

Baseline. The period of time before a change is introduced.

Behavior. Anything that a person does, such as talking, walking, thinking, or daydreaming.

Behavior Modification. An approach to motivation that uses the principles of operant conditioning.

Boundary-Spanning Role. The role of an individual who must relate to two different systems, usually an organization and some part of its environment.

Brainstorming. The generation of ideas in a group through noncritical discussion.

Cafeteria Fringe Benefits. The employee is allowed to develop and allocate a personally attractive fringe-benefit package. The employee is informed of what the total fringe benefits allowed will be and then distributes the benefits according to his or her preferences.

Centralization. A dimension of organizational structure that refers to the extent to which authority to make decisions is retained in top management.

Classical Design Theory. A body of literature that evolved from scientific management, classical organization, and bureaucratic theory. The theory emphasizes the design of a preplanned structure for doing work. It minimizes the importance of the social system.

Classical Organization Theory. A body of literature that developed from the writings of managers who proposed principles of organization. These principles were intended to serve as guidelines for other managers.

Coercive Power. Influence over others based on fear. A subordinate perceives that failure to comply with the wishes of a superior would lead to punishment or some other negative outcomes.

Cognition. This is basically what individuals know about themselves and their environment. Cognition implies a conscious process of acquiring knowledge.

Cognitive Dissonance. A mental state of anxiety that occurs when there is a conflict among an individual's various cognitions (for example, attitudes and beliefs) after a decision has been made.

Command Group. The group of subordinates who report to one particular manager constitutes the command group. The command group is specified by the formal organization chart.

Commitment. A sense of identification, involvement, and loyalty expressed by an employee toward the company.

Communication. The transmission of information and understanding through the use of common symbols.

Complexity. A dimension of organizational structure that refers to the number of different jobs and/or units within an organization.

Confrontation Conflict Resolution. A strategy that focuses on the conflict and attempts to resolve it through such procedures as the rotation of key group personnel, the establishment of superordinate goals, improving communications, and similar approaches.

Conscious Goals. The main goals that a person is striving toward and is aware of when directing behavior.

Consideration. Acts of the leader that show supportive concern for the followers in a group.

Content Motivation Theories. Theories that focus on the factors within a person that energize, direct, sustain, and stop behavior.

Contingency Approach to Management. This approach to management believes that there is no one best way to manage in every situation but that managers must find different ways that fit different situations.

Contingency Design Theory. An approach to designing organizations that states that the effective structure depends on factors in the situation.

Continuous Reinforcement. A schedule that is designed to reinforce behavior every time the behavior exhibited is correct.

Counterpower. Leaders exert power on subordinates, and subordinates exert power on leaders. Power is a two-way flow.

Decentralization. Basically, this entails pushing the decision-making point to the lowest managerial level possible. It involves the delegation of decision-making authority.

Decision. A means to achieve some result or to solve some problem. The outcome of a process that is influenced by many forces.

Decision Acceptance. An important criterion in the Vroom-Yetton model that refers to the degree of subordinate commitment to the decision.

Decision Quality. An important criterion in the Vroom-Yetton model that refers to the objective as-

pects of a decision that influence subordinates' performance aside from any direct impact on motivation.

Decoding. The mental procedure that the receiver of a message goes through to decipher the message.

Defensive Behavior. When an employee is blocked in attempts to satisfy needs to achieve goals, one or more defense mechanisms may be evoked. These defense mechanisms include withdrawal, aggression, substitution, compensation, repression, and rationalization.

Delegated Strategies. Strategies for introducing organizational change that allow active participation by subordinates.

Delegation. The process by which authority is distributed downward in an organization.

Delphi Technique. A technique used to improve group decision making that involves the solicitation and comparison of anonymous judgments on the topic of interest through a set of sequential questionnaires interspersed with summarized information and feedback of opinions from earlier responses.

Departmentalization. The manner in which an organization is structurally divided. Some of the more publicized divisions are by function, territory, product, customer, and project.

Development. A criterion of effectiveness that refers to the organization's ability to increase its responsiveness to current and future environmental demands. Equivalent or similar terms include institutionalization, stability, and integration.

Diagonal Communication. Communication that cuts across functions and levels in an organization.

Discipline. The use of some form of sanction or punishment when employees deviate from the rules.

Downward Communication. Communication that flows from individuals in higher levels of the organization's hierarchy to those in lower levels.

Dysfunctional Conflict. A confrontation or interaction between groups that harms the organization or hinders the achievement of organizational goals.

Dysfunctional Intergroup Conflict. Any confrontation or interaction between groups that hinders the achievement of organizational goals.

Effectiveness. In the context of organizational behavior, effectiveness refers to the optimal relationship among five components: production, efficiency, satisfaction, adaptiveness, and development.

Efficiency. A short-run criterion of effectiveness that refers to the organization's ability to produce outputs with minimum use of inputs. The measures of efficiency are always in ratio terms, such as benefit/cost, cost/output, and cost/time.

Encoding. The conversion of an idea into an understandable message by a communicator.

Environmental Certainty. A concept in the Lawrence and Lorsch research that refers to three characteristics of a subenvironment that determine the subunit's requisite differentiation. The three characteristics are the rate of change, the certainty of information, and the time span of feedback or results.

Environmental Diversity. A concept in the Lawrence and Lorsch research that refers to the differences among the three subenvironments in terms of certainty.

Environmental Forces. Forces for change beyond the control of the manager. These forces include marketplace actions, technological changes, and social and political changes.

Equity Theory of Motivation. A theory that examines discrepancies within a person after the person has compared his or her input/output ratio to that of a reference person.

Eustress. A term made popular by Dr. Hans Selye to describe good or positive stress.

Expectancy. The perceived likelihood that a particular act will be followed by a particular outcome.

Expectancy Theory of Motivation. In this theory, the employee is viewed as faced with a set of first-level outcomes. The employee will select an outcome based on how this choice is related to second-level outcomes. The preferences of the individual are based on the strength (valence) of desire to achieve a second-level state and the perception of the relationship between first- and second-level outcomes.

Experiment. To be considered an experiment, an investigation must contain two elements—manipulation of some variable (independent variable) and observation of the results (dependent variable).

Expert Power. Capacity to influence related to some expertise, special skill, or knowledge. Expert power is a function of the judgment of the less powerful person that the other person has ability or knowledge that exceeds his own.

Extinction. The decline in the response rate because of nonreinforcement.

Extrinsic Rewards. Rewards external to the job, such as pay, promotion, or fringe benefits.

Field Experiment. In this type of experiment, the investigator attempts to manipulate and control variables in the natural setting rather than in a laboratory.

Fixed Interval Reinforcement. A situation in which a reinforcer is applied only after a certain period of time has elapsed since the last reinforcer was applied.

Formal Group. A group formed by management to accomplish the goals of the organization.

Formalization. A dimension of organizational structure that refers to the extent to which rules, procedures, and other guides to action are written and enforced.

Friendship Group. An informal group that is established in the workplace because of some common characteristic of its members and that may extend the interaction of its members to include activities outside the workplace.

Functional Conflict. A confrontation between groups that enhances and benefits the organization's performance.

Functional Job Analysis. A method of job analysis that focuses attention on the worker's specific job activities, methods, machines, and output. The method is used widely to analyze and classify jobs.

General Adaptation Syndrome (GAS). A description of the three phases of the defense reaction that a person establishes when stressed. These phases are called alarm, resistance, and exhaustion.

Goal. A specific target that an individual is trying to achieve; a goal is the target (object) of an action.

Goal Approach to Effectiveness. A perspective on effectiveness that emphasizes the central role of goal achievement as the criterion for assessing effectiveness.

Goal Commitment. The amount of effort that is actually used to achieve a goal.

Goal Difficulty. The degree of proficiency or the level of goal performance that is being sought.

Goal Orientation. A concept that refers to the focus of attention and decision making among the members of a subunit.

Goal Participation. The amount of a person's involvement in setting task and personal development goals.

Goal Setting. The process of establishing goals. In many cases, goal setting involves a superior and subordinate working together to set the subordinate's goals for a specified period of time.

Goal Specificity. The degree of quantitative precision of the goal.

Graicunas' Model. The proposition that an arithmetic increase in the number of subordinates results in a geometric increase in the number of potential relationships under the jurisdiction of the superior. Graicunas set this up in a mathematical model:

$$C = N\left(\frac{2^N}{2} + N + 1\right)$$

Grapevine. An informal communication network that exists in organizations and short-circuits the formal channels.

Grid Training. A leadership development method proposed by Blake and Mouton that emphasizes the balance between production orientation and person orientation.

Group. Two or more employees who interact with one another in such a manner that the behavior and/or performance of one member is influenced by the behavior and/or performance of other members.

Group Cohesiveness. The strength of the members' desires to remain in the group and the strength of their commitment to the group.

Group Norms. Standards that are shared by the members of a group.

Groupthink. The deterioration of the mental efficiency, reality testing, and moral judgment of the individual members of a group in the interest of group solidarity.

Hardiness. A personality trait that appears to buffer an individual's response to stress. The hardy person assumes that he or she is in control, is highly committed to lively activities, and treats change as a challenge.

Hawthorne Studies. A series of studies undertaken at the Chicago Hawthorne Plant of Western Electric from 1924 to 1933. The studies made major contributions to the knowledge of the importance of the social system of an organization. They provided the impetus for the human relations approach to organizations.

History. A source of error in experimental results. It consists of events other than the experimental treatment that occur between pre- and post-measurement.

Horizontal Communication. Communication that flows across functions in an organization.

Horizontal Differentiation. The number of different units existing at the same level in an organization. The greater the horizontal differentiation, the more complex is the organization.

Incentive Plan Criteria. To be effective in motivating employees, incentives should (1) be related to specific behavioral patterns (for example, better performance), (2) be received immediately after the behavior is displayed, and (3) reward the employee for consistently displaying the desired behavior.

Influence. A transaction in which a person or a group acts in such a way as to change the behavior of another person or group. Influence is the demonstrated use of power.

Informal Group. Formed by individuals and developed around common interests and friendships rather than around a deliberate design.

Information Flow Requirements. The amount of information that must be processed by an organization, group or individual to perform effectively.

Initiating Structure. Leadership acts that imply the structuring of job tasks and responsibilities for followers.

Instrumentality. The relationship between first- and second-level outcomes.

Instrumentation. A source of error in experimental results. The error changes in the measure of participants' performance that are the result of changes in the measurement instruments or the conditions under which the measuring is done (for example, wear on machinery, fatigue on the part of observers).

Interaction. Any interpersonal contact in which one individual acts and one or more other individuals respond to the action.

Interaction Effects. The confounding of results that arises when any of the sources of errors in experimental results interact with the experimental treatment. For example, results may be confounded when the types of individuals withdrawing from any experiment (mortality) may differ for the experimental group and the control group.

Interest Group. A group that forms because of some special topic of interest. Generally, when the interest declines or a goal has been achieved, the group disbands.

Intergroup Conflict. Conflict between groups, which can be functional or dysfunctional.

Internal Forces. Forces for change that occur within the organization and that usually can be traced to *process* and to *behavioral* causes.

Interpersonal Communication. Communication that flows from individual to individual in face-to-face and group settings.

Interpersonal Orientation. A concept that refers to whether a person is more concerned with achieving good social relations as opposed to achieving a task.

Interpersonal Rewards. Extrinsic rewards such as receiving recognition or being able to interact socially on the job.

Interpersonal Style. The way in which an individual prefers to relate to others.

Interrole Conflict. A type of conflict that results from facing multiple roles. It occurs because individuals simultaneously perform many roles, some of which have conflicting expectations.

Intervention. The process by which either outsiders or insiders assume the role of a change agent in the OD program.

Intrapersonal Conflict. The conflict that a person faces internally, as when an individual experiences personal frustration, anxiety, and stress.

Intrarole Conflict. A type of conflict that occurs when different individuals define a role according to different sets of expectations, making it impossible for the person occupying the role to satisfy all of the expectations. This type of conflict is more likely to occur when a given role has a complex role set.

Intrinsic Rewards. Rewards that are part of the job itself. The responsibility, challenge, and feedback characteristics of the job are intrinsic rewards.

Job Analysis. The description of how one job differs from another in terms of the demands, activities, and skills required.

Job Content. The factors that define the general nature of a job.

Job Definition. The first subproblem of the organizing decision. It involves the determination of task requirements of each job in the organization.

Job Depth. The amount of control that an individual has to alter or influence the job and the surrounding environment.

Job Description. A summary statement of what an employee actually does on the job.

Job Descriptive Index. A popular and widely used 72-item scale that measures five job satisfaction dimensions.

Job Enlargement. An administrative action that involves increasing the range of a job. Supposedly, this action results in better performance and a more satisfied work force.

Job Enrichment. An approach developed by Herzberg that seeks to improve task efficiency and human satisfaction by means of building into people's jobs greater scope for personal achievement and recognition, more challenging and responsible work, and more opportunity for individual advancement and growth.

Job Evaluation. The assignment of dollar values to a job.

Job Range. The number of operations that a job occupant performs to complete a task.

Job Relationships. The interpersonal relationships that are required of or made possible by a job.

Job Rotation. A form of training that involves moving an employee from one work station to another. In addition to achieving the training objective, this procedure also is designed to reduce boredom.

Job Satisfaction. An attitude that workers have

about their jobs. It results from their perception of the jobs.

Laboratory Experiment. The key characteristic of laboratory experiments is that the environment in which the subject works is created by the researcher. The laboratory setting permits the researcher to control closely the experimental conditions.

Leader-Member Relations. A factor in the Fiedler contingency model that refers to the degree of confidence, trust, and respect that the leader obtains from the followers.

Learning. The process by which a relatively enduring change in behavior occurs as a result of practice.

Learning Transfer. An important learning principle that emphasizes the carry-over of learning into the workplace.

Legitimate Power. Capacity to influence derived from the position of a manager in the organizational hierarchy. Subordinates believe that they "ought" to comply.

Life Change Events. Major life changes that create stress for an individual. The work of Holmes and Rahe indicates that an excessive number of life change events in one period of time can produce major health problems in a subsequent period.

Linking-Pin Function. An element of System 4 organization that views the major role of managers to be that of representative of the group they manage to higher level groups in the organization.

Locus of Control. A personality characteristic that describes as *internalizers* people who see the control of their lives as coming from inside themselves. People who believe that their lives are controlled by external factors are *externalizers*.

Matrix Organizational Design. An organizational design that superimposes a product- or project-based design on an existing function-based design.

Maturation. A source of error in experimental studies. The error results from changes in the subject group with the passage of time that are not associated with the experimental treatment.

MBO. A process under which superiors and subordinates jointly set goals for a specified time period and then meet again to evaluate the subordinates' performance in terms of the previously established goals.

Mechanistic Model of Organizational Design. The type of organizational design that emphasizes the importance of production and efficiency. It is highly formalized, centralized, and complex.

Mission. The ultimate, primary purpose of an organization. An organization's mission is what society expects from the organization in exchange for its continuing survival.

Modeling. A method of administering rewards that relies on observational learning. An employee learns the behaviors that are desirable by observing how others are rewarded. It is assumed that behaviors will be imitated if the observer views a distinct link between performance and rewards.

Modified or Compressed Workweek. A shortened workweek. The form of the modified workweek that involves working four days a week, 10 hours each day, is called a 4/40. The 3/36 and 4/32 schedules also are being used.

Mortality. A source of error in experimental studies. This type of error occurs when participants drop out of the experiment before it is completed, resulting in the experimental and control groups not being comparable.

Motion Study. The process of analyzing a task to determine the preferred motions to be used in its completion.

Motivator-Hygiene Theory. The Herzberg approach that identifies conditions of the job that operate primarily to dissatisfy employees when they are not present (hygiene factors—salary, job security, work conditions, and so on). There also are job conditions that lead to high levels of motivation and job satisfaction. However, the absence of these conditions does not prove highly dissatisfying. The conditions include achievement, growth, and advancement opportunities.

Multiple Roles. The notion that most individuals play many roles simultaneously because they occupy many different positions in a variety of institutions and organizations.

Need for Power. A person's desire to have an impact on others. The impact can occur by such behaviors as action, the giving of help or advice, or concern for reputation.

Need Hierarchy Model. Maslow assumed that

the needs of a person depend on what he or she already has. This in a sense means that a satisfied need is not a motivator. Human needs are organized in a hierarchy of importance. The five need classifications are: physiological, safety, belongingness, esteem, and self-actualization.

Needs. The deficiencies that an individual experiences at a particular point in time.

Noise. Interference in the flow of a message from a sender to a receiver.

Nominal Group Technique (NGT). A technique to improve group decision making that brings people together in a very structured meeting that does not allow for much verbal communication. The group decision is the mathematically pooled outcome of individual votes.

Nonprogrammed Decisions. Decisions required for unique and complex management problems.

Nonverbal Communication. Messages sent with body posture, facial expressions, and head and eye movements.

Operant. Behaviors amenable to control by altering the consequences (rewards and punishments) that follow them.

Optimal Balance. The most desirable relationship among the criteria of effectiveness. Optimal, rather than maximum, balance must be achieved in any case of more than one criterion.

Organic Model of Organization. The organizational design that emphasizes the importance of adaptability and development. It is relatively informal, decentralized, and simple.

Organizational Behavior. The study of human behavior, attitudes, and performance within an organizational setting; drawing on theory, methods, and principles from such disciplines as psychology, sociology, and cultural anthropology to learn about *individual* perceptions, values, learning capacities, and actions while working in *groups* and within the total *organization;* analyzing the external environment's effect on the organization and its human resources, missions, objectives, and strategies.

Organizational Behavior Modification. An operant approach to organizational behavior. This term is used interchangeably with the term *behavior modification.*

Organizational Climate. A set of properties of the work environment, perceived directly or indirectly by the employees, that is assumed to be a major force in influencing employee behavior.

Organizational Culture. The pervasive system of values, beliefs, and norms that exists in any organization. The organizational culture can encourage or discourage effectiveness, depending on the nature of the values, beliefs, and norms.

Organizational Development. The process of preparing for and managing change in organizational settings.

Organizational Politics. The activities that are used to acquire, develop, and use power and other resources to obtain one's preferred outcome when there is uncertainty or disagreement about choices.

Organizational Processes. The activities that breathe life into the organizational structure. Among the common organizational processes are communication, decision making, socialization, and career development.

Organizational Structure. The formal pattern of how people and jobs are grouped in an organization. The organizational structure often is illustrated by an organization chart.

Organizations. Institutions that enable society to pursue goals that could not be achieved by individuals acting alone.

Participative Management. A concept of managing that encourages employees' participation in decision making and on matters that affect their jobs.

Path-Goal Leadership Model. A theory that suggests that it is necessary for a leader to influence the followers' perception of work goals, self-development goals, and paths to goal attainment. The foundation for the model is the expectancy motivation theory.

Perception. The process by which an individual gives meaning to the environment. It involves organizing and interpreting various stimuli into a psychological experience.

Performance. The desired results of behavior.

Person-Role Conflict. A type of conflict that occurs when the requirements of a position violate the basic values, attitudes, and needs of the individual occupying the position.

Personal-Behavioral Leadership Theories. A group of leadership theories that are based primarily on the personal and behavioral characteristics of leaders. The theories focus on *what* leaders do and/or *how* they behave in carrying out the leadership function.

Personality. A stable set of characteristics and tendencies that determine commonalities and differences in the behavior of people.

Personality Test. A test used to measure the emotional, motivational, interpersonal, and attitude characteristics that make up a person's personality.

Pooled Interdependence. Interdependence that requires no interaction between groups because each group, in effect, performs separately.

Position Analysis Questionnaire. A method of job analysis that takes into account the human, task, and technological factors of job and job classes.

Position Power. A factor in the Fiedler contingency model that refers to the power inherent in the leadership position.

Power. The ability to get things done in the way that one wants them to be done.

Power Illusion. The notion that a person with little power actually has significant power. The Miligram experiments indicated that the participants were obedient to commands given by an individual who seemed to have power (wore a white coat, was addressed as "doctor," and acted quite stern).

Process. In systems theory, the process element consists of technical and administrative activities that are brought to bear on inputs in order to transform them into outputs.

Process Motivation Theories. Theories that provide a description and analysis of the process by which behavior is energized, directed, sustained, and stopped.

Production. A criterion of effectiveness that refers to the organization's ability to provide the outputs that the environment demands of it.

Programmed Decisions. Situations in which specific procedures have been developed for repetitive and routine problems.

Progressive Discipline. Managerial use of a sequence of penalties for rule violations, each penalty being more severe than the previous one.

Punishment. Presenting an uncomfortable consequence for a particular behavior response or removing a desirable reinforcer because of a particular behavior response. Managers can punish by application or punish by removal.

Qualitative Overload. A situation in which a person feels that he or she lacks the ability or skill to do a job or that the performance standards have been set too high.

Quantitative Overload. A situation in which a person feels that he or she has too many things to do or insufficient time to complete a job.

Reciprocal Causation of Leadership. The argument that follower behavior has an impact on leader behavior and that leader behavior influences follower behavior.

Reciprocal Interdependence. Interdependence that requires the output of each group in an organization to serve as input to other groups in the organization.

Referent Power. Power based on a subordinate's identification with a superior. The more powerful individual is admired because of certain traits, and the subordinate is influenced because of this admiration.

Reward Power. An influence over others based on hope of reward; the opposite of coercive power. A subordinate perceives that compliance with the wishes of a superior will lead to positive rewards, either monetary or psychological.

Role. An organized set of behaviors.

Role Ambiguity. A person's lack of understanding about the rights, privileges, and obligations of a job.

Role Conflict. Arises when a person receives incompatible messages regarding appropriate role behavior.

Role Set. Those individuals who have expectations for the behavior of an individual in a particular role. The more expectations, the more complex is the role set.

Satisfaction. A criterion of effectiveness that refers to the organization's ability to gratify the needs of its participants. Similar terms include morale and voluntarism.

Scalar Chain. The graded chain of authority that is created through the delegation process.

Scientific Management. A body of literature that emerged during the period 1890–1930 and that reports the ideas and theories of engineers concerned with such problems as job definition, incentive systems, and selection and training.

Scope. The scale on which an organizational change is implemented (e.g., throughout the entire organization, level by level, or department by department).

Selection. A source of error in experimental studies. The error occurs when participants are assigned to experimental and control groups on any basis other than random assignment. Any other selection method will cause systematic biases that will result in differences between groups that are unrelated to the effects of the experimental treatment.

Sensitivity Training. A form of educational experience that stresses the process and emotional aspects of training.

Sequential Interdependence. Interdependence that requires one group to complete its task before another group can complete its task.

Shared Approach. An OD strategy that involves managers and employees in the determination of the OD program.

Shared Strategies. Strategies for introducing organizational change that focus on the sharing of decision-making authority among managers and subordinates.

Situational Theory of Leadership. An approach to leadership that advocates that leaders understand their own behavior, the behavior of their subordinates, and the situation before utilizing a particular leadership style. This approach requires diagnostic skills in human behavior on the part of the leader.

Skills. Task-related competencies.

Social Support. The comfort, assistance, or information that an individual receives through formal or informal contacts with individuals or groups.

Socialization Processes. The activities by which an individual comes to appreciate the values, abilities, expected behaviors, and social knowledge that are essential for assuming an organizational role and for participating as an organization member.

Span of Control. The number of subordinates reporting to a superior. The span is a factor that affects the shape and height of an organizational structure.

Status. In an organizational setting, status relates to positions in the formal or informal structure. Status is designated in the formal organization whereas in informal groups it is determined by the group.

Status Consensus. The agreement of group members about the relative status of members of the group.

Strategic Contingency. An event or activity that is extremely important for accomplishing organizational goals. Among the strategic contingencies of subunits are dependency, scarcity of resources, coping with uncertainty, centrality, and substitutability.

Stress. An adaptive response, mediated by individual differences and/or psychological processes, resulting from any environmental action, situation, or event that places excessive psychological and/or physical demands on a person.

Stressor. An external event or situation that is potentially harmful to a person.

Structure. The established patterns of interacting in an organization and of coordinating the technology and human assets of the organization.

Structure (in group context). Used in the context of groups, the term *structure* refers to the standards of conduct that are applied by the group, the communication system, and the reward and sanction mechanisms of the group.

Superordinate Goals. Goals that cannot be achieved without the cooperation of the conflicting groups.

Survey. A survey usually attempts to measure one or more characteristics in many people, usually at one point in time. Basically, surveys are used to investigate current problems and events.

System 4 Organization. The universalistic theory of organization design that has been proposed by Likert. The theory is defined in terms of overlapping groups, linking-pin management, and the principle of supportiveness.

Systems Theory. An approach to the analysis of organizational behavior that emphasizes the necessity for maintaining the basic elements of input-process-output and for adapting to the larger environment that sustains the organization.

Task Group.   A group of individuals who are working as a unit to complete a project or job task.

Task Structure.   A factor in the Fiedler contingency model that refers to how structured a job is with regard to requirements, problem-solving alternatives, and feedback on how correctly the job has been accomplished.

Technology.   An important concept that can have many definitions in specific instances but that generally refers to actions, physical and mental, that an individual performs upon some object, person, or problem in order to change it in some way.

Testing.   A source of error in experimental studies. The error occurs when changes in the performance of the subject arise because previous measurement of his performance made him aware that he was part of an experiment.

Time Orientation.   A concept that refers to the time horizon of decisions. Employees may have relatively short- or long-term orientations, depending on the nature of their tasks.

Time Study.   The process of determining the appropriate elapsed time for the completion of a task.

Timing.   The point in time that has been selected to initiate an organizational change method.

Tolerance of Ambiguity.   The tendency to perceive ambiguous situations or events as desirable. On the other hand, intolerance of ambiguity is the tendency to perceive ambiguous situations or events as sources of threat.

Trait Theory of Leadership.   An attempt to identify specific characteristics (physical, mental, personality) that are associated with leadership success. The theory relies on research that relates various traits to certain success criteria.

Type A Managers.   Managers who are aloof and cold toward others and are often autocratic leaders. Consequently, they are ineffective interpersonal communicators.

Type A Behavior Pattern.   Associated with research conducted on coronary heart disease. The Type A person is an aggressive driver who is ambitious, competitive, task-oriented, and always on the move.

Rosenman and Friedman, two medical researchers, suggest that Type As have more heart attacks than do Type Bs.

Type B Managers.   Managers who seek good relationships with subordinates but are unable to express their feelings. Consequently, they usually are ineffective interpersonal communicators.

Type B Behavior Pattern.   The Type B person is relaxed, patient, steady, and even-tempered. The opposite of the Type A.

Type C Managers.   Managers who are more interested in their own opinions than in those of others. Consequently, they usually are ineffective interpersonal communicators.

Type D Managers.   Managers who feel free to express their feelings to others and to have others express their feelings. Such managers are the most effective interpersonal communicators.

Unilateral Strategies.   Strategies for introducing organizational change that do not allow for participation by subordinates.

Universal Design Theory.   A point of view that states that there is "one best way" to design an organization.

Upward Communication.   Upward communication flows from individuals at lower levels of the organizational structure to those at higher levels. Among the most common upward communication flows are suggestion boxes, group meetings, and appeal or grievance procedures.

Valence.   The strength of a person's preference for a particular outcome.

Values.   The guidelines and beliefs that a person uses when confronted with a situation in which a choice must be made.

Vertical Differentiation.   The number of authority levels in an organization. The more authority levels an organization has, the more complex is the organization.

Vroom-Yetton Model.   A leadership model that specifies which leadership decision-making procedures will be most effective in each of several different situations. Two of the proposed leadership styles are autocratic (AI and AII); two are consultative (CI and CII); and one is oriented toward joint decisions (decisions made by the leader and the group, GII).

Whistle-Blowing. The process in which an employee, because of personal opinions, values, or ethical standards, concludes that an organization needs to change its behavior or practices and informs someone about that conclusion.

Work Module. An important characteristic of job redesign strategies. It involves the creation of whole tasks so that the individual senses the completion of an entire job.

Name Index

Subject Index